APPLICATION COMMENTARY
OF THE
GOSPEL OF MATTHEW
Final Edition

JOHN M. STROHMAN, J.D.

Published by:
Cross Centered Press
113 Village Drive
Pierre, SD 57501

Softcover ISBN 978-0-9859949-0-7
Hardcover ISBN 978-0-9859949-7-6
Kindle ISBN 978-0-9859949-1-4
E-Pub ISBN 978-0-9859949-2-1

Unless otherwise noted, most verses are cited from the *New American Standard Bible* 1977 edition and 1995 update with permission. *The New American Standard Bible®*, Copyright 1960,1962, 1963, 1968, 1971, 1972, 1973, 1975, 1977, 1995 La Habra, CA: The Lockman Foundation.

While efforts have been made to ensure accuracy, if you have identified an error in this publication, please send a notice to **john@CrossCenteredMissions.org**. Please identify your copy as: **Revision (9-20)**. Also include the page number and sentence, along with your suggested correction.

* Comments contained herein are the author's and are not meant to represent another or any institution/organization.

ABOUT THE AUTHOR

The most distinguishing feature of the Author is that he is a sinner who, in his early youth, was saved from the judgment to come by the grace of God. He continues to recognize his complete reliance on the mercy, forgiveness and grace of Jesus Christ <u>to this very moment</u>.

*Other matters:

John M. Strohman is a graduate of the University of Iowa College of Business and earned his Juris Doctor from the University of South Dakota School of Law. For approximately three decades he has served as an Assistant Attorney General for the State of South Dakota. As an attorney with over 30 years of experience, he has handled a variety of cases in state and federal courts, including serving as counsel for more than 200 cases before the South Dakota Supreme Court. John has also held faculty positions as an adjunct professor for South Dakota State University, Liberty University, Northern State University and Colorado Christian University. His teaching experience has spanned both the undergraduate and graduate level. In 2014 he authored *"The Fake Commission"* and in 2019 *"Does The Bible Really Say I am Good Enough for Heaven?"* He has served on mission boards and is the current chairman of Cross Centered Missions. John and his wife, Sarah, share a passion for equipping young people in Christian service through discipleship, Sunday school, Bible studies and leading short-term mission trips.

Oh yes… and at age 57, he could still do a backflip!

(The author does not receive any personal royalties from the sales of this book. All royalties go directly to further world missions.)

DEDICATION

I dedicate this commentary to my children Johannah and Elizabeth and write this note to them, their children, their children's children and all their family members to come.

Over the last 35 years I have noticed an expanding segment of the visible church that claims to speak for Christ, yet reflects little of the doctrines or discipleship we see in Scripture. Granted, we all fail daily in one way or another, yet our heart and desire should be to live unto Christ in all things. We learn how to do this <u>only</u> from knowing and applying the truths in God's infallible Word, the Bible. It is hoped that this commentary (merely the words of a very fallible man) will serve as an <u>aid</u> in your study of God's Word. During your life you will encounter many religious fads, movements, organizations, etc., with some even calling themselves "Christian," but they will prove not to be. My only concern for you is your eternal soul. My aim with this commentary is to provide you with an outline from my years of studying the Bible so that, *"... no one takes you captive through philosophy and empty deception, according to the tradition of men, according to the elementary principles of the world, rather than according to Christ."* <u>**Colossians 2:8**</u>.

Remember fathers and mothers (especially fathers) you have a duty before God to teach and train your children the truths of God (Deuteronomy 6:5–7). Do not delegate this responsibility to the church youth group or Sunday school. The church is there to supplement what you are already doing at home. Failure to fulfill your duty will result in pain for yourself and tragedy for generations to come.
> *"... and there arose another generation after them who did not know the Lord, nor yet the work which He had done for Israel. ¹¹ Then the sons of Israel did evil in the sight of the Lord..."* <u>**Judges 2:10–11**</u>

It is my sincere desire that all your family members will come to be part of the true church by being born again, which includes possessing a saving knowledge of Christ [to know more about what that means, read the entire comments section for Matt. 5:17-20]. It is my hope that you and your family will be serving God in your home, church, vocation and around the world via missions. My motivation for writing this commentary and my prayer for you is summed up in my favorite verse:
> *"Beloved, while I was making every effort to write you about our common salvation, I felt the necessity to write to you appealing that you <u>contend earnestly for the faith</u> which was once for all handed down to the saints."* <u>**Jude v.3**</u>

Remember, the second after you die, nothing else will matter but the King and His Kingdom. Live that truth now!

May the grace and peace of the Lord Jesus Christ be with you all.

Love,
Dad

PREFACE

This commentary is committed to Biblical Christianity. That is, a commitment to Biblical inerrancy, and salvation based solely on God's grace through faith in Jesus Christ's sacrificial death on the cross as the sole payment of a person's sin. A *general* list of the fundamentals of Biblical Christianity is set forth after this Preface.

This commentary is designed to be used in many different ways. <u>Do not let its length overwhelm you. It was not created to be read like an ordinary book,</u> but is a verse by verse study of the Gospel of Matthew that is divided into small sections. This method allows the reader to study and reflect on a section (or a part of a section) and then return the next day to do the same for the succeeding section. Each section contains a <u>Summary and Application</u> to help the reader consider how to take the truth of God's Word and live it out. This format lends itself to work well for personal or family devotions, preaching, as well as teaching a group Bible study or Sunday school. The commentary also has a Topical Index. <u>Finally, it is important that you check out the footnotes/endnotes as you read.</u> Many footnotes/endnotes may simply mention a source, but a considerable number contain in-depth information and commentary.

Let me explain the various applications in a little more detail. As you thumb through the commentary, you will note that the text of the Gospel of Matthew is divided up into smaller sections of the text. A group of sections constitutes an entire lesson. The end of a lesson will have a portion called <u>Summary and Application</u>. An entire lesson would represent something taught in a Sunday school or group Bible Study.

1. **Family or Personal Devotions**: Each day the family or an individual can study through the Book of Matthew by examining a selection of verses. For example, Dad can take a few minutes beforehand and read the verses and comments he will teach from that day. Since he has reviewed the text, he can decide how to present the lesson in a manner that all the family members can learn something, regardless of age. (Remember that you are daily sharing from just a few verses and not an entire lesson so aim for about 10-15 minutes.)

   In addition to teaching from the main text from Matthew, the commentary will have other supporting Bible verses that family members can look up and read. Since Dad has already studied that section, he can explain the Scriptures and then spur on a discussion by asking family members various questions about the verses and how they can apply the lesson to their lives. The family devotions can come to a close by asking family members what they would like to pray about. This becomes a great opportunity to stop and hear what is going on in everyone's life and heart. Conclude by having some prayer time together, taking turns so that each person in the family prays. If you do this, you will see a family unit that is greatly strengthened as it grows in God's Word and prays for each other's needs.

A couple of last thoughts. If you are shaking your head and thinking there is no way you could get everyone together for 15 minutes each day, then you must recognize that your family is out-of-control. Understand that your children's spiritual lives are being sacrificed by their endless activities and your obsession with work and money. One last word of caution, do not wait until your children are "old enough" to understand the Bible lessons. Sarah and I started having a little family devotion time right away when we brought our first child home from the hospital. I knew that if I did not start that habit right away, it would never happen. Also, it is amazing how even young children pick up on spiritual lessons that I would have considered way above them. Proverbs 22:6 tells us to:

> *"Train up a child in the way he should go,*
> *even when he is old he will not depart from it."*

2. **Bible study or Sunday school**: As mentioned above, the text of the Gospel of Matthew is divided up into sections of Scripture verses. A group of sections constitutes a complete lesson. The end of a lesson will have a portion called Summary and Application. You can teach an entire lesson at each meeting. Another option is for each member of the group to possess their own copy of the lesson. They can then spend the week reviewing the lesson on their own and then get together as a group to discuss it.

3. **Topical Index**: This section allows you to look up a particular Bible topics addressed in the commentary. The e-book version should allow you to click on the topic or other verses in that Topic Index and go directly to the text.

Remember that your chief objective is to walk in the truth of God's Word which will manifest itself in Holy Spirit born fruit.

> *"But prove yourselves doers of the word,*
> *and not merely hearers who delude themselves."* **James 1:22**

God's blessings as you study His Word!
John M. Strohman - (Jude v.3)

P.S. Other Issues: 1) Some issues/concepts are repeated throughout the commentary. The reason is that these issues reoccur in the Gospel of Matthew. Further, their repetition serves as an aid to learning via reinforcement. 2) Note that I have chosen not to belabor the reader with gender issues like (he or she) in my comments. The reasonable reader will recognize that when I use terms like "mankind" it also includes women. 3) If there is a matter you disagree with, feel free to contact me. Please understand that I will ultimately be persuaded only by Scripture in context (2 Tim. 2:15) and not simply by personal experience, denominational doctrine, or political agenda. As of the time of this publication, I can be contacted at **john@CrossCenteredMissions.org**

A GENERAL OUTLINE OF FUNDAMENTAL DOCTRINES OF CHRISTIANITY

True fundamental doctrines are derived from *Scripture alone* and do not originate from religious tradition or ecclesiastical groups/counsels. Oswald Chambers stated:

> "We are apt to forget that a man is not only committed to Jesus Christ for salvation; he is committed to Jesus Christ's view of God, of the world, of sin and of the devil, and this will mean that he must recognize the responsibility of being transformed by the renewing of his mind."[1]

A mature Christian is committed to the Bible to formulate their theological beliefs. From the study of Scripture, one will affirm the doctrines below. The list below forms a *general* **outline of true Christianity:**[2]

- **Inspiration, Inerrancy and Authority of Scripture:** Christ is the Word of God incarnate: John 1:1,14, 2 Peter 1:20-21, 2 Timothy 3:16, Proverbs 30:5-6, Revelation 22:18-19.
- **Virgin Birth:** Matthew 1:18-25, Luke 1:34-35, John 1:14,.
- **The Deity of Jesus Christ The Son of God:** He is God incarnate (God in a human flesh-and-blood body) Colossians 2:9, 1 John 5:20, Titus 2:13-14, John 8:58 and 10:30, Mark 14:61-62, John 20:28, Mark 15:39, John 21:14, Luke 22:70, John 20:31.
- **Jesus' Humanity:** (His incarnation) 1 John 4:2-3, He was tempted (Luke 4:1-13), hungry (Matthew 4:2), thirsty (John 19:28), slept (Matthew 8:24), died (Mark 15:39-45, Matthew 27:50).
- **Jesus' Sinlessness:** 2 Corinthians 5:21, Hebrews 4:15, 1 Peter 2:22, 1 John 3:5.
- **The Trinity:** Father, Son and Holy Spirit. There is one God who eternally exists in three persons. Each possesses the same nature and attributes but is distinct in office and activity: Deuteronomy 6:4, Matthew 28:19, John 10:30, John 17:21, John 10:38, 1 John 2:20-24, Jesus is the Son of God and Savior (John 20:31).
- **Jesus - Worker of Miracles, All Powerful and Creator of All Things:** John 11:32-45, Matthew 12:22, Luke 7:21-23, Matthew 15:30-31, Mark 9:23, 10:27, Luke 1:37, 18:27; Creator of all things, John 1:3, John 1:10, 1 Corinthians 8:6, Revelation 4:11, Genesis 1:1, Colossians 1:15-17, Hebrews 1:2.
- **Human Depravity:** Each person is morally corrupt and sinful which is the condition of being spiritually dead toward God: Romans 3:23, Ephesians 2:1-3, Ecclesiastes 7:20, Romans 5:12, Psalms 14:1-3, Romans 3:20, Psalms 143:2, Psalm 51:5.
- **Christ's Atoning Death and Bodily Resurrection:** Christ died on the cross as a substitutionary sacrifice for sinners: 1 Peter 3:18, 2 Corinthians 5:21, 1 Corinthians 15:1-7, Titus 2:13-14, Romans 5:12-21, Hebrews 2:14, John 11:25-27, John 4:25-26, 1 John 2:1-2, John 21:14.

[CONTINTUED ON THE NEXT PAGE]

---

[1] Chambers, O. (1993, c1935). *My Utmost for His Highest: Selections for the year* (September 9). Grand Rapids, MI: Discovery House Publishers.

[2] Generally but not exclusively from: MacArthur, J. (1994). *Reckless faith: When the church loses its will to discern* (102). Wheaton, Ill.: Crossway Books.

- **A Person is Saved from Eternal Damnation by God's Grace Through Faith in Jesus Christ and His Sacrificial Payment for Sin by His Death on The Cross (and nothing else):** One is not saved by works of righteousness, being a good person, or attempted obedience to the Law: Ephesians 2:8-10, Galatians 2:16 - 3:8, Romans 4:4-5, Romans 3:27-31, 5:11-21, Acts 10:43, Titus 2:13-14, John 3:15-18.
- **The Lordship of Christ:** Romans 10:9: *"that if you confess with your mouth Jesus as Lord, and believe in your heart that God raised Him from the dead, you will be saved;"* John 13:13: *"You call Me Teacher and Lord; and you are right, for so I am."* See also Philippians 2:8-11, 1 Corinthians 16:22-23, Romans 14:9, Acts 16:31, 1 Corinthians 12:3, Acts 2:21 and 36, Acts 1:21, Matthew 12:8, Matthew 22:37, Isaiah 45:23, Romans 14:11.
- **The Return of Christ:** Second Coming: John 14:1-3, Matthew 26:64, Luke 12:40, Matthew 24:27 and 42-51, Mark 14:62, John 21:21-23, Mark 13:26.
- **The Eternal Damnation in Hell for the Unsaved:** John 15:6, Revelation 20:10-15, Revelation 21:8, John 3:18, 1 Corinthians 6:9-11, 2 Thessalonians 1:8-9, John 5:22, Mark 9:43-48,.
- **Eternal Reign Of Christ in Heaven and Eternal Life for those He Redeemed:** John 14:1-3, Matthew 19:28-29, Matthew 25:46, John 3:15-16, Revelation 4:5-11, 1 John 5:20, Jude v.21, 1 Peter 4:11, 1 John 1:2-4, Titus 2:13-14.

WHAT MUST ONE BELIEVE TO BE SAVED FROM ETERNAL JUDGMENT?

Jesus states in the Bible that every single person is guilty of sin, which is punished by receiving *eternal judgment in the fires of hell.* Jesus preached that the only way to escape from hell is to *"repent and believe in the gospel."* **Mark 1:15**.
- To **REPENT** means to turn from your sins and forsake them by the power of God.
- To **BELIEVE THE GOSPEL** means that one who is "born again" by the Spirit of God (John 3:3-8) will:
  - Believe in Jesus Christ as Almighty God, who is without sin;
  - Believe in Jesus' sacrificial death on the cross as the only and complete payment for your sins;
  - Believe in Jesus' bodily resurrection from the dead on the third day;
  - Believe in Jesus as Lord over all things and confesses this fact to others.

It is that straightforward. It has nothing to do with your righteousness, good works or engaging in a religious ceremony or cleaning yourself up first to win God's acceptance. If you reject God's loving gift of forgiveness in Jesus Christ, you remain a guilty sinner waiting to be punished in eternal hell. The Bible says in **John 3:36:** *"He who believes in the Son has eternal life; but he who does not obey the Son will not see life, but the wrath of God abides on him."* Repent and believe the gospel TODAY, before it is too late!

---

* Fundamental doctrines are those that are essential to one making a claim to true Biblical Christianity. What are the fundamentals of the faith? Most restrict the list of fundamental doctrines to those that relate to the issue of salvation alone (soteriological—the theological doctrine of salvation in Christianity). "Historically, fundamentalism has been used to identify one holding to the five fundamentals of the faith adopted by the General Assembly of the Presbyterian Church in the U.S.A. in 1910. The five fundamentals were the miracles of Christ, the virgin birth of Christ, the substitutionary atonement of Christ, the bodily resurrection of Christ, and the inspiration of Scripture. Fundamentalism has stood for the historic fundamentals of Christianity, particularly as developed in *The Fundamentals*. These were initially issued as twelve booklets edited by R. A. Torrey and A. C. Dixon." Enns, P. P. (1997, c1989)." *The Moody Handbook of Theology* (613). Chicago, Ill.: Moody Press. The reason for limiting it to the doctrine of salvation is due to the awesome and wonderful simplicity to becoming a true Christian! **Romans 10:9** *"...that if you confess with your mouth Jesus as Lord, and believe in your heart that God raised Him from the dead, you will be saved;...."*

CONTENTS

TOPICS OF INTEREST

This is a topical index of *some* issues addressed in the Gospel of Matthew.
The page number (p.) indicates where the topic discussion begins.

Adultery: Matt. 5:27-32 (p. 101).

Apocrypha: See a footnote in Matt. 22:33 that discusses "Purgatory" because at the end of that footnote on Purgatory is a discussion regarding the *"Apocrypha."* (p. 449).

Apostasy: Judas (The Betrayer) (p.182): See *Apostasy* section in Matt. 10:2-4 (p.182) and 10:21-22 (p. 196). *End-Times Apostasy* - Matt. 24:9-10 (p.503). *Denial of Jesus:* Matt. 10:33 (p.208).

Apostles Creed: See comments in Summary and Application after Matt. 27:65-66 (p.661).

Are You A Good Enough Person To Go To Heaven? Matt. 5:17-20 (p.93).

Baptism: Read Summary and Application after Matt. 3:17 (p.64).

Beatitudes: Matt. 5:1-12 (p.80).

Bible Translations and Paraphrases: See footnote in Summary and Application after Matt. 4:8-11 (p.74).

Blasphemy Against The Holy Spirit: Matt. 12:30-32 (p.233) (May want to start at Matt. 12:22-32.) (p.232).

Burial of Jesus: Matt. 27:57-61 (p.653).

Children: Matt. 18:1-11 (p.353).

Christmas Story: Matt. 2:1-12 (p.36); *(Is Dec. 25 Christ's Earthly Birthday?* See footnote on p.36)

Church Discipline: Matt. 18:15-17 (p.361).

Civil Disobedience: Read Summary and Application after Matt. 22:22 (p.438).

Communion: Matt. 26:20-30 (p. 572).

Crucifixion of Jesus *(PART 1,* Matt. 27:32-37) (p.625); *(PART 2,* Matt. 27:38-44) (p.630); *(PART 3,* Matt. 27:45-50) (p.636); *(PART 4,* Matt. 27:51) (p.640); *(PART 5,* Matt. 27:52-56) (p.648).

Death: *What happens the moment you die?* See the section at the end of Matt. 22:33 titled "Doctrine of the Bodily Resurrection of Christ and the Saints." (p.446).

Decision-Making: Matt. 27:20-21. (p.616); *(God's Will:* – See verses in the footnote at the end of Matt. 6:7-8.) (p.121); *(Decision making using the 100 - Year Rule)* Matt 27:20-21.) (p.616).

Deity of Jesus Christ: See footnote in Matt. 1:19-23 and at the end of Matt. 13:31-32. (p.34).

Demon: See also *Satan cast out:* Matt. 8:28-34 (p.157).

Demonic Possession: Matt. 12:43-45 (p.243) and Matt. 8:28-34 (p.157) (See also **Devil.**)

Denial of Jesus: Matt. 10:33 (p.208); (See also **Apostasy.**)

Devil: Tempter – Matt. 4:1-11 (p.66). (See also **Demon.**)

Discipleship: Matt. 8:18-22 (p.154). *Harvest is plentiful, but the workers are few,* Matt. 9:35-38 (p.176). **Missionary Conduct** – Matt. 10:7-15 (p.189). *Take Up Your Cross,* Matt 10:38-39 (p.210). *Take up his cross, and follow Me,* Matt. 16:24-25 (p.330).

Discipline (in the church): Matt. 18:15-17 (p.361).

Divorce and Remarriage: See Matt. 5:27-32 (p.101) and 19:1-12 (p.371).

Education: See Summary and Application at the end of Matthew 19:23-24 (p.389). Note the footnote by Hodge (p.390). See also the Footnote comment in Matthew 4:8-11 (p.71.)

Election and Pre-Destination: (See footnote in Matt. 25:34-40) (p.547).

End Times: Good mini-outline in the Summary and Application section just after Matt. 25:41-46 (p.556). See also: *Signs of the End,* Matt. 24:3-14 (p.499). **Second Coming of Christ**, Matt. 24:15-22 (p.509), 24:23-28 (p.514), 24:29-31 (p.520). *Stay Alert As You Look For The Lord's Return,* Matt. 24:42-51 (p.530).

Enduring to the End *(i.e. Perseverance of the Saints)*: Matt. 10:21-22 (p.196) and Matt 24:12-13 (p.505).

Enemy: *(How are you to respond to your enemy?* Matt. 5:43-48.) (p.111).

Evangelism: Matt. 5:17-20 (p.92). (Must see Summary and Application at the end of Matt. 5:20) (p.97). See also **Great Commission**, Matt. 28:18-20 (p. 685). *See the story of Missionary John Paton in* Matt. 10:38-39 (p.211).

Eye For An Eye, And A Tooth For A Tooth: Matt 5:38-40 (p.108).

Faith: *Centurion's servant,* Matt. 8:5-13 (p.148). *Lack of faith* Matt. 17:19-21 (p.346). *" You say to this mountain,"* Matt. 21:20-22 (p.420).

False Prophets / False Converts: Matt 7:15-20 (p.140). *Lord-Lord,* Matt. 7:21-23 (p.143). *House built on the sand or rock,* Matt. 7:24-27 (p.144). *Do not persevere to the end:* Matt. 10:21-22 (p.196). Matt. 12:33-35 (p.237). *False Teachers,* Matt. 16:5-12 (p 316). *Eight Woes Addressed To The Pharisees / Hypocrites:* Matt 23:13-36 (p.472). Matt. 24:23-25 (p.514).

Family Divisions (Loyalty to Christ): Matt. 10:34-37 (p.209). *Who are Jesus' mother and brothers,* Matt. 12:46-50 (p.244).

Fasting: Matt. 6:16-18 (p.123).

Fear and Anxiousness Matt. 6:25-34 (p.129)

Feeding of the 4000: Matt 15:32-39 (p.310).

Feeding of the 5000: Matt. 14:13-21 (p.291).

Food: Matt. 15:15-20 (p.302).

Forgiveness: *Forgiveness of Sins by Jesus*, Matt 9:1-8 (p.161). *Forgiving others*: Matt.18:21-22 (p.366). See *The king who wished to settle accounts*, Matt. 18:23-35 (p.368).

Fruit-Bearing: Matt. 7:15-20 (p.140); Matt. 12:33-35 (p.237). See also **Sower and the Seed**, Matt. 13:1-23 (p.249).

Fundamental Doctrines: After the "Preface." See also Matt. 13:31-32 (p.273).

Giving: Matt. 6:1-4 (p.114) and Matt. 5:42 (p.111).

Government: *Execute justice* Matt. 5:38-40 p.108). (See also **Taxes** and **Civil Disobedience**).

Great Commission: Matt. 28:18-20 (p.685).

Greatest Commandment: Matt. 22:34-40 (p.457).

Healing (See also Miracles): Matt. 8:1-17 (p.147). (See also concepts regarding healing-at Summary and Application after Matt. 8:14-17.) (p.151).

Heart Attitude (not just external actions): Matt. 5:21-32 (p.100).

Heavenly Body: *New body upon resurrection:* Matt. 27:52-53 (p.648).

Hell: Matt. 13:24-30 – *description of hell* (p.266). See also **Purgatory**: - See more on the false doctrine of Purgatory at the end of Matt. 22:33 (p.447); see the footnote there also on the subject (p.447).

Herod: Matt. 2:3-8 (p.39). See footnotes there also (p.40).

JESUS:
> *Arrest of Jesus:* Matt. 26:47-56 (p.588).
> *Beatitudes:* Matt 5:1-12 (p.80).
> *Christ, Son of the Living God:* Matt. 16:15-18 (p.321).
> *Cleansing the Temple:* Matt. 21:12-17 (p.412).
> *Crucifixion of Jesus* (PART 1, Matt. 27:32-37) (p.625); (PART 2, Matt. 27:38-44) (p.630); (PART 3, Matt. 27:45-50) (p.636); (PART 4, Matt. 27:51) (p.640); (PART 5, Matt. 27:52-56) (p.648).
> *Cursing the fig tree:* Matt. 21:18-22 (p.419).
> *Divinity of Christ:* Matt. 11:27 (p.223); See footnote in Matt. 1:19-23 (p.34) and at end of Matt 13:31-32 (p. 273).
> *Feeding of the 4000:* Matt 15:32-39 (p. 310).
> *Feeding of the 5000:* Matt. 14:13-21 (p.291).

Mary: *Mary is not a co-redemptrix or co-mediator* (see footnote in Matt. 1:2-17) (p.28). See also **Virgin birth** Matt. 1:18 (p.30). *Jesus explains the spiritual family*, Matt. 12:46-50 (p.244).

Mercy: Matt. 5:7 (p.85).

Missionary Conduct: Matt 10:7-15.
- *Missionary Story - John Paton*, Matt. 10:38-39 (p.211).
- *Missionary Story - William Borden*, Matt. 19:21-22 (p.385).
- See also: **Great Commission,** Matt. 28:18-20 (p.685).

Money: Matt. 6:19-34 (p.126); 13:22 (p.258); and 19:21-22 (p.383).

Narrow Way: Matt. 7:13-14 (p.140).

Oaths/Promises: Matt 5:33-37 (p.106); Matt. 23:16-22 (p.475).

Oneness Theology: *(Re: heresies of Oneness theology*, Matt 28:19, and see footnote there) (p.697).

One Hundred Year Rule: *(Decision making using the 100 - Year Rule)* Matt 27:20-21 (p.616).

Parables: See *Parable* sections under **JESUS.**

Paradoxical Commandments: Matthew 10:29-31 (See Summary and Application.) (p.202).

Peacemakers: Matt 5:9 (p.87).

Persecution: Matt. 5:10-12 (p.88) and 10:16-23 (p.192); 10:24-31 (p.199).

Perseverance of the Saints: Matt. 10:21-22 (p.196) and Matt. 24:12-13 (p.505).

Peter's Denial: Matt. 26:69-75 (p.602).

Pharisees and Sadducees: Matt. 3:7 p.55).

Polygamy: Matt. 19:4-6 (see footnote there) (p.373).

Pope: Is Peter the first Pope? – No: Matt 16:15-18 (p.321).

Pornography: See **Adultery**

Prayer: Matt. 6:5-18 (p.117) (see several verses on prayer at the end of the Summary and Application for this section) (p.125). See also **Lord's Prayer**: Matt. 6:9-15 (p.122). *Pray only to God*: Matt. 6:9-15 (p.122). **Fasting** Matt. 6:16-18 (p.123). *Assurance of answered prayer*: Matt 7:7-12 (p.139)..

Predestination: (See footnote in Matt 25:34-40.) (p.547).

Pride: Matt. 5:3 (p.81).

Purgatory: See more on this false doctrine at the end of Matt. 22:33. See footnote on (p.447).

Remarriage: Matt. 19:1-12 (p.371) and 5:27-32 (p.101).

Repentance: Matt. 3:1-3 (p.47) and Matt. 4:17 (p.76).

Resurrection: *The doctrine of the resurrection;* Matt. 22:23-33 (p.446). *New Body upon resurrection:* Matt. 27:52-53 (p.648). See *Chronology of Resurrections* (p.451).

Revenge: Matt 5:38-40 (p.108).

Rewards: *To the believer:* 19:27-30 (p.392), 10:40-42 (p.212) and Matt. 16:27 (p.332), *Parable of the Talents – reward of faithful service:* Matt. 25:14-30 (p.538).

Riches: See Money.

Righteousness: Matt. 5:6 (p.84).

Sabbath: Matt. 12:1-14 (p.225).

Sadducees and Pharisees: Matt. 3:7 (p.55).

Salt and Light: Matt. 5:13-16 (p.91).

Satan: See **Devil.**

Second Coming of Christ: *(Second Coming of Christ:* Matt. 24:15-22 - 24:29-31) (p.509) Good mini outline at the Summary and Application section just after Matt. 25:41-46 (p.556).

Seeker Sensitive: See footnote at Matt. 19:21-22 (p.383).

Seeking the Lost: Matt 18:12-14 (p.360).

Sermon on the Mount: Matt. Ch. 5-7 (p.80).

Sickness: Concepts re: sickness/healing: see Summary and Application after Matt. 8:14-17 (p.151).

Sign-Seekers: Matt. 12:38-40 (p.240) and Matt. 16:1-12 (p.313).

Sorrow: *"Blessed are those who mourn:"* Matt 5:4 (p.83).

Sower and the Seed: Matt. 13:1-23 (p.249).

Speech: Matt. 12:36-37 (p.240) and Matt. 15:10-11 (p.301).

Substitutionary Death of Christ: Matt. 27:50 (p.637) and Summary and Application for that section. (p.639). Must also see Matt. 27:51 (p.640.)

Talents: *Reward of faithful service:* Matt. 25:14-30 (p.538).

Taxes: Matt. 22:15-22 (p.435); Matt. 17:24-27 (p.350).

Telling the Truth: Matt 12:34-35 (p.238).

Temples: *History of the Temples:* Matt. 24:1-2 (p.492).

Temptation: Matt. 4: 1-11 (p.66).

Thieves on the Cross with Jesus: Matt. 27:38-44 (p.630).

Three Days and Three Nights: Matt 12:38-40 (p.240).

Tithing: Matt 23:23 (p.477).

Transubstantiation: (Read footnote *Hodge on Transubstantiations,* located in Matt. 26:26-29) (p.576).

Trinity: Matt. 14:32-33 (p.297). (*Heresies of Oneness Theology,* Matt. 28:19, see footnote there) (p.697).

Twelve Disciples/Apostles: Matt. 10:1-4 (p.180).

The Law: See **Law**

U.S. Supreme Court Case: Matt. 5:17-20 see section on UNITED STATES v. GEORGE WILSON. (p.95).

Veil Is Torn in the Temple: Matt. 27:51 (p.640).

Virgin Birth: Matt. 1:18 (p.30).

Vows/Promises: Matt. 5:33-37 (p.106) and Matt. 23:16-22 (p.475).

Will of God: (See verses in the footnote at the end of Matt. 6:7-8 section) (p.121). *(Decision making using the 100 - Year Rule)* Matt 27:20-21 (p.616).

Wise Men: See **Christmas Story.**

Woes Addressed to the Pharisees / Hypocrites: Matt. 23:13-36 (p.472).

Women / Motherhood: See comments in Matt. 18:5-6 (p.357).

Worry / Fear: Matt. 6:25-34 (p.129).

Worship: Matt. 15:29-31 (p.308-309).

End of Topics of Interest

Please read the Preface.

Two matters to always remember as you study:

Nothing else matters but THE KING and HIS KINGDOM.
(cf. Matthew. 13:44-46)

and

Apart from Jesus Christ, you can do nothing.
(cf. John 15:5)

One last matter addressing all that Jesus taught:
"If you know these things, you are blessed if you do them."
(John 13:17 - see context John 13:10-20)

INTRODUCTION ON THE GOSPEL OF MATTHEW

"Say to the daughter of Zion,
'Behold your King is coming to you,
Gentle, and mounted on a donkey,
Even on a colt, the foal of a beast of burden.'"[3]
Matthew 21:5

The theme of the Gospel of Matthew is Christ the King. It was written to the Jews. Often Matthew quotes from the Old Testament showing how Jesus fulfills specific prophesies referring to the Messiah.

To start our examination of this Gospel we need to review some of the historical background. Matthew, an apostle of Christ, is the author of this Gospel.[4] Many conservative theologians believe that this Gospel was written somewhere in the 50's or 60's AD. This view is bolstered, in part, by the fact that Matthew contains no mention of the destruction of the Temple in Jerusalem, which occurred in 70 AD.

The book is one of the four Gospels. The term gospel means *good news*! What is this good news? The good news is that a sinner, destined to judgment, can be saved from eternal damnation by the grace of God through faith in the sacrificial work of Jesus Christ on the cross. Some commentators believe that each of the four gospels demonstrates the person of Jesus in a different way. Matthew show Jesus as King. Mark manifests Him as a Servant who sacrificed Himself for mankind. Luke proves Jesus is the Perfect Man. John reveals Jesus as the Divine Son of God. The first three New Testament books (Matthew, Mark and Luke) are referred to as the Synoptic Gospels. Synoptic comes from a Greek term that in essence means *view together*. When you examine Matthew in comparison to the other gospels, "Out of a total of 1071 verses, Matthew has 387 in common with Mark and Luke, 130 with Mark, 184 with Luke; only 387 being peculiar to itself." [5]

So what is the background of this person Matthew? He also went by the name Levi, and was a *publican* (i.e. a Jewish tax collector who worked for the Roman Empire.) Publicans were deeply despised by their fellow Jews. One must realize that during this time period the Jews were under Roman control and thus subject to Rome's taxes. Publicans were viewed as traitors because they made money for themselves by helping Rome tax fellow Jews. John MacArthur explains the tax system as follows:

---

[3] *The New American Standard Bible®*, Copyright 1960,1962, 1963, 1968, 1971, 1972, 1973, 1975, 1977, 1995 La Habra, CA: The Lockman Foundation. Most verses are cited from the 1977 edition with some verses from the 1995 update]. Biblical verses cited, with permission, are from the New American Standard Bible unless designated otherwise.

[4] Many early church fathers cited Matthew as its author, including Pseudo Barnabas, Clement of Rome, Polycarp, Justin Martyr, Clement of Alexandria, Tertullian, and Origen.
Walvoord, John F., and Zuck, Roy B., *The Bible Knowledge Commentary*. (Wheaton, Illinois: Scripture Press Publications, Inc.) 1983, 1985, [Online] Available: Logos Library System.

[5] Easton. *Eastons Bible Dictionary* (electronic ed.).

"Roman senators and various other high-ranking officials would buy from the central government at public auction the right of collecting the toll taxes in a given country, province, or region at a fixed rate for a period of five years. Whatever was collected above that amount was kept as profit. Those who held such taxing rights were called publicani. The publicani would hire others, usually citizens of the country being taxed, to do the actual collecting.

Those collectors had somewhat the same arrangement with the publicani that the publicani had with Rome. Whatever they managed to collect above the amount demanded by the publicani they kept as their own profit. Both the publicani and the tax-gatherers, therefore, had strong motivation to exact and collect as much tax as possible knowing they were backed by the full authority, including the military authority, of Rome. The tax-gatherers quite naturally were hated by their own people, not only as extortioners but as traitors. In Israel they were ranked with the lowest of human society—sinners, prostitutes, and Gentiles (Matt. 9:10-11; 18:17; 21:31-32; Mark 2:15-16; Luke 5:30; etc.)."[6]

Matthew describes in his Gospel how Jesus called him out of his corrupt tax-collecting life to one of discipleship:

Matthew 9:9-13: *"⁹ As Jesus went on from there, He saw a man called Matthew, sitting in the tax collector's booth; and He said to him, 'Follow Me!' And he got up and followed Him. ¹⁰ Then it happened that as Jesus was reclining at the table in the house, behold, many tax collectors and sinners came and were dining with Jesus and His disciples. ¹¹ When the Pharisees saw this, they said to His disciples, 'Why is your Teacher eating with the tax collectors and sinners?' ¹² But when Jesus heard this, He said, 'It is not those who are healthy who need a physician, but those who are sick. ¹³ But go and learn what this means: 'I desire compassion, and not sacrifice,' for I did not come to call the righteous, but sinners.'"*

From Luke's Gospel we find out that when Matthew (Levi) was called by Jesus, he, *"left everything behind, and rose and began to follow Him." Luke 5:28.* We also find out in Luke 5:29 that it was Matthew himself who hosted the big dinner in which, *"many tax-gatherers and sinners came and were dining with Jesus and His disciples." Matthew 9:10* (cf. Luke 5:27-32).

Summary and Application

The book of Matthew sets forth the Good News of salvation and forgiveness in Jesus Christ! Matthew, the person, serves as living proof of God's power to transform a corrupt man. As we read of his conversion in Matthew 9:9-13, it is clear that he recognized himself as a sinner before a Holy God. This is what every person who comes to Christ must understand. When Matthew ate in the presence of Jesus, he lumped himself in as a member of this group of sinners when he stated in verse 10, *"behold many tax-gatherers and sinners came and were dining with Jesus and His disciples."*

---

[6] MacArthur, John F., *The MacArthur New Testament Commentary*, Introduction (Chicago: Moody Press) 1985, Logos Library System.

Even if one has been saved for years, it is still healthy for that person to reflect on the state he was in prior to God's forgiveness and transformation. An example of this is in Matthew 10:2-4. In that section Matthew lists the apostles. When he names himself in v.3, he adds a little description:

> **Matthew 10:2-4:** *"Now the names of the twelve apostles are these: The first, Simon, who is called Peter, and Andrew his brother; and James the son of Zebedee, and John his brother;* [3] *Philip and Bartholomew; Thomas and Matthew the tax-gatherer; James the son of Alphaeus, and Thaddaeus;* [4] *Simon the Zealot, and Judas Iscariot, the one who betrayed Him."*

Even though Matthew had repented of the corrupt world of tax collecting decades before writing his Gospel, he mentions that he was, *"the tax-gatherer."* He never forgets that he is a sinner saved by the grace of God. We would do well to remember the same. We must look upon the unsaved with compassion and prayer rather than self-righteous judgment (cf. Titus 3:3-7, 1 Cor. 6:9-11). By remembering our constant need of grace we will be more effective servants of Almighty God and evangelists of the Gospel. We must realize that dedicated service to Christ is what God expects of all who name themselves *Christian.* Jesus instructs us regarding what our attitude should be when serving Him:

> **Luke 17:10:** *"So you too, when you do all the things which are commanded you, say, 'We are unworthy slaves; we have done only that which we ought to have done.'"*

J.C. Ryle summarized this concept when he stated that:

> "Sinners we are in the day we first come to Christ. Poor needy sinners we continue to be so long as we live…. We shall find ourselves sinners in the hour of our death, and shall die as much indebted to Christ's blood as on the day when we first believed."[7]

---

[7] Ryle, J.C., *Matthew (Expository Thoughts on the Gospels),* (Crossways Classic Commentaries: v.1) p.65.

MATTHEW 1:1-17
(THE GENEALOGY OF JESUS THROUGH JOSEPH)

"THE book of the genealogy of Jesus Christ, the son of David, the son of Abraham.

² To Abraham was born Isaac; and to Isaac, Jacob; and to Jacob, Judah and his brothers; ³ and to Judah were born Perez and Zerah by Tamar; and to Perez was born Hezron; and to Hezron, Ram; ⁴ and to Ram was born Amminadab; and to Amminadab, Nahshon; and to Nahshon, Salmon; ⁵ and to Salmon was born Boaz by Rahab; and to Boaz was born Obed by Ruth; and to Obed, Jesse; ⁶ and to Jesse was born David the king. And to David was born Solomon by her who had been the wife of Uriah;

⁷ and to Solomon was born Rehoboam; and to Rehoboam, Abijah; and to Abijah, Asa; ⁸ and to Asa was born Jehoshaphat; and to Jehoshaphat, Joram; and to Joram, Uzziah; ⁹ and to Uzziah was born Jotham; and to Jotham, Ahaz; and to Ahaz, Hezekiah; ¹⁰ and to Hezekiah was born Manasseh; and to Manasseh, Amon; and to Amon, Josiah; ¹¹ and to Josiah were born Jeconiah and his brothers, at the time of the deportation to Babylon.

¹² And after the deportation to Babylon, to Jeconiah was born Shealtiel; and to Shealtiel, Zerubbabel; ¹³ and to Zerubbabel was born Abihud; and to Abihud, Eliakim; and to Eliakim, Azor; ¹⁴ and to Azor was born Zadok; and to Zadok, Achim; and to Achim, Eliud; ¹⁵ and to Eliud was born Eleazar; and to Eleazar, Matthan; and to Matthan, Jacob; ¹⁶ and to Jacob was born Joseph the husband of Mary, by whom was born Jesus, who is called Christ.

¹⁷ Therefore all the generations from Abraham to David are fourteen generations; and from David to the deportation to Babylon fourteen generations; and from the deportation to Babylon to the time of Christ fourteen generations."

Introduction

This section sets out the lineage of Christ through His earthly father, Joseph. Often when I see genealogies in the Bible, my eyes start to glaze over and I begin skimming over the names (many of which I cannot even pronounce!). The reality is that God has an important truth for me to learn if I study the genealogical text.

As mentioned previously, Matthew was written to the Jews. The Jews knew the prophesies regarding the Messiah. Part of prophesies dealt with the lineage from which the Messiah would come. If Jesus did not fulfill those prophesies it would exclude Him from a claim to be the Messiah.

VERSE 1: *"THE book of the genealogy of Jesus Christ, the son of David, the son of Abraham."*

As mentioned above, in the Gospel of Matthew the genealogy of Jesus is set out through His earthly father Joseph. Jesus is introduced as, *"the son of David, the son of Abraham."* The importance of this statement is to demonstrate Jesus' fulfilling the scriptural mandate of God's promises both to David and Abraham. Scripture prophesied several centuries before Christ's birth that the Messiah would be a descendent of David:

> **Isaiah 9:6–7:** *⁶For a child will be born to us, a son will be given to us; And the government will rest on His shoulders; And His name will be called Wonderful Counselor, Mighty God, Eternal Father, Prince of Peace. ⁷There will be no end to the increase of His government or of peace, on*

the throne of David and over his kingdom, to establish it and to uphold it with justice and righteousness from then on and forevermore. The zeal of the Lord of hosts will accomplish this.

This prophesy of being a descendant of David was fulfilled in **Luke 2:4:** *"And Joseph also went up from Galilee, from the city of Nazareth, to Judea, to the city of David, which is called Bethlehem, because he was of the house and family of David,..."*

Jesus also fulfilled the great promise to Abraham that his descendant would be one to whom, *"all the families of the earth will be blessed."*

> <u>Genesis 12:1–3:</u>
>
> *¹Now the Lord said to Abram,*
> *"Go forth from your country,*
> *And from your relatives*
> *And from your father's house,*
> *To the land which I will show you;*
> *²And I will make you a great nation,*
> *And I will bless you,*
> *And make your name great;*
> *And so you shall be a blessing;*
> *³And I will bless those who bless you,*
> *And the one who curses you I will curse.*
> *And in you all the families of the earth will be blessed."*

Joseph is Jesus' "legal" father but His actual father is God the Father. (See **Luke 3:23:** *"...Jesus Himself was about thirty years of age, <u>being supposedly the son of Joseph</u>,"*). The Gospel of Luke sets out Jesus' genealogy through Mary (see Luke 3:23-38). It should be remembered that since the destruction of the Temple of Jerusalem in 70 AD, there no longer exist complete, documented genealogies that can trace a living Jew to a specific tribe of Israel. Jews who state that they are waiting for the Messiah have an insurmountable verification problem for their supposed future messiah. Anyone claiming to be the Messiah after 70 AD cannot be verified to have come through the lineage of King David. Jesus is the one and only Messiah for Israel and the world. He alone fulfills all the prophetic requirements.[8]

---

[8] John MacArthur states that, "Jesus was therefore the blood descendant of David through Mary and the legal descendant of David through Joseph. Genealogically, Jesus was perfectly qualified to take the throne of David. It is essential to note that in His virgin birth Jesus not only was divinely conceived but through that miracle was protected from regal disqualification because of Joseph's being a descendant of **Jeconiah** (v. 12). Because of that king's wickedness, God had declared of Jeconiah (also called Jehoiachin or Coniah) that, though he was in David's line, "no man of his descendants will prosper, sitting on the throne of David or ruling again in Judah" (Jeramiah 22:30). That curse would have precluded Jesus' right to kingship had He been the natural son of Joseph, who was in Jeconiah's line. Jesus' legal descent from David, which was always traced through the father, came through Jeconiah to Joseph. But His blood descent, and His human right to rule, came through Mary, who was not in Jeconiah's lineage. Thus the curse on Jeconiah's offspring was circumvented, while still maintaining the royal privilege." MacArthur, John F., *The MacArthur New Testament Commentary*, p.3 (Chicago: Moody Press) 1985.
[Note continued on the next page].

The name **Jesus** is not merely a name chosen by Mary. It is the name the Angel told her to call the child: **Matthew 1:21:** *"And she will bear a Son; and you shall call His name Jesus, for it is He who will save His people from their sins."* The Greek equivalent of "Jeshua, or Jehoshua" means "Jehovah (Yahweh) saves."[9] The term "Christ" is a Greek word which translates to Hebrew as "Messiah," which means "Anointed One." *"Son of David"* is a term used for the Messiah (i.e. a messianic title). Some of the people understood that He was The Messiah:

> **Matthew 9:27-30:** *"And as Jesus passed on from there, two blind men followed Him, crying out, and saying, 'Have mercy on us, Son of David!'* [28] *And after He had come into the house, the blind men came up to Him, and Jesus *said to them, 'Do you believe that I am able to do this?' They *said to Him, 'Yes, Lord.'* [29] *Then He touched their eyes, saying, 'Be it done to you according to your faith.'* [30] *And their eyes were opened...."*
> (See also Matthew 15:22, Matthew 20:30.)

> **Matthew 21:9:** *"And the multitudes going before Him, and those who followed after were crying out, saying,*
> *"...'Hosanna to the Son of David;*
> *Blessed is He who comes in the*
> *name of the Lord;*
> *Hosanna in the highest!'"*

VERSES 2-17: *"To Abraham was born Isaac; and to Isaac, Jacob; and to Jacob, Judah and his brothers;* [3] *and to Judah were born Perez and Zerah by Tamar; and to Perez was born Hezron; and to Hezron, Ram;* [4] *and to Ram was born Amminadab; and to Amminadab, Nahshon; and to Nahshon, Salmon;* [5] *and to Salmon was born Boaz by Rahab; and to Boaz was born Obed by Ruth; and to Obed, Jesse;* [6] *and to Jesse was born David the king. And to David was born Solomon by her who had been the wife of Uriah;* [7] *and to Solomon was born Rehoboam; and to Rehoboam, Abijah; and to Abijah, Asa;* [8] *and to Asa was born Jehoshaphat; and to Jehoshaphat, Joram; and to Joram, Uzziah;* [9] *and to Uzziah was born Jotham; and to Jotham, Ahaz; and to Ahaz, Hezekiah;* [10] *and to Hezekiah was born Manasseh; and to Manasseh, Amon; and to Amon, Josiah;* [11] *and to Josiah were born Jeconiah and his brothers, at the time of the deportation to Babylon.* [12] *And after the deportation to Babylon, to Jeconiah was born Shealtiel; and to Shealtiel, Zerubbabel;* [13] *and to Zerubbabel was born Abihud; and to Abihud, Eliakim; and to Eliakim, Azor;* [14] *and to Azor was born Zadok; and to Zadok, Achim; and to Achim, Eliud;* [15] *and to Eliud was born Eleazar; and to Eleazar, Matthan; and to Matthan, Jacob;* [16] *and to Jacob was born Joseph the husband of Mary, by*

[Note continued]

The Bible Knowledge Commentary explains this also: Matthew gave Jesus' lineage through His legal father, **Joseph** (v. 16). Thus this genealogy traced Jesus' right to the throne of **David**, which must come through **Solomon** and his descendants (v. 6). Of particular interest is the inclusion of **Jeconiah** (v. 11) of whom Jeremiah said, "Record this man as if childless" (Jer. 22:30). Jeremiah's prophecy related to the actual occupation of the throne and the reception of blessing while on the throne. Though Jeconiah's sons never occupied the throne, the line of rulership did pass through them. If Jesus had been a *physical* descendant of Jeconiah, He would not have been able to occupy David's throne. Luke's genealogy made it clear that Jesus was a physical descendant of David through another son named Nathan (Luke 3:31). But Joseph, a descendant of Solomon, was Jesus' *legal* father, so Jesus' right to the throne was traced through Joseph. Walvoord, J. F., Zuck, R. B., and Dallas Theological Seminary. (1983-). *The Bible Knowledge Commentary: An Exposition of the Scriptures* (Matt. 1:2–17) Vol. 2, p.18, Wheaton, IL: Victor Books.

[9] Ibid

whom was born Jesus, who is called Christ. [17] *Therefore all the generations from Abraham to David are fourteen generations; and from David to the deportation to Babylon fourteen generations; and from the deportation to Babylon to the time of Christ fourteen generations."*

These verses mention five women.

1) In verse 3 we read of Tamar. Her story is very scandalous. She disguised her identity and fooled her father-in-law Judah into thinking she was a prostitute. Incest was then committed resulting in the birth of Perez and Zerah (Genesis 38:6-30).

2) In verse 5 is Rahab. She was a harlot from Jericho (Joshua 2). Through faith in God she hid the two Israeli spies from the King of Jericho. Her faith in God is mentioned in **Hebrews 11:31:** *"By faith Rahab the harlot did not perish along with those who were disobedient, after she had welcomed the spies in peace..."*

3) Also in verse 5 is Ruth. Ruth was not a Jew but a Moabitess. Her story of repentance and becoming a follower of the One true God is set out in the Book of Ruth (see Ruth 1:3-22.)

4) In verse 6 we read a reference to Bathsheba. She committed adultery with King David. Later they were married and she gave birth to Solomon (2 Samuel 11). Her unsavory conduct is touched on in verse 6 as she is identified as, *"her who had been the wife of Uriah;...."*

5) In verse 16 Mary, the mother of Jesus is mentioned. Mary was a wonderful godly woman. With that said, it is unbiblical to claim she is divine or acts as co-redemptrix or co-mediator with Christ as some in the Roman church have claimed. If she were perfectly divine and without sin why would she need a savior? Mary herself declared her need for a Savior when she said in **Luke 1:46-47:** *"And Mary said: 'My soul exalts the Lord,* [47] *And my spirit has rejoiced in God my Savior'...."* [10]

---

[10] Concepts of Mary as co-redemptrix or as a co-mediator are contrary to scripture and thus heretical. They came into the church hundreds of years after Christ and have at their inception the mystery religions of the Babylonian's. Id. Please note the exact quote from the official Roman Catholic Catechism regarding Mary as co-redemptrix or as a co-mediator in 968 and 969:

968 Her role in relation to the Church and to all humanity goes still further. "In a wholly singular way she cooperated by her obedience, faith, hope, and burning charity in the Savior's work of restoring supernatural life to souls. For this reason she is a mother to us in the order of grace."

969 "This motherhood of Mary in the order of grace continues uninterruptedly from the consent which she loyally gave at the Annunciation and which she sustained without wavering beneath the cross, until the eternal fulfillment of all the elect. Taken up to heaven she did not lay aside this saving office but by her manifold intercession continues to bring us the gifts of eternal salvation . . . . Therefore the Blessed Virgin is invoked in the Church under the titles of Advocate, Helper, Benefactress, and Mediatrix."

[Note continued on the next page.]

Summary and Application

God made a promise to Abraham that the world's Messiah would come through his line in **Genesis 12:3:** *"...And in you all the families of the earth shall be blessed."* God promised to bring up the Savior from the family of David. J.C. Ryle states that these first 16 verses, *"prove that Jesus was the Son of David and the Son of Abraham, and that God's promise was fulfilled."* [11]

The application of this lesson to our life is that God will fulfill every promise He makes in His Word. We must also understand that *no one is so lost that he cannot be transformed by Christ.* Rahab, who was a harlot in Jericho, was lost in her sin like every other person before that person comes to Christ. But her story does not end there, and yours does not have to end there either. By the grace of God through faith, Rahab was forgiven and made a part of God's covenant family and the royal line of Christ. The Christian is not only released from his sin by Christ's sacrifice, he is also made part of His kingdom and family.

> **Revelation 1:5-6:** *"...and from Jesus Christ, the faithful witness, the first-born of the dead, and the ruler of the kings of the earth. To Him who loves us, and released us from our sins by His blood, 6 and He has made us to be a kingdom, priests to His God and Father; to Him be the glory and the dominion forever and ever. Amen."*

Jesus explained this concept of our belonging to the family of God when He stated:

> **Mark 3:33-35:** *"And answering them, He said, 'Who are My mother and My brothers?' 34 And looking about on those who were sitting around Him, He said, 'Behold, My mother and My brothers! 35 For whoever does the will of God, he is My brother and sister and mother.'"*

[Note continued.]

We are not taught in scripture to go to Mary, an angel, a saint, or a priest/pastor as an intercessory to Jesus or the Father. Scripture is clear that there is only one mediator between us and God, and that mediator is Jesus Christ. **1 Timothy 2:5:** *"For there is one God, and one mediator also between God and men, the man Christ Jesus, ..."* Jesus is our only intercessor: **Romans 8:34:** *"...Christ Jesus is He who died, yes, rather who was raised, who is at the right hand of God, who also intercedes for us."* **Hebrews 7:25:** *"Hence, also, He is able to save forever those who draw near to God through Him, since He always lives to make intercession for them."*

We are not to bow and give our praise to anyone or anything except almighty God. **Isaiah 42:8:** *"I am the Lord, that is My name; I will not give My glory to another, Nor My praise to graven images."* We see John being rebuked by a great angel when he bows before him. **Revelation 22:8-9:** *"And I, John, am the one who heard and saw these things. And when I heard and saw, I fell down to worship at the feet of the angel who showed me these things. 9 And he *said to me, 'Do not do that; I am a fellow servant of yours and of your brethren the prophets and of those who heed the words of this book; worship God.'"*

[11] Ryle, J.C. *Matthew (Expository Thoughts on the Gospels),* (Crossways Classic Commentaries: v.1) p.2.

MATTHEW 1:18-25
(THE VIRGIN BIRTH)

"Now the birth of Jesus Christ was as follows. When His mother Mary had been betrothed to Joseph, before they came together she was found to be with child by the Holy Spirit. [19] And Joseph her husband, being a righteous man, and not wanting to disgrace her, desired to put her away secretly. [20] But when he had considered this, behold, an angel of the Lord appeared to him in a dream, saying, 'Joseph, son of David, do not be afraid to take Mary as your wife; for that which has been conceived in her is of the Holy Spirit. [21] And she will bear a Son; and you shall call His name Jesus, for it is He who will save His people from their sins.' [22] Now all this took place that what was spoken by the Lord through the prophet might be fulfilled, saying, [23] 'BEHOLD, THE VIRGIN SHALL BE WITH CHILD, AND SHALL BEAR A SON, AND THEY SHALL CALL HIS NAME IMMANUEL,' which translated means, 'GOD WITH US.' [24] And Joseph arose from his sleep, and did as the angel of the Lord commanded him, and took her as his wife, [25] and kept her a virgin until she gave birth to a Son; and he called His name Jesus."

Introduction

The first 17 verses of Matthew detail Jesus' human genealogy. Verse 18 is the first to outline His divinity. In this section we will study the virgin birth of Christ. We will see why the virgin birth is a fundamental doctrine of the Christian faith. When studying this doctrine, one must also examine what the virgin birth does not mean. Often religious traditions and mythologies are in direct conflict with the Word of God. When that occurs, the Word of God prevails over the vain imaginations of men (2 Cor. 10:5; 1 Tim. 1:4). Many like to marginalize Christ as a, "great man of God." Scripture is very clear; Jesus was not merely a great spiritual leader, but God Himself who came in the form of a man.

> **John 1:14:** *"And the Word became flesh, and dwelt among us, and we beheld His glory, glory as of the only begotten from the Father, full of grace and truth."*

VERSE 18: *"Now the birth of Jesus Christ was as follows. When His mother Mary had been betrothed to Joseph, before they came together she was found to be with child by the Holy Spirit."*

This verse sets out the actual lineage of Jesus, "God's Son" (i.e. *"child by the Holy Spirit."*). As mentioned above, some would much rather think that Jesus was merely a man from God or some great prophet/teacher/spiritual leader/guru et al. Many cults will talk about Jesus, but not the Jesus of the Bible. Jehovah's Witnesses and Mormons both deny the deity of Christ.[12] Jehovah Witness' Jesus is not God and the Mormon Jesus is an elder spirit brother to Satan. Their Jesus is not the Jesus of Scripture. Paul warns us that there will be false teachers preaching about a false Jesus in **2 Corinthians 11:4:** *"For if one comes and preaches another Jesus whom we have not preached...."* The Jesus of the Bible was born of a virgin, *"by the Holy Spirit."* The virgin birth is also set out in **Luke 1:34-35:** *"And Mary said to the angel, 'How can this be, since I am a virgin?' [35] And the angel answered and said to her, 'The Holy Spirit will come upon you, and the power of the Most High will overshadow you; and for that reason the holy offspring shall be called the Son of God.'"*

---

[12] Sproul, R. C., *Essential Truths of the Christian faith*, Wheaton, Ill.: Tyndale House (1996, c1992).

The virgin birth was prophesied several hundred years before the birth of Christ (see Isaiah 7:14 - referenced in Matthew 1:23). "Virgin birth" means Mary was a virgin at Christ's conception (i.e. she was pregnant with Jesus but never had sexual relations with a man). The virgin birth demonstrates the preservation of the eternal Father-Son relationship of the first and second person of the Trinity.[13] This explains why the sin nature of Adam is not transmitted to Christ since Christ was not born of an earthly father like the rest of humanity; (*"The Holy Spirit will come upon you, and the power of the Most High will overshadow you; and for that reason the holy offspring shall be called the Son of God."* **Luke 1:35**). If Christ were fathered of human sexual origin (i.e. through Adam) He would be sinful and subject to His own death penalty, thus preventing Him from standing in as the substitutionary penalty bearer for sinful mankind. Since God was Christ's Father, it explains why Adam's sin and its consequences (death) could not be passed on to Christ. In other words, with God as Jesus' Father, it was impossible for the sinless Son to be born sinful (Acts 2:24). Paul explained it explicitly in **Galatians 4:4:** *"But when the fullness of the time came, God sent forth His Son, born of a woman,...."*

One should not get confused by some false teachings out there regarding this subject. One false teaching claims that sin runs only through the man and not the woman, thus Jesus could be born of Mary, but not Joseph. There is nothing in scripture that supports that claim. Scripture is very clear that women are just as sinful as men and equally tainted by the fall.[14] Paul points out that Eve also had a significant role in the fall of humanity.

> **1 Timothy 2:13–14:** *"For it was Adam who was first created, and then Eve.*
> [14]*And it was not Adam who was deceived, but the woman being deceived, fell into transgression."*

Some speculate whether Jesus had Mary's DNA? Again, these types of questions are not relevant as scripture does not claim that sin is something that reside specifically in blood or DNA. We are told that sin taints all humanity after Adam. In **Romans 8:3** we read

> *"For what the Law could not do, weak as it was through the flesh, God did: sending His own Son in the likeness of sinful flesh and as an offering for sin, He condemned sin in the flesh,...."*

There are some concepts that are important to remember regarding this subject:
1) God created a human body for Adam and Eve without a sin nature. **Genesis 1:31:** *"God saw all that He had made, and behold, it was very good...."* See also Genesis 2:20-25). Adam and Eve were tempted in that body and choose to sin, which defiled all humanity with sin and death.
2) Jesus as God, always existed with the Father before he took on a human body. God created a human body for Christ without a sin nature. Jesus (His fetus) that Mary carried had no taint of sin because God created Him that way. God can do this. Remember, Adam was created by God without a sin nature. Jesus was tempted in that body like Adam, *but Jesus did not sin:*

---

[13] Norman L. Geisler., *The Essential Doctrines of the Christian Faith (Part 2)*. Christian Research Journal Vol. 28, No.6 (2005)

[14] All the earth and creation also suffered as a result of Adam's sin – (See Romans 8:20-22 and Gen 3:17-19).

> **Hebrews 4:14–15**: *"Therefore, since we have a great high priest who has passed through the heavens, Jesus the Son of God, let us hold fast our confession. ¹⁵For we do not have a high priest who cannot sympathize with our weaknesses, but <u>One who has been tempted in all things as we are, yet without sin.</u>"*

Jesus is often referred to as the second Adam. It states in **1 Corinthians 15:45**: *So also it is written, "The first man, Adam, became a living soul." The last Adam became a life-giving spirit."* Jesus uses the title "Son of Man" for himself throughout the gospels expresses His humanity and messiahship (Daniel 7:13-14): **Matthew 18:11** *"For the Son of Man has come to save that which was lost."* This entire concept is summarized by the Apostle Paul:

> **Romans 5:12-19**: *"Therefore, just <u>as through one man sin entered into the world, and death through sin, and so death spread to all men, because all sinned</u>— ¹³for until the Law sin was in the world, but sin is not imputed when there is no law. ¹⁴Nevertheless death reigned from Adam until Moses, even over those who had not sinned in the likeness of the offense of Adam, who is a type of Him who was to come. ¹⁵But the free gift is not like the transgression. <u>For if by the transgression of the one the many died, much more did the grace of God and the gift by the grace of the one Man, Jesus Christ, abound to the many.</u> ¹⁶The gift is not like that which came through the one who sinned; for on the one hand the judgment arose from one transgression resulting in condemnation, but on the other hand the free gift arose from many transgressions resulting in justification. ¹⁷<u>For if by the transgression of the one, death reigned through the one, much more those who receive the abundance of grace and of the gift of righteousness will reign in life through the One, Jesus Christ. ¹⁸So then as through one transgression there resulted condemnation to all men, even so through one act of righteousness there resulted justification of life to all men. ¹⁹For as through the one man's disobedience the many were made sinners, even so through the obedience of the One the many will be made righteous</u>"*

MacArthur summarizes the concept of the virgin birth when he states "He was Son of Mary, Son of Joseph in the legal sense, but He was Son of God in the sense of His nature, in the sense of His essence. He was Son of God in human form."[15]

Roman Catholics agree with Scripture's claim that Mary was a virgin at Christ's conception, but then they have also added the unbiblical myth of the "miraculous virgin birth." This false doctrine maintains that the baby Jesus passed out of Mary's body in such a way as to leave her medically still a virgin.[16] This idea had its beginning in the *Protevangelium of James* (mid-2nd century–Syrian origin) and became a standard doctrine as part of the idea of the perpetual virginity of Mary.[17] We know

---

[15] MacArthur, John F, (Sermon: *The Virgin Birth: A Divine Miracle-Luke 1:34-38*; March 07, 1999 42-12).

[16] Note the non-scriptural based quote from the official Roman Catholic Catechism #499: "**499** The deepening of faith in the virginal motherhood led the Church to confess Mary's real and perpetual virginity even in the act of giving birth to the Son of God made man. In fact, <u>Christ's birth "did not diminish his mother's virginal integrity but sanctified it."</u> And so the liturgy of the Church celebrates Mary as Aeiparthenos, the "Ever-virgin." [See also: Mary is not a co-redemptrix or co-mediator; see footnote comments in Matthew 1:2-17.]

[17] *The New Bible Dictionary*, *"Virgin Birth"* (Wheaton, Illinois: Tyndale House Publishers, Inc.) 1996.

this concept is mythological because it is opposite of what the Scripture states. Scripture tells us Mary gave the sacrifice for the first child that, "opens the womb."

> **Luke 2:21-23:** *"And when eight days were completed before His circumcision, His name was then called Jesus, the name given by the angel before He was conceived in the womb. ²² And when the days for their purification according to the law of Moses were completed, they brought Him up to Jerusalem to present Him to the Lord ²³ (as it is written in the Law of the Lord, 'EVERY first-born MALE THAT OPENS THE WOMB SHALL BE CALLED HOLY TO THE LORD'),"*

Since her womb was opened (v.23), it cannot be said that the baby passed out of Mary's body so as to leave her medically a virgin. Additional textual proof denying the "perpetual virginity of Mary" is **Matthew 1:24-25** which states, *"And Joseph arose from his sleep, and did as the angel of the Lord commanded him, and took her as his wife, ²⁵ and <u>kept her a virgin until she gave birth to a Son;</u> and he called His name Jesus."* Finally, Scripture states Mary was not a virgin forever by the fact that Jesus had brothers and sisters as set out in **Mark 6:2-3** *"...Where did this man get these things, and what is this wisdom given to Him, and such miracles as these performed by His hands? ³ 'Is not this the carpenter, <u>the son of Mary, and brother of James, and Joses, and Judas, and Simon? Are not His sisters here with us?'</u> And they took offense at Him."*

VERSES 19-23: *"And Joseph her husband, being a righteous man, and not wanting to disgrace her, desired to put her away secretly. ²⁰ But when he had considered this, behold, an angel of the Lord appeared to him in a dream, saying, 'Joseph, son of David, do not be afraid to take Mary as your wife; for that which has been conceived in her is of the Holy Spirit. ²¹ And she will bear a Son; and you shall call His name Jesus, for it is He who will save His people from their sins.' ²² Now all this took place that what was spoken by the Lord through the prophet might be fulfilled, saying, ²³ 'BEHOLD, THE VIRGIN SHALL BE WITH CHILD, AND SHALL BEAR A SON, AND THEY SHALL CALL HIS NAME IMMANUEL,' which translated means, 'GOD WITH US.' ²⁴ And Joseph arose from his sleep, and did as the angel of the Lord commanded him, and took her as his wife, ²⁵ and kept her a virgin until she gave birth to a Son; and he called His name Jesus."*

Joseph's reaction to finding out that Mary was pregnant says a lot about his character. He assumed that her pregnancy was the result of adultery. The penalty for adulterous conduct could have resulted in Joseph having her stoned (Deuteronomy 22:23-24). Notice how gracious Joseph is in that his first reaction was to not disgrace her, but instead to *"put her away secretly."* To *"put her away ...."* means to divorce her, even though they were betrothed at the time. Being betrothed was a more serious step to marriage than our culture's concept of engagement. Before Joseph took any action, an angel from God appeared to him and told him what was really happening. In obedience to God's Word, Joseph took Mary as his wife.

In verse 21 we read that Joseph was instructed to name the child Jesus, but then verse 23 states that He will be called *"IMMANUEL."* The names Jesus and Immanuel each represent a different aspect of the Son of God:

> "One describes his office, the other his nature.... Jesus means 'Saviour' because 'He saves
> His people from their sins.'...The name 'Emmanuel'... is the name which is given to our

Lord from His nature as God-man, as 'God revealed in the body.' It means 'God with us."[18]

The importance of understanding Christ's divine and human nature cannot be neglected.

"[T]here was a union of two natures, the divine and the human, in the person of our Lord Jesus Christ…. We should settle it firmly in our minds that our Saviour is perfect man as well as perfect God, and perfect God as well as perfect man. If we once lose sight of this great foundational truth, we may run into fearful heresies."[19]

For more on the concept of human and divine nature of Christ see the footnote below.[20]

---

[18] Ryle, J.C., *Matthew (Expository Thoughts on the Gospels)*, (Crossways Classic Commentaries: v.1) p. 4.

[19] Ibid

[20] **DIVINE AND HUMAN NATURE OF CHRIST:** Here are some short notes of mine on Jesus' humanity and divine nature as shown in Scripture. Examples of His manhood are that He was: tempted (Luke 4:1-13), tired (John 4:6), hungry (Matthew 4:2), thirsty (John 19:28) slept (Matthew 8:24) and died (Mark 15:39-45, Matthew 27:50). Examples of His divine nature are that He was: born of a virgin (Luke 1:30-38), did miracles (John 11:38-44, Luke 7:21-23), never sinned (2 Corinthians 5:21), and rose from the dead (1 Corinthians 15:3-8, Matthew 28:5-15, John 21:14).

"Christ is God and man by a **hypostatic** or personal union, both natures, divine and human, remaining distinct without composition or confusion, in one and the same person."

Vincent, T. (1996). *A family instructional guide*. Index created by Christian Classics Foundation. (electronic edition based on the first Banner of Truth ed., 1980.) (p. 73). Simpsonville SC: Christian Classics Foundation.

Brakel explains the concept this way: "This union also was not established by mixing these two natures, with a third type of person coming forth. Rather, this union was established *without change and without mixture* each nature retaining its own attributes; each nature contributes its attributes to the Person. Thus, the same Christ has divine as well as human attributes by virtue of the union of these two natures in Him. However, the one nature does not have the attributes of the other nature. The union of these two natures in one Person has three consequences — *communication of: 1) gifts and honor, 2) attributes*, and *3) activity and office*. a Brakel, W. (1996, c1992)."

The Christian's reasonable service, Volumes 1 and 2. Published in electronic form by Christian Classics Foundation, 1996. (electronic ed. of the first publication in the English language, based on the 3rd edition of the original Dutch work.) (Vol. 1, pp. 505-506). Morgan PA: Soli Deo Gloria Publications.

(See also: THE HUMANITY AND DIVINITY OF CHRIST by Sproul, R. C. (1996, c1992). *Essential Truths of the Christian Faith*. Wheaton, Ill.: Tyndale House.

#27 The Humanity of Christ "That God the Son took upon Himself a real human nature is a crucial doctrine of historic Christianity. The great ecumenical Council of Chalcedon in A.D. 451 affirmed that Jesus is truly man and truly God and that the two natures of Christ are so united as to be without mixture, confusion, separation, or division, each nature retaining its own attributes. Christ's humanity was like ours. He became a man "for our sakes." He entered into our situation to act as our Redeemer. He became our substitute, taking upon Himself our sins in order to suffer in our place. He also became our champion, fulfilling the law of God on our behalf. In redemption there is a twofold exchange. Our sins are imparted to Jesus. His righteousness is imparted to us. He receives the judgment due to our imperfect humanity, while we receive the blessing due to His perfect humanity. In His humanity Jesus had the same limitations common to all human beings, except that He was without sin. As a human [Note continued on the next page.]

Summary and Application

We see here the importance of the doctrines of the virgin birth and the divinity of Christ. These are fundamental doctrines on which true Christianity does not compromise (see a review of fundamental doctrine in the comments for Matthew 13:31-32). There are many people who claim they are Christians and will even acknowledge that Jesus is the "Son of God," but they will not acknowledge that Jesus is "God the Son." There are others who will say things like, "Hey, we all are Christians, because we all believe in Jesus." It is not enough to believe whatever you want to about Jesus. If one does not believe the Word of God, that person neither knows God nor His will. One can give ceremonial allegiances to Jesus by calling Him "Lord" but that is not true faith. Jesus Himself said this in **Matthew 7:21:** *"Not everyone who says to Me, 'Lord, Lord,' will enter the kingdom of heaven; but he who does the will of My Father who is in heaven."*

[Note continued.]

being Jesus was restricted by time and space. Like all human beings He could not be in more than one place at the same time. He sweated. He hungered. He wept. He endured pain. He was mortal, capable of suffering death. In all these respects He was like us."

#25 THE DIVINITY OF CHRIST: "Faith in the deity of Christ is necessary to being a Christian. It is an essential part of the New Testament gospel of Christ. Yet in every century the church has been forced to deal with people who claim to be Christians while denying or distorting the deity of Christ.... As the Logos Incarnate, Christ is revealed as being not only pre-existent to creation, but eternal. He is said to be in the beginning *with* God and also that He *is* God (John 1:1-3). That He is *with* God demands a personal distinction within the Godhead. That He *is* God demands inclusion in the Godhead. Elsewhere, the New Testament ascribes terms and titles to Jesus that are clearly titles of deity. God bestows the preeminent divine title of *Lord* upon Him (Philippians 2:9-11). As the Son of Man, Jesus claims to be Lord of the Sabbath (Mark 2:28) and to have authority to forgive sins (Mark 2:1-12). He is called the *"Lord* of glory" (James 2:1) and willingly receives worship, as when Thomas confesses, "My Lord and my God!" (John 20:28). Paul declares that the fullness of the Godhead dwells in Christ bodily (Colossians 1:19) and that Jesus is higher than angels, a theme reiterated in the book of Hebrews." [Note: All of Creation was made by Jesus – Colossians. 1:16-17.]

MATTHEW 2:1-12
(HEROD and THE MAGI)

"NOW after Jesus was born in Bethlehem of Judea in the days of Herod the king, behold, magi from the east arrived in Jerusalem, saying, ² 'Where is He who has been born King of the Jews? For we saw His star in the east, and have come to worship Him.' ³ And when Herod the king heard it, he was troubled, and all Jerusalem with him. ⁴ And gathering together all the chief priests and scribes of the people, he began to inquire of them where the Christ was to be born. ⁵ And they said to him, 'In Bethlehem of Judea, for so it has been written by the prophet,'

⁶ 'AND YOU, BETHLEHEM, LAND OF JUDAH,
ARE BY NO MEANS LEAST AMONG THE LEADERS OF JUDAH;
FOR OUT OF YOU SHALL COME FORTH A RULER,
WHO WILL SHEPHERD MY PEOPLE ISRAEL.'

⁷ Then Herod secretly called the magi, and ascertained from them the time the star appeared. ⁸ And he sent them to Bethlehem, and said, "Go and make careful search for the Child; and when you have found Him, report to me, that I too may come and worship Him." ⁹ And having heard the king, they went their way; and lo, the star, which they had seen in the east, went on before them, until it came and stood over where the Child was. ¹⁰ And when they saw the star, they rejoiced exceedingly with great joy. ¹¹ And they came into the house and saw the Child with Mary His mother; and they fell down and worshiped Him; and opening their treasures they presented to Him gifts of gold and frankincense and myrrh. ¹² And having been warned by God in a dream not to return to Herod, they departed for their own country by another way."

Introduction

In this section we will study the event of the magi visiting the Christ child. Our objective is to look to scripture, and not legend, to guide us. Scripture will reveal common misconceptions regarding this event. For example, many believe the legendary view that there were *three* magi who visited Jesus. Another misconception is that the magi visited Jesus at the *manger on the night He was born* (see v.11).

VERSES 1-2: *"NOW after Jesus was born in Bethlehem of Judea in the days of Herod the king, behold, magi from the east arrived in Jerusalem, saying, ² 'Where is He who has been born King of the Jews? For we saw His star in the east, and have come to worship Him.'"*

Jesus was born in Bethlehem, which is located about six miles south of Jerusalem (see footnote on celebrating Christ's birth on December 25th).[21] Micah 5:2 prophesied that the Messiah would come

---

[21] **Is December 25 Christ's earthly birthday?** Scripture is very clear about the actual birth of Christ and even tells where He would be born. These facts were prophesied hundreds of years before. The actual year of Jesus' birth is believed to have been miscalculated by approximately four years by Dionysius Exiguus, a Scythian monk, "abbot of a Roman monastery. It is considered more likely that that Christ was born about 4-6 B.C. Green, J. B., McKnight, S., and Marshall, I. H. (1992). *Dictionary of Jesus and the Gospels.* Downers Grove, Ill.: InterVarsity Press
[Note continued on the next page.]

from Bethlehem. The name "Bethlehem" means "house of bread." Remember what Jesus said in **John 6:35:** "*...I am the bread of life; he who comes to Me shall not hunger, and he who believes in Me shall never thirst.*"

These verses talk about "magi" who came from the East. Magi were a priestly class of astrologers / magicians and scholars of science, agriculture, mathematics and history. They resided east of Palestine. They also possessed great political influence in Persia and had knowledge of the Old Testament Scripture.[22] Many believe that their knowledge of the Scriptures can be traced back to

---

.[Note continued.]

As to the day Christ was born, scripture is silent. Since it does not speak to the specific date, we know that it is not important for us to know. So where did December 25th come from? As early as A.D. 200 Hippolytus (A.D. 165–235) said Christ's birth was on December 25th. December 25th was also set by John Chrysostom (A.D. 345–407). Over 100 years after Hippolytus' date of December 25th, Pope Julius I in 320 A.D. specified the 25th of December as the official date of the birth of Jesus Christ. Some believe that Julius conveniently corresponded the date near a Roman pagan festival called Saturnalia in an attempt to Christianize the pagan holiday.

Clement of Alexandria speculated that Christ was born on November 17, 3 B.C. Some prefer speculating that the birth could not have occurred in December based on **Luke 2:8:** "*...some shepherds staying out in the fields and keeping watch over their flock by night.*" They say it would have been too cold to have sheep out grazing in late December. But before one just accepts this claim, it needs to be understood that the region of Bethlehem has at times been somewhat mild during December. Even "the Mishnah (*m. šeqal. 7.4*) suggests that sheep around Bethlehem might also be outside during the winter months (Hoehner)" Green, J. B., McKnight, S., and Marshall, I. H. (1992). *Dictionary of Jesus and the Gospels.* Downers Grove, Ill.: InterVarsity Press. *[The Mishnah is The first section of the Talmud, being a collection of early oral interpretations of the Scriptures as compiled about A.D. 200] – New American Heritage Dictionary.*

In colonial America many Puritans in the mid-to late-1600s typically did not celebrate Christmas, since they viewed it as heavy drinking and fleshly conduct. Yet the Reformer Martin Luther (1483–1546) took a very different view and loved to celebrate Christmas. Luther has been credited with starting the tradition of putting candles on Christmas trees to represent stars. Luther claimed his Biblical support for the Christmas tree was from **Isaiah 60:13:** "*The glory of Lebanon shall come unto thee, the fir-tree, the pine, and the box-tree together, to beautify the place of my sanctuary; ....*"

Since Scripture is silent on the matter of the actual birth date, we realize that it is of little significance. What is of eternal significance is that the Savior came! Paul makes it clear that we are free to celebrate any event or festival as long as it is done in a Christ-honoring way:

> **Colossians 2:16-17:** "*Therefore let no one act as your judge in regard to food or drink or in respect to a festival or a new moon or a Sabbath day—* [17] *things which are a mere shadow of what is to come; but the substance belongs to Christ.*"

It does not matter if one celebrates Christ's birth on December 25th, a different day or even not at all. What matters is that every day our heart is one of thankfulness and giving glory to God. Look at what God's Word says:

> **Romans 14:5-6:** "*One person regards one day above another, another regards every day alike. Each person must be fully convinced in his own mind.* [6]*He who observes the day, observes it for the Lord, and he who eats, does so for the Lord, for he gives thanks to God; and he who eats not, for the Lord he does not eat, and gives thanks to God.*"

[Note ended.]

[22] Morris, Henry, *The Defender's Study Bible,* World Publishing (1995).

Daniel of "Daniel in the Lion's Den." It was Daniel who had a great reputation as the chief Wiseman in Persia during his time. Look how Daniel was spoken of by the queen mother:

Daniel 5:11-12: *"There is a man in your kingdom in whom is a spirit of the holy gods; and in the days of your father, illumination, insight and wisdom like the wisdom of the gods were found in him. And King Nebuchadnezzar, your father, your father the king, appointed him chief of the magicians, conjurers, Chaldeans and diviners.* [12] *This was because an extraordinary spirit, knowledge and insight, interpretation of dreams, explanation of enigmas and solving of difficult problems were found in this Daniel, whom the king named Belteshazzar. Let Daniel now be summoned and he will declare the interpretation."*

There are Old Testament Scriptures and prophecies that make reference to a future Messiah. It is probable that Scripture in Numbers 24:17 is what the magi looked to when it was revealed to them that a new King, rising like a star, was born in Israel.

Numbers 24:17:

"I see him, but not now;
I behold him, but not near;
A star shall come forth from Jacob,
And a scepter shall rise from Israel,...." [23]

In Isaiah we know that nations and kings will come to this King.

Isaiah 60:3:

"And nations will come to your light,
And kings to the brightness of your rising."

The prophesies in both Numbers and Isaiah were accomplished by the magi's visit in Matthew 2:2. Much of the folklore that there were only "three kings" is based on the three gifts ,*"of gold and frankincense and myrrh."* Nowhere does Scripture tell us there were three wise men. It could have been two (*"magi* [plural] *from the east"*) or it could have been many. With that being said, if one were to speculate, there is good reason to guess that the magi group contained a large entourage. We know that they were carrying very expensive gifts. More than likely they dressed and traveled luxuriously as a reflection of their status. Both the carrying of cargo and beautiful attire would quickly catch the attention of the many highway robbers looking for a traveling victim alone in the desert (cf. Luke 10:30). It is further possible that the magi traveled with a personal army / protective entourage, large enough to discourage any would-be robbers. Another fact tending toward a large-group theory is reflected by how quickly and respectfully the magi caught the attention of Herod, his court, as well as the entire city. [24] Herod was not a cordial man who treated others with respect but when the magi arrived he pretended to be very cordial and respectful. Scripture tells us that, *"when Herod the king heard it, he was troubled, and all Jerusalem with him."* (v.3). He was very concerned about talk of a new king. In summary, although it is an interesting question, we have no idea how many magi came to worship the Christ-child.

---

[23] King David fulfills this verse (2 Sam. 8:2) but it is ultimately pointing to Jesus Christ.

[24] Morris states that, "These Persian magi were very important and powerful leaders in the great Persian empire, which had never been subjugated by Rome.... In fact, there are some historical indications that Persia was, at this time, threatening Rome along the eastern boundaries of the Roman Empire. No wonder Herod was 'troubled' and 'all Jerusalem with him' at the suggestion that Persia might be about to throw its support to a new Jewish king." Morris, Henry. The Defender's Study Bible, Note at Matthew 2:2, World Publishing (1995).

Note that these magi did not ask "*if*" there was a child born King of the Jews. Instead, they had the confidence of God's revelation when they asked, in verse 2, "*Where is He who has been born King of the Jews? For we saw His star in the east, and have come to worship Him ....*" Do not underestimate the great faith we see demonstrated by these men. As one commentator states, they believed in Christ before they had ever seen Him. They believed even though the scribes and Pharisees did not. They believed having seen no miracles performed by Him. They saw what appeared to be a helpless child with His mother.[25] They emptied themselves of their earthly treasures. They bowed and worshiped Him.

VERSES 3-8: *"And when Herod the king heard it, he was troubled, and all Jerusalem with him. [4] And gathering together all the chief priests and scribes of the people, he began to inquire of them where the Christ was to be born. [5] And they said to him, "In Bethlehem of Judea, for so it has been written by the prophet,*

> [6] *'AND YOU, BETHLEHEM, LAND OF JUDAH,*
>
> *ARE BY NO MEANS LEAST AMONG THE LEADERS OF JUDAH;*
>
> *FOR OUT OF YOU SHALL COME FORTH A RULER,*
>
> *WHO WILL SHEPHERD MY PEOPLE ISRAEL.'"*

[7] Then Herod secretly called the magi, and ascertained from them the time the star appeared. [8] And he sent them to Bethlehem, and said, "Go and make careful search for the Child; and when you have found Him, report to me, that I too may come and worship Him."

Herod wanted Jesus killed because one of the magi said they were looking for, "*He who has been born King of the Jews.*" Herod viewed himself as the only King of the Jews and would kill anyone who would threaten his throne. Herod reigned over Palestine from 37 B.C. to 4 B.C.[26] Herod was an Edomite (i.e. not a Jew), and thus did not have a legitimate claim to be King of the Jews. He served at the pleasure of Rome, who ruled at the time. His insatiable desire to maintain power made him extremely paranoid of those who surrounded him. He had his wife's brother, the high priest, Aristobulus,[27] drowned because he felt threatened by him. After committing the murder, he then held a big funeral for Aristobulus and pretended to weep at it. Herod had others killed, including his wife, mother-in-law, two of his sons, and five days before his death, he killed his third son.[28] MacArthur demonstrates the demonic insanity of Herod when he states:

> "Shortly before his death, he lured prominent Jewish leaders to Jericho where he imprisoned them. Knowing the people would not mourn his death, he ordered that these leaders be executed after he died. That way, he reasoned, there would at least be mourning going on at the time of his death. Fortunately, his mad scheme was not carried out." [29]

---

[25] Ryle, J.C. *Matthew (Expository Thoughts on the Gospels)*, (Crossways classic commentaries: v.1).

[26] Walvoord, John F., and Zuck, Roy B., *The Bible Knowledge Commentary*, (Wheaton, Illinois: Scripture Press Publications, Inc.) 1983, 1985, [Online] Available: Logos Library System.

[27] The high priest, Aristobulus, is not Herod's son, Aristobulus, who Herod also eventually killed.

[28] MacArthur, John F., *The MacArthur New Testament Commentary*, p. 319 (Chicago: Moody Press) 1983.

[29] Ibid.

Herod's homicidal style of hypocrisy is further manifested in verse 4 when he called in, *"all the chief priests and scribes of the people, he began to inquire of them where the Christ was to be born."* He pretended he had an interest in worshipping the newborn King, but he actually wanted to kill Him. To accomplish this murder, he turned his attention to finding the location and age of the child. The priests and scribes found the location of His birth through the prophesy in Micah 5:2 stating that the King would be born in Bethlehem.[30] To help determine the age of the child (*"Herod secretly called the magi, and ascertained from them the time the star appeared...."v.7*). We do not know what the magi told him regarding their first sighting of the star, but we can conclude that it was likely within two years of their meeting with Herod. This conclusion is based on the fact that Herod eventually responded by having all the baby boys of Bethlehem who were two years of age and younger killed (Matthew 2:16). Herod mistakenly believed that by killing all the baby boys, he was assured that the newborn king would be among the dead.[31]

VERSES 9-12: *"And having heard the king, they went their way; and lo, the star, which they had seen in the east, went on before them, until it came and stood over where the Child was. [10] And when they saw the star, they rejoiced exceedingly with great joy. [11] And they came into the house and saw the Child with Mary His mother; and they fell down and worshiped Him; and opening their treasures they presented to Him gifts of gold and frankincense and myrrh. [12] And having been warned by God in a dream not to return to Herod, they departed for their own country by another way."*

We know the visit by the magi took place sometime after the birth since it did not take place in the manger. Matthew 2:11 states that they entered the *"house."* The gifts were gold, frankincense and myrrh. Some speculate that the gifts were symbolic of the character of Christ: "gold might represent His deity or purity, incense the fragrance of His life, and myrrh His sacrifice and death (myrrh was used for embalming)."[32]

---

[30] It is estimated that this prophesy was written around 700 years before the birth of Christ.
Micah 5:2:
> *"But as for you, Bethlehem Ephrathah,*
> *Too little to be among the clans of Judah,*
> *From you One will go forth for Me to be ruler in Israel.*
> *His goings forth are from long ago,*
> *From the days of eternity."*

[31] "This Herod, known as "the Great," is the first of several Herods mentioned in the New Testament. Julius Caesar had appointed his father, Antipater, to be procurator, or governor, of Judea under the Roman occupation. Antipater then managed to have his son Herod appointed prefect of Galilee. In that office Herod was successful in quelling the Jewish guerilla bands who continued to fight against their foreign rulers. After fleeing to Egypt when the Parthians invaded Palestine, Herod then went to Rome and in 40 B.C. was declared by Octavian and Antony (with the concurrence of the Roman senate) to be the king of the Jews. He invaded Palestine the next year and, after several years of fighting, drove out the Parthians and established his kingdom. Because he was not Jewish, but Idumean (Edomite), Herod married Mariarune, heiress to the Jewish Hasmonean house, in order to make himself more acceptable to the Jews he now ruled." MacArthur, John F., *The MacArthur New Testament Commentary*, p. 25-26 (Chicago: Moody Press) 1983.

[32] Walvoord, John F., and Zuck, Roy B., *The Bible Knowledge Commentary*, v.2 p. 22 (Wheaton, Illinois: Scripture Press Publications, Inc.) 1983, 1985.

Upon seeing the child, the magi worshiped Him. The text states that the magi bowed down and worshiped, giving gifts to the child. They did not pay any homage like that to Herod when they saw him. It should also be noted they worshiped the Christ-child, not the child and His mother.

We also see God's divine protection in that the magi were warned to not return to Herod. The magi did not know that Herod wanted to kill the child but God knows the thoughts of every person. Evil men can make their plans but the Lord protects and will make foolishness of their evil schemes.

> **Psalm 2:2,4:** *"The kings of the earth take their stand,*
> *And the rulers take counsel together*
> *Against the Lord and against His Anointed…*
> *⁴He who sits in the heavens laughs,*
> *The Lord scoffs at them."*

Summary and Application

The story of the magi is one of revelation and faithful obedience to that revelation. They were given a word from God and they obeyed it. We have been given God's revelation through the Bible. We would do well to obey it faithfully like the magi.

We should also see the importance of knowing for ourselves what the Bible actually says and not blindly believe what others claim it says. For example, the comments in this book are just that, "comments," which should constantly be checked against the Bible, *"to see whether these things were so"* (Acts 17:11). Think of the myth of the magi appearing at the stable on the night the Christ-child was born. This myth has been passed down for generations. We must be careful to not love our traditions to the extent that we dismiss the truth. Jesus rebuked the Pharisees regarding this by stating in **Mark 7:9:** *"He was also saying to them, 'You are experts at setting aside the commandment of God in order to keep your tradition.'"*

Are there myths you allow to be part of your theology? If so, dismiss them.

> **1 Timothy 1:3-6:** *"As I urged you upon my departure for Macedonia, remain on at Ephesus, in order that you may instruct certain men not to teach strange doctrines, ⁴nor to pay attention to myths and endless genealogies, which give rise to mere speculation rather than furthering the administration of God which is by faith. ⁵But the goal of our instruction is love from a pure heart and a good conscience and a sincere faith. ⁶For some men, straying from these things, have turned aside to fruitless discussion,…."*

MATTHEW 2:13-23
(HEROD / MAGI CONTINUED and RESIDING IN NAZARETH)

"Now when they had departed, behold, an angel of the Lord *appeared to Joseph in a dream, saying, 'Arise and take the Child and His mother, and flee to Egypt, and remain there until I tell you; for Herod is going to search for the Child to destroy Him.' [14] *And he arose and took the Child and His mother by night, and departed for Egypt;* [15] *and was there until the death of Herod, that what was spoken by the Lord through the prophet might be fulfilled, saying, 'O*UT OF *E*GYPT DID *I* CALL *M*Y *S*ON.'*

[16] *Then when Herod saw that he had been tricked by the magi, he became very enraged, and sent and slew all the male children who were in Bethlehem and in all its environs, from two years old and under, according to the time which he had ascertained from the magi.* [17] *Then that which was spoken through Jeremiah the prophet was fulfilled, saying,*

[18] *'A* VOICE WAS HEARD IN *R*AMAH,
    *W*EEPING AND GREAT MOURNING,
    *R*ACHEL WEEPING FOR HER CHILDREN;
    *A*ND SHE REFUSED TO BE COMFORTED,
    *B*ECAUSE THEY WERE NO MORE.'

[19] *But when Herod was dead, behold, an angel of the Lord *appeared in a dream to Joseph in Egypt, saying,* [20] *'Arise and take the Child and His mother, and go into the land of Israel; for those who sought the Child's life are dead.'* [21] *And he arose and took the Child and His mother, and came into the land of Israel.* [22] *But when he heard that Archelaus was reigning over Judea in place of his father Herod, he was afraid to go there. And being warned by God in a dream, he departed for the regions of Galilee,* [23] *and came and resided in a city called Nazareth, that what was spoken through the prophets might be fulfilled, "He shall be called a Nazarene."*

Introduction
This section continues the story of the murderous Herod. It is also important to remember that despite the evil, God protects and provides for His own people.

VERSES 13-15: *"Now when they had departed, behold, an angel of the Lord *appeared to Joseph in a dream, saying, 'Arise and take the Child and His mother, and flee to Egypt, and remain there until I tell you; for Herod is going to search for the Child to destroy Him.'* [14] *And he arose and took the Child and His mother by night, and departed for Egypt;* [15] *and was there until the death of Herod, that what was spoken by the Lord through the prophet might be fulfilled, saying, 'O*UT OF *E*GYPT DID *I* CALL *M*Y *S*ON.'"*

In this section we see Herod, under demonic influence, still seeking to kill Jesus. It has always been Satan's desire to attempt to stifle God's redemption plan by killing Jesus. We see a reference to Satan's desire to kill Jesus in the book of Revelation.

Revelation 12:3-4: *"And another sign appeared in heaven: and behold, a great red dragon having seven heads and ten horns, and on his heads were seven diadems.* [4]*And his tail *swept away a third of the stars of heaven, and threw them to the earth. And the dragon stood before the woman who was about to give birth, so that when she gave birth he might devour her child."*

Matthew gives us another prophecy regarding the Lord, that was spoken seven centuries prior to its fulfillment: *"And out of Egypt I called My son."* (Hosea 11:1). "Hosea was writing of God's calling Israel out of Egypt into the Exodus."[33] But it had a second meaning: the prophecy of Jesus. Note the similarities between the two situations: The Jews originally went to Egypt to escape danger (i.e. the famine in Jacob's time), and Jesus was sent there to escape the danger of Herod.

VERSES 16-18: *"Then when Herod saw that he had been tricked by the magi, he became very enraged, and sent and slew all the male children who were in Bethlehem and in all its environs, from two years old and under, according to the time which he had ascertained from the magi.* [17] *Then that which was spoken through Jeremiah the prophet was fulfilled, saying,*

[18] *'A VOICE WAS HEARD IN RAMAH,*
WEEPING AND GREAT MOURNING,
RACHEL WEEPING FOR HER CHILDREN;
AND SHE REFUSED TO BE COMFORTED,
BECAUSE THEY WERE NO MORE.'"

Verses 16-18 represent another prophecy referred to by Matthew. This prophecy sets forth the hatred Herod had for the Savior of the world. He was consumed by homicidal anger and sought to slaughter as many as would assure him of the child's death.

Ramah was a town located five miles north of Jerusalem. In Jeremiah 40:1 we see it as the place where Jewish captives were located prior to their deportation to Babylon. Rachel was the wife of Jacob (who was also called Israel) and her tomb was close to Bethlehem. John MacArthur writes,

> "**Rachel weeping for her children** therefore represented the lamentation of all Jewish mothers who wept over Israel's great tragedy in the days of Jeremiah, and most specifically typified and prefigured the mothers of Bethlehem weeping bitterly over the massacre of their children by Herod in his attempt to kill the Messiah."[34]

Herod's murderous insanity was well known. The ancient, heathen historian Macrobius said that when Augustus Caesar heard that Herod may have slain his own young son along with the boys under two years old, he mocked Herod by saying, "That it was better to be Herod's swine than his son." [35]

VERSES 19-23: *"But when Herod was dead, behold, an angel of the Lord *appeared in a dream to Joseph in Egypt, saying,* [20] *'Arise and take the Child and His mother, and go into the land of Israel; for those who sought the Child's life are dead.'* [21] *And he arose and took the Child and His mother, and came into the land of Israel.* [22] *But when he heard that Archelaus was reigning over Judea in place of his father Herod, he was afraid to go there. And being warned by God in a dream, he departed for the regions of Galilee,* [23] *and came and resided in a city called Nazareth, that what was spoken through the prophets might be fulfilled, 'He shall be called a Nazarene.'"*

---

[33] Walvoord, John F., and Zuck, Roy B., *The Bible Knowledge Commentary*, (Wheaton, Illinois: Scripture Press Publications, Inc.) 1983, 1985, [Online] Available: Logos Library System.

[34] MacArthur, John F., *The MacArthur New Testament Commentary*, (Chicago: Moody Press) 1983.

[35] Henry, Matthew, *Matthew Henry's Commentary on the Bible*, (Peabody, MA: Hendrickson Publishers) 1997.

In verse 19, we see that Herod died. He was a powerful man who demanded control, but regardless of how powerful a man becomes, he has the same end as the lowliest slave. All people, great or small, will meet death. Regarding Herod's death, Matthew Henry wrote:

> "Note, Herod must die; proud tyrants, that were the terror of the mighty, and the oppressors of the godly, *in the land of the living,* their day must come to fall, and down to the pit they must go. *Who art thou then, that thou shouldest be afraid of a man that shall die?* (Isaiah 51:12, 13) especially considering that at death, not only their envy and hatred are perished (Ecclesiastes 9:6), and they cease from troubling (Job 3:17), but they are punished." [36]

There was a Jewish historian named Josephus who wrote a book called *Antiquities of the Jews.* In that book he discussed the death of Herod and said that Herod, "died of this, ulcerated entrails, putrefied and maggot-filled organs, constant convulsions, foul breath, and neither physicians nor warm baths led to recovery."[37]

The angel told Joseph to come out of Egypt since Herod was dead. Note that it was not just Herod that wanted the child dead. The angel said, "***those who sought the Child's life are dead.***" The angel said to "...*go into the land of Israel.*" He did not say to go back to Bethlehem. Joseph may have assumed the angel meant that he was to go back to Bethlehem, from where he fled. After they got into Israel, a new threat arose — Herod's oldest son, Archelaus, who ruled after his father's death. He became a murderer like his father. Joseph was warned in a dream and went to the, "***regions of Galilee,***" and resided in *Nazareth.* Matthew mentioned the prophecy concerning Jesus being a Nazarene, "***He shall be called a Nazarene.***" Some believe that the specific Old Testament reference to this prophecy is Isaiah 11:1:

> "However, the words **He will be called a Nazarene,** were not directly spoken by any Old Testament prophet, though several prophecies come close to this expression. Isaiah said the Messiah would be 'from [Jesse's] roots' like 'a Branch' (Isaiah 11:1). 'Branch' is

---

[36] Ibid

[37] *The Works of Josephus; The Antiquities of the Jews.* 17.146-199 [see specifically 168-170]. Note also that Josephus also wrote about Jesus in Antiquities of the Jews, Book 18, Chapter 3. paragraphs 3 (63-64). This section is known as the Testimonium Flavianum:

> "Now there was about this time Jesus, a wise man, if it be lawful to call Him a man: for He was a doer of wonderful works, a teacher of such men as receive the truth with pleasure. He drew over to Him both many of the Jews and many of the Gentiles. He was Christ. And when Pilate, at the suggestion of the principal men among us, had condemned Him to the cross, those that loved Him at the first did not forsake Him; for He appeared to them alive again the third day as the divine prophets had foretold these and ten thousand other wonderful things concerning Him. And the tribe of Christians so named from Him are not extinct at this day." (*Antiquities,* 18:63-64)

Obviously some like to attack the authenticity of this section. As a Christian, I know that Flavius Josephus was simply a secular historian. His writings are neither Scripture nor divine and thus it is irrelevant to me whether it is authentically written by Josephus in part or in its entirety (although there is very good evidence that it is authentic). Regardless, evidence has never gotten in the way of the hostile antichristian who is threatened by any mention of Christ apart from being used as a curse word.

the Hebrew word …which has consonants like those in the word 'Nazarene' and which carry the idea of having an insignificant beginning."[38]

The prophesy stating the Messiah would be a Nazarene must have been well-known among the Jews, who were the vast majority of the original readers of Matthew's Gospel. If Isaiah 11:1 is not the specific Old Testament reference, it should be understood that it is not unusual for something to be mentioned in the New Testament that does not have a specific Old Testament reference. Regardless of whether it is in the Old Testament or the New Testament, it is all God breathed and thus God's Word. John MacArthur says it this way:

> "Other sayings and events unrecorded in the Old Testament are nevertheless quoted or referred to in the New. Jude tells us that 'Enoch, in the seventh generation from Adam, prophesied, saying, 'Behold, the Lord came with many thousands of His holy ones, to execute judgment upon all, and to convict all the ungodly of all their ungodly deeds which they have done in an ungodly way" (Jude 14-15). Yet no such prophecy is mentioned in Genesis or in any other part of the Old Testament. In a similar way we know of Jesus' teaching that 'It is more blessed to give than to receive' only because of Paul's later reference to it (Acts 20:35). The saying is not mentioned by any of the gospel writers, including Luke, who reported the account in Acts. John tells us that he did not even attempt to record everything that Jesus said and did during His earthly ministry (John 21:25).

> Matthew does not tell us which prophets predicted the Messiah would be called a Nazarene, but only that more than one of them did so. The prophecy is said to be fulfilled when Jesus was taken to live in Nazareth, where Joseph and Mary had formerly lived. Matthew's original readers were largely Jewish, and it was probably common knowledge among them who the specific prophets were that had made the prediction. For later readers, the Holy Spirit obviously felt it was enough that we simply know that the prediction was made and that it was fulfilled as Matthew explains."[39]

The term "Nazarene" often had negative connotations. The city is located about 65 miles north of Jerusalem and had a reputation for rough-living people. Remember how Nathanael responded to Philip telling him about the Messiah, specifically about *"Jesus of Nazareth:"*

> **John 1:45-46:** *"Philip *found Nathanael and *said to him, 'We have found Him of whom Moses in the Law and also the Prophets wrote, Jesus of Nazareth, the son of Joseph.' [46] And Nathanael *said to him, 'Can any good thing come out of Nazareth?' Philip *said to him, 'Come and see.'"*

The negativism of being from Nazareth also fulfilled prophesies regarding how the Messiah would be despised by men.

> **Isaiah 53:3:** *"He was despised and forsaken of men,*
> *A man of sorrows, and acquainted with grief;*
> *And like one from whom men hide their face,*

---

[38] Walvoord, John F., and Zuck, Roy B., *The Bible Knowledge Commentary*, (Wheaton, Illinois: Scripture Press Publications, Inc.) 1983, 1985, [Online] Available: Logos Library System.

[39] MacArthur, John F., *The MacArthur New Testament Commentary*, (Chicago: Moody Press) 1983, [Online] Available: Logos Library System.

He was despised, and we did not esteem Him."

Isaiah 49:7: *"Thus says the LORD, the Redeemer of Israel, and its Holy One, To the despised One,…"*

John 9:22: *"His parents said this because they were afraid of the Jews; for the Jews had already agreed, that if anyone should confess Him to be Christ, he should be put out of the synagogue."*

Summary and Application

We must remember that man is to fear and obey God first and foremost. When God spoke to the magi, they obeyed. They were not concerned about Herod hunting them down. They were concerned about doing what God told them. This is true faith. What is your attitude regarding God's Word? Have you actually read the entire Bible? If not, you need to start by reading the New Testament. How can you obey God if you do not know what He requires?

Hebrews 11:6: *"And without faith it is impossible to please Him, for he who comes to God must believe that He is, and that He is a rewarder of those who seek Him."*

Romans 10:17: *"So faith comes from hearing, and hearing by the word of Christ."*

MATTHEW 3:1-12
(JOHN THE BAPTIST; PHARISEES, SADDUCEES and HYPOCRISY)

"Now in those days John the Baptist *came, preaching in the wilderness of Judea, saying, ² 'Repent, for the kingdom of heaven is at hand.' ³ For this is the one referred to by Isaiah the prophet, saying,
'THE VOICE OF ONE CRYING IN THE WILDERNESS, 'MAKE READY THE WAY OF THE LORD,
MAKE HIS PATHS STRAIGHT!'
⁴ Now John himself had a garment of camel's hair, and a leather belt about his waist; and his food was locusts and wild honey. ⁵ Then Jerusalem was going out to him, and all Judea, and all the district around the Jordan; ⁶ and they were being baptized by him in the Jordan River, as they confessed their sins. ⁷ But when he saw many of the Pharisees and Sadducees coming for baptism, he said to them, 'You brood of vipers, who warned you to flee from the wrath to come? ⁸ Therefore bring forth fruit in keeping with repentance; ⁹ and do not suppose that you can say to yourselves, 'We have Abraham for our father'; for I say to you, that God is able from these stones to raise up children to Abraham. ¹⁰ And the axe is already laid at the root of the trees; every tree therefore that does not bear good fruit is cut down and thrown into the fire. ¹¹ As for me, I baptize you with water for repentance, but He who is coming after me is mightier than I, and I am not fit to remove His sandals; He will baptize you with the Holy Spirit and fire. ¹² "And His winnowing fork is in His hand, and He will thoroughly clear His threshing floor; and He will gather His wheat into the barn, but He will burn up the chaff with unquenchable fire."

Introduction

We will start this section by discussing John the Baptist. We know that his father was Zacharias, a priest at the temple, and his mother was Elizabeth (see Luke 1:5-25 and Luke 1:57-80). Jesus said this of John in **Matthew 11:11:** *"Truly, I say to you, among those born of women there has not arisen anyone greater than John the Baptist; yet he who is least in the kingdom of heaven is greater than he."* Jesus also stated that John was a representation of Elijah (See Matthew 17:10-13, John 1:19-28, Luke 1:17, Acts 13:23-26). The end of John's earthly life came about as a result of being beheaded by an evil king (see Matthew 14:1-12).

In this section we will see the call to repentance for all believers as well as the judgment against religious hypocrisy.

VERSES 1-3: *"Now in those days John the Baptist *came, preaching in the wilderness of Judea, saying, ² 'Repent, for the kingdom of heaven is at hand.' ³ For this is the one referred to by Isaiah the prophet, saying,*
'THE VOICE OF ONE CRYING IN THE WILDERNESS,' 'MAKE READY THE WAY OF THE LORD,
MAKE HIS PATHS STRAIGHT!'"

The first part of John's message from God is stated in verse 2 (i.e. *"Repent, for the kingdom of heaven is at hand."*). The second part of John's message is the proclamation of the Messiah: *"MAKE READY THE WAY OF THE LORD."* John was the herald for this Great Announcement. The quote of Isaiah in Matthew 3:3 is taken from Isaiah 40:3-4.

John's message of repentance is often ignored in today's church or misdefined as works-based righteousness. Those who think this way ignore what the Lord told His disciples after He rose from the dead:

> *"Now He said to them, 'These are My words which I spoke to you while I was still with you, that all things which are written about Me in the Law of Moses and the Prophets and the Psalms must be fulfilled.' Then <u>He opened their minds to understand the Scriptures</u>, and He said to them, 'Thus it is written, that the Christ would suffer and rise again from the dead the third day, <u>and that repentance for forgiveness of sins would be proclaimed in His name to all the nations</u>, beginning from Jerusalem. You are witnesses of these things.'"* **Luke 24:44–48.**

Repentance is, "not just feeling sorry, or changing one's mind, but [is] a turning round, a complete alteration of the basic motivation and direction of one's life. This is why the best translation for *metanoeō* is often *to convert*, that is, *to turn round.*"[40] In summary it is turning and forsaking the sin. We need true, godly sorrow: *"For the sorrow that is according to the will of God produces a repentance without regret, leading to salvation; but the sorrow of the world produces death."* **2 Corinthians 7:10.**

The Pharisees (and we all) need to repent from *dead works*. *Dead works* can be defined as any conduct we do in an attempt to earn God's forgiveness. We often look to obtain righteousness by either,

- the good things we do,
- the bad things we don't do,
- or religious acts we engage in (e.g. baptism, communion, confirmation).

This is self-righteousness and it will not earn forgiveness, nor save anyone from hell.

> **Titus 3:5–7:** *"He saved us, not on the basis of deeds which we have done in righteousness, but according to His mercy, by the washing of regeneration and renewing by the Holy Spirit, whom He poured out upon us richly through Jesus Christ our Savior, so that being justified by His grace we would be made heirs according to the hope of eternal life."*
>
> **Ephesians 2:8–9:** *"For by grace you have been saved through faith; and that not of yourselves, it is the gift of God; not as a result of works, so that no one may boast."*

The *"gospel of God"*[41] that Jesus has called everyone to obey is two-pronged:

1) repent from sin/self-righteousness/man-made religion, and,
2) by faith, receive forgiveness by putting complete trust only in Jesus, as the divine Son of God who willingly bore the penalty for our sins on the cross and rose from the dead.

---

[40] Wood, D. R. W. and Marshall, I. H., *New Bible Dictionary* (3rd ed.) (Page 1007). Leicester, England; Downers Grove, Ill.: InterVarsity Press (1996).

[41] **Mark 1:14–15:** *"Now after John had been taken into custody, Jesus came into Galilee, preaching the gospel of God, and saying, 'The time is fulfilled, and the kingdom of God is at hand; repent and believe in the gospel.'"*

Some wrongfully claim repentance is legalism and has no place in salvation. What they fail to understand is that repentance is from God, just as faith is.

> **2 Tim 2:25-26:** "*...with gentleness correcting those who are in opposition, if perhaps God may grant them repentance leading to the knowledge of the truth, 26 and they may come to their senses and escape from the snare of the devil, having been held captive by him to do his will.*"

> **Acts 5:31:** "*He is the one whom God exalted to His right hand as a Prince and a Savior, to grant repentance to Israel, and forgiveness of sins.*"

> **Romans 2:4:** "*Or do you think lightly of the riches of His kindness and tolerance and patience, not knowing that the kindness of God leads you to repentance?*"

The true Gospel clearly includes repentance. Scripture tells us Jesus went out, "*preaching the gospel of God,*" and the message was to "*repent and believe in the gospel.*" **Mark 1:14–15**. Note that repentance was preached by Jesus; (see **Matthew 4:17** which says: "*From that time Jesus began to preach and say, "Repent, for the kingdom of heaven is at hand."*"). Jesus also sent His disciples out to spread the same message: **Mark 6:12:** "*They went out and preached that men should repent.*"; **Acts 2:38:** "*Peter said to them, 'Repent, and each of you be baptized in the name of Jesus Christ for the forgiveness of your sins; and you will receive the gift of the Holy Spirit.'*"; **Acts 17:30:** "*...God is now declaring to men that all people everywhere should repent,*" The Apostle Paul preached the Gospel in, "*solemnly testifying to both Jews and Greeks of repentance toward God and faith in our Lord Jesus Christ.*" **Acts 20:21.** In the Book of Revelation, the last book of the Bible, Jesus told the church in Ephesus to repent:

> **Revelation 2:5:** "*Therefore remember from where you have fallen, and repent and do the deeds you did at first; or else I am coming to you and will remove your lampstand out of its place—unless you repent.*"

He told the church in Pergamum to repent:

> **Revelation 2:16:** "*Therefore repent; or else I am coming to you quickly, and I will make war against them with the sword of My mouth.*"

He told the church in Thyatira to repent:

> **Revelation 2:21–22:** "*I gave her time to repent, and she does not want to repent of her immorality. 'Behold, I will throw her on a bed of sickness, and those who commit adultery with her into great tribulation, unless they repent of her deeds.*"

He told the church in Sardis to repent:

> **Revelation 3:3:** "*So remember what you have received and heard; and keep it, and repent....*"

He told the church in Laodicea to repent:

> **Revelation 3:19:** "*Those whom I love, I reprove and discipline; therefore be zealous and repent.*"

J. C. Ryle says, "...This is the old sermon which all the faithful witnesses of God have continually preached from the very beginning of the world. From Noah down to the present day the burden of their sermon has always been the same 'Repent and believe.'"[42]

---

[42] Ryle, J.C. *Mark (Expository thoughts on the Gospels),* p.5 (Crossways Classic Commentaries: v.2).

Ryle expanded by stating:

> "We are naturally dead and blind, and asleep in spiritual things; we are ready to content ourselves with a mere formal religion, and to flatter ourselves that if we go to church we shall be saved; we need to be told that, unless we 'repent…and turn to God' (Acts 3:19), we shall all perish…."[43]

One who relies on the fact that some years ago he was talked into muttering some pre-made prayer about, "asking Jesus into his heart," but never repented of his sin and placed his faith in Christ's substitutionary death on the cross, has no claim to conversion. [44][Please see this footnote.]

---

[43] Ryle, J.C. *Matthew (Expository Thoughts on the Gospels)*, (Crossways Classic Commentaries: v.1).

[44] It should be noted that nowhere in scripture does it inform us that the *method* in which a person is saved is by reciting or repeating a prayer to "ask Jesus into his heart." Modern evangelism has substituted *conversion by the power of God* (John 3:3-8), with *nominal decisionalism*. Scripture tells us Jesus preached that one is to, *"repent and believe the gospel"* **Mark 1:14-15;** (i.e. *"believe in the Lord Jesus Christ and you will be saved;"* **Acts 16:31**). I have found very few who at the time they, *"asked Jesus into their heart"* actually believed, with godly sorrow, that they had violated God's law and were *justly heading to an eternity of hell* (i.e. they never truly understood what they needed to be saved from). **John 3:36** states that *"… he who does not obey the Son will not see life, but the wrath of God abides on him."* If I have true saving faith, I will repent (turn from and forsake) my sin, false religion, and self-righteousness. It does not mean I will never fail or sin again (1 John 1:8-9). It does mean that the one who, by the power of God, is "born again" will have a true love for Jesus Christ, and faith in His Word. The truly converted will turn from sin, he will hate sin, and he will no longer practice sin (1 John 3:4-10, Galatians 5:19-21, Matthew 7:23, Revelation 22:15). Further, I have found very few who at the time they, *"asked Jesus into their heart"* really understood what *"believing in Jesus"* truly means. Sadly, many have been misled by being told they are saved by simply;

1. Acknowledging that they have done some wrong things;
2. Accept the good news that Jesus loves them just the way they are; and
3. Realize that God wants them to go to heaven when they die and that can happen
   by saying a prayer to "ask Jesus into their heart."

This mixes truth with error. One must be told that saving faith (i.e. *believing in Jesus*) really means that one believes with his whole heart that he is <u>saved ONLY by the grace of God through faith in the substitutionary death of Christ on the cross</u> (i.e. Jesus, as God and without any sin, paid my death and damnation penalty on the cross where He died as the sinless sacrifice, and then three days later He rose from the dead.) See Ephesians 2:8-10; 1 Corinthians 15:3-4. One who believes this (not merely intellectually, but truly surrenders his life to Christ as Lord and Savior) and is a true Christian (i.e. one whom is proven over time and fruitfulness). This is what it means when scripture states, *"that if you confess with your mouth Jesus as Lord, and believe in your heart that God raised Him from the dead, you will be saved;"* **Romans 10:9**. It must be remembered that the Gospel is very simple and can be summarized as follows:

Jesus states in the Bible that every single person is guilty of sin, which is punished by receiving *eternal judgment in the fires of hell*. Jesus preached that the only way to escape from hell is to *"repent and believe in the gospel."* **Mark 1:15**.

- To **REPENT** means to turn from your sins and forsake them by the power of God.
- To **BELIEVE THE GOSPEL** means that one who is "born again" by the Spirit of God (John 3:3-8) will:
  - Believe in Jesus Christ as Almighty God, who is without sin;
  - Believe in Jesus' sacrificial death on the cross as the only and complete payment for your sins;
  - Believe in Jesus' bodily resurrection from the dead on the third day;
  - Believe in Jesus as Lord over all things and confesses this fact to others.

[Note continued on next page.]

John MacArthur describes it this way:

"...the one who refuses to turn to God for forgiveness and salvation and therefore has no evidence, no good fruit, of genuine repentance. Salvation is not verified by a past act, but by present fruitfulness."[45]

So does repentance matter today? Absolutely! Jesus said *"... but unless you repent, you will all likewise perish."* **Luke 13:3**. As Peter taught in **Acts 2:38**: *"And Peter said to them, 'Repent, and let each of you be baptized in the name of Jesus Christ for the forgiveness of your sins; and you shall receive the gift of the Holy Spirit.'"* Repentance is not a "work" of man that can save you. One is not saved simply because he repents, or stops doing bad things, or even tries very hard to do good. The preaching of Christ tells us it is the only way to be saved from the *judgment to come:*

"... Jesus came into Galilee, preaching the gospel of God, [15]and saying, 'The time is fulfilled, and the kingdom of God is at hand; repent and believe in the gospel.'" **Mark 1:14–15.**

Repentance, comes *only* from God.

- **2 Timothy 2:25-26:** *"....with gentleness correcting those who are in opposition, if perhaps God may grant them repentance leading to the knowledge of the truth, [26] and they may come to their senses and escape from the snare of the devil, having been held captive by him to do his will."*
- **Romans 2:4:** *"Or do you think lightly of the riches of His kindness and tolerance and patience, not knowing that the kindness of God leads you to repentance?"*
- **Acts 5:31:** *"He is the one whom God exalted to His right hand as a Prince and a Savior, to grant repentance to Israel, and forgiveness of sins."*
- **Acts 11:18:** *"When they heard this, they quieted down and glorified God, saying, "Well then, God has granted to the Gentiles also the repentance that leads to life."*

We are saved ONLY by the grace of God through faith in the substitutionary death of Christ on the cross (Ephesians 2:8-10). If we have real saving faith, we will have repented from false religion, self-righteousness, and the love of sin.

Warren Wiersbe points out that the true believer understands *"sin is exceedingly sinful."*[46] The Puritan, Richard Baxter, set forth the seriousness of tolerating sin in our life:

"Use sin as it will use you; spare it not, for it will not spare you, it is your murderer, and the murderer of the world: use it, therefore, as a murderer should be used. Kill it before

---

[Note continued.]
It is that straightforward. It has nothing to do with your righteousness, good works or engaging in a religious ceremony or cleaning yourself up first to win God's acceptance. If you reject God's loving gift of forgiveness in Jesus Christ, you remain a guilty sinner waiting to be punished in eternal hell. The Bible says in **John 3:36:** *"He who believes in the Son has eternal life; but he who does not obey the Son will not see life, but the wrath of God abides on him."* Repent and believe the gospel TODAY, before it is too late!
[Note ended].

[45] MacArthur, J. F., Jr. (1985). Matthew. MacArthur New Testament Commentary (p. 70). Chicago: Moody Press.

[46] Wiersbe, W. W. (1996). *The Bible Exposition Commentary* (Romans 7:7). Wheaton, IL: Victor Books.

it kills you; and though it bring you to the grave, as it did your Head, it shall not be able to keep you there."[47]

As Christian's we often fail (1 John 1:8). When we do fail and fall into sin, we hate our sin and rebellion against God and His Word (Romans 7:14-25). We respond by repenting (turning from our sin) and asking God to forgive us, which He does! (1 John 1:9)[48]. The unrepentant are very different. They may be quick to say, "Lord forgive me" and even *feel bad* about their sin, but they have no intention of turning/repenting/ending their *practice* of sin and putting true faith in Christ. A. Hodge explained that true repentance is as follows:

"...to its essence, true repentance consists—(1) In a sincere hatred of sin, and sorrow for our own sin (Psalms 119:128, 136). Sin is seen to be exceeding*ly* sinful in the light of the divine holiness, of the law of God, and especially of the cross of Christ. The more we see of God in the face of Christ, the more we abhor ourselves and repent in dust and ashes. (Job 13:5, 6; Ezekiel 36:31)."[49]

J.C. Ryle summarized the true convert as follows:

"True repentance is no light matter: it is a thorough change of heart about sin, a change showing itself in godly sorrow for sin, in heartfelt confession of sin — in a complete breaking off from sinful habits, and a lasting hatred of all sin. Such repentance is inseparable companion of saving faith in Christ. Let us prize the doctrine highly. No Christian teaching can be called *understood* if it does not constantly bring us to 'turn to God in repentance and have faith in our Lord Jesus' (Acts 20:21)."[50]

"The person who hears Christian teaching and practices it is like 'a wise man who built his house on the rock'...He does not content himself with listening to exhortations to repent, believe in Christ and live a holy life. He actually repents; he actually believes. He actually ceases to do evil, learns to do good, abhors what is sinful, and clings to that which is good. He is a doer as well as a hearer."[51]

The warning of judgment is clear regarding the unrepentant who have not believed upon the Lord but instead willingly ***practice*** sin:

---

[47] Thomas, I. (1996). *The Golden Treasury of Puritan Quotations* (electronic ed.) (p. 281). Simpsonville SC: Christian Classics Foundation.

[48] **1 John 1:9:** *"If we confess our sins, He is faithful and righteous to forgive us our sins and to cleanse us from all unrighteousness."*

[49] Hodge, A., Hodge, C., and Hodge, A. (1996). *The Confession of faith: With Questions for Theological Students and Bible Classes*. With an appendix on Presbyterianism by Charles Hodge. Index created by Christian Classics Foundation. (electronic ed. based on the 1992 Banner of Truth reprint.) (p. 211). Simpsonville SC: Christian Classics Foundation. [Note: **Romans 7:13** (NASB95) *"so that through the commandment sin would become utterly sinful."*]

[50] Ryle, J.C., *Matthew (Expository Thoughts on the Gospels)*, (Crossways classic commentaries: v.1) p.27.

[51] Ryle, J.C., *Matthew / (Expository Thoughts on the Gospels)* (Crossways classic commentaries: v.1) p.54

- they are self-deceived,[52]
- they are slaves to sin,[53]
- they are not forgiven by God,[54]
- they are not Christians,[55]
- they are not going to heaven,[56]
- they are going to hell.[57]

Some scriptures regarding the *practicing* of sin are set out below:

Galatians 5:19–21: *"Now the deeds of the flesh are evident, which are: immorality, impurity, sensuality, [20] idolatry, sorcery, enmities, strife, jealousy, outbursts of anger, disputes, dissensions, factions, [21] envying, drunkenness, carousing, and things like these, of which I forewarn you, just as I have forewarned you, that those who practice such things will not inherit the kingdom of God."*

1 John 3:4–10: *"[4]Everyone who practices sin also practices lawlessness; and sin is lawlessness. [5]You know that He appeared in order to take away sins; and in Him there is no sin. [6]No one who abides in Him sins; no one who sins has seen Him or knows Him. [7] Little children, make sure no one deceives you; the one who practices righteousness is righteous, just as He is righteous; [8] the one who practices sin is of the devil; for the devil has sinned from the beginning. The Son of God appeared for this*

---

[52] **Titus 3:3:** *"For we also once were foolish ourselves, disobedient, deceived, enslaved to various lusts and pleasures, spending our life in malice and envy, hateful, hating one another."*

    2 Timothy 3:13: *"But evil men and impostors will proceed from bad to worse, deceiving and being deceived."*

[53] **John 8:34–35:** *"Jesus answered them, 'Truly, truly, I say to you, everyone who commits sin is the slave of sin. The slave does not remain in the house forever; the son does remain forever.'"* (See also Titus 3:3 in the footnote above.)

[54] **Hebrews 10:26–29:** *"For if we go on sinning willfully after receiving the knowledge of the truth, there no longer remains a sacrifice for sins, [27] but a terrifying expectation of judgment and the fury of a fire which will consume the adversaries. [28] Anyone who has set aside the Law of Moses dies without mercy on the testimony of two or three witnesses. [29] How much severer punishment do you think he will deserve who has trampled under foot the Son of God, and has regarded as unclean the blood of the covenant by which he was sanctified, and has insulted the Spirit of grace?"*

[55] **2 Timothy 2:25-26:** *"…with gentleness correcting those who are in opposition, if perhaps God may grant them repentance leading to the knowledge of the truth, [26] and they may come to their senses and escape from the snare of the devil, having been held captive by him to do his will ."*

[56] **Revelation 21:8:** *"But for the cowardly and unbelieving and abominable and murderers and immoral persons and sorcerers and idolaters and all liars, their part will be in the lake that burns with fire and brimstone, which is the second death."*

[57] See footnote above (Revelation 21:8).

purpose, to destroy the works of the devil. ⁹ No one who is born of God practices sin, because His seed abides in him; and he cannot sin, because he is born of God. ¹⁰ By this the children of God and the children of the devil are obvious: anyone who does not practice righteousness is not of God, nor the one who does not love his brother."

Matthew 7:23: *"And then I will declare to them, 'I never knew you; depart from Me, you who practice lawlessness.'"*

Revelation 22:15: *"Outside are the dogs and the sorcerers and the immoral persons and the murderers and the idolaters, and everyone who loves and practices lying."*

Will you repent of your sin and turn to faith in Christ? Or will you continue to hug, kiss and coddle your sin...like a giant anaconda snake that slowly wraps itself around you? You know something is not right about it, but you really enjoy the warm and secure feeling it gives you. It then starts to feel a little too tight so you decide to make a small adjustment, when suddenly you realize that you cannot move! Terror sets in as its grip on you tightens — you are unable to breath and the incredible bone-crushing slaughter begins! The last thing you see is the Serpent's mocking eyes over your head and its ugly mouth wide open ...anxious to devour you into hell forever. [And you thought your sin was your little feel-good friend that you got away with for years?]

VERSE 4: *"Now John himself had a garment of camel's hair, and a leather belt about his waist; and his food was locusts and wild honey."*

John's food should not be considered weird since under the Law locusts were considered *clean* to eat. Matthew Henry writes that, "Locusts were a sort of flying insect, very good for food, and allowed as clean (Leviticus 11:22); they required little dressing, and were light, and easy of digestion."[58]

Neither John's clothes nor his food were like those of the religious leaders of his time. The Pharisees and Scribes dressed and ate luxuriously. Jesus told His disciples in **Luke 20:46:** *"Beware of the scribes, who like to walk around in long robes, and love respectful greetings in the market places, and chief seats in the synagogues, and places of honor at banquets,....."* (See also Matthew 23:1-8.) John's plain food and clothes can be seen as a rebuke to the hypocritical and self-indulgent practices of religious leaders.

VERSES 5-6: *"Then Jerusalem was going out to him, and all Judea, and all the district around the Jordan; ⁶ and they were being baptized by him in the Jordan River, as they confessed their sins."*

John called the people to repentance and they responded. Note that even after he was dead, the people knew that they had a great prophet from God in John the Baptist.
  Luke 20:1-8: *"AND it came about on one of the days while He was teaching the people in the temple and preaching the gospel, that the chief priests and the scribes with the elders confronted Him, ² and they spoke, saying to Him, 'Tell us by what authority You are doing these things, or who is the one who gave You this authority?' ³ And He answered and said to them, 'I shall also ask you a question, and you tell Me: ⁴ Was the*

---

[58] Henry, M. (1994). *Matthew Henry's Commentary on the Whole Bible: Complete and Unabridged in One Volume* (Mt 3:1–6). Peabody: Hendrickson.

baptism of John from heaven or from men?' [5] *And they reasoned among themselves, saying, 'If we say, from heaven,' He will say, 'Why did you not believe him?'* [6] *'But if we say, 'From men, all the people will stone us to death, for they are convinced that John was a prophet.'* [7] *And they answered that they did not know where it came from.* [8] *And Jesus said to them, 'Neither will I tell you by what authority I do these things.'"*

VERSES 7: *"But when he saw many of the Pharisees and Sadducees coming for baptism, he said to them, 'You brood of vipers, who warned you to flee from the wrath to come?'"*

The companion verse for this section is found in Luke with more detail.

Luke 3:7-17: *"He therefore began saying to the multitudes who were going out to be baptized by him, 'You brood of vipers, who warned you to flee from the wrath to come?* [8] *Therefore bring forth fruits in keeping with repentance, and do not begin to say to yourselves, 'We have Abraham for our father,' for I say to you that God is able from these stones to raise up children to Abraham.* [9] *And also the axe is already laid at the root of the trees; every tree therefore that does not bear good fruit is cut down and thrown into the fire.'* [10] *And the multitudes were questioning him, saying, 'Then what shall we do?'* [11] *And he would answer and say to them, 'Let the man who has two tunics share with him who has none; and let him who has food do likewise.'* [12] *And some tax-gatherers also came to be baptized, and they said to him, 'Teacher, what shall we do?'* [13] *And he said to them, 'Collect no more than what you have been ordered to.'* [14] *And some soldiers were questioning him, saying, 'And what about us, what shall we do?' And he said to them, 'Do not take money from anyone by force, or accuse anyone falsely, and be content with your wages.'*

[15] *Now while the people were in a state of expectation and all were wondering in their hearts about John, as to whether he might be the Christ,* [16] *John answered and said to them all, 'As for me, I baptize you with water; but One is coming who is mightier than I, and I am not fit to untie the thong of His sandals; He will baptize you with the Holy Spirit and fire.* [17] *And His winnowing fork is in His hand to thoroughly clear His threshing floor, and to gather the wheat into His barn; but He will burn up the chaff with unquenchable fire.'"*

We see from verse 7 John was speaking to *"Pharisees and Sadducees."* Who are these people?

Definition of **SADDUCEES:** They were of the aristocracy of Israel (people with the money/land). "They denied the permanent validity of any but the written laws of the Pentateuch. They rejected the later doctrines of the soul and its after-life, the resurrection, rewards and retributions, angels and demons. They believed that there was no fate, men having a free choice of good and evil, prosperity and adversity being the outcome of their own course of action."[59] **Acts 23:8** states, *"For the Sadducees say that there is no resurrection, nor an angel, nor a spirit; but the Pharisees acknowledge them all."*

Definition of **PHARISEES:** They were known as the "separated ones." They thrived on self-righteousness. Jesus pointed that out in **Luke 18:9-14:**

---

[59] *The New Bible Dictionary*, (Wheaton, Illinois: Tyndale House Publishers, Inc.) 1962.

"And He also told this parable to certain ones who trusted in themselves that they were righteous, and viewed others with contempt: [10] 'Two men went up into the temple to pray, one a Pharisee, and the other a tax-gatherer. [11] The Pharisee stood and was praying thus to himself, 'God, I thank Thee that I am not like other people: swindlers, unjust, adulterers, or even like this tax-gatherer. [12] I fast twice a week; I pay tithes of all that I get.' [13] But the tax-gatherer, standing some distance away, was even unwilling to lift up his eyes to heaven, but was beating his breast, saying, 'God, be merciful to me, the sinner!' [14] I tell you, this man went down to his house justified rather than the other; for everyone who exalts himself shall be humbled, but he who humbles himself shall be exalted.'"

The Pharisees were also very proud of their detail in tithing, which Jesus pointed out in **Luke 11:42:** *"But woe to you Pharisees! For you pay tithe of mint and rue and every kind of garden herb, and yet disregard justice and the love of God; but these are the things you should have done without neglecting the others."* "They separated themselves not only from Gentiles but from tax collectors and any others whom they considered to be base 'sinners' (Luke 7:39). They even looked with disdain on the common Jewish people, whom a group of Pharisees in Jerusalem once referred to as *accursed* (John 7:49). After leaving the marketplace or any public gathering, they would as soon as possible perform ceremonial washings to purify themselves of possible contamination from touching some unclean person."[60]

Note that in Matthew 3:7 John described the Pharisees and Scribes as a *"brood of vipers."* Jesus used the same term for them in Matthew 23:33. *Brood* means "offspring or descendants" and "vipers" were a very poisonous desert snake. The serpent represents the Devil and we see him working through a serpent in Genesis 3:1-13 (see also Revelation 12:9). The religious leaders were very proud of their heritage from Abraham, but Jesus told them what their true spiritual heritage was. Jesus said plainly that they were sons of the Devil (John 8:39-44).

In the same way the desert viper's venom killed physically, the poisonous legalism of the Pharisees and Scribe's killed spiritually. They appeared to be concerned about the things of God, but it was merely a self-serving charade. When in Matthew 3:7, John said, *"who warned you to flee from the wrath to come?"* he attacked their ritualistic view of religion. The false-religious person is always willing to undergo superficial acts (such as baptism) to get his *fire insurance*, but will not repent of sin. Those who think water baptism guarantees salvation, conveniently forget that one of the thieves on the cross went to *paradise* unbaptized (Luke 23:41-43). External baptism alone often confers no benefit, as the case of Simon Magnus where we read that although baptized, he *"remained 'full of bitterness and captive to sin."* **Acts 8:23** NIV.[61] Look at what Jesus said of the unrepentant hypocrites concerned only with the externals of ritualism and not love for God:

Matthew 23:13-36: *"But woe to you, scribes and Pharisees, hypocrites, because you shut off the kingdom of heaven from men; for you do not enter in yourselves, nor do you allow those who are entering to go in. [14] [Woe to you, scribes and Pharisees, hypocrites,*

---

[60] MacArthur, John F., *The MacArthur New Testament Commentary*, p.61 (Chicago: Moody Press) 1985.

[61] Ryle, J.C. *Matthew (Expository Thoughts on the Gospels).* (Crossways Classic Commentaries: v.1) p. 294.

because you devour widows' houses, even while for a pretense you make long prayers; therefore you shall receive greater condemnation.] [15] *Woe to you, scribes and Pharisees, hypocrites, because you travel about on sea and land to make one proselyte; and when he becomes one, you make him twice as much a son of hell as yourselves.* [16]*Woe to you, blind guides, who say, 'Whoever swears by the temple, that is nothing; but whoever swears by the gold of the temple, he is obligated.'* [17] *You fools and blind men; which is more important, the gold, or the temple that sanctified the gold?* [18] *And, 'Whoever swears by the altar, that is nothing, but whoever swears by the offering upon it, he is obligated.'* [19] *You blind men, which is more important, the offering or the altar that sanctifies the offering?* [20] *Therefore he who swears by the altar, swears both by the altar and by everything on it.* [21] *And he who swears by the temple, swears both by the temple and by Him who dwells within it.* [22] *And he who swears by heaven, swears both by the throne of God and by Him who sits upon it.* [23] *Woe to you, scribes and Pharisees, hypocrites! For you tithe mint and dill and cummin, and have neglected the weightier provisions of the law: justice and mercy and faithfulness; but these are the things you should have done without neglecting the others.* [24] *You blind guides, who strain out a gnat and swallow a camel!* [25] *Woe to you, scribes and Pharisees, hypocrites! For you clean the outside of the cup and of the dish, but inside they are full of robbery and self-indulgence.* [26] *You blind Pharisee, first clean the inside of the cup and of the dish, so that the outside of it may become clean also.* [27] *Woe to you, scribes and Pharisees, hypocrites! For you are like whitewashed tombs which on the outside appear beautiful, but inside they are full of dead men's bones and all uncleanness.* [28] *Even so you too outwardly appear righteous to men, but inwardly you are full of hypocrisy and lawlessness.* [29]*Woe to you, scribes and Pharisees, hypocrites! For you build the tombs of the prophets and adorn the monuments of the righteous,* [30] *and say, 'If we had been living in the days of our fathers, we would not have been partners with them in shedding the blood of the prophets.'* [31] *Consequently you bear witness against yourselves, that you are sons of those who murdered the prophets.* [32] *Fill up then the measure of the guilt of your fathers.* [33] *You serpents, you brood of vipers, how shall you escape the sentence of hell?* [34] *Therefore, behold, I am sending you prophets and wise men and scribes; some of them you will kill and crucify, and some of them you will scourge in your synagogues, and persecute from city to city,* [35] *that upon you may fall the guilt of all the righteous blood shed on earth, from the blood of righteous Abel to the blood of Zechariah, the son of Berechiah, whom you murdered between the temple and the altar.* [36] *Truly I say to you, all these things shall come upon this generation."*

The Apostle Paul (an ex-Pharisee himself – Philippians 3:5) warns us about religious hypocrites in the New Testament church: **2 Timothy 3:5:** *"holding to a form of godliness, although they have denied its power; and avoid such men as these."* He makes reference to his own negative experience of having to deal with the religious hypocrite in the church when he speaks of *"dangers among false brethren..."* in **2 Corinthians 11:26.**

VERSE 8: In **Matthew 3:8** John said: *"Therefore bring forth fruit in keeping with repentance;"*

Paul also stated that he was to be, *"performing deeds appropriate to repentance"* in <u>Acts 26:20</u>. What are "fruits of repentance"? Some of the "fruits" are mentioned in **Luke 3:10-14:**

"And the multitudes were questioning him, saying, 'Then what shall we do?' ¹¹ And he would answer and say to them, 'Let the man who has two tunics share with him who has none; and let him who has food do likewise.' ¹² And some tax-gatherers also came to be baptized, and they said to him, 'Teacher, what shall we do?' ¹³ And he said to them, 'Collect no more than what you have been ordered to.' ¹⁴ And some soldiers were questioning him, saying, 'And what about us, what shall we do?' And he said to them, 'Do not take money from anyone by force, or accuse anyone falsely, and be content with your wages.'"

The fruit of repentance is not a mere change on the outside for appearance's sake, but it is the change on the inside. A heart that is converted by faith in Jesus Christ will result in good works for Christ's glory. This is where **James 2:17-18** says, *"Even so faith, if it has no works, is dead, being by itself. ¹⁸ But someone may well say, 'You have faith, and I have works; show me your faith without the works, and I will show you my faith by my works.'"* We often cite Ephesians 2:8-9 about not being saved by works. That view is correct, but when we are saved, good works will result as it says in the next verse, **Ephesians 2:10:** *"...For we are His workmanship, created in Christ Jesus for good works, which God prepared beforehand, that we should walk in them.* Remember what Jesus said:

> **Matthew 7:17-21:** *"Even so, every good tree bears <u>good fruit</u>; but the bad tree bears bad fruit. ¹⁸ A good tree cannot produce bad fruit, nor can a bad tree produce good fruit. ¹⁹ <u>Every tree that does not bear good fruit is cut down and thrown into the fire.</u> ²⁰ So then, you will know them by their fruits. ²¹ Not everyone who says to Me, 'Lord, Lord,' will enter the kingdom of heaven; but he who does the will of My Father who is in heaven."*

VERSES 9-10: *"and do not suppose that you can say to yourselves, 'We have Abraham for our father'; for I say to you, that God is able from these stones to raise up children to Abraham. ¹⁰ And the axe is already laid at the root of the trees; every tree therefore that does not bear good fruit is cut down and thrown into the fire."*

The religious leaders were confident of their salvation, based on the fleshly heritage of being a Jew (i.e. a child of Abraham). John points out that one's heritage is not the issue with God when he states God can make the stones into "sons of Abraham." In the same way, if we have a grandparent or parent who is a godly person, it does not mean we are saved.

The religious leaders did not want true repentance (turning to faith in Christ). They felt secure in their own "good works." From the scriptures they should have seen that the Abraham they boasted of was justified (i.e. declared righteous), not by his work but by his faith in God.

> **Romans 4:1-4:** *"WHAT then shall we say that Abraham, our forefather according to the flesh, has found? ² For if Abraham was justified by works, he has something to boast about; but not before God. ³ For what does the Scripture say? 'AND ABRAHAM BELIEVED GOD, AND IT WAS RECKONED TO HIM AS RIGHTEOUSNESS.'"*

Some Jews tried defending their physical heritage directly to Jesus. They claimed that they were children of Abraham, but Jesus told them their father was the Devil!

> **John 8:39-41, 44:** *"They answered and said to Him, 'Abraham is our father.' Jesus *said to them, 'If you are Abraham's children, do the deeds of Abraham. ⁴⁰ But as it is, you are seeking to kill Me, a man who has told you the truth, which I heard from God; this*

Abraham did not do. [41] *You are doing the deeds of your father....* [44] *You are of your father the devil, and you want to do the desires of your father.'"*

In verse 10, John states *"And the axe is already laid at the root of the trees; every tree therefore that does not bear good fruit is cut down and thrown into the fire."* Repentance will show its fruit. Jesus states this when He said, *"If anyone does not abide in Me, he is thrown away as a branch, and dries up; and they gather them, and cast them into the fire, and they are burned."* **John 15:6.** There is no doubt that the fire for those who do not *"abide"* in Christ is the fire of hell: *"And if your hand causes you to stumble, cut it off; it is better for you to enter life crippled, than having your two hands, to go into hell, into the unquenchable fire,...."* **Mark 9:43.** The summary point is made by John MacArthur as to a person,

> "...who refuses to turn to God for forgiveness and salvation and therefore has no evidence, no good fruit, of genuine repentance. Salvation is not verified by a past act, but by present fruitfulness."[62]

VERSE 11: *"As for me, I baptize you with water for repentance, but He who is coming after me is mightier than I, and I am not fit to remove His sandals; He will baptize you with the Holy Spirit and fire."*

The baptism of John was for repentance. What was the repentance of John? It was to turn from man-made religion and its hypocrisy to faith in the coming Messiah, Jesus. See how Paul described John's baptism in **Acts 19:4:** *"And Paul said, 'John baptized with the baptism of repentance, telling the people to believe in Him who was coming after him, that is, in Jesus.'"* Jesus' baptism is with the Holy Spirit (Matthew 3:11 and John 1:33).

John points out that he himself is not the Messiah (John 1:19-20). In addition, John states that the Messiah to come is much more than a great prophet, someone who even John would be unworthy to *"remove His sandals...."*

VERSE 12: *"And His winnowing fork is in His hand, and He will thoroughly clear His threshing floor; and He will gather His wheat into the barn, but He will burn up the chaff with unquenchable fire...."*

In Bible times, a farmer would take his wheat to a threshing floor, which was usually a small pit on a hilltop or someplace where the wind blew freely. The wheat was put into the pit and then the kernels were separated from the straw. The farmer would then take his winnowing fork and scoop up a pile and throw it in the air. The heavy wheat kernels would fall to the ground, but the light straw or chaff would blow off. He would continue this process until the pit contained nothing but wheat kernels.

John makes clear that Jesus will judge thoroughly and righteously to make a clear distinction between wheat and chaff. The "wheat" represents true believers who will dwell with Him in His Kingdom. The chaff are the "pretenders" who will dwell in the *unquenchable fire,* which is the same term Jesus used for hell, *"into hell, into the unquenchable fire,"* **Mark 9:43.** *Question:* Are you wheat or chaff? Do you love God with all your heart, or do you want certain people to think you love God?

---

[62] MacArthur, John F., *The MacArthur New Testament Commentary*, p.70 (Chicago: Moody Press) 1985.

Summary and Application:

One cannot claim that perfect righteousness comes from his own acts or from his spiritual/physical heritage. Do you look to yourself and the deeds you do to satisfy a holy God? Do you have a devout Christian among your family and friends? Are you thinking that your relationship with this person will help you get to heaven? Do you practice any religious rites or philosophies that are man-made and not set forth in Scripture? Are you willing to acknowledge that they are false and repent from them?

> **Colossians 2:8-11:** *"See to it that no one takes you <u>captive through philosophy and empty deception, according to the tradition of men, according to the elementary principles of the world, rather than according to Christ</u>. [9]For in Him all the fulness of Deity dwells in bodily form, [10]and in Him you have been made complete, and He is the head over all rule and authority; [11]and in Him you were also circumcised with a circumcision made without hands, in the removal of the body of the flesh by the circumcision of Christ;"*

If one has true faith in Christ, it will manifest in repentance from sin and doing good works for the glory of God. (James 2:26). Have you turned from your sin? Do you find great joy in serving Christ and working for His glory? The example we see from John the Baptist is one of confronting the false-religious. John preached that man-made ritualism and hypocritical self-righteousness have nothing to do with true Christianity.

MATTHEW 3:13-17
(BAPTISM OF JESUS)

"Then Jesus arrived from Galilee at the Jordan coming to John, to be baptized by him. ¹⁴ But John tried to prevent Him, saying, 'I have need to be baptized by You, and do You come to me?' ¹⁵ But Jesus answering said to him, 'Permit it at this time; for in this way it is fitting for us to fulfill all righteousness.' Then he permitted Him. ¹⁶ And after being baptized, Jesus went up immediately from the water; and behold, the heavens were opened, and he saw the Spirit of God descending as a dove, and coming upon Him, ¹⁷ and behold, a voice out of the heavens, saying, 'This is My beloved Son, in whom I am well-pleased.'"

Introduction

These verses set out the coronation of Jesus as King of Kings in a three-part manner:
1. His baptism,
2. The Spirit of God descending upon Him,
3. The declaration of the Father, *"This is My beloved Son, in whom I am well-pleased."*

VERSES 13-15: *"Then Jesus arrived from Galilee at the Jordan coming to John, to be baptized by him. ¹⁴ But John tried to prevent Him, saying, 'I have need to be baptized by You, and do You come to me?' ¹⁵ But Jesus answering said to him, 'Permit it at this time; for in this way it is fitting for us to fulfill all righteousness.' Then he permitted Him."*

In these verses we read of Jesus being baptized. We wonder why Jesus needed to be baptized since He had no need to be forgiven or to repent. Jesus said it was to, *"fulfill all righteousness."* Some believe His baptism was His identification with humankind and our sinfulness. It should be made clear that Jesus was sinless even in His identifying with us. (*e.g.* **2 Corinthians 5:21:** *"He made Him who knew no sin to be sin on our behalf, that we might become the righteousness of God in Him."*).

We need to also remember that Jesus set forth an example for us to follow: **1 Peter 2:21:** *"...For you have been called for this purpose, since Christ also suffered for you, leaving you an example for you to follow in His steps ...."* What is the example that baptism leaves us? It is an example of Jesus' death and resurrection to eternal life. Jesus refers to His "baptism" in relation to His work on the cross in **Luke 12:50:** *"But I have a baptism to undergo, and how distressed I am until it is accomplished!"* (See Mark 10:38). That *"distress"* is Jesus knowing that He would take on the world's sin and suffer on the cross (2 Corinthians 5:21). Here are two sections of scripture on the concept of Christ's baptism as a reflection of His death and resurrection:

> **Romans 6:3-5:** *"Or do you not know that all of us who have been baptized into Christ Jesus have been baptized into His death? ⁴ Therefore we have been <u>buried with Him through baptism into death, in order that as Christ was raised from the dead through the glory of the Father,</u> so we too might walk in newness of life. ⁵ For if we have become united with Him in the likeness of His death, certainly we shall be also in the likeness of His resurrection,...."*

Colossians 2:12: *"…having been buried with Him in baptism, in which you were also raised up with Him through faith in the working of God, who raised Him from the dead."*

VERSE 16: *"And after being baptized, Jesus went up immediately from the water; and behold, the heavens were opened, and he saw the Spirit of God descending as a dove, and coming upon Him,…."*

A Gnostic perversion is the heretical teaching that Jesus became God at the time He was baptized. [63] This is wrong. We see the angel telling Mary before Jesus was born that the child was the Son of God: **Luke 1:35:** *"And the angel answered and said to her, "The Holy Spirit will come upon you, and the power of the Most High will overshadow you; and for that reason the holy offspring shall be called the Son of God."* Jesus was God not only at His birth, but from the beginning of time. Jesus was not "created" but was the Creator of all things:

Colossians 1:15-19: *"And He is the image of the invisible God, the first-born of all creation. [16] For by Him all things were created, both in the heavens and on earth, visible and invisible, whether thrones or dominions or rulers or authorities—all things have been created by Him and for Him. [17] And He is before all things, and in Him all things hold together. [18] He is also head of the body, the church; and He is the beginning, the first-born from the dead; so that He Himself might come to have first place in everything. [19] For it was the Father's good pleasure for all the fulness to dwell in Him,…."*

It is very important to realize Jesus was with the Father from the beginning of creation as stated in **John 1:1-2:** *"In the beginning was the Word, and the Word was with God, and the Word was God. [2] He was in the beginning with God."* See also: **Revelation 22:13:** *"I am the Alpha and the Omega, the first and the last, the beginning and the end."*

---

[63] Gnosticism: This was an anti-christ philosophy which means "knowledge." More specifically they adored the concepts of "secret or hidden" knowledge that they possessed. Dualism was a pet doctrine of Gnosticism. Dualism maintains that everything "spiritual is good" and things physical are bad. Docetists, a Gnostic sect who claimed that flesh was evil, thus denied that Jesus came in the flesh. John denounced this anti-christ doctrine (1 John 4:2-3, 1 John 2:22-23, John 1:14). Because Gnostics claimed the flesh was bad, they did not want the spirit and the flesh to be reunited at the resurrection so they denied the concept of the resurrection of the dead or claimed that "resurrection was past already" (2 Timothy 2:17-18). They liked the concepts of secret knowledge that they received and would ascribe magical properties to rituals, as in done in witchcraft. One book celebrated by anti-christ religious leaders was the Gnostic work called the "Gospel of Thomas," which is a rambling of Gnostic thoughts claiming to be sayings of Jesus and attempting to sound like the legitimate gospels.

"From the standpoint of traditional Christianity, Gnostic thinking is quite alien. Its mythological setting of redemption leads to a depreciation of the historical events of the life, death and resurrection of Jesus. Its view of man's relationship to God leads to a denial of the importance of the person and work of Christ, while, in a Gnostic context, 'salvation' is not understood in terms of deliverance from sin, but as a form of existential self-realization." Wood, D. R. W., and Marshall, I. H. (1996). *New Bible Dictionary* (3rd ed.) (Page 416). Leicester, England; Downers Grove, Ill.: InterVarsity Press.

The word *baptized* means immersion.[64] The text states, *"Jesus went up immediately from the water;"* which means He had been in the water, not merely sprinkled.

We see in verse 16 the, *"Spirit of God descending as a dove."* Jesus did not lose His divinity when He became a man, but was, "anointed for service and granted strength for ministry. The Spirit anointed Him for His kingly service, as Isaiah had predicted:
> *" The Spirit of the Lord God is upon me, because the Lord has anointed me to bring good news to the afflicted; He has sent me to bind up the brokenhearted, to proclaim liberty to captives, and freedom to prisoners…."* **Isaiah 61:1**
> (cf. **Isaiah 11:2:** *And the Spirit of the LORD will rest on Him, The spirit of wisdom and understanding, The spirit of counsel and strength, The spirit of knowledge and the fear of the LORD.)"*

VERSE 17: *"and behold, a voice out of the heavens, saying, 'This is My beloved Son, in whom I am well-pleased.'"*

Here the Father testified of His Son: *"This is My beloved Son, in whom I am well-pleased."* (See also Matthew 17:5). Ryle points out that the statement,
> "…proclaimed the Father's full and complete approval of Christ's mission to seek and save the lost. It announced the Father's acceptance of the Son as the mediator, substitute and surety of the new covenant."[65]

Notice also that we have the Holy Trinity manifested at the baptism: the Son Jesus, the Holy Spirit and the Father. Many people have heard the term Holy Trinity, but seldom understand it. Here is an explanation: The word *Trinity* means, "a group of three." The "Trinity" can be explained, in part, by three concepts:
1. *that there is but one God,*
2. *that the Father, the Son and the Spirit is each God, and*
3. *that the Father, the Son and the Spirit is each a distinct Person.*[66]

Realize there are not three Gods **but ONE GOD** (Deuteronomy 6:4). In that unity of ONE God, there are three eternal and co-equal persons.[67]

---

[64] "The Greek word itself … means literally to dip an object into water or other liquid, not to have the liquid put on the object. If all the forms of this word in Scripture had been translated (as "immersed") instead of being simply transliterated (as "baptized") - first into Latin and then into modern languages - the confusion we now see regarding the mode of baptism would never have arisen. The Christian church knew no form of baptism but immersion until the Middle Ages, when the practice of sprinkling or pouring was introduced by the Roman Catholic church - which itself had previously always baptized by immersion." MacArthur, John F., *The MacArthur New Testament Commentary*, p. 79 (Chicago: Moody Press) 1985.

[65] Ryle, J.C. *Mark (Expository Thoughts on the Gospels)*, p.5 (Crossways Classic Commentaries: v.2).

[66] *The New Bible Dictionary*, 3rd edition, p.1209 (Wheaton, Illinois: Tyndale House Publishers, Inc.) 1996.

Summary and Application

The Holy Spirit seals us and baptizes us into the body of Christ.

1 Corinthians 12:13: *"For by one Spirit we were all baptized into one body, whether Jews or Greeks, whether slaves or free, and we were all made to drink of one Spirit."*

Ephesians 4:30: *"And do not grieve the Holy Spirit of God, by whom you were sealed for the day of redemption."*

The concept of being baptized into Christ and His body is set forth in:

Romans 6:2-11: *"May it never be! How shall we who died to sin still live in it? ³ Or do you not know that all of us who have been baptized into Christ Jesus have been baptized into His death? ⁴ Therefore we have been buried with Him through baptism into death, in order that as Christ was raised from the dead through the glory of the Father, so we too might walk in newness of life. ⁵ For if we have become united with Him in the likeness of His death, certainly we shall be also in the likeness of His resurrection, ⁶ knowing this, that our old self was crucified with Him, that our body of sin might be done away with, that we should no longer be slaves to sin; ⁷ for he who has died is freed from sin. ⁸ Now if we have died with Christ, we believe that we shall also live with Him, ⁹ knowing that Christ, having been raised from the dead, is never to die again; death no longer is master over Him. ¹⁰ For the death that He died, He died to sin, once for all; but the life that He lives, He lives to God. ¹¹ Even so consider yourselves to be dead to sin, but alive to God in Christ Jesus."*

Being baptized into the body of Christ is not a magical rite obtained through a special man with special water. Those who think water baptism is the means to secure salvation conveniently forget one of the thieves on the cross went to *paradise* unbaptized (Luke 23:41-43). External baptism alone often confers no benefit, as the case of Simon Magnus plainly shows: Although baptized he, *"remained 'full of bitterness and captive to sin."* **Acts 8:23** NIV.[68] Remember, baptism does not save you from your sins; only faith in Jesus Christ can bring salvation.

R. C. Sproul states it this way:

"Baptism was instituted by Christ and is to be administered in the name of the Father, Son, and Holy Spirit. The outward sign does not automatically or magically convey the realities that are signified. For example, though baptism signifies regeneration, or rebirth, it does not automatically convey rebirth. The power of baptism is not in the water but in the power of God."[69]

Some who are ritual-oriented argue that only an ordained pastor is authorized to baptize. I disagree. The Great Commission is not restricted to ordained clergy. Jesus commands all believers to, *"Go therefore and make disciples of all the nations, baptizing them in the name of the Father and the Son and the Holy Spirit,...."* **Matthew 28:19**.

---

[67] "The church has rejected the heresies of "modalism" and "tritheism." "Modalism" denies the distinction of persons within the Godhead, claiming that Father, Son, and Holy Spirit are just ways in which God expresses Himself. "Tritheism," on the other hand, falsely declares that there are three beings who together make up God." Sproul, R. C., *Essential Truths of the Christian Faith*, Wheaton, Ill.: Tyndale House (1996, c1992).

[68] Ryle, J.C. *Matthew (Expository Thoughts on the Gospels)*. (Crossways classic commentaries: v.1) p. 294.

[69] Sproul, R. C. (1996, c1992), *Essential Truths of the Christian Faith*, Baptism, Wheaton, Ill.: Tyndale House.

Just as some make the great error in believing the ritual of water baptism instills eternal salvation, others err in thinking water baptism is simply an insignificant rite. It should not go unnoticed that Jesus began His public ministry with His baptism (Matthew 3:13-17) and the Book of Matthew closes with Jesus commanding us to baptize His disciples (Matthew 28:19). Water baptism is very important for the Christian. During water baptism, an individual publicly identifies himself with Christ and the body of Christ (i.e. the church). It outwardly symbolizes the spiritual baptism/conversion that has taken place inwardly (see 1 Corinthians 12:13, Romans 6:2-11).

I do not see water baptism being the slightest bit optional for a truly converted person who desires to walk in obedience to Christ. In scripture we see that those who believed in Christ for salvation did not delay being baptized. Scripture does not support the concept of the Christian convert waiting six months until the annual church baptism; or waiting until he is spiritually mature, or even until he has mastered the theology of baptism. Once a person placed saving faith in Jesus Christ, the convert was baptized:

> **Acts 8:12:** *"But when they believed Philip preaching the good news about the kingdom of God and the name of Jesus Christ, they were being baptized, men and women alike."*

> **Acts 2:41:** *"So then, those who had received his word were baptized; and there were added that day about three thousand souls."*

The question is, have you been baptized since you have come to saving faith in Christ? If not, with prayer and obedience to the command of Christ, do so.

> **Acts 22:16:** *"And now why do you delay? Arise, and be baptized, and wash away your sins, calling on His name."*

<u>MATTHEW 4:1-11</u>
(THE TEMPTATION OF JESUS)

"Then Jesus was led up by the Spirit into the wilderness to be tempted by the devil. ² And after He had fasted forty days and forty nights, He then became hungry. ³ And the tempter came and said to Him, 'If You are the Son of God, command that these stones become bread.' ⁴ But He answered and said, 'It is written, "Man shall not live on bread alone, but on every word that proceeds out of the mouth of God."' ⁵ Then the devil *took Him into the holy city; and he had Him stand on the pinnacle of the temple, ⁶ and *said to Him, 'If You are the Son of God throw Yourself down; for it is written,

"He will give His angels charge concerning You";
and "On their hands they will bear You up,
Lest You strike Your foot against a stone."'

⁷ Jesus said to him, 'On the other hand, it is written, "You shall not put the Lord your God to the test."' ⁸ Again, the devil *took Him to a very high mountain, and *showed Him all the kingdoms of the world, and their glory; ⁹ and he said to Him, 'All these things will I give You, if You fall down and worship me.' ¹⁰ Then Jesus *said to him, 'Begone, Satan! For it is written, "You shall worship the Lord your God, and serve Him only."' ¹¹ Then the devil *left Him; and behold, angels came and began to minister to Him."

<u>Introduction</u>
Right after Jesus was baptized, He was tempted in the desert by the Devil. The Word of God tells us in **1 John 2:16:** *"For all that is in the world, the lust of the flesh and the lust of the eyes and the boastful pride of life, is not from the Father, but is from the world."* We will see below how Satan used these appeals to worldliness in his temptation of Jesus; (i.e. lust of the flesh; lust of the eyes; pride of life). Jesus overcame temptation by using the, *"sword of the Spirit, which is the word of God"* **Ephesians 6:17b**. From this lesson we will see that by the power of God we can overcome temptation in our lives.

> **1 Corinthians 10:13:** *"No temptation has overtaken you but such as is common to man; and God is faithful, who will not allow you to be tempted beyond what you are able, but with the temptation will provide the way of escape also, so that you will be able to endure it."*

VERSE 1: *"Then Jesus was led up by the Spirit into the wilderness to be tempted by the devil."*

Note that Jesus was tempted by the Devil. The term *devil* means, "false accuser or slanderer."[70] The Devil hoped to destroy God's plan of salvation for mankind by causing Jesus to sin. If Jesus sinned, He could not be our savior. He could not be our savior because He would be under the same sentence of death that man is under for his own sin. **Romans 6:23** says, *"For the wages of sin is death,…."*

---

[70] McGarvey, J. W., and Pendleton, P. Y. (1914). *The Four-Fold Gospel* (p. 90). Cincinnati, OH: The Standard Publishing Company.

Note also that the Holy Spirit *led* Jesus into the wilderness. The Father allowed the testing of Jesus, showing the world Jesus was sinless and the only worthy savior of the world. Jesus is the *"…One who has been tempted in all things as we are, yet without sin."* **Hebrews 4:15.**

VERSES 2-4 *"And after He had fasted forty days and forty nights, He then became hungry.* [3] *And the tempter came and said to Him, 'If You are the Son of God, command that these stones become bread.'* [4] *But He answered and said, 'It is written, "MAN SHALL NOT LIVE ON BREAD ALONE, BUT ON EVERY WORD THAT PROCEEDS OUT OF THE MOUTH OF GOD.'"*

Here Satan tempts Jesus to appeal to the, *"lust of the flesh."* Satan tempts the very hungry Jesus to perform a miracle to satisfy His bodily hunger. Do you remember what Jesus said was His true *food*? In **John 4:34** *"Jesus *said to them, "My food is to do the will of Him who sent Me, and to accomplish His work."* Notice the temptation includes a taunt by Satan through a slithery appeal to pride by saying, *"If You are the Son of God."* MacArthur states that,

> "Satan was hoping to persuade Jesus to demonstrate His power to verify that it was real. That would mean violating God's plan that He set that power aside in humiliation and used it only when the Father willed. Satan wanted Jesus to disobey God. Affirming His deity and rights as the Son of God would have been to act independently of God."

What was Jesus' response to the temptation? He quoted the Word of God! Notice verse 4, which says, *"But He answered and said, 'It is written, 'MAN SHALL NOT LIVE ON BREAD ALONE, BUT ON EVERY WORD THAT PROCEEDS OUT OF THE MOUTH OF GOD.'"* This is a quote from Deuteronomy 8:3.

VERSES 5-7: *"Then the devil *took Him into the holy city; and he had Him stand on the pinnacle of the temple,* [6] *and *said to Him, 'If You are the Son of God throw Yourself down; for it is written,*
> *'HE WILL GIVE HIS ANGELS CHARGE CONCERNING YOU';*
> *and 'ON their HANDS THEY WILL BEAR YOU UP,*
> *LEST YOU STRIKE YOUR FOOT AGAINST A STONE."*
[7] *Jesus said to him, 'On the other hand, it is written, 'YOU SHALL NOT PUT THE LORD YOUR GOD to the test.'"*

The second temptation of Satan was an appeal to the, "pride of life." Satan knows the destruction that can come from pride. [71] Satan's own destruction resulted from pride (Ezekiel 28:17 and Isaiah 14:14). Look at what the Word of God says about pride in **James 4:6-7:** *"…Therefore it says, 'GOD IS*

---

[71] More verses on "pride:"

> **1 Peter 5:5:** *"You younger men, likewise, be subject to your elders; and all of you, clothe yourselves with humility toward one another, for God is opposed to the proud, but gives grace to the humble."*
> **Proverbs 8:13:** *"The fear of the Lord is to hate evil;*
> *Pride and arrogance and the evil way,*
> *And the perverted mouth, I hate."*
> **Proverbs 11:2:** *"When pride comes, then comes dishonor, But with the humble is wisdom."*
> **Proverbs 16:18:** *"Pride goes before destruction, And a haughty spirit before stumbling."*
> **Proverbs 16:5:** *"Everyone who is proud in heart is an abomination to the Lord;*
> *Assuredly, he will not be unpunished."*

OPPOSED TO THE PROUD, BUT GIVES GRACE TO THE HUMBLE.' *Submit therefore to God. Resist the devil and he will flee from you."*

Notice that during the temptation, Satan again tries to solicit pride out of Jesus by questioning His position as the Son of God by saying, *"If You are the Son of God."* One of the basic attacks of the enemy is to question God and the authority of His Word. Back in the Garden of Eden, Eve told Satan that it was God who had instructed them to not eat the fruit from one particular tree. Do you remember what Satan said to Eve?

> **Genesis 3:1-4:** *"Now the serpent was more crafty than any beast of the field which the LORD God had made. And he said to the woman, 'Indeed, has God said, "You shall not eat from any tree of the garden?"' ²The woman said to the serpent, 'From the fruit of the trees of the garden we may eat; ³but from the fruit of the tree which is in the middle of the garden, God has said, "You shall not eat from it or touch it, or you will die."' ⁴The serpent said to the woman, 'You surely will not die!'"*

Trying to get people to question God and His Word is the Devil's frontline attack. Another trick of Satan's is to lie about what God said. Notice that God actually said that Adam and Eve could eat from all the trees of the garden <u>except one</u> (Genesis. 3:2). Satan tried to twist that to say God would not allow them to, *"eat from <u>any tree</u> in the garden."* Satan was attempting to make the all-loving God appear harsh and uncaring. If hard times come your way, Satan will try to convince you God does not care for you. He will suggest you need to take care of yourself, just like he suggested to Eve. He also likes to leave the impression that God is keeping you from something good. If you find yourself feeling that way, repent of it immediately or you will fall into his trap.

False prophets, religious leaders and some in authority often misuse and misquote the Word of God for their own purposes. This too originates with the Devil. They often will mock, misstate or question the Bible as authoritative and inerrant. Their deception is only possible because of the vast ignorance of the Bible in society. Because of this ignorance, anyone who claims to be a "religious expert" or a professor can say whatever he wants without any intellectual scrutiny.

An example of this occurred when high school students told me their school teacher said that the, "Bible says that the earth is flat." The students, who were raised in the church, sheepishly asked me if that was true. I told them the teacher is wrong. Year-in and year-out I would have a new group of youth tell me they were taking this teacher's class and he would tell them the Bible says that the world is flat. After some years of this, I finally had enough and went to the high school to meet with this teacher. I politely asked him to show me the verse in the Bible that says the, "world is flat." After listening to his claims of being "very religious" he fumbled around and went off on some scattered esoteric thoughts about Romanism and their history as well as how some might think the language could be interpreted differently. He soon realized that I was not impressed and that I was suspicious that he was making some of it up as he spoke. I pointed out that I had actually read the entire Bible, many times, and that there was no verse as he claimed. I then pointed out what the Bible stated in reference to God and the earth: **Isaiah 40:22:** *"It is He who sits above the <u>circle of the earth</u>,...."*

He then quickly acknowledged that the Bible may not say what he thought it did. I also pointed out how dangerous it was for him to speak so confidently about matters of scripture when he actually knew very little on that subject. He agreed he should be more careful. The conversation ended cordially, but the lesson was short-lived. The reason this teacher was able to continue unchallenged regarding his so-called quotes from the Bible, was due in large part to his students' Biblical ignorance.

We need to know the Word of God so we cannot be easily deceived by pseudo-intellectuals or so-called Bible scholars who attack the faith of young people. I wonder if this teacher ever read this warning in Scripture:

> **Mark 9:42:** *"Whoever causes one of these little ones who believe to stumble, it would be better for him if, with a heavy millstone hung around his neck, he had been cast into the sea."*

Note that during the second temptation (Matthew 4:5-7), Satan decided to use <u>some</u> of God's Word to further the temptation. He quoted inaccurately from Psalm 91:11-12. Satan omitted in verse 11, the phrase, *"in all your ways"* because that phrase changed the meaning Satan wanted to use it for (see also Luke 4:10). Matthew Henry explained this as follows:

> "The promise is, 'They shall keep thee;' but how? In all thy ways; not otherwise; if we go out of our way, out of the way of our duty, we forfeit the promise, and put ourselves out of God's protection. Now this word made against the tempter, and therefore he industriously left it out."

In our study text of Matthew 4:5-7, we notice Jesus answered Satan's temptation as before, He used the Word of God. Jesus quoted Deuteronomy 6:16, which states we are not to put God to the test. Do you put God to the test? Do you ever say, "God, if you are real then I want you to give me…." Or maybe you try to test God by saying, "God, I did all this for you and if you were truly a loving God, you would never have let this happen." Satan was trying to tempt Jesus into performing a sign. The unbelieving always demand signs, as Jesus states in **Matthew 12:38-39:**

> *"Then some of the scribes and Pharisees answered Him, saying, 'Teacher, we want to see a sign from You.' [39] But He answered and said to them, 'An evil and adulterous generation craves for a sign;….'"*

One must be careful to, *"NOT PUT THE LORD YOUR GOD TO THE TEST."* Matthew 4:7. In addition, we must be careful who we allow to be a Bible teacher over us. When you are told the Bible says, "such and such," you should go to the Bible and look it up yourself and see if what you are being told is true. Make sure you check to see if the verse quoted is in context. I call this checking process, *reading the verse with 20/20 Vision*. What I mean by *20/20 Vision* is when someone gives you a verse, read 20 verses before it and 20 verses after it, so that you get the real context of the verse. This method prevents someone from twisting a verse into what he wants it to say, instead of what it really says. Paul commended those who would go to the Word of God to check to see if what he taught was true.

> **Acts 17:10-11:** *"And the brethren immediately sent Paul and Silas away by night to Berea; and when they arrived, they went into the synagogue of the Jews. [11]Now these were more noble-minded than those in Thessalonica, for they received the word with great eagerness, <u>examining the Scriptures daily, to see whether these things were so.</u>"*

Any religious leader or so called "Bible teacher" who does not allow others to question him based on Scripture must be avoided:

> **1 John 4:1:** *"BELOVED, do not believe every spirit, <u>but test the spirits to see whether they are from God;</u> because many false prophets have gone out into the world."*

> **2 Corinthians 11:13-15:** *"For such men are false apostles, deceitful workers, disguising themselves as apostles of Christ. [14] And no wonder, <u>for even Satan disguises himself as an angel of light.</u> [15] Therefore it is not surprising if his servants also disguise themselves as servants of righteousness; whose end shall be according to their deeds."*

The godly man studies the Word of God and teaches it accurately in its context:

> **2 Timothy 2:15:** *"Be diligent to present yourself approved to God as a workman who does not need to be ashamed, <u>handling accurately the word of truth</u>."*

VERSES 8-11: *"Again, the devil *took Him to a very high mountain, and *showed Him all the kingdoms of the world, and their glory; [9] and he said to Him, 'All these things will I give You, if You fall down and worship me.' [10] Then Jesus *said to him, 'Begone, Satan! For it is written, "YOU SHALL WORSHIP THE LORD YOUR GOD, AND SERVE HIM ONLY."' [11] Then the devil *left Him; and behold, angels came and began to minister to Him."*

In this third temptation, the Devil tried to appeal to the, "lust of the eyes" by showing the glory of the kingdoms of this world. The Devil showed these kingdoms and then offered to give them to Jesus if the Lord would worship him. Satan's temptation to Jesus was a suggestion that Jesus could immediately have the kingdoms of the world, rather than experience the hard way of the cross. Of course, that shortcut would have removed salvation for mankind. For Jesus to sin in false worship would have destroyed Him from being the perfect sacrifice for the sins of others.

One may ask the following question: "If Jesus is the God of all things, how could Satan offer the *'kingdoms of the world'* to Him?" The Bible tells us that Satan is the, *"god of this world"* (NASV) or *"god of this age"* (NKJ), **2 Corinthians 4:4**. We are also told that the devil is the *"prince of the power of the air"* **Ephesians 2:2.** Understand that his designation as *"god of this age"* is <u>not</u> one of ultimate authority but rather is a temporary and limited power/authority. Satan's influence is manifest throughout the world: *"and that the whole world lies in the power of the evil one."* **1 John 5:19.** Satan works through the unconverted: *"During supper, <u>the devil having already put into the heart of Judas</u> Iscariot, the son of Simon, to betray Him,"* **John 13:2.**

Jesus states that Satan's primary attributes are that of lying and murder: *"… your father the devil, and you want to do the desires of your father. <u>He was a murderer from the beginning</u>, and does not stand in the truth because <u>there is no truth in him.</u> Whenever he speaks a lie, he speaks from his own nature<u>, for he is a liar and the father of lies</u>.* **John 8:44.** Satan obtained this temporary possession of the world system when it was forfeited by Adam through his sin in the Garden of Eden. This limited authority and influence of Satan is seen in every aspect of the world's systems including commerce, law, religion and education.

With that said, make no mistake about it, God is ultimately in control and Satan has already been completely defeated by Jesus on the Cross. **1 John 3:8:** *"…The Son of God appeared for this purpose, that He might destroy the works of the devil."* We also see judgment on Satan in **John 12:31** when Jesus said, *"Now judgment is upon this world; now the ruler of this world shall be cast out."* Although Satan (and his demonic kings on the earth) will appear to have been the great power so as to have *"shook kingdoms,"* he is crushed and thrown down by God to the lowest depths of the pit of hell. The Devil's will be exposed in his annihilated state. [72]

Isaiah 14: 12-17 (NKJV)
12   *"How you are fallen from heaven,*
     O Lucifer, son of the morning!
     How you are cut down to the ground,
     You who weakened the nations!
13   *For you have said in your heart:*
     'I will ascend into heaven,
     I will exalt my throne above the stars of God;
     I will also sit on the mount of the congregation
     On the farthest sides of the north;
14   *I will ascend above the heights of the clouds,*
     I will be like the Most High.'
15   *Yet you shall be brought down to Sheol,*
     To the lowest depths of the Pit.
16   *"Those who see you will gaze at you,*
     And consider you, saying:
     'Is this the man who made the earth tremble,
     Who shook kingdoms,
17   *Who made the world as a wilderness*
     And destroyed its cities,...?"

---

[72]   This limited authority and influence of Satan is seen in every aspect of the world's systems including commerce, law, religion and education. In **commerce**, lying and broken contracts are simply *doing business*. Money is god to most people whether they are rich or poor. In **law**, the Supreme Court declares that *privacy* means a mother's can kill her own child in the womb. In **religion**, some Hindus will let a rat eat from a pile of grain while denying it to a starving person who is supposedly working through his karma. We also have pulpits full of false ministers that deny the Bible as the Word of God, and abuse their position to pursue personal agendas like ordaining homosexuals, molesting children, and defrauding parishioners to get money. In **education**, most public school districts have banned many aspects of God from the classroom (with the exception of using His name in vain). Schools are afraid to post the Ten Commandments because they might offend someone. In an era of school shootings, explicit sex education, and academic dishonesty; how *dangerous* would it be for a student to read on the wall that God said you are not to: murder another person, fornicate, lie, cheat, or steal? Most science classes indoctrinate students to believe there is no God, and their existence is the result of a cosmic slime-ball that was transformed into a monkey without a tail. A school may claim that it teaches "character traits" without God. The problem is that teaching godly conduct—without God—results in a temporary, yet futile, attempt at behavior modification. It does not produce a transformed life that understands that one day the person will be ultimately accountable to Almighty God: *"The fear of the Lord is the beginning of wisdom, And the knowledge of the Holy One is understanding."* **Proverbs 9:10.** Paul explains the propagators of this false view of "character traits without God" as those *"holding to a form of godliness, although they have denied its power; and avoid such men as these."* **2 Timothy 3:5.** The end result of *godless morality* is a person who remains spiritually blind, and sees no reason for life except self-gratification. Having served approximately 28 years as a prosecutor, I can say to the parent who is raising a child void of the values and truths set forth in scripture, that they would do well to start saving now for a bail bondsman. If, by chance, the child has grown up and you did not have to deal with his legal/moral problems, do not be proud of how well you raised him; be thankful he did not get caught...yet.

In the Book of Revelation we see Jesus alone holds the "title deed" to the earth and rules it as the King of Kings. **Revelation 1:5:** *"Jesus Christ, … the ruler of the kings of the earth…."*

In our text regarding the temptation (Matthew 8:4-11), again we see Jesus crush the temptation of the Devil by using the Word of God, quoting Deuteronomy 6:13. Notice also how the Devil is under the complete domination of Christ. When Jesus said, *"Begone, Satan!"* he had to leave. Satan could not say, "No, I am not going to leave." Even though Satan has some power, only God is Almighty. We see Satan's end in **Revelation 20:10:**

> *"And the devil who deceived them was thrown into the lake of fire and brimstone, where the beast and the false prophet are also; and they <u>will be tormented day and night forever and ever."</u>*

Summary and Application

"To be tempted is in itself no sin; it is the yielding to temptation, and the giving it a place in our hearts, which we must fear."[73] Scripture warns us of this in **James 1:14–15:** *"But each one is tempted when he is carried away and enticed by his own lust. Then when lust has conceived, it gives birth to sin; and when sin is accomplished, it brings forth death."*

When fighting temptation, I need to:

A. Be in close communion/prayer with the Lord daily, and calling out to God for His protection. Jesus tells us in **Matthew 26:41:** *"Keep <u>watching and praying that you may not enter into temptation;</u> the spirit is willing, but the flesh is weak."* The concept of *watching* includes not being spiritually naïve, but understanding that the spiritual battle rages around you:

> **1 Peter 5:8–9:** *"Be of <u>sober spirit, be on the alert.</u> Your adversary, the devil, prowls around like a roaring lion, <u>seeking someone to devour.</u> 9 But <u>resist him, firm in your faith,</u> knowing that the same experiences of suffering are being accomplished by your brethren who are in the world."*

B. Not put myself in places and situations where I can be tempted, and when I am, *flee!*
- **1 Corinthians 6:18:** *"<u>Flee immorality.</u> Every other sin that a man commits is outside the body, but the immoral man sins against his own body."*
- **1 Corinthians 10:14:** *"Therefore, my beloved, <u>flee from idolatry."</u>*
- **1 Timothy 6:9–12:** *"But those <u>who want to get rich fall into temptation</u> and a snare and many foolish and harmful desires which plunge men into ruin and destruction. 10 For <u>the love of money is a root of all sorts of evil,</u> and some by longing for it have wandered away from the faith and pierced themselves with many griefs. 11 But <u>flee from these things, you man of God, and pursue righteousness, godliness, faith, love, perseverance and gentleness.</u> 12 <u>Fight the good fight of faith;</u> take hold of the eternal life to which you were called, and you made the good confession in the presence of many witnesses.*
- **2 Timothy 2:22:** *"<u>Now flee from youthful lusts</u> and pursue righteousness, faith, love and peace, with those who call on the Lord from a pure heart."*

---

[73] Ryle, J.C., *Matthew (Expository Thoughts on the Gospels)*, (Crossways Classic Commentaries: v.1) p.19.

C. Arm myself with the Word of God! Satan tries to get you to question God's Word, as well as God's love and faithfulness in providing for you. By not believing God, you will be doing what Satan did (i.e. exalting yourself as god). We are to fight temptation by the Word of God, that is, quoting it and believing what it says. The **quoting of the Scripture in a time of temptation is not like saying** *magic words*, **rather it is a faith-filled proclamation of what Almighty God has said on the subject.** Specifically, what He has said regarding sin, righteousness and judgment (John 16:8-12) ends all other speculation. In other words:

   i. When a Christian is being tempted, he is experiencing many fleshly impulses/desires and false messages from the world, and the Devil is telling the person to rebel against what God commands.[74]

   ii. The Christian should respond in faith by proclaiming the ultimate truth regarding the situation by stating what God has said in His Word.[75]

   iii. By believing what God has said, one is empowered by the Holy Spirit to submit to God, resist temptation and be restored to a sound mind: **Romans 8:6:** *"For the mind set on the flesh is death, but the mind set on the Spirit is life and peace,"*; **James 4:7:** *"Submit therefore to God. Resist the devil and he will flee from you."*; **2 Peter 2:9:** *"then the Lord knows how to rescue the godly from temptation, and to keep the unrighteous under punishment for the day of judgment,."* By truly believing what God's Word says, we should proclaim the same thing Joseph said when he was tempted: *"How then could I do this great evil and sin against God?"* **Genesis 39:9.**

If you do not study the Bible, you will not have this great weapon available in your time of need. As David wrote, in **Psalm 119:11:** *"Your word I have treasured in my heart, That I may not sin against You."*

Make sure you are well armed with the full armor of God on a daily basis:

Ephesians 6:10–18: *"Finally, be strong in the Lord and in the strength of His might. [11] Put on the full armor of God, so that you will be able to stand firm against the schemes of the devil. [12] For our struggle is not against flesh and blood, but against the rulers, against the powers, against the world forces of this darkness, against the spiritual forces of wickedness in the heavenly places. [13] Therefore, take up the full armor of God, so that you will be able to resist in the evil day, and having done everything, to stand firm. [14] Stand firm therefore, having girded your loins with truth, and having put on the breastplate of righteousness, [15] and having shod your feet with the preparation of the gospel of peace; [16] in addition to all, taking up the shield of faith with which you will be able to extinguish all the flaming arrows of the evil one. [17] And take the helmet of salvation, and the sword of the Spirit, which is the word of God. [18] With all prayer and petition pray at all times in*

---

[74] **1 John 2:16–17:** *"For all that is in the world, the lust of the flesh and the lust of the eyes and the boastful pride of life, is not from the Father, but is from the world. The world is passing away, and also its lusts; but the one who does the will of God lives forever."*

[75] I am not talking about the heretical "word-of-faith" teaching, also known as "name-it and claim-it / blab-it and grab-it." I am speaking of Holy Spirit-led faith and humble submission to God's Word:
Genesis 15:6: *"Then he believed in the Lord; and He reckoned it to him as righteousness."*
Romans 10:17: *"So faith comes from hearing, and hearing by the word of Christ."*
Romans 1:16–17: *"For I am not ashamed of the gospel, for it is the power of God for salvation to everyone who believes, to the Jew first and also to the Greek. For in it the righteousness of God is revealed from faith to faith; as it is written, 'But the righteous man shall live by faith.'"*

the Spirit, and with this in view, be on the alert with all perseverance and petition for all the saints,...." The concepts set out above are summarized in **James 4:7**: "*Submit therefore to God. Resist the devil and he will flee from you.*"[Please take a look footnote 76 regarding Bible translations.]

---

[76] **BIBLE TRANSLATIONS AND PARAPHRASES:** This author leans firmly to the NASB because it is known for being "*a monumental work of scholarship and a very accurate translation.*" Comfort, P. W. (1991). *The complete guide to Bible versions.* Wheaton, Ill.: Living Books. The foreword of the NASB states that, "The purpose of the Editorial Board in making this translation was to adhere as closely as possible to the original languages of the Holy Scriptures, and to make the translation in a fluent and readable style according to current English usage." *New American Standard Bible* 1995 by The Lockman Foundation. The NASB concept to, "adhere as closely as possible to the original languages of the Holy Scriptures" is called *formal equivalency*. Formal equivalency means that, it "attempts a word-for-word rendition, providing as literal a translation as possible." *Which Bible translation is best? by* John MacArthur. This is distinguishable from the NIV which is a *dynamic equivalent*. A dynamic equivalent translation is one in which the translators take a view of what was the "thought" behind the scripture rather than a more literal translation. The weakness in the "dynamic equivalent" is the possibility of the scholar having the wrong "thought" about a text and that thought becoming manifested in the text. I am much more interested in a more literal translation despite the difficulties it may cause in readability. When a person comments on scripture, it is merely that (i.e. writing and making comments regarding scripture). The comments are subject to error and misinterpretation. This fact does not give one the right to be sloppy in his research and handle divine scripture in a less than fearful manner. Indeed, commenting on scripture is an extremely serious matter, which will subject one to a stricter judgment (James 3:1). If this warning exists to teachers of God's Word, woe to the one who is tweaking with the actual text of scripture. Meddling with the text itself is always a very grave sin because scripture is perfect and does not need to be helped in its text - (*"**Do not add to His Words,**"* Proverbs 30:5-6, Deuteronomy 4:2, 12:32, Revelation 22:18-19, Ezekiel 13;). Although we may not have the original texts, only a fool would mess with God's word. If you look at the various Bibles in the market today, you will find an endless barrage of self-styled paraphrases or "study bibles." Some are "marketed" based on one's ethnicity, gender, gender neutrality, age, marital status, addiction recovery etc. The result of many of these is a church with a low regard for scripture and an inability to understand important biblical concepts. One commentator said that the concept behind a paraphrase is the height of arrogance and absurdity. His point is that one who writes a paraphrase is in essence saying, "God stated what He wants to tell man, but I [the paraphrase writer] can help God say it a little better by rewriting it." Paraphrase supporters will claim they are merely making scripture available to the masses. I disagree. Quality scholarship that is committed to the infallibility of scripture and adherence to "as closely as possible...the original languages" in the translation provides scripture to people in their own language. Paraphrase supporters would also claim that they are merely putting the words in a modern vernacular and slang. The failure of this argument turns on the fact that the Holy Spirit speaks to the person through the fidelity of scripture. The effect of slang inserted in scripture has resulted in much of the church having lost the importance of terms, which previously had great biblical/theological meaning. MacArthur states it this way, "Many translators today have also adopted the postmodern idea of elevating the experience of the reader over the intention of the author. They make the contemporary reader sovereign over the text and demote the intended meaning of the historic human writers who were carried along by one divine author (2 Peter 1:19-21)."

MATTHEW 4:12-25
(JESUS FULFILLS PROPHECY, PREACHES REPENTANCE, CALLS DISCIPLES and HEALS PEOPLE)

"Now when He heard that John had been taken into custody, He withdrew into Galilee; [13] *and leaving Nazareth, He came and settled in Capernaum, which is by the sea, in the region of Zebulun and Naphtali.* [14]*This was to fulfill what was spoken through Isaiah the prophet, saying,*

> [15] *'THE LAND OF ZEBULUN AND THE LAND OF NAPHTALI,*
>> *BY THE WAY OF THE SEA, BEYOND THE JORDAN, GALILEE OF THE GENTILES—*
> [16] *THE PEOPLE WHO WERE SITTING IN DARKNESS SAW A GREAT LIGHT,*
>> *AND TO THOSE WHO WERE SITTING IN THE LAND AND SHADOW OF DEATH,*
>> *UPON THEM A LIGHT DAWNED.'*

[17] *From that time Jesus began to preach and say, 'Repent, for the kingdom of heaven is at hand.'*

[18] *And walking by the Sea of Galilee, He saw two brothers, Simon who was called Peter, and Andrew his brother, casting a net into the sea; for they were fishermen.* [19] *And He *said to them, 'Follow Me, and I will make you fishers of men.'* [20] *And they immediately left the nets, and followed Him.* [21] *And going on from there He saw two other brothers, James the son of Zebedee, and John his brother, in the boat with Zebedee their father, mending their nets; and He called them.* [22] *And they immediately left the boat and their father, and followed Him.*

[23] *And Jesus was going about in all Galilee, teaching in their synagogues, and proclaiming the gospel of the kingdom, and healing every kind of disease and every kind of sickness among the people.* [24] *And the news about Him went out into all Syria; and they brought to Him all who were ill, taken with various diseases and pains, demoniacs, epileptics, paralytics; and He healed them.* [25] *And great multitudes followed Him from Galilee and Decapolis and Jerusalem and Judea and from beyond the Jordan."*

Introduction

In this section, we will see Jesus continue to fulfill prophesies that demonstrate He is the Messiah of Israel. Remember the Book of Matthew was written to the Jews. The Jewish readers were very familiar with prophesies the Messiah must fulfill. These prophesies were further fulfilled through His proclamation of the "good news" of the kingdom of God and His miraculous healing of others. We further read that Jesus called His listeners to "repentance." We will see below what it means to "repent."

VERSES 12-16: *"Now when He heard that John had been taken into custody, He withdrew into Galilee;* [13] *and leaving Nazareth, He came and settled in Capernaum, which is by the sea, in the region of Zebulun and Naphtali.* [14] *This was to fulfill what was spoken through Isaiah the prophet, saying,*

> [15] *'THE LAND OF ZEBULUN AND THE LAND OF NAPHTALI,*
>> *BY THE WAY OF THE SEA, BEYOND THE JORDAN, GALILEE OF THE GENTILES—*
> [16] *THE PEOPLE WHO WERE SITTING IN DARKNESS SAW A GREAT LIGHT,*
>> *AND TO THOSE WHO WERE SITTING IN THE LAND AND SHADOW OF DEATH,*
>> *UPON THEM A LIGHT DAWNED.'*

John the Baptist was arrested by Herod Antipas (a son of Herod the Great), for rebuking him for stealing his half-brother's wife (Luke 3:19-20). We next see that Jesus left Nazareth. This departure resulted from Him calmly leaving a group who desired to kill Him (Luke 4:16-30). He did not flee to protect Himself, but simply walked past those who desired to be His murderers (Luke 4:28-30). It is important to understand that no one could kill Him until His appointed time (John 10:17-18). He left that area because it was not His time yet.

In the Bible *light* and *darkness* had specific meanings as set out in:

> **Proverbs 4:18-19:** *"But the path of the righteous is like the light of dawn, that shines brighter and brighter until the full day. ¹⁹ The way of the wicked is like darkness;*
> *They do not know over what they stumble."*

Jesus came to bring people out of darkness into light.

> **John 8:12:** *"Again therefore Jesus spoke to them, saying, 'I am the light of the world; he who follows Me shall not walk in the darkness, but shall have the light of life.'"*

Jesus fulfilled the prophecy that He would minister to and bring a great *Light* to those of Zebulun and Naphtali. This prophecy, approximately 800 years before Christ, comes from Isaiah 9:1-7. This portion from Isaiah is prophesying about Jesus, The Coming Messiah.

> **Isaiah 9:1-7:** *"But there will be no more gloom for her who was in anguish; in earlier times He treated the land of Zebulun and the land of Naphtali with contempt, but later on He shall make it glorious, by the way of the sea, on the other side of Jordan, Galilee of the Gentiles.*
> *² The people who walk in darkness*
> *Will see a great light;*
> *Those who live in a dark land,*
> *The light will shine on them.*
> *³ Thou shalt multiply the nation,*
> *Thou shalt increase their gladness;*
> *They will be glad in Thy presence*
> *As with the gladness of harvest,*
> *As men rejoice when they divide the spoil.*
> *⁴ For Thou shalt break the yoke of their burden and the staff on their shoulders,*
> *The rod of their oppressor, as at the battle of Midian.*
> *⁵ For every boot of the booted warrior in the battle tumult,*
> *And cloak rolled in blood, will be for burning, fuel for the fire.*
> *⁶ For a child will be born to us, a son will be given to us;*
> *And the government will rest on His shoulders;*
> *And His name will be called Wonderful Counselor, Mighty God,*
> *Eternal Father, Prince of Peace.*
> *⁷ There will be no end to the increase of His government or of peace,*
> *On the throne of David and over his kingdom,*
> *To establish it and to uphold it with justice and righteousness*
> *From then on and forevermore.*
> *The zeal of the LORD of hosts will accomplish this."*

VERSE 17: *"From that time Jesus began to preach and say, 'Repent, for the kingdom of heaven is at hand.'"*

Jesus preached, *"Repent, for the kingdom of heaven is at hand."* Note that this is the same phrase that John the Baptist preached in Matthew 3:2. Jesus also sent His disciples out to spread the same message of repentance (see Mark 6:7-12). As we studied before, repentance means to change your mind, a complete turn from your sin to faith in Christ. It is "not just feeling sorry,…[but a] complete alteration of the basic motivation and direction of one's life."[77] So, does repentance matter today? Absolutely! People need to repent from dead works to true faith in God (see Heb. 6:1, Heb. 9:14). As Peter taught in <u>Acts 2:38:</u> *"And Peter said to them, 'Repent, and let each of you be baptized in the name of Jesus Christ for the forgiveness of your sins; and you shall receive the gift of the Holy Spirit.'"* Ryle stated the importance of repentance this way:

> "True repentance is no light matter: it is a thorough change of heart about sin, a change showing itself in godly sorrow for sin, in heartfelt confession of sin - in a complete breaking off from sinful habits, and a lasting hatred of all sin. Such repentance is inseparable companion of saving faith in Christ. Let us prize the doctrine highly. No Christian teaching can be called *understood* if it does not constantly bring us to 'turn to God in repentance have faith in our Lord Jesus' (Acts 20:21)."[78]

Repentance, *comes from God.* It says in <u>2 Timothy 2:25-26:</u> *"…with gentleness correcting those who are in opposition, <u>if perhaps God may grant them repentance</u> leading to the knowledge of the truth, 26 and they may come to their senses and escape from the snare of the devil, having been held captive by him to do his will."* (See also Acts 5:31 and 11:18.) We should pray that the Lord grant us repentance for sins in our life. Not just the sins we are aware of but also those we are unaware. [For a more detailed discussion about repentance review the notes in Matthew 3:1-3.]

<u>Section Application</u>

Are there areas in your life you need to repent of? Are there areas of unbelief, sinful conduct, or fears of losing your friends? Then you need to repent.

<u>VERSES 18-22:</u> *"And walking by the Sea of Galilee, He saw two brothers, Simon who was called Peter, and Andrew his brother, casting a net into the sea; for they were fishermen. 19 And He *said to them, "Follow Me, and I will make you fishers of men." 20 And they immediately left the nets, and followed Him. 21 And going on from there He saw two other brothers, James the son of Zebedee, and John his brother, in the boat with Zebedee their father, mending their nets; and He called them. 22 And they immediately left the boat and their father, and followed Him."*

Here Jesus called two sets of brothers (i.e. Peter and Andrew; James and John). Peter and Andrew were net-fishing when Jesus called them, v.18. James and John were with their dad, sitting in their fishing boat, repairing nets. James and John were named by Jesus the "Sons of Thunder." We do not know for sure about the spirituality of James' and John's dad, but we do know that they had a godly mother named Salome (Salome was one of the women at the cross, Mark 15:40 and Matthew 27:55-56; and she also went to the tomb Mark 16:1).

---

[77] Wood, D. R. W. and Marshall, I. H., *New Bible Dictionary* (3rd ed.) (Page 1007). Leicester, England; Downers Grove, Ill.: InterVarsity Press (1996).

[78] Ryle, J.C., Matthew *(Expository Thoughts on the Gospels)*, (Crossways Classic Commentaries: v.1) p.27.

The brothers James and John, along with Peter, became part of Jesus' inner circle as shown by their presence at: the resurrection of the girl (Mark 5:37-42); Jesus' transfiguration (Mark 9:2); and the garden of Gethsemane (Mark 14:32-42). James is not the same James who wrote the book of James. The book of James was written by Jesus' half-brother who appears to have become a believer after the resurrection.

Note that Jesus told them: *"Follow Me, and I will make you fishers of men."* v.19. They responded in that they *"immediately left the nets, and followed Him."*

<u>Section Application</u>

What is your response to Jesus' call to be His disciple and evangelize the world? Every Christian is called to be a witness:

- <u>Mark 16:15-16:</u> *"And He said to them, 'Go into all the world and preach the gospel to all creation. ¹⁶ He who has believed and has been baptized shall be saved; but he who has disbelieved shall be condemned.'"*

- <u>Romans 10:13-14:</u> *"...for 'WHOEVER WILL CALL UPON THE NAME OF THE LORD will be saved.' ¹⁴ How then shall they call upon Him in whom they have not believed? And how shall they believe in Him whom they have not heard?"*

- <u>2 Timothy 4:1-2,5:</u> *"I SOLEMNLY <u>charge you in the presence of God and of Christ Jesus, who is to judge</u> the living and the dead, and by His appearing and His kingdom: ² <u>preach the word</u>; be ready in season and out of season; reprove, rebuke, exhort, with great patience and instruction....⁵But you, be sober in all things, endure hardship, <u>do the work of an evangelist, fulfill your ministry."</u>*

- <u>Proverbs 11:30:</u> *"...And he who is wise wins souls."*

<u>VERSES 23-25:</u> *"And Jesus was going about in all Galilee, teaching in their synagogues, and proclaiming the gospel of the kingdom, and healing every kind of disease and every kind of sickness among the people. ²⁴ And the news about Him went out into all Syria; and they brought to Him all who were ill, taken with various diseases and pains, demoniacs, epileptics, paralytics; and He healed them. ²⁵ And great multitudes followed Him from Galilee and Decapolis and Jerusalem and Judea and from beyond the Jordan."*

Here we see the divine and compassionate Jesus. The text does not say He healed people with certain types of sicknesses. It says that Jesus went, *"<u>proclaiming the gospel</u> of the kingdom, and healing <u>every kind of disease</u> and <u>every kind of sickness</u> among the people."* Jesus is first concerned with the spiritual health of man because He went *"proclaiming the gospel"* and then He healed the physical needs of the people. Say that you observed a young neighbor-child riding his bike past your home when suddenly he fell very hard and started crying. You can tell he severely broke his arm. Which of the following two responses would you make?

1. Yell over to the kid, and tell him that you are heading into your house to have lunch but when you are done, you will come back out and see if he is doing any better, or
2. Run over to help and comfort him while you call for an ambulance?

The choice is obvious, but why is that not the way you look at the spiritual health of your neighbor? Jesus proclaimed the Gospel to people first. Jesus clearly states that one's spiritual condition is much more important than his physical condition.

- **MATTHEW 18:8-9:** *"If your hand or your foot causes you to sin cut it off and throw it away. It is better for you to enter life maimed or crippled than to have two hands or two feet and be thrown into eternal fire. ⁹ And if your eye causes you to sin, gouge it out and throw it away. It is better for you to enter life with one eye than to have two eyes and be thrown into the fire of hell."*

- Luke 12:4-5: *"And I say to you, My friends, do not be afraid of those who kill the body, and after that have no more that they can do. ⁵ But I will warn you whom to fear: fear the One who after He has killed has authority to cast into hell; yes, I tell you, fear Him!"*

If you act concerned for your neighbor's physical health, will you be more concerned about his spiritual health?

Summary and Application

The Great Commission (proclamation of the Gospel) is often exhorted from the pulpit, but very neglected in practice. The average committed churchman will be happy to get together with other guys to hammer and saw on a church-building project, but remains unavailable to carry the *sword of the Spirit* by going door-to-door to evangelize. Many of the dedicated women in the church are content to bring food to a potluck, but are likewise unavailable when it comes to public evangelism. This occurs for many reasons, running the spectrum from being inadequately trained, to the worst scenario, not really being a Christian in the first place. Where do you fall into this spectrum? Reread Luke 12:4-5 above and your fear of man will dissolve.

MATTHEW 5:1-12
(THE BEATITUDES)

5:1 "AND when He saw the multitudes, He went up on the mountain; and after He sat down, His disciples came to Him. ² And opening His mouth He began to teach them, saying,

³ 'Blessed are the poor in spirit, for theirs is the kingdom of heaven.

⁴ Blessed are those who mourn, for they shall be comforted.

⁵ Blessed are the gentle, for they shall inherit the earth.

⁶ Blessed are those who hunger and thirst for righteousness, for they shall be satisfied.

⁷ Blessed are the merciful, for they shall receive mercy.

⁸ Blessed are the pure in heart, for they shall see God.

⁹ Blessed are the peacemakers, for they shall be called sons of God.

¹⁰ Blessed are those who have been persecuted for the sake of righteousness, for theirs is the kingdom of heaven. ¹¹Blessed are you when men cast insults at you, and persecute you, and say all kinds of evil against you falsely, on account of Me. ¹²Rejoice, and be glad, for your reward in heaven is great, for so they persecuted the prophets who were before you.'"

Introduction

This section is known as the *Beatitudes,* which are part of the *Sermon on the Mount.* The *Sermon on the Mount* is contained in Matthew chapters 5-7. This great teaching from our Lord sets out the power of a Spirit-led life. It is the upside-down version of the world. In other words, our world thinks very highly of wealth, pride, personal power, and the "winner-take-all" mentality. But the kingdom of God is the exact opposite. As Jesus stated in **Luke 22:26**: *"... but let him who is the greatest among you become as the youngest, and the leader as the servant."*

The *Sermon on the Mount* has been often distorted by many false religious leaders who believe it supports their view of soft, weak-kneed sentimentalism. These false teachers love to appear on the outside as peaceful and kind. They never speak of truth and true righteousness. Often in their hypocritical, peacemaking appearances, they will stand up for evil, unrepentant men. For a photo opportunity they will embrace a murderous, communist dictator or terrorist. Claiming peace, they publically support the release of dangerous criminals into society. To show their open-mindedness they march for all sorts of immoral/perverted social agendas. They love the approval of others here on earth more than the approval of God in heaven. This glorification of spinelessness is not the truths our Lord set out in the Sermon on the Mount. As Charles Spurgeon stated,

> "Our peaceableness is never to be a compact with sin, or toleration of evil. We must set
> our faces like flints against everything which is contrary to God and his holiness: purity
> being in our souls a settled matter, we can go on to peaceableness.[79]

Martin Luther summed up this concept when he stated: "Peace if possible, truth at all costs."

---

[79] Spurgeon, C. H.. *Morning and Evening : Daily readings,* (March 17 PM) Oak Harbor (1995).

VERSES 1-2: *"AND when He saw the multitudes, He went up on the mountain; and after He sat down, His disciples came to Him. ² And opening His mouth He began to teach them, saying,…"*

The term *Beatitudes* is Latin in origin and means a "pronouncement of blessing… [and] has connotations of <u>happiness</u>, felicity, satisfaction and well-being."[80] The Beatitudes demonstrate that human effort to be righteous will never earn the blessings pronounced in the Lord's sermon. The *Sermon on the Mount* does not set out the way of salvation. It conveys the way of righteous living for those who are in God's family. One who reads it should be drawn to faith in God for forgiveness since the standard laid out in the *Beatitudes* is impossible for a human to obtain on his own. They do not apply to merely outward actions, but inward attitudes. One cannot behave like Christ until he has been converted by Christ. As stated in the *Introduction* section, there are those who will come up with their own view on how to engage in an illegitimate imitation of these attributes, but they are not the true Spirit-led life in Christ.

An example of a truly godly life would be John the Baptist. Jesus said that *"…among those born of women there has not arisen anyone greater than John the Baptist!.."* **Matthew 11:11**. We see John the Baptist, in godly humility and righteousness, being killed for confronting an ungodly king.

> **Matthew 14:3-5:** *"For when Herod had John arrested, he bound him, and put him in prison on account of Herodias, the wife of his brother Philip. ⁴ For John had been saying to him, 'It is not lawful for you to have her.' ⁵And although he wanted to put him to death, he feared the multitude, because they regarded him as a prophet."*

John MacArthur states the following regarding the Sermon on the Mount:
> "The ideals and principles in the Sermon on the Mount are utterly contrary to those of human societies and governments. <u>In Christ's kingdom the most exalted persons are those who are the lowliest in the world's estimation</u>, and vice versa. Jesus declared that John the Baptist was the greatest man who had ever lived until that time. Yet John had no possessions and no home, lived in the wilderness, dressed in a hair garment, and ate locusts and wild honey. He was not a part of the religious system, and he had no financial, military, or political power. In addition to that, he preached a message that in the world's eyes was completely irrelevant and absurd. By worldly standards he was a misfit and a failure. Yet he received the Lord's highest praise. In Jesus' kingdom the least are greater even than John the Baptist (Matthew 11:11). <u>They are characterized in this sermon as being humble, compassionate, meek, yearning for righteousness, merciful, pure in heart, peacemakers - and persecuted for the sake of the very righteousness they practice. In the world's eyes those characteristics are the marks of losers.</u> The world says, 'Assert yourself, stand up for yourself, be proud of yourself, elevate yourself, defend yourself, avenge yourself, serve yourself.' Those are the treasured traits of the world's people and the world's kingdoms."[81]

VERSE 3: *"Blessed are the poor in spirit, for theirs is the kingdom of heaven"*

---

[80] Ryken, L., Wilhoit, J., Longman, T., Duriez, C., Penney, D., and Reid, D. G. (2000). *Dictionary of Biblical imagery* (electronic ed.) (p. 82). Downers Grove, IL: InterVarsity Press.

[81] MacArthur, John F., *The MacArthur New Testament Commentary, Matthew* (Chicago: Moody Press) 1983.

The verse says blessed are the *"poor in spirit."* This blessing is not based on one's financial standing but rather his pride standing. One who is proud, self-reliant and self-righteous will not enter the kingdom of heaven because he sees no need for God.

> **Proverbs 16:5:** *"Everyone who is proud in heart is an abomination to the LORD; Assuredly, he will not be unpunished."*

> **Habakkuk 2:4:** *"Behold, as for the proud one, His soul is not right within him; But the righteous will live by his faith."*

> **1 Peter 5:5-6:** *"....clothe yourselves with humility toward one another, for 'GOD IS OPPOSED TO THE PROUD, BUT GIVES GRACE TO THE HUMBLE.' Humble yourselves, therefore, under the mighty hand of God, that He may exalt you at the proper time...."*

One who is *"poor in spirit"* is one who states like Paul, *"For I know that nothing good dwells in me, that is, in my flesh; for the willing is present in me, but the doing of the good is not."* **Romans 7:18**. That person, who in faith, calls upon the name of Jesus, will be granted forgiveness. God said in **Isaiah 66:2**: *"...But to this one I will look, To him who is humble and contrite of spirit, and who trembles at My word."*

This lesson can be summed up in the story Jesus told in **Luke 18:9-14**:
> *"And <u>He also told this parable to certain ones who trusted in themselves that they were righteous</u>, and viewed others with contempt: [10] 'Two men went up into the temple to pray, one a Pharisee, and the other a tax-gatherer. [11] The Pharisee stood and was praying thus to himself, "God, I thank Thee that I am not like other people: swindlers, unjust, adulterers, or even like this tax-gatherer. [12] I fast twice a week; I pay tithes of all that I get." [13] But the tax-gatherer, <u>standing some distance away, was even unwilling to lift up his eyes to heaven, but was beating his breast, saying, "God, be merciful to me, the sinner!"</u> [14] I tell you, this man went down to his house justified rather than the other; for everyone who exalts himself shall be humbled, but he who humbles himself shall be exalted.'"*

Section Application

The question to ask yourself is whether you are a self-righteous, religious hypocrite, or are you *poor in spirit*? The Pharisees of Jesus' day were consumed with looking good on the outside and did not care what their hearts were truly like. Do you want your life to look "Christian" on the outside or are you more concerned with what God sees on the inside? Do you cry out to God, knowing you have no hope for eternal life except from Him? Only you know the real answers to these questions. Do you need to repent and humble yourself before God?

One test of humility practiced by the great Puritan Thomas Watson was to:
> "… not complain about our situation, no matter how bad it may become. Because we know we deserve worse than anything we can experience in this life, we will consider no circumstance to be unfair. When tragedy comes we will not say, 'Why me, Lord?' When our suffering is for Christ's sake we not only will not complain or feel ashamed but will glorify God for it (1 Pet. 4:16), knowing that we will 'also be glorified with Him'

and realizing 'that the sufferings of this present time are not worthy to be compared with the glory that is to be revealed to us' (Rom. 8:17-18).'" [82]

VERSE 4: *"Blessed are those who mourn, for they shall be comforted."*

This verse does not glamorize self-pity, false humility/self-abasement (Colossians 2:18, 23). The mourning discussed here is the sorrow of a repentant heart that leads to salvation. Salvation is the happiness and comfort given to those who mourn. The Apostle Paul described it as follows:

> **2 Corinthians 7:9-11:** *"I now rejoice, not that you were made sorrowful, but that <u>you were made sorrowful to the point of repentance; for you were made sorrowful according to the will of God,</u> so that you might not suffer loss in anything through us. [10] For <u>the sorrow that is according to the will of God produces a repentance without regret, leading to salvation, but the sorrow of the world produces death.</u> [11] For behold what earnestness this very thing, this godly sorrow, has produced in you: what vindication of yourselves, what indignation, what fear, what longing, what zeal, what avenging of wrong! In everything you demonstrated yourselves to be innocent in the matter."*

Look in the Old Testament to see how the Messiah will comfort those who mourn. They will have the "good news" given to them:

> **Isaiah 61:1-3:**
> *"THE Spirit of the Lord GOD is upon me,*
> *Because the LORD has anointed me*
> *To bring good news to the afflicted;*
> <u>*He has sent me to bind up the brokenhearted,*</u>
> *To proclaim liberty to captives,*
> *And freedom to prisoners;*
> [2] *To proclaim the favorable year of the LORD,*
> *And the day of vengeance of our God;*
> <u>*To comfort all who mourn,*</u>
> [3] <u>*To grant those who mourn in Zion,*</u>
> <u>*Giving them a garland instead of ashes,*</u>
> <u>*The oil of gladness instead of mourning,….*"</u>

The great promise of the Messiah's comfort is set out in His word:

> **Revelation 21:4:** *"…<u>He shall wipe away every tear from their eyes; and there shall no longer be any death; there shall no longer be any mourning, or crying,</u> or pain; the first things have passed away."*

Section Application

Have you mourned over your sins to God and sought His forgiveness that comes only through Jesus Christ? If so, you are "comforted." Now that you have been comforted, you are able to comfort others by sharing with them the "good news" of the Gospel.

> **2 Corinthians 1:3-4:** *"Blessed be the God and Father of our Lord Jesus Christ, the Father of mercies and <u>God of all comfort;</u> [4] <u>who comforts us in all our affliction so that we may</u>*

---

[82] Ibid

be able to comfort those who are in any affliction with the comfort with which we ourselves are comforted by God."

VERSE 5: *"Blessed are the gentle, for they shall inherit the earth."*

The worldly, unbelieving man sees the earth being conquered by ruthless and murderous military power. Jesus' truth shows just the opposite in that the meek *"shall inherit the earth"* (see also Psalm 37:9-11). Meekness and gentleness do not mean weakness and powerlessness. On the contrary, gentleness is *great power under control,* like a powerful draft horse that can move heavy loads. The horse in itself has great power but once it has been broken, it is gentle enough for a person to ride on safely. Below are some verses on great power under control.

> **Proverbs 16:32:** *"He who is slow to anger is better than the mighty, and he who rules his spirit, than he who captures a city."*

> **Matthew 26:52-53:** *"Then Jesus *said to him, 'Put your sword back into its place; for all those who take up the sword shall perish by the sword. Or do you think that I cannot appeal to My Father, and He will at once put at My disposal more than twelve legions of angels?'"*

More verses on gentleness:

> **Numbers 12:3:** *"Now the man Moses was very humble, more than any man who was on the face of the earth."*

> **Ephesians 4:1-3:** *"I, THEREFORE, the prisoner of the Lord, entreat you to walk in a manner worthy of the calling with which you have been called, ² with all humility and gentleness, with patience, showing forbearance to one another in love, ³ being diligent to preserve the unity of the Spirit in the bond of peace."*

> **Colossians 3:12-13:** *"And so, as those who have been chosen of God, holy and beloved, put on a heart of compassion, kindness, humility, gentleness and patience; bearing with one another, and forgiving each other, whoever has a complaint against anyone; just as the Lord forgave you, so also should you."*

Section Application

Our Christian life must be marked by gentleness. How can you walk in gentleness? If you are to be an effective witness for Christ, you need to be gentle.

> **1 Peter 3:15:** *"…but sanctify Christ as Lord in your hearts, always being ready to make a defense to everyone who asks you to give an account for the hope that is in you, yet with gentleness and reverence;…."*

> **Philippians 4:5:** *"Let your gentle spirit be known to all men. The Lord is near."*

VERSE 6: *"Blessed are those who hunger and thirst for righteousness, for they shall be satisfied."*

We are to, *"hunger and thirst for righteousness."*   Hunger and thirst (food and water) are the most basic of human physical needs. A basic in the spiritual life is *righteousness*:

> **1 John 3:10:** *"By this the children of God and the children of the devil are obvious: <u>anyone who does not practice righteousness is not of God</u>, nor the one who does not love his brother."*

Just as we have a driving passion to eat or drink, we are to have a driving passion to live righteously to the glory of God. The term for growing in righteousness is "sanctification."

> **Hebrews 12:14:** *"Pursue peace with all men, <u>and the sanctification without which no one will see the Lord.</u>"*

Here is a true story of grace/salvation and then ongoing sanctification working out in the Christian's life.

> "Mel Trotter was a barber by profession and a drunkard by perversion. So debauched had he become that when his young daughter died, he stole the shoes she was to be buried in and pawned them for money to buy more drinks. One night he staggered into the Pacific Garden Mission in Chicago and was marvelously saved. Burdened for the men of skid row, he opened a rescue mission in Grand Rapids, Michigan. He went on to found more than sixty more missions and became supervisor of a chain of them stretching from Boston to San Francisco." [83]

VERSE 7: *"Blessed are the merciful, for they shall receive mercy."*

Our world thrives on self-oriented empowerment. Mercy does not exist in the dog-eat-dog mentality. Our society has turned so cruel that we are killing babies in the womb by abortion and treating the elderly as a nuisance. Even more curious is that many of the people who want the right to kill innocent babies in their mother's womb, also desire to be known for their "wonderful kindness" because they are so concerned about animals and "saving the earth." It is this type of hypocrisy that Jesus addressed when He said in **Matthew 23:23:**

> *"Woe to you, scribes and Pharisees, hypocrites! For you tithe mint and dill and cummin, and have <u>neglected the weightier provisions of the law: justice and mercy and faithfulness;</u> but these are the things you should have done without neglecting the others."*

Jesus is the merciful high priest who intercedes for us to the Father:

> **Hebrews 2:17-18:** *"Therefore, He had to be made like His brethren in all things, that He might become <u>a merciful and faithful high priest</u> in things pertaining to God, to make propitiation for the sins of the people. [18] For since He Himself was tempted in that which He has suffered, He is able to come to the aid of those who are tempted."*

> **Titus 3:5:** *"He saved us, not on the basis of deeds which we have done in righteousness, <u>but according to His mercy,</u> by the washing of regeneration and renewing by the Holy Spirit,"*

Those who show mercy by the Spirit of God will be given mercy by God. Those who do not show mercy (non-believers) will be shown judgment in hell:

---

[83] Elgin S. Moyer, *Who Was Who in Church History* [New Canaan, Conn.: Keats, 1974], p. 411).

Matthew 25:41-46: *"Then He will also say to those on His left, 'Depart from Me, accursed ones, into the eternal fire which has been prepared for the devil and his angels;* [42] *for I was hungry, and you gave Me nothing to eat; I was thirsty, and you gave Me nothing to drink;* [43] *I was a stranger, and you did not invite Me in; naked, and you did not clothe Me; sick, and in prison, and you did not visit Me.'* [44] *'Then they themselves also will answer, saying, "Lord, when did we see You hungry, or thirsty, or a stranger, or naked, or sick, or in prison, and did not take care of You?"* [45] *'Then He will answer them, saying, <u>"Truly I say to you, to the extent that you did not do it to one of the least of these, you did not do it to Me."</u>* [46] *And these will go away into eternal punishment, but the righteous into eternal life."*

James 2:13: *"For <u>judgment will be merciless to one who has shown no mercy;</u> mercy triumphs over judgment."*

Section Application

How can you extend mercy to others? Are you kind just to those who are kind to you? What if you sacrificially tried to help someone and he responded by mocking your kindness? Do you need to continue to be merciful to him? What about those who are evil?

Luke 6:32-36: *"And if you love those who love you, what credit is that to you? For even sinners love those who love them.* [33]*"And if you do good to those who do good to you, what credit is that to you? For even sinners do the same.* [34]*And if you lend to those from whom you expect to receive, what credit is that to you? Even sinners lend to sinners, in order to receive back the same amount.* [35]*But love your enemies, and do good, and lend, expecting nothing in return; and your reward will be great, and you will be sons of the Most High; for <u>He Himself is kind to ungrateful and evil men.</u>* [36]*<u>Be merciful, just as your Father is merciful.</u>"*

Proverbs 11:17: *"The <u>merciful man does himself good,</u>*
But the cruel man does himself harm."

VERSE 8: *"Blessed are the pure in heart, for they shall see God."*

A pure heart cannot come from the unsaved man.

Jeremiah 17:9: *"The heart is more deceitful than all else*
And is desperately sick; Who can understand it?"

Romans 3:9-12: *" What then? Are we better than they? Not at all; for we have already charged that both Jews and Greeks are all under sin;* [10] *as it is written, 'THERE IS NONE RIGHTEOUS, NOT EVEN ONE;*
   [11] *THERE IS NONE WHO UNDERSTANDS,*
      THERE IS NONE WHO SEEKS FOR GOD;
   [12] *ALL HAVE TURNED ASIDE, TOGETHER THEY HAVE*
      BECOME USELESS; THERE IS NONE WHO DOES GOOD,
      THERE IS NOT EVEN ONE.'"

If you walk by the Spirit of God, you will have the focus to which you are called. The result will not be comparing your righteousness to others', but to God's holy standard. By doing so, you will humbly see your constant need for His grace. You will joyfully follow Him and not the world. One who says he loves God but also loves the world and the things in it, is not pure in heart.

> **1 John 2:15 -17:** *"Do not love the world, nor the things in the world. If anyone loves the world, the love of the Father is not in him. [16]For all that is in the world, the lust of the flesh and the lust of the eyes and the boastful pride of life, is not from the Father, but is from the world. [17]And the world is passing away, and also its lusts; but the one who does the will of God abides forever."* (see also James 4:4)

Jesus said, *"No one can serve two masters; for either he will hate the one and love the other, or he will hold to one and despise the other. You cannot serve God and mammon."* **Matthew 6:24**.

A pure heart only comes from God!

> **Psalm 51:10:** *"Create in me a clean heart, O God, And renew a steadfast spirit within me."*

> **Ezekiel 36:26-27:** *"Moreover, I will give you a new heart and put a new spirit within you; and I will remove the heart of stone from your flesh and give you a heart of flesh. [27]And I will put My Spirit within you and cause you to walk in My statutes, and you will be careful to observe My ordinances."*

Section Application

Have you cried out to God to cleanse your heart? Repent of your sin and call out to God and confess your sin to Him. He promises that those who do will receive His forgiveness.

> **1 John 1:8-9:** *"If we say that we have no sin, we are deceiving ourselves, and the truth is not in us. [9]If we confess our sins, He is faithful and righteous to forgive us our sins and to cleanse us from all unrighteousness."*

VERSE 9: *"Blessed are the peacemakers, for they shall be called sons of God."*

The Bible tells us that the "sons of God" will be peacemakers. The Old Testament prophecy of Jesus tells us He is the "Prince of Peace."

> **Isaiah 9:6:** *"For a child will be born to us, a son will be given to us;*
> *And the government will rest on His shoulders;*
> *And His name will be called Wonderful Counselor, Mighty God, Eternal Father,*
> *Prince of Peace."*

Every Christian who is led by the Spirit of God will be a peacemaker:

> **Romans 8:14:** *"For all who are being led by the Spirit of God, these are sons of God."*

> **Galatians 5:22-24:** *"But the fruit of the Spirit is love, joy, peace, patience, kindness, goodness, faithfulness, [23]gentleness, self-control; against such things there is no law. [24] Now those who belong to Christ Jesus have crucified the flesh with its passions and desires."*

"The essential fact to comprehend is that the *peace* about which Jesus speaks is more than the absence of conflict and strife; it is the presence of righteousness." [84]   Being a peacemaker does not mean the godly person refuses to either confront evil or make a stand for truth. We see Jesus confronting the wicked money changers by making a whip and driving them out of the temple (John 2:14-16). We also see Him aggressively confronting the scribes and Pharisees who taught false doctrine (Matthew 23:13-36). Paul explains that some divisions in the church have their place to show the true from the false: **1 Corinthians 11:18–19:** *"...when you come together as a church, I hear that divisions exist among you; and in part I believe it. ¹⁹ For there must also be factions among you, so that those who are approved may become evident among you."* Anytime righteousness confronts an ungodly world, there will be conflict. It should be noted that Jesus himself said that He did not come to bring worldly peace (i.e. "hypocritical tolerance," John 14:27). Jesus said He would cause divisions between family members who love Him and those who do not.

> **Matthew 10:34-38:** *"Do not think that I came to bring peace on the earth; I did not come to bring peace, but a sword. ³⁵ For I came to SET A MAN AGAINST HIS FATHER, AND A DAUGHTER AGAINST HER MOTHER, AND A DAUGHTER-IN-LAW AGAINST HER MOTHER-IN-LAW; ³⁶ and A MAN'S ENEMIES WILL BE THE MEMBERS OF HIS HOUSEHOLD. ³⁷ He who loves father or mother more than Me is not worthy of Me; and he who loves son or daughter more than Me is not worthy of Me. ³⁸ And he who does not take his cross and follow after Me is not worthy of Me."*

Someone may ask why Jesus is called the Prince of Peace. Jesus is the Prince of Peace because He did what no person can do. He made peace between sinful/rebellious man and a Perfect/Holy God (Romans 5:1, Ephesians 2:13-21, Colossians 1:19-20). We as "sons of God" must tell others the gospel so that they too can be at peace with God through Christ. Note there is a huge difference between Spirit-led zeal for the truth of God (i.e. *"contend earnestly for the faith"* Jude 3-24) and fleshly, vengeful/violent behavior. The godly man does not seek his own revenge, but turns the other cheek (Matthew 5:39). Paul explained this in **Romans 12:18-21:**

> *"If possible, so far as it depends on you, be at peace with all men. ¹⁹ Never take your own revenge, beloved, but leave room for the wrath of God, for it is written, 'VENGEANCE IS MINE, I WILL REPAY,' says the Lord. ²⁰ 'BUT IF YOUR ENEMY IS HUNGRY, FEED HIM, AND IF HE IS THIRSTY, GIVE HIM A DRINK; FOR IN SO DOING YOU WILL HEAP BURNING COALS UPON HIS HEAD.' ²¹ Do not be overcome by evil, but overcome evil with good."*

Section Application

Are you a son or daughter of God? How can you seek peace for your friends and enemies? Are you telling a dying world of the love and peace with God that is found in Christ Jesus?

> **James 3:17-18:** *"But the wisdom from above is first pure, then peaceable, gentle, reasonable, full of mercy and good fruits, unwavering, without hypocrisy. ¹⁸And the seed whose fruit is righteousness is sown in peace by those who make peace."*

VERSES 10-12: *"Blessed are those who have been persecuted for the sake of righteousness, for theirs is the kingdom of heaven. ¹¹ Blessed are you when men cast insults at you, and persecute you, and say all kinds of evil against you falsely, on account of Me. ¹² Rejoice, and be glad, for your reward in heaven is great, for so they persecuted the prophets who were before you."*

---

[84] MacArthur, J. (1985). *Matthew* (p. 211). Chicago: Moody Press.

One must understand that persecution for the cause of Christ is part of the Christian life. **2 Timothy 3:12** says, *"And indeed, all who desire to live godly in Christ Jesus will be persecuted."* It does not say that you *may* be persecuted, but specifically says that the believer *will* be persecuted. Jesus Himself warned us about this:

> **John 15:18-19:** *"If the world hates you, you know that it has hated Me before it hated you. If you were of the world, the world would love its own; but because you are not of the world, but I chose you out of the world, therefore the world hates you."*

> **John 16:2-4:** *"They will make you outcasts from the synagogue, but an hour is coming for everyone who kills you to think that he is offering service to God. ³ And these things they will do, because they have not known the Father, or Me. ⁴But these things I have spoken to you, that when their hour comes, you may remember that I told you of them. And these things I did not say to you at the beginning, because I was with you."*

We should respond in love and prayer for those who persecute us.

> **Romans 12:14:** *"Bless those who persecute you; bless and curse not."*

> **Matthew 5:43-45:** *"You have heard that it was said, 'YOU SHALL LOVE YOUR NEIGHBOR, and hate your enemy.' ⁴⁴ But I say to you, love your enemies, and pray for those who persecute you ⁴⁵ in order that you may be sons of your Father who is in heaven; for He causes His sun to rise on the evil and the good, and sends rain on the righteous and the unrighteous."*

What should be our response to persecutions? It should not be self-pity; instead we should rejoice!

> **Acts 5:40-41:** *"And they took his advice; and after calling the apostles in, they flogged them and ordered them to speak no more in the name of Jesus, and then released them. ⁴¹ So they went on their way from the presence of the Council, rejoicing that they had been considered worthy to suffer shame for His name."*

Those who are persecuted will receive a reward from Christ. Our main study text, Matthew 5:10-12, tells us that our, *"reward in heaven is great."*

Summary and Application

Persecution for your faith is not the same as persecution for the wrong things that you do. You say you are a Christian? Put yourself to the test. Are you ever persecuted for your faith? If not, there is something very deficient about your spiritual life or your understanding of the Christian life. Persecution is not limited to those outside the church; it also comes from within the church through hypocrites, false brothers and the spiritually immature (cf. 2 Corinthians 11:26). One mark of a false Christian is his doctrine as it affects persecution. The false Christian will look, act, and sound very religious, but will compromise truth quickly to appear peaceful and inclusive of others. He will attack the true believers as "trouble makers" and "kooks" but this whole charade allows him to appear *good/reasonable* and avoid persecution. Paul had this very experience with the false teachers of Galatia.

> **Galatians 6:12:** *"Those who desire to make a good showing in the flesh try to compel you to be circumcised, simply that they may not be persecuted for the cross of Christ."*

Here, he points out that the false teachers do not suffer persecution (i.e. the mark of a true believer). A few verses later he summarizes his point by stating that he did not have to debate with the false teachers because the persecution he had received spoke volumes of his commitment to truth of the Cross of Christ:

> **Galatians 6:17:** " ...*let no one cause trouble for me, for <u>I bear on my body the</u>* <u>*brand-marks of Jesus.*</u>"

Paul's point is that his windbag critics would never have godly convictions that could result in serious bodily injury. Paul was saying that the church should not allow these false teachers to pick-on/argue with him (Paul), since for the cause of Christ, his body had been <u>beaten to the point of death</u> (see Acts 14:19, cf. 2 Corinthians 11:23-28).

Will you take a true stand for the cause of Christ and suffer the persecution which you have been called? (**Philippians 1:29:** *"For to you it has been granted for Christ's sake, not only to believe in Him, but also to suffer for His sake,....")* If you will not suffer for Christ, evaluate your faith in light of scripture and do not be one of the hypocrites who belittles the true brothers who do suffer for the gospel. The second-century church father Tertullian was once approached by a man with a problem that involved potential suffering:

> "...his business interests and Christianity conflicted. He ended [the conversation] by asking, 'What can I do? I must live!' Tertullian replied, 'Must you?'"[85]

---

[85] R. Kent Hughes, The Sermon on the Mount, p. 74.

MATTHEW 5:13-20
(THE CHRISTIANS IMPACT ON SOCIETY; FULFILLMENT OF THE LAW; TRUE RIGHTEOUSNESS)

"You are the salt of the earth; but if the salt has become tasteless, how will it be made salty again? It is good for nothing anymore, except to be thrown out and trampled under foot by men. ¹⁴ You are the light of the world. A city set on a hill cannot be hidden. ¹⁵ Nor do men light a lamp, and put it under the peck-measure, but on the lampstand; and it gives light to all who are in the house. ¹⁶ Let your light shine before men in such a way that they may see your good works, and glorify your Father who is in heaven. ¹⁷ Do not think that I came to abolish the Law or the Prophets; I did not come to abolish, but to fulfill. ¹⁸ For truly I say to you, until heaven and earth pass away, not the smallest letter or stroke shall pass away from the Law, until all is accomplished. ¹⁹ Whoever then annuls one of the least of these commandments, and so teaches others, shall be called least in the kingdom of heaven; but whoever keeps and teaches them, he shall be called great in the kingdom of heaven. ²⁰ For I say to you, that unless your righteousness surpasses that of the scribes and Pharisees, you shall not enter the kingdom of heaven."

Introduction

In this section, we see that the Christian is to bring *light and truth* to a *dark and deceived* world. This occurs by the power of the Holy Spirit moving through believers who proclaim the Truth and engage in *good works* for the glory of God.

We also will examine how the perfect Law of God shows us our sin. When we recognize our sinfulness, we should be driven to Christ to escape the eternal judgment in hell.

> **Romans 7:5–8:** *"For while we were in the flesh, the sinful passions, which were aroused by the Law, were at work in the members of our body to bear fruit for death. But now we have been released from the Law, having died to that by which we were bound, so that we serve in newness of the Spirit and not in oldness of the letter. What shall we say then? Is the Law sin? May it never be! On the contrary, I would not have come to know sin except through the Law; for I would not have known about coveting if the Law had not said, 'You shall not covet.' But sin, taking opportunity through the commandment, produced in me coveting of every kind; for apart from the Law sin is dead."*

VERSES 13-16: *"You are the salt of the earth; but if the salt has become tasteless, how will it be made salty again? It is good for nothing anymore, except to be thrown out and trampled under foot by men. ¹⁴ You are the light of the world. A city set on a hill cannot be hidden. ¹⁵ Nor do men light a lamp, and put it under the peck-measure, but on the lampstand; and it gives light to all who are in the house. ¹⁶Let your light shine before men in such a way that they may see your good works, and glorify your Father who is in heaven."*

Those who think that over time people are "getting better and better" are naive at best. Scripture says that humanity will go from *bad to worse* as time goes on: **2 Timothy 3:13:** *"But evil men and impostors will proceed from bad to worse, deceiving and being deceived."* Salt is not merely used as a flavoring, but it is also used as a preservative. As Christians, we are to be people of influence. The idea of Christians being *"salt of the earth"* is that we serve as a preserving element to an otherwise degenerating/godless society. We are to have a Sprit-led impact on society and not just be *"tasteless."*

Jesus said in <u>**John 9:5:**</u> *"<u>While I am in the world</u>, I am the <u>light of the world</u>."* Now that Jesus has left the world, His light shines through His people. Notice verse 14 says we are also the *"light of the world"* in that the Holy Spirit which dwells in us leads the Christian to tell others of the great plan of salvation for a lost and dying world. <u>**Ephesians 5:8-9**</u> says, *"for you were formerly darkness, but now you are light in the Lord; <u>walk as children of light</u> 9(for the fruit of the light consists in all goodness and righteousness and truth)...."* We cannot influence the world for God if we live like the world. Verse 15 states that we are not to, *"...light a lamp, and put it under the peck-measure...."* In the same way, we are not to take the truth regarding the way of salvation and "hide" it from the world. A person who hides the truth about Christ is usually ashamed of Him. Remember what Jesus said:

> *"Whosoever therefore shall be ashamed of me and of my words in this adulterous and sinful generation; of him also shall the Son of man be ashamed, when he cometh in the glory of his Father with the holy angels."* <u>**Mark 8:38.**</u>

One last thought about Christian service: We are not to be like the non-Christian or the false-religious who do their *good works* to get the attention and praise of others. Whenever possible, we are to do our good works in secret (Matthew 6:1-4). As Christians, we are to do good works (Ephesians 2:10) for the glory of God, not for our glory.

<u>Section Application</u>

Are you hiding your light? Are you ashamed of Christ? If the answer is, "yes" to either of these questions, repent and be a joyful servant, realizing that you have the most important information that has ever come to man: how to be eternally saved by Jesus.

<u>**VERSES 17-20:**</u> *"Do not think that I came to abolish the Law or the Prophets; I did not come to abolish, but to fulfill. 18For truly I say to you, until heaven and earth pass away, not the smallest letter or stroke shall pass away from the Law, until all is accomplished. 19Whoever then annuls one of the least of these commandments, and so teaches others, shall be called least in the kingdom of heaven; but whoever keeps and teaches them, he shall be called great in the kingdom of heaven. 20For I say to you, that unless your righteousness surpasses that of the scribes and Pharisees, you shall not enter the kingdom of heaven."*

Jesus said that He did not come *"to abolish the Law,"* but to fulfill it. Some people think that the Old Testament Law is something bad. This is wrong thinking. The Bible says, *"So then, the Law is holy, and the commandment is holy and righteous and good."* <u>**Roman 7:12.**</u> Jesus also said, *"But it is easier for heaven and earth to pass away than for one stroke of a letter of the Law to fail."* <u>**Luke 16:17**</u> (see our main text in Matthew 5:18).

God's law is holy and good, but the problem is that no man can obey it completely, and thus, every person is a sinner: <u>**Romans 3:23:**</u> *"...for <u>all have sinned</u> and fall short of the glory of God..."* Failure to perfectly obey everything in the law of God is sin: <u>**James 2:10:**</u> *"For whoever keeps the whole law and yet stumbles in one point, he has become guilty of all."*

In summary, the law of God shows us God's standard of perfection to enter heaven, but by showing us that standard it also shows us that we can never reach that standard. It is wrong to say the law is unfair or bad just because we cannot perfectly keep it. <u>**Romans 7:7:**</u> *"What shall we say then? Is the*

Law sin? May it never be! On the contrary, <u>I would not have come to know sin except through the Law</u>; for I would not have known about coveting if the Law had not said, "YOU SHALL NOT COVET." (See also 1 Timothy 1:8-11.)

We know God does not allow the perfection of heaven to be polluted by sin. We further know all humans are sinners. Combine that with the clear teaching from Scripture that each person will be judged for his or her own sin. The judgment against sin brings death and judgment in hell: *"...and when sin is accomplished, it brings forth death."* <u>James 1:15.</u> Once we see we are sinners, we realize we are doomed to hell. Understanding we are doomed to hell, we should then be drawn to Christ for forgiveness. In other words, you will either be judged by your "deeds" (*e.g.* whether you obeyed the law perfectly, which is impossible according to Romans 3:23 and Revelation 20:11-15), or you need to have someone who perfectly "fulfilled the Law" and paid your death penalty for you. Jesus is the only one who perfectly fulfilled the law: *"...One who has been tempted in all things as we are, yet without sin."* <u>Hebrew 4:15.</u> In Matthew 5:17 Jesus said He came to *"fulfill"* the Law. So the same Law that shows us we are doomed to hell should also draw us to Jesus to be forgiven and have eternal life: *"Therefore the Law has become our tutor to lead us to Christ, that we may be justified by faith ...."* <u>Galatians 3:24.</u>

To obtain this forgiveness, we must accept it from Christ by having faith in His sacrifice on the cross. We need to understand He did not die on the cross as a martyr or a great example of love. He died to pay the penalty of others' sins. One either puts his faith in the work of Christ on the cross, or that person will be judged for his own sin.

If you ask the average person on the street if he is a good person the typical answer is a confident "Yes!" Most people like to grade themselves on the curve (i.e. comparing themselves to others). Scripture tells us when one's righteousness is compared with the perfect law of God, the person's mouth is shut (i.e. he is prevented from talking about his own goodness and justifying himself.)
> <u>Romans 3:19-20:</u> *"Now we know that whatever the Law says, it speaks to those who are under the Law, that <u>every mouth may be closed, and all the world may become accountable to God;</u> [20]because by the works of the Law no flesh will be justified in His sight; for through the Law comes the knowledge of sin."*

Maybe you are one who considers yourself a *good person*. If you are not a Christian you will be judged by your deeds...and the standard will be the perfect law of God, The Ten Commandments (see Revelation 20:11-15, Jude verses 14-15, Romans 2:5-16). Do you think you have kept The Ten Commandments? Let's look at some of the Commandments:

- *"<u>Thou shalt not bear false witness....</u>"* Have you ever told a lie? What do you call someone who tells lies? So, what does that make you?
  [Answer: A **liar** – Exodus 20:16.]

- *"<u>Thou shalt not steal.</u>"* Have you ever taken anything that did not belong to you? (Remember it does not matter if it was of a small value, or took place a long time ago.) What do you call someone who has stolen? So, what does that make you?
  [Answer: A **thief** – Exodus 20:15.]

- *"Thou shall not take the name of the Lord your God in vain."* Have you ever used God's name in vain through swearing or saying "Oh my G_d!" Have you used Jesus' name as a curse word? If so, what does that make you?

    [Answer: A **blasphemer** – Exodus 20:7.]

- *"Thou shall not commit adultery."* Maybe you think that you have not committed the act of adultery, but have you ever looked at another person with lust? Jesus says the one who looks at another with lust *has already committed adultery* in his heart – Matt. 5:28. So, what does that make you?

    [Answer: At best, an **adulterer at heart** – Exodus 20:14.]

- *"Thou shall not murder."* Maybe you claim to not have murdered anyone, but have you every hated anyone? The Bible says that if you hate someone you are a murderer! **1 John 3:15:** *"Everyone who hates his brother is a murderer; and you know that no murderer has eternal life abiding in him."*] (Jesus said if you call someone a *fool* you are guilty of hell! – Matthew 5:22). So, what does that make you?

    [Answer: At best, a **murderer at heart**, Exodus 20:13.]

These questions involve only five of The Ten Commandments. There are five more for you to answer. Do you still think you are a truly "good person"?

If you died in the next five minutes would you be judged as <u>innocent or guilty</u> based on The Ten Commandments? Do you think you would go to heaven or hell? Let us look carefully at what the Bible states is the punishment for those who have simply told a lie: **Revelation 21:8:** *"… and all liars, their part will be in the lake that burns with fire and brimstone, which is the second death."*

Your answer of whether you are good enough to get into heaven, if honest, should greatly concern you. The answer is clear, by God's standard you are not even close to being *good enough* to get into heaven! Remember that eternity is not just another lifetime…it is forever and ever. Will you spend it in heaven with a loving God or will you spend it in fiery hell[86] because God judged you honestly for what you are?[87]

---

[86] In **Revelation 20:15** it says, *"And if anyone's name was not found written in the book of life, he was <u>thrown into the lake of fire."</u>* It must be understood that the judgment is <u>neither temporary,</u> nor does it end in annihilation so that you don't have to feel anything. The torment goes on and on *forever and ever.* Examine and carefully consider the description of hell from God's Word.

DESCRIPTION OF HELL: *Flames and Torment -* **Luke. 16:19-31;** *Lake of fire which burns with brimstone -* **Revelation 19:20;** *Lake of fire - Fire and brimstone and are tormented day and night forever and ever -* **Revelation 20:10;** *Eternal fire…the blackness of darkness forever -* **Jude v.7, 13;** *Everlasting destruction from the presence of the Lord -* **2 Thessalonians 1:9;** *Where their worm does not die, and the fire is not quenched -* **Mark 9:43-48;** *Weeping and gnashing of teeth -* **Matthew 24:51;** *Everlasting punishment -* **Matthew 25:46;** *Indignation, wrath, tribulation and anguish -* **Romans 2:8,9;** *Shame and everlasting contempt -* **Daniel 12:2;** *Unquenchable fire -* **Luke 3:17.**

[87] For instruction on evangelism using The Ten Commandments see R. Comfort and K. Cameron, The School of Biblical Evangelism (Bridge-Logos Publishers, 2004.)

When one judges himself by God's standard, that person quickly understands he is not the person he would like to believe he is. The response to Christ's sacrifice and forgiveness is either acceptance or rejection. In Hebrews 2:3 it states, *"how shall we escape if we neglect so great a salvation?...."* Many will neglect or even reject such salvation, even though there is no escape for them. For example, say you were convicted of a crime and rightfully sat on death row for that crime. According to the law, only one person has the authority to pardon you of that sentence. How would you respond if that person actually granted you a pardon? Would you just ignore it, or grab onto it, like your life depended on it (because it does!)? Let's look at a real Supreme Court case that involved those issues.

In 1833, during the January term of the United State Supreme Court, the case of United States v. George Wilson was decided.[88] One of the pertinent facts of the case was that Wilson had a Federal conviction that resulted in a death sentence.[89] Although doomed by the death sentence, he was saved when he was issued a pardon from the only person who could grant it, the President of the United States (Andrew Jackson).[90] One must realize the pardon gets sent directly to Wilson himself and not to the sentencing court. The Supreme Court specifically held that a pardon is a private communication by the President to the defendant, and not to the Court.

A bizarre turn of events occurred when Wilson refused to formally make the Court aware of his pardon! Technically, the Court was aware that the pardon was floating around out there, but Wilson did not actually produce it so that the Court could stop his execution. With that factual background, you can see that the issue before the Supreme Court was whether the Court could *force* a pardon upon someone. In answering that question, the Court first explained what a pardon is:

> "A pardon is an act of grace, proceeding from the power entrusted with the execution of the laws, which exempts the individual, on whom it is bestowed, from the punishment the law inflicts for a crime he has committed." [91]

The Court went on to explain that the pardon had no effect unless it was accepted by the criminal:

> "A pardon is a deed, to the validity of which, delivery is essential, and delivery is not complete without acceptance. It may then be rejected by the person to whom it is tendered; and if it be rejected, we have discovered no power in a court to force it on him." [92]

You are like George Wilson. You know you are guilty of violating God's law and that eternal judgment is coming soon. The only person in all creation who can pay for your sins is the perfect Son of God, Jesus Christ, who has died on the cross to pay your death penalty. He offers you a complete pardon because of His love for you. Will you, with great joy and appreciation, embrace that pardon

---

[88] UNITED STATES v. GEORGE WILSON 32 U.S. 150, 7 Pet. 150, 8 L.Ed. 640 (UNITED STATES SUPREME COURT January 1833 term).

[89] Id. 32 U.S. at 151

[90] President Andrew Jackson granted Wilson a pardon on June 14, 1830. Id at 153.

[91] Id. at 160.

[92] Id at 161.

and tell others? Or maybe you are like Wilson and say, "Yes, I may have done something wrong, but I am a tough guy, and I will take what's coming." That type of response shows complete ignorance of the justice and wrath of God. Such a person does not have a clue of the judgment that awaits him for all eternity, in the fiery hell!

It is my prayer that you will repent (turn from your sins and forsake them) and put your faith in The Lord Jesus Christ to be the total payment for your sins. Right now call upon Him to forgive you and save you from the judgment to come. He will receive you and forgive you. Jesus said:

> **John 6:37-40:** *"All that the Father gives Me shall come to Me, and the one who comes to Me I will certainly not cast out. ³⁸ For I have come down from heaven, not to do My own will, but the will of Him who sent Me. ³⁹ And this is the will of Him who sent Me, that of all that He has given Me I lose nothing, but raise it up on the last day. ⁴⁰ For this is the will of My Father, that everyone who beholds the Son and believes in Him, may have eternal life; and I Myself will raise him up on the last day."*

Those in Christ are no longer under the judgment of the Law because Jesus was the fulfillment of the Law:

> **Romans 8:1-4:** *"THERE is therefore now no condemnation for those who are in Christ Jesus. ² For the law of the Spirit of life in Christ Jesus has set you free from the law of sin and of death. ³ For what the Law could not do, weak as it was through the flesh, God did: sending His own Son in the likeness of sinful flesh and as an offering for sin, He condemned sin in the flesh, ⁴ in order that the requirement of the Law might be fulfilled in us, who do not walk according to the flesh, but according to the Spirit."*

More on VERSE 19: *"Whoever then annuls one of the least of these commandments, and so teaches others, shall be called least in the kingdom of heaven; but whoever keeps and teaches them, he shall be called great in the kingdom of heaven."*

God's moral law is a reflection of God's very character and is therefore changeless and eternal.[93] The Christian is to have the highest regard for God's Word. Jesus said, *"Heaven and earth will pass away, but my words will never pass away."* **Mark 13:31**. And those Christians who teach others to disregard some of the commands of God will be seen by God as least in His kingdom: *"Let not many of you become teachers, my brethren, knowing that as such we shall incur a stricter judgment."* **James 3:1.** In the Kingdom of God we do not want to lose our reward: *"Watch yourselves, that you might not lose what we have accomplished, but that you may receive a full reward."* **2 John 8.** We must live by the power of the Holy Spirit as a godly example to others: *"...but rather in speech, conduct, love, faith and purity, show yourself an example of those who believe."* **1 Timothy 4:12.**

VERSE 20: *"For I say to you, that unless your righteousness surpasses that of the scribes and Pharisees, you shall not enter the kingdom of heaven.*

This verse sums up much of what we have discussed. No man can earn his way to right standing before a holy and perfect God. The Pharisees not only thought that a man could be perfect on his own, but that they were perfect. See how Jesus described their hypocrisy in **Matthew 23:23-24:**

> *"Woe to you, scribes and Pharisees, hypocrites! For you tithe mint and dill and cummin, and have neglected the weightier provisions of the law: justice and mercy and*

---

[93] MacArthur, John F., *The MacArthur New Testament Commentary*, (Chicago: Moody Press) 1983.

faithfulness; but these are the things you should have done without neglecting the others. ²⁴ *You blind guides, who strain out a gnat and swallow a camel!"*
(Note: Look up and read the entire discourse in Matthew 23:22-36.)

See also **Luke 16:15:** *"And He said to them, 'You are those who justify yourselves in the sight of men, but God knows your hearts; for that which is highly esteemed among men is detestable in the sight of God.'"*

Jesus is the only way to salvation. Man-made religion or self-righteousness will never get one even close to the kingdom of heaven.
Titus 3:5-6: *"He saved us, not on the basis of deeds which we have done in righteousness, but according to His mercy, by the washing of regeneration and renewing by the Holy Spirit, ⁶ whom He poured out upon us richly through Jesus Christ our Savior,...."*

Ephesians 2:8-9: *"For by grace you have been saved through faith; and that not of yourselves, it is the gift of God; ⁹ not as a result of works, that no one should boast."*

Summary and Application

You need to have perfect righteousness to enter heaven. When you realize Jesus paid a price you could not, how does that impact your devotion to Him?

Why is the law a good *"tutor"* (Galatians 3:24) to lead people to saving knowledge of Christ?
Answer: For a person to be saved, the person needs to know how much he has rebelled against God. The person must also see that it is impossible for him to enter heaven on his own righteousness, because one cannot reach the perfect standard of God. A person can be saved only when he knows *what he needs to be saved from.* One does not get saved to be a better person. One needs to be saved because he is a complete reprobate in the sight of The Holy God and doomed for hell without the Savior Jesus Christ's payment for sin and forgiveness.

The Larger Catechism of the Westminster Confession Standards explains that:
"The moral law is of use to unregenerate men, to awaken their consciences to flee from wrath to come, and to drive them to Christ; or, upon their continuance in the estate and way of sin, to leave them inexcusable, and under the curse thereof." [94]

The Law shows our sinfulness. When some attempt to share their faith, they mistakenly feel a need to "market it." They want to make it attractive to their friends. This is the fundamental flaw with modern evangelism. The true Gospel is not appealing to the unbelieving world. We use the Law, not to save people, but to show them their need for a Saviour. As Warren Wiersbe stated: "The law is not the gospel, but the gospel is not lawless."[95]

---

[94] Smith, M. H. (1996, c1990). *Larger Catechism of the Westminster Confession Standards* Question 96. Index created by Christian Classics Foundation. (electronic ed.) (p. 2). Greenville: Greenville Presbyterian Theological Seminary Press.

[95] Wiersbe, W. W. (1996). *The Bible Exposition Commentary* (1 Timothy 1:1). Wheaton, Ill.: Victor Books.

Jesus said:

John 14:15: *"If you love Me, you will keep My commandments."*

1 John 2:3-6: *"And by this we know that we have come to know Him, if we keep His commandments. ⁴The one who says, 'I have come to know Him,' and does not keep His commandments, is a liar, and the truth is not in him; ⁵ but whoever keeps His word, in him the love of God has truly been perfected. By this we know that we are in Him: ⁶ the one who says he abides in Him ought himself to walk in the same manner as He walked."*

Martin Luther points out that the Law reveals our condemned state so we see our need for Christ: "The first duty of a preacher of the gospel is, through his revealing of the law and of sin…"[96] In another work he further explained, "Thou are killed by the law that through Christ thou mayest be quickened and restored to life."[97]

St. Augustine wrote:
"Sin cannot be overcome without the grace of God, so the law was given to convert the soul by anxiety about its guilt, so that it might be ready to receive grace." [98]

Charles Spurgeon explained why we should not avoid admonishing the lost regarding the law of God when he said:
"By lowering the law you weaken its power in the hands of God as a convincer of sin. It is the looking glass, which shows us our spots, and that is the most powerful thing, though nothing, but the gospel can wash them away…. Lower the law and you dim the light by which man perceives his guilt. This is a very serious loss to the sinner rather than a gain."[99]

Dr. D. Martin Lloyd-Jones stated the following regarding evangelism:
"This doctrine [what sin is], therefore, is absolutely vital in determining our conception of true evangelism. There is no true evangelism without the doctrine of sin, and without an understanding of what sin is. I do not want to be unfair, but I say that a gospel which merely says, 'Come to Jesus,' and offers Him as a Friend, and offers a marvelous new life, without convicting of sin, is not New Testament evangelism. The essence of evangelism is to start by preaching the law; and it is because the law has not been preached that we have had so much superficial evangelism. Go through the ministry of our Lord Himself and you cannot but get the impression that at times, far from pressing people to follow Him and to decide for Him, He put great obstacles in their way. He said in effect: 'Do you realize what you are doing? Have you counted the cost? Do you realize where it may lead you? Do you know that it means denying yourself, taking up your cross daily and following Me?' True evangelism, I say, because of this doctrine of sin, must always start by preaching the law. This means we must explain that mankind is confronted by the holiness of God, by His

---

[96] Martin Luther *Letter of St. Paul to the Romans* Translated by Bon Andrew Thomton, OS Bed Hans Volz and Heinz Blanke, Volume 2 p.iii.

[97] Martin Luther, Commentary on Galatians, p.212.

[98] Thomas C. Oden, *Ancient Christian Commentary on the Scriptures, Romans, Vol. VI*, p.182.

[99] Charles H. Spurgeon, *Metropolitan Tabernacle Pulpit, Vo. 28*, pp. 248, 285.

demands, and also by the consequences of sin. It is the Son of God Himself who speaks about being cast into hell. If you do not like the doctrine of hell you are just disagreeing with Jesus Christ. He, the Son of God, believed in hell; and it is in His exposure to the true nature of sin that He teaches that sin ultimately lands men in hell. <u>So evangelism must start with the holiness of God, the sinfulness of man, the demands of the law, the punishment meted out by the law, and the eternal consequences of evil and wrongdoing.</u> It is only the man who is brought to see his guilt in this way who flies to Christ for deliverance and redemption. Any belief in the Lord Jesus Christ which is not based on that is not a true belief in Him. You can have a psychological belief even in the Lord Jesus Christ; but a true belief sees in Him one who delivers us from the curse of the law. <u>True evangelism starts like that, and obviously is primarily a call to repentance, 'repentance toward God, and faith toward our Lord Jesus Christ.'"</u> [100]

Psalm 19:7: *"The law of the LORD is perfect, converting the soul: the testimony of the LORD is sure, making wise the simple."*

---

[100] Dr. D. Martin Lloyd-Jones *Studies in the Sermon on the Mount* (see his section on Matthew 5:27-30).

MATTHEW 5:21-32
(GOD EXAMINES THE HEART OF A PERSON AND NOT SIMPLY ONE'S EXTERNAL ACTIONS)
[ANGER/MURDER, LUST/ADULTERY, and DIVORCE]

[21] *"You have heard that the ancients were told, 'YOU SHALL NOT COMMIT MURDER' and 'Whoever commits murder shall be liable to the court.'* [22] *But I say to you that everyone who is angry with his brother shall be guilty before the court; and whoever shall say to his brother, 'Raca,' shall be guilty before the supreme court; and whoever shall say, 'You fool,' shall be guilty enough to go into the fiery hell.* [23] *If therefore you are presenting your offering at the altar, and there remember that your brother has something against you,* [24] *leave your offering there before the altar, and go your way; first be reconciled to your brother, and then come and present your offering.* [25] *Make friends quickly with your opponent at law while you are with him on the way, in order that your opponent may not deliver you to the judge, and the judge to the officer, and you be thrown into prison.* [26] *Truly I say to you, you shall not come out of there, until you have paid up the last cent.*

[27] *You have heard that it was said, 'YOU SHALL NOT COMMIT ADULTERY';* [28] *but I say to you, that everyone who looks on a woman to lust for her has committed adultery with her already in his heart.* [29] *And if your right eye makes you stumble, tear it out, and throw it from you; for it is better for you that one of the parts of your body perish, than for your whole body to be thrown into hell.* [30] *And if your right hand makes you stumble, cut it off, and throw it from you; for it is better for you that one of the parts of your body perish, than for your whole body to go into hell.* [31] *And it was said, 'WHOEVER SENDS HIS WIFE AWAY, LET HIM GIVE HER A CERTIFICATE OF DIVORCE';* [32] *but I say to you that everyone who divorces his wife, except for the cause of unchastity, makes her commit adultery; and whoever marries a divorced woman commits adultery."*

Introduction

These verses set out an important Biblical principle: Although one may think he or she is good by the external deeds one does (or the bad things one does not do), <u>God judges the heart</u>. **Proverbs 16:2:** *"All the ways of a man are clean in his own sight, But the LORD weighs the motives."*

The Pharisees and scribes were very careful about outward appearances. Despite that, we need to remember the verses we are studying (Matthew 5:21-32) come right after Matthew 5:20 which says, *"For I say to you, that unless your righteousness surpasses that of the scribes and Pharisees, you shall not enter the kingdom of heaven."* In Matthew 5:21-26 Jesus made reference to several sections of precepts and traditions derived from the Law. He then pressed the point to show their self-styled obedience was really hypocritical self-righteousness, and not out of love for God.

<u>**VERSES 21-26:**</u> *"You have heard that the ancients were told, 'YOU SHALL NOT COMMIT MURDER' and 'Whoever commits murder shall be liable to the court.'* [22] *But I say to you that everyone who is angry with his brother shall be guilty before the court; and whoever shall say to his brother, 'Raca,' shall be guilty before the supreme court; and whoever shall say, 'You fool,' shall be guilty enough to go into the fiery hell.* [23] *If therefore you are presenting your offering at the altar, and there remember that your brother has something against you,* [24] *leave your offering there before the altar, and go your way; first be reconciled to your brother, and then come and present your offering.* [25] *Make friends quickly with your opponent at law*

while you are with him on the way, in order that your opponent may not deliver you to the judge, and the judge to the officer, and you be thrown into prison. ²⁶ Truly I say to you, you shall not come out of there, until you have paid up the last cent."

God is concerned with us obeying the Spirit of the Law and not merely obeying mechanical rules. Many of the Pharisees took God's Law and added their own *traditions* to make it more palatable for themselves. An example of this would be that the Law of God does not say that one who commits murder is, ***"Liable to the court."*** The Law actually says the penalty for murder is *death*. (Genesis 9:6; Numbers 35:30-34).

Verses 21-26 also speak of the heart of man for his fellow man. The term ***"Raca"*** is a term of contempt for someone, "meaning 'empty' or 'ignorant,' [it was] a strong term of derision, second only to 'fool.'"[101] Jesus placed the term in the context of anger, and strongly condemned one who would use it in reference to another person. Jesus also points out that by calling your brother a "fool" (i.e. stupid and godless - see Psalm 14:1), you are subject to the judgment of hell by God.

The Lord tells us in these verses that if we have a dispute with a brother, we are to go to him and resolve it prior to engaging in fellowship with God. <u>Psalm 66:18:</u> *"If I regard wickedness in my heart, The Lord will not hear;...."*

> <u>1 John 3:14-15:</u> *"We know that we have passed out of death into life, because we love the brethren. He who does not love abides in death. ¹⁵ Everyone who hates his brother is a murderer; and you know that no murderer has eternal life abiding in him."*

> <u>1 John 2:9:</u> *"The one who says he is in the light and yet hates his brother is in the darkness until now."*

> <u>Romans 12:17-21:</u> *"Never pay back evil for evil to anyone. Respect what is right in the sight of all men. ¹⁸ If possible, so far as it depends on you, be at peace with all men. ¹⁹ Never take your own revenge, beloved, but leave room for the wrath of God, for it is written, 'VENGEANCE IS MINE, I WILL REPAY,' says the Lord. ²⁰ 'BUT IF YOUR ENEMY IS HUNGRY, FEED HIM, AND IF HE IS THIRSTY, GIVE HIM A DRINK; FOR IN SO DOING YOU WILL HEAP BURNING COALS UPON HIS HEAD.' ²¹ Do not be overcome by evil, but overcome evil with good."*

<u>VERSES 27-32</u> *"You have heard that it was said, 'YOU SHALL NOT COMMIT ADULTERY'; ²⁸ but I say to you, that everyone who looks on a woman to lust for her has committed adultery with her already in his heart. ²⁹ And if your right eye makes you stumble, tear it out, and throw it from you; for it is better for you that one of the parts of your body perish, than for your whole body to be thrown into hell. ³⁰And if your right hand makes you stumble, cut it off, and throw it from you; for it is better for you that one of the parts of your body perish, than for your whole body to go into hell. ³¹ And it was said, 'WHOEVER SENDS HIS WIFE AWAY, LET HIM GIVE HER A CERTIFICATE OF DIVORCE'; ³² but I say to you that everyone who divorces his wife,*

---

[101] Brand, C., Draper, C., England, A., Bond, S., Clendenen, E. R., Butler, T. C., and Latta, B. (2003). *Holman Illustrated Bible Dictionary* (p 1361). Nashville, TN: Holman Bible Publishers.

except for the cause of unchastity, makes her commit adultery; and whoever marries a divorced woman commits adultery."

Again Jesus addresses the heart attitude when discussing the sin of adultery. It is clear from verse 28 that an individual is committing adultery in his heart if he lusts after someone other than his wife. Obviously, engaging in pornography would likewise constitute committing adultery in your heart. Jesus makes it clear how eternally damaging this sin can be when He states it is much better to lose your eye than be thrown into hell (verse 29). The Christian, by the power of God, must keep his mind from lustful thoughts.

The Scribes and Pharisees thought committing adultery only occurred when two people had sexual relations and at least one of the sexual partners was married to someone else. In their man-made rules there was nothing wrong with lusting after those others than your spouse. The Pharisee maintained that if he first divorced his wife (for any reason), and then married the "other woman," he could have sexual relations with her and would not be committing adultery. Later on, if he got tired of his new wife, he would divorce her and then marry the next woman who was the current object of his lust. Thus he believed that he could engage in serial divorces and remarriages and never commit adultery. This very quick and easy divorce concept was based on the religious leaders' warped interpretation of Deuteronomy 24:1-4. In Matthew 19:3-9, Jesus addressed the fact that they were not pure men, but that they had adulterous hearts.

> **Matthew 19:3-9:** *"And some Pharisees came to Him, testing Him, and saying, 'Is it lawful for a man to divorce his wife for any cause at all?' ⁴ And He answered and said, 'Have you not read, that He who created them from the beginning MADE THEM MALE AND FEMALE, ⁵ and said, FOR THIS CAUSE A MAN SHALL LEAVE HIS FATHER AND MOTHER, AND SHALL CLEAVE TO HIS WIFE; AND THE TWO SHALL BECOME ONE FLESH? ⁶ Consequently they are no longer two, but one flesh. What therefore God has joined together, let no man separate.' ⁷ They *said to Him, 'Why then did Moses command to GIVE HER A CERTIFICATE OF DIVORCE AND SEND her AWAY?' ⁸ He *said to them, 'Because of your hardness of heart, Moses permitted you to divorce your wives; but from the beginning it has not been this way. ⁹ And I say to you, whoever divorces his wife, except for immorality, and marries another woman commits adultery.'"*

From Matthew 5:32 and Matthew 19:9 the only ground that I see for divorce and remarriage is in the case of *immorality/unchastity*. In both Matthew 5:32 and 19:9 the Greek word *porneia* is used which covers, *"any form of sexual relationship outside marriage."*[102] In other words, *immorality/unchastity* occurs when a spouse has been sexually unfaithful. With that being said, it is important to note that Jesus did NOT say that if one partner was immoral then the other *should* get a divorce. He explained that the allowing of divorce in this narrow exception was due to, *"your hardness of heart"* (i.e. you respond in an unforgiving manner, which is far from holy in the sight of God). If the *innocent* spouse chooses remarriage, that person is only to marry another Christian (i.e. *"only in the Lord"*). **1 Corinthians 7:39:** *"A wife is bound as long as her husband lives; but if her husband is dead, she is free to be married to whom she wishes, only in the Lord."* In summary, someone who says divorcing

---

[102] Alexander, T. D., and Rosner, B. S. (2001). *New dictionary of biblical theology, (Holiness, love and sexuality)* (electronic ed.). Downers Grove, IL: InterVarsity Press.

his spouse because that person, "does not love his spouse anymore" is clearly outside of God's Word.[103]

One question that often comes up in reference to the subject of divorce is whether there is any other Biblical basis for divorce apart from the case of *immorality/unchastity*? The only other time divorce is allowed is when there is *desertion by an unbeliever (non-Christian) spouse*. This can happen if a Christian is married to an unbeliever and the unbeliever divorces the believer (note: the Christian does not seek the divorce). In that situation, I do not see that Scripture allows the believer to go out and remarry.[104] The scriptures instruct the believer to either remain single or be reunited with the unbelieving spouse.

<u>1 Corinthians 7:10-16, 27, 39:</u> *"But to the married I give instructions, not I, but the Lord, that the wife should not leave her husband* [11] *(but if she does leave, let her remain unmarried, or else be reconciled to her husband), and that the husband should not send his wife away.* [12] *But to the rest I say, not the Lord, that if any brother has a wife who is an unbeliever, and she consents to live with him, let him not send her away.* [13] *And a woman who has an unbelieving husband, and he consents to live with her, let her not send her husband away.* [14] *For the unbelieving husband is sanctified through his wife, and the unbelieving wife is sanctified through her believing husband; for otherwise your children are unclean, but now they are holy.* [15] *Yet if the unbelieving one leaves, let him leave; the brother or the sister is not under bondage in such cases, but God has called us to peace.* [16] *For how do you know, O wife, whether you will save your husband? Or how do you know, O husband, whether you will save your wife?...."*
(verse. 27) *"Are you bound to a wife? Do not seek to be released. Are you released from a wife? Do not seek a wife...."*
(verse 39) *"A wife is bound as long as her husband lives; but if her husband is dead, she is free to be married to whom she wishes, only in the Lord."*

What if you are in a marriage where one of you comes from a divorced background and the divorce was not based on the Biblical grounds? In other words, the previously divorced spouse was not the innocent victim of the *immorality/unchastity* by his/her ex-spouse? Matthew 5:32 and Mark 10:11-12 maintain that the marriage remains in a guilty state of adultery. **That sin can be removed by God.** One must repent, confess and seek God's forgiveness. One who truly seeks that forgiveness from Christ will graciously receive it. Upon true repentance and forgiveness, the couple can live on with a clear conscience. More than simply a clear conscience, they can have a fruitful marriage, enjoying the blessings and mercy of God.

<u>1 John 1:9:</u> *"If we confess our sins, He is faithful and righteous to forgive us our sins and to cleanse us from all unrighteousness."*

---

[103] The Mosaic Law's (Old Testament) penalty for adultery was death. <u>Leviticus 20:10:</u> *"If there is a man who commits adultery with another man's wife, one who commits adultery with his friend's wife, the adulterer and the adulteress shall surely be put to death."*

[104] There are preeminent Bible teachers who believe the innocent Christian victim of desertion is free to remarry another Christian. I simply do not see that, although I have reviewed their reasoning. Our Lord sets out the exception in <u>Matthew 5:32:</u> *"...but I say to you that everyone who divorces his wife, <u>except for the cause of unchastity</u>, makes her commit adultery; and whoever marries a divorced woman commits adultery."*

One last issue: A person should not think the limitations on divorce in anyway prevent a spouse from seeking safety from a dangerous or abusive situation. Separation is an example of obtaining protection for a spouse and children while addressing the problems of an abusive spouse.

I am always amazed at the Biblical ignorance of those who think that abusive conduct is somehow tolerated in Scripture. The tyrant/thug who points out that somewhere in the Bible it says something about a wife *submitting* to the husband obviously did not actually read that section in its context. If he had read that section about submission in the book of Ephesians, he would have seen that a mere couple of verses after that subject, Paul directly instructs the husband on how to treat his wife. There he would see that he must care for his wife with the sacrifice, kindness and love that Jesus demonstrated by giving up His life for us! He is further instructed to nourish and cherish his wife and love her as much as he loves himself! This could not speak more contrary to the view of the ungodly-tyrant husband. Love is a decision, not a feeling. Husbands and wives are to choose love and kindness toward each other:

> **Ephesians 5:25-26, 28-29 and 33:** *"Husbands, love your wives, just as Christ also loved the church and gave Himself up for her;* [26] *that He might sanctify her, having cleansed her by the washing of water with the word, ...* [28] *So husbands ought also to love their own wives as their own bodies. He who loves his own wife loves himself;* [29] *for no one ever hated his own flesh, but nourishes and cherishes it, just as Christ also does the church, ...* [33] *Nevertheless let each individual among you also love his own wife even as himself; and let the wife see to it that she respect her husband."*

Divorce is a terrible matter and it is not part of God's plan. Jesus stated that divorce was not God's will: *"...but from the beginning it has not been this way."* **Matthew 19:8.** It must be remembered that *"...I hate divorce,' says the LORD, the God of Israel,...."* **Malachi 2:16.** Look very closely at that verse. God *does not say that He hates divorced people.* He says He *hates divorce.* If you ask most divorced people, they will tell you they hate divorce too. They will tell you of the shattered lives, confused children, the ongoing disputes over child custody and financial support. We need to be people who encourage and strengthen married couples to follow in the sacrificial and forgiving life of Christ so that they have healthy homes that are honoring to God. Likewise we need to encourage and strengthen our singles, divorced or abandoned, so they can see the healing and restoration of all things in Christ Jesus. Many of them have a very difficult job raising their children alone, both emotionally and financially. The Church must be there for them!

I encourage you to examine this subject of divorce further by reading the comments on divorce in Matthew 19:1-12.

Summary and Application

From the section above, the message is clear: God is not impressed with phony external actions or pretextual religious exercises. The Lord examines the heart attitude:

> *"For the word of God is living and active and sharper than any two-edged sword, and piercing as far as the division of soul and spirit, of both joints and marrow, and able to judge the thoughts and intentions of the heart.* **Hebrews 4:12.**

The unrepentant heart will eventually manifest his evil heart; *"For out of the heart come evil thoughts, murders, adulteries, fornications, thefts, false witness, slanders."* **Matthew 15:19.**

The reality is that we have all been ravaged by our own sin. The only way we can escape the judgment for our sins is by the grace of God. God will forgive and restore you no matter how wicked you have been, if you truly confess and believe upon Jesus Christ!

> **Romans 10:8–11:** *8 But what does it say? "The word is near you, in your mouth and in your heart"— that is, the word of faith which we are preaching, 9 <u>that if you confess with your mouth Jesus as Lord, and believe in your heart that God raised Him from the dead, you will be saved;</u> 10 for with the heart a person believes, resulting in righteousness, and with the mouth he confesses, resulting in salvation. 11 For the Scripture says, "Whoever believes in Him will not be disappointed."*

MATTHEW 5:33-48
(VOWS, REVENGE, and LOVE OF ENEMIES/NEIGHBORS)

"Again, you have heard that the ancients were told, 'YOU SHALL NOT MAKE FALSE VOWS, BUT SHALL FULFILL YOUR VOWS TO THE LORD.' [34] *But I say to you, make no oath at all, either by heaven, for it is the throne of God,* [35] *or by the earth, for it is the footstool of His feet, or by Jerusalem, for it is THE CITY OF THE GREAT KING.* [36] *Nor shall you make an oath by your head, for you cannot make one hair white or black.* [37] *But let your statement be, 'Yes, yes' or 'No, no'; and anything beyond these is of evil.*

[38] *You have heard that it was said, 'AN EYE FOR AN EYE, AND A TOOTH FOR A TOOTH.'* [39] *But I say to you, do not resist him who is evil; but whoever slaps you on your right cheek, turn to him the other also.* [40] *And if anyone wants to sue you, and take your shirt, let him have your coat also.* [41] *And whoever shall force you to go one mile, go with him two.* [42] *Give to him who asks of you, and do not turn away from him who wants to borrow from you.*

[43] *You have heard that it was said, 'YOU SHALL LOVE YOUR NEIGHBOR, and hate your enemy.'* [44] *But I say to you, love your enemies, and pray for those who persecute you* [45] *in order that you may be sons of your Father who is in heaven; for He causes His sun to rise on the evil and the good, and sends rain on the righteous and the unrighteous.* [46] *For if you love those who love you, what reward have you? Do not even the tax-gatherers do the same?* [47] *And if you greet your brothers only, what do you do more than others? Do not even the Gentiles do the same?* [48] *Therefore you are to be perfect, as your heavenly Father is perfect."*

Introduction

This section will cover the concept of vows. We as Christians are to be people of truth. We are also to be people of peace and the love of God. I find it amazing when I hear how one religion claims to be peaceful when some of its most vocal leaders maintain a tenant to, "kill their enemies." Christians are likewise instructed on how to deal with their enemies: Jesus said to, *"love your enemies, and pray for those who persecute you...."* **Matthew 5:44**. Throughout the world, it is true Christianity has set up shelters for the homeless, hospitals, orphanages, soup kitchens, elementary schools, universities, and raised the value of all people. Most importantly, Christianity has presented the good news of the kingdom of God. Despite that, Christianity is slandered and treated with utter disrespect. How are Christians to respond? Jesus tells His followers to, *"love your enemies, and pray for those who persecute you..."*

VERSES 33-37: *"Again, you have heard that the ancients were told, 'YOU SHALL NOT MAKE FALSE VOWS, BUT SHALL FULFILL YOUR VOWS TO THE LORD.'* [34] *But I say to you, make no oath at all, either by heaven, for it is the throne of God,* [35] *or by the earth, for it is the footstool of His feet, or by Jerusalem, for it is THE CITY OF THE GREAT KING.* [36] *Nor shall you make an oath by your head, for you cannot make one hair white or black.* [37] *But let your statement be, 'Yes, yes' or 'No, no'; and anything beyond these is of evil."*

Here, Jesus teaches on the concept of giving "oaths." The Law of Oaths is set out in the Old Testament in Numbers 30. Because people are not always truthful; they will swear an oath in the name of God. The point being that by swearing in the name of God, the person has bolstered his credibility/honesty regarding whatever he is promising or testifying about. In other words, the oath served to invite God to be the witness that what he was were saying was true. By asking God to be a witness to the truthfulness of what was said, the oath-taker is also inviting divine judgment upon himself if he is lying. The idea was that one would not take an oath and invite such judgment upon oneself if what he said was untrue. **Hebrews 6:16:** *"For men swear by one greater than themselves, and with them an oath given as confirmation is an end of every dispute."*

By the time of Jesus ministry, Jewish oaths were indiscriminately given. The religious leaders came up with the idea that if an oath was made in the name of something other than *"to the Lord,"* it was not required to be true or fulfilled.[105] In essence the religious leaders set up their own little "tradition" so they would not have to keep their word. The point of an oath was to support the truth and fulfillment of the promise. The religious leaders twisted the concept of an oath to support and further a lie. It must be remembered that lies come from Satan. Jesus told this to some who were listening to Him:

> **John 8:44:** *"You are of your father the devil, and you want to do the desires of your father. He was a murderer from the beginning, and does not stand in the truth, because there is no truth in him. Whenever he speaks a lie, he speaks from his own nature; for he is a liar, and the father of lies."*

God hates lying:

> **Proverbs 6:16, 19:** *"There are six things which the LORD hates....*[19] *A false witness who utters lies,...."*

> **Revelation 21:8:** *"...and all liars, their part will be in the lake that burns with fire and brimstone, which is the second death."*

Look back at the main text we are studying, Jesus said in **Matthew 5:34-37** that they were not to swear, *"...by heaven, for it is the throne of God,* [35] *or by the earth, for it is the footstool of His feet, or by Jerusalem, for it is THE CITY OF THE GREAT KING.* [36] *Nor shall you make an oath by your head, for you cannot make one hair white or black.* [37] *But let your statement be, 'Yes, yes' or 'No, no'; and anything beyond these is of evil."*

These man-made "traditions" of oaths undermined the true basis of an oath. An oath was supposed to support the truth, not a lie. Jesus taught, *"let your statement be, 'Yes, yes' or 'No, no'; and anything beyond these is of evil"* (see also James 5:12). Jesus is saying your speech must always be true and not encumbered by flowery oaths to help hide deception. Jesus further addresses the absurdity of this man-made oath system in Matthew 23:16-22.

Section Application

How can you be truthful in your daily life? Even in the small things? Do you lie to be polite or not offend people? Do you "swear" or "cross your heart" when you are stating something? You have no need to do this. Let your *Yes* [mean] *yes* and your *No* [mean] *no.* We must remember God hears and sees everything.

---

[105] This sounds like the junior high stunt of *crossing your fingers* when you make a promise. The claim was if you crossed your fingers while making a promise, your promise was null and void (i.e. a promise you did not have to keep).

VERSES 38-40: *"You have heard that it was said, 'AN EYE FOR AN EYE, AND A TOOTH FOR A TOOTH.' [39]But I say to you, do not resist him who is evil; but whoever slaps you on your right cheek, turn to him the other also. [40] And if anyone wants to sue you, and take your shirt, let him have your coat also."*

In these verses Jesus used the letter of Scripture, *"AN EYE FOR AN EYE, AND A TOOTH FOR A TOOTH…"* to set out the Spirit of God's Word as it applies to our personal obligation to not retaliate. We are to forgive, as well as to give to others.

The phrase, *"AN EYE FOR AN EYE, AND A TOOTH FOR A TOOTH…."* comes from **Leviticus 24:19-20,** which says, *"And if a man injures his neighbor, just as he has done, so it shall be done to him: [20] fracture for fracture, eye for eye, tooth for tooth; just as he has injured a man, so it shall be inflicted on him."* (see also Deuteronomy 19:21, Exodus 21:24). The concept was <u>not</u> about personal revenge but the execution of justice by the authorities. The phrase means that the punishment of the guilty must be in proportion to the crime (the principle of lex talionis). This law also protected the guilty from being <u>overly punished</u> for an incident (e.g. one knocks another's eye out, which results in him receiving the death penalty). Punishment by authorities is correct and God-ordained as set out in **Romans 13:1-7:**

> *"LET every person be in subjection to the governing authorities. For there is no authority except from God, and those which exist are established by God. [2] Therefore he who resists authority has opposed the ordinance of God; and they who have opposed will receive condemnation upon themselves. [3] For rulers are not a cause of fear for good behavior, but for evil. Do you want to have no fear of authority? Do what is good, and you will have praise from the same; [4] for it is a minister of God to you for good. But if you do what is evil, be afraid; <u>for it does not bear the sword for nothing; for it is a minister of God, an avenger who brings wrath upon the one who practices evil</u>. [5] Wherefore it is necessary to be in subjection, not only because of wrath, but also for conscience sake. [6] For because of this you also pay taxes, for rulers are servants of God, devoting themselves to this very thing. [7]Render to all what is due them: tax to whom tax is due; custom to whom custom; fear to whom fear; honor to whom honor."*

> **1 Peter 2:13-15:** *"Submit yourselves for the Lord's sake to every human institution, whether to a king as the one in authority, [14]or to governors as sent by him for the punishment of evildoers and the praise of those who do right. [15] For such is the will of God that by doing right you may silence the ignorance of foolish men."*

Jesus makes a distinction between our personal responsibility to forgive one who wrongs us as compared to the government's requirement to execute justice. The government's responsibility before God is to execute an, "eye for an eye" but that is not to be our individual Christian response. Forgiveness toward those who wrong us is not merely a New Testament concept. It has always been the law of God.

> **Proverbs 25:21-22:** *"If your enemy is hungry, give him food to eat; And if he is thirsty, give him water to drink; [22]For you will heap burning coals on his head, And the LORD will reward you."*

We are never to seek our own revenge:

> **Deuteronomy 32:35:** *"Vengeance is Mine, and retribution, In due time their foot will slip; For the day of their calamity is near,…."* (See also Proverbs 24:29).

Romans 12:19-21: *"Never take your own revenge, beloved, but leave room for the wrath of God, for it is written, 'VENGEANCE IS MINE, I WILL REPAY,' says the Lord. [20] 'BUT IF YOUR ENEMY IS HUNGRY, FEED HIM, AND IF HE IS THIRSTY, GIVE HIM A DRINK; FOR IN SO DOING YOU WILL HEAP BURNING COALS UPON HIS HEAD.' [21] Do not be overcome by evil, but overcome evil with good."*

In the text (Matthew 5:38-40), Jesus states: *"but whoever slaps you on your right cheek, turn to him the other also."* To be slapped was a great insult in Jewish culture (see Job 16:10; Lamentations 3:30; Micah 5:1). We are not to be angry and strike back in defense of ourselves. Jesus Himself did not retaliate when, *"they spat in His face and beat Him with their fists; and others slapped Him,"* **Matthew 26:67**. This personal non-retaliatory concept is not to be confused with standing by while evil is directed against others. Jesus did not stand by when evil was done to others. Remember Jesus' reaction when His Father's house was being desecrated by the money changers (Matthew 21:12-13)?

These sections can be summed up in **1 Peter 2:21-23** which states:
"For you have been called for this purpose, since Christ also suffered for you, leaving you an example for you to follow in His steps, [22] WHO COMMITTED NO SIN, NOR WAS ANY DECEIT FOUND IN HIS MOUTH; [23] and while being reviled, He did not revile in return; while suffering, He uttered no threats, but kept entrusting Himself to Him who judges righteously;" [106]

---

[106] The only time **civil disobedience** is allowed is when the governing authorities are clearly in violation of Scripture. This is not to be quickly claimed. Be very careful to not let your political agendas/philosophies be confused with true Biblical mandates (e.g. I am required to pay taxes even if the government uses tax money for things that are ungodly; see also Matthew 22:15-22 and comments). MacArthur states the following on the subject of civil disobedience and political activism:

"Many evangelicals believe that Christians should become active in political causes, relying on social action and pressure tactics to change laws and government policies and practices that are plainly evil and to protect cherished religious rights that are being encroached upon. In the name of such concepts as co-belligerency, some evangelicals are joining forces with individuals and organizations that are unchristian, heretical, and even cultic. The reasoning is that it is sometimes permissible to join forces with one evil in order to combat what is considered to be a greater evil. This zeal for preservation of the Christian faith, both culturally and individually, often gets blended in with strong views about economics, taxation, social issues, and partisanship, so that the Bible gets wrapped in the flag. Even social and political activities that are perfectly worthwhile can deplete the amount of a believer's time, energy, and money that is available for the central work of the gospel. The focus is shifted from the call to build the spiritual kingdom through the gospel to efforts to moralize culture—trying to change society from the outside rather than individuals from the inside. When the church is politicized, even in support of good causes, its spiritual power is vitiated and its moral influence diluted. And when such causes are supported in worldly ways and by worldly means, the tragedy is compounded. We are to be the conscience of the nation through faithful preaching and godly living, confronting it not with the political pressure of man's wisdom—including our own—but with the spiritual power of God's Word. Using legislation, adjudication, or intimidation to achieve a superficial, temporal 'Christian morality' is not our calling—and has no eternal value." MacArthur, J. F., Jr. (1991). *Romans.* MacArthur New Testament Commentary (p. 196). Chicago: Moody Press.
[Note continued on the next page.]

VERSE 41: *"And whoever shall force you to go one mile, go with him two."*

In this verse, one needs to understand that Rome was in control. MacArthur writes,
> "Roman law gave a soldier the right to **force** a civilian to carry his pack for a Roman **mile**, which was slightly shorter than our modern mile. The law, designed to relieve the soldier, not only caused great inconvenience to civilians but was made even more despicable by the fact that the oppressed were made to carry the equipment and weapons of their oppressors. Outside of combat the Roman soldier was probably never more hated than when he forced someone to carry his pack."[107]

Jesus again stressed the concept of submission and non-retaliation for personal violations by telling His followers to go twice the distance they were asked.

[Note continued.]

Look at some scriptural examples of civil disobedience, when believers were ordered not to worship the one true God, evangelize, etc. Notice that those who refused to obey, did not take up arms, but simply accepted the punishment. Look at what Jesus said when the evil mob came to arrest Him: *"Then Jesus said to him, 'Put your sword back into its place; for all those who take up the sword shall perish by the sword.'"* Matthew 26:52.

Acts 5:27–29: *"When they had brought them, they stood them before the Council. The high priest questioned them, saying, "We gave you strict orders not to continue teaching in this name, and yet, you have filled Jerusalem with your teaching and intend to bring this man's blood upon us." But Peter and the apostles answered, "We must obey God rather than men."*

Acts 5:40–41: *"They took his advice; and after calling the apostles in, they flogged them and ordered them not to speak in the name of Jesus, and then released them. So they went on their way from the presence of the Council, rejoicing that they had been considered worthy to suffer shame for His name."*

Daniel 3:14–18: *"Nebuchadnezzar responded and said to them, 'Is it true, Shadrach, Meshach and Abed-nego, that you do not serve my gods or worship the golden image that I have set up? Now if you are ready, at the moment you hear the sound of the horn, flute, lyre, trigon, psaltery and bagpipe and all kinds of music, to fall down and worship the image that I have made, very well. But if you do not worship, you will immediately be cast into the midst of a furnace of blazing fire; and what god is there who can deliver you out of my hands?' Shadrach, Meshach and Abed-nego replied to the king, 'O Nebuchadnezzar, we do not need to give you an answer concerning this matter. If it be so, our God whom we serve is able to deliver us from the furnace of blazing fire; and He will deliver us out of your hand, O king. But even if He does not, let it be known to you, O king, that we are not going to serve your gods or worship the golden image that you have set up.'"*

Wiersbe states, *"…* please note that, in each of these instances, *the people had a direct word from God that gave them assurance they were doing His will.* And further note that, in every instance, the believers were kind and respectful. They didn't start riots or burn down buildings 'for conscience sake.' Because civil authority is ordained of God (Romans 13), it's a serious thing for Christians to disobey the law; and if we're going to do it, we must know the difference between personal prejudices and biblical convictions." Wiersbe, W. W. (1993). *Be Committed.* "Be" Commentary Series (p 98). Wheaton, IL: Victor Books.

[107] MacArthur, John F., *The MacArthur New Testament Commentary*, p. 334-335 (Chicago: Moody Press) 1985.

VERSE 42: *"Give to him who asks of you, and do not turn away from him who wants to borrow from you."*

As Christians, we are to be very giving people. This generous heart is not simply to other Christians, but extends to our enemies.

> **Luke 6:34-36:** *"And if you lend to those from whom you expect to receive, what credit is that to you? Even sinners lend to sinners, in order to receive back the same amount. [35] But love your enemies, and do good, and <u>lend, expecting nothing in return</u>; and your reward will be great, and you will be sons of the Most High; for He Himself is kind to ungrateful and evil men. [36] Be merciful, just as your Father is merciful."*

The Lord also tells us how to give. Our giving style should be done very quietly. We should look to do kindness to those who cannot repay us. We should also realize that God sees our giving and will reward us in heaven.

> **Matthew 6:2-4:** *"When therefore you give alms, do not sound a trumpet before you, as the hypocrites do in the synagogues and in the streets, that they may be honored by men. Truly I say to you, they have their reward in full. [3] But when you give alms, do not let your left hand know what your right hand is doing [4] that your alms may be in secret; and your Father who sees in secret will repay you."*

> **Luke 14:13-14:** *"But when you give a reception, invite the poor, the crippled, the lame, the blind, [14] and you will be blessed, since they do not have the means to repay you; for you will be repaid at the resurrection of the righteous."*

> **Luke 12:33-34:** *"Sell your possessions and give to charity; make yourselves purses which do not wear out, an unfailing treasure in heaven, where no thief comes near, nor moth destroys. [34] For where your treasure is, there will your heart be also."*

VERSES 43-48: *"You have heard that it was said, 'YOU SHALL LOVE YOUR NEIGHBOR, and hate your enemy.' [44] But I say to you, love your enemies, and pray for those who persecute you [45] in order that you may be sons of your Father who is in heaven; for He causes His sun to rise on the evil and the good, and sends rain on the righteous and the unrighteous. [46] For if you love those who love you, what reward have you? Do not even the tax-gatherers do the same? [47] And if you greet your brothers only, what do you do more than others? Do not even the Gentiles do the same? [48] Therefore you are to be perfect, as your heavenly Father is perfect."*

As with the previous sections, we see the Pharisees mixing some truth with a lie. The truth of God was to *"love your neighbor,"* the lie was to *"hate your enemy."* Again and again we read of the Pharisees changing the Word of God to fit their own traditions and religious/political system. Notice they quoted, *"love your neighbor,"* but omitted the rest of the verse of the Law that said, *"as yourself."* It is one thing to say you love someone, and it is another thing to love that person with the same concern as you have for yourself. This type of sacrificial love would not fit well in the Pharisees' proud and self-righteous mindset. Pharisee or not, true sacrificial love, as defined by Jesus, is impossible for any person apart from the power of God.

Back in the Old Testament, God told His people, *"You shall not take vengeance, nor bear any grudge against the sons of your people, <u>but you shall love your neighbor as yourself;</u> I am the LORD."*

<u>Leviticus 19:18</u> (In the N.T., see also Matthew 19:19 and 22:39; Mark 12:31; Luke 10:27; Romans 13:9; Galatians 5:14; James 2:8). As for enemies, notice Leviticus 19:18 does not say you can hate your enemies, but instead it says you are to not take vengeance or hold a grudge against them. The only way to not hold a grudge is to forgive them. In addition, the Old Testament instructed the people to do good to their enemies and not hate them.

> **<u>Exodus 23:4-5</u>:** *"If you meet your enemy's ox or his donkey wandering away, you shall surely return it to him. ⁵ If you see the donkey of one who hates you lying helpless under its load, you shall refrain from leaving it to him, you shall surely release it with him."*

We know that our neighbor is *anyone* we have contact with in our daily life. Samaritans and Jews hated each other but look how one Samaritan fulfilled the law of God. In this story, Jesus tells a lawyer that he should love his neighbor. Looking for a technicality to justify his own lack of love, the lawyer asked, "And who is my neighbor?"

> **<u>Luke 10:30-37</u>:** *"Jesus replied and said, A certain man was going down from Jerusalem to Jericho; and he fell among robbers, and they stripped him and beat him, and went off leaving him half dead. ³¹ And by chance a certain priest was going down on that road, and when he saw him, he passed by on the other side. ³² And likewise a Levite also, when he came to the place and saw him, passed by on the other side. ³³ But a certain Samaritan, who was on a journey, came upon him; and when he saw him, he felt compassion, ³⁴ and came to him, and bandaged up his wounds, pouring oil and wine on them; and he put him on his own beast, and brought him to an inn, and took care of him. ³⁵ And on the next day he took out two denarii and gave them to the innkeeper and said, 'Take care of him; and whatever more you spend, when I return, I will repay you.' ³⁶ Which of these three do you think proved to be a neighbor to the man who fell into the robbers' hands? ³⁷ And he said, 'The one who showed mercy toward him.' And Jesus said to him, 'Go and do the same.'*

These verses sum up much of the Christian's attitude toward others. He is to love and pray for others, show them kindness, and give to them regardless of whether they are friends or enemies. Why should that be our response? Because your Father in heaven, *"is kind to ungrateful and evil men... [and is]... merciful."* (see Luke 6:35-36). This concept is specifically set out in **<u>1 John 4:20</u>:** *"If someone says, "I love God," and hates his brother, he is a liar; for the one who does not love his brother whom he has seen, cannot love God whom he has not seen."* It is not merely a flaw in one who states that he is a Christian but does not love others; it demonstrates that he is a child of the Devil.

> **<u>1 John 3:10</u>:** *"By this the children of God and the children of the devil are obvious: anyone who does not practice righteousness is not of God, nor the one who does not love his brother."*

Dietrich Bonhoeffer, a pastor who suffered and eventually was killed by the Nazis in Germany, wrote of Jesus' teaching in <u>Matthew 5:44</u>:

> "This is the supreme demand. Through the medium of prayer we go to our enemy, stand by his side, and plead for him to God."[108]

---

[108] *The Cost of Discipleship,* trans. R. H. Fuller [2d rev. ed.; New York: Macmillan, 1960], p. 166).

Summary and Application

Think of someone whom you consider an enemy. Do you seek revenge against him? [109] Have you forgiven him? Start praying for him and look for ways to bless him and demonstrate that you are a child of God.

---

[109]

a) The person who is a supporter of Islamic homicidal bombings believes that their prophet calls (and rewards) him when he hates and kills his enemies.

*Qur'an 8:12 "When your Lord revealed to the angels: I am with you, therefore make firm those who believe. I will cast terror into the hearts of those who disbelieve. Therefore <u>strike off their heads and strike off every fingertip of them</u>.."

*Qur'an 2:191 "And <u>kill them wherever you find them,</u> and drive them out from whence they drove you out, and <u>persecution is severer than slaughter,</u> and do not fight with them at the Sacred Mosque until they fight with you in it, but if they do fight you, then slay them; such is the recompense of the unbelievers."

*Qur'an 5:33 "The punishment of those who wage war against Allah and His messenger and strive to make mischief in the land is only this, that <u>they should be murdered or crucified or their hands and their feet should be cut off on opposite sides</u> or they should be imprisoned;...."

*Qur'an 9:5 "So when the sacred months have passed away, then <u>slay the idolaters wherever you find them,</u> and take them captives and besiege them and <u>lie in wait for them in every ambush,</u> then if they repent and keep up prayer and pay the poor-rate, leave their way free to them; surely Allah is Forgiving, Merciful."

*Qur'an 47: 4 "So when you meet in battle those who disbelieve, <u>then smite the necks until when you have overcome them, then make (them) prisoners,</u> and afterwards either set them free as a favor or let them ransom (themselves) until the war terminates....and (as for) <u>those who are slain in the way of Allah, He will by no means allow their deeds to perish.</u>"

* Taken from translator Muhammad Habib Shakir, (1866–1939) an Egyptian judge, born in Cairo and a graduate from Al Azhar University. You can find slight variances in some other English translations of the Qur'an that attempt to soften some of the violent language..

b) The followers of Christ are called to obey Jesus' words when He said, <u>**Matthew 5:44:**</u> *"But I say to you, <u>love your enemies , and pray for those who persecute you</u> [45] in order that you may be sons of your Father who is in heaven;...."*

c) In summary: The *god* of Islam is not the God of Christianity.

<u>MATTHEW 6:1-4</u>
(GIVING)

"BEWARE of practicing your righteousness before men to be noticed by them; otherwise you have no reward with your Father who is in heaven. ²When therefore you give alms, do not sound a trumpet before you, as the hypocrites do in the synagogues and in the streets, that they may be honored by men. Truly I say to you, they have their reward in full. ³ But when you give alms, do not let your left hand know what your right hand is doing ⁴ that your alms may be in secret; and your Father who sees in secret will repay you."

Introduction

In this section we will study the Christian's attitude when doing good or giving to others. Most people do good deeds so others will think well of them. Some may disagree and claim they do things because it gives them a good feeling inside. In pursuing that "good feeling" they are still doing good works for an audience who they desire will think well of them (the audience is themselves). They want to have the satisfaction of viewing themselves as very altruistic people. Others think that by doing something good they can offset some bad thing they have done. In neither case are they doing service to solely glorify God.

VERSE 1: *"BEWARE of practicing your righteousness before men to be noticed by them; otherwise you have no reward with your Father who is in heaven."*

The Pharisees, scribes and other religious leaders of Jesus' time loved the "approval of man" more than the "approval of God" (John 12:43). They would often do their good deeds with the hope that others would see them and think well of them.

Hypocrisy is all around us. Think of the activist who is anxiously concerned about a baby seal, but at the same time supports the slaughter of a baby child through abortion. Hypocrisy also flourishes among the religious fakes. A so-called religious leader wants people to think he is kind and helpful, but then we find out he uses his position of trust to molest children.

Religious hypocrisy has its roots way back to the first family. We see Cain, performing a ritualistically act of religious worship without faith and love for God (Genesis. 4:2-8, Hebrews 11:4). Cain's hypocrisy finally surfaced when he murdered his brother Abel. Abel was not a hypocrite but was a true and righteous follower of God, and that is why Cain killed him.

> **1 John 3:11-12:** *"For this is the message which you have heard from the beginning, that we should love one another; ¹² not as <u>Cain, who was of the evil one, and slew his brother. And for what reason did he slay him? Because his deeds were evil, and his brother's were righteous."</u>*

Another Biblical example of a religious fake is Judas Iscariot, who betrayed Jesus. Although he had others fooled, he never fooled Jesus. In **John 6:70-71:** *"Jesus answered them, 'Did I Myself not choose you, the twelve, and yet one of you is a devil?' ⁷¹ Now He meant Judas the son of Simon Iscariot, for* *he, one of the twelve, was going to betray Him."* Judas, the fake religious follower, sold Jesus to fake religious leaders, who wanted Him murdered. Look at the similarities of Cain and Judas. It is typical of false / hypocritical religious leaders to hate and attack the true followers of God.

A New Testament example of hypocritical giving is Ananias and Sapphira. They owned a piece of land and then sold it so they could give the money to the church. They held back some of the money but told the church they gave all they received for the land. They lied to the Holy Spirit by claiming they were giving more to the church than they really were. The church never asked for the money. Peter himself pointed out that both before and after the sale of the land Ananias and Sapphira were free to do whatever they wished with their money (Acts 5:4). Their motivation was to look good to others, and especially in the eyes of the church leadership (Acts 5:1-10). They were seeking honor for themselves and not God. They were interested in *imitating* the righteous giving of others without a heart for the Lord. We read in Acts 4 that some of the believers in the church, including a brother name Barnabas, had previously sold his land to assist the poor:

> **Acts 4:34–37:** *"For there was not a needy person among them, for all who were owners of land or houses would sell them and bring the proceeds of the sales* [35] *and lay them at the apostles' feet, and they would be distributed to each as any had need.* [36] *Now Joseph, a Levite of Cyprian birth, who was also called Barnabas by the apostles (which translated means Son of Encouragement),* [37] *and who owned a tract of land, sold it and brought the money and laid it at the apostles' feet."*

Hypocrisy is not the Christian's attitude. The Christian does good works out of love for God and is not interested in getting congratulated by others. Actually, the wise believer is interested in people not finding out about their good works.

VERSES 2-4: *"When therefore you give alms, do not sound a trumpet before you, as the hypocrites do in the synagogues and in the streets, that they may be honored by men. Truly I say to you, they have their reward in full.* [3] *But when you give alms, do not let your left hand know what your right hand is doing* [4] *that your alms may be in secret; and your Father who sees in secret will repay you."*

So what are "alms?" "The Gk. word signifies pity, prompting relief given in money or kind to the poor. Though not explicitly mentioned in the English OT, almsgiving is implied as an expression of compassion in the presence of God."[110] Ryle states, "Let us observe that our Lord takes it for granted that all who call themselves his disciples will give alms."[111]

Jesus makes it clear that your giving (whether money or service to God) is to be done in secret. It is actually to your advantage to hide your good works from others so that you do not get the praise for them. There is a very big difference between your good works glorifying you as compared to your good works getting others to glorify God. **Matthew 5:16:** *"Let your light shine before men in such a way that they may see your good works, and <u>glorify your Father who is in heaven.</u>"* This verse actually warns us against being cowardly and avoiding service to God. Our main text in Matthew 6:4 (about giving your alms in secret) is not about one being fearful from doing good works, but rather

---

[110] Wood, D. R. W., and Marshall, I. H. (1996). *New Bible dictionary* (3rd ed. /) (p. 25). Leicester, England; Downers Grove, Ill.: InterVarsity Press.

[111] Ryle, J.C. *Matthew (Expository thoughts on the Gospels).* (Crossways classic commentaries: v.1) p.36.

deals with one's motivation for doing good works. A. B. Bruce explains the distinction between Matthew 5:16 and 6:4 this way: "We are to show when tempted to hide and hide when tempted to show."[112]

Another concept in giving is that it is not a matter of how much you give <u>but how much you hold back</u>. Jesus always is examining the heart and not the mere external action. Notice how Jesus explained this concept:

> **Luke 21:1-4:** *"AND He looked up and saw the rich putting their gifts into the treasury. [2]And He saw a certain poor widow putting in two small copper coins. [3] And He said, 'Truly I say to you, this poor widow put in more than all of them; [4] for they all out of their surplus put into the offering; but she out of her poverty put in all that she had to live on.'"*

The godly are very giving and God promises to provide for this type of person:

> **Proverbs 11:25:** *"The generous man will be prosperous, And he who waters will himself be watered."*

> **2 Corinthians 9:6-7:** *"Now this I say, he who sows sparingly shall also reap sparingly; and he who sows bountifully shall also reap bountifully. [7] Let each one do just as he has purposed in his heart; not grudgingly or under compulsion; for God loves a cheerful giver."*

Summary and Application

When you do good works, is it your objective that others see you and think you are a good person? If so, repent of that and do your good work to glorify God (quietly and in secret). If you are told that something you did was very kind, you should tell that person you did it because you are a Christian. This will inform him that your motivation is from Christ and not of your own goodness. The end result will be that Christ is glorified and not yourself. At that moment you should also look for an opportunity to witness to him about salvation in Christ.

---

[112] MacArthur, J. (1985). *Matthew* (pp. 357–358). Chicago: Moody Press.

MATTHEW 6:5-18
(PRAYER and FASTING)

"And when you pray, you are not to be as the hypocrites; for they love to stand and pray in the synagogues and on the street corners, in order to be seen by men. Truly I say to you, they have their reward in full. ⁶ But you, when you pray, go into your inner room, and when you have shut your door, pray to your Father who is in secret, and your Father who sees in secret will repay you. ⁷ And when you are praying, do not use meaningless repetition, as the Gentiles do, for they suppose that they will be heard for their many words. ⁸ Therefore do not be like them; for your Father knows what you need, before you ask Him. ⁹ Pray, then, in this way:

> *'Our Father who art in heaven,*
> *Hallowed be Thy name.*
> ¹⁰ *Thy kingdom come.*
> *Thy will be done,*
> *On earth as it is in heaven.*

¹¹*Give us this day our daily bread.* ¹² *And forgive us our debts, as we also have forgiven our debtors.* ¹³*And do not lead us into temptation, but deliver us from evil. [For Thine is the kingdom, and the power, and the glory, forever. Amen.]'* ¹⁴ *For if you forgive men for their transgressions, your heavenly Father will also forgive you.* ¹⁵ *But if you do not forgive men, then your Father will not forgive your transgressions.* ¹⁶*And whenever you fast, do not put on a gloomy face as the hypocrites do, for they neglect their appearance in order to be seen fasting by men. Truly I say to you, they have their reward in full.* ¹⁷ *But you, when you fast, anoint your head, and wash your face* ¹⁸ *so that you may not be seen fasting by men, but by your Father who is in secret; and your Father who sees in secret will repay you."*

Introduction

These verses discuss the importance of prayer in the life of a Christian. [There is not one Christian who could not spend more time in prayer.] The business of life and even ministry can cause us to forget what Jesus tells us: *"...apart from Me you can do nothing."* **John 15:5**. William Wilberforce[113] recognized this when he said:

> "I must secure more time for private devotions. I have been living far too public for me.
> The shortening of private devotions starves the soul."[114]

We simply do not realize how much time and trouble we would be saving ourselves by praying about matters instead of running around trying to handle them by our own efforts.

---

[113] William Wilberforce, (1759-1833) a British politician who championed the opposition to the slave trade.

[114] Morgan, R. J. (2000). *Nelson's Complete Book of Stories, Illustrations, and Quotes* (electronic ed.) p. 175. Nashville: Thomas Nelson Publishers.

1 Thessalonians 5:16-18: *"Rejoice always; pray without ceasing; in everything give thanks; for this is God's will for you in Christ Jesus."*

VERSES 5-6: *"And when you pray, you are not to be as the hypocrites; for they love to stand and pray in the synagogues and on the street corners, in order to be seen by men. Truly I say to you, they have their reward in full.* [6] *But you, when you pray, go into your inner room, and when you have shut your door, pray to your Father who is in secret, and your Father who sees in secret will repay you."*

These verses continue the theme Jesus set out in previous sections. The point is that our relationship with God is not built on external actions, but our heart attitude while doing external actions (or private actions for that matter). That concept also applies to our prayer life. The Pharisees were hypocrites when it came to prayer. Their primary concern was for others to see them engaging in religious acts. The religious leaders wanted others to think highly of their piety. Why was that their concern? The answer is they were not true believers in God, and thus their view of prayer was that it could be used as a vehicle to have others think well of them. Scripture tells us people are rewarded according to their faith (Hebrews 11:6). Since they did not pray in faith, their prayers were not heard or answered. Matthew 6:5 states that their prayers were of no spiritual benefit: *"…they love to stand and pray in the synagogues and on the street corners, in order to be seen by men. Truly I say to you, they have their reward in full."*

After explaining how we are not to pray, Jesus tells believers the right way to pray: **Matthew 6:6:** *"But you, when you pray, go into your inner room, and when you have shut your door, pray to your Father who is in secret, and your Father who sees in secret will repay you."* This is not saying that you can never pray in public. For example, you can say grace before your meal at a restaurant. **1 Timothy 4:4-5** says, *"For everything created by God is good, and nothing is to be rejected, if it is received with gratitude;* [5] *for it is sanctified by means of the word of God and prayer."* (See also Matthew 14:19, where Jesus is praying to bless the food that He multiplied). Again, the issue is not the technicality of the prayer being in public, the issue is your heart attitude. Do you pray at the restaurant for others to see you and think good of you, or are you thanking God as the Giver of all good things?

One last thought, try not to have a great reputation of being a "prayer warrior,"… just be one. Let me explain. If you are praying in secret like Jesus instructs, how are people finding out you are a great "prayer warrior"? Sin and hypocrisy can be creeping at the door even when we pray. Martyn Lloyd-Jones[115] put it this way:

> "We tend to think of sin as we see it in rags and in the gutters of life. We look at a drunkard, poor fellow, and we say, there is sin. But that is not the essence of sin. To have a real picture and understanding of sin, you must look at some great saint, some unusually devout and devoted man, look at him there on his knees in the very presence of God. Even there self is intruding itself, and the temptation is for him to think about himself, to think pleasantly and pleasurably about himself and to really be worshiping

---

[115] Martyn Lloyd-Jones (1899-1981) was a Welsh Protestant minister and a medical doctor. He was well-known for his sound teaching and opposition to liberal theology.

himself rather than God. That, not the other, is the true picture of sin. The other is sin, of course, but there you do not see it at its acme, you do not see it in its essence. Or to put it in another form, if you really want to understand something about the nature of Satan and his activities, the thing is not to go to the dregs or the gutters of life. If you really want to know something about Satan, go away to that wilderness where our Lord spent forty days and forty nights. That's the true picture of Satan, where you see him tempting the very Son of God.[116]

VERSES 7-8: *"And when you are praying, do not use meaningless repetition, as the Gentiles do, for they suppose that they will be heard for their many words. [8]Therefore do not be like them; for your Father knows what you need, before you ask Him."*

Jesus goes back to what to not do during prayer (*"meaningless repetition"*). "Meaningless repetition" can take on many forms. Probably one of the most common would be the Catholic rosary. The rosary is heretical since it is not prayer to the One and only living God, but is done as a form of devotion to the Virgin Mary. Note that the Bible tells us Jesus Christ is the one and only mediator between God and mankind, *"For there is one God, and one mediator also between God and men, the man Christ Jesus."* <u>1 Timothy 2:5</u>. The rosary beads are used to count off prayers consisting of "three sets of five decades each of the Hail Mary with each decade preceded by the Lord's Prayer and ending with a doxology."[117] Some people are very satisfied with their spirituality because they have spent so much time *repeating* prayers. Scripture makes it clear that they are misled in that they, *"suppose that they will be heard for their many words."* <u>Matthew 6:7.</u>

Another form of "meaningless repetition" prayer that God has convicted me of involves giving thanks before mealtime. Sometimes I would just mumble out the same words of thanks for every meal in an almost mechanical and meaningless manner. I have repented of that. I now try to reflect on the many things I am thankful for at that moment, in addition to the meal.

Do not confuse "meaningless repetition" with the sincere, ongoing, pursuit of God in prayer. I have prayed to the Lord many times regarding the same matter. Scripture supports our pursuit of the Lord in prayer. In the Gospel of Luke, immediately after the section where Jesus is teaching the disciples how to pray, He states the following in <u>Luke 11:5–13:</u>

> *"Then He said to them, 'Suppose one of you has a friend, and goes to him at midnight and says to him, 'Friend, lend me three loaves; for a friend of mine has come to me from a journey, and I have nothing to set before him'; and from inside he answers and says, 'Do not bother me; the door has already been shut and my children and I are in bed; I cannot get up and give you anything.' I tell you, even though he will not get up and give him anything because he is his friend, yet because of his persistence he will get up and give him as much as he needs. So I say to you, ask, and it will be given to you; seek, and you will find; knock, and it will be opened to you. For everyone who asks, receives; and he who seeks, finds; and to him who knocks, it will be opened. Now suppose one of*

---

[116] Lloyd-Jones, Martyn D. *Studies in the Sermon on the Mount*, 2 vols. [Grand Rapids: Eerdmans, 1979], pp. 222–23).

[117] The American Heritage Dictionary.

you fathers is asked by his son for a fish; he will not give him a snake instead of a fish, will he? Or if he is asked for an egg, he will not give him a scorpion, will he? If you then, being evil, know how to give good gifts to your children, how much more will your heavenly Father give the Holy Spirit to those who ask Him?'"

So what is the result of our heartfelt prayers? Jesus gives us great assurance God hears and answers our prayers. Not only does He hear them, but He even, *"knows what you need, before you ask Him."* Matthew Henry said,

"It does not follow that therefore ye need not pray; for God requires you by prayer to own your need of him and dependence on him...." [118]

What an awesome, caring, and loving heavenly Father we have. His Word tells us in **Psalm 127:2** that *"...He gives to His beloved even in his sleep."*

When we say God always answers prayer, it should not be understood to mean that He always gives us what we want. Answered prayer does mean that He always gives us what is best. Sometimes the best for me is a "no" answer, sometimes it is "yes" and other times it may be "wait." We must always pray in the will of God. That comes by knowing His Word so we know His will. If we do not know His specific will on a matter, we should always end that prayer in Jesus' name by saying something like, "if it be your will Lord...not my will, but yours." This concept is set forth in
1 John 5:14–15:

"This is the confidence which we have before Him, that, if we ask anything <u>according to His will</u>, He hears us. And if we know that He hears us in whatever we ask, we know that we have the requests which we have asked from Him."

Remember what it says in **James 4:2-3**: *"...You do not have because you do not ask. ³ You ask and do not receive, because you ask with wrong motives, so that you may spend it on your pleasures."*

George Mueller, who was a great man of prayer, gave the following insights on how he sought out God's will for a matter. He said to:

- "Seek to get your heart in such a condition that it has no will of its own in regard to a given matter. Do not depend upon feelings or impressions.
- Seek the will of the Spirit of God through, or in connection with, the Word of God.
- Take into account providential circumstances.
- Ask God in prayer to reveal His will clearly.

Thus, through prayer to God, the study of His Word, and reflection, I come to a deliberate judgment, and if my mind is thus at peace, and continues so after two or three more petitions, I proceed accordingly. I have found this method always effective."[119]

See the footnote 120 regarding concepts and scriptures about THE WILL OF GOD.

---

[118] Henry, Matthew, *Matthew Henry's Commentary on the Bible*, Matt. 6:5-8 (Peabody, MA: Hendrickson Publishers) 1997.

[119] Osbeck, K. W. (1990). *Amazing grace : 366 inspiring hymn stories for daily devotions* (p 234). Grand Rapids, Mich.: Kregel Publications.

[120] **WILL OF GOD:**   Below are verses on God's will for us in: Faith, Sacrifice, Servanthood, Sexual Purity, Thanksgiving, Leading a Law-Abiding Life, Prayer, and being Heavenly Minded and not Materialistic.

- **Ephesians 5:15-17:**   *"Therefore be careful how you walk, not as unwise men but as wise, making the most of your time, because the days are evil. So then do not be foolish, but understand what the will of the Lord is. "*

- Jesus said in **Mark 3:35:** *"For whoever does the will of God, he is My brother and sister and mother."*   So what is the, "will of God?" There is only one place to find the answer, God's Word.

FAITH:

John 6:39-40: *"And this is the will of Him who sent Me, that of all that He has given Me I lose nothing, but raise it up on the last day. [40] For this is the will of My Father, that everyone who beholds the Son and believes in Him, may have eternal life; and I Myself will raise him up on the last day."*

SACRIFICE:

Romans 12:1-2: *"I urge you therefore, brethren, by the mercies of God, to present your bodies a living and holy sacrifice, acceptable to God, which is your spiritual service of worship. [2] And do not be conformed to this world, but be transformed by the renewing of your mind, that you may prove what the will of God is, that which is good and acceptable and perfect."*

2 Timothy 3:12-17: *"And indeed, all who desire to live godly in Christ Jesus will be persecuted. [13] But evil men and impostors will proceed from bad to worse, deceiving and being deceived. [14] You, however, continue in the things you have learned and become convinced of, knowing from whom you have learned them; [15] and that from childhood you have known the sacred writings which are able to give you the wisdom that leads to salvation through faith which is in Christ Jesus. [16] All Scripture is inspired by God and profitable for teaching, for reproof, for correction, for training in righteousness; [17] that the man of God may be adequate, equipped for every good work."*

SERVANTHOOD:

Ephesians 6:5-6: *"Slaves, be obedient to those who are your masters according to the flesh, with fear and trembling, in the sincerity of your heart, as to Christ; [6] not by way of eyeservice, as men-pleasers, but as slaves of Christ, doing the will of God from the heart."*

SEXUAL PURITY:

1 Thessalonians 4:3-8: *"For this is the will of God, your sanctification; that is, that you abstain from sexual immorality; [4] that each of you know how to possess his own vessel in sanctification and honor, [5] not in lustful passion, like the Gentiles who do not know God; [6] and that no man transgress and defraud his brother in the matter because the Lord is the avenger in all these things, just as we also told you before and solemnly warned you. [7] For God has not called us for the purpose of impurity, but in sanctification. [8] Consequently, he who rejects this is not rejecting man but the God who gives His Holy Spirit to you."*

THANKSGIVING:

1 Thessalonians 5:16-18: *"Rejoice always; [17] pray without ceasing; [18] in everything give thanks; for this is God's will for you in Christ Jesus."*

[Footnote on the WILL OF GOD continued on the next page.]

VERSES 9-15 [9] *"Pray, then, in this way: 'Our Father who art in heaven, Hallowed be Thy name.* [10] *Thy kingdom come. Thy will be done, On earth as it is in heaven.* [11] *Give us this day our daily bread.* [12] *And forgive us our debts, as we also have forgiven our debtors.* [13] *And do not lead us into temptation, but deliver us from evil. [For Thine is the kingdom, and the power, and the glory, forever. Amen.]'* [14] *For if you forgive men for their transgressions, your heavenly Father will also forgive you.* [15] *But if you do not forgive men, then your Father will not forgive your transgressions.'"*

This section is traditionally called the "Lord's Prayer" but it should be understood that <u>it was not a prayer that Jesus prayed</u>, nor was Jesus giving them a prayer to mechanically recite. Jesus was setting before them an outline of what their prayer time should consist of. [If you want to see the prayer Jesus prayed, examine Jesus' High Priestly Prayer in John 17.] By examining the prayer in outline form, we see what we are told to pray. Note the outline below (I through V):

I.   In reverent praise of the Holy and Most High God: ***"Our Father."*** Scripture tells us to pray in the name of Jesus (1Timothy 2:5). The Bible speaks directly to the fact that we are not to pray to saints, angels or the dead, etc.:

- **1 Timothy 2:5:** *"For there is one God, and <u>one mediator also between God and men, the man Christ Jesus,"</u>*
- **Revelation 22:8-9:** *"I, John, am the one who heard and saw these things. And when I heard and saw, I fell down to worship at the feet of the angel who showed me these things. But he said to me, '<u>Do not do that. I am a fellow servant of yours and of your brethren the prophets and of those who heed the words of this book. Worship God.'"</u>*
- **Romans 8:34:** *"Who is the one who condemns? Christ Jesus is He who died, yes, rather who was raised, who is at the right hand of God, who also intercedes for us."*
- **Leviticus 20:6:** *"As for the person who <u>turns to mediums and to spiritists, to play the harlot after them, I will also set My face against that person </u>and will cut him off from among his people."*

[Note continued.]

LEADING A LAW-ABIDING LIFE:

1 Peter 2:13-17: *"Submit yourselves for the Lord's sake to every human institution, whether to a king as the one in authority,* [14] *or to governors as sent by him for the punishment of evildoers and the praise of those who do right.* [15] <u>*For such is the will of God *</u>*that by doing right you may silence the ignorance of foolish men.* [16] *Act as free men, and do not use your freedom as a covering for evil, but use it as bondslaves of God.* [17] *Honor all men; love the brotherhood, fear God, honor the king."*

PRAYER:

1 John 5:14: *"And this is the confidence which we have before Him, that, if we ask anything <u>according to His will</u>, He hears us."*

BE HEAVENLY MINDED and NOT MATERIALISTIC, FLESHLY OR WORLDLY

1 John 2:15-17: *"Do not love the world, nor the things in the world. If anyone loves the world, the love of the Father is not in him.* [16] *For all that is in the world, the lust of the flesh and the lust of the eyes and the boastful pride of life, is not from the Father, but is from the world.* [17] *And the world is passing away, and also its lusts; <u>but the one who does the will of God abides forever.</u>"*

<u>End of footnote on the Will of God.</u>

- **Isaiah 42:8**: *"I am the Lord, that is My name; I will not give My glory to another, Nor My praise to graven images."*
- **Isaiah 8:19**: *"When they say to you, 'Consult the mediums and the spiritists who whisper and mutter,' should not a people consult their God? Should they consult the dead on behalf of the living?"*
- **1 Chronicles 10:13–14**: *"So <u>Saul died for his trespass which he committed against the Lord, because of the word of the Lord which he did not keep; and also because he asked counsel of a medium, making inquiry of it, and did not inquire of the Lord.</u> Therefore He killed him and turned the kingdom to David the son of Jesse."*

II.   For the coming kingdom and that people would obey His perfect will and not follow the way of this fallen world system.

III.   For daily provision of food and other needs by acknowledging that all things come from God.

IV.   For spiritual protection by being delivered from evil; again glorifying God for His awesome and complete Lordship.

V.   For forgiveness of our own sins, prayer for others and relinquishing them of any sin they may have committed against us.

John Bunyan once said, "Prayer will make a man cease from sin, or sin will entice a man to cease from prayer."[121]

VERSE 16-18: *"And whenever you fast, do not put on a gloomy face as the hypocrites do, for they neglect their appearance in order to be seen fasting by men. Truly I say to you, they have their reward in full. [17] But you, when you fast, anoint your head, and wash your face [18] so that you may not be seen fasting by men, but by your Father who is in secret; and your Father who sees in secret will repay you."*

Fasting involves denial [e.g. food] for a time period as you concentrate on prayer and seeking God. Ryle states that, "[the] abstinence from food in order to bring the body into subjection to the spirit, is a practice frequently mentioned in the Bible."[122] It is not done to try to manipulate or appease God but rather to seek Him more (Ezra 8:21). It is also a time of humility. **Psalm 35:13** says, *"...I humbled my soul with fasting...."*

In our main text of Matthew 6:5, Jesus states, *"And whenever you fast,...."* The verse makes it clear that fasting is not an option, but rather assumes that <u>you will fast</u>. We see prayer and fasting in the early church in **Acts 14:23**: *"When they had appointed elders for them in every church, having prayed with fasting, they commended them to the Lord in whom they had believed."*

---

[121] Thomas, I. (1996). *The Golden Treasury of Puritan Quotations* (electronic ed.) (p. 211). Simpsonville SC: Christian Classics Foundation.

[122] Ryle, J.C., *Matthew (Expository Thoughts on the Gospels)*, (Crossways Classic Commentaries: v.1) p.42.

As we have seen before, Jesus shows the condition of the heart is what matters when seeking God. The Pharisees saw fasting as an opportunity to get the approval of others who saw them. This is the same attitude they had about prayer. It was all external appearances. False humility is actually pride, and worthless in the sight of God:

> **Colossians 2:23:** *"Such regulations indeed have an appearance of wisdom, with their self-imposed worship, their false humility and their harsh treatment of the body, but they lack any value in restraining sensual indulgence."* (NIV)

> **1 Peter 5:5:** *"You younger men, likewise, be subject to your elders; and all of you, clothe yourselves with humility toward one another, for GOD IS OPPOSED TO THE PROUD, BUT GIVES GRACE TO THE HUMBLE."*

We must not forget that fasting has an important place in spiritual battle.

> **Matthew 17:18-21:** *"And Jesus rebuked him, and the demon came out of him, and the boy was cured at once. ¹⁹ Then the disciples came to Jesus privately and said, 'Why could we not drive it out?' ²⁰ And He said to them, 'Because of the littleness of your faith; for truly I say to you, if you have faith the size of a mustard seed, you will say to this mountain, Move from here to there, and it will move; and nothing will be impossible to you. ²¹But this kind does not go out except by prayer and fasting.'"*

Summary and Application

Are there times your prayers remain "meaningless repetition?" Do you say the same repeated prayer, with no heartfelt desire to speak to God at meal times, or before your go to bed? Repent of this ritualism and speak to God. Ritualism kills the ongoing relationship with God. Some think the best place to speak to God is at a church. Some think they need to be on their knees, hands folded and eyes closed in order to pray. They can have that view but Scripture does not give us a formula as to how we should look. External conduct is not the real issue that matters regarding prayer. The main issue is the attitude of the heart. You can walk down the street or be riding in your car and be praying to God in a reverent and holy way (even with your eyes wide open!). God wants you to tell Him everything. We limit the joy of our fellowship with God when we set up ritualistic regulations God never established.

So many times people feel guilty of their sins, so they do not look forward to coming before God in prayer. They look at prayer as something that makes them feel bad. If there is guilt or sin in our lives, we need to run to the cross and be released from our sins, not bound by them. **1 John 1:9-10:** *"If we confess our sins, He is faithful and righteous to forgive us our sins and to cleanse us from all unrighteousness."*

Another issue dealing with prayer has to do with our emotions after we have prayed. Some people are discouraged after praying because they don't feel like their prayers made it past the ceiling. The problem with that view is the word *feel*. It does not matter how we *feel* about our prayers, we are called to pray. He hears our prayers regardless of how we feel!

> **1 John 5:14-15:** *"And this is the confidence which we have before Him, that, if we ask anything according to His will, He hears us. ¹⁵And if we know that He hears us in whatever we ask, we know that we have the requests which we have asked from Him."*

More verses on PRAYER:

I would strongly encourage you to read through these verses on prayer:

PRAYER: Prayer in general-Matthew 6:5-15; Pray without doubting-Matthew 21:21-22, Mark 11:24-26; House of prayer-Matthew 21:12-13, Luke 19:45-46; Jesus prayed often-Luke 5:16; Pray and not faint-Luke 18:1-8; Pray you won't enter temptation-Luke 22:40, 46; Be anxious for nothing but pray instead-Philippians 4:6-8; Devote yourself to prayer-Colossians 4:2-3; Pray without ceasing-1 Thessalonians 5:17; Prayer for kings and those in authority, this is good in sight of God-1Timothy 2:1-3; Pray lifting holy hands without wrath-1Timothy 2:8; Everything created by God is good and not to be rejected if received with gratitude and sanctified with prayer-1Timothy 4:4-6; We do not have because we do not ask God-James 4:2-4; If suffering, then pray-James 5:13; Effective prayer of a righteous man can accomplish much-James 5:16 (see James 5:13-18 on prayer); God hears our prayers -1 John 5:14-15; Husband, live with your wife in an understanding way so your prayers will not be hindered-1 Peter 3:7; David prayed to God in the morning-Psalms 5:2-3; Prayer of the upright is God's delight-Proverbs 15:8; Prayer of the wicked: God does not hear the prayer of the non-believer-Isaiah 59:2; Lord is far from the wicked but hears the prayer of the righteous-Proverbs 15:29; He who turns away his ear from listening to the law, even his prayer is an abomination-Proverbs 28:9; The prayer of repentance and faith in Christ God does hear – Romans 10:13, Psalms 145:18-20.

MATTHEW 6:19-34
(MONEY and ANXIETY — FEAR OF THE FUTURE)

19 "Do not lay up for yourselves treasures upon earth, where moth and rust destroy, and where thieves break in and steal. 20 But lay up for yourselves treasures in heaven, where neither moth nor rust destroys, and where thieves do not break in or steal; 21for where your treasure is, there will your heart be also. 22 The lamp of the body is the eye; if therefore your eye is clear, your whole body will be full of light. 23 But if your eye is bad, your whole body will be full of darkness. If therefore the light that is in you is darkness, how great is the darkness! 24 No one can serve two masters; for either he will hate the one and love the other, or he will hold to one and despise the other. You cannot serve God and mammon. 25 For this reason I say to you, do not be anxious for your life, as to what you shall eat, or what you shall drink; nor for your body, as to what you shall put on. Is not life more than food, and the body than clothing? 26 Look at the birds of the air, that they do not sow, neither do they reap, nor gather into barns, and yet your heavenly Father feeds them. Are you not worth much more than they? 27 And which of you by being anxious can add a single cubit to his life's span? 28 And why are you anxious about clothing? Observe how the lilies of the field grow; they do not toil nor do they spin, 29 yet I say to you that even Solomon in all his glory did not clothe himself like one of these. 30 But if God so arrays the grass of the field, which is alive today and tomorrow is thrown into the furnace, will He not much more do so for you, O men of little faith? 31 Do not be anxious then, saying, 'What shall we eat?' or 'What shall we drink?' or 'With what shall we clothe ourselves?' 32 For all these things the Gentiles eagerly seek; for your heavenly Father knows that you need all these things. 33 But seek first His kingdom and His righteousness; and all these things shall be added to you. 34 Therefore do not be anxious for tomorrow; for tomorrow will care for itself. Each day has enough trouble of its own."

Introduction

These verses address the Christian view regarding material things and daily provisions for life on earth. Our view should be that material things and daily provisions are not to be looked upon with either greed or fear of lack. They are both under the sovereign hand of God, who will provide for us.

The warnings against greed or the love of money are not restricted to the rich; poor people (and those in-between) must heed them as well. One with riches must not be misled into thinking that his wealth serves as evidence of his spiritual superiority. On the other end of the economic spectrum is the false doctrine of *liberation theology.*[123] This view has been prevalent in some areas of South America. Liberation theology blends a teaching that upholds being poor as spiritually superior. The correct view I should have regarding possessions is that <u>everything I have has come from God and belongs to God</u>. (See Psalm 24:1). John MacArthur makes the following insightful comments regarding money and possessions:

> "Whether men are wealthy or poor-or somewhere in between-their attitude toward material possessions is one of the most reliable marks of their spiritual condition…. Sixteen of the thirty-eight parables of Jesus deal with money. One out of ten verses in

---

[123] *Liberation theology.* "A school of theology, especially prevalent in the Roman Catholic Church in Latin America, that finds in the Gospel a call to free people from political, social, and material oppression." *American Heritage Dictionary of the English Language Third Edition*, Houghton Mifflin Co., (1992).

the New Testament deals with that subject. Scripture offers about five hundred verses on prayer, fewer than five hundred on faith, and over two thousand on money. The believer's attitude toward money and possessions is determinative."[124]

VERSES 19-21: *"Do not lay up for yourselves treasures upon earth, where moth and rust destroy, and where thieves break in and steal. ²⁰ But lay up for yourselves treasures in heaven, where neither moth nor rust destroys, and where thieves do not break in or steal; ²¹ for where your treasure is, there will your heart be also."*

This section deals with the Christian's view of luxuries (material items over and above the necessities needed for life.) Luxuries are not evil, but it is our attitude about them that can be evil. We are to use things for our needs, for others, and for building the kingdom of God. A person should not, *"lay up for yourselves treasures upon earth."* These verses tell us that we are to view the material things in our life as very temporal (e.g. that which *"moth and rust destroy"*). We must remember that everything in this world will end up being destroyed by fire (2 Peter 3:7). Jesus demonstrates the pointlessness of material things here on earth compared to the Kingdom of God in **Mark 8:34-37:**

> *"And He summoned the multitude with His disciples, and said to them, 'If anyone wishes to come after Me, let him deny himself, and take up his cross, and follow Me. ³⁵ For whoever wishes to save his life shall lose it; but whoever loses his life for My sake and the gospel's shall save it. ³⁶ <u>For what does it profit a man to gain the whole world, and forfeit his soul?</u> ³⁷ For what shall a man give in exchange for his soul?'"*

> **Matthew 13:45-46:** *"Again, the kingdom of heaven is like a merchant seeking fine pearls, ⁴⁶ and upon finding one pearl of great value, he went and sold all that he had, and bought it."*

We need to understand that greed is not a mere flaw in our character, but it is just as bad as bowing down to idols. Colossians 3:5-6 defines greed as idolatry: *"...and <u>greed, which amounts to idolatry.</u> For it is on account of these things that the wrath of God will come,...."*

In our text of Matthew 6:21, Jesus says *"... for where your treasure is, there will your heart be also."* One cannot allow his job, car, or even his family to be more important than his relationship with Christ. Our heart's desire should be to serve Him first. Oh, how often we fail at this, but God is merciful. Only when we put God first in our lives are we able to love and care for our family members in a God-honoring way.

God's word sets forth the truth regarding the Pharisees view of money in **Luke 16:14:** *"Now the Pharisees, <u>who were lovers of money</u>...."* Is it your desire to get rich? If so, look what the Word of God says awaits you:

> **1 Timothy 6:9-10:** *"But those who want to get rich fall into temptation and a snare and many foolish and harmful desires which plunge men into ruin and destruction. ¹⁰ For the love of money is a root of all sorts of evil, and some by longing for it have wandered away from the faith, and pierced themselves with many a pang."*

---

[124] MacArthur, John F., *The MacArthur New Testament Commentary*, p.418 (Chicago: Moody Press) 1985.

Those who have riches are instructed to share and be generous, knowing that all that they have is on loan from God.

> **1 Timothy 6:17-19:** *"Instruct those who are rich in this present world not to be conceited or to fix their hope on the uncertainty of riches, but on God, who richly supplies us with all things to enjoy.* [18] *Instruct them to do good, to be rich in good works, to be generous and ready to share,* [19] *storing up for themselves the treasure of a good foundation for the future, so that they may take hold of that which is life indeed."*

Often times people borrow money to live above their means due to a lack of contentment. As one person observed, "Too many people spend money they haven't earned, to buy things they don't want, to impress people they don't like."[125] The bottom line is that we need to learn to be content in whatever situation the Lord has chosen for us.

> **Philippians 4:11-13:** *"Not that I speak from want; for I have learned to be content in whatever circumstances I am.* [12] *I know how to get along with humble means, and I also know how to live in prosperity; in any and every circumstance I have learned the secret of being filled and going hungry, both of having abundance and suffering need.* [13] *I can do all things through Him who strengthens me."*

> **1 Timothy 6:5-8:** *"...and constant friction between men of depraved mind and deprived of the truth, who suppose that godliness is a means of gain.* [6] *But godliness actually is a means of great gain, when accompanied by contentment.* [7] *For we have brought nothing into the world, so we cannot take anything out of it either.* [8] *And if we have food and covering, with these we shall be content."*

VERSES 22-24: *"The lamp of the body is the eye; if therefore your eye is clear, your whole body will be full of light.* [23] *But if your eye is bad, your whole body will be full of darkness. If therefore the light that is in you is darkness, how great is the darkness!* [24] *No one can serve two masters; for either he will hate the one and love the other, or he will hold to one and despise the other. You cannot serve God and mammon."*

These verses discuss the importance of not suffering from spiritual blindness. As **Ezekiel 12:2** says: *"Son of man, you live in the midst of the rebellious house, who have eyes to see but do not see, ears to hear but do not hear; for they are a rebellious house."* Jesus points out in our Matthew text that the lust for money will cause spiritual blindness: *"You cannot serve God and mammon."*

Have you ever been around a young child who had poor vision from birth? One of my daughters had poor vision. When she was about three years old, she was fitted for glasses. It was very interesting to observe her immediately after she got the glasses. When we returned home from the optometrist's office she went up to her bedroom. She looked around as if she had never been in the room before. She appeared awestruck and focused on things she didn't know were there. In a similar fashion, sin can cause spiritual blindness that we don't know exists until God opens our eyes and saves us. The tragedy is that sin's victim does not even know he is blind. As he continues down the road of destruction, the blindness will manifest itself when he no longer hides his sin but openly defends it.

---

[125] This quote is thought to have originated with Will Rogers.

Proverbs 28:22: *"A man with an evil eye hastens after wealth, and does not know that want will come upon him."*

The modern mentality is reflected on a bumper sticker I saw which states, "He who dies with the most toys wins!" The Biblical view of this statement would be, "He who dies with the most toys wins — NOTHING!" Go to any funeral director and ask him about the suits available to dress the deceased in. One interesting fact about those suits, they do not have pockets! They may be sewn to look like they have pockets, but they are not really there. Just another little reminder of what we already know: "You cannot take it with you." Look how Jesus explained this in **Luke 12:15-21:**

> *"And He said to them, 'Beware, and be on your guard against every form of greed; for not even when one has an abundance does his life consist of his possessions.' And He told them a parable, saying, 'The land of a certain rich man was very productive. And he began reasoning to himself, saying, What shall I do, since I have no place to store my crops? And he said, This is what I will do: I will tear down my barns and build larger ones, and there I will store all my grain and my goods. And I will say to my soul, 'Soul, you have many goods laid up for many years to come; take your ease, eat, drink and be merry.' But God said to him, 'You fool! This very night your soul is required of you; and now who will own what you have prepared?' So is the man who lays up treasure for himself, and is not rich toward God.'"*

VERSES 25-34: *"For this reason I say to you, do not be anxious for your life, as to what you shall eat, or what you shall drink; nor for your body, as to what you shall put on. Is not life more than food, and the body than clothing?* [26] *Look at the birds of the air, that they do not sow, neither do they reap, nor gather into barns, and yet your heavenly Father feeds them. Are you not worth much more than they?* [27] *And which of you by being anxious can add a single cubit to his life's span?* [28] *And why are you anxious about clothing? Observe how the lilies of the field grow; they do not toil nor do they spin,* [29] *yet I say to you that even Solomon in all his glory did not clothe himself like one of these.* [30] *But if God so arrays the grass of the field, which is alive today and tomorrow is thrown into the furnace, will He not much more do so for you, O men of little faith?* [31] *Do not be anxious then, saying, 'What shall we eat?' or 'What shall we drink?' or 'With what shall we clothe ourselves?'* [32] *For all these things the Gentiles eagerly seek; for your heavenly Father knows that you need all these things.* [33] *But seek first His kingdom and His righteousness; and all these things shall be added to you.* [34] *Therefore do not be anxious for tomorrow; for tomorrow will care for itself. Each day has enough trouble of its own."*

Earlier in this lesson we looked at Matthew 6:19-24. These verses dealt with what our Christian view should be toward luxuries (i.e. non-necessities that we store up). Now in verses 25-34, we look at our attitude toward necessities like food and clothes. In these verses, three times we are told, *"Do not be anxious"* (v.25, 31 and 34). That sums up what our attitude should be about necessities. Why should we not be anxious? Because God is our Father! He rules overall and controls all (1 Chronicles 29:12). Worry and anxiety can be devastating to us physically, as well as spiritually. We do not realize that worry is a manifestation of self-reliance. When we fret we are not trusting in our heavenly Father. Psalm 37:8 says, *"...Do not fret, it leads only to evildoing."* Instead of fear we are told to *"seek first His kingdom and His righteousness; and all these things shall be added to you."* To fight fear we should remember who God is and pray to Him.

> **Isaiah 41:10:** *"Do not fear, for I am with you; Do not anxiously look about you, for I am your God. I will strengthen you, surely I will help you, Surely I will uphold you with My righteous right hand."*

Philippians 4:6-7: *"Be anxious for nothing, but in everything by prayer and supplication with thanksgiving let your requests be made known to God. [7] And the peace of God, which surpasses all comprehension, shall guard your hearts and your minds in Christ Jesus."*

Psalm 91:5-7: *"You will not be afraid of the terror by night, or of the arrow that flies by day; of the pestilence that stalks in darkness, or of the destruction that lays waste at noon. A thousand may fall at your side and ten thousand at your right hand, But it shall not approach you."*

We are promised in **Philippians 4:19:** *"And my God shall supply all your needs according to His riches in glory in Christ Jesus."* Jesus promised that the very God who feeds the birds will feed His children. Jesus states plainly that you are more valuable than the birds: *"Are you not worth much more than they?"* **Matthew 6:26.** Do not let any "animal rights" person tell you humans and animals are equal in status, because God says they are not. He loves His children and will provide for their needs and bless them.

Commenting on Matthew 6:31-32, J.C. Ryle states:

"Over-carefulness about the things of this world is most unworthy of a Christian.
One great feature of paganism is living for the present." [126]

Summary and Application

What are the desires and fears of your life? Do you feel good only when you get the "toys" you want? Are you fearful of not having enough? Are your desires simply material ones, or are they to advance the kingdom of God? When we become concerned about worldly provisions and money we must remember who God is and what He promises. These concepts are summed up in **Hebrews 13:5-6:**

"Let your character be free from the love of money, being content with what you have; for He Himself has said 'I WILL NEVER DESERT YOU, NOR WILL I EVER FORSAKE YOU' [6] so that we confidently say, 'THE LORD IS MY HELPER, I WILL NOT BE AFRAID. What shall man do to me?'"

---

[126] Ryle, J.C., *Matthew (Expository thoughts on the Gospels)*, (Crossways Classic Commentaries: v.1) p.46.

MATTHEW 7:1-6
(JUDGING OTHERS)

"Do not judge lest you be judged. ² For in the way you judge, you will be judged; and by your standard of measure, it will be measured to you. ³ And why do you look at the speck that is in your brother's eye, but do not notice the log that is in your own eye? ⁴ Or how can you say to your brother, 'Let me take the speck out of your eye,' and behold, the log is in your own eye? ⁵ You hypocrite, first take the log out of your own eye, and then you will see clearly to take the speck out of your brother's eye. ⁶ Do not give what is holy to dogs, and do not throw your pearls before swine, lest they trample them under their feet, and turn and tear you to pieces."

Introduction

We are not to *judge*? Some think verse one above means we are never to judge anything as being right or wrong. Does verse one mean anything someone does is okay? Jesus is not saying that. Just look a little farther in that same chapter [Matthew 7:15-20] [127] and see that Jesus instructs us to judge the *fruit* so we are able to identify false prophets. The lesson to be understood from Matthew 7 regarding judging is what Jesus said in **John 7:24:** *"Do not judge according to appearance, **but judge with righteous judgment.**"* There is an eternal difference between self-righteous condemnation of another as compared with reproving a person with the desire of him coming into repentance.

VERSES 1-5: *"Do not judge lest you be judged. ² For in the way you judge, you will be judged; and by your standard of measure, it will be measured to you. ³ And why do you look at the speck that is in your brother's eye, but do not notice the log that is in your own eye? ⁴ Or how can you say to your brother, 'Let me take the speck out of your eye,' and behold, the log is in your own eye? ⁵ You hypocrite, first take the log out of your own eye, and then you will see clearly to take the speck out of your brother's eye."*

> To analyze this section, one needs to start by putting Matthew 7:1-6 in its correct context. The passage is a continuation of the *Sermon on the Mount* that began in the fifth chapter of Matthew. The *Sermon on the Mount* is constantly demonstrating the distinction between false/hypocritical religion and a true love for God. It must be remembered that among those in Jesus' audience were self-righteous Pharisees. Pharisees had set up a religion of their own by changing God's Word. They had no problem judging (i.e. condemning) others because they judged themselves superior to others. They felt very comfortable taking the place of God by condemning others who did not live up to their man-made religious standards. Evidence of their self-righteousness and hypocrisy is set out in verses 3-5

---

[127] **Matthew 7:15–20:** *"Beware of the false prophets, who come to you in sheep's clothing, but inwardly are ravenous wolves. ¹⁶You will know them by their fruits. Grapes are not gathered from thorn bushes nor figs from thistles, are they? ¹⁷So every good tree bears good fruit, but the bad tree bears bad fruit. ¹⁸A good tree cannot produce bad fruit, nor can a bad tree produce good fruit. ¹⁹Every tree that does not bear good fruit is cut down and thrown into the fire. ²⁰ So then, you will know them by their fruits."*

where it says:

> *"…why do you look at the speck that is in your brother's eye, but do not notice the log that is in your own eye? ⁴ Or how can you say to your brother, 'Let me take the speck out of your eye,' and behold, the log is in your own eye? ⁵ 'You <u>hypocrite</u>….'"*

Jesus exposed the Pharisees' hypocritical judgments when He said to them in **<u>Luke 16:15</u>:** *"You are those who justify yourselves in the sight of men, but God knows your hearts; …."* Their man-made religious standards even tried to condemn God for healing on the Sabbath:

> *"…are you angry with Me because I made an entire man well on the Sabbath? ²⁴ Do not judge according to appearance, but judge with righteous judgment."* **<u>John 7:23-24.</u>**

The false judge, like the Pharisees, assumes to usurp the place of God in judging.

> **<u>James 4:11-12</u>:** *"Do not speak against one another, brethren. He who speaks against a brother, or judges his brother, speaks against the law, and judges the law; but if you judge the law, you are not a doer of the law, but a judge of it. ¹² <u>There is only one Lawgiver and Judge, the One who is able to save and to destroy; but who are you who judge your neighbor?</u>"*

The false moralist is addressed in the book of Romans:

> **<u>Romans 2:1-3</u>:** *"THEREFORE you are without excuse, every man of you who passes judgment, for in that you judge another, you condemn yourself; for you who judge practice the same things. ² And we know that the judgment of God rightly falls upon those who practice such things. ³ And do you suppose this, O man, when you pass judgment upon those who practice such things and do the same yourself, that you will escape the judgment of God?"*

The verse in <u>Matthew 7:1</u> that says, *"Do not judge lest you be judged"* should not be understood by the Christian to mean he is never to discern, evaluate or criticize anyone or anything. Note that a few verses after Jesus makes that statement in verse 1, He tells the people, *"Do not give what is holy to dogs, and do not throw your pearls before swine, lest they trample them under their feet, and turn and tear you to pieces."* **<u>Matthew 7:6</u>**. Jesus expects us to discern and judge who the "dogs" are. Also, in chapter 7, Jesus warns us to watch out for false prophets and says we will know who they are by "their fruit" (i.e. you will have to judge their fruit).

> **<u>Matthew 7:15-20</u>:** *"<u>Beware of the false prophets</u>, who come to you in sheep's clothing, but inwardly are ravenous wolves. ¹⁶ <u>You will know them by their fruits</u>. Grapes are not gathered from thorn bushes, nor figs from thistles, are they? ¹⁷ Even so, every good tree bears good fruit; but the bad tree bears bad fruit. ¹⁸ A good tree cannot produce bad fruit, nor can a bad tree produce good fruit. ¹⁹ Every tree that does not bear good fruit is cut down and thrown into the fire. ²⁰ So then, <u>you will know them by their fruits</u>."*

In Matthew 18:15-17, Jesus explained the process of addressing a sinning brother (i.e. a person who claims to be a Christian but lives an ungodly life). If, after the process is complete, he does not repent, we are instructed to remove him from the church. Although many in the church would not dare admonish or rebuke another who is living in sin, this type of so-called *kindness* is actually not kind at all. God's Word tells us that not warning another to turn from his sin is the same as hating him:

> **<u>Leviticus 19:17</u>:** *"You shall not hate your fellow countryman in your heart; you may surely reprove your neighbor,…."*

Paul makes it clear that believers have the responsibility to judge matters within the church (i.e. among believers).

> **1 Corinthians 5:12-13:** *"For what have I to do with judging outsiders? Do you not judge those who are within the church?* ¹³ *But those who are outside, God judges. 'REMOVE THE WICKED MAN FROM AMONG YOURSELVES.'"*

When a Christian *judges* rightfully, the heart condition is completely different than that of the Pharisees. First, the Christian should not be judging the person based on his own man-made standard, but by the Word of God. The believer must also remember that he too is a servant who will eventually be judged by God. The Christian is never to judge another with the objective of exalting himself, but with a heart of love that desires the repentance of the wayward person. Finally, the correcting believer will fully examine his own frailty, which will result in compassion for the person he approaches.

> **Galatians 6:1-3:** *"BRETHREN, even if a man is caught in any trespass, you who are spiritual, <u>restore such a one in a spirit of gentleness</u>; each one looking to yourself, <u>lest you too be tempted. Bear one another's burdens, and thus fulfill the law of Christ.</u> ³ <u>For if anyone thinks he is something when he is nothing,</u> he deceives himself."*

J.C. Ryle summarizes Matthew 7:1-6 by saying:

> "What our Lord means to condemn is a censorious and fault-finding spirit. A readiness to blame others for trifling offenses or matters of indifference, a habit of passing rash and hasty judgments, a disposition to magnify the errors and infirmities of our neighbors and make worst of them – this is what our Lord forbids. It was common among the Pharisees."[128]

It is the person who lives by the Spirit of God who neither falls into:

1)   self-righteous condemning of others, nor
2)   false sentimentality/tolerance, which makes a mockery of God and His Word.

VERSE 6: *"Do not give what is holy to dogs, and do not throw your pearls before swine, lest they trample them under their feet, and turn and tear you to pieces."*

In verse 6, Jesus eliminates the view Matthew 7:1-5 means we are never to judge right from wrong. Obedience to verse six requires one to judge who is a dog or a swine.

We think of dogs as nice little house pets, but in Jesus' time dogs were anything but that:

> "...[dogs] were largely half-wild mongrels that acted as scavengers. They were dirty, greedy, snarling, and often vicious and diseased. They were dangerous and despised. It would have been unthinkable for a Jew to have thrown to those *dogs* a piece of *holy* meat that had been consecrated as a sacrifice in the Temple." [129]

This concept of *dogs* representing the wicked that are outside of the kingdom of God is set out in the

---

[128] Ryle, J.C., *Matthew / (Expository Thoughts on the Gospels)*, (Crossways Classic Commentaries: v.1) p.48.

[129] MacArthur, John F., *The MacArthur New Testament Commentary*, p. 437 (Chicago: Moody Press) 1985.

book of Revelation:

> **Revelation 22:15:** *"Outside are the dogs and the sorcerers and the immoral persons and the murderers and the idolaters, and everyone who loves and practices lying."*

Jesus also said, *"...do not throw your pearls before swine...."* Swine were also considered a rotten and "unclean" animal to the Jews. Look how the pig is described in the New Bible Dictionary:

> "The children of Israel were divinely prohibited from eating swine (...Leviticus 11:7; Deuteronomy 14:8). This was for two hygienic reasons. First, the pig, as a frequent scavenger, may pick up diseased material and either carry infection mechanically or itself become infected. Secondly, the pig is host of the tapeworm causing trichinosis; this passes one stage in the muscles of a pig and can be transmitted only by being eaten. The tape worms then invade various tissues in man and can even cause death. Thorough cooking kills the worms but this is not always possible when firewood is scarce, so that only a complete ban is safe. This relationship was proved only in the 20th century. This prohibition became a national loathing with the Jews, with the pig standing for what is despicable and hated."[130]

So when Jesus says that we are not to, *"give what is holy to dogs, and do not throw your pearls before swine,"* He is saying that we are not to continue to share the beautiful truths of God with those who treat them as garbage and blaspheme them. In **Matthew 10:14** Jesus said:

> *"And whoever does not receive you, nor heed your words, as you go out of that house or that city, shake off the dust of your feet. [15]Truly I say to you, it will be more tolerable for the land of Sodom and Gomorrah in the day of judgment, than for that city."*

Often we see people who have been exposed many times to the Gospel become hostile to it. The idea is that, *familiarity breeds contempt.* We saw that happen to Jesus when He taught among His own people.

> **Matthew 13:54-57:** *"...And coming to His hometown He began teaching them in their synagogue, so that they became astonished, and said, 'Where did this man get this wisdom, and these miraculous powers? Is not this the carpenter's son? Is not His mother called Mary, and His brothers, James and Joseph and Simon and Judas? And His sisters, are they not all with us? Where then did this man get all these things?' And they took offense at Him. But Jesus said to them, 'A prophet is not without honor except in his home town, and in his own household.'"*

Many of us are discouraged when it seems like those to whom we are closest are the ones who are least willing to listen to us. Many of these people think they are familiar with the Gospel and treat its *pearls* like swine would.

Ryle discusses it this way:

> "Do we wonder that the relatives, servants and neighbors of godly people are not always converted? Do we wonder that the parishioners of eminent ministers of the Gospel are often their hardest and most impenitent hearers? Let us wonder no more. Let us note the experience of our Lord at Nazareth, and learn wisdom."[131]

---

[130] Wood, D. R. W., and Marshall, I. H. (1996). *New Bible Dictionary (3rd ed.)* (p. 40). Leicester, England; Downers Grove, IL: InterVarsity Press.

[131] Ryle, J.C., *Matthew / (Expository Thoughts on the Gospels),* (Crossways Classic Commentaries: v.1) p.113.

The prohibition of casting spiritual pearls to dogs and swine does not apply only to those outside the church. There can be people in the church who are to be ignored also:

Titus 3:10: *"Reject a factious man after a first and second warning, ¹¹ knowing that such a man is perverted and is sinning, being self-condemned."*

Summary and Application

In our country of relativism[132] and political correctness, a person who makes any type of meaningful moral judgment is considered ignorant and intolerant. The relativist's view is that the highest form of morality is to maintain that there is no such thing as morality or judgment. Although the relativists will manifest great hostility to Biblical Christianity, it is amazing how many of them will quote their favorite Scripture: Matthew 7:1. Although they may not know the difference between the Apostle John and Johnny Appleseed, there is one Scripture that every non-believer loves to quote: *"Do not judge lest you be judged."* In their unregenerate minds, the verse means that one has no right to make a judgment on any ungodly or perverted behavior. What they fail to realize is that the Christian is not leveling a judgment against them, but rather the warning they are getting is from God Himself, as set forth from His Word:

Hebrews 9:27: *"And inasmuch as it is appointed for men to die once and after this comes judgment,...."*

1 Corinthians 6:9-11: *"Or do you not know that the unrighteous shall not inherit the kingdom of God? Do not be deceived; neither fornicators, nor idolaters, nor adulterers, nor effeminate, nor homosexuals, nor thieves, nor the covetous, nor drunkards, nor revilers, nor swindlers, shall inherit the kingdom of God. And such were some of you; but you were washed, but you were sanctified, but you were justified in the name of the Lord Jesus Christ, and in the Spirit of our God."*

John 3:36: *"He who believes in the Son has eternal life; but he who does not obey the Son will not see life, but the wrath of God abides on him."*

Notice that the *"wrath of God abides on him."* This means that he is under a state of God's anger.[133] Note the very same chapter in the Bible speaks of God's wrath also contains the well-known verses of God's love in **John 3:16**: *"For God so loved the world, that He gave His only begotten Son, that whoever believes in Him should not perish, but have eternal life.*

So which is it? Does God love them or is He angry at them? The answer is both. Through His love, He has provided the way of escape from the judgment to come through His Son, Jesus Christ. For those who put their faith in Christ's sacrificial death as their payment for sin, God's justice is satisfied and they are forgiven. This is explained in John 3:16-18. I must admit that I get a little concerned when people quote John 3:16 and remove the context by neglecting the verses that follow, which warn of the judgment to come. Look at John 3:16-18 and then you will see that John 3:36 is in perfect harmony.

---

[132] Relativism is a "theory that conceptions of truth and moral values are not absolute but are relative to the persons or groups holding them." *American Heritage Dictionary of the English Language Third Edition*, Houghton Mifflin Co., (1992).

[133] *Merriam-Webster Collegiate Dictionary, 11ᵗʰ edition* defines Abide and Wrath as follows: Abide: is defined in part as: To endure without yielding.... to remain stable or fixed in a state. Wrath: is defined as: 1. strong vengeful anger or indignation 2. retributory punishment for an offense or a crime....

John 3:16-18: *"For God so loved the world, that He gave His only begotten Son, that* <u>*whoever believes in Him should not perish, but have eternal life.*</u> *¹⁷ For God did not send the Son into the world to judge the world, but that the world should be saved through Him. ¹⁸ He who believes in Him is not judged;* <u>*he who does not believe has been judged already, because he has not believed in the name of the only begotten Son of God."*</u>

We would do well to warn people of the *wrath of God* abiding on them (John 3:36). To simply tell unbelievers that "God loves them," although true, can be misleading. The unbeliever, in his darkened understanding of God, can misinterpret that concept to mean that God accepts him as he continues to live in an unrepentant state of unbelief.

Another classic religious cliché is that "God loves the sinner and hates the sin." This phrase is often wrongfully attributed to the Bible. It has some of its origin with Augustine in his *Letter 211* (A.D. 424) where he writes the phrase (which in essence means), "love for the persons and a hatred for their vices." [134] The phrase was then co-opted by the Hindu, Mohandas Gandhi who wrote in his 1929 autobiography "Hate the sin and not the sinner." [135] Universalists[136] love this phrase, because they think no matter how evil a person continues to live, he will end up in heaven…because God loves him so much. They want to believe that God's view of the nonbelievers is one of simply ignoring their wicked and sinful conduct. It is true that **"God is love"** **1 John 4:8**, but it is not true that the unbeliever walks in God's forgiveness and has escaped the wrath of the judgment to come. The truth is that God does not separate the unsaved sinner from his sin…they are one and the same (Revelation 20:12-13).

Psalm 5:5–6: *"The boastful shall not stand before Your eyes;* <u>*You hate all who do iniquity.*</u> *You destroy those who speak falsehood;* <u>*The Lord abhors the man of bloodshed and deceit."*</u>

Psalm 11:5: *"The LORD tests the righteous and the wicked, And* <u>*the one who loves violence His soul hates."*</u>

---

[134] Before you are convinced that Augustine did not have a judgmental bone in his body, one should look into the context of the statement. He was writing to rebuke the nuns in the monastery at Hippo where his sister had been the head nun (prioress). It seems that there was dissatisfaction among the nuns regarding his sister's successor. In the letter that contains the famous statement, Augustine writes:

"11. …what I have said about making eyes at someone should also be observed with <u>love for the persons and a hatred for their vices</u> in discovering, prohibiting, reporting, proving, and punishing others sins. But if any sister who has gone so far in wrongdoing that she secretly receives a letter or any little gifts from a man should be forgiven if she confesses this on her own, and you should pray for her. But if she is caught and proven guilty, <u>she should be more severely corrected according to the judgment of the superior or of the priest or even of the bishop."</u> (emphasis added). Augustine, Saint, Bishop of Hippo. *Letters, The works of Saint Augustine,* Letter 211 p.25, Augustinian Heritage Institute, New City Press, Hyde Park, New York 2005.

[135] Gandhi's autobiography (1929), *Part IV, Chapter 9, A Tussle with Power.*

[136] Universalism teaches "universal reconciliation" which means that all are reconciled to God and no one goes to everlasting damnation.

Revelation 21:8: *"But for the cowardly and unbelieving and abominable and murderers and immoral persons and sorcerers and idolaters and all liars, their part will be in the lake that burns with fire and brimstone, which is the second death."*

What the unbeliever does not realize is that the Christian does not look down his pointy nose at how disgusting the sinner is. The true Christian realizes that prior to being forgiven by Christ, his sinful life was just as repugnant in the eyes of God. The Christian has found forgiveness and freedom from the bonds of sin and wants to share that *good news* (i.e. Gospel) with others. Look again at 1 Corinthians 6:9-11. It lists off a group of corrupt sins that the unrighteous practice. The judgment is also set out in verse 9, *"...that the unrighteous shall not inherit the kingdom of God."* Now notice the last sentence: *"<u>And such were some of you</u>; but you were washed, but you were sanctified, but you were justified in the name of the Lord Jesus Christ, and in the Spirit of our God."* <u>1 Corinthians 6:11</u>. Praise God for His forgiveness in Christ. Have you called upon Christ for that forgiveness? Do you care about others enough to tell them the truth about the judgment to come, even if they accuse you of being intolerant?

MATTHEW 7:7-29
(ASSURANCE OF ANSWERED PRAYER; THE NARROW WAY; FALSE PROPHETS; INSPECTING FRUIT; BUILDING ON A SOLID FOUNDATION)

"Ask, and it shall be given to you; seek, and you shall find; knock, and it shall be opened to you. [8] For everyone who asks receives, and he who seeks finds, and to him who knocks it shall be opened. [9] Or what man is there among you, when his son shall ask him for a loaf, will give him a stone? [10] Or if he shall ask for a fish, he will not give him a snake, will he? [11] If you then, being evil, know how to give good gifts to your children, how much more shall your Father who is in heaven give what is good to those who ask Him! [12] Therefore, however you want people to treat you, so treat them, for this is the Law and the Prophets.

[13] Enter by the narrow gate; for the gate is wide, and the way is broad that leads to destruction, and many are those who enter by it. [14] For the gate is small, and the way is narrow that leads to life, and few are those who find it.

[15] Beware of the false prophets, who come to you in sheep's clothing, but inwardly are ravenous wolves. [16] You will know them by their fruits. Grapes are not gathered from thorn bushes, nor figs from thistles, are they? [17] Even so, every good tree bears good fruit; but the bad tree bears bad fruit. [18] A good tree cannot produce bad fruit, nor can a bad tree produce good fruit. [19] Every tree that does not bear good fruit is cut down and thrown into the fire. [20] So then, you will know them by their fruits. [21] Not everyone who says to Me, 'Lord, Lord,' will enter the kingdom of heaven; but he who does the will of My Father who is in heaven. [22] Many will say to Me on that day, 'Lord, Lord, did we not prophesy in Your name, and in Your name cast out demons, and in Your name perform many miracles?' [23] And then I will declare to them, 'I never knew you; DEPART FROM ME, YOU WHO PRACTICE LAWLESSNESS.'

[24] Therefore everyone who hears these words of Mine, and acts upon them, may be compared to a wise man, who built his house upon the rock. [25] And the rain descended, and the floods came, and the winds blew, and burst against that house; and yet it did not fall, for it had been founded upon the rock. [26] And everyone who hears these words of Mine, and does not act upon them, will be like a foolish man, who built his house upon the sand. [27] And the rain descended, and the floods came, and the winds blew, and burst against that house; and it fell, and great was its fall.

[28] The result was that when Jesus had finished these words, the multitudes were amazed at His teaching; [29] for He was teaching them as one having authority, and not as their scribes."

Introduction

We are told to persevere in prayer. We are instructed that the way of the Lord is *narrow* by the world's standards. We are warned that the church will contain false prophets. The Lord concludes by assuring us that those who build their lives on the solid rock of His Word will not be deceived or moved. I am brought back to J.C. Ryle's summarization of how these concepts are manifest in the true believer:

> "The person who hears Christian teaching and practices it is like 'a wise man who built his house on the rock'…. He does not content himself with listening to exhortations to repent, believe in Christ and live a holy life. He actually repents; he actually believes. He actually ceases to do evil, learns to do good, abhors what is sinful, and clings to that which is good. He is a doer as well as a hearer."[137]

---

[137] Ryle, J.C., *Matthew (Expository Thoughts on the Gospels)* (Crossways Classic Commentaries: v.1) p.54.

VERSES 7-12: *"Ask, and it shall be given to you; seek, and you shall find; knock, and it shall be opened to you. ⁸ For everyone who asks receives, and he who seeks finds, and to him who knocks it shall be opened. ⁹ Or what man is there among you, when his son shall ask him for a loaf, will give him a stone? ¹⁰ Or if he shall ask for a fish, he will not give him a snake, will he? ¹¹ If you then, being evil, know how to give good gifts to your children, how much more shall your Father who is in heaven give what is good to those who ask Him! ¹² Therefore, however you want people to treat you, so treat them, for this is the Law and the Prophets."*

In a previous section (Matthew 6:9-13) Jesus was teaching us how to pray. In these verses (Matthew 7:7-12) He affirms our need to seek God in prayer. Jesus assures us that our prayers are heard and will be answered. *God always answers our prayers!* Sometimes the answer is yes, other times it is no, and even other times the answer is…wait. It is also important to consider what we are seeking and asking for. Just eight verses earlier in Matthew 6:33 Jesus says, *"…But seek first His kingdom and His righteousness; and all these things shall be added to you."* In 1 John 5:14-15, it speaks of us asking for things according to God's will:

> *"And this is the confidence which we have before Him, that, <u>if we ask anything according to His will, He hears us.</u> ¹⁵ And if we know that He hears us in whatever we ask, we know that we have the requests which we have asked from Him."*

Note in Matthew 7:9-11, Jesus points out that even evil men (all men are evil due to the fallen, evil nature of man) give good gifts to their children. He then makes clear that the believer's Father in heaven is abundantly more giving than our earthly fathers and will give us the good we ask. Often that "good" can include not getting things that we think are good for us, but are not. Only a father who is wishing death for his son would give him a new Ferrari the day the kid gets his driver's license. Why? Because most kids would go out to see if that Ferrari can really go 170 mph, when the kid's driving skills can barely get him around a residential neighborhood without an accident. In **James 4:3** it says: *"You ask and do not receive, because you ask with wrong motives, so that you may spend it on your pleasures."*

We all need the wisdom of God and should actively seek it. It says in **James 1:5-8**:

> *"But if any of you lacks wisdom, let him ask of God, who gives to all men generously and without reproach, and it will be given to him. ⁶ But let him ask in faith without any doubting, for the one who doubts is like the surf of the sea driven and tossed by the wind. ⁷ For let not that man expect that he will receive anything from the Lord, ⁸ being a double-minded man, unstable in all his ways."*

<u>Section Application</u>

What is the status of your prayer life? Do you ask God for things with the attitude that He is a celestial bellhop whose main objective is to make you happy? Does prayer time mean that you get out your list of what you want to happen or what you want to get that day? Understand that God's work is not to make you happy, but rather to make you holy:

> **1 Peter 1:14-16:** *"As obedient children, do not be conformed to the former lusts which were yours in your ignorance, ¹⁵ but like the Holy One who called you, be holy*

yourselves also in all your behavior; [16] *because it is written, 'You shall be holy, for I am holy.'"*

Do not misunderstand me. We are to take to God even the smallest problems and issues in our lives. When we spend time in communion with God through prayer, He conforms us to the image of His son (c.f. Romans 8:29) and thus changes our desires. When that occurs, our daily prayers change from being completely self-centered to seeking the will of God and being a servant in His kingdom. Sure, we need to bring to Him our requests about our daily needs, but that is not where it ends. We also start praying for missionaries, those who do not know the Lord, and even our enemies who persecute us. Another manifestation of a healthy prayer life is joy. The prayerful believer who is spending time with God is constantly thankful to God. The peace of the believer is not built on whether he is happy, but on the joy of knowing who God is and understanding the Lord's perfect care for him.

VERSES 13-14: *"Enter by the narrow gate; for the gate is wide, and the way is broad that leads to destruction, and many are those who enter by it.* [14] *For the gate is small, and the way is narrow that leads to life, and few are those who find it."*

These verses make it abundantly clear that not everyone goes to heaven (see also Matthew 7:21-23). It also debunks the idea that there are many ways to God. The way of life is narrow and few travel it and it is made possible by Jesus alone. In John 14:6 Jesus said: *"I am the way, and the truth, and the life; no one comes to the Father, but through Me."*

One reason why the narrow way is unattractive to the average person is because he prefers a self-absorbed lifestyle. The wide road says, "Come this way to get the materialism, power and the praise of people that you want." The narrow road represents servanthood, submission to God, and promised persecution for one's faith, and possibly death. Clearly, this road is not attractive, yet by the power of God the believer continues to travel on it. At the end of the narrow road is eternal life and endless joy. For those who laughed down the wide road, it is a life of extreme regret, deception and pain, ending in eternal death and judgment.

Section Application

Which road will you travel, the narrow way of life or the wide road to death?

> **Jeremiah 21:8:** *"You shall also say to this people, 'Thus says the LORD, Behold, I set before you the way of life and the way of death.'"*

Finding the road of life is done by putting your faith in the sacrificial work of Christ on the cross as the full payment for your sins. If you want to know more about how to find the narrow road, review the section of this commentary on Matthew 5:17-20.

VERSES 15-20: *"Beware of the false prophets, who come to you in sheep's clothing, but inwardly are ravenous wolves.* [16] *You will know them by their fruits. Grapes are not gathered from thorn bushes, nor figs from thistles, are they?* [17] *Even so, every good tree bears good fruit; but the bad tree bears bad fruit.* [18] *A good tree cannot produce bad fruit, nor can a bad tree produce good fruit.* [19] *Every tree that does not bear good fruit is cut down and thrown into the fire.* [20] *So then, you will know them by their fruits."*

We are warned to watch out for false prophets since they can look like *good Christians* (i.e. they *"come to you in sheep's clothing"*). In reality they are the devil's children:

> **2 Corinthians 11:13-15:** *"For such men are false apostles, deceitful workers, disguising themselves as apostles of Christ.* ¹⁴ *And <u>no wonder, for even Satan disguises himself as an angel of light.</u>* ¹⁵ <u>*Therefore it is not surprising if his servants also disguise themselves as servants of righteousness;*</u> *whose end shall be according to their deeds."*

So how can you tell the difference? Give it time, because just like the wheat and tares, as they mature it will quickly become apparent: **Matthew 13:26:** *"But when the wheat sprang up and bore grain, then the tares became evident also."* Jesus says this about false prophets in **Matthew 7:20:** *"You will know them by their fruits ...."* When you plant an apple tree sapling, you would not expect it to immediately produce apples; it takes time to see the fruit. Likewise, you would not expect the apple tree sapling to grow up simply to produce thorns and weeds. The thorns and weeds would both kill the tree and take life from all that is growing around it. That is what the false prophet does.

The false prophet or false brother is identified in Scripture:

> **1 John 3:10:** *"By this the children of God and the children of the devil are obvious: <u>anyone who does not practice righteousness is not of God, nor the one who does not love his brother."</u>*

> **1 John 5:2-3:** *"By this we know that we love the children of God, when we love God and observe His commandments.* ³ *For this is the love of God, that we keep His commandments; and His commandments are not burdensome."*

It is an often mistaken notion that doing miracles proves that one is a true man of God. These last two verses in 1 John demonstrate otherwise. One should not be taken in by false prophets who claim to do, or actually can do, miracles. The point of their miracles is the deception of others.

> **Matthew 24:24:** *"For false Christs and false prophets will arise and will <u>show great signs and wonders,</u> so as to mislead, if possible, even the elect."*

By knowing God's Word you will be equipped to discern false prophets. For example, if they teach that you need faith in Jesus but to really be saved you must also do certain religious rites and rituals or sacrifices, you will know that they are false teachers and are accursed.

> **Galatians 1:8-9:** *"But even though we, or an angel from heaven, should preach to you a gospel contrary to that which we have preached to you, let him be accursed.* ⁹ *As we have said before, so I say again now, if any man is preaching to you a gospel contrary to that which you received, let him be accursed."*

False teachers often have a message that appeals to the masses:

> **2 Timothy 4:3:** *"...but wanting to have their ears tickled, they will accumulate for themselves teachers in accordance to their own desires;..."*

The false teacher will talk about the mistakes and the faults we all have, but not the complete blackness of man's heart or the complete damnation awaiting us, but for the cross of Christ. He will include some Scripture, talk the "Christian talk" and even espouse certain doctrines, but he does not live what he says. He will be a person of greed (hungry for money, power, sex etc.):

> **2 Peter 2:1-3:** *"But false prophets also arose among the people, just as there will also be false teachers among you, who will secretly introduce destructive heresies, even denying the Master who bought them, bringing swift destruction upon themselves.* ² *And many <u>will follow their sensuality,</u> and because of them the way of the truth will be maligned;*

3 and in their greed they will exploit you with false words; their judgment from long ago is not idle, and their destruction is not asleep."

If there is a false prophet in your church, you should not be discouraged when division occurs over him. Remember popularity is not the determination of truth, God's Word is. As was shown above, the false prophet's message is often very popular. When you confront the false teaching of a false prophet, people will rebuke you for being divisive. They will make calls for unity (at all costs). False prophets have done that for thousands of years. Division should occur.

1 Corinthians 11:19: *"For there must also be factions among you, in order that those who are approved may have become evident among you."*

It is a noble and Biblical calling to expose false prophets and evil living.[138] John Calvin (1509-1564) said it well by pointing out that:

"Even a dog barks when his master is attacked. I would be a coward if
 I saw that God's truth is attacked and yet would remain silent. "

Paul references the false when he instructs us in **Ephesians 5:11:** *"And do not participate in the unfruitful deeds of darkness, but instead even expose them;."* Jesus commended the Ephesians church for this in **Revelation 2:2:**

"I know your deeds and your toil and perseverance, and that you cannot endure evil men, and you put to the test those who call themselves apostles, and they are not, and you found them to be false;"

Scripture teaches that we are not to even greet false prophets when they come to bring their teaching into our churches or homes:

2 John 1:10-11: *"If anyone comes to you and does not bring this teaching, do not receive him into your house, and do not give him a greeting; 11 for the one who gives him a greeting participates in his evil deeds."*

We are warned that false prophets are spiritually blind, fleshly, greedy for riches, deceivers, selfish, and desiring power over others. We are also told about their judgment.

Jude v.10–16: *But these men revile the things which they do not understand; and the things which they know by instinct, like unreasoning animals, by these things they are destroyed. 11 Woe to them! For they have gone the way of Cain, and for pay they have rushed headlong into the error of Balaam, and perished in the rebellion of Korah. 12 These are the men who are hidden reefs in your love feasts when they feast with you without fear, caring for themselves; clouds without water, carried along by winds; autumn trees without fruit, doubly dead, uprooted; 13 wild waves of the sea, casting up their own shame like foam; wandering stars, for whom the black darkness has been reserved forever. 14 It was also about these men that Enoch, in the seventh generation from Adam,*

---

[138] Ryle states that any claimed leader is to be evaluated by his doctrine and life (practice of that doctrine): "These things are written to show Christians that they must beware of depending too much on ordained ministers. They must not look up to ministers as Popes, or regard them as infallible. The orders of no church confer infallibility, whether they be episcopal, presbyterian or independent. Bishops, priests and deacons at their best are only flesh and blood, and may err both in doctrine and practice, as well as the chief priests and elders of the Jews. Their acts and teaching must always be tested by the Word of God. *They must be followed so far as they follow Scripture, and no further."* Ryle, J. C. (1993). *Mark.* Crossway Classic Commentaries (p. 177). Wheaton, IL: Crossway Books.

prophesied, saying, "Behold, the Lord came with many thousands of His holy ones, [15] to execute judgment upon all, and to convict all the ungodly of all their ungodly deeds which they have done in an ungodly way, and of all the harsh things which ungodly sinners have spoken against Him." [16] These are grumblers, finding fault, following after their own lusts; they speak arrogantly, flattering people for the sake of gaining an advantage.

Ryle points out the importance of every believer to be studying the Word of God himself: "What is the best safeguard against false teaching? Beyond all doubt the regular study of the Word of God, with prayer for the teaching of the Holy Spirit…the man who reads it aright will never be allowed greatly to err [i.e. error]. It is neglect of the Bible which makes so many a prey to the first false teacher whom they hear."[139]

VERSES 21-23: *"Not everyone who says to Me, 'Lord, Lord,' will enter the kingdom of heaven; but he who does the will of My Father who is in heaven. [22] Many will say to Me on that day, 'Lord, Lord, did we not prophesy in Your name, and in Your name cast out demons, and in Your name perform many miracles?' [23] And then I will declare to them, 'I never knew you; DEPART FROM ME, YOU WHO PRACTICE LAWLESSNESS.'"*

Many like to believe in *universalism*.[140] Universalism teaches that ultimately everyone ends up in heaven. Jesus clearly states in verses 21-23 above that everyone does not go to heaven. What is more difficult to understand is how some who call Him **Lord** will not enter into the kingdom (v.22 *"Many will say to Me on that day, 'Lord, Lord, did we not prophesy in Your name,…"*). Note that just a mere seven verses before, Jesus warned His followers in **Matthew 7:15**: *"Beware of the false prophets, who come to you in sheep's clothing, but inwardly are ravenous wolves."* Those who called Jesus *Lord* in verse 22 made great claims of being prophets but the reality is that they were false prophets. Verses 17 and 20 state that *"but the bad tree bears bad fruit… [20] So then, you will know them by their fruits."* They appear sincere in their claim of being prophets but Jesus says to them, *'I never knew you; DEPART FROM ME, YOU WHO PRACTICE LAWLESSNESS.'* This is not difficult to understand since the false prophet has deceived himself in addition to deceiving others. **2 Timothy 3:13**: *"But evil men and impostors will proceed from bad to worse, deceiving and being deceived."*

False believers and false prophets will also look to their own good works as the basis for earning salvation. We see these false prophets also made boasts of their own merit by pointing to their miracles they supposedly did, v.22. We discussed above that false miracles have been done by false prophets, but we also see in Acts nonbelievers performed a miracle in the *"name of Jesus who Paul preaches."* **Acts 19:13-16**. They also paid the price for it. Despite all their claims, Jesus said they were those *"WHO PRACTICE LAWLESSNESS."*

Those who say *"Lord, Lord"* are those who profess a relationship with God, but they really do not have one. One is not saved simply because he respectfully calls Him, *"Lord."* Jesus said in **John 13:13**: *"You call Me Teacher and Lord; and you are right, for so I am."* Those who are saved are those who

---

[139] Ryle, J.C., *Matthew / (Expository Thoughts on the Gospels)* (Crossways Classic Commentaries: v.1) p.52.

[140] _Universalism:_ is "a theological doctrine that all human beings will eventually be saved the principles and practices of a liberal Christian denomination founded in the 18th century orig. to uphold belief in universal salvation and now united with Unitarianism." *Merriam-Webster's Collegiate Dictionary,*

do the will of God. Jesus said in **Matthew 7:21:** *"Not everyone who says to Me, 'Lord, Lord,' will enter the kingdom of heaven; but he who does the will of My Father who is in heaven."*

Many think they are saved because they have a cold, intellectual belief in Jesus combined with a weekly religious ritual. But their lives have never been changed by Christ. They have never hated their sin or repented of it and are likewise misled. In **Matthew 4:17** it is written, *"From that time Jesus began to preach and say, 'Repent, for the kingdom of heaven is at hand.'"* Those who hold to religious ritual are like those, *"holding to a form of godliness, although they have denied its power; avoid such men as these."* **2 Timothy 3:5**. The godly man bears fruit. A supposed professing "Christian" who never reflects the Lord's righteousness is not of God. This type of profession of faith is what James speaks of as "faith without works" (i.e. dead faith); (James 2:17-20). A true Christian does not do good works to get saved; but as a result of salvation, good works (i.e. fruit) will be produced. This principle is set out in **Ephesians 2:8-10:**
> *"For by grace you have been saved through faith; and that not of yourselves, it is the gift of God;* [9] *not as a result of works, that no one should boast.* [10] *For we are His workmanship, created in Christ Jesus for good works, which God prepared beforehand, that we should walk in them."*

As Matthew Henry said,
> "At God's bar, a profession of religion will not bear out any man in the practice and indulgence of sin; therefore let everyone that names the name of Christ, depart from all iniquity."[141]

Many like using the name *Jesus* and then come up with their own theology and religion. They will say things like, "Well, my Jesus would not send anyone to hell." I am sure their "Jesus" would not. The problem is that their "Jesus" is a figment of their imagination. They have created a Jesus in their own image and thus violated the Second Commandment.[142] Their "Jesus" is not the Jesus who died on the cross to pay for the sins of those who would truly believe in Him for salvation. Paul warned the believers in Corinth of those who preach their own version of Jesus:
> **2 Corinthians 11:3-4:**   *"But I am afraid, lest as the serpent deceived Eve by his craftiness, your minds should be led astray from the simplicity and purity of devotion to Christ.* [4] *For if one comes and preaches another Jesus whom we have not preached..."*

By knowing and believing God's Word, we will not be deceived by the religious leader who has deceived himself and others. We will know the true *good shepherd.*
> **John 10:14:** *"I am the good shepherd; and I know My own, and My own know Me,"*

VERSES 24-27:   *"Therefore everyone who hears these words of Mine, and acts upon them, may be compared to a wise man, who built his house upon the rock.* [25] *And the rain descended, and the floods came, and the winds blew, and burst against that house; and yet it did not fall, for it had been founded upon the rock.* [26] *And everyone who hears these words of Mine, and does not act upon them, will be like a foolish man, who built his house upon the sand.* [27] *And the rain descended, and the floods came, and the winds blew, and burst against that house; and it fell, and great was its fall."*

---

[141] Henry, M. (1994). *Matthew Henry's Commentary on the Whole Bible: Complete and Unabridged in One Volume* (Matthew 7:21–29). Peabody: Hendrickson.

[142] Ray Comfort – Living Waters Ministries. See Comfort's video or audio "Hell's Best Kept Secret."

Here we have two people with a lot of similarities, but their end result is completely different. One house ends up with life and stability, whereas the other house results in complete destruction. The final result for each person depended on what he did with God's Word. Look at the similarities:

1. Both builders hear the words of the Lord.
2. Both build houses.
3. Both houses are near each other in proximity as shown in that the storm equally affects each home, i.e. *"the rain descended, and the floods came, and the winds blew, and burst against that house"* **v.25 and v.27**).

Both homes looked good on the outside, but what was unseen made all the difference. The one builder hears the, *"words of Mine, and acts upon them."* We read that he was *wise* and built his home on the solid rock (i.e. the words of Jesus); (see also Matthew 16:15-18). When the storm winds and floods came, the house (i.e. this man's life) was unmoved. The second builder represents the false professing "Christian" who will say, *"Lord, Lord"* but not obey the Lord's word. Jesus said that this builder *"hears these words of Mine, and does not act upon them,...."* Jesus said that this builder is *foolish.* When the storm winds and floods came, the house (i.e. this man's life) *"fell, and great was its fall."*

VERSES 28-29: *"The result was that when Jesus had finished these words, the multitudes were amazed at His teaching;* [29] *for He was teaching them as one having authority, and not as their scribes."*

We see that many were amazed by the teaching. We do not know how many repented and obeyed Him. It was Jesus Himself who pointed out to the crowd, *"Therefore everyone who hears these words of Mine, and acts upon them, may be compared to a wise man, who built his house upon the rock."* **Matthew 7:24**.

Jesus' teaching was clearly different than what they had heard from their religious leaders. He did not cite other writers or rabbis. Jesus did not speak in harsh tones about rules and regulations and self-righteousness. He spoke only the Word of God. The difference in authority was obvious to the people. Jesus was the Living Word of God.

> **John 1:14:** *"And the Word became flesh, and dwelt among us, and we beheld His glory, glory as of the only begotten from the Father, full of grace and truth."*

Summary and Application:

Are you in God's Word on a daily basis? False prophets are all over. By knowing God's Word you will be able to spot them. Think of the false religions that tell their followers to kill their enemies. Jesus makes it clear what God wants you to do to your enemies in **Luke 6:27-28:** *"But I say to you who hear, love your enemies, do good to those who hate you,* [28] *bless those who curse you, pray for those who mistreat you."* Can you detect the false prophets when they speak? Listen for them to explain how to be saved by engaging in a religious ritual or doing certain good works to earn heaven. Maybe the false religious leaders will assure you that all religious roads are good and all people will end up in heaven. We are not to be deceived but instead we are to listen and obey God's word. Those who listen and do not obey will call Jesus *'Lord Lord'* but they want to follow a Jesus they created. **James 1:22** says, *"But prove yourselves doers of the word, and not merely hearers who delude themselves."*

Have you built your life on the solid rock of Jesus Christ? If you have, even when the storms come, your life will, *"not fall, for it had been founded upon the rock."* As Job said:

> *"And as for me, I know that my Redeemer lives,*
> *And at the last He will take His stand on the earth."* __Job 19:25.__

MATTHEW 8:1-17
(THE HEALING MINISTRY OF CHRIST)

"AND when He had come down from the mountain, great multitudes followed Him. ² And behold, a leper came to Him, and bowed down to Him, saying, 'Lord, if You are willing, You can make me clean.' ³ And He stretched out His hand and touched him, saying, 'I am willing; be cleansed.' And immediately his leprosy was cleansed. ⁴ And Jesus *said to him, 'See that you tell no one; but go, show yourself to the priest, and present the offering that Moses commanded, for a testimony to them.'

⁵ And when He had entered Capernaum, a centurion came to Him, entreating Him, ⁶ and saying, 'Lord, my servant is lying paralyzed at home, suffering great pain.' ⁷ And He *said to him, 'I will come and heal him.' ⁸ But the centurion answered and said, 'Lord, I am not worthy for You to come under my roof, but just say the word, and my servant will be healed. ⁹ For I, too, am a man under authority, with soldiers under me; and I say to this one, 'Go!' and he goes, and to another, 'Come!' and he comes, and to my slave, 'Do this!' and he does it.' ¹⁰ Now when Jesus heard this, He marveled, and said to those who were following, 'Truly I say to you, I have not found such great faith with anyone in Israel. ¹¹ And I say to you, that many shall come from east and west, and recline at the table with Abraham, and Isaac, and Jacob, in the kingdom of heaven; ¹² but the sons of the kingdom shall be cast out into the outer darkness; in that place there shall be weeping and gnashing of teeth.' ¹³ And Jesus said to the centurion, 'Go your way; let it be done to you as you have believed.' And the servant was healed that very hour.

¹⁴ And when Jesus had come to Peter's home, He saw his mother-in-law lying sick in bed with a fever. ¹⁵ And He touched her hand, and the fever left her; and she arose, and waited on Him. ¹⁶ And when evening had come, they brought to Him many who were demon-possessed; and He cast out the spirits with a word, and healed all who were ill ¹⁷ in order that what was spoken through Isaiah the prophet might be fulfilled, saying, 'HE HIMSELF TOOK OUR INFIRMITIES, AND CARRIED AWAY OUR DISEASES.'"

Introduction

At chapter 8 we pick back up where we left off at chapter 4. The Sermon on the Mount was in-between Matthew chapter 4 and Matthew chapter 8. **Matthew 4:23-25** states:

> *"And Jesus was going about in all Galilee, <u>teaching in their synagogues, and proclaiming the gospel of the kingdom, and healing every kind of disease and every kind of sickness among the people.</u> ²⁴ And the news about Him went out into all Syria; and they brought to Him all who were ill, taken with various diseases and pains, demoniacs, epileptics, paralytics; and He healed them. ²⁵ <u>And great multitudes followed Him</u> from Galilee and Decapolis and Jerusalem and Judea and from beyond the Jordan."*

Note that a great multitude followed Him up the mountain (Matthew 5:1), and likewise a great multitude followed Him down after the Sermon on the Mount (Matthew 8:1). Early in Matthew chapter 8, we see Jesus engaging in His miraculous ministry of healing. It should not be thought that the miracles we read about in the Gospels are the sum total of all the miracles that Jesus did. **John 20:30** states, *"Many other signs therefore Jesus also performed in the presence of the disciples, which are not written in this book....;"* and **John 21:25** tells us that *"...there are also many other things which Jesus did, which if they *were written in detail, I suppose that even the world itself *would not contain the books which *were written."*

VERSES 1-4: *"AND when He had come down from the mountain, great multitudes followed Him. ² And behold, a leper came to Him, and bowed down to Him, saying, 'Lord, if You are willing, You can make me clean.' ³ And He stretched out His hand and touched him, saying, 'I am willing; be cleansed.' And immediately his leprosy was cleansed. ⁴ And Jesus *said to him, 'See that you tell no one; but go, show yourself to the priest, and present the offering that Moses commanded, for a testimony to them.'"*

Here we have a leper who was healed by Christ. A leper was about the lowest outcast of society and literally had to live "outside the camp," (Numbers 5:1-5). If a leper saw someone coming near him, he was required to yell out, "unclean, unclean!" so that people would be warned and not go near him. <u>Leviticus 13:45-46</u> states the following:

> *"As for the leper who has the infection, his clothes shall be torn, and the hair of his head shall be uncovered, and he shall cover his mustache and cry, 'Unclean! Unclean!' ⁴⁶ He shall remain unclean all the days during which he has the infection; he is unclean. He shall live alone; his dwelling shall be outside the camp."*

Leprosy was a life of isolation. They were not to dwell near healthy people, let alone be touched by them ever again. From our main text, we need to recognize the faith of this leper who dared to go through the crowd to get to Jesus. He bows and acknowledges Him as Lord and asks if Jesus would be <u>*willing*</u> to make him clean. The compassionate and loving Jesus could have spoken the Word to the leper to be healed, but He did not. Jesus did the unthinkable to any Jew who encountered a leper, <u>*"He stretched out His hand and touched him,*</u> *saying, 'I am willing; be cleansed.'"* I am sure the religious leaders were appalled when Jesus actually touched the man, since whoever touched a leper became unclean (Leviticus 5:3). Notice that the leper was healed *"immediately."* Jesus then instructed the man to go to the priests to be examined as the law required in Leviticus 14. He further said that it would be *"a testimony to them."* What a testimony it would be since there is "no record of any Israelite being healed from leprosy other than Miriam (Num. 12:10-15)."[143] Unfortunately, the leper did not obey Jesus. We read in **Mark 1:45** that,

> *"...he went out and began to proclaim it freely and to spread the news about, to such an extent that Jesus could no longer publicly enter a city, but stayed out in unpopulated areas; and they were coming to Him from everywhere."*

The Lord is compassionate, loving and all-powerful. We must learn to not just *bow* down when we need something from God, but also to *obey* His Word when all is well.

VERSES 5-13: *"And when He had entered Capernaum, a centurion came to Him, entreating Him, ⁶ and saying, 'Lord, my servant is lying paralyzed at home, suffering great pain.' ⁷ And He *said to him, 'I will come and heal him.' ⁸ But the centurion answered and said, 'Lord, I am not worthy for You to come under my roof, but just say the word, and my servant will be healed. ⁹ For I, too, am a man under authority, with soldiers under me; and I say to this one, 'Go!' and he goes, and to another, 'Come!' and he comes, and to my slave, 'Do this!' and he does it.' ¹⁰ Now when Jesus heard this, He marveled, and said to those who were following, 'Truly I say to you, I have not found such great faith with anyone in Israel. ¹¹ And I say to you, that many shall come from east and west, and recline at the table with Abraham, and Isaac, and Jacob, in the kingdom of heaven; ¹² but the sons of the kingdom shall be cast out into the outer darkness;*

---

[143] Walvoord, John F., and Zuck, Roy B., *The Bible Knowledge Commentary*, (Wheaton, Illinois: Scripture Press Publications, Inc.) 1983, 1985. [Note that Naaman was healed of leprosy by God through Elisha (2 Kings 5:8–14) but Naaman was not an Israelite. He was a captain of the army of the king of Aram.]

in that place there shall be weeping and gnashing of teeth.' [13] And Jesus said to the centurion, 'Go your way; let it be done to you as you have believed.' And the servant was healed that very hour."

Here we see a Roman soldier who is seeking Jesus to heal his servant boy. The Roman centurion, along with the Roman occupation of Israel, was a reminder to the Jews that they were a conquered people. Normally, this centurion would be hated by the Jewish people, but he was not. What do we know about this military man? We learn a little more detail about him in Luke's account. Luke tells us that he saw his unworthiness before God and sent the religious leaders to Jesus to see if Jesus would come and heal the servant boy. It is a common expression to say one "speaks" when he has someone else speak for him (i.e. an envoy). An example would be the spokesman for the President. The spokesman is to speak what the President wants said regarding a matter and not what the spokesman's personal opinion is.

> **Luke 7:2-5:** *"And a certain centurion's slave, who was highly regarded by him, was sick and about to die. And when he heard about Jesus, he sent some Jewish elders asking Him to come and save the life of his slave. [4] And when they had come to Jesus, they earnestly entreated Him, saying, 'He is worthy for You to grant this to him; [5] for he loves our nation, and it was he who built us our synagogue.'"*

We see further the centurion's reverence for the Lord in that when he hears that Jesus is coming to him, he then sends some friends to speak on his behalf again:

> **Luke 7:6-8:** *"Now Jesus started on His way with them; and when He was already not far from the house, the centurion sent friends, saying to Him, 'Lord, do not trouble Yourself further, for I am not worthy for You to come under my roof; [7] for this reason I did not even consider myself worthy to come to You, but just say the word, and my servant will be healed. [8] For I, too, am a man under authority, with soldiers under me; and I say to this one, 'Go!' and he goes; and to another, 'Come!' and he comes; and to my slave, 'Do this!' and he does it.'"*

Jesus responded by being marveled by the great faith of this man. Faith involves *understanding who God really is.* Jesus told the centurion that his servant would be healed just as the centurion believed: *"...let it be done to you as you have believed." And the servant was healed that very hour."* **Matthew 8:13**.

Jesus went on to rebuke Israel for its rejecting Him as Messiah, and confirms that there will be believing Gentiles who enter the Kingdom of God while those of Israel who reject Him will be sent to eternal judgment. Jesus said in **Matthew 8:11-12**:

> *"And I say to you, that many shall come from east and west, and recline at the table with Abraham, and Isaac, and Jacob, in the kingdom of heaven; [12] but the sons of the kingdom shall be cast out into the outer darkness; in that place there shall be weeping and gnashing of teeth."*

This statement had to be shocking to a lot of the Jews listening to Jesus. Many of the house of Israel at that time thought they were saved simply because they were Jews and not Gentiles (Matthew 3:8-9; John 8:39-44). Jesus points out that Gentile believers will be at the table with Abraham. This is not new; God told Abraham that back in Genesis. The covenant is set out in **Genesis 12:1-3**:

> *"Now the Lord said to Abram, 'Go forth from your country, and from your relatives And from your father's house, to the land which I will show you; and I will make you a great nation, And I will bless you, And make your name great; and so you shall be a blessing; and I will bless those who bless you, and the one who curses you I will curse. and in you all the families of the earth will be blessed.' "*

Until one is born again, he is not a direct heir of the covenant and promises that God made to Abraham.

> **Galatians 3:26-29:** *"For you are all sons of God through faith in Christ Jesus. ²⁷ For all of you who were baptized into Christ have clothed yourselves with Christ. ²⁸ There is neither Jew nor Greek, there is neither slave nor free man, there is neither male nor female; for you are all one in Christ Jesus. ²⁹ And if you belong to Christ, then you are Abraham's offspring, heirs according to promise."*

Are you walking in true faith in Christ? The centurion's actions were a manifestation of his faith. One person has defined true faith as:

1. A firm conviction, producing a full acknowledgment of God's revelation or truth....
2. A personal surrender to Him, [and]
3. Conduct inspired by such surrender, [that is Holy Spirit empowered conduct and fruit] ....[144]

As you can see, *saving faith* is much more than just having an opinion about Jesus. It is much more than simply acknowledging that He is the Son of God since Scripture tells us that even the demons do that: *"You believe that God is one. You do well; the demons also believe, and shudder,"* **James 2:19**. Jesus preached that people are to, *"repent and believe in the gospel."* **Mark 1:15**. The one who is saved is the one who turns from his sin by the power of God and believes the Gospel. *Believing the Gospel* means to put your faith in Jesus Christ (as God who is without sin) and believe in His sacrificial death on the cross for the sole and complete payment of your sins, and that He rose from the dead on the third day. It has nothing to do with your righteousness. It is that straightforward. You do not need to have a religious ceremony; you do not need to do charitable or religious work. Even if you dedicated your life to religious ceremony and good works you would still be guilty of sin and worthy of hell because you have rejected Christ as the only way for you to be saved. To be saved from the judgment to come, you must simply, *"repent and believe in the gospel."* **Mark 1:15**. It is this simplicity of the Gospel that so many find repugnant. Humans like to get things done the old-fashioned way, by *working hard and earning it.* One cannot earn salvation. Jesus sets forth that the only true godly work is to put your faith in Jesus Christ as the only way to be saved:

> **John 6:28-29:** *"Therefore they said to Him, 'What shall we do, so that we may work the works of God?' ²⁹Jesus answered and said to them, 'This is the work of God, that you believe in Him whom He has sent.'"*

The problem is that man does not comprehend how completely holy God is, and how completely sinful man is. Salvation by faith is so simple that even a very young child can understand it. It is the lack of complexity and self-reliance that makes *salvation by faith* appear *foolish*. That foolish appearance is exactly the way God wants it. The Apostle Paul said:

> **1 Corinthians 1:21-24:** *"...God was well-pleased through the foolishness of the message preached to save those who believe. ²² For indeed Jews ask for signs, and Greeks search for wisdom; ²³ but we preach Christ crucified, to Jews a stumbling block, and to Gentiles foolishness, ²⁴ but to those who are the called, both Jews and Greeks, Christ the power of God and the wisdom of God."*

---

[144] Vine, W., and Bruce, F., <u>Vine's Expository Dictionary of Old and New Testament Words,</u> Old Tappan NJ: Revell, (1981; Published in electronic form by Logos Research Systems, 1996) (p. 72)

VERSES 14-17: *"And when Jesus had come to Peter's home, He saw his mother-in-law lying sick in bed with a fever. 15 And He touched her hand, and the fever left her; and she arose, and waited on Him. 16 And when evening had come, they brought to Him many who were demon-possessed; and He cast out the spirits with a word, and healed all who were ill 17 in order that what was spoken through Isaiah the prophet might be fulfilled, saying, 'HE HIMSELF TOOK OUR INFIRMITIES, AND CARRIED AWAY OUR DISEASES.'"*

Here we see Jesus healing Peter's mother-in-law. Jesus healed wherever He went. The quote in verse 17 above is from Isaiah 53:4-5. The Scripture does not tell us that Jesus healed <u>some</u> of those that were brought to Him; it says that He *"healed <u>all</u> who were ill…"* He did not just heal physical problems but the spiritually sick and the demon-possessed: *"…when evening had come, they brought to Him many who were demon-possessed; and He cast out the spirits with a word, and<u> healed all who were ill</u>.."* The Lord cares for our wellbeing, even our emotional health. Paul states in **2 Corinthians 7:6:** *"<u>But God, who comforts the depressed</u>,…."*

Summary and Application

The Bible tells us that during Jesus' ministry, He healed every kind of sickness and disease (Matthew 9:35). Scripture also tells us in **1 Peter 2:24:** *"…and He Himself bore our sins in His body on the cross, that we might die to sin and live to righteousness; for by His wounds you were healed."*

We are to pray for one another when we are sick. **James 5:13-15** says:
> *"Is anyone among you suffering? Let him pray. Is anyone cheerful? Let him sing praises. 14Is anyone among you sick? Let him call for the elders of the church, and let them pray over him, anointing him with oil in the name of the Lord; 15and the prayer offered in faith will restore the one who is sick, and the Lord will raise him up, and if he has committed sins, they will be forgiven him."*

The Apostle John prayed for the health of his Christian brothers and sisters in **3 John 1:2:**
> *"Beloved, <u>I pray</u> that in all respects you may prosper and <u>be in good health</u>, just as your soul prospers."*

Are we to understand that God never allows us to be sick? Are we to believe some *faith healer* who claims that God does not want anyone sick, and if people simply have enough faith they would never suffer sickness or disease? Both of these views are not supported by Scripture. God can allow sickness in our lives for many reasons. Some of those reasons we may not know until heaven.

In the Bible we read of believers dealing with sickness. The very godly young man Timothy had *"frequent illnesses."* **1Tim. 5:23**. In 2 Corinthians 12:7-10 we read that the Apostle Paul also struggled with a possible physical problem in that God would not remove the thorn in his flesh. Obviously there are times when God lets us go through sickness. Other examples include Paul leaving Trophimus sick in Miletus (2 Timothy 4:19) and Epaphroditus being *"sick to the point of death…"* **Philippians 2:27.** Then there is the example of Job. The Bible describes Job as *"blameless, upright, fearing God, and turning away from evil."* **Job 1:1.** Despite Job being righteous, we read in Job 2 that he suffered greatly with *"boils from the sole of his foot to the crown of his head."* **Job 2:7.**

Job suffered sickness not as a result of sin, but endured it while his faith was being proved (although his friends wrongfully claimed it was a manifestation of his hidden sin). Often people jump to the conclusion that sickness proves the person is in sin. The disciples wrongfully assumed this when they encountered a particular man who was blind from birth. Jesus corrected their mistaken view and explained that the reason the man had been blind all his life was, *"that the works of God should be made manifest in him."* **John 9:3**. That *work of God* was his being healed of blindness by Jesus.

One should not go overboard the other way and say that sickness can never be a manifestation of sin. When sin came into the world so did sickness and death (Romans 5:12, 6:10). Jesus healed a man who *"who had been ill for thirty-eight years."* **John 5:5**. And then warned him, *"Behold, you have become well; do not sin anymore, so that nothing worse happens to you."* **John 5:14**. God can use sickness to get our attention. Some Christians in Corinth were disciplined by sickness and death for profaning the Lord's Supper (1 Corinthians. 11:26-30). These Corinthians never evaluated themselves before partaking in Communion. If they had examined themselves, it would have caused them to be humbled before God and enter confession and repentance of their sins (1 Corinthians 11:27-31). If you fear that your sickness may be due to sin, confess it to God and repent of it (review the verses in James 5:13-15). Know that God forgives you. **1 John 1:9**: *"If we confess our sins, He is faithful and righteous to forgive us our sins and to cleanse us from all unrighteousness."*

If after prayer and self-examination you are not aware of unconfessed/unrepented sin in your life, you must realize that we live in a fallen world where sickness, disease and death abound. That being said, it does not mean that you do not continue to pray about healing. When I pray for healing for myself or others, I always start my prayer by saying, "Dear Lord, until I know your perfect will, I pray for complete healing for _____." In this way I am being obedient to pray for the sick in faith and recognizing that the Lord's will is what is best. Sometimes we are called to endure sickness like Job. Both Job and Paul dealt with pain. God told Paul to endure an infliction even after Paul asked three times to have the *thorn* removed from his flesh. God told him that God's grace was sufficient for him in this situation. Paul writes of this in **2 Corinthians 12:8-10**:

> *"Concerning this I entreated the Lord three times that it might depart from me. ⁹ And He has said to me, 'My grace is sufficient for you, for power is perfected in weakness.' Most gladly, therefore, I will rather boast about my weaknesses, that the power of Christ may dwell in me. ¹⁰ Therefore I am well content with weaknesses, with insults, with distresses, with persecutions, with difficulties, for Christ's sake; for when I am weak, then I am strong."*

We need to remember that in the Lord's time He will bring *complete* healing from our body of flesh/death through the resurrection!

> **Romans 7:24-25:** *"Wretched man that I am! Who will set me free from the body of this death? ²⁵Thanks be to God through Jesus Christ our Lord! …."*

In the Kingdom of God we will never be subject to sickness, disease, pain, crying or death again! The curse will be removed forever!

> **Revelation 22:2-3:** *"…in the middle of its street. And on either side of the river was the tree of life, bearing twelve kinds of fruit, yielding its fruit every month; and the leaves of the tree were for the healing of the nations. ³ And there shall no longer be any curse; and the throne of God and of the Lamb shall be in it, and His bond-servants shall serve Him;"*

> **Revelation 21:3-4:** *"And I heard a loud voice from the throne, saying, 'Behold, the tabernacle of God is among men, and He shall dwell among them, and they shall be His people, and God Himself shall be among them, ⁴and He shall wipe away every tear from their eyes; and*

there *shall no longer be any death; there shall no longer be any mourning, or crying, or pain; the first things have passed away.'"*

MATTHEW 8:18-27
(JESUS' CALL TO DISCIPLESHIP AND TESTING OF THE DISCIPLES' FAITH)

"Now when Jesus saw a crowd around Him, He gave orders to depart to the other side. [19] And a certain scribe came and said to Him, 'Teacher, I will follow You wherever You go.' [20] And Jesus *said to him, 'The foxes have holes, and the birds of the air have nests; but the Son of Man has nowhere to lay His head.' [21] And another of the disciples said to Him, 'Lord, permit me first to go and bury my father.' [22] But Jesus *said to him, 'Follow Me; and allow the dead to bury their own dead.'

[23] And when He got into the boat, His disciples followed Him. [24] And behold, there arose a great storm in the sea, so that the boat was covered with the waves; but He Himself was asleep. [25] And they came to Him, and awoke Him, saying, 'Save us, Lord; we are perishing!' [26] And He *said to them, 'Why are you timid, you men of little faith?' Then He arose, and rebuked the winds and the sea; and it became perfectly calm. [27] And the men marveled, saying, 'What kind of a man is this, that even the winds and the sea obey Him?'

Introduction

Here we will see faith exemplified. Some claim to have that faith, but when the true call of discipleship comes, they leave. Later in the lesson, we will see the faith of the disciples tested in the calming of the sea. From that test, the Lord stated that their faith was "little" in measure. Despite their small amount of faith, we do see the power of God manifested. The very God who maintains absolute control of all things obviously can control the winds and the waves!

VERSES 18-22: *"Now when Jesus saw a crowd around Him, He gave orders to depart to the other side. [19]And a certain scribe came and said to Him, 'Teacher, I will follow You wherever You go.' [20] And Jesus *said to him, 'The foxes have holes, and the birds of the air have nests; but the Son of Man has nowhere to lay His head.' [21] And another of the disciples said to Him, 'Lord, permit me first to go and bury my father.' [22] But Jesus *said to him, 'Follow Me; and allow the dead to bury their own dead.'"*

In these verses Jesus examines the *heart* of those who would claim to faithfully follow Him. We read of one who says, *"Teacher, I will follow You wherever You go."* What was this man's attitude? We don't know because Scripture does not tell us. He may have been one who was a true disciple or he could have been the one of many who believed that Jesus was on the rise to political greatness and decided to follow Him in order to get in on the power early. Jesus' response to the man made it clear that there was no *vain glory* to be obtained by following Him. More specifically, Jesus explained that if you follow Him, you will not have a place to call your bed each night. In other words, if this man thought that being the Lord's disciple would result in being part of a kingly court, Jesus' response would have sent him back home quickly.

As the story of the scribe shows, a strong profession of faith does not always mean that there is a strong commitment. It is curious that we never read anything more in Scripture about this scribe. It may be fair to speculate that the price of discipleship was too high for him. It is a false gospel which claims that there is no price to be paid as a disciple. Jesus made it clear to His disciples that there was a great cost in following Him: *"And you will be hated by all on account of My name, but it is the one who has endured to the end who will be saved."* **Matthew 10:22.**

Next we see another man who claims that he wants to follow Jesus, just as soon as he buries his father. This seems like a reasonable request until Jesus exposes the spiritual heart of the matter. Jesus tells him that the spiritually dead can bury their own, but those who are God's children must follow him. Jesus told His disciples in **John 9:4:** *"We must work the works of Him who sent Me, as long as it is day; night is coming, when no man can work."* God demands complete allegiance to Him, even over family members. Jesus explains that our complete devotion to Him will make it appear that our love for our family or friends seems like hate in comparison to our love for Him.

> **Luke 14:26-28:** *"If anyone comes to Me, and does not hate his own father and mother and wife and children and brothers and sisters, yes, and even his own life, he cannot be My disciple. 27 Whoever does not carry his own cross and come after Me cannot be My disciple. 28 For which one of you, when he wants to build a tower, does not first sit down and calculate the cost, to see if he has enough to complete it?"*

Luke gives us a little more detail of this encounter Jesus has with these would-be disciples in Luke 9:57-62. There we read of another person who spoke to Jesus about following him.

> **Luke 9:61-62:** *"And another also said, 'I will follow You, Lord; but first permit me to say good-bye to those at home.' 62But Jesus said to him, 'No one, after putting his hand to the plow and looking back, is fit for the kingdom of God.'"*

Ryle summarizes this section by stating:

> "Nothing, in fact, has done more harm to Christianity than the practice of filling the ranks of Christ's army with every volunteer who is willing to make a little profession, and to talk fluently of his 'experience.' It has been painfully forgotten that numbers alone do not make strength, and that there may be a great quantity of mere outward religion, while there is very little real grace. Let us remember this. Let us keep back nothing from young believers and inquirers after Christ: let us not enlist them on false pretenses. Let us tell them plainly that there is a crown of glory at the end, but let us tell them no less plainly that there is a daily cross on the way."[145]

VERSES 23-27: *"And when He got into the boat, His disciples followed Him. 24 And behold, there arose a great storm in the sea, so that the boat was covered with the waves; but He Himself was asleep. 25 And they came to Him, and awoke Him, saying, 'Save us, Lord; we are perishing!' 26 And He *said to them, 'Why are you timid, you men of little faith?' Then He arose, and rebuked the winds and the sea; and it became perfectly calm. 27 And the men marveled, saying, 'What kind of a man is this, that even the winds and the sea obey Him?'"*

This section shows the humanity of Jesus in that He was tired and sleeping in the boat. Then, immediately the divinity of Christ was manifested by His complete control of everything, even the forces of nature!

---

[145] Ryle, J.C., *Matthew* (Expository Thoughts on the Gospels) (Crossways Classic Commentaries: v.1) p.59.

This was a very big storm and Matthew tells us *"...that the boat was covered with the waves ...."* Mark describes the same event as *"...a fierce gale of wind, and the waves were breaking over the boat so much that the boat was already filling up."* <u>Mark 4:37.</u> Those in the boat cried out, *"Save us, Lord; we are perishing!"* They were fearful and timid because Jesus said they were *"...men of little faith?"* Matthew tells us generally that Jesus, *"rebuked the winds and the sea...",* but Mark tells us exactly what Jesus said, *"Hush, be still."* <u>Mark 4:39.</u> Storms generally subside over time with the winds and rains gradually decreasing. That was not what happened here. Upon Jesus' command, the seas, *"became perfectly calm ...."* <u>Matthew 8:26</u>.

Summary and Application

We must be people of real faith, truly trusting God regardless of the storm and gales that blow on us and threaten our very lives. These trials are also part of the disciple's life. Although it is a life of trial and sacrifice, it is a life of great joy, such as the nonbeliever can never understand. We may have storms in our lives, but our God speaks to them, *"Hush, be still."* We must remember the words of the Psalmist:

"O LORD God of hosts, who is like Thee, O mighty LORD?
Thy faithfulness also surrounds Thee.
Thou dost rule the swelling of the sea;
When its waves rise, Thou dost still them." <u>Psalm 89:8-9.</u>

Thank God for His merciful protection of you!

MATTHEW 8:28-34
(JESUS' POWER OVER SATAN AND DEMONS)

"And when He had come to the other side into the country of the Gadarenes, two men who were demon-possessed met Him as they were coming out of the tombs; they were so exceedingly violent that no one could pass by that road. ²⁹ And behold, they cried out, saying, 'What do we have to do with You, Son of God? Have You come here to torment us before the time?' ³⁰ Now there was at a distance from them a herd of many swine feeding. ³¹ And the demons began to entreat Him, saying, 'If You are going to cast us out, send us into the herd of swine.' ³² And He said to them, 'Begone!' And they came out, and went into the swine, and behold, the whole herd rushed down the steep bank into the sea and perished in the waters. ³³ And the herdsmen ran away, and went to the city, and reported everything, including the incident of the demoniacs. ³⁴ And behold, the whole city came out to meet Jesus; and when they saw Him, they entreated Him to depart from their region."

Introduction

Earlier in Matthew chapter 8 we saw Jesus' power over physical deformity and disease. We also saw His power over nature by calming the storm. In Matthew 8:28-34, we see Jesus' power over the spiritual world by casting out demons. The corresponding accounts in Mark 5:2 and Luke 8:27 give the impression that there is one demoniac, but this is due to the fact that Mark and Luke are focusing on the dominant spokesman of the two. The more specific account of the number present in Matthew makes it clear that there were two demon-possessed men.

VERSE 28: *"And when He had come to the other side into the country of the Gadarenes, two men who were demon-possessed met Him as they were coming out of the tombs; they were so exceedingly violent that no one could pass by that road."*

Notice the demons were, *"exceedingly violent."* Scripture tells us about violent/evil men in **Psalm 140:1**: *"Deliver me, O LORD, from the evil man: preserve me from the violent man...."*

Matthew also tells us that these men were demon-possessed. This means that they were under the control of demonic spirits. We also know that there were many demons in control: *"And He was asking him, 'What is your name?' And he *said to Him, 'My name is Legion; for we are many.'"* **Mark 5:9**. This demonic control resulted in self-destruction as we read from the account in **Mark 5:5** *"...he was crying out and gashing himself with stones."* Their bizarre behavior included their living among the tombs. Tombs represent a place of death. Sin brings death. **Ezekiel 18:4** *"...The soul who sins will die."* The Bible states that those who reject God's wisdom love death. **Proverbs 8:36:** *"All those who hate me love death."*.

VERSE 29: *"And behold, they cried out, saying, 'What do we have to do with You, Son of God? Have You come here to torment us before the time?'"*

This shows that the demons immediately recognized Jesus and were in fear. It is amazing that there are many people who claim to believe in God but neither fear Him, nor shudder before Him. This is interesting because the demons, who are haters of God, understand who He is and quake in fear at the thought of Him. **James 2:19** tells us this too: *"You believe that God is one. You do well; the demons also believe, and shudder."*

We get a little more detail of Jesus' encounter with the demoniacs from Mark where we are told: *"Seeing Jesus from a distance, he ran up and bowed down before Him; and shouting with a loud voice, he said, 'What business do we have with each other, Jesus, Son of the Most High God? I implore You by God, do not torment me!'"* **Mark 5:6-7**. We should realize that even though the demons hate everything about God, they are powerless to do anything but bow down before Him. **Philippians 2:10** tells us, *"that at the name of Jesus EVERY KNEE SHOULD BOW, of those who are in heaven, and on earth, and under the earth, ..."* Notice that the demons ask Jesus, *"Have You come here to torment us before the time?"* **Matthew 8:29**. The demons know that God has appointed a time for eternal damnation.

VERSES 30-32: *"Now there was at a distance from them a herd of many swine feeding. 31 And the demons began to entreat Him, saying, 'If You are going to cast us out, send us into the herd of swine.' 32 And He said to them, 'Begone!' And they came out, and went into the swine, and behold, the whole herd rushed down the steep bank into the sea and perished in the waters."*

We learn from Mark 5:13 that the herd of pigs numbered about 2,000. It was clear to the demons that they were not going to be allowed to continue to possess the men. So, the demons may have been in fear of immediate judgment, we do not know for sure, but we know that they requested to go into the pigs. It must be remembered that pigs were a very disgusting and unclean animal to the Jews. Notice that Jesus just spoke one word, *"Begone"* (v.32) and the demons were powerless to resist Him.

VERSES 33-34: *"And the herdsmen ran away, and went to the city, and reported everything, including the incident of the demoniacs. 34 And behold, the whole city came out to meet Jesus; and when they saw Him, they entreated Him to depart from their region."*

The herdsman clearly understood that the mass suicide of the pigs was the result of Jesus casting the demons out of the men. Notice that the people of the city came out to see Jesus.

> **Mark 5:14-15:** *"And their herdsmen ran away and reported it in the city and out in the country. And the people came to see what it was that had happened. 15 And they *came to Jesus and *observed the man who had been demon-possessed sitting down, clothed and in his right mind, the very man who had had the 'legion'; and they became frightened."*

Notice that Mark tells us that, *"they became frightened."* The people wanted Jesus to leave, not because of some economic loss, but because they were frightened. They were unholy men who were confronted by the Holy God. Do you remember the response of fear that came from the disciples who were in the boat when Jesus calmed the sea? **Mark 4:41** states that, *"And they became very much afraid and said to one another, 'Who then is this, that even the wind and the sea obey Him?'"* Peter responded the same way when Jesus performed the miracle of filling their boat with fish.

> **Luke 5:6-8:** *"And when they had done this, they enclosed a great quantity of fish; and their nets began to break; 7and they signaled to their partners in the other boat, for them*

to come and help them. And they came, and filled both of the boats, so that they began to sink. [8] But when Simon Peter saw that, he fell down at Jesus' feet, saying, 'Depart from me, for I am a sinful man, O Lord!'"

Our understanding of our sinfulness is the first step to coming to a saving knowledge of God. If one does not know what he is saved from (i.e. the judgment of hell) he cannot be saved. Understanding one's own sinfulness is just the start. The next step is deciding what you are going to do with that realization. Some people try to ignore it but continue to live with a nagging conscience that brings to their mind their guilt every once in a while. Others come up with their own way to seek atonement. They may try to do good things or follow some religious teaching, all with the belief that they can earn their own salvation. Scripture tells us that their false religious ideas result in the *searing of their conscience* (1 Timothy 4:1-5). Some deal with the knowledge of their sinfulness by hating God. They hate God by trying to deny His existence, blaspheming His name and attacking those who are true followers of God. All of these responses do nothing to save a person. The only true response is to turn to the true and living God for salvation. It says in **Romans 10:13:** *"for 'Whoever will call upon the name of the Lord will be saved.'"*

In our main text we read that the people of the city responded by wanting Jesus to leave. What about the men who were healed? We learn more about their response in **Mark 5:18-20:**
> *"And as He was getting into the boat, the man who had been demon-possessed was entreating Him that he might accompany Him. [19] And He did not let him, but He *said to him, 'Go home to your people and report to them what great things the Lord has done for you, and how He had mercy on you.' [20] And he went away and began to proclaim in Decapolis what great things Jesus had done for him; and everyone marveled."*

Note the grace of Jesus. Even though the people of the city rejected Him by wanting Him to leave them, Jesus sent the healed men back to their own people to be living witnesses of the grace and goodness of God.

Summary and Application

This lesson shows us that the almighty, spiritual power of God easily conquers Satan and his demons. They are subject to the very word of Christ. Some may ask if a Christian can ever be possessed by a demon. The Christian by definition cannot be demon-possessed because the Christian is indwelt by the Holy Spirit of God. Although the Christian cannot be possessed by demons, he can be the target of demonic activity. A definition of Satan is set out in Vine's Dictionary as:
> "Being the malignant enemy of God and man, [the Devil] accuses man to God, Job 1:6-11; 2:1-5; Revelation 12:9, 10, and God to man, Genesis 3. He afflicts men with physical sufferings, Acts 10:38. Being himself sinful, 1 John 3:8, he instigated man to sin, Genesis 3, and tempts man to do evil, Ephesians 4:27; 6:11, encouraging him thereto by deception, Ephesians 2:2. Death having been brought into the world by sin, the Devil had the power of death, but Christ through His own Death, has triumphed over him, and will bring him to nought, Hebrews. 2:14...."[146]

We need to remember the awesome power of Christ's work on the Cross. **1 John 3:8:** *"...The Son of God appeared for this purpose, that He might destroy the works of the devil."*

---

[146] Vine, W., and Bruce, F. (1981; Published in electronic form by Logos Research Systems, 1996). *Vine's Expository Dictionary of Old and New Testament words* (p. 306). Old Tappan NJ: Revell.

How thankful those in Christ must be that they have God as their protective Father. God is infinitely more powerful than Satan and his demons, or anything else. The Lord will deliver us!

Psalm 18:48-49: *"He delivers me from my enemies;*
Surely Thou dost lift me above those who rise up against me;
Thou dost rescue me from the violent man.
[49] Therefore I will give thanks to Thee among the nations,
O Lord, And I will sing praises to Thy name."

Romans 8:37-39: *"But in all these things we overwhelmingly conquer through Him who loved us. [38] For I am convinced that neither death, nor life, nor angels, nor principalities, nor things present, nor things to come, nor powers, [39] nor height, nor depth, nor any other created thing, will be able to separate us from the love of God, which is in Christ Jesus our Lord."*

MATTHEW 9:1-8
(JESUS' POWER TO FORGIVE SINS!)

"AND getting into a boat, He crossed over, and came to His own city. ² And behold, they were bringing to Him a paralytic, lying on a bed; and Jesus seeing their faith said to the paralytic, 'Take courage, My son, your sins are forgiven.' ³ And behold, some of the scribes said to themselves, 'This fellow blasphemes.' ⁴ And Jesus knowing their thoughts said, 'Why are you thinking evil in your hearts? ⁵For which is easier, to say, Your sins are forgiven, or to say, Rise, and walk? ⁶ But in order that you may know that the Son of Man has authority on earth to forgive sins'—then He *said to the paralytic—'Rise, take up your bed, and go home.' ⁷ And he rose, and went home. ⁸ But when the multitudes saw this, they were filled with awe, and glorified God, who had given such authority to men."

Introduction

The core problem of people is not physical sickness or psychological disorders. The core problem of man is SIN. Every person has this same fatal disease of sin *("The soul who sins will die."* **Ezekiel 18:4**). Remember the statistic has not changed… "10 out of 10 will die." If an alcoholic would go to Alcoholics Anonymous and be able to quit drinking for the rest of his life, he would be a much improved man, but he is not any less sinful. The Bible also tells us that a non-Christian man who has lived a very clean life and helped a lot of people is just as destined for hell as the gutter drug dealer. God does not grade on a curve. To get into heaven, you have to be perfect (without sin). The Bible is clear; if you are not perfect, then you will go to hell: **Ezekiel 18:4** *"…The soul who sins will die."* Considering the fact that man is born with a sin nature, there has never been a perfect man…but one, Jesus the Son of God. Jesus sets out God's standard when He said: *"Therefore you are to be perfect, as your heavenly Father is perfect."* **Matthew 5:48.** The Bible tells us that everyone is a sinner and unless we are forgiven, we will not be allowed into heaven:

> **Romans 3:23:** *"for all have sinned and fall short of the glory of God."*

> **Romans 3:10:** *"as it is written: There is none righteous, no not one."*

The penalty for our sin is spending eternity in hell. Jesus said:

> **Matthew 10:28:** *"Do not fear those who kill the body but are unable to kill the soul; but rather fear Him who is able to destroy both soul and body in hell."*

> **Matthew 5:22:** *"…and whoever shall say, 'You fool,' shall be guilty enough to go into the fiery hell."*

> **2 Peter 2:4–6:** *For if God did not spare angels when they sinned, but cast them into hell and committed them to pits of darkness, reserved for judgment; ⁵ and did not spare the ancient world, but preserved Noah, a preacher of righteousness, with seven others, when He brought a flood upon the world of the ungodly; ⁶ and if He condemned the cities of Sodom and Gomorrah to destruction by reducing them to ashes, having made them an example to those who would live ungodly lives thereafter;*

Religious leaders who teach that an individual must do a certain amount of good deeds to find favor with God and earn salvation are not telling the truth of the Bible. The truth is that Jesus already purchased your forgiveness by dying on the cross Himself. It is like someone who was sentenced to death but right before the execution, another person, not subject to any punishment, tells the judge that he will take the punishment for the doomed man. The innocent taking the punishment of the guilty.

The difference between another person dying for us and Jesus dying for us is that Jesus alone was able to pay our penalty because he was sinless. God has accepted Jesus' sacrifice for our sins. This fact does not mean that every person is going to heaven. Just as if someone were to offer you a gift, it is not yours until you accept it. God's plan is that we simply repent and believe the Gospel.

> **Acts 20:21:** *"…solemnly testifying to both Jews and Greeks of repentance toward God and faith in our Lord Jesus Christ."*

> **Mark 1:14-15:** *"… Jesus came into Galilee, preaching the gospel of God, [15]and saying, 'The time is fulfilled, and the kingdom of God is at hand; repent and believe in the gospel.'"*

- To *REPENT* means to turn from your sins and forsake them by the power of God.
- To *BELIEVE THE GOSPEL* means that one who is "born again" by the Spirit of God (John 3:3-8) will:
    - Believe in Jesus Christ as Almighty God, who is without sin;
    - Believe in Jesus' sacrificial death on the cross as the only and complete payment for your sins;
    - Believe in Jesus' bodily resurrection from the dead on the third day;
    - Believe in Jesus as Lord over all things and confesses this fact to others.

It is that straightforward. It has nothing to do with your righteousness, good works or engaging in a religious ceremony or cleaning yourself up first to win God's acceptance. If you reject God's loving gift of forgiveness in Jesus Christ, you remain a guilty sinner waiting to be punished in eternal hell. The Bible says *in* **John 3:36:** *"He who believes in the Son has eternal life; but he who does not obey the Son will not see life, but the wrath of God abides on him."* Repent and believe the gospel TODAY, before it is too late!

We need to believe with our whole heart in Jesus' sacrificial work on the cross as the basis of our forgiveness and accept the gift of forgiveness of God because of what Jesus did on the cross. If one does not accept the gift of forgiveness, they are not forgiven. Even our human law recognizes this. In the United States Supreme Court case of United States v. George Wilson 7 P. 150 (1833), Wilson had been convicted of *"robbing the mail, and putting the life of the carrier in jeopardy, for which the punishment is death."* Id. at 160. The president granted a pardon. The Court defined a pardon as follows:

> "A pardon is an act of grace, proceeding from the power entrusted with the execution of the laws, which exempts the individual on whom it is bestowed from the punishment the law inflicts for a crime he has committed."

Although Wilson was granted this pardon, he refused it. The question presented to the Court was whether Wilson was still subject to the penalty if the President had provided the pardon that he refused? In other words, can one refuse to be pardoned if the pardon had been granted to him? The Court held as follows:

> "A pardon is a deed… and delivery is not complete without acceptance. It may then be rejected by the person to whom it is tendered; and if be rejected, we have discovered no power in a court to force it on him. It may be supposed that no being condemned to

death would reject a pardon; but the rule must be the same in capital cases and in misdemeanors." Id. at p161

In other words, forgiveness cannot be forced on someone who rejects it. The Court further commented it is incredible to think anyone condemned to die would reject a pardon. In summary, if he rejects the pardon, the Court cannot make him accept it. It is as if the pardon does not exist for that person.

In **1 Corinthians 15:3-4** the Apostle Paul writes:

> *"For I delivered to you as of first importance what I also received, that Christ died for our sins according to the Scriptures, and that He was buried, and that He was raised on the third day according to the Scriptures,"*

Christ died to grant you the pardon, but it is attached to you by God's grace through faith.

> **Ephesians 2:8-9:** *"For it is by grace you have been saved, through faith—and this not from yourselves, it is the gift of God—not by works, so that no one can boast."*

The concept of salvation is summarized in **John 3:18-19:**

> *"He who believes in Him is not judged; he who does not believe has been judged already, because he has not believed in the name of the only begotten Son of God. And this is the judgment, that the light is come into the world, and men loved the darkness rather than the light; for their deeds were evil."*

So, if I repent and believe the gospel, can I know that I am going to heaven? God's Word says, "yes!"

> **1 John 5:13:** *"These things I have written to you who believe in the name of the Son of God, in order that you may know that you have eternal life."*

The direct point is that your good deeds will never be enough to have your sins forgiven or to earn/buy your way into heaven. The only way for you to be saved from hell is to put complete faith in Christ as paying the penalty for you, and following Him.

VERSES 1-3: *"AND getting into a boat, He crossed over, and came to His own city. ² And behold, they were bringing to Him a paralytic, lying on a bed; and Jesus seeing their faith said to the paralytic, 'Take courage, My son, your sins are forgiven.' ³ And behold, some of the scribes said to themselves, 'This fellow blasphemes.'"*

In verse 1 we see Jesus, *"came to His own city."* Although Nazareth was the city Jesus grew up in as a child, the people there had rejected Him. Jesus' "own city" became Capernaum as we read in Mark 2:1. When He got there, a paralytic (one suffering from paralysis) was brought to Him.

In **Mark 2:3-5** we get a little more detail about how this paralytic man's friends got him before Jesus.

> *"And they *came, bringing to Him a paralytic, carried by four men. ⁴ And being unable to get to Him because of the crowd, they removed the roof above Him; and when they had dug an opening, they let down the pallet on which the paralytic was lying. ⁵ And Jesus seeing their faith *said to the paralytic, 'My son, your sins are forgiven.'"*

We read that his friends dug a hole through the roof that was big enough to lower him down to get him to Jesus. I am sure many were offended by the mess they were making and the uncouth manner in which they were conducting themselves. They were desperate! They did not care whether it met with others' approval; they knew that no one other than Jesus could save their friend. As others saw their actions as tacky, lowlife behavior, God saw great faith and granted forgiveness of sins. The man was saved spiritually and healed physically!

Oh, that we would see the desperate need of others and take the desperate measures needed. When we do so, expect some people to aggressively criticize. Especially expect it from the false religious inside the church. They will want to keep the church in a certain *comfort zone* and maintain their influence/position. They do not want to look extreme and they will not allow others to make the church look extreme. So if you have a heart for true evangelism or service, do not be discouraged when you run into these folks. They will talk about *balance*, which is their code word for status-quo dead religion. Dead religion never can meet the desperate need of man. Look at the paralytic. His desperate need required desperate action! Read the words of Charles Spurgeon in his comments regarding the friends who lowered the paralytic through the roof to Jesus:

> *"Faith is full of inventions.* The house was full, a crowd blocked up the door, but faith found a way of getting at the Lord and placing the palsied man before him. If we cannot get sinners where Jesus is by ordinary methods we must use extraordinary ones. It seems, according to Luke 5:19, that a tiling had to be removed, which would make dust and cause a measure of danger to those below, but where the case is very urgent we must not mind running some risks and shocking some proprieties. Jesus was there to heal, and therefore fall what might, faith ventured all so that her poor paralyzed charge might have his sins forgiven. O that we had more daring faith among us! Cannot we, dear reader, seek it this morning for ourselves and for our fellow-workers, and will we not try to-day to perform some gallant act for the love of souls and the glory of the Lord." [147]

Returning to the main text in Matthew 9:3 we see that the scribes accused Jesus of blasphemy when He stated that the man's sins were forgiven. To understand these verses we need to look at the meaning of <u>blasphemy</u>. In summary, to blaspheme is when:

> "[The] honor of God is insulted by man. The name of God, which is cursed or reviled instead of being honored…The penalty of the outrage of blasphemy is death by stoning (Leviticus 24:10-23; 1 Kings 21:9; Acts 6:11; 7:58)."[148]

The religious leaders accused Jesus of blasphemy for saying, ***"Take courage, My son, your sins are forgiven."*** The reason they accused Jesus of blasphemy is due to the fact that they did not know who He was. They did understand that only God could forgive sins. What they did not understand was that Jesus was God. In this section we specifically see the divinity of Christ. The religious leaders only needed to read the prophet Isaiah and they would have known who He was:

> *"For a child will be born to us, a son will be given to us;*
> *And the government will rest on His shoulders;*
> *And His name will be called Wonderful Counselor, <u>Mighty God</u>,*
> *Eternal Father, Prince of Peace."* <u>**Isaiah 9:6.**</u>

> *"For in Him all the fullness of Deity dwells in bodily form,"* <u>**Colossians 2:9**</u>

> *"…looking for the blessed hope and the appearing of the glory of <u>our great God and Savior,</u> <u>Christ Jesus</u>,…"* <u>**Titus 2:13**</u>

---

[147] Spurgeon, C. H. (2006). *Morning and Evening: Daily readings,* September 7- Morning; (Complete and unabridged; New modern edition.) Peabody, MA: Hendrickson Publishers.

[148] *The New Bible Dictionary,* (Wheaton, Illinois: Tyndale House Publishers, Inc.) 1962.

"But He kept silent and did not answer. Again the high priest was questioning Him, and saying to Him, 'Are You the Christ, the Son of the Blessed One?' And Jesus said, 'I am; and you shall see the Son of Man sitting at the right hand of Power, and coming with the clouds of heaven.'" **Mark 14:61–62**

"Jesus said to them, "Truly, truly, I say to you, before Abraham was born, I am." **John 8:58**

"And they all said, "Are You the Son of God, then?" And He said to them, "Yes, I am." **Luke 22:70**

Jesus said: *"I and the Father are one."* **John 10:30.** [149]

VERSES 4-8: *"And Jesus knowing their thoughts said, 'Why are you thinking evil in your hearts? [5] For which is easier, to say, Your sins are forgiven, or to say, Rise, and walk? [6]But in order that you may know that the Son of Man has authority on earth to forgive sins'—then He *said to the paralytic—'Rise, take up your bed, and go home.' [7] And he rose, and went home. [8] But when the multitudes saw this, they were filled with awe, and glorified God, who had given such authority to men."*

In verse 4 Jesus asks the religious leaders, *"Why are you thinking evil in your hearts?"* The evil they were thinking was the grave judgment of blasphemy they made against Jesus. Jesus responded by demonstrating that He was not speaking empty words. Jesus did not simply claim to be able to forgive sins; He showed His power by healing the paralyzed man. Praise God for providing a Savior who saves us from our sins!

In verse 8 we see the response of the multitude: *"they were filled with awe, and glorified God...."* Notice the difference in the response of this crowd compared to the people of the city where Jesus healed the two demoniacs. There they responded to the miracle they saw by asking Jesus to leave: **Matthew 8:34:** *"And behold, the whole city came out to meet Jesus; and when they saw Him, they entreated Him to depart from their region."* They did not want to deal with what they could not understand. They did not want to interrupt their normal lives or deal with their sinfulness. The

---

[149] R.C. Sproul writes the following on THE DIVINITY OF CHRIST: "Faith in the deity of Christ is necessary to being a Christian. It is an essential part of the New Testament gospel of Christ. Yet in every century the church has been forced to deal with people who claim to be Christians while denying or distorting the deity of Christ.... As the Logos Incarnate, Christ is revealed as being not only preexistent to creation, but eternal. He is said to be in the beginning *with* God and also that He *is* God (John 1:1-3). That He is *with* God demands a personal distinction within the Godhead. That He *is* God demands inclusion in the Godhead. Elsewhere, the New Testament ascribes terms and titles to Jesus that are clearly titles of deity. God bestows the preeminent divine title of *Lord* upon Him (Philippians 2:9-11). As the Son of Man, Jesus claims to be Lord of the Sabbath (Mark 2:28) and to have authority to forgive sins (Mark 2:1-12). He is called the *'Lord'* of glory' (James 2:1) and willingly receives worship, as when Thomas confesses, 'My Lord and my God!' (John 20:28). Paul declares that the fullness of the Godhead dwells in Christ bodily (Colossians 1:19) and that Jesus is higher than angels, a theme reiterated in the book of Hebrews. [Note that all of Creation was made by Jesus – Col. 1:15-17]" Sproul, R. C. (1996, c1992). *Essential Truths of the Christian Faith.* Wheaton, Ill.: Tyndale House.
Here are some short notes of mine on Jesus' humanity and divine nature as shown in Scripture. Examples of His manhood are that He was tempted (Luke 4:1-13), tired (John 4:6), hungry (Matthew 4:2), thirsty (John 19:28), slept (Matthew 8:24), and died (Mark 15:39-45, Matthew 27:50). Examples of His divine nature are that He was born of a virgin (Luke 1:30-38), did miracles (John 11:38-44, Luke 7:21-23), never sinned (2 Corinthians 5:21), and rose from the dead (1 Corinthians 15:3-8, Matthew 28:5-15, John 21:14).

people of the city made it clear that they would rather have the two men tortured and terrorizing others than be confronted with who Jesus is.

Summary and Application

Have you resolved who Jesus is? Do you see Him as just a great teacher or healer? If so, you still do not know Him. He is God incarnate (i.e. God became a man – Matthew 1:18-25). One defines "incarnate" as:

> "That act of grace whereby Christ took our human nature into union with his Divine Person, became man. Christ is both God and man. Human attributes and actions are predicated of Him, and He of whom they are predicated is God. A Divine Person was united to a human nature (Acts 20:28; Romans 8:32; 1 Corinthians 2:8; Hebrew 2:11-14; Timothy 3:16; Galatians 4:4 , etc.). The union is hypostatical, i.e., is personal; the two natures are not mixed or confounded, and it is perpetual." [150]

Christ became a man and because He was God, He was without sin. Because He was sinless, He could die as a sacrifice for others since He did not have to die for His own sins.

---

[150] Easton, M. G. (1996). *Easton's Bible dictionary*. (Incarnation) Oak Harbor, WA: Logos Research Systems, Inc.

MATTHEW 9:9-17
(JESUS CALLS DISCIPLES AND SINNERS and DENOUNCES EXTERNAL RITUALISM)

"And as Jesus passed on from there, He saw a man, called Matthew, sitting in the tax office; and He *said to him, 'Follow Me!' And he rose, and followed Him. *[10] And it happened that as He was reclining at the table in the house, behold many tax-gatherers and sinners came and were dining with Jesus and His disciples. [11] And when the Pharisees saw this, they said to His disciples, 'Why is your Teacher eating with the tax-gatherers and sinners?' [12] But when He heard this, He said, 'It is not those who are healthy who need a physician, but those who are sick. [13] But go and learn what this means, 'I DESIRE COMPASSION, AND NOT SACRIFICE,' for I did not come to call the righteous, but sinners.'*

[14] Then the disciples of John *came to Him, saying, 'Why do we and the Pharisees fast, but Your disciples do not fast?' [15] And Jesus said to them, 'The attendants of the bridegroom cannot mourn as long as the bridegroom is with them, can they? But the days will come when the bridegroom is taken away from them, and then they will fast. [16] But no one puts a patch of unshrunk cloth on an old garment; for the patch pulls away from the garment, and a worse tear results. [17] Nor do men put new wine into old wineskins; otherwise the wineskins burst, and the wine pours out, and the wineskins are ruined; but they put new wine into fresh wineskins, and both are preserved.'"

Introduction

In this portion we will see the difference between the love of "religion" and love for God. There are a lot of people who are like the Pharisees, who take satisfaction in adherence to their own religious rules. On the other hand, we see Matthew, who knew he was a sinner and responded to the call of God. Which are you?

VERSES 9-13: *"And as Jesus passed on from there, He saw a man, called Matthew, sitting in the tax office; and He *said to him, 'Follow Me!' And he rose, and followed Him.*

[10] And it happened that as He was reclining at the table in the house, behold many tax-gatherers and sinners came and were dining with Jesus and His disciples. [11] And when the Pharisees saw this, they said to His disciples, 'Why is your Teacher eating with the tax-gatherers and sinners?' [12] But when He heard this, He said, 'It is not those who are healthy who need a physician, but those who are sick. [13] But go and learn what this means, 'I DESIRE COMPASSION, AND NOT SACRIFICE,' for I did not come to call the righteous, but sinners.'"

Here we see Jesus calling Matthew, who is the author of the Gospel of Matthew. Who was this guy? We know that he was also called Levi and, "the son of Alphaeus" (Luke 5:27, Mark 2:14). Verse 9 tells us that he was a tax collector. One must remember how low a tax collector/publican was in those days. Although they were rich, they were considered very low class because they would collect taxes from their fellow Jews for the Roman empire. They were also viewed as traitors who joined with the controlling Roman Empire to profit off fellow Jews.

"Roman senators and various other high-ranking officials would buy from the central government at public auction the right of collecting the toll taxes in a given country, province, or region at a fixed rate for a period of five years. Whatever was collected above that amount was kept as profit. Those who held such taxing rights were called publicani. The publicani would hire others, usually citizens of the country being taxed, to do the actual collecting.

Those collectors had somewhat the same arrangement with the publicani that the publicani had with Rome. Whatever they managed to collect above the amount demanded by the publicani they kept as their own profit. Both the publicani and the tax-gatherers, therefore, had strong motivation to exact and collect as much tax as possible-knowing they were backed by the full authority, including the military authority, of Rome. The tax-gatherers (Greek telōnēs) quite naturally were hated by their own people, not only as extortionist but as traitors. In Israel they were ranked with the lowest of human society-sinners, prostitutes, and Gentiles (Matt. 9:10-11; 18:17; 21:31-32;Mark 2:15-16;Luke 5:30; etc.)." [151]

We also see Matthew's humility after he becomes a believer in Christ. Matthew explains when Jesus called him *"he rose, and followed Him."* Luke gives us a little more detail about what happened when Matthew was called. Luke states that this worldly rich man, *"left everything behind, and rose and began to follow Him,...."* (Luke 5:28). He did not gather up his bags of money and then follow Jesus. No, he *"left everything behind, and rose and began to follow Him,...."* (Luke 5:28). We also learn from Mark and Luke that the banquet where Jesus dined with *"many tax-gatherers and sinners"* (Matthew 9:10), was actually held at Matthew's own home (Mark 2:15, Luke 5:29).

Note that the Pharisees then asked "His disciples" why Jesus would eat with such rotten people as *"the tax-gatherers and sinners."* They did not have the guts to ask Jesus Himself. Jesus heard the Pharisees ask the question to the disciples. He responded that He had come to save sinners (i.e. those who were spiritually sick), not those who saw themselves as perfect. Unfortunately, the Pharisees did not know what Jesus knew (i.e. that every man is sick and needs to be saved from his sin). The Pharisees felt very good about how they had kept the rules and regulations they had set up. Based on their own standard, they assumed that they were superior morally and spiritually. Jesus points out the falsity of their view of themselves. He then obliterates their entire foundation of self-righteousness when He states in verse 13: *"But go and learn what this means, 'I DESIRE COMPASSION, AND NOT SACRIFICE,' for I did not come to call the righteous, but sinners."* Jesus was even more direct about their hypocritical self-righteousness when He said to them in **Matthew 23:23-24**:

> *"Woe to you, scribes and Pharisees, hypocrites! For you tithe mint and dill and cummin, and have neglected the weightier provisions of the law: justice and mercy and faithfulness; but these are the things you should have done without neglecting the others. 24 You blind guides, who strain out a gnat and swallow a camel!"*

Section Application

God is not interested in our ritualistic, religious activity. In other words, do you feel you have been made righteous because you go to church, sing in the choir, attend prayer meetings or give money? Maybe you think you are righteous because many people believe you are a real nice person or a great community leader. The problem is that even if you are all these things and more, the Bible is clear that you are still a sinner going to hell! (John 3:18) One cannot make any claim to righteousness based on any of his religious/good deeds (Ephesians 2:8-9). The only true claim that a person can make of

---

[151] MacArthur, John F., *The MacArthur New Testament Commentary*, Introduction (Chicago: Moody Press) 1985.

true righteousness is that given them by God through faith in Jesus Christ. As it says in **Romans 3:22:** *"even the righteousness of God through faith in Jesus Christ for all those who believe...."*

Another application of this section is whether you are witnessing to the lost. We are never to view anyone as "too evil" to be saved. All must hear the saving message of the gospel. Look at the example of John Newton who wrote the hymn "Amazing Grace":

> "At a young age, John Newton went to sea. Like most sailors of his day, he lived a life of rebellion and debauchery. For several years, he worked on slave ships, capturing slaves for sale to the plantations of the New World. So low did he sink that at one point he became a slave himself, captive of another slave trader. Eventually, he became the captain of his own slave ship. The combination of a frightening storm at sea, coupled with his reading of Thomas à Kempis's classic *Imitation of Christ,* planted the seeds that resulted in his conversion. He went on to become a leader in the evangelical movement in eighteenth century England, along with such men as John and Charles Wesley, George Whitefield, and William Wilberforce. On his tombstone is inscribed the following epitaph, written by Newton himself:
>
> > 'John Newton, clerk, once an infidel and Libertine, a servant of slavers in Africa, was, by the rich mercy of our Lord and Savior Jesus Christ, preserved, restored, pardoned, and appointed to preach the Faith he had long labored to destroy'."[152]

You will do well to remember that you were just as lost as any wicked sinner prior to God saving you. **1 Corinthians 6:9-11:** *"Or do you not know that the unrighteous shall not inherit the kingdom of God? Do not be deceived; neither fornicators, nor idolaters, nor adulterers, nor effeminate, nor homosexuals, nor thieves, nor the covetous, nor drunkards, nor revilers, nor swindlers, shall inherit the kingdom of God. And such were some of you; but you were washed, but you were sanctified, but you were justified in the name of the Lord Jesus Christ, and in the Spirit of our God."*

VERSES 14-17: *"Then the disciples of John *came to Him, saying, 'Why do we and the Pharisees fast, but Your disciples do not fast?' 15 And Jesus said to them, 'The attendants of the bridegroom cannot mourn as long as the bridegroom is with them, can they? But the days will come when the bridegroom is taken away from them, and then they will fast. 16 But no one puts a patch of unshrunk cloth on an old garment; for the patch pulls away from the garment, and a worse tear results. 17 Nor do men put new wine into old wineskins; otherwise the wineskins burst, and the wine pours out, and the wineskins are ruined; but they put new wine into fresh wineskins, and both are preserved.'"*

John's disciples ask Jesus why His disciples are not fasting. By the time of this event, John the Baptist was in prison (Matthew 4:12). Before his imprisonment, John had (in essence) told his disciples to quit following him and to follow Jesus. In John 3:30 John said, *"He must increase, but I must decrease."* Some of John's disciples did not do that but instead fell back to their external traditions after John's arrest. It was not God's Word that told them to fast twice a week (Luke 18:12) but the "traditions" they developed. The Old Testament required fasting once a year on Yom Kippur, the Day of Atonement (Leviticus. 16:29, 31).

---

[152] Kenneth W. Osbeck, *101 Hymn Stories* [Grand Rapids: Kregel, 1982], 28.

Jesus points out that His presence is a joyous time for His disciples. There will be a time for fasting when Jesus is rejected and crucified, but that time had not come yet. Now was the time of rejoicing like one enjoys at a wedding. When Jesus went to heaven, we know that the disciples did fast. It says in **Acts 13:2-3:**

> *"And while they were ministering to the Lord and <u>fasting</u>, the Holy Spirit said, 'Set apart for Me Barnabas and Saul for the work to which I have called them.' ³ Then, when they had <u>fasted and prayed</u> and laid their hands on them, they sent them away."*

The attitude of fasting here in Acts is very different than those of the Pharisees. The Pharisees were only concerned about the external appearance of religion, not pursuing God's will.

When Jesus says in **Matthew 9:17:** *"Nor do men put new wine into old wineskins; otherwise the wineskins burst...."* He is making an important statement to some of John's disciples (i.e. those who did not obey John to follow Christ). He was making it clear to them that He was not improving or even reforming their external ritual system. To work within that man-made system would be like putting, *"new wine into old wineskins;...."* (i.e. they are completely incompatible). Jesus made it clear that God has nothing to do with their external-traditional system and was renouncing it.

Renouncing man-made religious teaching is not to be understood as destroying the holy Law of God in the Old Testament. Jesus makes that clear in **Matthew 5:17-19:**

> *"Do not think that I came to abolish the Law or the Prophets; I did not come to abolish, but to fulfill. ¹⁸ For truly I say to you, until heaven and earth pass away, not the smallest letter or stroke shall pass away from the Law, until all is accomplished. ¹⁹ Whoever then annuls one of the least of these commandments, and so teaches others, shall be called least in the kingdom of heaven; but whoever keeps and teaches them, he shall be called great in the kingdom of heaven."*

Jesus did destroy the false religion of external self-righteousness so that people would see that the only way they could be saved is by faith in His sacrificial death on the cross. God's plan of salvation by faith in God is not something new that Jesus brought. The people of the Old Testament were saved the same way as those of the New Testament, having faith in God for their righteousness. Look at this Old Testament passage:

> *"Behold, as for the proud one,*
> *His soul is not right within him;*
> <u>*But the righteous will live by his faith*</u>*."* **Habakkuk 2:4**

Salvation by faith was God's way even before the Law was given to Moses. We read that Abraham received righteousness from God for believing what He said:

> *"Then he believed in the Lord; and He reckoned it to him as righteousness. "* **Genesis 15:6**

Section Application

Jesus is the only way to salvation and man-made religion or self-righteousness will never get one even close to the kingdom of heaven.

> **Titus 3:5-6:** *"He saved us, not on the basis of deeds which we have done in righteousness, but according to His mercy, by the washing of regeneration and renewing by the Holy Spirit, ⁶ whom He poured out upon us richly through Jesus Christ our Savior."*

> **Ephesians 2:8-9:** *"For by grace you have been saved through faith; and that not of yourselves, <u>it is the gift of God;</u> ⁹ <u>not as a result of works</u>, that no one should boast."*

Do you share with people the true Gospel of how to be saved? Many falsely believe that a religious ritual like baptism, confirmation or communion is what secures them a place in heaven. They are putting, *"new wine into old wineskins;..."* thus no true righteousness is accomplished. We must care enough about the eternal destiny of others to show them what the Bible says about salvation. Are you afraid to explain to a friend that he cannot be good enough or religious enough to earn a spot in heaven? If so, then you may have reason to question your understanding of Christ and His work on the cross. We must not deny Him before man! Jesus said in **Matthew 10:33:** *"But whoever denies Me before men, I will also deny him before My Father who is in heaven."* We must pray for boldness and step out in obedience to Christ. Even the great Apostle Paul asked for prayers to be bold in sharing the gospel!

> **Ephesians 6:19–20:** *"...and pray on my behalf, that utterance may be given to me in the opening of my mouth, to make known with boldness the mystery of the gospel, for which I am an ambassador in chains; that in proclaiming it I may speak boldly, as I ought to speak."*

MATTHEW 9:18-38
(MIRACLES OVER DEATH, BLINDNESS, DEMONS; and PROCLAIMING THE GOSPEL)

"While He was saying these things to them, behold, there came a synagogue official, and bowed down before Him, saying, 'My daughter has just died; but come and lay Your hand on her, and she will live.' [19] And Jesus rose and began to follow him, and so did His disciples. [20] And behold, a woman who had been suffering from a hemorrhage for twelve years, came up behind Him and touched the fringe of His cloak; [21] for she was saying to herself, 'If I only touch His garment, I shall get well.' [22] But Jesus turning and seeing her said, 'Daughter, take courage; your faith has made you well.' And at once the woman was made well. [23] And when Jesus came into the official's house, and saw the flute-players, and the crowd in noisy disorder, [24] He began to say, 'Depart; for the girl has not died, but is asleep.' And they began laughing at Him. [25] But when the crowd had been put out, He entered and took her by the hand; and the girl arose. [26] And this news went out into all that land.

[27] And as Jesus passed on from there, two blind men followed Him, crying out, and saying, 'Have mercy on us, Son of David!' [28] And after He had come into the house, the blind men came up to Him, and Jesus *said to them, 'Do you believe that I am able to do this?' They *said to Him, 'Yes, Lord.' [29] Then He touched their eyes, saying, 'Be it done to you according to your faith.' [30] And their eyes were opened. And Jesus sternly warned them, saying, 'See here, let no one know about this!' [31] But they went out, and spread the news about Him in all that land.

[32] And as they were going out, behold, a dumb man, demon-possessed, was brought to Him. [33] And after the demon was cast out, the dumb man spoke; and the multitudes marveled, saying, 'Nothing like this was ever seen in Israel.' [34] But the Pharisees were saying, 'He casts out the demons by the ruler of the demons.'

[35] And Jesus was going about all the cities and the villages, teaching in their synagogues, and proclaiming the gospel of the kingdom, and healing every kind of disease and every kind of sickness. [36] And seeing the multitudes, He felt compassion for them, because they were distressed and downcast like sheep without a shepherd. [37] Then He *said to His disciples, 'The harvest is plentiful, but the workers are few. [38] Therefore beseech the Lord of the harvest to send out workers into His harvest.'"

Introduction

This is an awesome section in which we see the miracles of Christ and His compassionate heart. We will also see the importance of our call to prayer and our service to the Lord, as He is the Lord of the Harvest!

VERSES 18-19: *"While He was saying these things to them, behold, there came a synagogue official, and bowed down before Him, saying, 'My daughter has just died; but come and lay Your hand on her, and she will live.' [19] And Jesus rose and began to follow him, and so did His disciples."*

Here we see a religious leader (i.e. *"synagogue official"*) who believes in the power of Jesus. His daughter has died and he is in such desperate need that he is unconcerned about how he looks to others or the Pharisees.

In other Gospels we are provided more background regarding this story. For example, in Luke we find out that this synagogue official's daughter was twelve years old (Luke 8:42). In Mark 5:22 we learn that the name of this synagogue official was Jairus (see also Luke 8:41). Mark also explains that shortly before Jairus found out that his daughter had died, Jairus had gone up to Jesus *"...and on seeing Him, fell at His feet* [23]*and implored Him earnestly, saying, 'My little daughter is at the point of death; please come and lay Your hands on her, so that she will get well and live.'"* **Mark 5:22-23**. Jairus is later told by someone who came from his house not to bother Jesus anymore since the girl is no longer sick but had died (Mark 5:35, Luke 8:49). Luke tells us that *"...when Jesus heard this, He answered him, 'Do not be afraid any longer; only believe, and she will be made well.'"* **Luke 8:50**. It is around this point in time that Matthew begins the story with Jairus' bowing down again before Jesus and *"saying, 'My daughter has just died; but come and lay Your hand on her, and she will live.'"* **Matthew 9:18**. Jesus responds by following Jairus to his home.

VERSES 20-22: *"And behold, a woman who had been suffering from a hemorrhage for twelve years, came up behind Him and touched the fringe of His cloak;* [21] *for she was saying to herself, 'If I only touch His garment, I shall get well.'* [22] *But Jesus turning and seeing her said, 'Daughter, take courage; your faith has made you well.' And at once the woman was made well."*

On the way to Jairus' house, we read in Mark 5:24 that *"...a great multitude was following Him and pressing in on Him."* From within that crowd, Jesus is sought by a woman who also has a desperate need: she had suffered from a *"hemorrhage for twelve years"* (Mark 5:25) and had spent all she had on doctors who not only did not help, but made her condition worse (Mark 5:26). Like Jairus, she too believes that Jesus has the power to heal her. Notice that the physician, Luke, gives us more detail of this encounter (Luke 8:43-48).

VERSES 23-26: *"And when Jesus came into the official's house, and saw the flute-players, and the crowd in noisy disorder,* [24] *He began to say, 'Depart; for the girl has not died, but is asleep.' And they began laughing at Him.* [25] *But when the crowd had been put out, He entered and took her by the hand; and the girl arose.* [26] *And this news went out into all that land."*

During this time period, one way to express grief was to hire flute players and professional mourners who make loud cries and sounds of devastation. The hypocrisy of these professional mourners is shown by how their cries quickly turn to laughing as Jesus tells them that the girl is not dead. He then commands them to leave the room.

Jesus says that the girl is *asleep* (i.e. that is her physical body was dead until Jesus resurrected it). At various places in the Bible, the term sleep is used in reference to the death of the physical body (e.g. see 1 Corinthians 15:51-57, 1 Corinthians 11:30). An example of this use of the term sleep is in the story of Lazarus as set forth in **John 11:11-15**:
> *"This He said, and after that He* *said to them, 'Our friend Lazarus has fallen asleep; but I go, that I may awaken him out of sleep.'* [12] *The disciples therefore said to Him, 'Lord, if he has fallen asleep, he will recover.'* [13] *Now Jesus had spoken of his death, but they thought that He was speaking of literal sleep.* [14] *Then Jesus therefore said to them plainly, 'Lazarus is dead,* [15] *and I am glad for your sakes that I was not there, so that you may believe; but let us go to him.'"*

This resurrection of Jairus' daughter (as well as others) further proves that Jesus is the Messiah. As Jesus said in **Revelation 1:17-18:**

> *"Do not be afraid; I am the first and the last,* ¹⁸ *and the living One; and I was dead, and behold, I am alive forevermore, and I have the keys of death and of Hades."*

It should be remembered that even though we see Jesus at weddings, dinners, etc., *we never see Him conduct a funeral.* We do read of Jesus being in contact with a funeral procession. The result of that contact was resurrection.

> **Luke 7:11-17:** *"Soon afterwards He went to a city called Nain; and His disciples were going along with Him, accompanied by a large crowd.* ¹²*Now as He approached the gate of the city, a dead man was being carried out, the only son of his mother, and she was a widow; and a sizeable crowd from the city was with her.* ¹³*When the Lord saw her, He felt compassion for her, and said to her, 'Do not weep.'* ¹⁴*And He came up and touched the coffin; and the bearers came to a halt. And He said, 'Young man, I say to you, arise!'* ¹⁵*The dead man sat up and began to speak. And Jesus gave him back to his mother.* ¹⁶*Fear gripped them all, and they began glorifying God, saying, 'A great prophet has arisen among us!' and, 'God has visited His people!'* ¹⁷*This report concerning Him went out all over Judea and in all the surrounding district."*

Never forget that Jesus is the resurrection and the life!

> **John 11:25-26:** *"Jesus said to her, "I am the resurrection and the life; he who believes in Me shall live even if he dies,* ²⁶ *and everyone who lives and believes in Me shall never die...."*

VERSES 27-31: *"And as Jesus passed on from there, two blind men followed Him, crying out, and saying, 'Have mercy on us, Son of David!'* ²⁸ *And after He had come into the house, the blind men came up to Him, and Jesus *said to them, 'Do you believe that I am able to do this?' They *said to Him, 'Yes, Lord.'* ²⁹ *Then He touched their eyes, saying, 'Be it done to you according to your faith.'* ³⁰ *And their eyes were opened. And Jesus sternly warned them, saying, 'See here, let no one know about this!'* ³¹ *But they went out, and spread the news about Him in all that land."*

Like Jairus and the woman with the bleeding, the blind men had a desperate need. They likewise believed that only Jesus could meet their need. Their desperate need is shown by their *"crying out, and saying, 'Have mercy on us....'"* Their faith is shown by their cry to Jesus as the, *"Son of David."* Declaring Him to be the *Son of David* was not a mere nice gesture of respect. By using that title, they were declaring that they believed that Jesus was the Messiah! These men surely knew what the prophet Isaiah said:

> *"For a child will be born to us, a son will be given to us;*
> *And the government will rest on His shoulders;*
> *And His name will be called Wonderful Counselor, Mighty God,*
> *Eternal Father, Prince of Peace.*
> ⁷ *There will be no end to the increase of His government or of peace,*
> *On the throne of David and over his kingdom,*
> *To establish it and to uphold it with justice and righteousness*
> *From then on and forevermore.*
> *The zeal of the LORD of hosts will accomplish this."*
> **Isaiah 9:6-7** (cf. Matthew 1:1)

Notice their appeal to God was not based on anything they had done to deserve His help. They made no claim as to why they were worthy of Him healing their eyes. Their plea is one crying out for *"mercy."* This is the only way one can approach the Perfect and Holy God. <u>**Titus 3:5**</u> says: *"He saved us, not on the basis of deeds which we have done in righteousness, but according to <u>His mercy,....</u>"*

After Jesus heals them, He tells them to not tell others about this. Specifically in verses 30-31, it says *"And Jesus sternly warned them, saying, 'See here, let no one know about this!' ³¹ But they went out, and spread the news about Him in all that land."* Jesus' command was not due to some desire to keep His miracle-working power a secret from others. He did many public miracles and had already become very famous for them. He was making reference to the men calling Him the, *"Son of David."* He did not want His true identity as Messiah proclaimed prematurely. (See Matthew 11:2-5, this healing of the blind is an attribute of the Messiah described in prophecy; see also Isaiah 35:5).

<u>**VERSES 32-34:**</u> *"And as they were going out, behold, a dumb man, demon-possessed, was brought to Him. ³³ And after the demon was cast out, the dumb man spoke; and the multitudes marveled, saying, 'Nothing like this was ever seen in Israel.' ³⁴ But the Pharisees were saying, 'He casts out the demons by the ruler of the demons.'"*

The King James version rendering of this verse translates it with a more specific reference. That specific reference indicates that the two blind men who were healed were the ones who brought the dumb/demon-possessed man to Jesus. The King James states in verse 32: *"As they went out, behold, <u>they brought</u> to him a dumb man possessed with a devil."* Despite the blind men's disobedience in telling others, they did do what real believers do: bring others to Jesus.

The term describing the man as *"dumb"* means that he could not talk. Jesus cast out the demon from that man and healed him so he could talk. This miracle of giving *speech* to the *dumb* is another fulfilled prophecy proving Jesus is the Messiah.
> <u>**Isaiah 35:5-6:**</u> *"Then the eyes of the blind will be opened,*
> *And the ears of the deaf will be unstopped.*
> *⁶Then the lame will leap like a deer,*
> <u>*And the tongue of the dumb will shout for joy.*</u>
> *For waters will break forth in the wilderness*
> *And streams in the Arabah."*

In Matthew 9:33 we see the reaction of the crowd to the healing of the man: *"And after the demon was cast out, the dumb man spoke; and the multitudes marveled, saying, 'Nothing like this was ever seen in Israel.'"* In verse 34, we see the response of the false religious leaders: *"But the Pharisees were saying, 'He casts out the demons by the ruler of the demons.'"* Notice the two different responses to the miracles of Jesus. The people were amazed and said, *"Nothing like this was ever seen in Israel."* (v.33). But the Pharisees, who hated Jesus, immediately denounced it. They were in great fear of losing their power over the people. They despised the fact that Jesus' following was increasing and that the people viewed Him, *"as one having authority, and not as their scribes."* <u>**Matthew 7:29**</u>. The Pharisees could not have cared less that a man bound and oppressed was set free; they cared about their political power and authority. Since they could not deny the awesome miracles of Jesus, they spoke the most evil, blasphemous lie they could. The godless Pharisees claimed that Jesus' power was really from the Devil. The Bible refers to this sin as blasphemy of the Holy Spirit (for more on that subject see the section for Matthew 12:30-32).

The true Christian must recognize that slander will come his way. As one commentator said: "Let it never surprise true Christians if they are slandered and misrepresented in this world. They must not expect to fare better than their Lord. Let them rather look forward to it, as a matter of course, and see in it a part of the cross which everyone must bear after conversion. Lies and false reports are among Satan's choicest weapons. When he cannot deter people from serving Christ, he labors to harass them and make Christ's service uncomfortable. Let us bear it patiently, and not count it a strange thing. The words of the Lord Jesus should often come to our minds: "Woe to you when all men speak well of you" (Luke 6:26). "Blessed are you when people insult you, persecute you and falsely say all kind of evil against you because of me" (Matthew 5:11)."[153]

How is the Christian to respond to slander? Jesus tells his followers to, *"love your enemies, and pray for those who persecute you...."* **Matthew 5:44.**

VERSES 35-38: *"And Jesus was going about all the cities and the villages, teaching in their synagogues, and proclaiming the gospel of the kingdom, and healing every kind of disease and every kind of sickness. [36] And seeing the multitudes, He felt compassion for them, because they were distressed and downcast like sheep without a shepherd. [37] Then He *said to His disciples, 'The harvest is plentiful, but the workers are few. [38] Therefore beseech the Lord of the harvest to send out workers into His harvest.'"*

The Scriptures tell us that Jesus taught in the *"synagogues."* The Babylonian exile began in 586 BC. Before the exile, Jewish worship was at the Jerusalem Temple. During the exile, they did not have access to the temple so they formed synagogues. The term *synagogue* means a, "place of assembly." If there were at least 10 Jewish men who lived in an area, they could form a synagogue.

In verse 1 we read that Jesus preached the *"gospel of the kingdom."* The term "gospel" means good news. Jesus proclaimed the new covenant in **Matthew 26:28** which says, *"for this is My blood of the covenant, which is poured out for many for forgiveness of sins."*

Notice also in verse 1 that Jesus had *compassion* for the people because they *"were distressed and downcast like sheep without a shepherd."* **Matthew 9:36.** Look who they had for supposed spiritual shepherds (i.e. the Pharisees and Scribes who hated Jesus). They were not merely ineffective shepherds, but Jesus clearly called them sons of the devil (John 8:44). Jesus describes them as hypocrites who prevent others from entering the kingdom of God in **Matthew 23:13:**
> "But woe to you, scribes and Pharisees, hypocrites, *because you shut off the kingdom of heaven from men; for you do not enter in yourselves, nor do you allow those who are entering to go in.*"

Jeremiah prophesied about the false shepherds, and Jesus coming and shepherding His own flock about 600 years before it happened in **Jeremiah 23:1-6:**
> "WOE *to the shepherds who are destroying and scattering the sheep of My pasture!' declares the* LORD. [2] *Therefore thus says the* LORD *God of Israel concerning the shepherds who are tending My people: 'You have scattered My flock and driven them*

---

[153] Ryle, J. C. (1993). *Mark.* Crossway Classic Commentaries (p. 242). Wheaton, IL: Crossway Books.

away, and have not attended to them; behold, I am about to attend to you for the evil of your deeds,' declares the LORD. ³ 'Then I Myself shall gather the remnant of My flock out of all the countries where I have driven them and shall bring them back to their pasture; and they will be fruitful and multiply. ⁴ I shall also raise up shepherds over them and they will tend them; and they will not be afraid any longer, nor be terrified, nor will any be missing,' declares the LORD.

⁵ *'Behold, the days are coming,' declares the LORD, When I shall raise up for David a righteous Branch;*
And He will reign as king and act wisely
And do justice and righteousness in the land.

⁶ *In His days Judah will be saved, And Israel will dwell securely; And this is His name by which He will be called, 'The LORD our righteousness.'''*

In verse 37 of the main text Jesus said to His disciples, *"The harvest is plentiful, but the workers are few. ³⁸ Therefore beseech the Lord of the harvest to send out workers into His harvest."* Almighty God is the Lord of the harvest. The harvest represents a time of final judgment. We see this analogy in **Matthew 13:36-43:**

"Then He left the multitudes, and went into the house. And His disciples came to Him, saying, 'Explain to us the parable of the tares of the field.' ³⁷ And He answered and said, 'The one who sows the good seed is the Son of Man, ³⁸ and the field is the world; and as for the good seed, these are the sons of the kingdom; and the tares are the sons of the evil one; ³⁹ and the enemy who sowed them is the devil, and the harvest is the end of the age; and the reapers are angels. ⁴⁰ Therefore just as the tares are gathered up and burned with fire, so shall it be at the end of the age. ⁴¹ The Son of Man will send forth His angels , and they will gather out of His kingdom all stumbling blocks , and those who commit lawlessness, ⁴² and will cast them into the furnace of fire; in that place there shall be weeping and gnashing of teeth . ⁴³ 'Then THE RIGHTEOUS WILL SHINE FORTH AS THE SUN' in the kingdom of their Father. He who has ears, let him hear .'" (See also Revelation 14:15-16.)*

It is our job to work the field until that Day of Judgment. Our first response is to not just get out to the field and get busy. We are to start in prayer. Verse 38 says we are to seek the Lord to send more workers: *"Therefore beseech the Lord of the harvest to send out workers into His harvest."* We need to be humble servants in the field. There are no superstars in the work. Everyone has a part and every effort starts with prayer for the Lord's blessing. Charles Spurgeon writes of the importance of prayer as the power in our labor:

"When our work is most promising this blight appears. We hoped for many conversions, and lo! a general apathy, an abounding worldliness, or a cruel hardness of heart! There may be no open sin in those for whom we are laboring, but there is a deficiency of sincerity and decision sadly disappointing our desires. We learn from this our dependence upon the Lord, and the need of prayer that no blight may fall upon our work." [154]

We are to do the reaping in the field. This job of ours is to not be confused with the reaping the angels will do at the end of the age in Matthew 13:36-43. Reaping is the cutting and gathering of ripened crops that have grown in the field. We work alongside other brothers and sisters who have already

---

[154] Spurgeon, C. H. *Morning and Evening: Daily Readings* (1995) (August 4 PM). Oak Harbor, WA: Logos Research Systems, Inc.

been laboring in the field. We may even be picking up where their labor ended. The point is that we work together for the joy and glory of our Lord. Look at **John 4:35-38:**

> *"Do you not say, 'There are yet four months, and then comes the harvest'? Behold, I say to you, lift up your eyes, and look on the fields, that they are white for harvest. *[36]* Already he who reaps is receiving wages, and is gathering fruit for life eternal; that he who sows and he who reaps may rejoice together. *[37]* For in this case the saying is true, 'One sows, and another reaps.' *[38]* I sent you to reap that for which you have not labored; others have labored, and you have entered into their labor."*

Notice the verse: *"Do you not say, 'There are yet four months, and then comes the harvest'? Behold, I say to you, lift up your eyes, and look on the fields, that they are white for harvest."* **John 4:35**. This verse tells us that we are not to take a view that the Great Commission is a job we can get to later (i.e. don't say, "I think we can be a witness later down the road and not right now."). We need to recognize that right now is the time to work the field. *"We must work the works of Him who sent Me as long as it is day; night is coming when no one can work."* **John 9:4**

What does it mean to work in His field? We are to proclaim His Gospel of salvation, pray for the sick, minister to the needs of others and warn all of the judgment to come for those who reject Christ's salvation and forgiveness. These concepts are set forth in **Luke 10:1-3, 8-12, and 16:**

> *"Now after this the Lord appointed seventy others, and sent them two and two ahead of Him to every city and place where He Himself was going to come. *[2]* And He was saying to them, 'The harvest is plentiful, but the laborers are few; therefore beseech the Lord of the harvest to send out laborers into His harvest. *[3]* Go your ways; behold, I send you out as lambs in the midst of wolves....*
> *[8]* And whatever city you enter , and they receive you, eat what is set before you; *[9]* and heal those in it who are sick , and say to them, 'The kingdom of God has come near to you.' *[10]* But whatever city you enter and they do not receive you, go out into its streets and say, *[11]* 'Even the dust of your city which clings to our feet, we wipe off in protest against you; yet be sure of this, that the kingdom of God has come near .' *[12]* I say to you, it will be more tolerable in that day for Sodom, than for that city....*
> *[16]* The one who listens to you listens to Me, and the one who rejects you rejects Me; and he who rejects Me rejects the One who sent Me.'"*

The results of our work are left with God. Often Christians are discouraged because they do not see positive results in the people to whom they have ministered. One of the biggest mistakes we can make is to determine our success and failure based on the response of the people we are serving. We often want to see the final result, but for there to be a final result, there had to be a seed planted long before. Maybe your work will be on the front side of the labor. You may be the first person to share the gospel with a particular person. Do not view your labor as a complete failure when that person's response is one of utter disinterest. You need to realize that you are just doing your job in the field for that person. We are to teach and minister, but we need to remember that we are not responsible for a person's spiritual growth. Spiritual growth is the work of God. Only He can open their eyes to the truth. Paul stated this in **1 Corinthians 3:6-9:**

> *"I planted, Apollos watered, but God was causing the growth. *[7]* So then neither the one who plants nor the one who waters is anything, but God who causes the growth. *[8]* Now he who plants and he who waters are one; but each will receive his own reward according to his own labor. *[9]* For we are God's fellow workers; you are God's field, God's building."*

Summary and Application

Jesus did not heal just some of the diseases people had, but Scripture says He went about, *"healing every kind of disease and every kind of sickness."* What a compassionate and loving God we have.

How fortunate we are to work in His field. Have you sought the Lord of the Harvest to send out workers? Are you ready to respond when He calls you? The reality is that, as a Christian, you have already been called to work in the field by Him (see Matthew 28:19-20). Pray for His Holy Spirit to empower you and carry out the work of God.

MATTHEW 10:1-4
(SUMMONING THE TWELVE DISCIPLES and ONE IS AN APOSTATE)

VERSES 1-4: *"AND having summoned His twelve disciples, He gave them authority over unclean spirits, to cast them out, and to heal every kind of disease and every kind of sickness. ² Now the names of the twelve apostles are these: The first, Simon, who is called Peter, and Andrew his brother; and James the son of Zebedee, and John his brother; ³ Philip and Bartholomew; Thomas and Matthew the tax-gatherer; James the son of Alphaeus, and Thaddaeus; ⁴ Simon the Zealot, and Judas Iscariot, the one who betrayed Him."*

Introduction

In this section of Scripture, we examine who the 12 apostles were. We will see that they were empowered to do ministry. Often people wonder what happened to Judas. They wonder how he went bad. Scripture tells us that Judas was not a good guy who went bad, but that Judas was never a man of God.

VERSE 1: *"AND having summoned His twelve disciples, He gave them authority over unclean spirits, to cast them out, and to heal every kind of disease and every kind of sickness."*

The term *disciple* means *learner* (i.e. the pupil of a teacher). [155] It is not until later in the book of Acts the term disciple is synonymous with a *believer* in Jesus Christ. Note in verse 1 that Jesus sent them out under His power to multiply the work of casting out unclean spirits and, *"to heal every kind of disease and every kind of sickness."* We read in **Acts 5:12:** *"And at the hands of the apostles many signs and wonders were taking place among the people; ...."*

VERSES 2-4: *"Now the names of the twelve apostles are these: The first, Simon, who is called Peter, and Andrew his brother; and James the son of Zebedee, and John his brother; ³ Philip and Bartholomew; Thomas and Matthew the tax-gatherer; James the son of Alphaeus, and Thaddaeus; ⁴ Simon the Zealot, and Judas Iscariot, the one who betrayed Him."*

Verses 2-4 set out the names of the *disciples* summoned by Jesus. In verse 2, we notice that instead of being called the *"twelve disciples"* they are called the *"twelve apostles."* The term *apostle* means "a person sent."[156]

Who are these men? The four New Testament lists of the apostles are in Matthew 10:2-4, Mark 3:16-19, Luke 6:14-16 and Acts 1:13 cf. v.26. Peter is named first in all the lists, not because he was chosen first, but because he was the leader. John MacArthur makes an important observation regarding the list of the disciples:

---

[155] *The New Bible Dictionary*, (Wheaton, Illinois: Tyndale House Publishers, Inc.) 1962.

[156] Ibid

"The four lists of the apostles are divided into the same three subgroups. The first group includes Peter, Andrew, James, and John; the second includes Philip, Bartholomew, Thomas, and Matthew; and the third includes James the son of Alphaeus, Thaddaeus, Simon the Zealot, and Judas Iscariot. The names are in different orders within the groups, but they always include the same four names, and the first name in each group is always the same, suggesting that each group had its own identity and leader. The first group includes those Jesus called first (though not in the individual order), the second includes those He called next, and the third group those He called last.

We know a great deal about the men in the first group, much less about those in the second, and almost nothing about those in the third—except for Judas, who betrayed Jesus, committed suicide, and was replaced by Matthias just before Pentecost (Acts 1:26). There is not only a decreasing amount of information about the members of each group but also a decreasing intimacy with Jesus. The first four constituted Jesus' inner circle of disciples; and of those four, Peter, James, and John were especially close to Him. Little is said about His direct instruction or work with the second group, and almost nothing about close contact with the third. He loved all the apostles equally, empowered them equally, and promised them equal glory;...." [157]

Note that the first group is composed of two sets of brothers, all of whom were fishermen. One set of brothers was Peter and Andrew, and the second set was James and John. Andrew was a follower of John the Baptist before he followed Christ. When John the Baptist said, "behold the Lamb of God" he left John to follow Jesus (John 1:36-37). Peter finds out about Jesus through his brother. Andrew went and told Peter that he found the Messiah (John 1:41). Soon thereafter, they both returned to their fishing business and Jesus called them and said, *"Follow Me, and I will make you fishers of men."* **Matthew 4:19**. Andrew is the one who tells Jesus that a boy has five barley loaves and two fish at the feeding of the five thousand (John 6:5-14).

The other set of brothers was James and John. They are pictured as passionate, zealous men. At times they exhibited zeal without sound knowledge (Romans 10:2), such as when the Samaritans did not accommodate Jesus, and they asked Him, *"Lord, do You want us to command fire to come down from heaven and consume them?"* **Luke 9:54**. It was James' and John's mother who asked Jesus if her boys could have thrones on His left and His right (Matthew 20:21-22). James (who, by the way, was not the writer of the Book of James), must have been one of the most influential, if not most influential, disciple at the infancy of the Church, because Herod went after James to have him killed. After Herod killed James he realized it made the non-Christians happy, so he then went after Peter as set forth in **Acts 12:1-3:**

> *"Now about that time Herod the king laid hands on some who belonged to the church, in order to mistreat them.* [2] *And he had James the brother of John put to death with a sword.* [3] *And when he saw that it pleased the Jews, he proceeded to arrest Peter also...."*

John (who was the writer of the *Gospel of John, The Epistles of John 1,2,and3* and the book of *Revelation*), died exiled on the island of Patmos. While Jesus was dying on the cross, He put John in charge of the care of His mother, Mary (John 19:26-27).

---

[157] MacArthur, J. F., Jr. (1985). *Matthew.* MacArthur New Testament Commentary (p. 111). Chicago: Moody Press.

Walvoord and Zuck provide an outline of the other disciples:

> "*Philip*, like Andrew and Peter, was from Bethsaida by the Sea of Galilee (John 1:44). Nothing is known about *Bartholomew*, except that he was possibly known as Nathanael (John 1:45-51). *Thomas* was called 'Didymus' (twin) in John 11:16; he was one who questioned Jesus' resurrection (John 20:24-27). *Matthew* referred to himself by his former dubious occupation of tax collecting (whereas Mark and Luke simply listed him as Matthew). *James, son of Alphaeus,* is mentioned only in the lists of apostles; *Thaddaeus* may be the same as Judas, son of James (Luke 6:16; Acts 1:13). *Simon the Zealot* had been a member of the revolutionary Jewish Zealots, a political party that sought to overthrow the Roman Empire."[158]

The opposite end of the spectrum was Judas. We do not know where or how he was called since it is not recorded in the Gospels. Judas was neither a good guy who went bad, nor was he some disappointment to Jesus. The Lord knew Judas was a devil, and knew from the beginning that Judas would betray Him:

> **John 6:64:** "'*But there are some of you who do not believe.' For Jesus knew from the beginning who they were who did not believe, and who it was that would betray Him.*"

> **John 6:70-71:** "*Jesus answered them, 'Did I Myself not choose you, the twelve, and yet one of you is a devil?'* [71] *Now He meant Judas the son of Simon Iscariot, for he, one of the twelve, was going to betray Him.*"

Jesus set forth that Judas' destiny was damnation in calling him the *"son of perdition"*:

> **John 17:12:** "*... and I guarded them and not one of them perished but the son of perdition, so that the Scripture would be fulfilled.*"

"Perdition" is defined as: a "sense of 'destruction' and with special reference to the fate of the wicked and their loss of eternal life...."[159]

Judas is the classic *apostate*. An *apostate* is one who knows the plan of salvation but never comes to a saving knowledge of it, and thus rejects it. For a time the apostate may look, talk and even claim to be a Christian, but he was never truly converted. Look at the definition of an apostate in Hebrews 10:26-27. There we see that the apostate is one who goes on sinning by living in unbelief of Jesus' sacrifice for sins. The difference between an apostate and a disobedient/carnal/fleshly Christian becomes obvious over time. The apostate never repents and returns to the faith. The carnal/fleshly Christian (1 Corinthians 3:1-3) will know in his heart that the life he is living *grieves* the Holy Spirit (Ephesians 4:30-32). Eventually the carnal/fleshly will be convicted with godly sorrow and repent (2 Corinthians 7:9-11), or they may be taken by death (*sin unto* death—1 John 5:16-17; some *sleep,* i.e. died, such as from partaking in the Lord's Supper in an unworthy manner, 1 Corinthians 11:29-34.)

The apostate may look somewhat similar to a fleshly Christian, but he is very different. The Puritan Timothy Cruso said: "*Apostasy is a perversion to evil after a seeming conversion from it.*" [160] An apostate

---

[158] Walvoord, J. F., Zuck, R. B., and Dallas Theological Seminary, *The Bible knowledge commentary: An Exposition of the Scriptures* (Mt. 10:1) Wheaton, IL: Victor Books (1983-c1985).

[159] Wood, D. R. W., and Marshall, I. H. (1996). *New Bible Dictionary* (3rd ed.) (p. 900). Leicester, England; Downers Grove, Ill.: InterVarsity Press.

will eventually openly disown Jesus after having learned the way of salvation. In other words, the Apostate will have made claims to have believed at one time but he will eventually reject Christ and His church.

There are many who claim that at one time they were Christians but now deny and denounce Christ. We should not be shocked or surprised. Judas was specifically chosen to serve as an example of the false brethren among the true. Matthew Henry states the following about Judas:

> "Christ knew what a wretch he [Judas] was, that he had a devil, and would prove a traitor; yet Christ took him among the apostles, that it might not be a surprise and discouragement to his church, if, at any time, the vilest scandals should break out...." [161]

As we study some of the parables of Jesus, we will see a recurring theme of the false masquerading among the true believers. We often ignore the warnings of Scripture about keeping an eye out for false brothers, apostles and prophets who will rise up to scatter the church. Time has a way of exposing the true believers from the look-alikes. The parable of the *"wheat and the tares"* is about false Christians (weeds/tares) who, for a while, look like real Christians (wheat), but over time it is shown that they were weeds from the beginning (Matthew 13:24-43). John explained this by pointing out the perseverance of the truly converted in **1 John 2:19**:

> *"They went out from us, but they were not really of us; for if they had been of us, they would have remained with us; but they went out, in order that it might be shown that they all are not of us."*

Look at the tricky hypocrite Judas was. He made himself look honest enough to be the treasurer for the disciples (**John 13:29** — *"Judas had the money box,...."*). True to his hypocrisy, Judas used his position as treasurer to steal from the group:

> **John 12:4-6:** *"But Judas Iscariot, one of His disciples, who was intending to betray Him, *said,* [5] *'Why was this perfume not sold for three hundred denarii, and given to poor people?'* [6] *Now he said this, not because he was concerned about the poor, but because he was a thief, and as he had the money box, he used to pilfer what was put into it."*

He was a very crafty hypocrite. Even though the disciples had been around Judas for about three years, they still did not identify him as the one who would betray Jesus. When Jesus told the disciples that one of them would betray Him, we do not read of all the disciples turning and looking at Judas. They clearly did not know who it was and began asking Jesus if it was themselves:

> **Matthew 26:20-22:** *"Now when evening had come, He was reclining at the table with the twelve disciples.* [21] *And as they were eating, He said, 'Truly I say to you that one of you will betray Me.'* [22] *And being deeply grieved, they each one began to say to Him, 'Surely not I, Lord?'"*

The disciples never had recognized Judas as the bad guy of the group until they were in the garden of Gethsemane (Matthew 26:47-52; Mark 14:32).

---

[160] I.D.E. Thomas, *The Golden Treasury of Puritan Quotations*, (Simpsonville, SC: Christian Classics Foundation) 1997.

[161] Henry, M. (1996, c1991). *Matthew Henry's Commentary on the Whole Bible: Complete and unabridged in One Volume* (Matthew 10:1). Peabody: Hendrickson.

Early on in Judas' association with Jesus it can be speculated that Judas was concerned about potential power, glory and money for himself. He saw Jesus clearly had incredible power and was becoming very popular. Like many political opportunists, Judas could see that his early attachment to Jesus could mean great things for himself later when Jesus became the King of Israel. Judas had no interest in being saved and regenerated by Christ.

Judas was like a businessman or politician who panders to you by discussing Christianity. He does not have the slightest sincere interest in the faith but is willing to talk *religion* in an attempt to charm you into a sale or something else. Judas was willing to put up with the spiritual talk of Jesus for three years because he thought it would be worth it for him politically/financially at the end. As mentioned above, time has a way of exposing the apostate.[162] After three years Judas could see that Jesus was not going to rid Israel of Roman control right then. With Rome still in control, he could assume that Jesus would not end up being king either. Judas obviously heard the talk on the street that Jesus' great popularity was waning and the religious leaders disdain for Him was becoming more public. Judas had invested three years into following Jesus and it was becoming clear that he was not going to get much out of it. It was time to figure out a way to cut his losses. He figured out a way to at least get some money out of this deal:

> **Matthew 26:14-16:** *"Then one of the twelve, named Judas Iscariot, went to the chief priests, ¹⁵ and said, 'What are you willing to give me to deliver Him up to you?' And they weighed out to him thirty pieces of silver. ¹⁶ And from then on he began looking for a good opportunity to betray Him."*

Judas' mocking contempt for Christ was fully shown when Judas chose to use a kiss as the betrayal sign.

> **Mark 14:44-45:** *"Now he who was betraying Him had given them a signal, saying, 'Whomever I shall kiss, He is the one; seize Him, and lead Him away under guard.' ⁴⁵And after coming, he immediately went to Him, saying, 'Rabbi!' and kissed Him."*

---

[162] Here is a general outline of Scriptures dealing with the subject of the false among the true:

Paul speaks of dangers among false brethren-2 Corinthians 11:26-28; Even Satan comes as an angel of light 2 Corinthians 11:13-15; They profess to know God but by their deeds they deny Him-Titus 1:16; Tares among the wheat-Matthew 13:24-30, 36-43; Sower/Seed-Matthew 13:1-23; False brethren went the way of Cain and Balaam, they are clouds without rain and wandering stars-Jude 1:11-19; Wolves will rise up from the flock-Acts 20:28-31; If one advocates a different doctrine then that of the Lord Jesus and conforming to godliness, he is false teacher-1 Timothy 6:3-5; Some peddling the word-2 Corinthians 2:17; False prophets inflate fleshly visions, worshiping angels-Colossians 2:18; They went out from us, but they were not really of us, for if they had been of us, they would have remained with us-1 John 2:19; Imposter...deceiving and being deceived-2 Timothy 3:13; False teachers teach for sordid gain-Titus 1:11; False prophets and teachers will secretly introduce destructive heresies-2 Peter 2:1-22; Do not greet one who comes to you with a false gospel otherwise you participate in his evil-2 John1:10-11; Ephesus church put to the test the false apostles-Revelation 2:2; Some preach out of selfish ambition-Philippians: 1:15-18; Some will fall from the faith; listening to doctrines of demons-1 Timothy 4:1-3; Let no one take you captive via philosophy, deception, elementary principles of the world-Colossians 2:8; Instruct not to teach strange doctrines-1 Timothy 1:3; They desire to be teachers of the law and make confident assertions about things they don't understand-1 Timothy 1:6-7; Avoid worldly and empty chatter and opposing argument falsely called knowledge-1 Timothy 6:20; Test false prophets-Deuteronomy 13; False brethren spy out our liberty-Galatians 2:4; Do not be carried by every wind of doctrine, trickery of man-Ephesians 4:14.

Scripture tells us in **James 1:15** *"…when sin is accomplished, it brings forth death."* Judas was no exception to this verse. He had remorse for what he did, but not godly repentance.

> **Matthew 27:5:** *"And he threw the pieces of silver into the sanctuary and departed; and he went away and hanged himself."*

As one writer put it, Judas *"…lives on the stage of Scripture as an awful warning to the uncommitted follower of Jesus who is in His company but does not share His Spirit (cf. Romans 8:9b)."* [163]

Summary and Application

There are two applications I want us to look at:

1. It is frightening to see someone like Judas who can walk, talk, and act the disciple's life but never be a Christian. Check your heart. You may have a lot of knowledge about Jesus, but in your heart do you think Jesus is a joke or just some great prophet or moral example? If so, you are just another Judas. If instead you trust completely in Jesus and His death on the cross as your only basis of forgiveness before God, you are His child.

   > **1 John 5:13:** *"These things I have written to you who believe in the name of the Son of God, in order that you may know that you have eternal life."*

2. If you look at the list of the true disciples, you do not see a group of talented, wealthy or brilliant individuals. Just as with many great men of God from the Old Testament, we find God uses those who would *not* be eminently qualified by earthly standards. **1 Corinthians 1:26–29:**

   > *"For consider your calling, brethren, that there were not many wise according to the flesh, not many mighty, not many noble;* [27] *but God has chosen the foolish things of the world to shame the wise, and God has chosen the weak things of the world to shame the things which are strong,* [28] *and the base things of the world and the despised God has chosen, the things that are not, so that He may nullify the things that are,* [29] *so that no man may boast before God."*

   When we see our weakness and lack of skill, we should never think that God cannot use us. On the contrary, you are the person He will use! Notice what God said to Paul in **2 Corinthians 12:9**: *"And He has said to me, 'My grace is sufficient for you, for power is perfected in weakness….'"* Look at Paul's response in the next sentences of **2 Corinthians 12:9-10**:

   > *"…Most gladly, therefore, I will rather boast about my weaknesses, that the power of Christ may dwell in me.* [10] *Therefore I am well content with weaknesses, with insults, with distresses, with persecutions, with difficulties, for Christ's sake; for when I am weak, then I am strong."*

---

[163] Wood, D. R. W., and Marshall, I. H. (1996). *New Bible dictionary (3rd ed.)* (p. 626). Leicester, England; Downers Grove, IL: InterVarsity Press.

MATTHEW 10:5-15
(THE MINISTRY OF THE MISSIONARY)

"These twelve Jesus sent out after instructing them, saying, 'Do not go in the way of the Gentiles, and do not enter any city of the Samaritans; ⁶ but rather go to the lost sheep of the house of Israel. ⁷And as you go, preach, saying, The kingdom of heaven is at hand.' ⁸ Heal the sick, raise the dead, cleanse the lepers, cast out demons; freely you received, freely give. ⁹ Do not acquire gold, or silver, or copper for your money belts, ¹⁰ or a bag for your journey, or even two tunics, or sandals, or a staff; for the worker is worthy of his support. ¹¹ And into whatever city or village you enter, inquire who is worthy in it; and abide there until you go away. ¹² And as you enter the house, give it your greeting. ¹³ And if the house is worthy, let your greeting of peace come upon it; but if it is not worthy, let your greeting of peace return to you. ¹⁴ And whoever does not receive you, nor heed your words, as you go out of that house or that city, shake off the dust of your feet. ¹⁵Truly I say to you, it will be more tolerable for the land of Sodom and Gomorrah in the day of judgment, than for that city."

Introduction

Here Jesus teaches the 12 disciples how to minister. A fundamental attribute of a faithful servant is the giving to others without any pretextual motive of accumulating for one's self. The true servant walks in faith knowing that God will provide for all his needs.

VERSES 5-6: *"These twelve Jesus sent out after instructing them, saying, 'Do not go in the way of the Gentiles, and do not enter any city of the Samaritans; ⁶ but rather go to the lost sheep of the house of Israel.'"*

Jesus is the Savior and promised Messiah. It must be remembered that the Jews are God's chosen people (Romans 11:1). It is through the Jews that the Messiah came (Romans 9:5). Jesus Himself said, *"...salvation is from the Jews"* (John 4:22). Some people do not understand why God chose Israel to be His people. We get a glimpse into the answer in **Deuteronomy 7:6-9:**

> *"For you are a holy people to the L*ORD *your God; the L*ORD *your God has chosen you to be a people for His own possession out of all the peoples who are on the face of the earth. ⁷ The L*ORD *did not set His love on you nor choose you because you were more in number than any of the peoples, for you were the fewest of all peoples, ⁸ but because the* L*ORD loved you and kept the oath which He swore to your forefathers, the* L*ORD brought you out by a mighty hand, and redeemed you from the house of slavery, from the hand of Pharaoh king of Egypt. ⁹ Know therefore that the L*ORD *your God, He is God, the faithful God, who keeps His covenant and His lovingkindness to a thousandth generation with those who love Him and keep His commandments;"*

It must be remembered that all that happens, has as its end, to glorify God. From this section of Deuteronomy we see three concepts come forth: 1) God's glory is demonstrated in our weakness, 2) God's love; and 3) God's faithfulness to His covenant (see verse 7-9).

The first concept deals with God being glorified. God is glorified in weakness (2 Corinthians 12:9-10). He did not choose the largest and most powerful empire in existence. God chose Israel, a people small in number. In **Deuteronomy 7:7** it says:

> *"The LORD did not set His love on you nor choose you because you were more in number than any of the peoples, for you were the fewest of all peoples,...."*

When we see God work in the weak areas of our lives, there is no way we can begin to claim credit for it. Paul points this out in both of his letters to the Corinthians:

> **1 Corinthians 1:26-29:** *"For consider your calling, brethren, that there were not many wise according to the flesh, not many mighty, not many noble;* [27]*but God has chosen the foolish things of the world to shame the wise, and God has chosen the weak things of the world to shame the things which are strong,* [28]*and the base things of the world and the despised, God has chosen, the things that are not, that He might nullify the things that are,* [29]*that no man should boast before God."*

> **2 Corinthians 12:9-10:** *"And He has said to me, 'My grace is sufficient for you, for power is perfected in weakness.' Most gladly, therefore, I will rather boast about my weaknesses, that the power of Christ may dwell in me.* [10]*Therefore I am well content with weaknesses, with insults, with distresses, with persecutions, with difficulties, for Christ's sake; for when I am weak, then I am strong."*

The second concept is God's love for Israel. In <u>Deuteronomy 7:8</u> it says that He put His love upon them: *"but because the LORD loved you...."* What a wonderful thing for God to love you. This is a difficult concept to understand. In our world, one may love someone because of what that other person does for him. When one no longer gets what he wants, he often will quit loving. This is not God's love. God's love is not soft sentimentalism. Scripture tells us that God disciplines those He loves (Hebrews 12:6). When God chooses to love, it is decisional, effectual, and powerful as stated in **1 John 4:8-10:**

> *"...for God is love.* [9]*By this the love of God was manifested in us, that God has sent His only begotten Son into the world so that we might live through Him.* [10]*In this is love, not that we loved God, but that He loved us and sent His Son to be the propitiation for our sins."*

Notice this verse (1 John 4:8) does not say that love is a mere attribute of God. It says that God <u>IS</u> <u>LOVE</u>. An attribute is defined as a characteristic or quality of a person. Love is not a part of Him (an attribute), but rather Jesus is the complete definition of love; ... *<u>for God is love.</u>*

The third concept that we see in God's choosing of Israel has to do with His covenant with them. A contract happens when two people make an agreement and exchange obligations and benefits. Vine states that a contract, "in its sense of an agreement on the part of each of two contracting parties cannot apply to a covenant between God and man. His covenant is essentially a matter of grace on His part (compare Galatians 3)." [164] The covenant that God entered into with Abraham was not a contract but a perpetual promise based not on the merit of Abram but on the mercy of God:

> **Genesis 12:1-3:**
> *"NOW the LORD said to Abram,*
> *"Go forth from your country,*
> *And from your relatives*

---

[164] Vine, W., and Bruce, F., *Vine's Expository Dictionary of Old and New Testament Words,* Old Tappan NJ: Revell (1981; Published in electronic form by Logos Research Systems, 1996). (p. 53).

And from your father's house,
To the land which I will show you;
[2]And I will make you a great nation,
And I will bless you,
And make your name great;
And so you shall be a blessing;
[3]And I will bless those who bless you,
And the one who curses you I will curse.
And in you all the families of the earth
  shall be blessed."

God's promise of salvation for other nations was present in that covenant. Notice in verse 3, God says to Abram *"And in you all the families of the earth shall be blessed."* That blessing is that Jesus, the Savior of the World, would be brought through his family line.

Israel has been the object of genocide by evil men/armies such as Haman,[165] Hitler and Hamas. Despite these attempts, Israel will survive and God will keep a remnant:

> **Jeremiah 23:3-4:** *"Then I Myself shall gather the remnant of My flock out of all the countries where I have driven them and shall bring them back to their pasture; and they will be fruitful and multiply. [4] I shall also raise up shepherds over them and they will tend them; and they will not be afraid any longer, nor be terrified, nor will any be missing, declares the LORD."*

It was God's plan that after the Jews rejected Christ that the Gospel would go to the Gentiles as set forth in **Acts 13:45-48:**

> *"But when the Jews saw the crowds, they were filled with jealousy, and began contradicting the things spoken by Paul, and were blaspheming. [46] And Paul and Barnabas spoke out boldly and said, 'It was necessary that the word of God should be spoken to you first; since you repudiate it, and judge yourselves unworthy of eternal life, behold, we are turning to the Gentiles. [47] For thus the Lord has commanded us,*
> *'I HAVE PLACED YOU AS A LIGHT FOR THE GENTILES,*
> *THAT YOU SHOULD BRING SALVATION TO THE END OF THE EARTH.''*
> *[48] And when the Gentiles heard this, they began rejoicing and glorifying the word of the Lord; and as many as had been appointed to eternal life believed."*

One reason for God's pursuit of the Gentiles is to make Israel jealous and eventually He will draw Israel back to Himself: **Romans 11:11:** *"I say then, they did not stumble so as to fall, did they? May it never be! But by their transgression salvation has come to the Gentiles, to make them jealous."* (See Romans 11:11-32, 10:16-21.)

In summary, Jesus sent His disciples to the lost sheep of Israel first and then to the rest of the nations. Note what Paul said:

> **Romans 1:16:** *"For I am not ashamed of the gospel, for it is the power of God for salvation to everyone who believes, to the Jew first and also to the Greek."*

---

[165] Regarding Haman see the Book of Esther Chapter 3.

Look also at what Jesus said:

> **Acts 1:8b:** *"...you shall be My witnesses both in Jerusalem, and in all Judea and Samaria, and even to the <u>remotest part of the earth</u>...."*

VERSES 7-10: *"And as you go, preach, saying, 'The kingdom of heaven is at hand.' ⁸ Heal the sick, raise the dead, cleanse the lepers, cast out demons; freely you received, freely give. ⁹ Do not acquire gold, or silver, or copper for your money belts, ¹⁰ or a bag for your journey, or even two tunics, or sandals, or a staff; for the worker is worthy of his support."*

The disciples were to minister to the people. First, they were to announce the salvation in Christ by stating that, *"The kingdom of heaven is at hand."* God also gave them the power to do miracles in the name of Christ.

The people of God are to not serve to acquire money; (*"Do not acquire gold, or silver, or copper for your money belts ...."*). They are to live the life of faith knowing that God will provide for them. Peter warned that pastors are to be men who do not try to exploit the ministry for their selfish gain: **1 Peter 5:2:** *"...shepherd the flock of God among you, exercising oversight not under compulsion, but voluntarily, according to the will of God; and <u>not for sordid gain</u>,...."* This should not be understood to mean that a church should not provide for their pastor. Scripture specifically states that those who are called of God and effectually labors for the Gospel should be provided for. With that said, one cannot just claim that he is in full-time ministry and expect support. He must be diligent, faithful and fruitful to the call:

> **1 Timothy 5:17-18:** *"Let the elders who rule well be considered worthy of double honor, especially those <u>who work hard at preaching and teaching</u>. ¹⁸ For the Scripture says, 'You shall not muzzle the ox while he is threshing,' and 'The laborer is worthy of his wages.'"*

There must also be a balance to the concept of "working hard." It can be tempting to be a *person-pleaser* who does anything, for anyone, at any time. Although this sounds like a great servant, there is a big difference in serving others so they think well of you, as compared to serving others solely out of the love of God. One immediately receives a fleeting reward of praise from people and the other receives his reward from God for all eternity. Faithful service does not mean that one makes himself available at a moment's notice for every person in the congregation at the great expense of one's own family. Although I have only functioned in lay ministries, I have had to deal with this issue of how to simultaneously serve God aggressively in His church and in my own home. Early on, I purposed that I would take my kids with me when I was involved in a ministry project. This served two purposes: 1) I would be an example to my children of service to God, and, 2) we would serve God together and it would not just be something dad and mom did. Every man's first ministry is with his own family, both in physical needs and nurturing. **1 Timothy 5:8:** *"But if anyone does not provide for his own, and especially for those of his household, he has denied the faith, and is worse than an unbeliever."*

Scripture supporting pastoral support is set out in **1 Corinthians 9:11-15:**

> *"<u>If we sowed spiritual things in you, is it too much if we should reap material things from you?</u> ¹²If others share the right over you, do we not more? Nevertheless, we did not use this right, but we endure all things, that we may cause no hindrance to the gospel of Christ. ¹³Do you not know that those who perform sacred services eat the food of the temple, and those who attend regularly to the altar have their share with the altar? ¹⁴<u>So also the Lord directed those who proclaim the gospel to get their living from the gospel.</u>*

15But I have used none of these things. And I am not writing these things that it may be done so in my case; for it would be better for me to die than have any man make my boast an empty one."

Note from verses 12 and 15 above that although Paul had the right to draw financial support from the church at Corinth, he refused to accept any. He did not want any person to claim that he was laboring in the Gospel to get financial gain. There is a big difference between providing comfortably for the needs of the pastor, and a spiritual leader who lives in luxury and excess. The so-called pastor who desires luxury and excess has disqualified himself from the position; (see the qualification for elder/pastor: He cannot be a lover of money (1 Timothy 3:3, Titus 1:7.) Needless to say, such desires or excesses are unbecoming to the calling of any Christian. Worse than that, we are told that greed is equal to idolatry, and idolaters will not enter the kingdom of God.

> **Colossians 3:5:** *"Therefore consider the members of your earthly body as dead to immorality, impurity, passion, evil desire, and <u>greed, which amounts to idolatry.</u>"*

> **Ephesians 5:5:** *"For this you know with certainty, that no immoral or impure person or <u>covetous man, who is an idolater,</u> has an inheritance in the kingdom of Christ and God."*

VERSES 11-15: *"And into whatever city or village you enter, inquire who is worthy in it; and abide there until you go away. 12 And as you enter the house, give it your greeting. 13 And if the house is worthy, let your greeting of peace come upon it; but if it is not worthy, let your greeting of peace return to you. 14 And whoever does not receive you, nor heed your words, as you go out of that house or that city, shake off the dust of your feet. 15 Truly I say to you, it will be more tolerable for the land of Sodom and Gomorrah in the day of judgment, than for that city."*

The disciples were to stay with a godly man when they got to a city or village. It is important that they stayed with one of good moral and spiritual character so as not to hinder their preaching (i.e. *"inquire who is worthy in it; and abide there."*) They were to bless the house with peace when they entered it. It was the common Jewish greeting of "shalom" (which means peace). If it was not really a house of peace, the blessing would be taken back.

Finally, Jesus states that if the disciples are not "received" by the village (i.e. they encounter rejection of their preaching on how to be saved) they were to, *"shake off the dust"* of their feet as a sign of God's judgment on that community. We see Paul and Barnabas do that in Iconium (Acts 13:51). It must be remembered what Jesus said:

> **John 15:18-20:** *"<u>If the world hates you, you know that it has hated Me before it hated you.</u> 19 If you were of the world, the world would love its own; but because you are not of the world, but I chose you out of the world, therefore the world hates you. 20 Remember the word that I said to you, 'A slave is not greater than his master.' <u>If they persecuted Me, they will also persecute you; if they kept My word, they will keep yours also.</u>"*

Summary and Application

God has a special place for the house of Israel. We are to preach the Gospel to the Jews as well as to all the nations. When functioning by the Spirit of God, one will not be motivated by material gain or the praise of man. The faithful servant is to be driven by the love of God, which translates into love for others.

Ask yourself if you have been a true servant to others. How many people do you minister to who have no way to give back to you? There should be many in that category. Maybe they are the elderly, children, the poor or the sick. Rich or poor, great or small, strong or weak, God calls all to repentance, and we need to be faithful servants in that work (Matthew 4:17).

MATTHEW 10:16-23
(WOLVES and ATTACKS WITHIN A FAMILY)

"Behold, I send you out as sheep in the midst of wolves; therefore be shrewd as serpents, and innocent as doves. ¹⁷ But beware of men; for they will deliver you up to the courts, and scourge you in their synagogues; ¹⁸ and you shall even be brought before governors and kings for My sake, as a testimony to them and to the Gentiles. ¹⁹ But when they deliver you up, do not become anxious about how or what you will speak; for it shall be given you in that hour what you are to speak. ²⁰ For it is not you who speak, but it is the Spirit of your Father who speaks in you. ²¹ And brother will deliver up brother to death, and a father his child; and children will rise up against parents, and cause them to be put to death. ²² And you will be hated by all on account of My name, but it is the one who has endured to the end who will be saved. ²³ But whenever they persecute you in this city, flee to the next; for truly I say to you, you shall not finish going through the cities of Israel, until the Son of Man comes."

Introduction

In this section we will study the concept that there are people who both hate God, and hate those who follow Him. Persecution sets apart the real believer from the claimed follower of God. We will study what is meant by the phrase *perseverance of the saints*. First and foremost we must realize that it is by the Lord's grace that we have the strength to **endure to the end.**[166]

VERSES 16: *"Behold, I send you out as sheep in the midst of wolves; therefore be shrewd as serpents, and innocent as doves."*

The Lord called His disciples (and us) "sheep." Sheep are quite defenseless animals. They are not cunning prowlers or fast runners. They don't possess sharp claws or a threatening bite. The wolf possesses all those qualities and more. Wolves are even more threatening when they run in a pack. The "wolves" in v.16 represent the non-believers of this world. They are not content to leave the sheep alone. They run in packs and it is their nature and desire to kill sheep. This is why the true believer must understand the cost of discipleship (self-preservation is not the Christian way—see comments for the sections of Matthew 18:18).

Why are wolves so hostile to sheep? **1 John 5:19** tells us that *"the whole world lies in the power of the evil one."* The one who disagrees with this is completely ignorant of the persecution of Christians around the world. One only needs to go to the university campus to find a cynical professor who is

---

[166] **Matthew 24:10–13:** *"At that time many will fall away and will betray one another and hate one another. ¹¹"Many false prophets will arise and will mislead many. ¹²"Because lawlessness is increased, most people's love will grow cold. ¹³"But the one who endures to the end, he will be saved.*

always mocking Christians.[167]   Jesus taught plainly that the unsaved are under the power and deluding influence of Satan. Jesus exposed the true evil of religious imposters when He said:

John 8:42-47: *"… If God were your Father, you would love Me; for I proceeded forth and have come from God, for I have not even come on My own initiative, but He sent Me. [43] Why do you not understand what I am saying? It is because you cannot hear My word. [44] You are of your father the devil, and you want to do the desires of your father. He was a murderer from the beginning, and does not stand in the truth, because there is no truth in him. Whenever he speaks a lie, he speaks from his own nature; for he is a liar , and the father of lies . [45] But because I speak the truth, you do not believe Me. [46] Which one of you convicts Me of sin? If I speak truth, why do you not believe Me? [47] He who is of God hears the words of God; for this reason you do not hear them, because you are not of God."*

We are to be wise when carrying out God's work, *"…therefore be shrewd as serpents…."* Part of being "shrewd" is not being naïve and realizing that the "wolves" are highly deceptive in that they will even try to disguise themselves by looking like sheep. Jesus said in **Matthew 7:15-16:** *"Beware of the false prophets, who come to you in sheep's clothing, but inwardly are ravenous wolves. [16] You will know them by their fruits. Grapes are not gathered from thorn bushes, nor figs from thistles, are they?"*   Paul also warned that the "wolves" would hang out at the church of the believers, trying to devour them from within. Often the wolves themselves are deceived thinking they are wonderful people as they attack and devour true doctrine and believers; **2 Timothy 3:13:** *"But evil men and impostors will proceed from bad to worse, deceiving and being deceived."* In **Acts 20:29-30** Paul said,

"I know that after my departure savage wolves will come in among you, not sparing the flock; [30] and from among your own selves men will arise, speaking perverse things, to draw away the disciples after them."

Yet we are to be blameless and holy people, *"innocent as doves …."* It is okay to have some *street smarts* when out ministering as long as you don't have *street evil* with it. We are told in **Colossians 4:5-6** to, *"Conduct yourselves with wisdom toward outsiders, making the most of the opportunity. [6] Let your speech always be with grace, seasoned, as it were, with salt, so that you may know how you should respond to each person."* We see Paul exhibiting that "shrewd-innocence" when he applied a strategy to reach the lost. His strategy never compromised the truth. He put it this way:

1 Corinthians 9:19-23: *"For though I am free from all men, I have made myself a slave to all, that I might win the more. [20] And to the Jews I became as a Jew, that I might win Jews; to those who are under the Law, as under the Law, though not being myself under*

---

[167] I find it interesting that so many atheists are obsessed with attacking a God they are 100% sure does not exist. Let me explain what I mean. For example: I do not believe that pink elephants are floating in my room. In addition, I am neither obsessed nor motivated by anger in convincing everyone else that I don't have pink elephants floating in my room. If the atheist is so sure that he possesses all knowledge, so as to be 100% positive that there is no God (and that he will never face the judgment to come) why does he get so furious that I believe in God? The reality is that the atheist loves his sin, and instead of repenting and turning to God to be saved, he takes the cowardly/anti-intellectual view of just *waving his magic wand* and saying with hostile-intolerance, "God does not exist." Unfortunately for the atheist, God has His own judgment of him: **Psalm 53:1:** *"The fool has said in his heart, "There is no God," They are corrupt, and have committed abominable injustice,…."*

the Law, that I might win those who are under the Law; ²¹ to those who are without law, as without law, though not being without the law of God but under the law of Christ, that I might win who are without law. ²² To the weak I became weak, that I might win the weak; I have become all things to all men, that I may by all means save some. ²³ And I do all things for the sake of the gospel, that I may become a fellow partaker of it."

MacArthur summed up this "shrewd-innocence" balance this way,
"To love our enemies and not return evil for evil is one thing;
to deny they are enemies is quite another."[168]

VERSES 17-20: *"But beware of men; for they will deliver you up to the courts, and scourge you in their synagogues; ¹⁸ and you shall even be brought before governors and kings for My sake, as a testimony to them and to the Gentiles. ¹⁹ But when they deliver you up, do not become anxious about how or what you will speak; for it shall be given you in that hour what you are to speak. ²⁰ For it is not you who speak, but it is the Spirit of your Father who speaks in you."*

We are promised persecution. Jesus told us that the expected outcome of being His disciple is persecution from the world. In **John 15:18-21** He stated:
"If the world hates you, you know that it has hated Me before it hated you. ¹⁹ If you were of the world, the world would love its own; but because you are not of the world, but I chose you out of the world, therefore the world hates you. ²⁰ Remember the word that I said to you, 'A slave is not greater than his master.' If they persecuted Me, they will also persecute you; if they kept My word, they will keep yours also. ²¹ But all these things they will do to you for My name's sake, because they do not know the One who sent Me."

When we are brought before people to be persecuted, we are to see it as an opportunity to preach (Matthew 10:18). Jesus further tells us to not fear what we will say, because He promises His Holy Spirit will give us the words!

One last comment regarding verses Matthew 10:19-20. I once encountered a Sunday school teacher who habitually would not prepare for his class. I confronted him about this. I tried to explain to him how unbiblical his teaching method was. He justified his lack of preparation by quoting *in part,* **Matthew 10:19-20:** *"…for it shall be given you in that hour what you are to speak. ²⁰For it is not you who speak, but it is the Spirit of your Father who speaks in you."* He claimed that he did not spend much time specifically studying and preparing for Sunday school so that the "Spirit would speak through him." He went on to say that his preparation was really a general [hodgepodge] reflection on the various experiences and spiritual thoughts and readings he had through the week. This same person who would put hours into preparing for a sales pitch to a client at work, would barely put 10 minutes into preparing for an hour-long Sunday school class. This view is not uncommon among some who teach Sunday schools, Bible studies, or help in other teaching ministries. Their hidden view is that the church should be thankful that they are volunteering any of their time at all. This perspective entails both erroneous Biblical interpretation, as well as a dereliction of duty. Let us

---

[168] MacArthur, J. F., Jr. (1985). *Matthew*. MacArthur New Testament Commentary (p. 199). Chicago: Moody Press.

examine the claim that one does not need to prepare because, "the Spirit will speak through him." To correctly interpret Scripture one needs to view it in its context. The context of Matthew 10:19-20 is in reference to a time of persecution. Review again that portion of Scripture starting a few verses prior, beginning at Matthew 10:16:

> "Behold, I send you out as sheep in the midst of wolves; therefore be shrewd as serpents, and innocent as doves. [17] But <u>beware of men; for they will deliver you up to the courts</u>, and scourge you in their synagogues; [18] and you shall even be brought before governors and kings for My sake, as a testimony to them and to the Gentiles. [19] <u>But when they deliver you up,</u> do not become anxious about how or what you will speak; for it shall be given you in that hour what you are to speak. [20] For it is not you who speak, but it is the Spirit of your Father who speaks in you. [21] <u>And brother will deliver up brother to death,</u> and a father his child; and children will rise up against parents, and cause them to be put to death. [22] <u>And you will be hated by all on account of My name,</u> but it is the one who has endured to the end who will be saved." <u>Matthew 10:16-22.</u>

When you read verses 19 and 20 regarding the Holy Spirit giving you the words to speak in *that hour,* it is clear that its interpretation relates to an hour of persecution. If we are suddenly put in a persecution situation, we are not to fear as to what we will say regarding our testimony for Christ because the Holy Spirit will give us the boldness and words at that moment.

The sudden testimonial event is very different from a situation involving a Sunday school or other similar teaching / preaching capacity where one knows days in advance that he will be called upon to testify of Christ and teach from the Word.[169] When we have been granted such an opportunity, we are to handle this great calling with an attitude of prayer, study and holy fear. Those who think they can just *wing it* do not understand their responsibility before God. They confuse passionate speeches containing a few Bible verses and good intentions with Spirit-led teaching. The problem of poor study and preparation is most commonly seen among those who are naturally good orators. Their ability to *speak well* serves to camouflage their lack of preparation...for the short term. Over time, the discerning members of the audience catch on and grow weary of it. Those who do not pray and study

---

[169] This problem of some not preparing properly before teaching the Bible is nothing new. Ryle writes about it in the late 1800s. He stated that:

"[There is a promise in this passage which is often much perverted. I allude to the implied promise contained in the words, "Do not worry beforehand about what to say. Just say whatever is given you at the time" (verse 11). The perversion I mean consists in supposing that this passage warrants ministers in getting up to preach unprepared every Sunday, and in expecting special help from the Holy Spirit in addressing regular congregations, when they have neither meditated, read nor taken pains about their subject. A moment's reflection must show any reader that such an application of this passage is utterly unjustifiable. The passage has no reference whatever to the regular Sabbath sermon of a minister, and only holds out the promise of special help in special times of need. It would be good for the church if this were more remembered than it is. At present it may be feared this promise is not infrequently made an excuse for ministerial idleness and undigested sermons. People seem to forget when they enter the pulpit that what costs nothing is worth nothing, and that the "foolishness" of preaching and foolish preaching are widely different things.]"

Ryle, J. C. (1993). *Mark.* Crossway Classic Commentaries (p. 206). Wheaton, IL: Crossway Books.

over a particular lesson fail to realize that they have substantially increased the possibility of erroneous interpretation and heretical doctrines.

> **2 Timothy 2:15-18:** "*Be diligent to present yourself approved to God as <u>a workman who does not need to be ashamed, handling accurately the word of truth.</u> [16]But avoid worldly and empty chatter, for it will lead to further ungodliness, [17]and their talk will spread like gangrene. Among them are Hymenaeus and Philetus, [18]men who have gone astray from the truth saying that the resurrection has already taken place, and thus they upset the faith of some.*"

Scripture states clearly that we are to work hard at studying the Word.

> **1 Timothy 5:17:** "*Let the elders who rule well be considered worthy of double honor, <u>especially those who work hard at preaching and teaching.</u>*"

Scripture soberly warns those who desire to be teachers of the seriousness of their responsibility. Specifically, it states that their judgment will be more severe.

> **James 3:1:** "*LET not many of you become teachers, my brethren, knowing that as such we shall incur a stricter judgment.*"

VERSES 21-22: "*And brother will deliver up brother to death, and a father his child; and children will rise up against parents, and cause them to be put to death. [22] And you will be hated by all on account of My name, but it is the one who has endured to the end who will be saved.*"

Here we see Jesus setting out the cost of discipleship. One can have "best friends" in grade school, high school, college, etc. but the relationship that goes on through life is the family relationship. There are few more basic bonds than the flesh-and-blood bond of a "father" and "his child." Yet an even more basic bond is the one that has descended spiritually (i.e. is their father God or the Devil?) Jesus warns His disciples that their obedience to Him will cause some family members to hate the believers so much as to want them dead! Skip ahead in this chapter and see that Jesus has more to say about the cost of discipleship and the effect it will have on family relationships in **Matthew 10:34-39:**

> "*Do not think that I came to bring peace on the earth; I did not come to bring peace, but a sword. [35] For I came to SET A MAN AGAINST HIS FATHER, AND A DAUGHTER AGAINST HER MOTHER, AND A DAUGHTER-IN-LAW AGAINST HER MOTHER-IN-LAW; [36] and A MAN'S ENEMIES WILL BE THE MEMBERS OF HIS HOUSEHOLD. [37] He who loves father or mother more than Me is not worthy of Me; and he who loves son or daughter more than Me is not worthy of Me. [38] And he who does not take his cross and follow after Me is not worthy of Me. [39] He who has found his life shall lose it, and he who has lost his life for My sake shall find it.*"

Matthew 10:22 says in-part, "*...but it is the one who has endured to the end who will be saved.*" Theologically, this phrase takes in the concept called *the perseverance of the saints*. It means that the truly saved are manifested by their endurance of persecution over time. Who are those who are saved? Jesus states that the ones who are saved are those who persevere to the end. This is not saying that the person who works hard to endure will earn salvation. Salvation and the ability to endure to the end comes only from the grace of God and is not something a person can generate. John MacArthur states it this way:

> "Endurance of persecution is the hallmark of genuine salvation: **It is the one who has endured to the end who will be saved.** Endurance does not produce or protect salvation, which is totally the work of God's grace. But endurance is evidence of

salvation, proof that a person is truly redeemed and a child of God…. The following Scriptures also emphasize perseverance: Matthew 24:13; John 8:31; 1 Corinthians 15:1-2; Colossians 1:21-23; Hebrews 2:1-3; 4:14; 6:11-12; 10:39; 12:14; 2 Peter 1:10."[170]

Note that Jesus spoke of this concept in the context of persecution. Persecution has a way of separating the *proud confessing churchman* from the true Christian who possesses eternal life. The *churchman* has never been converted. He has a place in his life for *religion* but not complete devotion to Christ. He would never let himself suffer for Christ on the job or be ostracized by society, let alone be killed!

This concept of the *perseverance of the saints* is repeated by Jesus in Matthew 24:13, where He says, *"But the one who endures to the end, he shall be saved."* The Apostle John speaks of the false Christian who for a little while appears to follow Christ but over time he abandons the faith:

> **1 John 2:19:** *"They went out from us, but they were not really of us; for if they had been of us, they would have remained with us; but they went out, in order that it might be shown that they all are not of us."*

Because of the mercy and call of God, we do not need to worry that we might later defect. A.A. Hodge states that:

> "This perseverance of the saints depends not upon their own free will, but upon the immutability of the decree of election, flowing from the free and unchangeable love of God the Father; upon the efficacy of the merit and intercession of Jesus Christ, the abiding of the Spirit, and of the seed of God within them; and the nature of the covenant of grace: from all which arises also the certainty and infallibility thereof."[171]

Jesus states plainly our security in Him:

> **John 10:27-30:** *"My sheep hear My voice, and I know them, and they follow Me; [28]and <u>I give eternal life to them, and they shall never perish; and no one shall snatch them out of My hand.</u> [29]My Father, who has given them to Me, is greater than all; <u>and no one is able to snatch them out of the Father's hand.</u> [30]I and the Father are one."*

How thankful we can be to God who keeps those who trust Him from falling away. This truth is set out in **Jude 24-25:** *"Now to Him who is able to keep you from stumbling, and to make you stand in the presence of His glory blameless with great joy, [25]to the only God our Savior, through Jesus Christ our Lord, be glory, majesty, dominion and authority, before all time and now and forever. Amen."*

> <u>**Romans 8:31-39:**</u> *"What then shall we say to these things? If God is for us, who is against us? [32]He who did not spare His own Son, but delivered Him up for us all, how will He not also with Him freely give us all things? [33]Who will bring a charge against God's elect? God is the one who justifies; [34]who is the one who condemns? Christ Jesus is He who died, yes, rather who was raised, who is at the right hand of God, who also intercedes for us. [35]Who shall separate us from the love of Christ? Shall tribulation, or distress, or persecution, or famine, or nakedness, or peril, or sword? [36]Just as it is written, 'FOR THY*

---

[170] MacArthur, J. F., Jr. (1985). *Matthew.* MacArthur New Testament Commentary (p. 199). Chicago: Moody Press.

[171] Hodge, A. (1996). *The Confession of Faith: With questions for Theological Students and Bible Classes.* With an appendix on Presbyterianism by Charles Hodge. Index created by Christian Classics Foundation. (electronic ed. based on the 1992 Banner of Truth reprint.). Simpsonville SC: Christian Classics Foundation.

SAKE WE ARE BEING PUT TO DEATH ALL DAY LONG; WE WERE CONSIDERED AS SHEEP TO BE SLAUGHTERED.' ³⁷*But in all these things we overwhelmingly conquer through Him who loved us.* ³⁸*For I am convinced that neither death, nor life, nor angels, nor principalities, nor things present, nor things to come, nor powers,* ³⁹*nor height, nor depth, nor any other created thing, shall be able to separate us from the love of God, which is in Christ Jesus our Lord."*

VERSE 23: *"But whenever they persecute you in this city, flee to the next; for truly I say to you, you shall not finish going through the cities of Israel, until the Son of Man comes."*

Part of being *"shrewd as serpents"* includes the concept of knowing when we are to flee to the next city. Fleeing to the next city is not cowardly. Cowardice is manifested in a fear to serve because of potential danger, or the denial of Christ to save your skin. Paul states in **Acts 20:24:** *'But I do not consider my life of any account as dear to myself, so that I may finish my course and the ministry which I received from the Lord Jesus, to testify solemnly of the gospel of the grace of God.'"* Paul underwent great persecutions such as beatings, stoning, imprisonment etc. (see 2 Corinthians 11:23-30), yet he followed this principle that Jesus sets out on "fleeing" to the next city (Acts 9:21-25).

Summary and Application

Do you take seriously the work that God has given you? Are you aware that there are wolves out to destroy your faith (e.g. evil people or *friends* who encourage you to sin by engaging in pornography or movies that glorify evil, murder, use illegal drugs, and mock God as they embrace materialism, drunkenness and false religious teaching - see Galatians 5:19-21). By pretending to look like sheep, these wolves may try to appear to be your friends at first, but in the end they will work their corruption in you.

1 Corinthians 15:33: *"Do not be deceived: Bad company corrupts good morals."*

James 1:14-15: *"But each one is tempted when he is carried away and enticed by his own lust.* ¹⁵*Then when lust has conceived, it gives birth to sin; and when sin is accomplished, it brings forth death."*

As to the issue of persecution: Have you resolved in your mind how far you will go in Christ by His power? We should see that the early-church believers and many around the world today persevered to the end even though it meant the forfeiture of their property and their own death.

<u>MATTHEW 10:24-31</u>
(PERSECUTION AND WHY WE NEED NOT FEAR)

"A disciple is not above his teacher, nor a slave above his master. ²⁵ It is enough for the disciple that he become as his teacher, and the slave as his master. If they have called the head of the house Beelzebul, how much more the members of his household! ²⁶ Therefore do not fear them, for there is nothing covered that will not be revealed, and hidden that will not be known. ²⁷ What I tell you in the darkness, speak in the light; and what you hear whispered in your ear, proclaim upon the housetops. ²⁸ And do not fear those who kill the body, but are unable to kill the soul; but rather fear Him who is able to destroy both soul and body in hell. ²⁹ Are not two sparrows sold for a cent? And yet not one of them will fall to the ground apart from your Father. ³⁰ But the very hairs of your head are all numbered. ³¹ Therefore do not fear; you are of more value than many sparrows."

Introduction

This section continues the concept of the believer's identity in Christ. Jesus teaches the disciple should expect to be subjected to the same slander He was. Despite the persecution, the believer is not to fear those who persecute him, because the Almighty Father in heaven knows all, sees all and will judge all one day.

<u>VERSES 24-25:</u> *"A disciple is not above his teacher, nor a slave above his master. ²⁵ It is enough for the disciple that he become as his teacher, and the slave as his master. If they have called the head of the house Beelzebul, how much more the members of his household!"*

A true disciple's (i.e. *learner*) desire is to become like his teacher. The disciple wants to master the material and then rightly apply it. The Christian disciple should desire to be like Christ:
> **<u>Romans 8:29:</u>** *"For whom He foreknew, He also predestined <u>to become conformed to the image of His Son,</u> that He might be the first-born among many brethren;...."*

Since Jesus was hated and despised by the world, we should expect the same treatment from the same godless world. Jesus reinforces these basics to His disciples through repetition. Over and over again Jesus sets forth the cost of true discipleship (i.e. persecution from the world). English Renaissance essayist Francis Bacon (1561-1626) wrote:
> "Prosperity is the blessing of the Old Testament, — adversity is the blessing of the New."[172]

The name "Beelzebul" was a Jewish epithet for Satan. How incredibly evil it was for sinful men to call the Almighty and Holy God by such a name! The Pharisees did exactly that earlier in Matthew 9:34 (you may want to review that outline). As Jesus' disciples, He warns us that we should expect such slander ourselves. One does not need to have been a follower of Christ for long to find out that if you engage in a good work with good motives, you will be attacked and slandered. The persecution does not just come from those outside the church. Jesus demonstrated in Matthew 9:34

---

[172] Wiersbe, W. W. (1996). *Be Satisfied* (p. 19). Wheaton, IL: Victor Books. [Not that I would look to Bacon for theology, it is still an interesting quote.]

that the attacks can come from *false brethren*[173] in the church. The problem lies in the fact that the non-believer/religious hypocrite engages in actions with pretense/ulterior motives to make themselves look good to others. They live in a world where they are much more concerned with how their *image* appears, rather than their true character. They slander those who truly do good because they assume everyone else thinks like they do. They assume that the true servant of God is doing good works for appearance's sake, because that is why they do good deeds.

VERSES 26-27: *"Therefore do not fear them, for there is nothing covered that will not be revealed, and hidden that will not be known. [27] What I tell you in the darkness, speak in the light; and what you hear whispered in your ear, proclaim upon the housetops."*

Here the true Christian is assured that God will totally vindicate him at the, *"revealing of the sons of God"* **Romans 8:19**. This will be exactly opposite of how the unbelieving world evaluates one's worth. The Bible explains how an unbelieving world views God's people as "losers" even, *"as the scum of the world"* **1 Corinthians 4:13**. God, who is the ultimate judge, sees His people as being clothed in the righteousness of Christ (Galatians 3:27). Although the world sees God's people as naïve trouble makers, God sees them as those *"whom the world was not worthy."*

> **Hebrews 11:35-39:** *"...and others were tortured, not accepting their release, in order that they might obtain a better resurrection; [36] and others experienced mockings and scourgings, yes, also chains and imprisonment. [37] They were stoned, they were sawn in two, they were tempted, they were put to death with the sword; they went about in sheepskins, in goatskins, being destitute, afflicted, ill-treated [38] (men of whom the world was not worthy), wandering in deserts and mountains and caves and holes in the ground. [39] And all these, having gained approval through their faith,...."*

VERSES 28: *"And do not fear those who kill the body, but are unable to kill the soul; but rather fear Him who is able to destroy both soul and body in hell.*

Jesus puts our earthly life in the correct perspective. Eternity is forever and this life on earth is a little blip on the screen. In this section Jesus teaches that a Christian should not be concerned with someone who can only kill the physical body but cannot touch his soul. God states that He is the possessor of all souls (**Ezekiel 18:4:** *"Behold, all souls are Mine;...the soul who sins will die."*). Instead of fearing *man*, one should fear God who can condemn the soul of a person to hell!

> **Revelation 20:6:** *"Blessed and holy is the one who has a part in the first resurrection; over these the <u>second death</u> has no power, but they will be priests of God and of Christ and will reign with Him for a thousand years."*

> **Revelation 20:14:** *"And death and Hades were thrown into the lake of fire. <u>This is the second death, the lake of fire.</u>"*

MacArthur states the following about persecution and fear of death:
> "The worst that can happen to a believer suffering unjustly is death, and that is the best that can happen because death means the complete and final end of all sins. If

---

[173] False brethren: Galatians 2:4; 2 Corinthians 11:13.

the Christian is armed with the goal of being delivered from sin, and that goal is achieved through his death, the threat and experience of death is precious (cf. Romans 7:5,18; 1 Corinthians 1:21; 15:42,49). Moreover, the greatest weapon that the enemy has against the Christian, the threat of death, is not effective."[174]

The missionary, Jim Elliot, who was killed by those he was trying to reach for Christ, understood the insignificance of earthly life in light of eternity when he said:
"He is no fool who gives what he cannot keep to gain what he cannot lose."[175]
When one dies to himself and his own desires, he can truly live for the cause of Christ. The evangelist George Mueller (1805-1898), whose Christian service included providing for thousands of orphans, said the following regarding the secret to his service to Christ:
"There was a day when I died, utterly died...died to George Muller, his opinions, preferences, tastes, and will—died to the world, its approval or censure—died to the approval or blame even of my brethren and friends—and since then I have studied only to show myself approved unto God."[176]

The Christian should serve the Lord diligently so as to hear the words of His master say: *"Well done, good and faithful slave....enter into the joy of your master."* <u>Matthew 25:21</u>.

<u>**VERSES 29-31:**</u> *"Are not two sparrows sold for a cent? And yet not one of them will fall to the ground apart from your Father.* [30] *But the very hairs of your head are all numbered.* [31] *Therefore do not fear; you are of more value than many sparrows."*

Jesus points out our great worth to God, as well as God's complete knowledge of literally everything. He also knows the number of *hairs on your head*. When we take an inventory of the important attributes of ourselves, we never consider something as insignificant as the number of hairs on our head. The point is that God knows *everything* (literally He knows *absolutely everything* = *omniscience*). God knows and cares when an insignificant bird falls. Verse 31 should also silence the "animal rights" activist who tries to equate the value of animals with humans. The Creator of all things states a person is of much, *"more value than many sparrows."* In Matthew 12:12 Jesus stated, *"Of how much more value then is a man than a sheep!"*

The fact that God is all-knowing is something that should strike fear into the unbeliever and provide great comfort to the child of God. Charles Spurgeon reflects on the omniscience of God this way:
"Divine omniscience affords no comfort to the ungodly mind, but to the child of God it overflows with consolation. God is always thinking upon us, never turns aside his mind from us, has us always before his eyes;... for it would be dreadful to exist for a moment beyond the observation of our heavenly Father. His thoughts are always tender, loving,

---

[174] *The MacArthur Study Bible.* 1997 (J. MacArthur, Jr., Ed.) (electronic ed.) (1 Peter 4:1). Nashville, TN: Word Pub.

[175] Douglas, J. D., Comfort, P. W., and Mitchell, D. (1992). *Who's Who in Christian history* (p. 230). Wheaton, IL. Tyndale House.

[176] Tan, P. L. (1996). *Encyclopedia of 7700 Illustrations: Signs of the Times. 6102 George Mueller's Secret* Garland, TX: Bible Communications, Inc.

wise, prudent, far-reaching, and they bring to us countless benefits: hence it is a choice delight to remember them."[177]

Summary and Application

We learn from this section that persecution is to be expected, and at the same time we need to remember we are in the Lord's care. How are you to respond to those who attack you? Paul explains that we are to endure, bless and be kind.

> **1 Corinthians 4:12-13:** *"...and we toil, working with our own hands; <u>when we are reviled, we bless</u>; when we are persecuted, we endure; [13]<u>when we are slandered, we try to conciliate</u>; we have become as the scum of the world, the dregs of all things, even until now."*

If a student is to be like his teacher, are you being *"conformed to the image of His Son?"* Are you being persecuted because you look and act like your teacher? When that happens we must remember that we are to *"Bless those who persecute you; bless and curse not."* <u>Romans 12:14</u>.

One last thought on staying focused when you are criticized and persecuted in your service for Christ comes from what one has called:

<u>The Paradoxical Commandments:</u> [178]

1. People are illogical, unreasonable, and self-centered. — *<u>Love them anyway.</u>*
2. If you do good, people will accuse you of selfish ulterior motives. — *<u>Do good anyway.</u>*
3. If you are successful, you will win false friends and true enemies. — *<u>Succeed anyway.</u>*
4. The good you do today will be forgotten tomorrow. — *<u>Do good anyway.</u>*
5. Honesty and frankness make you vulnerable. — *<u>Be honest and frank anyway.</u>*
6. The biggest men and women with the biggest ideas can be shot down by the smallest men and women with the smallest minds. — *<u>Think big anyway.</u>*
7. People favor underdogs but follow only top dogs. — *<u>Fight for some underdogs anyway.</u>*
8. What you spend years building may be destroyed overnight. — *<u>Build anyway.</u>*
9. People really need help but may attack you if you do help them. — *<u>Help people anyway.</u>*
10. Give the world the best you have and you'll get kicked in the teeth. — *<u>Give your best anyway.</u>*

---

[177] Spurgeon, C. H. (1995). *Morning and evening: Daily readings* (April 30 PM). Oak Harbor, WA: Logos Research Systems, Inc.

[178] Keith, Kent, *The Silent Revolution: Dynamic Leadership in the Student Council.* (Terrace Press) 2003. This is often mistakenly quoted as the work of Howard Ferguson. It appears to actually be the work of Kent Keith who authored it in 1968 while a sophomore at Harvard College. He entitled it "The Paradoxical Commandments."

MATTHEW 10:32-42
(LOYALTY TO CHRIST / FAMILY DIVISIONS — TRUE DISCIPLESHIP)

"Everyone therefore who shall confess Me before men, I will also confess him before My Father who is in heaven. [33] *But whoever shall deny Me before men, I will also deny him before My Father who is in heaven.*

[34] *Do not think that I came to bring peace on the earth; I did not come to bring peace, but a sword.* [35] *For I came to* SET A MAN AGAINST HIS FATHER, AND A DAUGHTER AGAINST HER MOTHER, AND A DAUGHTER-IN-LAW AGAINST HER MOTHER-IN-LAW; [36] *and* A MAN'S ENEMIES WILL BE THE MEMBERS OF HIS HOUSEHOLD. [37] *He who loves father or mother more than Me is not worthy of Me; and he who loves son or daughter more than Me is not worthy of Me.* [38] *And he who does not take his cross and follow after Me is not worthy of Me.* [39] *He who has found his life shall lose it, and he who has lost his life for My sake shall find it.* [40] *He who receives you receives Me, and he who receives Me receives Him who sent Me.* [41] *He who receives a prophet in the name of a prophet shall receive a prophet's reward; and he who receives a righteous man in the name of a righteous man shall receive a righteous man's reward.* [42] *And whoever in the name of a disciple gives to one of these little ones even a cup of cold water to drink, truly I say to you he shall not lose his reward."*

Introduction

Jesus' teaching on discipleship and commitment continues! Jesus sets out what it means to *confess* or *deny* Him. True confession is proven during the fires of persecution. That persecution can happen within one's own family. In this section, Jesus speaks clearly that discipleship can cost you everything (in this world only).

VERSES 32: *"Everyone therefore who shall confess Me before men, I will also confess him before My Father who is in heaven."*

Webster's dictionary defines the word *confess,* in part as: *"to declare faith in or adherence to."*[179] The true disciple will *confess* (i.e. openly declare and identify with Christ.):

> **Romans 10:9-10:** *"...that if you confess with your mouth Jesus as Lord, and believe in your heart that God raised Him from the dead, you shall be saved;* [10] *for with the heart man believes, resulting in righteousness, and with the mouth he confesses, resulting in salvation."*

A mere casual acknowledgement of God is not the manifestation of a person who understands the truth of Christ and has been saved. Scripture states that hell-bound demons also acknowledge the truth about God. One distinction between the person who makes a casual acknowledgment of God and that of demons is that the demons at least shake in fear at the thought of Almighty God's judgment! **James 2:19:** *"You believe that God is one. You do well; the demons also believe, and shudder."* Although the ungodly fear the punishment of God, they do not repent and submit to God.

---

[179] *Merriam-Webster's Collegiate Dictionary,* definition (3) of "Confess."

The Christian has a very different view of the *fear of God*. The Christian has a holy fear and reverence of God **Proverbs 9:10:** *"The fear of the LORD is the beginning of wisdom, And the knowledge of the Holy One is understanding."*

One who relies on the fact that some years ago he was talked into muttering a pre-made prayer about, "asking Jesus into his heart," but never repented of his sin and placed his faith in Christ's substitutionary death on the cross, has no claim to conversion. John MacArthur describes it this way:

> "...the one who refuses to turn to God for forgiveness and salvation and therefore has no evidence, no good fruit, of genuine repentance. Salvation is not verified by a past act, but by present fruitfulness."[180]

It should be noted that nowhere in scripture does it inform us that the way a person is saved is by, "asking Jesus into their heart." Modern evangelism has substituted *conversion by the power of God* (John 3:3-8), with *nominal decisionalism*. Scripture tells us that Jesus preached that one is to, *"repent and believe the gospel"* **Mark 1:14-15;** (i.e. *"believe in the Lord Jesus Christ and you will be saved;"* **Acts 16:31**). I have found very few who at the time they *"asked Jesus into their heart"* actually believed, with godly sorrow, that they had violated God's law and were *justly heading to an eternity of hell* (i.e. they never truly understood what they needed to be saved from). **John 3:36** states that *"... he who does not obey the Son will not see life, but the wrath of God abides on him."*

If I have true saving faith, I will repent (turn from and forsake my sin, false religion, and self-righteousness.) It does not mean that I will never fail or sin again (1 John 1:8-9). It does mean that the one who is "born again" will have a true love for Jesus Christ, and faith in His Word. The truly converted will turn from sin, he will hate sin, and he will no longer practice sin (1 John 3:4-10, Galatians 5:19-21, Matthew 7:23, Revelation 22:15).

I have also observed that very few who at the time they *"asked Jesus into their heart"* really understood what *"believing in Jesus"* truly means. Sadly, many have been misled by being told something to the effect that they: 1) need to acknowledge that they have done some wrong things; 2) they need to accept the good news that Jesus loves them "just the way they are;" and 3) realize that God wants them to go to heaven by saying a prayer to "ask Jesus into their heart." This mixes truth with error. In their darkened understanding, the unconverted mistakenly believes that if "Jesus loves them just the way they are" they can continue to live and practice unrighteous since God will forgive them anyway. The result of such teaching is heresy and false converts. To "believe in Jesus" means to believe what He says in His Word. The false convert is never truly warned that God is righteous and will judge wickedness. Jesus said in **Matthew 13:49-50:**

> *"So it will be at the end of the age; the angels will come forth and take out the wicked from among the righteous, and will throw them into the furnace of fire; in that place there will be weeping and gnashing of teeth.*

It is shocking to see a pastor or evangelists *promise* a person that he is going to heaven immediately after the person says a prayer to "ask Jesus into his heart." No one can claim to promise someone that he was converted because he repeated back a pre-made prayer. True conversion is proven over time and with fruitfulness (John 10:22, Mark 13:13, John 15:5-8, Matthew 13:3-23). Frankly, guaranteeing

---

[180] MacArthur, J. F., Jr. (1985). Matthew. MacArthur New Testament Commentary (p. 70). Chicago: Moody Press.

someone that he *truly believed and is forgiven,* 30 seconds after he read a pre-made prayer comes close to *evangelical papalism.* I cannot know his heart, maybe he was saved, maybe he was not, only God knows at that point (Acts 15:8, 1 Corinthians 2:11). Instead of utilizing modern evangelism methods, one must be told that saving faith (i.e. *believing in Jesus*) really means that one believes with his whole heart that he is <u>saved ONLY by the grace of God through faith in the substitutionary death of Christ on the cross</u> (i.e. Jesus, as God and without any sin, paid my death and damnation penalty on the cross where He died as the sinless sacrifice, and then three days later He rose from the dead Ephesians 2:8-10; 1 Corinthians 15:3-4). One who believes this (not merely intellectually, but truly surrenders his life to Christ as Lord and Savior) is a true Christian (i.e. one who is proven over time and fruitfulness). This is what it means when scripture states, **"that if you confess with your mouth Jesus as Lord, and believe in your heart that God raised Him from the dead, you will be saved;" Romans 10:9**. It must be remembered that the gospel is very simple: and be summarized as follows: Jesus states in the Bible that every single person is guilty of sin, which is punished by receiving eternal judgment in the fires of hell. Jesus preached that the only way to escape from hell is to ***"repent and believe in the gospel." Mark 1:15.***

- To **_REPENT_** means to turn from your sins and forsake them by the power of God.
- To **_BELIEVE THE GOSPEL_** means that one who is "born again" by the Spirit of God (John 3:3-8) will:
  - Believe in Jesus Christ as Almighty God, who is without sin;
  - Believe in Jesus' sacrificial death on the cross as the only and complete payment for your sins;
  - Believe in Jesus' bodily resurrection from the dead on the third day;
  - Believe in Jesus as Lord over all things and confesses this fact to others.

It is that straightforward. <u>It has nothing to do with your righteousness, good works or engaging in a religious ceremony or cleaning yourself up first to win God's acceptance.</u> If you reject God's loving gift of forgiveness in Jesus Christ, you remain a guilty sinner waiting to be punished in eternal hell. The Bible says *in* **John 3:36:** *"He who believes in the Son has eternal life; but he who does not obey the Son will not see life, but the wrath of God abides on him."* Repent and believe the gospel TODAY, before it is too late!

The main text we are studying, **Matthew 10:32-33** says: *"Everyone therefore who shall confess Me before men, I will also confess him before My Father who is in heaven. 33 But whoever shall deny Me before men, I will also deny him before My Father who is in heaven.* The one who think he is doing well because he will acknowledge that "his religion is Christianity," needs to read these verses in their context. The verses before Matthew 10:32-33, as well as the verses after it, speak directly about a confession and devotion to Christ, regardless of the persecution that comes for that confession. Note that the verses before Matthew 10:32-33 speak of persecution:

Matthew 10:24–31: *"A disciple is not above his teacher, nor a slave above his master. 25 It is enough for the disciple that he become like his teacher, and the slave like his master. If they have called the head of the house Beelzebul, how much more will they malign the members of his household! 26 Therefore do not fear them, for there is nothing concealed that will not be revealed, or hidden that will not be known. 27 What I tell you in the darkness, speak in the light; and what you hear whispered in your ear, proclaim upon the housetops. 28 Do not fear those who kill the body but are unable to kill the soul; but rather fear Him who is able to destroy both soul and body in hell. 29 Are not two sparrows sold for a cent? And yet not one of them will fall to the ground apart from your Father. 30 But the very hairs of your head are all numbered. 31 So do not fear; you are more valuable than many sparrows."*

Note that the verses after Matthew 10:32-33 speak of persecution:

> **Matthew 10:34–39:** *"Do not think that I came to bring peace on the earth; I did not come to bring peace, but a sword. [35] "For I came to set a man against his father, and a daughter against her mother, and a daughter-in-law against her mother-in-law; [36] and a man's enemies will be the members of his household. [37] "He who loves father or mother more than Me is not worthy of Me; and he who loves son or daughter more than Me is not worthy of Me. [38] "And he who does not take his cross and follow after Me is not worthy of Me. [39] "He who has found his life will lose it, and he who has lost his life for My sake will find it.*

The type of person referred to as making a confession for Christ in verses 32-33 is not engaging in a general *acknowledgment* of Him. The true disciple openly confesses Christ in the face of persecution. The truth of one's confession is proven when his faith is under the fires of persecution, not when he recites a church liturgy. A classic example of this is an evangelism outing that my family and some of our friends used to organize during the local Fourth of July parade. We would put together a float and then pass out gospel tracts, candy and beach-balls along the parade route. As we worked the route we would see and greet our neighbors, friends, family, colleagues from work, as well as those from the church. We did not see many adults from the church willing to join us distributing tracts. I suspect many are much more comfortable with *dignified* Christian service inside the walls of the church. Maybe that *dignified* service is being a deacon, teaching Sunday school, sitting on the mission committee, singing in the praise band or even baking a pie for a fellowship. The average church men's group will be happy to get together to swing hammers on a building project, but are unavailable to carry the *sword of the Spirit* by going on a door-to-door evangelizing outing. A lady may be known and respected for her praying for the lost, or giving to missions, but she never evangelizes. There is a huge disconnect of claimed faith and actions. As one man said, *"It is easier to talk to God about man than it is to talk to man about God."*[181]

The reality is that the church walls provide comfortable protection from persecution by the world. Unbelievers will think much better of you if you are an *Elder* inside the church, than a person who is out in the public warning them to escape the judgment to come. I have heard all kinds of arguments made about how one has a uniquely special work at the church that fulfills his Christian service. Scripture makes it clear that the true work of the church is the Great Commission (Matthew 28:16-20). For this to be accomplished, one must go *outside the church* and engage in the *"foolishness of preaching."*
> **1 Corinthians 1:21:** *"For since in the wisdom of God the world through its wisdom did not come to know God, God was well-pleased through the foolishness of the message preached to save those who believe."*
The church service is designed to be a gathering of believers to worship God and receive instruction from God's Word. Once instructed and built up, the church heads out to accomplish the work. The reality is that from church leadership on down, very few will truly take the Gospel outside the walls. It is for this reason that it remains a surprising small group in the church who can name five people in the last year who they have accurately shared the Gospel, either verbally or via written material like a gospel tract. For clarification, sharing the true gospel is not equivalent to inviting someone to church or having a general discussion regarding spiritual/Christian thoughts. (For a more extended

---

[181] Ray Comfort of Living Waters Ministry. His point is well taken. Obviously we are to do both i.e. talk to God about man and talk to man about God.

discussion on what the Great Commission is, go to the comments addressing **Matthew 28:18-20** in this commentary. A brief discussion is set out in the footnote below).[182]

Matthew 7:22-23 tells us that there are many who are content to make a general confession of Christ, yet they remain unsaved. Jesus stated that these people would call Him *Lord* and yet be damned. So what is the difference between those who confess Christ and are saved and those who confess Christ and are damned? The saved put their complete trust for salvation in Christ's sacrifice on the cross. They know that only His death can be the full payment for their sins. The damned are very different. The damned make a general confession of Christ, but they will also look to their own good works or religious service/rite to help them earn God's favor. Jesus' response to them is devastatingly direct. He will tell them: 1) He never knew them as His disciples, and, 2) that their sins remain on them:

> **Matthew 7:22-23:** *"Many will say to Me on that day, 'Lord, Lord, did we not prophesy in Your name, and in Your name cast out demons, and in Your name perform many*

---

[182] The Great Commission is set out in **Matthew 28:18-20:** *"And Jesus came up and spoke to them, saying, 'All authority has been given to Me in heaven and on earth. [19] Go therefore and make disciples of all the nations, baptizing them in the name of the Father and the Son and the Holy Spirit, [20] teaching them to observe all that I commanded you; and lo, I am with you always, even to the end of the age.'"* (emphasis added). We are to make disciples (i.e. followers of Christ). To accomplish this we must do more than just share with them the salvation message. From Matthew 28:20 Jesus tells us to be *"teaching them to observe all that I commanded you."* Jesus sums-up these commandments in that we are to love God first and foremost, and then love others as much as we love ourselves. **Matthew 22:36-40:** *"Teacher, which is the great commandment in the Law?' [37] And He said to him, 'You shall love the Lord your God with all your heart, and with all your soul, and with all your mind. [38] This is the great and foremost commandment. [39] The second is like it, You shall love your neighbor as yourself. [40] On these two commandments depend the whole Law and the Prophets.'"* In making disciples of Christ (not disciples of ourselves or our church), we are to be teaching and encouraging believers in service and true holiness. This teaching cannot simply come from one's words, but will have real meaning if the teacher is actually doing what he is encouraging others to do. It says in **James 1:27:** *"Pure and undefiled religion in the sight of our God and Father is this: to visit orphans and widows in their distress, and to keep oneself unstained by the world."* Good works will never help save anyone. **Ephesians 2:8-9:** *"For by grace you have been saved through faith; and that not of yourselves, it is the gift of God; [9]not as a result of works, so that no one may boast."* Those who God saves manifest good works, as demonstrated in the very next verse in: **Ephesians 2:10:** *"For we are His workmanship, created in Christ Jesus for good works, which God prepared beforehand so that we would walk in them."* The godless of Matthew 7:22-23 who look to their good works for some self-righteousness are damned. On the other hand, the true disciples manifest goods works and are not keeping an account of their works (nor are they trying to earn any righteousness). They are simply doing the, *"good works, which God prepared beforehand so that we would walk in them."* **Ephesians 2:10.** Jesus explains this concept in **Matthew 25:32-40:**

> *"All the nations will be gathered before Him; and He will separate them from one another, as the shepherd separates the sheep from the goats; [33]and He will put the sheep on His right, and the goats on the left. [34] Then the King will say to those on His right, 'Come, you who are blessed of My Father, inherit the kingdom prepared for you from the foundation of the world. [35]For I was hungry, and you gave Me something to eat; I was thirsty, and you gave Me something to drink; I was a stranger, and you invited Me in; [36]naked, and you clothed Me; I was sick, and you visited Me; I was in prison, and you came to Me.' [37] Then the righteous will answer Him, 'Lord, when did we see You hungry, and feed You, or thirsty, and give You something to drink? [38]And when did we see You a stranger, and invite You in, or naked, and clothe You? [39] When did we see You sick, or in prison, and come to You?' [40] The King will answer and say to them, 'Truly I say to you, to the extent that you did it to one of these brothers of Mine, even the least of them, you did it to Me.'"*

miracles?' [23] *And then I will declare to them, 'I never knew you; DEPART FROM ME, YOU WHO PRACTICE LAWLESSNESS.'"*

False believers often look to their own good works as the basis for earning salvation. People are very comfortable with the idea of working hard and getting what they deserve. The problem is that they apply that philosophy to the God of all Creation. Some will be shocked to find out that there is no Bible verse that says, "God helps those who help themselves."[183] Not only does that saying not exist in the Bible, Scripture states the exact opposite. Jesus said *"... apart from Me you can do nothing."* **John 15:5**. The unsaved person does not realize God's high standard of righteousness (i.e. perfection). He does not realize what perfection means. Sure, he may have tried to get rid of a few bad habits, but his life has never been changed by Christ. He has never hated his sin or repented of it. Jesus said in **Luke 13:3**: *"... but unless you repent, you will all likewise perish."* [184] Those who hold to religious rituals as a claim for salvation are those that Scripture refers to as, *"holding to a form of godliness, although they have denied its power."* **2 Timothy 3:5**.

If our own good works cannot help save us, why does Jesus teach about doing *good works*? A true Christian does not do good works to get saved; but instead understands that because God has saved you, He will now produce good works out of your life. The point is that good works are a manifestation of salvation. This principle is set out in **Ephesians 2:8-10:**
> *"For by grace you have been saved through faith; and that not of yourselves, it is the gift of God;* [9] *not as a result of works, that no one should boast.* [10] *For we are His workmanship, created in Christ Jesus for good works, which God prepared beforehand, that we should walk in them."*

VERSE 33: *But whoever shall deny Me before men, I will also deny him before My Father who is in heaven."*

Obviously one is not a Christian if he denies Christ.
> **2 Timothy 2:11-13:** *"It is a trustworthy statement:*
> *For if we died with Him, we shall also live with Him;*
> [12] *If we endure, we shall also reign with Him;*
> *If we deny Him, He also will deny us;*
> [13] *If we are faithless, He remains faithful; for He cannot deny Himself."*

People deny Christ by creating a Jesus of their own imagination; a Jesus who is not the Jesus of the Bible. Some create a Jesus who would never send anyone to hell. Others make up a Jesus who was a prophet, but is not God. There are those who want Jesus to be a hippy, or of a political ideology such as a communist, democrat or a republican. Still others fashion their Jesus in the form of a statue that

---

[183] The concept that "God helps those who help themselves" is not only unbiblical but originates from mythology. It can be found in *Aesop's Fables* (6th Century B.C.) in a story called "Hercules and the Waggoner." *Aesop. Fables*, retold by Joseph Jacobs. Vol. XVII, Part 1. The Harvard Classics. New York: P.F. Collier and Son, 1909–14; Bartleby.com, 2001. The modern version: "God helps those who help themselves....", was written by Algernon Sidney, (English political theorist) in *Discourses Concerning Government*, 1698, chapter 2 section 23. It became more widely known through Benjamin Franklin, who used the phrase in *Poor Richard's Almanac*—1736.

[184] The power to repent comes only from God: **2 Timothy 2:25:** *"... with gentleness correcting those who are in opposition, if perhaps God may grant them repentance leading to the knowledge of the truth,...."*

they can bow down to. All of these human creations of Christ are denials of the real Jesus and violate the Second Commandment by making God in our own image.[185] Paul warned that some would preach their own Jesus. **2 Corinthians: 11:4:** *"For if one comes and preaches <u>another Jesus whom we have not preached....</u>"* If you have a tendency to want to create a "god" in your own image, repent of such arrogance and examine the Scripture to see the real Lord and Savior.

> **2 Peter 3:18:** *"... but <u>grow in the grace and knowledge of our Lord and Savior Jesus Christ.</u> To Him be the glory, both now and to the day of eternity. Amen."*

When Jesus talks about denying Him in Matthew 10:33, it means much more than just a verbal denial. We must also take an inventory of our own lives to see if we are denying Him through our actions. We can deny the Lord by the way we live. **Titus 1:16:** *"They profess to know God, but <u>by their deeds they deny Him</u>, being detestable and disobedient, and worthless for any good deed.."* Let us not be hypocrites who merely say we love God. Let us encourage one another to carry that love out in the way we live our lives. The Apostle John said: *"...let us not love with word or with tongue, but in deed and truth."* **1 John 3:18.**

<u>Section Application</u>

When you claim to be a Christian, what are you really saying? Are you claiming to belong to a certain church or denomination? Maybe you are claiming to be a Christian because you have engaged in certain religious rituals such as baptism, communion or confirmation? To be saved one must see that there is no way he can have his sins forgiven except by Jesus Christ alone. To be saved from hell one must put his complete faith in Jesus' death as the sole payment of his sin. Jesus' resurrection is proof of His defeat of sin and death. Those who deny the resurrection have denied Christ.

> **John 3:16-18:** *"For God so loved the world, that He gave His only begotten Son, that whoever believes in Him should not perish, but have eternal life. 17 For God did not send the Son into the world to judge the world, but that the world should be saved through Him. 18 <u>He who believes in Him is not judged; he who does not believe has been judged already, because he has not believed in the name of the only begotten Son of God.</u>"*

VERSES 34-37: *"Do not think that I came to bring peace on the earth; I did not come to bring peace, but a sword. 35 For I came to SET A MAN AGAINST HIS FATHER, AND A DAUGHTER AGAINST HER MOTHER, AND A DAUGHTER-IN-LAW AGAINST HER MOTHER-IN-LAW; 36 and A MAN'S ENEMIES WILL BE THE MEMBERS OF HIS HOUSEHOLD. 37 He who loves father or mother more than Me is not worthy of Me; and he who loves son or daughter more than Me is not worthy of Me."*

This subject was addressed earlier in this study of Matthew 10:21 (you may want to review that section). Jesus makes it clear that He must be Lord of our life and never be relegated to second place in our allegiances.

---

[185] When one makes up his own version of "Jesus" he violates the Second Commandment by making God in his own image. **Deuteronomy 5:8-10:** *"You shall not make for yourself an idol, or any likeness of what is in heaven above or on the earth beneath or in the water under the earth. 9 You shall not worship them or serve them; for I, the Lord your God, am a jealous God, visiting the iniquity of the fathers on the children, and on the third and the fourth generations of those who hate Me, 10 but showing lovingkindness to thousands, to those who love Me and keep My commandments."*

Jesus states in verse 34, *"Do not think that I came to bring peace on the earth..."* He makes it clear that His first coming would not result in peace with an unbelieving world. Not until Christ's second coming, when He rules and reigns on the earth, can we expect peace. In **John 16:33** Jesus said to His disciples: *"These things I have spoken to you, that in Me you may have peace. In the world you have tribulation, but take courage; I have overcome the world."*

Someone may ask why Jesus is called the *Prince of Peace*, when He states that He did not come *"to bring peace on the earth."* Jesus is the *"Prince of Peace"* (Isaiah 9:6), because He did what no one else could do. He made peace between sinful mankind and a Holy God.

Despite the hostile surroundings the believer finds himself in, God promises a peace in his life unlike any other kind. In **John 14:27** Jesus said, *"Peace I leave with you; My peace I give to you; not as the world gives, do I give to you. Let not your heart be troubled, nor let it be fearful."* The peace we have is not derived from some *pie in the sky* or a *"don't worry-be happy"* attitude. The peace from God is based on the fact that even if all hell appears to be breaking loose on this earth, or in my life, the God of all creation is sovereign over all things and has me in His good care for all eternity. God is still in complete control, and the trials on this earth are a mere blip on the screen in comparison to spending eternity in heaven with God.

VERSES 38-39: *"And he who does not take his cross and follow after Me is not worthy of Me. [39] He who has found his life shall lose it, and he who has lost his life for My sake shall find it."*

Man's inward, main desire is for self-preservation. Protecting yourself is not the view of the true disciple of Christ. One must be totally devoted to Jesus and hold nothing back, including the life He *loaned*[186] you. When Jesus said, *"take his cross,"* the disciples knew exactly what He meant by that phrase (i.e. DEATH!).

> "Only a few years before Jesus spoke those words, a zealot named Judas had gathered together a band of rebels to fight the Roman occupation forces. The insurrection was easily quelled, and in order to teach the Jews a lesson, the Roman general Varus ordered the crucifixion of over 2,000 Jews. Their crosses lined the roads of Galilee from one end to the other." [187]

Look what Jesus said in **Mark 8:35-38:**

> *"For whoever wishes to save his life shall lose it; but whoever loses his life for My sake and the gospel's shall save it. [36] For what does it profit a man to gain the whole world, and forfeit his soul? [37] For what shall a man give in exchange for his soul? [38] For whoever is ashamed of Me and My words in this adulterous and sinful generation, the Son of Man will also be ashamed of him when He comes in the glory of His Father with the holy angels."*

---

[186] The Lord says in **Ezekiel 18:4:** *"Behold, all souls are Mine;...."* Upon death, immediately a person's physical body returns to dust and his soul returns to God (i.e. all souls belong to God). **Ecclesiastes 12:7:** *"...then the dust will return to the earth as it was, and the spirit will return to God who gave it."*

[187] MacArthur, John F., *The MacArthur New Testament Commentary*, (Chicago: Moody Press) 1983.

There is great insight to be gained when we understand the words of the Lord about the insignificance of our lives on earth in comparison to where we spend eternity.

> **Luke 12:4-5:** *"And I say to you, <u>My friends, do not be afraid of those who kill the body,</u> and after that have no more that they can do. 5 But I will warn you whom to fear: <u>fear the One who after He has killed has authority to cast into hell</u>; yes, I tell you, fear Him!"*

Often we think we are suffering for Christ when we are merely having a bad day. We need to toughen up and apply Luke 12:4-5 like the missionary John Paton. In 1858 he and his wife sailed to the New Hebrides islands in the South Pacific (they are now called the Vanuatu Islands). The islands are located between Australia and Fiji, and were full of idol-worshipping cannibals. Killing and revenge-killing served as the vicious circle that controlled their lives. One of their homicidal rituals required that upon a man's death, his wife was to be strangled to death also.[188]

The first Christian influence to the islands was in 1839 when John Williams and James Harris from the London Missionary Society landed there. Within minutes of arrival on the island of Erromanga, they were murdered and eaten. Paton knew this fact and still *felt a call to the islands*. When he told this to Christian friends and a respected spiritual elder, he did not get encouragement. He wrote,

> "The opposition was so strong from nearly all, and many of them warm Christian friends, that I was sorely tempted to question whether I was carrying out the divine will, or only some headstrong wish of my own."[189]

The elder, recalling what happened to Williams and Harris, responded by saying, "The cannibals! You will be eaten by cannibals." Paton's response was as follows:

> "Mr. Dickson, you are advanced in years now, and your own prospect is soon to be laid in the grave, there to be eaten by worms,…I confess to you, that if I can but live and die serving and honoring the Lord Jesus, it will make no difference to me whether I am eaten by Cannibals or by worms…" (Ibid at 56.)

[Now that is the response that reflects the Lords words in Luke 12:4-5.]

Paton finally arrived on Tanna Island in 1858 with his pregnant wife. Within the first year he would have to dig graves for his wife and newborn child who died from sickness. Alone on the island, he served the Lord. Many times he himself was sick and near death. Many times his life was threatened. Often the cannibal warriors sought to kill him. There was a time when the entire island arose and blamed him for an epidemic and wanted him dead. This was a constant way of life for Paton, who loved and ministered to them. He wrote of God's protection and sovereignty when he penned the following story:

> "A wild chief followed me around for four hours with his loaded musket, and though often directed towards me, God restrained his hand. I spoke kindly to him, and attended to my work as if he had not been there, fully persuaded that my God placed me there and would protect me till my allotted task was finished."[190]

---

[188] *John G. Paton: Missionary to the New Hebreds, An Autobiography Edited by His Brother* p. 69, 334 (Edinburgh: The Banner of Truth Trust, 1965, orig. 1889, 1891)

[189] Ibid at 56.

[190] Ibid at 117

Here is another example:

> "...at daybreak I found my house surrounded by armed men, and a chief intimated that they had assembled to take my life. Seeing that I was entirely in their hands, I knelt down and gave myself away body and soul to the Lord Jesus, for what seemed the last time on earth. Rising, I went out to them, and began calmly talking about their unkind treatment of me contrasting it with all my conduct toward them...[a chief then arose] and said 'Our conduct has been bad; but now we will fight for you...'"[191]

The trials were ongoing. He had worked very hard to obtain funds for a mission ship for use in the work, only to find it had sunk from a violent storm. But he lived on to a ripe old age, and despite years of trials and little apparent fruit, eventually the island of Aniwa turned to Christ!

Paton went on to publish the New Testament in the Islander's language. His influence is remembered to this day, as it is no coincidence that the motto of the Vanuatu islands is, "Long God yumi sitanap," which is translated, "In God we stand." This influence is also demonstrated in their national flag. The Vanuatu tourism bureau states that the bright yellow in the flag symbolizes, *"the light of Christ which shines over the whole of the Republic of Vanuatu."* [192]

May we all, like John Paton, actually live out and not just quote the words of Jesus:

> **Luke 12:4-5:** *"And I say to you, <u>My friends, do not be afraid of those who kill the body, and after that have no more that they can do.</u> 5 But I will warn you whom to fear: <u>fear the One who after He has killed has authority to cast into hell</u>; yes, I tell you, fear Him!"*

[I would encourage you to also read the story of William Borden at the end of the section for Matthew 19:21-22.]

The following sums up my thoughts on the concept of how a Christian should view fear, self-preservation, and faithfulness to his Creator: *A real disciple does not fear his own death, but rather his own disobedience.*

VERSES 40-42: *"He who receives you receives Me, and he who receives Me receives Him who sent Me. 41 He who receives a prophet in the name of a prophet shall receive a prophet's reward; and he who receives a righteous man in the name of a righteous man shall receive a righteous man's reward. 42 And whoever in the name of a disciple gives to one of these little ones even a cup of cold water to drink, truly I say to you he shall not lose his reward."*

The phrase, *"in the name of a..."* actually means, *"because he is a...."* So the phrase, *"in the name of a... prophet... righteous man... disciple,"* should be understood to mean *because he is a prophet... righteous man...disciple.* One of the marks of a believer is that he loves other Christians and warmly receives them.

> **1 John 3:14:** *"We know that we have passed out of death into life, because we love the brethren. He who does not love abides in death."*

---

[191] Ibid at 115

[192] As of 2014 - Vanuatu Tourism Office online: (See the Vanuatu National Flag section.)

Matthew 25:37-40: *"Then the righteous will answer Him, saying, 'Lord, when did we see You hungry, and feed You, or thirsty, and give You drink?* [38] *And when did we see You a stranger, and invite You in, or naked, and clothe You?* [39] *And when did we see You sick, or in prison, and come to You?'* [40] *And the King will answer and say to them, <u>'Truly I say to you, to the extent that you did it to one of these brothers of Mine, even the least of them, you did it to Me.'"</u>*

Section Application

Have you purposed in your heart to take up your cross and follow Him? It may cost you friends, or hurt you financially to stand for Christ. For some believers in this world, it costs them their lives. How are you responding to persecution? I can think of a *religion* that has the evil teaching of murdering your enemies. Compare that ugliness to the beauty of Christianity where our Lord tells us to, *"<u>...love your enemies, do good to those who hate you,</u>* [28] *<u>bless those who curse you, pray for those who mistreat you.</u>"* <u>**Luke 6:27-28.**</u>

How are you treating your brothers and sisters in Christ? Do you encourage them in the Lord's work? When they hear from you, are your words critical venom, or are they like a cool drink of water that refreshes and encourages? (Matthew 10:42.) Remember we will be judged for what we say. We are called to, *"**Let your speech always be with grace, seasoned, as it were, with salt, so that you may know how you should respond to each person.**"* <u>**Colossians 4:6.**</u>

MATTHEW 11:1-15
(JOHN THE BAPTIST)

"AND it came about that when Jesus had finished giving instructions to His twelve disciples, He departed from there to teach and preach in their cities.

² Now when John in prison heard of the works of Christ, he sent word by his disciples, ³ and said to Him, 'Are You the Expected One, or shall we look for someone else?' ⁴ And Jesus answered and said to them, 'Go and report to John what you hear and see: ⁵ the BLIND RECEIVE SIGHT and the lame walk, the lepers are cleansed and the deaf hear, and the dead are raised up, and the POOR HAVE THE GOSPEL PREACHED TO THEM. ⁶ And blessed is he who keeps from stumbling over Me.'

⁷ And as these were going away, Jesus began to speak to the multitudes about John, 'What did you go out into the wilderness to look at? A reed shaken by the wind? ⁸ But what did you go out to see? A man dressed in soft clothing? Behold, those who wear soft clothing are in kings' palaces. ⁹ But why did you go out? To see a prophet? Yes, I say to you, and one who is more than a prophet. ¹⁰ This is the one about whom it is written,

'BEHOLD, I SEND MY MESSENGER BEFORE YOUR FACE,
WHO WILL PREPARE YOUR WAY BEFORE YOU.'

¹¹ Truly, I say to you, among those born of women there has not arisen anyone greater than John the Baptist; yet he who is least in the kingdom of heaven is greater than he. ¹² And from the days of John the Baptist until now the kingdom of heaven suffers violence, and violent men take it by force. ¹³ For all the prophets and the Law prophesied until John. ¹⁴ And if you care to accept it, he himself is Elijah, who was to come. ¹⁵ He who has ears to hear, let him hear.'"

Introduction

This section involves John the Baptist sending his disciples to confirm what he had always believed. John's "doubt" is better characterized as confusion. Much of the Jewish *tradition* saw the Messiah coming to set them free from their enemies. At the time of Christ, Rome would have been considered Israel's enemy, but Jesus did not appear to be engaging in an agenda to free Israel from the Romans. What the Messiah granted was their real need—freedom from sin.

Not only is Jesus not leading an overthrow of Rome, but John knows that his own situation does not appear as one of strength. John is sitting in a rotting jail cell waiting to be executed. This does not make sense to him, so he sends his disciples to ask Jesus.

VERSES 1-6: "AND it came about that when Jesus had finished giving instructions to His twelve disciples, He departed from there to teach and preach in their cities. ² Now when John in prison heard of the works of Christ, he sent word by his disciples, ³ and said to Him, 'Are You the Expected One, or shall we look for someone else?' ⁴ And Jesus answered and said to them, 'Go and report to John what you hear and see: ⁵ the BLIND RECEIVE SIGHT and the lame walk, the lepers are cleansed and the deaf hear, and the dead are raised up, and the POOR HAVE THE GOSPEL PREACHED TO THEM. ⁶ And blessed is he who keeps from stumbling over Me.'"

We see here that Jesus departs, *"to teach and preach in their cities"* and that John was in prison. Josephus states that the prison where John was held was a fortress named Machaerus, located East of the Dead Sea.[193]   This fortress is the same place that John was eventually executed.[194]   John was imprisoned because he boldly confronted Herod regarding his adulterous marriage that resulted from him stealing his brother's wife (Matthew 14:3-4).

It is thought that John had been in prison for about a year when he sent his disciples to Jesus. As mentioned above, one might speculate that John is struggling because he was ready for the Messiah to rule and reign. Instead, John sees himself in prison at the hand of a wicked ruler, Herod Antipas, and the nation of Israel is still under Roman control. He is perplexed and seeks Jesus for confirmation on what he already knew (i.e. that Jesus was the Messiah). Remember it was John who:

> *"…*saw Jesus coming to him, and *said, '<u>Behold, the Lamb of God who takes away the sin of the world!</u>' 30 This is He on behalf of whom I said, 'After me comes a Man who has a higher rank than I, for He existed before me.'"* **John 1:29-30.**

We do not read of any direct contact that Jesus and John had after Jesus' baptism. In Matthew 11:2-3 we see that John sends his disciples to ask Jesus, *"Are You the Expected One, or shall we look for someone else?"* In Matthew 11:4-5 Jesus answers John's confusion directly with His Word. Jesus quotes from Isaiah 35:5 and 61:1. These verses address a prophecy of what the Messiah will do:

> *"And Jesus answered and said to them, 'Go and report to John what you hear and see: 5 the BLIND RECEIVE SIGHT and the lame walk, the lepers are cleansed and the deaf hear, and the dead are raised up, and the POOR HAVE THE GOSPEL PREACHED TO THEM.'"* **Matthew 11:4-5**.

Jesus tells John's disciples to inform John of all that had been done. Notice the gentle admonishment Jesus gives John and his disciples by telling them in verse 6: *"And blessed is he who keeps from stumbling over Me."* Jesus was telling John to not doubt. We know that after John was beheaded, his disciples buried him, and then they went right to Jesus to tell Him that John was dead (Matthew 14:12). That fact shows the supreme importance Jesus was in John's life.

<u>VERSES 7-11:</u> *"And as these were going away, Jesus began to speak to the multitudes about John, 'What did you go out into the wilderness to look at? A reed shaken by the wind? 8 But what did you go out to see? A man dressed in soft clothing? Behold, those who wear soft clothing are in kings' palaces. 9 But why did you go out? To see a prophet? Yes, I say to you, and one who is more than a prophet. 10 This is the one about whom it is written,*

> *'BEHOLD, I SEND MY MESSENGER BEFORE YOUR FACE,*
> *WHO WILL PREPARE YOUR WAY BEFORE YOU.'*

11 Truly, I say to you, among those born of women there has not arisen anyone greater than John the Baptist; yet he who is least in the kingdom of heaven is greater than he.'"

---

[193] Josephus, *Antiquities of the Jews* 18.112, 119 (See also *MACHAERUS The New Bible Dictionary*, Wheaton, Illinois: Tyndale House Publishers, Inc. 1962.)

[194] Ibid

How do most people measure "worldly greatness?" Many will look to political or military power, intelligence, athletic ability, or wealth. God does not see any of that as the basis of a great man. Jesus said in verse 11, *"Truly, I say to you, among those born of women there has not arisen anyone greater than John the Baptist...."* John was not a great, worldly king or a wealthy man of comfort, as we read from **Matthew 3:4**, where it states, *"Now John himself had a garment of camel's hair, and a leather belt about his waist; and his food was locusts and wild honey...."* John was a true man of God who possessed inspired conviction. In **Matthew 11:7-9:** Jesus said the following about John:

> *"...What did you go out into the wilderness to look at? A reed shaken by the wind? 8 But what did you go out to see? A man dressed in soft clothing? Behold, those who wear soft clothing are in kings' palaces. 9 But why did you go out? To see a prophet? Yes, I say to you, and one who is more than a prophet."*

John was not afraid to call religious hypocrisy what it was. Note what John said to the religious leaders of his day:

> *"But when he saw many of the Pharisees and Sadducees coming for baptism, he said to them, 'You brood of vipers, who warned you to flee from the wrath to come? 8 Therefore bring forth fruit in keeping with repentance; 9 and do not suppose that you can say to yourselves, We have Abraham for our father; for I say to you, that God is able from these stones to raise up children to Abraham. 10 And the axe is already laid at the root of the trees; every tree therefore that does not bear good fruit is cut down and thrown into the fire.'"* **Matthew 3:7-10.**

These are not the statements that one makes when he desires the approval of others. At the end of verse 11 Jesus says, *"...yet he who is least in the kingdom of heaven is greater than he...."* Jesus made it clear that among humans there was no one greater than John. This statement obviously does not mean that John is greater than Jesus, because Jesus was from above. In **John 3:31** it says, *"He who comes from above is above all, he who is of the earth is from the earth and speaks of the earth. He who comes from heaven is above all."* Jesus said in **John 8:23:** *"And He was saying to them, 'You are from below, I am from above; you are of this world, I am not of this world.'"*

When Jesus said, *"yet he who is least in the kingdom of heaven is greater than he...,"* MacArthur explained it to mean:

> "Although he was a spiritual giant among men, John's unique greatness was in his role in human history, not in his spiritual inheritance, in which he would be equal to every believer. Therefore, *the least in the kingdom of heaven*, the spiritual dimension, *is greater than he*, that is, than anyone in the human dimension, including John."[195]

VERSE 12: *"And from the days of John the Baptist until now the kingdom of heaven suffers violence, and violent men take it by force."*

The verse states that from the *"days of John the Baptist until now...."* That time period would have been about 18 months. As for the part of the verse that states, *"the kingdom of heaven suffers violence, and violent men take it by force."*; there are two commonly held interpretations: one positive and one negative:

---

[195] MacArthur, John F., *Matthew The MacArthur New Testament Commentary*, p. 235 (Chicago: Moody Press) 1983.

1) The positive view is that through John's preaching some heard the truth and were led to the Lord.

> <u>Luke 1:15-17</u>: *"For he will be great in the sight of the Lord, and he will drink no wine or liquor; and he will be filled with the Holy Spirit, while yet in his mother's womb. ¹⁶ And he will turn back many of the sons of Israel to the Lord their God . ¹⁷ And it is he who will go as a forerunner <u>before Him in the spirit and power of Elijah,</u> TO TURN THE HEARTS OF THE FATHERS BACK TO THE CHILDREN, and the disobedient to the attitude of the righteous; so as to make ready a people prepared for the Lord."*

2) The negative is that of being oppressed and treated evilly. John was attacked by Pharisees and scribes, as well as Herod had John killed. This interpretation takes on the idea that the kingdom of God is being violently denied and rejected.

There are good reasons to believe that the first interpretation is the most accurate when looking at the context. In Matthew 10 Jesus makes it clear that cowardly denial of Him is not a mark of those who are His disciples. He goes on to state that the mark of a true disciple includes courageous faith even in the face of death.

> <u>Matthew 10:38-39</u>: *"And he who does not take his cross and follow after Me is not worthy of Me. ³⁹He who has found his life shall lose it, and he who has lost his life for My sake shall find it."*

Another reason in support of the first interpretation is the fact that Jesus had previously taught that few would enter the kingdom (Matthew 7:13-14).

<u>VERSES 13-15:</u> *"For all the prophets and the Law prophesied until John. ¹⁴ And if you care to accept it, he himself is Elijah, who was to come. ¹⁵ He who has ears to hear, let him hear."*

This statement that John was Elijah is fulfillment of prophecy in <u>Malachi 4:5-6</u>:

> *"Behold, I am going to send you Elijah the prophet before the coming of the great and terrible day of the LORD. ⁶ And he will restore the hearts of the fathers to their children, and the hearts of the children to their fathers, lest I come and smite the land with a curse."*

This was not to mean that Elijah would be reincarnated, but rather that John would be as powerful and great a prophet as Elijah. Look at what the angel said to John's father, Zechariah, in <u>Luke 1:16-17</u>: *"And he will turn back many of the sons of Israel to the Lord their God. ¹⁷ And it is he who will go as a forerunner before Him in the spirit and power of Elijah,...."*

<u>Summary and Application</u>

God is gracious and He understands our weaknesses. With that said, we need to be careful when our faith begins to be clouded by doubt. God is not honored or pleased by our doubt. In <u>Romans 14:23</u> it says, *"...and everything that does not come from faith is sin."* James warns us about doubt when he states:

> *"But if any of you lacks wisdom, let him ask of God, who gives to all men generously and without reproach, and it will be given to him. ⁶ <u>But let him ask in faith without any doubting, for the one who doubts is like the surf of the sea driven and tossed by the wind. ⁷ For let not that man expect that he will receive anything from the Lord, ⁸</u> being a double-minded man, unstable in all his ways."* <u>James 1:5-8.</u>

One reason a person can fall into doubt about God is due to his incomplete understanding of Him. Many people have a little religion in their life or they see some Hollywood movie on Jesus and think they know about Him. We have God's complete revelation to us in His Word, the Bible. If we study it and know it, the revelation we get from the Holy Spirit will drive our doubts away.   In **John 8:31-32** Jesus said to the believers in Him:

> *"…If you abide in My word, then you are truly disciples of Mine;*
> *32 and you shall know the truth, and the truth shall make you free."*

If you are struggling in your faith, it can be safely assumed that you are not in prayerful daily study of God's Word. Change that today. Get into the Word and watch your faith grow. The Apostle Paul stated that: *"… faith comes from hearing, and hearing by the word of Christ."* **Romans 10:17.**

MATTHEW 11:16-30
(HYPOCRISY, JUDGMENT AND GOD REVEALING HIMSELF TO SOME)

[16] *"But to what shall I compare this generation? It is like children sitting in the market places, who call out to the other children, [17] and say, 'We played the flute for you, and you did not dance; we sang a dirge, and you did not mourn.' [18]For John came neither eating nor drinking, and they say, 'He has a demon!' [19]The Son of Man came eating and drinking, and they say, 'Behold, a gluttonous man and a drunkard, a friend of tax-gatherers and sinners!' Yet wisdom is vindicated by her deeds."*

[20]*Then He began to reproach the cities in which most of His miracles were done, because they did not repent. [21]'Woe to you, Chorazin! Woe to you, Bethsaida! For if the miracles had occurred in Tyre and Sidon which occurred in you, they would have repented long ago in sackcloth and ashes. [22]Nevertheless I say to you, it shall be more tolerable for Tyre and Sidon in the day of judgment, than for you. [23]And you, Capernaum, will not be exalted to heaven, will you? You shall descend to Hades; for if the miracles had occurred in Sodom which occurred in you, it would have remained to this day.*
[24] *Nevertheless I say to you that it shall be more tolerable for the land of Sodom in the day of judgment, than for you.'*

[25] *At that time Jesus answered and said, 'I praise Thee, O Father, Lord of heaven and earth, that Thou didst hide these things from the wise and intelligent and didst reveal them to babes. [26] Yes, Father, for thus it was well-pleasing in Thy sight. [27]All things have been handed over to Me by My Father; and no one knows the Son, except the Father; nor does anyone know the Father, except the Son, and anyone to whom the Son wills to reveal Him. [28] Come to Me, all who are weary and heavy-laden, and I will give you rest. [29] Take My yoke upon you, and learn from Me, for I am gentle and humble in heart; and YOU SHALL FIND REST FOR YOUR SOULS. [30]For My yoke is easy, and My load is light.'"*

Introduction

Here we see the Lord expose the hardness of man's heart. It does not matter that both John and Jesus called men to repentance by different styles, the people still refused to respond. It did not matter that they saw miracles or that they were very intelligent; their hearts were hardened and they would not repent. For those who did repent, they were forgiven by Jesus. They were set free from their old heavy load of sin. Jesus told those who followed Him that His *"...yoke is easy, and My load is light."* Some might counter by pointing out that Jesus spoke of the cost of discipleship including severe persecution and even death. They then might complain and argue that this type of life is not an easy yoke or light load. Their problem is that they do not understand the completely devastating effect of sin in their life. Not only does sin manifest its putrefying, corrupting impact in every area of their lives, but it also carries death and damnation to an eternity in hell. Now view Jesus' load as freeing us from sin, death and the eternal lake of fire. We are now able to love by the power of the Holy Spirit. Our *good deeds* are no longer hypocritical, self-centered acts, but instead are directed by the Holy Spirit to glorify God. Oh yes, indeed, Jesus did all the labor that we could never do! Oh yes, His *"yoke is easy"* and His *"load is light"*!

VERSES 16-19: *"But to what shall I compare this generation? It is like children sitting in the market places, who call out to the other children, [17] and say, 'We played the flute for you, and you did not dance; we sang a dirge, and you did not mourn.' [18] For John came neither eating nor drinking, and they say, 'He* *has a demon!'* [19] *The Son of Man came eating and drinking, and they say, 'Behold, a gluttonous man and a drunkard, a friend of tax-gatherers and sinners!' Yet wisdom is vindicated by her deeds."*

Often those who do not want to believe in God cover their hatred of God with criticism. In this section (verses 16-18), Jesus analogizes the unrepentant, as malcontent children, that are never happy with whatever is offered to them (i.e. children, play-acting either a wedding or a funeral.) It did not matter what was offered, some of the kids refused to play along and wanted something different. The analogy is a contrast of John the Baptist and Jesus' ministry style. Here John the Baptist can be viewed as the kids saying, *"we sang a dirge, and you did not mourn."* John's message of repentance and judgment, along with his ascetic[196] lifestyle, made some so mad that after a while they said, *'He has a demon!'* **Matthew 11:18**. Jesus also taught repentance, but His style was more like a marriage dance. An example of that is demonstrated by the time that John the Baptist's disciples asked Jesus why His disciples did not fast. Jesus answered them by saying,

> *"The attendants of the bridegroom cannot mourn as long as the bridegroom is with them, can they? But the days will come when the bridegroom is taken away from them, and then they will fast."* **Matthew 9:15**.

Jesus and John were a contrast in style. As mentioned above, John was a man who lived in the wilderness away from the people. Jesus was among the people. Yes, it was true that He was a friend of tax-gatherers and sinners because a sinner has not a greater friend than God who is the only one who can forgive him. Note that Jesus never participated in the sinful conduct of the people he associated with. Instead he preached to them deliverance from their sinful lifestyle. Jesus' critics tried to slander Him by falsely saying that He was *"…a gluttonous man and a drunkard."* The wicked are always the first to falsely judge and slander the godly, just as their father the devil does, but one day he too will be silenced:

> **Revelation 12:10:** *"…for the accuser of our brethren has been thrown down, who accuses them before our God day and night."*

Jesus' statement in **Matthew 11:19** says, *"Yet wisdom is vindicated by her deeds."* [197] This phrase means that given enough time, true wisdom will be proven. Over time it will be manifest that He is

---

[196] **as·cet·ic** (…-sŭt"ĭk) *n.* **1.** A person who renounces material comforts and leads a life of austere self-discipline, especially as an act of religious devotion. *adj.* **1.** Leading a life of self-discipline and self-denial, especially for spiritual improvement. *American Heritage Dictionary.*

[197] The NASB, **Matthew 11:19** states that *"Yet wisdom is vindicated by her deeds."* The KJV for Matthew 11:19 uses the phrase *"But wisdom is justified of her children…."* *"Children"* is also used in the parallel section in Luke 7:35 where it states that *"Yet wisdom is vindicated by all her children."* Both have the same meaning and the variance is explained below:

Matthew 11:19:
> *NASB, NRSV:* *"Yet wisdom is vindicated by her deeds"*
> *KJV:* *"But wisdom is justified of her children."*
> *Jerusalem Bible:* *"Yet wisdom has been proved right by her actions"* — "There is a Greek manuscript

variation here. 'Deeds' is found in the ancient Greek uncial manuscripts ℵ and B, while 'children' is found in the Corrector of Vaticanus (B²) and also C, D, K, and L. 'Children' is the parallel in **Luke 7:35** and seems to be added here by scribes to make the passages agree. The original Aramaic term may have meant 'future events.' The same truth is expressed in the phrase 'by their fruits you shall know them' (cf. **Matthew 7:16, 20; 12:33**). This is true of Jesus and of all people. The acts of Jesus in chapters 8–9 revealed to those who would see that He was the promised Messiah (cf. **Isaiah 29:18–19; 35:5–6; 61:1–2**)." Utley, R. J. D. (2000). *Vol. Volume 9: The First Christian Primer: Matthew*. Study Guide Commentary Series (p. 100). Marshall, Texas: Bible Lessons International.

the true Messiah. Despite the false and slanderous accusations against John and Jesus, the conduct of godly wisdom will one day silence all its critics.

So how do you handle these fault-finding hypocrites? Ryle states:
"The plain truth is that true believers must not expect unconverted men to be satisfied either with their faith or their practice.... They must be prepared for objections, cavils and excuses, however holy their own lives may be. As Quesnel so rightly says, 'Whatever measures good men take, they will never escape the censures of the world. The best way is not to be concerned at them.' After all, what does Scripture say? 'The sinful mind is hostile to God.' (Romans 8:7). 'The man without the Spirit does not accept the things from the Spirit of God' (1 Corinthians 2:14). This is the explanation of the whole matter."[198]

VERSES 20-24: *"Then He began to reproach the cities in which most of His miracles were done, because they did not repent.* [21] *'Woe to you, Chorazin! Woe to you, Bethsaida! For if the miracles had occurred in Tyre and Sidon which occurred in you, they would have repented long ago in sackcloth and ashes.* [22]*Nevertheless I say to you, it shall be more tolerable for Tyre and Sidon in the day of judgment, than for you.* [23]*And you, Capernaum, will not be exalted to heaven, will you? You shall descend to Hades; for if the miracles had occurred in Sodom which occurred in you, it would have remained to this day.* [24] *Nevertheless I say to you that it shall be more tolerable for the land of Sodom in the day of judgment, than for you.'"*

These cities represent those where miracles were done. These people simply did not respond in repentance. Look at Capernaum:
"Jesus made His headquarters in this beautiful, prosperous fishing village on the northern shore of the Sea of Galilee. He performed more miracles and preached more sermons in and around Capernaum than at any other place during His entire ministry. It was there that He raised Jairus's daughter from the dead and healed the nobleman's son. It was here that He healed the demoniac, Peter's mother-in-law, the woman with the hemorrhage, the two blind men, the centurion's servant, the dumb demoniac, and the paralytic who was lowered through the roof by his friends. Yet those marvels had little impact on most citizens of Capernaum; and because of their indifference they would not be exalted to heaven as they thought they deserved but would rather descend to Hades."[199]

We often underestimate the hardness and blindness of unbelievers. We think that if a nonbeliever simply heard the right message from the right preacher; or if he saw the power of God through a miracle, he surely would repent and believe the gospel. Ryle states:
"It is good for us all to take good note of this case of Capernaum. We are all too apt to suppose that it needs nothing but the powerful preaching of the Gospel to convert people's souls, and that if the Gospel is only brought into a place everybody *must* believe. We forge the amazing power of unbelief, and the depth of man's enmity

---

[198] *Matthew* / Ryle, J.C. p.84 (Expository Thoughts on the Gospels) (Crossways Classic Commentaries: v.1)

[199] MacArthur, John F., *Matthew, The MacArthur New Testament Commentary*, p. 261 (Chicago: Moody Press) 1983.

against God. We forget that the Capernaites heard the most faultless preaching, and saw it confirmed by the most surprising miracles, and yet remained dead in their transgressions and sins."[200]

VERSES 25-26: *"At that time Jesus answered and said, 'I praise Thee, O Father, Lord of heaven and earth, that Thou didst hide these things from the wise and intelligent and didst reveal them to babes. [26] Yes, Father, for thus it was well-pleasing in Thy sight.'"*

Notice the glory and praise God the Son gives to God the Father: *'I praise Thee, O Father, Lord of heaven and earth'....* We likewise must continually give God the glory He is worthy of.

Jesus then states, *"Thou didst hide these things from the wise and intelligent and didst reveal them to babes."* Those who see themselves as intelligent see no need to rely on the wisdom of God. It is not being intelligent that kept these people from God, but rather their pride (i.e. self-worship). Because of their sin, they are deaf to the Gospel and it makes no sense to them:

> **1 Corinthians 2:14:** *"But a natural man does not accept the things of the Spirit of God; for they are foolishness to him, and he cannot understand them, because they are spiritually appraised."*

Those who do not trust in themselves are the truly humble. They have put their trust in God and He then reveals Himself to them: *"didst reveal them to babes."*

In **Matthew 18:2-4** Jesus said:

> *"And He called a child to Himself and set him before them, [3]and said, 'Truly I say to you, <u>unless you are converted and become like children, you shall not enter the kingdom of heaven.</u> [4] <u>"Whoever then humbles himself as this child,</u> he is the greatest in the kingdom of heaven.'"*

Humans consider fame, wealth, power, prestige, and self-sufficiency to be desirable attributes to obtain. God deliberately chooses many who the world considers very inferior to glorify Himself and simultaneously discredit man's value system.

> **1 Corinthians 1:26-31:** *"For consider your calling, brethren, that there were not many wise according to the flesh, not many mighty, not many noble; [27] but God has chosen the foolish things of the world to shame the wise, and God has chosen the weak things of the world to shame the things which are strong, [28] and the base things of the world and the despised, <u>God has chosen, the things that are not, that He might nullify the things that are,</u> [29] <u>that no man should boast before God.</u> [30] But by His doing you are in Christ Jesus, who became to us wisdom from God, and righteousness and sanctification, and redemption, [31] that, just as it is written, 'LET HIM WHO BOASTS, BOAST IN THE LORD.'"*

---

[200] Ryle, J.C. *Mark (Expository Thoughts on the Gospels),* (Crossways Classic Commentaries: v.2) 1993.

VERSE 27: *"All things have been handed over to Me by My Father; and no one knows the Son, except the Father; nor does anyone know the Father, except the Son, and anyone to whom the Son wills to reveal Him."*

Jesus again makes clear His divinity, and equates Himself with God by calling God His Father.

> **John 14:9-10:** *"Jesus *said to him, 'Have I been so long with you, and yet you have not come to know Me, Philip? He who has seen Me has seen the Father; how do you say, Show us the Father? ¹⁰ Do you not believe that I am in the Father, and the Father is in Me....'"*

Verse 27 also sets forth that we do not get to the Father except through Jesus: *"nor does anyone know the Father, except the Son, and anyone to whom the Son wills to reveal Him."* No religious act, service, or priest can get you to the Father, only Jesus can:

> **John 14:6:** *"Jesus *said to him, 'I am the way, and the truth, and the life; no one comes to the Father, but through Me.'"*

VERSES 28-30: *"Come to Me, all who are weary and heavy-laden, and I will give you rest. ²⁹Take My yoke upon you, and learn from Me, for I am gentle and humble in heart; and YOU SHALL FIND REST FOR YOUR SOULS. ³⁰ For My yoke is easy, and My load is light."*

I have talked to *religious* people who are spending a lot of time and effort trying to make themselves acceptable to God. Some will give money to churches or charities. Others will decide to spend their life helping the poor. Still others believe that sacrificially going into a religious vocation will please God enough that they will earn a place in heaven. Scripture is clear that no person can earn his way to heaven:

> **Ephesians 2:8-9:** *"For by grace you have been saved through faith; and that not of yourselves, it is the gift of God; ⁹ not as a result of works, that no one should boast."*

The Lord can relieve us of our heavy burden of sin and worthless "religious" works. Putting our faith in His sacrificial death on the cross as the complete atonement for our sins is the only way to be saved.

> **John 3:16-18:** *"For God so loved the world , that He gave His only begotten Son, that whoever believes in Him should not perish, but have eternal life . ¹⁷ For God did not send the Son into the world to judge the world, but that the world should be saved through Him. ¹⁸ He who believes in Him is not judged; he who does not believe has been judged already, because he has not believed in the name of the only begotten Son of God."*

We need God's rest and it comes by putting our faith in Christ:

> **Hebrews 3:12, 18-19:** *"Take care, brethren, lest there should be in any one of you an evil, unbelieving heart, in falling away from the living God....*
> *¹⁸And to whom did He swear that they should not enter His rest, but to those who were disobedient? ¹⁹And so we see that they were not able to enter because of unbelief."*

In verse 30 Jesus says, *"For My yoke is easy, and My load is light."* The word **"yoke"** means: "The rendering of several Hebrew and Greek words, used either literally for the wooden frame joining two animals (usually oxen), or metaphorically as describing one individual's subjection to another."[201] The yoke of the Lord is not burdened with legalism[202] etc. He gives us the strength to obey Him, which makes it a light burden. The Apostle John states:

> **1 John 5:3:**   *"For this is the love of God, that we keep His commandments; and <u>His commandments are not burdensome</u>."*

<u>Summary and Application</u>

Are you one who is critical of Christ like the unrepentant who playact as children? Are you unrepentant before God because of a bad experience you had in a church? Maybe your excuse is that you have seen huge hypocrisy from people who claim to be Christian leaders. As legitimate as your complaint may be against another, it is meaningless when you stand before God's tribunal of judgment. At that moment you alone will be responsible for *your sin*. Christ has provided for your righteousness to enter heaven if you receive His grace by faith. For those who have been saved, there is no fear of their eternal future. God has purchased it and He will secure it. Do you experience the Lord's load in your life? It is light and easy because of the great joy of the Lord, the comfort of the Holy Spirit, and the knowledge that the eternal kingdom is soon to come. If your load is an endless burden and full of misery, you are carrying *religion's* load and not God's. If it were truly God's, it would be as Jesus told us: *"For My yoke is easy, and My load is light."*

---

[201] *The New Bible Dictionary*, (Wheaton, Illinois: Tyndale House Publishers, Inc.) 1962.

[202] <u>Legalism</u> teaches that *good works* and/or *religious rituals* etc. help get you saved or keep you saved. Legalism is a heretical doctrine because it attacks the central focus of the gospel — that salvation is 100% by God's grace through faith in the divine Christ's sacrifice on the cross and his resurrection. Sproul states that "…legalism exalts law above grace. The legalists of Jesus' day were the Pharisees, and Jesus reserved His strongest criticism for them. The fundamental distortion of <u>legalism is the belief that one can earn one's way into the kingdom of heaven.</u> The Pharisees believed that due to their status as children of Abraham, and to their scrupulous adherence to the law, they were the children of God. At the core, this was a denial of the gospel." Sproul, R. C. (1992). *Essential truths of the Christian faith*. <u>Article 91 Legalism,</u> Wheaton, IL: Tyndale House.

MATTHEW 12:1-14
(THE SABBATH)

"At that time Jesus went on the Sabbath through the grainfields, and His disciples became hungry and began to pick the heads of grain and eat. ² But when the Pharisees saw it, they said to Him, 'Behold, Your disciples do what is not lawful to do on a Sabbath.' ³ But He said to them, 'Have you not read what David did, when he became hungry, he and his companions; ⁴ how he entered the house of God, and they ate the consecrated bread, which was not lawful for him to eat, nor for those with him, but for the priests alone? ⁵ Or have you not read in the Law, that on the Sabbath the priests in the temple break the Sabbath, and are innocent? ⁶ But I say to you, that something greater than the temple is here. ⁷ But if you had known what this means, 'I DESIRE COMPASSION, AND NOT A SACRIFICE,' you would not have condemned the innocent. ⁸ For the Son of Man is Lord of the Sabbath.

*⁹ And departing from there, He went into their synagogue. ¹⁰ And behold, there was a man with a withered hand. And they questioned Him, saying, 'Is it lawful to heal on the Sabbath?'—in order that they might accuse Him. ¹¹ And He said to them, 'What man shall there be among you, who shall have one sheep, and if it falls into a pit on the Sabbath, will he not take hold of it, and lift it out? ¹² Of how much more value then is a man than a sheep! So then, it is lawful to do good on the Sabbath.' ¹³ Then He *said to the man, 'Stretch out your hand!' And he stretched it out, and it was restored to normal, like the other. ¹⁴ But the Pharisees went out, and counseled together against Him, as to how they might destroy Him."*

Introduction

The Pharisees did not have a clue what it meant to obey God as a result of love for Him. What they did love was their own claim of self-righteousness. They were proud of their rules, which they kept when it was convenient. Look at verses 12-14 of the text above and see that the Pharisees had hearts so darkened in sin that they wanted to murder Jesus because He healed a man!

This section deals with the Sabbath. To begin our study of the Sabbath we need to examine its meaning. SABBATH means to "cease or desist." It origins are found in **Genesis 2:1-3** which states:

> *"Thus the heavens and the earth were completed, and all their hosts. ² And by the seventh day God completed His work which He had done; and He rested on the seventh day from all His work which He had done. ³ Then God blessed the seventh day and sanctified it, because in it He rested from all His work which God had created and made."*

The Sabbath was a gift to man: *"See, the LORD <u>has given you the sabbath</u>; therefore He gives you bread for two days on the sixth day...."* **Exodus 16:29.** The point of the Sabbath was to give rest to man as well as a time to honor/focus on God (Exodus 16:29-30). The Sabbath is set out in the Ten Commandments in <u>**Deuteronomy 5:12-15:**</u>

> *"Observe the sabbath day to keep it holy, as the LORD your God commanded you. ¹³Six days you shall labor and do all your work, ¹⁴ but the seventh day is a sabbath of the LORD your God; in it you shall not do any work, you or your son or your daughter or your male servant or your female servant or your ox or your donkey or any of your cattle or your sojourner who stays with you, so that your male servant and your female servant may rest as well as you. ¹⁵ And you shall remember that you were a slave in the land of Egypt, and the LORD your God brought you out of there by a mighty hand and*

by an outstretched arm; therefore the LORD your God commanded you to observe the sabbath day."

VERSES 1-8: *"AT that time Jesus went on the Sabbath through the grainfields, and His disciples became hungry and began to pick the heads of grain and eat. ² But when the Pharisees saw it, they said to Him, 'Behold, Your disciples do what is not lawful to do on a Sabbath.' ³ But He said to them, 'Have you not read what David did, when he became hungry, he and his companions; ⁴ how he entered the house of God, and they ate the consecrated bread, which was not lawful for him to eat, nor for those with him, but for the priests alone? ⁵ Or have you not read in the Law, that on the Sabbath the priests in the temple break the Sabbath, and are innocent? ⁶ But I say to you, that something greater than the temple is here. ⁷ But if you had known what this means, 'I DESIRE COMPASSION, AND NOT A SACRIFICE,' you would not have condemned the innocent. ⁸ For the Son of Man is Lord of the Sabbath.'"*

Here we see the Pharisees claiming to catch Jesus violating the law. Specifically they made the false accusation that He violated the Sabbath. Although it was forbidden by Mosaic Law to do reaping on the Sabbath (Exodus 34:21), Jesus' disciples were not reaping. They were simply picking some heads of grain while they were walking (Mark 2:23). They were merely rubbing grain together in their hands (Luke 6:1) to satisfy their hunger. Their conduct was lawful under Deuteronomy 23:25. It was the Pharisees *man-made* traditions that determined that they were *reaping* (i.e. laboring) on the Sabbath. Many of these "traditions" and absurd *man-made* interpretations to the Mosaic Law were recorded in the Talmud:

> "One section alone of the Talmud, the major compilation of Jewish tradition, has twenty-four chapters listing Sabbath laws. One law specified that the basic limit for travel was 3,000 feet from one's house; but various exceptions were provided. If you had placed some food within 3,000 feet of your house, you could go there to eat it; and because the food was considered an extension of the house, you could then go another 3,000 feet beyond the food. If a rope were placed across an adjoining street or alley, the building on the other side, as well as the alley between, could be considered part of your house."[203]

One can see that the "yoke" of the Pharisees was heavy and hard. Jesus said in **Matthew 11:28-30:**

> *"Come to Me, all who are weary and heavy-laden, and I will give you rest. ²⁹ Take My yoke upon you, and learn from Me, for I am gentle and humble in heart; and YOU SHALL FIND REST FOR YOUR SOULS. ³⁰For My yoke is easy, and My load is light."*

The yoke of the Lord is not burdened with legalism, etc.[204] He gives us the strength to obey Him which makes it a light burden. The Apostle John said:

> *"For this is the love of God, that we keep His commandments;*
> *and His commandments are not burdensome."* **1 John 5:3.**

After the Pharisees claimed that Jesus and His disciples broke the Law (Matthew 12:2), Jesus exposes the Pharisees' hypocrisy with a three-pronged argument:

---

[203] MacArthur, John F., *Matthew, The MacArthur New Testament Commentary*, Page 275. (Chicago: Moody Press) 1983.

[204] See an explanation of llegalism in footnote 202 on page 224, in the Matthew 11:28-30 section.

1. In verses 3 and 4, Jesus cites David (King of Israel). Jesus points out that the Sabbath is not broken when one does good (cf. 1 Samuel 21:1-6).
2. The second argument points out that the priests engaged in labor on the Sabbath. Since the priest's work was doing God's calling it was not considered to be breaking the Sabbath. We see priests' working on the Sabbath in Numbers 28:9-10. Jesus Himself went and taught on the Sabbath in <u>Luke 4:16</u>: *"And He came to Nazareth, where He had been brought up; and as was His custom, He entered the synagogue on the Sabbath, and stood up to read."* (Paul spent many Sabbaths doing God's will: *"And he was reasoning in the synagogue every Sabbath and trying to persuade Jews and Greeks"* <u>Acts 18:4</u>).
3. The third argument deals with who Jesus is (v.6-8). He first points out that He is greater than the temple that the Jews took such pride in. More than that, He tells them plainly that He is *"Lord of the Sabbath."* This statement was an unequivocal proclamation by Jesus to declare Himself to be God.

Jesus said in <u>Matthew 12:7</u>: *"But if you had known what this means, 'I DESIRE COMPASSION, AND NOT A SACRIFICE,' you would not have condemned the innocent."* Jesus sums up the issue by pointing out that the law of God is not fulfilled through "robotic obedience" to rules and rituals. We fulfill the law of God when we have been converted by Christ, and then have a heart of compassion, love and service for others. Look what Paul says is the objective of godly teaching:

> <u>1 Timothy 1:5</u>: *"But the <u>goal of our instruction is love from a pure heart</u> and a good conscience and a sincere faith."*

<u>VERSES 9-14:</u> *"And departing from there, He went into their synagogue. 10 And behold, there was a man with a withered hand. And they questioned Him, saying, 'Is it lawful to heal on the Sabbath?'—in order that they might accuse Him. 11 And He said to them, 'What man shall there be among you, who shall have one sheep, and if it falls into a pit on the Sabbath, will he not take hold of it, and lift it out? 12 Of how much more value then is a man than a sheep! So then, it is lawful to do good on the Sabbath.' 13 Then He *said to the man, 'Stretch out your hand!' And he stretched it out, and it was restored to normal, like the other. 14 But the Pharisees went out, and counseled together against Him, as to how they might destroy Him."*

In verse 10, the Pharisees ask Jesus, *"Is it lawful to heal on the Sabbath?"* They acknowledged His supernatural ability to heal, but they did not care about any evidence of His Messiahship. The blind hatred led them only to hope that they *"might accuse Him."* Jesus exposes their hypocrisy by pointing out that they would never consider suffering economic loss by not doing the work needed to rescue one of their sheep, even if that happened on the Sabbath day. Jesus goes on to expound that if they would save a mere animal on the Sabbath, surely it is even more righteous to help a human being! In verse 12 Jesus says, *"Of how much more value then is a man than a sheep!"* (Note that this verse should also silence the "animal rights" activist who tries to equate animals on the same level as humans.)

In verse 13 we read that Jesus healed the man. This great miracle did not draw the Pharisees to Jesus, but rather exposed their evil hearts because their response was to work together to figure out a way to kill Jesus: *"But the Pharisees went out, and counseled together against Him, as to how they might destroy Him."* <u>Matthew 12:14</u>.

The incident in Matthew 12:9-14 is not the only time the Pharisees attacked Jesus for healing on the Sabbath.

> **Luke 13:10-17:** *"And He was teaching in one of the synagogues on the Sabbath. 11 And behold, there was a woman who for eighteen years had had a sickness caused by a spirit; and she was bent double, and could not straighten up at all. 12 And when Jesus saw her, He called her over and said to her, 'Woman, you are freed from your sickness.'13 And He laid His hands upon her; and immediately she was made erect again, and began glorifying God. 14 And the synagogue official, indignant because Jesus had healed on the Sabbath, began saying to the multitude in response, 'There are six days in which work should be done; therefore come during them and get healed, and not on the Sabbath day.' 15 But the Lord answered him and said, 'You hypocrites, does not each of you on the Sabbath untie his ox or his donkey from the stall, and lead him away to water him? 16 And this woman, a daughter of Abraham as she is, whom Satan has bound for eighteen long years, should she not have been released from this bond on the Sabbath day?' 17 And as He said this, all His opponents were being humiliated; and the entire multitude was rejoicing over all the glorious things being done by Him."*

Look how the religious leaders had no compassion for people when Jesus healed another man on the Sabbath:

> **John 5:5-11, 16-17:** *"And a certain man was there, <u>who had been thirty-eight years in his sickness</u>. 6 When Jesus saw him lying there, and knew that he had already been a long time in that condition, He *said to him, 'Do you wish to get well?' 7 The sick man answered Him, 'Sir, I have no man to put me into the pool when the water is stirred up, but while I am coming, another steps down before me.' 8 Jesus *said to him, 'Arise, take up your pallet, and walk.' 9 And immediately the man became well, and took up his pallet and began to walk. Now it was the Sabbath on that day. 10 Therefore the Jews were saying to him who was cured, 'It is the Sabbath, and it is not permissible for you to carry your pallet.' 11 But he answered them, 'He who made me well was the one who said to me, 'Take up your pallet and walk.'….*
>
> *16And for this reason the Jews were persecuting Jesus, because He was doing these things on the Sabbath. 17 But He answered them, 'My Father is working until now, and I Myself am working.'"*

Here is another example:

> **John 9:13-16:** *"They *brought to the Pharisees him who was formerly blind. 14 Now it was a Sabbath on the day when Jesus made the clay, and opened his eyes. 15 Again, therefore, the Pharisees also were asking him how he received his sight. And he said to them, 'He applied clay to my eyes, and I washed, and I see.' 16 Therefore some of the Pharisees were saying, 'This man is not from God, because He does not keep the Sabbath….'"*

Summary and Application

Some believe that it is wrong to have Sunday be your Sabbath day instead of Saturday. It is true that the Jewish Sabbath was on Saturday and that the Sabbath is part of the Ten Commandments (Exodus 20:9-11). But under the New Covenant we are free to have a specific Sabbath day just as much as we are free to enjoy and worship God every day of the week. John MacArthur writes regarding the Sabbath:

"...that law is the only one of the Ten Commandments that is nonmoral and purely ceremonial; and it was unique to the Old Covenant and to Israel. The other nine commandments, on the other hand, pertain to moral and spiritual absolutes and are repeated and expanded upon many places in the New Testament. But Sabbath observance is never recommended to Christians, much less given as a command in the New Testament." [205]

There is not an official *Christian day* that is mandated as a Sabbath for every Christian. That being the case, let no one tell you that if you were a *real Christian* you would have a certain day as your Sabbath. Below are Scriptures supporting the view that there is liberty as to the issue of a Sabbath day:

<u>Colossians 2:16-17:</u> *"<u>Therefore let no one act as your judge in regard</u> to food or drink or in respect to a festival or a new moon <u>or a Sabbath day</u>— ¹⁷ things which are a mere shadow of what is to come; but the substance belongs to Christ."*

<u>Romans 14:5-6:</u> *"One man regards one day above another, another regards every day alike. Let each man be fully convinced in his own mind. ⁶ He who observes the day, observes it for the Lord, and he who eats, does so for the Lord, for he gives thanks to God; and he who eats not, for the Lord he does not eat, and gives thanks to God."*

<u>Galatians 4:9-11:</u> *"But now that you have come to know God, or rather to be known by God, how is it that you turn back again to the weak and worthless elemental things, to which you desire to be enslaved all over again? ¹⁰ You observe days and months and seasons and years. ¹¹ I fear for you, that perhaps I have labored over you in vain."*

This freedom from ceremonial law should not be understood to mean that we do not need to fellowship with other believers. We are commanded to meet together and worship in **Hebrews 10:24-25:**

"...and let us consider how to stimulate one another to love and good deeds, ²⁵ not forsaking our own assembling together, as is the habit of some, but encouraging one another; and all the more, as you see the day drawing near."

In summary, we have been released from a ritualistic observation of one day a week for the Lord. Now that we walk in the newness of the Spirit of God, we can live <u>every day</u> and <u>every moment</u> in the joy of the Lord.

Romans 7:6: *"But now we have been released from the Law, having died to that by which we were bound, so that we serve in newness of the Spirit and not in oldness of the letter."*

---

[205] MacArthur, John F., *Matthew, The MacArthur New Testament Commentary*, p. 275 (Chicago: Moody Press) 1983.

MATTHEW 12:15-32
(BLASPHEMY AGAINST THE HOLY SPIRIT)

"But Jesus, aware of this, withdrew from there. And many followed Him, and He healed them all, 16 and warned them not to make Him known, 17 in order that what was spoken through Isaiah the prophet, might be fulfilled, saying,

18 *'BEHOLD, MY SERVANT WHOM I HAVE CHOSEN;*

    MY BELOVED IN WHOM MY SOUL is WELL -PLEASED;

    I WILL PUT MY SPIRIT UPON HIM,

    AND HE SHALL PROCLAIM JUSTICE TO THE GENTILES.

19 *HE WILL NOT QUARREL, NOR CRY OUT;*

    NOR WILL ANYONE HEAR HIS VOICE IN THE STREETS.

20 *A BATTERED REED HE WILL NOT BREAK OFF,*

    AND A SMOLDERING WICK HE WILL NOT PUT OUT,

    UNTIL HE LEADS JUSTICE TO VICTORY.

21 *AND IN HIS NAME THE GENTILES WILL HOPE.'*

22 *Then there was brought to Him a demon-possessed man who was blind and dumb, and He healed him, so that the dumb man spoke and saw. 23 And all the multitudes were amazed, and began to say, 'This man cannot be the Son of David, can he?' 24 But when the Pharisees heard it, they said, 'This man casts out demons only by Beelzebul the ruler of the demons.' 25 And knowing their thoughts He said to them, 'Any kingdom divided against itself is laid waste; and any city or house divided against itself shall not stand. 26 And if Satan casts out Satan, he is divided against himself; how then shall his kingdom stand? 27 And if I by Beelzebul cast out demons, by whom do your sons cast them out? Consequently they shall be your judges. 28 But if I cast out demons by the Spirit of God, then the kingdom of God has come upon you. 29 Or how can anyone enter the strong man's house and carry off his property, unless he first binds the strong man? And then he will plunder his house.*

30 *He who is not with Me is against Me; and he who does not gather with Me scatters. 31 Therefore I say to you, any sin and blasphemy shall be forgiven men, but blasphemy against the Spirit shall not be forgiven. 32 And whoever shall speak a word against the Son of Man, it shall be forgiven him; but whoever shall speak against the Holy Spirit, it shall not be forgiven him, either in this age, or in the age to come.'"*

Introduction

The previous lesson involved Jesus healing a man with a withered hand on the Sabbath. The Pharisees were angered that Jesus healed on the Sabbath. Their response to the healing is set out in verse 14 where it says:

> *"But the Pharisees went out, and counseled together against Him, as to how they might destroy Him."*

At this point the religious leaders had murder in their hearts. We read in this section that they went on to commit the unforgivable sin of blasphemy against the Holy Spirit.

VERSES 15-21: *"But Jesus, aware of this, withdrew from there. And many followed Him, and He healed them all, [16] and warned them not to make Him known, [17] in order that what was spoken through Isaiah the prophet, might be fulfilled, saying,*

[18] *'BEHOLD, MY SERVANT WHOM I HAVE CHOSEN;*

 MY BELOVED IN WHOM MY SOUL is WELL -PLEASED;

 I WILL PUT MY SPIRIT UPON HIM,

 AND HE SHALL PROCLAIM JUSTICE TO THE GENTILES.

[19] *HE WILL NOT QUARREL, NOR CRY OUT;*

 NOR WILL ANYONE HEAR HIS VOICE IN THE STREETS.

[20] *A BATTERED REED HE WILL NOT BREAK OFF,*

 AND A SMOLDERING WICK HE WILL NOT PUT OUT,

 UNTIL HE LEADS JUSTICE TO VICTORY.

[21] *AND IN HIS NAME THE GENTILES WILL HOPE.'"*

We see the demonic evil in the hearts of the Pharisees manifested by their plotting on how to kill Jesus (v.14). We also see the omniscience (all-knowingness) of Jesus in that He knew what they were plotting to do and so He left that area (verse15, *"But Jesus, aware of this, withdrew from there."*) Jesus was not "running away" to save Himself. He remained in complete control of all events. It was not His time to die at their hands, so He left them. There was a similar situation when Jesus declared himself the Messiah and then spoke to the crowd. They were so angry that they pushed Him to a cliff, preparing to throw Him to His death. Jesus, and not the angry mob had command over His life. He just walked through the middle of the murder-enraged crowd and *"...went His way."*

> **Luke 4:28-30:** *"And all in the synagogue were filled with rage as they heard these things; [29]and they rose up and cast Him out of the city, and led Him to the brow of the hill on which their city had been built, in order to throw Him down the cliff. [30] But passing through their midst, He went His way."*

Here is a direct statement by Jesus regarding His omnipotent control over all things, including His own life.

> **John 10:17-18:** *"For this reason the Father loves Me, because I lay down My life that I may take it again. [18] No one has taken it away from Me, but I lay it down on My own initiative. I have authority to lay it down, and I have authority to take it up again."*

> **Matthew 26:53:** *"Or do you think that I cannot appeal to My Father, and He will at once put at My disposal more than twelve legions of angels?"*

In the later portion of **Matthew 12:15**, it says, *"...And many followed Him, and He healed them all."* Notice that Jesus did not just heal the rich and famous or just the poor. Jesus *"...healed them all"* because of His great love and compassion. He gave instructions to those He healed by warning *"...them not to make Him known...."* This means that they were to not publicly reveal that He was the Messiah, since that would draw more opposition before the proper time. Along that theme, this was not the time set for His exaltation, which would occur later. Matthew Henry writes an additional thought on why Jesus told the people He healed to not make it known to others. "It may be looked upon as an act of righteous judgment upon the Pharisees, who were unworthy to hear of any more of his miracles, having made so light of those they had seen. By shutting their eyes against the light, they had forfeited the benefit of it."[206] There is merit to this view when examined in light of Matthew 12:24. In that verse the Pharisees see another miracle of Jesus' and then commit blasphemy of the Holy Spirit.

In **Matthew 12:18-21** we read the specific reason why the people were, *"not to make Him known."* The specific purpose was to fulfill prophecy which describes the Messiah in meekness and humility, as well as His complete victory over sin and the Devil. Note the great promise of mercy to the Gentiles in verses 18 and 21!

> [18] *"BEHOLD, MY SERVANT WHOM I HAVE CHOSEN;*
> *MY BELOVED IN WHOM MY SOUL is WELL -PLEASED;*
> *I WILL PUT MY SPIRIT UPON HIM,*
> *AND HE SHALL PROCLAIM JUSTICE TO THE GENTILES.*
> [19] *HE WILL NOT QUARREL, NOR CRY OUT;*
> *NOR WILL ANYONE HEAR HIS VOICE IN THE STREETS.*
> [20] *A BATTERED REED HE WILL NOT BREAK OFF,*
> *AND A SMOLDERING WICK HE WILL NOT PUT OUT,*
> *UNTIL HE LEADS JUSTICE TO VICTORY.*
> [21] *AND IN HIS NAME THE GENTILES WILL HOPE."*

[This prophecy is found in Isaiah 42:1-4.]

VERSES 22-29: *"Then there was brought to Him a demon-possessed man who was blind and dumb, and He healed him, so that the dumb man spoke and saw. [23] And all the multitudes were amazed, and began to say, 'This man cannot be the Son of David, can he?' [24] But when the Pharisees heard it, they said, 'This man casts out demons only by Beelzebul the ruler of the demons.' [25] And knowing their thoughts He said to them, 'Any kingdom divided against itself is laid waste; and any city or house divided against itself shall not stand. [26] And if Satan casts out Satan, he is divided against himself; how then shall his kingdom stand? [27] And if I by Beelzebul cast out demons, by whom do your sons cast them out? Consequently they shall be your judges. [28] But if I cast out demons by the Spirit of God, then the kingdom of God has come upon you. [29] Or how can anyone enter the strong man's house and carry off his property, unless he first binds the strong man? And then he will plunder his house.'"*

Here we have a man who is both physically and spiritually sick. Physically, he can neither see nor talk. Spiritually, he is possessed by demons. Jesus heals the man completely. The Pharisees see another awesome miracle which they know they cannot deny (*"…the multitudes were amazed"*). Despite the clear and undisputed evidence of Jesus being the Messiah, the Pharisees deliberately reject the evidence. The people were discerning that Jesus might be the Messiah. Note in verse 23 they asked each other if this could be, *"the Son of David."* The term *"Son of David"* was a scriptural title for the Messiah as found in Psalm 89:3-4 and Isaiah 9:6-7. The Pharisees concluded they must stop such talk among the people. They decided to attack the evidence the people saw with a demonic lie. That lie involved the attempt to persuade the people that Jesus was *Beelzebul*, the ruler of the demons (v.24). The Pharisees were making the ultimate slanderous comment by saying that the source of Jesus' power was from the devil.

---

[206] Henry, Matthew, *Matthew Henry's Commentary on the Bible*, (Matthew 12:14-21). (Peabody, MA: Hendrickson Publishers) 1997.

Jesus is *all knowing* (omniscient), so He knew what the Pharisees were saying to others as well as what they were thinking. *"And knowing their thoughts...."* **Matthew 12:25**. Jesus confronts them with their unforgivable, blasphemous statement and says:

> *"... Any kingdom divided against itself is laid waste; and any city or house divided against itself shall not stand. 26 And if Satan casts out Satan, he is divided against himself; how then shall his kingdom stand? 27 And if I by Beelzebul cast out demons, by whom do your sons cast them out? Consequently they shall be your judges. 28 But if I cast out demons by the Spirit of God, then the kingdom of God has come upon you. 29 Or how can anyone enter the strong man's house and carry off his property, unless he first binds the strong man? And then he will plunder his house."* **Matthew 12:25-29.**

It should be noted that the Biblically illiterate often mistakenly attribute the phrase, *"house divided against itself shall not stand ...."* to Abraham Lincoln. [207] Jesus points out the hypocrisy of the Pharisees in that some of the Pharisees' *disciples* (i.e. *"your sons"* v.27) performed exorcisms,[208] but the Pharisees never claimed those were demonically inspired.

The believer today should expect this same hatred and slander from the world. Ryle states that:
> "When the Christian's arguments cannot be answered, and the Christian's works cannot be denied, the last resource of the wicked is to blacken the Christian's character. If this is our lot, let us bear it patiently. Having Christ and a good conscience, we may be content; false charges will not keep us out of heaven. Our character will be cleared at the last day."[209]

VERSES 30-32: *"He who is not with Me is against Me; and he who does not gather with Me scatters. 31 Therefore I say to you, any sin and blasphemy shall be forgiven men, but blasphemy against the Spirit shall not be forgiven. 32 And whoever shall speak a word against the Son of Man, it shall be forgiven him; but whoever shall speak against the Holy Spirit, it shall not be forgiven him, either in this age, or in the age to come."*

The forgiveness of God is awesome. Can one think of a more evil deed than to mock and murder God's Son? Yet look how God responds: *"But Jesus was saying, 'Father, forgive them; for they do not know what they are doing.'"* We see God will even forgive a non-believer who blasphemed Him and later repents. Look what Paul said about himself before he was saved:

---

[207] "A speech made by Abraham Lincoln to the Illinois Republican convention [on June 16, 1858]. In the speech, Lincoln noted that conflict between North and South over slavery was intensifying. He asserted that the conflict would not stop until a crisis was reached and passed, for, in a biblical phrase Lincoln used, 'A house divided against itself cannot stand.' He continued: ' I believe this government cannot endure permanently half slave and half free. I do not expect the UNION to be dissolved — I do not expect the house to fall — but I do expect it will cease to be divided. It will become all one thing, or all the other.' *American Heritage Dictionary of Cultural Literacy.*

[208] Notice non-believers (seven sons of Chief priest named Sceva) attempting an exorcism in Acts 19:13—16.

[209] *Matthew* / Ryle, J.C. p.94 (Expository Thoughts on the Gospels) (Crossways Classic Commentaries: v.1)

1 Timothy 1:13-15: *"...even though <u>I was formerly a blasphemer</u> and a persecutor and a violent aggressor. And yet I was shown mercy, because <u>I acted ignorantly in unbelief</u>; [14] and the grace of our Lord was more than abundant, with the faith and love which are found in Christ Jesus. [15] It is a trustworthy statement, deserving full acceptance, that Christ Jesus came into the world to save sinners, among whom I am foremost of all."*

Matthew 12:32 states that one can be forgiven if that person had spoken against the name of Jesus (i.e. the Son of Man), but no man can be forgiven for blaspheming the Holy Spirit. John MacArthur demonstrates the distinction between this type of blasphemy and that of the Pharisees when they blasphemed the Holy Spirit:

"But to misjudge, belittle, and discredit Jesus from the vantage point of incomplete revelation or inadequate perception was forgivable, wrong as it was. As already mentioned, the apostle Paul had himself been an ignorant blasphemer of the Lord Jesus Christ of the worst sort and a fierce persecutor of His church. And many of those who had denied and rejected Christ during His earthly ministry later saw the truth of who He was and asked forgiveness and were saved. But the blasphemy against the Spirit was something more serious and irremediable. It not only reflected unbelief, but determined unbelief-the refusal, after having seen all the evidence necessary to complete understanding, even to consider believing in Christ. This was blasphemy against Jesus in His deity, against the Spirit of God who uniquely indwelt and empowered Him. It reflected determined rejection of Jesus as the Messiah against every evidence and argument. It reflected seeing the truth incarnate and then knowingly rejecting Him and condemning Him. It demonstrated an absolute and permanent refusal to believe, which resulted in loss of opportunity ever to be forgiven....either in this age, or in the age to come. Through this age (all of human history), such rejection is unforgivable. The age to come implies that through all of eternity there will be no forgiveness. In the age of human history and in the age of divine consummation, no forgiveness....Those who spoke against the Holy Spirit were those who saw His divine power working in and through Jesus but willfully refused to accept the implications of that revelation and, in some cases, attributed that power to Satan. Many people had heard Jesus teach and preach God's truth, as no man had ever taught before (Matt. 7:28-29), yet they refused to believe Him. They had seen him heal every kind of disease, cast out every kind of demon, and forgive every kind of sin, yet they charged Him with deceit, falsehood, and demonism. In the face of every possible evidence of Jesus' messiahship and deity, they said no. God could do nothing more for them, and they would therefore remain eternally unforgiven.....To unsaved Jews who had heard the full gospel message and had seen its evidence in supernatural power, and to all who would come after them with similar exposure to the truth and the biblical record of miraculous evidence, the writer of the book of Hebrews gave a stern warning: 'How shall we escape if we neglect so great a salvation? After it was at the first spoken through the Lord, it was confirmed to us by those who heard [that is, the apostles], God also bearing witness with them, both by signs and wonders and by various miracles and by gifts of the Holy Spirit according to His own will' (Hebrews 2:3-4)."[210]

---

[210] MacArthur, J. (1985). *Matthew* (p. 289). Chicago: Moody Press.

Below are some writing of other great Bible expositors on this issue.

Charles Hodge summarized the unpardonable sin as follows:
"This sin supposes, 1. Knowledge of the gospel. 2. Conviction of its truth. 3. Experience of its power. It is the rejection of the whole testimony of the Spirit and rejection of Him and His work, with malicious and outspoken blasphemy. It is by a comparison of (Matthew 12:31) and the parallel passages in Mark and Luke, with (Hebrews 6:6–10;10:26–29) that the true idea of the unpardonable sin is to be obtained." [211]

Morton H. Smith, in his work *Systematic Theology* writes:
"This context should be kept in mind as we seek to understand what the sin against the Holy Spirit is. Remember that the Jews were suggesting that his work done by the Spirit of God was the work of Satan. He showed them the unreasonableness of this line of argument. He then warns against sinning against the Spirit. In effect he said to them that their sin was the unreasonable and absurd rejection of the Son of God as Saviour in opposition to the plain and unanswerable testimony of the Spirit. This is the historical interpretation of this sin, based on the context. This understanding of the unpardonable sin then essentially identifies it with the rejection of Christ. This is warranted because it is the work of the Spirit to bear testimony of him (John 16:8–10). Thus when a person who has known the Gospel, and come under some conviction of the Gospel finally rejects it, he is, in effect, rejecting the testimony of the Holy Spirit. Abraham Kuyper cites not only the passages found in the Synoptics describing this sin, but also 1 John 5:16–18 and Hebrew 6:4–8. On the basis of the last passage he suggests that 'the sin against the Holy Spirit can be committed only by persons who, beholding the beauty and majesty of the Lord, turn the light into darkness and deem the highest glory of the Son of God's love to belong to Satan and his demons.' Again he says, 'To commit this sin two things are required, which absolutely belong together: First, close contact with the glory which is manifest in Christ or in His people. Second, not mere contempt of that glory, but the declaration that the Spirit which manifests itself in that glory, which is the Holy Spirit, is a manifestation of Satan.'"[212]

R. C. Sproul wrote in his book Essential Truths of the Christian Faith:
"Frequently the unforgiveable sin is identified with persistent and final unbelief in Christ. Since death brings the end of a person's opportunity to repent of sin and embrace Christ, the finality of unbelief brings the consequence of the termination of hope of forgiveness. Though persistent and final unbelief does bring about such consequences it does not adequately explain Jesus' warning concerning blasphemy against the Holy Spirit. Blasphemy is something one does with the mouth or the pen. It involves words. Though any form of blasphemy is a serious assault on the character of God, it is usually regarded as forgivable. When Jesus warned of the unforgivable sin, it was in the context of His accusers declaring that He was in

---

[211] Charles Hodge, *Sermon Outlines*, taken from Princeton sermons, p.2, Oct. 23, 1864 (Simpsonville, SC: Christian Classics Foundation) 1997.

[212] Morton H. Smith, *Systematic Theology, Volumes I and II*, p. 319 (Simpsonville, SC: Christian Classics Foundation) 1997.

league with Satan. His warning was sober and frightening. Yet, on the cross Jesus prayed for the forgiveness of those who blasphemed against Him on the grounds of their ignorance, *"Father, forgive them, for they do not know what they do"* (Luke 23:34). If, however, people are enlightened by the Holy Spirit to the degree that they know Jesus is truly the Christ, and then they accuse Him of being satanic, they have committed a sin for which there is no pardon. Christians left to their own devices are capable of committing the unpardonable sin, but we are confident that God in His preserving grace will restrain His elect from ever committing such a sin. When earnest Christians are fearful that perhaps they have actually committed this sin, it is probably an indication that they haven't. Those who do commit such a sin would be so hardened of heart and abandoned in their sin as to feel no remorse for it. Even in a pagan, secularized culture like our own, people seem to be reluctant to go too far in their blasphemy against God and Christ. Though the name of Christ is dragged through the mud as a common curse word and the gospel is ridiculed by irreverent jokes and comments, people still seem constrained to avoid linking Jesus with Satan. Though the occult and Satanism provide a context of perilous danger for the commission of the unpardonable sin, if radical blasphemy occurs here it may still be forgiven because it is committed in ignorance by those unenlightened by the Holy Spirit.

Summary:

1. Blasphemy against the Holy Spirit is not to be equated with murder or adultery.
2. Blasphemy is an offense against God involving words.
3. Christ's original warning was against attributing the works of God the Holy Spirit to Satan.
4. Jesus prayed for the forgiveness of blasphemers who were ignorant of His true identity.
5. Christians will never commit this sin because of the restraining grace of God.[213]

William Guthrie[214] speaks comforting truth to the believer who erroneously fears that he committed the unpardonable sin:

"Whatsoever thou hast done against God, if thou dost repent of it, and wish it were undone, thou can't not be guilty of this sin [blasphemy of the Holy Spirit]; for in…[the blasphemer of the Holy Spirit's] heart –malice and despite against God do still prevail." [215]

Summary and Application

Blasphemy against the Holy Spirit is the only unforgivable sin. It will not be committed by a Christian.

---

[213] Sproul, R. C., *Essential Truths of the Christian Faith, The Unforgivable Sin* (Wheaton, Illinois: Tyndale House Publishers, Inc.) 1992.

[214] A Scottish Puritan minister (1620–1665), known as the Puritan's Puritan.

[215] Rev. William Guthrie, *Your Salvation*, p. 176 (Simpsonville, SC: Christian Classics Foundation) 1997.

MATTHEW 12:33-50
(FRUIT BEARING; MIRACLE SEEKING; and THE SPIRITUAL FAMILY)

"'Either make the tree good, and its fruit good; or make the tree bad, and its fruit bad; for the tree is known by its fruit. [34] You brood of vipers, how can you, being evil, speak what is good? For the mouth speaks out of that which fills the heart. [35] The good man out of his good treasure brings forth what is good; and the evil man out of his evil treasure brings forth what is evil. [36] And I say to you, that every careless word that men shall speak, they shall render account for it in the day of judgment. [37] For by your words you shall be justified, and by your words you shall be condemned.'

[38] Then some of the scribes and Pharisees answered Him, saying, 'Teacher, we want to see a sign from You.' [39]But He answered and said to them, 'An evil and adulterous generation craves for a sign; and yet no sign shall be given to it but the sign of Jonah the prophet; [40] for just as JONAH WAS THREE DAYS AND THREE NIGHTS IN THE BELLY OF THE SEA MONSTER, so shall the Son of Man be three days and three nights in the heart of the earth. [41] The men of Nineveh shall stand up with this generation at the judgment, and shall condemn it because they repented at the preaching of Jonah; and behold, something greater than Jonah is here. [42] The Queen of the South shall rise up with this generation at the judgment and shall condemn it, because she came from the ends of the earth to hear the wisdom of Solomon; and behold, something greater than Solomon is here. [43] Now when the unclean spirit goes out of a man, it passes through waterless places, seeking rest, and does not find it. [44] Then it says, 'I will return to my house from which I came;' and when it comes, it finds it unoccupied, swept, and put in order. [45] Then it goes, and takes along with it seven other spirits more wicked than itself, and they go in and live there; and the last state of that man becomes worse than the first. That is the way it will also be with this evil generation.'

[46] While He was still speaking to the multitudes, behold, His mother and brothers were standing outside, seeking to speak to Him. [47] And someone said to Him, 'Behold, Your mother and Your brothers are standing outside seeking to speak to You.' [48] But He answered the one who was telling Him and said, 'Who is My mother and who are My brothers?' [49] And stretching out His hand toward His disciples, He said, 'Behold, My mother and My brothers! [50] For whoever does the will of My Father who is in heaven, he is My brother and sister and mother.'"

Introduction

It is important to keep context in mind when examining a Scripture. Just prior to the above Scripture, the Pharisees committed the unforgivable sin of blasphemy of the Holy Spirit. It is from that point we see Jesus teaching us that we can discern a lot about a person by his words and deeds. He then teaches about those who seek signs and not God. Jesus then teaches about the spiritual world. Jesus also tells us that a true member of God's family is one that does, *"the will of My Father who is in heaven."*

VERSE 33: *"Either make the tree good, and its fruit good; or make the tree bad, and its fruit bad; for the tree is known by its fruit."*

It must be remembered that Jesus just damned (*i.e. condemned to eternal punishment*) the Pharisees who blasphemed the Holy Spirit. He now teaches us that these evil religious leaders can be discerned by the fruit of their lives. Jesus taught this same concept about false teachers earlier in **Matthew 7:16-20**:

> *"You will know them by their fruits. Grapes are not gathered from thorn bushes, nor figs from thistles, are they?* [17] *Even so, every good tree bears good fruit; but the bad tree bears bad fruit.* [18] *A good tree cannot produce bad fruit, nor can a bad tree produce good fruit.* [19] *Every tree that does not bear good fruit is cut down and thrown into the fire.* [20] *So then, you will know them by their fruits."*

False teachers often have a message that appeals to the masses. Paul explained this in **2 Timothy 4:3**: *"...but wanting to have their ears tickled, they will accumulate for themselves teachers in accordance to their own desires;...."* One must carefully discern, since the false among us often disguise themselves in a way that hides their "bad fruit." **2 Corinthians 11:13-15** states that,

> *"For such men are false apostles, deceitful workers, disguising themselves as apostles of Christ.* [14] *And no wonder, for even Satan disguises himself as an angel of light.* [15] *Therefore it is not surprising if his servants also disguise themselves as servants of righteousness; whose end shall be according to their deeds."*

We are to have a zero tolerance for false teaching regarding the Gospel. Scripture states in **Galatians 1:8-9**:

> *"But even though we, or an angel from heaven, should preach to you a gospel contrary to that which we have preached to you, let him be accursed.* [9] *As we have said before, so I say again now, if any man is preaching to you a gospel contrary to that which you received, let him be accursed."*

By knowing God's Word you will be equipped to discern false prophets. Those who are not living Spirit-led lives, founded on God's Word, can easily be deceived when judging between good fruit and bad fruit. One thing is for sure, given enough time (sometimes several years), the false teacher's fruit will be obvious to all. Like the wheat and tares, as they mature it will quickly become apparent. **Matthew 13:26:** *"But when the wheat sprang up and bore grain, then the tares became evident also."* Often when a false teacher is questioned about his conduct or teaching, he will attack the person questioning as the one causing division. Although it is true that a believer must be careful to not cause disunity within the Church of God (cf. Ephesians 4:3), false teachers will take that truth and twist it to their own end. They will also line up others in the church to condemn the person questioning them. Do not be intimidated by the false teacher's accusations of disunity and calls for forgiveness, etc. They will often use these tactics as a cover of their own sin or false teaching. Unfortunately, you might even hear the false calling for unity from the church leadership when leadership does not have the backbone to address the issue. Remember that division *should* occur over issues involving the fundamental truths of God:

> **1 Corinthians 11:19:** *"For there must also be factions among you, in order that those who are approved may have become evident among you."*

VERSES 34-35: [34] *"You brood of vipers, how can you, being evil, speak what is good? For the mouth speaks out of that which fills the heart.* [35] *The good man out of his good treasure brings forth what is good; and the evil man out of his evil treasure brings forth what is evil."*

Speech is an indicator of what is going on within a person. An unsaved person may seem *super nice.* If you are with him for a long enough period of time, however, he will eventually start to let down that image, and you will see the ugly evil heart he has by the things he says. As Jesus said in verse 34, *"...For the mouth speaks out of that which fills the heart."*

The issue of speech also includes telling the truth. We are to be truthful people. **Ephesians 4:25** says, *"Therefore, laying aside falsehood, SPEAK TRUTH, EACH ONE of you, WITH HIS NEIGHBOR, for we are members of one another."* Lying also includes embellishing, flattery, false promises, and cheating on tests or taxes. In God's eye, there is no such thing as a *white lie*; there is the truth, and there are lies. Being truthful is essential in our life, regardless of whether it is convenient or not. There are those who think very little of lying. Take a look at what the Bible states is the punishment for having lied:

> **Revelation 21:8:** *"… and all liars, their part will be in the lake that burns with fire and brimstone, which is the second death."*

Examine the words or slang false teachers use. **Ephesians 4:29** instructs us by saying: *"Let no unwholesome word proceed from your mouth, but only such a word as is good for edification according to the need of the moment, that it may give grace to those who hear."* We are not to use foul language or dirty talk. Off-colored jokes and put-downs are not the way we are to talk. In like manner, we are not to talk in an angry, bitter or violent manner. Our words are to be seasoned with grace for those who hear them: **Colossians 4:6:** *"Let your speech always be with grace, seasoned, as it were, with salt, so that you may know how you should respond to each person."* James reiterates this concept that only a good tree produces good fruit. Read carefully this entire section addressing our speech:

> **James 3:2-12:** *"For we all stumble in many ways. If anyone does not stumble in what he says, he is a perfect man, able to bridle the whole body as well. ³ Now if we put the bits into the horses' mouths so that they may obey us, we direct their entire body as well. ⁴ Behold, the ships also, though they are so great and are driven by strong winds, are still directed by a very small rudder, wherever the inclination of the pilot desires. ⁵ So also the tongue is a small part of the body, and yet it boasts of great things. Behold, how great a forest is set aflame by such a small fire! ⁶ And the tongue is a fire, the very world of iniquity; the tongue is set among our members as that which defiles the entire body, and sets on fire the course of our life, and is set on fire by hell. ⁷ For every species of beasts and birds, of reptiles and creatures of the sea, is tamed, and has been tamed by the human race. ⁸ But no one can tame the tongue; it is a restless evil and full of deadly poison. ⁹ With it we bless our Lord and Father; and with it we curse men, who have been made in the likeness of God; ¹⁰ from the same mouth come both blessing and cursing. My brethren, these things ought not to be this way. ¹¹ Does a fountain send out from the same opening both fresh and bitter water? ¹² Can a fig tree, my brethren, produce olives, or a vine produce figs? Neither can salt water produce fresh."*

In summary, you can tell a true believer from a false one over time. He will not be able to hide what is in his heart. You will hear it out of his mouth here and there in his unguarded speech, and the doctrine he proclaims:

> **Colossians 3:8:** *"But now you also, put them all aside: anger, wrath, malice, slander, and abusive speech from your mouth."*

The Puritan, Richard Baxter, said:

> "Sound doctrine, makes sound judgment, a sound heart, a sound life, and a sound conscience - and if it was otherwise, then either the doctrine was not sound or it was not soundly understood."

VERSES 36-37: *"And I say to you, that every careless word that men shall speak, they shall render account for it in the day of judgment. 37 For by your words you shall be justified, and by your words you shall be condemned."*

The true believer must realize that his speech (and the heart from where his words come) is very serious to the Lord. **James 1:19:** *"This you know, my beloved brethren. But everyone must be quick to hear, <u>slow to speak</u> and slow to anger;...."* [216] The Lord gives us an example of the seriousness and condemnation that will be exacted when we use careless words.

> **Matthew 5:22:** *"But I say to you that everyone who is angry with his brother shall be guilty before the court; and whoever says to his brother, 'You good-for-nothing,' shall be guilty before the supreme court; and whoever says, '<u>You fool,' shall be guilty enough to go into the fiery hell.</u>"*

Matthew 12:37 also states the positive side of our words: *"For by your words you shall be justified...."* Obviously it is not referring to a word that results in *self-justification,* but rather speech that manifests the life of faith.

> **Romans 10:9-10:** *"...that <u>if you confess with your mouth Jesus as Lord, and believe in your heart that God raised Him from the dead, you will be saved;</u> 10 for with the heart a person believes, resulting in righteousness, and with the mouth he confesses, resulting in salvation."*

> **1 John 1:9:** *"If <u>we confess our sins,</u> He is faithful and righteous to forgive us our sins and to cleanse us from all unrighteousness."*

> **Revelation 12:11:** *"And they overcame him because of the <u>blood of the Lamb</u> and because <u>of the word of their testimony,</u> and they did not love their life even when faced with death."*

In summary we are to rid our life of ungodly speech:

> **Colossians 3:8:** *"But now you also, put them all aside: anger, wrath, malice, slander, and abusive speech from your mouth."*

We are to be people who speak words of truth and faith to the glory of God!

> **1 Timothy 6:12-16:** *"Fight the good fight of faith; take hold of the eternal life to which you were called, and you made the <u>good confession in the presence of many witnesses.</u> 13I charge you in the presence of God, who gives life to all things, and of Christ Jesus, who <u>testified the good confession before Pontius Pilate,</u> 14that you keep the commandment without stain or reproach until the appearing of our Lord Jesus Christ, 15which He will bring about at the proper time—He who is the blessed and only Sovereign, the King of kings and Lord of lords, 16who alone possesses immortality and dwells in unapproachable light, whom no man has seen or can see. To Him be honor and eternal dominion! Amen."*

VERSES 38-40: *"Then some of the scribes and Pharisees answered Him, saying, 'Teacher, we want to see a sign from You.' 39 But He answered and said to them, 'An evil and adulterous generation craves for a*

---

[216] See comments in Matthew 12:34-35 on speech.

sign; and yet no sign shall be given to it but the sign of Jonah the prophet; ⁴⁰ for just as JONAH WAS THREE DAYS AND THREE NIGHTS IN THE BELLY OF THE SEA MONSTER, so shall the Son of Man be three days and three nights in the heart of the earth.'"

Some mistakenly think that the only evidence of a man of God is his performing miracles. This is not true. Jesus teaches us that not all miracles are proof that the person is of God since even some false prophets will do miracles to deceive people.

> **Matthew 24:24:** *"For false Christs and false prophets will arise and will <u>show great signs and wonders,</u> so as to mislead, if possible, even the elect."*

The book of Revelation tells us that false miracles will be done by the Anti-christ to trick people in that he *"…performs great signs, so that he even makes fire come down out of heaven to the earth in the presence of men. ¹⁴ And <u>he deceives those who dwell on the earth because of the signs which it was given him to perform</u>…."* **Revelation 13:13-14.**

Christians should not spend their time chasing after signs or spiritual leaders who claim to be the one with *the power*. God owes no man proof of Himself, even though He gives it by His creation (Romans 1:19-20). We are to spend our time telling of the greatest miracle (i.e. that evil people can be saved and forgiven of their sins and spend eternity with God). As Paul said, we are to spend our time preaching the gospel.

> **1 Corinthians 1:22-23:** *"For indeed Jews ask for signs, and Greeks search for wisdom; but <u>we preach Christ crucified,</u>…."*

In our main text of Matthew 12:38 the false religious leaders demanded a "sign." Jesus refused to let His holy ministry be reduced to a circus act for these religious clowns. They had seen the miracles before, but they did not believe them then and they would not believe them now. But God in His grace said that there was one sign that He would give them (not just to them but to the whole world): Jesus' resurrection from the dead. That is what is meant in verse 40 when Jesus said, *"JONAH WAS THREE DAYS AND THREE NIGHTS IN THE BELLY OF THE SEA MONSTER, so shall the Son of Man be three days and three nights in the heart of the earth."* It should first be noted that this verse is Jesus' verification of the literal story of Jonah and the sea monster. Often unbelievers/theological liberals try to write off the book of Jonah as some allegory. Jesus' own words validate the literal swallowing of Jonah by the sea monster and thus obliterates their unbelieving theories. Likewise, other non-believing skeptics will try to take this verse and apply it to modern culture by saying that "three days and three nights" requires 72 hours to have transpired between Jesus' death and His resurrection. Again, they are trying to create error where it never existed. As Charles Ryrie states, "…Jews reckoned part of a day to be a whole day. [See more on the subject of **"three days and three nights"** in the footnote below.] Thus this prophecy can be properly fulfilled if the crucifixion occurred on Friday…" [217] The definitive truth of the counting of partial days is recorded on the road to Emmaus in **Luke 24:13–23:**

> *"And behold, two of them were going that very day to a village named Emmaus, which was about seven miles from Jerusalem. And they were talking with each other about all these things which had taken place. While they were talking and discussing, Jesus Himself approached and began traveling with them. But their eyes were prevented from recognizing Him. And He said to them, 'What are these words that you are exchanging with one another as you are walking?' And they stood still, looking sad. One of them, named Cleopas, answered and said to Him, 'Are You the only one visiting Jerusalem and*

---

[217] The Ryrie Study Bible -Expanded edition: New American Standard, comment to Matthew 12:40.

unaware of the things which have happened here in these days?' And He said to them, 'What things?' And they said to Him, 'The things about Jesus the Nazarene, who was a prophet mighty in deed and word in the sight of God and all the people, and how the chief priests and our rulers delivered Him to the sentence of death, and crucified Him. But we were hoping that it was He who was going to redeem Israel. Indeed, besides all this, <u>it is the third day since these things happened. But also some women among us amazed us. When they were at the tomb early in the morning, and did not find His body, they came, saying that they had also seen a vision of angels who said that He was alive.' "*

Note also that the Jewish Talmud held that "any part of a day is as the whole."[218]

VERSES 41-42: *"The men of Nineveh shall stand up with this generation at the judgment, and shall condemn it because they repented at the preaching of Jonah; and behold, something greater than Jonah is here. *42* The Queen of the South shall rise up with this generation at the judgment and shall condemn it, because she came from the ends of the earth to hear the wisdom of Solomon; and behold, something greater than Solomon is here."*

---

[218] MacArthur, John F., *Matthew, The MacArthur New Testament Commentary*, p. 289 (Chicago: Moody Press) 1983.

"The matter of **three days and three nights** is often used either to prove Jesus was mistaken about the time He would actually spend in the tomb or that He could not have been crucified on Friday afternoon and raised early on Sunday, the first day of the week. But as in modern usage, the phrase "day and night" can mean not only a full 24-hour day but any representative part of a day. To spend a day, or a day and night, visiting in a neighboring city does not require spending 24 hours there. It could refer to arriving in the late morning and leaving a few hours after dark. In the same way, Jesus' use of **three days and three nights** does not have to be interpreted as 72 hours, three full 24-hour days. The Jewish Talmud held that "any part of a day is as the whole." Jesus was simply using a common, well-understood generalization." **For a more detailed explanation read the rest of this footnote:** MacArthur, John F., *Matthew, The MacArthur New Testament Commentary*, (Chicago: Moody Press) 1983, "Matthew 28:1.

'A day and a night' was a Jewish colloquialism that could refer to any part of a day. When Queen Esther instructed Mordecai to tell the Jews to fast 'for three days' (Esther 4:16), it becomes obvious that she did not have in mind three full days. It was 'on the third day,' at the end of the fast, that she 'put on her royal robes and stood in the inner court of the king's palace to intercede for her people (5:1). The Talmud, the major Jewish commentary on Scripture and tradition, specifies that 'a day and a night makes one onah, and a part of an onah is as the whole.' In the same way, people today speak of visiting a certain place for three days, without necessarily meaning three full twenty-hour periods. To arrive on a Monday morning, for example, and leave on the following Wednesday afternoon is generally considered a three-day visit. That Jesus had in mind only a part of the first and third days is made clear by the numerous references to His rising on the third day (Matthew 16:21; 17:23; 20:19). It is also clear that the Jewish religious leaders themselves took Jesus to mean on the third day. Although they used the phrase **after three days** in giving Pilate the reason for their request, they asked Him to post a guard over the tomb **until the third day**, indicating that they used those two phrases synonymously. To insist on a full three-day burial not only precludes Jesus' rising on the third day but also requires pushing the day of crucifixion back to Wednesday, in order for Him to have been in the ground all of Thursday, Friday, and Saturday. In that case, parts of five consecutive days would have been involved—from Wednesday morning, when the crucifixion would have begun, until daybreak on Sunday which would have been some twelve hours after that day had begun at 6:00 P.M. the previous evening. But such an extended chronology cannot be squared with the Gospel accounts. The crucifixion is specifically said to have been on Friday, 'the day before the Sabbath' (Mark 15:42), and the resurrection to have been sometime before dawn on Sunday, "the first day of the week" (Mark 16:2; Luke 24:1; John 20:1). To argue for a full three-day burial is to presume serious, and very obvious, scriptural error."

Jesus continues on His theme about Jonah in verse 41. He points out that the city of Nineveh repented when Jonah spoke (cf. Jonah 3:10). He further points out the great lengths the *Queen of the South* traveled to hear Solomon (see 1 Kings 10:1-10). Jesus then sharpens His focus on the scribes and Pharisees by stating that they were called to repent by the Son of God and yet they refused. Because of their refusal to repent, they will be severely judged:

> *"The men of Nineveh shall stand up with this generation at the judgment, and shall condemn it because they repented at the preaching of Jonah; and behold, something greater than Jonah is here."* (v. 41).

VERSES 43-45: *"Now when the unclean spirit goes out of a man, it passes through waterless places, seeking rest, and does not find it. 44 Then it says, 'I will return to my house from which I came'; and when it comes, it finds it unoccupied, swept, and put in order. 45 Then it goes, and takes along with it seven other spirits more wicked than itself, and they go in and live there; and the last state of that man becomes worse than the first. That is the way it will also be with this evil generation."*

Jesus gives us insight into the spiritual world. He tells us that a man who is freed from demonic attack, but not regenerated by the blood of Christ, will find himself the target of even worse demonic possession. Reformation apart from the power of God is useless and will cause a deeper destruction.

While I was in college, many Christian young men would engage in open-air preaching at the campus square. One time when I had just finished speaking, a student came up to me and asked, "What would you say to a guy who quit being a drunk without the help of God?" I replied that it was great that a person quit drinking. The problem is that the drunk has not been delivered from alcohol; he has merely been able to stop drinking (i.e. control his behavior for a while). On top of all that, his not drinking does not suddenly make him righteous and without sin. He is still going to hell if he does not repent and turn to Christ for the forgiveness of his sins.

The term philosophy is the combination of two Greek words that means to *love wisdom.*[219] We live in a world of many *self-help* philosophies. Examples of these worldly philosophies include transcendental meditation, self–empowerment, positive thinking and New Age spiritualism. Unfortunately, these same worldly philosophies have infiltrated the Church with an endless barrage of so-called *christian* self-help books. They will use worldly wisdom and then sprinkle in some Bible verses (regardless of context) and claim that it is a Christian book. Paul warned the church of those who would try to pervert the truth of the gospel with man-made philosophies in **Colossians 2:8-10:**

> *"See to it that no one takes you captive through philosophy and empty deception, according to the tradition of men, according to the elementary principles of the world, rather than according to Christ. 9 For in Him all the fulness of Deity dwells in bodily form, 10 and in Him you have been made complete, and He is the head over all rule and authority;"*

---

[219] Philosophy "denotes the love and pursuit of wisdom, hence, philosophy, the investigation of truth and nature; in Colossians 2:8, the so–called philosophy of false teachers." Vine, W., and Bruce, F. (1981; Published in electronic form by Logos Research Systems, 1996). *Vine's Expository Dictionary of Old and New Testament words.* Old Tappan NJ: Revell.

[219] Spurgeon, C. H. (1995). *Morning and Evening: Daily readings* (September 25 PM). Oak Harbor, WA: Logos Research Systems, Inc.

Spurgeon explains how seducing it can be for people to turn from the simplicity of the gospel and be drawn to adding their own fleshly ideas.

> "Men of education are apt, even when converted, to look upon the simplicities of the cross of Christ with an eye too little reverent and loving. They are snared in the old net in which the Grecians were taken, and have a hankering to mix philosophy with revelation. The temptation with a man of refined thought and high education is to depart from the simple truth of Christ crucified, and to invent, as the term is, a more *intellectual* doctrine. This led the early Christian churches into Gnosticism, and bewitched them with all sorts of heresies."[220]

We must remember that the natural *wisdom* of this world is demonic at its base. You disagree? Need I remind you that some very intelligent and highly educated people in powerful positions of government and law have reasoned that it is a noble right to kill babies while in their mother's womb? James states that earthly wisdom is evil:

> **James 3:15-17:** *"This wisdom is not that which comes down from above, but is earthly, natural, demonic. 16 For where jealousy and selfish ambition exist, there is disorder and every evil thing. 17 But the wisdom from above is first pure, then peaceable, gentle, reasonable, full of mercy and good fruits, unwavering, without hypocrisy."*

Often people who resort to self-reformation may stop a problem in one area of their life only to develop an addiction in one or more other areas. For example, they may quit drinking and soon thereafter become addicted to gambling and overeating (or any other addiction). Man-made self-help is like plugging one leaky hole in a person's soul only to have seven others pop open (Matthew 12:43-45). Jesus states clearly that He is the only way to true freedom.

> **John 8:34-36:** *"Jesus answered them, 'Truly, truly, I say to you, everyone who commits sin is the slave of sin. 35 And the slave does not remain in the house forever; the son does remain forever. 36 If therefore the Son shall make you free, you shall be free indeed.'"*

VERSES 46-50: *"While He was still speaking to the multitudes, behold, His mother and brothers were standing outside, seeking to speak to Him. 47 And someone said to Him, 'Behold, Your mother and Your brothers are standing outside seeking to speak to You.' 48 But He answered the one who was telling Him and said, 'Who is My mother and who are My brothers?' 49 And stretching out His hand toward His disciples, He said, 'Behold, My mother and My brothers! 50 For whoever does the will of My Father who is in heaven, he is My brother and sister and mother.'"*

Here we see Jesus cutting past the physical and viewing things in truth via spiritual eyes. Jesus makes it clear that one is not a part of His family as a result of his lineage or bloodlines. A person is a child of God because God has opened his eyes and converted the man so that he, *"does the will of My Father"* (v.50). Take the example of a Christian in Russia who has an identical twin brother. Also assume that the identical twin is not a Christian. The spiritual reality is that a Christian man who lives in the U.S. is a truer brother to the Christian in Russia than his own identical twin brother. The spiritual family in Christ is a true family. Christians have God as their spiritual Father and

---

[220] Spurgeon, C. H. (2006). Morning and evening: Daily readings (Complete and unabridged; New modern edition.) (Sep 25 PM). Peabody, MA: Hendrickson Publishers.

unbelievers have the Devil as their spiritual father (see John 8:43-47). In reference to this in Matthew 12:46-50, Ryle states,

> "There is rich encouragement here for all believers. They are far more precious in their Lord's eyes than they are in their own. Their faith may be feeble, their repentance weak, their strength small: they may be poor and needy in this world; but there is a glorious 'Whoever' in the last verse of this chapter which ought to cheer them [v.50]. 'Whoever' believes is a near relative of Christ: the Elder Brother will provide for him in time and eternity, and never let *him be cast away.*" [221]

One last note: I have friends who are Roman Catholic. Some Roman Catholics espouse a doctrine of Mary that is contradicted by Scripture. Some try to exalt Mary beyond a position that Scripture supports. For example, Scripture does not support a view of Jesus being willing to do whatever His mother asks of Him. (Matthew 12:46-50... see also the Scriptures below.)

> **John 2:3-4:** *"And when the wine gave out, the mother of Jesus *said to Him, 'They have no wine.' ⁴And Jesus *said to her, 'Woman, what do I have to do with you? My hour has not yet come.'"*

> **Luke 11:27-28:** *"And it came about while He said these things, one of the women in the crowd raised her voice, and said to Him, 'Blessed is the womb that bore You, and the breasts at which You nursed.' ²⁸ But He said, 'On the contrary, blessed are those who hear the word of God, and observe it.'"*

With that said, it should be understood that Mary was a great woman of God. Mary was chosen by God to be the mother of our Lord. As stated in **Luke 1:28-30, 41-42:**

> *"And coming in, he said to her, 'Hail, favored one! The Lord is with you.' ²⁹ But she was greatly troubled at this statement, and kept pondering what kind of salutation this might be. ³⁰ And the angel said to her, 'Do not be afraid, Mary; for you have found favor with God.'....*
> v.41: *When Elizabeth heard Mary's greeting, the baby leaped in her womb; and Elizabeth was filled with the Holy Spirit. ⁴²And she cried out with a loud voice, and said, 'Blessed among women are you, and blessed is the fruit of your womb! ⁴³ And how has it happened to me, that the mother of my Lord should come to me?'"*

This is a wonderful proclamation about Mary! It is quite another thing to make the heretical claim that Mary is void of original sin, or that she never sinned, as stated in the official Roman Catholic catechism.[222] Scripture clearly speaks that Jesus alone is the only person without sin. We see that Mary herself claims a need for a Savior in **Luke 1:46-47:** *"And Mary said: 'My soul exalts the Lord, ⁴⁷And my spirit has rejoiced in God my Savior.'"* Notice that after the Birth of Jesus, Mary did as the Law commanded in that she give a sacrifice.

> **Luke 2:21-24:** *"And when eight days were completed before His circumcision, His name was then called Jesus, the name given by the angel before He was conceived in the womb. ²² And when the days for their purification according to the law of Moses were*

---

[221] *Matthew,* Ryle, J.C. p.102 (Expository Thoughts on the Gospels) (Crossways Classic Commentaries: v.1)

[222] Note the exact quotes from the Roman Catholic Catechism #493:

> **493** - The Fathers of the Eastern tradition call the Mother of God "the All-Holy" (Panagia), and celebrate her as "free from any stain of sin, as though fashioned by the Holy Spirit and formed as a new creature." By the grace of God Mary remained free of every personal sin her whole life long.

completed, they brought Him up to Jerusalem to present Him to the Lord [23] *(as it is written in the Law of the Lord, 'EVERY first-born MALE THAT OPENS THE WOMB SHALL BE CALLED HOLY TO THE LORD'),* [24] *and to offer a sacrifice according to what was said in the Law of the Lord, 'A PAIR OF TURTLEDOVES, OR TWO YOUNG PIGEONS.'"*

What was this offering of turtledoves or pigeons for? Leviticus 12:2-8 explains that it is a sin offering:

Leviticus 12:8: *"But if she cannot afford a lamb, then she shall take two turtledoves or two young pigeons, the one for a burnt offering and <u>the other for a sin offering</u>; and the priest shall make atonement for her, and she shall be clean."*

To claim that Mary was without original sin is nowhere supported in Scripture, but actually contradicts it.

Another heretical error some Roman Catholics make is to elevate Mary to a position of co-redemptrix or co-mediator with Christ.[223] We are not taught in Scripture to go to Mary, an angel, a *Saint*, or a priest/pastor as an intercessor to Jesus or the Father. Scripture is clear that there is only one mediator between us and God, and that mediator is Jesus Christ.

1 Timothy 2:5: *"For there is one God, and <u>one mediator</u> also between God and men, the man Christ Jesus,…."*

Jesus is our only intercessor:

Romans 8:34: *"…<u>Christ Jesus</u> is He who died, yes, rather who was raised, who is at the right hand of God, who also <u>intercedes for us</u>."*

Hebrews 7:25: *"Hence, also, He is able to save forever those who draw near to God through Him, since He always lives to make intercession for them."*

We are not to bow and give our praise to anyone or anything except almighty God.

Isaiah 42:8: *"I am the LORD, that is My name;*
I will not give My glory to another,
Nor My praise to graven images."

We see John being rebuked by an angel when he bows before him.

Revelation 22:8-9: *"And I, John, am the one who heard and saw these things. And when I heard and saw, I fell down to worship at the feet of the angel who showed me these things.* [9] *And he *said to me, 'Do not do that; I am a fellow servant of yours and of your brethren the prophets and of those who heed the words of this book; <u>worship God</u>.'"*

---

[223] Note the exact quote for the official Roman Catholic Catechism #968 and 969:

968 Her role in relation to the Church and to all humanity goes still further. "In a wholly singular way <u>she cooperated by her obedience, faith, hope, and burning charity in the Savior's work of restoring supernatural life to souls.</u> For this reason she is a mother to us in the order of grace."

969 "This motherhood of Mary in the order of grace continues uninterruptedly from the consent which she loyally gave at the Annunciation and which she sustained without wavering beneath the cross, until the eternal fulfillment of all the elect. Taken up to heaven <u>she did not lay aside this saving office but by her manifold intercession continues to bring us the gifts of eternal salvation</u> . . . . Therefore the <u>Blessed Virgin is invoked in the Church under the titles of Advocate, Helper, Benefactress, and Mediatrix.</u>"

For more on Mother/Son cult, see footnote below.[224]

Summary and Application

We are to be Christians. That means that after being saved by the grace of Christ, we are to bear fruit and do Spirit-led good works that God has for us (see Ephesians 2:10). These good works do not save us, but they are evidence that we have been saved. Are you bearing fruit in your life?

Having a correct view of God is vital to true Christianity. The unbelieving do not know God. When they pray, it is not the prayer of repentance and confession. It is a prayer to get what they want. If they do not get what they want, they are the first to lash out and charge God with fault. They will say something like, "Yeah, I tried praying, but it doesn't work because God did not give me what I asked for." They try to reduce God to some magic genie that sits up in the sky to grant wishes for our selfish pleasures. The true believer knows that he is never to make demands of God to prove Himself or perform miracles. Does God still do miracles? YES! Should we pray for supernatural miracles in time of need? YES! Should we demand God to do miracles for us? NO! The one miracle He has promised to do for the believer is to save his soul from sin, death and hell. He has adopted me into His family and calls me His child. Have you

---

[224] **Co-redemptrix / Co-mediator and Lent**:

John MacArthur writes: "The notions of her [Mary] being co-redemptrix and co-mediator with Christ are wholly unscriptural and were never a part of early church doctrine. Those heretical ideas came into the church several centuries later, through accommodations to pagan myths that originated in the Babylonian mystery religions.

Nimrod, a grandson of Ham, one of Noah's three sons, founded the great cities of Babel (Babylon), Erech, Accad, Calneh, and Nineveh (Genesis 10:10-11). It was at Babel that the first organized system of idolatry began with the tower built there. Nimrod's wife, Semiramis, became the first high priestess of idolatry, and Babylon became the fountainhead of all evil systems of religion. In the last days, 'the great harlot' will have written on her forehead, '**BABYLON THE GREAT, THE MOTHER OF HARLOTS AND OF THE ABOMINATIONS OF THE EARTH**' (Revelation 17:5). When Babylon was destroyed, the pagan high priest at that time fled to Pergamum (or Pergamos; called 'where Satan's throne is' in Revelation 2:13) and then to Rome. By the fourth century A.D. much of the polytheistic paganism of Rome had found its way into the church. It was from that source that the ideas of Lent, of Mary's immaculate conception, and of her being the 'queen of heaven' originated. In the pagan legends, Semiramis was miraculously conceived by a sunbeam, and her son, Tammuz, was killed and was raised from the dead after forty days of fasting by his mother (the origin of Lent). The same basic legends were found in counterpart religions throughout the ancient world. Semiramis was known variously as Ashtoreth, Isis, Aphrodite, Venus, and Ishtar. Tammuz was known as Baal, Osiris, Eros, and Cupid.

Those pagan systems had infected Israel centuries before the coming of Christ. It was to Ishtar, 'the queen of heaven,' that the wicked and rebellious Israelite exiles in Egypt insisted on turning (Jer. 44:17-19; cf. 7:18). While exiled in Babylon with his fellow Jews, Ezekiel had a vision from the Lord about the 'abominations' some Israelites were committing even in the Temple at Jerusalem—practices that included 'weeping for Tammuz' (Ezek. 8:13-14). Here we see some of the origins of the mother-child cult, which has drawn Mary into its grasp.

The Bible knows nothing of Mary's grace except that which she received from the Lord. She was the recipient, never the dispenser, of grace. The literal translation of 'favored one' (Luke 1:28) is 'one endued with grace.' Just as all the rest of fallen mankind, Mary needed God's grace and salvation. That is why she 'rejoiced in God [her] Savior' (Luke 1:47). She received a special measure of the Lord's grace by being chosen to be the mother of Jesus; but she was never a source of grace. God [by His] grace chose a sinful woman to have the unequaled privilege of giving birth to the Messiah." MacArthur, John F., *Matthew, The MacArthur New Testament Commentary*, p.4-6 (Chicago: Moody Press) 1983.

thanked Him for bringing you into His family forever? If you are a Christian, take a moment and dwell on the concept that you are a permanent member of His family.

MATTHEW 13:1-23
(THE SOWER AND THE SEED — FALSE CONVERTS / TRUE CONVERTS)

"ON *that day Jesus went out of the house, and was sitting by the sea.* [2] *And great multitudes gathered to Him, so that He got into a boat and sat down, and the whole multitude was standing on the beach.* [3] *And He spoke many things to them in parables, saying, 'Behold, the sower went out to sow;* [4] *and as he sowed, some seeds fell beside the road, and the birds came and ate them up.* [5] *And others fell upon the rocky places, where they did not have much soil; and immediately they sprang up, because they had no depth of soil.* [6] *But when the sun had risen, they were scorched; and because they had no root, they withered away.* [7] *And others fell among the thorns, and the thorns came up and choked them out.* [8] *And others fell on the good soil, and *yielded a crop, some a hundredfold, some sixty, and some thirty.* [9] *He who has ears, let him hear.'*

[10] *And the disciples came and said to Him, 'Why do You speak to them in parables?'* [11] *And He answered and said to them, 'To you it has been granted to know the mysteries of the kingdom of heaven, but to them it has not been granted.* [12] *For whoever has, to him shall more be given, and he shall have an abundance; but whoever does not have, even what he has shall be taken away from him.* [13] *Therefore I speak to them in parables; because while seeing they do not see, and while hearing they do not hear, nor do they understand.* [14] *And in their case the prophecy of Isaiah is being fulfilled, which says,*

> *'YOU WILL KEEP ON HEARING, BUT WILL NOT UNDERSTAND;*
> *AND YOU WILL KEEP ON SEEING, BUT WILL NOT PERCEIVE;*
> [15] *FOR THE HEART OF THIS PEOPLE HAS BECOME DULL,*
> *AND WITH THEIR EARS THEY SCARCELY HEAR,*
> *AND THEY HAVE CLOSED THEIR EYES*
> *LEST THEY SHOULD SEE WITH THEIR EYES,*
> *AND HEAR WITH THEIR EARS,*
> *AND UNDERSTAND WITH THEIR HEART AND RETURN,*
> *AND I SHOULD HEAL THEM.'*

[16] *But blessed are your eyes, because they see; and your ears, because they hear.* [17] *For truly I say to you, that many prophets and righteous men desired to see what you see, and did not see it; and to hear what you hear, and did not hear it.*

[18] *Hear then the parable of the sower.* [19] *When anyone hears the word of the kingdom, and does not understand it, the evil one comes and snatches away what has been sown in his heart. This is the one on whom seed was sown beside the road.* [20] *And the one on whom seed was sown on the rocky places, this is the man who hears the word, and immediately receives it with joy;* [21] *yet he has no firm root in himself, but is only temporary, and when affliction or persecution arises because of the word, immediately he falls away.* [22] *And the one on whom seed was sown among the thorns, this is the man who hears the word, and the worry of the world, and the deceitfulness of riches choke the word, and it becomes unfruitful.* [23] *And the one on whom seed was sown on the good soil, this is the man who hears the word and understands it; who indeed bears fruit, and brings forth, some a hundredfold, some sixty, and some thirty.'"

Introduction

This is the parable of the *Sower and the Seed*. The correct interpretation of this parable is absolutely necessary to accurately understand other parables. In the parallel passage in Mark, Jesus tells His disciples, *"...Do you not understand this parable? And how will you understand all the parables?"* **Mark 4:13.** Some theologians have said this parable is more accurately called the *"parable of the soils."* They point out that in each scenario the sower and the seed are the same—the only difference is the soil. Also note that each of the first three soils produce <u>no fruit</u> (not even a little fruit) . Only the "good soil" produces <u>any fruit</u>.

Some misinterpret this parable to mean that some people who become saved can later lose their salvation. Others misinterpret the parable to mean that there are different types of Christians (as represented by the different types of soil), and we should try to be the Christian with the "good soil" that bears fruit.

The reality is that it is not just the really good Christian who bears fruit, but that all true Christians produce good fruit. Those that do not bear any good fruit are not Christians at all. With that being said, it should be understood that not all believers bear fruit at the same rate/amount. An immature Christian will not be producing at the same rate a mature believer does. Jesus sets that principal out when He says *"some a hundredfold, some sixty, and some thirty."* The point is that a person who claims to be a Christian, but is devoid of Holy Spirit produced *good fruit,* proves that his alleged conversion is false and that the person was never a Christian.

The parable should be interpreted within the context of Jesus' own words on the subject of fruitfulness. In some verses prior to Jesus speaking the parable of the *Sower and the Seed,* He said, *"Either make the tree good, and its fruit good; or make the tree bad, and its fruit bad; for the tree is known by its fruit."* **Matthew 12:33.** In Matthew, right after Jesus gave the interpretation to the parable of the *"Sower and the Seed,"* He goes on to give a parable of the *"Wheat and the Tares."* The parable of the *"Wheat and the Tares"* is about false Christians who, for a while, look like real Christians, but over time, it is shown that they were weeds from the beginning. We must remember that Jesus is talking about fruitfulness in the parable of the *"Sower and the Seed."* In Matthew 7 we read what Jesus also taught about *fruit* and false Christians (i.e. those who claim conversion, but never were truly saved.)

> **Matthew 7:15-23:** *"Beware of the false prophets, who come to you in sheep's clothing, but inwardly are ravenous wolves.* [16] *<u>You will know them by their fruits</u>. Grapes are not gathered from thorn bushes, nor figs from thistles, are they?* [17] *Even so, every good tree bears good fruit; but the bad tree bears bad fruit.* [18] *A good tree cannot produce bad fruit, nor can a bad tree produce good fruit.* [19]*<u>Every tree that does not bear good fruit is cut down and thrown into the fire.</u>* [20] *So then, you will know them by their fruits.* [21] *<u>Not everyone who says to Me, 'Lord, Lord,' will enter the kingdom of heaven; but he who does the will of My Father who is in heaven.</u>* [22] *Many will say to Me on that day, 'Lord, Lord, did we not prophesy in Your name, and in Your name cast out demons, and in Your name perform many miracles?'* [23] *And then I will declare to them, 'I never knew you; DEPART FROM ME, YOU WHO PRACTICE LAWLESSNESS.'"*

VERSES 1-2: *"ON that day Jesus went out of the house, and was sitting by the sea.* [2] *And great multitudes gathered to Him, so that He got into a boat and sat down, and the whole multitude was standing on the beach."*

Note that, *"On that day,"* makes reference to the events that took place in the previous verses (i.e. Matthew 12). These events included the Pharisees' blasphemy of the Holy Spirit and when Jesus told the crowd, *"Either make the tree good, and its fruit good; or make the tree bad, and its fruit bad; for the tree is known by its fruit."* **Matthew 12:33**.

In Matthew 12:46-13:1 we read that Jesus was teaching in a house. In Matthew 13:1-2 we read that later *"on that day"* He leaves the house, gets in a boat and teaches the parable of the "Sower and the Seed" to those on the beach.

VERSES 3-9: *"And He spoke many things to them in parables, saying, 'Behold, the sower went out to sow; ⁴ and as he sowed, some seeds fell beside the road, and the birds came and ate them up. ⁵ And others fell upon the rocky places, where they did not have much soil; and immediately they sprang up, because they had no depth of soil. ⁶ But when the sun had risen, they were scorched; and because they had no root, they withered away. ⁷ And others fell among the thorns, and the thorns came up and choked them out. ⁸ And others fell on the good soil, and *yielded a crop, some a hundredfold, some sixty, and some thirty. ⁹ He who has ears, let him hear.'"*

Here Jesus tells the parable of the *"Sower and the Seed."* [225] He starts by stating that the *"sower went out to sow."* To understand this phrase, one needs to realize that this farmer did not plant his fields the way we do today. Back then, a farmer would have a bag full of seeds slung on him, and he would grab a handful of seeds and throw it on his field in a broadcasting fashion. The fields themselves were often divided by small paths (i.e. *"roads"*), which both the farmers and travelers used to reach their destination. As the roads were walked on, they would become packed and hard. The seed that fell on these roads did not penetrate into good soil *"...and the birds came and ate them up."* We know that the **birds** represent Satan and his demons (see v.19).

Jesus said that some of the seed fell on rocky soil. This is often visualized as seeds in rocky gravel, but that is not an accurate portrayal. MacArthur described it as follows:
> "It rather refers to underlying beds of solid rock deeper than the plow reached, mostly limestone, which **did not have much soil** covering them. The seeds that fell on such ground *"immediately ... sprang up, because they had no depth of soil."* When the seed began to germinate, its roots could not penetrate the rock that was just below the surface, and the little plant would instead start to **spring up** above ground much faster than it normally would. For a brief period these plants would look healthier and hardier than those in good soil, because more of them showed above ground and they grew faster. *"But when the sun had risen, they were scorched; and because they had no root, they withered away."* Lack of roots prevented the plants from reaching and absorbing moisture or nourishment. After *"the sun had risen"* in the morning, the plants that looked so promising *"were scorched"* and quickly *"withered away."*[226]

Jesus also taught that some of the seed fell *"among thorns"* (i.e. nasty thorny/prickly weed).[227]

---

[225] "'Parable' is ultimately derived from Greek [and literally means] 'putting things side by side.' Etymologically it is thus close to 'allegory', which by derivation means 'saying things in a different way.'"
The New Bible Dictionary, (Wheaton, Illinois: Tyndale House Publishers, Inc.) 1962.

[226] MacArthur, John F., *Matthew, The MacArthur New Testament Commentary*, p.289 (Chicago: Moody Press) 1983.

[227] Hebrew *kotz* (Genesis 3:18; Hosea 10:8), ... In the New Testament this word *akantha* is also rendered "thorns" (Matthew 7:16; 13:7; Hebrews 6:8). The word seems to denote any thorny or prickly plant (Jeremiah 12:13). It has been identified with the Ononis spinosa by some. Easton. (electronic ed.).

Often weeds will lay hidden in soil. Early in their growth they may appear harmless. Soon the weeds grow up and do their damage by swallowing up moisture and nutrients, thus denying from the good seed (*the thorns came up and choked them out....*). Jesus speaks of such weeds among true wheat in the very next parable (See Matthew 13:24-30 – parable of the Tares among the Wheat).

The last type of soil that Jesus teaches about in this section is the *good soil*. What made this soil *good*? This soil produced a real harvest —*"yielded a crop, some a hundredfold, some sixty, and some thirty."*

VERSES 10-17: *"And the disciples came and said to Him, 'Why do You speak to them in parables?'* [11] *And He answered and said to them, 'To you it has been granted to know the mysteries of the kingdom of heaven, but to them it has not been granted.* [12] *For whoever has, to him shall more be given, and he shall have an abundance; but whoever does not have, even what he has shall be taken away from him.* [13] *Therefore I speak to them in parables; because while seeing they do not see, and while hearing they do not hear, nor do they understand.* [14] *And in their case the prophecy of Isaiah is being fulfilled, which says,*

> *'YOU WILL KEEP ON HEARING, BUT WILL NOT UNDERSTAND;*
> *AND YOU WILL KEEP ON SEEING, BUT WILL NOT PERCEIVE;*
> [15] *FOR THE HEART OF THIS PEOPLE HAS BECOME DULL,*
> *AND WITH THEIR EARS THEY SCARCELY HEAR,*
> *AND THEY HAVE CLOSED THEIR EYES*
> *LEST THEY SHOULD SEE WITH THEIR EYES,*
> *AND HEAR WITH THEIR EARS,*
> *AND UNDERSTAND WITH THEIR HEART AND RETURN,*
> *AND I SHOULD HEAL THEM.'*

[16] *But blessed are your eyes, because they see; and your ears, because they hear.* [17] *For truly I say to you, that many prophets and righteous men desired to see what you see, and did not see it; and to hear what you hear, and did not hear it."*

Here Jesus uses a quote from Isaiah 6:9-10 and informs His disciples that they have been granted ears to hear (i.e. they will understand) the things about the kingdom of heaven. True spiritual revelation comes from the Holy Spirit.

> **John 14:26:** *"But the Helper, the Holy Spirit, whom the Father will send in My name, He will teach you all things, and bring to your remembrance all that I said to you."*

> **1 Corinthians 2:10-13:** *"For to us God revealed them through the Spirit; for the Spirit searches all things, even the depths of God.* [11] *For who among men knows the thoughts of a man except the spirit of the man, which is in him? Even so the thoughts of God no one knows except the Spirit of God.* [12] *Now we have received, not the spirit of the world, but the Spirit who is from God, that we might know the things freely given to us by God,* [13] *which things we also speak, not in words taught by human wisdom, but in those taught by the Spirit, combining spiritual thoughts with spiritual words."*

One does not receive God's revelation because he is "intelligent."

> **Matthew 11:25-26:** *"At that time Jesus answered and said, 'I praise Thee, O Father, Lord of heaven and earth, that Thou didst hide these things from the wise and intelligent and didst reveal them to babes.* [26] *Yes, Father, for thus it was well-pleasing in Thy sight.'"*

1 Corinthians 2:14: *"But a natural man does not accept the things of the Spirit of God; for they are foolishness to him, and he cannot understand them, because they are spiritually appraised."*

THE INTERPRETATION OF THE PARABLE

VERSES 18-19: *"Hear then the parable of the sower. ¹⁹ When anyone hears the word of the kingdom, and does not understand it, the evil one comes and snatches away what has been sown in his heart. This is the one on whom seed was sown beside the road."*

Scripture tells us what the seed represents in this parable. In the parallel passage of this parable in **Luke 8:11** we read that *"the seed is the word of God"* (i.e. the Truth about God, the sinfulness of man and the way of salvation).

Jesus does not specifically state the identity of the *sower* in this parable. It is interesting to point out that the parable following the *Sower and the Seed* is a parable commonly called the *Wheat and Tares*. In the context of interpreting the parable of the *"Wheat and Tares"* Jesus states that, *"The one who sows the good seed is the Son of Man,"* **Matthew 13:37.** In a more general sense, every believer, sharing the Gospel, is spreading the seed and functions as a "sower" under the headship of Christ.

The "birds" are the Devil (v.19 - *the evil one*) and his demons. They would swoop down on the seed and deceive/blind its recipient so as to snatch away the word of truth before it would take root (*"snatches away what has been sown in his heart"*).
> **2 Corinthians 4:3-4:** *"And even if our gospel is veiled, it is veiled to those who are perishing, ⁴ in whose case <u>the god of this world has blinded the minds of the unbelieving, that they might not see the light of the gospel of the glory of Christ, who is the image of God."</u>*

This is why there must be zero tolerance for false teachers of God's Word. There can be false teachers posing as Sunday school teachers, board members and even behind the pulpit. They can look very religious and good, but we are warned to examine them by the Biblical standard and not outward appearance.
> **1 John 4:1:** *"BELOVED, do not believe every spirit, <u>but test the spirits to see whether they are from God;</u> because many false prophets have gone out into the world."*

> **2 Corinthians 11:13-15:** *"For such men are false apostles, deceitful workers, disguising themselves as apostles of Christ. ¹⁴ And no wonder, <u>for even Satan disguises himself as an angel of light.</u> ¹⁵ Therefore it is not surprising if his servants also disguise themselves as servants of righteousness; whose end shall be according to their deeds."*

In summary, the good *seed* that fell *"beside the road"* could not be *understood* by the hearer and thus produced <u>no fruit</u> because *"the evil one... snatches away what has been sown in his heart."*

VERSES 20-21: *"And the one on whom seed was sown on the rocky places, this is the man who hears the word, and immediately receives it with joy; ²¹ yet he has no firm root in himself, but is only temporary, and when affliction or persecution arises because of the word, immediately he falls away."*

The rocky soil is one who thinks this "Christianity deal" is okay: He is glad to get his "fire insurance" from going to hell, and it fills a temporary need in his life. The problem begins when he finds out others are not too excited about this "Jesus" stuff and start to persecute him because of Christ. At that time, he may also be disappointed and embittered because God is not giving him the things he prayed for. Soon it shows that he had no root system to withstand the persecution. Since he is not getting out of this what he expected, *"immediately he falls away."* He never produces any fruit.

How many people do you know who came to Jesus to get some quick fix to their problems (i.e. help with their marriage, or they have trouble with the law, addictions, financial problems, etc.)? They make a confession for Christ, and even act very zealous. They may participate in Bible studies and demonstrate knowledge about the Bible. They may even be active in the church and public evangelism, but eventually it will show that they never truly came to Jesus because He is Lord and Savior (i.e. their soul was never converted). They came to get God to follow them and their desires, and not the other way around. As long as they get what they want they stay with it, but when the price is too high (i.e. persecution) they bail out of the faith never to be heard from again except to accuse the faith. Often these apostates become the most hostile opponents of Christianity.

> **2 Peter 2:20-22:** *"For if after they have escaped the defilements of the world by the knowledge of the Lord and Savior Jesus Christ, they are again entangled in them and are overcome, the last state has become worse for them than the first. ²¹ For it would be better for them not to have known the way of righteousness, than having known it, to turn away from the holy commandment delivered to them. ²² It has happened to them according to the true proverb, 'A DOG RETURNS TO ITS OWN VOMIT,' and, 'A sow, after washing, returns to wallowing in the mire.'"*

> **2 Timothy 3:1-7:** *"BUT realize this, that in the last days difficult times will come. ² For men will be lovers of self, lovers of money, boastful, arrogant, revilers, disobedient to parents, ungrateful, unholy, ³ unloving, irreconcilable, malicious gossips, without self-control, brutal, haters of good, ⁴ treacherous, reckless, conceited, lovers of pleasure rather than lovers of God; ⁵ holding to a form of godliness, although they have denied its power; and avoid such men as these. ⁶ For among them are those who enter into households and captivate weak women weighed down with sins, led on by various impulses, ⁷ always learning and never able to come to the knowledge of the truth."*

When some attempt to share their faith, they mistakenly feel a need to *market* the Gospel. When I use the term *market* I mean that they are trying to create a consumer-driven desire (i.e. appealing to the flesh as compared to being convicted by the Holy Spirit, *"...concerning sin and righteousness and judgment."* **John 16:8**). They want the Gospel to appear attractive to their unregenerate friends in the sense that the Gospel is socially acceptable. This form of *marketing* is the fundamental flaw with modern evangelism. The true Gospel is not appealing to the unbelieving world. The concept of death to selfish living and submission to Christ, is offensive and foolish to the unregenerate.

> **1 Corinthians 1:22-24:** *"For indeed Jews ask for signs, and Greeks search for wisdom; ²³ but we preach Christ crucified, to Jews a stumbling block, and to Gentiles foolishness, ²⁴ but to those who are the called, both Jews and Greeks, Christ the power of God and the wisdom of God."*

Thus the so-called *seeker-sensitive* church has error at its foundation, in that it attempts to change the offensiveness of the message so as to not turn off the non-believer. Steven J. Lawson stated:

"Step into the average church these days and you will likely see that the services are designed more to remove the fear of God than to promote it."[228]

Rather than entertaining the *goats* we should proclaim the true Gospel and leave the results with God. The modern standard for determining the spiritual success of a church or a crusade by counting the attendees is flawed. The numbers could be there because the message has been changed to their liking.

Dr. D. Martin Lloyd-Jones stated regarding evangelism:
"Evangelism must start with the holiness of God, the sinfulness of man,
the demands of the law, and the eternal consequences of evil."[229]

The false evangelist will talk about the "happier life and heaven too." This person speaks of the benefits of Christianity and ignores the cost of discipleship. The result is another false convert who is willing to "try Jesus." The false convert was never convicted by the Holy Spirit of his sin and his need for salvation from hell. Appealing to worldly flesh as the means to bring about conversion is a sure way to accomplish a false conversion. One can only pray that over time the false-convert will receive true teaching and truly be converted.

> **1 John 2:16-17**: *"For all that is in the world, the lust of the flesh and the lust of the eyes and the boastful pride of life, is not from the Father, but is from the world. 17 And the world is passing away, and also its lusts; but the one who does the will of God abides forever."*

> **1 Corinthians 2:14**: *"But a natural man does not accept the things of the Spirit of God; for they are foolishness to him, and he cannot understand them, because they are spiritually appraised."*

Why do some want to change the Gospel to make it appear socially acceptable? The answer is that they do not want to be persecuted. **Galatians 6:12**: *"Those who desire to make a good showing in the flesh…simply that they may not be persecuted for the cross of Christ."* This was as true for the false, legalistic teachers of Galatia, as it is today. Modern evangelism will say that you need to get a famous person like a sports hero in order to hold an effective evangelistic meeting. The sports hero will talk about being a "champion." He may even mention how he prays before he competes and wants to glorify God. Eventually he asks those listening to him if they want to be a "champion too." He will explain that they can be one if they just give their lives to God. Down to the front of the stage come 50 youth who are impressed with the sports hero and led in a prayer. After the meeting, the church congratulates itself and proclaims that 50 kids were *Saved*. The problem is that bits and pieces about God were talked about but the whole Gospel was never truly preached. The sports hero inadvertently made disciples after himself and not Christ. The proof of this becomes evident within a couple of months. The youth manifest no change in their lives, no passion for God, no repentance from sin and no fruit of the Spirit. Some may even be discouraged because they thought that after praying to accept Christ, God would make them better athletes. They soon realize they are never going to be a *champion* like the sports hero and then begin to think the whole *Christian thing* is an

---

[228] Steve. J. Lawson *Made in Our Image – What Shall We Do With a User-Friendly God?* p.194.

[229] Dr. D. Martin Lloyd-Jones *Studies in the Sermon on the Mount.* p.235

illusion. Their current state may become worse than before they attended the evangelism meeting. They may have been inoculated from hearing the true Gospel in the future. What I mean by "inoculated from the gospel" is that as soon as they start to hear the truth from someone else, they might reflect back to their previous experience and refuse to hear them out stating, "Yeah, yeah, I heard this all before."

> **Hebrews 6:4-8:** *"For in the case of those who have once been enlightened and have tasted of the heavenly gift and have been made partakers of the Holy Spirit, ⁵and have tasted the good word of God and the powers of the age to come, ⁶and then have fallen away, it is impossible to renew them again to repentance, since they again crucify to themselves the Son of God, and put Him to open shame. ⁷For ground that drinks the rain which often falls upon it and brings forth vegetation useful to those for whose sake it is also tilled, receives a blessing from God; ⁸but if it yields thorns and thistles, it is worthless and close to being cursed, and it ends up being burned."*

False teachers have always appealed to the flesh and not the Spirit as the determinant of truth. Look at the description of the false teachers in the early church, who slandered the great Apostle Paul:

> **2 Corinthians 10:10:** *"...but his personal presence is unimpressive, and his speech contemptible."*

The reality is that when the true Gospel is preached, it will be effective because the Holy Spirit is doing His work. It does not matter if it is spoken by a sports hero or the most ineloquent, because *God honors His Word,* not man or our techniques. **Isaiah 55:11:** *"So shall My word be which goes forth from My mouth; it shall not return to Me empty, without accomplishing what I desire, and without succeeding in the matter for which I sent it."* We should be very up-front that persecution is part of the Christian life. Paul sets this out in **2 Timothy 3:12:** *"And indeed, all who desire to live godly in Christ Jesus will be persecuted."* Jesus did not try to soften this issue when He preached. He said in **Matthew 10:37:**

> *"He who loves father or mother more than Me is not worthy of Me; and he who loves son or daughter more than Me is not worthy of Me."*

Jesus said in **Mark 8:34-35:**

> *"...He summoned the multitude with His disciples, and said to them, 'If anyone wishes to come after Me, let him deny himself, and take up his cross, and follow Me. ³⁵For whoever wishes to save his life shall lose it; but whoever loses his life for My sake and the gospel's shall save it.'"*

For a study on how to effectively share the Gospel, see an example in this book under the section identified as Matthew 5:17-20. In summary, realize that no "fruit" was produced from the joyful hearer of the word in **Matthew 13:20-21**, who, *"when affliction or persecution arises because of the word, immediately he falls away."* [230]

---

[230] I included the following note in the section of Matthew 28:18 but it has application here regarding modern evangelism. I have been involved with evangelism for over 40 years and I write this note in hopes that many might learn from my experiences. Specifically, I believe there are two lessons to keep in mind when engaging in true evangelism:

[Note continued on next the page.]

[Note continued.]

The first lesson to learn is to not be surprised at the fierceness of opposition you will face when you are involved in *true evangelism*. The attacks will occur from both outside and inside the visible church. The most discouraging attack will be from those within the church (and possibly even from church leadership). Sometimes it may be false-brethren (cf. Galatians 2:4). Don't be discouraged, remember that the Lord gave us Judas as the example of the false functioning (with great camouflage) among the elect. Other times it may be spiritually immature brothers/sisters who are leading the attack. You need to forgive them; remembering that you regret some of your own fleshly decisions that have indirectly hindered the Gospel. The important thing is to not be distracted by their comments or criticisms. Understand that in most cases, you will never satisfy your detractors by trying to answer all their *concerns*. Again, do not waste a lot of time discussing their complaints, but stay focused on the call you have been given (Matthew 28:19-20). Remember that in the end, you serve and answer an audience of one…the Lord. Despite the disappointment and discouragement, do not let your heart be troubled because there is a great peace the Holy Spirit will give to those who are obedient to the will of God.

The second lesson to learn, is that deep down, most of those in the church pews do not really want any part of suffering or persecution for the sake of the gospel. To avoid this persecution they default from the clear commands regarding evangelism/discipleship and create their own user-friendly version of evangelism. I see that the excuse called *friendship evangelism* is the technique of choice for most Christians who are either, untrained, fearful, immature, or false-christians within the church. *Friendship evangelism*, set forth in its simplest form, means you act real nice to someone so that over time he will trust you and like you. After you have his attention, *some year* down the road [hopefully before either of you die, move away, or he decides to end the friendship] you will have impressed them so much that he will ask you why you are so *nice* and *happy*. You then tell them it is because you are a Christian and then you either invite him to church or tell him how he can be happy too if he asks Jesus into his heart. Obviously there are different slants on this but the unspoken technique remains the same; that I am holding back the truth of the gospel until someone is so impressed with me that he will listen to me. When this cowardly view is espoused, it is often supported with the deep saying, *"Preach the gospel at all times; when necessary use words."* Not only does this statement have no basis in scripture, it is almost always wrongfully attributed to Francis of Assisi. Biographer Mark Galli authored the book **Francis of Assisi and His World** and he points out that "no biography written [about Francis] within the first 200 years of his death contains the saying. It's not likely that a pithy quote like this would have been missed by his earliest disciples." See *Speak the Gospel* by Mark Galli, *Christianity Today*, post 5/21/2009. Obviously scripture teaches that all believers are to live godly lives before unbelievers, but a godly life is to be lived out of love for Christ and not to escape the responsibility of telling others the truth of the gospel. "Good News can no more be communicated by deeds than can the nightly news." Id. This *silent preaching of the gospel* is a denial of the scriptural mandate to preach with words! God has chosen the foolishness of preaching to bring people to the knowledge of Him. **1 Corinthians 1:21:** *"For since in the wisdom of God the world through its wisdom did not come to know God, God was well-pleased through the foolishness of the message preached to save those who believe."* **Romans 10:13–15:** [13] *for "Whoever will call on the name of the Lord will be saved."* [14] *How then will they call on Him in whom they have not believed? How will they believe in Him whom they have not heard? And how will they hear without a preacher?* [15] *How will they preach unless they are sent? Just as it is written, "How beautiful are the feet of those who bring good news of good things!"* One writer points out that in Scripture, the Gospel is spread through proclamation. You really need to look up these verses and see this fact: Matthew 4:23, 9:35, 11:5, 24:14, 26:13; Mark 1:14, 13:10, 14:9, 16:15; Luke 9:6, 20:1, 3:18, 8:1, 4:15, 43, 16:16; Acts 8:12, 25, 40, 10:36, 14:7, 21, 15:7, 16:10; Romans 1:15, 10:15, 15:20,16:25; 1 Corinthians 1:17, 9:14-18, 15:1; 2 Corinthians 2:12, 8:18, 10:16, 11:4; Galatians 1:8-9, 11; 2:2, 3:8, 4:13; Ephesians 6:19; Colossians 1:23; 1 Thessalonians 1:5; 2:2, 9; 13; 1 Peter 4:6; Hebrews 4:2.

[Note continued on next the page.]

VERSE 22: *"And the one on whom seed was sown among the thorns, this is the man who hears the word, and the worry of the world, and the deceitfulness of riches choke the word, and it becomes unfruitful."*

This seed was planted in soil that was full of thorns. This is another who *"hears the word,"* but money, status and the preoccupation of the things that are important in this world *"choke the word."* In our society we must be careful of this. It is so easy to look to money for its false security instead of resting in the true security of Christ. MacArthur make a powerful analysis of money and one's spiritual condition:

> "Whether men are wealthy or poor-or somewhere in between-their attitude toward material possessions is one of the most reliable marks of their spiritual condition… Sixteen of the thirty-eight parables of Jesus deal with money. One out of ten verses in the New Testament deals with that subject. Scripture offers about five hundred verses on prayer, fewer than five hundred on faith, and over two thousand on money. The believer's attitude toward money and possessions is determinative."[231]

Is it your desire to get rich? If so, look what the Word of God says awaits you:

> **1 Timothy 6:9-10:** *"But those who want to get rich fall into temptation and a snare and many foolish and harmful desires which plunge men into ruin and destruction.* [10] *For the*

[Note Continued.] The true gospel informs the [friend, enemy, or stranger you just met] that he is a sinner to whom hell awaits unless he repents and believes in Christ's atoning death on the Cross as the only basis for him to be forgiven. [See comment for Matthew 5:17-20 on how to accurately share the Gospel.] Understand that when you do this (via conversation, gospel tract, etc.) the *friendship evangelism* people will berate you for *turning people away* and being *unloving*. They have this viewpoint because they are ultimately concerned on how they appear in public and not how they appear through the eyes of Christ. I cannot tell you the number of meaningful conversations about the Gospel I have had with complete strangers. If you simply talk to them, you find that most people are very concerned about what happens to them after they die. Maybe you struggle with talking to people; fine, give out high-quality tracts that accurately state the Gospel. Hand them out to the clerk at the check-out or drive through or wherever you go. After you do, you will wonder why you were so disobedient in the past.

I cannot think of anything more unloving than knowing the only truth for deliverance from eternal hell, but not telling anyone else about it because he might be offended. Let me provide you an example. Let us say that I am your neighbor and it is about 1:30 a.m. and I see your house is on fire. I know that if I go over and pound on your door yelling and screaming I will disturb your family's sleep and the neighborhood will wonder who is being so obnoxious in the middle of the night. To protect my image of being a good guy — who is not extreme, I just call the fire department. They arrive 15 minutes later. The firemen then break into the house and you barely survive. Unfortunately, the firemen were just a little too late to save your children who are 7, 3 and 6 months. They were burned to death along with your wife. What will you think of me when you find out that I was aware of the extreme danger the family was in 15 minutes before help arrived… *and said nothing.* You will not dismiss my lack of warning when I explain that I was surprised that the fire spread so fast, and that I thought you had more time. You will not accept my defense that I did not want to look like some neighborhood wacko yelling and screaming at 1:30 in the morning. This is the fallacy of *friendship evangelism.* Scripture does not instruct me to withhold the Gospel until I have proven to be either winsome/cute enough to earn the right to tell them how to be saved from the judgment to come. We are commanded to go and tell the truth in love.
[End of Note.]

[231] MacArthur, John F., *Matthew, The MacArthur New Testament Commentary*, p. 418 (Chicago: Moody Press) 1983.

love of money is a root of all sorts of evil, and some by longing for it have wandered away from the faith, and pierced themselves with many a pang."

1 John 2:15: *"Do not love the world, nor the things in the world. If anyone loves the world, the love of the Father is not in him."*

Spurgeon states:
> "Our danger is lest we grow rich and become proud, lest we give ourselves up to the fashions of this present evil world, and lose our faith. Or if wealth be not the trial, worldly care is quite as mischievous. If we cannot be torn in pieces by the roaring lion, if we may be hugged to death by the bear, the devil little cares which it is, so long as he destroys our love to Christ, and our confidence in him."[232]

Many people will spend much of their life focused on preparing for retirement. If they are so afforded, they may live long enough to enjoy a healthy and comfortable retirement of 5 to 15 years. Often they are proud of their forward-thinking and preparation, yet many of these same people do not consider preparing for…"after that." They will respond by saying, "after what?" After your retirement, of course. What preparations have you made for eternity? Sadly, some of these great planners will honestly respond by saying, "I try not to think about that." Jesus speaks of this person in **Luke 12:15-21:**
> *"And He said to them, 'Beware, and be on your guard against every form of greed; for not even when one has an abundance does his life consist of his possessions. ¹⁶And He told them a parable, saying, The land of a certain rich man was very productive. ¹⁷And he began reasoning to himself, saying, What shall I do, since I have no place to store my crops? ¹⁸ And he said, This is what I will do: I will tear down my barns and build larger ones, and there I will store all my grain and my goods. ¹⁹ And I will say to my soul, Soul, you have many goods laid up for many years to come; take your ease, eat, drink and be merry.' ²⁰"But God said to him, 'You fool! This very night your soul is required of you; and now who will own what you have prepared?' ²¹So is the man who lays up treasure for himself, and is not rich toward God.'"*

Jesus addresses the issue of pursuit of worldly riches and not God in **Matthew 16:25-26:**
> *"For whoever wishes to save his life shall lose it; but whoever loses his life for My sake shall find it. ²⁶"For what will a man be profited, if he gains the whole world, and forfeits his soul? Or what will a man give in exchange for his soul?"*

In summary, realize that no "fruit" was produced from this hearer of the Word who let, *"the worry of the world, and the deceitfulness of riches choke the word."*

VERSE 23: *"And the one on whom seed was sown on the good soil, this is the man who hears the word and understands it; who indeed bears fruit, and brings forth, some a hundredfold, some sixty, and some thirty."*

This is the only person who heard the Word, understood it and then bore fruit. This is the person who is a true disciple of Christ.

---

[232] Spurgeon, C. H. (1995). *Morning and evening: Daily readings* (April 26 PM). Oak Harbor, WA.

Colossians 1:5-6: *"…because of the hope laid up for you in heaven, of which you previously heard in the word of truth, the gospel, ⁶ which has come to you, just as in all the world also <u>it is constantly bearing fruit and increasing</u>, even as it has been doing in you also since the day you heard of it and understood the grace of God in truth;…."*

We know from this parable that "fruit" of the Christian's life includes evangelism and obedience to the Great Commission. Jesus said that the good soil, *"brings forth, some a hundredfold, some sixty, and some thirty."* **Matthew 13:23.** But there is more to producing fruit than simply evangelism. The true believer bears Sprit-led fruit. Remember what Paul said in **Galatians 5:22-24:**

"But the fruit of the Spirit is love, joy, peace, patience, kindness, goodness, faithfulness, ²³ gentleness, self-control; against such things there is no law. ²⁴ Now those who belong to Christ Jesus have crucified the flesh with its passions and desires."

In **Ephesians 5:9-11:** it says:

"(for the fruit of the light consists in all goodness and righteousness and truth),¹⁰ trying to learn what is pleasing to the Lord. ¹¹ And do not participate in the unfruitful deeds of darkness, but instead even expose them…."

The Bible tells us that fleshly conduct <u>is not fruit</u> of the Holy Spirit in **Galatians 5:16-21:**

"But I say, walk by the Spirit, and you will not carry out the desire of the flesh. ¹⁷ For the flesh sets its desire against the Spirit, and the Spirit against the flesh; for these are in opposition to one another, so that you may not do the things that you please. ¹⁸ But if you are led by the Spirit, you are not under the Law. ¹⁹ Now the deeds of the flesh are evident, which are: immorality, impurity, sensuality, ²⁰ idolatry, sorcery, enmities, strife, jealousy, outbursts of anger, disputes, dissensions, factions, ²¹ envying, drunkenness, carousing, and things like these, of which I forewarn you just as I have forewarned you that those who practice such things shall not inherit the kingdom of God."

R. C. Sproul points out that nonbelievers can pretend to have some of the fruits of the Spirit listed above. He answers that dilemma below when he says:

"We all know nonbelievers who exhibit more gentleness or patience than many Christians. If people can have the 'fruit of the Spirit' apart from the Spirit, how can we determine our spiritual growth in this manner? There is a qualitative difference between the virtues of love, joy, peace, patience, etc., engendered in us by the Holy Spirit and those exhibited by nonbelievers. <u>Nonbelievers operate from motives that are ultimately selfish.</u> But when believers exhibit the fruit of the Spirit, they are exhibiting characteristics that are ultimately directed toward God and others. Being filled with the Spirit means that one's life is controlled by the Holy Spirit; nonbelievers can only exhibit these spiritual virtues to the extent of human ability."[233]

---

[233] Sproul, R. C., *Essential Truths of the Christian Faith*, (Question 88 "Fruit of the Spirit) (Wheaton, Illinois: Tyndale House Publishers, Inc.) 1992.

Summary and Application

A true Christian has been sealed by the Holy Spirit (Ephesians 1:13-14, Romans 8:9). A true Christian is manifested by the production of fruit by the Holy Spirit (Ephesians 2:10, James 2:14-17). Note: I specifically mentioned fruit produced by the Holy Spirit, not manmade fruit (i.e. human "good works").

In modern evangelicalism, some claim that the evidence of conversion is that you can go back in time to a certain day that you said a particular prayer at a church or at a camp, etc. Unfortunately, the Scripture does not support that as the evidence of a converted soul. It is "fruitfulness" produced by the Holy Spirit that is the evidence of a converted soul. R. C. Sproul summarizes the issue of the assurance of our salvation this way:

> "…we must examine the fruit of our faith. We do not need perfect fruit to have assurance, but there must be some evidence of the fruit of obedience for our profession of faith to be credible. If no fruit is present, then no faith is present. Where saving faith is found, fruit of that faith is also found." [234]

This parable also provides an important explanation about those you know who once confessed Christ and now renounce Him. In the parable we read of some who, *"hears the word, and immediately receives it with joy"* (v.20) and yet they eventually fall away. Some wrongfully claim that verse 20 represents those who *"lost their salvation."* This parable states otherwise. The ones who fall away were never truly converted in the first place. They cannot lose a salvation they never had.

> **1 John 2:19:** *"They went out from us, but they were not really of us; <u>for if they had been of us, they would have remained with us; but they went out, in order that it might be shown that they all are not of us.</u>"*

Those who fall away are like those who called Jesus, "Lord." Jesus did not tell these people that He "no longer would know them" but He said He *"never knew"* them.

> **Matthew 7:20-23:** *"So then, you will know them by their fruits. [21] Not everyone who says to Me, 'Lord, Lord,' will enter the kingdom of heaven; but he who does the will of My Father who is in heaven. [22] Many will say to Me on that day, 'Lord, Lord, did we not prophesy in Your name, and in Your name cast out demons, and in Your name perform many miracles?' [23] And then I will declare to them, 'I never knew you; DEPART FROM ME, YOU WHO PRACTICE LAWLESSNESS.'"*

It is sorrowful when we see people who we thought were saved now denying the faith. Despite that sorrow, we do not need to be discouraged, worry or fear that we might later defect. Our confidence is based on the mercy and call of God. We do not keep ourselves saved. The Lord who saved us, keeps us saved. A.A. Hodge states that:

> "This perseverance of the saints depends not upon their own free will, but upon the immutability of the decree of election, flowing from the free and unchangeable love of God the Father; upon the efficacy of the merit and intercession of Jesus Christ, the abiding of the Spirit, and of the seed of God within them; and the nature of the covenant of grace: from all which arises also the certainty and infallibility thereof." [235]

Jesus states our security in Him:

> **John 10:27-30:** *"My sheep hear My voice, and I know them, and they follow Me; [28]and I give eternal life to them, and they shall never perish; and no one shall snatch them out*

---

[234] Ibid.

[235] Hodge, A. (1996). *The Confession of Faith: With questions for Theological students and Bible Classes.* p.232. With an appendix on Presbyterianism by Charles Hodge. Index created by Christian Classics Foundation. (electronic ed. based on the 1992 Banner of Truth reprint.). Simpsonville SC: Christian Classics Foundation.

of My hand. ²⁹*My Father, who has given them to Me, is greater than all; <u>and no one is able to snatch them out of the Father's hand.</u> ³⁰I and the Father are one."*

How thankful we can be to God who keeps those who trust Him from falling away.

<u>Jude 24-25:</u> *"Now to Him who is able to keep you from stumbling, and to make you stand in the presence of His glory blameless with great joy, ²⁵to the only God our Savior, through Jesus Christ our Lord, be glory, majesty, dominion and authority, before all time and now and forever. Amen."*

<u>Romans 8:31-39:</u> *"What then shall we say to these things? If God is for us, who is against us? ³²He who did not spare His own Son, but delivered Him up for us all, how will He not also with Him freely give us all things? ³³Who will bring a charge against God's elect? God is the one who justifies; ³⁴who is the one who condemns? Christ Jesus is He who died, yes, rather who was raised, who is at the right hand of God, who also intercedes for us. ³⁵Who shall separate us from the love of Christ? Shall tribulation, or distress, or persecution, or famine, or nakedness, or peril, or sword? ³⁶Just as it is written, 'For Thy sake we are being put to death all day long; We were considered as sheep to be slaughtered.' ³⁷But in all these things we overwhelmingly conquer through Him who loved us. ³⁸For I am convinced that neither death, nor life, nor angels, nor principalities, nor things present, nor things to come, nor powers, ³⁹nor height, nor depth, nor any other created thing, shall be able to separate us from the love of God, which is in Christ Jesus our Lord."*

One last caution on producing fruit and serving the Lord: Be careful to not confuse fruitfulness with legalism. Remember the heretical teaching of "legalism" says that it is *good works* or *religious rituals,* etc. that help get you saved or keeps you saved. Jesus tells us emphatically that we cannot do anything to earn our own salvation. <u>Those who are saved have put their complete trust for salvation in Christ's sacrifice on the cross. They know that only His death can be the full payment for their sins.</u> After we are converted, God begins to produce His fruit through us which includes good works for the glory of God (Ephesians 2:8-10) and a completely changed person.

<u>Galatians 5:22–25:</u> *"But the fruit of the Spirit is love, joy, peace, patience, kindness, goodness, faithfulness, ²³ gentleness, self-control; against such things there is no law. ²⁴ Now those who belong to Christ Jesus have crucified the flesh with its passions and desires. ²⁵ If we live by the Spirit, let us also walk by the Spirit."*

So what kind of soil has the *seed* (the Word of God) fallen on in your life?

MATTHEW 13:24-43
(PARABLES ABOUT THE KINGDOM OF HEAVEN)

"He presented another parable to them, saying, 'The kingdom of heaven may be compared to a man who sowed good seed in his field. 25 But while men were sleeping, his enemy came and sowed tares also among the wheat, and went away. 26 But when the wheat sprang up and bore grain, then the tares became evident also. 27 And the slaves of the landowner came and said to him, 'Sir, did you not sow good seed in your field? How then does it have tares?' 28 And he said to them, 'An enemy has done this!' And the slaves *said to him, 'Do you want us, then, to go and gather them up?' 29 But he *said, 'No; lest while you are gathering up the tares, you may root up the wheat with them. 30 Allow both to grow together until the harvest; and in the time of the harvest I will say to the reapers, First gather up the tares and bind them in bundles to burn them up; but gather the wheat into my barn.'

31He presented another parable to them, saying, 'The kingdom of heaven is like a mustard seed, which a man took and sowed in his field; 32and this is smaller than all other seeds; but when it is full grown, it is larger than the garden plants, and becomes a tree, so that THE BIRDS OF THE AIR come and NEST IN ITS BRANCHES.'

33He spoke another parable to them, 'The kingdom of heaven is like leaven, which a woman took, and hid in three pecks of meal, until it was all leavened.'

34All these things Jesus spoke to the multitudes in parables, and He did not speak to them without a parable, 35so that what was spoken through the prophet might be fulfilled, saying, 'I WILL OPEN MY MOUTH IN PARABLES; I WILL UTTER THINGS HIDDEN SINCE THE FOUNDATION OF THE WORLD.'

36Then He left the multitudes, and went into the house. And His disciples came to Him, saying, 'Explain to us the parable of the tares of the field.' 37And He answered and said, 'The one who sows the good seed is the Son of Man, 38and the field is the world; and as for the good seed, these are the sons of the kingdom; and the tares are the sons of the evil one; 39and the enemy who sowed them is the devil, and the harvest is the end of the age; and the reapers are angels. 40 Therefore just as the tares are gathered up and burned with fire, so shall it be at the end of the age. 41 The Son of Man will send forth His angels, and they will gather out of His kingdom all stumbling blocks, and those who commit lawlessness, 42and will cast them into the furnace of fire; in that place there shall be weeping and gnashing of teeth. 43 Then THE RIGHTEOUS WILL SHINE FORTH AS THE SUN in the kingdom of their Father. He who has ears, let him hear.'"

Introduction

Jesus continues to teach about the kingdom of heaven in parables. Why did He teach in parables? He fulfilled prophecy by revealing truths which have been hidden from the beginning of the creation of the earth. **Matthew 13:34-35** states that:

"All these things Jesus spoke to the multitudes in parables, and He did not speak to them without a parable, 35 so that what was spoken through the prophet might be fulfilled, saying, 'I WILL OPEN MY MOUTH IN PARABLES; I WILL UTTER THINGS HIDDEN SINCE THE FOUNDATION OF THE WORLD.'"

The prophecy quoted in Matthew 13:35 is from Psalm 78:2. Understanding of these deep truths regarding the Kingdom of God is not granted to everyone. Jesus states in **Matthew 13:10-11:**

"And the disciples came and said to Him, 'Why do You speak to them in parables?' 11And He answered and said to them, 'To you it has been granted to know the mysteries of the kingdom of heaven, but to them it has not been granted.'"

VERSES 24-30: *"He presented another parable to them, saying, 'The kingdom of heaven may be compared to a man who sowed good seed in his field. 25 But while men were sleeping, his enemy came and sowed tares also among the wheat, and went away. 26 But when the wheat sprang up and bore grain, then the tares became evident also. 27 And the slaves of the landowner came and said to him, 'Sir, did you not sow good seed in your field? How then does it have tares?' 28 And he said to them, 'An enemy has done this!' And the slaves *said to him, 'Do you want us, then, to go and gather them up?' 29 But he *said, 'No; lest while you are gathering up the tares, you may root up the wheat with them. 30 Allow both to grow together until the harvest; and in the time of the harvest I will say to the reapers, First gather up the tares and bind them in bundles to burn them up; but gather the wheat into my barn.'"*

This is the parable of the *Wheat and the Tares*. *Tares* is another word for weeds. The parable has *good seed* planted, but an enemy (i.e. the Devil) planted *tares* in the field. Note that while the crops were growing, there was very little difference in appearance between the wheat and the tares.

Once I was out touring a friend's wheat field in the heart of South Dakota. It was the time of year that some of the grain heads were coming in. As we walked he pointed down at a stalk and said, "that's not wheat." To me, it looked kinda like some of the other wheat plants that had not developed a head yet. The farmer called it "cheat grass" which is the same thing as a *tare*. "Cheat grass" is a weed that looks just like wheat while it is growing but when they both mature, the wheat has a head of grain on it and the "cheat grass" has none. This is exactly how Jesus described it when He said in verse 26 *"But when the wheat sprang up and bore grain, then the tares became evident also."* The problem with tares is that for them to grow they need to steal the moisture and nutrients from the soil and thus hinder the growth and production of the real crop. Not only do they hinder the good crop, but they are worthless. The interpretation of the parable of the *wheat and the tares* is given in **Matthew 13:36-43**:

> *"Then He left the multitudes, and went into the house. And His disciples came to Him, saying, 'Explain to us the parable of the tares of the field.' 37 And He answered and said, 'The one who sows the good seed is the Son of Man, 38 and the field is the world; and as for the good seed, these are the sons of the kingdom; and the tares are the sons of the evil one; 39 and the enemy who sowed them is the devil, and the harvest is the end of the age; and the reapers are angels. 40 Therefore just as the tares are gathered up and burned with fire, so shall it be at the end of the age. 41 The Son of Man will send forth His angels, and they will gather out of His kingdom all stumbling blocks, and those who commit lawlessness, 42 and will cast them into the furnace of fire; in that place there shall be weeping and gnashing of teeth. 43 Then THE RIGHTEOUS WILL SHINE FORTH AS THE SUN in the kingdom of their Father. He who has ears, let him hear.'"*

We see in these verses that Jesus plants the *sons of the kingdom* (v.38, i.e. all Christians) in this world. We also see the Devil doing his evil imitation by planting his evil children in the world also. This parable is often narrowly interpreted to be a lesson about the children of the devil coming into the church along with the children of God. Although that can be a part of it, the view is larger than that since Jesus tells us that the *"field is the world"* (v.38). Those who hate God cause corruption in this world. All creation awaits redemption from the judgment of corruption upon the earth resulting from man's sin:

> **Romans 8:19-21:** *"For the anxious longing of the creation waits eagerly for the revealing of the sons of God. 20 For the creation was subjected to futility, not of its own will, but because of Him who subjected it, in hope 21 that the creation itself also will be set free from its slavery to corruption into the freedom of the glory of the children of God."*

Jesus said the, *"sons of the evil one"* are *"stumbling blocks, and those who commit lawlessness,"* **Matthew 13:41**. The evil they commit is not restricted to simply inside the church but throughout the entire world because *"the field is the world."* They make others *stumble* in many ways. They attack others through their *lawless* acts of sin and abuse. They sometimes do their dirty work with a clean suit on by suing to make sure that students can never hear the name of God in school.[236]

I find it very paradoxical that the censors, who never want the mention of Christianity in a school, do not seem to have a big problem if the name of God and/or Jesus Christ is used in vain or as a curse word. Some lawyers make a very comfortable living off trying to keep God from being acknowledged almost anywhere. What are they so afraid of? The answer is they fear that if there is a God, they will be accountable to Him. Jesus made it clear that these *stumbling blocks* will be accountable to Him and they will suffer a severe judgment:

> **Matthew 18:5-6:** *"And whoever receives one such child in My name receives Me; 6but whoever causes one of these little ones who believe in Me to stumble, it is better for him that a heavy millstone be hung around his neck, and that he be drowned in the depth of the sea."*

Look back at the parable of the *wheat and the tares*. In Matthew 13:26 the tares looked like the wheat...until they matured: *"But when the wheat sprang up and bore grain, then the tares became evident also."* Evil can disguise itself, but eventually it is shown for what it is. False religions can appear peaceful, helpful, and even moral, but that is Satan's old deception:

> **2 Corinthians 11:13-15:** *"For such men are false apostles, deceitful workers, disguising themselves as apostles of Christ. 14 And no wonder, for even Satan disguises himself as an angel of light. 15 Therefore it is not surprising if his servants also disguise themselves as servants of righteousness; whose end shall be according to their deeds."*

> **Titus 1:16:** *"They profess to know God, but by their deeds they deny Him, being detestable and disobedient, and worthless for any good deed."*

Look how Jesus described the very outwardly religious scribes and Pharisees:

> **Matthew 23:27-28:** *"Woe to you, scribes and Pharisees, hypocrites! For you are like whitewashed tombs which on the outside appear beautiful, but inside they are full of dead men's bones and all uncleanness. 28 Even so you too outwardly appear righteous to men, but inwardly you are full of hypocrisy and lawlessness."*

We must know God's Word and have the Holy Spirit's discernment to not be deceived by false teachers, who are children of the Devil.

> **2 Timothy 3:13-17:** *"But evil men and impostors will proceed from bad to worse, deceiving and being deceived. 14 You, however, continue in the things you have learned and become convinced of, knowing from whom you have learned them; 15 and that from childhood you have known the sacred writings which are able to give you the wisdom*

---

[236] United States Supreme Court decision of Santa Fe Independent School Dist. v. Doe 120 S.Ct. 2266 (2000). In this case the School district had allowed a student-initiated and student-led prayer to be given prior to the start of football games. The Supreme Court ruled that this was not private speech and was too coercive and thus must be stopped.

that leads to salvation through faith which is in Christ Jesus. [16] All Scripture is inspired by God and profitable for teaching, for reproof, for correction, for training in righteousness; [17] that the man of God may be adequate, equipped for every good work."

1 Timothy 4:1: *"But the Spirit explicitly says that in later times some will fall away from the faith, paying attention to deceitful spirits and doctrines of demons,...."*

One should look at the final destiny of the children of the Devil. Jesus said that they *"will cast them into the furnace of fire; in that place there shall be weeping and gnashing of teeth..."* Often the wicked describe hell as some *good-time honky-tonk* where they are with all their buddies, drinking whiskey and dancing with loose women. They will go on to proclaim that they would rather be in hell with their buddies than stuck sitting on a cloud in heaven playing a harp. This type of thinking shows how deceived they are about heaven and hell. Jesus makes it clear in verse 42 that the wicked will be thrown into a *furnace of fire*. If one did not get Jesus' point about this, He repeats it shortly thereafter in the *parable of the dragnet*. In that parable Jesus states that the judgment of the wicked will be to *"...cast them into the furnace of fire; there shall be weeping and gnashing of teeth."* In **Revelation 20:15** it says, *"And if anyone's name was not found written in the book of life, he was thrown into the lake of fire."* It must be understood that the judgment is neither temporary, nor does it end in annihilation so that you don't have to feel anything. The torment goes on and on *forever and ever*. Examine and carefully consider the description of hell from God's Word.

> **DESCRIPTION OF HELL:** *Flames and torment* - Luke. 16:19-31; *Lake of fire which burns with brimstone* - Revelation 19:20; *Lake of fire - Fire and brimstone and are tormented day and night forever and ever* - Revelation 20:10; *Eternal fire...the blackness of darkness forever* - Jude v.7, 13; *Everlasting destruction from the presence of the Lord* - 2 Thessalonians 1:9; *Where their worm does not die, and the fire is not quenched* - Mark 9:43-48; *Weeping and gnashing of teeth* - Matthew 24:51; *Everlasting punishment* - Matthew 25:46; *Indignation, wrath, tribulation and anguish* - Romans 2:8,9; *Shame and everlasting contempt* - Daniel 12:2; *Unquenchable fire* - Luke 3:17.

The non-believer must be warned that he will end up in hell unless he is saved. I wince when I hear a weak-kneed pastor who will not say the word hell but simply says that the unsaved will end up *"separated from God."* This is very misleading to the unbeliever, who in his darkened understanding thinks he is currently living *separated from God*...and frankly likes it that way. It is also misleading theologically. It is true that a person in hell is separated from God's love, joy, forgiveness and salvation, but they are not *separated from God*. The person in hell is in the presence of God's judgment and wrath for all eternity. **Revelation 14:9–11:**

> [9] *Then another angel, a third one, followed them, saying with a loud voice, "If anyone worships the beast and his image, and receives a mark on his forehead or on his hand, [10] he also will drink of the wine of the wrath of God, which is mixed in full strength in the cup of His anger; and he will be tormented with fire and brimstone in the presence of the holy angels and in the presence of the Lamb.*
> [11] *"And the smoke of their torment goes up forever and ever; they have no rest day and night, those who worship the beast and his image, and whoever receives the mark of his name."*

Make no mistake about it, Satan is the not the ruler of hell; God is. Satan ends up a prisoner in God's hell. God made hell for Satan and his demonic angels. The unsaved are punished there too. Jesus said in **Matthew 25:41:** *"...Depart from Me, accursed ones, into the eternal fire which has been* *prepared for the devil and his angels;..."* In short, repent and believe the gospel so that you might be saved and escape the judgment of hell.

On the other hand, heaven is beyond what we are mentally capable of imagining. R. C. Sproul, applying Scripture, set out a *description of heaven* when he wrote:

"The New Jerusalem is described in terms of translucent streets of gold, a place with walls of precious gemstones, and a setting of perpetual and everlasting joy.

What is most notable about heaven is what is absent from it as well as what is present in it. Things that will be absent include: (1) tears, (2) sorrow, (3) death, (4) pain, (5) darkness, (6) ungodly people, (7) sin, (8) temples, (9) the sun or moon, and (10) the curse from Adam's sin (see Genesis 3:14-19).

What will be present in heaven includes: (1) the saints, (2) the river of the water of life, (3) healing fruit, (4) the Lamb of God, (5) worship, (6) the wedding feast of the Lamb and His bride, (7) the unveiled face of God, and (8) the Sun of Righteousness.

Heaven is where Christ is. It is the eternal bliss of communion with the God-man. Jonathan Edwards, in trying to give voice to the joy believers will find in heaven writes that the saints will swim in the ocean of love, and be eternally swallowed up in the infinitely bright, and infinitely mild and sweet beams of divine love; eternally receiving the light, eternally full of it, and eternally compassed round with it, and everlastingly reflecting it back again to its fountain. While the saints will delight in fellowship with their God and Savior, there is no reason to believe that they will not recognize and fellowship with saints they knew on earth. Heaven is the abode of all good things."[237] (see 1 Corinthians 15:50-57, 2 Corinthians 5:1-8, 1 Peter 1:3-9, Revelation chs. 21-22.)[238]

Section Application

This parable plainly tells us that there are evil people right alongside God's children in this world. Many of these evil people carry out their own self-deception, believing that they are wonderful people. They feel good about how they appear to those around them. They are proud that they serve as the chairperson for a charity or civic board. They have no true conviction of making sure they are obedient to Christ and His Word, especially if that would mean a loss of prestige. They are confident that they are *good people* because their friends and colleagues honor them with awards and affirmation. They not only deceive others, but they have deceived themselves:

1 John 1:8: *"If we say that we have no sin, we are deceiving ourselves, and the truth is not in us."*

They may look like children of God on the outside and may even attend church. But when the charade is removed, they are nothing but weeds. Like weeds they try to rob the wheat of the moisture and nutrients it needs. As religious imposters they will skillfully ridicule, mock and attack the children of God. They continue to deceive themselves and others:

2 Timothy 3:12-13: *"And indeed, all who desire to live godly in Christ Jesus will be persecuted. ¹³But evil men and impostors will proceed from bad to worse, deceiving and being deceived."*

---

[237] Sproul, R. C., *Essential Truths of the Christian Faith*, (Wheaton, Illinois: Tyndale House Publishers, Inc.) 1992.

[238] Ibid

The promise we have from the Lord in this parable is that righteousness will prevail and judgment is sure. Given enough time, it will be obvious who are the children of God (*wheat*) and who are the children of the evil one (*tares*). The children of God produce a crop (i.e. spiritual fruit) because Jesus dwells in them. The fakes produce no good crop but instead are, *"stumbling blocks, and those who commit lawlessness."*

> **1 John 3:7-10:** *"Little children, let no one deceive you; the one who practices righteousness is righteous, just as He is righteous; ⁸ the one who practices sin is of the devil; for the devil has sinned from the beginning. The Son of God appeared for this purpose, that He might destroy the works of the devil. ⁹ No one who is born of God practices sin, <u>because His seed abides in him</u>; and he cannot sin, because he is born of God. ¹⁰ <u>By this the children of God and the children of the devil are obvious: anyone who does not practice righteousness is not of God, nor the one who does not love his brother."</u>*

VERSES 31-32: *"He presented another parable to them, saying, 'The kingdom of heaven is like a mustard seed, which a man took and sowed in his field; ³²and this is smaller than all other seeds; but when it is full grown, it is larger than the garden plants, and becomes a tree, so that* THE BIRDS OF THE AIR *come and* NEST IN ITS BRANCHES.*'"*

Here Jesus demonstrates how something so small as a mustard seed can grow to a great height. [239] Although some varieties grow like bushes, the mustard seed variety used in Palestine grew much

---

[239] Nonbelievers often like to make a big deal of the mustard seed not being the smallest seed ever known to man and claim an error in the Bible. This is an absurd conclusion. Jesus did not say it was the smallest seed in all existence. Notice He is talking about seeds that are actually planted by the people to grow crops (see v.31, see also Mark 4:31), not merely some random seed of a weed or something else. One commentator put it this way:

> "But He was not comparing this seed to all other seeds in existence but only to the seeds of **garden plants** in Palestine. Many seeds, such as those of the wild orchid, are much smaller than the seed of the mustard plant. But of the many plants grown at that time in the gardens and fields of Palestine, the mustard plant has the smallest seeds, just as Jesus said. When (**seed**) is used in the New Testament in reference to plants, it is always used of agricultural plants, those intentionally grown for food. And of those **plants**, the mustard had seeds that were **smaller than all other seeds**. Dr. L. H. Shinners, director of the herbarium at Southern Methodist University in Dallas and lecturer at the Smithsonian Institution, stated in a conversation that the mustard seed would indeed have been the smallest of those to have been noticed by the people at the time of Christ. The principle field crops (barley, wheat, lentils, and beans) have much larger seeds, as do other plants which might have been present as weeds and so forth. There are various weeds and wild flowers belonging to the mustard, amaranth, pigweed, or chickweed families with seeds that are as small as or smaller than mustard; but they would not have been known or noticed by the inhabitants. They are wild and they certainly would not have been planted as a crop. ... The only modern crop plant in existence with smaller seeds than mustard is tobacco, and this plant of American origin was not grown in the old world until the sixteenth century or later." MacArthur, J. F., Jr. (1985). *Matthew. MacArthur New Testament Commentary* (p. 289). Chicago: Moody Press.

Often the nonbelievers, who like to call themselves, "religious scholars," are merely the sons of the Devil [Note continued on the next page.]

larger, which commentators verify as up to 12-15 feet in one season.[240] This parable teaches us that even the little seed of faith that God plants produces big results. From a human standpoint, the Lord's church had a small and insignificant beginning with a mere 120 people praying (Acts 1:14-15). When the Holy Spirit filled these people and the Gospel was preached, 3000 souls were saved on a single day (Acts 2:41). After that event, and on to today, we continue to experience **Acts 2:47:** *"...the Lord was adding to their number day by day those who were being saved."*

Notice that from such a little seed a plant grows to the size of a tree. Likewise, Christendom has exploded from such tiny beginnings. Jesus then speaks of the grown plant being sought after by the birds to make their nests: *"...so that THE BIRDS OF THE AIR come and NEST IN ITS BRANCHES"* (v.32). (We do not have a record of the interpretation of this parable.) Henry believes that the "birds" resting in it are God's people deriving rest and nourishment from God's kingdom:

> "The church is like a great tree, in which the fowls of the air do lodge; God's people have recourse to it for food and rest, shade and shelter. In particular persons, the principle of grace, if true, will persevere and be perfected at last: growing grace will be strong grace, and will bring much to pass. Grown Christians must covet to be useful to others, as the mustard-seed when grown is to the birds; that those who dwell near or under their shadow may be the better for them, Hos. 14:7." [241]

Probably the most commonly accepted interpretation is that the birds represent the gentiles (the nations) as part of the Kingdom of God. Old Testament scripture support this view:

[Note continued.]
who refuse to believe anything and deny everything God says. Scripture describes them like this:
> **Titus 1:15-16:** *"... but to those who are defiled and unbelieving, nothing is pure, but both their mind and their conscience are defiled. ¹⁶ They profess to know God, but by their deeds they deny Him, being detestable and disobedient, and worthless for any good deed."*

The mustard seed's smallness was also used by Jesus in another illustration:
> **Matthew 17:19-20:** *"Then the disciples came to Jesus privately and said, 'Why could we not cast it out?' ²⁰ And He *said to them, 'Because of the littleness of your faith; for truly I say to you, if you have faith as a mustard seed, you shall say to this mountain, 'Move from here to there,' and it shall move; and nothing shall be impossible to you.'"*

[End of note.]

[240] Walvoord, John F., and Zuck, Roy B., *The Bible Knowledge Commentary,* (Wheaton, Illinois: Scripture Press Publications, Inc.) 1983, 1985.

[241] Henry, M. (1994). *Matthew Henry's Commentary on the Whole Bible: Complete and Unabridged in One Volume* (Matthew. 13:24–43). Peabody: Hendrickson.
INTERPRETATIONS:
> "The figure of **birds** making nests normally calls to mind that which is positive and helpful. Nesting carries the idea of protection, safety, refuge, and sanctuary, which the mother bird provides for her young." MacArthur, John F., 1983 *The MacArthur New Testament Commentary,* (Chicago: Moody Press)

> [Birds] "probably they represent the incorporation of the Gentiles into God's kingdom program (cf. Ezekiel 17:22-24; 31:6)." Walvoord, J. F. (1983-c1985). *The Bible Knowledge Commentary: An Exposition of the Scriptures* (Mark 4:30). Wheaton, IL: Victor Books

Ezekiel 17:23–24: *"On the high mountain of Israel I will plant it, that it may bring forth boughs and bear fruit and become a stately cedar. And birds of every kind will nest under it; they will nest in the shade of its branches. "All the trees of the field will know that I am the Lord; I bring down the high tree, exalt the low tree, dry up the green tree and make the dry tree flourish. I am the Lord; I have spoken, and I will perform it."*

The promise God gave to Abraham stated that all the nations would be blessed through his line. Even though the covenant was made to Abraham and his descendants (the Jews), God also told him that those blessings would extend out to every nation.

Genesis 12:1-3:
"Now the LORD said to Abram,
Go forth from your country,
And from your relatives
And from your father's house,
To the land which I will show you;
² And I will make you a great nation,
And I will bless you,
And make your name great;
And so you shall be a blessing;
³ And I will bless those who bless you,
And the one who curses you I will curse.
And in you all the families of the earth shall be blessed."

The blessing to all *the families of the earth* is that Jesus would be the Savior to all nations. Simeon, who held baby Jesus, spoke about this when he said:

Luke 2:30-32: *"For my eyes have seen Thy salvation, ³¹ Which Thou hast prepared in the presence of all peoples, ³² A LIGHT OF REVELATION TO THE GENTILES,...."*

A less common interpretation is that the *birds* could represent evil. Remember the parable of the *Sower and the Seed*? In that parable we see the birds representing the Devil.

Matthew 13:3-4, 19: *"And He spoke many things to them in parables, saying, 'Behold, the sower went out to sow; ⁴and as he sowed, some seeds fell beside the road, and the birds came and ate them up....*
¹⁹ When anyone hears the word of the kingdom, and does not understand it, the evil one comes and snatches away what has been sown in his heart. This is the one on whom seed was sown beside the road.'"

This view sees the mustard seed parable as reflecting the Church and how Christendom has grown. The *birds* are viewed as the Devil placing his people in the church in an attempt to undermine its work. Walvoord states:

"Jesus did not directly interpret this parable. However, its meaning may be that the sphere of professing followers, sometimes called Christendom, which Jesus mentioned in the second parable, would have a small beginning but would grow rapidly into a large entity. This group could include both believers and unbelievers, as indicated by the birds lodging in the branches of the tree." [242]

---

[242] Walvoord, John F., and Zuck, Roy B., *The Bible Knowledge Commentary*, (Wheaton, Illinois: Scripture Press Publications, Inc.) 1983, 1985.

We do know that throughout the New Testament there are constant warnings of false teachers/apostles and false-brothers in the Church. For example, the parable just prior to the mustard seed parable is about the "wheat and the tares" in Matthew 13:24-30. The parable of the wheat and the tares teaches us that the enemy tries to put his people in the world and the church to undermine its work. There are plenty of examples of this. One only needs to look at some of the great Christian works such as that of the Wesley brothers in the building of the Methodist denomination. Consider the great work they did in comparison to some of the "birds" who now run the denomination. Very few are concerned with Biblical repentance and faith in Christ. A portion of their leaders believe that the issues that matter are abortion rights and ordaining homosexual pastors. There was a day when the Methodist church was built on Scripture and evangelism, but is now run by "ministers," many of which deny the inerrancy of the Scripture and thus are nonbelievers.

When I was in college I ran into one of these *religious leaders*. I worked in a grocery store during the summer at a lake resort area. My job was to sack the groceries for people as they checked out. There was a grandfatherly-looking, gray haired, Methodist minister who would often come to the store. He was on his third marriage, and loved to tell dirty jokes to the female checkers. Once while he was visiting with a checker, he proudly quoted from some article that he said he read in Playboy magazine. One Sunday I went to his church to see a false teacher in action. I watched him preach about all kinds of *nice* things. He even read from the Bible and prayed so very reverently. WHAT A FRAUD HE WAS! What was scary is that the unbeliever would never know the difference (and possibly even some believers – Matthew 24:24). He was a *tare*. He looked and sounded so….*religious…so Christian*. After the service I watched as he so enthusiastically, and with false kindness greeted everyone as they left the church. He was busy shaking hands with the men…but no handshakes for the women. All the women got hugs and if they were pretty and young, they got deep embraces. (One college girl I knew could barely get away from him!) It was sick to watch, but it was a great lesson on false teachers that I will not forget. J.C. Ryle stated it well when he said:

> "There is no one who does such injury to the cause of Christianity as unconverted, worldly ministers. They are a support to the unbeliever, a joy to the devil and an offense to God."[243]

When we speak of the false Christians, what does that mean? The false will always knowingly deny at least one of the fundamental doctrines of the faith. Fundamental doctrines are those that are essential for one making a claim to true Biblical Christianity. One can sound like a Christian and not be one. Some of the false can include Sunday school teachers, evangelists and even pastors. Over time you will run into people who consider themselves mature Christians, yet they deny scripture and remain unconverted. One is not a Christian if they deny the Word of God as true, claim Jesus was just a man, believe that they have to do good works to help earn their way into heaven, etc. One of the problems in the visible church is that we are very quick to accept a person as a Christian based solely on his claim that he has been saved. For example a person will be asked a general question such as if they believe they are saved by faith in Jesus. The person will say yes, and the enquiry ends. No one will ask him what it means to be "saved" or how he defines "faith." He may not even be asked who he believes Jesus is. I have run into Mormons who say they "believe in being saved by faith in Jesus." If you do a little more inquiry, you find out that their definition of terms are very different than the Bible's. For example, the Jesus of Mormonism is not the Jesus of the Bible (Mormons claims that Jesus is the brother of Satan!). The problem of the false Christian in the church

---

[243] Ryle, J.C. *Mark (Expository thoughts on the Gospels)*, p. 36 (Crossways Classic Commentaries: v.2) 1993.

is camouflaged because he may be vigorously involved in the church activities or programs. After some time, he will be asked to teach Sunday School, or serve on the board of deacons. Now the false convert has a platform and authority to undermine the truth, stumble the weak and attack true ministry.

What are the fundamentals of the faith? Most restrict the list of fundamental doctrines to those that relate to the issue of salvation alone; (soteriological – the theological doctrine of salvation in Christianity).[244] (Please review this footnote below). The reason for limiting it to the doctrine of salvation is due to the awesome and wonderful simplicity in becoming a true Christian! Romans 10:9 explains how to be saved from the judgment to come:

> **Romans 10:9:** *"that if you confess with your mouth Jesus as Lord, and believe in your heart that God raised Him from the dead, you will be saved…"*

True fundamental doctrines are derived from *Scripture alone* and not religious tradition or ecclesiastical counsels.[245] Oswald Chambers stated:

> "We are apt to forget that a man is not only committed to Jesus Christ for salvation; he is committed to Jesus Christ's view of God, of the world, of sin and of the devil, and this will mean that he must recognize the responsibility of being transformed by the renewing of his mind."[246]

---

[244] "Historically, fundamentalism has been used to identify one holding to the five fundamentals of the faith adopted by the General Assembly of the Presbyterian Church in the U.S.A. in 1910. The five fundamentals were the miracles of Christ, the virgin birth of Christ, the substitutionary atonement of Christ, the bodily resurrection of Christ, and the inspiration of Scripture. Fundamentalism has stood for the historic fundamentals of Christianity, particularly as developed in *The Fundamentals*. These were initially issued as twelve booklets edited by R. A. Torrey and A. C. Dixon. More than three million copies have been distributed to pastors and others." Enns, P. P. (1997, c1989). *The Moody Handbook of Theology* (613). Chicago, Ill.: Moody Press.

[245] Some wrongly claim that the so-called Apostles Creed is the standard for the fundamentals of the Christian faith.

> "The Creed is by no means a complete statement of all the doctrines essential to genuine Christianity. For example, since there is no statement about the deity of Christ, a Jehovah's Witness, who denies Christ's deity, could give full assent to the Creed as it stands. In fact, the ancient forerunners of Jehovah's Witnesses, the followers of a heretic named Arius, defended themselves by appealing to the Creed." MacArthur, J. (1994). *Reckless faith: When the church loses its will to discern* (103). Wheaton, Ill.: Crossway Books.

Note also that the Creed makes no mention of repentance and faith in Christ for salvation. This is why tens of thousands can stand up each week and mumble through the Creed and remain unsaved. As R.C. Sproul wrote: *"It is one thing to believe in God; it is another thing to believe God."*

Regarding the Apostles Creed: There is no evidence that Apostle's Creed was written by the apostles but there are unsubstantiated legends out there. One legend is that the Apostles wrote this creed on the 10th day after Christ's ascension into heaven. Another legend states that each of the 12 apostles composed a clause that composed the "apostles' creed." For more on the Apostles Creed see the section after the **Summary and Application** following Matthew 27:65-66.

[246] Chambers, O. (1993, c1935). *My Utmost for His Highest: Selections for the Year* (September 9). Grand Rapids, MI: Discovery House Publishers.

The list below forms a *general outline* of true **Christianity**. A mature Christian will have searched Scripture to formulate his theological beliefs and will affirm the following doctrines:

- **Inspiration, Inerrancy and Authority of Scripture:** Christ is the Word of God incarnate: John 1:1,14, 2 Peter 1:20-21, 2 Timothy 3:16, Proverbs 30:5-6, Revelation 22:18-19.
- **Virgin Birth:** Matthew 1:18-25, Luke 1:34-35, John 1:14.
- **The Deity of Jesus Christ The Son of God:** He is God incarnate (God in a human flesh-and-blood body): Colossians 2:9, 1 John 5:20, Titus 2:13-14, John 8:58 and 10:30, Mark 14:61-62, John 20:28, Mark 15:39, John 21:14, Luke 22:70, John 20:31.
- **Jesus' Humanity:** His incarnation (1 John 4:2-3), He was tempted (Luke 4:1-13), hungry (Matthew 4:2), thirsty (John 19:28), slept (Matthew 8:24), died (Mark 15:39-45, Matthew 27:50).
- **Jesus' Sinlessness:** 2 Corinthians 5:21, Hebrews 4:15, 1 Peter 2:22, 1 John 3:5.
- **The Trinity:** Father, Son and Holy Spirit. There is one God who eternally exists in three persons. Each possesses the same nature and attributes but is distinct in office and activity: Deuteronomy 6:4, Matthew 28:19, John 10:30, John 17:21, John 10:38, 1 John 2:20-24. Jesus is the Son of God and Savior (John 20:31).
- **Jesus—Worker of Miracles, All-Powerful and Creator of All Things:** John 11:32-45, Matthew 12:22, Luke 7:21-23, Matthew 15:30-31, Mark 9:23, 10:27, Luke 1:37, 18:27; Creator of All Things, John 1:3, John 1:10, 1 Corinthians 8:6, Revelation 4:11, Genesis 1:1, Colossians 1:15-17, Hebrews 1:2.
- **Human Depravity:** Each person is morally corrupt and sinful which is the condition of being spiritually dead toward God: Romans 3:23, Ephesians 2:1-3, Ecclesiastes 7:20, Romans 5:12, Psalms 14:1-3, Romans 3:20, Psalms 143:2, Psalm 51:5.
- **Christ's Atoning Death and Bodily Resurrection:** Christ died on the cross as a substitutionary sacrifice for sinners: 1 Peter 3:18, 2 Corinthians 5:21, 1 Corinthians 15:1-7, Titus 2:13-14, Romans 5:12-21, Hebrews 2:14, John 11:25-27, John 4:25-26, 1 John 2:1-2, John 21:14.
- **A Person is Saved from Eternal Damnation by God's Grace Through Faith in Jesus Christ and His Sacrificial Payment for Sin by His Death on The Cross (and nothing else):** One is not saved by works of righteousness, being a good person, or attempted obedience to the Law: Ephesians 2:8-10, Galatians 2:16-3:8, Romans 4:4-5, Romans 3:27-31, 5:11-21, Acts 10:43, Titus 2:13-14, John 3:15-18.
- **The Lordship of Christ:** Romans 10:9: *"that if you confess with your mouth Jesus as Lord, and believe in your heart that God raised Him from the dead, you will be saved;"* John 13:13: *"You call Me Teacher and Lord; and you are right, for so I am."* See also Philippians 2:8-11, 1 Corinthians 16:22-23, Romans 14:9, Acts 16:31, 1 Corinthians 12:3, Acts 2:21, 36, Acts 1:21, Matthew 12:8, Matthew 22:37, Isaiah 45:23, Romans 14:11.
- **The Return of Christ:** Second Coming: John 14:1-3, Matthew 26:64, Luke 12:40, Matthew 24:27 and 42-51, Mark 14:62, John 21:21-23, Mark 13:26.
- **The Eternal Damnation in Hell for the Unsaved:** John 15:6, Revelation 20:10-15, Revelation 21:8, John 3:18, 1 Corinthians 6:9-11, 2 Thessalonians 1:8-9, John 5:22, Mark 9:43-48.
- **Eternal Reign Of Christ in Heaven and Eternal Life for those He Redeemed:** John 14:1-3, Matthew 19:28-29, Matthew 25:46, John 3:15-16, Revelation 4:5-11, 1 John 5:20, Jude v.21, 1 Peter 4:11, 1 John 1:2-4, Titus 2:13-14.[247]

---

[247] Generally but not exclusively from: MacArthur, J. (1994). *Reckless faith: When the Church Loses Its Will to discern* (p. 102). Wheaton, Ill.: Crossway Books.

Do you attend a church that allows those who are in leadership to deny the fundamentals of the faith? In love, directly confront the false leadership to repent, and if it will not, leave and find a different church. I have seen Christians stay in dead churches for years in hopes of turning them around. The consistent result of that approach has been injury to their individual spiritual lives, that of their children, and the religious institution remaining completely unchanged. Puritan John Owen demonstrated the difference between the religious hypocrite and the real Christian this way:

> "There is no visible difference, as unto light, between the light of the morning and the sunlight of the evening; yea, … But herein they differ: the first goes on gradually unto more light until it comes to perfection; the other gradually gives place unto darkness until it comes to be midnight. So is it as unto the light of the just and of the hypocrite."[248]

VERSE 33: *"He spoke another parable to them, 'The kingdom of heaven is like leaven, which a woman took, and hid in three pecks of meal, until it was all leavened.'"*

Like the previous parable, Jesus does not give the interpretation. The term leaven means "yeast." Leaven causes bread to rise. Some see leaven in this parable as an analogy that says: "Just like leaven causes the increasing size of the bread, so does the Kingdom of God expand from its apparently small beginnings."

Others see the leaven in the parable representing the many false doctrines that permeate the churches in an attempt to corrupt it. This interpretation is derived from the fact that on another occasion Jesus made reference to leaven as the false doctrine of the Pharisees when He said:

> **Matthew 16:5-7, 11-12:** *"And the disciples came to the other side and had forgotten to take bread. ⁶ <u>And Jesus said to them, 'Watch out and beware of the leaven of the Pharisees and Sadducees.'</u> ⁷ And they began to discuss among themselves, saying, 'It is because we took no bread.'….*
> *¹¹ 'How is it that you do not understand that I did not speak to you concerning bread? But beware of the leaven of the Pharisees and Sadducees.' ¹² <u>Then they understood that He did not say to beware of the leaven of bread, but of the teaching of the Pharisees and Sadducees.</u>"*

When Paul is talking about false doctrine in Galatians he refers to it as *leaven* which could impact the entire church.

> **Galatians 5:7-9:** *"You were running well; who hindered you from obeying the truth? ⁸ This persuasion did not come from Him who calls you. ⁹ <u>A little leaven leavens the whole lump of dough.</u>"*

In addressing someone who was sinning in the church Paul again used the term *leaven* in a negative sense. The context of Paul's statement is that if you allow this unrepentant sinner to go on uncensored, the entire church will be infected by the sin.

> **1 Corinthians 5:4-8:** *"In the name of our Lord Jesus, when you are assembled, and I with you in spirit, with the power of our Lord Jesus, ⁵ I have decided to deliver such a one to Satan for the destruction of his flesh, that his spirit may be saved in the day of the Lord Jesus. ⁶ Your boasting is not good. <u>Do you not know that a little leaven leavens the whole lump of dough?</u> ⁷ <u>Clean out the old leaven, that you may be a new lump, just</u>*

---

[248] Thomas, I. (1996). *The Golden Treasury of Puritan Quotations.* p. 151. Includes index of authors. General index created by Christian Classics Foundation. (electronic ed.). Simpsonville SC: Christian Classics Foundation.

as you are in fact unleavened. For Christ our Passover also has been sacrificed. ⁸ Let us therefore celebrate the feast, not with old leaven, nor with the leaven of malice and wickedness, but with the unleavened bread of sincerity and truth."

VERSES 34-35: *"All these things Jesus spoke to the multitudes in parables, and He did not speak to them without a parable, ³⁵ so that what was spoken through the prophet might be fulfilled, saying, 'I WILL OPEN MY MOUTH IN PARABLES; I WILL UTTER THINGS HIDDEN SINCE THE FOUNDATION OF THE WORLD.'"*

The quotation here is from Psalm 78:2, which was written by Asaph. We are told by Matthew that he was a prophet (see also 2 Chronicles 29:30 where Asaph[249] is called a "seer".) The *"THINGS HIDDEN SINCE THE FOUNDATION OF THE WORLD...."* is in reference to the mysteries of the kingdom of heaven. When telling these mysteries to the multitude He did it by parable. In other words, He did not give the secrets of the kingdom to the unbelieving people who were there. But He did explain the meaning to the believers (i.e. the disciples). Remember what Jesus said earlier in Matthew 13:

> **Matthew 13:10-11:** *"And the disciples came and said to Him, 'Why do You speak to them in parables?' ¹¹ And He answered and said to them, 'To you it has been granted to know the mysteries of the kingdom of heaven, but to them it has not been granted.'"*

In Matthew 7:6 Jesus teaches us that we are not to go on sharing the beautiful truths of God to those who treat them as garbage and blaspheme them.

> **Matthew 7:6:** *"Do not give what is holy to dogs, and do not throw your pearls before swine, lest they trample them under their feet, and turn and tear you to pieces."*

Section Application

Few people can say that they have encountered a person they should quit sharing with because they were throwing their *pearls before swine*. This type of blasphemer referred to in the verse is not simply a person who is arguing and disagreeing with you. Most people are initially hostile to the gospel when they first hear it. It is referring to those who are mocking Christ, or blaspheming in other ways. One of the reasons few have experienced this type of person is because they are not engaged in ongoing witnessing. Pray and ask the Lord how you can be a more effective witness.

Verses 36-43: *"Then He left the multitudes, and went into the house. And His disciples came to Him, saying, 'Explain to us the parable of the tares of the field.' ³⁷And He answered and said, 'The one who sows the good seed is the Son of Man, ³⁸and the field is the world; and as for the good seed, these are the sons of the kingdom; and the tares are the sons of the evil one; ³⁹and the enemy who sowed them is the*

---

[249] *New Bible Dictionary* "ASAPH (Heb.). 1. A descendant of Gershom, son of Levi (1 Chronicles 6:39); nominated by the chief Levites as a leading singer, using cymbals, when the ark was brought to Jerusalem (1 Chronicles 15:17, 19). David made him leader of the choral worship (16:4-5). The 'sons of Asaph' remained the senior family of musicians until the Restoration (1 Chronicles 25; 2 Chronicles 20:14; 35:15; Ezra 3:10; Nehemiah 11:17, 22; 12:35), primarily as singers and cymbalists. Asaph himself had a reputation as a seer, and was recognized as the author of psalms used when Hezekiah revived the Temple-worship (2 Chronicle. 29:30; *cf.* the traditional ascriptions of Psalms 50, 73-83; *cf.* also the prophecy of Jahaziel, 2 Chronicles 20:14ff.). It is not clear whether Asaph lived to see the Temple consecrated, or if 2 Chronicles 5:12 simply means 'the families of Asaph', *etc.* 2. Warden of forests in Palestine under the Persian king Artaxerxes (Nehemiah 2:8)." .

devil, and the harvest is the end of the age; and the reapers are angels. ⁴⁰ *Therefore just as the tares are gathered up and burned with fire, so shall it be at the end of the age.* ⁴¹ *The Son of Man will send forth His angels, and they will gather out of His kingdom all stumbling blocks, and those who commit lawlessness,* ⁴²*and will cast them into the furnace of fire; in that place there shall be weeping and gnashing of teeth.* ⁴³ *Then* THE RIGHTEOUS WILL SHINE FORTH AS THE SUN *in the kingdom of their Father. He who has ears, let him hear.'"*

The analysis of these verses can be found above, in the section identified as <u>VERSES 24-30</u>.

MATTHEW 13:44-58
(PARABLES: HIDDEN TREASURE, PEARL OF GREAT PRICE, DRAGNET)

"'The kingdom of heaven is like a treasure hidden in the field, which a man found and hid; and from joy over it he goes and sells all that he has, and buys that field.

45 Again, the kingdom of heaven is like a merchant seeking fine pearls, 46and upon finding one pearl of great value, he went and sold all that he had, and bought it.

47 Again, the kingdom of heaven is like a dragnet cast into the sea, and gathering fish of every kind; 48and when it was filled, they drew it up on the beach; and they sat down, and gathered the good fish into containers, but the bad they threw away. 49 So it will be at the end of the age; the angels shall come forth, and take out the wicked from among the righteous, 50and will cast them into the furnace of fire; there shall be weeping and gnashing of teeth.

51 Have you understood all these things?' They *said to Him, 'Yes.' 52And He said to them, 'Therefore every scribe who has become a disciple of the kingdom of heaven is like a head of a household, who brings forth out of his treasure things new and old.'

53 And it came about that when Jesus had finished these parables, He departed from there. 54And coming to His home town He began teaching them in their synagogue, so that they became astonished, and said, 'Where did this man get this wisdom, and these miraculous powers? 55 Is not this the carpenter's son? Is not His mother called Mary, and His brothers, James and Joseph and Simon and Judas? 56 And His sisters, are they not all with us? Where then did this man get all these things?' 57And they took offense at Him. But Jesus said to them, 'A prophet is not without honor except in his home town, and in his own household.' 58And He did not do many miracles there because of their unbelief."

Introduction

Jesus continues to instruct via parables. The overall theme is the priceless value of the kingdom of heaven. To the unconverted, the idea of heaven is nice but they would rather just live here forever. To the person to whom The Lord has *revealed* the kingdom of heaven, nothing else matters. In that context, Jesus reiterates the severity of the judgment for the wicked (*"…and will cast them into the furnace of fire; there shall be weeping and gnashing of teeth."* v.50).

VERSE 44: *"The kingdom of heaven is like a treasure hidden in the field, which a man found and hid; and from joy over it he goes and sells all that he has, and buys that field."*

Again, this is a parable in which Jesus does not give us the interpretation. One thing is clear: The kingdom of heaven is not obvious for everyone to see, it is, *"like a treasure hidden."* In **Matthew 7:14** Jesus said, *"For the gate is small, and the way is narrow that leads to life, and <u>few are those who find it</u>."* He also said, *"My kingdom is not of this world"* — **John 18:36**. The religious leaders could not see the *treasure* of the kingdom of God even when it was right before their eyes.

> **Luke 17:20-21:** *"Now having been questioned by the Pharisees as to when the kingdom of God was coming, He answered them and said, 'The kingdom of God is not coming with signs to be observed; 21 nor will they say, 'Look, here it is!' or, 'There it is!' <u>For behold, the kingdom of God is in your midst</u>.'"*

This parable of the hidden treasure is often viewed as having two possible meanings.

1. One interpretation (which I believe is the most accurate interpretation) sees this from the viewpoint of the believer. Once a person has been given the revelation of salvation, nothing else matters to him except the kingdom of God. The parable is not saying that a man can purchase salvation. It explains what happens to one after he enters into the knowledge of God. From that point on, his life, his finances and everything else is wrapped up and invested in the Kingdom. Nothing else begins to matter like the Kingdom. Jesus shows us a young man who did not yet have that revelation of how valuable the Kingdom was in comparison to his life here on earth:

    Matthew 19:21-22: *"Jesus said to him, 'If you wish to be complete, go and sell your possessions and give to the poor, and you shall have treasure in heaven; and come, follow Me.'* [22] *But when the young man heard this statement, he went away grieved; for he was one who owned much property."*

    Compare that young man's response to that of the Apostle Paul who had a real knowledge of the Kingdom:

    Philippians 3:7-8: *<u>"But whatever things were gain to me, those things I have counted as loss for the sake of Christ. More than that, I count all things to be loss in view of the surpassing value of knowing Christ Jesus my Lord,</u> for whom I have suffered the loss of all things, and count them but rubbish in order that I may gain Christ,...."*

    In the Old Testament, Moses understood this concept too:

    Hebrews 11:24-26: *"By faith Moses, when he had grown up, refused to be called the son of Pharaoh's daughter;* [25] *choosing rather to endure ill-treatment with the people of God, than to enjoy the passing pleasures of sin;* [26] *considering the reproach of Christ greater riches than the treasures of Egypt; for he was looking to the reward."*

    Nothing else will matter to the man who knows Jesus as Savior (the only way to the Kingdom). The man in the parable of the hidden treasure is not trying to earn or buy his way into God's approval (see <u>Hebrews 11:6</u>). He does represent the manifestation of one who has been converted by God in that all that he used to hold dear, including his own life, becomes meaningless compared to the love and devotion he has for his Savior. Like Moses and Paul in the previous verses, there is no focus on what was given up, but rather what was gained!

    Matthew 16:24-26: *"Then Jesus said to His disciples, 'If anyone wishes to come after Me, let him deny himself, and take up his cross, and follow Me.* [25] *<u>For whoever wishes to save his life shall lose it; but whoever loses his life for My sake shall find it.</u>* [26] *<u>For what will a man be profited, if he gains the whole world, and forfeits his soul? Or what will a man give in exchange for his soul?"'</u>*

2. Another interpretation is that Israel is God's treasure and Jesus is seen as the One who gives everything (i.e. comes into the world and gives His own life) "to redeem Israel."[250] This redemptive work obviously applies to all believers.

> **Philippians 2:5-8:** *"Have this attitude in yourselves which was also in Christ Jesus, [6] who, although He existed in the form of God, did not regard equality with God a thing to be grasped, [7] but emptied Himself, taking the form of a bond-servant, and being made in the likeness of men. [8] And being found in appearance as a man, He humbled Himself by becoming obedient to the point of death, even death on a cross."*

> **Mark 10:45:** *"For even the Son of Man did not come to be served, but to serve, and to give His life a ransom for many."*

> **Romans 11:25-26:** *"For I do not want you, brethren, to be uninformed of this mystery, lest you be wise in your own estimation, that a partial hardening has happened to Israel until the fullness of the Gentiles has come in; [26] and thus all Israel will be saved; just as it is written, 'THE DELIVERER WILL COME FROM ZION, HE WILL REMOVE UNGODLINESS FROM JACOB.'"*

VERSES 45-46: *"Again, the kingdom of heaven is like a merchant seeking fine pearls, [46] and upon finding one pearl of great value, he went and sold all that he had, and bought it."*

This parable is very similar to the previous one. Review interpretation number 1 above. Matthew Henry said:

> "All the children of men are busy, seeking goodly pearls: one would be rich, another would be honorable, another would be learned; but the most are imposed upon, and take up with counterfeits for pearls."[251]

Men will invest their lives into obtaining counterfeit pearls like money, fame, etc. The pearl that is not counterfeit is Christ and His kingdom. A man who has a revelation of the *"pearl of great value"* does not care about counterfeit pearls ever again. He will liquidate himself of all that is counterfeit. He does not do that as some religious sacrifice, but simply as a natural manifestation of his coming to the knowledge of God. His view of the world is boiled down to an accurate understanding that *"nothing else matters but the King and His Kingdom."*

> "All pleasure must be bought at the price of pain.
> The price of legitimate pleasures are paid before the pleasure,
> the price of illegitimate pleasures is paid after,"[252]

(and I may add are much more costly than ever expected).

---

[250] Walvoord, John F., and Zuck, Roy B., *The Bible Knowledge Commentary*, v.2 p.51 (Wheaton, Illinois: Scripture Press Publications, Inc.) 1983, 1985.

[251] Henry, Matthew, *Matthew Henry's Commentary on the Bible*, Matthew 13:44-52 (Peabody, MA: Hendrickson Publishers) 1997.

[252] John W. Foster, Attorney, (born March 2, 1836, Pike county, Ind., U.S.—died Nov. 15, 1917, Washington, D.C.), diplomat and U.S. secretary of state (1892–93). (The last portion of the quote was made by Ravi Zacharias.)

VERES 47-50: *"Again, the kingdom of heaven is like a dragnet cast into the sea, and gathering fish of every kind; ⁴⁸ and when it was filled, they drew it up on the beach; and they sat down, and gathered the good fish into containers, but the bad they threw away. ⁴⁹ So it will be at the end of the age; the angels shall come forth, and take out the wicked from among the righteous, ⁵⁰ and will cast them into the furnace of fire; there shall be weeping and gnashing of teeth."*

Again Jesus returns to the truth about the Judgment to come. It is very interesting how those who do not believe the Bible like to talk about the "love" of God but never His judgment. They also try to create a type of Jesus who would never really send anyone to hell. Unfortunately, Scripture says differently. MacArthur points this out when he writes:

> "Jesus spoke more of hell than any of the prophets or apostles did-perhaps for the reason that its horrible truth would be all but impossible to accept had not the Son of God Himself absolutely affirmed it. It had special emphasis in Jesus' teaching from the beginning to the end of His earthly ministry. He said more about hell than about love. More than all other teachers in the Bible combined, He warned men of hell, promising no escape for those who refused His gracious, loving offer of salvation."²⁵³ (emphasis added).

For more on the Biblical description of hell, see the footnote below.²⁵⁴

Earlier in this chapter Jesus taught parables on similar themes as this parable, *The Parable of the Dragnet*. The theme of this parable addresses the separation of the children of God from the children of the devil. For a more in-depth discussion, please review the comments for the section delineated in Matthew 13:24-30. Scripture saliently explains to us how to tell the difference between the children of God from the children of the devil.

> **1 John 3:10:** *By this the children of God and the children of the devil are obvious: anyone who does not practice righteousness is not of God, nor the one who does not love his brother.*

VERSES 51-52: *"'Have you understood all these things?' They *said to Him, 'Yes.' ⁵² And He said to them, 'Therefore every scribe who has become a disciple of the kingdom of heaven is like a head of a household, who brings forth out of his treasure things new and old.'"*

The disciples are asked if they understand the parables that were given to them. They said, "Yes." What are some of the things to have been learned from the previous parables?

> "They knew the kingdom would include righteousness, but they did not know it would also include evil. Jesus pointed out a new truth that the period between His rejection

---

²⁵³ MacArthur, John F., *The MacArthur New Testament Commentary*, p. 289 (Chicago: Moody Press) 1983.

²⁵⁴ **DESCRIPTION OF HELL:** *Flames and torment* - <u>Luke. 16:19-31</u>; *Lake of fire which burns with brimstone* - <u>Revelation 19:20</u>; *Lake of fire - Fire and brimstone and are tormented day and night forever and ever* - <u>Revelation 20:10</u>; *Eternal fire...the blackness of darkness forever* - <u>Jude v.7, 13</u>; *Everlasting destruction from the presence of the Lord* - <u>2 Thessalonians 1:9</u>; *Where their worm does not die, and the fire is not quenched* - <u>Mark 9:43-48</u>; *Weeping and gnashing of teeth* - <u>Matthew 24:51</u>; *Everlasting punishment* - <u>Matthew 25:46</u>; *Indignation, wrath, tribulation and anguish* - <u>Romans 2:8,9</u>; *Shame and everlasting contempt* - <u>Daniel 12:2</u>; *Unquenchable fire* - <u>Luke 3:17</u>.

and His second coming would be characterized by professing followers, both good and evil. This era would have a small beginning, but it would grow into a great 'kingdom' of professors.... This interadvent period will end with a time of judgment in which God will separate the wicked from the righteous and the righteous will then enter the earthly kingdom to rule and reign with Christ." [255]

Now the disciples would be responsible to teach what they had learned to others, so as to be, *"like a head of a household"* (i.e. apostles of the church). They would teach others the revelation they were given while they were with Jesus (*brings forth out of his treasure...old*). Jesus also told them the Holy Spirit would teach them, as well as remind them of things they already had been taught:

John 14:25-26: *"These things I have spoken to you, while abiding with you. [26]But the Helper, the Holy Spirit, whom the Father will send in My name, He will teach you all things, and bring to your remembrance all that I said to you."*

They would also be responsible to share new revelations they would be taught later (*"...treasure things new..."*). What we see in John 14:26 is that the Holy Spirit will both teach us regarding what was written in the Bible and remind us of what we have been taught from the Bible.[256]

One of the most awesome experiences in the life of a Christian disciple is when God reveals spiritual truth to him through His Word (i.e. the Bible). It does not matter how many times a Christian reads a certain portion of Scripture, there is something new the Holy Spirit can reveal from it. In addition, the Holy Spirit will also bring back to remembrance something the Christian may have been taught by God decades earlier.

VERSES 53-58: *"And it came about that when Jesus had finished these parables, He departed from there. [54]And coming to His home town He began teaching them in their synagogue, so that they became astonished, and said, 'Where did this man get this wisdom, and these miraculous powers? [55] Is not this the carpenter's son? Is not His mother called Mary, and His brothers, James and Joseph and Simon and Judas? [56] And His sisters, are they not all with us? Where then did this man get all these things?' [57]And they took offense at Him. But Jesus said to them, 'A prophet is not without honor except in his home town, and in his own household.' [58]And He did not do many miracles there because of their unbelief."*

How sad it is that those in Jesus' hometown of Nazareth, *"took offense at Him"* despite the fact that they were aware of His *"...wisdom, and these miraculous powers...."*. What this teaches us is how spiritually dead and unbelieving the unregenerate heart can be. Those in Nazareth got to hear and see Jesus, but that was not enough. These are people to whom the "seed" fell on the road as in **Matthew 13:19:** *"When anyone hears the word of the kingdom, and does not understand it, the evil one comes and snatches away what has been sown in his heart. This is the one on whom seed was*

---

[255] Walvoord, John F., and Zuck, Roy B., *The Bible Knowledge Commentary*, v.2 p.52-53, (Wheaton, Illinois: Scripture Press Publications, Inc.) 1983, 1985.

[256] Some Bible scholars maintain that the promise of the Holy Spirit in John 14:25-26 only applies to the disciples that would write the New Testament. There is little question that it applied to those disciples. But it also applies to us in that the Holy Spirit will both teach us from what is written in the Bible and remind us of what we have been taught from the Bible.

sown beside the road."

On a previous visit to Nazareth, the people of His hometown wanted to kill Him by pushing Him off a cliff (Luke 4:16-29). The rejection of Jesus is part of what was prophesied about the Messiah:

<u>Isaiah 53:3:</u> *"He was despised and forsaken of men,*
A man of sorrows, and acquainted with grief;
And like one from whom men hide their face,
<u>*He was despised, and we did not esteem Him*</u>.*"*

The people of Nazareth complained that they knew Jesus' family and there was nothing special about them. *"Is not this the carpenter's son? Is not His mother called Mary, and His brothers, James and Joseph and Simon and Judas? ⁵⁶And His sisters, are they not all with us?...."* (Matthew 13:55-56). It is important to note that Mary had other children, a concept that Catholics reject.[257] They try to say these brothers and sisters were really "close relations" of Jesus, like a cousin. The text says otherwise, as well as other Scriptures such as Matthew 12:46, Galatians 1:19, Acts 1:14, John 7:5, John 2:12. (For more on the Roman Catholic view of the Perpetual Virginity of Mary, see the comments under the section for Matthew 1:18.)

Often we see people who have been exposed many times to the Gospel become increasingly hostile to it. The idea is that *familiarity breeds contempt.* We see this played out with Jesus being among His own people. Ryle states,

"Do we wonder that the relatives, servants and neighbors of godly people are not always converted? Do we wonder that the parishioners of eminent ministers of the Gospel are often their hardest and most impenitent hearers? Let us wonder no more. Let us note the experience of our Lord at Nazareth, and learn wisdom."[258]

Many of these people *think* they are familiar with the Gospel and treat it as good for nothing.

<u>Matthew 7:6:</u> *"Do not give what is holy to dogs, and do not throw your pearls before swine, lest they trample them under their feet, and turn and tear you to pieces."*

---

[257] Read below the exact quotes form the <u>Roman Catholic Catechism</u> #499 and #500:

499 The deepening of faith in the virginal motherhood led the Church to confess Mary's real and perpetual virginity even in the act of giving birth to the Son of God made man. In fact, <u>Christ's birth "did not diminish his mother's virginal integrity</u> but sanctified it." And so the liturgy of the Church celebrates Mary as *Aeiparthenos*, the "Ever-virgin."

500 Against this doctrine the objection is sometimes raised that the Bible mentions brothers and sisters of Jesus. The Church has always understood these passages as not referring to other children of the Virgin Mary. In fact James and Joseph, "brothers of Jesus," are the sons of another Mary, a disciple of Christ, whom St. Matthew significantly calls "the other Mary." They are close relations of Jesus, according to an Old Testament expression.

[258] *Matthew* / Ryle, J.C. p.113 (Expository Thoughts on the Gospels) (Crossways Classic Commentaries: v.1)

Summary and Application

What is your view of the Kingdom of God? What is your view of the King, Jesus Christ, and His Kingdom? Hopefully you realize the priceless value of both.

MATTHEW 14:1-12
(JOHN THE BAPTIST BEHEADED)

"At that time Herod the tetrarch heard the news about Jesus, ²and said to his servants, 'This is John the Baptist; he has risen from the dead; and that is why miraculous powers are at work in him.' ³For when Herod had John arrested, he bound him, and put him in prison on account of Herodias, the wife of his brother Philip. ⁴For John had been saying to him, 'It is not lawful for you to have her.' ⁵And although he wanted to put him to death, he feared the multitude, because they regarded him as a prophet. ⁶But when Herod's birthday came, the daughter of Herodias danced before them and pleased Herod. ⁷Thereupon he promised with an oath to give her whatever she asked. ⁸And having been prompted by her mother, she *said, 'Give me here on a platter the head of John the Baptist.' ⁹And although he was grieved, the king commanded it to be given because of his oaths, and because of his dinner guests. ¹⁰And he sent and had John beheaded in the prison. ¹¹And his head was brought on a platter and given to the girl; and she brought it to her mother. ¹²And his disciples came and took away the body and buried it; and they went and reported to Jesus."

Introduction

To review the matter of who John the Baptist was and the details of his earlier ministry, see the comments in Matthew 3:1-12. John's message from the beginning is stated in Matthew 3:2 (i.e. *"Repent, for the kingdom of heaven is at hand."*). Repentance is, "not just...feeling sorry, or changing one's mind, but as a turning round, a complete alteration of the basic motivation and direction of one's life."[259] John's life was Christ-centered and he was killed for telling the truth to a wicked King.

VERSES 1-5: *"AT that time Herod the tetrarch heard the news about Jesus, ²and said to his servants, 'This is John the Baptist; he has risen from the dead; and that is why miraculous powers are at work in him.' ³For when Herod had John arrested, he bound him, and put him in prison on account of Herodias, the wife of his brother Philip. ⁴For John had been saying to him, 'It is not lawful for you to have her.' ⁵And although he wanted to put him to death, he feared the multitude, because they regarded him as a prophet."*

Verses 1-5 tell the story of why John the Baptist was put into prison. When people hear the name Herod they often think of the King Herod who ruled at the time Jesus was born. The Herod mentioned here in Matthew 14 is not that King Herod.

The Herod we read about here in Matthew 14:1-11 is a son of Herod the Great,[260] — Herod Antipas. He is referred to as *"Herod the tetrarch"* (v.1). The word *tetrarch* "was used in classical Greek to

---

[259] Wood, D. R. W. and Marshall, I. H., *New Bible Dictionary* (3rd ed.) (p. 1007). Leicester, England; Downers Grove, Ill.: InterVarsity Press (1996).

[260] For a more detailed outline of the family line of Herod the Great (which includes murder, incest and other evils) see the extra segment after the **Summary and Application** section to this lesson (Matthew 14:1-12).

denote the 'ruler of a fourth part of a region',...."[261] Herod Antipas' had a half-brother named Phillip. Phillip had a wife named Herodias [262] who left him and became Herod Antipas' wife. Both Herod Antipas and Herodias hated John because he told Herod Antipas that it was, *"not lawful for"* him to have his brother Philip's wife.

Herodias fit very nicely into this group being that she was a very evil woman who plotted to have John killed: *"And Herodias had a grudge against him and wanted to put him to death and could not do so;"* **Mark 6:19.** The reason she could not get the job done is set out in the next verse in **Mark 6:20:** *"for Herod was afraid of John, knowing that he was a righteous and holy man, and kept him safe. And when he heard him, he was very perplexed; but he used to enjoy listening to him."* This should not be understood to say that Herod Antipas was a follower of John. Antipas wanted John killed, but the only thing holding him back was, *"...Herod was afraid of John, ..."* **Mark 6:20** . This is also mentioned in the text we are studying, where it says that Herod Antipas wanted to kill John for this but, *"he feared the multitude, because they regarded him as a prophet...."* **Matthew 14:5**. Matthew Henry explained it this way: *"Wicked men are restrained from the most wicked practices, merely by their secular interest, and not by any regard to God."* [263]

In Matthew 14:1 we read that when Herod Antipas hears about Jesus, he fears that Jesus is really John the Baptist resurrected. His fear is based on the fact that he ordered John's murder. Although Antipas had a *fear* of God because of John, it was not a *belief* that resulted in repentance and salvation. The Bible tells us that, *"God is one."* Even demons know that truth in such a way that they *"believe, and shudder...."* **James 2:19**. The demons are not saved, and neither is a person who has an interest in God and even at times is afraid, but will not repent. We see in Mark 6:20 that Herod Antipas enjoyed listening to John. In the same manner, we later read that Herod Antipas is excited to meet Jesus, but instead of repenting and being saved at that meeting, Herod Antipas' evil heart was exposed in his attack on Jesus:

> Luke 23:8-12: *"Now Herod was very glad when he saw Jesus; for he had wanted to see Him for a long time, because he had been hearing about Him and was hoping to see*

---

[261] *The New Bible Dictionary*, (Wheaton, Illinois: Tyndale House Publishers, Inc.) 1962. See also:

Vine, W. E., *Vine's Expository Dictionary of Old and New Testament Words*, (Grand Rapids, MI: Fleming H. Revell) 1981

(tetraarcevw , (5075), to be a tetrarch, occurs in Luke 3:1 (thrice), of Herod Antipas, his brother Philip and Lysanias. Antipas and Philip each inherited a fourth part of his father's dominions. Inscriptions bear witness to the accuracy of Luke's details.

[262] This is one bizarre family. Phillip was actually Herodias' uncle as was Antipas! F.F Bruce wrote that Herodias was the, "daughter to Aristobulus (son of Herod the Great by Mariamne). She married, first, her uncle Herod Philip (son of Herod the Great by a second Mariamne, and not to be confused with Philip the tetrarch), and secondly, her uncle Herod Antipas. By her first husband she had a daughter Salome, who married her grand-uncle Philip the tetrarch...When Antipas was exiled in AD 39 Herodias chose to accompany him rather than accept the favour which Gaius was willing to show to the sister of his friend Agrippa...." Wood, D. R. W., and Marshall, I. H. (1996). *New Bible Dictionary (3rd ed.)* Herodias (p. 472). Leicester, England; Downers Grove, IL: InterVarsity Press.

[263] Henry, Matthew, *Matthew Henry's Commentary on the Bible*, Matthew 14:1-12, (Peabody, MA: Hendrickson Publishers) 1997.

some sign performed by Him. [9] And he questioned Him at some length; but He answered him nothing. [10] And the chief priests and the scribes were standing there, accusing Him vehemently. [11] _And Herod with his soldiers, after treating Him with contempt and mocking Him, dressed Him in a gorgeous robe and sent Him back to Pilate._ [12] Now Herod and Pilate became friends with one another that very day; for before they had been at enmity with each other."

Here is a little more in-depth look at Herod Antipas:

"Herod the tetrarch' (Luke 3:19, etc.), who bore the distinctive name of <u>Antipas</u>. He was Herod's younger son by Malthace, and inherited the Galilean and Peraean portions of his father's kingdom. <u>In the Gospels he is conspicuous chiefly for his part in the imprisonment and execution of John the Baptist</u> (Mark 6:14-28) and for his brief encounter with Jesus when the latter was sent to him by Pilate for judgment (Luke 23:7.). Jesus is recorded as having once described him as 'that fox' (Luke 13:31). He was the ablest of Herod's sons, and like his father was a great builder; the city of Tiberias on the Lake of Galilee was built by him (AD 22) and named in honor of the Emperor Tiberius. <u>He married the daughter of the Nabataean king Aretas IV, but divorced her in order to marry Herodias, the wife of his half-brother Herod Philip. ... John the Baptist incurred the wrath of Antipas for denouncing his second marriage as unlawful.</u> _Josephus_ (Ant. 18. 118) says that Antipas was afraid that John's great public following might develop into a revolt. Aretas naturally resented the insult offered to his daughter, and seized the opportunity a few years later to wage war against Antipas (AD 36). The forces of Antipas were heavily defeated, and Josephus says that many people regarded the defeat as divine retribution for Antipas' killing of John the Baptist. In AD 39 Antipas was denounced to the Emperor Gaius by his nephew Agrippa as a plotter; he was deposed from his tetrarchy and ended his days in exile." [264]

VERSES 6-11:   _"But when Herod's birthday came, the daughter of Herodias danced before them and pleased Herod. [7]Thereupon he promised with an oath to give her whatever she asked. [8]And having been prompted by her mother, she *said, 'Give me here on a platter the head of John the Baptist.' [9]And although he was grieved, the king commanded it to be given because of his oaths, and because of his dinner guests. [10]And he sent and had John beheaded in the prison. [11]And his head was brought on a platter and given to the girl; and she brought it to her mother."_

Herod's birthday party was typical of those times. "Roman nobles frequently held stag birthday parties in which gluttony, excessive drinking, erotic dancing, and sexual indulgence were common."[265] Clearly Herodias' daughter performed a lewd dance.[266] The statement that Herod was **"pleased"** (v.6), was a "euphemism for 'sexually aroused,' and the drunken king was so enamored of his stepdaughter that he rashly **promised with an oath to give her whatever she asked**, even up to half his kingdom (Mark 6:23)." [267]

---

[264] _The New Bible Dictionary_, p. 472 (Wheaton, Illinois: Tyndale House Publishers, Inc.) 1962.

[265] MacArthur, John F., _The MacArthur New Testament Commentary_, p. 417 (Chicago: Moody Press) 1983.

[266] The Ryrie Study Bible—Expanded Edition: New American Standard, comment to Matthew 14:6.

[267] MacArthur, John F., _The MacArthur New Testament Commentary_, p. 417 (Chicago: Moody Press) 1983.

It was pointed out previously that Herodias hated John and wanted him killed (Mark 6:19). The reason Antipas had not killed John before was due to his own political self-interest (Mark 6:20, Matthew 14:5). One can speculate why Herodias was so hateful to John. Remember that the lustful Herod seduced her from his brother Philip while on a visit to Rome.[268] One theory might be that she was afraid she could someday be dumped by Herod, just as Herod dumped his first wife. While Herodias was young, she was able to seduce Herod, but now that she had become older, her youthful beauty was fleeting. (As with every woman who prostitutes her beauty when she is young, the day will come when the beauty is gone and she is no longer sought after, but merely laughed at as being an "old whore.")[269] One might speculate that she was afraid Herod could pretend to obey John, thus giving him a reason to get rid of her.

Herodias knew Herod Antipas was a lustful man. She knew that she was not able to get Herod to kill John just for her. She needed more than she had. She set up her plan well. Note that Herodias waited for the right moment and then used her young, seductive daughter to get what she could not get on her own. Mark explains this:

> *"And Herodias had a grudge against him and wanted to put him to death and could not do so; 20 for Herod was afraid of John, … 21 And a strategic day came when Herod on his birthday gave a banquet for his lords and military commanders and the leading men of Galilee; 22 and when the daughter of Herodias herself came in and danced, she pleased Herod and his dinner guests;…."* **Mark 6:19-22**

Herod Antipas then promises to give her what she wants. Note that the daughter goes directly to her mother to see what she should ask for and then quickly returns to the king with the request.

> *"… 'what shall I ask for?' And she said, 'The head of John the Baptist.' 25 And immediately she came in haste before the king and asked, saying, 'I want you to give me right away the head of John the Baptist on a platter.'"* **Mark 6:24-25**

Note that Herodias tells her to ask for John's head *"right away."* Herodias wants to take advantage of Herod Antipas' drunken state as well as his pride by holding him to the promise he made in front of *"his lords and military commanders and the leading men of Galilee."* **Mark 6:21** (Man-pleasing pride has destroyed many a person.)

Herodias' daughter, although not named in Scripture, is identified by Josephus as Salome. (Josephus, *Antiquities of the Jews* 18. 136f.) [270] The perversion of this family is immense, especially when you realize that Salome was the daughter of Herodias' first marriage to Herod Philip.

The Bible tells us that *"God is not mocked; for whatever a man sows, this he will also reap."* **Galatians 6:7**. Herod Antipas is no exception. Look at his end after a lifetime of political scheming: "… some years after this, his jealous and scheming nephew, Agrippa (the brother of Herodias), convinced the emperor Caligula that Herod was planning a rebellion…Herod and Herodias suffered exile to Gaul (modern France)…."[271]

---

[268] Ibid

[269] Oh, but how God can restore all things to those who turn to HIM!

[270] *The New Bible Dictionary*, (Wheaton, Illinois: Tyndale House Publishers, Inc.) 1962.

[271] MacArthur, John F., *The MacArthur New Testament Commentary*, p.417 (Chicago: Moody Press) 1983.

<u>**VERSE 12:**</u> *"And his disciples came and took away the body and buried it; and they went and reported to Jesus."*

Jesus was the most important person in John's life. This is exemplified by the fact that upon John's death, his disciples went directly to tell Jesus of his passing.[272] John the Baptist was the first martyr for Christ.[273]

Matthew Henry comments about John being martyred by saying that:

"Note, (1.) Faithful reproofs, if they do not profit, usually provoke; if they do not do good, they are resented as affronts, and they that will not bow to the reproof, will fly in the face of the reprover and hate him, as Ahab hated Micaiah, 1 Kings 22:8. See Proverbs 9:8; 15:10, 12. *Veritas odium parit*—Truth produces hatred. (2.) It is no new thing for God's ministers to suffer ill for doing well. Troubles abide those most that are most diligent and faithful in doing their duty, Acts 20:20." [274]

Summary and Application

John represents the truly faithful follower of Christ (i.e. one who lived for God and served Him even to death). It is very difficult to rebuke others for the sin in their life. John did that and we should do likewise. The admonishment should not be done in a self-righteous, manner but out of love for them and a true concern regarding their eternal destiny. When we warn others of the judgment to come, we are not

---

[272] (One should not take this to mean that the divine Jesus did not already know that John was dead before being told by John's disciples. Jesus knows everything. Remember the story of Lazarus? Jesus knew Lazarus was dead and nobody had to tell Him. See John 11:11-15.)

[273] MacArthur states that John is the first martyr for Christ. MacArthur, J. F., Jr. (1985). *Matthew*. MacArthur New Testament Commentary (p 417). Chicago: Moody Press.

Note that some will say Stephen was the first martyr of the church, which is true, Acts 7:55-57. John was the first martyr of Jesus. Note that Scripture sets forth the beginning of the Gospel being preached at the baptism of Jesus: *"…beginning with the baptism of John until the day that He was taken up from us—one of these must become a witness with us of His resurrection."* **Acts 1:22.** We see from *Nelson's Quick Reference Topical Bible Index* how much John was involved in the ministry of Jesus.

"Identifies Jesus as the Messiah: John 1:29–36
Bears witness to Christ: John 5:33
Exalts Christ: John 3:25–36
Baptizes Christ: Matthew 3:13–16
Identified with Elijah: Matthew 11:13, 14
Public reaction to: Matthew 11:16–18
Christ's testimony concerning: Matthew 11:9–13
Reproves Herod for adultery: Mark 6:17, 18
Imprisoned by Herod: Matthew 4:12
Beheaded by Herod: Matthew 14:3–12
Thomas Nelson Publishers. (1996). *Nelson's quick reference topical Bible index*. Nelson's Quick reference (p. 348). Nashville, TN: Thomas Nelson Publishers.

[274] Henry, M. (1994). *Matthew Henry's commentary on the whole Bible: Complete and unabridged in one volume* (Mt 14:1–12). Peabody: Hendrickson.

judging them based on our views or standards, but God's. [Consider reading the comments for Matthew 18:12-17]. We are warning them about what God has already said about their unbelieving/unrepentant state: that His wrath abides on them.

> **John 3:36:** *"He who believes in the Son has eternal life; but he who does not obey the Son shall not see life, but the wrath of God abides on him."*

Below is a basic outline of "HEROD THE GREAT" and his family. [275]

"Herod The Great" — HEROD was of Edomite descent. He rebuilt the Temple in Jerusalem. He was the murderous king that killed the baby boys in Bethlehem who were two years old and younger (Matthew 2:16-18). His family was an evil, incestuous mess. Start by looking at his wives and children. His **wife, Mariamne,** was the granddaughter of the former Jewish high priest, Hyrcanus II of the Hasmonaean family. Mariamne's Hasmonaean descent made her and their two sons, Alexander and Aristobulus, more acceptable to the Jews. The two boys were raised in Rome and at that time were the designated heirs of their father Herod. Herod was suspicious of the Hasmonaeans so he killed them all, including his wife Mariamne in 29 BC and his boys in 7 BC. Herod killed the boys because his **2ⁿᵈ wife, Doris'** oldest son, Antipater, was envious of them. Antipater convinced Herod that Alexander and Aristobulus were plotting against Herod and should not to be trusted. Even though Antipater got the boys killed, Herod would later kill Antipater in 4 BC (just a few days before Herod's own death). Herod's kingdom was split (per ratification by Caesar Augustus), between three sons: 1) **Archelaus** got Judaea and Samaria (Matthew 2:22), 2) **Herod Antipas-(Herod Tetrarch)** got Galilee and Peraea (Luke 3:1); and 3) **Philip** got the territories east and northeast of the Sea of Galilee (Luke 3:1). Some details of each of these sons of Herod The Great are set out below:

- **Archelaus** married Alexander's widow Glaphyra. The Jews did not like this man because he was the son of a Samaritan. Some of the aristocratic Jews went to Rome and complained to Caesar Augustus about him and got him removed and banished.
- **Herod Antipas (Herod Tetrarch)** was confronted by John the Baptist (Luke 3:19-20), and he later killed John (Mark 6:14-29). Jesus was told that Antipas wanted to kill him and Jesus called him a *fox* (Luke 13:31-32). He later had an encounter with Jesus (Luke 23:7-12). Herod Antipas' first wife was daughter of the Nabataean king, Aretas IV. After Herod Antipas divorced her, he married Herodias. The Nabataean king Aretas IV was very mad about this and declared a successful war on Herod Antipas in AD 36. Herod Antipas was deposed in exile with Herodias because Agrippa talked Emperor Gaius into the idea that Herod Antipas was not to be trusted (see more on Herod Agrippa below).
- **Philip (Herod Philip)** was married to Herodias and they had a daughter Salome. Herodias left Philip for his half-brother Herod Antipas. Salome is the one who performed a lewd dance at Herod Antipas' birthday party (Mark 6:21-22).

Herod Agrippa (a.k.a. Herod the King in Acts 12:1) was heavily in debt while living in Rome so he moved in with his sister Herodias and her new husband, Herod Antipas. He later had arguments with Herod Antipas and went back to Rome where he angered the Emperor Tiberius, which landed him in prison. When Gaius (Caligula) became Emperor he released Agrippa and gave him a territory. When Herod Antipas was exiled, Agrippa got Herod Antipas' Galilee and Peraea territories. In A.D. 41 Emperor

---

[275] Main source for family tree, *The New Bible Dictionary*, (Wheaton, Illinois: Tyndale House Publishers, Inc.) p.178, 1962.

Claudius also gave him Judea and Samaria. Jews generally liked him because his grandmother **Mariamne** was of Hasmonaeans descent. Agrippa was another evil man. He had the **Apostle James,** the brother of John, killed by the sword (Acts 12:2). He also had the **Apostle Peter** arrested (Acts 12:3). Herod Agrippa, while giving a speech, was struck by an angel and died a gruesome death, *"being eaten by worms"* (Acts 12:21-23).

Herod Agrippa II (<u>son of Herod Agrippa</u>) got the title "King" from Claudius. Nero increased his kingdom by adding a portion of north and northeast Palestine. The **Apostle Paul** made his defense before Herod Agrippa II and his sister Bernice in Acts 25:13 through 26:32. **Bernice** married her uncle Herod of Chalcis. When he died, she went to live with Herod Agrippa II, her brother. Her relationship with her brother was thought to be incestuous (see Juvenal, *Sat.* 6. 156-160). Later she married Polemon, king of Cilicia, but left him to go back to her brother Herod Agrippa II. The two of them listened to Apostle Paul's defense in Acts 25:13-26. Later she was a mistress to Titus, who became emperor.

MATTHEW 14:13-36
(HEALING THE SICK; FEEDING THE 5,000 MEN; WALKING ON THE WATER)

"Now when Jesus heard it, He withdrew from there in a boat, to a lonely place by Himself; and when the multitudes heard of this, they followed Him on foot from the cities. [14] And when He went ashore, He saw a great multitude, and felt compassion for them, and healed their sick. [15] And when it was evening, the disciples came to Him, saying, 'The place is desolate, and the time is already past; so send the multitudes away, that they may go into the villages and buy food for themselves.' [16] But Jesus said to them, 'They do not need to go away; you give them something to eat!' [17] And they *said to Him, 'We have here only five loaves and two fish.' [18] And He said, 'Bring them here to Me.' [19] And ordering the multitudes to recline on the grass, He took the five loaves and the two fish, and looking up toward heaven, He blessed the food, and breaking the loaves He gave them to the disciples, and the disciples gave to the multitudes, [20] and they all ate, and were satisfied. And they picked up what was left over of the broken pieces, twelve full baskets. [21] And there were about five thousand men who ate, aside from women and children. [22] And immediately He made the disciples get into the boat, and go ahead of Him to the other side, while He sent the multitudes away. [23] And after He had sent the multitudes away, He went up to the mountain by Himself to pray; and when it was evening, He was there alone. [24] But the boat was already many stadia away from the land, battered by the waves; for the wind was contrary. [25] And in the fourth watch of the night He came to them, walking on the sea. [26] And when the disciples saw Him walking on the sea, they were frightened, saying, 'It is a ghost!' And they cried out for fear. [27] But immediately Jesus spoke to them, saying, 'Take courage, it is I; do not be afraid.' [28] And Peter answered Him and said, 'Lord, if it is You, command me to come to You on the water.' [29] And He said, 'Come!' And Peter got out of the boat, and walked on the water and came toward Jesus. [30] But seeing the wind, he became afraid, and beginning to sink, he cried out, saying, 'Lord, save me!' [31] And immediately Jesus stretched out His hand and took hold of him, and *said to him, 'O you of little faith, why did you doubt?' [32] And when they got into the boat, the wind stopped. [33] And those who were in the boat worshiped Him, saying, 'You are certainly God's Son!'

[34] And when they had crossed over, they came to land at Gennesaret. [35] And when the men of that place recognized Him, they sent into all that surrounding district and brought to Him all who were sick; [36] and they began to entreat Him that they might just touch the fringe of His cloak; and as many as touched it were cured."

Introduction:

The feeding of the 5,000 men (plus women and children; v.21), is the only miracle of Jesus' that is recorded in all four Gospels (see Mark 6:33-42, Luke 9:12-17, John 6:1-14, Matthew 14:13-21). It occurred at Bethsaida (Luke 9:10). The timing of the miracle was shortly before Passover (John 6:4).[276] We will also look at the miracle of Jesus walking on the water, which caused Jesus' disciples to exclaim, *"You are certainly God's Son!"* **Matthew 14:33**.

---

[276] Walvoord, John F., and Zuck, Roy B., *The Bible Knowledge Commentary*, p. 239 (Wheaton, Illinois: Scripture Press Publications, Inc.) 1983, 1985.

There are important distinctions between this story and the story in Matthew 15:32-39 which is the feeding of the *4,000*. Here, in Matthew 14:13-21, the feeding of the *5,000* was among the Jews, the very people that Jesus was first called to.[277] One commentator points-out that it is interesting that there were 12 basketsful left over. This could be analogues to the 12 tribes of Israel.

In the feeding of the 4,000 (Matthew 15:32-39), the work of the Lord was among Gentiles, those who Christ also came to save. Jesus said in reference to the Gentiles:

> *"I have other sheep, which are not of this fold; I must bring them also, and they will hear*
> *My voice; and they will become one flock with one shepherd."* John 10:16.

In the feeding of the 4,000 there are seven baskets leftover. Seven represents a number of completeness in Scripture.[278]

Both events are summed up in the words of Simeon who spoke in the Spirit about Jesus saying:

> *"...A LIGHT OF REVELATION TO THE GENTILES,*
> *And the glory of Your people Israel."* Luke 2:32

VERSES 13-14: *"Now when Jesus heard it, He withdrew from there in a boat, to a lonely place by Himself; and when the multitudes heard of this, they followed Him on foot from the cities. 14 And when He went ashore, He saw a great multitude, and felt compassion for them, and healed their sick."*

Verse 13 starts out, *"...Now when Jesus heard it...."* This is referring to John's disciples telling Jesus that John the Baptist had been killed. One verse before, in verse 12, it said; *"And his disciples came and took away the body and buried it; and they went and reported to Jesus."* Matthew 14:12. One should not take this to mean that the divine Jesus had no idea that John was dead before being told by John's disciples. Jesus knows everything. Remember the story of Lazarus? Jesus knew Lazarus was dead and nobody had to tell Him.

> John 11:11-15: *"This He said, and after that He *said to them, 'Our friend Lazarus has fallen asleep; but I go, that I may awaken him out of sleep.' 12 The disciples therefore said to Him, 'Lord, if he has fallen asleep, he will recover.' 13 Now Jesus had spoken of his death, but they thought that He was speaking of literal sleep. 14 Then Jesus therefore said to them plainly, 'Lazarus is dead, 15 and I am glad for your sakes that I was not there, so that you may believe; but let us go to him.'"*

In the rest of Matthew 14:13, we see that, *"He withdrew from there in a boat, to a lonely place by Himself...."* (Matthew 14:13). This is an important reminder that we must go and spend time with the Father alone.

---

[277] Paul said: *"For I am not ashamed of the gospel, for it is the power of God for salvation to everyone who believes, to the Jew first and also to the Greek."* Romans 1:16.

[278] Wiersbe states: "The number seven is important in this book because it signifies fullness and completeness. In Revelation, God tells us how He is going to complete His great work and usher in His eternal kingdom. In Revelation, you will find seven seals (Revelation 5:1), seven trumpets (Revelation 8:6), seven vials (Revelation 16:1), seven stars (Revelation 1:16), and seven lampstands (Revelation 1:12, 20)." Wiersbe, W. W. (1996). *The Bible Exposition Commentary* (Revelation 1:3). Wheaton, Ill.: Victor Books.

Matthew 6:6: *"But you, when you pray, <u>go into your inner room, and when you have</u> <u>shut your door,</u> pray to your Father who is in secret, and <u>your Father who sees in secret</u> <u>will repay you."</u>*

Immediately after Jesus fed the 5,000 men, He went to be alone with the Father: **Matthew 14:23:** *"And after He had sent the multitudes away, He went up to the mountain by Himself to pray...."* If Jesus modeled continual communion with the Father, we should do so all the more. It is easier for us to be busy with church or other *ministry* activities than to stop and be engaged in prayer. We often feel better *doing and helping* rather than being prayerful. That mentality will result in running from one *crisis* to another *need*, forgetting that our ability to truly minister is the result of being empowered by the Holy Spirit. Jesus demonstrates prayerful communion with the Father both before and after He healed and fed the multitude (Matthew 14:13 and 23). Note also that Jesus, who was full of *compassion* (v.14), actually sent the people away so He could spend time with the Father in prayer: **Matthew 14:23:** *"And after He had sent the multitudes away, He went up to the mountain by Himself to pray...."*

Compassion and love is the heart of our Savior. In verse 14 we read: *"He saw a great multitude, and felt compassion for them, and healed their sick."* **Matthew 14:14**. It does not say that He did *"a"* miracle for the multitude by healing *"a"* person. No, the compassionate Savior healed all those in the multitude who were sick. Jesus' compassionate heart was also demonstrated in Matthew chapter 9:

> **Matthew 9:35-36:** *"And Jesus was going about all the cities and the villages, teaching in their synagogues, and proclaiming the gospel of the kingdom, and <u>healing every kind of</u> <u>disease and every kind of sickness.</u> 36 And seeing the multitudes, <u>He felt compassion for</u> <u>them</u>...."*

VERSES 15-16: *"And when it was evening, the disciples came to Him, saying, 'The place is desolate, and the time is already past; so send the multitudes away, that they may go into the villages and buy food for themselves.' 16 But Jesus said to them, 'They do not need to go away; you give them something to eat!'"*

The disciples were still seeing through merely human eyes. They saw it was getting late, the people were getting hungry, and they wanted Jesus to send the people into town to get some food. Jesus challenges them to walk in faith by telling them, *"you give them something to eat."*

How many times do we see a problem through only our human eyes? When we do this we get fearful and try to figure out how we are going to solve the problem. We plan, scheme and manipulate to get what we think will give us peace. Again, I find myself constantly being taught that my first response is to seek the Lord in prayer and let Him guide me as to what to do *(if anything at all!)*. Jesus spoke of the difference between seeing things with only our human eyesight as compared to seeing with spiritual vision when He said in **Matthew 13:16:** *"But blessed are your eyes, because they see; and your ears, because they hear."* The servant of Elisha the prophet was in great fear because he could see with his eyes that they were surrounded by an army. Then God gave the servant spiritual eyes to see the reality of the situation and demonstrate His protection.

> **2 Kings 6:15-17:** *"Now when the attendant of the man of God had risen early and gone out, behold, an army with horses and chariots was circling the city. And his servant said to him, 'Alas, my master! What shall we do?' 16 So he answered, 'Do not fear, for those who are with us are more than those who are with them.' 17 <u>Then Elisha prayed</u> <u>and said, 'O Lord, I pray, open his eyes that he may see.'</u> And the Lord opened the*

servant's eyes, and he saw; and behold, the mountain was full of horses and chariots of fire all around Elisha."

VERSES 17-21: *"And they *said to Him, 'We have here only five loaves and two fish.' ¹⁸ And He said, 'Bring them here to Me.' ¹⁹ And ordering the multitudes to recline on the grass, He took the five loaves and the two fish, and looking up toward heaven, He blessed the food, and breaking the loaves He gave them to the disciples, and the disciples gave to the multitudes, ²⁰ and they all ate, and were satisfied. And they picked up what was left over of the broken pieces, twelve full baskets. ²¹ And there were about five thousand men who ate, aside from women and children."*

After Jesus tells the disciples to feed the multitude of people, they explain to Him that all they have is five loaves and two fish. We know that it was a boy who gave them the loaves and fish (John 6:9). No doubt the disciples themselves were hungry, but Jesus tells them to, *"Bring them here to Me."* The Lord wants us to always lay our talents, provisions, etc. before Him to use for His glory (remembering that the talents and provision come only from God!). We must remember that apart from Jesus, we are not able to do anything of eternal value. Jesus said in **John 15:5:** *"I am the vine, you are the branches; he who abides in Me, and I in him, he bears much fruit; <u>for apart from Me you can do nothing</u>."*

The illustration of Jesus giving the disciples the bread and them distributing it to others was a reflection of their future ministry. As the Apostles, they would eventually take the words and teachings of Christ and distribute them to spiritually feed others. Jesus said:

> **John 6:48-51:** *"I am the bread of life. ⁴⁹ Your fathers ate the manna in the wilderness, and they died. ⁵⁰ This is the bread which comes down out of heaven, so that one may eat of it and not die. ⁵¹ I am the living bread that came down out of heaven; if anyone eats of this bread, he shall live forever; and the bread also which I shall give for the life of the world is My flesh."*

After the miracle of Jesus multiplying the food, there was more than enough for everyone to eat until they were filled. Note the verse says, *"about five thousand men who ate…."* We tend to call this event *the feeding of the 5,000*, which is actually inaccurate. The Scripture tells us that the "5,000" only represents the men. The verse said that in addition to the 5,000 men there were, *"women and children"* who were fed. People had large families in Jesus' time and children were considered a blessing. It has been estimated that the actual number in the crowd easily could have exceeded 25,000 people.[279] Note also that after all the people had eaten, each disciple had a basket full of leftover food for himself. (v.20). Remember that when this started, the disciples, as a group, had only what they were given, two fish and five loaves. When it ended, each disciple ended up with more than the two fish and five loaves. The godly man is very generous and God gives to that type of man.

> **Proverbs 11:25:** *"The generous man will be prosperous, And he who waters will himself be watered."*

> **2 Corinthians 9:6-7:** *"Now this I say, he who sows sparingly shall also reap sparingly; and he who sows bountifully shall also reap bountifully. ⁷ Let each one do just as he has purposed in his heart; not grudgingly or under compulsion; for God loves a cheerful giver."*

---

[279] MacArthur, John F., *The MacArthur New Testament Commentary*, p. 429 (Chicago: Moody Press) 1983.

VERSE 22: *"And immediately He made the disciples get into the boat, and go ahead of Him to the other side, while He sent the multitudes away."*

Jesus sent the disciples out into the boat and He also, *"sent the multitudes away."* John tells us a little more about why Jesus sent them away.

John 6:14-15: *"When therefore the people saw the sign which He had performed, they said, 'This is of a truth the Prophet who is to come into the world.'* [15] *Jesus therefore perceiving that they were intending to come and take Him by force, to make Him king, withdrew again to the mountain by Himself alone."*

It was not yet Jesus' time and He would not allow the crowd to try to make Him king. Many in the crowd must have seen the Messiah simply as their deliverer from Rome and a giver of food. They did not see that their eternal soul was more important than Roman control or daily bread. The Messiah came to give what they really needed, to be saved from the judgment of hell.

Matthew 1:21: *"...you shall call His name Jesus, for it is He who will save His people from their sins."*

VERSES 23-24: *"And after He had sent the multitudes away, He went up to the mountain by Himself to pray; and when it was evening, He was there alone.* [24] *But the boat was already many stadia away from the land, battered by the waves; for the wind was contrary."*

Again we see Jesus going alone to pray. We need to realize that if Jesus spent time in prayer, we too need to be continuously in prayer.

1 Thessalonians 5:16-18: *"Rejoice always; pray without ceasing; in everything give thanks; for this is God's will for you in Christ Jesus."*

The verse tells us that the disciples, were *"many stadia"* away from land when the storm was raging. "A stadia is the same as a furlong. It takes eight stadia to equal a Roman mile—(a Roman mile is a little less than our standard mile)." [280] John states that they were about 25-30 stadia out (John 6:19 KJV), which is about three or four U.S. miles (NASV 95 Update).

The disciples had just seen Jesus perform a great miracle of feeding and providing for thousands of people. Now they are in the boat three to four miles out to sea when they found themselves caught in the middle of a storm. Remember also that it was Jesus who *"...made the disciples get into the boat, and go ahead of Him...."* Obviously Jesus knew they were going to run into this storm, but the trial they would go through would be worth it. They were desperately in trouble and they saw Jesus walking on the water to be there during their time of trouble. He also stopped the storm and gave them a revelation of who He was: *"...You are certainly God's Son!"* **Matthew 14:33.** We must remember this lesson when we go through hard times and trials. God has allowed trials in our lives and He promises to be with us during them. After having gone through the trial, we will have a greater revelation of God's love and protection for His people!

James 1:2-4: *"Consider it all joy, my brethren, when you encounter various trials, knowing that the testing of your faith produces endurance. And let endurance have its perfect result, that you may be perfect and complete, lacking in nothing."*

---

[280] *Enhanced Strong's Lexicon,* (Oak Harbor, WA: Logos Research Systems, Inc.) 1995.

VERSES 25-27: *"And in the fourth watch of the night He came to them, walking on the sea. [26] And when the disciples saw Him walking on the sea, they were frightened, saying, 'It is a ghost!' And they cried out for fear. [27] But immediately Jesus spoke to them, saying, 'Take courage, it is I; do not be afraid.'"*

We read in verse 22 that Jesus had sent the disciples out in the boat to go, *"to the other side."* After Jesus spent time in prayer, He came to them, *"walking on the sea."* Verse 25 tells us that this occurred during the *"fourth watch of the night"* (between 3-6 a.m. in the morning).[281] The disciples could not believe what they saw and became afraid. (Note: All the disciples saw Jesus walking on the water - Mark 6:50). Jesus comforted them and told them to not be afraid. We should remember when we are confronted by the unknown that it may be unknown to us, but it is not unknown to God. We would do well at times of fear to look to Jesus and thus, *"not be afraid."*

> **Psalm 43:5:**
> *"Why are you in despair, O my soul?*
> *And why are you disturbed within me?*
> *Hope in God, for I shall again praise Him,*
> *The help of my countenance, and my God."*

VERSES 28-31: *"And Peter answered Him and said, 'Lord, if it is You, command me to come to You on the water.' [29] And He said, 'Come!' And Peter got out of the boat, and walked on the water and came toward Jesus. [30] But seeing the wind, he became afraid, and beginning to sink, he cried out, saying, 'Lord, save me!' [31] And immediately Jesus stretched out His hand and took hold of him, and *said to him, 'O you of little faith, why did you doubt?'"*

We often speak of the great miracle of Jesus walking on the water. Ryle points out that the story is more miraculous than we often realize. He states that, "To walk on the sea Himself was a mighty miracle; but to enable a poor weak disciple to do the same, was a mightier miracle still."[282]

Here we see Peter doubting by saying, *"Lord, if it is You, command me to come to You on the water."* We can learn from this that we should take the Lord at His Word and not ask Him to prove Himself. Note how after Peter heads out on the water, he soon takes his eyes off Jesus and quickly sinks in the water. Peter, without any strength or ability of his own, cries out *"Lord, save me!"* Ryle states:

> "We see him stretching out his hand immediately to save Peter, as soon as Peter cried to him. He does not leave him to reap the fruit of his own unbelief, and to sink in the deep waters: He only seems to consider his trouble, and to think of nothing so much as delivering him from it."[283]

Our Lord, forgiving and gracious, reached out and pulled Peter up and asked him, *"O you of little faith, why did you doubt?"* The question remains: why do we doubt when we have the Master of the universe protecting our souls?

---

[281] *Enhanced Strong's Lexicon*, (Oak Harbor, WA: Logos Research Systems, Inc.) 1995.

[282] Matthew / Ryle, J.C. p.121 (Expository Thoughts on the Gospels) (Crossways Classic Commentaries: v.1)

[283] Ibid p.122.

VERSES 32-33: *"And when they got into the boat, the wind stopped. ³³ And those who were in the boat worshiped Him, saying, 'You are certainly God's Son!'"*

Here we again see the divinity of Christ. He controlled nature by stopping the wind. The disciples knew what they saw and worshipped Him saying, *"You are certainly God's Son!"* The Father in heaven said this at Jesus' baptism (Matthew 3:17). Man is not to worship anyone but God. Jesus is God!

> **John 14:9-10:** *"Jesus *said to him, 'Have I been so long with you, and yet you have not come to know Me, Philip? He who has seen Me has seen the Father; how do you say, Show us the Father?' ¹⁰ Do you not believe that I am in the Father, and the Father is in Me?'...."*

Many people have heard the term *Holy Trinity* but seldom understand it. The word "Trinity" means "a group of three." The "Trinity" can be explained in part by three concepts:

1) there is but one God,
2) the Father, the Son and the Spirit is each God,
3) the Father, the Son and the Spirit is each a distinct Person.[284]

Realize that there are not three Gods <u>but ONE GOD</u>. But in that unity of ONE God there are three eternal and co-equal persons. See if you can identify each member of the Trinity in this verse:

> **Matthew 3:16-17:** *"And after being baptized, Jesus went up immediately from the water; and behold, the heavens were opened, and he saw the Spirit of God descending as a dove, and coming upon Him, ¹⁷ and behold, a voice out of the heavens, saying, 'This is My beloved Son, in whom I am well-pleased.'"*

VERSES 34-36: *"And when they had crossed over, they came to land at Gennesaret. ³⁵ And when the men of that place recognized Him, they sent into all that surrounding district and brought to Him all who were sick; ³⁶ and they began to entreat Him that they might just touch the fringe of His cloak; and as many as touched it were cured."*

Jesus was sought after by the people. They recognized Jesus as a great healer but they did not have the deeper truth of who Jesus actually was. Those in *Gennesaret* realized that their friends who were sick must be brought to Him, and by simply touching the, *"fringe of His cloak"* they were *"cured."*
We are to be concerned about helping those among us who are sick, but how much more concerned should we be for those who are spiritually sick. They may enjoy good physical health now, but they are staring at an eternity in hell if they do not repent and believe the Gospel. Jesus said it like this:

> **Mark 9:47-48:** *"And if your eye causes you to stumble, cast it out; it is better for you to enter the kingdom of God with one eye, than having two eyes, to be cast into hell, ⁴⁸ where THEIR WORM DOES NOT DIE, AND THE FIRE IS NOT QUENCHED."*

---

[284] Wood, D. R. W., and Marshall, I. H. (1996). *New Bible Dictionary (3rd ed.)* (p. 1209). Leicester, England; Downers Grove, IL: InterVarsity Press.

Summary and Application

We have been granted the knowledge that Jesus is the Son of God. We must take the, "bread of heaven" that we have been given and distribute it among the people who are spiritually sick by bringing them to the knowledge of who Jesus really is. Jesus told a group of people in **John 6:48-51:**

> *"I am the bread of life. 49 Your fathers ate the manna in the wilderness, and they died. 50 This is the bread which comes down out of heaven, so that one may eat of it and not die. 51 I am the living bread that came down out of heaven; if anyone eats of this bread, he shall live forever; and the bread also which I shall give for the life of the world is My flesh."*

Have you been given some false teaching that claims when you come to Christ, you will no longer have problems? The word of God says that we will have *many* afflictions. Do the trials you have in your life leave you depressed and feeling like there is little hope? We should not be overcome or bewildered when trials and afflictions come our way. We need to remember that our Lord is, *"God's Son!"* (v. 33). He is not simply with you in trial but will deliver you according to His perfect will.

Psalm 34:19:

> *"Many are the afflictions of the righteous;*
> *But the Lord delivers him out of them all."*

MATTHEW 15:1-20
(CEREMONIAL WASHINGS and SPIRITUAL DEFILEMENT)

"Then some Pharisees and scribes came to Jesus from Jerusalem, saying,
2 'Why do Your disciples transgress the tradition of the elders? For they do not wash their hands when they eat bread.' 3 And He answered and said to them, 'And why do you yourselves transgress the commandment of God for the sake of your tradition? 4 For God said, 'Honor your father and mother,' and, 'He who speaks evil of father or mother, let him be put to death.' 5 But you say, 'Whoever shall say to his father or mother, Anything of mine you might have been helped by has been given to God, 6 he is not to honor his father or his mother.' And thus you invalidated the word of God for the sake of your tradition . 7 You hypocrites, rightly did Isaiah prophesy of you, saying,
> *8 'This people honors Me with their lips,*
> *But their heart is far away from Me.*
> *9 But in vain do they worship Me,*
> *Teaching as doctrines the precepts of men.''*
10 And after He called the multitude to Him, He said to them, 'Hear, and understand. 11 Not what enters into the mouth defiles the man, but what proceeds out of the mouth, this defiles the man.' 12 Then the disciples *came and *said to Him, 'Do You know that the Pharisees were offended when they heard this statement?' 13 But He answered and said, 'Every plant which My heavenly Father did not plant shall be rooted up. 14 Let them alone; they are blind guides of the blind. And if a blind man guides a blind man, both will fall into a pit.' 15 And Peter answered and said to Him, 'Explain the parable to us.' 16 And He said, 'Are you still lacking in understanding also? 17'Do you not understand that everything that goes into the mouth passes into the stomach, and is eliminated? 18 But the things that proceed out of the mouth come from the heart, and those defile the man. 19 For out of the heart come evil thoughts, murders, adulteries, fornications, thefts, false witness, slander. 20 These are the things which defile the man; but to eat with unwashed hands does not defile the man.'"

Introduction:

Here the Pharisees attack Christ because He is a threat to their man-made religion. They confront Jesus on the fact that His disciples will not respect and obey the religious rituals that their forefathers created (it is important to note that these are not rituals that God required). They pretend to obey God but they really are exploiting God's Word to use it as a pretext for their own anti-christ religion. Although these Pharisees considered themselves to be true Jews, Jesus pointed out that they were not. True Jews would read and obey God's word over other people's traditions. Jesus specifically said they were *hypocrites* who invalidated the Word of God for their traditions.

VERSES 1-2: *"THEN some Pharisees and scribes *came to Jesus from Jerusalem, saying, 'Why do Your disciples transgress the tradition of the elders? For they do not wash their hands when they eat bread.'"*

Look at how driven by a hatred of God these men were. They did not simply ask Him a question about something they did not understand. In verse one we read that they sought Him out to confront Him (i.e. *"some Pharisees and scribes <u>came to Jesus from Jerusalem saying</u>"*). What was the charge they made against Jesus? They were offended that Jesus let His disciples *"transgress the tradition of* *the elders....*" Although there were some ceremonial washings God gave to Moses, they were to be outward symbols of an internal heart after God. The washings discussed in Matthew 15:1-2 were an <u>expansion</u> of what the law said applied to the priests only (Leviticus 22:1-16). The O.T. never taught that outward washing provided spiritual purity. The book of Hebrews explains that God gave Israel the ceremonial law to, *"serve a copy and shadow of the heavenly things..."* <u>Hebrews 8:5;</u> (see also Hebrews 9:8-14). Unfortunately, the false teachers did not see these laws for the purposes that God intended, but rather made the false assumption that obedience to them would make them spiritually holy:

> <u>Hebrews 10:1:</u> *"For the Law, since it <u>has only a shadow of the good things to come</u> and not the very form of things, can never by the same sacrifices year by year, which they offer continually, make perfect those who draw near."*

The religious leaders were upset because Jesus attacked their entire man-made religious system of being saved by works (i.e. legalism). True Christianity teaches that we are saved by grace through faith in Jesus only:

> *"For by grace you have been saved through faith; and that not of yourselves, it is the gift of God; ⁹not as a result of works, that no one should boast."* <u>Ephesians 2:8-9.</u>

Most false religions (including false sects that claim to be Christian) teach that you enter heaven by one or all of the following: 1) not doing bad things, 2) doing "good works," or 3) performing certain religious rituals. These perversions of the truth can appear slight, such as a "church" which "says" you are saved by God's grace, but then changes the meaning of God's grace to mean something *owned* by the church and is given out through a religious ritual performed by an official church priest. A more obvious perversion is a Moslem teaching which claims if a Moslem is killed while engaged in a "holy war" (i.e. while killing his enemies), he will have earned a place in heaven. No matter how slight or extreme, the perversion that claims you bring merit before God to *earn your way* into heaven is what Paul refers to as a *"doctrine of demons."* Paul explains this concept when addressing the doctrine of false teachers who claimed that in order to be saved a person cannot eat certain foods or get married.

> <u>1 Timothy 4:1-3:</u> *"But the Spirit explicitly says that in later times some will fall away from the faith, paying attention to deceitful spirits and <u>doctrines of demons</u>, ² by means of the hypocrisy of liars seared in their own conscience as with a branding iron, ³ men who forbid marriage and advocate abstaining from foods, which God has created to be gratefully shared in by those who believe and know the truth."*

<u>VERSES 3-6:</u> *"And He answered and said to them, 'And why do you yourselves transgress the commandment of God for the sake of your tradition? ⁴ For God said, 'Honor your father and mother,' and, 'He who speaks evil of father or mother, let him be put to death.' ⁵ But you say, 'Whoever shall say to his father or mother, Anything of mine you might have been helped by has been given to God, ⁶ he is not to honor his father or his mother.' And thus you invalidated the word of God for the sake of your tradition.'"*

Jesus' reply exposes the Pharisees' hypocrisy. The Fifth Commandment says that one is to, *"Honor your father and mother,"* (Exodus 20:12). He further points out that anyone who curses his parents is to be put to death (Exodus 21:17). Honoring your parents included taking care of your parents when they become elderly. This is also set out in the New Testament:

1 Timothy 5:4: *"...but if any widow has children or grandchildren, let them first learn to practice piety in regard to their own family, and to make some return to their parents; for this is acceptable in the sight of God."*

The false religious leaders wanted to come up with a way to avoid any financial responsibility of taking care of their parents. To accomplish this, they set up a little religious rite whereby they could declare their money was "dedicated to God" (i.e. Corban - Mark 7:11). They could then say that since they made this vow to God, they could not break it by giving their parents financial support. Jesus points out their hypocrisy and how they really have no regard for God's word, but great regard for their man-made traditions (i.e. *"thus you invalidated the word of God for the sake of your tradition."*).

VERSES 7-9: *"You hypocrites, rightly did Isaiah prophesy of you, saying,*
⁸ 'This people honors Me with their lips,
But their heart is far away from Me.
⁹ But in vain do they worship Me, Teaching
as doctrines the precepts of men.' "

In the verses above, Jesus here quotes the prophet Isaiah (Isaiah 29:13). He points out that religious hypocrites can say the right "religious words" (i.e. "THIS PEOPLE HONORS ME WITH THEIR LIPS") but they do not have a heart for God ("BUT THEIR HEART IS FAR AWAY FROM ME."). They have all the outward appearances of worshiping God, but they are really worshiping their own man-made doctrines while claiming that their views are more important than God's word. Look at the words of the great Puritan, Thomas Adams, regarding hypocrisy:

"The hypocrite, certainly, is a secret atheist; for if he did believe there was a God, he [would] not be so bold as to deceive Him to His face." [285]

VERSES 10-11: *"And after He called the multitude to Him, He said to them, 'Hear, and understand. ¹¹ Not what enters into the mouth defiles the man, but what proceeds out of the mouth, this defiles the man.'"*

From verses 15:1-2 above we see the Pharisees and scribes complaining to Jesus that His disciples are not making sure they wash their hands in a ceremonial manner before they eat. In verses 10-11, Jesus explains that external ceremonial acts like washings neither prevents the soul from defilement nor purifies it. Jesus specifically points out that one's soul is not defiled by the food he eats. A person is defiled by what comes out of the mouth because it speaks of where the heart is. Our words reveal our character. Some people can hide behind false words but eventually their true character will come through their speech. Look at what Jesus said to the false religious leaders that blasphemed the Holy Spirit:

Matthew 12:33-37: *"Either make the tree good, and its fruit good; or make the tree bad, and its fruit bad; for the tree is known by its fruit. ³⁴ You brood of vipers, how can you, being evil, speak what is good? For the mouth speaks out of that which fills the heart. ³⁵ The good man out of his good treasure brings forth what is good; and the evil man out of his evil treasure brings forth what is evil. ³⁶ And I say to you, that every careless*

---

[285]   I.D.E. Thomas, *The Golden Treasury of Puritan Quotations*, (Simpsonville, SC: Christian Classics Foundation) 1997.

word that men shall speak, they shall render account for it in the day of judgment. ³⁷ For by your words you shall be justified, and by your words you shall be condemned."

VERSES 12-14: *"Then the disciples *came and *said to Him, 'Do You know that the Pharisees were offended when they heard this statement?' ¹³ But He answered and said, 'Every plant which My heavenly Father did not plant shall be rooted up. ¹⁴ Let them alone; they are blind guides of the blind. And if a blind man guides a blind man, both will fall into a pit.'"*

The message Jesus gives His disciples is that they do not need to worry about what false teachers think of them: *"Let them alone; they are blind guides of the blind."* We need to remember that God will deal with false teachers and we are not to fear them or what they think of us. One should not misinterpret this to mean that we do not confront false teachers. Jesus confronted and exposed false teachers at every corner throughout the gospels.

VERSES 15-20: *"And Peter answered and said to Him, 'Explain the parable to us.' ¹⁶ And He said, 'Are you still lacking in understanding also? ¹⁷'Do you not understand that everything that goes into the mouth passes into the stomach, and is eliminated? ¹⁸ But the things that proceed out of the mouth come from the heart, and those defile the man. ¹⁹ For out of the heart come evil thoughts, murders, adulteries, fornications, thefts, false witness, slander. ²⁰ These are the things which defile the man; but to eat with unwashed hands does not defile the man.'"*

In verse 11 Jesus said: *"Not what enters into the mouth defiles the man, but what proceeds out of the mouth, this defiles the man."* It is here in verses 15-20 that He explains in more detail what He meant. He points out that ceremonial foods or dietary requirements are not what gives you spiritual wholeness. Mark writes more directly on that point when he states:

Mark 7:19: *"...'because it does not go into his heart, but into his stomach, and is eliminated?' (Thus He declared all foods clean.)"*

The Holy Spirit warns us that false teachers will set up dietary requirements claiming that it brings holiness. God tells us that He created all foods and we are to receive them with *thankfulness,* and they are *sanctified by prayer* and the *word of God.* I might suggest that sanctification by the *word of God* includes dining conversation which is edifying and builds each other up in the truths of God.

1 Timothy 4:1-5: *"BUT the Spirit explicitly says that in later times some will fall away from the faith, paying attention to deceitful spirits and doctrines of demons, ² by means of the hypocrisy of liars seared in their own conscience as with a branding iron, ³<u>men who forbid marriage and advocate abstaining from foods, which God has created to be gratefully shared in by those who believe and know the truth. ⁴ For everything created by God is good, and nothing is to be rejected, if it is received with gratitude; ⁵ for it is sanctified by means of the word of God and prayer.</u>"*

Colossians 2:16-17: *"Therefore <u>let no one act as your judge in regard to food or drink</u> or in respect to a festival or a new moon or a Sabbath day— ¹⁷ things which are a mere shadow of what is to come; but the substance belongs to Christ."*

1 Corinthians 10:31: *"Whether, then, you eat or drink or whatever you do, do all to the glory of God."*

Jesus points out that evil does not come from food. Evil in the heart is what defiles a person, <u>Matthew 15:18-20</u>. We see that God looks not to what we eat, but examines our heart.

> **1 Samuel 16:7:** *"But the L*ORD *said to Samuel, 'Do not look at his appearance or at the height of his stature, because I have rejected him; <u>for God sees not as man sees, for man looks at the outward appearance, but the L*ORD *looks at the heart.'"*

Summary and Application

The Bible teaches that man cannot bring anything before God to earn salvation. The scribes and Pharisees thought otherwise. God is not interested in our outward, ritualistic religious activity. In other words, do you feel you have been made righteous because you have undergone a church ritual, done a good deed, given financially to the poor, or been confirmed by your church? If so, you remain a sinner going to hell. One cannot make any claim to righteousness based on his religious rituals or good deeds. (Read Ephesians 2:8-9 if you question that statement.) The problem is that you are comparing yourself to others and not to the perfection of God. The only claim that a person can make of true righteousness is that given him by God through faith in Jesus Christ. As it says in **Romans 3:22:** *"even the righteousness of God through faith in Jesus Christ for all those who believe; for there is no distinction;...."*

MATTHEW 15:21-28

(HEALING AND FAITH)

"And Jesus went away from there, and withdrew into the district of Tyre and Sidon. ²² And behold, a Canaanite woman came out from that region, and began to cry out, saying, 'Have mercy on me, O Lord, Son of David; my daughter is cruelly demon-possessed.' ²³ But He did not answer her a word. And His disciples came to Him and kept asking Him, saying, 'Send her away, for she is shouting out after us.' ²⁴ But He answered and said, 'I was sent only to the lost sheep of the house of Israel.' ²⁵ But she came and began to bow down before Him, saying, 'Lord, help me!' ²⁶ And He answered and said, 'It is not good to take the children's bread and throw it to the dogs.' ²⁷ But she said, 'Yes, Lord; but even the dogs feed on the crumbs which fall from their masters' table.' ²⁸ Then Jesus answered and said to her, 'O woman, your faith is great; be it done for you as you wish.' And her daughter was healed at once."

Introduction:

When people first read this story, some make the serious mistake in believing Jesus is being cruel to the Canaanite[286] woman. Here we see Jesus testing the faith of this woman, who comes from one of the most evil lines of people (i.e. the Canaanites). In the process, He is also showing His disciples that He is the Savior of the entire world, not just the Jews.

VERSES 21-23: *"And Jesus went away from there, and withdrew into the district of Tyre and Sidon. ²²And behold, a Canaanite woman came out from that region, and began to cry out, saying, 'Have mercy on me, O Lord, Son of David; my daughter is cruelly demon-possessed.' ²³But He did not answer her a word. And His disciples came to Him and kept asking Him, saying, 'Send her away, for she is shouting out after us.'"*

It is important to know that the Canaanite people were some of the most wicked idolaters on the earth.[287] When this woman approached Jesus, I am sure the disciples were appalled. The disciples

---

[286] **Mark 7:26** states, *"Now the woman was a Gentile, of the Syrophoenician race."* Note that Syrophoenician is the same as the ancient name Canaanite.

"SYROPHOENICIAN: An inhabitant of Phoenicia, which in New Testament times was part of the Roman province of Cilicia and Syria. It was a Syrophoenician woman, a Greek from the region of Tyre and Sidon, who pleaded with Jesus to heal her daughter (Mark 7:26; *cf.* Matthew 15:21-28). The parallel verse in Matthew 15:22 calls the woman a Canaanite, using the ancient name by which these people were known. The name Syrophoenician combines the area of Phoenicia which included Tyre and Sidon, and the larger Roman province of Syria. Phoenicians who lived in Carthage were called Libyphoenicians."
The New Bible Dictionary, (Wheaton, Illinois: Tyndale House Publishers, Inc.) 1962.

[287] "The Canaanites had an extensive pantheon, headed by El. More prominent in practice were *Baal (lord'), *i.e.* Hadad the storm-god, and *Dagon, with temples in Ugarit and elsewhere. The goddesses *Asherah, Astarte (*Ashtaroth) and Anath—like Baal—had multi-coloured personalities and violent characters; they were goddesses of sex and war. Kothar-and-Hasis was artificer-god (*cf.* Vulcan)." *The New Bible Dictionary*, (Wheaton, Illinois: Tyndale House Publishers, Inc.) 1962.

wanted to get rid of her, so they said to Jesus, *"Send her away, for she is shouting out after us."* Note that Jesus does not tell her to leave, but speaks to her (see verses 24-28 below). We see her faith starting to emerge. She has turned her back on idolatry when she calls Jesus, *"Lord"* and *"Son of David."* Faith in Christ is a gift from God. It is not something you inherit from Christian parents. In like manner, faith in Christ is not cultural. This woman, who lives among an evil people, is told by Jesus that, *"your faith is great;"* Ryle states it this way:

> "[I]t is grace, not place, which makes people believers. We may live in a prophet's family, like Gehazi, the servant of Elisha, and yet continue impenitent, unbelieving and fond of the world. We may dwell in the midst of superstition and dark idolatry, like the girl in Naaman's house, and yet be faithful witnesses for God and his Christ. Let us not despair of anyone's soul merely because his lot is cast in an unfavorable position."[288]

VERSES 24-26: *"But He answered and said, 'I was sent only to the lost sheep of the house of Israel.' *[25]* But she came and began to bow down before Him, saying, 'Lord, help me!' *[26]* And He answered and said, 'It is not good to take the children's bread and throw it to the dogs.'"*

Jesus' response to the woman was, *"I was sent only to the lost sheep of the house of Israel."* It is true that Jesus was sent to Israel because He was their King and from them would come the Savior of the whole world. Paul explains it this way:

> **Romans 1:16-17:** *"For I am not ashamed of the gospel, for it is the power of God for salvation to everyone who believes, to the Jew first and also to the Greek. *[17]* For in it the righteousness of God is revealed from faith to faith; as it is written, 'BUT THE RIGHTEOUS man SHALL LIVE BY FAITH.'"*

It is important to realize that the Jews are God's chosen people and Jesus was sent through them.

> **Romans 9:4-5:** *"…Israelites, to whom belongs the adoption as sons and the glory and the covenants and the giving of the Law and the temple service and the promises, *[5]* whose are the fathers, and from whom is the Christ according to the flesh, who is over all, God blessed forever. Amen."*

Even though Israel rejected Jesus, the time will come when God will bring revival among them in keeping with His covenant, for His glory.

> **Romans 11:25-27:** *"For I do not want you, brethren, to be uninformed of this mystery, lest you be wise in your own estimation, that a partial hardening has happened to Israel until the fulness of the Gentiles has come in; *[26]* and thus all Israel will be saved; just as it is written,*
>
> > *'THE DELIVERER WILL COME FROM ZION,*
> > *HE WILL REMOVE UNGODLINESS FROM JACOB.*
> *[27] AND THIS IS MY COVENANT WITH THEM,'*
> > *When I take away their sins."*

In verse 25 this woman bows down to Jesus and calls Him Lord. She is demonstrating an outward manifestation of an inward understanding that Jesus is Lord and not just a great teacher or a "miracle man." Next, Jesus tests that outward manifestation by saying, *"It is not good to take the children's*

---

[288] Matthew / Ryle, J.C. (Expository thoughts on the Gospels) (Crossways Classic Commentaries: v.1) p.130

bread and throw it to the dogs." Jesus is saying that He was sent to Israel, and should not ignore Israel by spending His works on others first.

VERSES 27-28: *"But she said, 'Yes, Lord; but even the dogs feed on the crumbs which fall from their masters' table.'* [28] *Then Jesus answered and said to her, 'O woman, your faith is great; be it done for you as you wish.' And her daughter was healed at once."*

The woman humbles herself before God. She acknowledges Jesus' lordship and call to Israel. She further admits her great need of Him by calling herself a "dog." Notice that true faith does not quit when tested. Jesus tells us to persevere:

> Luke 11:5-13: *"And He said to them, 'Suppose one of you shall have a friend, and shall go to him at midnight, and say to him, 'Friend, lend me three loaves;* [6] *for a friend of mine has come to me from a journey, and I have nothing to set before him;'* [7] *and from inside he shall answer and say, 'Do not bother me; the door has already been shut and my children and I are in bed; I cannot get up and give you anything.'* [8] *I tell you, even though he will not get up and give him anything because he is his friend, yet because of his persistence he will get up and give him as much as he needs.* [9] *And I say to you, ask, and it shall be given to you; seek, and you shall find; knock, and it shall be opened to you.* [10] *For everyone who asks, receives; and he who seeks, finds; and to him who knocks, it shall be opened.* [11] *Now suppose one of you fathers is asked by his son for a fish; he will not give him a snake instead of a fish, will he?* [12] *Or if he is asked for an egg, he will not give him a scorpion, will he?* [13] *If you then, being evil, know how to give good gifts to your children, how much more shall your heavenly Father give the Holy Spirit to those who ask Him?'"*

It is true that those, who are not Jews by physical birth, have enjoyed the overflow of the covenant to Abraham. In other words, even though the covenant was made to Abraham and his descendants (the Jews), God also told him that those blessings would extend out to every nation.

> **Genesis 12:1-3:**
> *"NOW the LORD said to Abram,*
> *Go forth from your country,*
> *And from your relatives*
> *And from your father's house,*
> *To the land which I will show you;*
> [2] *And I will make you a great nation,*
> *And I will bless you,*
> *And make your name great;*
> *And so you shall be a blessing;*
> [3] *And I will bless those who bless you,*
> *And the one who curses you I will curse.*
> *And in you all the families of the earth shall be blessed."*

The blessing to all *the families of the earth* is that Jesus would be the Savior to all nations. Simeon, who held baby Jesus, spoke about this when he said:

> Luke 2:30-32: *"For my eyes have seen Thy salvation,* [31] *Which Thou hast prepared in the presence of all peoples,* [32] *A LIGHT OF REVELATION TO THE GENTILES,...."*

Let us go back to our main text in Matthew 15:27-28. Look at Jesus' response in verse 28: *"O woman, your faith is great; be it done for you as you wish."* He does not reluctantly grant her request but instead rejoices in her faith. She understood her great need for Christ. She also understood that she could not bring her heritage or good works to earn His favor. She put her faith completely in His loving-kindness. This is not the only non-Jew Jesus said that about.

Matthew 8:5-13: *"And when He had entered Capernaum, a centurion came to Him, entreating Him, ⁶ and saying, 'Lord, my servant is lying paralyzed at home, suffering great pain.' ⁷ And He *said to him, 'I will come and heal him.' ⁸ But the centurion answered and said, 'Lord, I am not worthy for You to come under my roof, but just say the word, and my servant will be healed. ⁹ For I, too, am a man under authority, with soldiers under me; and I say to this one, 'Go!' and he goes, and to another, 'Come!' and he comes, and to my slave, 'Do this!' and he does it.' ¹⁰ Now when Jesus heard this, He marveled, and said to those who were following, 'Truly I say to you, I have not found such great faith with anyone in Israel. ¹¹ And I say to you, that many shall come from east and west, and recline at the table with Abraham, and Isaac, and Jacob, in the kingdom of heaven; ¹² but the sons of the kingdom shall be cast out into the outer darkness; in that place there shall be weeping and gnashing of teeth.' ¹³ And Jesus said to the centurion, 'Go your way; let it be done to you as you have believed.' And the servant was healed that very hour."*

Summary and Application

Jesus shows us that His mission was first to the lost house of Israel. In **Matthew 10:5-6** it states:

"These twelve Jesus sent out after instructing them, saying, 'Do not go in the way of the Gentiles, and do not enter any city of the Samaritans; but rather go to the lost sheep of the house of Israel.'"

After that mission was completed, He sent His disciples to all the nations to spread the truth of salvation in Christ. Jesus said this in **Luke 24:45-47:**

"Then He opened their minds to understand the Scriptures, ⁴⁶ and He said to them, 'Thus it is written, that the Christ should suffer and rise again from the dead the third day; ⁴⁷ and that repentance for forgiveness of sins should be proclaimed in His name to all the nations, beginning from Jerusalem. ⁴⁸You are witnesses of these things.'"

The Canaanite woman did not fail when her faith was being tested. She did not come to Christ with self-righteousness or her own worthiness but realized she was merely a *dog* compared to the Almighty God and had to fall completely on His mercy. That should be the attitude of every Christian.

How do you respond to the testing of your faith? When you pray about something and do not get the answer you want right away, it might be a time of silence from the Lord, just like the Canaanite woman experienced. When God remains silent, do you try to judge God or complain? Notice that the Canaanite woman did not complain but instead worshiped Jesus *more*. This worship is the result of faith in the fact that He loves you and will do whatever is best for you.

James 1:2-4: *"Consider it all joy, my brethren, when you encounter various trials, ³ knowing that the testing of your faith produces endurance. ⁴ And let endurance have its perfect result, that you may be perfect and complete, lacking in nothing."*

MATTHEW 15:29-39
(JESUS CONTINUES HEALING AMONG THE GENTILES; and
FEEDS THE CROWD OF WOMEN AND CHILDREN, IN ADDITION TO 4,000 MEN)

"And departing from there, Jesus went along by the Sea of Galilee, and having gone up to the mountain, He was sitting there. [30] And great multitudes came to Him, bringing with them those who were lame, crippled, blind, dumb, and many others, and they laid them down at His feet; and He healed them, [31] so that the multitude marveled as they saw the dumb speaking, the crippled restored, and the lame walking, and the blind seeing; and they glorified the God of Israel.

[32] And Jesus called His disciples to Him, and said, 'I feel compassion for the multitude, because they have remained with Me now three days and have nothing to eat; and I do not wish to send them away hungry, lest they faint on the way.' [33] And the disciples *said to Him, 'Where would we get so many loaves in a desolate place to satisfy such a great multitude?' [34] And Jesus *said to them, 'How many loaves do you have?' And they said, 'Seven, and a few small fish.' [35] And He directed the multitude to sit down on the ground; [36] and He took the seven loaves and the fish; and giving thanks, He broke them and started giving them to the disciples, and the disciples in turn, to the multitudes. [37] And they all ate, and were satisfied, and they picked up what was left over of the broken pieces, seven large baskets full. [38] And those who ate were four thousand men, besides women and children. [39] And sending away the multitudes, He got into the boat, and came to the region of Magadan."

Introduction

In the above verses we see Jesus having compassion and mercy on both the physical and spiritual needs of people in a region where many Gentiles lived.

VERSES 29-31: *"And departing from there, Jesus went along by the Sea of Galilee, and having gone up to the mountain, He was sitting there. [30] And great multitudes came to Him, bringing with them those who were lame, crippled, blind, dumb, and many others, and they laid them down at His feet; and He healed them, [31] so that the multitude marveled as they saw the dumb speaking, the crippled restored, and the lame walking, and the blind seeing; and they glorified the God of Israel."*

Jesus had gone up on to the mountain, but the word had spread among the Gentiles that He was doing great miracles of healing. We know that the crowd was large because we read in verse 38 that over *4,000 men*, plus women and children, were there after three days. People had large families in Jesus' time and children were considered a blessing. It can be estimated that the actual number in the crowd could easily have exceeded 20,000 people. The people brought, *"those who were lame, crippled, blind, dumb, and many others"* to Jesus and, *"He healed them."* Note that He did not heal just certain diseases or people, but He healed them all. We read that the Gentiles, *"saw the dumb speaking, the crippled restored, and the lame walking, and the blind seeing...."* v.31. The people knew that their pagan idols had never brought healing to them, so they rightfully, *"glorified the God of Israel"* v.31. Compare these Gentiles' reaction, to that of the self-righteous Pharisees. The Pharisees' reaction was not one that, *"glorified the God of Israel,"* but instead they began blaspheming (see Matthew 12:24).

God desires true worshipers, irrespective of their race, gender or culture. All true worship is led by the Holy Spirit and thus manifests itself with conduct that conforms to Scripture. The concept of *conduct in conformity to Scripture* has to do with what is *true* and pleasing to the Lord (***"the true worshipers shall worship the Father in spirit and truth."*** **John 4:23**). Over time I have witnessed many movements trying to claim that any bizarre conduct is *worship*. They justify their conduct on the claim that *"the spirit led them"* or even *"Jesus told them."* They think that these statements result in an incontrovertible claim that they are right. There have actually been some false teachers who claim that the more bizarre a person's behavior is during worship is proof that the person is spiritual. To justify the conduct, many of these fakes will make simplistic arguments like, *"you can't put God in a box."* What they are really saying is, "Who are you to say what is right or not?" Yes, it is true that no one can limit God, but it is not true that God's character changes. For example, Scripture tells us that it is impossible for God to lie (Hebrews 6:18). So if someone comes up to me and claims that God told him to cheat on a test and lie to his teacher, I can have complete assurance he never heard from God. Why? Because his conduct violates God's character and commands as He has revealed them in His Word. Thus, if someone claims God sanctioned all the chaos and confusion that occurred in a church service, I can confidently say that he is wrong. My response is not based on my personal views, feelings, or worship-style preference. My response is based on the Word of God. When writing about Spirit-led worship in the Church, Paul states in **1 Corinthians 14:33:** *"for God is not a God of confusion but of peace, as in all the churches of the saints."*

We all have different personalities and come from different cultures but worship must be God-centered and not focused on how it makes us *feel*. If this were followed, I am confident that most of the disputes about worship styles would dissolve. Remember that the object of our worship is God and not our feelings. We are to say, *"Bless the Lord,"* not "bless my flesh."

> **Psalm 103:1:**
> *"Bless the Lord, O my soul;*
> *And all that is within me, bless His holy name."*

While worshiping, some might sing,[289] clap their hands,[290] dance,[291] or play guitars or loud instruments[292] to the Lord. All of these forms of worship are set out in Scripture. Other worshipers may quietly lift their hands to God in praise.[293] But all this worship falls within the order and peace set out in 1 Corinthians 14:33. Worship is not a ritual one engages in during a church service.

---

[289] **Hebrews 2:12:** *"...saying, 'I will proclaim Thy name to My brethren, In the midst of the congregation I will sing Thy praise.'"*

[290] **Psalm 47:1:** *"O Clap your hands, all peoples; Shout to God with the voice of joy."*

[291] **Psalm 150:4:** *"Praise Him with timbrel and dancing;...."*

2 Samuel 6:14: *"And David was dancing before the Lord with all his might...."*

[292] **Psalm 150:3-6:** ³ *"Praise Him with trumpet sound; Praise Him with harp and lyre.* ⁴ *Praise Him with timbrel and dancing; Praise Him with* stringed instruments *and pipe.* ⁵ *Praise Him with loud cymbals; Praise Him with resounding cymbals.* ⁶ *Let everything that has breath praise the Lord. Praise the Lord!"*

Worship is a Holy Spirit led life which manifests itself in thankfulness and the Fruit of the Spirit, for the glory of God ("...*love, joy, peace, patience, kindness, goodness, faithfulness, gentleness, self-control;....*" <u>Galatians 5:22</u>).

This whole concept of worship is summed up in <u>John 4:23-24:</u>
> "*But an hour is coming, and now is, when the <u>true worshipers shall worship the Father in spirit and truth; for such people the Father seeks to be His worshipers.</u> ²⁴ God is spirit, and those who worship Him must worship in spirit and truth.*"

<u>VERSES 32-39:</u> "*And Jesus called His disciples to Him, and said, 'I feel compassion for the multitude, because they have remained with Me now three days and have nothing to eat; and I do not wish to send them away hungry, lest they faint on the way.'* ³³ *And the disciples *said to Him, 'Where would we get so many loaves in a desolate place to satisfy such a great multitude?'* ³⁴ *And Jesus *said to them, 'How many loaves do you have?' And they said, 'Seven, and a few small fish.'* ³⁵ *And He directed the multitude to sit down on the ground;* ³⁶ *and He took the seven loaves and the fish; and giving thanks, He broke them and started giving them to the disciples, and the disciples in turn, to the multitudes.* ³⁷ *And they all ate, and were satisfied, and they picked up what was left over of the broken pieces, seven large baskets full.* ³⁸ *And those who ate were four thousand men, besides women and children.* ³⁹ *And sending away the multitudes, He got into the boat, and came to the region of Magadan.*"

There are important distinctions between this story and the story in Matthew 14:16-17 which is the feeding of the 5,000. The feeding of the 5,000 was among the Jews, the very people that Jesus was first called to.[294] As one commentator points out, it is more than a little interesting that that there were 12 baskets lefts over. This could be analogous to the twelve tribes of Israel.

In the feeding of the 4,000 (Matthew 15:32-39), the work of the Lord was among Gentiles, those who Christ also came to save. Jesus said in reference to the gentiles:
> "*I have other sheep, which are not of this fold; I must bring them also, and they will hear My voice; and they will become one flock with one shepherd.*" <u>John 10:16</u>.

---

[293] <u>1 Timothy 2:8:</u> "*Therefore I want the men in every place to pray, <u>lifting up holy hands</u>, without wrath and dissension.*"

> <u>Psalm 37:7:</u> "*Be still before the Lord and wait patiently for him; fret not yourself over the one who prospers in his way, over the man who carries out evil devices!*"

> <u>Psalm 46:10:</u> "*<u>Be still, and know that I am God</u>; I will be exalted among the nations, I will be exalted in the earth.*"

[294] <u>Matthew 10:5–6:</u> "*These twelve Jesus sent out after instructing them: "Do not go in the way of the Gentiles, and do not enter any city of the Samaritans; but rather go to the lost sheep of the house of Israel."*"
Paul said: "*For I am not ashamed of the gospel, for it is the power of God for salvation to everyone who believes, to the Jew first and also to the Greek.*" <u>Romans 1:16</u>.

In the feeding of the 4,000 there are seven baskets leftover. Seven represents a number of completeness in Scripture.[295] Both events are summed up in the words of Simeon who spoke in the Spirit about Jesus saying:

> "... A LIGHT OF REVELATION TO THE GENTILES, And the glory of Your people Israel." **Luke 2:32.**

Going back to the main text of the feeding of the 4,000 we see that the God of All Creation is compassionate and concerned with our daily needs. We see that the crowd had been with Jesus for three days and was in a place where food was not readily available. Jesus says to His disciples, *"I feel compassion for the multitude."* Look at some other verses that remind us of God's compassion:

> **Lamentations 3:22-23:**
> *"The LORD's <u>lovingkindnesses</u> indeed never cease,*
> *For His <u>compassions</u> never fail.*
> *23 They are new every morning;*
> *Great is Thy faithfulness."*

> **Matthew 9:36-38:** *"And seeing the multitudes, He felt <u>compassion</u> for them, because they were distressed and downcast like sheep without a shepherd. 37 Then He *said to His disciples, 'The harvest is plentiful, but the workers are few. 38 Therefore beseech the Lord of the harvest to send out workers into His harvest.'"*

> **Psalms 103:8:** *"The LORD is <u>compassionate and gracious</u>,*
> *Slow to anger and abounding in lovingkindness."*

The story in Matthew 15:32-39 is about Jesus feeding the multitude. He tells His disciples that He does not want to send the people away hungry. The disciples' weak faith is shown by the failure to remember the fact that Jesus had created food for another multitude about a month or so before (Matthew 14:16-17 – feeding the 5,000 men). Instead of viewing the situation through eyes of faith, they choose to respond based only on what they could see right at the moment, saying, *"Where would we get so many loaves in a desolate place to satisfy such a great multitude?"* How many times are we guilty of the same thing? We speak of a great miracle that God did in our lives, but it does not take long for a little problem to rise up and we are looking about with human eyes trying to figure out how we are going to solve the issue. We must learn that our response in time of trouble should always be to look to God to answer our needs, whether big or small.

Notice the lessons Jesus had for His disciples and for us.
1. Jesus explains that He had compassion on the people, *and so should we.*
2. Although God does not need anyone to do His work, He has chosen His disciples to participate in His work, *and so should we.* The disciples were told by Jesus to distribute the

---

[295] "The number seven is important in this book because it signifies fullness and completeness. In Revelation, God tells us how He is going to complete His great work and usher in His eternal kingdom. In Revelation, you will find seven seals (Revelation 5:1), seven trumpets (Revelation 8:6), seven [bowls] vials (Revelation. 16:1), seven stars (Revelation 1:16), and seven lampstands (Revelation 1:12, 20)." Wiersbe, W. W. (1996). *The Bible Exposition Commentary* (Revelation 1:3). Wheaton, Ill.: Victor Books.

miracle-bread that Jesus created: *"He broke them and started giving them to the disciples, and the disciples in turn, to the multitudes."*

As believers we are to be concerned for others' basic daily needs and their spiritual eternity. As followers of Jesus we are to be vessels God works through to accomplish His work. Jesus instructed His disciples to look to God for both their physical and spiritual needs when He taught them to pray:

Luke 11:2-4:
"And He said to them, 'When you pray, say:
Father, hallowed be Thy name. Thy kingdom come
³ Give us each day our daily bread. ⁴ And forgive us our sins,
For we ourselves also forgive everyone who is indebted to us.'"

We read that after, *"all ate, and were satisfied, and they picked up what was left over of the broken pieces, seven large baskets full."* After the disciples gave out all that people wanted, there was still a lot left over. The term for baskets used in Matthew 15:37 refers to seven "large baskets." It is the same term used for the type of basket that Paul was put in when he was lowered down the wall in Damascus in Acts 9:25.[296] God gives abundantly as stated in **Luke 6:38:**

"Give, and it will be given to you; good measure, pressed down, shaken together, running over, they will pour into your lap. For by your standard of measure it will be measured to you in return."

Summary and Application

The Lord is compassionate and generous. He is concerned about people's daily physical and spiritual needs. The Lord will work through His people to minister to others, whether those in need are believers or not. We must have the same compassion as our Savior does, *"... for He Himself is kind to ungrateful and evil men."* **Luke 6:35**. Paul instructs this in **Galatians 6:10:** *"while we have opportunity, let us do good to all men, and especially to those who are of the household of the faith."*

---

[296] *Vine's Expository Dictionary of Old and New Testament Words* defines it as follows:
"(spuriv, (4711),... signifies something round, twisted or folded together (connected with ... anything rolled into a circle; Eng., sphere); hence a reed basket, plaited, a capacious kind of hamper, sometimes large enough to hold a man, Matthew 15:37; 16:10; Mark 8:8, 20 (R.V., basketfuls); Acts 9:25."
(Note: The twelve baskets of food left over in Matthew 14:20 were regular, small hand-baskets.)

MATTHEW 16:1-12
(SIGN-SEEKERS and FALSE TEACHING)

"And the Pharisees and Sadducees came up, and testing Him asked Him to show them a sign from heaven. ² But He answered and said to them, 'When it is evening, you say, 'It will be fair weather, for the sky is red.' ³ And in the morning, 'There will be a storm today, for the sky is red and threatening.' Do you know how to discern the appearance of the sky, but cannot discern the signs of the times? ⁴ An evil and adulterous generation seeks after a sign; and a sign will not be given it, except the sign of Jonah. And He left them, and went away.

⁵ And the disciples came to the other side and had forgotten to take bread. ⁶ And Jesus said to them, 'Watch out and beware of the leaven of the Pharisees and Sadducees.' ⁷ And they began to discuss among themselves, saying, 'It is because we took no bread.' ⁸ But Jesus, aware of this, said, 'You men of little faith, why do you discuss among yourselves that you have no bread? ⁹ Do you not yet understand or remember the five loaves of the five thousand, and how many baskets you took up? ¹⁰ Or the seven loaves of the four thousand, and how many large baskets you took up? ¹¹ How is it that you do not understand that I did not speak to you concerning bread? But beware of the leaven of the Pharisees and Sadducees.' ¹² Then they understood that He did not say to beware of the leaven of bread, but of the teaching of the Pharisees and Sadducees."

Introduction

I have encountered people who proudly refer to themselves as *"signs and wonders people."* The reality is they are *sign-seekers*. *Sign-seekers* are those who go from *meeting to meeting,* wanting to see some miracle or so-called *manifestation*. On TV I witnessed a hocus-pocus false *evangelist* who was trying to get people to believe he had this great power from God because he had a very special relationship with God. What a fraud! When you watch a guy like that, I will guarantee that within one hour he will be hounding you for money. When a guy like this asks for your money, realize that it would be better spent if you just flushed it down the toilet. God will judge those who try to exploit the Gospel for their own selfish greed (2 Peter 2:1-22).

Do not misunderstand me. The God of the Bible still does miracles today. We, likewise, can call out to Him to miraculously intervene in our daily affairs. When true believers call out to God in prayer they understand that God's answer will be either: *yes, no, or wait.*

VERSE 1: *"AND the Pharisees and Sadducees came up, and testing Him asked Him to show them a sign from heaven."*

True faith does not attempt to put God to the test. Here we see the Pharisees pretending to be open to the fact that Jesus is the Messiah. In reality, they were hoping to discredit Jesus when they asked Him to do a miraculous sign in the sky. Jesus Himself was the, *"sign from heaven."* In **John 6:38** Jesus said, *"For I have come down from heaven, not to do My own will, but the will of Him who sent Me."* This sign (Jesus coming to earth) would be opposed by some men, as prophesied in **Luke 2:34:**
> *"And Simeon blessed them, and said to Mary His mother, 'Behold, this Child is appointed for the fall and rise of many in Israel, and <u>for a sign to be opposed.</u>'"*

Jesus knew the heart of the Pharisees and Sadducees who demanded a *sign*. He knew they were not seekers of God but that Satan was working through them, trying to tempt Jesus into proving Himself to them. Satan had previously tried to tempt Jesus in the very same way:

> **Matthew 4:2-7:** *"And after He had fasted forty days and forty nights, He then became hungry. ³ And the tempter came and said to Him, 'If You are the Son of God, command that these stones become bread.' ⁴ But He answered and said, 'It is written, Man shall not live on bread alone, but on every word that proceeds out of the mouth of God.' ⁵ Then the devil *took Him into the holy city; and he had Him stand on the pinnacle of the temple, ⁶ and *said to Him, 'If You are the Son of God throw Yourself down; for it is written,*
>
> > *'He will give His angels charge concerning You;*
> > *and On their hands they will bear You up,*
> > *Lest You strike Your foot against a stone.''*
>
> ⁷ *Jesus said to him, 'On the other hand, it is written , 'You shall not put the Lord your God to the test" .''*

In Satan's temptation in Matthew 4, we note the temptation includes a taunt by Satan to appeal to pride by saying, *"If You are the Son of God...."* John MacArthur states that,

> "Satan was hoping to persuade Jesus to demonstrate His power to verify that it was real. That would mean violating God's plan that He set that power aside in humiliation and use it only when the Father willed. Satan wanted Jesus to disobey God. Affirming His deity and rights as the Son of God would have been to act independently of God."

What was Jesus' response to the temptation? — The Word of God! Notice that verse 4 says, *"But He answered and said, 'It is written, 'MAN SHALL NOT LIVE ON BREAD ALONE, BUT ON EVERY WORD THAT PROCEEDS OUT OF THE MOUTH OF GOD.'"* This is a quote from Deuteronomy 8:3.

It should be remembered that this is not the first time Jesus ran into a group who demanded of Him to do miracles. A few chapters back in Matthew, we read of another group of Pharisees that demanded a sign from Jesus:

> **Matthew 12:38-40:** *"Then some of the scribes and Pharisees answered Him, saying, 'Teacher, we want to see a sign from You.' ³⁹ But He answered and said to them, 'An evil and adulterous generation craves for a sign; and yet no sign shall be given to it but the sign of Jonah the prophet; ⁴⁰ for just as JONAH WAS THREE DAYS AND THREE NIGHTS IN THE BELLY OF THE SEA MONSTER, so shall the Son of Man be three days and three nights in the heart of the earth.'"*

VERSES 2-4: *"But He answered and said to them, 'When it is evening, you say, 'It will be fair weather, for the sky is red. ³ And in the morning, There will be a storm today, for the sky is red and threatening.' Do you know how to discern the appearance of the sky, but cannot discern the signs of the times? ⁴ An evil and adulterous generation seeks after a sign; and a sign will not be given it, except the sign of Jonah.' And He left them, and went away."*

Here we see Jesus' response to their demand for a miraculous sign. Jesus points out that they are able to look at the sky in the morning and see that it is *"red and threatening"* and then deduce the obvious forecast that *"There will be a storm today."* Jesus points out how spiritually blind the Pharisees are. Even though the evidence was blatantly clear that Jesus had fulfilled prophecy and did the miraculous works that the Messiah would do, the Pharisees still claimed that they were not sure if Jesus was of God.

In verse four Jesus states that, *"An evil and adulterous generation seeks after a sign;"* This *evil and adulterous generation* exists today. There are many people who care greatly to see power, but care little about the power source. It is disturbing to hear of "Christians" who will get in their cars and drive to some place to see a *"miracle man"* or *"be where the power is."* These people are sign-seekers and often deceive themselves into thinking that they are God-seekers.

Jesus refused to let His holy ministry be reduced to a circus act for religious clowns like the Pharisees. They had seen the miracles before, and chose not to believe. Even today it is a common attribute of sign seekers that they are never satisfied; they always want another sign, miracle, manifestation or experience. Underneath the surface zeal is really a heart harboring unbelief. In Luke, Jesus points out how some would not believe the warnings of God, even if one came back from the dead to tell them.

> **Luke 16:27-31:** *"And he said, 'Then I beg you, Father, that you send him to my father's house— ²⁸ for I have five brothers—that he may warn them, lest they also come to this place of torment.' ²⁹ 'But Abraham *said, 'They have Moses and the Prophets; let them hear them.' ³⁰ "But he said, 'No, Father Abraham, but if someone goes to them from the dead, they will repent!' ³¹ "But he said to him, 'If they do not listen to Moses and the Prophets, neither will they be persuaded if someone rises from the dead.'"*

It should be remembered that Jesus taught that miracles were not the *final proof* of a man of God, since false prophets will do miracles to deceive people.

> **Matthew 24:24:** *"For false Christs and false prophets will arise and will show great signs and wonders, so as to mislead, if possible, even the elect."*

The book of Revelation tells us that false miracles will be done by the Anti-christ to deceive people. The Anti-christ:

> **Revelation 13:13-14:** *"...performs great signs, so that he even makes fire come down out of heaven to the earth in the presence of men. ¹⁴ And he deceives those who dwell on the earth because of the signs which it was given him to perform..."*

Finally, God owes no man proof of Himself, even though He provides proof through His creation (Romans 1:19-20). We are to spend our time telling of the greatest miracle (i.e. that evil man can be saved and forgiven of his sin and spend eternity with God). As Paul said, we are to be spending our time preaching the gospel.

> **1 Corinthians 1:22-23:** *"For indeed Jews ask for signs, and Greeks search for wisdom; but we preach Christ crucified,..."*

Despite not owing them a sign, Jesus said He would give them one: *"... the sign of Jonah."* **Matthew 16:4.** This sign would not just be given to them, but to the whole world. The sign would be Jesus' resurrection from the dead. (See more on the subject of the, *"sign of Jonah,"* in the comments for Matthew 12:38-42).

The pretense of intellectual skepticism was alive and well among the religious leaders of Jesus' time. They claimed they needed just a sign for verification. The reality is that no sign would satisfy them because they had hearts of stone. Even though they were given eyewitness accounts from their guards about Jesus' resurrection, their darkened hearts rejected it. Despite the fact they received the *sign of Jonah* (i.e. Jesus resurrection), they immediately bribed the guards to get them to lie so as to prevent others from knowing the truth:

> <u>Matthew 28:11-13:</u> *"Now while they were on their way, behold, some of the guard came into the city and reported to the chief priests all that had happened. [12] And when they had assembled with the elders and counseled together, <u>they gave a large sum of money to the soldiers, [13] and said, 'You are to say, His disciples came by night and stole Him away while we were asleep.'</u>"*

<u>VERSES 5-12:</u> *"And the disciples came to the other side and had forgotten to take bread. [6] And Jesus said to them, 'Watch out and beware of the leaven of the Pharisees and Sadducees.' [7] And they began to discuss among themselves, saying, 'It is because we took no bread.' [8] But Jesus, aware of this, said, 'You men of little faith, why do you discuss among yourselves that you have no bread? [9] Do you not yet understand or remember the five loaves of the five thousand, and how many baskets you took up? [10] Or the seven loaves of the four thousand, and how many large baskets you took up? [11] How is it that you do not understand that I did not speak to you concerning bread? But beware of the leaven of the Pharisees and Sadducees.' [12] Then they understood that He did not say to beware of the leaven of bread, but of the teaching of the Pharisees and Sadducees."*

Jesus warns the disciples to watch out for false teachers. Unfortunately, the disciples were weak in faith. They thought that Jesus was talking about not having enough bread to eat. In verses 8-9 Jesus points out that they have no business worrying about food, especially since they saw Him feed thousands on two different occasions (see Matthew 14:13-21; 15:32-38).

The term leaven[297] is similar to "yeast." Leaven (yeast) causes bread to rise. Here Jesus speaks of leaven as false doctrine that permeates the churches and tries to corrupt it. When Paul is talking about false doctrine in Galatians, he also refers to leaven as false doctrine impacting the entire church.

> <u>Galatians 5:7-9:</u> *"You were running well; who hindered you from obeying the truth? [8]This persuasion did not come from Him who calls you. [9] <u>A little leaven leavens the whole lump of dough.</u>"*

In addressing someone who was sinning in the church, Paul again used the analogy of leaven in a negative sense:

> <u>1 Corinthians 5:4-8:</u> *"In the name of our Lord Jesus, when you are assembled, and I with you in spirit, with the power of our Lord Jesus, [5] I have decided to deliver such a one to Satan for the destruction of his flesh, that his spirit may be saved in the day of the Lord Jesus. [6] Your boasting is not good. Do you not know that a little leaven*

---

[297] "<u>Leaven</u> (Heb. 'śᵉ'ōr, 'leaven', 'leavened bread' in Deuteronomy 16:4; ḥāmēṣ, 'anything leavened or fermented'; *cf.* maṣṣâ, 'without leaven', Leviticus 10:12; Gk. *zymē*, 'leaven'; *cf.* Lat. *levare*, 'to raise'). In Hebrew life leaven came to play an important part, not only in bread-making, but also in law, ritual and religious teaching. It was made originally from fine white bran kneaded with must; from the meal of certain plants such as fitch or vetch; or from barley mixed with water and then allowed to stand till it turned sour. As baking developed, leaven was produced from bread flour kneaded without salt and kept till it passed into a state of fermentation." Wood, D. R. W., and Marshall, I. H. (1996). *New Bible Dictionary* (3rd ed.) (p. 679). Leicester, England; Downers Grove, IL: InterVarsity Press.

leavens the whole lump of dough? ⁷Clean out the old leaven, that you may be a new lump, just as you are in fact unleavened. For Christ our Passover also has been sacrificed. ⁸Let us therefore celebrate the feast, not with old leaven, nor with the leaven of malice and wickedness, but with the unleavened bread of sincerity and truth."

Jesus points out directly that the *leaven of the Pharisees* is *hypocrisy*:
Luke 12:1: *"...He began saying to His disciples first of all, 'Beware of the leaven of the Pharisees, which is <u>hypocrisy</u>.'"*

One must be careful who he allows to be a teacher of the Word over him. When you are told the Bible says *such and such*, you should go to the Bible and look it up yourself and see if what you are told is true and whether the verse quoted is in the context that it was written. Paul commended those who went to the Word of God to see if what he was teaching was true.
Acts 17:10-11: *"And the brethren immediately sent Paul and Silas away by night to Berea; and when they arrived, they went into the synagogue of the Jews. ¹¹ Now these were more noble-minded than those in Thessalonica, for they received the word with great eagerness, examining the Scriptures daily, to see whether these things were so."*

Any "Bible teacher" who does not tolerate being questioned based on Scripture must be rejected!
1 John 4:1: *"*Beloved*, do not believe every spirit, <u>but test the spirits to see whether they are from God;</u> because many false prophets have gone out into the world."*

Do not let the pretense of humility or outward good works be determination of truth. Scripture tells us that even the Devil can disguise himself to look very *good*.
2 Corinthians 11:13-15: *"For such men are false apostles, deceitful workers, disguising themselves as apostles of Christ. ¹⁴ And no wonder, <u>for even Satan disguises himself as an angel of light.</u> ¹⁵ Therefore it is not surprising if his servants also disguise themselves as servants of righteousness; whose end shall be according to their deeds."*

The godly man studies the Word of God and teaches it accurately, in its context, to the glory of God.
2 Timothy 2:15: *"Be diligent to present yourself approved to God as a workman who does not need to be ashamed, <u>handling accurately the word of truth</u>."*

Puritan preacher John Flavel warns us about listening to false teachers when he said;
"By entertaining of strange persons, men sometimes entertain angels unawares: but by entertaining of strange doctrines, many have entertained devils unaware."[298]

Ryle further expands this warning when he stated,
"Let us remember that we live in a world where Pharisaism and Sadduceeism are continually striving for the mastery in the church of Christ. Some want to add to the Gospel, and some want to take away from it; some would bury it, and some would pare it down to nothing; some would stifle it by heaping on additions, and some would bleed it to death by subtraction from its truths. Both parties agree only in one respect: both would kill and destroy the life of Christianity if they succeeded in having their own way. Against both errors let us watch and pray, and stand on guard. Let us not add to

---

[298] I.D.E. Thomas, *The Golden Treasury of Puritan Quotations*, (Simpsonville, SC: Christian Classics Foundation) 1997.

the Gospel, to please the modern Pharisee; let us not subtract from the Gospel, to please the modern Sadducee." [299]

Summary and Application

We are warned not to engage in *sign seeking*. Jesus said, ***"An evil and adulterous generation seeks after a sign...."*** One must be careful in wasting a lot of time with those who pretend to be seeking God when they really are playing a *shell game*. It is amazing how you can run into people who claim to have a particular question about the faith that, they claim, keeps them from becoming a Christian. It is my experience, that in most cases, if you answer their question they still will not repent. It will take just a few days after you answer their question that they will claim to have a new *question* or a new *objection* to Christianity. I have found that the best way to respond to someone's *pet theological question* is to ask him, "If I am able to answer that question, are you saying you will repent of your sin and turn to Christ?" Almost always the person will pause for a moment and then tell you,... "No." This is a self-righteous person who is not posing sincere questions. He loves his sin and hypocritically hides behind the facade of theological and intellectual questions.

The other main point in this text has to do with false doctrine. Unfortunately some want to be involved in *religion* for a lot of the wrong reasons. Anyone who claims to be a Bible teacher must be scrutinized as to his doctrine and his life. Both life and doctrine must line up with Scripture. The false teacher is very content to *look, act, and sound very religious*. Their heart is full of hypocrisy (*leaven*). The best defense you can have from this type of person is continued personal Bible study time. The more familiar you are with God's Word, the less chance you can be fooled by a fake. The fake religious leader may quote Scripture, but you won't be impressed because you know the real context from which the Scripture came...and if you don't, you will look it up to find out!

---

[299] Matthew / Ryle, J.C. p.138 (Expository Thoughts on the Gospels) (Crossways classic commentaries: v.1)

MATTHEW 16:13-20

(WHO JESUS REALLY IS.)

"Now when Jesus came into the district of Caesarea Philippi, He began asking His disciples, saying, 'Who do people say that the Son of Man is?' ^{14} *And they said, 'Some say John the Baptist; and others, Elijah; but still others, Jeremiah, or one of the prophets.'* ^{15} *He *said to them, 'But who do you say that I am?'* ^{16} *And Simon Peter answered and said, 'Thou art the Christ, the Son of the living God.'* ^{17} *And Jesus answered and said to him, 'Blessed are you, Simon Barjona, because flesh and blood did not reveal this to you, but My Father who is in heaven.* ^{18} *And I also say to you that you are Peter, and upon this rock I will build My church; and the gates of Hades shall not overpower it.* ^{19} *I will give you the keys of the kingdom of heaven; and whatever you shall bind on earth shall be bound in heaven, and whatever you shall loose on earth shall be loosed in heaven.'* ^{20} *Then He warned the disciples that they should tell no one that He was the Christ."*

Introduction

Jesus states plainly to His disciples that He is the Messiah, the Son of God. This concept is fundamental to Christianity. There are many people and religions who try to create a Jesus of their own liking, but not according to Scripture.

Galatians 1:7-9: *"…some who are disturbing you, and want to distort the gospel of Christ. But even though we, or an angel from heaven, should preach to you a gospel contrary to that which we have preached to you, let him be accursed.* ^{9} *As we have said before, so I say again now, if any man is preaching to you a gospel contrary to that which you received, let him be accursed."*

We are warned to guard against the beliefs of false teachers and false Christians who speak of some other type of Jesus. Paul wrote in bewilderment of how the Corinthians could embrace false teaching about Jesus and the Gospel.

2 Corinthians 11:4: *"For if one comes and preaches another Jesus whom we have not preached, or you receive a different spirit which you have not received, or a different gospel which you have not accepted, you bear this beautifully."*

VERSES 13-14: *"Now when Jesus came into the district of Caesarea Philippi, He began asking His disciples, saying, 'Who do people say that the Son of Man is?'* ^{14} *And they said, 'Some say John the Baptist; and others, Elijah; but still others, Jeremiah, or one of the prophets.'"*

Jesus asks His disciples, *"Who do people say that the Son of Man is?"* The term *"Son of Man"* was recognized by Jews as a title for the Messiah:

Daniel 7:13:

"I kept looking in the night visions,
And behold, with the clouds of heaven
One like a Son of Man was coming,
And He came up to the Ancient of Days
And was presented before Him."

We also see Jesus use the title, *"Son of Man"* as it identifies Him with mankind for whom He is the sacrifice.

> **Matthew 20:28:** *"… just as the Son of Man did not come to be served, but to serve, and to give His life a ransom for many."*

Notice from Matthew 16:14 that some of the people thought that Jesus was John the Baptist resurrected. Herod the Tetrarch was one who held to this view. He is the one who had John arrested and later beheaded.

> **Matthew 14:1-2:** *"At that time Herod the tetrarch heard the news about Jesus, and <u>said to his servants, 'This is John the Baptist; he has risen from the dead; and that is why miraculous powers are at work in him.'"</u>*

Others thought Jesus might be the resurrected Elijah. Their reasoning for that view was based on an Old Testament prophesy saying that Elijah would come:

> **Malachi 4:5-6:** *"Behold, I am going to <u>send you Elijah the prophet before the coming of the great and terrible day of the LORD.</u> ⁶ And he will restore the hearts of the fathers to their children, and the hearts of the children to their fathers, lest I come and smite the land with a curse."*

Jesus explains the prophecy of Malachi in Mark 9:10-13 and Matthew 11:11-14. Specifically:

> **Mark 9:10-13:** *"And they seized upon that statement, discussing with one another what rising from the dead might mean. ¹¹ And they asked Him, saying, 'Why is it that the scribes say that Elijah must come first?' ¹² And He said to them, <u>'Elijah does first come and restore all things.</u> And yet how is it written of the Son of Man that He should suffer many things and be treated with contempt? ¹³ But I say to you, that <u>Elijah has indeed come,</u> and they did to him whatever they wished, just as it is written of him.'"*

> **Matthew 11:11-14:** *"Truly, I say to you, among those born of women there has not arisen anyone greater than John the Baptist; yet he who is least in the kingdom of heaven is greater than he. ¹² And from the days of John the Baptist until now the kingdom of heaven suffers violence, and violent men take it by force. ¹³ For all the prophets and the Law prophesied until <u>John.</u> ¹⁴ <u>And if you care to accept it, he himself is Elijah, who was to come."</u>*

This statement in Matthew 11:11-14 tells us that John the Baptist was the *Elijah* who fulfilled the prophecy of Malachi 4:5-6. This prophecy was not intended to mean Elijah would be reincarnated but rather that John would be a great prophet like Elijah. Look at what the angel said to John's father Zecharias:

> **Luke 1:16-17:** *"And he will turn back many of the sons of Israel to the Lord their God. ¹⁷And it is he who will go as a forerunner before Him <u>in the spirit and power of Elijah,</u>…."*

Some thought Jesus might be Jeremiah, which might have been based on a prophesy in Jeremiah.

> **Jeremiah 1:10:** *"See, I have appointed you this day over the nations and over the kingdoms, To pluck up and to break down, To destroy and to overthrow, To build and to plant."*

It is clear that some people had different ideas about Jesus. What would your answer be if I asked you, "who do you think Jesus is?" <u>Your answer is fundamental to your eternity</u>. Some people will say Jesus was a prophet or teacher. Others say He was a giving person, or a great martyr. All of these answers are from the pit of hell. Any explanation that tries to take Jesus away from being the divine almighty God is a damning error. Look at a few of the verses in the Bible that address the fact that Jesus is God.

Jesus says in **John 10:30:** *"I and the Father are one."*

Colossians 2:8-10: *"See to it that no one takes you captive through philosophy and empty deception, according to the tradition of men, according to the elementary principles of the world, rather than according to Christ. ⁹ For in Him all <u>the fullness of Deity dwells in bodily form</u>, ¹⁰ and in Him you have been made complete, and <u>He is the head over all rule and authority;</u>"*

Titus 2:13: *"…looking for the blessed hope and the <u>appearing of the glory of our great God and Savior, Christ Jesus;</u>"*

Philippians 2:9-11: *"Therefore also God highly exalted Him, and bestowed on Him the <u>name which is above every name</u>, ¹⁰ that <u>at the name of Jesus</u> <small>EVERY KNEE SHOULD BOW</small>, of those who are in heaven, and on earth, and under the earth, ¹¹ and that every tongue should confess that Jesus Christ is Lord, to the glory of God the Father."*

Colossians 1:15-19: *"And He is the image of the invisible God, the first-born of all creation. ¹⁶ For <u>by Him all things were created, both in the heavens and on earth</u>, visible and invisible, whether thrones or dominions or rulers or authorities—all things have been created by Him and for Him. ¹⁷ <u>And He is before all things, and in Him all things hold together.</u> ¹⁸ He is also head of the body, the church; and He is the beginning, the first-born from the dead; so that He Himself might come to have first place in everything. ¹⁹ For it was the Father's good pleasure for all the fullness to dwell in Him,"*

VERSES 15-18: *"He *said to them, 'But who do you say that I am?' ¹⁶ And Simon Peter answered and said, 'Thou art the Christ, the Son of the living God.' ¹⁷ And Jesus answered and said to him, 'Blessed are you, Simon Barjona, because flesh and blood did not reveal this to you, but My Father who is in heaven. ¹⁸ And I also say to you that you are Peter, and upon this rock I will build My church; and the gates of Hades shall not overpower it.'"*

In this passage Jesus takes His general question to Peter (i.e. *"Who do people say that the Son of Man is?"*) to a direct question (i.e. *"But who do you say that I am?"*). Peter answered by saying: *"<u>Thou art the Christ, the Son of the living God.</u>"* The term *Christ* in the Greek is equivalent to the Hebrew word "Messiah." Peter's answer was not the result of his learning or natural intellectual ability. His answer was given to him directly by the Holy Spirit of God (*"because flesh and blood did not reveal this to you, but My Father who is in heaven."*). It is a great blessing to be given a true revelation (understanding) by God (i.e. *"Blessed are you, Simon Barjona"*). The revelation of Jesus, as the Christ, is proclaimed throughout the world but not everyone receives it. This revelation is truly heard and understood only when that understanding is given by the Holy Spirit. This is why Jesus stated in **Mark 4:23:** *"If any man has ears to hear, let him hear."* He is not talking about physical ears. Jesus is saying that if you have been given spiritual understanding by the Holy Spirit, then listen carefully as to what God is stating. The unconverted man is spiritually dead. On his own he is neither able to seek after God, nor understand spiritual truths.

> **Romans 3:10:** *"...as it is written, 'There is none righteous, not even one;* [11] *There is none who understands, There is none who seeks for God....'"*

A person's pride, sinfulness and self-righteousness consigns him to a view that spiritual matters are mere foolishness.

> **1 Corinthians 2:13-14:** *"...which things we also speak, not in words taught by human wisdom, but in those taught by the Spirit, combining spiritual thoughts with spiritual words.* [14] *But a natural man does not accept the things of the Spirit of God; for they are foolishness to him, and he cannot understand them, because they are spiritually appraised."*

The lesson to be learned in this section is how humble and grateful we should be when God, in His mercy, has allowed us to know Him. The truth that the Christian has learned has been revealed to him by God through His Word (the Bible). This instruction is not the result of cold academic achievement, but revelation by the Sprit. The person who studies God's Word, simply to appear smarter than others, is engaged in a prideful endeavor that will not produce spiritual fruit.

> **1 Corinthians 8:1-3:** *"....Knowledge makes arrogant, but love edifies.* [2] *If anyone supposes that he knows anything, he has not yet known as he ought to know;* [3] *but if anyone loves God, he is known by Him."*

This is why some so-called pastors who have gone to seminary and studied for years still do not have the truth of God in their heart. On Sunday morning these false pastors might read from the Bible and tell you all kinds of interesting thoughts they have learned, but it is all academic and vocational. They apply what they want when it fits their view of the world and disregard what does not. Their hearts are not set on seeking and serving the Lord. They just want to be viewed by others as *religious and kind.* Despite their religious veneer, they often will attack those who truly believe and preach the Gospel as naive and uneducated. Scripture describes these imposters as:

> *"...always learning and never able to come to the knowledge of the truth.* [8] *And just as Jannes and Jambres opposed Moses, so these men also oppose the truth, men of depraved mind, rejected as regard to the faith."* **2 Timothy 3:7-8**

Do not misunderstand me — we are to diligently seek God and His truth through the study of His Word.

> **2 Timothy 2:15:** *"Be diligent to present yourself approved to God as a workman who does not need to be ashamed, handling accurately the word of truth."*

This can at times be a very rigorous academic pursuit.

> **Proverbs 25:2:** *"It is the glory of God to conceal a matter,*
> *But the glory of kings is to search out a matter."*

The distinction is that the converted person studies and pursues the revelation of God out of love for God. His objective is not to know more than others, but to know, love and obey God.

> **1 Timothy 1:5:** *"But the goal of our instruction is love from a pure heart and a good conscience and a sincere faith."*

The Bible tells us that, *"God is Love."* Note that love is not a mere attribute of God, but it is who He is. The definition of love...is God!

> **1 John 4:16:** *"And we have come to know and have believed the love which God has for us. God is love, and the one who abides in love abides in God, and God abides in him."*

The believer's desire is to be conformed to the image of Christ *for the glory of God.*

Romans 8:29: *"For whom He foreknew, He also predestined to <u>become conformed to the image of His Son</u>, that He might be the first-born among many brethren;...."*

Return back to the section of text we were studying (Matthew 16:15-18). Note that Jesus is the Messiah, *"the Son of the living God."* Jesus then said in verse 18, *"...you are Peter, and upon this rock I will build My church; and the gates of Hades shall not overpower it."* This statement has been distorted by the Roman Catholic church. Roman Catholics argue that this passage supports their claim that the "church" would be built on Peter as the "first pope" of the church. Romanists also claim that this divine authority would follow through popes who succeeded Peter as the head of the church (papal succession). If you read Matthew 16:15-18 in its context, it is clear that Jesus is building His church on the statement that He is, *"the Son of the living God"* (i.e. the Messiah), not on the person of Peter.

"For more than fifteen hundred years the Roman Catholic church has maintained that this passage teaches the church was built on the person of Peter, who became the first pope and bishop of Rome and from whom the Catholic papacy has since descended. Because of this supposed divinely ordained apostolic succession, the pope is considered to be the supreme and authoritative representative of Christ on earth. When a pope speaks ex cathedra,[300] that is, in his official capacity as head of the church, he is said to speak with divine authority equal to that of God in Scripture. Such an interpretation, however, is presumptuous and unbiblical, because the rest of the New Testament makes abundantly clear that Christ alone is the foundation and only head of His church."[301]

The church's sole foundation is built on the statement that, *"Thou art the Christ, the Son of the living God."* Although God had a special work and teaching He did through the apostles, Jesus alone is the cornerstone of the church.

Ephesians 2:20: *"...having been built upon the foundation of the apostles and prophets, <u>Christ Jesus Himself being the corner stone</u>...."*

Scripture makes it clear that Jesus is the sole head of the church:

Colossians 1:18-19: *"He is also <u>head of the body, the church</u>; and He is the beginning, the first-born from the dead; so that He Himself might come to have first place in everything. 19 For it was the Father's good pleasure for all the fullness to dwell in Him...."*

Jesus did not say that Peter would build the church, but Jesus said, *"I will build My church."* Jesus will build His church on Himself as the divine Messiah. Those who think verse 18 states that Jesus crowned Peter as the foundation of all the church forget that, but a few verses later, Jesus rebukes Peter for being used by Satan to discourage Him from going to the cross for mankind.

Matthew 16:21-23: *"From that time Jesus Christ began to show His disciples that He must go to Jerusalem, and suffer many things from the elders and chief priests and scribes, and be killed, and be raised up on the third day. 22 And Peter took Him aside and began to rebuke Him, saying, 'God forbid it, Lord! This shall never happen to You.' 23*

---

[300] *Merriam-Webster's Collegiate Dictionary*, defines <u>ex cathedra</u> as, "by virtue of or in the exercise of one's office or position" [as pope]. Webster also defines <u>papal infallibility as</u>: "the Roman Catholic doctrine that the pope cannot err when speaking ex cathedra in defining a doctrine of Christian faith or morals."

[Holy Scripture alone is infallible. When there is a conflict between a person's doctrine and Holy Scripture, Scripture alone stands as absolutely correct, not the opinions of man.]

[301] MacArthur, John F., *The MacArthur New Testament Commentary*, p.441 (Chicago: Moody Press) 1983.

But He turned and said to Peter, 'Get behind Me, Satan! You are a stumbling block to Me; for you are not setting your mind on God's interests, but man's.'"

Obviously neither Peter nor the other disciples took Jesus' words as meaning that He was building His church on the person of Peter. On one occasion the disciples asked Jesus which of them would be the greatest. Such a question would not have been asked if Jesus had previously set Peter aside as the one on whom He would build His church.

> **Matthew 18:1-4:** *"A*T *that time the disciples came to Jesus, saying, 'Who then is greatest in the kingdom of heaven?'* 2 *And He called a child to Himself and set him before them,* 3 *and said, 'Truly I say to you, unless you are converted and become like children, you shall not enter the kingdom of heaven.* 4 *Whoever then humbles himself as this child, he is the greatest in the kingdom of heaven.'"* (See also the request of James and John's mother in Matthew 20:20-21.)

Although Peter clearly had leadership he:

> "...recognized himself as an apostle (see e.g., 1 Peter 1:1; 2 Peter 1:1), he never claimed a superior title, rank, or privilege over the other apostles. He even referred to himself as a *'fellow elder'* (1 Peter 5:1) and as *'a bond-servant'* of Christ (2 Peter 1:1). Far from claiming honor and homage for himself, he soberly warns his fellow elders to guard against lording it over those under their pastoral care (1 Peter 5:3). The only glory he claimed for himself was that which is shared by all believers and which is yet, *'to be revealed,... when the Chief Shepherd appears'*."[302]

In Acts we see Peter being used by God to do a miracle, but we also see him go to great lengths to make sure people did not think that the miracle came from any special power or holiness that he obtained on his own.

> **Acts 3:11-16:** *"While he was clinging to Peter and John, all the people ran together to them at the so-called portico of Solomon, full of amazement. But when Peter saw this, he replied to the people, 'Men of Israel, why are you amazed at this, or <u>why do you gaze at us, as if by our own power or piety we had made him walk?</u> The God of Abraham, Isaac and Jacob, the God of our fathers, has glorified His servant Jesus, the one whom you delivered and disowned in the presence of Pilate, when he had decided to release Him. But you disowned the Holy and Righteous One and asked for a murderer to be granted to you, but put to death the Prince of life, the one whom God raised from the dead, a fact to which we are witnesses. And on the basis of faith in His name, it is the name of Jesus which has strengthened this man whom you see and know; and the faith which comes through Him has given him this perfect health in the presence of you all.'"*

VERSES 19-20: *"'I will give you the keys of the kingdom of heaven; and whatever you shall bind on earth shall be bound in heaven, and whatever you shall loose on earth shall be loosed in heaven.'* 20 *Then He warned the disciples that they should tell no one that He was the Christ."*

God's Word tells us what is true and what is not. We do not have to determine on our own what is wrong or right; we have the Bible. The church must handle its discipline according to God's Word,

---

[302] MacArthur, J. F., Jr. (1985). *Matthew.* MacArthur New Testament Commentary (p. 441). Chicago: Moody Press.

and thus we bind and loose based upon what God has spoken, not on our own authority. Look at the context in which Jesus used the concept of "binding and loosing" in Matthew 18 in regards to handling an unrepentant member (i.e. treat him as a non-believer):

> **Matthew 18:15-20:** *"And if your brother sins, go and reprove him in private; if he listens to you, you have won your brother. [16] But if he does not listen to you, take one or two more with you, so that BY THE MOUTH OF TWO OR THREE WITNESSES EVERY FACT MAY BE CONFIRMED. [17] And if he refuses to listen to them, tell it to the church; and if he refuses to listen even to the church, let him be to you as a Gentile and a tax-gatherer." [18] Truly I say to you, whatever you shall bind on earth shall be bound in heaven; and whatever you loose on earth shall be loosed in heaven. [19] Again I say to you, that if two of you agree on earth about anything that they may ask, it shall be done for them by My Father who is in heaven. [20] For where two or three have gathered together in My name, there I am in their midst."*

The Bible is the final authority on faith and doctrine. Our judgments of doctrine and conduct will be accurate if they align with God's Word and not our own ideas or traditions. For example, what if a person tells me that he is going to heaven because he did enough "good things" during his life? I know that Scripture states that his view is a completely false doctrine. I respond by telling him that he is wrong about earning his way into heaven. I go on to explain that he will enter the judgment of hell because he is holding to his own self-righteousness and not Christ's forgiveness. He responds by telling me that I am narrow-minded and judgmental. It bothers him that I do not get upset or take offense at his accusation. I explain that I am not judging him, I am merely telling him what God's Word says. He does not realize that his argument is with God. Perhaps he would let me show him what Scripture says about getting into heaven:

> **Ephesians 2:8-9:** *"For by grace you have been saved through faith; and that not of yourselves, it is the gift of God; [9] not as a result of works, that no one should boast."*

The point of the example is that the church has been given the authority to address discipline and doctrine under the authority of Scripture. We can confidently state the truth when it comes from God's Word and not man's. It is at this point that the church must be careful and see that its opinions are indeed based on Scripture and not a beloved tradition or man-made religion. If an opinion is not clearly set forth in Scripture, we must leave room for conscience and liberty (1 Corinthians 10:27-33);

> **Galatians 2:4:** *"But it was because of the false brethren who had sneaked in to spy out our liberty which we have in Christ Jesus, in order to bring us into bondage."* To take any other view is in essence to be claiming some form of "papal infallibility" (i.e. the heretical view of trying to make your opinions equal in authority with Scripture.).[303]

---

[303] As mentioned above, Webster defines *papal infallibility;* *"the Roman Catholic doctrine that the pope cannot err when speaking ex cathedra in defining a doctrine of Christian faith or morals."* I have always found it curious how Catholics reconcile a conflict that arises between a papal ex cathedra proclamation and Scripture. In other words, Scripture is without error and Romanism claims that the Pope's ex cathedra statements are without error; so what happens if the Pope's view contradicts Scripture? It appears that in the past they have resolved those conflicts in favor of the Pope. Kind of a "tie goes to the runner," approach I suppose. Note the quotes below . [Note continued on the next page.]

Summary and Application

The deity and Messiahship of Jesus is the foundation of the church. Man cannot be saved believing that Jesus is a great man, prophet or, "one sent by God." You have to believe that He is God incarnate (i.e. *"Thou art the Christ, the Son of the living God."*). To reject this leaves you unconverted. Look how Jesus is described in the book of Colossians:

> <u>Colossians 1:17-19:</u> *"And He is before all things, and in Him all things hold together. [18] He is also head of the body, the church; and He is the beginning, the first-born from the dead; so that He Himself might come to have first place in everything. [19] For it was the Father's good pleasure for all the fullness to dwell in Him,...."*

[Note continued.]

from the official Catholic Catechism #891 regarding papal infallibility:

> *891 "The Roman Pontiff, head of the college of bishops, <u>enjoys this infallibility in virtue of his office,</u> when, as supreme pastor and teacher of all the faithful - who confirms his brethren in the faith he proclaims by a definitive act a doctrine pertaining to faith or morals.... <u>The infallibility promised to the Church is also present in the body of bishops when, together with Peter's successor,</u> they exercise the supreme Magisterium, above all in an Ecumenical Council. When the Church through its supreme Magisterium proposes a doctrine for belief as being divinely revealed, and as the teaching of Christ, the definitions must be adhered to with the obedience of faith." <u>This infallibility extends as far as the deposit of divine Revelation itself.</u>"*

MATTHEW 16:21-27
(WALKING BY HUMAN SIGHT; COST OF DISCIPLESHIP)

"From that time Jesus Christ began to show His disciples that He must go to Jerusalem, and suffer many things from the elders and chief priests and scribes, and be killed, and be raised up on the third day. [22] And Peter took Him aside and began to rebuke Him, saying, 'God forbid it, Lord! This shall never happen to You.' [23] But He turned and said to Peter, 'Get behind Me, Satan! You are a stumbling block to Me; for you are not setting your mind on God's interests, but man's.' [24] Then Jesus said to His disciples, 'If anyone wishes to come after Me, let him deny himself , and take up his cross , and follow Me. [25] For whoever wishes to save his life shall lose it; but whoever loses his life for My sake shall find it. [26] For what will a man be profited, if he gains the whole world, and forfeits his soul? Or what will a man give in exchange for his soul? [27] For the Son of Man is going to come in the glory of His Father with His angels; and will then recompense every man according to his deeds."

Introduction

We must be careful when viewing things only through our human eyes and intellect instead of being led by the Spirit of God. In this section, we see the view of Christ's coming crucifixion through Peter's human eyes instead of by the Spirit of God. Also in this section Jesus sets out that the cost of discipleship includes the necessity of death to self and the real possibility of physical death.

VERSES 21-23: *"From that time Jesus Christ began to show His disciples that He must go to Jerusalem, and suffer many things from the elders and chief priests and scribes, and be killed, and be raised up on the third day. [22] And Peter took Him aside and began to rebuke Him, saying, 'God forbid it, Lord! This shall never happen to You.' [23] But He turned and said to Peter, 'Get behind Me, Satan! You are a stumbling block to Me; for you are not setting your mind on God's interests, but man's.'"*

We read in Matthew 16:15-17 how Peter was given a revelation, by the Holy Spirit, of who Jesus is. Now we see Peter speaking by his own fleshly opinion, which Jesus states was received by the suggestion of Satan. Satan was always attempting to keep Jesus from the cross. Remember that at the temptation Satan suggested Jesus could be ruler of everything without going to the cross.

> **Luke 4:5-8 and 13:** *"And he led Him up and showed Him all the kingdoms of the world in a moment of time. [6] And the devil said to Him, 'I will give You all this domain and its glory; for it has been handed over to me, and I give it to whomever I wish. [7] Therefore if You worship before me, it shall all be Yours.' [8] And Jesus answered and said to him, 'It is written, 'YOU SHALL WORSHIP THE LORD YOUR GOD AND SERVE HIM ONLY.' .....'*
> *[13] And when the devil had finished every temptation, he departed from Him until an opportune time."*

Notice in verse 13 that Satan left but was also waiting *"until an opportune time"* to tempt Jesus again. Could it be that Matthew 16:21-23 was such a time? We see Jesus' response was directed at Satan when Peter suggested that it would be bad if Jesus were to *"suffer many things from the elders and chief priests and scribes, and be killed."* Peter was looking at the situation purely from human eyes and not spiritual ones.

Galatians 5:16-17: *"But I say, walk by the Spirit, and you will not carry out the desire of the flesh. ¹⁷ <u>For the flesh sets its desire against the Spirit, and the Spirit against the flesh; for these are in opposition to one another,</u> so that you may not do the things that you please."*

Often times we hear part of a statement but as our mind gets going, we don't hear the complete statement (review Matthew 16:21). Peter obviously heard Jesus say, *"...that He must go to Jerusalem, and suffer many things from the elders and chief priests and scribes,...."* One has to wonder if Peter actually heard everything that Jesus said, because at the end of that statement He said He would be, *"raised up on the third day."* Peter's response was simply, *"God forbid it, Lord! This shall never happen to You."* (v.22). How often do we only hear part of what the Lord speaks to us? This occurs when we view his Word through our own agendas or worldviews rather than His. This is why daily Bible study is vital for the Christian walk. As we study His word, we learn to think and act more Christ-like. When issues or events cross our daily lives, we are able to quickly sift them through the grid of Scripture and make wise decisions.

Psalm 19:7: *"The law of the Lord is perfect, restoring the soul; The testimony of the Lord is sure, making wise the simple."*

Hebrews 5:14: *"But solid food is for the mature, who because of practice <u>have their senses trained to discern good and evil.</u>"*

1 Corinthians 2:14–15: *"But a natural man does not accept the things of the Spirit of God, for they are foolishness to him; and he cannot understand them, because they are spiritually appraised. ¹⁵But he who is spiritual appraises all things, yet he himself is appraised by no one."*

We know that Peter would later love the Cross. He understood and taught the truth regarding the righteousness the believer receives from Jesus' death on the cross:

1 Peter 2:24: *"...<u>and He Himself bore our sins in His body on the cross,</u> that we might die to sin and live to righteousness; <u>for by His wounds you were healed.</u>"*

Jesus knew that going to the cross was the only way mankind could be saved from his sins. Look at what He told His disciples in <u>Luke 18:31-34:</u>

"And He took the twelve aside and said to them, 'Behold, we are going up to Jerusalem , and all things which are written through the prophets about the Son of Man will be accomplished . ³² For He will be delivered to the Gentiles , and will be mocked and mistreated and spit upon, ³³ and after they have scourged Him, they will kill Him; and the third day He will rise again.' ³⁴ And they understood none of these things, and this saying was hidden from them, and they did not comprehend the things that were said."

Scripture is clear that the only atonement for sins is the sacrificial, substitutionary work of Christ's death on the Cross:

Ephesians 2:13-16: *"But now in Christ Jesus <u>you who formerly were far off have been brought near by the blood of Christ.</u> ¹⁴ For He Himself is our peace, who made both groups into one, and broke down the barrier of the dividing wall, ¹⁵ <u>by abolishing in His flesh the enmity, which is the Law of commandments</u> contained in ordinances, that in Himself He might make the two into one new man, thus establishing peace, ¹⁶ <u>and might reconcile them both in one body to God through the cross, by it having put to death the enmity.</u>"*

Christ's *substitutionary atonement*[304] had been prophesied by Isaiah hundreds of years before the Cross.

<u>Isaiah 53:5-6:</u>

> *"But He was pierced through for our transgressions,*
>> *He was crushed for our iniquities;*
>> *The chastening for our well-being fell upon Him,*
>> *And by His scourging we are healed.*
> [6] *All of us like sheep have gone astray,*
>> *Each of us has turned to his own way;*
>> <u>*But the Lord has caused the iniquity of us all*</u>
>> <u>*To fall on Him."*</u>

It is the substitutionary death for our sins by Christ that we remember when we take the Lord's Supper (*communion*). Jesus said in <u>**Matthew 26:26-28:**</u>

> *"And while they were eating, Jesus took some bread, and after a blessing, He broke it and gave it to the disciples, and said, 'Take, eat; this is My body.'*[27] *And when He had taken a cup and given thanks, He gave it to them, saying, 'Drink from it, all of you;* [28] *for this is My blood of the covenant, which is poured out for many for forgiveness of sins.'"*

One theologian notes:

> "That the Lord's Supper was given as a memorial is clear from the words, 'This do in remembrance of me.' What is it that is remembered? It is specifically the death of Christ. One might think that the Resurrection would be the object of memorial, but instead it is the death. More particularly, it is the death as a substitutionary sacrifice. 'This is my body which is given for you.' 'This is my blood of the New Covenant, which is shed for many for the remission of sins.' Charles Hodge says: 'Redemption, therefore, is not by power, or by teaching, or by moral influence, but by expiation. It is this truth which the Lord's Supper exhibits and authenticates. Still further, as Christ affirms that His body was to be broken and his blood shed for the remission of sin, this from the nature of the case involves on His part the promise and pledge, that the sins of those who receive and trust Him, shall certainly be forgiven. The sacrament thus becomes not only a sign but also a seal. It is the handwriting and signet of the Son of God attached to the promise of redemption.' "[305]

The Cross has always been foolish to the unregenerate.

---

[304] <u>Substitutionary Atonement:</u> "The death of Christ was substitutionary—He died in the stead of sinners and in their place. This is also described as *vicarious* from the Latin word *vicarius* meaning 'one in place of another.' The death of Christ 'is vicarious in the sense that Christ is the Substitute who bears the punishment rightly due sinners, their guilt being imputed to Him in such a way that He representatively bore their punishment.' There are many passages that emphasize Christ's substitutionary atonement in the place of mankind. Christ was a substitute in being made sin for others (2 Corinthians 5:21); He bore the sins of others in His body on the cross (1 Peter 2:24); He suffered once to bear the sins of others (Hebrews 9:28); He experienced horrible suffering, scourging, and death in place of sinners (Isaiah 53:4–6)." Enns, P. P. (1997). *The Moody Handbook of Theology.* p.323 Chicago, Ill.: Moody Press.

[305] Smith, M. H. (1994; Published in electronic form by Christian Classics Foundation, 1996). *Systematic Theology, Volume One: Prolegomena, Theology, Anthropology, Christology* p.683. Index created by Christian Classics Foundation. (electronic ed.). Greenville SC: Greenville Presbyterian Theological Seminary Press.

1 Corinthians 1:18: *"For the word of the cross is to those who are perishing foolishness, but to us who are being saved it is the power of God."*

Faith in Christ's work on the cross as the basis of our righteousness seems foolish to them because it seems too easy. We live in a world where our efforts *appear* to control the outcome of events. For example, if a student studies hard, he will probably do well on a test. If an employee works hard on the job, he is more likely to get the promotion. The kingdom of God is not like this. Man's best efforts at righteousness are not able to earn him salvation.

Romans 9:16: *"So then it does not depend on the man who wills or the man who runs, but on God who has mercy."*

This entire section can be summarized as Paul stated:

2 Corinthians 9:15: *"Thanks be to God for His indescribable gift!"* (cf. Romans 5:12-21.)

VERSES 24-25: *"Then Jesus said to His disciples, 'If anyone wishes to come after Me, let him deny himself, and take up his cross, and follow Me. 25 For whoever wishes to save his life shall lose it; but whoever loses his life for My sake shall find it."*

In this portion of Scripture Jesus continues to teach about the Cross. This time the Cross is not just pointing to the one He will carry, but more specifically to the Cross that His disciples will bear. In verses 24-25 Jesus makes it clear that there is a cost associated with discipleship. This cost should not be confused with salvation. Jesus paid the entire cost of our salvation. We cannot earn it, and we cannot pay Him back for it. Although salvation is a free gift, true discipleship will manifest Holy Spirit led thankfulness, allegiance and service as a result of that gift. The motto we repeat in my Sunday School class is, "Nothing else matters but the King and His Kingdom!" We must realize that after He has saved us, God will perform good works through us for His glory.

James 2:17-18: *"Even so faith, if it has no works, is dead, being by itself. 18But someone may well say, 'You have faith, and I have works; show me your faith without the works, and I will show you my faith by my works.'"*

This entire concept is summed up in **Ephesians 2:8-10:**

"For by grace you have been saved through faith; and that not of yourselves, it is the gift of God; 9 not as a result of works, that no one should boast. 10 For we are His workmanship, created in Christ Jesus for good works, which God prepared beforehand, that we should walk in them."

It is a false gospel that claims that there is no cost in true *discipleship*. The Apostle Paul makes it clear that persecution is expected for the true disciple: **2 Timothy 3:12:** *"And indeed, all who desire to live godly in Christ Jesus will be persecuted."* Jesus said of His disciples, *"And you will be hated by all on account of My name, but it is the one who has endured to the end who will be saved."* **Matthew 10:22.** It should further be understood that a false general confession of Jesus is not *saving faith* as Jesus said in **Matthew 7:21:** *"Not everyone who says to Me, 'Lord, Lord,' will enter the kingdom of heaven; but he who does the will of My Father who is in heaven."* *Faith* is much greater than just having an opinion about Jesus. It is more than acknowledging that He is the Son of God since Scripture tells us even the demons do that: *"You believe that God is one. You do well; the demons also believe, and shudder."* **James 2:19.** Jesus preached that people are to, *"repent and believe in the gospel."* **Mark 1:15.** The one who is saved is the one who turns from his sin by the power of God and believes the Gospel. *Believing the Gospel* means to put your faith in Jesus Christ (as God and without sin) and believe in His sacrificial death on the cross for the sole and complete payment of your sins, and that He rose from the dead on the third day. It has nothing to do with your righteousness. It is that straightforward. You do not need to have a religious ceremony; you do not need to do charitable or religious work. You must simply, *"repent and believe in the gospel."* **Mark 1:15.**

In Matthew 16:24-28, Jesus continues on the subject of the Cross by explaining to His disciples that the true follower will have to, *"deny himself, and take up his cross, and follow Me."* The disciples knew exactly what Jesus meant (i.e. that they were called to die to themselves which included the possibility of physical death for their identification with Christ).

> "Only a few years before Jesus spoke those words, a zealot named Judas had gathered together a band of rebels to fight the Roman occupation forces. The insurrection was easily quelled, and in order to teach the Jews a lesson, the Roman general Varus ordered the crucifixion of over 2,000 Jews. Their crosses lined the roads *of* Galilee from one end to the other."[306]

Note that Jesus made a very similar statement about the cross earlier in **Matthew 10:38:** *"And he who does not take his cross and follow after Me is not worthy of Me."* We should not think that Jesus' statement about taking up your cross applied only to the disciples of that time. Although you may never be called to die for Christ, it is clear that if you are a disciple of Jesus you must be willing to be a martyr. Please see this footnote as to what martyr means from the Christian perspective.[307]

---

[306] MacArthur, J. F., Jr. (1985). *Matthew.* MacArthur New Testament Commentary. Chicago: Moody Press. (p. 199)

[307] Unfortunately we live in a time when the term *MARTYR* has to be defined. In 2004 some Muslims had explosives strapped to them and went into an area populated by their enemies blowing up themselves and their enemies. Their Muslim leaders called them *"martyrs."* Their religion may call them martyrs, but Christianity calls them murderers. God's Word says in **1 John 3:15:** *"Everyone who hates his brother is a murderer; and you know that no murderer has eternal life abiding in him."* These homicidal bombers have absolutely nothing to do with the Christian definition of martyrdom. The Christian martyr is, "one who bears witness of the truth, and suffers death in the cause of Christ (Acts 22:20; Revelation 2:13; 17:6)." Easton, M. G. (1996). *Easton's Bible Dictionary* "martyr." Webster defines martyr as, "a person who voluntarily suffers death as the penalty of witnessing to and refusing to renounce a religion." Merriam-Webster's 11th Collegiate Dictionary. Jesus warned his disciples: **Matthew 24:9:** *"Then they will deliver you to tribulation, and will kill you, and you will be hated by all nations on account of My name."* In other words, the true Christian remains faithful to Christ in the face of torment, torture and death at the hands of evil men who hate Christ. Christians are not to retaliate but must obey Jesus' words: **Matthew 5:44:** *"But I say to you, love your enemies , and pray for those who persecute you[45] in order that you may be sons of your Father who is in heaven;...."* In summary: The **god** of Islam **is not** the God of Christianity.

Within Islam, there are some who believe they are rewarded when they hate and kill their enemies. Their book, the Qur'an states as follows: ***Qur'an 8:12*** "When your Lord revealed to the angels: I am with you, therefore make firm those who believe. I will cast terror into the hearts of those who disbelieve. Therefore strike off their heads and strike off every fingertip of them.." ***Qur'an 2:191*** "And kill them wherever you find them, and drive them out from whence they drove you out, and persecution is severer than slaughter, and do not fight with them at the Sacred Mosque until they fight with you in it, but if they do fight you, then slay them; such is the recompense of the unbelievers." ***Qur'an 5:33*** "The punishment of those who wage war against Allah and His messenger and strive to make mischief in the land is only this, that they should be murdered or crucified or their hands and their feet should be cut off on opposite sides or they should be imprisoned;...." ***Qur'an 9:5*** "So when the sacred months have passed away, then slay the idolaters wherever you find them, and take them captives and besiege them and lie in wait for them in every ambush, then if they repent and keep up prayer and pay the poor-rate, leave their way free to them; surely Allah is Forgiving, Merciful." ***Qur'an 47: 4*** "So when you meet in battle those who disbelieve, then smite the necks until when you have overcome them, then make (them) [Note continued on the next page.]

God demands complete allegiance to Him, even over family members. Jesus explains that our devotion to Him should be so much greater than to anyone else that even our sincere love for family would appear to be hate in comparison to our love for God.

> **Luke 14:26-28:** *"If anyone comes to Me, and does not hate his own father and mother and wife and children and brothers and sisters, yes, and even his own life, he cannot be My disciple. ²⁷ Whoever does not carry his own cross and come after Me cannot be My disciple. ²⁸ For which one of you, when he wants to build a tower, does not first sit down and calculate the cost, to see if he has enough to complete it?"*

VERSE 26: *"For what will a man be profited, if he gains the whole world, and forfeits his soul? Or what will a man give in exchange for his soul?"*

Jesus points out that one cannot buy his way into heaven. Even if one were to own everything on earth, it would not even begin to buy redemption for his own soul.

> **Psalm 49:7-8:** *"No man can by any means redeem his brother, Or give to God a ransom for him — For the redemption of his soul is costly,..."*
> **Proverbs 11:4:** *"Riches do not profit in the day of wrath, But righteousness delivers from death."*

Only Christ can pay our way into heaven. His payment was made with His own sinless blood.

> **Romans 5:9:** *"Much more then, having now been justified by His blood, we shall be saved from the wrath of God through Him."*

VERSE 27: *"For the Son of Man is going to come in the glory of His Father with His angels; and WILL THEN RECOMPENSE EVERY MAN ACCORDING TO HIS DEEDS."*

Most non-Christians think that the way to get into heaven is by doing good deeds. That way of thinking is terribly wrong because the Bible makes it clear that it is impossible for a non-Christian to do anything truly *"good."*

> **Romans 3:20:** *"...because by the works of the Law no flesh will be justified in His sight; for through the Law comes the knowledge of sin."*

The unredeemed person may do nice things on the outside, but inside him there is still a self-centered motive when shone under the light of God's perfect standard. Even the Christian's *good works* are tainted by selfishness unless he is completely led by the Holy Spirit.

> **Isaiah 64:6 KJV:** *"But we are all as an unclean thing, and all our righteousnesses are as filthy rags;...."*

Matthew Henry in addressing Isaiah 64:6 said:

> "We have all by sin become not only obnoxious to God's justice, but odious to his holiness; for sin is that abominable thing which the Lord hates, and cannot endure to look upon. Even all our righteousnesses are as filthy rags.... Our best duties are so

---

[Note continued.]

prisoners, and afterwards either set them free as a favor or let them ransom (themselves) until the war terminates ....and (as for) those who are slain in the way of Allah, He will by no means allow their deeds to perish."

> * Taken from translator Muhammad Habib Shakir, (1866–1939) an Egyptian judge, born in Cairo and a graduate from Al Azhar University. You can find slight variances in some other English translations of the Qur'an that attempt to soften some of the violent language.

defective, and so far short of the rule, that they are as rags, and so full of sin and corruption cleaving to them that they are as filthy rags. When we would do good, evil is present with us;...."[308]

All non-Christians will be judged to hell based on the deeds they did while on earth. Although these deeds may be applauded by their friends today, they will not be by God at the judgment.

> **Revelation 20:12-13:** *"And I saw the dead, the great and the small, standing before the throne, and books were opened; and another book was opened, which is the book of life; <u>and the dead were judged from the things which were written in the books, according to their deeds.</u> 13 And the sea gave up the dead which were in it, and death and Hades gave up the <u>dead which were in them; and they were judged, every one of them according to their deeds.</u>"*

If you still think you are a good person as a result of you own righteousness, please take the "good person" test below in footnote 309. Christians' eternal destiny is made secure not based upon their

---

[308] Henry, Matthew, *Matthew Henry's Commentary on the Bible*, Isaiah 64:6-12 (Peabody, MA: Hendrickson Publishers) 1997.

[309] If you ask the average person on the street if he is a good person the typical answer is a confident "Yes!" Most people like to grade themselves on the curve (i.e. comparing themselves to others). Scripture tells us that when one's righteousness is compared with the perfect law of God, the person's mouth is shut (i.e. he is prevented from talking about his own goodness and justifying himself).

> **Romans 3:19-20:** *"Now we know that whatever the Law says, it speaks to those who are under the Law, that <u>every mouth may be closed, and all the world may become accountable to God;</u> 20because by the works of the Law no flesh will be justified in His sight; for through the Law comes the knowledge of sin."*

Maybe you are one who considers yourself a *good person*. If you are not a Christian you will be judged by your deeds...and the standard will be the perfect law of God, The Ten Commandments (Revelation 20:11-15, Jude verses 14-15, Romans 2:5-16). Do you think you have kept The Ten Commandments? Let's look at some of the Commandments:

- *"Thou shalt not bear false witness..."* Have you ever told a lie? What do you call someone who tells lies? So, what does that make you? [**Answer:** a **liar** – Exodus 20:16.]

- *"Thou shalt not steal."* Have you ever taken anything that did not belong to you? (Remember it does not matter if it was of a small value, or took place a long time ago.) What do you call someone who has stolen? So, what does that make you? [**Answer:** a **thief** – Exodus 20:15]

- *"Thou shall not take the name of the Lord your God in vain."* Have you ever used God's name in vain through swearing or saying, "Oh my G_d!" Have you used Jesus' name as a curse word? If so, what does that make you? [**Answer:** a **blasphemer** – Exodus 20:7.] [

- *"Thou shall not commit adultery."* Maybe you think that you have not committed the act of adultery, but have you ever looked at another person with lust? Jesus says the one who looks at another with lust *has **already committed adultery** in his heart* – Matthew 5:28. So, what does that make you? [**Answer:** At best, an **adulterer at heart** – Exodus 20:14.]

[Note continued on the next page.]

own righteousness but that of Christ, through faith in Him. Jesus said that those who believe in Him will not be part of the judgment of sending nonbelievers to hell.

> **John 3:16-18:** *"For God so loved the world, that He gave His only begotten Son, that <u>whoever believes in Him should not perish, but have eternal life</u>. ¹⁷ For God did not send the Son into the world to judge the world, but that the world should be saved through Him. ¹⁸ <u>He who believes in Him is not judged; he who does not believe has been judged already, because he has not believed in the name of the only begotten Son of God."</u>*

The main text that we were looking at (Matthew 16:27), says *"For the Son of Man is going to come in the glory of His Father with His angels; and* WILL THEN RECOMPENSE EVERY MAN ACCORDING TO HIS DEED.* This verse says that every man will be judged by his deeds, but John 3:18 says that the believer will not be judged. How can both be true? They are both true as follows:

1. The <u>non-Christian</u> is judged to hell based on his evil works (Revelation 20:12-13).
2. The <u>Christian</u> avoids the judgment of hell based on his saving faith in Christ (John 3:18).
3. The Christian, dwelling in heaven, will be subject to a judgment of rewards or lack of rewards for the deeds he did in Christ *after* becoming a believer.

> **1 Corinthians 3:11-15:** *"For no man can lay a foundation other than the one which is laid, which is Jesus Christ. ¹² Now if any man builds upon the foundation with gold, silver, precious stones, wood, hay, straw, ¹³ each man's work will become evident; for the day will show it, because it is to be revealed with fire; and the fire itself will test the quality of each man's work. ¹⁴ If any <u>man's work which he has built upon it remains, he shall receive a reward</u>. ¹⁵ <u>If any man's work is burned up, he shall suffer loss; but he himself shall be saved, yet so as through fire."</u>*

[Note continued.]

- *"Thou shalt not murder."* Maybe you claim to not have murdered anyone, but have you ever hated anyone? The Bible says that if you hate someone you are a murderer! **1 John 3:15:** *"Everyone who hates his brother is a murderer; and you know that no murderer has eternal life abiding in him."*] (Jesus said if you call someone a *fool* you are guilty of hell – Matthew 5:22). So, what does that make you? [**Answer:** At best, a **murderer at heart**, Exodus 20:13.]

These questions involve only four of the Ten Commandments. There are six more for you to answer. Do you still think you are a truly "good person?" If you died in the next five minutes would you be judged as <u>innocent or guilty</u> based on the Ten Commandments? Do you think you would go to heaven or hell? Let us look carefully at what the Bible states is the punishment for those who have simply told a lie: **Revelation 21:8:** *"... and all liars, their part will be in the lake that burns with fire and brimstone, which is the second death."*

Your answer of whether you are good enough to get into heaven, if honest, should greatly concern you. The answer is clear: by God's standard you are not even close to being *good enough* to get into heaven! Remember that eternity is not just another lifetime,…it is forever and ever. Will you spend it in heaven with a loving God or will you spend it in fiery hell because God judged you honestly for what you are?

When one judges himself by God's standard, that person quickly understands that he is not the person he would like to think he is. The response to Christ's sacrifice and forgiveness is either acceptance or rejection. In **Hebrews 2:3** it states, *"how shall we escape if we neglect so great a salvation?...."*

(See also: Ray Comfort – Living Waters Ministries. See Comfort's video or audio, *"Hell's Best Kept Secret."*)

2 Corinthians 5:9-10: *"Therefore also we have as our ambition, whether at home or absent, to be pleasing to Him. [10] For we must all appear before the judgment seat of Christ, that each one may be recompensed for his deeds in the body, according to what he has done, whether good or bad."*

1 Corinthians 3:7-8: *"So then neither the one who plants nor the one who waters is anything, but God who causes the growth. [8] Now he who plants and he who waters are one; but each will receive his own reward according to his own labor."*

Summary and Application

As believers in Christ, we must remember that we must serve Him, from simply giving someone a cool glass of water, to dying for the faith. Our "deeds" will be judged by Jesus for rewards. We are not saved by any "good works," but they will be manifested from the true believer's life.

Matthew 10:42: *"And whoever in the name of a disciple gives to one of these little ones even a cup of cold water to drink, truly I say to you he shall not lose his reward."*

Matthew 10:38: *"And he who does not take his cross and follow after Me is not worthy of Me."*

MATTHEW 17 (16:28-17:9)
(THE TRANSFIGURATION)

16:28: "'Truly I say to you, there are some of those who are standing here who shall not taste death until they see the Son of Man coming in His kingdom.'

17:1 AND six days later Jesus *took with Him Peter and James and John his brother, and *brought them up to a high mountain by themselves. ² And He was transfigured before them; and His face shone like the sun, and His garments became as white as light. ³ And behold, Moses and Elijah appeared to them, talking with Him. ⁴ And Peter answered and said to Jesus, 'Lord, it is good for us to be here; if You wish, I will make three tabernacles here, one for You, and one for Moses, and one for Elijah.' ⁵ While he was still speaking, behold, a bright cloud overshadowed them; and behold, a voice out of the cloud, saying, 'This is My beloved Son, with whom I am well-pleased; listen to Him!' ⁶ And when the disciples heard this, they fell on their faces and were much afraid. ⁷ And Jesus came to them and touched them and said, 'Arise, and do not be afraid.' ⁸And lifting up their eyes, they saw no one, except Jesus Himself alone. ⁹ And as they were coming down from the mountain, Jesus commanded them, saying, 'Tell the vision to no one until the Son of Man has risen from the dead.'"

Introduction

This section is called the transfiguration. The term "transfiguration" is often mistakenly taken for a mere change in appearance. A man who takes off his dirty work clothes, washes his face, combs his hair and then puts on a suit and tie has undergone a change in appearance. Jesus did not have a mere change in "appearance." He had a transformation into His glorified state. The transformation took place about a week after the Holy Spirit revealed to Peter the Messiahship of Jesus (Matthew 17:1), when he said that Jesus was the, ***"Christ, the Son of the living God."*** (Matthew 16:16). The transfiguration is also recorded in Mark 9:2-8; Luke. 9:28-36. Throughout the gospel of John there is an ongoing emphasis of Jesus as the Divine Son of God. Surely John had thoughts of Jesus in His glorified state when he wrote in **John 1:14:** *"And the Word became flesh, and dwelt among us, and we beheld His glory, glory as of the only begotten from the Father, full of grace and truth."* We also know that the gospels do not contain all the acts or miracles that Jesus did. John said it this way:

> **John 21:24-25:** *"This is the disciple who bears witness of these things, and wrote these things; and we know that his witness is true. ²⁵ And there are also many other things which Jesus did, which if they *were written in detail, I suppose that even the world itself *would not contain the books which *were written."*

CHAPTER 16 VERSE 28: *"Truly I say to you, there are some of those who are standing here who shall not taste death until they see the Son of Man coming in His kingdom."*

> In this verse we see Jesus stating to His disciples that some of them would not die until they saw Him in His glory. The glory that would be revealed to them would be the transformation which

we read about in the first eight verses of Matthew 17. The Greek word for *"kingdom"* in Matthew 16:28 means "royal majesty."[310]

In addition to the gospel accounts, Peter himself states that he is a personal witness to this event described in Matthew 16:28 when he writes in his epistle:

2 Peter 1:16: *"For we did not follow cleverly devised tales when we made known to you the power and coming of our Lord Jesus Christ, but we were eyewitnesses of His majesty."*

CHAPTER 17:1 *"AND six days later Jesus *took with Him Peter and James and John his brother, and *brought them up to a high mountain by themselves."*

Jesus took Peter, James and John, His three closest disciples, up a mountain. We know from Matthew 16:13 that Jesus was in the area of Caesarea Philippi and thus the mountain that they went up was "probably Hermon, which rises to a height of 2,814 m above sea-level."[311]

Note that Scripture tells us that this event took place *"six days later."* The question is six days later from what? The answer is six days after Peter made the statement that Jesus was the *"Christ, the Son of the living God"* (Matthew 16:16). Those who do not carefully review this text in its context try to point to Luke 9:28 where Luke says *"some eight days after these sayings,…."* If read in its context, one notes that Luke goes on to recite all the events that took place and the days it took to complete them and not merely the start of the assent up the mountain which took place on day six (i.e. Matthew 17:1). Luke accounts for the time of the *entire event* (i.e. the events started on day six and then add one day going up the mountain and one day coming down, for a total of eight days, *"after these sayings."*). [312]

VERSE 2: *"And He was transfigured before them; and His face shone like the sun, and His garments became as white as light."*

---

[310] *Enhanced Strong's Lexicon*, (Oak Harbor, WA: Logos Research Systems, Inc.) 1995. Defines "Kingdom" as follows:
    1)   royal power, kingship, dominion, rule
        1a) not to be confused with an actual kingdom but rather the right or authority to rule over a kingdom,
        1b) of the royal power of Jesus as the triumphant Messiah,
        1c) of the royal power and dignity conferred on Christians in the Messiah's kingdom;
    2) a kingdom, the territory subject to the rule of a king;
    3) used in the N.T. to refer to the reign of the Messiah;

[311] Wood, D. R. W., and Marshall, I. H. (1996). *New Bible Dictionary (3rd ed.) (p. 1200). Leicester, England; Downers Grove, IL: InterVarsity Press.*

[312] The Ryrie Study Bible — Expanded edition: New American Standard, comment to Matthew 17:1.

Jesus had previously demonstrated His divinity by the powerful miracles that He performed (i.e. deeds). **John 2:11:** *"This beginning of His signs Jesus did in Cana of Galilee, <u>and manifested His glory</u>, and His disciples believed in Him."* But His transfiguration is the first time they saw His glory physically.

As was just mentioned, Jesus' transfiguration was not just a mere change in appearance, as if one had put on different clothes. Jesus underwent a change in form and gave the disciples a glimpse of Him in His glorified state as Messiah. The term *"transfigured"* comes from the Greek word that means, "to change into another form – *morphē* implying change, … Matthew 17:2; Mark 9:2." [313] It is from this Greek word that we get the word "metamorphosis." The disciples had always seen Jesus physically as a human man, but for this short moment they had a display of His divine glory. The Apostle John got another glimpse of the Almighty Son of God when he received the Revelation:

> **Revelation 1:12-18:** *"And I turned to see the voice that was speaking with me. And having turned I saw seven golden lampstands; [13] and in the middle of the lampstands one like a son of man, clothed in a robe reaching to the feet, and girded across His breast with a golden girdle. [14] And His head and His hair were white like white wool, like snow; and His eyes were like a flame of fire; [15] and His feet were like burnished bronze, when it has been caused to glow in a furnace, and His voice was like the sound of many waters. [16] And in His right hand He held seven stars; and out of His mouth came a sharp two-edged sword; and His face was like the sun shining in its strength. [17] And when I saw Him, I fell at His feet as a dead man. And He laid His right hand upon me, saying, 'Do not be afraid; I am the first and the last, [18] and the living One; and I was dead, and behold, I am alive forevermore, and I have the keys of death and of Hades.'"*

The writer of Hebrews wrote of Jesus' divinity when he said:

> **Hebrews 1:1-3:** *"GOD, after He spoke long ago to the fathers in the prophets in many portions and in many ways, [2] <u>in these last days has spoken to us in His Son</u>, whom He appointed heir of all things, through whom also He made the world. [3] And <u>He is the radiance of His glory and the exact representation of His nature, and upholds all things by the word of His power</u>. When He had made purification of sins, He sat down at the right hand of the Majesty on high;"*

VERSE 3: *"And behold, Moses and Elijah appeared to them, talking with Him."*

The appearance of Moses and Elijah also served as further confirmation to the disciples of Jesus' Messiahship. Moses represented God's work through the Old Covenant (i.e. the Old Testament law). As for the Prophets of the Old Testament, Elijah stands out as the great defender of God and one through whom God worked miracles. Remember that Elijah did not die but was taken up by God in a chariot of fire (2 Kings 2:11).

---

[313] Vine, W. E., *Vine's Expository Dictionary of Old and New Testament Words*, (Grand Rapids, MI: Fleming H. Revell) 1981.

In summary Moses and Elijah are Old Testament representatives of the "Law and the Prophets."

> **John 1:45:** *"Philip *found Nathanael and *said to him, 'We have found Him of whom <u>Moses in the Law and also the Prophets</u> wrote, Jesus of Nazareth, the son of Joseph.'"*

Jesus said:

> **Matthew 5:17:** *"Do not think that I came to abolish the <u>Law or the Prophets</u>; I did not come to abolish, but to fulfill."*

Jesus explained that the law and prophets all pointed to Him!

> **John 5:39:** *"You search the Scriptures, because you think that in them you have eternal life; and <u>it is these that bear witness of Me</u>;"*

Moses and Elijah did not just show up and stand by Jesus. Luke tells us that they discussed Jesus' coming death for the salvation of mankind. **Luke 9:30-31:** *"And behold, two men were talking with Him; and they were Moses and Elijah, 31 who, appearing in glory, were <u>speaking of His departure which He was about to accomplish at Jerusalem</u>."* The disciples often got upset when Jesus would speak of His death (Matthew 16:21-23), but these three disciples should have taken from this event that the divine plan was unfolding just as God would have it. The disciples did not need to fear that God's work was somehow being wrecked by the religious rulers.

One might recall the story when Moses spent time with God. Moses underwent a reflection of God's glory and his face shone brightly.

> **Exodus 34:29-33:** *"And it came about when Moses was coming down from Mount Sinai (and the two tablets of the testimony were in Moses' hand as he was coming down from the mountain), that Moses did not know that the skin of his face shone because of his speaking with Him. 30 So when Aaron and all the sons of Israel saw Moses, behold, the skin of his face shone, and they were afraid to come near him. 31 Then Moses called to them, and Aaron and all the rulers in the congregation returned to him; and Moses spoke to them. 32 And afterward all the sons of Israel came near, and he commanded them to do everything that the LORD had spoken to him on Mount Sinai. 33 When Moses had finished speaking with them, he put a veil over his face."*

Charles Spurgeon, wrote on the difference between the transformation of Jesus and that of Moses when he said:

> "How great the difference between Moses and Jesus! When the prophet of Horeb had been forty days upon the mountain, he underwent a kind of transfiguration, so that his countenance shone with exceeding brightness, <u>and he put a veil over his face, for the people could not endure to look upon his glory. Not so our Saviour. He had been transfigured with a greater glory than that of Moses, and yet, it is not written that the people were blinded by the blaze of his countenance, but rather they were amazed, and running to him they saluted him. The glory of the law repels, but the greater glory of Jesus attracts. Though Jesus is holy and just, yet blended with his purity there is so much of truth and grace, that sinners run to him amazed at his goodness, fascinated by his love;</u> they salute him, become his disciples, and take him to be their Lord and Master. Reader, it may be that just now you are blinded by the dazzling brightness of the law of God. You feel its claims on your conscience, but you cannot keep it in your life. Not that you find fault with the law, on the

contrary, it commands your profoundest esteem, still you are in nowise drawn by it to God; you are rather hardened in heart, and are verging towards desperation. Ah, poor heart! turn thine eye from Moses, with all his repelling splendor, and look to Jesus, resplendent with milder glories. Behold His flowing wounds and thorn-crowned head! He is the Son of God, and therein He is greater than Moses, but He is the Lord of love, and therein more tender than the lawgiver. He bore the wrath of God, and in His death revealed more of God's justice than Sinai on a blaze, but that justice is now vindicated, and henceforth it is the guardian of believers in Jesus. Look, sinner, to the bleeding Saviour, and as thou feelest the attraction of His love, fly to His arms, and thou shalt be saved." [314]

VERSE 4: *"And Peter answered and said to Jesus, 'Lord, it is good for us to be here; if You wish, I will make three tabernacles here, one for You, and one for Moses, and one for Elijah.'"*

Have you ever had something happen to you and you were so taken by surprise that the first thing that came out of your mouth may not have been the smartest thing you ever said? That is what may have happened to Peter here. Luke points that out in **Luke 9:33:**
> *"And it came about, as these were parting from Him, Peter said to Jesus, 'Master, it is good for us to be here; and let us make three tabernacles: one for You, and one for Moses, and one for Elijah'—not realizing what he was saying."*

One explanation for Peter's response is as follows:
> "New Testament chronologists have determined that the Jewish month in which the transfiguration took place was Tishri (October), the sixth month before Passover and therefore six months before Jesus' crucifixion. During this month the Jews celebrated the feast of Tabernacles, or Booths, and it is possible that at this very time the feast was being observed in Jerusalem. During a period of seven days the people lived in small shelters, or booths, made of boughs, symbolizing the temporary dwellings of their forefathers in the wilderness. It was a memorial to God's preserving His chosen and redeemed people (see Leviticus 23:33-44).
>
> Zechariah predicted that during the Millennium, when 'the Lord will be king over all the earth; in that day the Lord will be the only one, and His name the only one. Then it will come about that any who are left of all the nations that went against Jerusalem will go up from year to year to worship the King, the Lord of hosts, and to celebrate the Feast of Booths' (Zechariah 14:9, 16). That is the only week-long Old Testament festival that will be celebrated during the millennial reign of Christ. The feast of Tabernacles will be remembered every year for 1,000 years as a picture of God's deliverance and preservation of His people.
>
> The feast's being close at hand may therefore have caused Peter to suggest building the **three tabernacles** on the mountain. That possibility is even more likely in light of the fact that this festival commemorated the exodus from

---

[314] Spurgeon, Charles H., *Morning and Evening*, (Evening- August 26) (Oak Harbor, WA: Logos Research Systems, Inc.) 1995.

slavery in Egypt and the wilderness wanderings of Israel under Moses. As noted above, Moses and Elijah were talking with Jesus 'of His departure,' or exodus (Luke 9:31), the soon-coming and infinitely greater deliverance of believing mankind from sin."[315]

VERSES 5-8: *"While he was still speaking, behold, a bright cloud overshadowed them; and behold, a voice out of the cloud, saying, 'This is My beloved Son, with whom I am well-pleased; listen to Him!' [6] And when the disciples heard this, they fell on their faces and were much afraid. [7] And Jesus came to them and touched them and said, 'Arise, and do not be afraid.' [8] And lifting up their eyes, they saw no one, except Jesus Himself alone."*

First we have the witness of Jesus as Messiah by His transformation, and then we have the Old Testament witness via the presence of Moses and Elijah. Now we have the Father's statement confirming that Jesus was His **"beloved Son"** and thus the Messiah. Remember that the Father also said this when Jesus was being baptized (Matthew 3:17).

Matthew 17:5 states, *"a bright cloud overshadowed them...."* God had manifested Himself to His people by a cloud during the days while they were walking in the wilderness. **Exodus 13:21:** *"And the LORD was going before them in a pillar of cloud by day to lead them on the way,...."*
By the Father testifying of Jesus as His Son, He also was declaring the divinity of Jesus. Jesus was not just a great prophet or the best example of how a person should live; He is God. The writer of Hebrews said:

> **Hebrews 1:1-3, 5, 8:** *"GOD, after He spoke long ago to the fathers in the prophets in many portions and in many ways, [2] in these last days has spoken to us in His Son, whom He appointed heir of all things, through whom also He made the world. [3] And He is the radiance of His glory and the exact representation of His nature, and upholds all things by the word of His power. When He had made purification of sins, He sat down at the right hand of the Majesty on high; ....*
> *[v.5] For to which of the angels did He ever say,*
> *'THOU ART MY SON,*
> *TODAY I HAVE BEGOTTEN THEE'? And again, 'I WILL BE A FATHER TO HIM AND HE SHALL BE A SON TO ME'?....*
> *[v.8] But of the Son He says,*
> *'THY THRONE, O GOD, IS FOREVER AND EVER,*
> *AND THE RIGHTEOUS SCEPTER IS THE SCEPTER OF HIS KINGDOM.'"*

In Matthew 17:7 we again see the awesomeness of God compared to the puniness of man when the fear of God fell upon the disciples. At that fearful moment, we also see the loving grace of God to His children when He, *"...touched them and said, 'Arise, and do not be afraid.'"* (v.7). Compare the response at the transfiguration to the response the Lord gave John when he saw the glorified Christ in **Revelation 1:17-18:**

> *"And when I saw Him, I fell at His feet as a dead man. And He laid His right hand upon me, saying, 'Do not be afraid; I am the first and the last, [18] and the living One;*

---

[315] MacArthur, John F., *The MacArthur New Testament Commentary*, p.441 (Chicago: Moody Press) 1983.

and I was dead, and behold, I am alive forevermore, and I have the keys of death and of Hades.'"

In verse 7, there is also the statement of the Father which tells us that when Jesus speaks, we are to *"listen to Him."* Oh, how much trouble we would save ourselves if we only did!

VERSE 9: *"And as they were coming down from the mountain, Jesus commanded them, saying, 'Tell the vision to no one until the Son of Man has risen from the dead.'"*

Jesus tells His disciples not to tell others about what they just witnessed. We also remember Him telling His disciples not to tell others just yet that He was the Messiah (Matthew 16:20). The people had a fixed view that the Messiah would come to bring them military victory over Rome and any other enemies. If they found out that He indeed was the Messiah, would they try to make Him king? John tells us that after one of Jesus' miracles, the crowd was thinking about doing that very thing:

> **John 6:14-15:** *"When therefore the people saw the sign which He had performed, they said, 'This is of a truth the Prophet who is to come into the world.'* ¹⁵ *Jesus therefore perceiving that <u>they were intending to come and take Him by force</u>, to make Him king, withdrew again to the mountain by Himself alone."*

The true Messiah would come to defeat man's greatest enemy (i.e. sin and death). Since it would only be after Jesus' death and resurrection that some would understand this, they were told to not tell about what they saw until then.

Summary and Application

Jesus is the Messiah of mankind. It was confirmed by His transformation, as well as by Moses, Elijah, and the Father. When you die, will you be a believer whom Jesus puts His hand on and says, *"<u>...Do not be afraid; I am the first and the last</u>,* ¹⁸ *and the living One; and I was dead, and behold, I am alive forevermore, and I have the keys of death and of Hades."* **Revelation 1:17-18.** If not, you are of the unbelieving, who will be left in great fear and judgment. Repent now and put your faith in the great salvation work of Jesus Christ on the cross as the only basis for you to be forgiven.

> **Romans 3:21-24:** *"But now apart from the Law the righteousness of <u>God has been manifested, being witnessed by the Law and the Prophets</u>,* ²² *even the righteousness of <u>God through faith in Jesus Christ</u> for all those who believe; for there is no distinction;* ²³ *for all have sinned and fall short of the glory of God,* ²⁴ <u>*being justified as a gift by His grace through the redemption which is in Christ Jesus;*</u>*"*

MATTHEW 17:10-21
(INTERPRETATION OF PROPHESY;
FAITH THAT MOVES MOUNTAINS)

"And His disciples asked Him, saying, 'Why then do the scribes say that Elijah must come first?' [11] And He answered and said, 'Elijah is coming and will restore all things; [12] but I say to you, that Elijah already came, and they did not recognize him, but did to him whatever they wished. So also the Son of Man is going to suffer at their hands.' [13] Then the disciples understood that He had spoken to them about John the Baptist.

[14] And when they came to the multitude, a man came up to Him, falling on his knees before Him, and saying, [15] 'Lord, have mercy on my son, for he is a lunatic, and is very ill; for he often falls into the fire, and often into the water. [16] And I brought him to Your disciples, and they could not cure him.' [17] And Jesus answered and said, 'O unbelieving and perverted generation, how long shall I be with you? How long shall I put up with you? Bring him here to Me.' [18] And Jesus rebuked him, and the demon came out of him, and the boy was cured at once.

*[19] Then the disciples came to Jesus privately and said, 'Why could we not cast it out?' [20] And He *said to them, 'Because of the littleness of your faith; for truly I say to you, if you have faith as a mustard seed, you shall say to this mountain, 'Move from here to there,' and it shall move; and nothing shall be impossible to you. [21] [But this kind does not go out except by prayer and fasting.]"*

Introduction

In this section, we will see how necessary it is to have Holy Spirit-led wisdom when reading and understanding Scripture. Without the illumination of the Spirit, we are like the scribes who may have thought they understood the words of prophecy about Elijah, but did not recognize it when it was fulfilled before their eyes.

Also in this section we will examine the concept of faith. Jesus told His disciples they were ineffective because of *"the littleness of your faith;...."* What kind of faith is Jesus speaking of? Is it different than saving faith? No, they are the same faith. The faith for salvation or any other matter in the Christian life is faith purely set on God: only His power, only His righteousness, only His glory!

VERSES 10-13: *"And His disciples asked Him, saying, 'Why then do the scribes say that Elijah must come first?' [11] And He answered and said, 'Elijah is coming and will restore all things; [12] but I say to you, that Elijah already came, and they did not recognize him, but did to him whatever they wished. So also the Son of Man is going to suffer at their hands.' [13] Then the disciples understood that He had spoken to them about John the Baptist."*

These verses must be read in their context. Go back and read about the transfiguration in Matthew 17:1-9 first. In Matthew 17:3 we read, *"And behold, Moses and Elijah appeared to them, talking with Him."* Obviously, their seeing Elijah (v.3) spurred on the question that the disciples asked in verse 10, which says, *"Why then do the scribes say that Elijah must come first?"* The reason the scribes claimed this was based on an Old Testament prophecy that said Elijah would come:

>**Malachi 4:5-6:** *"Behold, I am going to <u>send you Elijah the prophet before the</u> <u>coming of the great and terrible day of the</u> LORD. 6 And he will restore the hearts of the fathers to their children, and the hearts of the children to their fathers, lest I come and smite the land with a curse."*

Jesus then tells them that, *"Elijah already came, and they did not recognize him,... Then the disciples understood that He had spoken to them about John the Baptist."* In Matthew 11 Jesus tells the disciples point blank that John the Baptist was the Elijah to come, as prophesied in Malachi 4:5-6:

>**Matthew 11:11-14:** *"Truly, I say to you, among those born of women there has not arisen anyone greater than John the Baptist; yet he who is least in the kingdom of heaven is greater than he. 12 And from the days of John the Baptist until now the kingdom of heaven suffers violence, and violent men take it by force. 13 For all the prophets and the Law prophesied until <u>John. 14 And if you</u> <u>care to accept it, he himself is Elijah, who was to come."</u>*

This was not to mean that Elijah was reincarnated. John himself denied being the resurrected Elijah (John 1:21). The verse means that John would be as powerful and great a prophet as Elijah. Look at what the angel said to John's father, Zechariah.

>**Luke 1:16-17:** *"And he will turn back many of the sons of Israel to the Lord their God. 17 "And it is he who will go as a forerunner before Him <u>in the spirit</u> <u>and power of Elijah, ..."</u>*

In **Matthew 17:12** Jesus says *"... but I say to you, that Elijah already came, and they did not recognize him, but did to him whatever they wished. So also the Son of Man is going to suffer at their hands."* Jesus is making reference to the murder of John the Baptist, which is recorded for us in Matthew 14:1-12. (See comments for Matthew 14:1-12 for more detail on this subject.)

Jesus prophesied that just as they mistreated and murdered John, so they would do to Him. We see that abuse did occur later on.

>**Matthew 27:27-31:** *"Then the soldiers of the governor took Jesus into the Praetorium and gathered the whole Roman cohort around Him. 28 And they stripped Him, and put a scarlet robe on Him. 29 And after weaving a crown of thorns, they put it on His head, and a reed in His right hand; and they kneeled down before Him and mocked Him, saying, 'Hail, King of the Jews!' 30 And they spat on Him, and took the reed and began to beat Him on the head. 31 And after they had mocked Him, they took His robe off and put His garments on Him, and led Him away to crucify Him."*

We must remember that as Christ's followers we should expect the same treatment. Jesus said:

>**John 15:18-20:** *"If the world hates you, you know that it has hated Me before it hated you. 19 If you were of the world, the world would love its own; but because you are not of the world, but I chose you out of the world, therefore the world hates you. 20 Remember the word that I said to you, <u>'A slave is not</u> <u>greater than his master.' If they persecuted Me, they will also persecute you; if</u> <u>they kept My word, they will keep yours also."</u>*

VERSES 14-18: *"And when they came to the multitude, a man came up to Him, falling on his knees before Him, and saying, 15 'Lord, have mercy on my son, for he is a lunatic, and is very ill; for he often falls into the fire, and often into the water. 16 And I brought him to Your disciples, and they could not cure him.' 17 And Jesus answered and said, 'O unbelieving and perverted generation, how long shall I be with you? How long shall I put up with you? Bring him here to Me.' 18 And Jesus rebuked him, and the demon came out of him, and the boy was cured at once."*

Note that the disciples who, *"could not cure him,"*(v.16) did **not** include the three who saw the transfiguration (i.e. Peter, James and John, His three closest disciples). It was the remaining nine disciples.

We read that this man who came to Jesus had a son (his only son — Luke 9:38). We also know that the son suffered from an evil spirit which made him *"mute"* (Mark 9:17), *"deaf"* (Mark 9:25), and *"dashes him to the ground and he foams at the mouth, and grinds his teeth, and stiffens out...."* (Mark 9:18). The demon also *"...has often thrown him both into the fire and into the water to destroy him...."* (Mark 9:22; Matthew 17:15). How painful this must have been for the father to watch his son suffer like this from *"childhood"* (Mark 9:21).

The disciples were bewildered about why they could not heal the boy. Jesus had sent the disciples out before and they had seen the power of God work through them in the past.

> **Mark 6:7, 12-13:** *"And He *summoned the twelve and began to send them out in pairs; and He was giving them authority over the unclean spirits;....*
> *12 And they went out and preached that men should repent. 13 And they were casting out many demons and were anointing with oil many sick people and healing them."*

Maybe some of the disciples became used to God working through them and had neglected prayer. Maybe they were less thoughtful of the fact that it was God's power and not their own that resulted in the miracles. We know Jesus told them they were not able to be used by God to heal because they were not spiritually built up in *"prayer and fasting"* (v.21).

Jesus is amazed at the lack of faith of the disciples, who have been with Him all this time, and the crowd that was there (v.17). We read from the account in Mark that the father of this boy was struggling with His own faith. This man did what we should do when our faith is weak — turn to God to help us!

> **Mark 9:22-24:** *"'And it has often thrown him both into the fire and into the water to destroy him. But if You can do anything, take pity on us and help us!'*
> *23 And Jesus said to him, 'If You can! All things are possible to him who believes.' 24 Immediately the boy's father cried out and began saying, 'I do believe; help my unbelief.'"*

The man of this boy said to Jesus,*"...But if You can do anything"* Christ was shocked at this man's statement and said, *"If You can!"* Of course Jesus can. He is God and has total power and control over absolutely everything!

We see in verse 18 that Jesus rebuked the demon. Mark's account gives us more detail on what was said:

> **Mark 9:25-27:** *"...He rebuked the unclean spirit, saying to it, 'You deaf and dumb spirit, I command you, come out of him and do not enter him again.' 26*

And after crying out and throwing him into terrible convulsions, it came out; and the boy became so much like a corpse that most of them said, 'He is dead!' [27] But Jesus took him by the hand and raised him; and he got up."

VERSES 19-21: *"Then the disciples came to Jesus privately and said, 'Why could we not cast it out?' [20] And He *said to them, 'Because of the littleness of your faith; for truly I say to you, if you have faith as a mustard seed, you shall say to this mountain, 'Move from here to there,' and it shall move; and nothing shall be impossible to you. [21] [But this kind does not go out except by prayer and fasting.]'"*

Notice that after the healing, the disciples went into a house (Mark 9:28), and then the *"…disciples came to Jesus privately and said, 'Why could we not cast it out?'"* **Matthew 17:19.** Jesus told them that it was the *"littleness of your faith."* Jesus had confronted them before about the littleness of their faith:

> **Matthew 8:24-26:** *"And behold, there arose a great storm in the sea, so that the boat was covered with the waves; but He Himself was asleep. [25] And they came to Him, and awoke Him, saying, 'Save us, Lord; we are perishing!' [26] And He *said to them, <u>'Why are you timid, you men of little faith?'</u> Then He arose, and rebuked the winds and the sea; and it became perfectly calm."*

> **Matthew 14:29-32:** *"And Peter got out of the boat, and walked on the water and came toward Jesus. [30]But seeing the wind, he became afraid, and beginning to sink, he cried out, saying, 'Lord, save me!' [31]And immediately Jesus stretched out His hand and took hold of him, and *said to him, <u>'O you of little faith, why did you doubt?'</u> [32]And when they got into the boat, the wind stopped."*

Littleness of faith not only distorts our view of God, it also prevents us from clearly hearing His Word and rightly discerning it.

> **Matthew 16:6-8, 11-12:** *"And Jesus said to them, 'Watch out and beware of the leaven of the Pharisees and Sadducees.' [7] And they began to discuss among themselves, saying, 'It is because we took no bread.' [8] But Jesus, aware of this, said, <u>'You men of little faith</u>, why do you discuss among yourselves that you have no bread? ….*
> *[11] <u>How is it that you do not understand that I did not speak to you concerning bread?</u> But beware of the leaven of the Pharisees and Sadducees.' [12] Then they understood that He did not say to beware of the leaven of bread, but of the teaching of the Pharisees and Sadducees."*

In Matthew 17:20 Jesus says, *"…if you have faith as a mustard seed, you shall say to this mountain, 'Move from here to there,' and it shall move; and nothing shall be impossible to you."*
It says in **Hebrews 11:6:** *"And <u>without faith it is impossible to please Him</u>, for he who comes to God must believe that He is, and that He is a rewarder of those who seek Him."*

When Jesus is talking about faith, he means having faith in God— not *faith in faith*.[316]

One should not think that being "saved by faith" is a different faith than employed in being used by God to do miracles. The faith for salvation or anything in the Christian life is faith purely set on God.

> **Romans 4:1-3:** *"What then shall we say that Abraham, our forefather, discovered in this matter? ²If, in fact, Abraham was justified by works, he had something to boast about—but not before God. ³What does the Scripture say? 'Abraham believed God, and it was credited to him as righteousness.'"*

> **Luke 10:17-20:** *"And the seventy returned with joy, saying, 'Lord, even the demons are subject to us in Your name.' ¹⁸And He said to them, 'I was watching Satan fall from heaven like lightning. ¹⁹Behold, I have given you authority to tread upon serpents and scorpions, and over all the power of the enemy, and nothing shall injure you. ²⁰Nevertheless do not rejoice in this, that the spirits are subject to you, but rejoice that your names are recorded in heaven.'"*

> **1 John 3:8:** *"...The Son of God appeared for this purpose, that He might destroy the works of the devil."*

What does it mean to "have faith?" Does it merely mean that you have an opinion in which you will agree that Jesus lived and died and rose from the dead? The answer to that question is, "No!" Even the demons acknowledge the facts of Jesus' perfect work on the cross, yet they are not saved.

> **James 2:19:** *"You believe that God is one. You do well; the demons also believe, and shudder."*

R.C. Sproul wrote:

> "Faith includes believing in God. Yet that kind of faith is not particularly praiseworthy. James writes, 'You believe that there is one God. You do well. Even the demons believe—and tremble!' (James 2:19). Here sarcasm drips from James's pen. To believe in the existence of God merely qualifies us to be demons. It is one thing to believe in God; it is another thing to believe God. To believe God, to trust in Him for our very life, is the essence of the Christian faith."[317]

---

[316] When I use the term, "faith in faith" I am referencing to the heretical "word of faith" teaching: i.e. "prosperity gospel" or also called "name it and claim it" or "blab it and grab it." In my generation there are many false prophets who teach this seductive view who include the infamous Benny Hinn, Kenneth Copeland and many others (Matthew 7:15-23). Their false gospel has spread around the world. I have personally witnessed the spiritual cancer this teaching has implanted in America and through exploitation of the poor in Africa. When I speak of true faith, it means faith only in God and not ourselves or any power of our own. I am speaking of Holy Spirit led faith and humble submission to God's Word: **Genesis 15:6:** *"Then he believed in the Lord; and He reckoned it to him as righteousness."* **Romans 10:17**: *"So faith comes from hearing, and hearing by the word of Christ."*

As you can see, *saving faith* is much more than just having an opinion about Jesus. Jesus preached that the only way to escape from hell is to *"repent and believe in the gospel."* **Mark 1:15**

- To *REPENT* means to turn from your sins and forsake them by the power of God.
- To **BELIEVE THE GOSPEL** means that one who is "born again" by the Spirit of God (John 3:3-8) will:
  - Believe in Jesus Christ as Almighty God, who is without sin;
  - Believe in Jesus' sacrificial death on the cross as the only and complete payment for your sins;
  - Believe in Jesus' bodily resurrection from the dead on the third day;
  - Believe in Jesus as Lord over all things and confesses this fact to others.

It is that straightforward. It has nothing to do with your righteousness, good works or engaging in a religious ceremony or cleaning yourself up first to win God's acceptance. If you reject God's loving gift of forgiveness in Jesus Christ, you remain a guilty sinner waiting to be punished in eternal hell. The Bible says *in* **John 3:36:** *"He who believes in the Son has eternal life; but he who does not obey the Son will not see life, but the wrath of God abides on him."* Repent and believe the gospel TODAY, before it is too late!

It is this simplicity of the Gospel that so many find repugnant. Repentance is not works-based righteousness. Repentance comes from God (**2 Timothy 2:25:** *"God may grant them repentance leading to the knowledge of the truth,"*). In this world, the true believer will continue to battle the sinful flesh and temptations. At times he will fail (Romans 7:14-25, 1 John 1:10), but one cannot say he truly believes in God and not turn from sin to God.

> **John 14:21:** *"He who has My commandments and keeps them is the one who loves Me; and he who loves Me will be loved by My Father, and I will love him and will ᶜdisclose Myself to him."*

Summary and Application

So the question becomes, "How can I increase my faith?" It does not come as a result of being intellectual: **1 Corinthians 2:5:** *"...that your faith should not rest on the wisdom of men, but on the power of God."* **2 Corinthians 5:7:** *"...for we walk by faith, not by sight."* Faith is not self-generated as some heretics have tried to teach. Faith is a *"gift of God;"* **Ephesians 2:8**. As it says in **Romans 12:3:** *"...as God has allotted to each a measure of faith."* We also know that studying God's Word increases our faith: **Romans 10:17:** *"faith comes from hearing, and hearing by the word of Christ."* We have learned from the lesson in Matthew 17:19-21 that we need to also pray and fast. [Please see also the comments on *fasting* set out in Matthew 6:16-18 of this commentary.]

---

[317] Sproul, R. C., *Essential Truths of the Christian Faith*, Topic 64 – Faith (Wheaton, Illinois: Tyndale House Publishers, Inc.) 1992.

MATTHEW 17:22-27
(CONCERNING HIS DEATH/RESURRECTION; AND TAXES)

"And while they were gathering together in Galilee, Jesus said to them, 'The Son of Man is going to be delivered into the hands of men; ²³ *and they will kill Him, and He will be raised on the third day.' And they were deeply grieved.*

²⁴ *And when they had come to Capernaum, those who collected the two-drachma tax came to Peter, and said, 'Does your teacher not pay the two-drachma tax?'* ²⁵ *He *said, 'Yes.' And when he came into the house, Jesus spoke to him first, saying, 'What do you think, Simon? From whom do the kings of the earth collect customs or poll-tax, from their sons or from strangers?'* ²⁶ *And upon his saying, 'From strangers,' Jesus said to him, 'Consequently the sons are exempt.* ²⁷ *But, lest we give them offense, go to the sea, and throw in a hook, and take the first fish that comes up; and when you open its mouth, you will find a stater. Take that and give it to them for you and Me.'"*

Introduction

When we hear the Lord speak to us through the Bible, we need to examine carefully all that He says. We need to pray for God to give us His Holy Spirit-led wisdom so that we can comprehend His truths and obey them. If we view His words from a fleshly point of view, we will miss the great truth and victory in them. We will fail to see that the Cross represents victory and not defeat.

Another issue addressed in this section is the Christian's responsibility to government, especially to pay our taxes. The issue is one of submission to God.

VERSES 22-23: *"And while they were gathering together in Galilee, Jesus said to them, 'The Son of Man is going to be delivered into the hands of men;* ²³ *and they will kill Him, and He will be raised on the third day.' And they were deeply grieved."*

In these verses Jesus again reminds His disciples of His mission. It was not to come and overthrow Rome, but rather to die for mankind. Jesus was the sinless, almighty God who would be raised from the dead. This was not the first time they had heard about this, because Jesus began to explain to the disciples about His death and resurrection back in **Matthew 16:21**:

> *"From that time Jesus Christ began to show His disciples* *that He must go to Jerusalem, and suffer many things from the elders and chief priests and scribes, and be killed, and be raised up on the third day."*

It must also be remembered that Jesus was not some helpless victim at the hands of evil men. Jesus willingly laid down His life for our sins.

> **John 10:17-18:** *"For this reason the Father loves Me, because I lay down My life that I may take it again.* ¹⁸ *No one has taken it away from Me, but I lay it down on My own initiative. I have authority to lay it down, and* *I have authority to take it up again. This commandment I received from My Father."*

Notice from the text in Matthew 17:2-23 how selective the disciples' hearing was. They heard the part about death but they either did not understand or ignored the part that, *"He will be raised on the third day."* We know that they did not understand the power of the resurrection, because their response to all that Jesus said was, *"...they were deeply grieved."* (Matthew 17:23). Luke gives us more insight into their response when finding out that Jesus would be handed over to evil men when he wrote in **Luke 9:45:**

> *"But they did not understand this statement, and it was concealed from them so that they might not perceive it; and they were afraid to ask Him about this statement."*

How many times do we let our preconceived views about God get in the way of what His word really says? Many of the people in Jesus' time saw the Messiah as simply their deliverer from Rome and other enemies. They did not see that their eternal soul was much more important than independence from Rome. The Messiah came to save them from hell.

> **Matthew 1:21:** *"...you shall call His name Jesus, for it is He who will save His people from their sins."*

What preconceived and unbiblical attitudes do you bring to the Bible that hinder you from understanding what God is saying? For example, if you are one who was told early in your church life that God does not do miracles in modern times, you will not read the Bible with a complete faith in God. You will not know that the same miracle-working power God demonstrated as Jesus walked the earth still exists today.

> **Hebrews 13:8-9:** *"Jesus Christ is the same yesterday and today, yes and forever. 9 Do not be carried away by varied and strange teachings; for it is good for the heart to be strengthened by grace,...."*

> **Romans 11:29:** *"...for the gifts and the calling of God are irrevocable."*

> **Romans 14:23:** *"...and whatever is not from faith is sin."*

We should pray before we read God's word, asking Him to enlighten us by His Holy Spirit that we might know His will for our lives.

> **John 14:26:** *"But the Helper, the Holy Spirit, whom the Father will send in My name, He will teach you all things, and bring to your remembrance all that I said to you."*

VERSES 24-27: *"And when they had come to Capernaum, those who collected the two-drachma tax came to Peter, and said, 'Does your teacher not pay the two-drachma tax?' 25 He *said, 'Yes.' And when he came into the house, Jesus spoke to him first, saying, 'What do you think, Simon? From whom do the kings of the earth collect customs or poll-tax, from their sons or from strangers?' 26 And upon his saying, 'From strangers,' Jesus said to him, 'Consequently the sons are exempt. 27 But, lest we give them offense, go to the sea, and throw in a hook, and take the first fish that comes up; and when you open its mouth, you will find a stater. Take that and give it to them for you and Me.'"*

The tax collectors in Capernaum went to Peter and asked him if Jesus paid the tax. These tax collectors were not the publican tax collectors appointed by Rome. The tax involved here was also referred to as the temple tax. "[E]very Jew 20 years old and above was required to pay a **temple tax** of half a shekel or two drachmas each year to help support the temple."[318]

The tax collectors in verse 24 may have been trying to trap Jesus as a person who was not following the law (cf. Exodus 30:13-15; Nehemiah 10:32). The religious leaders made a more direct attempt at entrapping Jesus regarding taxes later as we read in **Matthew 22:15-22:**

> *"Then the Pharisees went and counseled together how they might trap Him in what He said. 16 And they *sent their disciples to Him, along with the Herodians, saying, 'Teacher, we know that You are truthful and teach the way of God in truth, and defer to no one; for You are not partial to any. 17 Tell us therefore, what do You think? Is it lawful to give a poll-tax to Caesar, or not?'18 But Jesus perceived their malice, and said, 'Why are you testing Me, you hypocrites? 19 Show Me the coin used for the poll-tax.' And they brought Him a denarius. 20 And He *said to them, 'Whose likeness and inscription is this?' 21 They *said to Him, 'Caesar's.' Then He *said to them, 'Then render to Caesar the things that are Caesar's; and to God the things that are God's.' 22 And hearing this, they marveled, and leaving Him, they went away."*

In Matthew 17:25 Jesus asked Peter if kings collected taxes from the royal family or whether taxes were collected from subjects who were not *royals*. In other words, should the king of the temple have to pay taxes to the temple? The answer is, "No"! The next question is, who is the King of the Temple of God? Remember what Jesus said about the temple when he was a young boy?

> **Luke 2:49:** *"And He said to them, 'Why is it that you were looking for Me? Did you not know that I had to be in My Father's house?'"*

Look also at what He said to the Pharisees about His presence on earth in **Matthew 12:6:** *"But I say to you, that something greater than the temple is here."*

Peter acknowledged that it was not from the royal family that taxes were to be raised, but from others. Jesus had explained earlier that the temple had been defiled and turned into *"a ROBBERS DEN"* (Mark 11:17). Despite the conduct that occurred at the temple, Jesus told Peter that He still would pay the tax, *"lest we give them offense."* If Jesus willingly paid a tax that He was completely exempt from to a very corrupt group, no Christian can claim that he is exempt from paying taxes because of the evil the government ends up doing with their money. Christians are not endorsing ungodly behavior or ungodly leadership when they pay taxes, but instead are submitting to a higher authority, God Himself:

> **Romans 13:1-2, 6-7:** *"LET every person be in subjection to the governing authorities. For there is no authority except from God, and those which exist are established by God. 2 Therefore he who resists authority has opposed the ordinance of God; and they who have opposed will receive condemnation upon themselves....*
> *6 For because of this you also pay taxes, for rulers are servants of God, devoting themselves to this very thing. 7 Render to all what is due them: tax to whom tax is due; custom to whom custom; fear to whom fear; honor to whom honor."*

As we study the lesson here, let us not miss the great miracle that took place. In verse 27, it tells us how Jesus was going to pay for the tax.

---

[318] Walvoord, John F., and Zuck, Roy B., *The Bible Knowledge Commentary*, p. 61 (Wheaton, Illinois: Scripture Press Publications, Inc.) 1983, 1985.

Matthew 17:27:   27 *"But, lest we give them offense, go to the sea, and throw in a hook , and take the first fish that comes up; and when you open its mouth, you will find a stater. Take that and give it to them for you and Me."*

Here we see the divinity of Christ in providing the fish with the coin. This was surely a great faith lesson to Peter. Peter was a professional fisherman, who never caught a fish that had a coin in its mouth! He now had to walk in faith and obey when Jesus told him to *"take the first fish that comes up; and when you open its mouth"* get the needed money. One of the faith lessons we can learn here is that God is our all-sufficient provider. He is the creator of all things and has even given fish for man to rule over:

Psalm 8:6-8:
"Thou dost make him to rule over the works of Thy hands;
  Thou hast put all things under his feet,
 7 All sheep and oxen,
  And also the beasts of the field,
 8 The birds of the heavens, and the fish of the sea,
  Whatever passes through the paths of the seas.*"*

Summary and Application

We must read God's Word in complete faith, being led by the Holy Spirit, so that we do not hear just part of what God speaks to us. Likewise, our conduct to an on-looking world must be exemplary in our submission to God as the ultimate authority.

MATTHEW 18:1-11
(SERVANT LEADERSHIP; CHILDREN; STUMBLING FROM SIN)

"AT that time the disciples came to Jesus, saying, 'Who then is greatest in the kingdom of heaven?' ² And He called a child to Himself and set him before them, ³ and said, 'Truly I say to you, unless you are converted and become like children, you shall not enter the kingdom of heaven. ⁴ Whoever then humbles himself as this child, he is the greatest in the kingdom of heaven. ⁵ And whoever receives one such child in My name receives Me; ⁶ but whoever causes one of these little ones who believe in Me to stumble, it is better for him that a heavy millstone be hung around his neck, and that he be drowned in the depth of the sea.

⁷ Woe to the world because of its stumbling blocks! For it is inevitable that stumbling blocks come; but woe to that man through whom the stumbling block comes! ⁸ And if your hand or your foot causes you to stumble, cut it off and throw it from you; it is better for you to enter life crippled or lame, than having two hands or two feet, to be cast into the eternal fire. ⁹ And if your eye causes you to stumble, pluck it out, and throw it from you. It is better for you to enter life with one eye, than having two eyes, to be cast into the fiery hell. ¹⁰ See that you do not despise one of these little ones, for I say to you, that their angels in heaven continually behold the face of My Father who is in heaven. ¹¹ [For the Son of Man has come to save that which was lost.]'"

Introduction

As you read through Matthew 18, look to see how this chapter discusses our conduct as believers in the church. A couple of specific church issues you will see addressed are power struggles in 18:1-6 and false teaching in 18:7-9. The middle of the chapter (18:12-14) sets forth the importance of reaching out to the weak and backslidden. Matthew 18:15-20 addresses church discipline and prayer. The chapter concludes by discussing the important issue of forgiving others who have sinned against us in 18:21-35.

In our earthly world, great leaders and kings are often proud, arrogant and exalt themselves. The kingdom of heaven is just the opposite. One cannot enter the kingdom of heaven unless he humbles himself and comes to God like a child, seeking forgiveness in Christ. This is very different than appearing as a self-exalting conqueror. This world says, "get it for yourself," but God says that the one who is rich is the one who gives. This world says that the leader is the one who everyone serves, but God says that the leader is the one who serves everybody else. What a tragedy it will be for many who die and find out that the world system and ideals that they were living under were a lie from Satan himself. The Bible tells us that Satan runs the world system:

> **1 John 5:19:** *"We know that we are of God, and the whole world lies in the power of the evil one."*

Those in Christ are not of this world's system:

> **John 15:19:** *"If you were of the world, the world would love its own; but <u>because you are not of the world, but I chose you out of the world</u>, therefore the world hates you."*

How thankful we are to God for His mercy on us that He has not left us under the world system: **John 14:18:** *"I will not leave you as orphans; I will come to you...."* We are also thankful that Christ has conquered this world's system:

> **1 John 3:8:** *"...The Son of God appeared for this purpose, that <u>He might destroy the works of the devil</u>."*

VERSES 1-4 *"At that time the disciples came to Jesus, saying, 'Who then is greatest in the kingdom of heaven?'* [2] *And He called a child to Himself and set him before them,* [3] *and said, 'Truly I say to you, unless you are converted and become like children, you shall not enter the kingdom of heaven.* [4] *Whoever then humbles himself as this child, he is the greatest in the kingdom of heaven.'"*

The disciples are seen jockeying for position in the kingdom of heaven. We read from Luke 9:46 that the disciples were actually arguing about which one of them would be the *greatest*. Mark 9:33-34 tells us that when Jesus asked them what they were talking about, they were embarrassed about their attitudes. Here in Matthew 18 Jesus destroys their view of leadership by setting a child in front of them. A child does not represent a great warrior or a king who commands fear and respect. A child represents one that has not seared his heart, but instead comes with faith and humility before God with his needs. As for the proud and self-righteous, he sees no need for a savior, thus his place will be in hell. Truly the Kingdom of God operates opposite to this world, as Jesus said in **Matthew 20:16:** *"Thus the last shall be first, and the first last."*

This is a lesson for the church. The believers are called children of God:

John 1:12: *"But as many as received Him, to them He gave the <u>right to become children of God</u>, even to those who believe in His name."*

We are not to fight for position, power, or self-importance in the house of God since **1 Corinthians 8:6** tells us that:

"...for us there is but one God, the Father, from whom are all things, and we exist for Him; and one Lord, Jesus Christ, by whom are all things, and we exist through Him."

Matthew Henry points out that:

"Converting grace makes us like little children, not foolish as children (1 Corinthians 14:20), nor fickle (Ephesians 4:14), nor playful (ch. 11:16); but, as children, we must desire the sincere milk of the word (1 Peter 2:2); as children, we must be careful for nothing, but leave it to our heavenly Father to care for us (ch. 6:31); we must, as children, be harmless and inoffensive, and void of malice (1 Corinthians 14:20), governable, and under command (Galatians 4:2); and (which is here chiefly intended) we must be humble as little children." [319]

In our world, almost all institutions work in a corporate structure. The corporation has some workers it considers of lowest value and it also has others that it considers skilled and thus more valuable. The corporation then has bosses who are even more important and can yell out orders that others must do or be fired. Then there are bosses over the bosses. On top of all that is a president of the corporation in whom everyone in the organization must obey. The structure of the Lord's work on earth is very different from the corporate structure. The church is considered a body: **Colossians 1:24:** *"...I do my share on behalf of His body, which is the church...."* Even the smallest function of the body is very important for the good of all:

1 Corinthians 12:24-25: *"...But God has so composed the body, giving more abundant honor to that member which lacked,* [25] *that there should be no division in the body, but that the members should have the same care for one another."*

---

[319] Henry, M. (1994). *Matthew Henry's Commentary on the Whole Bible: Complete and Unabridged in One Volume* (Matthew 18:1–6). Peabody: Hendrickson.

We do not have bosses, but elders. Elders are to conduct themselves as *shepherds* and not corporate *board members*. They are supposed to take care of people spiritually, and never enrich or empower themselves. The church is not a democracy. Elders/Deacons are not representatives of the people; they are representatives of God. Their opinions are not to be influenced by what a segment in the congregation wants, or what a wealthy contributor wants, or what the pastor wants, or what their own family members want, etc. They are not to exalt themselves nor pander to people's flesh; like a politician solidifying his political base. They are to be men leading the church to do the will of Christ, as revealed in His Word. They are bound by the Word of God. Opinions, ideas or programs; as wonderful as they may sound, are rejected when they are contrary to the Word of God. Elders are accountable to God:

> **1 Peter 5:2-3:** *"...shepherd the flock of God among you, <u>exercising oversight not under compulsion, but voluntarily</u>, according to the will of God; and not for sordid gain, but with eagerness; ³ <u>nor yet as lording it over those allotted to your charge,</u> but proving to be examples to the flock."*

We are a family and are to address each other as such:

> **1 Timothy 5:1-2:** *"Do not sharply rebuke an older man, but rather <u>appeal to him as a father, to the younger men as brothers, ² the older women as mothers, and the younger women as sisters</u>, in all purity."*

VERSES 5-6: *"And whoever receives one such child in My name receives Me; ⁶ but whoever causes one of these little ones who believe in Me to stumble, it is better for him that a heavy millstone be hung around his neck, and that he be drowned in the depth of the sea."*

God is very protective of His children. This section applies to causing a young believer to stumble *regardless of his physical age.* Jesus points out in Matthew 25 that sharing Christian love and kindness to one who may be considered unimportant to the world, is the same as showing love to Christ Himself.

> **Matthew 25:40:** *"And the King will answer and say to them, 'Truly I say to you, <u>to the extent that you did it to one of these brothers of Mine, even the least of them, you did it to Me.'"*

Jesus also declared in **Matthew 10:42:** *"And whoever in the name of a <u>disciple gives to one of these little ones even a cup of cold water to drink, truly I say to you he shall not lose his reward."*

The young believer is so valuable to Christ that if a person discourages a child from believing in Christ and/or encourages him to sin, there is a very severe judgment to come: *"...it is better for him that a heavy millstone be hung around his neck, and that he be drowned in the depth of the sea."* (v.6). It is often taught that God uses His angels on behalf of His children. Scripture validates that view as we read in **Matthew 18:10:** *"See that you <u>do not despise one of these little ones</u>, for I say to you, that <u>their angels in heaven continually behold the face of My Father</u> who is in heaven."*

God is very protective of His children. It is for that reason that we must be very careful who we put in positions of teaching and authority in the church. Many churches appear comfortable putting unqualified people in positions of authority over children/young believers. I have watched those in leadership suggest an individual be placed as a Sunday School teacher to get that person, *"involved in the church."* If you protest, you will be accused of being unloving. The Devil knows that an unqualified Christian or non-believer is the perfect person to have misleading children about God. In the same manner, one should be equally concerned about who educates his children. I mention this because I teach the Bible to teenagers and I have had students tell me of experiences in school where a teacher has spent class time denigrating the Bible, their faith, or God's creation of the world.

Warren Wiersbe explains Matthew 18:5-6 by stating:

"It is a dangerous thing to look down on the children, because God values them highly. When we welcome a child (or a Christian believer), we welcome Christ (Matthew 18:5). The Father cares for them and the angels watch over them (Matthew 18:10). Like the good shepherd, God seeks the lost and saves them; and we must not cause them to perish. If the shepherd goes after an adult sheep, how much more important is it that he protect the lambs!

In these days of child neglect and child abuse, we need to take Christ's warning seriously. It is better to drown with a heavy millstone around one's neck, than to abuse a child and face the judgment of God (Matthew 18:6)." [320]

(Addendum 1 of 2)

Additional thoughts on children…

We live in a very evil time. Children are severely devalued. In this world, many children are abused both physically and sexually. Some politicians sell-out children believing they can get more votes if they promise to allow mothers to kill their children through abortion. Many young parents see children as kind of a "necessary nuisance," while others have chosen to forgo parenting altogether. They would much rather have bigger houses and nicer cars than assume the responsibility of completely caring for the child that God created and gave them. Our society warehouses its children in daycares. The daycares are packed, but these kids are not all children of struggling moms who are forced to work to feed their family. Drive by a daycare from 7:30-8:00 a.m. any Monday through Friday. You will see well-dressed women dashing out of very expensive vehicles to quickly dispose of their sleepy, irritable and sometimes crying children. Some kids do not even have their hair combed. The career-oriented parents may own a big, beautiful home, but during the day it is not full of the sounds of children laughing and playing. The home is empty, while the parents mortgage their children's care, and their parental influence, to someone else.

We can encourage our daughters to pursue a truly godly and great education and career, but when the time comes for her and her husband to bring a child into the world, they must realize the seriousness of parenting before God. It is then that a couple must quit living only for themselves and the wife can now use her quality education to help her be an excellent mother in the home, raising healthy and well-adjusted children. [As a prosecutor of approximately 28 years I have seen the consequences when this does not happen, irrespective of the socio-economic class the child grew up in.]

---

[320] Wiersbe, W. W. (1996). *The Bible exposition commentary* (Matthew 18:1). Wheaton, IL: Victor Books.

Another mistake of modern parenting is that *good parents* have their child in an endless array of sports, fine arts, and other activities so that the family's life is constantly racing around from one event to another. I know of a pastor who for years would not firmly preach from the pulpit against families being gone from church on Sunday mornings to attend youth sporting events. When you live like that, you are teaching your child that his pee-wee soccer (or any other activity) is more important than worshiping God. You are causing, "... *one of these little ones who believe in Me to stumble.*" <u>Matthew 18:6.</u>

These thoughts are definitely not directed at the dear single mom, or the women married to a healthy but irresponsible husband (i.e. one who is not disabled, yet remains unwilling to work). My heart goes out deeply for the woman who would love to be at home with her kids, but basic necessities have forced her to work. These are all very difficult situations.

My concern is for the mother of children who works outside of the home simply to elevate or maintain a materialistic lifestyle. My objective is not to condemn, but it is rather a call to repentance in a society that has devalued its children to warehouse status, and a church that has abandoned Scripture for materialism.

> <u>Titus 2:4-5:</u> "*...so that they may <u>encourage the young women to love their husbands, to love their children, 5 to be sensible, pure, workers at home,</u> kind, being subject to their own husbands, that the word of God may not be dishonored.*"

(Addendum 2 of 2)

Christianity's high value of women and motherhood.

Feminist theology mock traditional motherhood and distort the term "submission." <u>Scripture never teaches that women are in anyway second class in the church, home or God's eyes</u>. A different role in ministry is not a difference in value. Two thousand years ago Jesus was the true liberator of all, especially women. He upheld the great value of women in a culture that did not. It was to a woman that Jesus first revealed Himself after His resurrection. The true Christian man knows that the raising of children by a godly mother is a higher calling with more eternal consequences than his paperwork at the office. He also knows that <u>the Bible does NOT say that a man is more important than a woman</u>. The Bible says they are equal in the sight of God (Galatians 3:28**). <u>What it does say is that there is an order of headship</u> (1 Corinthians 11:3-16). Ephesians 5:25-29 commands that the husband treat his wife with love and tenderness. What Scripture teaches is that the man is to love his wife in a way that <u>he views her life more important than his own</u> (Ephesians 5:25). The godly man knows that he must treat his wife well, not only because God commands it, <u>but because his wife is God's daughter and must be treated with royal dignity.</u> As a matter of fact, Scripture explains that a husband's prayer life is directly connected to his treatment of his wife. God does not hear the prayers of the man who is not kind and understanding to his wife. **1 Peter 3:7:** *"You husbands likewise, live with your wives in an understanding way, as with a weaker vessel, since she is a woman; and grant her honor as a fellow heir of the grace of life, so that your prayers may not be hindered."*

(End of addendums)

VERSES 7-9: *"Woe to the world because of its stumbling blocks! For it is inevitable that stumbling blocks come; but woe to that man through whom the stumbling block comes! ⁸ And if your hand or your foot causes you to stumble, cut it off and throw it from you; it is better for you to enter life crippled or lame, than having two hands or two feet, to be cast into the eternal fire. ⁹ And if your eye causes you to stumble, pluck it out, and throw it from you. It is better for you to enter life with one eye, than having two eyes, to be cast into the fiery hell."*

Jesus warns about stumbling blocks coming our way and warns of the judgment that comes on those who send them out. These stumbling blocks come to us in many ways, whether through things we watch, read, listen to, or the people we associate with. It can also come through the church via false teaching. The mature Christian must be careful to not exercise his liberty in such a way as to cause to stumble one who is weaker in faith.

> **Romans 14:13-17:** *"Therefore let us not judge one another anymore, but rather determine this—<u>not to put an obstacle or a stumbling block in a brother's way</u>. ¹⁴ I know and am convinced in the Lord Jesus that nothing is unclean in itself; but to him who thinks anything to be unclean, to him it is unclean. ¹⁵ For if because of food your brother is hurt, you are no longer walking according to love. Do not destroy with your food him for whom Christ died. ¹⁶ Therefore do not let what is for you a good thing be spoken of as evil; ¹⁷ for the kingdom of God is not eating and drinking, but righteousness and peace and joy in the Holy Spirit."*

The judgment of those who send out stumbling blocks is set out by Jesus in **Matthew 13:41-42:** *"The Son of Man will send forth His angels, and <u>they will gather out of His kingdom all stumbling blocks, and those who commit lawlessness, ⁴² and will cast them into the furnace of fire;</u> in that place there shall be weeping and gnashing of teeth."*

Jesus is not just using an interesting allegory in Matthew 18:9-10, but is demonstrating the eternal seriousness of sin. Many would like to pretend there is not a hell. They like the lie that the Devil told Eve in **Genesis 3:4:** *"And the serpent said to the woman, 'You surely shall not die!'"* How horrendously wrong they are. One would think that losing a hand, foot, or eye would be a devastating matter. Jesus points out that sin and hell is so extremely bad that, in comparison, losing a hand, foot, or eye would be very insignificant. Jesus is not saying that mutilation will remove sin, but He is pointing out how terrible are the consequences of stumbling into sin. Jesus made it clear that sin does not originate in our hands or eyes, but in our heart.

> **Matthew 15:19:** *"For out of the heart come evil thoughts, murders, adulteries, fornications, thefts, false witness, slanders."*

How thankful we are that our God keeps us from stumbling in an eternal sense so that we can stand before Him in the grace of Christ.

> **Jude v.24-25:** *"Now to Him <u>who is able to keep you from stumbling, and to make you stand in the presence of His glory blameless</u> with great joy, ²⁵ to the only God our Savior, through Jesus Christ our Lord, be glory, majesty, dominion and authority, before all time and now and forever. Amen."*

VERSES 10-11: *"See that you do not despise one of these little ones, for I say to you, that their angels in heaven continually behold the face of My Father who is in heaven. ¹¹ [For the Son of Man has come to save that which was lost.]"*

Believers are the children of God. We are not to despise one another. One example would be by making distinctions between believers based on wealth.

> **James 2:2-4:** *"For if a man comes into your assembly with a gold ring and dressed in fine clothes, and there also comes in a poor man in dirty clothes,* [3] *and you pay special attention to the one who is wearing the fine clothes, and say, 'You sit here in a good place,' and you say to the poor man, 'You stand over there, or sit down by my footstool,'* [4] <u>*have you not made distinctions among yourselves, and become judges with evil motives?*</u>*"*

As mentioned, God uses His angels to protect His children and carry out His instructions.

> **Matthew 18:10:** *"See that you <u>do not despise one of these little ones,</u> for I say to you, that <u>their angels in heaven continually behold the face of My Father</u> who is in heaven."*

Oh, what a wonderful promise of protection there is for all of us who are children of God as it says in, **Psalm 91:11:** *"For <u>He will give His angels charge concerning you, To guard you</u> in all your ways."* Look also at **Psalm 34:7:** *"The angel of the LORD encamps around those who fear Him, And rescues them."*

Matthew 18:11 says, *"For the Son of Man has come to save that which was lost."* Jesus also made a very similar statement in Luke 19:10.

Summary and Application

Let us love children (and each other as children of God) with the same concern that God has for us.

> **Isaiah 49:15-16:**
> *"Can a woman forget her nursing child,*
> *And have no compassion on the son of her womb?*
> *Even these may forget, but I will not forget you.*
> *Behold, <u>I have inscribed you on the palms of</u>*
> <u>*My hands*</u>*; Your walls are continually before Me."*

If you have put your faith in Christ, you have been inscribed in His nail-scarred hands.

MATTHEW 18:12-17
(SEEKING THE LOST; CHURCH DISCIPLINE)

"What do you think? If any man has a hundred sheep, and one of them has gone astray, does he not leave the ninety-nine on the mountains and go and search for the one that is straying? ¹³ *And if it turns out that he finds it, truly I say to you, he rejoices over it more than over the ninety-nine which have not gone astray.* ¹⁴ *Thus it is not the will of your Father who is in heaven that one of these little ones perish.*

¹⁵ *And if your brother sins, go and reprove him in private; if he listens to you, you have won your brother.* ¹⁶ *But if he does not listen to you, take one or two more with you, so that* BY THE MOUTH OF TWO OR THREE WITNESSES EVERY FACT MAY BE CONFIRMED. ¹⁷ *And if he refuses to listen to them, tell it to the church; and if he refuses to listen even to the church, let him be to you as a Gentile and a tax-gatherer."*

Introduction

Here we see the great joy God has in the restoration of even one of His children who strays from the truth. In that context of restoration, the Lord sets out how we are to confront a sinning brother/sister. The objectives of the confrontation are not to humiliate the person or (self-righteously) exalt yourself. The two constant objectives are: 1) to protect the church from false doctrine/hypocrisy and, 2) simultaneously, to seek spiritual restoration for the sinner.

VERSES 12-14: *"What do you think? If any man has a hundred sheep, and one of them has gone astray, does he not leave the ninety-nine on the mountains and go and search for the one that is straying?* ¹³ *And if it turns out that he finds it, truly I say to you, he rejoices over it more than over the ninety-nine which have not gone astray.* ¹⁴ *Thus it is not the will of your Father who is in heaven that one of these little ones perish."*

These verses show God's view of the value of a single soul. He does not view humanity as some big ocean of people, but sees each person individually. He saves people individually. Scripture tells us that Jesus is the Good Shepherd. **John 10:11:** *"I am the good shepherd; the good shepherd lays down His life for the sheep."* Psalm 23 starts out, *"THE LORD is my shepherd,...."* Notice the mercy of the Good Shepherd. He protects us from ourselves. If we wander off He comes and finds us and takes us home.

Verse 13 of the main text says, *"And if it turns out that he finds it, truly I say to you, he rejoices over it more than over the ninety-nine which have not gone astray."* Luke tells us more detail of what Jesus taught regarding the "rejoicing" over one lost sheep.

    Luke 15:7: *"I tell you that in the same way, there will be more joy in heaven over one sinner who repents, than over ninety-nine righteous persons who need no repentance."*

It must be remembered that the section of Matthew 18:1-11 deals with children and how special they are to God. We see that all the more in this illustration, where Jesus speaks so caringly about saving a single lamb. In **Matthew 18:14** it says, *"Thus it is not the will of your Father who is in heaven that one of these little ones perish."*

VERSES 15-17: *"And if your brother sins, go and reprove him in private; if he listens to you, you have won your brother. 16 But if he does not listen to you, take one or two more with you, so that* BY THE MOUTH OF TWO OR THREE WITNESSES EVERY FACT MAY BE CONFIRMED. *17 And if he refuses to listen to them, tell it to the church; and if he refuses to listen even to the church, let him be to you as a Gentile and a tax-gatherer."*

Verses 15-17 set out the manner of handling a sinning brother. Often the church today refuses to execute its responsibility to handle church discipline. The lack of Biblical discipline subjects the church and the Lord's name to being slandered by the world as they see hypocrisy in the church.

> **Romans 2:23-24:** *"You who boast in the Law, through your breaking the Law, do you dishonor God? 24 For 'THE NAME OF GOD IS BLASPHEMED AMONG THE GENTILES BECAUSE OF YOU,' just as it is written."*

MacArthur states the problem plainly:

> "Yet in many churches where there is no tolerance for sin in principle there is much tolerance for it in practice. And when preaching becomes separated from living, it becomes separated both from integrity and from spiritual and moral effectiveness. It promotes hypocrisy instead of holiness." [321]

It should be remembered that there are **TWO MAIN OBJECTIVES WHEN DISCIPLINE IS INITIATED:**

1) **THE PROTECTION OF THE REST OF THE CHURCH FROM UNGODLY BEHAVIOR AND FALSE TEACHING.**

> **1 Corinthians 5:6, 12-13:** *"Your boasting is not good. Do you not know that a little leaven leavens the whole lump of dough?...*
>
> *12 ...Do you not judge those who are within the church? 13 But those who are outside, God judges. 'REMOVE THE WICKED MAN FROM AMONG YOURSELVES.'"*
>
> **2 Timothy 2:16-18, 19:** *"But avoid worldly and empty chatter, for it will lead to further ungodliness, 17 and their talk will spread like gangrene. Among them are Hymenaeus and Philetus, 18 men who have gone astray from the truth. ...*
>
> *19 Nevertheless, the firm foundation of God stands, having this seal, 'The Lord knows those who are His,' and, 'Let everyone who names the name of the Lord abstain from wickedness.'"*

2) **THE SPIRITUAL RESTORATION OF THE SINNING BROTHER / SISTER.**

> **2 Corinthians 2:6-9:** *"Sufficient for such a one is this punishment which was inflicted by the majority, 7 so that on the contrary you should rather forgive and comfort him, lest somehow such a one be overwhelmed by excessive sorrow. 8 Wherefore I urge you to reaffirm your love for him. 9 For to this end also I wrote that I might put you to the test, whether you are obedient in all things."*

---

[321] MacArthur, John F., *The MacArthur New Testament Commentary*, p. 441 (Chicago: Moody Press) 1983.

~ 361 ~

Unfortunately, restoration does not always take place and removal must occur in order to protect the rest of the church. Only the Lord can open one's eyes and grant him the needed repentance.

> **2 Timothy 2:25-26:** *"with gentleness correcting those who are in opposition, <u>if perhaps God may grant them repentance leading to the knowledge of the truth,</u> ²⁶ and they may come to their senses and escape from the snare of the devil, having been held captive by him to do his will."*

Paul sums up our response to the unrepentant in **1 Corinthians 5:9-13:**

> *"I wrote you in my letter not to associate with immoral people; ¹⁰ I did not at all mean with the immoral people of this world, or with the covetous and swindlers, or with idolaters; for then you would have to go out of the world. ¹¹ But actually, <u>I wrote to you not to associate with any so-called brother if he should be an immoral person, or covetous, or an idolater, or a reviler, or a drunkard, or a swindler—not even to eat with such a one.</u> ¹² For what have I to do with judging outsiders? Do you not judge those who are within the church? ¹³ But those who are outside, God judges. 'REMOVE THE WICKED MAN FROM AMONG YOURSELVES.'"*

Jesus sets out in Matthew 18:15-17 the four steps in confronting a sinning brother or sister in Christ.
1. Speak to him in private about it. If you get nowhere then…
2. Bring another with you who serves as a witness to the sinful conduct. If he still won't listen to you then…
3. Take him before the church (i.e. rebuke him publicly). If he won't listen to the church…
4. Remove him from the church.

Our attitude when entering a situation where we must correct someone is to be one of humility and love for the other person. **1 Corinthians 10:12:** *"Therefore let him who thinks he stands take heed lest he fall."* You should never think that you are so good that you would never sin like the person you are correcting:

Galatians 6:1-2: *"BRETHREN, even if a man is caught in any trespass, you who are spiritual, restore such a one in a spirit of gentleness; each one looking to yourself, lest you too be tempted. ² Bear one another's burdens, and thus fulfill the law of Christ."*

Godly correction is a beautiful thing in the sight of the Lord:

> **James 5:19-20:** *"My brethren, if any among you strays from the truth, and one turns him back, ²⁰ let him know that he who turns a sinner from the error of his way will save his soul from death, and will cover a multitude of sins."* (See the explanation of this verse in the footnote below). [322]

If it is an elder/pastor who continues in sin, it is even a more serious matter (see **James 3:1**). Scripture specifically tells us how to handle the sinning conduct of an elder/pastor in **1 Timothy 5:19-21:**

---

[322] Walvoord, John F., and Zuck, Roy B., *The Bible Knowledge Commentary*, p. 835 (Wheaton, Illinois: Scripture Press Publications, Inc.) 1983, 1985.

> *"James referred here not to evangelism but to restoration. Revival, not redemption, is in view. The rescue action is of great significance. A lost sheep is saved from destruction [see sin unto death 1 John 5:16, [see also 1 Corinthians 5:5, 11:30 and 1 Timothy 1:20] and his sins (the sins of the restored one, not the restorer) are covered as if a veil were thrown over them (cf. 1 Peter 4:8). He can move ahead again on the path toward spiritual maturity."*

"Do not receive an accusation against an elder except on the basis of two or three witnesses. ²⁰ Those who continue in sin, rebuke in the presence of all, so that the rest also may be fearful of sinning. ²¹ I solemnly charge you in the presence of God and of Christ Jesus and of His chosen angels, to <u>maintain these principles without bias</u>, doing nothing in a spirit of partiality."

John MacArthur quotes Augustine as saying,

"'Tis not advantageous to correct in secret an error which occurred publicly.' Unless the public sin of a believer is dealt with publicly, people will think the church does not take sin seriously and therefore gives tacit approval of it. A church that does not discipline sinning members (including the most prominent members) loses its credibility, because it does not take seriously its own doctrines and standards. A child who is not disciplined when he does wrong soon concludes that his parent's standards are not really very important, because they are not enforced. After taking care to determine by several witnesses that a charge against an elder is true, Paul told Timothy, the elder should be rebuked 'in the presence of all, so that the rest also may be fearful of sinning' (1 Timothy 5:20). Paul's rebuke of Peter shows that no Christian leader, regardless of his stature, is beyond discipline by the Body. Public sin demands public rebuke." [323]

Summary and Application

True church discipline is something that most churches believe is optional (or just skillfully ignored). It will be spoken of positively from the pulpit and even claimed to be applied at times. In reality I cannot say that I have been in a church where I have really seen discipline handled biblically. Often times the reason discipline is not applied is the result of the church either putting a premium on the prominence of the offender, or it propagates a false view of *unity / love* over truth and holiness.

I once attended a church where the song leader was engaging in an adulterous affair with a woman in the church. The woman happened to be the wife of a friend of mine. The politically sensitive pastor pointed out that the song leader admitted (after he was caught) that it was wrong so we must forgive and *not remove him from his leadership position*. Needless to say, the lack of godly discipline made it clear to the congregation that this conduct was no big deal. Soon other adultery problems began popping up in the church. The lack of discipline not only hurt the church but also the song leader, as exemplified by the fact that he later entered into a different adulterous affair. This kind of unrepentant, false love/forgiveness and unity will result in the spread of corruption which will deny holiness and sound doctrine in the congregation. Paul warns that such conduct by the church is actually *"arrogant"* and boastful.

1 Corinthians 5:1–6: *"It is actually reported that there is immorality among you, and immorality of such a kind as does not exist even among the Gentiles, that someone has his father's wife. ²You have become <u>arrogant</u> and have not mourned instead, so that the one who had done this deed would be removed from your midst. ³For I, on my part, though absent in body but present in spirit, have already judged him who has so committed this, as though I were present. ⁴In the name of our Lord Jesus, when you are assembled, and I with you in spirit, with the power of our Lord Jesus, ⁵I have decided to deliver such a one to Satan for the destruction of his flesh, so that his spirit may be saved in the day of the Lord Jesus. ⁶ Your <u>boasting</u> is not good. Do you not know that a little leaven leavens the whole lump of dough?"*

---

[323] MacArthur, John F., *The MacArthur New Testament Commentary*, p. 54 (Chicago: Moody Press) 1983.

The lack of godly church discipline facilitates a very anemic church that is proud of how loving it is, but in reality it functions in a lukewarm status. It will deceive itself into believing that as long as the offerings are strong, God is pleased with all that they do. Unfortunately, a true church that does not execute godly discipline will eventually experience an *"earthquake"* from a sudden revelation of hypocrisy by a church leader. This will result in the stumbling of young believers and injury to the church's testimony in the community. (The sad part is that long before the *earthquake* hits, other church leaders are generally aware of the problem and choose not to deal with it, or deal with it unbiblically.)

> **Revelation 3:16–19:** *"So because you are lukewarm, and neither hot nor cold, I will spit you out of My mouth. Because you say, 'I am rich, and have become wealthy, and have need of nothing,' and you do not know that you are wretched and miserable and poor and blind and naked, I advise you to buy from Me gold refined by fire so that you may become rich, and white garments so that you may clothe yourself, and that the shame of your nakedness will not be revealed; and eye salve to anoint your eyes so that you may see. Those whom I love, I reprove and discipline; therefore be zealous and repent."*

The great puritan John Owen stated that,

> "The nature and end of judgment or sentence must be corrective,
> not vindictive; for healing, not destruction." [324]

---

[324] I.D.E. Thomas, *The Golden Treasury of Puritan Quotations*, (Simpsonville, SC: Christian Classics Foundation) 1997.

MATTHEW 18:18-35
(FORGIVENESS)

"'Truly I say to you, whatever you shall bind on earth shall be bound in heaven; and whatever you loose on earth shall be loosed in heaven. ¹⁹ Again I say to you, that if two of you agree on earth about anything that they may ask, it shall be done for them by My Father who is in heaven. ²⁰ For where two or three have gathered together in My name, there I am in their midst.'

²¹"Then Peter came and said to Him, 'Lord, how often shall my brother sin against me and I forgive him? Up to seven times?' ²² Jesus *said to him, 'I do not say to you, up to seven times, but up to seventy times seven. ²³ For this reason the kingdom of heaven may be compared to a certain king who wished to settle accounts with his slaves. ²⁴ And when he had begun to settle them, there was brought to him one who owed him ten thousand talents. ²⁵ But since he did not have the means to repay, his lord commanded him to be sold, along with his wife and children and all that he had, and repayment to be made. ²⁶ The slave therefore falling down, prostrated himself before him, saying, 'Have patience with me, and I will repay you everything.' ²⁷ And the lord of that slave felt compassion and released him and forgave him the debt. ²⁸ But that slave went out and found one of his fellow slaves who owed him a hundred denarii; and he seized him and began to choke him, saying, 'Pay back what you owe.' ²⁹ So his fellow slave fell down and began to entreat him, saying, 'Have patience with me and I will repay you.' ³⁰ He was unwilling however, but went and threw him in prison until he should pay back what was owed. ³¹ So when his fellow slaves saw what had happened, they were deeply grieved and came and reported to their lord all that had happened. ³² Then summoning him, his lord *said to him, 'You wicked slave, I forgave you all that debt because you entreated me. ³³ Should you not also have had mercy on your fellow slave, even as I had mercy on you?' ³⁴ And his lord, moved with anger, handed him over to the torturers until he should repay all that was owed him. ³⁵ So shall My heavenly Father also do to you, if each of you does not forgive his brother from your heart."

Introduction
We will look at the subjects of prayer and corporate discipline in the body of Christ (v.20). We also will look at Jesus' teaching on the subject of forgiveness. To keep this in context, it must be remembered that Jesus was not teaching this section to a large crowd, but to His own disciples (Matthew 18:1).

VERSES 18-20: *"Truly I say to you, whatever you shall bind on earth shall be bound in heaven; and whatever you loose on earth shall be loosed in heaven. ¹⁹ Again I say to you, that if two of you agree on earth about anything that they may ask, it shall be done for them by My Father who is in heaven. ²⁰ For where two or three have gathered together in My name, there I am in their midst."*

These verses speak to us about the responsibility of the church to discipline its own and the power of prayer. Some misinterpret v.18-19 to mean that a person gets to decide (based on his own ideas) what is right or wrong, or what should be *bound* or *loosed*. The verses should be read in their context. Immediately before verses 18-20, the issue of church discipline is addressed:

> **Matthew 18:15-19:** *"And if your brother sins, go and reprove him in private; if he listens to you, you have won your brother. ¹⁶ But if he does not listen to you, take one or two more with you, so that* BY THE MOUTH OF TWO OR THREE WITNESSES EVERY FACT MAY BE

CONFIRMED. 17 And if he refuses to listen to them, tell it to the church; and if he refuses to listen even to the church, let him be to you as a Gentile and a tax-gatherer. 18 Truly I say to you, whatever you shall bind on earth shall be bound in heaven; and whatever you loose on earth shall be loosed in heaven. 19 Again I say to you, that if two of you agree on earth about anything that they may ask, it shall be done for them by My Father who is in heaven."

We do not have to determine on our own what is wrong or right; we have the Bible. The church must handle its discipline according to God's Word, and thus we bind and loose based upon what God has spoken, not on our own authority. The authority originates from God in heaven (not man) as Jesus told Peter earlier in **Matthew 16:19:** *"I will give you the keys of the kingdom of heaven; and whatever you shall bind on earth shall be bound in heaven, and whatever you shall loose on earth shall be loosed in heaven."*

Since any authority we have comes from God, the believers of the church are to function together in properly exercising it. It also must be remembered that they operate in the Lord's presence. **Matthew 18:20:** *"For where two or three have gathered together in My name, there I am in their midst."* This verse often is cited as one that tells us of the Lord's presence at corporate prayer (i.e. when Christians get together to pray the Lord is present.) Although it is true that the Lord is in the presence of His church, He is also in the constant presence of the lone believer (e.g. Matthew 28:20 "... lo, I am with you always, even to the end of the age."). The accurate context of Matthew 18:20 is not regarding corporate prayer but church discipline. Remember that in Matthew 18:16 Jesus said that when discipline is executed it must be done with two or three witnesses: **Matthew 18:16:** *"But if he does not listen to you, take one or two more with you, so that BY THE MOUTH OF TWO OR THREE WITNESSES EVERY FACT MAY BE CONFIRMED."* Likewise, verse 20 says, *"For where two or three have gathered together in My name, there I am in their midst."* When the church *witnesses* declare either the discipline or the repentance and restoration of one of its members, we are told that this is done in the Lord's presence. This concept of the Lord's presence causes the *witnesses* to proceed with humility and godly fear. When this is done, there is no place for self-righteousness or hypocrisy.

VERSES 21-22: *"Then Peter came and said to Him, 'Lord, how often shall my brother sin against me and I forgive him? Up to seven times?' 22 Jesus *said to him, 'I do not say to you, up to seven times, but up to seventy times seven.'"*

Here we have the issue of *personal forgiveness*. This is a separate and distinct issue from church discipline or the *government's responsibility to punish wrongdoers*. As set out before, the church is responsible to discipline its own (see comments on Matthew 18:1-17). Likewise, the government is responsible to execute public justice (see Romans 13:1-6, 1 Peter 2:13-15, Titus 3:1). We as *individuals* are responsible to forgive every wrong done to us. Jesus said in **Matthew 6:14-15:**

> *"For if you forgive men for their transgressions, your heavenly Father will also forgive you. 15 But if you do not forgive men, then your Father will not forgive your transgressions."*

If a crime is committed against me, the government must execute fair judgment and *I must forgive*. These concepts are not mutually exclusive. I must forgive personal offenses to me irrespective of the government executing justice.

Peter thought he, *"was being generous here, for the traditional Rabbinic teaching was that an offended person needed to forgive a brother only three times."* [325] The Lord annihilated Peter's self-righteous view by telling him **"seventy times seven."** We should be quick to forgive and not think so well of ourselves for forgiving. Matthew Henry put it this way:

> "There is a proneness in our corrupt nature... [of being concerned about] forgiving too much, though we have so much forgiven us. ...It does not look well for us to keep count of the offences done against us by our brethren. There is something of ill-nature in scoring up the injuries we forgive, as if we would allow ourselves to be revenged when the measure is full." [326]

We are not to seek our own revenge when we suffer unfair or harsh treatment by others:

> **Romans 12:19:** *"Never take your own revenge, beloved, but leave room for the wrath of God, for it is written, 'Vengeance is Mine, I will repay,' says the Lord."*

> **1 Peter 2:20:** *"... But if when you do what is right and suffer for it you patiently endure it, this finds favor with God."*

What if I am not quick to forgive? What are the results? Obviously I am actively and knowingly sinning, but on top of that, I will become a bitter and angry person.[327] This bitterness will boil over and cause others to be victims of my unforgiveness.

> **Hebrews 12:15:** *"See to it that no one comes short of the grace of God; that no root of bitterness springing up causes trouble, and by it many be defiled;"*

Bitterness is not the only manifestation of an unforgiving and hateful person. It also manifests a murderous heart of one who is not really converted:

> **1 John 3:14–15:** *"We know that we have passed out of death into life, because we love the brethren. He who does not love abides in death. Everyone who hates his brother is a murderer; and you know that no murderer has eternal life abiding in him."*

Some people teach that you need to forgive only if the person repents or only if he is a Christian (i.e. only a **brother**). That is a wrong view of Scripture. First, Jesus defines that we are to love our

---

[325] Walvoord, John F., and Zuck, Roy B., *The Bible Knowledge Commentary*, v.2 (p.62) (Wheaton, Illinois: Scripture Press Publications, Inc.) 1983, 1985.

[326] Henry, Matthew, *Matthew Henry's Commentary on the Bible*, Matthew18:21-35 (Peabody, MA: Hendrickson Publishers) 1997.

[327] Ryle states that,"The quantity of malice, bitterness and party-spirit among Christians is fearfully great. No wonder so many prayers seem to be thrown away and unheard. It is a subject which ought to come home to all classes of Christians. All have not equal gifts of knowledge and speech in their approaches to God. But all can forgive other people. It is a subject which our Lord Jesus Christ has taken special pains to impress on our minds. He has given it a prominent place in that pattern of prayers, the Lord's prayer. We are all familiar from our infancy with the words, 'Forgive us our trespasses, as we forgive those who trespass against us.' It would be good for many people if they would consider what those words mean!" Ryle, J. C. (1993). *Mark.* Crossway Classic Commentaries (p. 175). Wheaton, IL: Crossway Books.

"neighbor," who represents all people, whether we like them or not.[328] Secondly, Jesus tells us that we are to forgive *anyone*.

> **Mark 11:25-26:** *"And whenever you stand praying, <u>forgive, if you have anything against anyone</u>; so that your Father also who is in heaven may forgive you your transgressions. [26] [But if you do not forgive, neither will your Father who is in heaven forgive your transgressions.]"*

One last thought on the distinction between forgiveness and trust. I am required to forgive a person, but that does not require me to immediately put him back into a position of trust (1 Timothy 5:19-21). It is an atrocity for churches to have found out that their leaders have greatly violated the trust of their position, and yet leave them in that position. Forgiveness must be free, but trust in church leadership is earned over time (1 Timothy 3:1-13) (*e.g.* true forgiveness of a bank robber does not require you to hire him as a teller at the bank!).

VERSES 23-35: *"For this reason the kingdom of heaven may be compared to a certain king who wished to settle accounts with his slaves. [24] And when he had begun to settle them, there was brought to him one who owed him ten thousand talents. [25] But since he did not have the means to repay, his lord commanded him to be sold, along with his wife and children and all that he had, and repayment to be made. [26] The slave therefore falling down, prostrated himself before him, saying, 'Have patience with me, and I will repay you everything.' [27] And the lord of that slave felt compassion and released him and forgave him the debt. [28] But that slave went out and found one of his fellow slaves who owed him a hundred denarii; and he seized him and began to choke him, saying, 'Pay back what you owe.' [29] "So his fellow slave fell down and began to entreat him, saying, 'Have patience with me and I will repay you.' [30] He was unwilling however, but went and threw him in prison until he should pay back what was owed. [31] So when his fellow slaves saw what had happened, they were deeply grieved and came and reported to their lord all that had happened. [32] Then summoning him, his lord *said to him, 'You wicked slave, I forgave you all that debt because you entreated me. [33] Should you not also have had mercy on your fellow slave, even as I had mercy on you?' [34] And his lord, moved with anger, handed him over to the torturers until he should repay all that was owed him. [35] So shall My heavenly Father also do to you, if each of you does not forgive his brother from your heart."*

---

[328] <u>Luke 10:27–37</u>: *"And he answered, 'You shall love the Lord your God with all your heart, and with all your soul, and with all your strength, and with all your mind; and your neighbor as yourself.' And He said to him, 'You have answered correctly; do this and you will live.' But wishing to justify himself, he said to Jesus, <u>'And who is my neighbor?'</u> Jesus replied and said, 'A man was going down from Jerusalem to Jericho, and fell among robbers, and they stripped him and beat him, and went away leaving him half dead. And by chance a priest was going down on that road, and when he saw him, he passed by on the other side. Likewise a Levite also, when he came to the place and saw him, passed by on the other side. But a Samaritan, who was on a journey, came upon him; and when he saw him, he felt compassion, and came to him and bandaged up his wounds, pouring oil and wine on them; and he put him on his own beast, and brought him to an inn and took care of him. On the next day he took out two denarii and gave them to the innkeeper and said, 'Take care of him; and whatever more you spend, when I return I will repay you.' <u>Which of these three do you think proved to be a neighbor to the man who fell into the robbers' hands?'</u> And he said, 'The one who showed mercy toward him.' <u>Then Jesus said to him, 'Go and do the same.'"</u>*

This is a story of a slave who owes a debt that he could never pay. "[He] *owed a large amount, 10,000 talents...a talent was probably a measure of gold....*"[329] A talent represents a weight measure of about "*75 pounds.*"[330] (See this footnote below re: the amount in today's dollars.) The slave was granted infinite mercy and forgiveness. Even though he was the recipient of such overwhelming forgiveness, he refused to forgive one who owed him a small amount. We are told that he refused to forgive one who owed him a mere 100 denarius. "*A denarius was a Roman silver coin, worth about 16 cents; it represented a laborer's daily wages.*" [331] As a result of his unforgiveness, he was accountable for his debts and the king, "*handed him over to the torturers until he should repay all that was owed him.*" Scripture tells us in **James 2:13:** "*For judgment will be merciless to one who has shown no mercy; mercy triumphs over judgment.*"

We must remember that the "smallest sin" is a horrible sin against God himself. **James 2:10:** "*For whoever keeps the whole law and yet stumbles in one point, he has become guilty of all.*" Since God forgave us to a level that we could never begin to comprehend, we must likewise forgive others. That means we do not wait for them to say they are sorry or something similar. Our forgiveness is not to be a mere external act. Nor should our act of forgiveness serve as an opportunity to get a *whack* on the other person. For example, when one says, "I want you to know that I am forgiving you for all the terrible hurts you have caused me", this statement can be more of a condemning judgment than true forgiveness. Another common pseudo-christian[332] statement is to tell someone that you are *trying hard to forgive him.* You do not get to *try hard.* Forgiveness is a decision. You either forgive or do not. Remember Scripture tells us that we are to, "*forgive... from your heart....*" (Matthew 18:35).

There is no sin that anyone could commit that would be as unjust and evil as the murdering of the perfect Son of God. Remember Jesus' response to the evil and murderous men:
Luke 23:34: "*Father, forgive them; for they do not know what they are doing.*"

---

[329] Walvoord, John F., and Zuck, Roy B., *The Bible Knowledge Commentary*, v.2 (p. 62) (Wheaton, Illinois: Scripture Press Publications, Inc.) 1983, 1985.

[330] Elwell, W. A., and Comfort, P. W. (2001). *Tyndale Bible dictionary*. p. 1298, Tyndale reference library. Wheaton, Ill.: Tyndale House Publishers.

NOTE: I am not a math whiz but *if* my math is correct, the slave owed the king (in today's US dollars / July 20, 2012) about $18,984,000,000 which is **[18 billion 984 million dollars].** Below is the formula I used:
   a) On July 20, 2012 gold closed right around $1,582 an oz. So if there are 16 ozs. in a pound, a pound of gold is worth about $25,312; Formula used: (16 ozs. x $1,582 an oz. = $25,312 for 1 pound).
   b) If a talent is about 75 pounds. Each talent is worth in today's dollars = $1,898,400. Formula used: (75 pounds x $25,312 per pound = one million, eight hundred and ninety-eight thousand, four hundred dollars).
   c) Now we know he owed the king 10,000 talents so 10,000 talents x $1,898,400 (dollars per talent) = $18,984,000,000 (18 billion 984 million dollars).

[331] Ibid.

[332] A *pseudo-christian* is one who goes by the name Christian but has never truly been converted. They distort or deny fundamental doctrines of the Christian faith. They are neither saved from the judgment to come nor a Christian.

Look also at the response of Stephen when he was stoned in **Acts 7:60:** *"And falling on his knees, he cried out with a loud voice, 'Lord, do not hold this sin against them!' And having said this, he fell asleep."* We must do as it says in **Ephesians 4:32:** *"And be kind to one another, tender-hearted, forgiving each other, just as God in Christ also has forgiven you."*

Summary and Application

Take a moment and think of a person who you need to forgive *from your heart.* Not only forgive him from your heart, but then pray for God to bless them. Pray for them the things you pray for yourself. Now also pray for the Lord to forgive you for all the time you wasted holding on to this unforgiveness.

> **Luke 6:35-36:** *"But love your enemies, and do good, and lend, expecting nothing in return; and your reward will be great, and you will be sons of the Most High; for He Himself is kind to ungrateful and evil men. 36 Be merciful, just as your Father is merciful."*

Later on you may be tempted to get angry when you think about that person. I have found that if I immediately change my thoughts and think of the things God has forgiven me and then start again praying blessings for that other person, I will keep from falling back into unforgiveness, bitterness and anger.

> **Ephesians 4:31-32:** *"Let all bitterness and wrath and anger and clamor and slander be put away from you, along with all malice. 32 And be kind to one another, tender-hearted, forgiving each other, just as God in Christ also has forgiven you."*

Dietrich Bonhoeffer was a German Lutheran pastor who opposed the Nazi party and was eventually killed by them. Bonhoeffer wrote:

> "This is the supreme demand. Through the medium of prayer
>   we go to our enemy, stand by his side, and plead for him to God"[333]

Finally, it is important to realize that if you think the sin committed against you was bad, it is much worse in God's eyes. His standard is not man's, it is much higher.[334] God will hold accountable those who sin against you unless they sincerely seek His forgiveness (Romans 12:19). *You are not God;* you do not have any right to hold *anything* against anyone — no matter how heinous the offense or crime. You must completely forgive your enemy, pray for them and truly leave it with the Lord, being, *"kind to one another, tender-hearted, forgiving each other, just as God in Christ also has forgiven you."* **Ephesians 4:32.**

---

[333] *The Cost of Discipleship,* trans. R. H. Fuller [2d rev. ed.; New York: Macmillan, 1960], p. 166.

[334] **Matthew 5:48:** *"Therefore you are to be perfect, as your heavenly Father is perfect."*

MATTHEW 19:1-12
(DIVORCE and REMARRIAGE)

*"AND it came about that when Jesus had finished these words, He departed from Galilee, and came into the region of Judea beyond the Jordan; ² and great multitudes followed Him, and He healed them there. ³ And some Pharisees came to Him, testing Him, and saying, 'Is it lawful for a man to divorce his wife for any cause at all?' ⁴ And He answered and said, 'Have you not read, that He who created them from the beginning MADE THEM MALE AND FEMALE, ⁵ and said, 'FOR THIS CAUSE A MAN SHALL LEAVE HIS FATHER AND MOTHER, AND SHALL CLEAVE TO HIS WIFE; AND THE TWO SHALL BECOME ONE FLESH'? ⁶ Consequently they are no longer two, but one flesh. What therefore God has joined together, let no man separate.' ⁷ They *said to Him, 'Why then did Moses command to GIVE HER A CERTIFICATE OF DIVORCE AND SEND her AWAY?' ⁸ He *said to them, 'Because of your hardness of heart, Moses permitted you to divorce your wives; but from the beginning it has not been this way. ⁹ And I say to you, whoever divorces his wife, except for immorality, and marries another woman commits adultery.' ¹⁰ The disciples *said to Him, 'If the relationship of the man with his wife is like this, it is better not to marry.' ¹¹ But He said to them, 'Not all men can accept this statement, but only those to whom it has been given. ¹² For there are eunuchs who were born that way from their mother's womb; and there are eunuchs who were made eunuchs by men; and there are also eunuchs who made themselves eunuchs for the sake of the kingdom of heaven. He who is able to accept this, let him accept it.'"*

Introduction

The issue of divorce and remarriage in the *visible church* occurs almost as often as those who claim no Christian affiliation.[335] Unfortunately, divorce is often viewed as acceptable conduct for those who claim to be Christians. The church should never look down upon or treat the divorced as second-rate believers because <u>God does not</u>. There are many who are the victims of divorce. A victim of divorce would be the one whose spouse has ran off on him or her. With that being said, it is clear from Scripture that divorce should *never be held up as the resolution to marital difficulties.*[336] The response of the church to those who

---

[335] Note that I use the term *"visible church"* to mean all church buildings and those who are present in the public congregation and claim to be Christians. This *visible church* group includes true Christians in addition to many unbelievers, false-believers and self-deceived. The reality is that the inflated divorce rate in the visible church is largely contributed by the many unconverted present. When the Bible refers to the true Church, the term only includes the redeemed.

[336] Every believer has equal standing before God in Christ. That does not mean that each person in the body of Christ is equipped or called to every ministry in the church. One's status can impact a person's qualification to minister in a certain capacity or office. For example, 1 Timothy 2:12 teaches that women are not to be teachers/leaders over men in the church. Likewise, I believe that a divorced man or a man with unruly children is also disqualified from the biblical position of "elder." **1 Timothy 3:2, 4-5:** (v.2): *"An overseer, then, must be above reproach, <u>the husband of one wife</u>, temperate, prudent, respectable, hospitable, able to teach,...* (v..4-5): *⁴ <u>He must be one who manages his own household</u> well, keeping his children under control with all dignity ⁵ <u>(but if a man does not know how to manage his own household, how will he take care of the church of God?)</u>:"*
[Note continued on the next page.]

have undergone the immense pain of divorce must be that of Christ, which is a response of love, healing and compassion (especially if the individual is the victim in the divorce). Unfortunately, many Christians do not realize that the ministry of restoration can be accomplished without compromising the scriptural truth on the subject. Divorce is sin, and for the perpetrator of the divorce, confession and repentance must be part of the person's spiritual restoration (just as it is with any other sin that may not be as public). Regardless of what the sin is, the church must not tolerate the unrepentant flaunting of it. This often is seen when an individual divorces his or her spouse to pursue another and then returns to the church with the new girlfriend/boyfriend or spouse. If the person is unrepentant about his or her sin and the devastation it has caused the family, there should be no place for that person to serve in ministry. Obviously, that person should not enjoy full standing in the body, but rather should be handled in the disciplinary manner set out in Matthew 18:15-17.[337]

> **1 Corinthians 5:11:** *"But now I have written to you not to keep company with anyone named a brother, who is sexually immoral, or covetous, or an idolater, or a reviler, or a drunkard, or an extortioner — not even to eat with such a person."*

VERSES 1-2: *"AND it came about that when Jesus had finished these words, He departed from Galilee, and came into the region of Judea beyond the Jordan; 2 and great multitudes followed Him, and He healed them there."*

Verse 1 says, *"when Jesus had finished these words,..."* The words being referred to are those in Matthew chapter 18. From the previous lessons we see that Jesus taught about the sin of power struggles in 18:1-6; the stumbling blocks of sin and false teaching in 18:7-9; reaching out for the weak and backslider in 18:12-14; church discipline and prayer in 18:15-20; and forgiveness in 18:21-35. After Jesus taught on these subjects we see that He, *"He departed from Galilee, and came into the region of Judea beyond the Jordan; 2 and great multitudes followed Him, and He healed them there."* Notice how compassionate Jesus is in that He healed those who followed Him (Matthew 19:2).

[Note continued.]
Although I am aware of various arguments contrary to that opinion, I remain satisfied that 1 Timothy 3:2 is self-explanatory. Another example of disqualification from eldership comes from verses 4-5 of 1 Timothy 3 cited above. Here we see that one could be a sound Christian man but have children who are either unbelievers (see Titus 1:5-6) or rebellious. That man is likewise disqualified from the position of Biblical eldership during that time period. That does not mean that he is disqualified from other ministries or is to be looked down upon. What we should grasp is that when the Bible sets out the requirements of a ministry position, the church must listen and obey. It is much easier to look at one's talent, giftedness, worldly status or wealth when selecting leadership, but that is not the Bible's way.

[337] Jesus sets out in Matthew 18:15-17 the four steps in confronting a sinning brother or sister in Christ.
1. Speak to him in private about it. If you get nowhere then…
2. Bring another with you who serves as a witness to the sinful conduct. If he still won't listen to you then…
3. Take him before the church (i.e. rebuke him publicly). If he won't listen to the church…
4. Remove him from the church.

[End of note.]

VERSE 3: *"And some Pharisees came to Him, testing Him, and saying, 'Is it lawful for a man to divorce his wife for any cause at all?'"*

The Pharisees were known for their false holiness. Some in their sect believed that if a man would lust after another women, he could remain perfectly holy if he simply divorced his current wife and married the one he now wanted. In other words, some taught they were not committing adultery based on the legal technicality of divorcing and remarrying. In practice, the Pharisee would write his wife a letter of divorce, for any reason *(for any cause at all...v.3)* so that he would be free to go marry whoever he wanted. This type of treacherous conduct to one's wife is what God rebuked Israel for through the prophet Malachi.

> **Malachi 2:13-16:** *"And this is another thing you do: you cover the altar of the LORD with tears, with weeping and with groaning, because He no longer regards the offering or accepts it with favor from your hand. [14] Yet you say, 'For what reason?' <u>'Because the LORD has been a witness between you and the wife of your youth, against whom you have dealt treacherously, though she is your companion and your wife by covenant.</u> [15] But not one has done so who has a remnant of the Spirit. And what did that one do while he was seeking a godly offspring? Take heed then, to your spirit, and let no one deal treacherously against the wife of your youth. [16] <u>'For I hate divorce,' says the LORD, the God of Israel, 'and him who covers his garment with wrong,'</u> says the LORD of hosts. So take heed to your spirit, that you do not deal treacherously."*

The Pharisees not only wanted to justify themselves, but they were even more interested in trying to discredit Jesus in front of the crowd. The question they asked Jesus was a trap in which they attempted to make it appear that Jesus taught contrary to the Law of Moses. In verse 3 of Matthew 19 it says, *"And some Pharisees came to Him, testing Him, and saying, 'Is it lawful for a man to divorce his wife <u>for any cause at all</u>?'"* Note that the Pharisees slipped in the phrase *"<u>for any cause at all.</u>"*

Note Jesus' response in verses Matthew 19:4-6 (set out in the next section). The verses state that when two people are married, they are *one in the sight of God*. This ends excuses for divorce such as claims that a person no longer loves his/her spouse, or that the person may have married too young and did not realize what he/she was doing. A married couple is *one before God* and not two individuals any longer.

VERSES 4-6: *"And He answered and said, 'Have you not read, that He who created them from the beginning MADE THEM MALE AND FEMALE, [5] and said, FOR THIS CAUSE A MAN SHALL LEAVE HIS FATHER AND MOTHER, AND SHALL CLEAVE TO HIS WIFE; AND THE TWO SHALL BECOME ONE FLESH? [6]Consequently they are no longer two, but one flesh. What therefore God has joined together, let no man separate.'"*

Jesus goes back to creation as the foundation for the ordination of the marriage institution. Jesus addresses the Pharisees' religious pride by asking, *"Have you not read...."* Jesus is making the point to the Pharisees that if they think they are so religious/smart, surely they would have read the book of Genesis? His point is that if you read the text, you obviously would know what it says. The quotes Jesus uses are taken from Genesis 1:27 and 2:24.

Some argue that the act of sex makes two people "ONE FLESH" and thus they are automatically married. This is not true. If that was the case, it would be impossible for a non-married man or women to commit fornication because that person would *automatically* be married instead of committing sin before God. Further proof of this is in Exodus 22:16-17, which says,

> *"And if a man seduces a virgin who is not engaged, and lies with her, he must pay a dowry for her to be his wife. ¹⁷ If her father absolutely refuses to give her to him, he shall pay money equal to the dowry for virgins."*

The law did not consider them married just because they had sex.

Some people misunderstand and think that somehow the Bible endorses polygamy because some Old Testament men had more than one wife. This is not the case. Way back at Creation[338] God said that the TWO will become ONE. Only one man and only one woman (obviously homosexual marriage / and homosexuality is Biblically forbidden).[339] It does not say the three of them will become one. Look again at **Matthew 19:5-6**: *"'FOR THIS CAUSE A MAN SHALL LEAVE HIS FATHER AND MOTHER, AND SHALL CLEAVE TO HIS WIFE; AND THE TWO SHALL BECOME ONE FLESH'? ⁶ Consequently they are no longer two, but one flesh..."*

---

[338] Note that the parallel passage in Mark 10:6 states: *"But from the beginning of creation,...."* Note the entire parallel section in **Mark 10:5-12**: *"But Jesus said to them, "Because of your hardness of heart he wrote you this commandment. "But from the beginning of creation, God MADE THEM MALE AND FEMALE. "FOR THIS REASON A MAN SHALL LEAVE HIS FATHER AND MOTHER, AND THE TWO SHALL BECOME ONE FLESH; so they are no longer two, but one flesh. "What therefore God has joined together, let no man separate." In the house the disciples began questioning Him about this again. And He said to them, "Whoever divorces his wife and marries another woman commits adultery against her; and if she herself divorces her husband and marries another man, she is committing adultery."*

[339] Obviously Matthew 19:4-6 speaks against homosexuality and homosexual marriage. Those who claim that Jesus never spoke against homosexuality not only willingly reject the Bible's clear teaching, but these very words of Jesus: *"He who created them from the beginning made them male and female, ⁵ and said, 'For this cause a man shall leave his father and mother, and shall cleave to his wife; and the two shall become one flesh?'"* The Old Testament law spoke strongly against homosexual conduct: **Leviticus 20:13**: *"If there is a man who lies with a male as those who lie with a woman, both of them have committed a detestable act; they shall surely be put to death. Their bloodguiltinessis upon them."* Here are some New Testament verses that address homosexuality:

Romans 1:26-32: *"For this reason God gave them over to degrading passions; for their women exchanged the natural function for that which is unnatural, and in the same way also the men abandoned the natural function of the woman and burned in their desire toward one another, men with men committing indecent acts and receiving in their own persons the due penalty of their error. And just as they did not see fit to acknowledge God any longer, God gave them over to a depraved mind, to do those things which are not proper, being filled with all unrighteousness, wickedness, greed, evil; full of envy, murder, strife, deceit, malice; they are gossips, slanderers, haters of God, insolent, arrogant, boastful, inventors of evil, disobedient to parents, without understanding, untrustworthy, unloving, unmerciful; and although they know the ordinance of God, that those who practice such things are worthy of death, they not only do the same, but also give hearty approval to those who practice them."*

1 Corinthians 6:9-11: *"Or do you not know that the unrighteous will not inherit the kingdom of God? Do not be deceived; neither fornicators, nor idolaters, nor adulterers, nor effeminate, nor homosexuals, nor thieves, nor the covetous, nor drunkards, nor revilers, nor swindlers, will inherit the kingdom of God. Such were some of you; but you were washed, but you were sanctified, but you were justified in the name of the Lord Jesus Christ and in the Spirit of our God."*

The husband and wife are one and no longer individuals. Paul sets this principal out in **1 Corinthians 7:4:** *"The wife does not have authority over her own body, but the husband does; and likewise also the husband does not have authority over his own body, but the wife does."*

In verse 6 it says: *"What therefore God has joined together, let no man separate."* MacArthur clarifies the meaning of this verse as follows:

> "To destroy a marriage is to destroy a creation of Almighty God... Jesus' point is that marriage is always the work of **God**, whereas divorce is always the work of man, and that no man — whoever he is, or wherever he is, or for whatever reason he may have — has the right to separate what **God has joined together**. A pagan husband and wife who divorce break God's law just as surely as believers who divorce. In the ultimate sense, every marriage is ordained of God and every divorce is not. ... Jesus said that God permits it only on the basis of sexual immorality and even then as a gracious concession to man's sinfulness (Matthew 19:8-9). To claim, as some professing Christians do, that the Lord led them out of a marriage is to lie and to make God a liar."[340]

VERSES 7-8: *"They *said to Him, 'Why then did Moses command to* GIVE HER A CERTIFICATE OF DIVORCE AND SEND *her* AWAY?' [8] *He *said to them, 'Because of your hardness of heart, Moses permitted you to divorce your wives; but from the beginning it has not been this way.'"*

The Pharisees think they have caught Jesus by pointing out Moses' *"command to* GIVE HER A CERTIFICATE OF DIVORCE AND SEND *her* AWAY?" But Moses never *commanded* them to divorce as they claimed. The Scripture that the Pharisees misstate is Deuteronomy 24:1-4. That section actually addresses a prohibition in <u>one area</u> of remarriage. Specifically it says that remarriage would be prohibited if one were divorced from another and then remarried to a different person, and the second spouse either dies or divorces her. In that situation the person is prohibited from remarrying the original spouse.

> **Deuteronomy 24:1-4:** *"WHEN a man takes a wife and marries her, and it happens that she finds no favor in his eyes <u>because he has found some indecency in her,</u> and he writes her a certificate of divorce and puts it in her hand and sends her out from his house, [2] and she leaves his house and goes and becomes another man's wife, [3] and if the latter husband turns against her and writes her a certificate of divorce and puts it in her hand and sends her out of his house, or if the latter husband dies who took her to be his wife, [4] then her former husband who sent her away is not allowed to take her again to be his wife, since she has been defiled; for that is an abomination before the LORD, and you shall not bring sin on the land which the LORD your God gives you as an inheritance."*

Deuteronomy 24:1-4 addresses what would be permitted if a man marries a woman whom he soon finds out has been sexually impure prior to marriage or sexually immoral after marriage. It must have been immoral conduct less than the loss of virginity prior to marriage, or less than adultery after marriage, since the Mosaic penalty for sexual intercourse in either case (i.e. outside of marriage) was death — Deuteronomy 22:20-22.

---

[340] MacArthur, John F., *The MacArthur New Testament Commentary*, p.167 (Chicago: Moody Press) 1983.

Notice that Jesus corrects their twisting of what the Law said by telling them that divorce was "permitted" because a person's heart was so hardened such that one would not forgive. With that said, Jesus is quick to point out that divorce was not God's plan from the beginning of time. In essence, a Christian should not take the position that if his spouse commits adultery against them, he/she should *automatically* respond by divorcing the offending spouse. One would be permitted to divorce only because of the "hardness" of his/her own heart, *which is a very poor spiritual condition to be in.* [Please see the subject of *forgiveness* in Matthew 18:21-35.]

VERSE 9: *"And I say to you, whoever divorces his wife, except for immorality, and marries another woman commits adultery."*

Scripture is clear that if a divorce occurs for reasons other than sexual *"immorality"* a remarriage to anyone other than the original spouse results in adultery.

From Matthew 5:32 and Matthew 19:9 I see that the only grounds for divorce and remarriage are in the case of **immorality/unchastity**. Matthew 5:32 and 19:9 both use the Greek term *porneia* which covers *"any form of sexual relationship outside marriage."*[341] In other words, **immorality/unchastity** is when a spouse has been sexually unfaithful. Now with that being said, it is important to note that Jesus did NOT say that if one partner was immoral then the other should get a divorce. Even though it was mentioned above, it is worthy to repeat that the allowing of divorce in this narrow exception is due to *"your hardness of heart"* (*i.e.* you respond in an unforgiving manner). I see that after divorce one should still try to reconcile with the hope of remarriage with the repentant ex-spouse. Obviously if the ex-spouse remarries someone else, the idea of restoration through remarriage is over. If remarriage takes place by the innocent spouse, that person is only to marry another Christian (i.e. *"only in the Lord"*). **1 Corinthians 7:39:** *"A wife is bound as long as her husband lives; but if her husband is dead, she is free to be married to whom she wishes, only in the Lord."* [342] In summary, those who say they are divorcing their spouse because they "do not love their spouse any more" are clearly outside of God's word.

One question that comes up along with the subject of divorce is whether there is any other Biblical basis for divorce apart from the case of **immorality/unchastity**. The only other time that divorce may occur is when there is desertion by an unbelieving spouse (non-Christian spouse). This can happen if a Christian is married to an unbeliever and the unbeliever divorces the believer (note: the Christian does not seek the divorce). In that situation, I do not see that Scripture allows the believer to go out

---

[341] Alexander, T. D., and Rosner, B. S. (2001). *New Dictionary of Biblical Theology* (electronic ed.). Downers Grove, IL: InterVarsity Press.

See also: *Enhanced Strong's Lexicon* defined the Greek word of immorality as:

4202 { por-ni'-ah} AV - fornication GK - 4518 { porneiva } 1) illicit sexual intercourse 1a) adultery, fornication, homosexuality, lesbianism, intercourse with animals etc., 1b) sexual intercourse with close relatives; Leviticus 18, 1c) sexual intercourse with a divorced man or woman; Mark 10:11,12.

[342] The Mosaic Law (Old Testament) penalty for adultery was death. **Leviticus 20:10:** *"If there is a man who commits adultery with another man's wife, one who commits adultery with his friend's wife, the adulterer and the adulteress shall surely be put to death."*

and remarry.[343]   The Scriptures instruct the believer to either remain single or be reunited with the unbelieving spouse.

> **1 Corinthians 7:10-16, 27, 39:** *"But to the married I give instructions, not I, but the Lord, that the wife should not leave her husband [11] (but if she does leave, let her remain unmarried, or else be reconciled to her husband), and that the husband should not send his wife away. [12] But to the rest I say, not the Lord, that if any brother has a wife who is an unbeliever, and she consents to live with him, let him not send her away. [13] And a woman who has an unbelieving husband, and he consents to live with her, let her not send her husband away. [14] For the unbelieving husband is sanctified through his wife, and the unbelieving wife is sanctified through her believing husband; for otherwise your children are unclean, but now they are holy. [15] Yet if the unbelieving one leaves, let him leave; the brother or the sister is not under bondage in such cases, but God has called us to peace. [16] For how do you know, O wife, whether you will save your husband? Or how do you know, O husband, whether you will save your wife?...*
> *v.27 Are you bound to a wife? Do not seek to be released. Are you released from a wife? Do not seek a wife...."*
> *v.39 A wife is bound as long as her husband lives; but if her husband is dead, she is free to be married to whom she wishes, only in the Lord."*

One last issue: What if you are in a marriage where one of you comes from a divorced background and the divorce was not based on the Biblical grounds? In other words, the previously divorced spouse was not the innocent victim of *immorality/unchastity* by the ex-spouse? Matthew 5:32 and Mark 10:11-12 maintain that the marriage remains in a guilty state of adultery. That sin, like all sin, can be forgiven and removed by God. One must repent, confess and seek God's forgiveness. One who truly seeks that forgiveness from Christ will graciously receive it. Upon true repentance and forgiveness, the couple can live on with a clear conscience. More than simply a clear conscience, they can have a fruitful marriage, enjoying the blessings and mercy of God.

> **1 John 1:9:** *"If we confess our sins, He is faithful and righteous to forgive us our sins and to cleanse us from all unrighteousness."*

VERSES 10-12: *"The disciples *said to Him, 'If the relationship of the man with his wife is like this, it is better not to marry.' [11] But He said to them, 'Not all men can accept this statement, but only those to whom it has been given. [12] For there are eunuchs who were born that way from their mother's womb; and there are eunuchs who were made eunuchs by men; and there are also eunuchs who made themselves eunuchs for the sake of the kingdom of heaven. He who is able to accept this, let him accept it.'"*

We read in Mark that at this time the disciples went into a house with Jesus (Mark 10:10). It was there that the disciples started talking to Jesus about what He had said to the Pharisees. They were accustomed to a society of easy divorce and realized that Jesus made it clear that God's plan is that marriage is for life, until one spouse dies. This type of commitment might have seemed difficult, just as some today see marriage as a constraint rather than a blessing. A Biblically based marriage is a

---

[343] There are preeminent Bible teachers who believe that the innocent Christian victim of desertion is free to remarry another Christian. I simply do not see that, although I have reviewed their reasoning. Our Lord sets out the exception in **Matthew 5:32:** *"...but I say to you that everyone who divorces his wife, <u>except for the cause of unchastity</u>, makes her commit adultery; and whoever marries a divorced woman commits adultery."*

wonderful and blessed institution ordained by God. The Bible also points out the blessings of singleness.

Summary and Application

Divorce rips at the very fabric of one's soul. That is why God created marriage for life. You may want to review this subject further by reading additional comments on divorce in Matthew 5:27-32.

There are many things young people who look to be married someday can do to help divorce-proof their marriage. First, Scripture is clear that a believer is permitted to only marry a true believer (not simply one who claims to be Christian).

> **2 Corinthians 6:14-16:** *" Do not be bound together with unbelievers; for what partnership have righteousness and lawlessness, or what fellowship has light with darkness? [15] Or what harmony has Christ with Belial, or what has a believer in common with an unbeliever? [16] Or what agreement has the temple of God with idols? For we are the temple of the living God; just as God said, "I will dwell in them and walk among them; And I will be their God, and they shall be My people."*

Be very careful in pursuing someone who is a young or new believer. The immature believer may be interested (or pretend to be interested) in Christ because that person is really interested in you. I have seen this happen. A Christian young lady will tell her boyfriend that she cannot marry him because he is not a believer. Next thing you know, she will be so excited that her boyfriend received the Lord! The boyfriend dutifully goes to church with her and even wants to attend Bible studies! They get married. After a while, he skips some of the Bible studies because he is busy with work. Soon he is not coming to church because he claims that Sunday is the only day he has to relax (or some other excuse). After a couple of years of marriage, she is so upset because he just does not seem interested in the Lord. The reality is that he never was. One should seriously consider marrying only a mature believer who has had years of proven faithfulness to Christ. If that person has not been faithful to the one he/she claims is their God for a term of a few years, how can you expect that person to be faithful to you for the next 60?

> **1 John 2:19:** *"They went out from us, but they were not really of us; for if they had been of us, they would have remained with us; but they went out, in order that it might be shown that they all are not of us."*

Marriage should be entered into with great prayer and godly counsel.

MATTHEW 19:13-26
(BRING THE CHILDREN TO JESUS; and THE RICH YOUNG RULER)

"Then some children were brought to Him so that He might lay His hands on them and pray; and the disciples rebuked them. ¹⁴ But Jesus said, 'Let the children alone, and do not hinder them from coming to Me; for the kingdom of heaven belongs to such as these.' ¹⁵And after laying His hands on them, He departed from there.

¹⁶ And behold, one came to Him and said, 'Teacher, what good thing shall I do that I may obtain eternal life?' ¹⁷ And He said to him, 'Why are you asking Me about what is good? There is only One who is good; but if you wish to enter into life, keep the commandments.' ¹⁸ He *said to Him, 'Which ones?' And Jesus said, 'YOU SHALL NOT COMMIT MURDER; YOU SHALL NOT COMMIT ADULTERY; YOU SHALL NOT STEAL; YOU SHALL NOT BEAR FALSE WITNESS; ¹⁹ HONOR YOUR FATHER AND MOTHER; and YOU SHALL LOVE YOUR NEIGHBOR AS YOURSELF.' ²⁰ The young man *said to Him, 'All these things I have kept; what am I still lacking?' ²¹ Jesus said to him, 'If you wish to be complete, go and sell your possessions and give to the poor, and you shall have treasure in heaven; and come, follow Me.' ²² But when the young man heard this statement, he went away grieved; for he was one who owned much property.

²³ And Jesus said to His disciples, 'Truly I say to you, it is hard for a rich man to enter the kingdom of heaven. ²⁴ And again I say to you, it is easier for a camel to go through the eye of a needle, than for a rich man to enter the kingdom of God.' ²⁵ And when the disciples heard this, they were very astonished and said, 'Then who can be saved?' ²⁶ And looking upon them Jesus said to them, 'With men this is impossible, but with God all things are possible.'"

Introduction

Here we see a contrast in worldly stature. On the one hand we have little babies, and on the other hand we have a distinguished and wealthy young ruler (Luke 18:18, 23). In the eyes of some, the wealthy and powerful are clearly more important than a helpless child. This is not how Jesus viewed them. He loved them *both* (Mark 10:21, Matthew 19:14). What are the factors that you look at when you evaluate a person?

1 Samuel 16:7: *"But the Lord said to Samuel, 'Do not look at his appearance or at the height of his stature, because I have rejected him; <u>for God sees not as man sees, for man looks at the outward appearance, but the Lord looks at the heart.'"</u>*

Also in this section we will see the impossibility for people to be righteous by their own efforts. Even when we feel we have done all the right things, we have still failed miserably. We like to compare ourselves to others, but God's standard for us is complete perfection: **Matthew 5:48:** *"Therefore you are to be perfect, as your heavenly Father is perfect."* Who then can be saved? We will find that, *"With men this is impossible, but with God all things are possible."* (Matthew 19:26).

VERSES 13-15: *"Then some children were brought to Him so that He might lay His hands on them and pray; and the disciples rebuked them. ¹⁴ But Jesus said, 'Let the children alone, and do not hinder them from coming to Me; for the kingdom of heaven belongs to such as these.' ¹⁵ And after laying His hands on them, He departed from there."*

Here we have the story of some parents[344] wanting Jesus to "bless" their toddlers and babies (Luke 18:15). The disciples thought this would be an unimportant disturbance to Jesus. They were wrong! We find out a little more detail about Jesus' reaction to the disciples preventing the parents from bringing their babies to Him in Mark 10:14, where it says, ***"But when Jesus saw this, He was indignant and said to them...."*** "Indignant" means *"Anger aroused by something unjust."*[345] Remember what Jesus said in **Matthew 18:10:** ***"See that you do not despise one of these little ones, for I say to you, that their angels in heaven continually behold the face of My Father who is in heaven."*** [You may want to see the comments on children in Matthew 18:5-6 and 18:10-11.] In **Matthew 19:14,** Jesus, referring to children, said, ***"for the kingdom of heaven belongs to such as these."*** Most children will have uninhibited faith in God, and so should we. Often as people get older they put faith in their own efforts, abilities or the "connections" they have. We should always have an attitude that all we really need comes from our spiritual Father. This is the humble attitude Jesus referred to in **Matthew 18:4:** ***"Whoever then humbles himself as this child, he is the greatest in the kingdom of heaven."***

As parents we must remember that we have the responsibility to bring our children before Jesus:

> **Ephesians 6:4:** ***"And, fathers, do not provoke your children to anger; but bring them up in the discipline and instruction of the Lord."***

> **Deuteronomy 6:6-9:** ***"And these words, which I am commanding you today, shall be on your heart; 7 and you shall teach them diligently to your sons and shall talk of them when you sit in your house and when you walk by the way and when you lie down and when you rise up. 8 And you shall bind them as a sign on your hand and they shall be as frontals on your forehead. 9 And you shall write them on the doorposts of your house and on your gates."***

VERSE 16: *"And behold, one came to Him and said, 'Teacher, what good thing shall I do that I may obtain eternal life?'"*

What do we know about this man? We know that he was *"extremely rich"* (Luke 18:23). Luke also tells us that he was a *"ruler"* of sorts (Luke 18:18). Mark tells us that the man conducted himself respectfully when he came to Jesus. We read that he knelt down before Him: **Mark 10:17:** *"...a man ran up to Him and knelt before Him, and began asking Him,..."*

It is very unusual when someone actually approaches us to ask how he, *"may obtain eternal life."* Even when that does happen, how many of these people are truly sincere? We will see that this man did not approach Jesus because he wanted to desperately serve God, but wanted to justify himself and/or find out what *"good thing"* he had yet to do to earn eternal life.

Note that his question encompasses the viewpoint of many non-Christians. They believe that they can "earn" their salvation by doing something "good." The heretical teaching of "legalism" says that it is good works or religious rituals that get you saved or keep you saved. The truth tells us that we

---

[344] I say *parents* because neither the text here nor the parallel passages says that it was simply mothers who brought their children.

[345] The American Heritage Dictionary.

cannot do anything to earn our salvation. God tells us that we are saved by grace through faith in Jesus. It is after we are saved that He produces fruit (good works) through us (Ephesians 2:8-10).

VERSES 17: *"And He said to him, 'Why are you asking Me about what is good? There is only One who is good; but if you wish to enter into life, keep the commandments.'"*

Jesus asks him why he was calling Him good and why he was asking Him about what is good (Mark 10:18, Luke 18:19, Matthew 19:17). Jesus' response confronts the man with the question as to whether or not He even knew who Jesus was. Jesus points out that only God is good (Mark 10:18; Luke 18:19; Matthew 19:17). Jesus is not denying His divinity; He is confronting this man with the fact that the man does not know who he is talking to. Jesus exposed that this man did not know that he was indeed talking to God. (You may want to see the comments for Matthew 16:13-14 on the divinity of Christ). A person cannot know God unless he is given that knowledge by God. Remember when Jesus asks Peter who he believed Jesus to be? Peter replied: *"Thou art the Christ, the Son of the living God."* Jesus then tells Peter that he was not able to figure that out on his own, but that was only from divine revelation of the Holy Spirit:

> **Matthew 16:16-17:** *"And Simon Peter answered and said, 'Thou art the Christ, the Son of the living God.' ¹⁷ And Jesus answered and said to him, 'Blessed are you, Simon Barjona, because flesh and blood did not reveal this to you, but My Father who is in heaven.'"*

A point to be made here is that one cannot truly know Jesus unless it is permitted by God.

> **John 6:64-65:** *"...For Jesus knew from the beginning who they were who did not believe, and who it was that would betray Him. ⁶⁵ And He was saying, 'For this reason I have said to you, that <u>no one can come to Me, unless it has been granted him from the Father.</u>'"*

Remember earlier in Matthew when Jesus explained to His disciples that one could not understand the Kingdom of God unless it was given him to know.

> **Matthew 13:10-11:** *"And the disciples came and said to Him, 'Why do You speak to them in parables?' ¹¹ And He answered and said to them, '<u>To you it has been granted to know the mysteries of the kingdom of heaven, but to them it has not been granted.</u>'"*

Jesus answered the young man's question about obtaining eternal life by telling him, *"...but if you wish to enter into life, keep the commandments."* For people to attempt to enter heaven on their own efforts they need to be perfect (i.e. they will have needed to have kept <u>all</u> the commandments.). The problem is that the Word of God tells us that it is impossible for a man to be righteous on his own. **Romans 3:10:** *"...as it is written, 'THERE IS NONE RIGHTEOUS, NOT EVEN ONE;'"* (see also Psalm 53:1-3). The Christian is *not* saved by his own "earned" righteousness (i.e. by obedience to the Law) but through faith in Christ:

> **Philippians 3:9:** *"...and not having a righteousness of my own derived from the Law, but <u>that which is through faith in Christ</u>, the righteousness which comes from God on the basis of faith,"*

> **Romans 1:17:** *"For in it the righteousness of God is revealed from faith to faith; as it is written, 'BUT THE RIGHTEOUS man SHALL LIVE BY FAITH.'"*

Let there be no mistake. The Christian does practice righteousness through faith in Christ after he has been saved:

> **1 John 3:7-8, 10:** *"Little children, let no one deceive you; the one who practices righteousness is righteous, just as He is righteous; ⁸ the one who practices sin is of the devil; for the devil has sinned from the beginning. The Son of God appeared for this purpose, that He might destroy the works of the devil....*
> *¹⁰ By this the children of God and the children of the devil are obvious: anyone who does not practice righteousness is not of God, nor the one who does not love his brother."*

Some try to teach that since we are saved by grace we do not have to keep the Commandments of God. Jesus says the opposite:

> **John 14:21:** *"He who has My commandments and keeps them, he it is who loves Me; and he who loves Me shall be loved by My Father, and I will love him, and will disclose Myself to him."*

VERSES 18-19: *"He *said to Him, 'Which ones?' And Jesus said, 'YOU SHALL NOT COMMIT MURDER; YOU SHALL NOT COMMIT ADULTERY; YOU SHALL NOT STEAL; YOU SHALL NOT BEAR FALSE WITNESS; ¹⁹ HONOR YOUR FATHER AND MOTHER; and YOU SHALL LOVE YOUR NEIGHBOR AS YOURSELF.'"*

Jesus said to the man *"...if you wish to enter into life, keep the commandment."* This resulted in the man asking, *"Which ones?"* Notice in verses 18-19 Jesus lists five of the Ten Commandments (Exodus 20) and then added the second greatest commandment to, *"...LOVE YOUR NEIGHBOR AS YOURSELF"* (Leviticus 19:18; Matthew 22:39). All of these have to do with man's relationship with other people. Notice that Jesus has not even begun to mention the first four of the Ten Commandments, which deal with man's relationship with God (Exodus 20:3-8). It is these commandments that encompass the Greatest Commandment:

> **Matthew 22:37-38:** *"And He said to him, 'YOU SHALL LOVE THE LORD your GOD WITH ALL YOUR HEART, AND WITH ALL YOUR SOUL, AND WITH ALL YOUR MIND.' ³⁸ This is the great and foremost commandment."*

VERSE 20: *"The young man *said to Him, 'All these things I have kept; what am I still lacking?'"*

Notice his response in verse 20. He confidently responds that he kept the commandments. Typically we view ourselves as much more righteous than we really are. It seems we are quick to remember a "good thing" we did two months ago and quickly dismiss from our memory the lie we told yesterday. False religion, with its *works of righteousness*, deceives a person regarding his sin. Often people will do something "good" in hopes of clearing their conscience and atoning their sin. The Bible is clear that if we break one of the Commandments we are guilty of breaking them all.

> **James 2:10-12:** *"For whoever keeps the whole law and yet stumbles in one point, he has become guilty of all. ¹¹ For He who said, 'DO NOT COMMIT ADULTERY,' also said, 'DO NOT COMMIT MURDER.' Now if you do not commit adultery, but do commit murder, you have become a transgressor of the law. ¹² So speak and so act, as those who are to be judged by the law of liberty."*

This young man is deceived by thinking that he has kept God's law. Like most people he saw adultery and murder only as physical acts. Jesus made it clear that God's standard of fulfillment of these two commandments runs much deeper than outward acts, going to one's heart and mind.

Matthew 5:21-22, 27: *"You have heard that the ancients were told, 'YOU SHALL NOT COMMIT MURDER' and 'Whoever commits murder shall be liable to the court.'* 22 *But I say to you that everyone who is angry with his brother shall be guilty before the court; and whoever shall say to his brother, 'Raca,' shall be guilty before the supreme court; and whoever shall say, 'You fool,' shall be guilty enough to go into the fiery hell....* 27 *You have heard that it was said, 'YOU SHALL NOT COMMIT ADULTERY'; 28 but I say to you, that everyone who looks on a woman to lust for her has committed adultery with her already in his heart."*

Although this man is confident that he kept the commandments, his conscience still does not assure him that he is righteous because he asks Jesus, *"what am I still lacking?"* Many people are more than willing to do a religious rite or act to fill what they are lacking, but they are not willing to submit to God's Word in faith. Do you remember Naaman who had leprosy? He went to Elisha to see if he could be healed by God. Elisha told him what to do, but Naaman was not happy because it was too simple an act of faith.

2 Kings 5:10-12: *"And Elisha sent a messenger to him, saying, 'Go and wash in the Jordan seven times, and your flesh shall be restored to you and you shall be clean.'* 11 *But Naaman was furious and went away and said, 'Behold, I thought, He will surely come out to me, and stand and call on the name of the LORD his God, and wave his hand over the place, and cure the leper.* 12 *Are not Abanah and Pharpar, the rivers of Damascus, better than all the waters of Israel? Could I not wash in them and be clean?' So he turned and went away in a rage."*

Naaman's pride prevented him from being healed. He wanted a dramatic sign or a "work" to obtain his healing. His servant pointed out that he would have done some big work if the prophet had told him to, but he should instead have the faith to just wash in the river.

*"Then his servants came near and spoke to him and said, 'My father, had the prophet told you to do some great thing, would you not have done it? How much more then, when he says to you, 'Wash, and be clean?'*14 *So he went down and dipped himself seven times in the Jordan, according to the word of the man of God; and his flesh was restored like the flesh of a little child, and he was clean."* **(v.13-14)**

VERSES 21-22: *"Jesus said to him, 'If you wish to be complete, go and sell your possessions and give to the poor, and you shall have treasure in heaven; and come, follow Me.'* 22 *But when the young man heard this statement, he went away grieved; for he was one who owned much property."*

Here Jesus cut down this man's belief that he had already fully obeyed God. Jesus showed him that money was his god. Jesus exposed the fact that the man really did not care about the poor and thus did not fulfill the commandment, *"YOU SHALL LOVE YOUR NEIGHBOR AS YOURSELF."* Yes, he was a very eager "seeker" of God, but not on God's terms.[346]

---

[346] The modern version of a *seeker* is dubious in its own right. Scripture makes it clear that apart from God's intervention, a person left to himself is spiritually dead (Ephesians 2:1-3) and does not *seek* after God. **Psalm 14:2–3:** *"The Lord has looked down from heaven upon the sons of men To see if there are any who understand, Who seek after God. They have all turned aside, together they have become corrupt; There is no one who does good, not even one. "* (See also Psalm 53:2-3.).
[Note continued on the next page.]

This man's life reflects that of many who are comfortably rich. Since he already had his wealth and prestige, he decided to start being concerned about his afterlife. The answer he got from Jesus messed with his life's plan. Obeying Jesus would mean that he would no longer have the comfort and prestige he was used to. That was too high of a price. This is not an issue of just "money," but of the heart. Compare the reaction of this man with that of Zaccheus who on his own offered to give to the poor.

> **Luke 19:8-9:** *"And Zaccheus stopped and said to the Lord, 'Behold, Lord, half of my possessions I will give to the poor, and if I have defrauded anyone of anything, I will give back four times as much.' ⁹ And Jesus said to him, 'Today salvation has come to this house, because he, too, is a son of Abraham.'"*

Who will be your god…money or the true God? Jesus said in **Matthew 6:24:**

> *"No one can serve two masters; for either he will hate the one and love the other, or he will be devoted to one and despise the other. You cannot serve God and wealth."*

When Jesus told the parable of the "Sower and the Seed" He explained the dangers to one's spiritual life when he focuses on money:

> **Matthew 13:22:** *"And the one on whom seed was sown among the thorns, this is the <u>man who hears the word</u>, and the worry of the world, and <u>the deceitfulness of riches choke the word, and it becomes unfruitful.</u>"*

Compare the rich young ruler's desire to have his wealth over the *kingdom of God* with that of the men in the parables of the "Hidden Treasure" and "Pearl of Great Price" in Matthew 13.

> **Matthew 13:44-46:** *"The kingdom of heaven is like a treasure hidden in the field, which a man found and hid; and from joy over it he goes <u>and sells all that he has, and buys that field.</u> ⁴⁵ Again, the kingdom of heaven is like a merchant seeking fine pearls, ⁴⁶ and upon finding one pearl of great value, <u>he went and sold all that he had, and bought it.</u>"*

Remember what Paul thought of his worldly possessions in comparison to knowing Christ?

> **Philippians 3:7-9:** *"But whatever things were gain to me, those things I have counted as loss for the sake of Christ. ⁸ More than that, <u>I count all things to be loss in view of the surpassing value of knowing Christ Jesus my Lord,</u> for whom I have suffered the loss of*

[Note continued.]

Unfortunately some churches have attempted to be more attractive to so-called *seekers* and refer to themselves as *seeker-sensitive* or *seeker-friendly* churches. To meet the comfort level of the non-Christian seeker, such groups have dispensed with sound doctrine and expositional teaching and preaching. They have also eliminated from the sermon concepts of repentance, God's judgment, hell, Christ's shed blood on the Cross, and personal discipleship. The seeker-sensitive movement focuses on a therapeutic view of church which is designed to appeal to the audience's desires, comfort, personal needs and fulfillment. This is not seeking after the true God. The true *seeker* seeks after God, on God's terms, and not his own.

Hebrews 11:6: *"And without faith it is impossible to please Him, for he who comes to God must believe that He is and that He is a rewarder of those who seek Him."* The true Church is a <u>gathering of converted believers</u> who praise God in Spirit and Truth, are instructed from the Word of God, and encourage each other through Christ-centered fellowship. It is not about whether the church service met my *felt needs* but whether I blessed the God who created me. Scripture tells us what we are to do:

Psalm 106:48: *"Blessed be the LORD, the God of Israel, From everlasting even to everlasting. And let all the people say, 'Amen.' Praise the LORD!"*

all things, and count them but rubbish in order that I may gain Christ, ⁹ and may be found in Him, not having a righteousness of my own derived from the Law, but that which is through faith in Christ, the righteousness which comes from God on the basis of faith….."

John MacArthur states in his commentary on Matthew:
"Whether men are wealthy or poor—or somewhere in between—their attitude toward material possessions is one of the most reliable marks of their spiritual condition…. Sixteen of the thirty-eight parables of Jesus deal with money. One out of ten verses in the New Testament deals with that subject. Scripture offers about five hundred verses on prayer, fewer than five hundred on faith, and over two thousand on money. The believer's attitude toward money and possessions is determinative." [347]

In Luke 14:25-35 Jesus teaches the importance of understanding the cost involved in being one of his disciples. In that lesson He makes this very sobering statement: *"So therefore, no one of you can be My disciple who does not give up all his own possessions."* **Luke 14:33**

Note what Jesus also said to the rich young ruler, *"…come, follow Me."* Jesus did not just say to give your money to the poor. Some may be willing to give up some money, but they are not willing to follow Jesus. Remember early in the encounter, the man asked Jesus, *"Teacher, what good thing shall I do that I may obtain eternal life?"* **Matthew 19:16**. We should remember what Jesus said is the *"work of God."*

John 6:28-29: *"They said therefore to Him, 'What shall we do, that we may work the works of God?' ²⁹ Jesus answered and said to them, 'This is the work of God, that you believe in Him whom He has sent.'"*

Compare the story of the rich young ruler with that of William Borden. Borden lived a short life, having died at the age of 25. He lived a life following Jesus. Below is the entire article entitled: **"NO RESERVES, NO RETREATS, NO REGRETS,"** of which portions were reprinted from *Daily Bread*, December 31, 1988, and *The Yale Standard*, Fall 1970 edition.[348]

"NO RESERVES, NO RETREATS, NO REGRETS."

"In 1904 William Borden graduated from a Chicago high school. As heir to the Borden… estate,[349] he was already a millionaire. For his high school graduation present, his parents gave 16-year-old Borden a trip around the world. As the young man traveled through Asia, the Middle East, and Europe, he felt a growing burden for the world's hurting people. Finally, Bill Borden wrote home about his 'desire to be a missionary.'(1). One friend expressed surprise that he was 'throwing himself away as a missionary.' In response, Bill wrote two words in the

---

[347] MacArthur, John F., *The MacArthur New Testament Commentary*, p. 418 (Chicago: Moody Press) 1983.

[348] I apologize that I cannot cite the specific author of the article but it does mention sources in the article's own footnotes.

[349] Borden's father made his fortune in silver mining and not dairies as the original article states. See also: Wiersbe, Warren W., (2009) *50 People Every Christian Should Know*, (p.341) Grand Rapids, MI: Baker Books.

back of his Bible: *'No reserves.'* Even though young Borden was wealthy, he arrived on the campus of Yale University in 1905 trying to look like just one more freshman. Very quickly, however, Borden's classmates noticed something unusual about him and it wasn't his money. One of them wrote: 'He came to college far ahead, spiritually, of any of us. He had already given his heart in full surrender to Christ and had really done it. We who were his classmates learned to lean on him and find in him a strength that was solid as a rock, just because of this settled purpose and consecration.'(2)

During his college years, Bill Borden made one entry in his personal journal that defined what his classmates were seeing in him. That entry said simply: *'Say 'no' to self and 'yes' to Jesus every time.'*(3) Borden's first disappointment at Yale came when the university president spoke on the students' need of 'having a fixed purpose.' After hearing that speech, Borden wrote: *'He neglected to say what our purpose should be, and where we should get the ability to persevere and the strength to resist temptations.'*(4) Surveying the Yale faculty and much of the student body, Borden lamented what he saw as the end result of this empty philosophy: moral weakness and sin-ruined lives.

During his first semester at Yale, Borden started something that would transform campus life. One of his friends described how it happened: 'It was well on in the first term when Bill and I began to pray together in the morning before breakfast. I cannot say positively whose suggestion it was, but I feel sure it must have originated with Bill. We had been meeting only a short time when a third student joined us and soon after a fourth. The time was spent in prayer after a brief reading of Scripture. Bill's handling of Scripture was helpful...He would read to us from the Bible, show us something that God had promised and then proceed to claim the promise with assurance.'(5)

Borden's small morning prayer group gave birth to a movement that spread across the campus. By the end of his first year, 150 freshmen were meeting for weekly Bible study and prayer. By the time Bill Borden was a senior, one thousand of Yale's 1,300 students were meeting in such groups. Borden made it his habit to seek out the most "incorrigible" students and try to bring them to salvation. 'In his sophomore year we organized Bible study groups and divided up the class of 300 or more, each man interested taking a certain number, so that all might, if possible, be reached. The names were gone over one by one, and the question asked, 'Who will take this person?' When it came to someone thought to be a hard proposition, there would be an ominous pause. Nobody wanted the responsibility. Then Bill's voice would be heard, 'Put him down to me.''(6)

Borden's outreach ministry was not confined to the Yale campus. He cared about widows and orphans and cripples. He rescued drunks from the streets of New Haven. To rehabilitate them, he founded the Yale Hope Mission. One of his friends wrote that he 'might often be found in the lower parts of the city at night, on the street, in a cheap lodging house or some restaurant to which he had taken a poor hungry fellow to feed him, seeking to lead men to Christ.'(7)

Borden's missionary call narrowed to the Muslim Kansu people in China. Once that goal was in sight, Borden never wavered. He also inspired his classmates to consider missionary service. One of them said: 'He certainly was one of the strongest characters I have ever known, and he put backbone into the rest of us at college. There was real iron in him, and I always felt he was of the stuff martyrs were made of, and heroic missionaries of more modern times.'(8)

Although he was a millionaire, Bill seemed to 'realize always that he must be about his Father's business, and not wasting time in the pursuit of amusement.'(9) Although Borden refused to join a fraternity, 'he did more with his classmates in his senior year than ever before.' He presided over the huge student missionary conference held at Yale and served as president of the honor society Phi Beta Kappa.

Upon graduation from Yale, Borden turned down some high paying job offers. In his Bible, he wrote two more words: *'No retreats.'*

William Borden went on to graduate work at Princeton Seminary in New Jersey. When he finished his studies at Princeton, he sailed for China. Because he was hoping to work with Muslims, he stopped first in Egypt to study Arabic. While there, he contracted spinal meningitis. Within a month, 25-year-old William Borden was dead.

When news of William Whiting Borden's death was cabled back to the U.S., the story was carried by nearly every American newspaper. 'A wave of sorrow went round the world . . . Borden not only gave (away) his wealth, but himself, in a way so joyous and natural that it (seemed) a privilege rather than a sacrifice' wrote Mary Taylor in her introduction to his biography.(10) Was Borden's untimely death a waste? Not in God's plan. Prior to his death, Borden had written two more words in his Bible. Underneath the words *'No reserves'* and *'No retreats,'* he had written: *'No regrets.'''*

(1) Taylor, Mrs. Howard. Borden of Yale '09. Philadelphia: China Inland Mission, 1926, p. 75.
(2) Ibid., page 98.
(3) Ibid., page 122.
(4) Ibid., page 90.
(5) Ibid., page 97.
(6) Ibid., page 150.
(7) Ibid., page 148.

(8) Ibid., page 149.
(9) Ibid., page 149.
(10) Ibid., page ix.
Portions reprinted from Daily Bread, December 31, 1988, and The Yale Standard, Fall 1970 edition."

VERSES 23-24: *"And Jesus said to His disciples, 'Truly I say to you, it is hard for a rich man to enter the kingdom of heaven.* [24] *And again I say to you, it is easier for a camel to go through the eye of a needle, than for a rich man to enter the kingdom of God.'"*

In verse 23 Jesus states, *"...it is hard for a rich man to enter the kingdom of heaven."* In verse 24 He explains just how hard it is. Everyone knows how small is the "eye of a needle." You have to squint to see it when you thread a needle. Likewise everyone knows how large a camel is. It does seem impossible for a camel to go through an eye of a needle, but as Jesus points out in verse 26, nothing is impossible for God. One more thought on the subject.

Some liberals have tried to teach that this analogy is not as dramatic as it sounds. They (unbelievers as they are) say that a camel going through the eye of a needle was a reference to a small gate called "needle's eye" and for a camel to go through it was somewhat difficult because it would have to get down and crawl through on its knees. This is again another liberal, "make it up as you go" statement about the Bible that has no historical basis and is completely false. **(For more on that subject, see footnote 350 below.)**

Please go back to verse 23. One needs to ask why it is hard for a rich man to enter the kingdom of heaven. It is not evil or bad to be rich. God gave great riches to the father of faith, Abraham. Job was

---

[350] Vine, W. E., *Vine's Expository Dictionary of Old and New Testament Words*, (Grand Rapids, MI: Fleming H. Revell) 1981. *"Note:* The idea of applying 'the needle's eye' to small gates seems to be a modern one; there is no ancient trace of it. The Lord's object in the statement is to express human impossibility and there is no need to endeavor to soften the difficulty by taking the needle to mean anything more than the ordinary instrument. Mackie points out (Hastings' Bib.Dic.) that 'an attempt is sometimes made to explain the words as a reference to the small door, a little over 2 feet square, in the large heavy gate of a walled city. This mars the figure....and receives no justification from the language and traditions of Palestine.'"

The New Bible Dictionary, (Wheaton, Illinois: Tyndale House Publishers, Inc.) 1962. Some scholars interpret 'needle's eye' as a reference to a narrow gateway for pedestrians, but <u>there is no historical evidence to support this</u>. See F. W. Farrar, 'The Camel and the Needle's Eye', *The Expositor* 3, 1876, pp. 369-380.

Another point that has to be made involves the disciples' response to the statement about a camel passing though the eye of a needle. They knew that this was not a hassle that took some time. No, they knew Jesus was talking of a literal eye of a needle and that a camel passing though it would be impossible for man. In verse 25 they said, *"And when the disciples heard this, they were very astonished and said, 'Then who can be saved?'"*

McArthur says: "Some propose that there was a very small gate in the ancient wall of Jerusalem called the Needle's Eye. In order for a camel to go through it, they surmised, the animal would have to be completely unloaded and then crawl through on its knees. But neither the Persian nor the Jewish saying used the term gate, and no Jerusalem gate by that name is mentioned in any extant historical or archeological record. In any case, no sensible person would go to such trouble when he could take his camel a few hundred yards down the wall and go through a larger gate." MacArthur, J. F., Jr. (1985). *Matthew.* MacArthur New Testament Commentary (p. 167). Chicago: Moody Press.

also a rich man and God said of him, *"...For there is no one like him on the earth, a blameless and upright man, fearing God and turning away from evil." Job 1:8.* The problem of riches comes when one looks to them for provision and protection and not to God. (See the parable in Luke 12:16-21.) They do not see the need for God because of their trust in riches. The attitude of self-reliance of the wealthy is set out in Proverbs.

<u>Proverbs 18:11:</u> *"A rich man's wealth is his strong city,*
And <u>like a high wall in his own imagination</u>."

Even though the "rich man" is wrongfully deceived that his money is protection for him, the "righteous" man looks to the Lord for his protection.

<u>Proverbs 18:10:</u> *"The name of the LORD is a strong tower;*
The righteous runs into it and is safe."

Remember it is not money that is the, *"root of all sorts of evil."* Rather, *"<u>the love of money</u> is a root of all sorts of evil."*

<u>1 Timothy 6:9-10:</u> *"But those who want to get rich fall into temptation and a snare and many foolish and harmful desires which plunge men into ruin and destruction. ¹⁰ For <u>the love of money is a root of all sorts of evil</u>, and some by longing for it have wandered away from the faith, and pierced themselves with many a pang."*

Often we look at a wealthy person and think that person represents "the rich." The reality is that the average American is very rich compared to much of the population of the earth. So how should we look at our wealth from a Christian perspective?

<u>1 Timothy 6:17-19:</u> *"Instruct those who are rich in this present world <u>not</u> to be conceited <u>or to fix their hope on the uncertainty of riches</u>, but on God, who richly supplies us with all things to enjoy. ¹⁸ Instruct them to do good, to be rich in good works, to be generous and ready to share, ¹⁹ storing up for themselves the treasure of a good foundation for the future, so that they may take hold of that which is life indeed."*

<u>VERSES 25-26:</u> *"And when the disciples heard this, they were very astonished and said, 'Then who can be saved?' ²⁶ And looking upon them Jesus said to them, 'With men this is impossible, but with God all things are possible.'"*

There is nothing to comment here. What Jesus said is very straightforward: *"...with God all things are possible."*

Summary and Application

At the beginning of this section we read of the importance of bringing our children to the Lord. Jesus stated, *"...for the kingdom of heaven belongs to such as these."* A rhetorical question for any parent would be: Am I bringing my child up in Christ and fulfilling Deuteronomy 6:6-9, or simply taking him to church a couple of hours a week? Obviously we are to be teaching them the truths of God at home, at play, through daily living and during family Bible time. Another rhetorical question: Am I bringing my child up in Christ and fulfilling Deuteronomy 6:6-9 by sending them to 17,000 hours of life instruction (kindergarten through 12th grade) if they attend a school system that is devoid of the truths of God? Is it a system where they are told prayer is illegal? Is it a system where they are told that God did not create them but they are the result of *millions and millions of years* of random chance that started with a celestial slime-ball flying around...somewhere? What are two conclusions that can be drawn by a child who believes this?

1) That life is all about himself getting as many material things as he can in a dog-eat-dog world (i.e. survival of the fittest).
2) When he dies, nothing matters anyway since his meaningless life was the result of millions of years of random chance.

In most schools they are never taught the very important fact that, *"... it is appointed for men to die once and __after this comes judgment....__"* **Hebrews 9:27.** Your child's eternal soul is too valuable to abandon him/her to a godless format of life instruction. A high-quality academic education is *very important* for your child and should be aggressively pursued. The quality education cannot be devoid of a Biblical ethos and worldview. If it is devoid of Godly instruction then your result will be as Hodge stated more than 150 years ago:

> "If a man is not religious, he is irreligious; if he is not a believer, he is an unbeliever. This is as true of organizations and institutions, as it is of individuals. Byron uttered a profound truth when he put into the mouth of Satan the words 'He that does not bow to God, has bowed to me.' If you banish light, you are in darkness. If you banish Christianity from the schools, you thereby render them infidel. If a child is brought up in ignorance of God, he becomes an atheist. If never taught the moral law, his moral nature is as undeveloped as that of a pagan."[351]

> *"The fool has said in his heart, 'There is no God.'"* **Psalm 14:1.** [352]

---

[351] Hodge, C. (1997). *Systematic Theology* (V 3, pp. 355–356). Oak Harbor, WA: Logos Research Systems, Inc.

[352] Professor Charles Hodge (1797-1878) taught at Princeton Theological Seminary for 50 years. He wrote the following regarding Deuteronomy 6:6-9:

"...the Bible does require that education should be religiously conducted. 'These words which I command thee this day, shall be in thine heart: and thou shalt teach them diligently unto thy children, and shalt talk of them when thou sittest in thine house, and when thou walkest by the way, and when thou liest down, and when thou risest up.' (Deuteronomy 6:6, 7 and Deuteronomy 11:19.) 'He established a testimony in Jacob, and appointed a law in Israel, which He commanded our fathers, that they should make them known to their children; that the generation to come might know them, even the children which should be born, who should arise and declare them to their children; that they might set their hope in God, and not forget the works of God, but keep His commandments.' (Psalms 78:5, 6, 7.) 'Train up a child in the way he should go; and when he is old he will not depart from it.' (Proverbs 22:6.) Fathers bring up your children, 'in the nurture and admonition of the Lord.' (Ephesians 6:4.) These are not ceremonial or obsolete laws. They bind the consciences of men just as much as the command, 'Thou shalt not steal.' If parents themselves conduct the education of their children, these are the principles upon which it must be conducted. If they commit that work to teachers, they are bound, by the law of God, to see that the teachers regard these divine prescriptions; if they commit the work to the state, they are under equally sacred obligation to see that the state does not violate them. This is an obligation which they cannot escape."

Hodge, C. (1997). *Systematic Theology* (V 3, pp. 354–355). Oak Harbor, WA: Logos Research Systems, Inc.

The second part of this lesson addressed the subjects of false righteousness and money. We must watch out for the constant emphasis our society puts on money and power. We can convince ourselves that we are followers of Christ, but does our checkbook call us a liar? We need to cry out to the Lord to help us overcome the temptations of our flesh. He can deliver us! Jesus said it straight on: *"...with God all things are possible."* Do you believe this?

> **Jeremiah 32:17:** *"Ah Lord God! Behold, Thou hast made the heavens and the earth by Thy great power and by Thine outstretched arm! Nothing is too difficult for Thee...."*

MATTHEW 19:27-30

(REWARDS IN HEAVEN)

[27] *"Then Peter answered and said to Him, 'Behold, we have left everything and followed You; what then will there be for us?' [28] And Jesus said to them, 'Truly I say to you, that you who have followed Me, in the regeneration when the Son of Man will sit on His glorious throne, you also shall sit upon twelve thrones, judging the twelve tribes of Israel. [29] And everyone who has left houses or brothers or sisters or father or mother or children or farms for My name's sake, shall receive many times as much, and shall inherit eternal life. [30] But many who are first will be last; and the last, first.'"*

Introduction

This section touches on the individual rewards of the believer. It is clear that the believer's Spirit-led service is richly rewarded by God.

VERSE 27: *"Then Peter answered and said to Him, 'Behold, we have left everything and followed You; what then will there be for us?'"*

> The contexts of this passage must be remembered. Right before this verse, Jesus had His confrontation with the "rich young ruler." In that confrontation Jesus told the rich young ruler in **Matthew 19:21-22**:
>
> > *"...'If you wish to be complete, go and sell your possessions and give to the poor, and you shall have treasure in heaven; and come, follow Me.' But when the young man heard this statement, he went away grieved; for he was one who owned much property."*
>
> Now in verse 27 we see Peter pointing out that they left everything to follow Jesus (see Matthew 4:18-20). Peter's direct question to Jesus asks what they will receive for their sacrifice.

VERSE 28: *"And Jesus said to them, 'Truly I say to you, that you who have followed Me, in the regeneration when the Son of Man will sit on His glorious throne, you also shall sit upon twelve thrones, judging the twelve tribes of Israel.'"*

> Jesus refers to a time period called the *"regeneration."* It is the time period when the earth is made new during the Millennium.[353] *The New Bible Dictionary* says that the term *"regeneration"* is used eschatologically to refer to the restoration of all things, reminding us that the renewal of the individual is part of a wider and cosmic renewal.[354] It is during this time that the disciples will

---

[353] The Ryrie Study Bible - Expanded edition: New American Standard, comment to Matthew 19:28.

[354] Wood, D. R. W., and Marshall, I. H. (1996). *New Bible Dictionary (3rd ed.)* (p 1005). Leicester, England; Downers Grove, IL: InterVarsity Press.

sit as judges over the 12 tribes of Israel. (Note: The term "regeneration" in verse 28 has a different meaning than in Titus 3:5, where it refers to the new birth of the Christian.)

VERSE 29: *"And everyone who has left houses or brothers or sisters or father or mother or children or farms for My name's sake, shall receive many times as much, and shall inherit eternal life."*

Our service for the Lord is not irrelevant to Him. The Scripture is clear that the Lord multiplies back to us what we give Him.

> **Luke 6:38:** *"Give, and it will be given to you; good measure, pressed down, shaken together, running over, they will pour into your lap. For by your standard of measure it will be measured to you in return."*

Since everything we have ever had has come from God's hand, we must remember that it is the power of God that is doing the good work through us for His glory.

> **Ephesians 2:10:** *"For we are His workmanship, created in Christ Jesus for good works, which God prepared beforehand, that we should walk in them."*

It is amazing. God does the work through us by His power, blesses the result, and then rewards us. He is truly the gracious and almighty God. R.C. Sproul wrote:

> "Our reward in the kingdom will be according to our good works, which is, as Augustine noted, a case of God's gracious crowning of His own gifts."[355]

We must remember that we are the Lord's servants. He is not our servant that we call on just to get things we want. We serve Him because we love Him. He has done so much for us; it is an honor to be His lowest servant. Jesus told His disciples what their attitudes should be in the service of Him:

> **Luke 17:7-10:** *"But which of you, having a slave plowing or tending sheep, will say to him when he has come in from the field, 'Come immediately and sit down to eat'? [8] But will he not say to him, 'Prepare something for me to eat, and properly clothe yourself and serve me until I have eaten and drunk; and afterward you will eat and drink?' [9] He does not thank the slave because he did the things which were commanded, does he? [10] So you too, when you do all the things which are commanded you, say, 'We are unworthy slaves; we have done only that which we ought to have done.'"*

The concept of rewards is set out in other places in Scripture:

> **1 Corinthians 3:12-15:** *"Now if any man builds upon the foundation with gold, silver, precious stones, wood, hay, straw, [13] each man's work will become evident; for the day will show it, because it is to be revealed with fire; and the fire itself will test the quality of each man's work. [14] If any man's work which he has built upon it remains, he shall receive a reward. [15] If any man's work is burned up, he shall suffer loss; but he himself shall be saved, yet so as through fire."*

---

[355] Sproul, R. C., *Essential Truths of the Christian Faith*, #67 *Faith and Works* (Wheaton, Illinois: Tyndale House Publishers, Inc.) 1992.

2 Corinthians 5:9-10: *"Therefore also we have as our ambition, whether at home or absent, to be pleasing to Him. [10] For we must all appear before the judgment seat of Christ, <u>that each one may be recompensed for his deeds in the body, according to what he has done, whether good or bad."</u>*

Proverbs 11:18: *"The wicked earns deceptive wages, But <u>he who sows righteousness gets a true reward."</u>*

Colossians 3:23-25: *"Whatever you do, do your work heartily, as for the Lord rather than for men; [24] knowing that from the Lord <u>you will receive the reward of the inheritance.</u> It is the Lord Christ whom you serve. [25] For he who does wrong will receive the consequences of the wrong which he has done, and that without partiality."*

Luke 6:22-23: *"Blessed are you when men hate you, and ostracize you, and cast insults at you, and spurn your name as evil, for the sake of the Son of Man. [23] <u>Be glad in that day, and leap for joy, for behold, your reward is great in heaven;</u> for in the same way their fathers used to treat the prophets."*

Luke 6:35: *"But love your enemies, and do good, and lend, expecting nothing in return; <u>and your reward will be great,</u> and you will be sons of the Most High; for He Himself is kind to ungrateful and evil men."*

2 John v.8: *"Watch yourselves, that you might not lose what we have accomplished, <u>but that you may receive a full reward."</u>*

Revelation 22:12-13: *"<u>Behold, I am coming quickly, and My reward is with Me, to render to every man according to what he has done.</u> [13] I am the Alpha and the Omega, the first and the last, the beginning and the end."*

J.C. Ryle said:

"Let us settle it in our minds that the Christian fight is a good fight—really good, truly good, emphatically good. We see only part of it yet. We see the struggle, but not the end; we see the campaign, but not the reward; we see the cross, but not the crown. We see a few humble, broken–spirited, penitent, praying people, enduring hardships and despised by the world; but we see not the hand of God over them, the face of God smiling on them, the kingdom of glory prepared for them. These things are yet to be revealed. Let us not judge by appearances. There are more good things about the Christian warfare than we see."[356]

VERSE 30: *"But many who are first will be last; and the last, first."*

This verse will be addressed in the next section since Jesus gives an illustration of it in Matthew 20:1-16.

---

[356] *Holiness*, J.C. Ryle, p. 62, Simpsonville, SC: Christian Classics Foundation) 1995.

Summary and Application

After you have been saved, are you desiring to live a Christ-honoring life? Are you doing good works which will receive a reward? You should be.

I once met a person who proclaimed that it was very unspiritual to desire to have rewards in heaven. His view is not supported by scripture but rather is one of *"false humility"* (NIV) that has, *"...the appearance of wisdom in self-made religion...."* **Colossians 2:23**. Scripture teaches that you were saved to do good works: *"...For we are His workmanship, created in Christ Jesus for good works, which God prepared beforehand so that we would walk in them."* **Ephesians 2:9–10**. Obviously, if you are not serving out of love for Christ, it profits nothing (1 Corinthians 13:3). The desire to please the Lord and glorify only Him, should always be our aim. If we were not to have any desire for rewards, why would Jesus warn us on how good works can result in no heavenly reward? *"BEWARE of practicing your righteousness before men to be noticed by them; otherwise you have no reward with your Father who is in heaven."* **Matthew 6:1.** Jesus also states that when giving to the poor, praying etc., do not announce it to others and lose your heavenly reward. *"When therefore you give alms, do not sound a trumpet before you, as the hypocrites do in the synagogues and in the streets, that they may be honored by men. Truly I say to you, they have their reward in full. ³ But when you give alms, do not let your left hand know what your right hand is doing ⁴ that your alms may be in secret; and your Father who sees in secret will repay you."* **Matthew 6:2-4.** There is a very big difference between your good works glorifying you as compared to your good works inspiring others to glorify God. *"Let your light shine before men in such a way that they may see your good works, and glorify your Father who is in heaven."* **Matthew 5:16.** This verse actually warns us against being cowardly and avoiding service to God. The text in Matthew 6:4 (about giving your alms in secret) is not about one being fearful from doing good works, but rather deals with one's motivation for doing good works. A. B. Bruce explains the distinction between Matthew 5:16 and 6:4 this way: "We are to show when tempted to hide and hide when tempted to show."[357]

Scripture tells us that we are to have an *ambition* to serve and please Christ (2 Corinthians 5:9). The next verse after that ties that ambition with the concept of rewards: *"For we must all appear before the judgment seat of Christ, so that each one may be recompensed for his deeds in the body, according to what he has done, whether good or bad."* **2 Corinthians 5:10.** Moses himself was noted for his obedience to Christ and that he kept an eye on the reward to come: **Hebrews 11:24–26:**

> *"By faith Moses, when he had grown up, refused to be called the son of Pharaoh's daughter, choosing rather to endure ill-treatment with the people of God than to enjoy the passing pleasures of sin, considering the reproach of Christ greater riches than the treasures of Egypt; for he was looking to the reward."*

Let us not serve out of slavish legalism, but out of sincere joy and love for Christ who will reward us in heaven. **Mark 9:41:** *"For whoever gives you a cup of water to drink because of your name as followers of Christ, truly I say to you, he shall not lose his reward."* What Christian does not want to hear the words:

> *"...Well done, good and faithful slave. You were faithful with a few things, I will put you in charge of many things; enter into the joy of your master."* **Matthew 25:23**

---

[357] MacArthur, J. (1985). *Matthew* (pp. 357–358). Chicago: Moody Press.

<u>MATTHEW 20:1-16</u>
(THE FIRST WILL BE LAST — PARABLE OF THE LABORERS IN THE VINEYARD)

20:1 *"For the kingdom of heaven is like a landowner who went out early in the morning to hire laborers for his vineyard. ² And when he had agreed with the laborers for a denarius for the day, he sent them into his vineyard. ³ And he went out about the third hour and saw others standing idle in the market place; ⁴ and to those he said, 'You too go into the vineyard, and whatever is right I will give you.' And so they went. ⁵Again he went out about the sixth and the ninth hour, and did the same thing. ⁶And about the eleventh hour he went out, and found others standing; and he *said to them, 'Why have you been standing here idle all day long?' ⁷"They *said to him, 'Because no one hired us.' He *said to them, 'You too go into the vineyard.' ⁸ And when evening had come, the owner of the vineyard *said to his foreman, 'Call the laborers and pay them their wages, beginning with the last group to the first.' ⁹ And when those hired about the eleventh hour came, each one received a denarius. ¹⁰ And when those hired first came, they thought that they would receive more; and they also received each one a denarius. ¹¹ And when they received it, they grumbled at the landowner, ¹² saying, 'These last men have worked only one hour, and you have made them equal to us who have borne the burden and the scorching heat of the day.' ¹³ But he answered and said to one of them, 'Friend, I am doing you no wrong; did you not agree with me for a denarius? ¹⁴ Take what is yours and go your way, but I wish to give to this last man the same as to you. ¹⁵ Is it not lawful for me to do what I wish with what is my own? Or is your eye envious because I am generous?' ¹⁶ Thus the last shall be first, and the first last."*

Introduction

At the end of the previous chapter, Jesus was discussing individual rewards for His disciples (Matthew 19:27-30). We can be sure that the Lord rewards all of His disciples extremely generously. He then tells them this parable, which points out that when it comes to salvation, everyone is equal no matter when they come to the Lord, be it early in life or late.

<u>VERSES 1-2</u>: *"For the kingdom of heaven is like a landowner who went out early in the morning to hire laborers for his vineyard. ² And when he had agreed with the laborers for a denarius for the day, he sent them into his vineyard."*

We see in this parable that the kingdom of heaven is represented by the vineyard. Notice that the "landowner" represents the Lord.

The landowner and the laborers **"agreed"** to work for one **"denarius."** The denarius was the principle Roman silver coin used in New Testament times and represented the wage an ordinary worker would make for a day's labor.[358]

---

[358] *Enhanced Strong's Lexicon*, (Oak Harbor, WA: Logos Research Systems, Inc.) 1995.
[Note continued on next page.]

VERSES 3-7: *"And he went out about the third hour and saw others standing idle in the market place; [4] and to those he said, 'You too go into the vineyard, and whatever is right I will give you.' And so they went. [5] Again he went out about the sixth and the ninth hour, and did the same thing. [6] And about the eleventh hour he went out, and found others standing; and he *said to them, 'Why have you been standing here idle all day long?' [7] They *said to him, 'Because no one hired us.' He *said to them, 'You too go into the vineyard.'"*

Throughout the day the landowner sees others who are unemployed and he sends them out to his field. The *third hour* means 9 a.m., the *sixth hour* is noon, the *ninth hour* is 3 p.m., and the *eleventh hour* is 5 p.m. From verse 12 we see that those he hired near the eleventh hour worked only one hour.

VERSES 8-9: *"And when evening had come, the owner of the vineyard *said to his foreman, 'Call the laborers and pay them their wages, beginning with the last group to the first.' [9] And when those hired about the eleventh hour came, each one received a denarius."*

Now we see the payment and rewards. What is unusual is that the landowner calls in those who have worked the least amount to be paid first. Note that when he hired the extra workers he did not set an agreed wage like he did for the first group, but instead told them, *"whatever is right I will give you."* Notice also in verse 9 that even though they worked only a little bit, they were paid the same amount as those who worked all day. This is a very gracious and generous landowner.

VERSES 10-12: *"And when those hired first came, they thought that they would receive more; and they also received each one a denarius. [11] And when they received it, they grumbled at the landowner, [12] saying, 'These last men have worked only one hour, and you have made them equal to us who have borne the burden and the scorching heat of the day.'"*

The men who were hired first found out that those who worked only an hour got paid a whole day's wage, *a denarius*. They assumed that since they worked longer, they would get paid much more than the agreed upon denarius. When they got paid a single denarius, they complained that they labored long and during the hot time of the day and were treated as equals with those who worked only an hour.

Matthew Henry believes that the parable;
> "[S]ignifies the jealousy which the Jews were provoked to by the admission of the Gentiles into the kingdom of heaven. As the elder brother, in the parable of the prodigal, repined at the reception of his younger brother, and complained of his father's generosity to him; so these laborers quarreled with their master, and

---

[Note continued.]

1220 { day-nar'-ee-on} of Latin origin; AV - penny 9, pence 5, pennyworth 2; 16 GK - 1324 { dhnavrion }denarius = "containing ten" 1) A Roman silver coin in NT time. It took its name from it being equal to ten "asses" a number after 217 B.C. increased to sixteen (about 3.898 grams or .1375 oz.). It was the principal silver coin of the Roman empire. From the parable of the laborers in the vineyard, it would seem that a denarius was then the ordinary pay for a day's wages. (Matthew 20:2-13)

found fault, not because they had not enough, so much as because others were made equal with them. They boast, as the prodigal's elder brother did, of their good services; *We have borne the burden and heat of the day;* that was the most they could make of it." [359]

John MacArthur also explains the parable in terms of salvation. He writes that the lesson is not addressing the issue of the believers "individual rewards" but rather salvation.

"The laborers are believers, and the denarius is eternal life, which all received equally for trusting in Christ. The work day is the believer's lifetime of service to his Lord and the evening is eternity.

God's sovereign principle for salvation is that every person who comes in faith to His Son, Jesus Christ, receives the same gracious salvation prepared by the Father and given by the Son. There are no exceptions or variations. Whether a person comes to God as a small child and lives a long life of faithful, obedient service, or whether he comes to Him on his deathbed, all come into the kingdom on the same basis and receive the same glorious, eternal blessings. The penitent thief who turned to Jesus on the cross with his last breath received the same salvation and heavenly glory as the apostles. He died justly as a criminal, whereas most of them died unjustly because of their faithfulness to Christ. He did not have even one hour to serve Christ, whereas some of them served Him far into old age." [360]

VERSES 13-16: *"But he answered and said to one of them, 'Friend, I am doing you no wrong; did you not agree with me for a denarius?* [14] *Take what is yours and go your way, but I wish to give to this last man the same as to you.* [15] *Is it not lawful for me to do what I wish with what is my own? Or is your eye envious because I am generous?'* [16] *Thus the last shall be first, and the first last."*

The landowner responds by stating that he is completely fair in paying them what they had agreed to be paid. He points out that he can give his money to whoever he wants to. He further points out that his generosity has exposed their envy.

In verse 16 Jesus says, *"Thus the last shall be first, and the first last."* A very similar statement is also made by Jesus to His disciples just before this story (see Matthew 19:30) when He assures them that they will be rewarded for their service.

Summary and Application

Salvation is available to all on an equal basis. Paul even explains that there will be those who are saved at the last moment of their lives. Even though they have no individual rewards to show, their entrance into the kingdom of God is no less legitimate than anyone else's. Why? Because nobody can earn entrance into the Kingdom of God. God is the one who pays it all.

---

[359] Henry, Matthew, *Matthew Henry's Commentary on the Bible*, Matthew 20:1-16 (Peabody, MA: Hendrickson Publishers) 1997.

[360] MacArthur, John F., *The MacArthur New Testament Commentary*, p. 167 (Chicago: Moody Press) 1983.

1 Corinthians 3:14-15: *"If any man's work which he has built upon it remains, he shall receive a reward.* [15] *If any man's work is burned up, he shall suffer loss; but he himself shall be saved, yet so as through fire."*

2 Timothy 4:7-8: *"I have fought the good fight, I have finished the course, I have kept the faith;* [8] *in the future there is laid up for me the crown of righteousness, which the Lord, the righteous Judge, will award to me on that day; and not only to me, but also to all who have loved His appearing."*

The Lord's rewards are not arbitrary and capricious. He is sovereign and just in His judgments. We see that as to individual rewards, His evaluation of our works is all that matters. Men may applaud our "religious work," but only the eye of the Lord matters (see Matthew 6:1-6). Review Matthew 6:1-6 and pray for the Lord to reveal any hypocritical "service" you have been engaged in and ask Him to grant you repentance. May we receive the ultimate reward as it is set out in the parable below. That reward is for the Lord to say, *"Well done, good and faithful slave;...."*

Matthew 25:14-30: *"For it is just like a man about to go on a journey, who called his own slaves, and entrusted his possessions to them.* [15] *And to one he gave five talents, to another, two, and to another, one, each according to his own ability; and he went on his journey.* [16] *Immediately the one who had received the five talents went and traded with them, and gained five more talents.* [17] *In the same manner the one who had received the two talents gained two more.* [18] *But he who received the one talent went away and dug in the ground, and hid his master's money.* [19] *Now after a long time the master of those slaves *came and *settled accounts with them.* [20] *And the one who had received the five talents came up and brought five more talents, saying, 'Master, you entrusted five talents to me; see, I have gained five more talents.'* [21] *His master said to him, 'Well done, good and faithful slave; you were faithful with a few things, I will put you in charge of many things, enter into the joy of your master.'* [22] *The one also who had received the two talents came up and said, 'Master, you entrusted to me two talents; see, I have gained two more talents.'* [23] *His master said to him, 'Well done, good and faithful slave; you were faithful with a few things, I will put you in charge of many things; enter into the joy of your master.'* [24] *And the one also who had received the one talent came up and said, 'Master, I knew you to be a hard man, reaping where you did not sow, and gathering where you scattered no seed.* [25] *And I was afraid, and went away and hid your talent in the ground; see, you have what is yours.'* [26] *But his master answered and said to him, 'You wicked, lazy slave, you knew that I reap where I did not sow, and gather where I scattered no seed.* [27] *Then you ought to have put my money in the bank, and on my arrival I would have received my money back with interest.* [28] *Therefore take away the talent from him, and give it to the one who has the ten talents.'* [29] *For to everyone who has shall more be given, and he shall have an abundance; but from the one who does not have, even what he does have shall be taken away.* [30] *And cast out the worthless slave into the outer darkness; in that place there shall be weeping and gnashing of teeth."*

<u>MATTHEW 20:17-28</u>
(JESUS REMINDS THE DISCIPLES OF HIS COMING CRUCIFIXION;
and
A MOTHER REQUESTS PREFERENTIAL TREATMENT FOR HER SONS)

"And as Jesus was about to go up to Jerusalem, He took the twelve disciples aside by themselves, and on the way He said to them, ¹⁸ 'Behold, we are going up to Jerusalem; and the Son of Man will be delivered to the chief priests and scribes, and they will condemn Him to death, ¹⁹ and will deliver Him to the Gentiles to mock and scourge and crucify Him, and on the third day He will be raised up.'

²⁰ Then the mother of the sons of Zebedee came to Him with her sons, bowing down, and making a request of Him. ²¹ And He said to her, 'What do you wish?' She *said to Him, 'Command that in Your kingdom these two sons of mine may sit, one on Your right and one on Your left.' ²² But Jesus answered and said, 'You do not know what you are asking for. Are you able to drink the cup that I am about to drink?' They *said to Him, 'We are able.' ²³ He *said to them, 'My cup you shall drink; but to sit on My right and on My left, this is not Mine to give, but it is for those for whom it has been prepared by My Father.' ²⁴ And hearing this, the ten became indignant with the two brothers. ²⁵ But Jesus called them to Himself, and said, 'You know that the rulers of the Gentiles lord it over them, and their great men exercise authority over them. ²⁶ It is not so among you, but whoever wishes to become great among you shall be your servant, ²⁷ and whoever wishes to be first among you shall be your slave; ²⁸ just as the Son of Man did not come to be served, but to serve, and to give His life a ransom for many.'"

<u>Introduction</u>
Often the Lord will speak an important truth to us and we will hear the words but not truly listen to what is being said. Here the disciples are told by Jesus an important truth of what will happen to Him. How willing were they to take that important revelation to heart? God has given us His revelation in His Word, but how quickly do we go to it for the true answers…especially when it does not fit comfortably into our lifestyle or point of view? Remember, it is always easier to seek the advice of well-meaning friends or so-called "Christian" self-help books, but if you want truthful answers, go to God's Word (the Bible) and prayer.

This section will also look at the mistake of viewing "Christian service" as a means to obtain personal power and glory. The leader is to be a slave.

VERSES 17-19: *"And as Jesus was about to go up to Jerusalem, He took the twelve disciples aside by themselves, and on the way He said to them, ¹⁸ 'Behold, we are going up to Jerusalem; and the Son of Man will be delivered to the chief priests and scribes, and they will condemn Him to death, ¹⁹ and will deliver Him to the Gentiles to mock and scourge and crucify Him, and on the third day He will be raised up.'"*

Jesus again tells His disciples about His soon-coming crucifixion. We do not read about a response from the disciples this time but there had been responses on earlier occasions.
> **Matthew 17:22-23:** *"And while they were gathering together in Galilee, Jesus said to them, 'The Son of Man is going to be delivered into the hands of men;*

²³ *and they will kill Him, and He will be raised on the third day.' <u>And they</u>* <u>*were deeply grieved."*</u>

Could it be that they still did not want to believe what Jesus told them would really happen? Or could it be that they remembered what Peter was told the last time he tried to counter the Lord's information?

> **Matthew 16:21-23**: *"From that time Jesus Christ <u>began to show His disciples</u>* <u>*that He must go to Jerusalem, and suffer many things from the elders and chief*</u> <u>*priests and scribes, and be killed, and be raised up on the third day.*</u> *²² And Peter took Him aside and began to rebuke Him, saying, 'God forbid it, Lord! This shall never happen to You.' ²³ But He turned and said to Peter, 'Get behind Me, Satan! You are a stumbling block to Me; for you are not setting your mind on God's interests, but man's.'"*

Notice in the text we are studying (Matthew 20:17-19) it says that Jesus will *"...be delivered to the chief priests and scribes, and they will condemn Him to death, ¹⁹ and will deliver Him to the Gentiles to mock and scourge and crucify...."* That is exactly what took place. Remember that it was the Jewish counsel that judged Jesus to death (Mark 15:1). Roman law did not allow anyone to be put to death except by Rome's authority and approval (John 18:31, Luke 23:23-24). So it was the "gentiles" (i.e. Rome) that also went on to, *"mock and scourge and crucify...."* We see this in more detail in **Matthew 27:27-31:**

> *"Then the soldiers of the governor took Jesus into the Praetorium and gathered the whole Roman cohort around Him. ²⁸ And they stripped Him, and put a scarlet robe on Him. ²⁹ And after weaving a crown of thorns, they put it on His head, and a reed in His right hand; and they kneeled down before Him and mocked Him, saying, 'Hail, King of the Jews!' ³⁰ And they spat on Him, and took the reed and began to beat Him on the head. ³¹ And after they had mocked Him, they took His robe off and put His garments on Him, and led Him away to crucify Him."*

Jesus tells His disciples about His death in Matthew 20:17-19, but He also tells them about His resurrection in verse 19: *"...and on the third day He will be raised up."*

VERSES 20-21: *"Then the mother of the sons of Zebedee came to Him with her sons, bowing down, and making a request of Him. ²¹ And He said to her, 'What do you wish?' She *said to Him, 'Command that in Your kingdom these two sons of mine may sit, one on Your right and one on Your left.'"*

Here we see James and John and their mother[361] in front of Jesus, asking that the boys would be seated on His right and on His left in the Kingdom. One has to wonder if her actions resulted

---

[361] "The mother of James and John was named Salome and was a sister of Mary, the Mother of Jesus (see Matthew 27:56; Mark 15:40; John 19:25), making her Jesus' aunt and James and John His first cousins. ...From the Mark passage [Mark 10:35] it is clear that **the mother** was speaking at the behest of her **two sons**. In fact, Mark makes no mention of her at all. The three obviously came with a common purpose and plan they had discussed among themselves beforehand. The mother probably spoke first, and then James and John spoke for themselves." MacArthur, John F., *The MacArthur New Testament Commentary*, Matthew p.167 (Chicago: Moody Press) 1983.

from what Jesus told the disciples in **Matthew 19:28** when He said, *"...Truly I say to you, that you who have followed Me, in the regeneration when <u>the Son of Man will sit on His glorious throne, you also shall sit upon twelve thrones, judging the twelve tribes of Israel.</u>"* Their request revealed their spiritual blindness in the area of leadership, since they continued to compete for personal glory.

VERSES 22-23: *"But Jesus answered and said, 'You do not know what you are asking for. Are you able to drink the cup that I am about to drink?' They *said to Him, 'We are able.' 23 He *said to them, 'My cup you shall drink; but to sit on My right and on My left, this is not Mine to give, but it is for those for whom it has been prepared by My Father.'"*

Notice that Jesus turns to the two men and responds to their request by asking them, *"Are you able to drink the cup that I am about to drink?"* He is asking if they are able to drink the <u>cup of death.</u> When Jesus was being arrested, He referred to this "cup" as His death when He said to Peter, *"Put the sword into the sheath; <u>the cup which the Father has given Me, shall I not drink it?</u>"* **John 18:11.** Jesus' death was to redeem us from sin:

> **Titus 2:13-14:** *"...looking for the blessed hope and the appearing of the glory of our great God and Savior, Christ Jesus; 14 who gave Himself for us, <u>that He might redeem us</u> from every lawless deed and purify for Himself a people for His own possession, zealous for good deeds."*

James and John responded to Jesus by saying they could drink the cup. They said this without completely knowing what that meant. Jesus then tells them that they would indeed drink the <u>cup of death</u> for the truth of the Gospel. James was killed (Acts 12:2) and John (author of the Gospel of John, Epistles of John and the Revelation) was exiled to the island of Patmos. John wrote of his willingness to accept persecution for the Lord Jesus Christ:

> **Revelation 1:9:** *"I, John, your brother and <u>fellow partaker in the tribulation and kingdom and perseverance which are in Jesus,</u> was on the island called Patmos, because of the word of God and the testimony of Jesus."*

In verse 23 of the text Jesus says, *"...but to sit on My right and on My left, this is not Mine to give, but it is for those for whom it has been prepared by My Father."* Jesus tells them that the Father has ordained who will have those positions.

VERSES 24-28: *"And hearing this, the ten became indignant with the two brothers. 25 But Jesus called them to Himself, and said, 'You know that the rulers of the Gentiles lord it over them, and their great men exercise authority over them. 26 It is not so among you, but whoever wishes to become great among you shall be your servant, 27 and whoever wishes to be first among you shall be your slave; 28 just as the Son of Man did not come to be served, but to serve, and to give His life a ransom for many.'"*

We see that the other disciples, were *"indignant with the two brothers."* No one knows the real reason they were upset with them. Often in a work-place environment we see people getting upset when they are afraid that someone is getting ahead of them. Although the other disciples were "indignant" they were not so holy as to not be thinking about their own glory. We read of an earlier occasion in which the other disciples entertained the same selfish and self-exalting ideas that James and John had.

> **Mark 9:33-35:** *"And they came to Capernaum; and when He was in the house, He began to question them, 'What were you discussing on the way?'* [34] *But they kept silent, for on the <u>way they had discussed with one another which of them was the greatest.</u>* [35] *And sitting down, He called the twelve and *said to them, 'If anyone wants to be first, he shall be last of all, and servant of all.'"*

Jesus points out that leadership in this world is based on who gets to boss around others and make them serve. That is not the way for the believer. The greatest is not the one who gets to be the boss of others, but rather is the one who is a *"slave"* to others.

> **Colossians 3:23-24:** *"Whatever you do, do your work heartily, as for the Lord rather than for men;* [24] *knowing that from the Lord you will receive the reward of the inheritance. <u>It is the Lord Christ whom you serve.</u>"*

Ryle summarizes Matthew 20:24-28 as follows:

> "The standard of the world and the standard of the Lord Jesus are completely different. They are more than different: they are totally contradictory to each other. Among the children of this world a person is thought the greatest if he has the most land, most money, most servants, most rank and most earthly powers; among the children of God a person is reckoned the greatest who does most to promote the spiritual and temporal happiness of his fellow-creatures. True greatness consists not in receiving but in giving; not in selfish absorption of good things but in imparting good to others; not in being served but in serving; not in sitting still and being served but in going about and serving others. The angels of God see far more beauty in the work of the missionary than in the work of the Australian gold-digger. They take far more interest in the labors of men like Howard and Judson than in the victories of generals, the political speeches of statesmen, or the council-chambers of kings. Let us remember these things. Let us beware of seeking false greatness; let us aim at that greatness which alone is true."[362]

Summary and Application

What is the basis of the requests we bring before the Lord? Are our prayers to glorify ourselves or to glorify the Lord? James (not the James who was John's brother) explains why many of our prayers go unanswered.

> **James 4:3:** *"You ask and do not receive, because you ask with wrong motives, so that you may spend it on your pleasures."*

Remember what our attitude should be about service. We are not to seek a name for ourselves but be thankful we even get the opportunity to be slaves for Christ.

> **Luke 17:7-10:** *"But which of you, having a slave plowing or tending sheep, will say to him when he has come in from the field, 'Come immediately and sit down to eat'?* [8] *But will he not say to him, 'Prepare something for me to eat, and properly clothe yourself*

---

[362] *Matthew* / Ryle, J.C. p.184-185 (Expository Thoughts on the Gospels) (Crossways Classic Commentaries: v.1)

and serve me until I have eaten and drunk; and afterward you will eat and drink?' [9] He does not thank the slave because he did the things which were commanded, does he? [10] So you too, when you do all the things which are commanded you, <u>say, 'We are unworthy slaves; we have done only that which we ought to have done.'"</u>

<u>Acts 20:24:</u> *"But <u>I do not consider my life of any account as dear to myself, in order that I may finish my course,</u> and the ministry which I received from the Lord Jesus, to testify solemnly of the gospel of the grace of God."*

We are to serve without any regard for how others view us or treat us. In other words, do not serve so that others recognize or approve of you as the Pharisees did. Our service is first to God, to whom we will give account. As one man told me, "You know you are a servant...when you are treated like one."

MATTHEW 20:29-34
(HEALING THE BLIND MEN)

"And as they were going out from Jericho, a great multitude followed Him. [30] And behold, two blind men sitting by the road, hearing that Jesus was passing by, cried out, saying, 'Lord, have mercy on us, Son of David!' [31] And the multitude sternly told them to be quiet; but they cried out all the more, saying, 'Lord, have mercy on us, Son of David!' [32] And Jesus stopped and called them, and said, 'What do you want Me to do for you?' [33] They *said to Him, 'Lord, we want our eyes to be opened.' [34] And moved with compassion, Jesus touched their eyes; and immediately they regained their sight and followed Him."

Introduction

Here we see Jesus compassionately healing two blind men. When Jesus asked them, *"What do you want Me to do for you?"*, they answered that they wanted the Lord to open their eyes. Even though these men had a physical need, their plea should also be ours. We need the Lord to open our eyes spiritually, so that we can know and understand His Word even more. The unbeliever cannot *see* (i.e. comprehend) the truth of God's Word because of his spiritually blind state:

> **2 Corinthians 4:3-4:** *"And even if our gospel is veiled, it is veiled to those who are perishing, [4] <u>in whose case the god of this world has blinded the minds of the unbelieving,</u> that they might not see the light of the gospel of the glory of Christ, who is the image of God."*

VERSES 29-31: *"And as they were going out from Jericho, a great multitude followed Him. [30] And behold, two blind men sitting by the road, hearing that Jesus was passing by, cried out, saying, 'Lord, have mercy on us, Son of David!' [31] And the multitude sternly told them to be quiet; but they cried out all the more, saying, 'Lord, have mercy on us, Son of David!'"*

Matthew tells us that there were two blind men involved in this incident. The parallel accounts in Mark and Luke speak of a blind man. Undoubtedly there were two of them as we get more detail from Matthew, but the other writers focus on the dominant spokesman of the two, a man named Bartimaeus, the son of Timaeus who also was a beggar (Mark 10:46). Some have speculated that the possible reason Mark was so specific about mentioning Bartimaeus (i.e. *Bartimaeus, the <u>son of Timaeus</u>*), is due to the possibility that this Barimaeus later became well-known among the believers of that time period.

Those who refuse to believe the Bible try to falsely claim that the Bible has errors because "Matthew and Mark said the men were healed when Jesus left Jericho, but Luke said the healing occurred when Jesus approached Jericho. This [is] explained by the fact that there were two Jerichos then, an old city and a new one. Jesus was leaving old Jericho (Matthew and Mark) and approaching new Jericho (Luke) when the miracle occurred."[363]

---

[363] Walvoord, John F., and Zuck, Roy B., *The Bible Knowledge Commentary*, v.2 p.67 (Wheaton, Illinois: Scripture Press Publications, Inc.) 1983, 1985.

Note that these men were calling Jesus the *"Son of David."* The term *"Son of David"* was a title used for the Messiah. By referring to Jesus by this title they were declaring Jesus as the Messiah.

The people saw these two blind men as unimportant, annoying and an embarrassment. In verse 31 we read that the crowd, *"sternly told them to be quiet; but they cried out all the more, saying, 'Lord, have mercy on us, Son of David!'"* The blind men were not intimidated by the crowd and started to yell even louder. We should not let others discourage us when we pray. Jesus says in Luke 18:1 that at all times His people, *"ought to pray and not to lose heart,...."*

VERSES 32-34: *"And Jesus stopped and called them, and said, 'What do you want Me to do for you?'* ³³ *They *said to Him, 'Lord, we want our eyes to be opened.'* ³⁴ *And moved with compassion, Jesus touched their eyes; and immediately they regained their sight and followed Him."*

Unlike the crowd, Jesus sees great value in these two men. He asks them, *"What do you want Me to do for you?"* If Jesus asked you that question, how would you answer it? Would you ask for money, power or some other self-centered greed? These men wanted to be healed. We read that Jesus had compassion on the men and touched their eyes. The healing did not take days or weeks but, *"immediately they regained their sight."*

Notice the response of the men after they were healed. Verse 34 tells us that they *"followed"* Jesus. Luke even goes a little deeper with reference to their reaction in **Luke 18:43:** *"And immediately he regained his sight, and began following Him, <u>glorifying God; and when all the people saw it, they gave praise to God.</u>"*

After all that He did for them they did not care about anything but following Jesus. That should be our response after all He has done for us by saving our souls from eternal damnation.

Summary and Application

We need to walk by spiritual eyesight and not by human sight. We must ask God to open our spiritual eyes, and then we will see what really is going on. This will bring us peace and security in the Lord because we will know the truth, *"and the truth shall make you free"* (John 8:32). Look at the example of Elisha when an army surrounded the city trying to arrest him. Elisha's servant was scared to death but Elisha prayed to the Lord to give his servant spiritual eyes to see the real situation.

> **2 Kings 6:14-18:** *"And he sent horses and chariots and a great army there, and they came by night and surrounded the city.* ¹⁵ *Now when the attendant of the man of God had risen early and gone out, behold, an army with horses and chariots was circling the city. And his servant said to him, 'Alas, my master! What shall we do?'* ¹⁶ *So he answered, 'Do not fear, <u>for those who are with us are more than those who are with them.</u>'* ¹⁷ *Then Elisha prayed and said, <u>'O LORD, I pray, open his eyes that he may see.'</u> <u>And the LORD opened the servant's eyes, and he saw; and behold, the mountain was full of horses and chariots of fire all around Elisha."</u>*

MATTHEW 21:1-11
(JESUS' TRIUMPHAL ENTRY INTO JERUSALEM)

"*AND when they had approached Jerusalem and had come to Bethphage, to the Mount of Olives, then Jesus sent two disciples,* ² *saying to them, 'Go into the village opposite you, and immediately you will find a donkey tied there and a colt with her; untie them, and bring them to Me.* ³*And if anyone says something to you, you shall say, 'The Lord has need of them,' and immediately he will send them.'* ⁴ *Now this took place that what was spoken through the prophet might be fulfilled, saying,*

> ⁵ *'SAY TO THE DAUGHTER OF ZION,*
>> *BEHOLD YOUR KING IS COMING TO YOU,*
>> *GENTLE, AND MOUNTED ON A DONKEY,*
>> *EVEN ON A COLT, THE FOAL OF A BEAST OF BURDEN.'*

⁶ *And the disciples went and did just as Jesus had directed them,* ⁷ *and brought the donkey and the colt, and laid on them their garments, on which He sat.* ⁸ *And most of the multitude spread their garments in the road, and others were cutting branches from the trees, and spreading them in the road.* ⁹ *And the multitudes going before Him, and those who followed after were crying out, saying,*

> *'Hosanna to the Son of David;*
> *BLESSED IS HE WHO COMES IN THE NAME OF THE LORD;*
> *Hosanna in the highest!'*

¹⁰ *And when He had entered Jerusalem, all the city was stirred, saying, 'Who is this?'* ¹¹ *And the multitudes were saying, 'This is the prophet Jesus, from Nazareth in Galilee.'"*

Introduction

In this passage there is a snapshot of Jesus' omniscience when He tells His disciples where to find the donkey. We also observe the humility of Christ as He rides on a donkey. Some in the crowd simply wanted a king to deliver them from Roman occupation. They were not concerned with their slavery to sin. Many today, are like the false worshipers of Jesus' day, they want to have a God that fits their own desires. They will bow and pretend allegiance to Christ as long as it is popular and He provides what they want.

VERSES 1-5: "*AND when they had approached Jerusalem and had come to Bethphage, to the Mount of Olives, then Jesus sent two disciples,* ² *saying to them, 'Go into the village opposite you, and immediately you will find a donkey tied there and a colt with her; untie them, and bring them to Me.* ³ *And if anyone says something to you, you shall say, 'The Lord has need of them,' and immediately he will send them.* ⁴ Now this took place that what was spoken through the prophet might be fulfilled, saying,*

> ⁵ *'SAY TO THE DAUGHTER OF ZION, 'BEHOLD YOUR KING IS COMING TO YOU, GENTLE, AND MOUNTED ON A DONKEY, EVEN ON A COLT, THE FOAL OF A BEAST OF BURDEN.'"*

Jesus had just left Jericho after healing the blind men (Matthew 20:29-34). From Jericho they were going to Jerusalem. On the way there they stopped at a village called *Bethphage*, which is less than a mile from Jerusalem. It was at *Bethphage* that Jesus sent two of His disciples to get the donkey and its colt. [364]   Jesus warns them that if anyone protests, they are simply to say that, *'The Lord has need of them,'* and Jesus assures them that this would be a satisfactory answer for the one questioning.   In the parallel passages written by Mark and Luke, we find out that the disciples were questioned about taking the colt.

> **Mark 11:5-6:** *"And some of the bystanders were saying to them, 'What are you doing, untying the colt?' And they spoke to them just as Jesus had told them, and they gave them permission."* (See also Luke 19:32-34).

The other Gospels refer to the *colt*, whereas John says a *young donkey* (John 12:14).   We read from Mark and Luke that the colt had never been ridden on before (Mark 11:2 and Luke 19:30).   From Matthew 21:7 we read that the disciples took some of their clothes and laid them on the back of the donkey and on the colt as a riding pad for Jesus.   They obviously did not know which one Jesus would ride on.   Jesus rode the colt and its mother went along with her colt as Matthew 21:2 tells us.

It was necessary that Jesus came riding on a colt so that prophecy could be fulfilled.   Matthew is quoting from Zechariah 9:9 when he wrote in **Matthew 21:5:**

> *"SAY TO THE DAUGHTER OF ZION, 'BEHOLD YOUR KING IS COMING TO YOU, GENTLE, AND MOUNTED ON A DONKEY, EVEN ON A COLT, THE FOAL OF A BEAST OF BURDEN.'"*

VERSES 6-9: *"And the disciples went and did just as Jesus had directed them, [7] and brought the donkey and the colt, and laid on them their garments, on which He sat. [8] And most of the multitude spread their garments in the road, and others were cutting branches from the trees, and spreading them in the road. [9] And the multitudes going before Him, and those who followed after were crying out, saying,*
> *'Hosanna to the Son of David;*
> *BLESSED IS HE WHO COMES IN THE NAME OF THE LORD;*
> *Hosanna in the highest!'"*

The disciples brought back the donkey and Jesus began His triumphal entry into Jerusalem.   The act of Jesus riding on a donkey fulfilled prophesy and also demonstrated His humbleness.

Typically in those days a conquering king would have more likely appeared on a white stallion, with his powerful army marching alongside.   There will be that day for Jesus:

> **Revelation 19:11-16:**   *"And I saw heaven opened; and <u>behold, a white horse, and He who sat upon it is called Faithful and True; and in righteousness He judges and wages war.</u> [12] And His eyes are a flame of fire, and upon His head are many diadems; and He has a name written upon Him which no one knows except Himself. [13] And He is clothed with a robe dipped in blood; and His name is called The Word of God. [14] <u>And the armies which are in heaven, clothed in fine linen, white and clean, were following Him on white horses.</u> [15] <u>And from His mouth comes a sharp sword, so that with it He may smite the nations; and He will rule them with a rod of iron;</u> and He treads the wine press of the fierce*

---

[364] "Less than a mile southeast of Jerusalem was the village of Bethphage (lit., 'house of unripe figs') and about two miles out was Bethany (lit., 'house of dates or figs'), on the eastern side of the Mount of Olives, a high ridge about two miles long known for its many olive trees. In Bethany, the last stopping place on the desolate and unsafe road from Jerusalem to Jericho."   Walvoord, J. F., Zuck, R. B., and Dallas Theological Seminary. (1985). *The Bible Knowledge Commentary: An Exposition of the Scriptures* (V 2, p. 155). Wheaton, IL: Victor Books.

wrath of God, the Almighty. *16 And on His robe and on His thigh He has a name written, 'KING OF KINGS, AND LORD OF LORDS.'"*

This time, Jesus rode a colt. This would continue to confound the unbelieving, but as for the believing, His humility would bear their heavy burden of sin.

> **Matthew 11:25-30:** *"At that time Jesus answered and said, 'I praise Thee, O Father, Lord of heaven and earth, that Thou didst hide these things from the wise and intelligent and didst reveal them to babes. 26 Yes, Father, for thus it was well-pleasing in Thy sight. 27 All things have been handed over to Me by My Father; and no one knows the Son, except the Father; nor does anyone know the Father, except the Son, and anyone to whom the Son wills to reveal Him. 28 Come to Me, all who are weary and heavy-laden, and I will give you rest. 29 Take My yoke upon you, and learn from Me, for I am gentle and humble in heart; and YOU SHALL FIND REST FOR YOUR SOULS. 30 For My yoke is easy, and My load is light.'"*

The people laid some of their garments in front of His path in respect and as a sign of outward submission to their King. The people also cut tree branches and spread them on the road for Jesus to ride over. In John 12:13 we are told that the branches were from palm trees. There is another place in Scripture that we see palm branches being used in worship. In the Book of Revelation the branches are not being laid on the road but were in the hands of worshipping believers who went through the great tribulation.

> **Revelation 7:9-10, 13-14:** *"After these things I looked, and behold, a great multitude, which no one could count, from every nation and all tribes and peoples and tongues, standing before the throne and before the Lamb, clothed in white robes, and palm branches were in their hands; 10 and they cry out with a loud voice, saying, 'Salvation to our God who sits on the throne, and to the Lamb.'....*
> *13 And one of the elders answered, saying to me, 'These who are clothed in the white robes, who are they, and from where have they come?' 14 And I said to him, 'My lord, you know.' And he said to me, 'These are the ones who come out of the great tribulation, and they have washed their robes and made them white in the blood of the Lamb.'"*

In Matthew 21:9 we read that the crowd was crying out:

> *"...Hosanna to the Son of David;*
> BLESSED IS HE WHO COMES IN THE NAME OF THE LORD;
> *Hosanna in the highest!"*

They were quoting from **Psalms 118:25-26:**

> 25 *"O LORD, do save, we beseech Thee;*
> *O LORD, we beseech Thee, do send prosperity!*
> 26 *Blessed is the one who comes in the name of the LORD;*
> *We have blessed you from the house of the LORD."*

The term *Hosanna* in the Hebrew means *save us now* or *save, we pray*.[365] The disciples were proclaiming that Jesus was the Messiah, and the Pharisees did not like that. Notice how Jesus pointed out to the Pharisees that His Messiahship was an undeniable truth that creation proclaims!

> **Luke 19:37-40:** *"And as He was now approaching, near the descent of the Mount of Olives, the whole multitude of the disciples began to praise God joyfully with a loud voice for all the miracles which they had seen, [38] saying,*
>> *'Blessed is the King who comes in the name of the Lord;*
>> *Peace in heaven and glory in the highest!'*
>
> *[39] And some of the Pharisees in the multitude said to Him, 'Teacher, rebuke Your disciples.' [40] <u>And He answered and said, 'I tell you, if these become silent, the stones will cry out!'"</u>*

Creation does declare the glory of God!

> **Psalm 148:3:** *"Praise Him, sun and moon; Praise Him, all stars of light!"*

The spiritual blindness of the Pharisees resulted in their unwillingness to worship God. Paul addresses this mentality in all of the unsaved:

> **Romans 1:20-22:** *"For since the creation of the world His invisible attributes, His eternal power and divine nature, have been clearly seen, being understood through what has been made, so that they are without excuse. [21] <u>For even though they knew God, they did not honor Him as God, or give thanks; but they became futile in their speculations, and their foolish heart was darkened.</u> [22] <u>Professing to be wise, they became fools.</u>"*

We read from Luke how Jesus wept over Jerusalem while riding on the colt:

> **Luke 19:41-44:** *"And when He approached, He saw the city and wept over it, [42] saying, 'If you had known in this day, even you, the things which make for peace! But now they have been hidden from your eyes. [43] For the days shall come upon you when your enemies will throw up a bank before you, and surround you, and hem you in on every side, [44] and will level you to the ground and your children within you, and they will not leave in you one stone upon another, because you did not recognize the time of your visitation.'"*

The people were proclaiming Jesus as their Messiah, but their concept of the work the Messiah would do at that time was wrong. They saw the Messiah coming to set them free from Rome and defeat all other enemies they had. Jesus came to set them free from sin. They did not realize that His kingdom was not of this world (John 18:36). It would only take a matter of days and they would see that He did not come to defeat Rome. This same crowd proclaiming Him Messiah as He entered Jerusalem, would disown Him as its king and demand that Pilate have Him put to death.

---

[365] "… hōsanna (ὡσαννά, (5614), in the Hebrew, means 'save, we pray.' The word seems to have become an utterance of praise rather than of prayer, though originally, probably, a cry for help. The people's cry at the Lord's triumphal entry into Jerusalem (Matthew 21:9, 15; Mark 11:9, 10; John 12:13) was taken from Psalms 118, which was recited at the Feast of Tabernacles (see Feast) in the great Hallel (Psalms 113 to 118) in responses with the priest, accompanied by the waving of palm and willow branches. The last day of the feast was called 'the great Hosanna;' the boughs also were called hosannas." Vine, W. E., *Vine's Expository Dictionary of Old and New Testament Words*, (Grand Rapids, MI: Fleming H. Revell) 1981.

John 19:14-15: *"Now it was the day of preparation for the Passover; it was about the sixth hour. And he *said to the Jews, 'Behold, your King!'* [15] *They therefore cried out, 'Away with Him, away with Him, crucify Him!' Pilate *said to them, 'Shall I crucify your King?' The chief priests answered, 'We have no king but Caesar.'"* (See also Luke 23:20-23)

Many people today are like the crowd. They will come to Jesus because they are after "something." They may want God to fix a problem or give them financial success. They may want a spouse or pray for healing from a disease. They desire to create a "god" in the likeness of their own imagination or greed. Some want a God who winks at sin and functions as a celestial Santa Clause to give the toys they want. When they don't get what they want, these apostates are the first to mock and blaspheme God by saying, "Yeah, I tried that Jesus stuff, but it did not work." What they are saying is that they will appear to bow the knee if they get what they want. Scripture makes it clear that the time will come when everyone will bow the knee to Jesus.

Philippians 2:10-11: *"...that at the name of Jesus EVERY KNEE SHOULD BOW, of those who are in heaven, and on earth, and under the earth,* [11] *and that every tongue should confess that Jesus Christ is Lord, to the glory of God the Father."*

The true Christian knows that no matter what happens, his God is in ultimate control. Because of the confidence we have in the Lord and His love for us, we can say like Job,

"Though he slay me, yet will I trust in him..." **Job 13:15** (KJV)

VERSES 10-11: *"And when He had entered Jerusalem, all the city was stirred, saying, 'Who is this?'* [11] *And the multitudes were saying, 'This is the prophet Jesus, from Nazareth in Galilee.'"*

Even though the people were calling Jesus the Messiah (see v.9), they did not really know who He was. It did not take much time to pass for the same crowd that was calling Him, *"the Son of David,"* to be referring to Him simply as, *"the prophet Jesus, from Nazareth."*

Summary and Application

So who is your King Jesus? Is it the one you have created in your mind, or is it the Jesus of the Bible, the Almighty God of Glory and Ruler of all of His creation? We are not to be Christians who will bow the knee when it is easy because everyone else is (such as when we are at church). We are to be the true believers who are calling Him Lord when others are crying "Crucify!" Make no mistake about it, the humble King who came the first time riding on a donkey will come again as the glorified Lord who rules and reigns with an iron rod (Revelation 19:11-16).

MATTHEW 21:12-17
(CLEANSING THE TEMPLE; HEALING THE SICK; and BEING GLORIFIED)

"And Jesus entered the temple and cast out all those who were buying and selling in the temple, and overturned the tables of the moneychangers and the seats of those who were selling doves. [13] *And He *said to them, 'It is written, 'MY HOUSE SHALL BE CALLED A HOUSE OF PRAYER'; but you are making it a ROBBERS' DEN.'* [14] *And the blind and the lame came to Him in the temple, and He healed them.* [15] *But when the chief priests and the scribes saw the wonderful things that He had done, and the children who were crying out in the temple and saying, 'Hosanna to the Son of David,' they became indignant,* [16] *and said to Him, 'Do You hear what these are saying?' And Jesus *said to them, 'Yes; have you never read, 'OUT OF THE MOUTH OF INFANTS AND NURSING BABES THOU HAST PREPARED PRAISE FOR THYSELF?''* [17] *And He left them and went out of the city to Bethany, and lodged there."*

Introduction

It is important to have the correct timeline of events as we begin to look into the days before Jesus' crucifixion. Many mistakenly think that right after the triumphal entry Jesus went and cleansed the temple. On the day of the triumphal entry, Jesus simply looked around the temple, and after that He went to Bethany[366] for the night. It was on the next day that He returned to Jerusalem and cleansed the temple as Mark sets out below:

> **Mark 11:9-12, 15-16:** *"And those who went before, and those who followed after, were crying out,*
>
>> *'Hosanna!*
>>> *BLESSED IS HE WHO COMES IN THE NAME OF THE LORD;*
>> [10] *Blessed is the coming kingdom of our father David;*
>>> *Hosanna in the highest!'*
>
> [11] *And He entered Jerusalem and came into the temple; and after looking all around, He departed for Bethany with the twelve, since it was already late.* [12] *And on the next day, when they had departed from Bethany,.... v. 15: And they *came to Jerusalem. And He entered the temple and began to cast out those who were buying and selling in the temple, and overturned the tables of the moneychangers and the seats of those who were selling doves;* [16] *and He would not permit anyone to carry goods through the temple."*

VERSES 12-13: *"And Jesus entered the temple and cast out all those who were buying and selling in the temple, and overturned the tables of the moneychangers and the seats of those who were selling doves.* [13] *And He *said to them, 'It is written, 'MY HOUSE SHALL BE CALLED A HOUSE OF PRAYER'; but you are making it a ROBBERS' DEN.'"*

---

[366] Note that after Jesus' triumphal entry He went to Bethany which was about two miles from Jerusalem (John 11:18). Bethany is a different place than Bethphage, which was about ¾ of a mile from Jerusalem. For more on Bethphage see footnote in lesson of Matthew 21:1-11. Bethany was the home of Mary, Martha and Lazarus, John 12:1-3.

This incident is the second time that Jesus cleansed the temple. Both cleansings took place during Passover. The first time Jesus cleansed the temple was three years before this incident recorded in Matthew 21. The first cleansing was recorded by John:[367]

> **John 2:13-16:** *"And the Passover of the Jews was at hand, and Jesus went up to Jerusalem. ¹⁴And He found in the temple those who were selling oxen and sheep and doves, and the moneychangers seated. ¹⁵ And He made a scourge of cords, and drove them all out of the temple, with the sheep and the oxen; and He poured out the coins of the moneychangers, and overturned their tables; ¹⁶ and to those who were selling the doves He said, 'Take these things away; stop making My Father's house a house of merchandise.'"*

These temple salesmen would have argued, under pretext, that they were providing a "necessary religious service" for people. They would sell to the people animals that were satisfactory for a sacrificial offering, such as an "unblemished lamb" or a dove, etc. They would falsely claim that all they were doing was helping the priests and the people uphold God's law.

> **Leviticus 22:17-22:** *"Then the LORD spoke to Moses, saying, ¹⁸ 'Speak to Aaron and to his sons and to all the sons of Israel, and say to them, Any man of the house of Israel or of the aliens in Israel who presents his offering, whether it is any of their votive or any of their freewill offerings, which they present to the LORD for a burnt offering— ¹⁹ for you to be accepted—it <u>must be a male without defect from the cattle, the sheep, or the goats. ²⁰ Whatever has a defect, you shall not offer, for it will not be accepted for you.</u> ²¹ And when a man offers a sacrifice of peace offerings to the LORD to fulfill a special vow, or for a freewill offering, of the herd or of the flock, it must be perfect to be accepted; <u>there shall be no defect in it.</u> ²² Those that are blind or fractured or maimed or having a running sore or eczema or scabs, you shall not offer to the LORD, nor make of them an offering by fire on the altar to the LORD.'"*

The reality is that these salesmen were running a financial racket complete with kick-backs, extortion and corruption. The temple salesmen would buy the right to sell livestock in the Court of the Gentiles from the priests. To make sure the business was good for them and the kick-backs

---

[367] "This is the first of two temple cleansings [John 2:13-16]—one at the beginning and the other at the end of Jesus' ministry (cf. Matthew 21:12–17)." Hughes, R. B., and Laney, J. C. (2001). *Tyndale Concise Bible commentary.* The Tyndale reference library (p 468). Wheaton, IL: Tyndale House Publishers.

MacArthur also believes the evidence is strongly in favor of two separate "cleansings of the temple." He states: "As John recorded this cleansing of the temple at the beginning of Jesus' ministry, the synoptic gospels record a temple cleansing at the end of Jesus' ministry during the final Passover week before Jesus' crucifixion (Matthew 21:12–17; Mark 11:15–18; Luke 19:45, 46). The historical circumstances and literary contexts of the two temple cleansings differ so widely that attempts to equate the two are unsuccessful. Furthermore, that two cleansings occurred is entirely consistent with overall context of Jesus' ministry, for the Jewish nation as a whole never recognized Jesus' authority as Messiah (Matthew 23:37–39)." *The MacArthur Study Bible.* 1997 (J. MacArthur, Jr., Ed.) (electronic ed.) (John 2:15). Nashville, TN: Word Publishing.

kept coming, the priests routinely would find a *defect* in an animal that was not purchased by the temple salesman. So if a person brought his own lamb for offering and the priest claimed it had a defect, the person would be forced to either go home, or purchase an animal from the salesmen at an inflated rate.

Jesus cleansed the temple during Passover. Passover had to be a very profitable event for the temple salesmen since many people would have traveled great distances to attend. When traveling far distances, many worshippers found it easier to bring money rather than bring a sacrificial animal on the trip. The salesmen understood the traveler's dilemma and would exploit it by inflating their rates during that time.

The money used in the temple was not the common Roman or Greek currencies since those coins featured the face of a man, and thus were considered idolatrous. The Greek and Roman currencies were required to be converted to the temple currency.[368] Money changers would sell the required Tyrian (Jewish coin) that was used for all males who were at least 20 years old to pay the annual half-shekel temple tax that was prescribed in Exodus 30:12-16. To purchase an animal deemed acceptable for sacrifice, one was required to use the temple currency. To obtain temple currency one had to take his money to the *moneychangers* who would set an exchange rate that was very profitable to them. They would hide their greed behind spirituality. This spirit of greed is no different than the businessman who goes to church because he hopes to develop business contacts or thinks it will help his image in the community. Scripture speaks of this:

> **1 Timothy 6:5:** *"...and constant friction between men of depraved mind and deprived of the truth, who suppose that godliness is a means of gain."*

From our text in Matthew 21:13 Jesus says to the salesmen and moneychangers, *"...It is written, 'MY HOUSE SHALL BE CALLED A HOUSE OF PRAYER'; but you are making it a ROBBERS' DEN."* Jesus is quoting portions from Isaiah 56:7 and Jeremiah 7:11.

We should be very careful about merchandizing in the "Christian" market. It is offensive to see what some booksellers or those in the "Christian" music industry will do to make money under a spiritual cloak. There have been times when a big-name Christian leader uses a "ghost writer" (which means that the prominent leader's name is put on the book as the author, even though he never wrote the book). This type of conduct is deception in the name of God. Christian booksellers used to focus on making sure they sold only books containing solid theology, along with commentaries and Bibles. Now they will hawk about anything to get a buck. If you make a product and slap the word "Christian" or "inspirational" somewhere on its cover, it can pass muster to be sold in a "Christian" bookstore. Go into a large Christian bookstore and you will see display stands that are full of "Christian" romance novels and pseudo-psychology self-help books. One of the lowest levels of marketing I have seen was a so-called spooky "Christian" book series which was marketed to compete with a popular secular horror series.

---

[368] "The money-changers in Matthew 21:12; Mark 11:15; John. 2:14-15 converted Roman money into orthodox coinage for the Temple half-shekel (Matthew 17:24)." Wood, D. R. W., and Marshall, I. H. (1996). *New Bible dictionary (3rd ed.)* (p. 119). Leicester, England; Downers Grove, IL: InterVarsity Press.

It is also troubling when a "Christian music artist" is heavily marketed in the identical techniques of the world. It does not seem the artist's main concern is that people hear a truly Christ-centered message based on sound theology. Many use techniques that are designed for one purpose: sell more records and get more air time on the radio. This mentality is not much different than the salesmen and moneychangers of the temple in Jesus' day. May we return to the example of Keith Green. He was a man who produced very Christ-centered music. He did not focus on profits. In the early 1980's he produced an album and his philosophy was that if one could not afford to buy it, the person could write him a note to that effect and he would send it to him, free, no strings attached!

We must be very careful when the work of the church is crossed with the making of money, whether it is on the church's behalf or an individual's. It is a very thin line that can be quickly crossed even with the claim of a spiritual cloak. We see from our text that the moneychangers at the temple would surcharge the people who brought money to the temple to exchange it for the temple currency. This resulted in a quick financial profit for the moneychangers at the expense of those who came to worship.

What about the reverse situation? The reverse situation would be when those who are members of the church loan (not give) money to the church, as long as they get paid interest on the loan! I have watched this occur (and protested…to no avail.). If we look at the issue of borrowing under the Law of love (James 2:8), we see that Jesus does not bother addressing the technical aspects of a loan. Interest is not even discussed. Jesus focuses on what our view should be regarding the principle! Again, He raises the standard and examines the heart condition:

> Luke 6:33-35: *"And if you do good to those who do good to you, what credit is that to you? For even sinners do the same.* [34] *And if you lend to those from whom you expect to receive, what credit is that to you? Even sinners lend to sinners, in order to receive back the same amount.* [35] *But love your enemies, and do good, and lend, expecting nothing in return; and your reward will be great, and you will be sons of the Most High; for He Himself is kind to ungrateful and evil men."*

VERSE 14: *"And the blind and the lame came to Him in the temple, and He healed them."*

In verses 12-13 we see Jesus very aggressively attack the desecration of His Father's House. The only ones threatened by His attack are those who hated Him (i.e. the moneychangers, religious rulers and salesmen). Mark tells us that upon Jesus cleaning the temple, the chief priests and scribes *"…began seeking how to destroy Him; for they were afraid of Him,…."* Mark 11:18. The blind and lame were instead drawn to Him and were healed. Here we see a time of judgment on some, but we also see His mercy on others.

VERSES 15-16: *"But when the chief priests and the scribes saw the wonderful things that He had done, and the children who were crying out in the temple and saying, 'Hosanna to the Son of David,' they became indignant,* [16] *and said to Him, 'Do You hear what these are saying?' And Jesus *said to them, 'Yes; have you never read, OUT OF THE MOUTH OF INFANTS AND NURSING BABES THOU HAST PREPARED PRAISE FOR THYSELF?'"*

When the children saw the healings of the blind and lame, they broke out in spontaneous praise saying, *"Hosanna to the Son of David."* What they were saying was, "Save us now Messiah!"[369] The chief priests and scribes did not like what the children were saying and demanded that Jesus tell the children to immediately stop! Jesus instead rebukes the chief priests and scribes and affirms what the children were saying in verse 15 by making reference to Psalm 8:2:

> *"...Out of the mouth of infants and nursing babes Thou hast prepared praise for Thyself?"* <u>Matthew 21:16.</u>

A day before, during His triumphal entry, the Pharisees tried to make Jesus have the disciples quit calling Him the Messiah. Jesus told the Pharisees that the stones on the ground would not tolerate such silence about the truth of who He was:

> <u>Luke 19:39-40:</u> *"And some of the Pharisees in the multitude said to Him, 'Teacher, rebuke Your disciples.'* [40] *And He answered and said, <u>'I tell you, if these become silent, the stones will cry out!'"</u>*

Note that those who hated God thought they were very religious and intelligent, yet they did not have a clue who Jesus really was. On the other hand, the children knew that He was the Messiah. Remember what Jesus said before?

> <u>Matthew 11:25-26:</u> *"At that time Jesus answered and said, 'I praise Thee, O Father, Lord of heaven and earth, that <u>Thou didst hide these things from the wise and intelligent and didst reveal them to babes.</u>* [26] *Yes, Father, for thus it was well-pleasing in Thy sight.'"*

The false religious leaders were trying to destroy the faith of the children. This is a terrible evil. Remember what Jesus said earlier about children and the kingdom of heaven:

> <u>Matthew 19:14:</u> *"But Jesus said, 'Let the children alone, and do not hinder them from coming to Me; for the kingdom of heaven belongs to such as these.'"*

<u>VERSE 17:</u> *"And He left them and went out of the city to Bethany, and lodged there."*
This verse is self-explanatory.

Summary and Application

In this section you see three classic attributes of the false religious:
1. A greedy desire for money/power.
2. Attempts to rob God of His true glory and prevent others from worshipping Him.
3. Attempts to inflict spiritual injury on others, especially the young.

The falsely religious ignore the warning that judgment awaits those who cause others to spiritually stumble, especially children:

> <u>Matthew 18:5-6:</u> *"And whoever receives one such child in My name receives Me;* [6] *but whoever causes one of these little ones who believe in Me to stumble, it would be better*

---

[369] The term *Hosanna* in the Hebrew means "save us now" or "save, we pray." They were quoting from Psalms 118:25-26. For more on this term see the footnote in the lesson for Matthew 21:1-11.

for him to have a heavy millstone hung around his neck, and to be drowned in the depth of the sea."

<u>MATTHEW 21:18-32</u>
(CURSING OF THE FIG TREE;
LESSON ON FAITH;
JESUS' AUTHORITY CHALLENGED)

"Now in the morning, when He returned to the city, He became hungry. [19] *And seeing a lone fig tree by the road, He came to it, and found nothing on it except leaves only; and He *said to it, 'No longer shall there ever be any fruit from you.' And at once the fig tree withered.* [20] *And seeing this, the disciples marveled, saying, 'How did the fig tree wither at once?'* [21] *And Jesus answered and said to them, 'Truly I say to you, if you have faith, and do not doubt, you shall not only do what was done to the fig tree, but even if you say to this mountain, 'Be taken up and cast into the sea,' it shall happen.* [22] *And all things you ask in prayer, believing, you shall receive.'*

[23] *And when He had come into the temple, the chief priests and the elders of the people came to Him as He was teaching, and said, 'By what authority are You doing these things, and who gave You this authority?'* [24] *And Jesus answered and said to them, 'I will ask you one thing too, which if you tell Me, I will also tell you by what authority I do these things.* [25] *The baptism of John was from what source, from heaven or from men?' And they began reasoning among themselves, saying, 'If we say, From heaven, He will say to us, 'Then why did you not believe him?'* [26] *But if we say, 'From men,' we fear the multitude; for they all hold John to be a prophet.'* [27] *And answering Jesus, they said, 'We do not know.'' He also said to them, 'Neither will I tell you by what authority I do these things.'*

[28] *But what do you think? A man had two sons, and he came to the first and said, 'Son, go work today in the vineyard.'* [29] *And he answered and said, 'I will not'; but afterward he regretted it and went.* [30] *The man came to the second and said the same thing; and he answered, 'I will, sir' but he did not go.* [31] *Which of the two did the will of his father? They *said, 'The first.' Jesus *said to them, 'Truly I say to you that the tax-collectors and prostitutes will get into the kingdom of God before you.* [32] *For John came to you in the way of righteousness and you did not believe him; but the tax collectors and prostitutes did believe him; and you, seeing this, did not even feel remorse afterward so as to believe him.'''*

<u>Introduction</u>

Here is a visual lesson of the state of the hypocrite, and more specifically, the unfruitfulness of Israel. The fig tree had beautiful leaves but lacked fruit. Israel's religious leaders had all the appearances of being servants of God (i.e. the beautiful temple, priests, sacrifices, etc.) but they produced no true, godly fruit.

One needs to understand the time sequence of the event of the cursing of the fig tree. It is mistakenly thought by some that this event took place after Jesus cleansed the temple. Matthew is not setting out a chronological order, but is writing topically. The chronological order is set out by Mark. Mark tells us that Jesus cursed the fig tree on the way to Jerusalem to cleanse the temple (Mark 11:12-15). The next morning after cleansing the temple, the disciples comment on the fig tree and Jesus teaches on faith (Mark 11:19-26).

God moved each of the Gospel writers to write without error. God also presents a different emphasis from each writer. For example, Matthew typically writes in a narrative form that arranges material in a topical order rather than an emphasis on chronological order. Often when Matthew begins a topic, he will stay with it until he brings it to its conclusion. We see an example of that here with the cursing of the fig tree. Matthew begins the story and then brings it to its conclusion, addressing the topic of faith rather than delaying its point by breaking it up for chronological order. Mark and Luke are the gospel writers who tend to write in more of a chronological order.

VERSES 18-19: *"Now in the morning, when He returned to the city, He became hungry.* ¹⁹ *And seeing a lone fig tree by the road, He came to it, and found nothing on it except leaves only; and He *said to it, 'No longer shall there ever be any fruit from you.' And at once the fig tree withered."*

> *"Now in the morning, when He returned to the city,..."* v.18. This is the morning that Jesus went to cleanse the temple (Mark 11:20). *"He became hungry...."* Here we see Jesus manifesting His humanity. ³⁷⁰

> Verse 19 says: *"And seeing a lone fig tree by the road, He came to it, and found nothing on it except leaves only; and He *said to it, 'No longer shall there ever be any fruit from you.' And at once the fig tree withered."* Mark explains that it was not the season for figs. (Mark 11:13). Note how the tree had plenty of foliage but no fruit. *"Fig trees **bear fruit** first and then the leaves appear, or both appear about the same time. Since the tree was in leaf, figs should have been on it."* ³⁷¹ Obviously it was not Jesus who failed to understand the season of fruit but the nation of Israel that *"...did not recognize the time of your visitation."* **Luke 19:44**. Their Messiah appeared right before them and they did not know it.

> Israel can be seen here as the tree with terrific leaves. The big and broad fig leaves that are, *"still sewn together in the East and used as wrappings for fresh fruit sent to the markets, where they are a valuable item of commerce."*³⁷² Recall that we read in Genesis 3:7 that it was fig leaves that Adam and Eve used to cover themselves after the fall. Like the fig tree Jesus went up to, the nation of Israel had all the appearances of true religion before God (i.e. beautiful foliage). Israel had the great temple (Mark 13:1) and was *"...entrusted with the oracles of God."* **Romans 3:2**. Despite all this, true spiritual fruit was not produced. Their service to God, as exemplified by their religious leaders, was mere hypocrisy. Jesus stated this in **Mark 7:6-8:**
> > *"...Rightly did Isaiah prophesy of you hypocrites, as it is written,*
> > *'THIS PEOPLE HONORS ME WITH THEIR LIPS,*
> > *BUT THEIR HEART IS FAR AWAY FROM ME.*
> > ⁷ *BUT IN VAIN DO THEY WORSHIP ME,*
> > *TEACHING AS DOCTRINES THE PRECEPTS OF MEN.'*
> > ⁸ *Neglecting the commandment of God, you hold to the tradition of men."*

Jesus cursed the fig tree and said, *"No longer shall there ever be any fruit from you."* Likewise, there was no more fruit from that generation of Israel. We also read that the tree started to wither immediately, v.19. It was the next day that the tree was seen *"...withered from its roots up."*

---

³⁷⁰ For another example of the humanity and divinity of Jesus being manifested, see Matthew 8:23-27. The humanness is seen in that He was tired and sleeping in the boat; the divine in His calming the sea.

³⁷¹ Walvoord, John F., and Zuck, Roy B., *The Bible Knowledge Commentary*, v.2 p.69 (Wheaton, Illinois: Scripture Press Publications, Inc.) 1985.

³⁷² Wood, D. R. W., and Marshall, I. H. (1996). *New Bible Dictionary (3rd ed.)* (p. 368). Leicester, England; Downers Grove, IL: InterVarsity Press.

Mark 11:20. Likewise, the "foliage" of Israel (like its great temple) would soon be laid waste because the people did not know *"that something greater than the temple is here."* **Matthew 12:6.**

> **Mark 13:1-2:** *"AND as He was going out of the temple, one of His disciples *said to Him, 'Teacher, behold what wonderful stones and what wonderful buildings!'* ²And Jesus said to him, 'Do you see these great buildings? Not one stone shall be left upon another which will not be torn down.'"*

We know that this passage has the dual perspective of referring to the End Times as well as the complete destruction of the temple in 70 A.D.

We need to be careful of having all the appearances of Christianity but without any fruit. There are mainline denominations that have all kinds of rituals/rites and liturgy, but remain spiritually dead. Instead of pursuing the will of God, they are consumed with issues of homosexual clergy and attacking the fidelity of the Bible. It has been stated:

> "High profession of Christianity, without holiness among a people—
> overweening confidence in councils, bishops, liturgies, and ceremonies,
> while repentance and faith have been neglected —have ruined many
> a visible church in time past, and may yet ruin many more."[373]

VERSES 20-22: *"And seeing this, the disciples marveled, saying, 'How did the fig tree wither at once?' ²¹ And Jesus answered and said to them, 'Truly I say to you, if you have faith, and do not doubt, you shall not only do what was done to the fig tree, but even if you say to this mountain, 'Be taken up and cast into the sea,' it shall happen. ²² And all things you ask in prayer, believing, you shall receive.'"*

Here we see the disciples asking how the tree withered so fast after He cursed it. Jesus takes the opportunity to teach His disciples about faith. When Jesus says, *"you say to this mountain..."* He is referring to the Mount of Olives. When He says, *"Be taken up and cast into the sea"* He is referring to the Dead Sea. The faith Jesus is referring to is not self-generated or some "faith in faith." It is faith in Almighty God.

> **John 14:12-14:** *"Truly, truly, I say to you, he who believes in Me, the works that I do shall he do also; and greater works than these shall he do; because I go to the Father. ¹³ And whatever you ask in My name, that will I do, that the Father may be glorified in the Son. ¹⁴ If you ask Me anything in My name, I will do it."*

Obviously, the prayer made in true faith is one that is in accordance with God's will.

> **1 John 5:14-15:** *"And this is the confidence which we have before Him, that, if we ask anything according to His will, He hears us. ¹⁵ And if we know that He hears us in whatever we ask, we know that we have the requests which we have asked from Him."*

---

[373]*Matthew* / Ryle, J.C. p.195 (Expository Thoughts on the Gospels) (Crossways Classic Commentaries: v.1)

VERSE 23: *"And when He had come into the temple, the chief priests and the elders of the people came to Him as He was teaching, and said, 'By what authority are You doing these things, and who gave You this authority?'"*

We see here that the day after Jesus cleansed the temple He was confronted by the chief priests, scribes and elders (Mark 11:15-29). At the time they confronted Him, He was teaching the people in the temple (Luke 20:1). They challenged Him regarding His "authority." Even though they were questioning Him regarding His authority to teach, they clearly were confronting Him regarding His authority in receiving praise during His triumphal entry (Luke19:33-39) and His authority in cleansing the temple (Mark 11:15-18).

The religious leaders took great pride in their educational backgrounds and who they studied under (cf. Paul alludes to this when he states that he was *"...educated under Gamaliel,"* <u>Acts 22:3</u>). They were pointing out that Jesus did not have the authority to teach or do what He did in the temple. Because they were spiritually blind, they refused to acknowledge that Jesus' authority came from God. Look how they previously responded in *rage* when Jesus had healed a man's hand:

> <u>Luke 6:7-11:</u> *"And the scribes and the Pharisees were watching Him closely, to see if He healed on the Sabbath, in order that they might find reason to accuse Him. 8 But He knew what they were thinking, and He said to the man with the withered hand, 'Rise and come forward!' And he rose and came forward. 9 And Jesus said to them, 'I ask you, is it lawful on the Sabbath to do good, or to do harm, to save a life, or to destroy it?' 10 And after looking around at them all, He said to him, 'Stretch out your hand!' And he did so; and his hand was restored. 11 <u>But they themselves were filled with rage, and discussed together what they might do to Jesus.</u>"*

The scribes and Pharisees possessed very hard and unbelieving hearts that prevented them from seeing the source of Jesus' authority. Even though the religious leaders said that they did not know the source of His power, it was obvious to the average person that Jesus was from God.

> <u>Matthew 9:8:</u> *"But when the multitudes saw this, they were filled with awe, and glorified God, who had given such authority to men."*

VERSES 24-27: *"And Jesus answered and said to them, 'I will ask you one thing too, which if you tell Me, I will also tell you by what authority I do these things. 25 The baptism of John was from what source, from heaven or from men?' And they began reasoning among themselves, saying, 'If we say, 'From heaven,' He will say to us, 'Then why did you not believe him?' 26 But if we say, 'From men,' we fear the multitude; for they all hold John to be a prophet. 27 And answering Jesus, they said, 'We do not know.'' He also said to them, 'Neither will I tell you by what authority I do these things.'"*

Remember that the religious leaders were challenging Jesus on the basis of His "authority." Jesus responds to them by asking whether John the Baptist's authority was merely from man or if John was indeed a prophet from God. We know that they did not believe the message of John (Matthew 21:32). Remember what John the Baptist said to the Pharisees and Sadducees when they came to him pretending that they wanted to be baptized?

> <u>Matthew 3:7-10:</u> *"But when he saw many of the Pharisees and Sadducees coming for baptism, he said to them, '<u>You brood of vipers, who warned you to</u>*

flee from the wrath to come? ⁸*Therefore bring forth fruit in keeping with repentance;* ⁹*and do not suppose that you can say to yourselves 'We have Abraham for our father'; for I say to you, that God is able from these stones to raise up children to Abraham.* ¹⁰*And the axe is already laid at the root of the trees; every tree therefore that does not bear good fruit is cut down and thrown into the fire.'"*

The religious leaders knew they were between a rock and a hard place by Jesus' question to them about John the Baptist. If they acknowledged that John's authority was ***"from heaven"***, then the question became why did they not listen and obey John's declaration of who Jesus was?

<u>John 1:29:</u> *"The next day he *saw Jesus coming to him, and *said, '<u>Behold, the Lamb of God who takes away the sin of the world!</u>'"*

If the religious leaders tried to claim that John the Baptist's authority was merely of man, they knew they would face outrage from common people. Luke gives us more insight into their thoughts:

<u>Luke 20:6:</u> *"But if we say, 'From men,' <u>all the people will stone us to death</u>, for they are convinced that John was a prophet."*

(cf. Herod was afraid to put John to death because the multitude regarded John as a prophet; <u>Matthew 14:5.</u>)

The religious leaders finally answered Jesus' question by telling Him that they were unable to determine whether John's authority was from God or man. Jesus responds by refusing to answer their question about His source of authority. In essence, Jesus is saying that since they are not able to discern God's ordination on John, they obviously are not able to see it on Him, the only begotten Son of God. They are not able to make this discernment because they did not know God or believe on Him.

<u>John 5:36-37:</u> *"<u>But the witness which I have is greater than that of John;</u> for the works which the Father has given Me to accomplish, the very works that I do, bear witness of Me, that the Father has sent Me.* ³⁷ *And the Father who sent Me, He has borne witness of Me. You have neither heard His voice at any time, nor seen His form.* ³⁸ *<u>And you do not have His word abiding in you, for you do not believe Him whom He sent.</u>"*

The reality is that the religious leaders did not come to Jesus with any sincere desire to find out the authority of His ministry. What they really were after was another declaration from Jesus that He was the Son of God so that they could put Him to death. Note that the various religious groups that were assembled to confront Jesus included chief priests, scribes, elders, and Pharisees (Mark 11:15-29 and Matthew 21:45). This was not the time appointed for Jesus' death and thus the religious leaders evil plans were foiled.

<u>**VERSES 28-32:**</u> *"But what do you think? A man had two sons, and he came to the first and said, 'Son, go work today in the vineyard.'* ²⁹ *And he answered and said, 'I will not'; but afterward he regretted it and went.* ³⁰ *The man came to the second and said the same thing; and he answered, 'I will, sir' but he did not go.* ³¹ *Which of the two did the will of his father? They *said, 'The first.' Jesus *said to them, 'Truly I say to you that the tax-collectors and prostitutes will get into the kingdom of God before you.* ³² *For John came to you in the way of righteousness and you did not believe him; but the tax collectors and*

prostitutes did believe him; and you, seeing this, did not even feel remorse afterward so as to believe him."'

This parable is the first in a trilogy of parables that Jesus gives regarding the hypocrisy of the religious leaders. In this story Jesus brings home the point about those who repented and obeyed God as compared to those who pretended to obey God.

The first son initially disobeys his father's command, but later repents. The first son in the parable represents the *" tax-gatherers and harlots"* (v.32), who believed John the Baptist and became children of God. The apostle Paul speaks of us, who were wicked rebels, but were later granted repentance by God.

> <u>1 Corinthians 6:9-11:</u> *"Or do you not know that the unrighteous shall not inherit the kingdom of God? Do not be deceived; neither fornicators, nor idolaters, nor adulterers, nor effeminate, nor homosexuals, [10] nor thieves, nor the covetous, nor drunkards, nor revilers, nor swindlers, shall inherit the kingdom of God. [11] <u>And such were some of you; but you were washed, but you were sanctified, but you were justified in the name of the Lord Jesus Christ, and in the Spirit of our God."</u>*

The religious leaders are those represented by the second son who states that he will obey the Father, but never really does. Notice how the second son (like the religious hypocrite) appears so respectful and righteous in his response, saying *"I will, <u>sir</u>."* They are the ones who would not believe John the Baptist's preaching (v.32). Their hypocrisy is shown by the contradiction between their words and deeds. Unfortunately there are many so called "Christians" like that today.

> <u>Titus 1:15-16:</u> *"...but to those who are <u>defiled and unbelieving</u>, nothing is pure, but both their mind and their conscience are defiled. [16] <u>They profess to know God, but by their deeds they deny Him</u>, being detestable and disobedient, and worthless for any good deed."*

> <u>Matthew 7:21:</u> *"Not everyone who says to Me, 'Lord, Lord,' will enter the kingdom of heaven; but he who does the will of My Father who is in heaven."*

Summary and Application

A common attribute of the wolves/false religious people in the church is their pious appearance and their attack on the Word of God. They hate the authority of God's Word. We see this is nothing new. Religious hypocrites have always attacked the authority of God's word, even when it is staring them in their face! (Matthew 21:23).

We learn from the parable of the two sons that we are not to be like the second son. He is the one who talked a big story of service, but in reality did not believe the Word of God so as to obey!

> <u>1 John 2:3-5:</u> *"By this we know that we have come to know Him, if we keep His commandments. [4] The one who says, 'I have come to know Him,' and does not keep His commandments, is a liar, and the truth is not in him; [5] but whoever keeps His word, in him the love of God has truly been perfected. By this we know that we are in Him: the one who says he abides in Him ought himself to walk in the same manner as He walked."*

Please read the sections addressing Matthew 21:33 - 22:14 as Jesus continues to give the second and third parables in this trilogy. In those parables (i.e. The Landowner and The Marriage Feast) Jesus continues the theme that He began with the parable of the two sons in Matthew 21:28-32.

MATTHEW 21:33-46
(THE PARABLE OF THE LANDOWNER)

"Listen to another parable. There was a landowner who PLANTED A VINEYARD AND PUT A WALL AROUND IT AND DUG A WINE PRESS IN IT, AND BUILT A TOWER, *and rented it out to vine-growers, and went on a journey.* [34] *And when the harvest time approached, he sent his slaves to the vine-growers to receive his produce.* [35] *And the vine-growers took his slaves and beat one, and killed another, and stoned a third.* [36] *Again he sent another group of slaves larger than the first; and they did the same thing to them.* [37] *But afterward he sent his son to them, saying, 'They will respect my son.'* [38] *But when the vine-growers saw the son, they said among themselves, 'This is the heir; come, let us kill him, and seize his inheritance.'* [39] *And they took him, and threw him out of the vineyard, and killed him.* [40] *Therefore when the owner of the vineyard comes, what will he do to those vine-growers?'* [41] *They *said to Him, 'He will bring those wretches to a wretched end, and will rent out the vineyard to other vine-growers, who will pay him the proceeds at the proper seasons.'* [42] *Jesus *said to them, 'Did you never read in the Scriptures,*

'THE STONE WHICH THE BUILDERS REJECTED,
THIS BECAME THE CHIEF CORNER stone;
THIS CAME ABOUT FROM THE LORD,
AND IT IS MARVELOUS IN OUR EYES'?

[43] *Therefore I say to you, the kingdom of God will be taken away from you, and be given to a nation producing the fruit of it.* [44] *And he who falls on this stone will be broken to pieces; but on whomever it falls, it will scatter him like dust.'* [4] *And when the chief priests and the Pharisees heard His parables, they understood that He was speaking about them.* [46] *And when they sought to seize Him, they feared the multitudes, because they held Him to be a prophet."*

Introduction

We need to review the setting in which Jesus gave this parable. Matthew 21:23 tells us that Jesus was teaching in the temple when the religious leaders confronted Him:

> **Matthew 21:23:** *"And when He had come into the temple, the chief priests and the elders of the people came to Him as He was teaching, and said, 'By what authority are You doing these things, and who gave You this authority?'"*

The religious leaders clearly were confronting Him regarding His authority in receiving praise during His triumphal entry (Luke 19:33-39), and His authority in cleansing the temple (Mark 11:15-18). [To review Jesus' response, see the comments for Matthew 21:18-32.]. Below we will look at the second of this trilogy of parables that Jesus gives about the nation of Israel and the hypocrisy of her religious leaders.

VERSES 33: *"Listen to another parable. There was a landowner who* PLANTED A VINEYARD AND PUT A WALL AROUND IT AND DUG A WINE PRESS IN IT, AND BUILT A TOWER, *and rented it out to vine-growers, and went on a journey."*

We see that a landowner developed a vineyard, did all that was necessary to produce good fruit, put a tower in it, and then he rented it out. Those renting it were to give the landowner a portion of the produce each season.

This parable demonstrates Israel's rejection of God. God provided everything that Israel needed spiritually. Israel bore the name of God. The Psalmist tells us in **Proverbs 18:10**: *"The name of the LORD is a strong tower;...."* Paul points out that Israel was also given the precious Word of God:

> **Romans 3:1-2:** *"THEN what advantage has the Jew? Or what is the benefit of circumcision? ² Great in every respect. First of all, that they were entrusted with the oracles of God."*

VERSES 34-36: *"And when the harvest time approached, he sent his slaves to the vine-growers to receive his produce. ³⁵ And the vine-growers took his slaves and beat one, and killed another, and stoned a third. ³⁶ Again he sent another group of slaves larger than the first; and they did the same thing to them."*

The treatment of the landowner's slaves was brutal. Many times God sent His prophets to the rebellious people and they were mocked and killed. Jesus points this out:

> **Matthew 23:37:** *"O Jerusalem, Jerusalem, who kills the prophets and stones those who are sent to her!...."*

Here is another verse where Jesus indicts the false religious leaders:

> **Luke 11:48-51:** *"Consequently, you are witnesses and approve the deeds of your fathers; because it was they who killed them, and you build their tombs. ⁴⁹ For this reason also the wisdom of God said, 'I will send to them prophets and apostles, and some of them they will kill and some they will persecute, ⁵⁰ in order that the blood of all the prophets, shed since the foundation of the world, may be charged against this generation, ⁵¹ from the blood of Abel to the blood of Zechariah, who perished between the altar and the house of God; yes, I tell you, it shall be charged against this generation.'"*

VERSES 37-39: *"But afterward he sent his son to them, saying, 'They will respect my son.' ³⁸ But when the vine-growers saw the son, they said among themselves, 'This is the heir; come, let us kill him, and seize his inheritance.' ³⁹ And they took him, and threw him out of the vineyard, and killed him."*

The greed of the renters grew when they saw that the heir had come (i.e. the son). Instead of seeing that by the grace of the landowner they were allowed to be the renters, they began to see themselves as owners of the vineyard. It is important to remember the context in which Jesus told this parable. The religious leaders were spitefully questioning Jesus' authority after he had cleansed His Father's temple. It was God's temple, but the renters (i.e. the religious leaders) thought it was their temple. The religious leaders did not like anyone getting in the way of the control and financial profits they were making while running the temple. They disregarded God's headship and authority, just as the renters disregarded the fact that the landowner was the one who had the title to the land and, *"PLANTED A VINEYARD AND PUT A WALL AROUND IT AND DUG A WINE PRESS IN IT, AND BUILT A TOWER, and rented it...."*

In verse 38 we see that the renters saw the son coming and decided that if they could get rid of him, they could completely control the place. This is exactly the attitude that the religious leaders had about Jesus. He was threatening their religious/financial racketeering, so they needed to kill him. Jesus had earlier pointed out that these would be His murderers despite their claims to be God's people. Jesus made it clear that they were really sons of the Devil:

> **John 8:42-44:** *"Jesus said to them, 'If God were your Father, you would love Me; for I proceeded forth and have come from God, for I have not even come on My own initiative, but He sent Me. ⁴³ Why do you not understand what I am saying? It is because you cannot hear My word. ⁴⁴ <u>You are of your father the devil, and you want to do the desires of your father. He was a murderer from the beginning,</u> and does not stand in the truth, because there is no truth in him. Whenever he speaks a lie, he speaks from his own nature; for he is a liar, and the father of lies.'"*

Later on we see their true evil attitude come through.

> **Matthew 26:3-4:** *"Then the chief priests and the elders of the people were gathered together in the court of the high priest, named Caiaphas; ⁴ and they <u>plotted together to seize Jesus by stealth, and kill Him.</u>"*

VERSES 40-41: *"'Therefore when the owner of the vineyard comes, what will he do to those vine-growers?' ⁴¹ They *said to Him, 'He will bring those wretches to a wretched end, and will rent out the vineyard to other vine-growers, who will pay him the proceeds at the proper seasons.'"*

God is a God of love and justice. Here we see the justice and judgment that God leveled against Israel. Approximately 40 years after they murdered Jesus (AD 70)[374], Jerusalem and the temple were completely destroyed. Jesus told His disciples that one day this would happen.

> **Luke 21:5-6:** *"And while some were talking about the temple, that it was adorned with beautiful stones and votive gifts, He said, ⁶ 'As for these things which you are looking at, <u>the days will come in which there will not be left one stone upon another which will not be torn down.</u>'"*

VERSES 42-43: *"Jesus *said to them, 'Did you never read in the Scriptures,*
  'THE STONE WHICH THE BUILDERS REJECTED,
  THIS BECAME THE CHIEF CORNER stone;
  THIS CAME ABOUT FROM THE LORD,
  AND IT IS MARVELOUS IN OUR EYES'?
⁴³ *Therefore I say to you, the kingdom of God will be taken away from you, and be given to a nation producing the fruit of it. ⁴⁴"And he who falls on this stone will be broken to pieces; but on whomever it falls, it will scatter him like dust.'"*

The quote Jesus uses about the cornerstone comes from Psalm 118:22. Here Jesus sets forth the whole point of the parable, namely that He is the cornerstone that they had rejected. Peter pointed this out when he preached after the resurrection:

> **Acts 4:10-12:** *"...let it be known to all of you, and to all the people of Israel, that by the name of <u>Jesus Christ</u> the Nazarene, whom you crucified, whom God raised from the dead—by this name this man stands here before you in good health. ¹¹ He is the <u>STONE WHICH WAS REJECTED</u> by you, THE BUILDERS, but WHICH*

---

[374] Caesar ordered his general Titus Vespasian to annihilate Jerusalem.

BECAME THE VERY CORNER stone. [12] And there is salvation in no one else; for there is no other name under heaven that has been given among men, by which we must be saved." (cf. 1 Peter 2:4-10).

Remember that the parable speaks of the landowner of a <u>vineyard</u>. The religious leaders did not produce *fruit* because they had rejected Jesus and thus were not part of the vine.

> <u>John 15:1-6:</u> "*I AM the true vine, and My Father is the vinedresser. [2] <u>Every branch in Me that does not bear fruit, He takes away;</u> and every branch that bears fruit, He prunes it, that it may bear more fruit. [3] You are already clean because of the word which I have spoken to you. [4] <u>Abide in Me, and I in you. As the branch cannot bear fruit of itself, unless it abides in the vine, so neither can you, unless you abide in Me.</u> [5] I am the vine, you are the branches; he who abides in Me, and I in him, he bears much fruit; for apart from Me you can do nothing. [6] <u>If anyone does not abide in Me, he is thrown away as a branch, and dries up; and they gather them, and cast them into the fire, and they are burned.</u>*"

This generation would now be rejected by God. Israel had not produced the spiritual fruit that it should have (remember the cursing of the fig tree, Matthew 21:18-20), and now God would let the Gentiles produce fruit for Him. Paul references this when he teaches how God is drawing the Gentiles near to Him.

> <u>Ephesians 2:11,13, 19-20:</u> "*Therefore remember, that formerly you, the Gentiles in the flesh,....*
> [13] *But now in Christ Jesus you who formerly were far off have been brought near by the blood of Christ....*
> [19] *So then you are no longer strangers and aliens, but you are fellow citizens with the saints, and are of God's household, [20] having been built upon the foundation of the apostles and prophets, Christ Jesus Himself being the <u>corner stone</u>,*"

<u>VERSES 45-46:</u> "*And when the chief priests and the Pharisees heard His parables, they understood that He was speaking about them. [46] And when they sought to seize Him, they feared the multitudes, because they held Him to be a prophet.*"

Here is the manifestation of the evil hearts of the religious leaders. When Jesus confronts them with their sin, they do not repent. Their reaction is true to their evil spiritual foundation, they desire to kill Jesus (cf. John 8:42-44).

Some erroneously teach that God has nothing to do with Israel anymore. Even though God judged Israel, it should be clearly understood that He is not done with her. In the book of Romans, Paul sets forth that God has an eternal covenant with Israel:

> <u>Romans 11:1:</u> "*I say then, God has not rejected His people, has He? May it never be!....*"

Paul goes on in that same chapter and explains that God's calling of the Gentiles to salvation serves to make Israel jealous.

> <u>Romans 11:11-12, 25-26:</u> "*I say then, they did not stumble so as to fall, did they? May it never be! But by their <u>transgression salvation has come to the</u>*

Gentiles, to make them jealous. ¹² *Now if their transgression be riches for the world and their failure be riches for the Gentiles, how much more will their fulfillment be!* ... ²⁵ *For I do not want you, brethren, to be uninformed of this mystery, lest you be wise in your own estimation, that a partial hardening has happened to Israel until the fulness of the Gentiles has come in;* ²⁶ <u>*and thus all Israel will be saved;*</u> *just as it is written,*

> '*THE DELIVERER WILL COME FROM ZION,*
> *HE WILL REMOVE UNGODLINESS FROM JACOB.*
> ²⁷ *AND THIS IS MY COVENANT WITH THEM,*
> *WHEN I TAKE AWAY THEIR SINS.*'"

Summary and Application

Again, the lesson for us is on hypocrisy. As believers, we need to produce fruit. Do not look around and compare yourself with others and then decide that you are either doing good or that you are not producing as much as someone else. Appearances can be very misleading as demonstrated by the religious leaders that Jesus condemned (cf. Matthew 6:1-7). Instead, pray to the Lord and ask Him to produce fruit through you and He will.

There is another lesson here involving ministry. Never underestimate the ability of unbelievers, false believers, or even immature/fleshly believers to slip into ministry to control and destroy the true work of God. You do not have to look too far to see many denominations that used to produce fruit for the glory of God, but now deny the inerrancy of the Bible and install sexual perverts to be their pastors. Remember, the religious hypocrites of Jesus' time asked Him what "authority" He had in the temple (i.e. His own temple!). The religious hypocrites around you will do the same. You should never be discouraged if you are truly following God's Word in ministry and find some in "authority" who subtly harass you or try to stop your service to Christ...in the name of godliness. Just continue to pray and do not look for the approval of man to encourage you in ministry. Continue to examine your heart against the Word of God and press on with the task you have been given.

One last thought: Notice how God warned Israel through the prophet Isaiah of this very same lack of fruitfulness more than 950 years before Jesus taught the parable of the landowner.

> <u>Isaiah 5:1-7:</u> "*Let me sing now for my well-beloved A song of my beloved concerning His vineyard. My well-beloved had a vineyard on a fertile hill.* ² *He dug it all around, removed its stones, And planted it with the choicest vine. And He built a tower in the middle of it And also hewed out a wine vat in it; Then He expected it to produce good grapes, But it produced only worthless ones.* ³ *And now, O inhabitants of Jerusalem and men of Judah, Judge between Me and My vineyard.* ⁴ *What more was there to do for My vineyard that I have not done in it? Why, when I expected it to produce good grapes did it produce worthless ones?* ⁵ *So now let Me tell you what I am going to do to My vineyard: I will remove its hedge and it will be consumed; I will break down its wall and it will become trampled ground.* ⁶ *I will lay it waste; It will not be pruned or hoed, But briars and thorns will come up. I will also charge the clouds to rain no rain on it.* ⁷ *For the vineyard of the Lord of hosts is the house of Israel And the men of Judah His delightful plant. Thus He looked for justice, but behold, bloodshed; For righteousness, but behold, a cry of distress.*"

MATTHEW 22:1-14
(THE PARABLE OF THE KING'S WEDDING FEAST)

"AND Jesus answered and spoke to them again in parables, saying, ²'The kingdom of heaven may be compared to a king, who gave a wedding feast for his son. ³ And he sent out his slaves to call those who had been invited to the wedding feast, and they were unwilling to come. ⁴ Again he sent out other slaves saying, 'Tell those who have been invited, Behold, I have prepared my dinner; my oxen and my fattened livestock are all butchered and everything is ready; come to the wedding feast.' ⁵ But they paid no attention and went their way, one to his own farm, another to his business, ⁶ and the rest seized his slaves and mistreated them and killed them. ⁷ But the king was enraged and sent his armies, and destroyed those murderers, and set their city on fire. ⁸ Then he *said to his slaves, 'The wedding is ready, but those who were invited were not worthy. ⁹ Go therefore to the main highways, and as many as you find there, invite to the wedding feast.' ¹⁰ And those slaves went out into the streets, and gathered together all they found, both evil and good; and the wedding hall was filled with dinner guests. ¹¹ But when the king came in to look over the dinner guests, he saw there a man not dressed in wedding clothes, ¹² and he *said to him, 'Friend, how did you come in here without wedding clothes?' And he was speechless. ¹³ Then the king said to the servants, 'Bind him hand and foot, and cast him into the outer darkness; in that place there shall be weeping and gnashing of teeth. ¹⁴ For many are called, but few are chosen.'"

Introduction

This is the third parable in a trilogy Jesus gave after He was confronted by the chief priests and the elders. They challenged Jesus regarding the basis of His authority to cleanse and teach in the temple (Matthew 21:23). The first story was the parable of "two sons" (Matthew 21:28-32). It showed the religious hypocrisy of Israel's leaders. The second story was the parable of the "landowner." It showed the rebellion of Israel as well as the murderous hostility of the religious leaders against God and His son (Matthew 21:33-46). It was after the second parable that the chief priests and the Pharisees realized that Jesus was talking about them (Matthew 21:45). That set the stage for the third parable about the King holding a wedding feast in Matthew 22:1-14.

VERSES 1-3: *"AND Jesus answered and spoke to them again in parables, saying, ² 'The kingdom of heaven may be compared to a king, who gave a wedding feast for his son. ³ And he sent out his slaves to call those who had been invited to the wedding feast, and they were unwilling to come.'"*

Notice in verse one it says that Jesus, *"spoke to them again...."* As mentioned above, this is the third parable the Lord gives on the temporary "setting aside" of Israel. In this parable, the Lord tells us something about the "kingdom of heaven" (v.2). In this context the *"kingdom of heaven"* represents the redeemed (i.e. the saved). The Jews believed that the "kingdom of heaven" was their exclusive domain. In this parable the *king* represents God the Father. The *"son"* represents Jesus, the person for whom the king is having a wedding feast. The *"slaves"* represent the prophets, just as they did in the second parable (Matthew 21:34).

In verse three the king's slaves went out and called those who were invited but they would not come. Notice that there was nothing special about those who were invited. We do not read that they were rich, powerful, or of nobility. They were worthy to be invited only because the king declared them worthy. It was his grace that let them be invited. What an honor it would be to receive an invitation to a royal wedding. What an insult to the king that the invited guests did not even make polite excuses. They simply *"were unwilling to come."*

VERSES 4-6: *"Again he sent out other slaves saying, 'Tell those who have been invited, Behold, I have prepared my dinner; my oxen and my fattened livestock are all butchered and everything is ready; come to the wedding feast.'* [5] *But they paid no attention and went their way, one to his own farm, another to his business,* [6] *and the rest seized his slaves and mistreated them and killed them."*

The invited guests here are being sought a <u>second time</u>. When we read the Old Testament we see God the Father, time and time again, calling out to Israel to repent and enjoy the blessings of obedience to Him. But time and time again they reject His call.

> <u>Deuteronomy 30:15-20:</u> *"See, I have set before you today life and prosperity, and death and adversity;* [16] *in that I command you today to love the LORD your God, to walk in His ways and to keep His commandments and His statutes and His judgments, that you may live and multiply, and that the LORD your God may bless you in the land where you are entering to possess it.* [17] *But if your heart turns away and you will not obey, but are drawn away and worship other gods and serve them,* [18] *I declare to you today that you shall surely perish. You shall not prolong your days in the land where you are crossing the Jordan to enter and possess it.* [19] *I call heaven and earth to witness against you today, that <u>I have set before you life and death, the blessing and the curse. So choose life in order that you may live, you and your descendants,</u>* [20] *<u>by loving the LORD your God, by obeying His voice, and by holding fast to Him; for this is your life and the length of your days, that you may live in the land which the LORD swore to your fathers, to Abraham, Isaac, and Jacob, to give them."</u>*

We also see that some of those invited a second time were too preoccupied with their immediate affairs to enjoy the good that the king had for them. In verse five of the main text we read that, *"they paid no attention and went their way, one to his own farm, another to his business...."*

In today's world people often go after money, popularity or some other frivolous pursuits and in the process ignore the call of God.

> **Mark 4:18-19:** *"And others are the ones on whom seed was sown among the thorns; these are the ones who have heard the word,* [19] *and the <u>worries of the world, and the deceitfulness of riches, and the desires for other things</u> enter in and choke the word, and it becomes unfruitful."*

> <u>1 Timothy 6:9-10:</u> *"But those who <u>want to get rich fall into temptation and a snare and many foolish and harmful desires</u> which plunge men into ruin and destruction.* [10] *For the love of money is a root of all sorts of evil, and <u>some by longing for it have wandered away from the faith, and pierced themselves with many a pang."</u>*

Not only are there those who ignore God's call, but the parable teaches that there are also those who will respond with violent hatred, insults and murder (i.e. *"and the rest seized his slaves and mistreated them and killed them."*). This was the type of treatment that the slaves received in the parable of the landowner (Matthew 21:34-36). Many times God sent His prophets to the rebellious people only to be mocked and killed. Jesus points this out:

> **Matthew 23:37:** *"O Jerusalem, Jerusalem, who kills the prophets and stones those who are sent to her!"*

These same responses to the Word of God exist today. The spectrum can span from ignoring God's Word to murdering His people. There are many Christians around the world who are being persecuted and killed for their faith by those who hate the true and living God. Some Moslems will teach that Christians are infidels and must be killed. But Christianity teaches the exact opposite regarding our enemies:

> **Luke 6:27-31:** *"But I say to you who hear, love your enemies, do good to those who hate you, 28 bless those who curse you, pray for those who mistreat you. 29 Whoever hits you on the cheek, offer him the other also; and whoever takes away your coat, do not withhold your shirt from him either. 30 Give to everyone who asks of you, and whoever takes away what is yours, do not demand it back. 31 Treat others the same way you want them to treat you."*

VERSE 7: *"But the king was enraged and sent his armies, and destroyed those murderers, and set their city on fire."*

The king, acting with patience and kindness, gave two callings to the invitees to the wedding. In like fashion God has given man many opportunities to repent, but eventually there will be a just judgment. Here in verse seven we read the king's response: *"...and sent his armies, and destroyed those murderers, and set their city on fire."*

> **Ephesians 5:6:** *"Let no one deceive you with empty words, for because of these things the wrath of God comes upon the sons of disobedience."*

> **Nahum 1:2-3:** *"A jealous and avenging God is the LORD; The LORD is avenging and wrathful. The LORD takes vengeance on His adversaries, And He reserves wrath for His enemies. The LORD is slow to anger and great in power, 3 And the LORD will by no means leave the guilty unpunished...."*

In verse seven Jesus again alludes to the destruction of Jerusalem which would take place a mere 40 years after He was murdered (AD 70). During AD 70, Caesar ordered his general, Titus Vespasian, to annihilate Jerusalem. The city and its great temple were completely destroyed.

VERSES 8-10: *"Then he *said to his slaves, 'The wedding is ready, but those who were invited were not worthy. 9 Go therefore to the main highways, and as many as you find there, invite to the wedding feast.' 10 And those slaves went out into the streets, and gathered together all they found, both evil and good; and the wedding hall was filled with dinner guests."*

As mentioned previously, there is nothing stated that leads us to believe that the original invitees were worthy to be invited on their own merit. They were found worthy only by the grace of the king. What an insult, when in response to that grace they murdered the king's messengers. Even though they did nothing to make themselves worthy to be invited, they did make themselves unworthy because they refused the grace of the king (v.8). We see that grace served as the basis of all those invited as exhibited by the calling of the new invitees: "...*gathered together all they found, both evil and good;....*"

From a New Testament prospective, we are the Lord's messengers. Remember the Great Commission!

> **Mark 16:15-16:** *"And He said to them, 'Go into all the world and preach the gospel to all creation.* [16] *He who has believed and has been baptized shall be saved; but he who has disbelieved shall be condemned.'"* [See also Matthew 28:19-20.]

Just like the messengers in this parable, we are to go and call the evil and the good to the salvation of the Father through faith in Jesus Christ. We call the evil to escape the judgment to come, because their deeds are clearly wicked (Ephesians 5:6). We are likewise to call the "good" because, like the Pharisees, they have deceived themselves into believing that their own righteousness will earn them heaven.

> **Ephesians 2:8-9:** *"For by grace you have been saved through faith; and that not of yourselves, it is the gift of God;* [9] *not as a result of works, so that no one may boast."*

VERSES 11-13: *"But when the king came in to look over the dinner guests, he saw there a man not dressed in wedding clothes,* [12] *and he *said to him, 'Friend, how did you come in here without wedding clothes?' And he was speechless.* [13] *Then the king said to the servants, 'Bind him hand and foot, and cast him into the outer darkness; in that place there shall be weeping and gnashing of teeth.'"*

Since the king called everyone so quickly, he obviously provided for their wedding clothes. It is Jesus who purchased our salvation.

> **Galatians 3:26-28:** *"For you are all sons of God through faith in Christ Jesus.* [27] *For all of you who were baptized into Christ have clothed yourselves with Christ.* [28] *There is neither Jew nor Greek, there is neither slave nor free man, there is neither male nor female; for you are all one in Christ Jesus."*

> **Isaiah 61:10:** *"I will rejoice greatly in the* LORD,
> *My soul will exult in my God;*
> *For He has clothed me with garments of salvation,*
> *He has wrapped me with a robe of righteousness,*
> *As a bridegroom decks himself with a garland,*
> *And as a bride adorns herself with her jewels."*

Still there are those who believe they will be accepted by God on their own terms. Cain was the first to do this. His sacrifice to God was not accepted because it was not done in faith like his brother Abel's (Hebrews 11:4). In like manner, we see in verse 12 that one man came to the wedding feast clothed as he wanted to be. He came in his own dirty clothes, thinking they looked good enough.

> **Isaiah 64:6:** *"For all of us have become like one who is unclean, And all our righteous deeds are like a filthy garment;"*

The man in verse 12 was not clothed in Christ and so had no place in the kingdom. Verse 13 tells us that he was removed from the king's presence and thrown into judgment with darkness and *"weeping and gnashing of teeth."* When we read this phrase, *"weeping and gnashing of teeth,"* it refers to judgment in hell (Matthew 13:50). Jesus had previously stated that those who would be invited to His table are those who come by faith alone:

> **Matthew 8:10-13:** *"Now when Jesus heard this, He marveled, and said to those who were following, 'Truly I say to you, <u>I have not found such great faith with anyone in Israel.</u> 11 And I say to you, that <u>many shall come</u> from east and west, and <u>recline at the table</u> with Abraham, and Isaac, and Jacob, in the kingdom of heaven; 12 <u>but the sons of the kingdom shall be cast out into the outer darkness; in that place there shall be weeping and gnashing of teeth.</u>' 13 And Jesus said to the centurion, 'Go your way; let it be done to you as you have believed.' And the servant was healed that very hour."*

VERSE 14: *"For many are called, but few are chosen."*

In this verse we see that all men are called to repentance by God (2 Peter 3:9). It is the responsibility of man to repent. But man is spiritually dead and cannot cause his own repentance. It is God who grants repentance (2 Timothy 2:25-26). Those who are *"chosen,"* God grants repentance and salvation.

> **2 Thessalonians 2:13:** *"But we should always give thanks to God for you, brethren beloved by the Lord, because <u>God has chosen you from the beginning for salvation</u> through sanctification by the Spirit and faith in the truth."*

Summary and Application

Israel rejected the grace that the Father provided them in His Son Jesus. Even though God judged Israel, one must realize that He is not done with the nation: **Romans 11:29:** *"…for the gifts and the calling of God are irrevocable."* Paul explains that God's calling of the Gentiles to salvation serves to make Israel jealous, and one day *"all Israel will be saved;…."* (Romans 11:11-12, 25-26). We are to view our election with great humility and thankfulness (Romans 11:17-24), remembering that it was not by any merit of our own that we are invited into God's presence. Martin Luther has been attributed with saying, "God does not love us because we are valuable, we are valuable because God loves us."

Always be thankful that God has chosen us to be invited to the marriage supper of His Son.

> **Revelation 19:7-9:** *"Let us rejoice and be glad and give the glory to Him, for the marriage of the Lamb has come and His bride has made herself ready. It was given to her to clothe herself in fine linen, bright and clean; for the fine linen is the righteous acts of the saints. Then he said to me, 'Write, Blessed are those who are invited to the marriage supper of the Lamb.' " And he said to me, 'These are true words of God.'"*

MATTHEW 22:15-22
(DO WE PAY TAXES TO THE GOVERNMENT?)

*"Then the Pharisees went and counseled together how they might trap Him in what He said. ¹⁶ And they *sent their disciples to Him, along with the Herodians, saying, 'Teacher, we know that You are truthful and teach the way of God in truth, and defer to no one; for You are not partial to any. ¹⁷ Tell us therefore, what do You think? Is it lawful to give a poll-tax to Caesar, or not?' ¹⁸ But Jesus perceived their malice, and said, 'Why are you testing Me, you hypocrites? ¹⁹ Show Me the coin used for the poll-tax.' And they brought Him a denarius. ²⁰ And He *said to them, 'Whose likeness and inscription is this?' ²¹ They *said to Him, 'Caesar's.' Then He *said to them, 'Then render to Caesar the things that are Caesar's; and to God the things that are God's.' ²² And hearing this, they marveled, and leaving Him, they went away."*

Introduction

Take a look at the context of this event. Remember that right before this encounter with the Pharisee's disciples, Jesus had delivered three scathing judgments in the form of parables to Israel and its religious leaders. Now we see the religious leaders engaged in three "questions" back to Jesus, which were designed to trap Him into looking bad and fall into the wrath of either Rome or the people of Israel. Matthew 22:15-22 represents the first question asked by the Pharisee's disciples. The second question is presented by the Sadducees (22:23-33), and the third question is brought by the Pharisees directly (22:34-40).

VERSE 15: *"Then the Pharisees went and counseled together how they might trap Him in what He said."*

Here again we see the unbelieving, hard-heartedness of the Pharisees. They did not have as their objective to learn "Truth" from Jesus. Verse 15 tells us that the Pharisees got together to devise what they saw as the perfect plan to put Jesus in a "catch 22" (*"...the Pharisees went and counseled together how they might trap Him in what He said."*). The planned question would end in one of two results, either: 1) Jesus would say that the Jews did not have to pay taxes to Rome, which would result in Rome arresting Him as a rebellious political leader, or 2) Jesus would say that the Jews were to pay a tax to Rome and thus be completely discredited to the Jews.

What is interesting is that the Pharisees hated the Herodians, but they had a common goal of getting rid of Jesus. They had worked together before on trying to "destroy" Jesus.

> **Mark 3:1-6:** *"AND He entered again into a synagogue; and a man was there with a withered hand. ² And they were watching Him to see if He would heal him on the Sabbath, in order that they might accuse Him. ³ And He *said to the man with the withered hand, 'Rise and come forward!' ⁴ And He *said to them, 'Is it lawful on the Sabbath to do good or to do harm, to save a life or to kill?' But they kept silent. ⁵ And after looking around at them with anger, grieved at their hardness of heart, He *said to the man, 'Stretch out your hand.' And he stretched it out, and his hand was restored. ⁶ And the Pharisees went out and*

immediately began taking counsel with the Herodians against Him, as to how they might destroy Him."

The **Pharisees** were known as the "separated ones." Jesus points out in Luke 18:9-14 that they thrived on self-righteousness. The Pharisees were also proud of the extreme detail they applied to their tithing. Jesus exposed their hypocrisy regarding tithing in **Luke 11:42:** *"But woe to you Pharisees! For you pay tithe of mint and rue and every kind of garden herb, and yet disregard justice and the love of God; but these are the things you should have done without neglecting the others."* The Pharisees hated tax collectors[375] as demonstrated in **Matthew 9:11:** *"And when the Pharisees saw this, they said to His disciples, 'Why is your Teacher eating with the tax-gatherers and sinners?'"*

The **Herodians**: Who were they? In 40 B.C. the Romans made the father of Herod the Great, king of Judea.[376] There became a succession of members of the Herod family that held positions of power at the will of Rome (See information on the Herodian family tree at the **Summary and Application** portion after the **Matthew 14:12** section.) Herod the Great was not Jewish but Idumean. The Idumean were descendants of the Edomites. He is infamously known for his ordering the murder of all the male children under the age of two in Bethlehem (Matthew 2:16). The Herodians were a Jewish party who favored Herodian's dynasty and thus were sympathetic to Rome. The Herodians had no love for Jesus, as we read that Herod Antipas (son of Herod the Great) once sought to kill Jesus (Luke 13:31).

VERSE 16: *"And they *sent their disciples to Him, along with the Herodians, saying, 'Teacher, we know that You are truthful and teach the way of God in truth, and defer to no one; for You are not partial to any.'"*

Notice that the Pharisees knew that any question that they gave Jesus would be obvious to Jesus and anyone else that they were out to get Him. They did not want to foil their plan so they sent their disciples and the Herodians. Their disciples would be the witnesses against Jesus if He said they should pay a tax to Rome. The Herodians were there to be witnesses to Rome if Jesus stated that they were not to pay the tax. Luke gives us a little more detail on why they sent their disciples when he wrote:

> **Luke 20:20:** *"And they watched Him, and sent spies who pretended to be righteous, in order that they might catch Him in some statement, so as to deliver Him up to the rule and the authority of the governor."*

---

[375] A *publican* was a Jewish tax collector who worked for the Roman Empire. Publicans were deeply despised by their fellow Jews. One must realize that at that time the Jews were under Roman control and thus subject to Rome's taxes. Publicans were viewed as traitors because they made money for themselves by helping Rome tax fellow Jews.

[376] *Enhanced Strong's Lexicon,* (Oak Harbor, WA: Logos Research Systems, Inc.) 1995.
The name Herod represented a "royal family that flourished among the Jews in the times of Christ and the Apostles. Herod the Great was the son of Antipater of Idumaea." Antipater was appointed king of Judaea B.C. 40 "by the Roman Senate at the suggestion of Antony and with the consent of Octavian," (the first Roman Emperor, later named Augustus).

Under pretext, the Pharisees' disciples pretended to be interested in what was the "truth." They also resorted to flattery to "butter-up" Jesus before they asked their question: **Matthew 22:16:** *"Teacher, we know that You are truthful and teach the way of God in truth, and defer to no one; for You are not partial to any."* The Pharisees hated Jesus and He did not believe a word of their false flattery.[377] One person correctly defined flattery as, "saying something to one's face that you would never say behind his back."

VERSE 17: *"Tell us therefore, what do You think? Is it lawful to give a poll-tax to Caesar, or not?"*

Here is their loaded question. As mentioned above, the question was designed to end in one of two results: 1) Jesus would say that the Jews did not have to pay taxes to Rome which would result in Rome arresting Him as a rebellious political leader, or 2) Jesus would say that the Jews were to pay a tax to Rome and thus be completely discredited to the Jews.

Here is a little history regarding this tax. The poll tax was instigated by Rome on those they had conquered. The coin used to pay the poll-tax was the Roman denarius which was about the daily wage of a laborer. Modern archeology has given us more information about this coin. The "silver denarii of the time have been discovered which carry the laureate head of the emperor Tiberius on the obverse, with his mother, Livia, in the role of Pax, holding a branch and scepter, on the reverse."[378] It was the "poll tax" that Joseph and Mary went to Bethlehem to pay when Jesus was born (Luke 2:1-4).

VERSE 18: *"But Jesus perceived their malice, and said, 'Why are you testing Me, you hypocrites?'"*

Jesus did not let their false flattery go unchecked, he rather called them what they were, *"hypocrites."* Webster's Dictionary defines a hypocrite as:
    "1: a person who puts on a false appearance of virtue or religion; 2: a person who
    acts in contradiction to his or her stated beliefs or feelings."[379]
Notice the word *"malice"* is used to describe the hearts of those asking the question. The American Heritage Dictionary defines malice this way:
    "**1.** A desire to harm others or to see others suffer; extreme ill will or spite. **2.** *Law*
    The intent, without just cause or reason, to commit a wrongful act that will result in
    harm to another."

---

[377] What the Pharisees said about Jesus was true: *"You are truthful and teach the way of God in truth, and defer to no one; for You are not partial to any."* But what is not true is that the Pharisees, who hated Jesus, truly believed this. They made this statement as a form of false/mocking flattery as a set up for the question that they hoped would force Jesus to defer or be partial to either the Jews or the Roman government.

[378] *The New Bible Dictionary*, (Wheaton, Illinois: Tyndale House Publishers, Inc.) 1962.

[379] *Merriam-Webster Collegiate Dictionary, 11ᵗʰ edition.*

VERSE 19-21: *"'Show Me the coin used for the poll-tax.' And they brought Him a denarius. ²⁰ And He *said to them, 'Whose likeness and inscription is this?' ²¹ They *said to Him, 'Caesar's.' Then He *said to them, 'Then render to Caesar the things that are Caesar's; and to God the things that are God's.'"*

> Jesus destroys their plan by telling them that if something has Caesar's likeness on it, give it to him, but you need to give to God all that is His. What belongs to God? The answer is that *everything and everyone belongs to God.*

VERSE 22: *"And hearing this, they marveled, and leaving Him, they went away."*

> The hypocrites were stunned by the brilliant answer Jesus gave them. Their only response was to leave.

Summary and Application

This lesson brings up the sub-issue of whether Christians should pay taxes. Let us review a portion taken from this author's comments on Matthew 17:24-27. In that section I state that Jesus had explained earlier that the temple had been defiled and turned into *"a ROBBERS' DEN"* (Mark 11:17). Despite the conduct that occurred at the temple, Jesus told Peter that He still would pay the tax *"lest we give them offense."* If Jesus willingly paid a tax that He was completely exempt from (to a very corrupt group) no Christian can claim that He is not required to pay taxes. Those who say we are not to pay taxes often point out immoral government programs or socially unjust use of tax money. That does not remove our obligation to pay taxes. By paying taxes, one is not endorsing ungodly behavior or leadership, but instead we are submitting to a higher authority, God Himself.

> **Romans 13:1-2, 6-7:** *"Let every person be in subjection to the governing authorities. For there is no authority except from God, and those which exist are established by God. ² Therefore he who resists authority has opposed the ordinance of God; and they who have opposed will receive condemnation upon themselves. ...*
> *⁶ For because of this you also pay taxes, for rulers are servants of God, devoting themselves to this very thing. ⁷ Render to all what is due them: tax to whom tax is due; custom to whom custom; fear to whom fear; honor to whom honor."*

Civil Disobedience?

The only time civil disobedience is allowed is when the governing authorities are clearly in violation of Scripture. *This is not to be quickly claimed.* Be very careful to not let your political agendas or philosophies be confused with true Biblical mandates (e.g. I am required to pay taxes even if the government uses tax money for things that are ungodly—see Matthew 22:15-22). MacArthur states the following on the subject of civil disobedience and political activism:

> "Many evangelicals believe that Christians should become active in political causes, relying on social action and pressure tactics to change laws and government policies and practices that are plainly evil and to protect cherished religious rights that are being encroached upon. In the name of such concepts as co-belligerency, some evangelicals are joining forces with individuals and organizations that are unchristian, heretical, and even cultic. The reasoning is that it is sometimes permissible to join forces with one evil in order to combat what is considered to be a greater evil. This zeal for preservation of the Christian faith, both culturally and individually, often gets blended in with strong

~ 438 ~

views about economics, taxation, social issues, and partisanship, so that the Bible gets wrapped in the flag.

Even social and political activities that are perfectly worthwhile can deplete the amount of a believer's time, energy, and money that is available for the central work of the gospel. The focus is shifted from the call to build the spiritual kingdom through the gospel to efforts to moralize culture—trying to change society from the outside rather than individuals from the inside. When the church is politicized, even in support of good causes, its spiritual power is vitiated and its moral influence diluted. And when such causes are supported in worldly ways and by worldly means, the tragedy is compounded. We are to be the conscience of the nation through faithful preaching and godly living, confronting it not with the political pressure of man's wisdom—including our own—but with the spiritual power of God's Word. Using legislation, adjudication, or intimidation to achieve a superficial, temporal 'Christian morality' is not our calling—and has no eternal value." MacArthur, J. F., Jr. (1991). *Romans*. MacArthur New Testament Commentary (p. 196). Chicago: Moody Press.

Look at a couple examples of civil disobedience in scripture. They are directly ordering a person to not worship the one true God, evangelize, etc. Notice that those who refused to obey, did not take up arms, but simply accepted the punishment. Listen to what Jesus said when the evil mob came to arrest Him: ***"Then Jesus said to him, 'Put your sword back into its place; for all those who take up the sword shall perish by the sword.'"*** **Matthew 26:52.**

> **Acts 5:27-29:** *"When they had brought them, they stood them before the Council. The high priest questioned them, saying, "We gave you strict orders not to continue teaching in this name, and yet, you have filled Jerusalem with your teaching and intend to bring this man's blood upon us." But Peter and the apostles answered, "We must obey God rather than men..."* **Acts 5:40–41:** *"They took his advice; and after calling the apostles in, they flogged them and ordered them not to speak in the name of Jesus, and then released them. So they went on their way from the presence of the Council, rejoicing that they had been considered worthy to suffer shame for His name."*

> **Daniel 3:14–18:** *"Nebuchadnezzar responded and said to them, 'Is it true, Shadrach, Meshach and Abed-nego, that you do not serve my gods or worship the golden image that I have set up? Now if you are ready, at the moment you hear the sound of the horn, flute, lyre, trigon, psaltery and bagpipe and all kinds of music, to fall down and worship the image that I have made, very well. But if you do not worship, you will immediately be cast into the midst of a furnace of blazing fire; and what god is there who can deliver you out of my hands?' Shadrach, Meshach and Abed-nego replied to the king, 'O Nebuchadnezzar, we do not need to give you an answer concerning this matter. If it be so, our God whom we serve is able to deliver us from the furnace of blazing fire; and He will deliver us out of your hand, O king. But even if He does not, let it be known to you, O king, that we are not going to serve your gods or worship the golden image that you have set up.'"*

(See also Daniel praying when it was against the law - Daniel 6:1–23.)

Wiersbe states "... please note that, in each of these instances, *the people had a direct word from God that gave them assurance they were doing His will.* And further note that, in every instance, the believers were kind and respectful. They didn't start riots or burn down buildings 'for conscience sake.' Because civil authority is ordained of God (Romans 13), it's a serious thing for Christians to disobey the law; and if we're going to do it, we must know the difference between personal prejudices and biblical convictions." Wiersbe, W. W. (1993). *Be Committed*. "Be" Commentary Series (p 98). Wheaton, IL: Victor Books.

MATTHEW 22:23-33
(JESUS — GOD OF THE LIVING;
THE DOCTRINE OF THE RESURRECTION;
CHRONOLOGY OF THE RESURRECTIONS)

"On that day some Sadducees (who say there is no resurrection) came to Him and questioned Him, [24] *saying, 'Teacher, Moses said, 'IF A MAN DIES, HAVING NO CHILDREN, HIS BROTHER AS NEXT OF KIN SHALL MARRY HIS WIFE, AND RAISE UP AN OFFSPRING TO HIS BROTHER.'* [25] *Now there were seven brothers with us; and the first married and died, and having no offspring left his wife to his brother;* [26] *so also the second, and the third, down to the seventh.* [27] *And last of all, the woman died.* [28] *In the resurrection therefore whose wife of the seven shall she be? For they all had her.'* [29] *But Jesus answered and said to them, 'You are mistaken, not understanding the Scriptures, or the power of God.* [30] *For in the resurrection they neither marry, nor are given in marriage, but are like angels in heaven.* [31] *But regarding the resurrection of the dead, have you not read that which was spoken to you by God, saying,* [32] *'I AM THE GOD OF ABRAHAM, AND THE GOD OF ISAAC, AND THE GOD OF JACOB?' He is not the God of the dead but of the living.'* [33] *And when the multitudes heard this, they were astonished at His teaching."*

Introduction

In the previous lesson on Matthew 22:15-22, we read of how the disciples of the Pharisees sought to entrap Jesus with a trick question regarding paying taxes to Rome. Now in Matthew 22:23-33 we see the Sadducees setting up a question in hopes of humiliating Jesus and justifying their false religion that denies the resurrection.

VERSES 23-24: *"On that day some Sadducees (who say there is no resurrection) came to Him and questioned Him,* [24] *saying, 'Teacher, Moses said, 'IF A MAN DIES, HAVING NO CHILDREN, HIS BROTHER AS NEXT OF KIN SHALL MARRY HIS WIFE, AND RAISE UP AN OFFSPRING TO HIS BROTHER'.'"*

Right away Matthew tells us where the Sadducees are coming from (i.e. they deny any resurrection). **Acts 23:8** states, *"For the Sadducees say that there is no resurrection, nor an angel, nor a spirit; but the Pharisees acknowledge them all."* The Sadducees were of the aristocracy of Israel (people with the money/land).

"They denied the permanent validity of any [Scripture] but the written laws of the Pentateuch. They rejected the later doctrines of the soul and its after-life, the resurrection, rewards and retributions, angels and demons. They believed that there was no fate, men having a free choice of good and evil, prosperity and adversity being the outcome of their own course of action."[380]

---

[380] *The New Bible Dictionary*, (Wheaton, Illinois: Tyndale House Publishers, Inc.) 1962, [Online] Available: Logos Library System.

To set up their trick question, they pointed to the Law in Deuteronomy, which said that if a man dies before he gave birth to a son, the dead man's brother must marry the woman, and the first son she has is to be named after the dead man. If the brother refuses to do this, he is to be summoned before the elders of the city to correct him. If he refuses to accept the correction of the elders, the dead man's wife will take the man's sandal and spit in his face! The action was done as a public humiliation/repudiation of the man for not caring for his dead brother's heritage. This type of marriage was called the law of levirate (Lat. *levir*, 'husband's brother').[381] The point of this law was to keep one's family name and inheritance from being eliminated. Here is the section in Deuteronomy that explains this:

> **Deuteronomy 25:5-10:** *"When brothers live together and one of them dies and has no son, the wife of the deceased shall not be married outside the family to a strange man. Her husband's brother shall go in to her and take her to himself as wife and perform the duty of a husband's brother to her. ⁶ And it shall be that the first-born whom she bears shall assume the name of his dead brother, that his name may not be blotted out from Israel. ⁷ But if the man does not desire to take his brother's wife, then his brother's wife shall go up to the gate to the elders and say, 'My husband's brother refuses to establish a name for his brother in Israel; he is not willing to perform the duty of a husband's brother to me.' ⁸ Then the elders of his city shall summon him and speak to him. And if he persists and says, 'I do not desire to take her,' ⁹ then his brother's wife shall come to him in the sight of the elders, and pull his sandal off his foot and spit in his face; and she shall declare, 'Thus it is done to the man who does not build up his brother's house.' ¹⁰ And in Israel his name shall be called, 'The house of him whose sandal is removed.'"*

For an example of the law of levirate marriage, see Ruth 4:1-10.

VERSES 25-28: *"Now there were seven brothers with us; and the first married and died, and having no offspring left his wife to his brother; ²⁶ so also the second, and the third, down to the seventh. ²⁷ And last of all, the woman died. ²⁸ In the resurrection therefore whose wife of the seven shall she be? For they all had her."*

After reviewing Deuteronomy 25:5-10 you can see the trick question. They were trying to make the resurrection look absurd by asking who this woman would be married to in heaven. Remember, the Sadducees were infamous for their denial of the resurrection, so you can almost hear their snickering when they pretend to believe there is a resurrection by saying in verse 28, *"In the resurrection therefore whose wife of the seven shall she be? For they all had her."*

VERSE 29: *"But Jesus answered and said to them, 'You are mistaken, not understanding the Scriptures, or the power of God.'"*

What a direct and devastating response to receive from God. It is important that we rightly interpret Scripture because in doing so we will know the power of God.

---

[381] *The New Bible Dictionary*, (Wheaton, Illinois: Tyndale House Publishers, Inc.) 1962.

1 Timothy 4:16: *"Pay close attention to yourself and to your teaching; persevere in these things, for as you do this you will ensure salvation both for yourself and for those who hear you."*

Paul spoke of those who pretend to be great teachers of the Law but are actually false teachers.

1 Timothy 1:6-7: *"For some men, straying from these things, have turned aside to fruitless discussion, ⁷ wanting to be teachers of the Law, even though they do not understand either what they are saying or the matters about which they make confident assertions."*

VERSE 30: *"For in the resurrection they neither marry, nor are given in marriage, but are like angels in heaven."*

Here the Lord tells us more about heaven. We find out that marriage does not exist in heaven since we are all children of God and brothers and sister to each other. Just because there is not the formal institution of marriage in heaven, it should not be understood that our relationships on earth are irrelevant. We develop important spiritual relationships here on earth, especially in the God-ordained institution of marriage. Jesus summarizes it by saying that we **will be like the angels.** Note that He did not say we become angels, but in regard to marriage we will be like them. Angels in heaven neither have marriage, nor do they reproduce (see this footnote regarding issues regarding angels/demons and sons of God in the Old Testament as it applies to Genesis 6:1-14).[382]

---

[382] Matthew 22:30 states: *"For in the resurrection they neither marry, nor are given in marriage, but are like angels in heaven."* This verse is often cited as authority for the position that the incident in Genesis 6:1-15 did not involve fallen angels (i.e. demons). I disagree and believe that incident did involve fallen angels. Genesis 6:1-15 states that there were "sons of God" who took women as wives and produced *"mighty men who were of old, men of renown."* Start by reviewing the text in Genesis:

> **Genesis 6:1-7, 11-14:** *"Now it came about, when men began to multiply on the face of the land, and daughters were born to them, ² that the sons of God saw that the daughters of men were beautiful; and they took wives for themselves, whomever they chose. ³ Then the Lord said, 'My Spirit shall not strive with man forever, because he also is flesh; nevertheless his days shall be one hundred and twenty years.' ⁴ The Nephilim were on the earth in those days, and also afterward, when the sons of God came in to the daughters of men, and they bore children to them. Those were the mighty men who were of old, men of renown.⁵ Then the Lord saw that the wickedness of man was great on the earth, and that every intent of the thoughts of his heart was only evil continually. ⁶ And the Lord was sorry that He had made man on the earth, and He was grieved in His heart. ⁷ And the Lord said, 'I will blot out man whom I have created from the face of the land, from man to animals to creeping things and to birds of the sky; for I am sorry that I have made them.' ⁸ But Noah found favor in the eyes of the Lord....*
> *¹¹ Now the earth was corrupt in the sight of God, and the earth was filled with violence. ¹² And God looked on the earth, and behold, it was corrupt; for all flesh had corrupted their way upon the earth. ¹³ Then God said to Noah, 'The end of all flesh has come before Me; for the earth is filled with violence because of them; and behold, I am about to destroy them with the earth. ¹⁴ Make for yourself an ark of gopher wood; you shall make the ark with rooms, and shall cover it inside and out with pitch.'"*
> [Note continued on the next page.]

[Note continued.]

"Sons of God"   In the New Testament, we read that the term "sons of God" refers to converted human believers (Galatians 3:26-27).   In the Old Testament (like Genesis 6) the term "sons of God" is used almost exclusively for angelic beings.   Look how the Hebrew and English Lexicon of the Old Testament addresses the term "sons of God":

בני (ה) אלהים = (*the*) *sons of God* , or *sons of gods* = **angels.**

> Whitaker, R., Brown, F., Driver, S. (. R., and Briggs, C. A. (. A. (1997, c1906). *The Abridged Brown-Driver-Briggs Hebrew-English Lexicon of the Old Testament: From A Hebrew and English Lexicon of the Old Testament by Francis Brown, S.R. Driver and Charles Briggs, based on the lexicon of Wilhelm Gesenius.* Edited by Richard Whitaker (Princeton Theological Seminary). Text provided by Princeton Theological Seminary. (44.1). Oak Harbor WA: Logos Research Systems, Inc.

> **Job 1:6-7**:   *"Now there was a day when the sons of God came to present themselves before the LORD, and Satan also came among them.* [7]*And the LORD said to Satan, 'From where do you come?' Then Satan answered the LORD and said, 'From roaming about on the earth and walking around on it.'"*

> **Job 2:1**:   *"Again there was a day when the sons of God came to present themselves before the Lord, and Satan also came among them to present himself before the Lord."*

"In Genesis 6:1–2 the 'sons of God' are contrasted with human women in a way which seems to preclude their identification with the line of Cain. …Others argue that the phrase denotes demon-possessed men or fallen angels (cf. 1 Peter 3:19–20; Jude 6)." Wood, D. R. W., and Marshall, I. H. (1996). *New Bible dictionary* (3rd ed.) (p. 1122).   Leicester, England; Downers Grove, Ill.: InterVarsity Press.

Vines Dictionary says: *"The Nephilim mentioned above are found in two passages, in Genesis 6:4 R.V. which indicates the existence of giants born in a manner contrary to nature (the word may be derived from the Hebrew verb nāphal, to fall). These perished in the Flood with the rest of the race (except for Noah's family), Genesis 7:21-23. The other passage, Numbers 13:33 R.V., indicates a similar kind of being identical with the Anakim. These are to be distinguished from those before the Flood."*   Vine, W., and Bruce, F. (1981; Published in electronic form by Logos Research Systems, 1996). *Vine's Expository Dictionary of Old and New Testament Words* (p. 17). Old Tappan NJ: Revell.

These **_mighty men who were of old, men of renown_** (if not demonic themselves) were heavily demon-possessed as were their offspring.   Some say that they cannot be demons who procreated with women because demons cannot reproduce based on **Matthew 22:30**:   *"For in the resurrection they neither marry, nor are given in marriage, but are like angels in heaven."*   Note that the demons who procreated are no longer like the *"angels in heaven."*   Scripture tells us that those demons had left their boundaries – *"domain."*   I believe that part of the domain that those demons violated includes the desire for women and procreation with them.   Because they did that, they have been kept in bonds awaiting final judgment.

> **Jude 6:** *"And angels who did not keep their own domain, but abandoned their proper abode, He has kept in eternal bonds under darkness for the judgment of the great day."*

[Note continued on next page]

VERSES 31-32: *"But regarding the resurrection of the dead, have you not read that which was spoken to you by God, saying, [32] 'I AM THE GOD OF ABRAHAM, AND THE GOD OF ISAAC, AND THE GOD OF JACOB'? He is not the God of the dead but of the living."*

The Sadducees looked with false respect to the written laws of the Pentateuch. Jesus takes them back to the law, where Moses saw the burning bush and God affirmed that He was the God of Abraham, Isaac and Jacob, men who had long since passed from this world (see Exodus 3:5-6). Jesus goes directly to the real point of the Sadducees' question and points out that unequivocally there is a resurrection...*"He is not the God of the dead but of the living."*

Jesus spoke plainly about the resurrection and who He was:
> **John 11:25-26:** *"Jesus said to her, 'I am the resurrection and the life; he who believes in Me shall live even if he dies, [26] and everyone who lives and believes in Me shall never die. Do you believe this?'"*

VERSE 33: *"And when the multitudes heard this, they were astonished at His teaching."*

Verse 33 tells us that the people who had gathered around and listened to the questioning of Jesus by the Sadducees where **"astonished"** by Jesus' answer. Luke tells us a little more detail about the response from the scribes who were standing by having listened to the Sadducees' trick

---

[Note continued]
Peter makes reference to demons from the time period of Noah being in prison.
1 Peter 3:18: *"For Christ also died for sins once for all, the just for the unjust, in order that He might bring us to God, having been put to death in the flesh, but made alive in the spirit; [19] in which also He went and made proclamation to the spirits now in prison, [20] who once were disobedient, when the patience of God kept waiting in the days of Noah, during the construction of the ark, in which a few, that is, eight persons, were brought safely through the water."*
Notice that in Second Peter, he writes again making reference to the judgment of *"angels"*/demons who were condemned to hell during the time of Noah.
> **2 Peter 2:4-5:** *" For if God did not spare angels when they sinned, but cast them into hell and committed them to pits of darkness, reserved for judgment; [5] and did not spare the ancient world, but preserved Noah, a preacher of righteousness, with seven others, when He brought a flood upon the world of the ungodly;"*

MacArthur similarly states the following about Genesis 6:2:
> "The sons of God, identified elsewhere almost exclusively as angels (Job 1:6; 2:1; 38:7), saw and took wives of the human race. This produced an unnatural union which violated the God-ordained order of human marriage and procreation (Genesis 2:24). Some have argued that the sons of God were the sons of Seth who cohabited with the daughters of Cain; others suggest they were perhaps human kings wanting to build harems. But the passage puts strong emphasis on the angelic vs. human contrast. The NT places this account in sequence with other Genesis events and identifies it as involving fallen angels who indwell men (see notes on 2 Peter 2:4,5; Jude 6). Matthew 22:30 does not necessarily negate the possibility that angels are capable of procreation, but just that they do not marry. To procreate physically, they had to possess human, male bodies." *The MacArthur Study Bible.* 1997 (J. MacArthur, Jr., Ed.) (electronic ed.) (Genesis 6:2). Nashville, TN: Word Pub.

[End of note.]

question: <u>Luke 20:39-40:</u> *"And some of the scribes answered and said, 'Teacher, You have spoken well.' [40] <u>For they did not have courage to question Him any longer about anything."</u>*

Jesus' teaching amazed the crowds. Remember earlier when Matthew described how the crowds responded to Jesus' teaching?

<u>Matthew 7:28-29:</u> *"The result was that when Jesus had finished these words, the multitudes were amazed at His teaching; [29] for He was teaching them as one having authority, and not as their scribes."*

The Doctrine of the Bodily Resurrection of Christ and the Saints

The bodily resurrection of Christ is not just a foundation of Christianity but a hallmark of the faith.

<u>1 Corinthians 15:3-8:</u> *"For I delivered to you <u>as of first importance</u> what I also received, that Christ died for our sins according to the Scriptures, [4] and that He was buried, and that He was raised on the third day according to the Scriptures, [5] and that He appeared to Cephas, then to the twelve. [6] After that He <u>appeared to more than five hundred brethren at one time, most of whom remain until now,</u> but some have fallen asleep; [7] then He appeared to James, then to all the apostles; [8] and last of all, as it were to one untimely born, He appeared to me also."*

Those who deny the resurrection are not Christian, no matter what they call themselves. Although other religions speak of reincarnation or mythological new beginnings, Christianity claims a literal bodily resurrection. Some people do not like the thought of resurrection. They would prefer to pretend that life is meaningless rather than face a judgment of accountability. We see some of these types sneering when Paul taught of the resurrection in Acts.

<u>Acts 17:32-34:</u> *"Now when they heard of the resurrection of the dead, some began to sneer, but others said, 'We shall hear you again concerning this.' [33] So Paul went out of their midst. [34] But some men joined him and believed, among whom also were Dionysius the Areopagite and a woman named Damaris and others with them."*

What happens to a person who dies? We start by examining what the Bible tells us about man. Scripture states that God made man out of the **dust** of the earth, but He <u>breathed into him a living **spirit**</u> as we see in <u>Genesis 2:7:</u>

"Then the LORD God formed man of dust from the ground, and breathed into his nostrils the breath of life; and man became a living being."

Upon death, the physical body of humans <u>returns to "dust"</u> (i.e. undergoes decay). We read about this in the curse of man in <u>Genesis 3:19</u> which states, *"...For you are dust, And to dust you shall return."* Immediately upon death, the <u>soul returns to God</u> (i.e. all souls belong to God – Ezekiel 18:4). The soul does not sleep as some falsely claim. Jesus Himself told the criminal on the cross that, *"...Truly I say to you, <u>today</u> you shall be with Me in Paradise."* <u>Luke 23:43</u>. The believer's soul goes to the presence of God in Paradise and then at last to live forever in the new heaven - Revelation 21:1-5. The unbeliever's soul is justly ordered by God to go into torment in Hades. Jesus speaks of a man sent to a very painful judgment in <u>Luke 16:23:</u> *"And in Hades he lifted up his eyes, being in torment, and saw Abraham far away, and Lazarus in his bosom."* In the end, the unbeliever ends up in hell (i.e. the Lake of Fire - Revelation 20:14-15).

This whole concept of the body's decay and the soul's return to the Lord is set out in **Ecclesiastes 12:7:** *"...then the dust will return to the earth as it was, and the spirit will return to God who gave it."* We see Jesus returning the spirit back to the girl He resurrected from the dead in **Luke 8:53-56:** *"And they began laughing at Him, knowing that she had died. 54 He, however, took her by the hand and called, saying, 'Child, arise!' 55 And <u>her spirit returned</u>, and she rose immediately; and He gave orders for something to be given her to eat. 56 And her parents were amazed; but He instructed them to tell no one what had happened."*

A.A. Hodge explains the concept of the bodily death and resurrection and *Purgatory* as follows:

> "The souls of the righteous, being then made perfect in holiness, are received into the highest heavens, where they behold the face of God in light and glory, waiting for the full redemption of their bodies (Hebrews 12:23; 2 Corinthians 5:1,6,8; Philippians 1:23; Acts 3:21; Ephesians 4:10.); and the souls of the wicked are cast into hell where they remain in torments and utter darkness, reserved to the judgment of the great day. (Luke 16:23,24; Acts 1:25; Jude 6,7; 1 Peter 3:19.) Besides these two places for souls separated from their bodies, the Scripture acknowledges none.
>
> <u>Concerning purgatory</u>, the Council of Trent teaches—
>
> (a) That there is a purifying fire through which imperfect Christians must pass.
>
> (b) That souls in purgatory may be benefited by the prayers and masses offered on their behalf on earth. (Council of Trent, sess. 25.)
>
> <u>This doctrine is false, because</u>—
>
> (1) It is nowhere taught in Scripture.
>
> (2) It is opposed to the teaching of Scripture as to the intermediate state, as above shown.
>
> (3) It rests upon anti-christian principles as to the efficacy of the atonement of Christ, as to the sin–expiating and soul–purifying efficacy of temporary suffering, as to the sacrifice of the mass, and as to prayers for the dead etc."[383] (See the footnote below for an expanded explanation of purgatory).

---

[383] A. A. Hodge, *The Confession of Faith*, (Simpsonville, SC: Christian Classics Foundation) 1997.

More on Purgatory:

The great theologian, A.A. Hodge, summarizes the concept of purgatory this way: 1) nowhere is purgatory mentioned in the Bible, 2) Scripture teaches that when you die you go immediately to Hades or Paradise and there is no holding place or waiting station (i.e. there is no *timeout-chair* in which you pay your penalty and then you get to go to heaven), 3) the idea of purgatory also attacks the truth that Jesus paid the complete price of our sins on the cross. Christ's atoning death was not a partial payment that requires you to get the rest paid for by roasting in purgatory or the payment of indulgences to buy your way out.

The heresy of purgatory is not some little difference that Christians have, but instead is a very anti-Christian view that must be rejected by all who truly believe what God said in His Word.

The judgment takes place as soon as you die:

Hebrews 9:27: *"And inasmuch as it is appointed for men to die once and after this comes judgment,"*

[Note continued on the next page.]

[Note continued.]

Jesus does not cleanse us from *some* of our sins, but ALL of them.

> **1 John 1:9:** "*If we confess our sins, He is faithful and righteous to forgive us our sins and to cleanse us from <u>all unrighteousness</u>.*" Obviously a verse that obliterates the concept of Purgatory is that of the criminal on the cross next to Jesus.

The Lord told him where he would be yet that day after he died:

> **Luke 23:39-43:** "*And one of the criminals who were hanged there was hurling abuse at Him, saying, 'Are You not the Christ? Save Yourself and us!' [40] But the other answered, and rebuking him said, 'Do you not even fear God, since you are under the same sentence of condemnation? [41] And we indeed justly, for we are receiving what we deserve for our deeds; but this man has done nothing wrong.' [42] And he was saying, 'Jesus, remember me when You come in Your kingdom!' [43] And He said to him, <u>'Truly I say to you, today you shall be with Me in Paradise.'</u>*"

Where the Catholic Church comes up with purgatory:

The following are quotes from the *Catechism of the Catholic Church*,

> ¶ **1471** "The doctrine and <u>practice of indulgences in the Church are closely linked to the effects of the sacrament of Penance.</u>"

What is an indulgence?

> "<u>An indulgence is a remission before God of the temporal punishment due to sins whose guilt has already been forgiven, which the faithful Christian who is duly disposed gains under certain prescribed conditions through the action of the Church which, as the minister of redemption,</u> dispenses and applies with authority the treasury of the satisfactions of Christ and the saints."
>
> "<u>An indulgence is partial or plenary according as it removes either part or all of the temporal punishment due to sin. The faithful can gain indulgences for themselves or apply them to the dead.</u>" (emphasis added)

The punishments of sin

> ¶ **1472** "To understand this doctrine and practice of the Church, it is necessary to understand that sin has a *double consequence*. Grave sin deprives us of communion with God and therefore makes us incapable of eternal life, the privation of which is called the 'eternal punishment' of sin. <u>On the other hand every sin, even venial, entails an unhealthy attachment to creatures, which must be purified either here on earth, or after death in the state called Purgatory. This purification frees one from what is called the 'temporal punishment' of sin. These two punishments must not be conceived of as a kind of vengeance inflicted by God from without, but as following from the very nature of sin.</u> A conversion which proceeds from a fervent charity can attain the complete purification of the sinner in such a way that no punishment would remain."
>
> ¶ **1473** "The forgiveness of sin and restoration of communion with God entail the remission of the eternal punishment of sin, but temporal punishment of sin remains. While patiently <u>bearing sufferings and trials of all kinds and, when the day comes, serenely facing death, the Christian must strive to accept this temporal punishment of sin as a grace. He should strive by works of mercy and charity, as well as by prayer and the various practices of penance,</u> to put off completely the 'old man' and to put on the 'new man.'" (emphasis added).

[Note continued on the next page.]

\

[Note continued.]

The Catholic church also claims that the Apocrypha book of 2 Maccabees 12:42-45 is an authority for the concept of the sins being removed after one dies by either prayers or money given as a sin offering (i.e. indulgences).

"Betook <u>themselves unto prayer, and besought him that the sin committed might wholly be put out of remembrance.</u> Besides, that noble Judas exhorted the people to keep themselves from sin, forsomuch as they saw before their eyes the things that came to pass for the sins of those that were slain. [43] And when he had <u>made a gathering throughout the company to the sum of two thousand drachms of silver, he sent it to Jerusalem to offer a sin offering,</u> doing therein very well and honestly, in that he was mindful of the resurrection: [44] <u>For if he had not hoped that they that were slain should have risen again, it had been superfluous and vain to pray for the dead.</u> [45] And also in that he perceived that there was great favour laid <u>up for those that died godly, it was an holy and good thought. Whereupon he made a reconciliation for the dead, that they might be delivered from sin.</u>" *The Apocrypha: King James Version.* 1995. (emphasis added)

It is important to understand that the Apocrypha is not Scripture. Below is a short analysis of the subject.

APOCRYPHA

While Roman Catholics and Protestants agree as to which book were to be included in the New Testament there is extremely serious disagreement as to the Old Testament cannon. Roman Catholics include the books of the Apocrypha and historic Protestantism does not. [Sproul, R. C., *Essential Truths of the Christian Faith,* (Wheaton, Illinois: Tyndale House Publishers, Inc.) 1992.] The Apocrypha books can be found between the Old and New Testaments in the "Catholic Bible" and are books that were written after the Old Testament was completed and before the New Testament began. The term Apocrypha means "**hidden.**" Theologian A.A. Hodge stated: "The books commonly called Apocrypha, not being of divine inspiration, are no part of the canon of the Scripture, and therefore are of no authority in the Church of God, nor to be any otherwise approved or made use of than other human writings." [A. A. Hodge, The Confession of Faith, (Simpsonville, SC: Christian Classics Foundation) 1997.] Even the Roman Catholic church did not admit them to the cannon until the 16th century at the Council of Trent, where 12 works were included in the Catholic canon. [The New Bible Dictionary, (Wheaton, Illinois: Tyndale House Publishers, Inc.) 1962.] "That these books have no right to a place in the canon is proved by the following facts:

(1) They never formed a part of the Hebrew Scriptures. They have always been rejected by the Jews, to whose guardianship the Old Testament Scriptures were committed.

(2) None of them were ever quoted by Christ or the apostles.

(3) They were never embraced in the list of the canonical books by the early Fathers; and even in the Roman Church their authority was not accepted by the most learned and candid men until after it was made an article of faith by the Council of Trent, late in the sixteenth century.

(4) The internal evidence presented by their contents disproves their claims. None of them make any claim to inspiration, while the best of them disclaim it. Some of them consist of childish fables, and inculcate bad morals." [A. A. Hodge, The Confession of Faith, (Simpsonville, SC: Christian Classics Foundation) 1997.]

One final thought has to do with the Apocrypha's false and heretical teaching of salvation by man's effort (i.e. good works). The foundation of God's Word (Old and New Testament) specifically tells us that we are saved by the grace of God through faith in Him and not good works.

- **Ephesians 2:8-9:** *"For by grace you have been saved through faith; and that not of yourselves, it is the gift of God; 9 not as a result of works, that no one should boast."*

- **Galatians 2:16:** *"...nevertheless knowing that a man is not justified by the works of the Law but through faith in Christ Jesus, even we have believed in Christ Jesus, that we may be justified by faith in Christ, and not by the works of the Law; since by the works of the Law shall no flesh be justified."*

[Note continued on the next page.]

We know that scripture teaches that a body of flesh cannot live in heaven, so God gives us glorified bodies.

> **1 Corinthians 15:50-53:** *"Now I say this, brethren, <u>that flesh and blood cannot inherit the kingdom of God;</u> nor does the perishable inherit the imperishable. ⁵¹ Behold, I tell you a mystery; we shall not all sleep, <u>but we shall all be changed,</u> ⁵² in a moment, in the twinkling of an eye, at the last trumpet; for the trumpet will sound, and the dead will be raised imperishable, and we shall be changed. ⁵³ For this perishable must put on the imperishable, and this mortal must put on immortality."*

Hodge explains the glorified body this way,

> "The very same bodies that are buried in the earth shall be raised and reunited to their souls—their identity preserved, although their qualities are changed. This is explicitly declared in Scripture: 'Our vile body is to be changed.' (Philippians 3:21.)
> 'This corruptible is to put on incorruption.' (1 Corinthians 15:53,54.) 'All that are in the graves shall hear His voice, and shall come forth.' John 5:28. 'They who are asleep, . . . the dead in Christ shall rise.' (1 Thessalonians 4:13–17.) Our bodies are now members of Christ, and they are to be raised in a manner analogous to His resurrection, which we know to have been of His identical body by the print of the nails and of the spear. It was seen and handled for the space of forty days in order to establish this very fact. (Luke 24:39; Acts 1:3; 1 Corinthians 15:4.)…There are many changes in the material elements and form of the human body between birth and death, and yet no one can for a moment doubt that the body remains one and the same throughout all. There is no difficulty in believing, upon the authority of God's Word, that, in spite of the lapse of time and of all the changes, whether of matter or of form, it undergoes, the body of the resurrection will be in the same sense and to the same degree one with the body of death as the body of death is one with the body of birth…These changes will doubtless be very great. The body of the believer is to be made 'like unto Christ's glorious body.' Philippians 3:21…not a new body substituted for the old, but the old changed into the new." ³⁸⁴

View Hodge's comments above in the light of 1 Corinthians 15 and Philippians 3.

> **1 Corinthians 15:40-44, 50-55:** *"There are also heavenly bodies and earthly bodies, but the glory of the heavenly is one, and the glory of the earthly is another. ⁴¹ There is one glory of the sun, and another glory of the moon, and another glory of the stars; for star*

[Note continued.]
- **Romans 3:20:** *"…because by the works of the Law no flesh will be justified in His sight; for through the Law comes the knowledge of sin."*
- **Habakkuk 2:4:** *"…But the righteous will live by his faith…."*
- **Genesis 15:6:** [Speaking of Abraham] *"Then he believed in the Lord; and He reckoned it to him as righteousness."*

With God's Word telling us how to be saved, one should realize that the <u>Jewish apocryphal books teach salvation by "works" to the contrary of God's Word.</u> For example we read such things as,
- *"…It is better to give alms than to lay up gold: ⁹ For alms doth deliver from death, and shall purge away all sin…."* (Tobit 12:8-9) and,
- *"Water will quench a flaming fire; and alms maketh an atonement for sins."* (Sirach 3:30.)

[End of note.]

³⁸⁴ Hodge, A. A., and Hodge, C. (1996). *The Confession of Faith: With Questions for Theological Students and Bible Classes* (p. 387). Simpsonville, SC: Christian Classics Foundation.

differs from star in glory. [42] *So also is the resurrection of the dead. It is sown a perishable body, it is raised an imperishable body;* [43] *it is sown in dishonor, it is raised in glory; it is sown in weakness, it is raised in power;* [44] *it is sown a natural body, it is raised a spiritual body.*

...[50] *Now I say this, brethren, that flesh and blood cannot inherit the kingdom of God; nor does the perishable inherit the imperishable.* [51] *Behold, I tell you a mystery; we shall not all sleep, but we shall all be changed,* [52] *in a moment, in the twinkling of an eye, at the last trumpet; for the trumpet will sound, and the dead will be raised imperishable, and we shall be changed.* [53] *For this perishable must put on the imperishable, and this mortal must put on immortality.* [54] *But when this perishable will have put on the imperishable, and this mortal will have put on immortality, then will come about the saying that is written, 'DEATH IS SWALLOWED UP in victory.* [55] *O DEATH, WHERE IS YOUR VICTORY? O DEATH, WHERE IS YOUR STING?'"*

Philippians 3:20-21: *"For our citizenship is in heaven, from which also we eagerly wait for a Savior, the Lord Jesus Christ;* [21] *who will transform the body of our humble state into conformity with the body of His glory, by the exertion of the power that He has even to subject all things to Himself."*

There are several resurrections that take place over time. Below is the list of the various resurrections that scripture tells about.

CHRONOLOGY OF RESURRECTIONS

Resurrection begins with Jesus Christ. After Christ's resurrection we see different groups resurrected, starting with the people of God and ending with non-believers. Below is not to be viewed as a chronology of eschatology (i.e. end times theology), but rather deals with the chronology of various resurrections that take place. The sequence of resurrections is as follows:

1) Resurrection of Christ: Resurrection concepts are set forth in 1 Corinthians 15:20-49. From verse 20 we read that Jesus' resurrection is the first as well as the hallmark of all resurrections.
    1 Corinthians 15:20: *"But now Christ has been raised from the dead, the first fruits of those who are asleep."* One might ask, "Did not the resurrections of Jarius' daughter, Lazarus, or the widow's son occur before Jesus' resurrection?" The answer is no, they are not the same resurrections as Jesus'. These other people would eventually die again. Jesus is the resurrection that was to eternal life (i.e. the first resurrection of one who would never die again).

2) Resurrection of some Old Testament saints immediately after Jesus' resurrection: Immediately after the resurrection of Christ was "the token resurrection of a number of saints..."
    Matthew 27:50-53: *"And Jesus cried out again with a loud voice, and yielded up His spirit.* [51] *And behold, the veil of the temple was torn in two from top to bottom, and the earth shook; and the rocks were split,* [52] *and the tombs were opened; and many bodies of the saints who had fallen asleep were raised;* [53] *and coming out of the tombs after His resurrection they entered the holy city and appeared to many."*

Note that the resurrection of all Old Testament believers is later, as set out in number seven below. [385]

3) <u>Resurrection of Christians who died before the Rapture:</u> The resurrection of the church. This resurrection will be the Christians who had died from the point of Pentecost to the rapture of the church.

> **1 Thessalonians 4:16:** *"For the Lord Himself will descend from heaven with a shout, with the voice of the archangel, and with the trumpet of God; and the dead in Christ shall rise first."*

4) <u>Rapture of those who are alive at the time Jesus comes for His Church:</u> Next we see that the Christians who are alive at the time of the rapture will be taken up and joined in the air with those who were raised in the first group. Notice the next verse after what was quoted above:

> **1 Thessalonians 4:17:** *"Then <u>we who are alive and remain shall be caught up together with them in the clouds</u> to meet the Lord in the air, and thus we shall always be with the Lord."*

> **John 14:1–3:** *"Do not let your heart be troubled; believe in God, believe also in Me. In My Father's house are many dwelling places; if it were not so, I would have told you; for I go to prepare a place for you. If I go and prepare a place for you, <u>I will come again and receive you to Myself,</u> that where I am, there you may be also."*

> **1 Corinthians 15:51–52:** *"Behold, I tell you a mystery; we will not all sleep, but we will all be changed, in a moment, in the twinkling of an eye, at the last trumpet; for the trumpet will sound, and the dead will be raised imperishable, and we will be changed."*

> **Revelation 3:10:** *"Because you have kept the word of My perseverance, I also will keep you from the hour of testing, that hour which is about to come upon the whole world, to test those who dwell on the earth."*

5) <u>Resurrection of the Two Tribulation Prophets:</u> Next we see the resurrection of the two witnesses of God during the Tribulation.

> **Revelation 11:3-12:** *"And I will grant authority to my two witnesses, and they will prophesy for twelve hundred and sixty days, clothed in sackcloth. [4] These are the two olive trees and the two lampstands that stand before the Lord of the earth. [5] And if anyone desires to harm them, fire proceeds out of their mouth and devours their enemies; and if anyone would desire to harm them, in this manner he must be killed. [6] These have the power to shut up the sky, in order that rain may not fall during the days of their prophesying; and they have power over the waters to turn them into blood, and to smite the earth with*

---

[385] Walvoord, J. F., Zuck, R. B., and Dallas Theological Seminary. (1985). *The Bible Knowledge Commentary: An Exposition of the Scriptures* (v. 2, p 980). Wheaton, IL: Victor Books.. "Many others, however, say that since Christ is the first-fruits of the dead (1 Corinthians 15:23), their resurrection did not occur till He was raised. In this view, the phrase 'after Jesus' resurrection' goes with the words *were raised to life* and *came out of the tombs.* This is possible in the Greek, and is suggested in the KJV and the NASB. The tombs, then, *broke open* at Christ's death, probably by the earthquake, thus heralding Christ's triumph in death over sin, but the bodies were not raised till Christ was raised. These people returned to Jerusalem, (the Holy City) where they were recognized by friends and family."

every plague, as often as they desire. [7] And when they have finished their testimony, the beast that comes up out of the abyss will make war with them, and overcome them and kill them. [8] And their dead bodies will lie in the street of the great city which mystically is called Sodom and Egypt, where also their Lord was crucified. [9] And those from the peoples and tribes and tongues and nations will look at their dead bodies for three and a half days, and will not permit their dead bodies to be laid in a tomb. [10] And those who dwell on the earth will rejoice over them and make merry; and they will send gifts to one another, because these two prophets tormented those who dwell on the earth. [11] And after the three and a half days the breath of life from God came into them, and they stood on their feet; and great fear fell upon those who were beholding them. [12] And they heard a loud voice from heaven saying to them, 'Come up here.' And they went up into heaven in the cloud, and their enemies beheld them."

6) <u>Resurrection of the Tribulation Saints (i.e. those who became believers and were killed during the Tribulation):</u> The next resurrection will be at the end of the tribulation, which is the beginning of the Millennial reign of Christ. This resurrection will be of those who become believers during the Tribulation, (the "Tribulation saints"). Many will, "come to trust in Christ during the Tribulation, that unimaginably horrible seven–year ordeal during which many godly people will be put to death for their faith. At the end of that period, however, all those who will have come to faith in Christ will be raised up to reign with Him during the Millennium..."[386] We see this in **Revelation 20:4:**

> *"And I saw thrones, and they sat upon them, and judgment was given to them. And I saw the souls of those who had been beheaded because of the testimony of Jesus and because of the word of God, and those who had not worshiped the beast or his image, and had not received the mark upon their forehead and upon their hand; and they came to life and reigned with Christ for a thousand years."*

7) <u>Resurrection of the Old Testament Saints:</u> Next is the resurrection of the Old Testament saints. MacArthur believes that simultaneously with the resurrection of the Tribulation saints in (6), there will be the resurrection of Old Testament saints.[387] He points this out from **Daniel 12:1-2:**

> *"Now at that time Michael, the great prince who stands guard over the sons of your people, will arise. And <u>there will be a time of distress such as never occurred</u> since there was a nation until that time; and at that time your people, everyone who is found written in the book, will be rescued. [2] And many of those who sleep in the dust of the ground will awake, these to everlasting life, but the others to disgrace and everlasting contempt."*

MacArthur speculates the following regarding the death of believers during the millennium:

> "Then during the millennial Kingdom there will, of necessity, be the resurrection of those who die during that time. It is interesting to think that

---

[386] MacArthur, J. F., Jr. (1984). *1 Corinthians*. MacArthur New Testament Commentary (p. 418). Chicago: Moody Press.

[387] Ibid.

they may well be raised as soon as they die, no burial being necessary. It would make death for a believer during the Kingdom nothing more than an instant transformation into his eternal body and spirit." [388]

One may ask, isn't everyone a Christian who is alive during the millennium? Maybe not. There is reason to believe that during the millennium there will be those who obey and submit to God's rule, but not from a true heart.[389] We read of the release of the Devil after the 1000-year reign. At his release, the Devil will have his short and final attempt of an insurrection in **Revelation 20:7-9:**

> *"And when the thousand years are completed, Satan will be released from his prison, [8] and will come out to deceive the nations which are in the four corners of the earth, Gog and Magog, to gather them together for the war; the number of them is like the sand of the seashore. [9] And they came up on the broad plain of the earth and surrounded the camp of the saints and the beloved city, and fire came down from heaven and devoured them."*

Regarding this passage Charles Ryrie writes: "The large number of rebels will come from the many people born during the Millennium who, though giving outward obedience to the King, never accept Him."[390]

8) Resurrection of the damned (i.e. non-Christians): The final resurrection will be of the damned. These are all non-Christians who are raised at the end of the 1000-year reign of Christ after the Tribulation. We will see in the verses below that these individuals will be judged to hell before the Great White Throne of Judgment.

> **Revelation 20:4-5:** *"And I saw thrones, and they sat upon them, and judgment was given to them. And I saw the souls of those who had been beheaded because of the testimony of Jesus and because of the word of God, and those who had not worshiped the beast or his image, and had not received the mark upon their forehead and upon their hand; and they came to life and reigned with Christ for a thousand years. [5] The rest of the dead did not come to life until the thousand years were completed. This is the first resurrection."* [391]

---

[388] MacArthur, J. F., Jr. (1984). *1 Corinthians.* MacArthur New Testament Commentary (p. 418). Chicago: Moody Press.

[389] For an example of those who "believe" in Jesus but are damned look at **James 2:19,** *"You believe that God is one. You do well; the demons also believe, and shudder."*

See also: **Matthew 7:21–23:** *"Not everyone who says to Me, 'Lord, Lord,' will enter the kingdom of heaven, but he who does the will of My Father who is in heaven will enter. Many will say to Me on that day, 'Lord, Lord, did we not prophesy in Your name, and in Your name cast out demons, and in Your name perform many miracles?' And then I will declare to them, 'I never knew you; depart from Me, you who practice lawlessness.' "*

[390] The Ryrie Study Bible — Expanded edition: New American Standard, comment to Revelation 20:8.

[391] The end of verse five in Revelation chapter 20, refers to the *"first resurrection."* Verse six mentions the blessings of those of the first resurrection. The term "first resurrection is referring to the resurrection of the tribulation saints of verse four, not the *"rest of the dead"* who are the damned.

After the resurrection of the damned, we then see the judgment of the Devil. At the end of the 1000-year millennial reign of Christ, the Devil is released and he engages in one last attempted insurrection against God, and then is judged to hell.

> **Revelation 20:7-10:** *"And when the thousand years are completed, Satan will be released from his prison, [8] and will come out to deceive the nations which are in the four corners of the earth, Gog and Magog, to gather them together for the war; the number of them is like the sand of the seashore. [9] And they came up on the broad plain of the earth and surrounded the camp of the saints and the beloved city, and fire came down from heaven and devoured them. [10] And the devil who deceived them was thrown into the lake of fire and brimstone, where the beast and the false prophet are also; and they will be tormented day and night forever and ever."*

Notice that the next verse (verse 11) explains that the nonbelievers who were resurrected are now subject to the Great White Throne of Judgment before they are cast into hell for eternity.

> **Revelation 20:11-15:** *"And I saw <u>a great white throne and Him who sat upon it</u>, from whose presence earth and heaven fled away, and no place was found for them. [12] And I saw the dead, the great and the small, standing before the throne, and books were opened; and another book was opened, which is the book of life; and the dead were judged from the things which were written in the books, according to their deeds. [13] And the sea gave up the dead which were in it, and death and Hades gave up the dead which were in them; and they were judged, every one of them according to their deeds. [14] <u>And death and Hades were thrown into the lake of fire. This is the second death, the lake of fire.</u> [15] And <u>if anyone's name was not found written in the book of life, he was thrown into the lake of fire.</u>"*

The judgment and punishment on nonbelievers is set out again in the book of Revelation.

> **Revelation 21:8:** *"But for the cowardly and unbelieving and abominable and murderers and immoral persons and sorcerers and idolaters and all liars, their part will be in the lake that burns with fire and brimstone, which is the second death."*

We then see the re-creation of heaven and earth by God. This is where the believers will dwell forever.

> **Revelation 21:1-5:** *"AND I saw <u>a new heaven and a new earth; for the first heaven and the first earth passed away, and there is no longer any sea.</u> [2] And I saw the holy city, new Jerusalem, coming down out of heaven from God, made ready as a bride adorned for her husband. [3] And I heard a loud voice from the throne, saying, 'Behold, the tabernacle of God is among men, and He shall dwell among them, and they shall be His people, and God Himself shall be among them, [4] and He shall wipe away every tear from their eyes; and there shall no longer be any death; there shall no longer be any mourning, or crying, or pain; the first things have passed away.' [5] And He who sits on the throne said, 'Behold, I am making all things new.' And He *said, 'Write, for these words are faithful and true.'"*

Summary and Application

Jesus makes it clear that all mankind will be resurrected, some to eternal life and most to eternal damnation. **Matthew 7:14:** *"For the gate is small and the way is narrow that leads to life, and there are few who find it. "* One must turn to Him for salvation to escape the eternal judgment to hell.

John 5:25-29: *"Truly, truly, I say to you, an hour is coming and now is, when the dead shall hear the voice of the Son of God; and those who hear shall live. [26]For just as the Father has life in Himself, even so He gave to the Son also to have life in Himself; [27]and He gave Him authority to execute judgment, because He is the Son of Man. [28] Do not marvel at this; for an hour is coming, in which all who are in the tombs shall hear His voice,"*

John 11:25-28: *"Jesus said to her, 'I am the resurrection and the life; he who believes in Me shall live even if he dies , [26] and everyone who lives and believes in Me shall never die . Do you believe this?' [27] She *said to Him, 'Yes, Lord; I have believed that You are the Christ, the Son of God, even He who comes into the world.' [28] And when she had said this, she went away, and called Mary her sister, saying secretly, 'The Teacher is here, and is calling for you.'"*

MATTHEW 22:34-40
(THE GREATEST COMMANDMENT)

"But when the Pharisees heard that Jesus had silenced the Sadducees, they gathered themselves together. ³⁵ *One of them, a lawyer, asked Him a question, testing Him,* ³⁶ *'Teacher, which is the great commandment in the Law?'* ³⁷ *And He said to him, 'You shall love the Lord your God with all your heart, and with all your soul, and with all your mind.* ³⁸ *This is the great and foremost commandment.* ³⁹ *The second is like it, You shall love your neighbor as yourself.* ⁴⁰ *On these two commandments depend the whole Law and the Prophets.'"*

Introduction

In this section we see the ongoing questioning of Jesus. The questions were not asked to obtain truth, but in hopes of tricking or humiliating Jesus. Let us review the sequence of the questions. In Matthew 22:15-22, we read of how the disciples of the Pharisees sought to entrap Jesus with a trick question regarding paying taxes to Rome. Then in Matthew 22:23-33 the Sadducees set up a ridiculous question to justify their mocking of the concept of a resurrection. Now they are trying to catch Him in a misstep regarding the commandments of God.

VERSES 34-35: *"But when the Pharisees heard that Jesus had silenced the Sadducees, they gathered themselves together.* ³⁵ *One of them, a lawyer, asked Him a question, testing Him,"*

Jesus had just humiliated the Sadducees when He exposed their ignorance of the things of God by saying,

> *"But regarding the resurrection of the dead, have you not read that which was spoken to you by God, saying,* ³² *'I AM THE GOD OF ABRAHAM, AND THE GOD OF ISAAC, AND THE GOD OF JACOB'? He is not the God of the dead but of the living."* **Matthew 22:31-32.**

The Pharisees gathered together to come up with their best question. They sent in a lawyer. When we hear the word lawyer, we immediately think of an attorney as we know it. This is an incorrect view. ³⁹² A lawyer here means one who is an expert in Jewish law. The term *lawyer* is

---

³⁹² A more traditional view of an attorney in the Bible is found in **Acts 24:1–6:**

> *"After five days the high priest Ananias came down with some elders, with an attorney named Tertullus, and they brought charges to the governor against Paul.* ² *After Paul had been summoned, Tertullus began to accuse him, saying to the governor, 'Since we have through you attained much peace, and since by your providence reforms are being carried out for this nation,* ³ *we acknowledge this in every way and everywhere, most excellent Felix, with all thankfulness.* ⁴ *But, that I may not weary you any further, I beg you to grant us, by your kindness, a brief hearing.* ⁵ *For we have found this man a real pest and a fellow who stirs up dissension among all the Jews throughout the world, and a ringleader of the sect of the Nazarenes.* ⁶ *And he even tried to desecrate the temple; and then we arrested him. [We wanted to judge him according to our own Law...."*

synonymous with the term *scribe*. In fact, in the parallel account in Mark 12:28 the term *scribe* is used instead of *lawyer*.

> **"One of the scribes came and heard them arguing, and recognizing that He had answered them well, asked Him, 'What commandment is the foremost of all?'"**
> **Mark 12:28.**

A lawyer or scribe is defined as a "teacher of the law"[393] As noted from the account in Mark, this lawyer recognized that Jesus had effectively struck down the Sadducees' bogus question. But that did not stop him!

VERSE 36: *"Teacher, which is the great commandment in the Law?"*

When we hear the term *"commandments of the Law,"* we immediately think of the Ten Commandments. This mindset can miss the question being raised here. He is not simply asking which of the Ten Commandments is the most important, but rather which among all the laws should be emphasized. Warren Wiersbe explains it this way:

> "This was not a new question, for the scribes had been debating it for centuries. They had documented 613 commandments in the Law, 248 positive and 365 negative. No person could ever hope to know and fully obey all of these commandments. So, to make it easier, the experts divided the commandments into "heavy" (important) and "light" (unimportant). A person could major on the "heavy commandments" and not worry about the trivial ones. The fallacy behind this approach is obvious: You need only break *one law*, heavy or light, to be guilty before God. 'For whosoever shall keep the whole Law, and yet offend in one point, he is guilty of all' (James 2:10)."[394]

VERSES 37-38: *"And He said to him, 'You shall love the Lord your God with all your heart, and with all your soul, and with all your mind. ³⁸ This is the great and foremost commandment.'"*

Here Jesus takes them to the First Commandment as the most important. We are to love God. This is not a soft sentimental love, but is a love that permeates all that we are: *"...all your heart, and with all your soul, and with all your mind."* Jesus was quoting from **Deuteronomy 6:4–5:**

> **"Hear, O Israel! The LORD is our God, the LORD is one! ⁵You shall love the LORD your God with all your heart and with all your soul and with all your might."**

"This verse has been called 'the *Shema,*' from the Hebrew word translated 'hear.' The statement in this verse is the basic confession of faith in Judaism. The verse means

---

[393] Wood, D. R. W., and Marshall, I. H. (1996). *New Bible Dictionary* (3rd ed.) (p. 677). Leicester, England; Downers Grove, Ill.: InterVarsity Press.

[394] Wiersbe, W. W. (1996). *The Bible Exposition Commentary* (Matthew 22:34). Wheaton, Ill.: Victor Books.

that the LORD (Yahweh) is totally unique. He alone is God." [395]

It is important that we see how God defines this term love:

<u>John 14:15</u>: *"If you love Me, you will keep My commandments."*

<u>John 15:10</u>: *"If you keep My commandments, you will abide in My love; just as I have kept My Father's commandments and abide in His love."*

<u>Matthew 10:37</u>: *"He who loves father or mother more than Me is not worthy of Me; and he who loves son or daughter more than Me is not worthy of Me."*

<u>Luke 7:47–49</u>: *"For this reason I say to you, her sins, which are many, have been forgiven, for she loved much; but he who is forgiven little, loves little. [48] Then He said to her, 'Your sins have been forgiven.' [49] Those who were reclining at the table with Him began to say to themselves, 'Who is this man who even forgives sins?'"*

<u>VERSES 39-40</u>: *"The second is like it, You shall love your neighbor as yourself. [40] On these two commandments depend the whole Law and the Prophets."*

Remember that the lawyer asked *which* was the greatest commandment. He did not ask what was the second greatest. Jesus answers it anyway by going to: <u>Leviticus 19:18</u>:

"You shall not take vengeance, nor bear any grudge against the sons of your people, but you shall love your neighbor as yourself; I am the Lord."

The point Jesus makes here is that the two commandments, loving God and loving others, are inseparable. One cannot claim to be a follower of God and yet not love others.

<u>1 John 3:14-15</u>: *"We know that we have passed out of death into life, because we love the brethren. He who does not love abides in death. [15] Everyone who hates his brother is a murderer; and you know that no murderer has eternal life abiding in him."*

<u>1 John 2:9</u>: *"The one who says he is in the light and yet hates his brother is in the darkness until now."*

<u>Romans 13:8</u>: *"Owe nothing to anyone except to love one another; for he who loves his neighbor has fulfilled the law."*

<u>Luke 6:32-36</u>: *"And if you love those who love you, what credit is that to you? For even sinners love those who love them. [33] And if you do good to those who do good to you, what credit is that to you? For even sinners do the same. [34] And if you lend to those from whom you expect to receive, what credit is that to you? Even sinners lend to sinners, in order to receive back the same amount. [35] But love your enemies, and do good, and lend, expecting nothing in return;*

---

[395] Walvoord, J. F., Zuck, R. B., and Dallas Theological Seminary. (1983). *The Bible Knowledge Commentary: An Exposition of the Scriptures* (v. 1, p. 274). Wheaton, IL: Victor Books.

and your reward will be great, and you will be sons of the Most High; for <u>He</u> <u>*Himself is kind to ungrateful and evil men.*</u> [36]<u>*Be merciful, just as your Father is*</u> <u>*merciful.*</u>*"*

The Pharisees studied hard but they missed the whole point of studying the Word of God:

> <u>1 Timothy 1:5</u>: *"But the goal of our instruction is love from a pure heart and a good conscience and a sincere faith."*

We get some more information from Mark regarding the answers Jesus gave. Specifically, we find out how the lawyer responded.

> <u>Mark 12:32–34</u>: *"The scribe said to Him, 'Right, Teacher; You have truly stated that He is One, and there is no one else besides Him;* [33] *and to love Him with all the heart and with all the understanding and with all the strength, and to love one's neighbor as himself, is much more than all burnt offerings and sacrifices.'* [34] *When Jesus saw that he had answered intelligently, He said to him, 'You are not far from the kingdom of God.' After that, no one would venture to ask Him any more questions."*

The lawyer knew that Jesus had answered in truth and that nothing could be twisted to accuse Him. Notice that Jesus said that the lawyer answered *"intelligently."* Jesus did not say that the lawyer answered by the Holy Spirit, like He said to Peter. The lawyer was not a member of the kingdom but he was, *"not far from the kingdom of God."* The lawyer had the head knowledge, but not the converted heart. His lack of conversion is manifested by the way he addressed Jesus as *"Teacher"* and not **Lord**. When the Lord asked Peter who he believed Jesus to be, Peter said by revelation of God:

> <u>Matthew 16:16–17</u>: *"…'You are the Christ, the Son of the living God.'* [17] *And Jesus said to him, 'Blessed are you, Simon Barjona, because flesh and blood did not reveal this to you, but My Father who is in heaven.'"*

There are many who will acknowledge Jesus as a moral/religious leader, but they are not saved. Many others will say that Jesus is a great teacher, but they are not saved. There are even some who will call Jesus *Lord* and they too are not saved.

> <u>Matthew 7:21–23</u>: *"Not everyone who says to Me, 'Lord, Lord,' will enter the kingdom of heaven, but he who does the will of My Father who is in heaven will enter.* [22] *Many will say to Me on that day, 'Lord, Lord, did we not prophesy in Your name, and in Your name cast out demons, and in Your name perform many miracles?'* [23] *And then I will declare to them, 'I never knew you; depart from Me, you who practice lawlessness.'"*

At first blush it seems difficult to understand how some who call Him *Lord* will not enter into the Kingdom (Matthew 7:21-23). It should be realized that they confess with their mouth that Jesus is Lord, but do not believe with their heart unto salvation (Romans 10:9-10). Note that just a mere seven verses before in <u>Matthew 7:15</u> Jesus warned His followers, *"Beware of the false prophets, who come to you in sheep's clothing, but inwardly are ravenous wolves."* Those who called Jesus Lord in verse 22 made great claims of being prophets, but in reality they were false prophets. Just a couple verses before that Jesus states, [17]*"…the bad tree bears bad fruit…* [20]*So then, you will know them by their fruits."* The appearance of sincerity is their claim to be prophets. This is not difficult to understand since the false prophet has deceived himself in addition to deceiving others: *"But evil men and impostors will proceed from bad to worse, deceiving and being deceived." 2 Timothy 3:13.* False believers and false prophets will also look to their own good works as the basis for earning salvation. We see these false prophets also made boasts of their own merit by pointing to the miracles they did (v.22). Despite all their claims, Jesus said they were those, *"WHO PRACTICE LAWLESSNESS."* Oswald Chambers pointed out that the difference between fake fruit and Spirit-led fruit is as follows:

> "The expression of Christian character is not good doing, but Godlikeness:
> If the Spirit of God has transformed you within, you will exhibit Divine characteristics in your life, not good human characteristics. God's life in us expresses itself as *God's* life, not as human life trying to be godly."[396]

People are not saved simply because they respectfully call Jesus *Teacher* or *Lord*. Jesus is Lord; so simply speaking that truth is not meritorious per se. Jesus said in **John 13:13:** *"You call Me Teacher and Lord; and you are right, for so I am."* Those who are saved are those who do the will of God. Jesus said in **Matthew 7:21:** *"Not everyone who says to Me, 'Lord, Lord,' will enter the kingdom of heaven, but he who does the will of My Father who is in heaven will enter."* What is it that He commands? **1 John 3:23:** *"This is His commandment, that we believe in the name of His Son Jesus Christ, and love one another, just as He commanded us."*

A true Christian does not do good works to get saved, but as a result of his salvation through faith, good works (i.e. fruit) will be produced. This principle is set out in **Ephesians 2:8-10:**

> *"For by grace you have been saved through faith; and that not of yourselves, it is the gift of God; ⁹ not as a result of works, that no one should boast. ¹⁰ For we are His workmanship, created in Christ Jesus for good works, which God prepared beforehand, that we should walk in them."*

Summary and Application

Scripture says that God is love. **1 John 4:8:** *"The one who does not love does not know God, for God is love."* Note that it does not say that love is an attribute of God, but that God *is* LOVE. Since God is love, a manifesting attribute of His children will be love. This is love for God and all people, whether friend or enemy:

> **Matthew 5:44–45:** *"But I say to you, love your enemies and pray for those who persecute you, ⁴⁵ so that you may be sons of your Father who is in heaven;...."*

> **1 John 4:7–11:** *"Beloved, let us love one another, for love is from God; and everyone who loves is born of God and knows God. ⁸ The one who does not love does not know God, for God is love. ⁹ By this the love of God was manifested in us, that God has sent His only begotten Son into the world so that we might live through Him. ¹⁰ In this is love, not that we loved God, but that He loved us and sent His Son to be the propitiation for our sins. ¹¹ Beloved, if God so loved us, we also ought to love one another."*

We must obey His commandments to love God with all that we are and thus love others.

---

[396] Chambers, O. (1993, c1935). *My Utmost for His Highest: Selections for the Year* (September 20). Grand Rapids, MI: Discovery House Publishers.

MATTHEW 22:41-46
(WHOSE SON IS THE CHRIST?)

"Now while the Pharisees were gathered together, Jesus asked them a question: ⁴²*'What do you think about the Christ, whose son is He?' They said to Him, 'The son of David.'* ⁴³ *He said to them, 'Then how does David in the Spirit call Him 'Lord,' saying,* ⁴⁴ *The Lord said to my Lord, 'Sit at My right hand, Until I put Your enemies beneath Your feet'?* ⁴⁵ *If David then calls Him 'Lord,' how is He his son?'* ⁴⁶ *No one was able to answer Him a word, nor did anyone dare from that day on to ask Him another question."*

Introduction

This section is a continuation of the questioning that started back at Matthew 22:15. By way of review, the questions began with the Pharisee's disciples asking about governmental authority and taxes. Then, the Sadducees question on theology/resurrection. Finally, the lawyer questions regarding the commandments. Now, Jesus turns the tables on these hypocrites and asks them a few questions. His fundamental question is similar to the one asked of Peter: *"...who do you say that I am."* As mentioned in the notes from the previous lesson (see notes for Matthew 22:39-40) the lawyer recognized Jesus as a *teacher* and not the divine Messiah. Jesus attacks their false view of Him through His series of questions.

VERSES 41-42: *"Now while the Pharisees were gathered together, Jesus asked them a question: 'What do you think about the Christ, whose son is He?' They said to Him, 'The son of David.'"*

> The term "Christ" is a Greek word, which translated to Hebrew is "Messiah" and means "Anointed One." The term ***"Son of David"*** is likewise a messianic title. Every Jew knew that the Christ would come from the lineage of David. Soon after Jesus performed public miracles, even the common people began to wonder if He might be the Son of David.
>> **Matthew 12:22–23:** *"Then a demon-possessed man who was blind and mute was brought to Jesus, and He healed him, so that the mute man spoke and saw.* ²³ *All the crowds were amazed, and were saying, 'This man cannot be the Son of David, can he?'"*
>
> The religious leaders could have shut down any speculation that Jesus was the Messiah by simply proving that Jesus was not of the lineage of David. It is certain that they would have already checked this matter out. Their problem was that Jesus was indeed from the house of David.
>> **Matthew 1:6:** *"Jesse was the father of David the king. David was the father of Solomon by Bathsheba who had been the wife of Uriah."*
>
> Here are a couple of examples in Matthew where Jesus is referred to as the Son of David:
>> **Matthew 9:27–30:** *"As Jesus went on from there, two blind men followed Him, crying out, 'Have mercy on us, Son of David!'* ²⁸ *When He entered the house, the blind men came up to Him, and Jesus said to them, 'Do you believe that I am able to do this?' They said to Him, 'Yes, Lord.'* ²⁹ *Then He touched their eyes, saying, 'It shall be done to you according to your faith.'* ³⁰ *And their eyes were opened. And Jesus sternly warned them: 'See that no one knows about this!'"*

Matthew 21:6–11: *"The disciples went and did just as Jesus had instructed them, ⁷ and brought the donkey and the colt, and laid their coats on them; and He sat on the coats. ⁸ Most of the crowd spread their coats in the road, and others were cutting branches from the trees and spreading them in the road. ⁹ The crowds going ahead of Him, and those who followed, were shouting, 'Hosanna to the Son of David; Blessed is He who comes in the name of the Lord; Hosanna in the highest!' ¹⁰ When He had entered Jerusalem, all the city was stirred, saying, 'Who is this?' ¹¹ And the crowds were saying, 'This is the prophet Jesus, from Nazareth in Galilee.'"*

VERSES 43-45: *"He said to them, 'Then how does David in the Spirit call Him 'Lord,' saying, ⁴⁴ 'The Lord said to my Lord, Sit at My right hand, Until I put Your enemies beneath Your feet'? ⁴⁵ If David then calls Him 'Lord,' how is He his son?'"*

It needs to be understood that the religious leaders did not believe in a divine Messiah. They believed that the Messiah would merely be a human descendent of David. Jesus confronts their wrong view of The Messiah. He points out that God the Father said to the divine Son, **"Sit at My right hand, Until I put Your enemies beneath Your feet."** In verse 45 Jesus also points out that David refers to the divine Son as his **Lord.** Walvoord states that it is indisputable that Jesus spoke of Himself as the divine Messiah:

> "If the Messiah were simply an earthly son of David, why did David ascribe deity to Him? Jesus quoted from a messianic psalm (Psalms 110:1)[397], in which David referred to the Messiah as **my Lord.** 'Lord' translates the Hebrew *'ădōnāy,* [is] used only of God (e.g., Genesis 18:27; Job 28:28)." [398]

> [See also Blomberg: "Not surprisingly, Psalms 110:1–4 becomes the Old Testament passage quoted more than any other in the New Testament. It points to Jesus' Messiahship and His exaltation, and the first Christians take their cue from its effectiveness here for use in their later apologetic? (See, e.g., Acts 2:34–35; Hebrew 1:13; 5:6, 10; 7:17, 21)."][399]

When I was in college there was a liberal religion professor, and many freshmen took his class. Each year he would tell the naïve freshmen that "Jesus never said he was the son of God." He would explain that the divinity of Jesus was something made up later in time. The naïve freshmen would often regurgitate their professor's claim during a debate on Christianity.

---

[397] **Psalm 110:1–4:** *"The Lord says to my Lord: 'Sit at My right hand Until I make Your enemies a footstool for Your feet.' ² The Lord will stretch forth Your strong scepter from Zion, saying, 'Rule in the midst of Your enemies.' ³ Your people will volunteer freely in the day of Your power; In holy array, from the womb of the dawn, Your youth are to You as the dew. ⁴ The Lord has sworn and will not change His mind, 'You are a priest forever According to the order of Melchizedek.'"*

[398] Walvoord, J. F., Zuck, R. B., and Dallas Theological Seminary. (1983). *The Bible Knowledge Commentary: An Exposition of the Scriptures* (v. 2, p. 73). Wheaton, IL: Victor Books.

[399] Blomberg, C. (2001). *Vol. 22: Matthew* (electronic ed.). Logos Library System; The New American Commentary (p. 337). Nashville: Broadman and Holman Publishers.

Unfortunately, both the students and the professor failed to read the Bible. If they had, they would have seen one of many verses that supported Jesus asserting His divinity as The Christ. An example of this is found in **Luke 22:70:** *"And they all said, 'Are You the Son of God, then?' And He said to them, 'Yes, I am.'"*

VERSE 46: *"No one was able to answer Him a word, nor did anyone dare from that day on to ask Him another question."*

Jesus answered the question in a way that was very clear to these experts of the law. They understood without any ambiguity that He was declaring Himself the Son of God.

Mark gives us additional information regarding the conclusion of this event when he states, *"...the large crowd enjoyed listening to Him"* **Mark 12:37.** No wonder none of the religious leaders, *"dare from that day on to ask Him another question."* Not only did they fail in their attempt to expose Him with their questions, but He exposed them as false/hypocritical religious leaders with His questions. We see this detailed in Mark's conclusion of the encounter:

> *"'David himself calls Him 'Lord'; so in what sense is He his son?' And the large crowd enjoyed listening to Him. 38 In His teaching He was saying: 'Beware of the scribes who like to walk around in long robes, and like respectful greetings in the market places, 39 and chief seats in the synagogues and places of honor at banquets, 40 who devour widows' houses, and for appearance's sake offer long prayers; these will receive greater condemnation.'"* **Mark 12:37–40.**

Summary and Application

The Bible does not allow a person to take the view that Jesus was either a great teacher, moral example or anything less than the divine son of God. The divinity of Christ is a fundamental doctrine derived from the Bible. Many of today's so-called Christian religious leaders deny the deity of Christ. They are not unlike the religious leaders of Jesus' day. The Bible makes it clear that those who reject the deity of Christ have not only denied the faith, but they are antichrists themselves.

> **1 John 2:22–23:** *"Who is the liar but the one who denies that Jesus is the Christ? This is the antichrist, the one who denies the Father and the Son. 23 Whoever denies the Son does not have the Father; the one who confesses the Son has the Father also."*

Paul had a true view of the glory of the Messiah. From this truth, he realized that any type of hardship suffered was insignificant compared to people knowing Christ and being saved. We should have that same attitude.

> **2 Timothy 2:8–10:** *"Remember Jesus Christ, risen from the dead, descendant of David, according to my gospel, 9 for which I suffer hardship even to imprisonment as a criminal; but the word of God is not imprisoned. 10 For this reason I endure all things for the sake of those who are chosen, so that they also may obtain the salvation which is in Christ Jesus and with it eternal glory."*

MATTHEW 23:1-12
(FALSE/HYPOCRITICAL SPIRITUAL LEADERSHIP)

"THEN Jesus spoke to the multitudes and to His disciples, ² saying, 'The scribes and the Pharisees have seated themselves in the chair of Moses; ³ therefore all that they tell you, do and observe, but do not do according to their deeds; for they say things, and do not do them. ⁴ And they tie up heavy loads, and lay them on men's shoulders; but they themselves are unwilling to move them with so much as a finger. ⁵ But they do all their deeds to be noticed by men; for they broaden their phylacteries, and lengthen the tassels of their garments. ⁶ And they love the place of honor at banquets, and the chief seats in the synagogues, ⁷ and respectful greetings in the market places, and being called by men, Rabbi. ⁸ But do not be called Rabbi; for One is your Teacher, and you are all brothers. ⁹ And do not call anyone on earth your father; for One is your Father, He who is in heaven. ¹⁰ And do not be called leaders; for One is your Leader, that is, Christ. ¹¹But the greatest among you shall be your servant. ¹² And whoever exalts himself shall be humbled; and whoever humbles himself shall be exalted.'"

Introduction

Here Jesus tells the people they are to follow God's message given through Moses. He also makes it very clear that judgment awaits the hypocritical false teachers (i.e. the Pharisees—see later in the chapter 23:13-17). This chapter is Jesus' last public sermon and it focuses on the great condemnation of false teachers. The Pharisees never saw themselves as false teachers, which is typical of false teachers. False teachers are always self-deceived, in addition to deceiving others. Paul points this out in **2 Timothy 3:13:** *"But evil men and impostors will proceed from bad to worse <u>deceiving and being deceived.</u>"* Jesus teaches this crowd that they are not to have anything to do with religious hypocrisy. A religious hypocrite seeks his own grandeur and honor from man instead of humbly submitting to God.

VERSES 1-2: *"THEN Jesus spoke to the multitudes and to His disciples, ² saying, 'The scribes and the Pharisees have seated themselves in the chair of Moses;...'"*

Jesus points out that the, *"scribes and the Pharisees have seated themselves in the chair of Moses."* Notice Jesus said that these false teachers *"seated themselves."* In other words, they were not called of God or in any way qualified, but rather took the seat upon themselves. The term "seat" means a place of authority. This type of conduct is not found simply in Biblical times. Today there are many in "church leadership" who have *"seated themselves"* and were never called by God. Many take a simplistic view of eldership and believe that since an individual has been voted or appointed into position by the pastor, they are in fact, "God's anointed." This mindset results in an unbiblical theology of submission in which one is not evaluated by his biblical qualifications, theology, lifestyle, speech and love, but simply by the title.

God has relegated to His people the decision of who will be leaders—with one unalterable exception. The exception is that anyone considered for the position must meet the <u>minimum</u> requirements set out in Titus and 1 Timothy. Many church constitutions do lip service to the qualification sections but quickly water them down in practice. When this occurs, leadership is obtained by political means, wealth, business experience or other fleshly ways with the ultimate end being a very weak or even apostate church which is run by some immature/unqualified believers, false-brethren or unbelievers.

Another manifestation of the unqualified or false believers taking a seat of ecclesiastical authority is their hostility for the truly qualified and called. Remember that it was the Pharisees who sought to kill Jesus because He so threatened their power structure. We read in **Matthew 26:3-4:** *"Then the chief priests and the elders of the people were gathered together in the court of the high priest, named Caiaphas; 4 and they plotted together to seize Jesus by stealth, and kill Him."* In the modern church the spiritually immature, unqualified or false church leader will often persecute, harass, and slander those who are God's anointed leaders because they represent a threat to his power. It is important to note that it is possible that a church can wrongly install unqualified Christians as church leaders. It is also important to note that these unqualified believers will eventually do great damage to the church.

In Matthew 23:1-2, Jesus states that the people are to listen to the truths that God gave to Moses. His point is that these truths are no less the Word of God even when they are recited from the perverted mouths of the Pharisees and scribes. Notice Jesus told the multitude to do what the Pharisees said (i.e. what Moses said), but to not act like the Pharisees. I have heard many try to dismiss their accountability to Christ by pointing out the hypocrisy of one who claims to be a believer. For example, they may point to some so-called priest who is a heinous child molester as the reason they won't listen to the Gospel or follow Christ. One does not escape his accountability to God by reducing the perfect example of Christ to that of the lowest example of anyone who makes a claimed affiliation to Christianity. One does not get to compare himself to whomever he thinks makes him look good. Spiritual honesty requires one to compare his life to that of Christ's (who was *always perfect* in thought, deed and action). The result should be that the person recognizes the desperate and sinful state of his soul, and then cries out with faith to Christ for forgiveness.

VERSES 3-4: *"…therefore all that they tell you, do and observe, but do not do according to their deeds; for they say things, and do not do them. 4 And they tie up heavy loads, and lay them on men's shoulders; but they themselves are unwilling to move them with so much as a finger."*

Again Jesus points out the importance of listening to Moses, but not the false teaching of the hypocritical scribes and Pharisees:

> **Luke 12:1-2:** *"*UNDER *these circumstances, after so many thousands of the multitude had gathered together that they were stepping on one another, He began saying to His disciples first of all, 'Beware of the leaven of the Pharisees, which is hypocrisy. 2 But there is nothing covered up that will not be revealed, and hidden that will not be known.'"*

God spoke of these false teachers in the Old Testament:

> **Malachi 2:7-9:** *"For the lips of a priest should preserve knowledge, and men should seek instruction from his mouth; for he is the messenger of the* LORD *of hosts. 8 But as for you, you have turned aside from the way; you have caused many to stumble by the instruction; you have corrupted the covenant of Levi, says the* LORD *of hosts. 9 So I also have made you despised and abased before*

all the people, just as you are not keeping My ways, but are showing partiality in the instruction."

False teachers always make up their own rules of religion and the Pharisees were no exception. *"And they tie up heavy loads, and lay them on men's shoulders; but they themselves are unwilling to move them with so much as a finger."* Many of these "traditions" and absurd manmade interpretations of the Mosaic Law were recorded in the Talmud:

> "One section alone of the Talmud, the major compilation of Jewish tradition, has twenty-four chapters listing Sabbath laws. One law specified that the basic limit for travel was 3,000 feet from one's house; but various exceptions were provided. If you had placed some food within 3,000 feet of your house, you could go there to eat it; and because the food was considered an extension of the house, you could then go another 3,000 feet beyond the food. If a rope were placed across an adjoining street or alley, the building on the other side, as well as the alley between, could be considered part of your house."[400]

Here are some examples of manmade righteousness that we see in false religions today:

> **1 Timothy 4:1-3:** *"But the Spirit explicitly says that in later times some will fall away from the faith, paying attention to deceitful spirits and <u>doctrines of demons</u>, 2 by means of the hypocrisy of liars seared in their own conscience as with a branding iron, 3 <u>men who forbid marriage and advocate abstaining from foods</u>, which God has created to be gratefully shared in by those who believe and know the truth."*

Jesus points out that the Pharisees engaged in hyper-technical/false obedience to the law of God—manifesting no interest in true justice and love for God.

> **Luke 11:42:** *"But woe to you Pharisees! For you pay tithe of mint and rue and every kind of garden herb, and <u>yet disregard justice and the love of God</u>; but these are the things you should have done without neglecting the others."*

A few verses down from our main text in Matthew 23, we see that Jesus warns of the danger of subjecting yourself to false teaching:

> **Matthew 23:15:** *"Woe to you, scribes and Pharisees, hypocrites, because you travel about on sea and land to make one proselyte; and <u>when he becomes one, you make him twice as much a son of hell as yourselves</u>."*

One sure sign of false religious leadership is a continual fleshly lifestyle. Even though false leaders care very much that people see them as good, eventually their true nature will slip out. Since they are not able to live by the Spirit, they live by the flesh which will eventually manifest itself (Galatians 5:19-21). One can imitate spiritual fruit for a while, but not for the long term.

VERSE 5: *"But they do all their deeds to be noticed by men; for they broaden their phylacteries, and lengthen the tassels of their garments."*

---

[400] MacArthur, J. F., Jr. (1985). *Matthew.* MacArthur New Testament Commentary (p 275). Chicago: Moody Press. MacArthur, John F.

Here Jesus exposes the true intentions of the false religious leaders. They are not concerned about people being drawn to God, but rather, *"they do all their deeds to be noticed by men...."* They do not want to truly repent of their sin and be good workers that are *"approved to God."* Instead, their desire is that people would THINK that they are *"approved to God."*

> **2 Timothy 2:15:** *"Be diligent to present yourself approved to God as a workman who does not need to be ashamed, handling accurately the word of truth."*

Jesus tells us in verse 5 that the Pharisees would *"broaden their phylacteries."* The phylacteries are defined below by the *New Bible Dictionary*:

> "Their present form became standardized by the early years of the 2nd century AD and consists of two hollow cubes made of the skin of clean animals. They vary between 1.25 cm and 4 cm a side. That for the head is divided into four equal compartments; that for the hand has no divisions. In them are placed the four passages Exodus 13:1–10; 13:11–16; Deuteronomy 6:4–9; 11:13–21 written by hand on parchment (on four pieces for the head, on one for the hand). The phylacteries are attached to leather straps by which they are fastened to the left hand and the centre of the forehead by the men before morning prayers, whether in the home or the synagogue, except on the sabbath and high festivals. They are put on after the praying shawl, that for the hand coming first. Both they and the straps are always colored black. The phylactery for the head can be recognized by a three- and four-armed šin on its right and left sides."[401]

We also see in verse 5 that the Pharisees would *"lengthen the tassels of their garments."* The tassels were commanded by God (Deuteronomy 22:12) for the people to remember to obey His Word:

> **Numbers 15:37-41:** *"The LORD also spoke to Moses, saying, [38] 'Speak to the sons of Israel, and tell them that they shall make for themselves tassels on the corners of their garments throughout their generations, and that they shall put on the tassel of each corner a cord of blue. [39] And it shall be a tassel for you to look at and remember all the commandments of the LORD, so as to do them and not follow after your own heart and your own eyes, after which you played the harlot, [40] in order that you may remember to do all My commandments, and be holy to your God. [41] I am the LORD your God who brought you out from the land of Egypt to be your God; I am the LORD your God.'"*

The Pharisees saw these verses as an opportunity to publicly proclaim their righteousness. They made a religious fashion statement out of the tassels by lengthening theirs more than the average person. This type of conduct is not a whole lot different than the guy who walks around the church on Sunday with a Bible that he never reads the rest of the week. Another modern day example would be the perverted rock star who makes a hypocritical and blasphemous fashion statement when he banters around the cross of Christ as a dangling earring.

---

[401] Wood, D. R. W. (1996). *New Bible dictionary* (3rd ed.) (p. 927). Leicester, England; Downers Grove, Ill.: InterVarsity Press.

VERSES 6-9: *"And they love the place of honor at banquets, and the chief seats in the synagogues, [7] and respectful greetings in the market places, and being called by men, Rabbi. [8] But do not be called Rabbi; for One is your Teacher, and you are all brothers. [9] And do not call anyone on earth your father; for One is your Father, He who is in heaven."*

Here Jesus exposes the heart of the false religious leader. He or she wants to be honored both in the church and the world (i.e. *market place*). In the parallel passage in Luke, we are told that these religious hypocrites would steal from widows and then be seen in public making long pious prayers!

> **Luke 20:46-47:** *"Beware of the scribes, who like to walk around in long robes, and love respectful greetings in the market places, and chief seats in the synagogues, and places of honor at banquets, [47] who devour widows' houses, and for appearance's sake offer long prayers; these will receive greater condemnation."*

The type of person spoken of here does not pursue service to God and others, but instead seeks titles such as Rabbi, Teacher, Elder, Deacon or Leader, etc. You can see this in church today. When a church is very short on true theology (i.e. Biblical doctrine), it will be long on "organization" and "programming." It will substitute corporate structure instead of sound theology, and activities instead of service. Along with the corporate structure will come grand titles (i.e. Head of Women's Education, or President of the Board, or as the Roman Catholic church calls their leaders, "Father", etc.). Matthew 23:8 tells us that we are not to use titles such as Rabbi or Father. Hypocrites will seek these titles instead of seeking after the work that the position calls for. When the church does not apply the minimum standards for its deacons and elders as set out in Timothy and Titus it will end up with this type of leader. It is truly an ugly sight to behold! Those who claim that God must want this type of guy on the board based on the fact that he was voted to the position are misled. It is the ignoring of God's Word that results in hypocritical leadership. Matthew Henry wrote,

> "People must be told of the wolves (Acts 20:29, 30), the dogs (Philippians 3:2), the deceitful workers (2 Corinthians 11:13), that they may know where to stand upon their guard." [402]

Look what Paul wrote concerning being on guard against false leadership:

> **2 Corinthians 11:13-15:** *"For such men are false apostles, deceitful workers, disguising themselves as apostles of Christ. [14] And no wonder, for even Satan disguises himself as an angel of light. [15] Therefore it is not surprising if his servants also disguise themselves as servants of righteousness; whose end shall be according to their deeds."*

God has assigned the church to select its leadership only from among those who meet the minimal standards. There may only be one who qualifies. It is better to have one Spirit-led elder than 12 who are led by their flesh and enjoy the prestige of their position.

It is important to realize that the church is not to function as a corporation with bosses who are allowed to spitefully threaten and control others. The church is to function as a family and address each other as such:

---

[402] Henry, M. (1994). *Matthew Henry's Commentary on the Whole Bible: Complete and Unabridged in One Volume* (Mathew 23:1–12). Peabody: Hendrickson.

> **1 Timothy 5:1-2:** *"Do not sharply rebuke an older man, but rather <u>appeal to him as a father, to the younger men as brothers, ² the older women as mothers, and the younger women as sisters</u>, in all purity."*

Notice that this verse in Timothy does not in any way contradict Matthew 23:8. 1 Timothy 5:1 does not tell us to "call" older men *father*, but instead, as we function in a family manner, the older men in the church are to be addressed with humble respect and we are to, *"<u>appeal to him as a father,</u>…."* "Timothy was to appeal to the older men as he would his own father—not with rough rebukes but with gentle exhortations." [403] The context in Timothy is very different than the religious leader context of the term "spiritual father" in Matthew 23:8. We have only one spiritual father; the Lord.

<u>VERSES 10-12:</u> *"And do not be called leaders; for One is your Leader, that is, Christ. ¹¹ But the greatest among you shall be your servant. ¹² And whoever exalts himself shall be humbled; and whoever humbles himself shall be exalted."*

Look at the verses below which point out that Jesus is our one and only leader.

> **<u>1 Timothy 2:5:</u>** *"For there is one God, and <u>one mediator</u> also between God and men, the man Christ Jesus, .."*

> **<u>Colossians 1:18:</u>** *"He is also <u>head of the body</u>, the church; and He is the beginning, the first-born from the dead; so that He Himself might come to <u>have first place in everything</u>."*

> **<u>Ephesians 1:22-23:</u>** *"And He put all things in subjection under His feet, and gave Him <u>as head over all things to the church</u>, ²³ which is His body, the fullness of Him who fills all in all."*

> **<u>Ephesians 4:4-6:</u>** *"There is one body and one Spirit, just as also you were called in one hope of your calling; ⁵ one Lord, one faith, one baptism, ⁶ one God and Father of all who <u>is over all and through all and in all.</u>"*

We must remember that we are the servants of the Lord and He is not our servant. We don't just call on Him to get things. We serve Him because we love Him. He has done so much for us that it is an honor to be His servant. Jesus told His disciples what their attitudes should be:

> **<u>Luke 17:7-10:</u>** *"But which of you, having a slave plowing or tending sheep, will say to him when he has come in from the field, 'Come immediately and sit down to eat?' ⁸ But will he not say to him, 'Prepare something for me to eat, and properly clothe yourself and serve me until I have eaten and drunk; and afterward you will eat and drink'? ⁹ He does not thank the slave because he did the things which were commanded, does he? ¹⁰ So you too, when you do all the things which are commanded you, say, <u>'We are unworthy slaves; we have done only that which we ought to have done.'"</u>*

---

[403] Walvoord, J. F., Zuck, R. B., and Dallas Theological Seminary. (1985). *The Bible Knowledge Commentary: An Exposition of the Scriptures* (v. 2, p. 742). Wheaton, IL: Victor Books.

Summary and Application

Ask yourself, are there times when you play the hypocrite? Are there times when you are engaging in a false outward appearance of godliness so that others will think well of you? Maybe you claim to be Christian because of all the work you do at the church or some other ministry. Maybe you are the type who enjoys the special titles and recognition you have been given by the church. If so, and you are a Christian, repent and ask the Lord to forgive you. If you are not a Christian, you must cry out to the Lord to save your s soul. Otherwise you will face a severe eternal judgment.

Even though hypocrisy/pretense can win you the approval of others, God judges the heart.
James 3:1: *"Let not many of you become teachers, my brethren,*
knowing that as such we will incur a stricter judgment."

<u>MATTHEW 23:13-36</u>
(THE EIGHT WOES ADDRESSED TO THE PHARISEES / HYPOCRITES)

¹³ *"But woe to you, scribes and Pharisees, hypocrites, because you shut off the kingdom of heaven from men; for you do not enter in yourselves, nor do you allow those who are entering to go in.* ¹⁴ *[Woe to you, scribes and Pharisees, hypocrites, because you devour widows' houses, even while for a pretense you make long prayers; therefore you shall receive greater condemnation.]*

¹⁵ *Woe to you, scribes and Pharisees, hypocrites, because you travel about on sea and land to make one proselyte; and when he becomes one, you make him twice as much a son of hell as yourselves.*

¹⁶ *Woe to you, blind guides, who say, 'Whoever swears by the temple, that is nothing; but whoever swears by the gold of the temple, he is obligated.'* ¹⁷ *You fools and blind men; which is more important, the gold, or the temple that sanctified the gold?* ¹⁸ *And, 'Whoever swears by the altar, that is nothing, but whoever swears by the offering upon it, he is obligated.'* ¹⁹ *You blind men, which is more important, the offering or the altar that sanctifies the offering?* ²⁰ *Therefore he who swears by the altar, swears both by the altar and by everything on it.* ²¹ *And he who swears by the temple, swears both by the temple and by Him who dwells within it.* ²² *And he who swears by heaven, swears both by the throne of God and by Him who sits upon it.*

²³ *Woe to you, scribes and Pharisees, hypocrites! For you tithe mint and dill and cummin, and have neglected the weightier provisions of the law: justice and mercy and faithfulness; but these are the things you should have done without neglecting the others.* ²⁴ *You blind guides, who strain out a gnat and swallow a camel!*

²⁵ *Woe to you, scribes and Pharisees, hypocrites! For you clean the outside of the cup and of the dish, but inside they are full of robbery and self-indulgence.* ²⁶ *You blind Pharisee, first clean the inside of the cup and of the dish, so that the outside of it may become clean also.*

²⁷ *Woe to you, scribes and Pharisees, hypocrites! For you are like whitewashed tombs which on the outside appear beautiful, but inside they are full of dead men's bones and all uncleanness.* ²⁸ *Even so you too outwardly appear righteous to men, but inwardly you are full of hypocrisy and lawlessness.* ²⁹ *Woe to you, scribes and Pharisees, hypocrites! For you build the tombs of the prophets and adorn the monuments of the righteous,* ³⁰ *and say, 'If we had been living in the days of our fathers, we would not have been partners with them in shedding the blood of the prophets.'* ³¹ *Consequently you bear witness against yourselves, that you are sons of those who murdered the prophets.* ³² *Fill up then the measure of the guilt of your fathers.* ³³ *You serpents, you brood of vipers, how shall you escape the sentence of hell?* ³⁴ *Therefore, behold, I am sending you prophets and wise men and scribes; some of them you will kill and crucify, and some of them you will scourge in your synagogues, and persecute from city to city,* ³⁵ *that upon you may fall the guilt of all the righteous blood shed on earth, from the blood of righteous Abel to the blood of Zechariah, the son of Berechiah, whom you murdered between the temple and the altar.* ³⁶ *Truly I say to you, all these things shall come upon this generation."*

Introduction

In the previous lesson we saw Jesus speaking to the multitude about the Pharisees. Jesus' message is one of condemnation for their false teachings. Jesus affirms God's message given through Moses but makes very clear that judgment awaits the hypocritical false teachers.

In the section we are about to study, we see Jesus take His message which was spoken to the multitude and turn directly to the Scribes and Pharisees and set out why they will be judged so harshly. There are eight "woes" in verses 13-33. The *New Bible dictionary* defines the term *"woe"* as Jesus,

> "deploring the miserable condition in God's sight of those he is addressing. Their wretchedness lies not least in the fact that they are living in a fool's paradise, unaware of the misery that awaits them."[404]

VERSE 13: *"But woe to you, scribes and Pharisees, hypocrites, because you shut off the kingdom of heaven from men; for you do not enter in yourselves, nor do you allow those who are entering to go in."*

Here is the first woe. This is the classic action of the false teacher. Not only is he godless, but he is a huge stumbling block to others. To put it another way, it is because of his false teaching, life, and religion others are kept from the truth. Of course these types think they are very good and godly. Paul explained to Timothy about the false teachers and their own self-deception when he wrote in **2 Timothy 3:13:** *"But evil men and impostors will proceed from bad to worse, deceiving and being deceived."*

When Jesus says they, *"shut off the kingdom of heaven from men...."* He is referring to their hostility to the Messiah and the Gospel. Recall how they opposed Jesus at every corner and did not want anyone else to follow Him.

VERSE 14: [*"Woe to you, scribes and Pharisees, hypocrites, because you devour widows' houses, even while for a pretense you make long prayers; therefore you shall receive greater condemnation."*]

Here the Pharisees, sitting as judicial members, would pass decrees regarding the transfer of land. Jesus confronted them with their abuse of power by using the unfortunate circumstance of a new widow's distress to purchase her dead husband's estate at a discount. We read of God's view and judgment of such conduct in the Old Testament:

Isaiah 10:1-3:
"WOE to those who enact evil statutes,
And to those who constantly record unjust decisions,
2 So as to deprive the needy of justice,
And rob the poor of My people of their rights,
In order that widows may be their spoil,
And that they may plunder the orphans.
3 Now what will you do in the day of punishment,
And in the devastation which will come from afar?
To whom will you flee for help?
And where will you leave your wealth?"

---

[404] Wood, D. R. W. (1996). *New Bible Dictionary* (3rd ed.) (p. 1246). Leicester, England; Downers Grove, Ill.: InterVarsity Press.

God will defend the widow:

> **Proverbs 15:25:** *"The LORD will tear down the house of the proud, but He will establish the boundary of the widow."*

In verse 14 we read that after robbing from widows, the Pharisees' covering for their evil deeds is public displays of religion—specifically prayer. This type of hypocritical conduct is not simply reserved for Biblical times. It is commonplace today. Often you can go to a church service and hear a religious leader praying to his audience in the congregation, not to God. The hypocrite is willing to engage in public ceremonial prayers, while others watch, but it is not a discipline he engages in much when only God is watching. It was Jonathan Edwards who stated that:

> "Hypocrites [are] deficient in the duty of prayer...." [405]

Notice Jesus says in verse 14 that these hypocrites would *"receive greater condemnation."* One should realize that all non-believers face the terrible and unending judgment of hell, but there are those whose judgment will be even more devastating than others. Wilhelmus 'a Brakel, in his book *The Christian's Reasonable Service*, states that: "In Luke 12:47 and 48 few or many stripes are mentioned in relation to the degree of sin." [406] In other words, these verses make it clear that there are degrees of judgment.

VERSE 15: *"Woe to you, scribes and Pharisees, hypocrites, because you travel about on sea and land to make one proselyte; and when he becomes one, you make him twice as much a son of hell as yourselves."*

The term *"proselyte"* in this context is defined as "a Gentile who, through conversion, committed [themself] to the practice of the Jewish law, exclusive devotion to Yahweh and integration into the Jewish community." [407]

The result of false teaching is false converts. The false converts then go about and zealously produce more false converts, all of whom are heading to judgment in hell. Jesus referred to a false-teaching scribe or Pharisee as *"a son of hell"* and that the convert he creates would end up as *"twice as much a son of hell as yourselves* [i.e. scribes / Pharisees]." Matthew Henry points out that the false teaching and hatred of God in the Pharisees was even more evident in their converts. "The most bitter enemies the apostles met with in all places were the Hellenist Jews, who were mostly proselytes, Acts 13:45; 14:2–19; 17:5; 18:6." [408] Henry points out the example of the murderous heart of the young Pharisee Saul prior to his conversion. Saul was often in the

---

[405] *The Works of Jonathan Edwards,* vol. 2 [Carlisle, PA.: Banner of Truth, 1986 reprint], pp. 71-77.

[406] a Brakel, W. (17th Century Dutch theologian). Reformed theology.
(1992; Published in electronic form by Christian Classics Foundation, 1996). *The Christian's Reasonable Service, Volumes 1 and 2* - based on the 3rd edition of the original Dutch work.). Morgan PA: Soli Deo Gloria Publications.

[407] Wood, D. R. W. (1996). *New Bible Dictionary* (3rd ed.) (p. 976). Leicester, England; Downers Grove, Ill.: InterVarsity Press.

[408] Henry, M. (1996). *Matthew Henry's Commentary on the Whole Bible: Complete and Unabridged in One Volume* (Matthew 23:13–33). Peabody: Hendrickson.

company of false hypocritical teachers.[409]   Scripture tells us that he was among false-teachers when they stoned Stephen to death. Look what Paul himself said in **Acts 22:19-20**:

> *"... in one synagogue after another I used to imprison and beat those who believed in You. [20] And when the blood of Your witness Stephen was being shed, I also was standing by approving, and watching out for the coats of those who were slaying him."*

VERSES 16-17: *"Woe to you, blind guides, who say, 'Whoever swears by the temple, that is nothing; but whoever swears by the gold of the temple, he is obligated.' [17] You fools and blind men; which is more important, the gold, or the temple that sanctified the gold?"*

False teachers are very dangerous with their man-made ideas. Ryle states:

> "It is bad enough to be blind ourselves; it is a thousand times worse to be a blind guide. Of all people none is so culpably wicked as an unconverted minister, and none will be judged so severely. It is a solemn saying about such a person that 'he resembles an unskilled ship captain: he does not perish alone.'"[410]

Jesus points out not only the false religious leaders' hypocrisy, but also the ridiculousness of their man-made rules. They came up with their own rules concerning when a promise was really a promise. In other words, they taught that there were times when a promise really was not enforceable. This is kind of like the elementary school kid who promises to tell the truth but thinks that by crossing his fingers behind his back it is alright to lie.

Scripture tells us in **Hebrews 6:16:** *"For men swear by one greater than themselves, and with them an oath given as confirmation is an end of every dispute."* When I was a kid, if you told someone that you thought he was lying, he would respond by saying, "I am telling you the truth, I swear on a stack of Bibles." What he is doing is making an attempt to show the sincerity of the truth of his statement. Since his own promise to tell the truth may not be convincing enough, he turns to something higher and more truthful in an attempt to bolster his credibility. In verse 16 we see that the religious leaders turned to the Holy Temple of God as something to bolster their credibility. Obviously at some point someone wanted out of a promise he made in which he swore by the temple. So they re-wrote the rules and in essence said that to swear by the temple was meaningless, *"but whoever swears by the gold of the temple"* — now that would really mean something. Jesus points out the absurdity of their rule, which said that mere gold is more important than the Holy Temple of God. In verse 17 Jesus says, *"You fools and blind men; which*

---

[409] Look at how Stephen in the Book of Acts describes the false religious leaders and compare it to what Jesus said to the scribes and Pharisees in Matthew 23:29-36.

Acts 7:51-53: *"You men who are stiff-necked and uncircumcised in heart and ears are always resisting the Holy Spirit; you are doing just as your fathers did. [52] 'Which one of the prophets did your fathers not persecute? And they killed those who had previously announced the coming of the Righteous One, whose betrayers and murderers you have now become; [53]you who received the law as ordained by angels, and yet did not keep it.'"*

[410] *Matthew* / Ryle, J.C. p.220-21 (Expository Thoughts on the Gospels) (Crossways Classic Commentaries: v.1)

is more important, the gold, or the temple that sanctified the gold?" It must be remembered that Jesus had taught earlier on the whole issue of oaths made by men:

> **Matthew 5:33-37:** *"Again, you have heard that the ancients were told, 'YOU SHALL NOT MAKE FALSE VOWS, BUT SHALL FULFILL YOUR VOWS TO THE LORD.' ³⁴ But I say to you, make no oath at all, either by heaven, for it is the throne of God, ³⁵ or by the earth, for it is the footstool of His feet, or by Jerusalem, for it is THE CITY OF THE GREAT KING. ³⁶ Nor shall you make an oath by your head, for you cannot make one hair white or black. ³⁷ But let your statement be, 'Yes, yes' or 'No, no'; and anything beyond these is of evil."*

One may want to review the comments for the section addressing Matthew 5:33-37 for further insight into the issue of oaths. (See also James 5:12.)

Note that God is the ultimate authority on keeping His word:

> **Hebrews 6:13-14:** *"For when God made the promise to Abraham, since He could swear by no one greater, He swore by Himself, ¹⁴ saying, 'I WILL SURELY BLESS YOU, AND I WILL SURELY MULTIPLY YOU.'"*

A person is to be truthful in what he says. The false religious leaders created a system that allowed them to lie, even when making great statements and oaths claiming that they were telling the truth. Lying is a serious matter before God:

> **Proverbs 6:16, 19:** *"There are six things which the LORD hates,.... ¹⁹ A false witness who utters lies,...."*

> **Revelation 21:8:** *"...and all liars, their part will be in the lake that burns with fire and brimstone, which is the second death."*

Lying is one of the two classic attributes of the Devil (the other is murder). Look what Jesus said about Satan:

> **John 8:44:** *"You are of your father the devil, and you want to do the desires of your father. He was a murderer from the beginning, and does not stand in the truth, because there is no truth in him. Whenever he speaks a lie, he speaks from his own nature; for he is a liar, and the father of lies."*

There is no such thing as "a little white lie." Further, a religious system that facilitates a lie is from the Devil. God and His Kingdom are built on truth. Jesus said in **John 14:6:** *"...I am the way, and the truth, and the life; no one comes to the Father, but through Me."* Earlier in John 8:31-32: Jesus said, *"...If you abide in My word, then you are truly disciples of Mine; ³² and you shall know the truth, and the truth shall make you free."*

VERSES 18-19: *"And, 'Whoever swears by the altar, that is nothing, but whoever swears by the offering upon it, he is obligated. ¹⁹You blind men, which is more important, the offering or the altar that sanctifies the offering?'"*

Again Jesus gives another example of the hypocrisy of the religious leaders' system which they invented in order to somehow tell a lie, yet not be guilty for telling that lie. Review the comments for verses 16-17 above.

VERSES 20-22: *"Therefore he who swears by the altar, swears both by the altar and by everything on it. ²¹ And he who swears by the temple, swears both by the temple and by Him who dwells within it. ²² And he who swears by heaven, swears both by the throne of God and by Him who sits upon it."*

Jesus points out that your promise is a promise no matter what you have sworn by. Jesus is saying in verse 21 that those who think that swearing by the temple does not obligate them to tell the truth or fulfill a promise (see verse 16) do not realize that they are swearing *"both by the temple and by Him who dwells within it."* (v.21) Even though they think something is an insignificant vow, they do not realize that they are swearing by God as their witness. It is only a fool who takes this warning lightly. How many times do people take a vow before God and then find a reason to get out of it. Look at our 50 percent plus divorce rate. Most of those people took a vow before God to be married to that person for life (see Malachi 2:13-16).

> **Ecclesiastes 5:4:** *"When you make a vow to God, do not be late in paying it, for He takes no delight in fools...."*

VERSES 23: *"Woe to you, scribes and Pharisees, hypocrites! For you tithe mint and dill and cummin, and have neglected the weightier provisions of the law: justice and mercy and faithfulness; but these are the things you should have done without neglecting the others."*

Here are the scribes and Pharisees again taking a truth (tithing), twisting it and making their own religion out of it. They emphasize the less significant and ignore the essentials of a godly life, *"justice and mercy and faithfulness...."* When I say "less significant," I do not mean "unimportant." Regarding the tithe, the Lord told them that it is something that they, *"should have done,"* but not at the expense of the, *"weightier provisions of the law: justice and mercy and faithfulness...."* It is humanly possible to be a non-believer and be very careful to accurately tithe: *"For you tithe mint and dill and cummin...."* It is impossible for a non-Christian to truly obey, *"justice and mercy and faithfulness."*

To start a discussion on *justice and mercy* there needs to be a defining of the words *"justice"* and *"mercy."* If you ask a very small segment of attorneys,[411] they will tell you that justice is done when a defendant is acquitted, irrespective of whether that acquittal is obtained by flamboyant lawyering or less than honest testimony. *True justice* is not limited to a decision by a jury but is anchored in TRUTH. If a person is truly guilty of the crime of robbery but slips by a jury, one cannot say that *true justice* was served. He can say that under our justice system a decision of "not guilty" was rendered, not a determination of *innocence.*

God is a God of true justice, centered solely on the truth and not sleight of hand: *"...Yet you have turned justice into poison...."* **Amos 6:12.** The American Heritage Dictionary, defines (in part) justice this way:

> **jus·tice** 1. The quality of being just; fairness. 2. a. The principle of moral rightness; equity. b. Conformity to moral rightness in action or attitude; righteousness. 3. a. The upholding of what is just, especially <u>fair treatment and due reward in</u>

---

[411] Note that I say a "small segment." I have run into attorneys who do an honest and good job of defense for their clients, under the Constitution.

accordance with honor, standards, or law. **b.** *Law* The administration and procedure of law. 4. Conformity to truth, fact, or sound reason.

Mercy is defined (in part) as:

mer·cy 1. Compassionate treatment, especially of those under one's power; clemency. 2. A disposition to be kind and forgiving: *a heart full of mercy.*

In summary:
1. *Justice* results in you getting what you deserve.
2. *Mercy* results in you not getting what you deserve.

One can falsely imitate the characteristics of justice and mercy for a while, but it is impossible for the non-believer to obey these from a pure heart.

> **Psalm 14:2-3:**
> *"The LORD has looked down from heaven upon the sons of men,*
> *To see if there are any who understand, Who seek after God.*
> *³They have all turned aside; together they have become corrupt;*
> *There is no one who does good, not even one."*

To execute justice and mercy and faithfulness by its true definition requires the work of the Holy Spirit in the believer's life.

> **Galatians 5:18, 22-25:** *"But if you are led by the Spirit, you are not under the Law.....*
> ²² *But the fruit of the Spirit is love, joy, peace, patience, kindness, goodness, faithfulness,* ²³ *gentleness, self-control; against such things there is no law.* ²⁴*Now those who belong to Christ Jesus have crucified the flesh with its passions and desires.* ²⁵ *If we live by the Spirit, let us also walk by the Spirit."*

Tithing:

Note that the false religious leaders would *"tithe mint and dill and cummin."* Scripture did not teach that these little herbs were to be tithed. They were told to tithe oil, wine, grain, and fruits.

> **Numbers 18:12-13:** *"All the best of the fresh oil and all the best of the fresh wine and of the grain, the first fruits of those which they give to the LORD, I give them to you.* ¹³ *The first ripe fruits of all that is in their land, which they bring to the LORD, shall be yours; everyone of your household who is clean may eat it."* [See also Deuteronomy14:22-23.]

Tithing the herbs came out of a hyper-twisted interpretation of **Leviticus 27:30:**

> *"Thus all the tithe of the land, of the seed of the land or of the fruit of the tree,*
> *is the LORD'S; it is holy to the LORD."*

The seed of the land actually meant the crops[412] and "not garden herbs used as kitchen spices" [413] like *"mint and dill and cumin."* The false religious leader said that when tithing the "seed" you should include the garden herbs even if they were not farm crops in order to really "correctly"

---

[412] Wood, D. R. W. (1996). *New Bible Dictionary* (3rd ed.) (p. 1193). Leicester, England; Downers Grove, Ill.: InterVarsity Press.

[413] MacArthur, J. (1989). *Matthew* (Matthew 23:34). Chicago: Moody Press.

tithe. The *New Bible Dictionary* states the following regarding the corrupt religious leaders who thought their obedience to their own interpretations of the law would earn them salvation:

> "To these comparatively simple laws in the Pentateuch governing tithing there were added a host of minutiae which turned a beautiful religious principle into a grievous burden. These complex additions are recorded in the Mishnaic and Talmudic literature. This unfortunate tendency in Israel undoubtedly contributed to the conviction that acceptance with God could be merited through such ritual observances as tithing (Luke 11:42), without submitting to the moral law of justice, mercy and faith (Matthew 23:23f.)."[414]

Look at the verses below and see if God is concerned with people giving Him a part of the property that He previously gave them, or whether He requires us to walk in His holiness.

Micah 6:6-8:

> 6 *"With what shall I come to the LORD*
> *And bow myself before the God on high?*
> *Shall I come to Him with burnt offerings,*
> *With yearling calves?*
> 7 *Does the LORD take delight in thousands of rams,*
> *In ten thousand rivers of oil?*
> *Shall I present my first-born for my rebellious acts,*
> *The fruit of my body for the sin of my soul?*
> 8 *He has told you, O man, what is good;*
> *And what does the LORD require of you*
> *But to do justice, to love kindness,*
> *And to walk humbly with your God?"*

The person who does justice, loves kindness, and walks humbly before God will be a person who gives to God's work and to others. What the false religious person does not understand is that one can give all his property or even his life and it is irrelevant to God if it is not done with the love of God.

> **1 Corinthians 13:3:** *"And if I give all my possessions to feed the poor, and if I deliver my body to be burned, but do not have love, it profits me nothing."*

So how does tithing affect us under the New Testament? MacArthur explains it this way:

> "The tithe, however, was strictly a requirement of the Old Covenant. It is mentioned only six times in the New Testament, three times each in the gospels and in the book of Hebrews. In the gospels it is always used, as here, in regard to its abuse by the scribes and Pharisees (see also Luke 11:42; 18:12). In the book of Hebrews the Mosaic tithe is mentioned only in regard to its use in ancient Israel (Hebrews 7:8–9; vv. 5–6). At no time in the New Testament is tithing mentioned as binding on the church or even recommended as the standard for Christian giving. This is easy to understand if one recognizes that tithes were a form of

---

[414] Wood, D. R. W. (1996). *New Bible Dictionary* (3rd ed.) (p. 1193). Leicester, England; Downers Grove, Ill.: InterVarsity Press.

taxation to support the national life of Israel …. The closest New Testament parallel is the requirement to pay taxes indicated in Romans 13:6–7."[415]

When we speak of the New Testament believer not being under the legal requirement to tithe, that concept can often become twisted by some and used as an excuse to give very little. The New Testament position is that now we are free to give even more generously (*"as he may prosper…"* <u>1 Corinthians 16:2</u>), with a cheerful heart, rather than begrudgingly giving our ten percent. Look at the verses below:

<u>2 Corinthians 9:6-7:</u> *"Now this I say, he who sows sparingly shall also reap sparingly; and he who sows bountifully shall also reap bountifully. 7 Let each one do just as he has purposed in his heart; not grudgingly or under compulsion; for God loves a cheerful giver."*

<u>Hebrews 13:16:</u> *"And do not neglect doing good and sharing; for with such sacrifices God is pleased."*

<u>1 Timothy 6:18-19:</u> *"Instruct them to do good, <u>to be rich in good works, to be generous and ready to share,</u> 19 storing up for themselves the treasure of a good foundation for the future, so that they may take hold of that which is life indeed."*

<u>Luke 6:38:</u> *"Give, and it will be given to you. They will pour into your lap a good measure—pressed down, shaken together, and running over. For by your standard of measure it will be measured to you in return."*

<u>2 Corinthians 8:1-5, 12:</u> *"Now, brethren, we wish to make known to you the grace of God which has been given in the churches of Macedonia, 2 that in a great ordeal of affliction their abundance of joy and their deep poverty overflowed in the wealth of their liberality. 3 For I testify that according to their ability, and beyond their ability they gave of their own accord, 4 begging us with much entreaty for the favor of participation in the support of the saints, 5 and this, not as we had expected, <u>but they first gave themselves to the Lord</u> and to us by the will of God….*
12 For if the readiness is present, it is acceptable according to what a man has, not according to what he does not have."

The Lord also tells us how to give:
<u>Matthew 6:2-4:</u> *"When therefore you give alms, do not sound a trumpet before you, as the hypocrites do in the synagogues and in the streets, that they may be honored by men. Truly I say to you, they have their reward in full. 3 But when you give alms, <u>do not let your left hand know what your right hand is doing</u> <u>4 that your alms may be in secret;</u> and your Father who sees in secret will repay you."*

---

[415] MacArthur, J. F., Jr. (1985). *Matthew*. MacArthur New Testament Commentary (p. 249). Chicago: Moody Press..

> **Luke 12:33-34:** *"Sell your possessions and give to charity; make yourselves purses which do not wear out, an <u>unfailing treasure in heaven</u>, where no thief comes near, nor moth destroys.* [34] *For where your treasure is, there will your heart be also."*

> **Luke 14:13-14:** *"But when you give a reception, <u>invite the poor, the crippled, the lame, the blind,</u>* [14] *and you will be blessed, since they do not have the means to repay you; for you will be repaid at the resurrection of the righteous."*

> **Luke 21:1-4:** *"And He looked up and saw the rich putting their gifts into the treasury.* [2] *And He saw a certain poor widow putting in two small copper coins.* [3] *And He said, 'Truly I say to you, this poor widow put in more than all of them;* [4] *for they all out of their surplus put into the offering; <u>but she out of her poverty put in all that she had to live on.'"</u>*

Over my Christian life I have met many a proud tither, who may not be willing to give his time to serve God, but is very pleased with how he tithes. Others wrongfully see their tithe as an insurance policy in which they keep God on their side financially. Still others use their supposed "gift to God" as a means of political control / influence in the church. An example of this would be the wealthy businessman who feels he should be an elder in the church because his *contribution* is one of the largest in the church; [notice I said contribution—not gift to God].

Our gifts are to support the real ministry of God. So after rereading Matthew 23:23-24, ask yourself if you have ever bought into that lie that if you just keep writing that check for ten percent of your income (no more and no less) you have fulfilled your service to God. Equally misguided is the stingy individual, or one who has little to give because he is paying thousands of dollars in interest to the bank/credit card company to finance his debt-ridden lifestyle. Just think of the personal freedom and money that could be available for true ministry if professed Christians lived within their means, instead of financing a lifestyle. Remember, the godly man is very giving, and God gives to that type of man.

> **Proverbs 11:25:** *"The generous man will be prosperous,*
> *And he who waters will himself be watered."*

VERSES 24: *"You blind guides, who strain out a gnat and swallow a camel!"*

Here Jesus illustrates the absurdity of the Pharisees' external actions attempting to prove their own righteousness. They knew that the Law told them what animals were unclean. One of the largest of those unclean animals mentioned in Scripture is the camel. An animal that was declared "unclean" meant that it was not to be eaten.

> **Leviticus 11:4:** *"Nevertheless, you are not to eat of these, among those which chew the cud, or among those which divide the hoof: the camel, for though it chews cud, it does not divide the hoof, it is unclean to you."*

The portion of verse 24 that states *"who strain out a gnat"* makes reference to the technical care the Pharisee would take while drinking his wine or water. He would drink in such a manner as to use his teeth to strain out any bugs or other impurities that may have gotten into the liquid. Another straining technique that was used involved a separate straining cloth. See how Strong's Lexicon defines gnats—*kōnōps*:

2971 κώνωψ [konops /ko·nopes/] "...AV translates as 'gnat' once. **1** a wine gnat or midge that is bred in fermenting and evaporating wine."[416]

Jesus points out in verse 24 how perverted their manmade religion was in that they went to great lengths to prevent a gnat from accidentally being swallowed, yet they were not concerned about swallowing a camel (i.e. something huge and unclean). In other words, they had elevated unimportant matters and ignored the things that did matter. In the Pharisees' view, they were holy by being hyper-technical on a matter that had nothing to do with righteousness. In reality, they were more than willing to indulge in huge amounts of sin, and dismiss it as irrelevant.

Jesus explains this concept in **Matthew 15:10-20:**
> *"And after He called the multitude to Him, He said to them, 'Hear, and understand. [11] Not what enters into the mouth defiles the man, but what proceeds out of the mouth, this defiles the man.' [12] Then the disciples *came and *said to Him, 'Do You know that the Pharisees were offended when they heard this statement?' [13] But He answered and said, 'Every plant which My heavenly Father did not plant shall be rooted up. [14] Let them alone; they are blind guides of the blind. And if a blind man guides a blind man, both will fall into a pit.' [15] And Peter answered and said to Him, 'Explain the parable to us.' [16] And He said, 'Are you still lacking in understanding also? [17] Do you not understand that everything that goes into the mouth passes into the stomach, and is eliminated? [18] But the things that proceed out of the mouth come from the heart, and those defile the man. [19] For out of the heart come evil thoughts, murders, adulteries, fornications, thefts, false witness, slanders. [20] These are the things which defile the man; but to eat with unwashed hands does not defile the man.'"*

This passage takes on the whole false religious system that is based in "form" over true worship of God. This can be seen in a church today that has "ritual" as its cornerstone, and not Christ. In the false, ritualistic church you will see the "minister" and the people very concerned and careful that the rituals are correctly performed in detail. There is not a true objective to, "Bless the Lord, O my soul." Just like the Pharisees of old, these religious leaders do not care about God, but they are very concerned with their rituals that are the standard to declare themselves righteous.

Matthew Henry points out that the ultimate example of "swallowing a camel" (doing the unclean) is when the religious leaders gave Judas the 30 pieces of silver to help them identify Jesus so they could kill Him. Henry then points out that the "straining of the gnat" is when Judas gave the money back to them, and they were very concerned that it would be unlawful to put the money back in the treasury.
> **Matthew 27:6-7:** *"And the chief priests took the pieces of silver and said, 'It is not lawful to put them into the temple treasury, since it is the price of blood.' [7] And they counseled together and with the money bought the Potter's Field as a burial place for strangers."*

---

[416] Strong, J. (1996). *Enhanced Strong's Lexicon*. Ontario: Woodside Bible Fellowship.

VERSES 25-26: *"Woe to you, scribes and Pharisees, hypocrites! For you clean the outside of the cup and of the dish, but inside they are full of robbery and self-indulgence. ²⁶ You blind Pharisee, first clean the inside of the cup and of the dish, so that the outside of it may become clean also."*

Could you imagine your mom serving you a great bowl of chili and after you got done eating she just wiped off the *outside* of the bowl and then put it back in the cupboard? A week later you wake up in the morning, and reach in the cupboard and get a box of cereal, and then grab that exact bowl. To your horror you see it filthy with crusted week-old chili and even some mold growing on it. You would not pour your cereal in it or use it for anything even though it was clean and pretty on the outside.

The putrid rottenness inside the bowl is an allegory of how the Lord sees the inside of the non-believer/false religious leader. Oh sure it is easy to clean up on the outside, but God knows what is really going on in the inside. Review what we just read in **Matthew 15:18-20:**
> *"But the things that proceed out of the mouth come from the heart, and those defile the man. ¹⁹ For out of the heart come evil thoughts, murders, adulteries, fornications, thefts, false witness, slanders. ²⁰ These are the things which defile the man; but to eat with unwashed hands does not defile the man."*

Verse 25: *"...inside they are full of robbery and self-indulgence."*
A mark of the false religious leader is his obsession with money and fleshly desires. Look at the Mormon's founder explaining how holy he was to have multiple wives (i.e. using his own religion to justify his desire for multiple sex partners). Just turn on the T.V. and it will not be long until you will see a false teacher begging for money, etc. Note that the Scripture points out that these types are full of robbery inside. Recall how earlier Jesus explained the way these guys would steal from helpless widows, but to look clean on the outside they would engage in public prayers.
> **Matthew 23:14:** *"Woe to you, scribes and Pharisees, hypocrites, because you devour widows' houses, even while for a pretense you make long prayers; therefore you shall receive greater condemnation."*

The false religious leaders did not acknowledge Jesus for who He was. We read a description of the unrighteousness that fills those who do not acknowledge God for who He is:
> **Romans 1:28-32:** *"And just as they did not see fit to acknowledge God any longer, God gave them over to a depraved mind, to do those things which are not proper, ²⁹ being filled with all unrighteousness, wickedness, greed, evil; full of envy, murder, strife, deceit, malice; they are gossips, ³⁰ slanderers, haters of God, insolent, arrogant, boastful, inventors of evil, disobedient to parents, ³¹ without understanding, untrustworthy, unloving, unmerciful; ³² and, although they know the ordinance of God, that those who practice such things are worthy of death, they not only do the same, but also give hearty approval to those who practice them."*

VERSES 27-28: *"Woe to you, scribes and Pharisees, hypocrites! For you are like whitewashed tombs which on the outside appear beautiful, but inside they are full of dead men's bones and all uncleanness. ²⁸ Even so you too outwardly appear righteous to men, but inwardly you are full of hypocrisy and* *lawlessness."*

Whitewash was a type of paint/plaster that was made from limestone. [417] People in Jerusalem would whitewash graves near the time of Passover. This served two functions: 1) whitewash made buildings, tombs, etc. look nice, 2) it also designated a tomb. The reason this mattered is set out in Numbers 19:16, which explains that one would be ceremonially unclean if he touched the dead or tombs. One would not want this to happen during Passover and then be ceremonially unclean for seven days and be unable to participate in the Passover. Thus, the whitewash would clearly mark a tomb.[418]

The nice-looking tomb that was whitewashed on the outside still contained the decaying rot, maggots, and foul stench of death on the inside. Jesus' point is that the nice covering of the Pharisees was purely external since their real person (the inside person that God sees) was full of rottenness and death.

VERSES 29-33: *"Woe to you, scribes and Pharisees, hypocrites! For you build the tombs of the prophets and adorn the monuments of the righteous, ³⁰ and say, 'If we had been living in the days of our fathers, we would not have been partners with them in shedding the blood of the prophets.' ³¹ Consequently you bear witness against yourselves, that you are sons of those who murdered the prophets. ³² Fill up then the measure of the guilt of your fathers. ³³ You serpents, you brood of vipers, how shall you escape the sentence of hell?"*

Here we see Jesus exposing the hypocrisy of the scribes and Pharisees as to their false identification with the righteous. The religious leaders are claiming that they would never have done what their forefathers did by killing the prophets. Jesus points out that their claims are an admission that they are the sons of the murderers of the prophets. Jesus tells them that their murderous family line has not yet finished what it began, *"Fill up then the measure of the guilt of your fathers."* Jesus knew their hearts were full of murder and that they desired to kill Him. This time it was not just a prophet, but the Son of God! **Matthew 12:14:** *"But the Pharisees went out, and counseled together against Him, as to how they might destroy Him."* (See also **Luke 22:2:** *"And the chief priests and the scribes were seeking how they might put Him to death; for they were afraid of the people."*)

Note that Jesus tells them what the final result will be regarding their plot in **Matthew 23:33:** *"You serpents, you brood of vipers, how shall you escape the sentence of hell?"* John the Baptist called these hypocritical religious leaders "vipers" way back in the beginning of the book of Matthew. **Matthew 3:7:** *"But when he saw many of the Pharisees and Sadducees coming for*

---

[417] Wood, D. R. W. (1996). *New Bible Dictionary* (3rd ed.) (p. 691). Leicester, England; Downers Grove, Ill.: InterVarsity Press. "Chemically, lime is calcium oxide, made by heating limestone in a kiln, of which there must have been many in ancient Palestine. The Hebrew Bible uses three words,..'plaster', 'lime' or 'whitewash' (Deuteronomy 27:2, 4; Isaiah 33:12; Amos 2:1), '...chalk' or 'lime' (Daniel 5:5) and '... stones of lime' (Isaiah 27:9, RSV 'chalkstones'). Limestone is abundant in Palestine. Geologically it was formed from the compacting together of shells, *etc.*, on the sea bed, which was then thrust up by earth movement. Palestine was under the sea more than once, at least in part. The bulk of the limestone visible today on both sides of the Jordan is from the Cretaceous period."

[418] MacArthur, J. (1989). *Matthew* (Mathew 23:34). Chicago: Moody Press.

baptism, he said to them, 'You brood of vipers, who warned you to flee from the wrath to come?'" Look at the term viper as it was used by John the Baptist in Matthew 3:7 and Jesus in Matthew 23:33.

> "An echidna is a 'poisonous serpent' (adder or viper). The only New Testament instances are in Acts 28:3 and Matthew 3:7; 12:34; 23:33. …Poison is essential to the comparisons in Matthew, and since the viper is by nature destructive…."[419]

How deadly are the vipers that come into churches today! We are warned throughout the New Testament to watch out for these types who at times can be cleverly disguised, but oh so poisonous.

> **2 Corinthians 11:13-15:** *"For such men are false apostles, deceitful workers, disguising themselves as apostles of Christ. 14 And no wonder, for even Satan disguises himself as an angel of light. 15 Therefore it is not surprising if his servants also disguise themselves as servants of righteousness; whose end shall be according to their deeds."*

VERSES 34-36: *"Therefore, behold, I am sending you prophets and wise men and scribes; some of them you will kill and crucify, and some of them you will scourge in your synagogues, and persecute from city to city, 35 that upon you may fall the guilt of all the righteous blood shed on earth, from the blood of righteous Abel to the blood of Zechariah, the son of Berechiah, whom you murdered between the temple and the altar. 36 Truly I say to you, all these things shall come upon this generation."*

Notice that Jesus stated that He will be sending the prophets: *"I am sending you prophets."* Again, this shows plainly that He was God, for it is only God who sends true prophets. These prophets would be rejected and evilly treated, and thus serve a place in the evidence of the divine judgment God had against the scribes and Pharisees.

Jesus had previously warned His disciples of the treatment they would face. **Matthew 10:17:** *"But beware of men; for they will deliver you up to the courts, and scourge you in their synagogues;…"* Look at the Apostles who were scourged and killed by these murderous false religious leaders. It goes on today as we see Christian martyrs being butchered for their faith in many parts of the world.

> **Psalm 116:15:** *"Precious in the sight of the LORD Is the death of His godly ones."*

Notice that in Matthew 23:35 it states that this bloodthirsty generation that murdered the Son of God will be judged. The verse also points out that Abel was the first martyr for righteousness.

> **Hebrews 11:4:** *"By faith Abel offered to God a better sacrifice than Cain, through which he obtained the testimony that he was righteous, God testifying about his gifts, and through faith, though he is dead, he still speaks."*

Jesus said that the judgment on this generation was from Abel to, *"the blood of Zechariah, the son of Berechiah, whom you murdered between the temple and the altar."* MacArthur explains the meaning of this passage:

---

[419] Kittel, G. (1995, c1985). *Theological Dictionary of the New Testament.* Translation of: Theologisches Worterbuch zum Neuen Testament. (p. 286). Grand Rapids, Mich.: W.B. Eerdmans.

"Because Jesus was pointing out the extensiveness of persecution of righteous people, beginning with **Abel** and ending with **Zechariah**, it would suggest that He was covering the whole of Old Testament history, from creation to the end of the prophetic period. It is also significant that **Zechariah** wrote more of the coming Messiah than did any other prophet except Isaiah.

The prophet **Zechariah**, whose father's name was **Berechiah** (Zechariah 1:1), was among the last prophets of Israel and apparently the last to be martyred. And although the Old Testament does not report his being **murdered between the temple and the altar**, it seems certain he was the **Zechariah** to whom Jesus referred.

It is significant that Jesus said, **whom you murdered**, speaking directly to the scribes and Pharisees but including all unbelieving Israel (v. 36). Although the murder of the prophet had been over 500 years earlier, the wicked leaders the Lord now addressed had participated in it. By their murdering Jesus, the incarnation of righteousness, they proved their complicity in and solidarity with the persecution and murder of every righteous person who has ever suffered at the hands of evil men." [420]

Paul, a former persecutor of the church, would become one who was severely persecuted for the faith in that he was beaten, stoned, and chased from city to city.

> **2 Corinthians 11:23-28:** *"Are they servants of Christ? (I speak as if insane) I more so; in far more labors, in far more imprisonments, beaten times without number, often in danger of death. [24] Five times I received from the Jews thirty-nine lashes. [25] Three times I was beaten with rods, once I was stoned, three times I was shipwrecked, a night and a day I have spent in the deep. [26] I have been on frequent journeys, in dangers from rivers, dangers from robbers, dangers from my countrymen, dangers from the Gentiles, dangers in the city, dangers in the wilderness, dangers on the sea, dangers among false brethren; [27] I have been in labor and hardship, through many sleepless nights, in hunger and thirst, often without food, in cold and exposure. [28] Apart from such external things, there is the daily pressure upon me of concern for all the churches."*

Summary and Application

What we saw from the *eight woes* addressed above is the seriousness of religious hypocrisy. Israel's evil and rejection of God also resulted in their judgment by God, as set out in Matthew 23:34-36.

The Christian must take very seriously the hypocrisy he tolerates in his own life and repent of it. Scripture makes it clear that the church is not immune to the cleansing judgment of God. Specifically, Scripture states that a purging judgment will *start first* in the church:

> **1 Peter 4:15-18:** *"Make sure that none of you suffers as a murderer, or thief, or evildoer, or a troublesome meddler; [16] but if anyone suffers as a Christian, he is not to be ashamed, but is to glorify God in this name. [17] For it is time for judgment to begin with*

---

[420] MacArthur, J. F., Jr. (1985). *Matthew*. MacArthur New Testament Commentary (p. 249). Chicago: Moody Press..

the household of God; and if it begins with us first, what will be the outcome for those who do not obey the gospel of God? [18] *And if it is with difficulty that the righteous is saved, what will become of the godless man and the sinner?"*

MATTHEW 23:37-39

(JESUS' LAMENT OVER JERUSALEM FOR REJECTION OF GOD.)

[37] *"O Jerusalem, Jerusalem, who kills the prophets and stones those who are sent to her! How often I wanted to gather your children together, the way a hen gathers her chicks under her wings, and you were unwilling.* [38] *Behold, your house is being left to you desolate!* [39]*For I say to you, from now on you shall not see Me until you say, 'BLESSED IS HE WHO COMES IN THE NAME OF THE LORD!'"*

Introduction

Here we see Jesus lament over Jerusalem (and all of Israel) as its people rejected God. He also made it clear that Israel would face its judgment, but in the end the Lord will also return and save Israel (Romans 11:26).

VERSE 37: *"O Jerusalem, Jerusalem, who kills the prophets and stones those who are sent to her! How often I wanted to gather your children together, the way a hen gathers her chicks under her wings, and you were unwilling."*

False religious leaders have always hated the true prophets of God. Jesus points out how this city served as the killing field of the prophets that God had sent the nation of Israel. The Sanhedrin met in Jerusalem.[421] The Sanhedrin had a history of condemning those sent by God and worse yet, they tried to use the word of God to justify it. Deuteronomy 13:5-10 required that false prophets and those who seduced the Jews to not follow God were to be killed. It was the false religious leaders' twisted application of these verses that they used to kill the true prophets of God.

Jesus made it clear that the murder of the Son of God would take place in Jerusalem.
> **Luke 13:33:** *"Nevertheless I must journey on today and tomorrow and the next day; for it cannot be that a prophet should perish outside of Jerusalem."*

Jesus set out a parable about how Israel would kill those who God had sent to her in **Matthew 21:33-46:**
> *"Listen to another parable. There was a landowner who PLANTED A VINEYARD AND PUT A WALL AROUND IT AND DUG A WINE PRESS IN IT, AND BUILT A TOWER, and rented*

---

[421] "Both before and at the time of Christ, it was the name of the highest tribunal of the Jews which met in Jerusalem and also for various lesser tribunals. In EVV the term is often translated 'council'.... In New Testament times the Great Sanhedrin in Jerusalem comprised the high priests (*i.e.* the acting high priest and those who had been high priest), members of the privileged families from which the high priests were taken, the elders (tribal and family heads of the people and the priesthood), and the scribes, *i.e.* the legal experts. The whole comprised both Sadducees and Pharisees." Wood, D. R. W. (1996). *New Bible Dictionary* (3rd ed.) (p. 1060). Leicester, England; Downers Grove, Ill.: InterVarsity Press.

it out to vine-growers, and went on a journey. *34 And when the harvest time approached, he sent his slaves to the vine-growers to receive his produce. *35 And the vine-growers took his slaves and beat one, and killed another, and stoned a third. *36 Again he sent another group of slaves larger than the first; and they did the same thing to them. *37 But afterward he sent his son to them, saying, 'They will respect my son.' *38 But when the vine-growers saw the son, they said among themselves, 'This is the heir; come, let us kill him, and seize his inheritance.' *39 And they took him, and threw him out of the vineyard, and killed him. *40 Therefore when the owner of the vineyard comes, what will he do to those vine-growers? *41 They *said to Him, 'He will bring those wretches to a wretched end, and will rent out the vineyard to other vine-growers, who will pay him the proceeds at the proper seasons.' *42 Jesus *said to them, 'Did you never read in the Scriptures,*

> 'THE STONE WHICH THE BUILDERS REJECTED,
> THIS BECAME THE CHIEF CORNER stone;
> THIS CAME ABOUT FROM THE LORD,
> AND IT IS MARVELOUS IN OUR EYES'?

*43 Therefore I say to you, the kingdom of God will be taken away from you, and be given to a nation producing the fruit of it. *44 And he who falls on this stone will be broken to pieces; but on whomever it falls, it will scatter him like dust.' *45 And when the chief priests and the Pharisees heard His parables, they understood that He was speaking about them. *46 And when they sought to seize Him, they feared the multitudes, because they held Him to be a prophet."*

In the main text of Matthew 23:37, Jesus said: "*How often I wanted to gather your children together, the way a hen gathers her chicks under her wings, and you were unwilling.*" Here we see the compassion of God. Many times He reached out to Israel and was rejected. The response of chicks is to run to their mother hen when they are in need or fearful, but Israel refused to seek God's protection and the help which He offered.

Psalm 36:7: "*How precious is Thy lovingkindness, O God! And the children of men take refuge in the shadow of Thy wings.*"

VERSE 38: "*Behold, your house is being left to you desolate!*"

Jerusalem and Israel rejected God and thus God would reject her. The religious leaders would not listen to God. They would pretend to obey God, but they really hated Him.

Psalm 81:11-15:
11 "But My people did not listen to My voice; And Israel did not obey Me.
12 So I gave them over to the stubbornness of their heart,
*   To walk in their own devices.*
13 Oh that My people would listen to Me,
*   That Israel would walk in My ways!*
14 I would quickly subdue their enemies,
*   And turn My hand against their adversaries.*
15 Those who hate the LORD would pretend obedience to Him;
*   And their time of punishment would be forever.*"
[See also Matthew 23:15.]

The Jews took great pride in their temple. Jesus said earlier that the temple had become a den of thieves. When Jesus proclaimed the judgment we read of in verse 38: *"Behold, your house is being left to you desolate!"* their temple would be part of that desolation. Remember that a mere 40 years after they murdered Jesus (AD 70)[422], Jerusalem and the temple were completely destroyed. Jesus told His disciple, that one day this would happen:

> **Matthew 24:1-2:** *"AND Jesus came out from the temple and was going away when His disciples came up to point out the temple buildings to Him. ² And He answered and said to them, 'Do you not see all these things? Truly I say to you, not one stone here shall be left upon another, which will not be torn down.'"*

VERSE 39: *"For I say to you, from now on you shall not see Me until you say, 'BLESSED IS HE WHO COMES IN THE NAME OF THE LORD!'"*

God has stated His departure from Israel…for a time. Back in Matthew 21 we read of Jesus' triumphal entry into Jerusalem:

> *"And the multitudes going before Him, and those who followed after were crying*
> *out, saying,*
> *'Hosanna to the Son of David;*
> *BLESSED IS HE WHO COMES IN THE NAME OF THE LORD;*
> *Hosanna in the highest!'"* **Matthew 21:9.**

The people were proclaiming Jesus the Messiah, but their concept of the Messiah's rule at that time was wrong. They saw the Messiah as coming to set them free from Rome and defeat any other enemies they had. Jesus came to set them free from sin. They did not realize that His kingdom was not of this world (John 18:36). When they realized that He did not come to defeat Rome, some of those who were proclaiming Him Messiah as He entered Jerusalem, disowned Him as their king, and demanded that Pilate have Him put to death. Now we see in Matthew 23:39 that Jesus tells them that they will not see Him until they say, *"BLESSED IS HE WHO COMES IN THE NAME OF THE LORD!"* This will occur at His second coming. There should be no mistake. God's partial hardening toward Israel <u>does not</u> mean He is done with them:

> **Romans 11:25-26:** *"For I do not want you, brethren, to be uninformed of this mystery, lest you be wise in your own estimation, that a partial hardening has happened to Israel until the fullness of the Gentiles has come in; ²⁶ and <u>thus all Israel will be saved</u>; just as it is written, 'The Deliverer will come from Zion, He will remove ungodliness from Jacob.'"*

Summary and Application

The Lord loves and cares for His people. Remember how the Lord illustrates His care for His people: *"How often I wanted to gather your children together, the way a hen gathers her chicks under her wings…."* How often do we neglect the great love and protection of almighty God by seeking worldly security in work, money or people? Let us learn from this section to reject the folly of rebellious self-seeking, and instead take shelter in the Lord alone.

---

[422] Caesar ordered his general Titus Vespasian to annihilate Jerusalem.

Psalm 61:3-4: *"For You have been a refuge for me, a tower of strength against the enemy. [4] Let me dwell in Your tent forever; let me take refuge in the shelter of Your wings."*

MATTHEW 24:1-2

(DESTRUCTION OF THE TEMPLE AND OTHER FUTURE EVENTS)

"AND Jesus came out from the temple and was going away when His disciples came up to point out the temple buildings to Him. ² And He answered and said to them, 'Do you not see all these things? Truly I say to you, not one stone here shall be left upon another, which will not be torn down.'"

Introduction

This section begins what is known as the "Olivet Discourse" because Jesus spoke this to His disciples on the Mount of Olives. This section discusses the second coming of Christ.

VERSES 1-2: *"AND Jesus came out from the temple and was going away when His disciples came up to point out the temple buildings to Him. ² And He answered and said to them, 'Do you not see all these things? Truly I say to you, not one stone here shall be left upon another, which will not be torn down.'"*

History of the Temples:

Here we see the disciples marveling over the temple. Before reviewing this passage, it would be helpful to examine the history of the temples in Jerusalem. It must be remembered that the tabernacle was used by the Jews prior to Solomon's Temple being built in Jerusalem. God's instructions on the building of the tabernacle were given to Moses and set out in Exodus 25. We see in the book of Acts that this tabernacle and Solomon's Temple were mentioned by Stephen at his great defense of the faith before he was stoned:

> **Acts 7:44-50:** *"Our fathers had the tabernacle of testimony in the wilderness, just as He who spoke to Moses directed him to make it according to the pattern which he had seen. ⁴⁵ And having received it in their turn, our fathers brought it in with Joshua upon dispossessing the nations whom God drove out before our fathers, until the time of David. ⁴⁶ And David found favor in God's sight, and asked that he might find a dwelling place for the God of Jacob. ⁴⁷ But it was Solomon who built a house for Him. ⁴⁸ However, the Most High does not dwell in houses made by human hands; as the prophet says:*
>> *⁴⁹ 'HEAVEN IS MY THRONE, AND EARTH IS THE FOOTSTOOL OF MY FEET;*
>> *WHAT KIND OF HOUSE WILL YOU BUILD FOR ME?' says the Lord;*
>> *'OR WHAT PLACE IS THERE FOR MY REPOSE?*
>> *⁵⁰ WAS IT NOT MY HAND WHICH MADE ALL THESE THINGS?'"*

We will look at the Tabernacle of Moses, Solomon's Temple, The Second Temple and Herod's Temple.

1) Mosaic Tabernacle:

"The tabernacle was the precursor of the temple during most of the period between the formation of Israel at Sinai and its final establishment in the Promised Land in the early period of the monarchy. A portable sanctuary in keeping with the demand for easy mobility, it was the symbol of God's presence with His people and, therefore, of His availability, as well as a place where His will was communicated."[423]

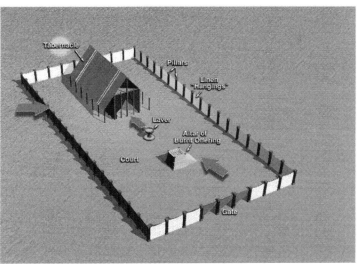

The Mosaic Tabernacle.

2) Solomon's Temple:
The first temple is known as **Solomon's Temple**. This is the great temple that King Solomon built. This area is known today as the "Temple Mount" area. The highest part of the rock is controlled by the Moslems who have covered the rock with a mosque called the "Dome of the Rock." *"'The Dome of the Rock' may have been the site of the innermost sanctuary or of the altar of burnt-offering outside (2 Chronicles 3:1)."*[424]

The Temple Mount is a holy site to the Jews for a couple of reasons: 1) It is the place where Abraham began to offer Isaac (Genesis 22). 2) It is believed to be the threshing floor of Araunah (who is also called Ornan). So who is Araunah? If you read 2 Samuel 24:15-24 you will see that David had sinned against God by taking a census of the people. This was sin because David was putting his faith in the number of fighting men he had in his army instead of God. As a result of David's sin, God gave him a choice of three punishments and he took the third one. This third punishment was three days of pestilence in the land.

> **2 Samuel 24:15-16:** *"So the LORD sent a pestilence upon Israel from the morning until the appointed time; and seventy thousand men of the people from Dan to Beersheba died. [16] When the angel stretched out his hand toward*

---

[423] Elwell, W. A., and Comfort, P. W. (2001). *Tyndale Bible Dictionary.*, Tabernacle. Tyndale reference library (p. 1233). Wheaton, IL: Tyndale House Publishers.

[424] Wood, D. R. W. (1996). *New Bible Dictionary* (3rd ed.) (p. 1156). Leicester, England; Downers Grove, Ill.: InterVarsity Press.

Jerusalem to destroy it, the LORD relented from the calamity, and said to the angel who destroyed the people, 'It is enough! Now relax your hand!' And the angel of the LORD was by the threshing floor of Araunah the Jebusite."

We then see that the prophet Gad told David to build an altar to the Lord *"...on the threshing floor of Araunah the Jebusite...."* **2 Samuel 24:18.** When you read the rest of the text you find that David wanted to buy the threshing floor from Araunah for the altar, but Araunah offered it for free. David replied in verse 24 by saying: *"No, but I will surely buy it from you for a price, for I will not offer burnt offerings to the LORD my God which cost me nothing."*[425] We then read that David made his offering to the Lord and the plague was stopped. Solomon's Temple was built at this spot.

David wanted to build a great temple to the Lord but God told him that he would not build the temple but his son (Solomon) would. The Lord did not have David build the temple because David was a warrior who had killed many people.

> **1 Chronicles 22:6-10:** *"Then he called for his son Solomon, and charged him to build a house for the Lord God of Israel. ⁷ And David said to Solomon, 'My son, I had intended to build a house to the name of the Lord my God. ⁸ But the word of the Lord came to me, saying, 'You have shed much blood, and have waged great wars; you shall not build a house to My name, because you have shed so much blood on the earth before Me. ⁹ Behold, a son shall be born to you, who shall be a man of rest; and I will give him rest from all his enemies on every side; for his name shall be Solomon, and I will give peace and quiet to Israel in his days. ¹⁰ He shall build a house for My name,....'"*

Solomon put together a large work force to do this great work of building the temple.

> **2 Chronicles 2:1-2:** *"NOW Solomon decided to build a house for the name of the LORD, and a royal palace for himself. ² So Solomon assigned 70,000 men to carry loads, and 80,000 men to quarry stone in the mountains, and 3,600 to supervise them."*

This was an incredible complex. Look up chapter 6 of 1 Kings to get more of the details. Here is just a portion from that chapter:

> **1 Kings 6:21-22:** *"So Solomon <u>overlaid the inside of the house with pure gold</u>. And he drew <u>chains of gold across the front of the inner sanctuary; and he overlaid it with gold</u>. ²² And <u>he overlaid the whole house with gold</u>, until all the house was finished. Also the <u>whole altar which was by the inner sanctuary he overlaid with gold</u>."*

---

[425] 2 Samuel 24:24. Note that **"Araunah** therefore sold him the **threshing floor** and **oxen** for **50 shekels of silver** (the 600 shekels of gold in 1 Chronicles 21:25 includes, however, "the site," more than just the threshing floor). Fifty shekels was about 1 1/2 pounds of silver. The silver David paid was only for the oxen and the threshing floor, and the 600 shekels (15 pounds of gold) mentioned in 1 Chronicles 21:25 was for the lot of land surrounding the threshing floor." Walvoord, J. F. (1983-c1985). *The Bible Knowledge Commentary: An Exposition of the Scriptures* (2 Samuel 24:10). Wheaton, IL: Victor Books.

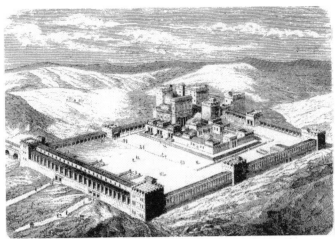

**Artist's sketch of Solomon's Temple looking Northwest.
Fortress Antonia is immediately to the right of the temple compound.**
(Drawing from Ryrie Study Bible)

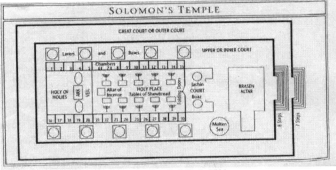

(Drawing from Ryrie Study Bible)

Israel sinned against the Lord and suffered judgment which resulted in it being invaded by Babylon. In 587 B.C. Solomon's Temple was looted by Nebuchadnezzar, King of Babylon and burned (2 Kings 25:8-17).[426] The temple was completely destroyed.

3) **Second Temple:**

In 539 B.C. Cyrus, king of Persia, overthrew Babylon. In 537 B,C. exiles from Babylonia returned with the vessels that were stolen from Solomon's temple by Nebuchadnezzar. [427] The Second Temple was built by order of Cyrus king of Persia, as we read in the book of Ezra.

---

[426] Wood, D. R. W. (1996). *New Bible Dictionary* (3rd ed. /) (p. 1157). Leicester, England; Downers Grove, Ill.: InterVarsity Press.

[427] Ibid.

Ezra 1:1-4: *"Now in the first year of Cyrus king of Persia, in order to fulfill the word of the Lord by the mouth of Jeremiah, the Lord stirred up the spirit of Cyrus king of Persia, so that he sent a proclamation throughout all his kingdom, and also put it in writing, saying,* [2] *'Thus says Cyrus king of Persia, The Lord, the God of heaven, has given me all the kingdoms of the earth, and He has appointed me to build Him a house in Jerusalem, which is in Judah.* [3] *Whoever there is among you of all His people, may his God be with him! Let him go up to Jerusalem which is in Judah, and rebuild the house of the Lord, the God of Israel; He is the God who is in Jerusalem.* [4] *And every survivor, at whatever place he may live, let the men of that place support him with silver and gold, with goods and cattle, together with a freewill offering for the house of God which is in Jerusalem.'"*

This Second Temple was built by Zerubbabel (Ezra 5:2) and was completed in 515 B.C. during the reign of Darius, king of Persia. The temple was not as grand as Solomon's Temple (Ezra 3:12). This Second Temple never contained the Ark of the Covenant since it was believed to have been lost or destroyed during the sacking of Jerusalem by the Babylonians (Josephus, *BJ* 5.219). The Second Temple was defiled by:

> "Antiochus IV, the Syrian king who ruled Palestine from 175–165 B.C. as a surrogate of the Greek empire. He took to himself the title Theos Epiphanes, which means "manifest god," but his enemies nicknamed him Epimanes, which means "madman" or "the insane one." Ironically, when he died in 163, he was totally insane, outraged to the point of madness because of his military defeats by the Jewish rebel Judas Maccabaeus. The text of Daniel 11:21–35 perfectly describes the rule of Antiochus, who gained his throne "by intrigue" (v. 21), made numerous excursions into Egypt (vv. 24–27), broke his covenant with Israel (v. 28), and desecrated the Temple in Jerusalem (v. 31).
>
> The apocryphal books of 1 and 2 Maccabees vividly portray the time of Antiochus and the Jews' zealous resistance to his brutal and sacrilegious tyranny. He slaughtered countless thousands of Jewish men, sold many of their wives and children into slavery, and tried to completely obliterate the Jewish religion. He desecrated the Temple by sacrificing a pig, the most ceremonially unclean of all animals, on the altar and forcing the priests to eat its flesh. He then set up in the Temple an idol of Zeus, the pagan deity he fancied himself as manifesting. That horrible defilement by Antiochus was a preview of the even greater abomination of desolation to be committed by the Antichrist in the end time."[428]

After the temple defilement by Antiochus Epiphanes in B.C. 168, the temple was cleansed and rededicated by Judas Maccabaeus in 165 B.C. This celebration is called the Feast of the Dedication as we see in John 10:22. The Feast of Dedication is known today as Hanukkah or the Feast of Lights.[429] The Maccabees built a new altar and restored the incense altar (1 Maccabees

---

[428] MacArthur, J. F., Jr. (1985). *Matthew.* MacArthur New Testament Commentary (p. 249). Chicago: Moody Press.

[429] Walvoord, J. F. (1983-c1985). *The Bible Knowledge Commentary: An Exposition of the Scriptures* (2 Samuel 24:10). Wheaton, IL: Victor Books.

4:44–49), and these continued to be in use when Herod enlarged the temple in the latter part of the 1st century B.C. [430]

4) Herod's Temple Mount:

The building that became known as Herod's temple began construction in 19 B.C. It was rightfully called Herod's temple because his work on it was viewed as both an opportunity to make himself (an Idumaean) more appealing to the Jews, as well as to glorify himself. The "main structure was finished within 10 years (c. 9 B.C.), but work continued until A.D. 64."[431]

You will note that the temple is located in the center and the rest of the structure became known as Herod's Temple Mount.

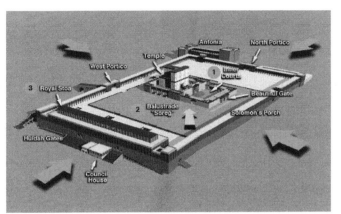

Herod's Temple Mount.

Very large stones were used in the building, normally sized about one meter high and five meters long. [432] Yet others were extremely large: "…measured 40 feet by 12 by 12 and weighed up to a hundred tons, quarried as a single piece and transported many miles to the building site." [433] The Jews were very proud of the temple and its stones. We see this in the comments of a disciple in **Matthew 24:1-2:**

> "AND Jesus came out from the temple and was going away when His disciples
> came up to point out the temple buildings to Him. ² And He answered and said
> to them, "Do you not see all these things? Truly I say to you, not one stone
> here shall be left upon another, which will not be torn down."

---

[430] Wood, D. R. W. (1996). *New Bible Dictionary* (3rd ed.) (p. 27). Leicester, England; Downers Grove, Ill.: InterVarsity Press.

[431] Wood, D. R. W. (1996). *New Bible Dictionary* (3rd ed.) (p. 1158). Leicester, England; Downers Grove, Ill.: InterVarsity Press. See also: Bimson, J. J., and Kane, J. P. (2000). *New Bible Atlas* (electronic ed.) (p. 110). Wheaton, IL: InterVarsity Press.

[432] Ibid.

[433] MacArthur, J. (1989). *Matthew* (Mathew 24:4). Chicago: Moody Press.

Remember that approximately 40 years after they murdered Jesus (around A.D. 70)[434], Jerusalem and the temple were completely destroyed. Note that it was also just a matter of years after construction was completed on the temple in A.D. 64.

> "Josephus relates that Titus, after he had taken Jerusalem, ordered his soldiers to demolish it [the city], except three of the largest and most beautiful towers, and the western wall of the city [which <u>were not part</u> of the Temple edifice proper]; all the rest was leveled, so that they who had never before seen it, could scarcely persuade themselves it had been inhabited. The Jewish writers also inform us, that Turnus Rufus, whom Titus had left in command, ploughed up the very foundations of the temple."[435]

5) **The New Jerusalem:** The Temple Is The Lord and The Lamb — not a building!

The Christian is looking forward to the temple of the New Jerusalem (see Revelation 21:22).

> **Revelation 21:10, 22-27:** *"And he carried me away in the Spirit to a great and high mountain, and showed me the holy city, Jerusalem, coming down out of heaven from God, ...*
> [22] <u>*And I saw no temple in it, for the Lord God, the Almighty, and the Lamb, are its temple.*</u> *[23] And the city has no need of the sun or of the moon to shine upon it, for the glory of God has illumined it, and its lamp is the Lamb. [24] And the nations shall walk by its light, and the kings of the earth shall bring their glory into it. [25] And in the daytime (for there shall be no night there) its gates shall never be closed; [26] and they shall bring the glory and the honor of the nations into it; [27] and nothing unclean and no one who practices abomination and lying, shall ever come into it, but only those whose names are written in the Lamb's book of life."*

Summary and Application

God's Holy Spirit dwells in the Christian. This fact should cause us to take very seriously the importance of living holy lives to His glory! **1 Corinthians 3:16:** *"Do you not know that you are a temple of God, and that the Spirit of God dwells in you?"*

---

[434] Caesar ordered his general Titus Vespasian to annihilate Jerusalem.

[435] *The Treasury Of Scripture Knowledge: Five Hundred Thousand Scripture References and Parallel Passages.* 1995. Introduction by R.A. Torrey. (Jeremiah 26:18). Oak Harbor: Logos Research Systems, Inc.

MATTHEW 24:3-14
(SIGNS OF THE END)

"And as He was sitting on the Mount of Olives, the disciples came to Him privately, saying, 'Tell us, when will these things be, and what will be the sign of Your coming, and of the end of the age?' ⁴ And Jesus answered and said to them, 'See to it that no one misleads you. ⁵ For many will come in My name, saying, 'I am the Christ,' and will mislead many. ⁶ And you will be hearing of wars and rumors of wars; see that you are not frightened, for those things must take place, but that is not yet the end. ⁷ For nation will rise against nation, and kingdom against kingdom, and in various places there will be famines and earthquakes. ⁸ But all these things are merely the beginning of birth pangs. ⁹ Then they will deliver you to tribulation, and will kill you, and you will be hated by all nations on account of My name. ¹⁰ And at that time many will fall away and will deliver up one another and hate one another. ¹¹ And many false prophets will arise, and will mislead many. ¹² And because lawlessness is increased, most people's love will grow cold. ¹³ But the one who endures to the end, he shall be saved. ¹⁴ And this gospel of the kingdom shall be preached in the whole world for a witness to all the nations, and then the end shall come.'"

Introduction

Here we see Jesus explaining to the disciples when the end will come. This is called the "Olivet Discourse" because it took place on the Mount of Olives (v.3). One must realize that the end Jesus is talking about is not the "rapture" of the church. "The end" is the Second Coming of Christ. It is also referred to in the Bible as the *Day Of The Lord* (1Thessalonians 5:2).

VERSES 3-4: *"And as He was sitting on the Mount of Olives, the disciples came to Him privately, saying, 'Tell us, when will these things be, and what will be the sign of Your coming, and of the end of the age?' ⁴ And Jesus answered and said to them, 'See to it that no one misleads you.'"*

To understand the context of what brought on the Olivet Discourse, we need to go back to Matthew 24:1-2.

> **Matthew 24:1-2:** *"And Jesus came out from the temple and was going away when His disciples came up to point out the temple buildings to Him. ² And He answered and said to them, 'Do you not see all these things? Truly I say to you, not one stone here shall be left upon another, which will not be torn down.'"*

The disciples were so amazed, even bewildered, by Jesus' claim that this mighty structure (the glory of the nation) would be destroyed! We see in verse 3 that the disciples waited until they were out of the presence of the people to ask Jesus when this event would take place. The parallel passage in Mark tells us specifically who the disciples were that asked Jesus the question:

> **Mark 13:3:** *"And as He was sitting on the Mount of Olives opposite the temple, <u>Peter and James and John and Andrew</u> were questioning Him privately,...."*

They wanted to know what would be the tell-tale signs leading up to this event. Jesus answered the disciples with the most important premise when studying end times by stating: *"See to it that no one misleads you."* What is it one could be misled on? Jesus tells us in verse 5: *"For many will come in My name, saying, 'I am the Christ,' and will mislead many."* The warning is about being misled on who the *Messiah* really is. Realize that many religions teach a Jesus who is not the Jesus of Scripture. We would do well today to walk in that same wisdom so as not to be deceived by false-christs.

> **2 Corinthians 11:4:** *"For if one comes and preaches another Jesus whom we have not preached, or you receive a different spirit which you have not received, or a different gospel which you have not accepted, you bear this beautifully."*

Many people today are very interested in "end times" discussions, but few are interested in following Christ. There are many self-proclaimed experts in "end times" matters who have been proven to be false prophets. I remember in 1988 many Christians were fascinated by a book called *88 Reasons Why the Rapture Will Be in 1988*, by Edgar C. Whisenant. The book sold about 4.5 million copies. People would hail that Whisenant was a NASA engineer: (which some claimed made him intellectually qualified to deal with the mathematic difficulties used to arrive at his prediction date). I did not bother to read the book because I knew that Scripture stated that this type of guy was a fraud: **Matthew 25:13:** *"Be on the alert then, for you do not know the day nor the hour."* But what amazed me was how any people believed in Whisenant's book. Many folks arranged their financial interests based on this false prophet's teaching. That year I witnessed how quickly people were deceived, including some of whom I would have considered to be mature Christians. [436] Some who claimed to be Christians were not able to discern because they were not being fed daily by God's Word. If they simply would have read God's Word, they would have known that these *date-setters* are charlatans.

> **Matthew 25:13:** *"Be on the alert then, for you do not know the day nor the hour."*
> **Matthew 24:42:** *"Therefore be on the alert, for you do not know which day your Lord is coming."*
> **Matthew 24:44:** *"For this reason you also must be ready; for the Son of Man is coming at an hour when you do not think He will."*

Instead of seeking the Lord in His Word, people will rely on some pop-culture "Christian book" or some great religious leader on television to tell them what the Lord requires of them. The true believer is the one whom the Word of God abides in:

> **John 8:31:** *"Jesus therefore was saying to those Jews who had believed Him, 'If you abide in My word, then you are truly disciples of Mine;....'"*

---

[436] [This falls under the guise of, "You can't make this stuff up," — but then again, the false prophets can!] In the spring of 2011, there was this guy Harold Camping – [who is the founder of a radio network called FAMILY RADIO]. Camping claimed that the world will end on May 21, 2011. The basis of his claim was that the earth will be exactly 7,000 years old on that date and thus it was the exact Day of Judgment. Camping must have missed that little section where Jesus says: **Matthew 24:42:** *"Therefore be on the alert, for you do not know which day your Lord is coming."* Oh by the way, Camping made predictions in 1994 about the end that did not pan out so well either. Again scripture proved true. **Romans 3:4:** *"… let God be found true, though every man be found a liar…."*

Oh, as a little side note: After Whisenant enjoyed such great success with his book, *88 Reasons Why the Rapture Will Be in 1988,* he decided to write a sequel the next year. That book predicted the rapture in 1989. The book entitled, *The Final Shout: Rapture Report 9* did not sell very well — for obvious reasons. Sales were also very poor in 1993 for his book, *23 Reasons Why A Pre-tribulation Rapture Looks Like It Will Occur On Rosh-Hashanah 1993* and it only got worse with his 1994 prediction book; *And Now The Earth's Destruction By Fire, Nuclear Bomb Fire* — sales for that book also bombed.

VERSES 5-8: *"For many will come in My name, saying, 'I am the Christ,' and will mislead many. ⁶ And you will be hearing of wars and rumors of wars; see that you are not frightened, for those things must take place, but that is not yet the end. ⁷ For nation will rise against nation, and kingdom against kingdom, and in various places there will be famines and earthquakes. ⁸ But all these things are merely the beginning of birth pangs.'"*

In verse 5 Jesus warns us that there will be "false Christs." These "antichrists" will be those who claim that they are the Messiah, the Savior, or even specifically claim to be Jesus. The Apostle John warns of these "antichrists":

> **1 John 2:18-20:** *"Children, it is the last hour; and just as you heard that antichrist is coming, even now many antichrists have arisen; from this we know that it is the last hour. ¹⁹ They went out from us, but they were not really of us; for if they had been of us, they would have remained with us; but they went out, in order that it might be shown that they all are not of us. ²⁰ But you have an anointing from the Holy One, and you all know."*

We read later in Matthew 24:23-24 that these antichrists will use "great signs and wonders" to entice people to follow their lies.

> **Matthew 24:23-24:** *"Then if anyone says to you, 'Behold, here is the Christ,' or 'There He is,' do not believe him. ²⁴ For false Christs and false prophets will arise and will show great signs and wonders, so as to mislead, if possible, even the elect."*

We live in a time when many in the church would rather have an emotional "spiritual experience" (i.e. something they can see and feel) rather than a true faith that is built squarely on God's word. The undiscerning, who walk by sight, will be the type that quickly follow someone who calls fire down from heaven or some other great feat.

> **Revelation 13:13-14:** *"And he performs great signs, so that he even makes fire come down out of heaven to the earth in the presence of men. ¹⁴ And he deceives those who dwell on the earth because of the signs which it was given him to perform in the presence of the beast, telling those who dwell on the earth to make an image to the beast who *had the wound of the sword and has come to life."*

The Church will have been raptured[437] before "the end." [It must be recognized that there are Christian brothers who are preeminent theologians who hold different views on the subject of eschatology (end times and chronology of the end time).] After the rapture of the church, there will be a great increase in evil and deception.

> **2 Thessalonians 2:7-12:** *"For the mystery of lawlessness is already at work; only he who now restrains will do so until he is taken out of the way. ⁸ And then that lawless one will be revealed whom the Lord will slay with the breath of His mouth and bring to an end by the appearance of His coming;*
> *⁹ that is, the one whose coming is in accord with the activity of Satan, with all power and signs and false wonders, ¹⁰ and with all the deception of wickedness for those who perish, because they did not receive the love of the truth so as to be saved. ¹¹ And for this reason God will send upon them a deluding influence so that they might believe what is false, ¹² in order that they all may be judged who did not believe the truth, but took pleasure in wickedness."*

Another way people are being misled regarding the end times is when they hear of *"wars and rumors of wars."* The statement *"wars and rumors of war"* is wrongfully quoted by some as a sign of *the end*. It is not. Jesus specifically tells us if we hear of "wars and rumors of wars," we are not to be afraid because the end is not yet. More specifically, in verse **Matthew 24:6** Jesus said: *"And you will be hearing of wars and rumors of wars; see that you are not frightened, for those things must take place, but that is not yet the end."*

We are told what some of the early signs of the end will be: **Matthew 24:7-8:** *"For nation will rise against nation, and kingdom against kingdom, and in various places there will be famines and earthquakes. ⁸ But all these things are merely the beginning of birth pangs."* Note that the chaos on the earth will be in the form of famines and earthquakes, and we also see in the parallel passage in Luke that there will be plagues.

---

[437] Rapture of those who are alive at the time Jesus comes for His Church: Next we see that the Christians who are alive at the time of the rapture will be taken up and joined in the air with those who were raised in the first group. Notice the verses below in this footnote:

1 Thessalonians 4:17: *"Then we who are alive and remain shall be caught up together with them in the clouds to meet the Lord in the air, and thus we shall always be with the Lord."*

John 14:1–3: *"Do not let your heart be troubled; believe in God, believe also in Me. In My Father's house are many dwelling places; if it were not so, I would have told you; for I go to prepare a place for you. If I go and prepare a place for you, I will come again and receive you to Myself, that where I am, there you may be also."*

1 Corinthians 15:51–52: *"Behold, I tell you a mystery; we will not all sleep, but we will all be changed, in a moment, in the twinkling of an eye, at the last trumpet; for the trumpet will sound, and the dead will be raised imperishable, and we will be changed."*

Revelation 3:10: *"Because you have kept the word of My perseverance, I also will keep you from the hour of testing, that hour which is about to come upon the whole world, to test those who dwell on the earth."*

"Then He continued by saying to them, 'Nation will rise against nation, and kingdom against kingdom, [11] and there will be great earthquakes, and in various places plagues and famines; and there will be terrors and great signs from heaven.'"

Other signs of the end times are severe persecution of believers, along with apostasy of the "false brethren" (i.e. pretending to be Christians). These signs are discussed more in the next section.

VERSES 9-10: *"Then they will deliver you to tribulation, and will kill you, and you will be hated by all nations on account of My name. [10] And at that time many will fall away and will deliver up one another and hate one another."*

In verse 9 we see severe persecution of the believers. After the rapture of the church there will be those who become converted during the Tribulation. Christians will be hated by the nations of the world. The nonbelievers' hatred for us will be so severe that they will kill us. The fires of persecution will also show who are the real believers. Persecution for the cause of Christ is part of the Christian life: **2 Timothy 3:12:** *"And indeed, all who desire to live godly in Christ Jesus will be persecuted."* It does not say that true Christians "may" be persecuted, but rather that they WILL BE persecuted. Jesus warns us about this:

> John 15:18-19: *"If the world hates you, you know that it has hated Me before it hated you. [19] If you were of the world, the world would love its own; but because you are not of the world, but I chose you out of the world, therefore the world hates you."*

> John 16:2-4: *"They will make you outcasts from the synagogue, but an hour is coming for everyone who kills you to think that he is offering service to God. [3] And these things they will do, because they have not known the Father, or Me. [4] But these things I have spoken to you, that when their hour comes, you may remember that I told you of them. And these things I did not say to you at the beginning, because I was with you."*

We see in Matthew 24:10 that there will be a great "apostasy" that will take place at that time. Apostasy means to "fall away" (i.e. renounce the faith). Note from verse 10 that the apostates, who at one time were hanging around the Christians, will be among those who hate the believers and deliver them up for persecution *(v.10 "...many will fall away and will deliver up one another and hate one another.")* The Puritan, Timothy Cruso, stated that, "Apostasy is a perversion to evil after a seeming conversion from it."[438]

Paul explains that this must take place before the end in **2 Thessalonians 2:3:** *"Let no one in any way deceive you, for it will not come unless the apostasy comes first, and the man of lawlessness is revealed, the son of destruction,...."* Even in the church today (as has been the case throughout

---

[438] Thomas, I. (1996). *The Golden Treasury Of Puritan Quotations.* Includes index of authors. General index created by Christian Classics Foundation. (electronic ed.). Simpsonville SC: Christian Classics Foundation.

time) there are false Christians. R.C. Sproul states:

> "We know it is possible for people to be enamored by certain elements of Christianity without ever embracing Christ Himself. Perhaps a young person is attracted to a fun and stimulating youth group that has an appealing program. The person may be *converted* to the program without being converted to Christ. Such a person may be like those pictured in the parable of the sower:[439]
>> [Consider reviewing the comments on the parable of the Sower and the Seed in Matthew 13:2-23]

As we see above, persecution is not limited to those outside the church; it also comes from hypocrites, false brothers and the spiritually immature from within the church (2 Corinthians 11:26). A mark of a false Christian is his poor response to persecution for the faith. The false Christian will look, act, and sound very religious, but he will compromise Biblical truth very quickly so that he appears peaceful and inclusive of others. He will attack the true believers as "trouble makers" and kooks. But this whole charade keeps him appearing "good" so that he can avoid persecution. Paul had this experience with the false teachers of Galatia.

> **Galatians 6:12:** *"Those who desire to make a good showing in the flesh try to compel you to be circumcised, simply that they may not be persecuted for the cross of Christ."*

Who in the Bible is the classic example of an apostate? The answer is Judas Iscariot. He was around Jesus and acted like a disciple, yet he hated Christ. When he saw there was nothing in the deal for him, he defected and handed over Jesus to the religious leaders to be persecuted and killed. Judas was not a good guy who went bad, or even a slight disappointment to Jesus. Jesus knew from the beginning that Judas would betray Him:

> **John 6:64:** *"'But there are some of you who do not believe.' For Jesus knew from the beginning who they were who did not believe, and who it was that would betray Him."*

> **John 6:70-71:** *"Jesus answered them, 'Did I Myself not choose you, the twelve, and yet one of you is a devil?' 71 Now He meant Judas the son of Simon Iscariot, for he, one of the twelve, was going to betray Him."*

Judas is the classic apostate in that he knew the plan of salvation, never believed it, and thus rejected it. In Hebrews 10:26 we see that an apostate is one who goes on sinning by living in unbelief of Jesus' sacrifice for sins. The difference between an apostate and a backslidden/disobedient Christian is obvious over time. The apostate will claim to have been a Christian, but at some point down the road disowns Jesus and Christianity. Many do this today. **1 John 2:19** says it this way:

> *"They went out from us, but they were not really of us; for if they had been of us, they would have remained with us; but they went out, in order that it might be shown that they all are not of us."*

---

[439] Sproul, R. C. (1996, c1992). *Essential Truths of the Christian Faith.* (#70 Perseverance Of The Saints) Wheaton, Ill.: Tyndale House.

Look at the parallel section in Mark that tells us more about the persecution and how it will exist in one's own home!

> **Mark 13:9-13:** *"But be on your guard; for they will deliver you to the courts, and you will be flogged in the synagogues, and you will stand before governors and kings for My sake, as a testimony to them. [10] And the gospel must first be preached to all the nations. [11] And when they arrest you and deliver you up, do not be anxious beforehand about what you are to say, but say whatever is given you in that hour; for it is not you who speak, but it is the Holy Spirit. [12] And brother will deliver brother to death, and a father his child; and children will rise up against parents and have them put to death. [13] And you will be hated by all on account of My name, but the one who endures to the end, he shall be saved."*

VERSE 11: *"And many false prophets will arise, and will mislead many."*

False prophets do not speak from God but from the evil one. One sign of the end times is the number of false prophets who will rise up and mislead many. These people will continue to come in the form of a college professor who preaches his evolution theology and ridicules the God who created him. In pop culture, the false prophet is the rock star who goes about preaching "love and tolerance," yet is openly hostile and mocking of Christianity. False prophets can also be in the church and behind the pulpits. They will talk religion and tell you that God will forgive you if you do enough good works or engage in some special religious ritual. Paul warns us of these hypocrites:

> **1 Timothy 4:1-5:** *"But the Spirit explicitly says that in later times some will fall away from the faith, paying attention to deceitful spirits and doctrines of demons, [2] by means of the hypocrisy of liars seared in their own conscience as with a branding iron, [3] men who forbid marriage and advocate abstaining from foods, which God has created to be gratefully shared in by those who believe and know the truth. [4] For everything created by God is good, and nothing is to be rejected, if it is received with gratitude; [5] for it is sanctified by means of the word of God and prayer."*

VERSES 12-13: *"And because lawlessness is increased, most people's love will grow cold. [13] But the one who endures to the end, he shall be saved."*

In verse 12 Jesus tells us that at the end times, *"most people's love will grow cold."* Paul warns of the heart condition and affections of people in the end times.

> **2 Timothy 3:1-5:** *"But realize this, that in the last days difficult times will come. [2] For men will be lovers of self, lovers of money, boastful, arrogant, revilers, disobedient to parents, ungrateful, unholy, [3] unloving, irreconcilable, malicious gossips, without self-control, brutal, haters of good, [4] treacherous, reckless, conceited, lovers of pleasure rather than lovers of God; [5] holding to a form of godliness, although they have denied its power; and avoid such men as these."*

In verse 13 Jesus states that, *"the one who endures to the end, he shall be saved."* (See also Matthew 10:22.) This is not a self-generated endurance, but rather the endurance and preservation that God gives us. Theologically, this is called *"the perseverance of the saints."* What it means is that the truly saved are manifested by their endurance of persecution. Who are those who are saved? Those who persevere to the end. This is not saying that the person who works hard to endure will earn salvation. Salvation and the ability *to endure to the end* comes only from the grace of God and is not something a man can generate. John MacArthur states it this way:

> "Endurance of persecution is the hallmark of genuine salvation: It is the one who has endured to the end who will be saved. Endurance does not produce or protect salvation, which is totally the work of God's grace. But endurance is evidence of salvation, proof that a person is truly redeemed and a child of God.... The following Scriptures also emphasize perseverance: Matthew 24:13; John 8:31; 1 Corinthians 15:1-2; Colossians 1:21-23; Hebrews 2:1-3; 4:14; 6:11-12; 10:39; 12:14; 2 Peter 1:10."[440]

We see there are believers who endured *"to the end"* and come through the great tribulation in **Revelation 7:13-17:**

> *"And one of the elders answered, saying to me, 'These who are clothed in the white robes, who are they, and from where have they come?' [14] And I said to him, 'My lord, you know.' And he said to me, 'These are the ones who come out of the great tribulation, and they have washed their robes and made them white in the blood of the Lamb. [15] For this reason, they are before the throne of God; and they serve Him day and night in His temple; and He who sits on the throne shall spread His tabernacle over them. [16] They shall hunger no more, neither thirst anymore; neither shall the sun beat down on them, nor any heat; [17] for the Lamb in the center of the throne shall be their shepherd, and shall guide them to springs of the water of life; and God shall wipe every tear from their eyes.'"*

VERSE 14: *"And this gospel of the kingdom shall be preached in the whole world for a witness to all the nations, and then the end shall come."*

Another sign right before the end will be the supernatural worldwide proclamation of the Gospel. We read of this in the book of Revelation.

> **Revelation 14:6-7:** *"And I saw another angel flying in midheaven, having an eternal gospel to preach to those who live on the earth, and to every nation and tribe and tongue and people; [7] and he said with a loud voice, 'Fear God, and give Him glory, because the hour of His judgment has come; and worship Him who made the heaven and the earth and sea and springs of waters.'"*

This even marks the ultimate fulfillment of the Great Commission. MacArthur states that this event,

> "...will be the final and total evangelization of the world, miraculously proclaimed from heaven. After that proclamation man's day will be finished, his rebellion will

---

[440] MacArthur, J. F., Jr. (1985). *Matthew.* MacArthur New Testament Commentary (p. 199). Chicago: Moody Press.

be over, and his opportunity for salvation will be over, because **then the end shall come**."[441]

Summary and Application

In examining the end times signs, the Lord warns us in Matthew 24:4-14:

1. <u>We are not to be misled.</u> This will require us to be in the Word and on our knees so we can discern the Lord's voice. " *⁴See to it that no one misleads you.*"

2. There will be <u>false messiahs and wars and rumors of wars.</u> Believers ought not to be *"frightened,"* and should realize that the *"end is not yet"* (v.6). So when your friend tells you that "wars and rumors of wars" is a sign of the end, tell him it is not, and that the *"end is not yet."*

3. More of the <u>very early signs</u> leading up to the end include <u>wars, famines and earthquakes</u>: " *⁷For nation will rise against nation, and kingdom against kingdom, and in various places there will be famines and earthquakes. ⁸ <u>But all these things are merely the beginning of birth pangs.</u>*"

4. After the early signs are past, we start into the <u>signs of the end times.</u> These signs include <u>extreme persecution, hatred and murder committed against Christians</u>: " *⁹Then they will deliver you to tribulation, and will kill you, and you will be hated by all nations on account of My name.*

5. Also a sign of the end times is the <u>great falling away or apostasy</u> of those who claimed to be Christians but were not (it will be composed of those whose are deceivers and the self-deceived [2 Timothy 3:13, 2 John v.7]. When persecution and death hits the Church, the fakes will have nothing to do with it. They will not only deny the faith, but they will take their knowledge of who the believers are and <u>hand it over to the persecutors</u>: " *¹⁰ And at that time many will fall away and will deliver up one another and hate one another.*"

6. As it moves closer to the end there will be <u>a lot of false prophets</u> and <u>lawlessness,</u> along with <u>very little love</u> left in the world: " *¹¹ And many false prophets will arise, and will mislead many. ¹² And because lawlessness is increased, most people's love will grow cold. ¹³ But the one who endures to the end, he shall be saved.*"

7. The last sign before the end will be the <u>worldwide preaching of the Gospel</u>: ¹⁴ *"And this gospel of the kingdom shall be preached in the whole world for a witness to all the nations,*

8. Then the end will come! ¹⁴ *"…and then the end shall come.'"*

---

[441] MacArthur, J. F., Jr. (1985). *Matthew*. MacArthur New Testament Commentary (p. 249). Chicago: Moody Press.

How will you prepare for the end times? It is not about having enough food and water stored up. The way to prepare is to be feeding on the Word of God and being filled with the Holy Spirit so that by faith you can discern the times, and by the power of God be the *"one who endures to the end"* because it is that person who *"shall be saved."* v. 13.

MATTHEW 24:15-22
(END TIMES—SECOND COMING OF CHRIST)

¹⁵ *"Therefore when you see the* ABOMINATION OF DESOLATION *which was spoken of through Daniel the prophet, standing in the holy place (let the reader understand),* ¹⁶*then let those who are in Judea flee to the mountains;* ¹⁷ *let him who is on the housetop not go down to get the things out that are in his house;* ¹⁸ *and let him who is in the field not turn back to get his cloak.* ¹⁹ *But woe to those who are with child and to those who nurse babes in those days!* ²⁰*But pray that your flight may not be in the winter, or on a Sabbath;* ²¹*for then there will be a great tribulation, such as has not occurred since the beginning of the world until now, nor ever shall.* ²²*And unless those days had been cut short, no life would have been saved; but for the sake of the elect those days shall be cut short."*

Introduction

This section continues the emphasis on the end times which began at Matthew 24:3. It must be remembered that these end times are referencing the Second Coming of Christ, not the rapture. This time period occurs after the rapture of the church, and is known as the Tribulation.

VERSE 15: *"Therefore when you see the* ABOMINATION OF DESOLATION *which was spoken of through Daniel the prophet, standing in the holy place (let the reader understand),"*

The "ABOMINATION OF DESOLATION" occurs halfway through the Tribulation. Here is the timeline:

1. First, there is the rapture of the church.
2. Then the Tribulation begins and lasts for a total of seven years.
3. Halfway through those seven years the Anti-Christ will go into the temple in Jerusalem and desecrate it by declaring that he is God. Because it is such an utter lie and blasphemy, it is called the Abomination of Desolation. *The American Heritage Dictionary* defines *"Abomination"* as *"A cause of abhorrence or disgust."* It also defines *"Desolation"* as, *"… Devastation; ruin: a drought that brought desolation to the region. 4. a. The state of being abandoned or forsaken…b. Wretchedness; misery."* The phrase "the Abomination of Desolation" referred to the presence of an idolatrous person or object so detestable that it caused the temple to be abandoned and left desolate.[442]

We read more about this incident in **2 Thessalonians 2:3-5:**
> *"Let no one in any way deceive you, for it will not come unless the apostasy comes first, and the man of lawlessness is revealed, the son of destruction,* ⁴ *who opposes and exalts himself above every so-called god or object of worship, so that he takes his seat in the temple of God, displaying himself as*

---

[442] Walvoord, J. F., Zuck, R. B., and Dallas Theological Seminary. (1985). *The Bible Knowledge Commentary: An Exposition of the Scriptures* (v. 2, p. 169). Wheaton, IL: Victor Books..

being God. 5 Do you not remember that while I was still with you, I was telling you these things?"

The main text of **Matthew 24:15** stated, *"Therefore when you see the ABOMINATION OF DESOLATION which was spoken of through Daniel the prophet, standing in the holy place (let the reader understand)."* Three times in Scripture, the prophet Daniel makes reference to the "abomination of desolation" (Daniel 9:27, 11:31 and 12:11).

> **Daniel 11:30-39:** *"For ships of Kittim will come against him; therefore he will be disheartened, and will return and become enraged at the holy covenant and take action; so he will come back and show regard for those who forsake the holy covenant. 31 And forces from him will arise, desecrate the sanctuary fortress, and do away with the regular sacrifice. And they will set up the abomination of desolation. 32 And by smooth words he will turn to godlessness those who act wickedly toward the covenant, but the people who know their God will display strength and take action. 33 And those who have insight among the people will give understanding to the many; yet they will fall by sword and by flame, by captivity and by plunder, for many days. 34 Now when they fall they will be granted a little help, and many will join with them in hypocrisy. 35 And some of those who have insight will fall, in order to refine, purge, and make them pure, until the end time; because it is still to come at the appointed time. 36 Then the king will do as he pleases, and he will exalt and magnify himself above every god, and will speak monstrous things against the God of gods; and he will prosper until the indignation is finished, for that which is decreed will be done. 37 And he will show no regard for the gods of his fathers or for the desire of women, nor will he show regard for any other god; for he will magnify himself above them all. 38 But instead he will honor a god of fortresses, a god whom his fathers did not know; he will honor him with gold, silver, costly stones, and treasures. 39 And he will take action against the strongest of fortresses with the help of a foreign god; he will give great honor to those who acknowledge him, and he will cause them to rule over the many, and will parcel out land for a price."*

This prophesy of Daniel's (Daniel 11:21-35) can be viewed as first being fulfilled during "the desecration of the temple in 167 B.C. by the Syrian ruler Antiochus Epiphanes. He erected an altar to the pagan Greek god Zeus over the altar of burnt offering and sacrificed a pig on it (cf. apocryphal 1 Maccabees 1:41-64; 6:7; and Josephus The Antiquities of the Jews 12. 5. 4)."[443] After the temple defilement by Antiochus Epiphanes the temple was cleansed and rededicated by Judas Maccabaeus in 165 B.C. This celebration is called the Feast of the Dedication as we see in John 10:22. The Feast of Dedication is known today as Hanukkah or the Feast of Lights.[444]

Some see a fulfillment of Daniel's prophecy with the destruction of the temple in A.D. 70.
> "Josephus relates that Titus, after he had taken Jerusalem, ordered his soldiers to demolish it [the city], except three of the largest and most beautiful towers,

---

[443] Walvoord, J. F. (1983-c1985). *The Bible Knowledge Commentary: An Exposition of the Scriptures* (Mark 13:14). Wheaton, IL: Victor Books.

[444] Ibid at (2 Samuel 24:10).

and the western wall of the city [which <u>were not part</u> of the Temple edifice proper]; all the rest was leveled, so that they who had never before seen it, could scarcely persuade themselves it had been inhabited. The Jewish writers also inform us, that Turnus Rufus, whom Titus had left in command, ploughed up the very foundations of the temple."[445]

The complete fulfillment of Daniel's prophecies, and the focus of Jesus' instruction in Matthew 24 is set for the future.

> "This person is the end-time Antichrist (Daniel. 7:23-26; 9:25-27; 2 Thessalonians 2:3-4, 8-9; Revelation 13:1-10, 14-15). He will make a covenant with the Jewish people at the beginning of the seven-year period preceding Christ's second coming (Daniel 9:27). The temple will be rebuilt and worship reestablished (Revelation 11:1). In the middle of this period (after three and a half years) the Antichrist will break his covenant, stop temple sacrifices, desecrate the temple (cf. Daniel 9:27), and proclaim himself to be God (Matthew 24:15; 2 Thessalonians 2:3-4; Revelation 11:2). This launches the terrible end-time events of the Great Tribulation (Revelation 6; 8-9; 16). Those who refuse to be identified with the Antichrist will suffer severe persecution and be forced to flee for refuge (Revelation 12:6, 13-17). Many—both Jews and Gentiles—will be saved during this period (Revelation 7) but many will also be martyred (Revelation 6:9-11)."[446]

VERSES 16-20: *"...then let those who are in Judea flee to the mountains;* [17] *let him who is on the housetop not go down to get the things out that are in his house;* [18] *and let him who is in the field not turn back to get his cloak.* [19] *But woe to those who are with child and to those who nurse babes in those days!* [20] *But pray that your flight may not be in the winter, or on a Sabbath;"*

Verses 16 through 20 need to be read in light of verse 15. Verse 15 says: *"...when you see the ABOMINATION OF DESOLATION... standing in the holy place...."* In essence, when the event of the Abomination of Desolation takes place in the temple, the people in Judea are instructed to literally run for their lives, and not even stop to get something out of their houses before they escape. The verse speaks of the location of Judea because that will be closest to the defiled temple in Jerusalem which will be the central location for the Antichrist. Those in that location will have the least amount of time to start their escape. The reason they must run for their lives is set out in verses 21-22 (i.e. *"there will be great tribulation"*). In verse 19 Jesus points out that the pregnant and those with young children will have great difficulty trying to make the escape. The Judean winter would also make travel hard.

---

[445] Canne, J., Browne, Blayney, B., Scott, T., and Torrey, R. (2009). *The Treasury of Scripture Knowledge* (v. 1, p. 484). Bellingham, WA: Logos Bible Software.

[446] Walvoord, J. F., Zuck, R. B., and Dallas Theological Seminary. (1985). *The Bible Knowledge Commentary: An Exposition of the Scriptures* (v. 2, p. 170). Wheaton, IL: Victor Books.

VERSES 21-22: *"...for then there will be a great tribulation, such as has not occurred since the beginning of the world until now, nor ever shall. ²² And unless those days had been cut short, no life would have been saved; but for the sake of the elect those days shall be cut short."*

In verse 21, Jesus tells us of a *"great tribulation."* The term "tribulation" as defined by The American Heritage Dictionary means:

"1. Great affliction, trial, or distress; suffering: *the tribulations of the persecuted... at* **trial.** 2. An experience that tests one's endurance, patience, or faith...."

Jesus makes it clear that this will be the worst time of suffering and death that this world has ever seen. This is the time of "Jacob's trouble" as spoken of in Jeremiah 30:7:

"From Zechariah we learn that not every Jew will be successful in the attempt to escape. And it will come about in all the land,' declares the Lord, 'that two parts in it will be cut off and perish; but the third will be left in it. And I will bring the third part through the fire, refine them as silver is refined, and test them as gold is tested' (Zechariah 13:8–9a)." [447]

That third part will include the 144,000 Jews (12,000 from each of the 12 tribes) who are God's chosen evangelists. See Revelation 7:4-8 and 14:1-5.

Matthew 24:22 plainly states that if God allowed the Great Tribulation to continue on, every person would die. God's mercy for His people (*"for the sake of the elect"*) results in His limiting the amount of time the Great Tribulation will last. [448]

Summary and Application

Those who maintain a pre-tribulation view of eschatology believe that those who are *in Christ* at the time of the rapture will not have to endure the "Great Tribulation." Despite the avoidance of the Great Tribulation, all Christians will experience tribulation in various degrees here on earth.

2 Timothy 3:12: *"And indeed, all who desire to live godly in Christ Jesus will be persecuted."*

Romans 5:3-5: *"And not only this, but we also exult in our tribulations, knowing that tribulation brings about perseverance; ⁴ and perseverance, proven character; and proven character, hope; ⁵ and hope does not disappoint, because the love of God has been poured out within our hearts through the Holy Spirit who was given to us."*

1 Thessalonians 1:6: *"You also became imitators of us and of the Lord, having received the word in much tribulation with the joy of the Holy Spirit,"*

---

[447] MacArthur, J. F., Jr. (1985). *Matthew.* MacArthur New Testament Commentary (p. 249). Chicago: Moody Press.

[448] Some have also speculated that the phrase, *"And unless those days had been cut short,"* means a supernatural shortening of the amount of daylight during the regular 24-hour period day. This view believes that with less daylight there would be an easier chance to escape and move under the cover of darkness. Again that is merely a theory.

Revelation 1:9: *"I, John, your brother and fellow partaker in the tribulation and kingdom and perseverance which are in Jesus, was on the island called Patmos, because of the word of God and the testimony of Jesus."*

John 15:20: *"Remember the word that I said to you, 'A slave is not greater than his master.' If they persecuted Me, they will also persecute you; if they kept My word, they will keep yours also."*

MATTHEW 24:23-28
(FALSE CHRISTS AND THE SECOND COMING OF CHRIST)

[23] *"Then if anyone says to you, 'Behold, here is the Christ,' or 'There He is,' do not believe him.* [24] *For false Christs and false prophets will arise and will show great signs and wonders, so as to mislead, if possible, even the elect.* [25] *Behold, I have told you in advance.* [26] *If therefore they say to you, 'Behold, He is in the wilderness,' do not go forth, or, 'Behold, He is in the inner rooms,' do not believe them.* [27] *For just as the lightning comes from the east, and flashes even to the west, so shall the coming of the Son of Man be.* [28] *Wherever the corpse is, there the vultures will gather."*

Introduction

God is gracious to us in that we are not left ignorant about the future and His return. Although the Bible is clear that we do not know the day or hour of that event; the Lord tells us about signs to be on the lookout for. Note that in verse 25 He says, *"Behold, I have told you in advance."* The church is also warned about the deceptions that will abound and how we are not to be seduced by them. Finally, in verses 29-31 we are told what will occur at The End when the Lord returns (i.e. His Second Coming). Remember that Jesus' Second Coming is different than the rapture of the church.[449] The rapture takes place just before the tribulation and it is when Jesus returns for His Church. It is at the end of the tribulation that The Second Coming of Christ takes place.

VERSES 23-25: *"Then if anyone says to you, 'Behold, here is the Christ,' or 'There He is,' do not believe him.* [24] *For false Christs and false prophets will arise and will show great signs and wonders, so as to mislead, if possible, even the elect.* [25] *Behold, I have told you in advance."*

Those who become Christians during the tribulation are warned in verses 22-26 to not listen to false prophets. How does one know a false prophet? A false prophet will not truthfully and accurately teach from the Word of God. Notice that I did not say a false prophet will not teach from the Bible. There are many false prophets and false Christians who are actually disciples of Satan who teach from or about the Bible. We must know God's Word and have Holy Spirit discernment so as to not be deceived by false teachers who are children of the Devil.

> **2 Timothy 3:13-17:** *"But <u>evil men and impostors</u> will proceed from bad to worse, <u>deceiving and being deceived</u>.* [14] *You, however, continue in the things you have learned and become convinced of, knowing from whom you have learned them;* [15] *and that from childhood <u>you have known the sacred writings which are able to give you the wisdom that leads to salvation through faith which is in Christ Jesus</u>.* [16] *All Scripture is inspired by God and profitable for teaching, for reproof, for correction, for training in righteousness;* [17] *that the man of God may be adequate, equipped for every good work."*

---

[449] It is recognized that there are many preeminent theologians who have different views on the subject of eschatology.

False teachers often will quote parts of the Bible, but not the Truth in its context. They talk about a Jesus of their own creation, not the Jesus of the Bible. Many people will say, "Well, my Jesus is a God of love and would never send anyone to hell!" This is a classic example of where a truth is mixed with a lie. The truth is that God *is* love (1 John 4:16). The lie is that God would never send anyone to hell. As R.C. Sproul points out: *"Almost all the biblical teaching about hell comes from the lips of Jesus."*[450] For example Jesus said:

> **Luke 12:4-5:** *"And I say to you, <u>My friends, do not be afraid of those who kill the body</u>, and after that have no more that they can do. ⁵ But I will warn you whom to fear: <u>fear the One who after He has killed has authority to cast into hell</u>; yes, I tell you, fear Him!"*

Note from the text we are studying in **Matthew 24:24** Jesus said: *"For false Christs and false prophets will arise and will show great signs and wonders, so as to mislead, if possible, even the elect."* We are also told about these false wonders in the end times:

> **2 Thessalonians 2:8-10:** *"And then that <u>lawless one will be revealed</u> whom the Lord will slay with the breath of His mouth and bring to an end by the appearance of His coming; ⁹ <u>that is, the one whose coming is in accord with the activity of Satan, with all power and signs and false wonders</u>, ¹⁰ and with all <u>the deception of wickedness</u> for those who perish, because they did not receive the love of the truth so as to be saved."*

The book of Revelation tells us that false miracles will be done by the Antichrist to trick people. The antichrist *"...performs great signs, so that he even makes fire come down out of heaven to the earth in the presence of men. ¹⁴ And <u>he deceives those who dwell on the earth because of the signs which it was given him to perform</u>..."* **Revelation 13:13-14.** We must be reminded that Truth is taught by God's Word, and that those who live by their emotions instead of scripture are very susceptible to false prophets. Many people enjoy "emotionally based" religion. This is the reason some love the emotion they feel from intense ritualism in a very liturgical church. Others enjoy religious emotion in a church service that is lacking any sense of order. Often in that scenario, "truth" can supposedly be whatever someone says or does, no matter how bizarre, as long as the person claims that God told him to say or do it.

Matthew 24:24 says false prophets will do great miracles to prove what they are saying is *true*. We have been warned by Jesus that these signs should not mislead us. Whether one does miracles or not, the determination of whether he is from God comes from applying a two-prong test which evaluates both his 1) doctrine and 2) the fruit of his life. These tests are set out below:

1. The **Doctrine Test** is to always evaluate what is being said against the truth of Scripture.

    > **1 Timothy 6:3–5:** *"If anyone advocates a different doctrine and does not agree with sound words, those of our Lord Jesus Christ, and with the doctrine conforming to godliness, he is conceited and understands nothing; but he has a morbid interest in controversial questions and disputes about words, out of which arise envy, strife, abusive language, evil suspicions, and constant friction between men of depraved mind and deprived of the truth, who suppose that godliness is a means of gain."*

---

[450] Sproul, R. C. (1996, c1992). *Essential Truths of the Christian Faith; 102 Hell*. Wheaton, Ill.: Tyndale House.

We read in Acts how those who lived in Berea were considered "noble"[451] because they checked what Paul was teaching against Scripture and did not just accept it.

> **Acts 17:11:** *"Now these were more noble-minded than those in Thessalonica, for they received the word with great eagerness, examining the Scriptures daily, to see whether these things were so."*

Any so called "Bible teacher" who does not tolerate being questioned based on scripture must be completely avoided.

> **1 John 4:1:** *"BELOVED, do not believe every spirit, but test the spirits to see whether they are from God; because many false prophets have gone out into the world."*

> **2 Corinthians 11:13-15:** *"For such men are false apostles, deceitful workers, disguising themselves as apostles of Christ. ¹⁴ And no wonder, for even Satan disguises himself as an angel of light. ¹⁵ Therefore it is not surprising if his servants also disguise themselves as servants of righteousness; whose end shall be according to their deeds."*

> **Galatians 1:8–9:** *"But even if we, or an angel from heaven, should preach to you a gospel contrary to what we have preached to you, he is to be accursed! As we have said before, so I say again now, if any man is preaching to you a gospel contrary to what you received, he is to be accursed!"*

2. The **Fruit Of One's Life Test** is explained by Jesus. The true believer produces Holy Spirit-led fruit in his life. That is not so with the false prophet.

> **Galatians 5:18-25:** *"But if you are led by the Spirit, you are not under the Law. ¹⁹ Now the deeds of the flesh are evident, which are: immorality, impurity, sensuality, ²⁰ idolatry, sorcery, enmities, strife, jealousy, outbursts of anger, disputes, dissensions, factions, ²¹ envying, drunkenness, carousing, and things like these, of which I forewarn you just as I have forewarned you that those who practice such things shall not inherit the kingdom of God. ²² But the fruit of the Spirit is love, joy, peace, patience, kindness, goodness, faithfulness, ²³ gentleness, self-control; against such things there is no law. ²⁴ Now those who belong to Christ Jesus have crucified the flesh with its passions and desires. ²⁵ If we live by the Spirit, let us also walk by the Spirit.*

Oswald Chambers pointed out that the difference between fake fruit and Spirit-led fruit is as follows:

"The expression of Christian character is not good doing, but Godlikeness:
If the Spirit of God has transformed you within, you will exhibit Divine

---

[451] **"Noble"** is defined in part., "**2. a.** Having or showing qualities of high moral character, such as courage, generosity, or honor: *a noble spirit.*" American Heritage Dictionary electronic edition.

characteristics in your life, not good human characteristics. God's life in us expresses itself as *God's* life, not as human life trying to be godly."[452]

The fakes may appear to be doing "good things" in the Lord's name, but they are false prophets who *"PRACTICE LAWLESSNESS."* (Note: Matthew 7:21-23.)

> **Matthew 7:15-23:** *"Beware of the false prophets, who come to you in sheep's clothing, but inwardly are ravenous wolves. [16]You will know them by their fruits. Grapes are not gathered from thorn bushes, nor figs from thistles, are they? [17] Even so, every good tree bears good fruit; but the bad tree bears bad fruit. [18] A good tree cannot produce bad fruit, nor can a bad tree produce good fruit. [19] Every tree that does not bear good fruit is cut down and thrown into the fire. [20] So then, you will know them by their fruits. [21] Not everyone who says to Me, 'Lord, Lord,' will enter the kingdom of heaven; but he who does the will of My Father who is in heaven. [22] Many will say to Me on that day, 'Lord, Lord, did we not prophesy in Your name, and in Your name cast out demons, and in Your name perform many miracles?' [23] "And then I will declare to them, 'I never knew you; DEPART FROM ME, YOU WHO PRACTICE LAWLESSNESS.'"*

Jude summarizes the doctrine and fruit of the false prophet. He makes clear that the false prophets are spiritually blind, fleshly, greedy for riches, deceivers, selfish, and desiring power over others. We are also told about their judgment.

> **Jude v.10–16:** *But these men revile the things which they do not understand; and the things which they know by instinct, like unreasoning animals, by these things they are destroyed. [11] Woe to them! For they have gone the way of Cain, and for pay they have rushed headlong into the error of Balaam, and perished in the rebellion of Korah. [12] These are the men who are hidden reefs in your love feasts when they feast with you without fear, caring for themselves; clouds without water, carried along by winds; autumn trees without fruit, doubly dead, uprooted; [13] wild waves of the sea, casting up their own shame like foam; wandering stars, for whom the black darkness has been reserved forever. [14] It was also about these men that Enoch, in the seventh generation from Adam, prophesied, saying, "Behold, the Lord came with many thousands of His holy ones, [15] to execute judgment upon all, and to convict all the ungodly of all their ungodly deeds which they have done in an ungodly way, and of all the harsh things which ungodly sinners have spoken against Him." [16] These are grumblers, finding fault, following after their own lusts; they speak arrogantly, flattering people for the sake of gaining an advantage.*

---

[452] Chambers, O. (1993, c1935). *My Utmost for His Highest: Selections for the Year* (September 20). Grand Rapids, MI: Discovery House Publishers.

The apostle John sums up the analysis between the true and the false this way:

> **1 John 3:10:** *"By this the children of God and the children of the devil are obvious: anyone who does not practice righteousness is not of God, nor the one who does not love his brother."*

We have been warned about false prophets by Jesus so that we won't be tricked by the enemy. Our Lord is not one who just leaves us out there to stumble around in the dark. He tells us what will happen. Notice in <u>Matthew 24:25,</u> He says, *"Behold, I have told you in advance."* Since He has already told us, we can take His Word, apply it, and by His working in us we are made wise and discerning.

VERSES 26-27: *"If therefore they say to you, 'Behold, He is in the wilderness,' do not go forth, or, 'Behold, He is in the inner rooms,' do not believe them . ²⁷ For just as the lightning comes from the east, and flashes even to the west, so shall the coming of the Son of Man be."*

Jesus makes it very clear to His children that they do not have to go around trying to find Him. The person who tells you that Jesus is some guru out in the wilderness is a liar, just as the one who tells you Jesus is at some secret temple. Those who go into the mountains to escape (Matthew 24:15-22) are specifically warned to not leave their hideout to go see the "Messiah" based on someone's claim that he has found Him. His appearing will be plain to see as stated in verse 27, *"For just as the lightning comes from the east, and flashes even to the west, so shall the coming of the Son of Man be."*

Acts 1:9-11 tells us more about Christ's awesome appearing:

> **Acts 1:9-11:** *"And after He had said these things, He was lifted up while they were looking on, and a cloud received Him out of their sight. ¹⁰ And as they were gazing intently into the sky while He was departing, behold, two men in white clothing stood beside them; ¹¹ and they also said, 'Men of Galilee, why do you stand looking into the sky? This Jesus, who has been taken up from you into heaven, will come in just the same way as you have watched Him go into heaven.'"*

Remember, you will not have to be told that Jesus has come back since everyone will see Him.

> **Revelation 1:7:** *"BEHOLD, HE IS COMING WITH THE CLOUDS, and every eye will see Him, even those who pierced Him; and all the tribes of the earth will mourn over Him. Even so. Amen."*

VERSE 28: *"Wherever the corpse is, there the vultures will gather."*

Dr. Walvoord states his view of the meaning of this verse:

> **"Wherever there is a carcass** (physical corruption), **vultures will** go there to eat it. Similarly, where there is spiritual corruption judgment will follow. The world will have become the domain of Satan's man, the Antichrist, the lawless one (2 Thessalonians 2:8), and many people will have been corrupted by false

prophets (Matthews 24:24). But **the Son of Man** will come quickly in judgment (v. 27)."[453]

Summary and Application

Jesus taught in Matthew 16:4 that, *"An evil and adulterous generation seeks after a sign..."* Even today we see people who only care that they see some great power, but care little about the power source. It is disturbing to hear of *Christians* who will get in their cars and drive to some place to see a "miracle man" or "be where the action is." These people are sign-seekers and not God-seekers. In the text of Matthew 24:23-27 we see that we must not let our emotions or our eyes (i.e. seeing miracles) be what dictates truth, but rather the Word of God. We further know that we do not need to follow some person who says he knows where the Lord is located. We who are in Christ will see Him clearly!

[453] Walvoord, J. F., Zuck, R. B., and Dallas Theological Seminary. (1985). *The Bible Knowledge Commentary: An Exposition of the Scriptures* (v 2, p. 78). Wheaton, IL: Victor Books..

MATTHEW 24:29-31

(CHRIST'S SECOND COMING)

²⁹ *"But immediately after the tribulation of those days* THE SUN WILL BE DARKENED, AND THE MOON WILL NOT GIVE ITS LIGHT, AND THE STARS WILL FALL *from the sky, and the powers of the heavens will be shaken,* ³⁰ *and then the sign of the Son of Man will appear in the sky, and then all the tribes of the earth will mourn, and they will see the* SON OF MAN COMING ON THE CLOUDS OF THE SKY *with power and great glory.* ³¹ *And He will send forth His angels with* A GREAT TRUMPET *and* THEY WILL GATHER TOGETHER *His elect from the four winds, from one end of the sky to the other."*

Introduction

Many people are comfortable and unthreatened by the Bible story of Jesus' coming as a baby in a manger (Matthew 1:18–2:23). Few people know about his second coming, which will be with great power and glory! This will be the most spectacular event ever in the history of the earth! From the text above, we see that after the tribulation, supernatural changes will take place in the heavens. After everyone's attention is toward the sky and its radically changed condition, the Lord will return with great power and glory.

VERSES 29: *"But immediately after the tribulation of those days* THE SUN WILL BE DARKENED, AND THE MOON WILL NOT GIVE ITS LIGHT, AND THE STARS WILL FALL *from the sky, and the powers of the heavens will be shaken,...."*

> In understanding this, we need to remember the sequence of events. First the church is raptured. Then the seven years of tribulation begins. Halfway through the tribulation (three and one-half years), the Abomination of Desolation takes place — the Antichrist defiles the temple by declaring himself God and setting up an idol in the temple. It is after the last three and one-half years (of the seven years) when verse 29 takes place (i.e. the shaking of the heavens).
>
> Notice the supernatural changes in the heavens: *"THE SUN WILL BE DARKENED, AND THE MOON WILL NOT GIVE ITS LIGHT, AND THE STARS WILL FALL from the sky, and the powers of the heavens will be shaken...."* These events have never taken place before. When it says the stars will fall from the sky, it does not mean there will be a lot of pretty "shooting stars." A so-called "shooting star" is a mere meteoroid[454] that gets so hot as a result of friction with the earth's atmosphere that it begins to glow. Verse 29 speaks of a completely different matter. It tells us that the stars will fall and the sun and moon will not give off light. Without the sun giving its light by day and the stars and moon not giving light by night, the earth will experience complete darkness. Remember, the sun has a huge effect on the earth's temperature. Consider at night how the outdoor temperature cools due to the lack of sunshine. Imagine how cold it will be when the sun is not heating the earth during the day. We also know that the sun and moon have an enormous gravitational effect on the tides. Luke say there will be a huge disturbance in the sea and its waves:

---

[454] **me·te·or·oid 1.** A solid body, moving in space, that is smaller than an asteroid and at least as large as a speck of dust. <u>American Heritage Dictionary.</u>

> **Luke 21:25-27:** *"And there will be signs in sun and moon and stars, and upon the earth dismay among nations, <u>in perplexity at the roaring of the sea and the waves,</u> ²⁶ men fainting from fear and the expectation of the things which are coming upon the world; for the powers of the heavens will be shaken. ²⁷ And then they will see the Son of Man coming in a cloud with power and great glory."*

Scripture foretells an absolute catastrophic change in the celestial body. Several centuries before Jesus' first coming, the prophet Isaiah prophesied about this with a dual fulfillment. The first fulfillment concerned the destruction of Babylon, but the prophecy's full impact is set for the End Times:

> **Isaiah 13:6-13:** *"Wail, for the <u>day of the Lord is near!</u>*
> *It will come as destruction from the Almighty.*
> *⁷ Therefore all hands will fall limp,*
> *And <u>every man's heart will melt.</u>*
> *⁸ <u>And they will be terrified,</u>*
> *Pains and anguish will take hold of them;*
> *They will writhe like a woman in labor,*
> *<u>They will look at one another in astonishment,</u>*
> *<u>Their faces aflame.</u>*
> *⁹ Behold, the day of the Lord is coming,*
> *Cruel, with fury and burning anger,*
> *To make the land a desolation;*
> *And He will exterminate its sinners from it.*
> *¹⁰ <u>For the stars of heaven and their constellations</u>*
> *<u>Will not flash forth their light;</u>*
> *<u>The sun will be dark when it rises,</u>*
> *<u>And the moon will not shed its light.</u>*
> *¹¹ Thus I will punish the world for its evil,*
> *And the wicked for their iniquity;*
> *I will also put an end to the arrogance of the proud,*
> *And abase the haughtiness of the ruthless. I will make mortal man scarcer than pure gold,*
> *¹² And mankind than the gold of Ophir.*
> *¹³ <u>Therefore I shall make the heavens tremble,</u>*
> *<u>And the earth will be shaken from its place</u>*
> *At the fury of the Lord of hosts*
> *In the day of His burning anger."*

It is in the midst of complete darkness that the return of the Lord will be made evident in this dramatic return from the sky.

VERSE 30: *"…and then the sign of the Son of Man will appear in the sky, and then all the tribes of the earth will mourn, and they will see the Son of Man coming on the clouds of the sky with power and great glory."*

This is the Second Coming! While the earth is experiencing complete darkness, a great sign will appear in the sky that the people will see. The sign will be the Lord Jesus. The response of the unbelievers will be to *"mourn."* The dictionary definition for "mourn" means to *"feel or express grief or sorrow…. to feel or express deep regret for: mourned the wasted years."*[455] Why will they mourn? There is a sorrow that leads to repentance (2 Corinthians 7:9), and there is the mourning of the unregenerate who realize that the One who they made their enemy by rejecting, attacking and killing Him, is now going to rule and reign as Lord and God. The unregenerate will mourn over their doom and possibly some may repent. We get more details about the unrepentant reaction in Revelation 6:16.

> **Revelation 6:12-17:** *"And I looked when He broke the sixth seal, and there was a great earthquake; and the sun became black as sackcloth made of hair, and the whole moon became like blood;* ¹³ *and the stars of the sky fell to the earth, as a fig tree casts its unripe figs when shaken by a great wind.* ¹⁴ *And the sky was split apart like a scroll when it is rolled up; and every mountain and island were moved out of their places.* ¹⁵ *And the kings of the earth and the great men and the commanders and the rich and the strong and every slave and free man, hid themselves in the caves and among the rocks of the mountains;* ¹⁶ *and they *said to the mountains and to the rocks, 'Fall on us and hide us from the presence of Him who sits on the throne, and from the wrath of the Lamb;* ¹⁷ *for the great day of their wrath has come; and who is able to stand?'"*

> **Revelation 1:7:** *"BEHOLD, HE IS COMING WITH THE CLOUDS, and every eye will see Him, even those who pierced Him; and all the tribes of the earth will mourn over Him. Even so. Amen."*

Clearly the call to repent comes from the angel who has the, *"eternal gospel to preach to those who live on the earth…."*

> **Revelation 14:6–7:** *"And I saw another angel flying in midheaven, having an eternal gospel to preach to those who live on the earth, and to every nation and tribe and tongue and people; and he said with a loud voice, 'Fear God, and give Him glory, because the hour of His judgment has come; worship Him who made the heaven and the earth and sea and springs of waters.'"*

Everyone will see the Lord's coming in an awesomely spectacular flash of light against the dark sky as we read from **Matthew 24:27:** *"For just as the lightning comes from the east, and flashes even to the west, so shall the coming of the Son of Man be."* Verse 30 tells us that we, *"will see the SON OF MAN COMING ON THE CLOUDS OF THE SKY with power and great glory."*

Another section of Scripture makes reference to the Lord's coming on the clouds:

> **Acts 1:9-11:** *"And after He had said these things, He was lifted up while they were looking on, and a cloud received Him out of their sight.* ¹⁰ *And as they were gazing intently into the sky while He was departing, behold, two men in white clothing stood beside them;* ¹¹ *and they also said, 'Men of Galilee, why do you stand looking into the sky? This Jesus, who has been taken up from you*

---

[455] The American Heritage Dictionary.

into heaven, will come in just the same way as you have watched Him go into heaven.'"

VERSE 31: *"And He will send forth His angels with A GREAT TRUMPET and THEY WILL GATHER TOGETHER His elect from the four winds, from one end of the sky to the other."*

After the Second Coming, the angels will gather the Christians who are still alive on the earth because they survived the Great Tribulation. These were converted through the preaching of the 144,000 witnesses and the angelic preaching set out in Revelation 14:6-7. Wiersbe points out that "Revelation 7:1–8 teaches that God will choose and seal 144,000 Jewish evangelists who will carry the kingdom message to the ends of the earth."[456]

Summary and Application

Matthew 16:1 states, *"The Pharisees and Sadducees came up, and testing Jesus, they asked Him to show them a sign from heaven."* Jesus responded in **Matthew 16:4** that, *"An evil and adulterous generation seeks after a sign...."* The hypocrites will end up getting an astronomical sign from Jesus! It will not be the sign they wanted. In Matthew 16 they claimed to want a sign so they could sit as judges against Jesus' claim that He was from God. Instead, the sign they will receive is one of absolute judgment on them, and the undisputed Lordship of Christ, The Messiah. This will be the most awesome sign of power and glory ever manifested on the earth. **Matthew 24:30** states:

> *"...and <u>then the sign of the Son of Man will appear</u> in the sky, and then all the tribes of the earth will mourn, and they will see the SON OF MAN COMING ON THE CLOUDS OF THE SKY <u>with power and great glory.</u>"*

Everyone will witness this event, whether you are alive on this earth or you have already entered eternity. The question for you is whether that day will be one of great joy and glory for your Lord and Savior, or will it be the ultimate horrifying realization of eternal judgment? Repent and turn to Christ as Savior and Lord.

> **Romans 10:12-13:** *" For there is no distinction between Jew and Greek; for the same Lord is Lord of all, abounding in riches for all who call on Him; [13] for Whoever will call on the name of the Lord will be saved."*

---

[456] Wiersbe, W. W. (1996). *The Bible Exposition Commentary* (Matthew 24:4–15). Wheaton, IL: Victor Books.

<u>MATTHEW 24:32-41</u>
(PARABLE OF THE FIG TREE and MORE ON THE END TIMES)

"Now learn the parable from the fig tree: when its branch has already become tender, and puts forth its leaves, you know that summer is near; 33 even so you too, when you see all these things, recognize that He is near, right at the door. 34 Truly I say to you, this generation will not pass away until all these things take place. 35 Heaven and earth will pass away, but My words shall not pass away. 36 But of that day and hour no one knows, not even the angels of heaven, nor the Son, but the Father alone. 37 For the coming of the Son of Man will be just like the days of Noah. 38 For as in those days which were before the flood they were eating and drinking, they were marrying and giving in marriage, until the day that Noah entered the ark, 39 and they did not understand until the flood came and took them all away; so shall the coming of the Son of Man be. 40 Then there shall be two men in the field; one will be taken, and one will be left. 41 Two women will be grinding at the mill; one will be taken, and one will be left."

<u>Introduction</u>

Here the Lord instructs us about the End Times. In His grace He has made us aware of the future events so we will not be confused when they occur. We also can take great comfort in the fact that He is in complete control and will always rule over the affairs of men.

VERSES 32-33: *"Now learn the parable from the fig tree: when its branch has already become tender, and puts forth its leaves, you know that summer is near; 33 even so you too, when you see all these things, recognize that He is near, right at the door."*

Jesus set forth many signs of the end in Matthew 24:1-31. We are instructed to take note of the signs leading to the end so it will not take us by surprise. Jesus uses the analogy of the fig tree. He explains that when the leaves appear on the fig tree, you realize that summer is very near. In the same way, when you see the signs Jesus warned of, you will know the end is very near. Verse 33 states, *"He is near,"* meaning the Second Coming of Christ is near. You can review the signs leading to the end starting with the "birth pains" and going through the changes in the heavens in Matthew 24:4-29.

VERSE 34: *"Truly I say to you, this generation will not pass away until all these things take place."*

The *generation* refers to those who are alive at the beginning of the End-Time signs. It is not referring to the generation that Jesus was addressing. This is shown by the fact that all the signs we read of in v.7-31 did not take place during that generation. All the signs will take place within one generation. We know that the total time of the Tribulation is seven-years. The time period of the signs beginning with the Abomination of Desolation (v. 15) occurs during the last three and one-half years of the seven-year period. It is this last three and one-half years of the seven year

Tribulation that is known as the "Great Tribulation" (Revelation 11:2-3). [457]

VERSE 35: *"Heaven and earth will pass away, but My words shall not pass away."*

Jesus is not using a hyperbole when He says that, *"Heaven and earth will pass away,"* because we know from scripture that one day they will. That event will occur 1000 years after Christ's Second Coming. The heavens and earth will be replaced with a new heaven and earth.

> **2 Peter 3:10-13:** *"But the day of the Lord will come like a thief, in which the heavens will pass away with a roar and the elements will be destroyed with intense heat, and the earth and its works will be burned up. [11] Since all these things are to be destroyed in this way, what sort of people ought you to be in holy conduct and godliness, [12] looking for and hastening the coming of the day of God, on account of which the heavens will be destroyed by burning, and the elements will melt with intense heat! [13] But according to His promise we are looking for new heavens and a new earth, in which righteousness dwells."*

> **Revelation 21:1:** *"And I saw a new heaven and a new earth; for the first heaven and the first earth passed away, and there is no longer any sea."*

---

[457] MacArthur states that:

"Some of those who believe Jesus was speaking of the disciples' generation claim the terrible events He mentions here refer to the destruction of Jerusalem by the Romans in A.D. 70. But as we have noted before, the events of Matthew 24 are much too universal and cataclysmic to represent the dreadful but geographically limited devastation of Jerusalem. That did not involve "'famines and earthquakes' (Matthew 24:7), believers' being 'hated by all nations' (v. 9), false Christs and false prophets (vv. 5, 11), the preaching of the gospel to the whole world (v. 14), or the abomination of desolation (v. 15). Nor were the sun darkened, the moon extinguished, or the stars dislodged from their places (v. 29). Most important of all, Jesus certainly did not appear then. It is strange logic to argue that Jesus could accurately foretell the destruction of Jerusalem some forty years hence but be mistaken about His returning at that time. Or if, as some suggest, the teaching here was merely symbolic and allegorical, with the limited destruction of Jerusalem representing the vastly greater destruction of the end time, what event in A.D. 70 could possibly have symbolized Jesus' return, which is the main subject of the discourse?

Those who hold that the fig tree is Israel usually affirm that **this generation** refers to the Jewish people, indicating they would **not pass away** as a race **until these things take place**. That idea is true, and the perpetuity of the Jews is clearly taught elsewhere in Scripture, but it does not seem to fit this context, All Jews firmly believed in God's promise of an everlasting kingdom of David, and for Jesus to have meant that the Jews would survive until the Messiah ushered in His kingdom would have been superfluous and pointless. And if Jesus had intended that meaning, He could easily have referred to the Jews as 'My people,' 'God's people,' or the like. To allude to them as **this generation** would seem obtuse and confusing."

MacArthur, J. F., Jr. (1985). Matthew. MacArthur New Testament Commentary (p. 249). Chicago: Moody Press.

The Word of God is unmovable. It will never fade away. It can be counted on more than anything. This is great assurance to the believer. When God tells us in His Word that we are forgiven by His grace, we can have complete assurance that we are forgiven. We do not have to feel forgiven or even be "pretty sure that we are." By God's Word, we know that we are forgiven and have a place in heaven with Him.

> **Hebrews 4:12:** *"For the word of God is living and active and sharper than any two-edged sword, and piercing as far as the division of soul and spirit, of both joints and marrow, and able to judge the thoughts and intentions of the heart."*

> **Isaiah 40:8:** *"The grass withers, the flower fades,*
> *But the word of our God stands forever."*

VERSE 36: *"But of that day and hour no one knows, not even the angels of heaven, nor the Son, but the Father alone."*

No one can ever tell you that Jesus is coming on a certain day or hour. No human knows. The one who claims to know this would be a false prophet because he violated what Scripture states plainly in verse 37. We are told to keep an eye on the signs pointing to the End Times. When a matter is repeated, it is usually done so for emphasis. Many times during this section Jesus reiterates that we do not know the day of His coming, but must always be ready. Look at the following verses:

> **Matthew 24:42-44:** *"<u>Therefore be on the alert, for you do not know which day your Lord is coming.</u> 43 But be sure of this, that if the head of the house had known at what time of the night the thief was coming, he would have been on the alert and would not have allowed his house to be broken into. 44 <u>For this reason you be ready too; for the Son of Man is coming at an hour when you do not think He will.</u>"*

In the parable of the Ten Virgins in **Matthew 25:13** we read:
> *"Be on the alert then, <u>for you do not know the day nor the hour."</u>*

In Matthew 24:36 Jesus states that He does not know the day assigned for His Return, but only the Father knows. Note that after Jesus' resurrection, He does not explicitly state that He does not know the *times or epochs* (Acts 1:6-7) but rather that it is not for the *disciples* to know the *times or epochs*. He does not include Himself in that limited knowledge.
> **Acts 1:6-7:** *"And so when they had come together, they were asking Him, saying, 'Lord, is it at this time You are restoring the kingdom to Israel?' 7 He said to them, '<u>It is not for you to know times or epochs which the Father has fixed</u> by His own authority;....'"*

It must be remembered that Jesus was fully man and fully God.
> **John 1:1, 14:** *"IN the beginning was the Word, and the Word was with God, and the Word was God....*
> *14 And the Word became flesh, and dwelt among us, and we beheld His glory, glory as of the only begotten from the Father, full of grace and truth."*

While Jesus was on earth there were times that He would restrict Himself of some of His divine authority…(*"no one knows, not even the angels of heaven, nor the Son, but the Father alone." v.36*). But after the resurrection we read that He walks in His full divine authority… He is the risen Lord.[458] *"And Jesus came up and spoke to them, saying, 'All authority has been given to Me in heaven and on earth.'"* **Matthew 28:18**. The *resurrected* Jesus, does know the exact day and hour the Father has set for His return (Acts 1:6-7).

> **Ephesians 1:20-23:** *"… which He brought about in Christ, when He raised Him from the dead, and seated Him at His right hand in the heavenly places, 21 far above all rule and authority and power and dominion, and every name that is named, not only in this age, but also in the one to come. 22 And He put all things in subjection under His feet, and gave Him as head over all things to the church, 23 which is His body, the fullness of Him who fills all in all."*

VERSES 37-39: *"For the coming of the Son of Man will be just like the days of Noah. 38 For as in those days which were before the flood they were eating and drinking, they were marrying and giving in marriage, until the day that Noah entered the ark, 39 and they did not understand until the flood came and took them all away; so shall the coming of the Son of Man be."*

Scripture makes it clear that right up to the end people will be consumed with their regular affairs such as *"… eating and drinking, they were marrying"* (v. 38). These were the same activities that were going on at the time Noah entered the ark, just before the Great Flood. The story of Noah can be found in Genesis 6:9-9:17.

---

[458] Here are some examples of Jesus' humanity and divine nature as shown in scripture. Examples of His manhood are that He was: tempted (Luke 4:1-13), tired (John 4:6), hungry (Matthew 4:2), thirsty (John 19:28), slept (Matthew 8:24), and died (Mark 15:39-45, Matthew 27:50). Examples of His divine nature are that He was: born of a virgin (Luke 1:30-38), did miracles, (John 11:38-44, Luke 7:21-23), never sinned (2 Corinthians 5:21), and rose from the dead (1 Corinthians 15:3-8, Matthew 28:5-15, John 21:14).

"Christ is God and man by a hypostatic or personal union, both natures, divine and human, remaining distinct without composition or confusion, in one and the same person."
> Vincent, T. (1996). *A Family Instructional Guide*. Index created by Christian Classics Foundation. (electronic edition based on the first Banner of Truth ed., 1980.) (P. 73). Simpsonville SC: Christian Classics Foundation.

"This union also was not established by mixing these two natures, with a third type of person coming forth. Rather, this union was established *without change and without mixture*, each nature retaining its own attributes; each nature contributes its attributes to the Person. Thus, the same Christ has divine as well as human attributes by virtue of the union of these two natures in Him. However, the one nature does not have the attributes of the other nature. The union of these two natures in one Person has three consequences— *communication of: 1) gifts and honor, 2) attributes*, and *3) activity and office*. a Brakel, W. (1996, c1992)." *The Christian's Reasonable Service, Volumes 1 and 2*. Published in electronic form by Christian Classics Foundation, 1996. (electronic ed. of the first publication in the English language, based on the 3rd edition of the original Dutch work.) (Vol. 1, pp. 505-506). Morgan PA: Soli Deo Gloria Publications.

2 Peter 3:3-13: *"Know this first of all, that in the last days mockers will come with their mocking, following after their own lusts, ⁴ and saying, 'Where is the promise of His coming? For ever since the fathers fell asleep, all continues just as it was from the beginning of creation.' ⁵ <u>For when they maintain this, it escapes their notice that by the word of God the heavens existed long ago and the earth was formed out of water and by water, ⁶ through which the world at that time was destroyed, being flooded with water.</u> ⁷ But the present heavens and earth by His word are being reserved for fire, kept for the day of judgment and destruction of ungodly men. ⁸ But do not let this one fact escape your notice, beloved, that with the Lord one day is as a thousand years, and a thousand years as one day. ⁹ The Lord is not slow about His promise, as some count slowness, but is patient toward you, not wishing for any to perish but for all to come to repentance. ¹⁰ But the day of the Lord will come like a thief, in which the heavens will pass away with a roar and the elements will be destroyed with intense heat, and the earth and its works will be burned up. ¹¹ Since all these things are to be destroyed in this way, what sort of people ought you to be in holy conduct and godliness, ¹² looking for and hastening the coming of the day of God, on account of which the heavens will be destroyed by burning, and the elements will melt with intense heat! ¹³ But according to His promise we are looking for new heavens and a new earth, in which righteousness dwells."*

VERSES 40-41: *"Then there shall be two men in the field; one will be taken, and one will be left. ⁴¹ Two women will be grinding at the mill; one will be taken, and one will be left."*

These verses are not about the rapture. The ones "taken" are the wicked who are "taken" into judgment. Often verses 40-41 are mistakenly interpreted to mean that the believers are taken away. Remember that during the days of Noah it was the wicked who were taken away into judgment. Likewise those taken in verses 40 and 41 are those who go into judgment.

The righteous will be left on the earth with Jesus as He rules and reigns in His millennial kingdom. The story of the *sheep and the goats* in Matthew 25 demonstrates this point. Review that story which demonstrates that the righteous will dwell in the kingdom and the wicked will be taken away.

> **Matthew 25:33-34:** *"…and He will put the sheep on His right, and the goats on the left. ³⁴ Then the King will say to those on His right, 'Come, you who are blessed of My Father, inherit the kingdom prepared for you from the foundation of the world.'"*

But as for the goats, judgment:

> **Matthew 25:46:** *"And these will go away into eternal punishment, but the righteous into eternal life."*

Summary and Application

In Matthew 24:32-41 Jesus reinforces the importance of seeing the signs of the End. How gracious of the Lord to let us know ahead of time about this terrible era. If one is aware of what is going to happen, he will be more comforted during it. The great comfort is that despite all of the judgment occurring, the Christian knows that he is in the ever-loving arms of our Lord, who will rule and reign in the end.

Job 19:25: *"As for me, I know that my Redeemer lives,*
And at the last He will take His stand on the earth."

<u>MATTHEW 24:42-51</u>
(THE BELIEVERS' RESPONSIBILITY TO BE FAITHFUL
AND ALERT IN LOOKING FOR THE LORD'S RETURN)

[42] *"Therefore be on the alert, for you do not know which day your Lord is coming.* [43] *But be sure of this, that if the head of the house had known at what time of the night the thief was coming, he would have been on the alert and would not have allowed his house to be broken into.* [44] *For this reason you be ready too; for the Son of Man is coming at an hour when you do not think He will.*

[45] *Who then is the faithful and sensible slave whom his master put in charge of his household to give them their food at the proper time?* [46] *Blessed is that slave whom his master finds so doing when he comes.* [47] *Truly I say to you, that he will put him in charge of all his possessions.* [48] *But if that evil slave says in his heart, 'My master is not coming for a long time,'* [49] *and shall begin to beat his fellow slaves and eat and drink with drunkards;* [50] *the master of that slave will come on a day when he does not expect him and at an hour which he does not know,* [51] *and shall cut him in pieces and assign him a place with the hypocrites; weeping shall be there and the gnashing of teeth."*

Introduction

In these verses the Lord reinforces the importance of His people looking for His return. Remember that the *times* specifically addressed in Matthew 24 deal with the Second Coming of Christ and not the rapture of the church. With that said, I would note that there are many great theologians who have different eschatological viewpoints (i.e. different theological views on the end times order of events.).

Even though this section of Scripture is not the teaching on the time period of the rapture, it remains very important for all Christians, at all times, to be alert, faithful, and, *"looking for the blessed hope and the appearing of the glory of our great God and Savior, Christ Jesus;...."* **Titus 2:13**. Regardless of which end-times view you hold to, scripture is clear, no man knows the day of the Lord's return. Because of that fact, we are to be ready to meet the Lord whether it is by His unexpected return or our sudden death.

<u>VERSE 42:</u> *"Therefore be on the alert, for you do not know which day your Lord is coming."*

> This verse sets forth the point Jesus is making. We are not to be slack in our service to Him. In previous verses Jesus explained some of the signs of His return. Here, He makes it clear we do not know the day that the Lord is coming.

<u>VERSES 43-44:</u> *"But be sure of this, that if the head of the house had known at what time of the night the thief was coming, he would have been on the alert and would not have allowed his house to be broken into.* [44] *For this reason you be ready too; for the Son of Man is coming at an hour when you do not think He will."*

> In verses 43 and 44 Jesus gives the illustration of how important it is that we are alert to His return. Few images can be as frightening as to be laying in your bed, sound asleep, while a criminal is quietly entering your home. Not only are your possessions at risk, but so is your very

life. Think how vulnerable you are lying unconscious while the burglar is wide awake, armed, and ready to attack. Obviously, Jesus is not comparing Himself to a thief, but the analogy is similar in the unexpectedness of that type of occurrence. Look at the verses below:

> **Revelation 3:3:** *"Remember therefore what you have received and heard; and keep it, and repent. If therefore you will not wake up, <u>I will come like a thief, and you will not know at what hour</u> I will come upon you."*

> **Revelation 16:15:** *"<u>Behold, I am coming like a thief.</u> Blessed is the one who stays awake and keeps his garments, lest he walk about naked and men see his shame."*

> **2 Peter 3:10-13:** *"But the day of the <u>Lord will come like a thief,</u> in which the heavens will pass away with a roar and the elements will be destroyed with intense heat, and the earth and its works will be burned up. [11] Since all these things are to be destroyed in this way, what sort of people ought you to be in holy conduct and godliness, [12] looking for and hastening the coming of the day of God, on account of which the heavens will be destroyed by burning, and the elements will melt with intense heat! [13] But according to His promise we are looking for new heavens and a new earth, in which righteousness dwells."*

In summary, what would you do to protect yourself, your family and your property if you knew <u>for a fact</u> that a robber was going to try to break into your home tonight? The bottom line is that you would be ready for him. We are to have that same expectant attitude toward Jesus' return. We should be busy doing His work for His glory. It is all about the King and His Kingdom!

VERSES 45-51: *"Who then is the faithful and sensible slave whom his master put in charge of his household to give them their food at the proper time? [46] Blessed is that slave whom his master finds so doing when he comes. [47] Truly I say to you, that he will put him in charge of all his possessions. [48] But if that evil slave says in his heart, 'My master is not coming for a long time,' [49] and shall begin to beat his fellow slaves and eat and drink with drunkards; [50] the master of that slave will come on a day when he does not expect him and at an hour which he does not know, [51] and shall cut him in pieces and assign him a place with the hypocrites; weeping shall be there and the gnashing of teeth."*

Jesus gives another example of how important it is that we are obedient and faithful disciples until His return. Scripture makes it clear, there are rewards for those who are found faithful as His servants in every aspect of their lives. Faithful servanthood is especially important to those God has put under your ministry care:

> **1 Peter 5:1-4:** *"Therefore, I exhort the elders among you, as your fellow elder and witness of the sufferings of Christ, and a partaker also of the glory that is to be revealed, [2] shepherd the flock of God among you, <u>exercising oversight not under compulsion</u>, but voluntarily, according to the will of God; and <u>not for sordid gain</u>, but with eagerness; [3] <u>nor yet as lording it over</u> those allotted to your charge, but proving to <u>be examples to the flock</u>. [4] And when the Chief Shepherd appears, you will receive the unfading crown of glory."*

Part of that faithfulness is remembering that the money earned from our employment is really the Lord's money on loan to us, to use for His glory.

> **Luke 16:10-11:** *"He who is faithful in a very little thing is faithful also in much; and he who is unrighteous in a very little thing is unrighteous also in much. ¹¹ If therefore you have not been faithful in the use of unrighteous mammon, who will entrust the true riches to you?"*

Jesus also makes it clear that the unbeliever does not really concern himself with when the master returns. There are many today who are like that "evil slave" who have a view that they are going to live by the flesh while they are young, and when they get older they will "get religion." Their destruction will come upon them before they can anticipate it. Those who think they will take care of this "God thing" later are like the foolish ones we read about in Matthew 25 who were not ready:

> **Matthew 25:1-13:** *"Then the kingdom of heaven will be comparable to ten virgins, who took their lamps, and went out to meet the bridegroom. ² And five of them were foolish, and five were prudent. ³ For when the foolish took their lamps, they took no oil with them, ⁴ but the prudent took oil in flasks along with their lamps. ⁵ Now while the bridegroom was delaying, they all got drowsy and began to sleep. ⁶ But at midnight there was a shout, 'Behold, the bridegroom! Come out to meet him.' ⁷ Then all those virgins rose, and trimmed their lamps. ⁸ And the foolish said to the prudent, 'Give us some of your oil, for our lamps are going out.' ⁹ But the prudent answered, saying, 'No, there will not be enough for us and you too; go instead to the dealers and buy some for yourselves.' ¹⁰ And while they were going away to make the purchase, the bridegroom came, and those who were ready went in with him to the wedding feast; and the door was shut. ¹¹ And later the other virgins also came, saying, 'Lord, lord, open up for us.' ¹² But he answered and said, 'Truly I say to you, I do not know you.' ¹³ Be on the alert then, for you do not know the day nor the hour."*

We must always have an attitude of readiness and anticipation for the Lord's return. Jesus reinforces and warns us about this matter in many places in Scripture. We will study more about these warnings in Matthew 25.

Summary and Application

How can you live your life at a higher level of faithfulness to the Lord in anticipation of His return? As I mentioned previously, regardless of which end-times view you hold, Scripture is clear, no man knows exactly the day of the Lord's return. Because of that fact, our meeting of the Lord, whether by His unexpected return, or our sudden death, should be one in which we are ready, faithful, and diligently being about the Father's business as good slaves of Christ (Luke 12:37-38). One last verse that encompasses this entire issue is penned by Paul to the Thessalonians.

> **1 Thessalonians 5:2-9:** *"For you yourselves know full well that the day of the Lord will come just like a thief in the night. ³ While they are saying, 'Peace and safety!' then destruction will come upon them suddenly like birth pangs upon a woman with child; and they shall not escape. ⁴ But you, brethren, are not in darkness, that the day should overtake you like a thief; ⁵ for you are all sons of light and sons of day. We are not of night nor of darkness; ⁶ so then let us not sleep as others do, but let us be alert and*

sober. [7] For those who sleep do their sleeping at night, and those who get drunk get drunk at night. [8] But since we are of the day, let us be sober, having put on the breastplate of faith and love, and as a helmet, the hope of salvation. [9] For God has not destined us for wrath, but for obtaining salvation through our Lord Jesus Christ,"

Jesus tells us to take advantage of the moment and do His work as faithful slaves:

John 9:4: *"We must work the works of Him who sent Me as long as it is day; night is coming when no one can work."*

MATTHEW 25:1-13
(THE PARABLE OF THE TEN VIRGINS – PREPAREDNESS FOR THE LORD'S RETURN)

"THEN the kingdom of heaven will be comparable to ten virgins, who took their lamps, and went out to meet the bridegroom. ² And five of them were foolish, and five were prudent. ³ For when the foolish took their lamps, they took no oil with them, ⁴ but the prudent took oil in flasks along with their lamps. ⁵ Now while the bridegroom was delaying, they all got drowsy and began to sleep. ⁶ But at midnight there was a shout, 'Behold, the bridegroom! Come out to meet him.' ⁷ Then all those virgins rose, and trimmed their lamps. ⁸ And the foolish said to the prudent, 'Give us some of your oil, for our lamps are going out.' ⁹ But the prudent answered, saying, 'No, there will not be enough for us and you too; go instead to the dealers and buy some for yourselves.' ¹⁰ And while they were going away to make the purchase, the bridegroom came, and those who were ready went in with him to the wedding feast; and the door was shut. ¹¹ And later the other virgins also came, saying, 'Lord, lord, open up for us.' ¹² But he answered and said, 'Truly I say to you, I do not know you.' ¹³ Be on the alert then, for you do not know the day nor the hour."

Introduction

The closing verses in Matthew 24 reemphasized the importance of being ready, alert and faithful for the Lord's return. In chapter 25 Jesus continues on the subject of the End Times. The time period that Jesus is speaking of here is during the tribulation. After the tribulation, Jesus will return to earth, which is the Second Coming of Jesus. The parable of the 10 virgins reinforces the importance of preparedness for the Lord's return.

VERSES 1-4: *"THEN the kingdom of heaven will be comparable to ten virgins, who took their lamps, and went out to meet the bridegroom. ² And five of them were foolish, and five were prudent. ³ For when the foolish took their lamps, they took no oil with them, ⁴ but the prudent took oil in flasks along with their lamps."*

Jesus continues to give us insight into the kingdom of heaven. We have seen in previous parables that often there is a contrast among the real Christians and the *look-alikes* (wheat and the tares, different soils in the sower and the seed, etc.). Notice here that the distinguishing difference between the true Christians and the false believers (i.e. fakes). Those who are true are *"prudent"* and the fakes are *"foolish."* We see that the prudent made preparations for the bridegroom's arrival but the foolish thought they would take care of the need for oil later. Many people today think they can take care of spiritual matters later in life, but will find that they are too late.

VERSES 5-9: *"Now while the bridegroom was delaying, they all got drowsy and began to sleep. ⁶ But at midnight there was a shout, 'Behold, the bridegroom! Come out to meet him.' ⁷ Then all those virgins rose, and trimmed their lamps. ⁸ And the foolish said to the prudent, 'Give us some of your oil, for our lamps are going out.' ⁹ But the prudent answered, saying, 'No, there will not be enough for us and you too; go instead to the dealers and buy some for yourselves.'"*

The bridegroom in this story is the Lord Jesus. His arrival is His Second Coming. In Jesus' day, it was a common custom that on the wedding day the bridegroom went and retrieved his wife from her parents' home. Often it was unknown when that day would be until the bridegroom began his march to his bride-elect's home. Those who were part of the wedding party were picked up on the way to get the bride. The "virgins" would be the bridesmaids and thus part of the wedding party. The lamps were actually a form of a torch. *New Bible Dictionary* explains the term "lamp" as follows:

> "In the parable of the virgins (Matthew 25:1–13). The conventional lamp was for indoor use, and what was needed (and what is still sometimes used) at a wedding was a TORCH. The rags which formed its wick needed to be soaked in oil. It seems that the foolish virgins had no oil at all (v. 3), and therefore when they lit their torches they went out instantly (v. 8). The wise had taken oil in separate containers ready for use at the appropriate moment. The difference between them seems to have been not in the quantity of oil that they possessed but in the fact of their possessing or not possessing any at all."[459]

The foolish women's problem was not one of having enough oil, but more basic than that, they did not possess any oil at all (v.3 *"For when the foolish took their lamps, they took no oil with them...."*). The fake Christian also has this problem. He may dress like, speak like, and participate in the church just like the real believers, but he has never been converted. The problem is not a small amount of the Holy Spirit in him, but rather the complete lack of the Spirit in him. One cannot have "some" of God. Either he is possessed by the Holy Spirit and thus saved, or he is not possessed by the Holy Spirit and thus damned. Dr. Walvoord put it this way:

> "Though this passage does not specifically interpret the meaning of the oil, many commentators see it as representing the Holy Spirit and His work in salvation. Salvation is more than mere profession for it involves regeneration by the Holy Spirit. Those who will merely profess to be saved, and do not actually possess the Spirit, will be excluded from the feast, that is, the kingdom." [460]

Reread verses 8-9: *"And the foolish said to the prudent, 'Give us some of your oil, for our lamps are going out.' ⁹But the prudent answered, saying, 'No, there will not be enough for us and you too;'...."* The foolish think that they can have God passed on to them from others. Scripture makes it clear that a person is saved by God. Likewise the saved person cannot go out and save someone else. God alone is the Author of Salvation. It is true that one can share the truth of the Gospel with another, who then believes and is saved. Sharing the message is a completely different matter than being a person's savior. One cannot intrinsically get saved by having it passed on to him. One does not become a true Christian just because he has parents who are believers. In the same way, a church cannot transform you into a Christian by having you participate in its religious rituals or rites.

---

[459] Wood, D. R. W. (1996). *New Bible Dictionary* (3rd ed.) (p. 663). Leicester, England; Downers Grove, Ill.: InterVarsity Press.

[460] Walvoord, J. F., Zuck, R. B., and Dallas Theological Seminary. (1985). *The Bible Knowledge Commentary: An Exposition of the Scriptures* (v. 2, p. 80). Wheaton, IL: Victor Books..

In verse 9 it states, "…*go instead to the dealers and buy some for yourselves.*" Jesus is not saying that one can purchase the Holy Spirit or God's Salvation. Remember in Acts when Simon the Sorcerer wanted to buy the power of God?

> **Acts 8:17-24:** *"Then they began laying their hands on them, and they were receiving the Holy Spirit. [18] Now when Simon saw that the Spirit was bestowed through the laying on of the apostles' hands, he offered them money, [19] saying, 'Give this authority to me as well, so that everyone on whom I lay my hands may receive the Holy Spirit.' [20] But Peter said to him, 'May your silver perish with you, because you thought you could obtain the gift of God with money! [21] You have no part or portion in this matter, for your heart is not right before God. [22] Therefore repent of this wickedness of yours, and pray the Lord that if possible, the intention of your heart may be forgiven you. [23] For I see that you are in the gall of bitterness and in the bondage of iniquity.' [24] But Simon answered and said, 'Pray to the Lord for me yourselves, so that nothing of what you have said may come upon me.'"*

When the prudent virgins told the foolish to go buy some oil themselves, it should be understood that there was a time when the oil was available for the foolish virgins to buy, but they just put it off until later. Now it is too late in the night and the oil salesmen have long since closed their shops for the day. This is the same way with salvation. It is available for all, but all do not receive it. Some think they will wait for another day to get serious about God, but the reality is what Jesus says:

> **Matthew 24:44:** *"For this reason you be ready too;*
> *for the Son of Man is coming at an hour*
> *when you do not think He will."*
> (See also: Hebrews 4:6–7.)

VERSES 10-12: *"And while they were going away to make the purchase, the bridegroom came, and those who were ready went in with him to the wedding feast; and the door was shut. [11] And later the other virgins also came, saying, 'Lord, lord, open up for us.' [12] But he answered and said, 'Truly I say to you, I do not know you.'"*

We see the bridegroom's arrival, and that those who were ready went into the wedding party.

> **Revelation 19:7-9:** *"Let us rejoice and be glad and give the glory to Him, for the marriage of the Lamb has come and His bride has made herself ready. [8] And it was given to her to clothe herself in fine linen, bright and clean; for the fine linen is the righteous acts of the saints. [9] And he *said to me, 'Write, 'Blessed are those who are invited to the marriage supper of the Lamb.' And he *said to me, 'These are true words of God.'"*

In verse 11 we hear the virgins begging to be let in: *"Lord, lord, open up for us."* The bridegroom's response was, *"I do not know you."* What a terrible thing to hear from the mouth of Almighty God. Those who do not come to Him in faith will hear those words. They may point out the things they claim to have done for Him or their religious pedigrees, but His answer is the same:

> **Matthew 7:21-23:** *"Not everyone who says to Me, 'Lord, Lord,' will enter the kingdom of heaven; but he who does the will of My Father who is in heaven. [22]*

Many will say to Me on that day, 'Lord, Lord, did we not prophesy in Your name, and in Your name cast out demons, and in Your name perform many miracles?' [23] And then I will declare to them, 'I never knew you; DEPART FROM ME, YOU WHO PRACTICE LAWLESSNESS.'"

<u>Luke 13:25-28:</u> *"Once the head of the house gets up and shuts the door, and you begin to stand outside and knock on the door, saying, 'Lord, open up to us!' then He will answer and say to you, 'I do not know where you are from.' [26] Then you will begin to say, 'We ate and drank in Your presence, and You taught in our streets'; [27] and He will say, 'I tell you, I do not know where you are from; depart from Me, all you evildoers.' [28] There will be weeping and gnashing of teeth there when you see Abraham and Isaac and Jacob and all the prophets in the kingdom of God, but yourselves being cast out."*

<u>VERSE 13:</u> *"Be on the alert then, for you do not know the day nor the hour."*

This verse summarizes the entire point of the lesson: *True Christians must be prepared to see the Lord's return.* The Lord's return is not to take us by surprise like it will the false believers. The true believer knows that it could occur at any moment and is busy about the Father's business. We must work and serve the Lord today, tomorrow, and until we die or He returns. Since we do not know when that is, we should take advantage of every opportunity.

<u>John 9:4:</u> *"We must work the works of Him who sent Me, as long as it is day; night is coming, when no man can work."*

Summary and Application

The Christian life is one of death to self and service to God. One cannot earn his salvation as is pointed out in Ephesians 2:8-9, but after he is saved, good works will flow out of us as a result of that salvation (Ephesians 2:10). The parable of the 10 virgins points out again the importance of being prepared for the Lord's return. It is also important for all believers to remember that they do not know when their time on earth is up, and thus they should do the work of the Lord.

<u>Hebrews 9:27:</u> *"And inasmuch as it is appointed for men to die once and after this comes judgment,.... "*

<u>MATTHEW 25:14-30</u>
(PARABLE OF THE TALENTS; and REWARD OF FAITHFUL SERVICE)

"For it is just like a man about to go on a journey, who called his own slaves, and entrusted his possessions to them. ¹⁵ And to one he gave five talents, to another, two, and to another, one, each according to his own ability; and he went on his journey. ¹⁶ Immediately the one who had received the five talents went and traded with them, and gained five more talents. ¹⁷ In the same manner the one who had received the two talents gained two more. ¹⁸ But he who received the one talent went away and dug in the ground, and hid his master's money. ¹⁹ Now after a long time the master of those slaves *came and *settled accounts with them. ²⁰ And the one who had received the five talents came up and brought five more talents, saying, 'Master, you entrusted five talents to me; see, I have gained five more talents.' ²¹ His master said to him, 'Well done, good and faithful slave; you were faithful with a few things, I will put you in charge of many things, enter into the joy of your master.' ²² The one also who had received the two talents came up and said, 'Master, you entrusted to me two talents; see, I have gained two more talents.' ²³ His master said to him, 'Well done, good and faithful slave; you were faithful with a few things, I will put you in charge of many things; enter into the joy of your master.' ²⁴ And the one also who had received the one talent came up and said, 'Master, I knew you to be a hard man, reaping where you did not sow, and gathering where you scattered no seed. ²⁵ And I was afraid, and went away and hid your talent in the ground; see, you have what is yours.' ²⁶ But his master answered and said to him, 'You wicked, lazy slave, you knew that I reap where I did not sow, and gather where I scattered no seed. ²⁷ Then you ought to have put my money in the bank, and on my arrival I would have received my money back with interest. ²⁸ Therefore take away the talent from him, and give it to the one who has the ten talents.' ²⁹ For to everyone who has shall more be given, and he shall have an abundance; but from the one who does not have, even what he does have shall be taken away. ³⁰ And cast out the worthless slave into the outer darkness; in that place there shall be weeping and gnashing of teeth."

Introduction

This parable is called the parable of the talents. MacArthur points out that this parable is separate and distinct from the parable of the minas in the book of Luke:

> "It should be noted that, despite some resemblances, the parable of the talents and the parable of the minas (Luke 19:11–27) are not variations of the same story. The mina parable was given several days earlier, and the two accounts have as many differences as similarities."[461]

Let us first review the context of this parable. If we go back to the previous 23 verses (Matthew 24:42-51 – 25:13), we see Jesus emphasize the theme of being faithful, ready and alert for the Lord's return. In Matthew 25:1-13 Jesus specifically tells us that we are to be the true Christians who are prepared to see the Lord's return. His return is not to take us by surprise like it will the false believer. The true believer knows and believes that the Lord is coming and is busy being about the Father's business. We must work and serve the Lord today, tomorrow, and onward until we leave this earth. Since we do not know when our time is done, we should take advantage of every opportunity. That theme should serve as the

---

[461] MacArthur, J. F., Jr. (1985). *Matthew.* MacArthur New Testament Commentary (p. 249). Chicago: Moody Press.

backdrop for this next parable, which is called the parable of the talents. It is often mistakenly taught to mean that we are to use our natural talents well. The parable means much more than that. All three servants claim devotion to the Master. Two of them prove that they are true servants of the Master by being about his business while he is gone. The third, who claimed to be a servant, proves that he is not. His own mouth confesses what he really thinks of the Master when he says, *"Master, I knew you to be a hard man, reaping where you did not sow, and gathering where you scattered no seed."* This parable also speaks of rewards for the believer measured in quality, not quantity.

VERSES 14-15: *"For it is just like a man about to go on a journey, who called his own slaves, and entrusted his possessions to them. 15 And to one he gave five talents, to another, two, and to another, one, each according to his own ability; and he went on his journey."*

Verse 14 starts out, *"For it."* The "it" is the *"kingdom of heaven."* As mentioned earlier, the parable must be read in its context. We see that this parable occurs right after the parable of the 10 virgins. The parable of the 10 virgins starts out in Matthew 25:1 by stating: *"Then the kingdom of heaven will be comparable to ten virgins, who took their lamps, and went out to meet the bridegroom."* The parable of the 10 virgins teaches, among other things, that there will be both true Christians and false ones here on earth. This group of both the true and false Christians is the outward appearing church, or otherwise referred to as the *visible* kingdom of heaven. MacArthur explains that the *invisible* kingdom of heaven is composed only of those who are the real Christians (i.e. those who have been converted). Remember that all 10 bridesmaids *claimed to know the bridegroom*, but only five truly did (more specifically, only five were known by the bridegroom). The parable of the talents is similar. In it the Master has three people who claim to be His servants, but only two are true servants.

In Matthew 25:14 we see that the Master in this parable is Jesus and He has entrusted His servants with His possessions to watch over while He is gone. The concept of *entrustment* [462] is to not simply "guard and return" like the "worthless slave" did. Godly entrustment means to use and prosper the Master's interest. In other words, the servants are to do what the Master Himself would do with His own possessions (i.e. prosper and multiply them). In the parable the term talent refers to money: "...the talents were of silver (money in Matthew 25:18 is argyrion, which means silver money). A talent weighed between 58 and 80 pounds."[463]

VERSES 16-18: *"Immediately the one who had received the five talents went and traded with them, and gained five more talents. 17 In the same manner the one who had received the two talents gained two more. 18 But he who received the one talent went away and dug in the ground, and hid his master's money."*

Here we see what each servant did with what was entrusted to him. Notice in verse 16 that the one who received five talents did not sit around for a while and then start to put them to work. The verse says, *"**Immediately,**"* he went out and traded and obtained a profit. The second

---

[462] A *trustee* is defined in part by Webster as, "a natural or legal person to whom property is legally committed to be administered for the benefit of a beneficiary."

[463] Walvoord, J. F. (1983-c1985). *The Bible Knowledge Commentary: An Exposition of the Scriptures* (Matthew 25:14). Wheaton, IL: Victor Books.

servant also went right to work, *"In the same manner...."* The third one removed himself from the others and hid the money, *"...went away and dug in the ground, and hid his master's money."*

VERSES 19-23: *"Now after a long time the master of those slaves *came and *settled accounts with them.* ²⁰*And the one who had received the five talents came up and brought five more talents, saying, 'Master, you entrusted five talents to me; see, I have gained five more talents.'* ²¹ *His master said to him, 'Well done, good and faithful slave; you were faithful with a few things, I will put you in charge of many things, enter into the joy of your master.'* ²² *The one also who had received the two talents came up and said, 'Master, you entrusted to me two talents; see, I have gained two more talents.'* ²³ *His master said to him, 'Well done, good and faithful slave; you were faithful with a few things, I will put you in charge of many things; enter into the joy of your master.'"*

Here we see the rewards given for faithful service. The one with five talents doubled them. The servant with two talents doubled them as well. So the one who made five extra talents produced two and one-half times as much as the one who had two talents, but when viewed in raw percentage of increase, they both produced the same by doubling what they each had been given. Notice that both of them were given the same compliment: *"...Well done, good and faithful slave; you were faithful with a few things, I will put you in charge of many things, enter into the joy of your master."* (v.21 and 23). God looks at the <u>quality</u> of our work and not just the quantity. Quality also takes on the issue of our heart attitude. Are we serving God so others think well of us? This is a pharisaical view from which we must repent. We are to serve with a view to please God.

VERSES 24-27: *"And the one also who had received the one talent came up and said, 'Master, I knew you to be a hard man, reaping where you did not sow, and gathering where you scattered no seed.* ²⁵ *And I was afraid, and went away and hid your talent in the ground; see, you have what is yours.'* ²⁶ *But his master answered and said to him, 'You wicked, lazy slave, you knew that I reap where I did not sow, and gather where I scattered no seed.* ²⁷ *Then you ought to have put my money in the bank, and on my arrival I would have received my money back with interest.'"*

Here we see the response of the wicked slave. He is a false servant. He may say the right things when the Master is around, but he does not love him in his heart. The truth is that the wicked slave is like a false Christian who on the outside makes all kinds of claims of loyalty, but actually despises the Master in his heart: *"I knew you to be a hard man, reaping where you did not sow, and gathering where you scattered no seed."* This is how many view Christ today. They may say they are God's servants, but they do not believe and love Him from their hearts. They see God as hard and one who keeps them from having fun. They do not understand a true love for their Master because they have never been converted. The true believer knows that whatever God says is best for him or her.

The Master is not agreeing with the slave's assessment of himself when he says, *"...you knew that I reap where I did not sow, and gather where I scattered no seed.* ²⁷ *Then you ought to have put my money in the bank, and on my arrival I would have received my money back with interest."* Notice that the Master does not agree with the servant by saying, "Yes, that is true." Instead, the Master's reply is an accurate evaluation of the servant's heart and attitude: *"You wicked, lazy slave....*" The Master then goes on to ask, if he thought him so hard, why he didn't simply put the money in the bank to get interest? Notice that this false servant did not produce a little, but rather he produced <u>nothing</u>.

Recall the parable of the sower and the seed in Matthew 13:3. That parable explained that all true Christians will have "good fruit" produced by the Holy Spirit. Note: it is fruit produced by the Holy Spirit, not manmade fruit (i.e. human "good works"). Those that do not bear good fruit are not Christians at all. It does not mean that everyone will bear fruit at the same rate. An immature Christian will not be producing at the same rate as a mature believer. Jesus sets out that principal when He says, "*...some a hundredfold, some sixty, and some thirty.*" A person who claims to be a Christian, but is devoid of Holy Spirit-produced "good fruit," is not a Christian in the first place. R. C. Sproul summarizes the issue of the assurance of our salvation this way:

> "...we must examine the fruit of our faith. We do not need perfect fruit to have assurance, but there must be some evidence of the fruit of obedience for our profession of faith to be credible. If no fruit is present, then no faith is present. Where saving faith is found, fruit of that faith is also found." [464]

The heretical teaching of "legalism" says that good works or religious rituals help you get saved or keep you saved. Jesus tells us that we cannot do anything to earn our salvation, but rather we are saved by grace through faith in Jesus, and then He produces fruit through us (Ephesians 2:8-10).

The concepts discussed above can be summed up in what Jesus stated in <u>**John 15:5–6:**</u>

> "*I am the vine, you are the branches; he who abides in Me and I in him, he bears much fruit, <u>for apart from Me you can do nothing</u> If anyone does not abide in Me, he is thrown away as a branch and dries up; and they gather them, and cast them into the fire and they are burned.*"

<u>**VERSES 28-29:**</u> "*Therefore take away the talent from him, and give it to the one who has the ten talents. 29 For to everyone who has shall more be given, and he shall have an abundance; but from the one who does not have, even what he does have shall be taken away.*"

> People seem to forget that although the true believer does not undergo a judgment for salvation, he will be judged as to his works done for the Lord.
>
> <u>**2 Corinthians 5:9-10:**</u> "*Therefore also we have as our ambition, whether at home or absent, to be pleasing to Him. 10 <u>For we must all appear before the judgment seat of Christ, that each one may be recompensed for his deeds in the body, according to what he has done, whether good or bad.</u>*"
>
> <u>**1 Corinthians 3:7-8:**</u> "*So then neither the one who plants nor the one who waters is anything, but God who causes the growth. 8 Now he who plants and he who waters are one; <u>but each will receive his own reward according to his own labor.</u>*"

---

[464] Sproul, R. C., *Essential Truths of the Christian Faith*, #71. *The Assurance of Salvation* (Wheaton, Illinois: Tyndale House Publishers, Inc.) 1992.

In verse 29 it says, *"For to everyone who has shall more be given, and he shall have an abundance; but from the one who does not have, even what he does have shall be taken away."* Among other things, this verse points out that those who are His disciples die to themselves, and end up with even more—dwelling eternally in the presence of God in His Kingdom.

> **Matthew 16:25-28:** *"For whoever wishes to save his life shall lose it; but whoever loses his life for My sake shall find it. 26 For what will a man be profited, if he gains the whole world, and forfeits his soul? Or what will a man give in exchange for his soul? 27For the Son of Man is going to come in the glory of His Father with His angels; and will then recompense every man according to his deeds. 28Truly I say to you, there are some of those who are standing here who shall not taste death until they see the Son of Man coming in His kingdom."*

Those who take what God has given them (i.e. the gift of human life) and use it for themselves, will lose what they have and undergo the second death.

> **Revelation 21:8:** *"But for the cowardly and unbelieving and abominable and murderers and immoral persons and sorcerers and idolaters and all liars, their part will be in the lake that burns with fire and brimstone, which is the second death."*

VERSE 30: *"And cast out the worthless slave into the outer darkness; in that place there shall be weeping and gnashing of teeth."*

The false believer will get his reward: judgment in hell. This verse states plainly that hell will be a place of complete isolation, darkness and unending anguish and pain: *"...the outer darkness; in that place there shall be weeping and gnashing of teeth."*

Summary and Application

We learn a lot from this parable. First we see that there is a difference between true believers and those who just say they are God's servants. The true believers are doing what He told them to do. John 14:15: *"If you love Me, you will keep My commandments."* False believers will do what they think is best or at least, looks best to others. They do not serve God out of love from their hearts, because they were never converted in the first place.

> **James 2:14-19:** *"What use is it, my brethren, if a man says he has faith, but he has no works? Can that faith save him? 15 If a brother or sister is without clothing and in need of daily food, 16 and one of you says to them, 'Go in peace, be warmed and be filled,' and yet you do not give them what is necessary for their body, what use is that? 17 Even so faith, if it has no works, is dead, being by itself. 18 But someone may well say, 'You have faith, and I have works; show me your faith without the works, and I will show you my faith by my works.' 19 You believe that God is one. You do well; the demons also believe, and shudder."*

We also have learned there are rewards for the Christian as to the quality of his service to the Lord. The evangelist George Mueller (1805-1898), whose Christian service included providing for thousands of orphans, said the following regarding the secret to his service to Christ:

"There was a day when I died, utterly died...died to George Muller, his opinions, preferences, tastes, and will—died to the world, its approval or censure—died to the approval or blame even of my brethren and friends—and since then I have studied only to show myself approved unto God."[465]

The Christian should serve the Lord diligently so as to hear His Master say: *"Well done, good and faithful slave...enter into the joy of your master."*

---

[465] Tan, P. L. (1996). *Encyclopedia of 7700 Illustrations: Signs of the Times. 6102 George Mueller's Secret* Garland, TX: Bible Communications, Inc.

MATTHEW 25:31-46
(JUDGMENT OF THE NATIONS)

"But when the Son of Man comes in His glory, and all the angels with Him, then He will sit on His glorious throne. ³² And all the nations will be gathered before Him; and He will separate them from one another, as the shepherd separates the sheep from the goats; ³³ and He will put the sheep on His right, and the goats on the left. ³⁴ Then the King will say to those on His right, 'Come, you who are blessed of My Father, inherit the kingdom prepared for you from the foundation of the world. ³⁵ For I was hungry, and you gave Me something to eat; I was thirsty, and you gave Me drink; I was a stranger, and you invited Me in; ³⁶naked, and you clothed Me; I was sick, and you visited Me; I was in prison, and you came to Me.' ³⁷Then the righteous will answer Him, saying, 'Lord, when did we see You hungry, and feed You, or thirsty, and give You drink? ³⁸And when did we see You a stranger, and invite You in, or naked, and clothe You? ³⁹And when did we see You sick, or in prison, and come to You?' ⁴⁰And the King will answer and say to them, 'Truly I say to you, to the extent that you did it to one of these brothers of Mine, even the least of them, you did it to Me.' ⁴¹Then He will also say to those on His left, 'Depart from Me, accursed ones, into the eternal fire which has been prepared for the devil and his angels; ⁴² for I was hungry, and you gave Me nothing to eat; I was thirsty, and you gave Me nothing to drink; ⁴³ I was a stranger, and you did not invite Me in; naked, and you did not clothe Me; sick, and in prison, and you did not visit Me.' ⁴⁴Then they themselves also will answer, saying, 'Lord, when did we see You hungry, or thirsty, or a stranger, or naked, or sick, or in prison, and did not take care of You?' ⁴⁵Then He will answer them, saying, 'Truly I say to you, to the extent that you did not do it to one of the least of these, you did not do it to Me.' ⁴⁶And these will go away into eternal punishment, but the righteous into eternal life."

Introduction

This portion is the conclusion of the Olivet Discourse. This section is called by some the *Judgment of the Nations*.[466] The people being judged are those who survive the Great Tribulation. There are Christians and non-Christians among those who survive (i.e. sheep and goats [v.32]). It occurs after the tribulation and immediately before Jesus' millennium reign on earth.

> **Matthew 24:29-31:** *"But <u>immediately after the tribulation</u> of those days the sun will be darkened, and the moon will not give its light, and the stars will fall from the sky, and the powers of the heavens will be shaken, ³⁰ and then the sign of the Son of Man will appear in the sky, and then all the tribes of the earth will mourn, and they will see the Son of Man coming on the clouds of the sky with power and great glory. ³¹ And He will send forth His angels with a great trumpet and they will gather together His elect from the four winds, from one end of the sky to the other."*

This judgment is not to be confused with the Great White throne judgment mentioned in Revelation 20:11-15. Likewise, it should not be confused with the Judgment Seat of Christ, where the believers are judged

---

[466] Some refer to it as the Judgment of the Nations: Smith, J. H. (1992). *The New Treasury of Scripture Knowledge:* (p. 1050). Nashville TN: Thomas Nelson. MacArthur, J. F., Jr. (1985). *Matthew*. MacArthur New Testament Commentary (p. 249). Chicago: Moody Press. Weber, S. K. (2000). *Vol. 1: Matthew*. Holman New Testament Commentary (p. 424). Nashville, TN: Broadman and Holman Publishers.

and rewarded for their work in the Lord (1 Corinthians 3:12-15). This judgment in Matthew 25:31-46 is for those alive at the time of Jesus' Second Coming. It is composed of believers and non-believers who survive the Great Tribulation. They will be judged by Christ based on their conduct toward Jesus' *"brothers."* The sheep do not earn their position (*"inherit the kingdom"* v. 34) from their good deeds, but rather, because they are true Christians, their good works are a mere manifestation of their conversion.

The two parables prior to this (10 virgins and talents) emphasized the distinction between the visible church and the invisible church. The visible church[467] is comprised of all those who confess loyalty to Christ. The invisible church is comprised of all who are truly converted. The truly converted do not merely perform lip-service to Christ, but are loyal servants going about His business. Likewise, the story of the sheep and the goats demonstrates there are those who will call Him *"Lord"* (v.44), but are not true Christians.

VERSES 31-33: *"But when the Son of Man comes in His glory, and all the angels with Him, then He will sit on His glorious throne. 32 And all the nations will be gathered before Him; and He will separate them from one another, as the shepherd separates the sheep from the goats; 33 and He will put the sheep on His right, and the goats on the left."*

As mentioned above, there will be some who live through the Great Tribulation. It must also be remembered that there will be those who will die during those seven years. Many believers will be killed by the Antichrist (Matthew 24:9-22). Many unbelievers will die from plagues, as well as by Christ during the battle of Armageddon (Revelation 19:21). Jesus tells us that if the tribulation continued on, there would be no life left on the earth:

> **Matthew 24:22:** *"And unless those days had been cut short, no life would have been saved; but for the sake of the elect those days shall be cut short."*

Those who are alive at the time of Christ's return will immediately be subject to His judgment, as to whether they will enter the millennial kingdom and eternal life or eternal damnation (v.46-51).

In Matthew 25:31, Jesus speaks of His coming, *"in His glory,"* which is His Second Coming. It is clear that Jesus returns as "King of Kings and Lord of Lords." Verse 31 tells us that, *"He will sit on His glorious throne."* Enoch, who the Bible tells us, "walked with God" (Genesis 5:24), prophesied about this day:

> **Jude v.14-15:** *"And about these also Enoch, in the seventh generation from Adam, prophesied, saying, 'Behold, the Lord came with many thousands of His holy ones, 15 to execute judgment upon all, and to convict all the ungodly of all their ungodly deeds which they have done in an ungodly way, and of all the harsh things which ungodly sinners have spoken against Him.'"*

In the book of Revelation, John gives even more detail of that moment:

> **Revelation 6:12-17:** *"And I looked when He broke the sixth seal, and there was a great earthquake; and the sun became black as sackcloth made of hair, and*

---

[467] Note that I use the term *visible church* to mean all church buildings and those who are present in the public congregation and claim to be Christians. This *visible church* group includes true Christians in addition to many unbelievers, false-believers and self-deceived. When the Bible refers to the true Church, the term only includes the redeemed.

the whole moon became like blood; ¹³ and the stars of the sky fell to the earth, as a fig tree casts its unripe figs when shaken by a great wind. ¹⁴ And the sky was split apart like a scroll when it is rolled up; and every mountain and island were moved out of their places. ¹⁵ And the kings of the earth and the great men and the commanders and the rich and the strong and every slave and free man, hid themselves in the caves and among the rocks of the mountains; ¹⁶ and they *said to the mountains and to the rocks, 'Fall on us and <u>hide us from the presence of Him who sits on the throne, and from the wrath of the Lamb; ¹⁷ for the great day of their wrath has come; and who is able to stand?</u>'"

Matthew 25:32 says that the, *"nations will be gathered before Him."* The word *"nations"* is the same as "Gentiles." For that reason this section is referred to by some as the Judgment of the Gentiles. The angels will come with Christ and then the righteous and unrighteous will be separated from each other. Jesus spoke earlier of the angels being used in separating the saved from the damned.

> **Matthew 13:38-43 and verses 47-49:** *"...and the field is the world; and as for the good seed, these are the sons of the kingdom; and the tares are the sons of the evil one; ³⁹ and the enemy who sowed them is the devil, and the harvest is the end of the age<u>; and the reapers are angels.</u> ⁴⁰ Therefore just as the tares are gathered up and burned with fire, so shall it be at the end of the age. ⁴¹ <u>The Son of Man will send forth His angels, and they will gather out of His kingdom all stumbling blocks, and those who commit lawlessness, ⁴² and will cast them into the furnace of fire</u>; in that place there shall be weeping and gnashing of teeth. ⁴³ Then the righteous will shine forth as the sun in the kingdom of their Father. He who has ears, let him hear...*
>
> *⁴⁷ Again, the kingdom of heaven is like a dragnet cast into the sea, and gathering fish of every kind; ⁴⁸ and when it was filled, they drew it up on the beach; and they sat down, and gathered the good fish into containers, but the bad they threw away. ⁴⁹ <u>So it will be at the end of the age; the angels shall come forth, and take out the wicked from among the righteous,</u>...."*

Notice in Matthew 25:33 Jesus calls those who are His, *sheep*. He calls His disciples *sheep* in other Scripture passages.

> **John 10:26-28:** *"But you do not believe, because you are not of My sheep. ²⁷ <u>My sheep hear My voice, and I know them, and they follow Me; ²⁸ and I give eternal life to them</u>, and they shall never perish; and no one shall snatch them out of My hand."*

Jesus is the "Good Shepherd."

> **John 10:14-16:** *"<u>I am the good shepherd</u>; and I know My own, and My own know Me, ¹⁵ even as the Father knows Me and I know the Father; <u>and I lay down My life for the sheep</u>. ¹⁶ And I have other sheep, which are not of this fold; I must bring them also, and they shall hear My voice; and they shall become one flock with one shepherd."*

VERSES 34-40: *"Then the King will say to those on His right, 'Come, you who are blessed of My Father, inherit the kingdom prepared for you from the foundation of the world. ³⁵For I was hungry, and you gave Me something to eat; I was thirsty, and you gave Me drink; I was a stranger, and you invited Me in; ³⁶*

naked, and you clothed Me; I was sick, and you visited Me; I was in prison, and you came to Me.' 37 Then the righteous will answer Him, saying, 'Lord, when did we see You hungry, and feed You, or thirsty, and give You drink? 38 And when did we see You a stranger, and invite You in, or naked, and clothe You? 39 And when did we see You sick, or in prison, and come to You?' 40 And the King will answer and say to them, 'Truly I say to you, to the extent that you did it to one of these brothers of Mine, even the least of them, you did it to Me.'"

Verse 34 continues the concept of election.[468] Jesus makes it clear that these people are *not* admitted into the Kingdom because of their hard work, but rather the Kingdom has been *"...prepared for you from the foundation of the world."* Verse 34, states that the sheep did not earn this right but they were, *"blessed of My Father."* Note also that out of the believer flows righteous and good works that *God had ordained* for him to do:

<u>Ephesians 2:10:</u> *"For we are His workmanship, created in Christ Jesus for good works, which God prepared beforehand, that we should walk in them."*

We were created by Christ to do these good works. In the main text (Matthew 25:34-40), Jesus makes it clear that when we serve others in His name, we are serving Him. Many times we are not even aware of the good works Jesus is doing through us by His Holy Spirit.

The self-righteous think that "good deeds" will earn favor with God. Compare them to the sheep here, who are doing good works and at times not even realizing they are glorifying Christ. Why are the Sheep not keeping track of all the good they are doing? The true believer's (i.e. sheep) response is not an act of false humility, but simply the manifestation of being led by the Spirit. In verse 40 Jesus says, *"to the extent that you did it to one of these brothers of Mine, even the least of them, you did it to Me."* It is natural for them to serve God and others. This is the true faith of the believer. He is not saved by his own works of righteousness, but by faith in Christ (Ephesians 2:8-9). The truth of his conversion is manifested by his service to Christ. It is this faith that James writes about when he says:

<u>James 2:14-21:</u> *"What use is it, my brethren, if a man says he has faith, but he has no works? Can that faith save him? 15 If a brother or sister is without clothing and in need of daily food, 16 and one of you says to them, 'Go in peace, be warmed and be filled,' and yet you do not give them what is necessary for their body, what use is that? 17 Even so faith, if it has no works, is dead, being by itself. 18 But someone may well say, 'You have faith, and I have works; show me your faith without the works, and I will show you my faith by my works.' 19 You believe that God is one. You do well; the demons also believe,*

---

[468] <u>**Election and Predestination:**</u> Here are some verses on the concept of election and pre-destination: Few are chosen - Matthew 22:14; One cannot come to Christ unless granted by the Father - John 6:65; God chose us and we did not choose Him - John 15:16; Those chosen of God - **Titus 1:1; No** one can come to Christ unless the Father draws him - John 6:44; Not by will of man - John 1:12-13; Those He predestined He called - Romans 8:29-30; Salvation not by the person who wills or runs but God's mercy - Romans 9:16-18; Those who are of God can hear Him - John 8:47; Appointed to eternal life - Acts. 13:48; Before birth - Jacob I loved-Romans 9:10-13; Mercy on who God wishes to give it - Romans 9:14-21; God's choice of you – 1 Thessalonians 1:4; God chose you from the beginning - 2 Thessalonians 2:13; God saved us and called us - 2 Timothy 1:9; [God gives each man a measure of faith - Romans 12:3 (so since we are saved by grace through faith—note who gives the faith)]; Consider your calling - 1 Corinthians 1:26; Been granted for Christ's sake to believe and suffer - Philippians 1:29; Lord has made everything for a purpose, the wicked for the day of evil - Proverbs 16:4; God blinded some - John 12:37-40.

and shudder. ²⁰ But are you willing to recognize, you foolish fellow, that faith without works is useless? ²¹ Was not Abraham our father justified by works, when he offered up Isaac his son on the altar?"

In **Matthew 25:40** Jesus says:
> "And the King will answer and say to them, 'Truly I say to you, to the extent that you did it to one of these brothers of Mine, even the least of them, you did it to Me.'"

Who are Jesus' brothers? Jesus says they are those who do the will of God:
> **Matthew 12:48-50:** "But He answered the one who was telling Him and said, 'Who is My mother and who are My brothers?' ⁴⁹ And stretching out His hand toward His disciples, He said, 'Behold, My mother and My brothers! ⁵⁰ For whoever does the will of My Father who is in heaven, he is My brother and sister and mother.'"

Look also at this verse in Hebrews, which tells us that Jesus is not ashamed to call us His brothers:
> **Hebrews 2:9-12:** "But we do see Him who has been made for a little while lower than the angels, namely, _Jesus, because of the suffering of death crowned with glory and honor, that by the grace of God He might taste death for everyone._ ¹⁰For it was fitting for Him, for whom are all things, and through whom are all things, in bringing many sons to glory, to perfect the author of their salvation through sufferings. ¹¹ For both He who sanctifies and those who are sanctified are all from one Father; _for which reason He is not ashamed to call them brethren,_ ¹² saying, 'I will proclaim Thy name to My brethren, in the midst of the congregation I will sing Thy praise.'"

In Matthew 25:40 the *brothers* are the Christians. The Christians are both Jews and Gentiles who have put their faith in Christ and endured the Tribulation.[469] Jesus *"...said to them, "My mother and My brothers are these who hear the word of God and do it."* **Luke 8:21**.

---

[469] One commentator states, "Who are these brothers? The majority view throughout church history has taken them to be some or all of Christ's disciples since the word "least" (*elachistōn*) is the superlative form of the adjective "little [ones]" (*mikroi*), which without exception in Matthew refers to the disciples (10:42; 18:6, 10, 14; cf. also 5:19; 11:11), while "brothers" in this Gospel (and usually in the New Testament more generally) when not referring to literal, biological siblings, always means *spiritual kin* (5:22–24, 47; 7:3–5; 12:48–50; 18:15 (2X),21, 35; 23:8; 28:10)." Blomberg, C. (1992). *Vol. 22: Matthew*. The New American Commentary (pp. 377–378). Nashville: Broadman and Holman Publishers. Other commentators believe that the term *brothers* is referring exclusively to believing Jews during the Tribulation. Wiersbe states the following regarding the term *brothers*: "Who are these people that the King dares to call 'My brethren'? It seems likely that they are the believing Jews from the Tribulation period. These are people who will hear the message of the 144,000 and trust Jesus Christ. Since these believing Jews will not receive the 'mark of the beast' (Revelation 13:16–17), they will be unable to buy or sell. How, then, can they survive? Through the loving care of the Gentiles who have trusted Christ and who care for His brethren." Wiersbe, W. W. (1996). *The Bible Exposition Commentary* (Matthew 25:31). Wheaton, IL: Victor Books.

VERSES 41-46: *"Then He will also say to those on His left, 'Depart from Me, accursed ones, into the eternal fire which has been prepared for the devil and his angels; ⁴² for I was hungry, and you gave Me nothing to eat; I was thirsty, and you gave Me nothing to drink; ⁴³ I was a stranger, and you did not invite Me in; naked, and you did not clothe Me; sick, and in prison, and you did not visit Me.' ⁴⁴ Then they themselves also will answer, saying, 'Lord, when did we see You hungry, or thirsty, or a stranger, or naked, or sick, or in prison, and did not take care of You?' ⁴⁵ Then He will answer them, saying, 'Truly I say to you, to the extent that you did not do it to one of the least of these, you did not do it to Me.' ⁴⁶ And these will go away into eternal punishment, but the righteous into eternal life."*

The social-gospel crowd often will cite Matthew 25:45 in their fundraising material: *"…to the extent that you did not do it to one of the least of these, you did not do it to Me."* This verse is their proof-text to infer that feeding, clothing, healing, and visiting others, is what Jesus is *really* concerned about…not verbally preaching the gospel so that people can be save from eternal judgement. Their promotional material can even carry a veiled implication that if you are not interested in supporting their social effort, you do not care about, **"the least of these."** The implication is often carried one step further to infer that you may not even care about helping Jesus (i.e. **"did not do it to Me"**). The most serious misinterpretation of Matthew 25:31-46 is that one obtains salvation because of the good *works* he does for, *"one of the least of these."* [470]

A thorough examination of Matthew 25:31-46 *does not teach* that doing good works is the real way to earn salvation. Further, it *does not teach* that one is a "brother" of Jesus (i.e. part of the family of God) simply because he is poor, hungry, thirsty, sick, imprisoned or lacking adequate clothing.[471] Again, the context and timetable is important. The sheep and the goats are those who are alive immediately after the tribulation (v. 31-32). The sheep are true followers of Jesus who are providing love and comfort to fellow Christians (Jesus' brothers) during the terrible tribulation time. The reality of their faith and love for Christ is manifest in their care and love for fellow believers (Jesus' brothers—even the least of them). Jesus said in **John 13:34-35**:

> *"A new commandment I give to you, that you love one another, even as I have loved you, that you also love one another. ³⁵By this all men will know that you are My disciples, if you have love for one another."*

The goats are the hypocrites. Hypocrites (especially religious hypocrites) always view themselves in a light more positive than reality. The goats call Jesus *"Lord"* (Matthew 25:44) and claim they would have done the right thing if they were given the chance (v. 44). The reality is that they have no love for Christ or His followers. The goats are the *"accursed ones"* (v. 41), condemned to *"eternal punishment"* (v. 46), and sentenced to the *"eternal fire which has been prepared for the devil and his angels"* (v. 41). The judgment in Matthew 25:31-46 of the goats demonstrates there are plenty of goats who will call Jesus *"Lord"* (v. 44), yet are not true Christians. They try to justify themselves by saying they too *would have* provided food/drink, shelter, and clothes to Jesus, if given the opportunity. If they had the chance, they would have visited Him when He was sick or in prison! These *goats* are like the false believers we read about in the parable of the 10 virgins

---

[470] Much of this section is taken from the author's book *The Fake Commission*. Strohman, John (2014) *The Fake Commission* p. 99-110 (Cross Centered Press).

[471] Litfin, Duane (2012) *Words vs Deeds* p.192- 193 (Crossway Press).

and the parable of the talents (Matthew 25:1-30). The false believers give deceptive (even self-deceived) appearances that they are real servants of God, except for the fact that they did not produce any Holy Spirit-led good works.

>**2 Timothy 3:13:** *"But evil men and impostors will proceed from bad to worse, deceiving and being deceived."*

>**2 Timothy 3:5:** *"…holding to a form of godliness, although they have denied its power; Avoid such men as these."*

>**2 Corinthians 11:13–15:** *"For such men are false apostles, deceitful workers, disguising themselves as apostles of Christ. No wonder, for even Satan disguises himself as an angel of light. Therefore it is not surprising if his servants also disguise themselves as servants of righteousness, whose end will be according to their deeds."*

The sheep (Christians)[472] do not earn their position from their good deeds, but by the grace of God. The sheep's good works are a mere manifestation of truly being Christians. Ephesians 2:8-10 sums both concepts up as follows:

>**Ephesians 2:8–10:** *"For by grace you have been saved through faith; and that not of yourselves, it is the gift of God; [9]not as a result of works, so that no one may boast. For we are His workmanship, created in Christ Jesus for good works, which God prepared beforehand so that we would walk in them."*

Recall that in Matthew 25:45, Jesus is speaking to the goats (the unsaved/damned) when they are condemned for their lack of mercy toward "the least of these." Who are the people that Jesus is referring to that he calls "the least of these?" The definition of the **"least of these"** is set out five verses before, when Jesus addresses the sheep (i.e. Christians) in verse 40: *"And the King will answer and say to them, 'Truly I say to you, to the extent that you did it to one of these brothers of Mine, even the least of them, you did it to Me.'"* The "least of these" are Jesus' brothers (i.e. true Christians). Jesus said that his real brothers, sisters and mother are those who do the will of God:

>**Matthew 12:48-50:** **"But He answered** *the one who was telling Him and said, 'Who is My mother and who are My brothers?' [49]And stretching out His hand toward His disciples, He said, 'Behold, My mother and My brothers! [50]For whoever does the will of My Father who is in heaven, he is My brother and sister and mother.'"*

Jesus personally identifies with the afflictions of His children. When one is persecuting you, for the cause of Christ, the person is actually persecuting Jesus. This is exemplified when Jesus spoke directly to Saul on his way to Damascus to attack believers.

---

[472] Jesus calls His disciples *sheep* in other passages of scripture. John 10:26-28: *"But you do not believe, because you are not of My sheep. [27] My sheep hear My voice, and I know them, and they follow Me; [28]and I give eternal life to them, and they shall never perish; and no one shall snatch them out of My hand."* Jesus is the "Good Shepherd." John 10:14-16: *"I am the good shepherd; and I know My own, and My own know Me, [15]even as the Father knows Me and I know the Father; and I lay down My life for the sheep. [16]And I have other sheep, which are not of this fold; I must bring them also, and they shall hear My voice; and they shall become one flock with one shepherd."*

<u>Acts 9:1–6</u>: *"Now Saul, still breathing threats and murder against the disciples of the Lord, went to the high priest, [2]and asked for letters from him to the synagogues at Damascus, so that if he found any belonging to the Way, both men and women, he might bring them bound to Jerusalem. [3]As he was traveling, it happened that he was approaching Damascus, and suddenly a light from heaven flashed around him; [4]and he fell to the ground and heard a voice saying to him, '<u>Saul, Saul, why are you persecuting Me?</u>' [5]And he said, 'Who are You, Lord?' And He said, 'I am Jesus whom you are persecuting, [6]but get up and enter the city, and it will be told you what you must do.'"*

A correct interpretation and application of Matthew 25:31-46 will not make you popular with non-believers, false disciples, and the social-gospel crowd. Those groups are interested in a gospel that recognizes their efforts at self-righteousness.[473] Duane Litfin[474] accurately summarizes Matthew 25:31-46 when he writes:

"When Jesus speaks there of 'the least of these my brothers,' he is not referring to just any poor person. There is no biblical warrant for supposing that people become Jesus' brothers or one of his "little ones" simply by becoming hungry, or thirsty, or impoverished, or incarcerated in prison (see also Matthew 12:49-50; 28:10; Hebrews 2:10-18). Nor does the Bible teach that such individuals somehow embody Jesus in the world. Jesus surely is embodied in the world…in His followers (Colossians 2:19), His brothers, His disciples, His little ones who believe, even 'the least of them.'…. [B]y broadening it out to include all human suffering, however well-intentioned, does not merely miss Jesus's point; it undermines and falsifies it."[475]

A heart that is converted by Jesus Christ will result in good works for Christ's glory, not one's own glory. This is part of being a true disciple.

<u>James 2:17-18</u>: *"Even so faith, if it has no works, is dead, being by itself. [18]But someone may well say, 'You have faith, and I have works; show me your faith without the works, and I will show you my faith by my works.'"*

---

[473] Scripture does not advocate throwing money at just *anyone* who says he is poor. Whether one is a Christian, or not, if he is healthy and refuses to work, the church is not to aimlessly waste resources on him. The following verses set this out.

<u>2 Thessalonians 3:10</u>: *"For even when we were with you, we used to give you this order: if anyone is not willing to work, then he is not to eat, either."*

<u>1 Timothy 5:8</u>: *"But if anyone does not provide for his own, and especially for those of his household, he has denied the faith and is worse than an unbeliever."*

<u>Proverbs 23:21</u>: *"For the heavy drinker and the glutton will come to poverty, And drowsiness will clothe one with rags."*

[474] Dr. A. Duane Litfin served as the seventh president at Wheaton College.

[475] Litfin, Duane (2012) *Words vs Deeds* p.192- 193 (Crossway Press).

The Lord Jesus is compassionate and generous. He is concerned about people's daily spiritual and physical needs (Matthew 9:36, 15:32). The Lord will work through His people to minister to others, whether those in need are believers or not. This is God's common grace to all. This common grace keeps us all from immediate justice the moment we sin. This concept is reflected in 1 Timothy 4:10 where it states, *"…because we have fixed our hope on the living God, who is the Savior of all men, especially of believers."* That common grace also allows us to be the beneficiary of good things in this life, which we do not deserve. Christians are to be like their heavenly Father in showing grace, since they have been shown infinite mercy and saving grace:

> **Matthew 5:44–45:** *"But I say to you, love your enemies and pray for those who persecute you, ⁴⁵so that you may be sons of your Father who is in heaven; for He causes His sun to rise on the evil and the good, and sends rain on the righteous and the unrighteous."*

> **Acts 14:16-17:** *"In the generations gone by He permitted all the nations to go their own ways; ¹⁷and yet He did not leave Himself without witness, in that He did good and gave you rains from heaven and fruitful seasons, satisfying your hearts with food and gladness."*

We must have the same compassion as our Savior does, *"… for He Himself is kind to ungrateful and evil men."* **Luke 6:35**. We are to do *"good to all"* but there is also a very special place for our brothers and sisters in Christ. Paul instructs this in:

> **Galatians 6:10:** *"…while we have opportunity, let us do good to all men, and especially to those who are of the household of the faith."*

> **1 Corinthians 12:26–27:** *"And if one member suffers, all the members suffer with it; if one member is honored, all the members rejoice with it. ²⁷Now you are Christ's body, and individually members of it."*

John admonishes Christians to be especially caring for fellow Christians in need: **1 John 3:16–17:** *"We know love by this, that He laid down His life for us; and we ought to lay down our lives for the brethren. ¹⁷But whoever has the world's goods, and sees his brother in need and closes his heart against him, how does the love of God abide in him?"* We see the example of Paul sending financial support from the Christians in Macedonia and Achaia, to the Christians in Jerusalem (the saints): *"For Macedonia and Achaia have been pleased to make a contribution for the poor among the saints in Jerusalem."* **Romans 15:26**. In Acts, we see Christians giving according to their financial ability. They were "determined" to provide relief to fellow believers in Judea: **Acts 11:29:** *"And in the proportion that any of the disciples had means, each of them determined to send a contribution for the relief of the brethren living in Judea."* The author of Hebrews writes of the great value of Christians caring for one another when in prison for the gospel. **Hebrews 13:1–3:** *"Let love of the brethren continue. ²Do not neglect to show hospitality to strangers, for by this some have entertained angels without knowing it. ³Remember the prisoners, as though in prison with them, and those who are ill-treated, since you yourselves also are in the body."* Paul also mentions the great value of Christian care when he was in prison: **2 Timothy 1:16–18:** *"The Lord grant mercy to the house of Onesiphorus, for he often refreshed me and was not ashamed of my chains; ¹⁷but when he was in Rome, he eagerly searched for me and found me— ¹⁸the Lord grant to him to find mercy from the Lord on that day—and you know very well what services he rendered at Ephesus."*

One should examine the list of causes that many secular and religious activists claim that they are zealous about. The list for some of those groups includes hunger, orphans, climate change, trafficking, income equality, social justice, homosexual rights, immigration and even abortion rights. There is one cause that is often at the bottom of the list (if ever mentioned at all) — *the persecution of Christians for evangelizing the gospel.* The "Christian human rights" cause does not bring out the big corporate contributors and secular organizations to assist. We (Christians) must watch out for our own. The true Christians must champion care and concern for all but *"especially to those who are of the household of the faith"* <u>Galatians 6:10</u>.

So what is the end for "goats" who care nothing for Jesus or His children? In Matthew 25:41 we hear their judgement: *"Then He will also say to those on His left, 'Depart from Me, accursed ones, into the eternal fire which has been prepared for the devil and his angels;* <u>Matthew 25:41</u>. The goats then try to justify themselves by saying they would have given Jesus food/drink, shelter, and clothes, and visited Him when sick or in prison, if they had been given the opportunity. These goats are like the false believers we read about in the parable of the 10 virgins and the parable of the talents (Matthew 25:14-30). They try to appear as servants of God, except for the fact that they did not produce any Holy Spirit-led good works.

Cults and false Christians like to point to supposed "good deeds" as to why they deserve heaven. The problem is that the non-believer does not realize that he can do nothing "good." This is in addition to the fact that there is no good work he can do to remove his sin. <u>Isaiah 64:6</u>: *"For all of us have become like one who is unclean, <u>and all our righteous deeds are like a filthy garment</u>;"* I have been told by some non-believers, that in the end, they believe they have done more good than bad. They are often proud of the good they think they have done and want to be judged by their deeds. Unfortunately, they will get what they want. We see that in the Great White Throne Judgment, the non-Christian will be judged by his deeds and then condemned to hell. The Great White Throne Judgment is the final judgment of the damned.

> <u>Revelation 20:11-15</u>: *"And I saw a great white throne and Him who sat upon it, from whose presence earth and heaven fled away, and no place was found for them. [12] And I saw the dead, the great and the small, standing before the throne, and books were opened; and another book was opened, which is the book of life; <u>and the dead were judged from the things which were written in the books, according to their deeds.</u> [13] And the sea gave up the dead which were in it, and death and Hades gave up the dead which were in them; and they were judged, every one of them according to their deeds. [14] And death and Hades were thrown into the lake of fire. This is the second death, the lake of fire. [15] And if anyone's name was not found written in the book of life, he was thrown into the lake of fire."*

Where do the goats/non-believers/false Christians go for *"eternal punishment?"* Jesus gives the answer in <u>Matthew 25:41</u>: *"...into the eternal fire which has been prepared for the devil and his angels...."* That verse makes it clear that the eternal fire (hell) was not made for man but it was, *"prepared for the devil and his angels."* Although hell was made for the Devil and his demons, man's sin likewise brings him to eternal death: <u>James 1:15</u>: *"Then when lust has conceived, it gives birth to sin; and <u>when sin is accomplished, it brings forth death."</u>* Scripture tells us that everyone is a sinner and worthy of death: <u>Romans 3:23</u>: *"...for all have sinned and fall short of the glory of God,"* thus, man has no hope except turning to Christ to be forgiven and saved: <u>Romans 8:2</u>: *"For the law of the Spirit of life in Christ Jesus has set you free from the law of sin* *and of death."* Even though hell was not made for man, he earns and deserves hell by rejecting God's salvation through the atonement of Jesus Christ.

> <u>Hebrews 2:2-3:</u> *"For if the word spoken through angels proved unalterable, and every transgression and disobedience received a just recompense, ³ how shall we escape if we neglect so great a salvation? After it was at the first spoken through the Lord, it was confirmed to us by those who heard,…."*

It must be understood that this judgment is <u>neither temporary,</u> nor does it end in annihilation so that you don't have to "feel" any pain or suffering. The torment goes on and on *forever and ever*. Examine and carefully consider the description of hell from God's Word.

> **DESCRIPTION OF HELL:** *Flames and Torment* - <u>Luke 16:19-31</u>; *Lake of fire which burns with brimstone* - <u>Revelation 19:20</u>; *Lake of fire - Fire and brimstone and are tormented day and night forever and ever* - <u>Revelation 20:10</u>; *Eternal fire…the blackness of darkness forever* - <u>Jude v.7, 13</u>; *Everlasting destruction from the presence of the Lord* - <u>2 Thessalonians 1:9</u>; *Where their worm does not die, and the fire is not quenched* - <u>Mark 9:43-48</u>; *Weeping and gnashing of teeth* - <u>Matthew 24:51</u>; *Everlasting punishment* - <u>Matthew 25:46</u>; *Indignation, wrath, tribulation and anguish* - <u>Romans 2:8,9</u>; *Shame and everlasting contempt* - <u>Daniel 12:2</u>; *Unquenchable fire* - <u>Luke 3:17</u>.

The non-believer must be warned that he will end up in hell unless he is saved. I wince when I hear a weak-kneed pastor who will not say the word hell, but simply says that the unsaved will end up *"separated from God."* This is very misleading to the unbeliever, who in his darkened understanding thinks he is currently living *separated from God*…and frankly likes it that way. It is also misleading theologically. It is true that a person in hell is separated from God's love, joy, forgiveness and salvation, but they are not *separated from God*.[476] The person in hell is in the absolute presence of God's judgment, wrath and punishment for all eternity. **Revelation 14:9–11:**

> ⁹ *Then another angel, a third one, followed them, saying with a loud voice, "If anyone worships the beast and his image, and receives a mark on his forehead or on his hand, ¹⁰ he also will <u>drink of the wine of the wrath of God, which is mixed in full strength in the cup of His anger; and he will be tormented with fire and brimstone in the presence of the holy angels and in the presence of the Lamb.</u> ¹¹ "And the smoke of their torment goes up forever and ever; they have no rest day and night, those who worship the beast and his image, and whoever receives the mark of his name."*

Make no mistake about it, Satan is the not the ruler of hell; God is. Satan ends up a prisoner in God's hell. God made hell for Satan and his demonic angels (Matthew 25:41). In short, repent and believe the gospel so that you might be saved and escape the judgment of hell.

Summary and Application

This section concludes the Olivet Discourse which began in Matthew 24:3. In this discourse, Jesus teaches on the end times. It must be remembered that this "end times" is the Second Coming of Christ, not His rapture of the Church. Even though the Olivet Discourse applies to a specific time period in history, there

---

[476] In death one is still in the presence of God. **Psalm 139:7–8:** *"Where can I go from Your Spirit? Or where can I flee from Your presence? If I ascend to heaven, You are there; If I make my bed in Sheol, behold, You are there. "*

are still many lessons every Christian can learn and apply to his/her life. From the Olivet discourse, all Christians should see:

- Those who are in Christ at the time of the rapture will not have to endure the "Great Tribulation." Despite the avoidance of the Great Tribulation, all Christians will experience tribulation in various degrees here on earth (2 Timothy 3:12).

- We are to be Christians who are faithfully prepared to see the Lord's return. It should not take us by surprise like it will the false believers. The true believer always knows He is coming. The Christian realizes that he is called to be about the Father's business. We must work and serve the Lord today, tomorrow, and until we either die or are taken up with Him. Since we do not know when that is, we should take advantage of every opportunity.

- The difference between true believers and false believers who say they are God's servants is that the true believers are doing what He told them to do. **John 14:15:** *"If you love Me, you will keep My commandments."* False believers will do what they think is best and looks good to others. They do not love Him from their hearts because they have never been converted.

- Neither Matthew 25:32-46, nor any other scripture in context, supports the view that a person can earn one's own righteousness/forgiveness. One does not obtain/earn salvation by either suffering physical hardship, or engaging in acts to relieve others who are suffering from them. Providing aid to another's physical condition is not spiritually superior to preaching the gospel of Christ to that person. The Great Commissions (Matthew 28:16-20) calls us to worldwide evangelism, along with good works and mercy which follow the true disciple. Jesus did not come to earth with the objective to set up a homeless shelter. The eternal need of man is much greater than even the basic necessities of daily life. Jesus states clearly that He came to preach the gospel and pay the sacrifice for our sins on the cross.

  > **Luke 4:43–44:** *"But He said to them, 'I must preach the kingdom of God to the other cities also, for I was sent for this purpose.' ⁴⁴So He kept on preaching in the synagogues of Judea."*

  > **1 John 3:5:** *"You know that He appeared in order to take away sins; and in Him there is no sin."*

MacArthur states well why we should not get so caught up in end-times eschatology that we miss living a fruitful Christian life today.

> "The study of the end times is the consuming passion of many in the church today. Sensational best-selling authors argue that current events fulfill their often dubious interpretations of biblical prophecy. ...Tragically, some people get so caught up in the study of eschatology that they neglect the basic principles of spiritual growth and evangelism that the Second Coming is designed to motivate." [477]

Here is a mini-timeline of some of the events at the end times from a Pre-tribulation/Premillennial view. (It should be clearly understood that within orthodox Christianity there are other views of eschatology.)

---

[477] MacArthur, J. F., Jr. (2002). *1 and 2 Thessalonians. MacArthur New Testament Commentary* (pp, 123–124). Chicago: Moody Press.

Mini End-Times Timeline:

1. Age of Grace – or "Church Age" beginning after the Cross of Christ.

2. Rapture of the church — 1 Thessalonians 4:13-18 states that believers go to heaven with Christ. On earth, it is the start of the seven years of tribulation.

3. Halfway through the tribulation (three and one-half years) the "Abomination of Desolation" occurs. That is where the Antichrist declares himself god and sets up an idol in the temple to be worshiped; 2 Thessalonians 2:3-5, Matthew 24:15.

4. Near the end of the seven years of tribulation there will be the battle of Armageddon (Revelation 16:16). Jesus will return with the believers in Revelation 19:11-16 (i.e. The Second Coming of Christ).

5. Satan is bound and cast into the Pit (Revelation 20:1-3) and Jesus begins His Millennium kingdom on earth for 1000 years.

6. After the 1000 years, Satan is released from the Pit and the final rebellion against God begins (Revelation 20:7-10).

7. God destroys His enemies with fire and Satan, the false prophet, and the beast are thrown into the lake of fire (Revelation 20:9-10).

8. The Great White Throne of Judgment is the final judgment for unbelievers prior to their being damned to the lake of fire (Revelation 20:11-15).

9. Believers dwell for eternity in the new heaven and new earth (Revelation 22:1-5).

More general verses on the End Times:

Matthew 24:3-31, Luke 21:5-38; Rapture 1 Thessalonians 4:16-17, Revelation 4:1; No man knows when the end is - Matthew 24:36, Mark 13, Luke 12:40 - but Jesus knew after resurrection when He would come back - Acts 1:6-7. When He comes back - Mark 13:32. Man of lawlessness revealed and apostasy occurs - 2 Thessalonians 2:3-12. Men will be lovers of self, money, boastful, arrogant etc. - 2 Timothy 3:1-5. In the last days men will be mocking the idea of His coming, conveniently forgetting the first worldwide judgment (i.e. the flood) - 2 Peter 3:3-13. With a roar - elements will be destroyed with intense heat and earth will be burned up - 2 Pet. 3:10-12. Tribulation and Second Coming. Jesus rescued us from the wrath to come - 2 Thessalonians 1:5-10, Revelation 3:10, see also Matthew 24:15-31. Day of the Lord - 1 Thessalonians 5:1-11. Come Lord Jesus - Revelation 22:20. At the end only God will stand - Job 19:25.

MATTHEW 26:1-5
(RELIGIOUS LEADERS PLOT TO ARREST AND KILL JESUS)

"AND it came about that when Jesus had finished all these words, He said to His disciples, ²'You know that after two days the Passover is coming, and the Son of Man is to be delivered up for crucifixion.' ³ Then the chief priests and the elders of the people were gathered together in the court of the high priest, named Caiaphas; ⁴ and they plotted together to seize Jesus by stealth, and kill Him. ⁵ But they were saying, 'Not during the festival, lest a riot occur among the people.'"

Introduction

The time period of Matthew 26:1-16 occurred on Wednesday. [478] In the second verse of Matthew 26, Jesus draws the disciples' attention to the purpose of His coming—His crucifixion:

> John 12:27: *"Now My soul has become troubled; and what shall I say, 'Father, save Me from this hour'? But for this purpose I came to this hour."*

VERSE 1: *"And it came about that when Jesus had finished all these words, He said to His disciples...."*

This sentence refers back to Matthew 24:3-25:46, which is known as the Olivet Discourse. The Olivet Discourse deals with the end times and the Second Coming of Christ.

VERSE 2: *"You know that after two days the Passover is coming, and the Son of Man is to be delivered up for crucifixion."*

On previous occasions Jesus told His disciples that He would be going to the cross:

> Matthew 16:21-23: *"From that time Jesus Christ began to show His disciples that He must go to Jerusalem, and suffer many things from the elders and chief priests and scribes, and be killed, and be raised up on the third day. ²² And Peter took Him aside and began to rebuke Him, saying, 'God forbid it, Lord! This shall never happen to You.' ²³ But He turned and said to Peter, 'Get behind Me, Satan! You are a stumbling block to Me; for you are not setting your mind on God's interests, but man's.'"*

> Matthew 17:22-23: *"And while they were gathering together in Galilee, Jesus said to them, 'The Son of Man is going to be delivered into the hands of men; ²³ and they will kill Him, and He will be raised on the third day.' And they were deeply grieved."*

> Matthew 20:17-19: *"And as Jesus was about to go up to Jerusalem, He took the twelve disciples aside by themselves, and on the way He said to them,*

---

[478] Walvoord, J. F. (1983-c1985). *The Bible Knowledge Commentary: An Exposition of the Scriptures* (Matthew 26:1). Wheaton, IL: Victor Books.

¹⁸ *'Behold, we are going up to Jerusalem; and the Son of Man will be delivered to the chief priests and scribes, and they will condemn Him to death, ¹⁹ and will deliver Him to the Gentiles to mock and scourge and crucify Him, and on the third day He will be raised up.'"*

In our main text of Matthew 26, we read of the days before Jesus' crucifixion. Verse 2 states that two days before the Passover, He reminded His followers that He would be crucified. As you will recall, the origin of Passover was in Egypt when God told His people, through Moses, to sprinkle the blood of the Passover lamb on their, *"two doorposts and on the lintel of the houses"* **Exodus 12:7**. The blood of the lamb would serve as a sign: *"And the blood shall be a sign for you on the houses where you live; and when I see the blood I will pass over you, and no plague will befall you to destroy you when I strike the land of Egypt."* **Exodus 12:13**. The judgment against Egypt was clear— God would, *"...strike down all the first-born in the land of Egypt, both man and beast; and against all the gods of Egypt I will execute judgments...."* **Exodus 12:12**. Here is that entire section regarding the Passover:

> **Exodus 12:1-13:** *"Now the Lord said to Moses and Aaron in the land of Egypt, ² 'This month shall be the beginning of months for you; it is to be the first month of the year to you. ³ Speak to all the congregation of Israel, saying, On the tenth of this month they are each one to take a lamb for themselves, according to their fathers' households, a lamb for each household. ⁴ Now if the household is too small for a lamb, then he and his neighbor nearest to his house are to take one according to the number of persons in them; according to what each man should eat, you are to divide the lamb. ⁵ Your lamb shall be an unblemished male a year old; you may take it from the sheep or from the goats. ⁶ And you shall keep it until the fourteenth day of the same month, then the whole assembly of the congregation of Israel is to kill it at twilight. ⁷ Moreover, they shall take some of the blood and put it on the two doorposts and on the lintel of the houses in which they eat it. ⁸ And they shall eat the flesh that same night, roasted with fire, and they shall eat it with unleavened bread and bitter herbs. ⁹ Do not eat any of it raw or boiled at all with water, but rather roasted with fire, both its head and its legs along with its entrails. ¹⁰ And you shall not leave any of it over until morning, but whatever is left of it until morning, you shall burn with fire. ¹¹ Now you shall eat it in this manner: with your loins girded, your sandals on your feet, and your staff in your hand; and you shall eat it in haste—it is the Lord's Passover. ¹² For I will go through the land of Egypt on that night, and will strike down all the first-born in the land of Egypt, both man and beast; and against all the gods of Egypt I will execute judgments—I am the Lord. ¹³ And the blood shall be a sign for you on the houses where you live; and when I see the blood I will pass over you, and no plague will befall you to destroy you when I strike the land of Egypt.'"*

Many of the Old Testament concepts served as a mere shadow of their completion/fulfillment in Christ.

> **Colossians 2:16-17:** *"Therefore let no one act as your judge in regard to food or drink or in respect to a festival or a new moon or a Sabbath day— ¹⁷ <u>things which are a mere shadow of what is to come; but the substance belongs to Christ."</u>*

Jesus is the Passover Lamb for us who have been saved by God from the judgment of hell:

> **1 Corinthians 5:7:** *"Clean out the old leaven, that you may be a new lump, just as you are in fact unleavened. For Christ our Passover also has been sacrificed."*

> **1 Peter 1:18-19:** *"...knowing that you were not redeemed with perishable things like silver or gold from your futile way of life inherited from your forefathers,* [19] *but with precious blood, as of a lamb unblemished and spotless, the blood of Christ."*

Jesus is the only true and complete sacrifice for our sins. John the Baptist recognized this when he said:

> **John 1:29:** *"The next day he *saw Jesus coming to him, and *said, 'Behold, the Lamb of God who takes away the sin of the world!'"*

It is no coincidence that He was crucified during Passover. As we see in both Matthew 26:5 and Mark 14:1-2, Jesus' murderers did not want Him killed during Passover:

> **Mark 14:1-2:** *"Now the Passover and Unleavened Bread was two days off; and the chief priests and the scribes were seeking how to seize Him by stealth, and kill Him;* [2] *for they were saying, 'Not during the festival, lest there be a riot of the people.'"*

Regardless of what the religious leaders wanted, God was and is in complete control. Remember that Jesus did not get overrun and killed. Even though they plotted to kill Him on many occasions (see John 7:1), Jesus was in complete control of when and how He would die.

> **John 10:17-18:** *"For this reason the Father loves Me, because I lay down My life that I may take it again.* [18] *No one has taken it away from Me, but I lay it down on My own initiative. I have authority to lay it down, and I have authority to take it up again. This commandment I received from My Father."*

VERSE 3-5: *"Then the chief priests and the elders of the people were gathered together in the court of the high priest, named Caiaphas;* [4] *and they plotted together to seize Jesus by stealth, and kill Him.* [5] *But they were saying, 'Not during the festival, lest a riot occur among the people.'"*

Here we see the powerful religious leaders working together in a conspiracy to have Jesus killed. They gathered in Caiaphas' court. Caiaphas was not some neutral judge. He had been arguing in favor of and plotting how to murder Jesus for some time:

> **John 11:49-50:** *"But a certain one of them, Caiaphas, who was high priest that year, said to them, 'You know nothing at all,* [50] *nor do you take into account that it is expedient for you that one man should die for the people, and that the whole nation should not perish.'"*

Here is a little more information on the murderous conspirators: Joseph Caiaphas was high priest from AD 18 to 36, and prior to that, his father-in-law Annas served as the high priest from 6 A.D until he was removed by the Romans in 15 A.D. [479] Even though Caiaphas was the Roman

---

[479] Wood, D. R. W. (1996). *New Bible Dictionary* (3rd ed. /) (p. 155). Leicester, England; Downers Grove, Ill.: InterVarsity Press.

installed high priest, Jewish tradition suggested that once an individual was a high priest, he always was a high priest.[480] We see this in Acts 4:5-6, where Annas is called the high priest:

> *"And it came about on the next day, that their rulers and elders and scribes were gathered together in Jerusalem; 6 and Annas the high priest was there, and Caiaphas and John and Alexander, and all who were of high-priestly descent."*

"Annas had great personal influence with succeeding high priests. Five of his sons and Caiaphas, his son-in-law became high priest."[481] Annas conducted his own interrogation of Jesus prior to sending him to Caiaphas (John 18:13-24). Caiaphas, upon receiving Jesus, interrogated Him and then the chief priests and elders delivered Jesus to Pilate (Matthew 26:57–68; Matthew 27:1-2; John 11:49).

Notice in **Matthew 26:4** it says that they, *"plotted together to seize Jesus by stealth, and kill Him."* This means they were trying to figure out how to quietly/secretly take Jesus by surprise. Verse 5 tells us why they did not want to make a public scene about it: *"...Not during the festival, lest a riot occur among the people...."* (See also Mark 14:1-2.) Understand that their concern about a riot was not simply a fear of civil unrest. Their real concern was that the people would directly attack them for arresting Jesus. "They were awed, not by the fear of God, but by the fear of the people; all their concern was for their own safety, not God's honor." [482] Luke sets this out plainly:

> **Luke 22:1-2:** *"Now the Feast of Unleavened Bread, which is called the Passover, was approaching. 2 And the chief priests and the scribes were seeking how they might put Him to death; for they were afraid of the people."*

There was good reason for them to be afraid of the people because a mere few days before, these people were declaring Jesus as the Messiah!

> **Matthew 21:8-9:** *"And most of the multitude spread their garments in the road, and others were cutting branches from the trees, and spreading them in the road. 9 And the multitudes going before Him, and those who followed after were crying out, saying,*
> *'Hosanna to the Son of David;*
> *Blessed is He who comes in the name of the Lord;*
> *Hosanna in the highest!'"*

Summary and Application

Here we see the great ugliness of religious hypocrites. Their concern is for their own power and control of other people. What they do not realize is that God's will is going to be done regardless. Take a look at Psalm 2 and see how vainly people think they can fight against God.

---

[480] "The Mishnah (*Horayoth* 3. 4) says: 'A high priest in office differs from the priest that is passed from his high priest, hood only in the bullock that is offered on the Day of Atonement and the tenth of the ephah.' Secondly, the title 'high priest' is given in Acts and Josephus to members of the few priestly families from which most high priests were drawn, as well as to those exercising the high-priestly office." Wood, D. R. W. (1996). *New Bible dictionary* (3rd ed.) (p. 155). Leicester, England; Downers Grove, Ill.: InterVarsity Press.

[481] Wood, D. R. W. (1996). *New Bible Dictionary* (3rd ed.) (p. 49). Leicester, England; Downers Grove, Ill.: InterVarsity Press.

[482] Henry, M. (1996, c1991). *Matthew Henry's Commentary on the Whole Bible: Complete and Unabridged in One Volume* (Matthew 26:1). Peabody: Hendrickson.

Psalm 2:

"Why are the nations in an uproar,
And the peoples devising a vain thing?
[2] *The kings of the earth take their stand,*
And the rulers take counsel together
Against the Lord and against His Anointed:
[3] *'Let us tear their fetters apart,*
And cast away their cords from us!'
[4] *He who sits in the heavens laughs,*
The Lord scoffs at them.
[5] *Then He will speak to them in His anger*
And terrify them in His fury:
[6] *But as for Me, I have installed My King*
Upon Zion, My holy mountain.
[7] *I will surely tell of the decree of the Lord:*
He said to Me, 'Thou art My Son,
Today I have begotten Thee.
[8] *Ask of Me, and I will surely give the nations as Thine inheritance,*
And the very ends of the earth as Thy possession.
[9] *Thou shalt break them with a rod of iron,*
Thou shalt shatter them like earthenware.'
[10] *Now therefore, O kings, show discernment;*
Take warning, O judges of the earth.
[11] *Worship the Lord with reverence,*
And rejoice with trembling.
[12] *Do homage to the Son, lest He become angry, and you perish in the way,*
For His wrath may soon be kindled.
How blessed are all who take refuge in Him!"

<u>MATTHEW 26:6-13</u>
(ALABASTER OF PERFUME TO ANOINT FOR BURIAL)

"Now when Jesus was in Bethany, at the home of Simon the leper, ⁷ a woman came to Him with an alabaster vial of very costly perfume, and she poured it upon His head as He reclined at the table. ⁸ But the disciples were indignant when they saw this, and said, 'Why this waste? ⁹ For this perfume might have been sold for a high price and the money given to the poor.' ¹⁰ But Jesus, aware of this, said to them, 'Why do you bother the woman? For she has done a good deed to Me. ¹¹ For the poor you have with you always; but you do not always have Me. ¹² For when she poured this perfume upon My body, she did it to prepare Me for burial. ¹³ Truly I say to you, wherever this gospel is preached in the whole world, what this woman has done shall also be spoken of in memory of her.'"

Introduction

First let us get orientated with the timetable: "Matthew here presents a flashback to the previous Saturday, when Jesus came into the area of **Bethany** and Bethphage, just east of Jerusalem near the Mount of Olives (see Matthew 21:1; Mark 11:1)."[483] The parallel passages for this story are found in Mark 14:3-9, John 12:1-8 and Luke 10:38-42. The story of the woman in Luke 7:37-39 is a different event, but is similar in that it was an act of love for the Savior.

VERSE 6: *"Now when Jesus was in Bethany, at the home of Simon the leper...."*

Who was Simon the leper? We really do not know for sure. Most commentators believe that he was a leper that Jesus healed. The support for that view is that if Simon continued to suffer from leprosy, he would not have been welcome in the community by it residents.

VERSE 7: *"...a woman came to Him with an alabaster vial of very costly perfume, and she poured it upon His head as He reclined at the table."*

We see in John 12:3 that the woman who did this was Mary, whose siblings were Martha and Lazarus. Mary came to Jesus and broke open a bottle of expensive perfume and anointed Him. When it says that it was *"costly,"* we get a more exact value from John, who tells us that Judas believed that it could be sold for 300 denarii (John 12:4-5). Since a denarii was equivalent to a laborer's daily wage, 300 denarii would be approximately 10 months' work. According to Mark, the perfume was made of "spikenard" (KJV), which is also called "nard." A more specific definition is as follows: "Nardostochys jatamansi an herb, related to valerian, was imported from northern India and used widely by Hebrews and Romans alike in the anointing of the dead."[484]

---

[483] MacArthur, J. (1989). *Matthew* (Matthew 26:17). Chicago: Moody Press.

[484] Wood, D. R. W. (1996). *New Bible Dictionary* (3rd ed.) (p. 844). Leicester, England; Downers Grove, Ill.: InterVarsity Press.

John also gives us more detail regarding the anointing. He tells us that she anointed His feet and then wiped them with her hair (John 12:3).

VERSES 8-9: *"But the disciples were indignant when they saw this, and said, 'Why this waste? ⁹ For this perfume might have been sold for a high price and the money given to the poor.'"*

Notice the critical attitude of the disciples: *"But the disciples were <u>indignant</u> when they saw this...."* v.8. Webster defines *"indignation"* as, "anger aroused by something unjust, unworthy, or mean."[485] This same judgmental attitude of the disciples is unfortunately found in some churches today. A person may be actively serving God in a Biblically sound ministry, while others around him are focusing their time and energy criticizing the work. This attitude can come from a myriad of origins[486] including judging externals and not the heart that God sees. *"...for God sees not as man sees, for man looks at the outward appearance, but the Lord looks at the heart."* <u>1 Samuel 16:7</u>.

Where did the suggestion for the disciples' critical attitude come from? Deeper study of this event sheds light on the fact that it was Judas who poisoned their viewpoint. This is another example of why one must be alert to the false-christian's presence among the true believers. The false-religious/unbeliever often will throw out slander against true ministry to distract, discourage, and destroy it. The slander is usually disguised as some "righteous purpose."
An example of this is Judas who feigns a concern for the poor when he really is upset that it is a lost opportunity to steal more money from the disciples' treasury. In <u>John 12:4-6</u>:

> *"But Judas Iscariot, one of His disciples, who was intending to betray Him, *said, ⁵ 'Why was this perfume not sold for three hundred denarii, and given to poor people?' ⁶ Now he said this, not because he was concerned about the poor, but because he was a thief, and as he had the money box, he used to pilfer what was put into it."*

By this time Judas realized that he was not going to get power, glory, and wealth out of being a disciple of Jesus, so he began to look for ways to make up for it. We read that he stole money from the disciples' treasury (John 12:6). No doubt he was thinking that if that perfume was sold and the money put into the money box, he could steal some of it. We read in Matthew that financial gain was on the mind of Judas as he went to the religious leaders to get some money to betray Jesus.

> <u>Matthew 26:14-16:</u> *"Then one of the twelve, named Judas Iscariot, went to the chief priests, ¹⁵ and said, 'What are you willing to give me to deliver Him up to*

---

[485] *Merriam-Webster Collegiate Dictionary, 11ᵗʰ edition.*

[486] Immature believers, and even mature believers can succumb to the temptation of engaging in this type of nitpicking conduct. The most common origin is demonic, in which the unbeliever or false-believer persecutes the children of promise: *"And you brethren, like Isaac, are children of promise. But as at that time he who was born according to the flesh persecuted him who was born according to the Spirit, so it is now also."* <u>Galatians 4:28–29.</u> (See also John 15:19-20, John 16:2, 1 Peter 4:12-14.)

you?' And they weighed out to him thirty pieces of silver. [16] And from then on he began looking for a good opportunity to betray Him."

VERSES 10-11: *"But Jesus, aware of this, said to them, 'Why do you bother the woman? For she has done a good deed to Me. [11]For the poor you have with you always; but you do not always have Me.'"*

What Jesus declares good, is what is truly good—end of discussion. Here we see that Jesus declares *"good"* what Mary does by anointing Him with perfume.

In verse 11, Jesus points out that the poor will always be in existence. No welfare system or socialistic system will truly resolve poverty. Verse 11 is not to be understood as giving anyone an excuse not to have a deep care for the poor.[487] What Jesus is pointing out is that His presence and true worship of Him is much more important than the poor who will always be there. Jesus further explains that this event represents the anointing of Him for His burial. Jesus came to give His life as a ransom for many.

VERSES 12-13: *"For when she poured this perfume upon My body, she did it to prepare Me for burial. [13]Truly I say to you, wherever this gospel is preached in the whole world, what this woman has done shall also be spoken of in memory of her."*

The anointing was done for Jesus' burial. Jesus spoke of His upcoming crucifixion on other occasions (Matthew 16:21, 17:22-23, and 20:18-19). Obviously Mary was a woman of faith who believed what Jesus said. Her act was one of love and worship. Jesus told His disciples that her act will be spoken of everywhere the Gospel is preached. As with all that comes from the mouth of God, this too has proven true. J.C. Ryle put it this way:

> "We may be laughed at and ridiculed by the world. Our motives may be misunderstood; our conduct may be misrepresented; our sacrifices for Christ's sake may be called 'waste'—waste of time, waste of money, waste

---

[487] God has great concern for the poor as exhibited in the chapter before.

> **Matthew 25:34–40:** *"Then the King will say to those on His right, 'Come, you who are blessed of My Father, inherit the kingdom prepared for you from the foundation of the world. For I was hungry, and you gave Me something to eat; I was thirsty, and you gave Me something to drink; I was a stranger, and you invited Me in; naked, and you clothed Me; I was sick, and you visited Me; I was in prison, and you came to Me.' Then the righteous will answer Him, 'Lord, when did we see You hungry, and feed You, or thirsty, and give You something to drink? And when did we see You a stranger, and invite You in, or naked, and clothe You? When did we see You sick, or in prison, and come to You?' The King will answer and say to them, 'Truly I say to you, to the extent that you did it to one of these brothers of Mine, even the least of them, you did it to Me.'"*

> **Proverbs 14:31:** *"He who oppresses the poor taunts his Maker, But he who is gracious to the needy honors Him."*

of strength. Let none of these things move us. The eye of Him who sat in Simon's house at Bethany is upon us; He notes all we do, and is well pleased."[488]

1 Corinthians 15:58: *"Therefore, my beloved brethren, be steadfast, immovable, always abounding in the work of the Lord, <u>knowing that your toil is not in vain in the Lord.</u>"*

Summary and Application

As with everything we do, Jesus sees the heart. Mary did not do this act in some cold, religious and ritualistic manner, but out of true love for the Savior. We must likewise be those who worship in spirit and truth. We do not worship or conduct ourselves to win the approval of man, but so we bless God. Notice how Mary gave that which was of great value in her act of worship. Is that the way you worship? Do you instead decide if the cost is more than you want to give? Are you afraid the time commitment is too much for you when you have other things to do? Repent and re-prioritize so that your lifestyle is one of loving worship of Christ.

> **John 4:23-24:** *"But an hour is coming, and now is, when the true worshipers shall worship the Father in spirit and truth; for such people the Father seeks to be His worshipers. 24 God is spirit, and those who worship Him must worship in spirit and truth."*

---

[488] *Matthew* / Ryle, J.C. p.251 (Expository Thoughts on the Gospels) (Crossways Classic Commentaries: v.1)

<u>MATTHEW 26:14-19</u>
(BETRAYAL OF JESUS BY JUDAS)

"Then one of the twelve, named Judas Iscariot, went to the chief priests, ¹⁵ *and said, 'What are you willing to give me to deliver Him up to you?' And they weighed out to him thirty pieces of silver.* ¹⁶ *And from then on he began looking for a good opportunity to betray Him.*

¹⁷ *Now on the first day of Unleavened Bread the disciples came to Jesus, saying, 'Where do You want us to prepare for You to eat the Passover?'* ¹⁸ *And He said, 'Go into the city to a certain man, and say to him, The Teacher says, My time is at hand; I am to keep the Passover at your house with My disciples.''* ¹⁹ *And the disciples did as Jesus had directed them; and they prepared the Passover."*

Introduction

Here we see Judas beginning his betrayal of Jesus. We are also entering into the Passover celebration. As they continue in the final days before the crucifixion, we look at the events that took place on Thursday.[489]

---

[489] MacArthur writes: "It is clear from this passage in Matthew, as well from many others in all four gospel records, that Jesus and the disciples ate the Passover meal on Thursday evening. Certain other passages, however, such as the one cited below from John's gospel, indicate that some Jews celebrated the Passover on Friday, which seems to create a contradiction and has given some scholars what they think is proof of scriptural error.

The apostle John notes that after the Passover meal Jesus took His disciples out of the city to the Garden of Gethsemane, which was on the western slope of the Mount of Olives. He was arrested there and taken first to the high priest Annas (John 18:13) and then to the house of his father-in-law, Caiaphas, who also still held the title of high priest (v. 24). A few hours later, while it was still early on Friday morning, Jesus was taken to Pilate. But the Jewish leaders would 'not enter into the Praetorium in order that they might not be defiled, but might eat the Passover' (v. 28). Unlike Jesus and the disciples, those Jews obviously had not yet eaten the Passover.

Some interpreters suggest that because those religious leaders would surely have celebrated the Passover at the proper time, Jesus must have moved His observance up a day. But Jesus was meticulous in His observance of the Mosaic law and would not have desecrated such an important feast by observing it at the wrong time. Even had He wanted to do such a thing, however, He could not have, because the lamb eaten at the Passover meal first had to be slaughtered by a priest in the Temple and have its blood sprinkled on the altar. No priest would have performed that ritual a day earlier, or even an hour earlier, than the law prescribed.

Other scholars suggest that the chief priests and elders involved in Jesus' arrest were a day late in their observance. But in spite of their control of the Temple, even those ungodly men would not have dared make an exception for themselves for this most celebrated of all feasts. Not only that, but John recognized Friday as the legitimate Passover day, reporting that when Pilate finally agreed to Jesus' crucifixion 'it was the day of preparation for the Passover' (John 19:14). In the same verse he states that 'it was about the sixth hour,' that is, noon on Friday.

Some three hours later, 'about the ninth hour,' Jesus cried out from the cross, 'My God, My God, why hast Thou forsaken Me?' (Matthew 27:46). Shortly after that, 'Jesus cried out again with a loud voice, and yielded up His spirit' (v. 50). John therefore specifically recounts that our Lord died within the prescribed time of sacrifice for the Passover lambs, from three to five o'clock in the afternoon of Passover day. At the very time those lambs were being sacrificed in the Temple, 'Christ our Passover also [was] sacrificed on Calvary (1 Corinthians 5:7). [Note continued on the next page]

VERSES 14-16: *"Then one of the twelve, named Judas Iscariot, went to the chief priests, ¹⁵ and said, 'What are you willing to give me to deliver Him up to you?' And they weighed out to him thirty pieces of silver. ¹⁶ And from then on he began looking for a good opportunity to betray Him."*

Remember in Matthew 26:6-13 we read how the disciples were concerned about the waste of the perfume? The Apostle John gave us some more detail on the disciples' concern for the poor in John 12:4-6. That section explained that it was Judas who started the discussion about the perfume being wasted on Jesus. His complaint was that it could have been sold and given to the poor. John explained why Judas complained about the supposed waste: *"Now he said this, not because he was concerned about the poor, but because he was a thief, and as he had the money box, he used to pilfer what was put into it."* **John 12:6.**

In our text of Matthew 26:14-16, we continue to see Judas' love for money. He goes to the chief priests and asks them what they will give him to get Jesus. Money and materialism are often bait that the devil uses on people. Remember what Satan told Jesus during the temptation: *"...All these things will I give You, if You fall down and worship me."* **Matthew 4:9.** The Puritan William Jenkyn said:

[Note continued.]

In addition to that evidence for a Friday Passover and crucifixion is the fact that, just as the tenth of Nisan was on a Monday the year Jesus was crucified, the fourteenth (the day of Passover, Exodus. 12:6) was on the following Friday. Still further evidence is Joseph of Arimathea's taking Jesus' body down from the cross on 'the preparation day, that is, the day before the Sabbath' (Mark 15:42; cf. John 19:42). That day of preparation referred to the weekly preparation for the Sabbath, not preparation for the Passover, as in John 19:14. Unless it was qualified (such as being for the Passover), the day of preparation always referred to preparation for the Sabbath and was commonly used to designate Friday, the day before the Sabbath (Saturday).

Why, then, did Jesus observe the Passover on the previous evening? The answer lies in a difference among the Jews in the way they reckoned the beginning and ending of days. From Josephus, the Mishna, and other ancient Jewish sources we learn that the Jews in northern Palestine calculated days from sunrise to sunrise. That area included the region of Galilee, where Jesus and all the disciples except Judas had grown up. Apparently most, if not all, of the Pharisees used that system of reckoning. But Jews in the southern part, which centered in Jerusalem, calculated days from sunset to sunset. Because all the priests necessarily lived in or near Jerusalem, as did most of the Sadducees, those groups followed the southern scheme.

That variation doubtlessly caused confusion at times, but it also had some practical benefits. During Passover time, for instance, it allowed for the feast to be celebrated legitimately on two adjoining days, thereby permitting the Temple sacrifices to be made over a total period of four hours rather than two. That separation of days may also have had the effect of reducing both regional and religious clashes between the two groups.

On that basis the seeming contradictions in the gospel accounts are easily explained. Being Galileans, Jesus and the disciples considered Passover day to have started at sunrise on Thursday and to end at sunrise on Friday. The Jewish leaders who arrested and tried Jesus, being mostly priests and Sadducees, considered Passover day to begin at sunset on Thursday and end at sunset on Friday. By that variation, predetermined by God's sovereign provision, Jesus could thereby legitimately celebrate the last Passover meal with His disciples and yet still be sacrificed on Passover day.

Once again we see how God sovereignly and marvelously provides for the precise fulfillment of His redemptive plan. Jesus was anything but a victim of men's wicked schemes, much less of blind circumstance. Every word He spoke and every action He took were divinely directed and secured. Even the words and actions by others against Him were divinely controlled (see, e.g., John 11:49–52; 19:11)."

MacArthur, J. (1989). Matthew (Matthew 26:21). Chicago: Moody Press.

"The devil shapes himself to the fashions of all men. If he meet with a proud man, or a prodigal man, then he makes himself a flatterer; if a covetous man, then he comes with a reward in his hand. He hath an apple for Eve, a grape for Noah, a change of raiment for Gehazi, a bag for Judas. He can dish out his meat for all palates; he hath a last to fit every shoe; he hath something to please all conditions."[490]

Scripture warns us that <u>greed is idolatry</u> (Colossians 3:5). We see this same apostasy working in Demas by his desertion of Paul for the sake of worldly pursuits: *"... for Demas, having loved this present world, has deserted me and gone to Thessalonica...."* <u>**2 Timothy 4:10**</u>.

Notice Judas and the religious leaders did not negotiate. Judas was willing to take their first offer. We next read that the false religious leaders are right there on the spot counting out 30 pieces of silver. Take note of the fact that the Mosaic Law set the value of a slave at 30 pieces of silver (Exodus 21:32). Approximately 550 years earlier, God showed through the prophet Zechariah that the Good Shepherd would be mocked and considered to be worth nothing more than a slave (30 pieces of silver) to the people of Israel (Zechariah 11:12-14).

> <u>**Zechariah 11:12–14:**</u> *"I said to them, 'If it is good in your sight, give me my wages; but if not, never mind!' So they weighed out thirty shekels of silver as my wages. Then the Lord said to me, 'Throw it to the potter, that magnificent price at which I was valued by them.' So I took the thirty shekels of silver and threw them to the potter in the house of the Lord. Then I cut in pieces my second staff Union, to break the brotherhood between Judah and Israel."*

We are starting to get a glimpse of the real Judas. He was not a good guy who went bad, or even a disappointment to Jesus. Jesus knew from the beginning Judas would betray Him:

> <u>**John 6:64:**</u> *"'But there are some of you who do not believe.' <u>For Jesus knew from the beginning</u> who they were who did not believe, and <u>who it was that would betray Him.</u>"*

> <u>**John 6:70-71:**</u> *"Jesus answered them, 'Did I Myself not choose you, the twelve, and <u>yet one of you is a devil?</u>' [71] Now He meant Judas the son of Simon Iscariot, for he, one of the twelve, was going to betray Him."*

Judas was not interested in being regenerated by Christ. His only concern was to obtain power and money for himself. Judas could see that Jesus was not going to rid Israel of Roman rule and thus not become a powerful earthly ruler. Judas also realized that he was not going to get any political power or money for himself as a result of all the time he spent following Jesus. He then decided to cut his losses and at least get something out of it:

> <u>**Matthew 26:14-16:**</u> *"Then one of the twelve, named Judas Iscariot, went to the chief priests, [15] <u>and said, 'What are you willing to give me to deliver Him up to you?'</u> And they weighed out to him thirty pieces of silver. [16] And from then on he began looking for a good opportunity to betray Him."*

His mocking contempt for Christ is fully shown when Judas uses a kiss as the betrayal sign:

---

[490] Thomas, I. D. E. (1999). *The Golden Treasury of Puritan Quotations* (electronic ed.) (p. 76). Simpsonville, SC: Christian Classics Foundation.

Mark 14:44-45: *"Now he who was betraying Him had given them a signal, saying, 'Whomever I shall kiss, He is the one; seize Him, and lead Him away under guard.' *45* And after coming, he immediately went to Him, saying, 'Rabbi!' and kissed Him."*

Scripture tells us in **James 1:15:** *"...when sin is accomplished, it brings forth death."* Judas was not an exception to this verse. He had remorse for what he did, but not repentance.

Matthew 27:5: *"And he threw the pieces of silver into the sanctuary and departed; and he went away and hanged himself."*

As one writer said, Judas "...lives on the stage of Scripture as an awful warning to the uncommitted follower of Jesus who is in His company but does not share His Spirit (cf. Romans 8:9b)." [491]

Judas is the classic apostate. An apostate is one who knows the plan of salvation yet never truly believes it and thus rejects it. The definition of an apostate is one who goes on sinning by living in unbelief of Jesus' sacrifice for sins (Hebrews 10:26). The difference between an apostate and a backslidden/disobedient Christian becomes obvious in that the apostate will make claims to know the way of salvation in Christ, but will inevitably reject Him. Many do that today.

1 John 2:19: *"They went out from us, but they were not really of us; for if they had been of us, they would have remained with us; but they went out, in order that it might be shown that they all are not of us."*

We have seen that Judas made himself a very tricky apostate. He appeared honest enough to be the treasurer for the disciples (John 12:6). But true to his hypocrisy, Judas used his position as treasurer to steal from the group (John 12:4-6). His stealth hypocrisy also is shown by the fact that the other disciples, who had been around Judas for about three years, still did not have him pegged to be the one who would betray Jesus:

Matthew 26:20-22: *"Now when evening had come, He was reclining at the table with the twelve disciples. *21* And as they were eating, He said, 'Truly I say to you that one of you will betray Me.' *22* <u>And being deeply grieved, they each one began to say to Him, 'Surely not I, Lord?'"</u>*

VERSES 17-19: *"Now on the first day of Unleavened Bread the disciples came to Jesus, saying, 'Where do You want us to prepare for You to eat the Passover?' *18* And He said, 'Go into the city to a certain man, and say to him, 'The Teacher says, My time is at hand; I am to keep the Passover at your house with My disciples.'' *19* And the disciples did as Jesus had directed them; and they prepared the Passover."*

Here we see the preparations being made for what has traditionally been known as the *Last Supper*. Notice that Jesus told John and Peter to go and tell a certain man that the Passover dinner would be held at his house (Luke 22:8). We get more detail about this event from the parallel passage in Mark:

Mark 14:13-16: *"And He *sent two of His disciples, and *said to them, 'Go into the city, and a man will meet you carrying a pitcher of water; follow him; *14**

---

[491] Wood, D. R. W., and Marshall, I. H. (1996). *New Bible Dictionary (3rd ed.)* (p. 626). Leicester, England; Downers Grove, IL: InterVarsity Press.

and wherever he enters, say to the owner of the house, The Teacher says, 'Where is My guest room in which I may eat the Passover with My disciples?' *15 And he himself will show you a large upper room furnished and ready; and prepare for us there.* *16 And the disciples went out, and came to the city, and found it just as He had told them; and they prepared the Passover."*

Again we see the deity of Christ, as demonstrated by His omniscience. R.C. Sproul explains that the word omniscience "means to have all (omni) knowledge (science). It is a term that is properly applied to God alone. Only a being who is infinite and eternal is capable of knowing everything. The knowledge of a finite creature is always limited by a finite being."[492] Jesus knew that the man with the pitcher of water would be at the right place, at the right time for the disciples to see him.

Summary and Application

There are two applications to take away from this passage:

1. How scary it is to see someone like Judas who can walk, talk, and act the disciple's life, but never have been converted (i.e. never was a Christian). Check your heart. You may have a lot of knowledge about Jesus, but in your heart do you think Jesus is just some great prophet or a moral example? Maybe you view the church as an avenue to make business contacts, get attention, or obtain a position of authority. If so, you are another Judas. On the other hand, if you trust completely in Jesus Christ and His death on the cross as your only basis of forgiveness before God, you are His child.

2. We also learn an important fact about Jesus from the Passover preparations story. We see He has everything under His complete control. This is an important reminder to us when we start to fall into fear about our needs. We need to remember that it was the Lord God who said:

    Matthew 6:25-34: *"For this reason I say to you, do not be anxious for your life, as to what you shall eat, or what you shall drink; nor for your body, as to what you shall put on. Is not life more than food, and the body than clothing? 26 Look at the birds of the air, that they do not sow, neither do they reap, nor gather into barns, and yet your heavenly Father feeds them. Are you not worth much more than they? 27 And which of you by being anxious can add a single cubit to his life's span? 28 And why are you anxious about clothing? Observe how the lilies of the field grow; they do not toil nor do they spin, 29 yet I say to you that even Solomon in all his glory did not clothe himself like one of these. 30 But if God so arrays the grass of the field, which is alive today and tomorrow is thrown into the furnace, will He not much more do so for you, O men of little faith? 31 Do not be anxious then, saying, 'What shall we eat?' or 'What shall we drink?' or 'With what shall we clothe ourselves?' 32 For all these things the Gentiles eagerly seek; for your heavenly Father knows that you need all these things. 33 But seek first His kingdom and His righteousness; and all these things shall be added to you. 34*

---

[492] Sproul, R. C. (1996, c1992). *Essential truths of the Christian Faith; #15 The Omniscience of God.* Wheaton, Ill.: Tyndale House.

Therefore do not be anxious for tomorrow; for tomorrow will care for itself. Each day has enough trouble of its own."

MATTHEW 26:20-30
(THE LAST SUPPER)

"Now when evening had come, He was reclining at the table with the twelve disciples. ²¹ And as they were eating, He said, 'Truly I say to you that one of you will betray Me.' ²² And being deeply grieved, they each one began to say to Him, 'Surely not I, Lord?' ²³ And He answered and said, 'He who dipped his hand with Me in the bowl is the one who will betray Me. ²⁴ The Son of Man is to go, just as it is written of Him; but woe to that man by whom the Son of Man is betrayed! It would have been good for that man if he had not been born.' ²⁵And Judas, who was betraying Him, answered and said, 'Surely it is not I, Rabbi?' He *said to him, 'You have said it yourself.'

²⁶ And while they were eating, Jesus took some bread, and after a blessing, He broke it and gave it to the disciples, and said, 'Take, eat; this is My body.' ²⁷ And when He had taken a cup and given thanks, He gave it to them, saying, 'Drink from it, all of you; ²⁸ for this is My blood of the covenant, which is poured out for many for forgiveness of sins. ²⁹ But I say to you, I will not drink of this fruit of the vine from now on until that day when I drink it new with you in My Father's kingdom.'

³⁰ And after singing a hymn, they went out to the Mount of Olives."

Introduction

Here we read about the event known as the "Last Supper." The parallel accounts are in Mark 14:17-30, Luke 22:14-38, and John 13. This event was not an ordinary meal, but rather the Passover meal. At that dinner the Lord invoked the institution of "communion," which is now part of Christian practice. Scripture is clear that our participation in communion should be taken seriously. It must be approached with the right frame of mind because of the awesomeness of the event that we are remembering— God Almighty coming and dying to take the penalty of our sins.

VERSES 20-21: *"Now when evening had come, He was reclining at the table with the twelve disciples. ²¹ And as they were eating, He said, 'Truly I say to you that one of you will betray Me.'"*

What a terrible fright the disciples must have experienced after hearing the Lord state that one of their own would betray Him. Their response begs the question of whether we have the same sense of concern when we are challenged by others about our faith or lifestyle. There is many a proud Christian who will tell other believers how unashamed he is of the faith, but when he is out in the world it becomes obvious that making money or getting a promotion is his first priority.

VERSES 22-25: *"And being deeply grieved, they each one began to say to Him, 'Surely not I, Lord?' ²³ And He answered and said, 'He who dipped his hand with Me in the bowl is the one who will betray Me. ²⁴ The Son of Man is to go, just as it is written of Him; but woe to that man by whom the Son of Man is betrayed! It would have been good for that man if he had not been born.' ²⁵ And Judas, who was betraying Him, answered and said, 'Surely it is not I, Rabbi?' He *said to him, 'You have said it yourself.'"*

We see the disciples grieved about there being a betrayer among them. Mark gives us more details of this event by stating that each disciple began asking Jesus if he was the betrayer. **Mark 14:19:** *"They began to be grieved and to say to Him one by one, 'Surely not I?'"* This may explain why we read in Matthew that Judas also asks*"...Surely it is not I, Rabbi?"* **Matthew 26:25.** It is clear that Judas' question was not one of concern or even curiosity, but rather a necessary inquiry so as not to blow his cover as the betrayer. If everyone in the group asked Jesus if he were the betrayer and Judas did not, it would become obvious that he was the betrayer. Judas was hoping that Jesus did not know he had already cut a deal with the religious leaders. When Judas asked the question, he probably was watching Jesus carefully to determine how much He knew. Jesus' response to Judas was direct when *"He *said to him, 'You have said it yourself.'"*

Judas' response to that statement of Jesus' is not one of shock, grief or repentance. One could speculate from the text that Judas does not really care that his cover has been blown. Judas was never a believer and when it appeared that he was not going to get a good deal out of following Jesus, he became even more embolden to take care of himself. Judas is the ultimate example of an apostate. From the study of Matthew 26:14-19 we see Judas is the traitor. Judas was not a good guy who went bad or even a disappointment to Jesus. Jesus knew from the beginning Judas would betray Him:

> **John 6:64:** *"'But there are some of you who do not believe.' For Jesus knew from the beginning who they were who did not believe, and who it was that would betray Him."*

> **John 6:70-71:** *"Jesus answered them, 'Did I Myself not choose you, the twelve, and yet one of you is a devil?' 71 Now He meant Judas the son of Simon Iscariot, for he, one of the twelve, was going to betray Him."*

Jesus set forth Judas' destiny as damnation in calling him the *"son of perdition"*:
> **John 17:12:** *"... and I guarded them and not one of them perished but the son of perdition, so that the Scripture would be fulfilled."*

"Perdition" is defined as: a *"sense of 'destruction,' and with special reference to the fate of the wicked and their loss of eternal life...."*[493]

The fact that Judas was not a believer is highlighted in this verse, because the highest title Judas uses for Jesus is "Rabbi" (Matthew 26:25). We never read of Judas, calling Jesus "Lord."[494] Do not be confused by the verse in John 14:22. The Judas who calls Jesus Lord in that verse, is not Judas Iscariot. This is made plain in the text: **John 14:22:** *"Judas (not Iscariot) *said to Him, 'Lord, what then has happened that You are going to disclose Yourself to us, and not to the world?'"*

It is an interesting side note how Scripture identifies Judas. When we read of him being named among the 12 disciples, "the name of Judas always appears last, and usually with some

---

[493] Wood, D. R. W., and Marshall, I. H. (1996). *New Bible Dictionary* (3rd ed.) (p. 900). Leicester, England; Downers Grove, Ill.: InterVarsity Press.

[494] Wood, D. R. W. (1996). *New Bible Dictionary* (3rd ed.) (p. 626). Leicester, England; Downers Grove, Ill.: InterVarsity Press. Nowhere do we see Judas addressing Jesus as Lord.

description which brands him with an infamous stigma (e.g. 'who betrayed him,' Mark 3:19; Matthew 10:4; Luke 6:16; cf. John 18:2, 5)."[495]

We read from John that during the Passover meal, Judas is sent out from the group and Jesus finishes this important fellowship with His true disciples.

> **John 13:26-30:** *"Jesus therefore *answered, 'That is the one for whom I shall dip the morsel and give it to him.' So when He had dipped the morsel, He *took and *gave it to Judas, the son of Simon Iscariot. 27 And after the morsel, Satan then entered into him. Jesus therefore *said to him, 'What you do, do quickly.' 28 Now no one of those reclining at the table knew for what purpose He had said this to him. 29 For some were supposing, because Judas had the money box, that Jesus was saying to him, 'Buy the things we have need of for the feast'; or else, that he should give something to the poor. 30 And so after receiving the morsel he went out immediately; and it was night."*

Jesus makes it clear that Judas will get the punishment due him in **Matthew 26:24:**

> *"...but woe to that man by whom the Son of Man is betrayed! It would have been good for that man if he had not been born."*

VERSES 26-29: *"And while they were eating, Jesus took some bread, and after a blessing, He broke it and gave it to the disciples, and said, 'Take, eat; this is My body.' 27 And when He had taken a cup and given thanks, He gave it to them, saying, 'Drink from it, all of you; 28 for this is My blood of the covenant, which is poured out for many for forgiveness of sins. 29 But I say to you, I will not drink of this fruit of the vine from now on until that day when I drink it new with you in My Father's kingdom.'"*

Here we see the institution of the Lord's Supper. Jesus explains that the broken bread (i.e. torn from the loaf) represents His body. "The fact that He **broke** the bread does not symbolize a broken body, because John makes clear that, in fulfillment of prophecy, *'...Not a bone of Him shall be broken.'* (John 19:36; cf. Psalm 34:20), just as no bones of the original Passover lambs in Egypt were broken (Exodus 12:46)."[496] Often one will quote from the King James and New King James where in 1 Corinthians 11:24 it says the bread being broken represents Jesus body which was "broken."

> "The word broken (as in the KJV of verse 24) does not appear in the best manuscripts or in most modern translations. Though the Romans frequently broke the legs of crucified victims in order to hasten death as an act of mercy John specifically tells us that Jesus' legs were not broken. In order 'that the Scripture might be fulfilled, not a bone of Him shall be broken' (John 19:33, 36). The best reading therefore is simply *'This is My body, which is for you.'"*[497]

---

[495] Ibid at 624.

[496] MacArthur, J. (1989). *Matthew* (Matthew 26:28). Chicago: Moody Press.
KJV King James Version.

[497] MacArthur, J. (1996, c1984). *1 Corinthians.* Includes indexes. (1 Corinthians 11:23). Chicago: Moody Press.

Note how The New American Standard Bible states it in **1 Corinthians 11:24:** *"...and when He had given thanks, He broke it, and said, 'This is My body , which is for you; do this in remembrance of Me.'"*

It should be remembered that earlier in His earthly ministry, Jesus told the disciples, *"I am the bread of life; he who comes to Me shall not hunger, and he who believes in Me shall never thirst."* **John 6:35**.

Although bones were not broken, one should not understate the tremendous physical beating His body underwent in the punishment for our sins:

>**Isaiah 53:5:** *"But He was pierced through for our transgressions, He was crushed for our iniquities; The chastening for our well-being fell upon Him, And by His scourging we are healed."*

Jesus also explains in Matthew 26:27-28 that the wine represents His blood that was shed for us. We see more regarding the sacrificial blood of Jesus in Scripture:

>**Romans 5:9-10:** *"Much more then, having now been justified by His blood, we shall be saved from the wrath of God through Him. 10 For if while we were enemies, we were reconciled to God through the death of His Son, much more, having been reconciled, we shall be saved by His life."*

>**Revelation 5:8-9:** *"And when He had taken the book, the four living creatures and the twenty-four elders fell down before the Lamb, having each one a harp, and golden bowls full of incense, which are the prayers of the saints. 9 And they *sang a new song, saying, 'Worthy art Thou to take the book, and to break its seals; for Thou wast slain, and didst purchase for God with Thy blood men from every tribe and tongue and people and nation.'"*

In Matthew 26:29, Jesus says, *"But I say to you, I will not drink of this fruit of the vine from now on until that day when I drink it new with you in My Father's kingdom."* He is saying that He will not drink earthly produced wine again until He is joined with His disciples in the Kingdom of God. Luke points out that Jesus said, *"...until the kingdom of God comes."* This Kingdom to come refers to the millennium kingdom here on earth after His second coming.

>**Luke 22:19:** *"And when He had taken some bread and given thanks, He broke it, and gave it to them, saying, 'This is My body which is given for you; do this in remembrance of Me.'"*

We celebrate communion because it is an institution that Jesus instructed His disciples to do. It is very important how we approach the Lord's Supper when we participate. Some in the church suffered physical weakness, sickness and even death because they came to the Lord's table in an ungodly manner. The Apostle Paul explains this to the Corinthians:

>**1 Corinthians 11:23-34:** *"For I received from the Lord that which I also delivered to you, that the Lord Jesus in the night in which He was betrayed took bread; 24 and when He had given thanks, He broke it, and said, 'This is My body, which is for you; do this in remembrance of Me.' 25 In the same way He took the cup also, after supper, saying, 'This cup is the new covenant in My blood; do this, as often as you drink it, in remembrance of Me.' 26 For as often as you eat this bread and drink the cup, you proclaim the Lord's death until He comes. 27 Therefore whoever eats the bread or drinks the cup of the Lord in an*

unworthy manner, shall be guilty of the body and the blood of the Lord. 28 But let a man examine himself, and so let him eat of the bread and drink of the cup. 29 For he who eats and drinks, eats and drinks judgment to himself, if he does not judge the body rightly. 30 For this reason many among you are weak and sick, and a number sleep. 31 But if we judged ourselves rightly, we should not be judged. 32 But when we are judged, we are disciplined by the Lord in order that we may not be condemned along with the world. 33 So then, my brethren, when you come together to eat, wait for one another. 34 If anyone is hungry, let him eat at home, so that you may not come together for judgment. And the remaining matters I shall arrange when I come."

In Hebrews, the writer explains there is severe punishment for those who do not hold in highest regard the precious blood of Christ.

Hebrews 10:29: *"How much severer punishment do you think he will deserve who has trampled under foot the Son of God, and has regarded as unclean the blood of the covenant by which he was sanctified, and has insulted the Spirit of grace?"*

We need to have the right attitude and theology when we come to the Lord's table. An example of bad doctrine is a heretical concept called transubstantiation. This false doctrine maintains that the *"whole substance of the bread is changed into the literal body* [of Christ], *and the whole substance of the wine is changed into the literal blood* [of Christ]...." [498] We know that Jesus was speaking of the bread and wine as symbols. This is obvious because at the Last Supper Jesus continued to recline at the table with His disciples after making the statement in **Matthew 26:26-28**:

"...He broke it and gave it to the disciples, and said, 'Take, eat; this is My body.' 27 And when He had taken a cup and given thanks, He gave it to them, saying, 'Drink from it, all of you; 28 for this is My blood of the covenant, which is poured out for many for forgiveness of sins.'"

In other words, He did not disappear and become the bread and wine. This is an important lesson on how to interpret a passage of Scripture. We are to read the Bible literally unless the portion is clearly not to be read that way. Here the bread and the wine are symbolic, just like when Jesus said, "I am the door," in John 10:7. To better understand transubstantiation, I encourage you to read the footnote below by the great theologian A.A. Hodge addressing the subject of transubstantiation. [499]

---

[498] Hodge, A. A., and Hodge, C. (1996). *The confession of faith: With questions for theological students and Bible classes* (p. 359). Simpsonville, SC: Christian Classics Foundation.

[499] Hodge – his lengthy quote on **Transubstantiation**: "The Papal errors condemned in these sections are:

(1) Their doctrine of transubstantiation, or conversion of substance. The Council of Trent teaches (sees. 13. cans. 1–4) that the whole substance of the bread is changed into the literal body, and the whole substance of the wine is changed into the literal blood, of Christ; so that only the appearance or sensible properties of the bread and wine remain, and the only substances present are the true body and blood, soul and divinity, of our Lord. And thus He is objectively presented to, and is eaten and drunk by, every recipient, believer and unbeliever indifferently; and thus he remains before and after the communion, His very body and blood, Godhead and manhood, shut up in a vessel, carried about, elevated, worshipped, etc.

The Lutherans hold that while the bread and the wine remain, nevertheless at the words of consecration the real body and blood of Christ, though invisible, are really present in, with and under the bread and wine. [Hodge quote continued on the next page.]

[Hodge quote continued.]

The only ground of this doctrine is the word of our Lord, 'This is my body.' They hold the word 'is' is literal: all the Reformed Churches hold it must mean 'represents,' 'symbolizes.' This is a frequent usage of the word in Scripture. 'The seven good kine [cows] are seven years; and the seven good ears are seven years.' (Genesis 41:26,27; Ezekiel 37:11; Daniel 7:24; Luke 12:1; Revelation 1:20.) Besides, when our Lord said this, and gave them the bread to eat He was sitting by them in His sound, undivided flesh, eating and drinking with them.

This doctrine, then, is false—(a) Because it is not taught in Scripture. (b) Because it confounds the very idea of sacrament, making the sign identical with the thing it signifies. (c) It contradicts our senses, since we see, smell, taste, and feel bread and wine, and do never either see, or smell, or taste, or feel flesh and blood. (d) It contradicts reason; for reason teaches that qualities cannot exist except as they inhere in some substance, and that substance cannot be known and cannot act except by its qualities. But this doctrine supposes that the qualities of bread and wine remain without any substance, and that the substance of flesh and blood remains without any qualities. (e) It is absurd and impossible; because Christ's glorified body is still material and therefore finite, and therefore not omnipresent in all places on earth, but absent at the right hand of God in heaven.

(2) Their doctrine as to the mass as a sacrifice. The Council of Trent teaches (sees. 22., cans. 1–3) that the Eucharist is both a sacrament and a sacrifice. As a sacrament, the soul of the recipient is nourished by the real body, blood, soul and divinity of Christ, which he eats in the form of a wafer. As a sacrifice, it is 'an external oblation of the body and blood of Christ offered to God, in recognition of his supreme lordship, under the appearance of bread and wine visibly exhibited by a legitimate minister, with the addition of certain prayers and ceremonies prescribed by the Church, for the greater worship of God and edification of the people,' This is not a mere act in commemoration of the one sacrifice upon the cross, but a constantly repeated real, although bloodless, expiatory sacrifice, atoning for sin and propitiating God. (Council. Trent, sess. 22., can. 3.)

This doctrine is false, because—(a) It is nowhere taught in Scripture. (b) The Christian ministry are never called or spoken of as priests, but as 'teachers' and 'rulers.' (c) The one sacrifice of Christ on the cross was perfect, and excludes all others. (Hebrews 9:25–28; 10:10–27.) (d) The same ordinance cannot be both a sacrament and a sacrifice. Christ says that by eating and drinking we are to 'shew forth his death,' and to 'do this in remembrance of him'. The same act cannot be a commemoration of one sacrifice, and itself an actual sacrifice having intrinsic sin–expiating efficacy.

(3) Since the Papists hold that the entire substance of the bread and wine is permanently changed into the body, blood, soul and divinity of Christ, they consequently maintain that the principal intention of the ordinance is accomplished when the words of consecration are pronounced and the change effected. Hence they preserve the host carefully shut up in the pyx, elevate and adore and carry it about in their processions.

All this stands or falls with the doctrine of transubstantiation, before refuted.

(4) After the establishment of the doctrine of transubstantiation there arose the natural fear lest some of the august person of the Lord should be spoiled or lost from the crumbling of the bread or the spilling of the wine. Hence the bread is prepared in little wafers which cannot crumble, and the cup is denied to the laity and confined to the priests. To comfort the laity, they teach that as the blood is in the flesh, and as the soul is in the body, and as the divinity is in the soul of Christ, the whole person—body, blood, soul and divinity—of Christ is equally in every particle of the bread; so that he who receives the bread receives all. (Council Trent, sess. 21., cans. 1–3.)

(5) In opposition to the manifold abuses of this ordinance which prevail among the Romanists our Standards, in common with the general judgment of the Reformed Churches, teach that the Lord's Supper is essentially a communion, in which the fellowship of the believer with Christ and with his fellow–Christians is set forth by eating and drinking of the bread and the same cup. It follows that it should not be sent to persons not present at the administration, nor administered by the officiating priest to himself alone. In particular cases, however, it may be administered in private houses, for the benefit of Christians long confined by sickness

[Hodge quote continued on the next page.]

We get additional information about the Last Supper from Luke. Luke explains that while dining, the disciples became fleshly and began debating with each other on which of them was to be seen as the greatest disciple! How typical of our fallen flesh. At this great and holy event, they began looking to themselves instead of Christ.

> **Luke 22:24-30:** *"And there arose also a dispute among them as to which one of them was regarded to be greatest. 25 And He said to them, 'The kings of the Gentiles lord it over them; and those who have authority over them are called Benefactors. 26 But not so with you, but let him who is the greatest among you become as the youngest, and the leader as the servant. 27 For who is greater, the one who reclines at the table, or the one who serves? Is it not the one who reclines at the table? But I am among you as the one who serves. 28 And you are those who have stood by Me in My trials; 29 and just as My Father has granted Me a kingdom, I grant you 30 that you may eat and drink at My table in My kingdom, and you will sit on thrones judging the twelve tribes of Israel.'"*

We read from John that during the Last Supper, Jesus set the example that the greatest among them was to be a servant.

> **John 13:4-6 and 12-17:** *"....rose from supper, and *laid aside His garments; and taking a towel, He girded Himself about. 5 Then He *poured water into the basin, and began to wash the disciples' feet, and to wipe them with the towel with which He was girded. 6 And so He *came to Simon Peter....*
>
> *12 And so when He had washed their feet, and taken His garments, and reclined at the table again, He said to them, 'Do you know what I have done to you? 13 You call Me Teacher and Lord; and you are right, for so I am. 14 If I then, the Lord and the Teacher, washed your feet, you also ought to wash one another's feet. 15 For I gave you an example that you also should do as I did to you. 16 Truly, truly, I say to you, a slave is not greater than his master; neither is one who is sent greater than the one who sent him. 17 If you know these things, you are blessed if you do them.'"*

VERSE 30: *"And after singing a hymn, they went out to the Mount of Olives."*

Here we read that after the supper, they go to the Mount of Olives, which is the location where the Lord is betrayed and apprehended.

[Hodge quote continued.]

provided that the officers and a sufficient number of the members of the Church be present to preserve the true character of the ordinance as a communion.

SECTION 7 OF THE CONFESSION:

WORTHY receivers, outwardly partaking of the visible elements in this sacrament, do then also inwardly, by faith, really and indeed, yet not carnally and corporally, but spiritually, receive and feed upon Christ crucified, and all benefits of His death: the body and blood of Christ being then not corporally or carnally in, with, or under the bread and wine; yet as really, but spiritually, present to the faith of believers in that ordinance, as the elements themselves are to their outward senses."

[End of Hodge quote.]

Summary and Application

The Lord's Supper teaches us to constantly remember that our forgiveness is completely dependent on the sacrifice of Jesus Christ (Matthew 26:26-27, 1 Corinthians 11:23-26). We also learn the importance of humility and service toward each other (John 13:12-17). Finally, before participating, we must examine ourselves and conduct ourselves in a manner that does not disgrace the gospel.

> **1 Corinthians 11:27-30:** *"Therefore whoever eats the bread or drinks the cup of the Lord in an unworthy manner, shall be guilty of the body and the blood of the Lord. 28 But let a man examine himself, and so let him eat of the bread and drink of the cup. 29 For he who eats and drinks, eats and drinks judgment to himself, if he does not judge the body rightly. 30 For this reason many among you are weak and sick, and a number sleep."*

<u>MATTHEW 26:31-35</u>
(MISTAKEN CONFIDENCE IN ONE'S OWN STRENGTH)

"Then Jesus *said to them, 'You will all fall away because of Me this night, for it is written, I will strike down the shepherd, and the sheep of the flock shall be scattered. ³² But after I have been raised, I will go before you to Galilee.' ³³ But Peter answered and said to Him, 'Even though all may fall away because of You, I will never fall away.' ³⁴ Jesus said to him, 'Truly I say to you that this very night, before a cock crows, you shall deny Me three times.' ³⁵ Peter *said to Him, 'Even if I have to die with You, I will not deny You.' All the disciples said the same thing too."

Introduction
We need to begin by setting forth the location and time of this event. In the verses prior to this section, Matthew 26:20-29, we read of the Last Supper. In verse 30 we see that after the Last Supper, *"...they went out to the Mount of Olives."*

The lesson to derive from Matthew 26:31-35 is how we can make the mistake of putting trust in our flesh. When reading this section of Scripture, we often focus on Peter's denial and then we like to believe that his actions are a very rare event. The reality is that often Christians deny the Lord in word and deed so that they are not rejected by others. If you look at verse 35 closely, you will see that all the disciples said they would not deny Him and would be willing to die with Him. Yet shortly after the arrest of Jesus, the disciples ran to protect themselves. This raises the question, how do we keep from becoming "fair-weather Christians?" By "fair-weather Christians," I mean the type who proclaims Christ at church and among other believers, but denies Christ when faced with persecution from the world. Let's try to answer that question below.

VERSE 31: *"Then Jesus *said to them, 'You will all fall away because of Me this night, for it is written, I will strike down the shepherd, and the sheep of the flock shall be scattered."*

Here we see Jesus with the disciples at the Mount of Olives (v. 30) telling them what will happen in the near future. In verse 31 He made the statement, *"I will strike down the shepherd, and the sheep of the flock shall be scattered."* The verse that Jesus was quoting from can be found in Zechariah 13:7. Jesus was telling the disciples that this Scripture was about to be fulfilled because the disciples would flee from Jesus when it appeared that He was going to be destroyed by the religious leaders.

Note that in Zechariah 13:7 the verse says, "Strike the Shepherd." In Matthew 26:31 Jesus says, *"I will strike down the shepherd."* "The interpretive change from the command 'Strike' (Zechariah 13:7) to the assertion 'I will strike' suggests that Jesus [is]...God's suffering Servant...."[500] In other words the term *"I will"* refers to the Father as the one who will have the Son struck. *"I (God the Father) will strike (put to death) the Shepherd (Jesus), and the sheep (the*

---

[500] Walvoord, J. F. (1983-c1985). *The Bible Knowledge Commentary: An Exposition of the Scriptures* (Mark 14:27). Wheaton, IL: Victor Books.

*disciples) **will be scattered** (in all directions)."*[501] One might ask why the Father would do that. It must be remembered that Jesus did not come to earth to be a good example or simply to show God's love to us. He came here to suffer and die to pay the penalty of our sins.

> **Romans 5:9-10:** *"Much more then, having now been justified by His blood, we shall be saved from the wrath of God through Him. ¹⁰ For if while we were enemies, we were reconciled to God through the death of His Son, much more, having been reconciled, we shall be saved by His life."*

We see that the Father called His own Son, Jesus, to be the suffering servant, as prophesied in:

Isaiah 53:10 and 12:

> *"But the LORD was pleased*
> *To crush Him, putting Him to grief;*
> *If He would render Himself as a guilt offering….*
> ¹² *Therefore, I will allot Him a portion with the great, And He will divide the booty with the strong; Because He poured out Himself to death, And was numbered with the transgressors; Yet He Himself bore the sin of many, And interceded for the transgressors."*

VERSE 32: *"But after I have been raised, I will go before you to Galilee."*

Jesus tells the disciples that even though the group will be scattered, He will be raised from the dead and they are to meet Him in Galilee. Later in Matthew chapter 28, we see the angel at the tomb give the disciples instructions to go to Galilee to meet Jesus. Jesus also tells the women to send the disciples to Galilee.

> **Matthew 28:5-10:** *"And the angel answered and said to the women, 'Do not be afraid; for I know that you are looking for Jesus who has been crucified. ⁶ He is not here, for He has risen, just as He said. Come, see the place where He was lying. ⁷ And go quickly and tell His disciples that He has risen from the dead; and behold, He is going before you into Galilee, there you will see Him; behold, I have told you.' ⁸ And they departed quickly from the tomb with fear and great joy and ran to report it to His disciples. ⁹ And behold, Jesus met them and greeted them. And they came up and took hold of His feet and worshiped Him. ¹⁰ Then Jesus *said to them, 'Do not be afraid; go and take word to My brethren to leave for Galilee, and there they shall see Me.'"*

VERSES 33-34: *"But Peter answered and said to Him, 'Even though all may fall away because of You, I will never fall away.' ³⁴ Jesus said to him, 'Truly I say to you that this very night, before a cock crows, you shall deny Me three times.'"*

In these verses Peter, looking to his own strength and ability, boldly states that even if the rest of the men abandon Christ, he will not! Peter makes the mistake that we often are tempted to do. We are deceived into giving ourselves credit for our virtuous *intentions*. We often view ourselves as more noble than what our conduct reveals. For example, if you are not a drinker, don't let pride slip in and say, "I could never become a drunk."   It is that sort of pride in oneself that Peter

---

[501] Ibid (Mark 14:27).

exhibits, and he falls. Despite Peter's claims of faithfulness, Jesus states the reality in verse 34: *"Truly I say to you that this very night, before a cock crows, you shall deny Me three times."*

We must walk by faith and not in our own abilities and "will power." Paul made it clear that he did not put trust in himself to produce righteousness.

> **Philippians 3:3:** *"…for we are the true circumcision, who worship in the Spirit of God and glory in Christ Jesus and <u>put no confidence in the flesh</u>, …."*

This verse in Philippians 3 begins to answer the question of how one keeps from becoming a "fair-weather Christian." The answer is to not trust yourself or your own ability to fight against sin. We must lean completely on Christ. It is God alone who makes us stand (Romans 14:4). We are instructed to put on the armor of God because it is not our power or talents that make us stand firm against the enemy. We see from the section on the armor of God that knowing God's Word and praying helps us to see the schemes of the Devil before the strike.

> **Ephesians 6:10-20:** *"Finally, be strong in the Lord, and in the strength of His might. [11] Put on the full armor of God, that you may be able to stand firm against the schemes of the devil. [12] For our struggle is not against flesh and blood, but against the rulers, against the powers, against the world forces of this darkness, against the spiritual forces of wickedness in the heavenly places. [13] Therefore, take up the full armor of God, that you may be able to resist in the evil day, and having done everything, to stand firm. [14] Stand firm therefore, HAVING GIRDED YOUR LOINS WITH TRUTH, and HAVING PUT ON THE BREASTPLATE OF RIGHTEOUSNESS, [15] and having shod YOUR FEET WITH THE PREPARATION OF THE GOSPEL OF PEACE; [16] in addition to all, taking up the shield of faith with which you will be able to extinguish all the flaming missiles of the evil one. [17] And take THE HELMET OF SALVATION, <u>and the sword of the Spirit, which is the word of God.</u> [18] <u>With all prayer and petition pray at all times in the Spirit,</u> and with this in view, be on the alert with all perseverance and petition for all the saints, [19] and pray on my behalf, that utterance may be given to me in the opening of my mouth, to make known with boldness the mystery of the gospel, [20] for which I am an ambassador in chains; that in proclaiming it I may speak boldly, as I ought to speak."*

VERSE 35: *"Peter *said to Him, 'Even if I have to die with You, I will not deny You.' All the disciples said the same thing too."*

Again we see Peter's pride. In verse 34 Jesus tells Peter he will deny Him. Peter then argues with Jesus in verse 35, and makes even greater boasts of not denying Him, in addition to claiming that he will follow Jesus to death. Note also in verse 35 that the rest of the disciples jump in and make the same claim of following Jesus even to death. As we will see in later studies, all the disciples do abandon Jesus shortly after His arrest. Again the point we must take from this is to walk as humble servants and not proud warriors. As Paul points out, if we have any bragging to do, it is not in ourselves, but Christ only.

> **Galatians 6:14:** *"But may it never be that I should boast, except in the cross of our Lord Jesus Christ, through which the world has been crucified to me, and I to the world."*

2 Corinthians 10:17-18: *"But he who boasts is to boast in the Lord. For it is not he who commends himself that is approved, but he whom the Lord commends."*

Summary and Application

Oh how scary it would be if we had to try to keep ourselves saved. God's standard is perfection, which no one can come close to. Because of that, Christ came and paid the price to purchase our forgiveness so that we could be made children of God. Because He made us His children, He also will preserve us. We must remember it is not our strength or abilities that make us faithful disciples, but the power of God and His forgiveness.

From the lesson above we see that the disciples thought very highly of their abilities and commitment in standing strong in the time of trial. The result was that they ended up running for their lives. But the story was not over. Here is the incredible thing, by the power of the Holy Spirit these same weak men, who were afraid and in hiding, were transformed into bold, uncompromising witnesses of Christ! We read in Acts that they truly did not fear beatings, imprisonment, or even death for the name of Christ.

> **Acts 5:40-42:** *"And they took his advice; and after calling the apostles in, they flogged them and ordered them to speak no more in the name of Jesus, and then released them. 41 So they went on their way from the presence of the Council, <u>rejoicing that they had been considered worthy to suffer shame for His name.</u> 42 And every day, in the temple and from house to house, they kept right on teaching and preaching Jesus as the Christ."*

What made the difference? Jesus promised them after He rose from the dead He would send them the Holy Spirit.

> **John 14:25-26:** *"These things I have spoken to you, while abiding with you. 26 But the Helper, the Holy Spirit, whom the Father will send in My name, He will teach you all things, and bring to your remembrance all that I said to you."*

We can have peace knowing the Holy Spirit helps us in our time of trouble. In summary, we must praise God and put our trust in Him alone, and not trust in our abilities or well-meaning intentions.

MATTHEW 26:36-46
(WATCH AND PRAY — "THE SPIRIT IS WILLING, BUT THE FLESH IS WEAK.")

"Then Jesus *came with them to a place called Gethsemane, and *said to His disciples, 'Sit here while I go over there and pray.' [37] And He took with Him Peter and the two sons of Zebedee, and began to be grieved and distressed. [38] Then He *said to them, 'My soul is deeply grieved, to the point of death; remain here and keep watch with Me.' [39] And He went a little beyond them, and fell on His face and prayed, saying, 'My Father, if it is possible, let this cup pass from Me; yet not as I will, but as Thou wilt.' [40] And He *came to the disciples and *found them sleeping, and *said to Peter, 'So, you men could not keep watch with Me for one hour? [41] Keep watching and praying, that you may not enter into temptation; the spirit is willing, but the flesh is weak.' [42] He went away again a second time and prayed, saying, 'My Father, if this cannot pass away unless I drink it, Thy will be done.' [43] And again He came and found them sleeping, for their eyes were heavy. [44] And He left them again, and went away and prayed a third time, saying the same thing once more. [45] Then He *came to the disciples, and *said to them, 'Are you still sleeping and taking your rest? Behold, the hour is at hand and the Son of Man is being betrayed into the hands of sinners. [46] Arise, let us be going; behold, the one who betrays Me is at hand!'"

Introduction

The time table is "near midnight on the Thursday of Passover week...."[502] The setting is the Garden of Gethsemane. After the Last Supper, Jesus takes His disciples up the Mount of Olives. On the mount there was a garden where Jesus went to pray. The principal lesson we learn from this section of Scripture is the importance of staying alert and praying. In addition, we see a lesson regarding the power of the Holy Spirit indwelling the believer. In this section we see the disciples functioning with spiritually dull eyes. Even though Jesus told the disciples, *"My soul is deeply grieved, to the point of death...."* the disciples still fell asleep instead of staying up and praying. Yet after Pentecost these same weak and unreliable disciples become great, uncompromising apostles. What was the difference? After Pentecost they were filled with the Holy Spirit.

VERSE 36: *"Then Jesus *came with them to a place called Gethsemane, and *said to His disciples, 'Sit here while I go over there and pray.'"*

Let's follow the time table set out in Matthew 26. In verse 20 Jesus has the Passover dinner with His disciples (i.e. the Last Supper). In verse 30 they head to the Mount of Olives. Then in verse 36 we see that Jesus and the disciples go to the Garden of Gethsemane that was on the Mount of Olives.

The garden of Gethsemane was "a garden...East of Jerusalem beyond the Kidron valley and near the Mount of Olives."[503] See also **John 18:1** which says, *"When Jesus had spoken these words, He*

---

[502] MacArthur, J. (1989). *Matthew* (Matthew 26:36). Chicago: Moody Press.

[503] Wood, D. R. W. (1996). *New Bible dictionary* (3rd ed.) (p. 407). Leicester, England; Downers Grove, Ill.: InterVarsity Press.

went forth with His disciples over the ravine of the Kidron, where there was a garden, into which He Himself entered, and His disciples." John also tells us that Jesus and His disciples often went to this garden:

> **John 18:2:** *"Now Judas also, who was betraying Him, knew the place; for Jesus had often met there with His disciples."*

VERSE 37: *"And He took with Him Peter and the two sons of Zebedee, and began to be grieved and distressed."*

Remember in verse 36 He told all but three disciples to sit and wait for Him. Not all the disciples go with Jesus to pray. Jesus takes with Him Peter, James, and John. These three were part of Jesus' inner-sanctum. When Jesus raises from the dead the daughter of the synagogue ruler, the only disciples He allows to go with Him into the room are Peter, James, and John.

> **Mark 5:36-43:** *"But Jesus, overhearing what was being spoken, *said to the synagogue official, 'Do not be afraid any longer, only believe.' 37 And He allowed no one to follow with Him, except Peter and James and John the brother of James. 38 And they *came to the house of the synagogue official; and He *beheld a commotion, and people loudly weeping and wailing. 39 And entering in, He *said to them, 'Why make a commotion and weep? The child has not died, but is asleep.' 40 And they began laughing at Him. But putting them all out, He *took along the child's father and mother and His own companions, and *entered the room where the child was. 41 And taking the child by the hand, He *said to her, 'Talitha kum!' (which translated means, 'Little girl, I say to you, arise!'). 42 And immediately the girl rose and began to walk; for she was twelve years old. And immediately they were completely astounded. 43 And He gave them strict orders that no one should know about this; and He said that something should be given her to eat."*

It is Peter, James, and John that are taken with Jesus up the mountain when He is transfigured.

> **Matthew 17:1-3:** *"AND six days later Jesus *took with Him Peter and James and John his brother, and *brought them up to a high mountain by themselves. 2 And He was transfigured before them; and His face shone like the sun, and His garments became as white as light. 3 And behold, Moses and Elijah appeared to them, talking with Him."*

Jesus' grief and distress is not based on the pain of the cross, but rather that He, who knew no sin, would become sin on our part.

VERSE 38: *"Then He *said to them, 'My soul is deeply grieved, to the point of death; remain here and keep watch with Me.'"*

Here we read of the tremendous grieving Jesus undergoes. He is about to be separated from the Father and bear all the sin of the world. The One who was in perfect union with the Father and without sin will take on our sin and receive our punishment.

> **2 Corinthians 5:21:** *"He made Him who knew no sin to be sin on our behalf, that we might become the righteousness of God in Him."*

VERSE 39: *"And He went a little beyond them, and fell on His face and prayed, saying, 'My Father, if it is possible, let this cup pass from Me; yet not as I will, but as Thou wilt.'"*

Here we see Jesus' prayer to the Father. Our prayers should always draw to a close with the heartfelt statement, *"yet not as I will, but as Thou wilt."* Luke tells us that the Father responds to Jesus by sending an angel to encourage Him. We also read that the agony was so great that He sweat blood.

> **Luke 22:43-45:** *"Now an angel from heaven appeared to Him, strengthening Him. 44 And being in agony He was praying very fervently; and His sweat became like drops of blood, falling down upon the ground. 45 And when He rose from prayer, He came to the disciples and found them sleeping from sorrow,...."*

MacArthur explains Matthew 26:39 this way:

> "Jesus implored the Father, *'If it is possible, let this cup pass from Me.'* By asking, *'If it is possible;'* Jesus did not wonder if escaping the cross was within the realm of possibility. He knew He could have walked away from death at any time He chose. *'I lay down My life that I may take it again,'* .... Jesus was here asking if avoiding the cross were **possible** within the Father's redemptive plan and purpose. The agony of becoming sin was becoming unendurable for the sinless Son of God, and He wondered aloud before His Father if there could be another way to deliver men from sin. God's wrath and judgment are often pictured in the Old Testament as a cup to be drunk (see, e.g., Ps. 75:8; Isa. 51:17; Jer. 49:12). **This cup** symbolized the suffering Jesus would endure on the cross, the **cup** of God's fury vented against all the sins of mankind, which the Son would take upon Himself as the sacrificial Lamb of God."[504]

VERSES 40-43: *"And He *came to the disciples and *found them sleeping, and *said to Peter, 'So, you men could not keep watch with Me for one hour? 41 Keep watching and praying, that you may not enter into temptation; the spirit is willing, but the flesh is weak.' 42 He went away again a second time and prayed, saying, 'My Father, if this cannot pass away unless I drink it, Thy will be done.' 43 And again He came and found them sleeping, for their eyes were heavy."*

Here we see an example of the disciples in their flesh. They are tired and fall asleep. Luke seems to insinuate that the disciples were made sleepy from sadness. Sometimes a person can get sad and depressed and all he wants to do is sleep.

> **Luke 22:45:** *"And when He rose from prayer, He came to the disciples and found them <u>sleeping from sorrow</u>,...."*

Jesus wants them to keep watch and pray with Him for an hour (v.40) but they are not able. Notice how we can have good intentions (*"the spirit is willing"*) but when we try to serve God from our flesh, it is worthless (*"but the flesh is weak"*). When we review the previous lesson (Matthew 26:31-35), we see the proud claims Peter makes in the flesh about his devotion. Yet it will be the indwelling of the Holy Spirit at Pentecost that changes the fearful into bold, uncompromising witnesses for Christ.

---

[504] MacArthur, J. F., Jr. (1985). *Matthew.* MacArthur New Testament Commentary (p. 249). Chicago: Moody Press.

VERSES 44-46: *"And He left them again, and went away and prayed a third time, saying the same thing once more. 45 Then He *came to the disciples, and *said to them, 'Are you still sleeping and taking your rest? Behold, the hour is at hand and the Son of Man is being betrayed into the hands of sinners. 46 Arise, let us be going; behold, the one who betrays Me is at hand!'"*

> We again see that Jesus' disciples were not there at His time of need. Jesus is alone and about to bear the world's sin. In addition, Judas is approaching and about to betray the Son of God with a hypocritical kiss as a greeting.

Summary and Application

We see here the mistake we make when we put confidence in the flesh. When we put confidence in the flesh, we walk by the flesh and not the Spirit. The disciples were at this time so spiritually blind that they could not pray and be with Jesus in His hour of distress.

Even though Peter is a completely different man after He is filled with the Spirit at Pentecost, it does not mean that the believer will never walk in the flesh ever again. In Galatians 2:11-17 we read of Peter temporarily falling into the flesh by bowing to the pressure of the legalists. Even Barnabas (whose name meant the son of encouragement) was drawn into the man-pleasing hypocrisy—Galatians 2:13. The lesson for us is that we are very weak and we continually need God's strength to survive. May God grant us the heart and strength to walk by His Spirit!

> **Galatians 5:16-26:** *"But I say, walk by the Spirit, and you will not carry out the desire of the flesh. 17 For the flesh sets its desire against the Spirit, and the Spirit against the flesh; for these are in opposition to one another, so that you may not do the things that you please. 18 But if you are led by the Spirit, you are not under the Law. 19 Now the deeds of the flesh are evident, which are: immorality, impurity, sensuality, 20 idolatry, sorcery, enmities, strife, jealousy, outbursts of anger, disputes, dissensions, factions, 21 envying, drunkenness, carousing, and things like these, of which I forewarn you just as I have forewarned you that those who practice such things shall not inherit the kingdom of God. 22 But the fruit of the Spirit is love, joy, peace, patience, kindness, goodness, faithfulness, 23 gentleness, self-control; against such things there is no law. 24 Now those who belong to Christ Jesus have crucified the flesh with its passions and desires. 25 If we live by the Spirit, let us also walk by the Spirit. 26 Let us not become boastful, challenging one another, envying one another."*

MATTHEW 26:47-56
(THE ARREST OF JESUS)

"And while He was still speaking, behold, Judas, one of the twelve, came up, accompanied by a great multitude with swords and clubs, from the chief priests and elders of the people. ⁴⁸ Now he who was betraying Him gave them a sign, saying, 'Whomever I shall kiss, He is the one; seize Him.' ⁴⁹ And immediately he went to Jesus and said, 'Hail, Rabbi!' and kissed Him. ⁵⁰ And Jesus said to him, 'Friend, do what you have come for.' Then they came and laid hands on Jesus and seized Him. ⁵¹ And behold, one of those who were with Jesus reached and drew out his sword, and struck the slave of the high priest, and cut off his ear. ⁵² Then Jesus *said to him, 'Put your sword back into its place; for all those who take up the sword shall perish by the sword. ⁵³ Or do you think that I cannot appeal to My Father, and He will at once put at My disposal more than twelve legions of angels? ⁵⁴ How then shall the Scriptures be fulfilled, that it must happen this way?' ⁵⁵ At that time Jesus said to the multitudes, 'Have you come out with swords and clubs to arrest Me as against a robber? Every day I used to sit in the temple teaching and you did not seize Me. ⁵⁶ But all this has taken place that the Scriptures of the prophets may be fulfilled.' Then all the disciples left Him and fled."

Introduction

This section deals with Jesus' arrest by the religious leaders. We should notice Jesus responds by seeing all things as being God the Father's sovereign will (v. 54 and 56). One action that stands out is the hypocrisy of Judas' kiss (v.49). The section concludes in verse 56 with the disciples fleeing for fear of their lives. These are the same disciples that, in the previous section of Matthew 26:20-35, were making statements of their loyalty and commitment.

Without a doubt the major principal to grasp in this section is that despite all the chaos, injustice, hypocrisy, perversion, abandonment and evil that can encircle and tempt us, the Father's sovereign will always prevails and will ultimately result in holiness, justice, truth, and godly fellowship. As we read of evil men and the Devil determining how they can put an end to Jesus, we see that the sovereign will of the Father dominantly triumphs. Christ's death will purchase the forgiveness and eternal salvation of His people.

VERSE 47: *"And while He was still speaking, behold, Judas, one of the twelve, came up, accompanied by a great multitude with swords and clubs, from the chief priests and elders of the people."*

This *"great multitude with swords and clubs,"* were sent by the *"chief priests and elders of the people."* From Mark 14:43 we read that the Scribes were also involved. Luke tells us that there were also temple officers present (Luke 22:52). John tells us there was a Roman cohort present (John 18:3) (a cohort is composed of several hundred solders).[505] We read in verse 55 that Jesus

---

[505] "The **detachment of** Roman **soldiers** was a cohort (*speiran*, 10th part of a legion), which here included about 600 men." Walvoord, J. F., Zuck, R. B., and Dallas Theological Seminary. (1983-). *The Bible Knowledge Commentary: An Exposition of the Scriptures* (v. 2, p 334). Wheaton, IL: Victor Books.
[Note continued on the next page.]

confronts them with the questions of why they came armed with swords and clubs, as if they were arresting a dangerous robber. Jesus points out that they could have arrested Him anytime He was teaching in the temple.

Who else showed up in this evil mob? The answer is Judas. We read earlier in Matthew 26:14-16 that Judas had been paid by the religious leaders to betray Jesus so that they could arrest Him in a non-public situation. Right after Judas was paid, *"…he began looking for a good opportunity to betray Him."* **Matthew 26:16**. As we have pointed out before, Judas was not a good guy who went bad, or even a disappointment to Jesus. Judas never believed in Christ as Messiah and Savior, as evident by the fact that the highest title we hear of him calling Jesus is, *"Rabbi"* (Matthew 26:25).[506] Jesus knew from the beginning that Judas was a devil and would betray Him (John 6:64).

> **John 6:70-71:** *"Jesus answered them, 'Did I Myself not choose you, the twelve, and yet one of you is a devil?' 71 Now He meant Judas the son of Simon Iscariot, for he, one of the twelve, was going to betray Him."*

It is important to remember that as we read about the arrest of Jesus in Matthew 26:46, the mob does not trap Jesus, but rather He allows them to arrest Him.

VERSES 48-49: *"Now he who was betraying Him gave them a sign, saying, 'Whomever I shall kiss, He is the one; seize Him.' 49 And immediately he went to Jesus and said, 'Hail, Rabbi!' and kissed Him."*

Judas sets up a sign to tell the mob which person is the subject of its attack. How perverse that the kiss of *greeting* would be given by one seeking Jesus' murder. Scripture teaches us about the righteous and holy affection we should have for one another in that it admonishes us to *"Greet one another with a holy kiss."* **2 Corinthians 13:12**; (see also Romans 16:16, 1 Corinthians 16:20, 1 Thessalonians 5:26).[507] Typical of an apostate, Judas takes what is made for good and uses it for evil.

[Note continued.]
See also MacArthur: "The term 'detachment of troops' refers to a cohort of Roman troops. A full auxiliary cohort had the potential strength of 1,000 men (i.e., 760 foot soldiers and 240 cavalry led by a *chiliarch* or 'leader of a thousand'). Usually, however, in practice a cohort normally numbered 600 men, but could sometimes refer to as little as 200 (i.e., a 'maniple'). MacArthur, J. J. (1997). *The MacArthur Study Bible* (electronic ed.) (John 18:3). Nashville: Word Pub.

[506] Nowhere do we see Judas addressing Jesus as Lord. Do not be confused by the verse in John 14:22. The Judas in that verse, that calls Jesus Lord, is not Judas Iscariot. That verse specifically points that out. **John 14:22:** *"Judas (not Iscariot) *said to Him, 'Lord, what then has happened that You are going to disclose Yourself to us, and not to the world?'"*

[507] *"PHILEMA (φιλημα , (5370)), a kiss (akin to B), Luke 7:45; 22:48, was a token of Christian brotherhood, whether by way of welcome or farewell, 'a holy kiss,' Romans 16:16; 1 Corinthians 16:20; 2 Cor. 13:12; 1 Thessalonians 5:26, 'holy' (hagios), as free from anything inconsistent with their calling as saints (hagioi); 'a kiss of love' 1 Peter 5:14. There was to be an absence of formality and hypocrisy, a freedom from prejudice arising from social distinctions, from discrimination against the poor, from partiality towards the well–to–do. In the churches masters and servants would thus salute one another without any attitude of condescension on the one part or disrespect on the other."*
Vine, W. (1981; Published in electronic form by Logos Research Systems, 1996). *Vine's Expository Dictionary of Old and New Testament Words* (p. 297). Old Tappan NJ: Revell.

> **Matthew 7:6:** *"Do not give what is holy to dogs, and do not throw your pearls before swine, lest they trample them under their feet, and turn and tear you to pieces."*

This is not just evil murder that Judas is a conspirator in, but murder for hire. Judas is fulfilling his agreed role in the murder of Jesus for the 30 pieces of silver that the religious leaders paid him.

> **Matthew 26:14-16:** *"Then one of the twelve, named Judas Iscariot, went to the chief priests, 15 and said, 'What are you willing to give me to deliver Him up to you?' And they weighed out to him thirty pieces of silver. 16 And from then on he began looking for a good opportunity to betray Him."*

VERSE 50: *"And Jesus said to him, 'Friend, do what you have come for.' Then they came and laid hands on Jesus and seized Him."*

The term *"Friend"* is not used here in a deep, close relationship. The term used here has a general meaning of "comrade, companion, friend of one's neighbor." [508] The same term for *friend* that Jesus used for Judas in verse 50 is found in four other verses. Each of them does not include a close friendship.[509] "The Lord did not use the usual word (*philos*) for **friend**, which He used of the Twelve in John 15:14."[510]

Jesus' response to Judas' treachery is one of complete omniscience of what was going on. He lets Judas know He is not deceived by the kiss of greeting. We read from Luke that Jesus directly confronts Judas:

> **Luke 22:48:** *"But Jesus said to him, 'Judas, are you betraying the Son of Man with a kiss?'"*

---

[508] Arndt, W. (1996, c1979). *A Greek-English lexicon of the New Testament and other early Christian literature: A Translation and Adaption of the Fourth Revised and Augmented Edition of Walter Bauer's Griechisch-deutsches Worterbuch zu den Schrift en des Neuen Testaments und der ubrigen urchristlichen Literatur* (Page 314). Chicago: University of Chicago Press.

[509] The term "Friend" as used in Matthew 26:50 is also used in two other verses. In both those examples, we see Jesus telling a story and the "friend" has in one way or another been evil (i.e. greedy or self-righteous).

Matthew 20:13-15 (NASB): *"But he answered and said to one of them, 'Friend, I am doing you no wrong; did you not agree with me for a denarius? 14 Take what is yours and go your way, but I wish to give to this last man the same as to you. 15 Is it not lawful for me to do what I wish with what is my own? Or is your eye envious because I am generous?'"*

Matthew 22:12-15 (NASB): *"...and he *said to him, 'Friend, how did you come in here without wedding clothes?' And he was speechless. 13Then the king said to the servants, 'Bind him hand and foot, and cast him into the outer darkness; in that place there shall be weeping and gnashing of teeth.' 14 "For many are called, but few are chosen."*

[510] MacArthur, J. (1989). *Matthew* (Matthew 26:48). Chicago: Moody Press.

The book of Proverbs points out the deceptiveness of the apparent affection of evil people.

> **Proverbs 27:6:** *"Faithful are the wounds of a friend,*
> *But deceitful are the kisses of an enemy."*

Jesus tells Judas in **Matthew 26:50:** *"...do what you have come for."* At that point the mob grabs and arrests Jesus. One commentator points out that the apostate Judas brought a multitude to Jesus, but it was not to bring them to the source of salvation. Instead, Judas brought people to Jesus to have Him killed. This is the conduct of the unbeliever in the church. They will lead people into sin, attack the true saints, and at the same time claim they are part of the church.

John gives us more detail about the composition of the mob. In addition to the religious leaders, there is a Roman cohort.[511]

> **John 18:3:** *"Judas then, having received the Roman cohort, and officers from the chief priests and the Pharisees, *came there with lanterns and torches and weapons."*

Jesus is not overpowered by this group. He shows a glimpse of His power which results in the crowd falling to the ground.

> **John 18:4-9:** *"Jesus therefore, knowing all the things that were coming upon Him, went forth, and *said to them, 'Whom do you seek?' 5 They answered Him, 'Jesus the Nazarene.' He *said to them, 'I am He.' And Judas also who was betraying Him, was standing with them. 6 When therefore He said to them, 'I am He,' they drew back, and fell to the ground. 7 Again therefore He asked them, 'Whom do you seek?' And they said, 'Jesus the Nazarene.' 8 Jesus answered, 'I told you that I am He; if therefore you seek Me, let these go their way,' 9 that the word might be fulfilled which He spoke, 'Of those whom Thou hast given Me I lost not one.'"*

Jesus' proclamation of Himself as Messiah brought forth a little glimpse of His power, in that the mob was forced to the ground simply by his statement: *"'I am He'" translates egō eimi, which literally means 'I am,' the covenant name of God* (see Exodus 3:14)."[512]

VERSE 51-54: *"And behold, one of those who were with Jesus reached and drew out his sword, and struck the slave of the high priest, and cut off his ear. 52 Then Jesus *said to him, 'Put your sword back into its place; for all those who take up the sword shall perish by the sword. 53 Or do you think that I cannot appeal to My Father, and He will at once put at My disposal more than twelve legions of angels? 54 How then shall the Scriptures be fulfilled, that it must happen this way?"*

Again John gives us more detail of this event. Specifically, he tells us it is was Simon Peter who cuts the ear off of the high priest's slave. John also tells us the slave's name is Malchus.

> **John 18:10-11:** *"Simon Peter therefore having a sword, drew it, and struck the high priest's slave, and cut off his right ear; and the slave's name was Malchus.*

---

[511] "A 'cohort'" was composed of approximately 600 men commanded by a tribune." Vine, W. (1981; Published in electronic form by Logos Research Systems, 1996). *Vine's Expository Dictionary of Old and New Testament Words* (p. 96). Old Tappan NJ: Revell.

[512] MacArthur, J. (1989). *Matthew* (Matthew 26:55). Chicago: Moody Press.

[11] Jesus therefore said to Peter, 'Put the sword into the sheath; the cup which the Father has given Me, shall I not drink it?'"

Luke, the physician, also points out Jesus supernaturally heals the man's ear.

> **Luke 22:49-51:** *"And when those who were around Him saw what was going to happen, they said, 'Lord, shall we strike with the sword?' [50] And a certain one of them struck the slave of the high priest and cut off his right ear. [51] But Jesus answered and said, 'Stop! No more of this.' <u>And He touched his ear and healed him.</u>"*

In our main text of Matthew 26:52-54, Jesus states He does not need men with swords to protect Him. If He wants, He can have the Father send 12 legions of angels. A Roman legion was composed of approximately 6,000 men.[513] So if you use the 6,000 figure, Jesus is stating that He could easily have 72,000 angels there to defend Him if He chose. We see in the Old Testament that the angel of the Lord killed over 185,000 at one time.

> **2 Kings 19:35:** *"Then it happened that night that the angel of the Lord went out, and struck 185,000 in the camp of the Assyrians; and when men rose early in the morning, behold, all of them were dead."*

In **Matthew 26:54** Jesus again points out the sovereignty of God and that all is going according to plan even though it may appear to the disciples that evil is prevailing. *"How then shall the Scriptures be fulfilled, that it must happen this way?"*

One last thought from J.C. Ryle who in 1856 stated the following about force/violence and the Christian life:

> "We would do well to remember this in all our attempts to extend the kingdom of true religion. It is not to be propagated by violence, or by bodily strength. 'The weapons we fight with are not the weapons of the world' (<u>2 Corinthians 10:4</u>). 'Not by might nor by power, but by my Spirit,' says the Lord Almighty' (<u>Zechariah 4:6</u>). The cause of truth does not need force to maintain it. False religions, like Islam, have often been spread by the sword. False Christianity, like that of the Roman church, has often been enforced on people by bloody persecutions. But the real Gospel of Christ requires no such aids as these. It stands by the power of the Holy Spirit. It grows by the hidden influence of the Holy Spirit on people's hearts and consciences. There is no clearer sign of a bad cause in religion than a readiness to appeal to the sword."[514]

VERSE 55: *"At that time Jesus said to the multitudes, 'Have you come out with swords and clubs to arrest Me as against a robber? Every day I used to sit in the temple teaching and you did not seize Me.'"*

---

[513] Wood, D. R. W. (1996). *New Bible Dictionary* (3rd ed.) (Page 682). Leicester, England; Downers Grove, Ill.: InterVarsity Press.

[514] Ryle, J. C. (1993). *Mark*. Crossway Classic Commentaries (pp. 236–237). Wheaton, IL: Crossway Books.

Jesus does not let the evil religious leaders define who He is, but confronts them with truth. By pointing out that they came to arrest Him with swords and clubs, He demonstrates their murderous motives. Instead of trying to arrest Jesus at the temple while He was teaching, they came at night, hoping to hide their evil agenda.

> **Matthew 26:3-5:** *"Then the chief priests and the elders of the people were gathered together in the court of the high priest, named Caiaphas; ⁴ and they plotted together to seize Jesus by stealth, and kill Him. ⁵ But they were saying, Not during the festival, lest a riot occur among the people."*

VERSE 56: *"But all this has taken place that the Scriptures of the prophets may be fulfilled. Then all the disciples left Him and fled."*

This sums it all up. This is not a situation out of control. Despite all the evil being done by men and the Devil, God is still on the throne, and all of it fulfills Scripture.

Notice the sentence that says, *"Then all the disciples left Him and fled."* Jesus had explained to the disciples earlier that evening they would abandon Him.

> **Matthew 26:31:** *"Then Jesus *said to them, 'You will all fall away because of Me this night, for it is written, I WILL STRIKE DOWN THE SHEPHERD, AND THE SHEEP OF THE FLOCK SHALL BE SCATTERED.'"*

We see even this occurs that Scripture might be fulfilled.

> **John 18:8-9:** *"Jesus answered, 'I told you that I am He; if therefore you seek Me, let these go their way, ⁹ that the word might be fulfilled which He spoke, 'Of those whom Thou hast given Me I lost not one.'"*

Summary and Application

Allow me to repeat what was written at the introduction of this section. Despite all the chaos, injustice, hypocrisy, perversion, abandonment and evil that can encircle us, the Father's *sovereign will* always prevails and ultimately results in holiness, justice, truth, and godly fellowship. Because of God's promise of love and provision, we do not need to fear any lack, or even death.

> **Luke 12:22–32:** *"And He said to His disciples, 'For this reason I say to you, do not worry about your life, as to what you will eat; nor for your body, as to what you will put on. For life is more than food, and the body more than clothing. Consider the ravens, for they neither sow nor reap; they have no storeroom nor barn, and yet God feeds them; how much more valuable you are than the birds! And which of you by worrying can add a single hour to his life's span? If then you cannot do even a very little thing, why do you worry about other matters? Consider the lilies, how they grow: they neither toil nor spin; but I tell you, not even Solomon in all his glory clothed himself like one of these. But if God so clothes the grass in the field, which is alive today and tomorrow is thrown into the furnace, how much more will He clothe you? You men of little faith! And do not seek what you will eat and what you will drink, and do not keep worrying. For all these things the nations of the world eagerly seek; but your Father knows that you need these things. But seek His kingdom, and these things will be added to you. Do not be afraid, little flock, for your Father has chosen gladly to give you the kingdom.'"*

The Lord is sovereign over all…even when it is all over.

Job 19:25: *"As for me, I know that my Redeemer lives, And at the last He will take His stand on the earth."*

MATTHEW 26:57-68
(JESUS' TRIAL BEFORE CAIAPHAS)

"And those who had seized Jesus led Him away to Caiaphas, the high priest, where the scribes and the elders were gathered together. [58] But Peter also was following Him at a distance as far as the courtyard of the high priest, and entered in, and sat down with the officers to see the outcome. [59] Now the chief priests and the whole Council kept trying to obtain false testimony against Jesus, in order that they might put Him to death; [60] and they did not find any, even though many false witnesses came forward. But later on two came forward, [61] and said, 'This man stated, I am able to destroy the temple of God and to rebuild it in three days.' [62] And the high priest stood up and said to Him, 'Do You make no answer? What is it that these men are testifying against You?' [63] But Jesus kept silent. And the high priest said to Him, 'I adjure You by the living God, that You tell us whether You are the Christ, the Son of God.' [64] Jesus *said to him, 'You have said it yourself; nevertheless I tell you, hereafter you shall see THE SON OF MAN SITTING AT THE RIGHT HAND OF POWER, and COMING ON THE CLOUDS OF HEAVEN.' [65] Then the high priest tore his robes, saying, 'He has blasphemed! What further need do we have of witnesses? Behold, you have now heard the blasphemy; [66] what do you think?' They answered and said, 'He is deserving of death!' [67] Then they spat in His face and beat Him with their fists; and others slapped Him, [68] and said, 'Prophesy to us, You Christ; who is the one who hit You?'"

Introduction

After Jesus' arrest at the Garden of Gethsemane, He was taken to Caiaphas. We see a complete kangaroo court[515] here in that Caiaphas is going to conduct a technical trial but has no interest in seeking justice. This is an orchestrated trial complete with false witnesses (v.60).

VERSE 57: *"And those who had seized Jesus led Him away to Caiaphas, the high priest, where the scribes and the elders were gathered together."*

In the previous lesson, we looked at the arrest of Jesus. It is interesting to point out that both the arrest and the trial were held in the cover of night. Jesus directly asks those arresting Him why they did not apprehend Him while He was teaching at the temple.

> **Luke 22:53:** *"While I was with you daily in the temple, you did not lay hands on Me; but this hour and the power of darkness are yours."*

The reason the "trial" was held at night is obvious—they were doing evil and evil never likes to be exposed to the light.

> **1 Thessalonians 5:5-8:** *".... We are not of night nor of darkness; [6]so then let us not sleep as others do, but let us be alert and sober. [7] For those who sleep do*

---

[515] A *kangaroo court* is one that is set up to appear to be a legitimate court session but in reality is phony and pretextual. Instead of seeking the truth and justice, it is a sham session in which the outcome has been predetermined before evidence is actually heard. Webster defines a "kangaroo court" as: "...a mock court in which the principles of law and justice are disregarded or perverted." *Merriam-Webster Collegiate Dictionary, 11th edition.*

their sleeping at night, and those who get drunk get drunk at night. 8 But since we are of the day, let us be sober, having put on the breastplate of faith and love, and as a helmet, the hope of salvation."

In Matthew 26:57 they led Jesus to *"...Caiaphas, the high priest...."* So who is Caiaphas? Joseph Caiaphas was a high priest of the Jews appointed "by Valerius Gratus, governor of Judaea, after removal of Simon, son of Camith, A.D. 18." [516] Caiaphas himself was removed from office in A.D. 36 by the governor of Syria, Vitellius. Caiaphas' father-in-law, Annas, also had previously served as high priest (John 18:13). [517] Annas' son, Jonathan, replaced Caiaphas. These appointments were politically based, having nothing to do with the individual being a proven spiritual leader.

Matthew's gospel goes directly to the main questioning by Caiaphas. John gives us more detail by telling us that before Jesus was taken to Caiaphas, He was questioned by Annas[518] (Caiaphas' father-in-law). Annas may not have been the current High Priest, but he carried great clout, as shown by the fact that many of his family members served as High Priests.

> **John 18:12-14:** *"So the Roman cohort and the commander, and the officers of the Jews, arrested Jesus and bound Him, 13 and led Him to Annas first; for he was father-in-law of Caiaphas, who was high priest that year. 14 Now Caiaphas was the one who had advised the Jews that it was expedient for one man to die on behalf of the people."*

John tells us about the questioning in front of Annas before Jesus was sent to Caiaphas.

> **John 18:19-24:** *"The high priest therefore questioned Jesus about His disciples, and about His teaching. 20 Jesus answered him, 'I have spoken openly to the world; I always taught in synagogues, and in the temple, where all the Jews come together; and I spoke nothing in secret. 21 Why do you question Me? Question those who have heard what I spoke to them; behold, these know what I said.' 22 And when He had said this, one of the officers standing by gave Jesus a blow, saying, 'Is that the way You answer the high priest?' 23 Jesus answered him, 'If I have spoken wrongly, bear witness of the wrong; but if rightly, why do you strike Me?' 24 Annas therefore sent Him bound to Caiaphas the high priest."*

Luke refers to both Annas and Caiaphas as high priest (Luke 3:2). Why did Annas carry such a title and power even though he was out of office?

> "This may be for one of three reasons. First, though the Romans deposed high priests and appointed new ones, the Jews thought of the high priesthood as a life office. The Mishnah (Horayoth 3. 4) says: 'A high priest in office differs from the priest that is passed from his high priesthood only in the bullock that is offered on the Day of Atonement and the tenth of the ephah.' Secondly, the

---

[516] Strong, J. (1996). *Enhanced Strong's Lexicon.* Ontario: Woodside Bible Fellowship.

[517] Ibid.

[518] Annas "...high priest of the Jews, elevated to the priesthood by Quirinius the governor of Syria c. 6 or 7 A.D., but afterwards deposed by Valerius Gratus, the procurator of Judaea, who put in his place, first Ismael, son of Phabi, and shortly after Eleazar, son of Annas. From the latter, the office passed to Simon; from Simon c. 18 A.D. to Caiaphas; but Annas even after he had been put out of office, continued to have great influence." Strong, J. (1996). *Enhanced Strong's Lexicon.* Ontario: Woodside Bible Fellowship.

title 'high priest' is given in Acts and Josephus to members of the few priestly families from which most high priests were drawn, as well as to those exercising the high-priestly office. Thirdly, Annas had great personal influence with succeeding high priests. Five of his sons and Caiaphas his son-in-law became high priest. At the trial of Jesus we find Annas conducting a preliminary investigation before the official trial by Caiaphas (John 18:13–24). When Luke 3:2 says that the high priest was Annas and Caiaphas, the singular is probably deliberate, indicating that, though Caiaphas was the high priest officially appointed by Rome, his father-in-law shared his high-priestly power, both de facto by his personal influence and, according to strict Jewish thought, also de jure (cf. Acts 4:6)." [519]

Caiaphas, without knowing what he was doing, prophesied about Jesus.

> **John 11:47-53:** *"Therefore the chief priests and the Pharisees convened a council, and were saying, 'What are we doing? For this man is performing many signs. [48] If we let Him go on like this, all men will believe in Him, and the Romans will come and take away both our place and our nation.' [49] But a certain one of them, Caiaphas, who was high priest that year, said to them, 'You know nothing at all, [50] nor do you take into account that it is expedient for you that one man should die for the people, and that the whole nation should not perish.' [51] Now this he did not say on his own initiative; but being high priest that year, he prophesied that Jesus was going to die for the nation, [52] and not for the nation only, but that He might also gather together into one the children of God who are scattered abroad. [53] So from that day on they planned together to kill Him."*

VERSE 58: *"But Peter also was following Him at a distance as far as the courtyard of the high priest, and entered in, and sat down with the officers to see the outcome."*

Again we get a little more information on this event from the Apostle John. John personally knew the high priest and was admitted into the court. John used his influence to get Peter admitted also.

> **John 18:15-16:** *"And Simon Peter was following Jesus, and so was another disciple. Now that disciple was known to the high priest, and entered with Jesus into the court of the high priest, [16] but Peter was standing at the door outside. So the other disciple, who was known to the high priest, went out and spoke to the doorkeeper, and brought in Peter."*

VERSE 59-61: *"Now the chief priests and the whole Council kept trying to obtain false testimony against Jesus, in order that they might put Him to death; [60] and they did not find any, even though many false witnesses came forward. But later on two came forward, [61] and said, 'This man stated, I am able to destroy the temple of God and to rebuild it in three days.'"*

---

[519] Wood, D. R. W. (1996). *New Bible Dictionary* (3rd ed.) (p. 49). Leicester, England; Downers Grove, Ill.: InterVarsity Press.

Mark tells us about the false testimony:

> **Mark 14:55-59:** *"Now the chief priests and the whole Council kept trying to obtain testimony against Jesus to put Him to death; and they were not finding any. [56] For many were giving false testimony against Him, and yet their testimony was not consistent. [57] And some stood up and began to give false testimony against Him, saying, [58] 'We heard Him say, I will destroy this temple made with hands, and in three days I will build another made without hands.'[59] And not even in this respect was their testimony consistent."*

It is interesting that the Jewish leaders did not use Judas as a witness against Jesus. Judas hated Jesus from his heart and was a devil from the beginning (John 6:70-71). Ryle points out that:

> "If there was any living witness who could give evidence against our Lord Jesus Christ, Judas Iscariot was the man. A chosen apostle of Jesus, a constant companion in all his journeying, a hearer of all his teaching, both in public and private – he must have known well if our Lord had done any wrong, either in word of deed. As a deserter form our Lord's company, a betrayer of him into the hands of his enemies, it was in his interest for his own character's sake, to prove Jesus guilty….[Judas] knew he could prove nothing against Christ…The absence of Judas Iscariot at our Lord's trial is one among many proofs that the Lamb of God was without blemish, a sinless man." [520]

Judas later admits Jesus' complete innocence in **Matthew 27:3-5:** *"Then when Judas, who had betrayed Him, saw that He had been condemned, he felt remorse and returned the thirty pieces of silver to the chief priests and elders, [4] saying, 'I have sinned by betraying innocent blood.' But they said , 'What is that to us? See to that yourself!' [5] And he threw the pieces of silver into the sanctuary and departed; and he went away and hanged himself."*

Matthew explains how this "court" was pursuing one objective: *"that they might put Him to death."* The religious leaders were pretending to go through the technical procedures of a trial, but not for the reason that a trial is held. A true trial's objective is to exact truth, justice, light, and life. Jesus' trial was all about falsehood, injustice, darkness, and murder. Verse 59 points out that the religious leaders were unsuccessful in their attempt to find a false witness. The Mosaic Law required that if a person turned out to be a false witness, the false witness was subject to the punishment he had hoped to be inflicted on the person he lied about.

> **Deuteronomy 19:16-20:** *"If a malicious witness rises up against a man to accuse him of wrongdoing, [17] then both the men who have the dispute shall stand before the LORD, before the priests and the judges who will be in office in those days. [18] And the judges shall investigate thoroughly; and if the witness is a false witness and he has accused his brother falsely, [19] then you shall do to him just as he had intended to do to his brother. Thus you shall purge the evil from among you. [20] And the rest will hear and be afraid, and will never again do such an evil thing among you."*

At this trial, the false witnesses had nothing to worry about because they knew it was the judges themselves who wanted the false testimony.

---

[520] *Matthew* / Ryle, J.C. p.272 (Expository Thoughts on the Gospels) (Crossways Classic Commentaries: v.1)

As the Council continued in their religious hypocrisy, they ironically were trying to use the law of God…against God. Notice that they were trying to secure more than one witness because they knew that the law of Moses did not let them put someone to death on the testimony of just one witness for blasphemy (Deuteronomy 17:2-7).

> **Deuteronomy 17:6-7**: *"On the evidence of two witnesses or three witnesses, he who is to die shall be put to death; he shall not be put to death on the evidence of one witness. ⁷ The hand of the witnesses shall be first against him to put him to death, and afterward the hand of all the people. So you shall purge the evil from your midst."*

Eventually they found a witness who testified that Jesus stated that He was, *"able to destroy the temple of God and to rebuild it in three days."* This is neither what Jesus said nor what He meant. We read of the account in John and see that Jesus was referring to His bodily resurrection.

> **John 2:18-22**: *"The Jews therefore answered and said to Him, 'What sign do You show to us, seeing that You do these things?' ¹⁹ Jesus answered and said to them, 'Destroy this temple, and in three days I will raise it up.' ²⁰ The Jews therefore said, 'It took forty-six years to build this temple, and will You raise it up in three days?' ²¹ But He was speaking of the temple of His body. ²² When therefore He was raised from the dead, His disciples remembered that He said this; and they believed the Scripture, and the word which Jesus had spoken."*

VERSE 62: *"And the high priest stood up and said to Him, 'Do You make no answer? What is it that these men are testifying against You?'"*

The temple represented God's presence with the Jews. It was an awesome structure. The building that became known as Herod's temple began construction in 19 B.C. It was called Herod's temple because he commissioned the work on it and viewed it as politically expedient. Herod used the construction of the temple as an opportunity to make himself (an Idumaean) more appealing to the Jews and glorify himself at the same time. The "main structure was finished within 10 years (c. 9 B.C.), but work continued until A.D. 64."[521] Very large stones were used in the building. The normal-sized stones were about one meter high and 5 meters long. [522] Some extremely large stones, "measured 40 feet by 12 by 12 and weighed up to a hundred tons, quarried as a single piece and transported many miles to the building site."[523] (For more on the Temple, see the section on Matthew 24:1-2.) Look what Jesus said earlier to the Pharisees about the Temple in which they took such great pride. **Matthew 12:6:** *"But I say to you, that something greater than the temple is here."*

In our main text of Matthew 26:62, we see that Caiaphas is trying to create a charge based on blasphemy so that he will feel righteous about the murder he desires to commit on Jesus.

---

[521] Wood, D. R. W. (1996). *New Bible Dictionary* (3rd ed. /) (p. 1158). Leicester, England; Downers Grove, Ill.: InterVarsity Press.

[522] Ibid.

[523] MacArthur, J. F., Jr. (1985). *Matthew*. MacArthur New Testament Commentary (p. 249). Chicago: Moody Press..

Leviticus 24:16: *"Moreover, the one who blasphemes the name of the LORD shall surely be put to death; all the congregation shall certainly stone him. The alien as well as the native, when he blasphemes the Name, shall be put to death."*

VERSES 63-64: *"But Jesus kept silent. And the high priest said to Him, 'I adjure You by the living God, that You tell us whether You are the Christ, the Son of God.' 64 Jesus *said to him, 'You have said it yourself; nevertheless I tell you, hereafter you shall see THE SON OF MAN SITTING AT THE RIGHT HAND OF POWER, and COMING ON THE CLOUDS OF HEAVEN.'"*

Here we see Caiaphas engaging in courtroom acting as he stands up and states: *"I adjure You by the living God, that You tell us whether You are the Christ, the Son of God."* What a moral and spiritual reprobate, that this murderer Caiaphas would dare use the name of God to make a demand of God incarnate! No one can seriously think that Caiaphas really was interested in the answer beyond using it to justify his murderous scheme. Note Jesus' response in verse Matthew 26:64, where He declares unequivocally that He is the Messiah, the Son of God:

> *"Jesus said to him, 'You have said it yourself; nevertheless I tell you, hereafter you shall see THE SON OF MAN SITTING AT THE RIGHT HAND OF POWER, and COMING ON THE CLOUDS OF HEAVEN.'"*

When I was in college there was a religion professor who loved to explain to his naive freshman students that Jesus never declared He was the Son of God. Verse 64 points out that the religion professor was dead wrong. If he would have actually read his Bible instead of pretending to be an expert about all things religious, he would have read Jesus' own words:

> Luke 22:70: *"And they all said, 'Are You the Son of God, then?' And He said to them, 'Yes, I am.'"*

VERSES 65-66: *"Then the high priest tore his robes, saying, 'He has blasphemed! What further need do we have of witnesses? Behold, you have now heard the blasphemy; 66 what do you think?' They answered and said, 'He is deserving of death!'"*

They were claiming that it was blasphemy because Jesus stated that He was the Messiah. It would be blasphemy for anyone to make that claim other than Jesus. Caiaphas' claim to kill Jesus for blasphemy was based on a Mosaic Law Scripture (see Leviticus 24:16).

As we mentioned earlier, the Law of Moses required two witnesses to condemn someone to death. In Matthew 26:65-66, Caiaphas claims that Jesus' statement made the whole counsel a witness to the alleged blasphemy. Caiaphas is your classic false religious leader who did not recognize God even when He was standing right in front of him. In reality, Caiaphas wanted to move his case along so he could get to the murder of Jesus.

VERSES 67-68: *"Then they spat in His face and beat Him with their fists; and others slapped Him, 68 and said, 'Prophesy to us, You Christ; who is the one who hit You?'"*

Here we see the brutal treatment of Jesus for our sins. How evil it was for puny man to beat and mock almighty God. Jesus had prophesied about this much earlier.

> **Mark 10:32-34:** *"And they were on the road, going up to Jerusalem, and Jesus was walking on ahead of them; and they were amazed, and those who followed were fearful. And again He took the twelve aside and began to tell them what was going to happen to Him, [33] saying, 'Behold, we are going up to Jerusalem, and the Son of Man will be delivered to the chief priests and the scribes; and they will condemn Him to death, and will deliver Him to the Gentiles. [34] And they will mock Him and spit upon Him, and scourge Him, and kill Him, and three days later He will rise again.'"*

Today many people still try to mock God. They use His name in vain, belittle His Word and view Him as just another version of Santa Clause or the Easter Bunny. They will suffer judgment for that.

> **Galatians 6:7-8 (NKJV):** *"Do not be deceived, <u>God is not mocked</u>; for whatever a man sows, that he will also reap. [8] For he who sows to his flesh will of the flesh reap corruption, but he who sows to the Spirit will of the Spirit reap everlasting life."*

Summary and Application

If you have ever seen a movie set of an old western town, you will understand the meaning of the term *facade*. As you walk down the main street of the town you will see the general store, the blacksmith's shop and the saloon. They look real from the front, but if you go around to the back of the buildings you find out...that there are no buildings! The building fronts are simply held up by support beams. Facade has been defined as, "a deceptive outward appearance."[524] Facade is the best way to define Caiaphas' trial. He wanted it to *appear* that he fairly weighed the witness's testimony, followed the law and cautiously rendered judgment. What he really wanted was to use the trial as a means to accomplish the murder of Jesus. As with all religious hypocrites, Caiaphas was self-deceived. He thought he was putting on a good show, but there were some onlookers who knew they were watching a fraud.

What about your spiritual life? When people walk down the *main street of your life* do they see the church sanctuary over here, the choir loft next to it and the Sunday school over there? But what happens when they go around back behind the building? Does any of that really exist from God's viewpoint? Do you actually think you are an effective Christian simply because you help in the church and pay a tithe? Is your spiritual life a *facade*, "a deceptive outward appearance?" If so, then REPENT! The hypocrite is always self-deceived because he does not recognize what many already know, that he is a fraud.

---

[524] Soanes, C., and Stevenson, A. (2004). *Concise Oxford English Dictionary* (11th ed.). Oxford: Oxford University Press.

<u>MATTHEW 26:69-75</u>
(PETER'S DENIAL)

"Now Peter was sitting outside in the courtyard, and a certain servant-girl came to him and said, 'You too were with Jesus the Galilean.' 70 But he denied it before them all, saying, 'I do not know what you are talking about.' 71 And when he had gone out to the gateway, another servant-girl saw him and *said to those who were there, 'This man was with Jesus of Nazareth.' 72 And again he denied it with an oath, 'I do not know the man.' 73 And a little later the bystanders came up and said to Peter, 'Surely you too are one of them; for the way you talk gives you away.' 74 Then he began to curse and swear, 'I do not know the man!' And immediately a cock crowed. 75 And Peter remembered the word which Jesus had said, 'Before a cock crows, you will deny Me three times.' And he went out and wept bitterly."

Introduction

We read of the parallel accounts of Peter's denial in Mark 14:66-72, Luke 22:55-62, and John 18:16-18, 25-27. One of the lessons we draw from Peter is to not trust in our flesh. In Matthew 26 it is Peter who boldly tells Jesus that he will never deny Him even if the other disciples do. Jesus then replies by prophesying to Peter that he will deny Him three times that very night. In response, Peter claims that he will never deny Jesus, even if it costs him his life!

> **Matthew 26:33-35:** *"But Peter answered and said to Him, 'Even though all may fall away because of You, I will never fall away.' 34 Jesus said to him, 'Truly I say to you that this very night, before a cock crows, you shall deny Me three times.' 35 Peter *said to Him, 'Even if I have to die with You, I will not deny You.' All the disciples said the same thing too."*

VERSES 69-72: *"Now Peter was sitting outside in the courtyard, and a certain servant-girl came to him and said, 'You too were with Jesus the Galilean.' 70 But he denied it before them all, saying, 'I do not know what you are talking about.' 71 And when he had gone out to the gateway, another servant-girl saw him and *said to those who were there, 'This man was with Jesus of Nazareth.' 72 And again he denied it with an oath, 'I do not know the man.'"*

Mark 14:66 tells us Peter was warming himself by a fire when he is confronted by the servant girl. We see Peter, the big rough and tough fisherman, being intimidated by a little servant girl. The servant girl accuses Peter of being one who was with Jesus. Peter brushes it off by saying, *"I do not know what you are talking about."* (v.71)

The second confrontation Peter has is also initiated by a servant girl. In Mark she tells a group of bystanders that Peter is one of those who followed Jesus. The group then responds by stating that they too believe he is a follower (Mark 14:69-70). Peter's denial intensifies in that this time he gives an oath that he does not know Jesus. The term "oath" means something similar to an oath that one gives in a courtroom. The courtroom-style oath serves as a promise that you are telling the truth. Scripture tells us in **Hebrews 6:16:** *"For men swear by one greater than themselves, and with them an oath given as confirmation is an end of every dispute."* Have you ever heard one say, "I swear on a stack of Bibles."? What he is attempting to do is bolster the sincerity of his statement. Since one's own promise to tell the truth may not be convincing enough, he turns to something higher and very truthful, in an attempt to bolster his own credibility. That is what Peter is doing here by giving an oath.

VERSES 73-74: *"And a little later the bystanders came up and said to Peter, 'Surely you too are one of them; for the way you talk gives you away.'* [74] *Then he began to curse and swear, 'I do not know the man!' And immediately a cock crowed."*

Here is the third encounter Peter has with someone accusing him of being Jesus' disciple. In Matthew and Mark we are told that the man in the third confrontation says he can tell Peter is a Galilian by his accent. John gives us more details about this guy. John states that this bystander was a relative of the person whose ear was cut off by Peter (John 18:26). Again we see an escalation in the fervency of Peter's denials. Remember that the first denial was a mere statement of not knowing what the girl was talking about. The second denial came with oaths. During this third denial, we see that frustration and the flesh is taking over and he begins using rough language by beginning to *"curse and swear."* To understand what those terms mean in their context, MacArthur states that:

> "...(**to curse**) is a very strong term that involved pronouncing death upon oneself at the hand of God if one were lying. In perhaps the most serious taking of the Lord's name in vain that is conceivable, Peter said, in essence, 'May God kill and damn me if I am not speaking the truth.' Omnumi (to **swear**) was a less extreme pledge of truthfulness but was nevertheless a strong affirmation."[525]

VERSE 75: *"And Peter remembered the word which Jesus had said, 'Before a cock crows, you will deny Me three times.' And he went out and wept bitterly."*

Peter is struck by what he has just done and, *"went out and wept bitterly."* Luke gives us more detail by explaining that Peter realizes what he had done when Jesus looks at him! What a completely crushing moment in Peter's life.

> **Luke 22:61:** *"And the Lord turned and looked at Peter. And Peter remembered the word of the Lord, how He had told him, 'Before a cock crows today, you will deny Me three times.'"*

Summary and Application

In our text of Matthew 26:69-72, we see Peter's failure and denial came so quickly after his bold statements of allegiance. A lesson for all of us is to never put trust in ourselves to withstand spiritual attack. Remember Peter was not a man of prayer as exhibited by his continual falling asleep in the garden (Matthew 26:40-41, 43, 45). Spiritual warfare is won on the knees in prayer. Don't take great comfort in the fact that you have been a believer for decades, or that you have a very fruitful ministry, or maybe that you are a deacon, elder, or pastor. I was deeply sorrowed by news I received of a pastor I knew who fell

---

[525] MacArthur, J. F., Jr. (1985). *Matthew*. MacArthur New Testament Commentary (p. 249). Chicago: Moody Press.

from ministry. While visiting with an assistant pastor at the church, he explained that the pastor who fell was one who did not practice accountability at all. He controlled all the finances, discussion, decisions, etc. He further stated that the fallen pastor held the view that the elders were simply to pray and were neither a part of the decision-making body, nor were they to help with the oversight of the church. This is a classic example of a man who put trust in himself to minister, rather than leaning wholly on the Holy Spirit. The apostle Paul made it clear that he did not think he was able to do anything apart from God.

> **Romans 7:18:** *"For I know that nothing good dwells in me, that is, in my flesh; for the wishing is present in me, but the doing of the good is not."*

Jesus told us that all our strength and fruitfulness come directly from Him alone!

> **John 15:4-5:** *"Abide in Me, and I in you. As the branch cannot bear fruit of itself, unless it abides in the vine, so neither can you, unless you abide in Me. ⁵ I am the vine, you are the branches; he who abides in Me, and I in him, he bears much fruit; for apart from Me you can do nothing."*

Peter's story is a reminder to us all of our fleshly weakness. What J. C. Ryle wrote in the mid 1800's is still true today:

> "Great illnesses seldom attack the body without warning symptoms coming first; great falls seldom happen to a saint without a previous course of secret backsliding. The church and the world are sometimes shocked by the sudden misconduct of some great Christian; believers are discouraged and stumbled by it; the enemies of God rejoice and mock; but if the truth could be known, the explanation of such cases would generally be found to have been private departure from God. People fall in private long before they fall in public."[526]

There is another great lesson to be drawn from Peter's failure: there is great forgiveness and restoration given by God to those who repent and turn to Him for it. We will study that later.

---

[526] *Matthew* / Ryle, J.C. p.270 (Expository Thoughts on the Gospels) (Crossways Classic Commentaries: v.1)

MATTHEW 27:1-10
(JESUS IS TAKEN BEFORE PILATE; JUDAS' DESTRUCTION)

"Now when morning had come, all the chief priests and the elders of the people took counsel against Jesus to put Him to death; ² and they bound Him, and led Him away, and delivered Him up to Pilate the governor .

³ Then when Judas, who had betrayed Him, saw that He had been condemned, he felt remorse and returned the thirty pieces of silver to the chief priests and elders, ⁴ saying, 'I have sinned by betraying innocent blood .' But they said, 'What is that to us? See to that yourself!' ⁵ And he threw the pieces of silver into the sanctuary and departed; and he went away and hanged himself. ⁶ And the chief priests took the pieces of silver and said, 'It is not lawful to put them into the temple treasury, since it is the price of blood.' ⁷ And they counseled together and with the money bought the Potter's Field as a burial place for strangers. ⁸ For this reason that field has been called the Field of Blood to this day. ⁹ Then that which was spoken through Jeremiah the prophet was fulfilled, saying, 'AND THEY TOOK THE THIRTY PIECES OF SILVER, THE PRICE OF THE ONE WHOSE PRICE HAD BEEN SET by the sons of Israel ; ¹⁰ AND THEY GAVE THEM FOR THE POTTER'S FIELD, AS THE LORD DIRECTED ME.'"

Introduction

Here we see what happens when evil men are in charge of the justice system. Scripture speaks of evil lawmakers and judges:

> **Isaiah 10:1-4:** *"Woe to those who enact evil statutes, And to those who constantly record unjust decisions, ² So as to deprive the needy of justice, And rob the poor of My people of their rights, In order that widows may be their spoil, And that they may plunder the orphans. ³ Now what will you do in the day of punishment, And in the devastation which will come from afar? To whom will you flee for help? And where will you leave your wealth? ⁴ Nothing remains but to crouch among the captives Or fall among the slain. In spite of all this His anger does not turn away, And His hand is still stretched out."*

Matthew 27:1-10 also sets out the destruction of Judas. The Bible is clear that sin leads to death.

VERSES 1-2: *"Now when morning had come, all the chief priests and the elders of the people took counsel against Jesus to put Him to death; ² and they bound Him, and led Him away, and delivered Him up to Pilate the governor."*

> The Chief priests and elders met early in the morning to pronounce their verdict of death. Again we see their perverse application of justice. Since they did not allow trials and verdicts to occur at night, they simply waited until it was technically day (i.e. morning) and gave their verdict.[527]

---

[527] The Sanhedrin was composed of 71 members. Note that the formal decision was not rendered until morning light so as to not violate procedure that prohibited night-time trials. See Mark 15:1.

One needs to remember that this was a kangaroo court where the verdict was determined before the trial. In Matthew 26, Jesus was taken before Caiaphas. Caiaphas was not holding a hearing to seek the truth, but he instead was using the justice system as a vehicle to murder Jesus.

> **Matthew 26:59:** *"Now the chief priests and the whole Council kept trying to obtain false testimony against Jesus, in order that they might put Him to death;"*

The council had one problem, it was not allowed to put someone to death. Remember that the Romans were in control at this time and they did not allow anyone to be put to death without their consent. In verse 2 of the main text, we see the religious leaders headed to Pilate, the Roman governor. They needed Pilate's permission to crucify Jesus. We will read more about Jesus' trial before Pilate later in the sections covering Matthew 27:11-26.

VERSES 3-5: *"Then when Judas, who had betrayed Him, saw that He had been condemned, he felt remorse and returned the thirty pieces of silver to the chief priests and elders, 4 saying, 'I have sinned by betraying innocent blood .' But they said, 'What is that to us? See to that yourself!' 5 And he threw the pieces of silver into the sanctuary and departed; and he went away and hanged himself."*

The term "repentance" can have different meanings in its application. One example would be the response of a child who gets caught stealing out of the cookie jar. When he finds out that he will be punished, out comes the tears and promises never to do it again. The child is sorry that he was caught and not necessarily that he did wrong by disobeying and stealing. There are many confessing Christians who take this view. They think just because they say they are sorry to God, everything is alright. They can keep living their lives the way they want to, just as long as they say, "sorry," or participate in a religious ritual to get themselves cleansed. This is typical of the "antinomianists." [528]

---

[528] Christ has fulfilled the law and we are saved by grace alone. Unfortunately, there are some in the evangelical ranks that have perverted that truth to mean Christians can actively, willfully and unrepentantly participate in sin because we are under grace and not the law. That false teaching is called the heresy of *Antinomianism,* which literally means "anti-lawism." These people say we do not have to obey the moral law of God. The Word of God teaches the opposite of Antinomianism:

> **Romans 6:15:** *What then? Shall we sin because we are not under law but under grace? May it never be!*
>
> **Romans 3:31:** *Do we then nullify the Law through faith? May it never be! On the contrary, we establish the Law.*
>
> Jesus says in **John 14:15:** *"If you love Me, you will keep My commandments.*

Here is the formal definition: "<u>Antinomianism</u>. An ethical system that denies the binding nature of any supposedly absolute or external laws on individual behavior. Some antinomianists argue that Christians need not preach or practice the laws of the Old Testament because Christ's merits have freed Christians from the law. Others, like the early Gnostics, teach that spiritual perfection comes about through the attainment of a special knowledge rather than by obedience to law. Generally, Christian theology has rejected antinomianism on the basis that although Christians are not saved through keeping the law, we still have a responsibility to live uprightly, that is, in obedience to God's law of love in service to one another (Galatians 5:13–14) as we walk by the Spirit (Galatians 5:16) who continually works to transform us into the image of Christ the Creator (Colossians, 7–10)." Grenz, S., Guretzki, D., and Nordling, C. F. (1999). *Pocket Dictionary of Theological Terms* (p. 12). Downers Grove, Ill.: InterVarsity Press.

Paul makes it clear that an unrepentant practitioner of unrighteousness will be judged:

> **Galatians 5:19-21:** *"Now the deeds of the flesh are evident, which are: immorality, impurity, sensuality,[20] idolatry, sorcery, enmities, strife, jealousy, outbursts of anger, disputes, dissensions, factions,[21] envying, drunkenness, carousing, and things like these, of which I forewarn you just as I have forewarned you <u>that those who practice such things shall not inherit the kingdom of God.</u>"*

> **1 Corinthians 6:9-11:** *"Or do you not know that the unrighteous shall not inherit the kingdom of God? Do not be deceived; neither fornicators, nor idolaters, nor adulterers, nor effeminate, nor homosexuals, [10] nor thieves, nor the covetous, nor drunkards, nor revilers, nor swindlers, shall inherit the kingdom of God. [11] And such were some of you; but you were washed, but you were sanctified, but you were justified in the name of the Lord Jesus Christ, and in the Spirit of our God."*

R. C. Sproul writes, "When repentance is offered to God in a spirit of true contrition, He promises to forgive us and to restore us to fellowship with Him:"[529]

> **1 John 1:9:** *"If we confess our sins, He is faithful and righteous to forgive us our sins and to cleanse us from all unrighteousness."*

A. Hodge wrote that:

> "As to its essence, true repentance consists—(1) In a sincere hatred of sin, and sorrow for our own sin (Psalms 119:128, 136). Sin is seen to be exceeding sinful in the light of the divine holiness, of the law of God, and especially of the cross of Christ. The more we see of God in the face of Christ, the more we abhor ourselves and repent in dust and ashes. (Job 13:5, 6 ; Ezekiel 36:31)."[530]

Judas' sorrow is not based in a love for God, but merely an awareness of the great sinfulness of his act. He did not desire to do right, but greatly regretted that he did wrong. He responded to the exposure of his sin by killing himself, not by repenting and turning to God. Sometimes non-Christians will say they feel better if they confess to another person something they did wrong. That confession does absolutely nothing toward the removal of one's sins. In verse 4, we read that Judas told the Chief Priest, *"I have sinned by betraying innocent blood."* They responded by saying, *"What is that to us? See to that yourself!"* Judas' confession to the priests did nothing to absolve him of his sin.

---

[529] Sproul, R. C. (1996, c1992). *Essential Truths of the Christian Faith*. Wheaton, Ill.: Tyndale House.

[530] Hodge, A., Hodge, C., and Hodge, A. (1996). *The Confession of Faith: With Questions for Theological Students and Bible Classes*. With an appendix on Presbyterianism by Charles Hodge. Index created by Christian Classics Foundation. (electronic ed. based on the 1992 Banner of Truth reprint.) (p. 211). Simpsonville SC: Christian Classics Foundation.

If one has true, godly sorrow, it will result in repentance.[531] Paul speaks of this type of sorrow that results in salvation.

> **2 Corinthians 7:9-10:** *"I now rejoice, not that you were made sorrowful, but that you were made sorrowful to the point of repentance; for you were made sorrowful according to the will of God, in order that you might not suffer loss in anything through us. [10] For the sorrow that is according to the will of God produces a repentance without regret, leading to salvation; but the sorrow of the world produces death."*

True repentance comes only from God. We cannot generate it ourselves.

> **2 Timothy 2:25-26:** *"…with gentleness correcting those who are in opposition, if perhaps <u>God may grant them repentance</u> leading to the knowledge of the truth, [26] and they may come to their senses and escape from the snare of the devil, having been held captive by him to do his will ."*

Our prayers to the Father should include a plea that He would grant us repentance for our sins. One reason we should ask God to give us repentance is due to the fact that we commit many sins we may be unaware of, or we do not think they are that big of a deal. Despite our ignorance, they are still sinful acts or attitudes.

The foolish person may be flirting with sin and at the same time seem to have things going his way. He does not realize God's patience serves as a draw for him to repent. His grace should not be understood to mean God thinks lightly of the sin.

> **Romans 2:4-5:** *"Or do you think lightly of the riches of His kindness and forbearance and patience , <u>not knowing that the kindness of God leads you to repentance</u>? [5]But because of your stubbornness and unrepentant heart you are storing up wrath for yourself in the day of wrath and revelation of the righteous judgment of God,"*

In verse 5 it mentions that Judas hung himself. We read from the book of Acts that while Judas was being hung, his rope broke or something else happened that resulted in his falling in such a way that his stomach was cut open and his bowels came out.

> **Acts 1:18-19:** *"(Now this man acquired a field with the price of his wickedness; and falling headlong, he burst open in the middle and all his bowels gushed out. [19]And it became known to all who were living in Jerusalem; so that in their own language that field was called Hakeldama, that is, Field of Blood.)"*

J.C. Ryle summarizes the unprofitability of gain obtained through evil;

> "Let us be sure that of all trades, sin is the most unprofitable. Judas, Achan, Gehazi, Ananias and Sapphria all found it so to their cost."[532]

---

[531] Repentance is, "not just feeling sorry, or changing one's mind, but [is] a turning round, a complete alteration of the basic motivation and direction of one's life. This is why the best translation for *metanoeō* is often *to convert*, that is, *to turn round*. [In summary it is turning and forsaking the sin.] Wood, D. R. W. and Marshall, I. H., *New Bible dictionary* (3rd ed.) (p. 1007). Leicester, England; Downers Grove, Ill.: InterVarsity Press (1996).

[532] *Matthew* / Ryle, J.C. p.275 (Expository Thoughts on the Gospels) (Crossways Classic Commentaries: v.1)

VERSES 6-10: *"And the chief priests took the pieces of silver and said, 'It is not lawful to put them into the temple treasury, since it is the price of blood.' ⁷And they counseled together and with the money bought the Potter's Field as a burial place for strangers. ⁸ For this reason that field has been called the Field of Blood to this day. ⁹ Then that which was spoken through Jeremiah the prophet was fulfilled, saying, 'AND THEY TOOK THE THIRTY PIECES OF SILVER, THE PRICE OF THE ONE WHOSE PRICE HAD BEEN SET by the sons of Israel; ¹⁰ AND THEY GAVE THEM FOR THE POTTER'S FIELD, AS THE LORD DIRECTED ME.'"*

The priests had the money Judas threw at them (30 pieces of silvers), and they were trying to figure out what they would do with it. When they said, *"It is not lawful to put them into the temple treasury, since it is the price of blood,"* they meant that they could not take the money and put it back into the treasury because it was money that was used to have someone killed.[533] They were so concerned about keeping "God's money clean" (i.e. the temple treasury money), they failed to realize that they were covered in blood for the murder of God.

Verses 7 and 8 tell us that the chief priests decided to buy a graveyard for strangers who died while visiting Jerusalem.[534] The reason it is called a potter's field is because a potter (i.e. one who made vessels out of clay) would dig in this area to find clay to make his pottery. The holes left could also be used for graves.

Verses 9 and 10 are very similar to passages from Zechariah 11:12-13. When Matthew mentions Jeremiah the prophet, one needs to remember that Jeremiah prophetically mentions this event also:

> "But there are also similarities between Matthew's words and the ideas in Jeremiah 19:1, 4, 6, 11. Why then did Matthew refer only to Jeremiah? The solution to this problem is probably that Matthew had both prophets in mind but only mentioned the 'major' prophet by name. (A similar situation is found in Mark 1:2-3, where Mark mentioned the Prophet Isaiah but quoted directly from both Isaiah and Malachi.) In addition, another explanation is that Jeremiah, in the Babylonian Talmud (Baba Bathra 14b), was placed first among the prophets, and his book represented all the other prophetic books."[535]

---

[533] "Mathew 27:9 . τιμὴ αἵματος *the money paid for a bloody deed* ."
Arndt, W., Gingrich, F. W., Danker, F. W., and Bauer, W. (1996, c1979). *A Greek-English lexicon of the New Testament and other early Christian literature: A translation and adaption of the fourth revised and augmented edition of Walter Bauer's Griechisch-deutsches Worterbuch zu den Schrift en des Neuen Testaments und der ubrigen urchristlichen Literatur* (p. 817). Chicago: University of Chicago Press.

[534] *"And this field was to be a burying-place for strangers, that is, proselytes to the Jewish religion, who were of other nations, and, coming to Jerusalem to worship, happened to die there."* Henry, M. (1996, c1991). *Matthew Henry's Commentary on the Whole Bible: Complete and Unabridged in One Volume* (Matthew 27:1). Peabody: Hendrickson.

[535] Walvoord, J. F., Zuck, R. B., and Dallas Theological Seminary. (1983-c1985). *The Bible Knowledge Commentary: An exposition of the scriptures* (Mt 27:3). Wheaton, IL: Victor Books.

Summary and Application

In this section of Scripture, we see the false follower's legalism and its end result. The religious leaders utilized their hypocritical legalism to accomplish Jesus' murder, via a false trial. We see the religious leaders doing what their father the Devil does (i.e. lie and murder—John 8:44).

The death of Judas is an example of the end of life for the false follower of Jesus. He plays the Christian game, but never repents to Christ for his salvation. His end is guilt, condemnation, destruction and damnation.

MATTHEW 27:11-14
(FIRST TRIAL BEFORE PILATE)

"Now Jesus stood before the governor, and the governor questioned Him, saying, 'Are You the King of the Jews?' And Jesus said to him, 'It is as you say.' 12 *And while He was being accused by the chief priests and elders, He made no answer.* 13 *Then Pilate *said to Him, 'Do You not hear how many things they testify against You?'* 14 *And He did not answer him with regard to even a single charge, so that the governor was quite amazed."*

Introduction

After the religious leaders held their bogus trial, they went to the Roman governor to get the permission to carry out the execution of Jesus (Matthew 27:1-2). Pontius Pilate was the Roman governor and he attempted to examine the situation himself.

What we learn from this lesson is the huge amount of evil a person can be persuaded to do if he is a "man-pleasers." A man-pleaser is one who is more concerned that others think well of him than doing the right thing. Pilate had the authority to prevent this murder, but when he realized that his own political future could suffer, he quickly caved in. We see many people making their moral judgments based on what is acceptable to others rather than applying God's standard. We are not to be spineless individuals, but people of principal and conviction. Our confidence in these unmoving principles is not based in ourselves, or even the way we were raised, but the Word of God.

VERSES 11-14: *"Now Jesus stood before the governor, and the governor questioned Him, saying, 'Are You the King of the Jews?' And Jesus said to him, 'It is as you say.'* 12 *And while He was being accused by the chief priests and elders, He made no answer.* 13 *Then Pilate *said to Him, 'Do You not hear how many things they testify against You?'* 14 *And He did not answer him with regard to even a single charge, so that the governor was quite amazed."*

The governor was Pilate. The Jewish leaders knew they needed to go through him to get Jesus killed. "The procurator had full powers of life and death, and could reverse capital sentences passed by the Sanhedrin, which had to be submitted to him for ratification."[536]

To get more detail on this entire incident before Pilate, we need to look to the Apostle John:

> **John 18:29-38:** *"Pilate therefore went out to them, and said, 'What accusation do you bring against this Man?' They answered and said to him, 'If this Man were not an evildoer, we would not have delivered Him up to you.' Pilate therefore said to them, 'Take Him yourselves, and judge Him according to your law.' The Jews said to him, 'We are not permitted to put anyone to death,' that the word of Jesus might be fulfilled, which He spoke, signifying by what kind of death He was about to die.*

---

[536] Wood, D. R. W., and Marshall, I. H. (1996). *New Bible Dictionary* (3rd ed.) (p. 929). Leicester, England; Downers Grove, Ill.: InterVarsity Press.

Pilate therefore entered again into the Praetorium, and summoned Jesus, and said to Him, 'Are You the King of the Jews?' Jesus answered, 'Are you saying this on your own initiative, or did others tell you about Me?' Pilate answered, 'I am not a Jew, am I? Your own nation and the chief priests delivered You up to me; what have You done?' Jesus answered, 'My kingdom is not of this world. If My kingdom were of this world, then My servants would be fighting, that I might not be delivered up to the Jews; but as it is, My kingdom is not of this realm.' Pilate therefore said to Him, 'So You are a king?' Jesus answered, 'You say correctly that I am a king . For this I have been born, and for this I have come into the world, to bear witness to the truth. Everyone who is of the truth hears My voice.' Pilate said to Him, 'What is truth?' And when he had said this, he went out again to the Jews, and said to them, 'I find no guilt in Him.'"

Notice that Jesus does not make a defense for the charges made against Him, just as Scripture said (Matthew 27:14). Jesus' conduct before Pilate fulfilled Isaiah's prophesy, which was made several hundred hears before.

Isaiah 53:7:
"He was oppressed and He was afflicted,
Yet He did not open His mouth;
Like a lamb that is led to slaughter,
And like a sheep that is silent before its shearers,
So He did not open His mouth."

We read from Luke what some of the charges against Him were:

Luke 23:2: *"And they began to accuse Him, saying, 'We found this man misleading our nation and forbidding to pay taxes to Caesar, and saying that He Himself is Christ, a King.'"*

The religious leaders tried to fashion their charges in such a way as to appeal to the interest of Pilate. This is in sharp contrast to the charges/accusations they claimed when they were before the Sanhedrin. Before the Sanhedrin, the initial charge they raised claimed Jesus said He would destroy their temple in three days. After the initial charge failed before the Sanhedrin, they shifted to the charge of blasphemy.

Matthew 26:60-65: *"...and they did not find any, even though many false witnesses came forward. But later on two came forward, and said, 'This man stated, I am able to destroy the temple of God and to rebuild it in three days.' And the high priest stood up and said to Him, 'Do You make no answer? What is it that these men are testifying against You? But Jesus kept silent. And the high priest said to Him, 'I adjure You by the living God, that You tell us whether You are the Christ, the Son of God.' Jesus said to him, 'You have said it yourself; nevertheless I tell you, hereafter you shall see the Son of Man sitting at the right hand of Power, and coming on the clouds of heaven.' Then the high priest tore his robes, saying, 'He has blasphemed! What further need do we have of witnesses? Behold, you have now heard the blasphemy;....'"*

But now that Jesus is in front of the Roman governor, their big accusations are fashioned so as to allege a threat to Rome. They now are claiming that Jesus is leading a rebellion to not pay taxes and that He is challenging the Roman government for the kingship of the country.

Paul wrote to Timothy about Jesus' trial before Pilate. In that letter he encourages Timothy to stand strong in testifying to the truth that Jesus is King and Messiah.

> **1 Timothy 6:13:** *"I charge you in the presence of God, who gives life to all things, and of Christ Jesus, who testified the good confession before Pontius Pilate,..."*

MacArthur writes the following about that "good confession" of Jesus:

> "Knowing that it would cost Him His life, Jesus confessed that He was indeed the King and Messiah. He never equivocated in the face of danger, having committed Himself to the God who raises the dead (cf. Colossians 2:12). No wonder that Revelation calls Him 'the faithful witness' (Revelations 1:5; cf. . 3:14)." [537]

As Paul tells Timothy, all of us must be people who are not afraid of the fires of persecution and stand up even in the face of death to make the good confession.

At this first appearance before Pilate, Jesus was found innocent:

> **Luke 23:3-4:** *"And Pilate asked Him, saying, 'Are You the King of the Jews?' And He answered him and said, 'It is as you say.' And Pilate said to the chief priests and the multitudes, 'I find no guilt in this man.'"*

This finding was not good enough for the religious leaders who wanted to kill Jesus. They continued to protest, and when Pilate heard that Jesus was from Galilee, he sent Jesus there to be judged by Herod.

> **Luke 23:5-7:** *"But they kept on insisting, saying, 'He stirs up the people, teaching all over Judea, starting from Galilee, even as far as this place.' But when Pilate heard it, he asked whether the man was a Galilean. And when he learned that He belonged to Herod's jurisdiction, he sent Him to Herod, who himself also was in Jerusalem at that time."*

Summary and Application

We will see later Pilate crumble. His failure was his desire for worldly approval. What is the failure of so many today? To be approved by the world. James states it as follows:

> **James 4:3-4:** *"You ask and do not receive, because you ask with wrong motives, so that you may spend it on your pleasures. You adulteresses, do you not know that friendship with the world is hostility toward God? Therefore whoever wishes to be a friend of the world makes himself an enemy of God."*

Let us be the true believers who make the *good confession* Jesus made. Let us declare truth in the threat of any circumstance by the power of the Holy Spirit.

---

[537] MacArthur, J. (1995). *1 Timothy* (1 Timothy 6:13). Chicago: Moody Press.

<u>MATTHEW 27:15-26</u>
(MANKIND CHOOSES A MURDERER OVER THE SON OF GOD
AND WANTS TO MURDER THE SON OF GOD)

"Now at the feast the governor was accustomed to release for the multitude any one prisoner whom they wanted . [16] And they were holding at that time a notorious prisoner, called Barabbas . [17] When therefore they were gathered together, Pilate said to them, 'Whom do you want me to release for you? Barabbas, or Jesus who is called Christ?' [18] For he knew that because of envy they had delivered Him up. [19] And while he was sitting on the judgment seat, his wife sent to him, saying, 'Have nothing to do with that righteous Man; for last night I suffered greatly in a dream because of Him.' [20] But the chief priests and the elders persuaded the multitudes to ask for Barabbas, and to put Jesus to death . [21] But the governor answered and said to them, 'Which of the two do you want me to release for you?' And they said, 'Barabbas.' [22] Pilate * said to them, 'Then what shall I do with Jesus who is called Christ?' They all * said, 'Let Him be crucified!' [23] And he said, 'Why, what evil has He done?' But they kept shouting all the more, saying, 'Let Him be crucified!' [24] And when Pilate saw that he was accomplishing nothing, but rather that a riot was starting, he took water and washed his hands in front of the multitude, saying, 'I am innocent of this Man's blood; see to that yourselves.' [25] And all the people answered and said, 'His blood be on us and on our children!' [26] Then he released Barabbas for them; but after having Jesus scourged, he delivered Him to be crucified."

Introduction

Jesus' first trial was before the Sanhedrin. The religious leaders then took Jesus to Pilate for a trial, and Pilate found Him not guilty. Pilate then sent Jesus to Herod (Herod Antipas),[538] who likewise found Him not guilty (Luke 23:14-15) and returned Jesus to Pilate, who held a second trial in which He was found not guilty (Luke 23:13-15). Luke records a review of those events:

> <u>Luke 23:4-25</u>: *"And Pilate said to the chief priests and the multitudes, 'I find no guilt in this man.' [5] But they kept on insisting, saying, 'He stirs up the people, teaching all over Judea, starting from Galilee, even as far as this place.' [6] But when Pilate heard it, he asked whether the man was a Galilean. [7] And when he learned that He belonged to Herod's jurisdiction, he sent Him to Herod, who himself also was in Jerusalem at that time.*
>
> *[8] Now Herod was very glad when he saw Jesus; for he had wanted to see Him for a long time, because he had been hearing about Him and was hoping to see some sign performed by Him.[9] And he questioned Him at some length; but He answered him nothing.[10] And the chief priests and the scribes were standing there, accusing Him vehemently.[11] And Herod with his soldiers, after treating Him with contempt and mocking Him, dressed Him in a gorgeous robe and sent Him back to Pilate. [12] Now*

---

[538] Herod Antipas (Tetrarch of Galilee Luke 3:1). He wanted to kill Jesus earlier: <u>Luke 13:31-33:</u> *"Just at that time some Pharisees came up, saying to Him, 'Go away and depart from here, for Herod wants to kill You.' [32] And He said to them, 'Go and tell that fox, Behold, I cast out demons and perform cures today and tomorrow, and the third day I reach My goal . [33] Nevertheless I must journey on today and tomorrow and the next day; for it cannot be that a prophet should perish outside of Jerusalem.'"*

Herod and Pilate became friends with one another that very day; for before they had been at enmity with each other.

*   ¹³ And Pilate summoned the chief priests and the rulers and the people, ¹⁴ and said to them, 'You brought this man to me as one who incites the people to rebellion, and behold, having examined Him before you, I have found no guilt in this man regarding the charges which you make against Him.¹⁵ No, nor has Herod, for he sent Him back to us; and behold, nothing deserving death has been done by Him. ¹⁶ I will therefore punish Him and release Him.' ¹⁷ [Now he was obliged to release to them at the feast one prisoner.]¹⁸ But they cried out all together, saying, 'Away with this man, and release for us Barabbas!' ¹⁹ (He was one who had been thrown into prison for a certain insurrection made in the city, and for murder.) ²⁰ And Pilate, wanting to release Jesus, addressed them again, ²¹ but they kept on calling out, saying, 'Crucify, crucify Him!' ²² And he said to them the third time, 'Why, what evil has this man done? I have found in Him no guilt demanding death; I will therefore punish Him and release Him.' ²³ But they were insistent, with loud voices asking that He be crucified. And their voices began to prevail. ²⁴ And Pilate pronounced sentence that their demand should be granted.²⁵ And he released the man they were asking for who had been thrown into prison for insurrection and murder, but he delivered Jesus to their will."*

Here we see the evil of mankind. They chose a murderer (Luke 23:17-25, Mark 15:7-15) over God Almighty as the favored one. This section also fulfills Scripture when it speaks of Jesus being rejected by His own people.

    Isaiah 53:3: *"He was despised and forsaken of men, A man of sorrows and acquainted with grief; And like one from whom men hide their face He was despised, and we did not esteem Him. "*

Note that Pilate says, *"Then what shall I do with Jesus who is called Christ?"* **Matthew 27:22.** This is the essential question that every person must answer. For those who reject the Messiah, an eternity of judgment and damnation awaits them. For those who receive Him, they will be saved for an eternity in the presence of God.

VERSES 15-18: *"Now at the feast the governor was accustomed to release for the multitude any one prisoner whom they wanted. ¹⁶ And they were holding at that time a notorious prisoner, called Barabbas . ¹⁷ When therefore they were gathered together, Pilate said to them, 'Whom do you want me to release for you? Barabbas, or Jesus who is called Christ ?' ¹⁸ For he knew that because of envy they had delivered Him up."*

During the Passover the governor customarily set free a prisoner. Mark tells us the crowd reminded Pilate of that tradition (Mark 15:6-8). Pilate knew Jesus was a prisoner only because the religious leaders were extremely jealous of Him. This is demonstrated in Matthew 27:18 where it says, *"For he knew that because of envy they had delivered Him up."* To save his political face and not condemn an innocent man, Pilate tries to bypass the religious leaders and go directly to the people, and asks who they want to have released (v.17). Pilate is confident if the people are given the choice between Barabbas and Jesus, they will clearly choose Jesus. He was stunned by their demand for Barabbas.

We know who Jesus is, but who is this man named Barabbas? Mark tells us that Barabbas had been arrested and placed with those who committed murder during a rebellion against the governing authorities.

> **Mark 15:7:** *"And the man named Barabbas had been imprisoned with the insurrectionists who had committed murder in the insurrection ."*

Peter points out Barabbas was a murderer (Acts 314). It should also be mentioned that Barabbas was known as a robber (John 18:40). There is a difference between a robber and a thief. A thief takes what does not belong to him. In contrast, a robber takes what does not belong to him, but does it through force or threat.

VERSE 19: *"And while he was sitting on the judgment seat, his wife sent to him, saying, 'Have nothing to do with that righteous Man; for last night I suffered greatly in a dream because of Him.'"*

Here Pilate receives his last warning regarding the person of Jesus Christ, *"that righteous Man."* The warning comes from his wife, but that is not enough for a man-pleaser. The man-pleaser will do what keeps more people happy with him, rather than standing alone to do what is right.

VERSES 20-21: *"But the chief priests and the elders persuaded the multitudes to ask for Barabbas, and to put Jesus to death. 21 But the governor answered and said to them, 'Which of the two do you want me to release for you?' And they said, 'Barabbas .'"*

Pilate thought that his way out of this was to take the decision to the people, but he did not realize that the religious leaders already had convinced the people to ask for Barabbas.

It is important in your ministry to remember that you are not trying to please the masses. You serve an audience of ONE – the Lord Jesus Christ. When you are faced with a difficult decision, first seek the Lord in His Word and prayer. If you are not sure after that because Scripture does not specifically address the matter, then seek truly godly counsel[539] and apply what I call the 100 Year Rule. The 100 Year Rule means that 100 years from now, when all the things and people around me have passed, what is the decision I will wish I had made? This should eliminate the man-pleasing and keep an eternal, Christ-glorifying, perspective in making the decision. Remember…the mob is hardly ever right, and *even fewer times seeking the will of God.*

VERSES 22-23: *"Pilate * said to them, 'Then what shall I do with Jesus who is called Christ?' They all * said, 'Let Him be crucified!' 23 And he said, 'Why, what evil has He done?' But they kept shouting all the more, saying, 'Let Him be crucified!'"*

Pilate is surprised by their response of wanting the criminal Barabbas released over Jesus! He then asks the crowd what should be done to Jesus. He is further shocked by their desire to have

---

[539] When I speak of seeking godly counsel, I mean truly godly counsel. Often people will run to a Christian friend or even a pastor who may give them a worldly/reasonable answer. Worse yet, they may tell you what you want to hear. I would discuss the matter with one who will truly pray over the matter before he speaks, and has a proven life of godliness and is not simply following the current pop-culture trends. In other words, a person who truly fears God and not man.

Him executed. We can derive from verse 23 and Luke 23:14-15 that Pilate had found Jesus innocent of any wrongdoing and so he inquired of the crowd what they believed Jesus did that was worthy of death. The mob would not answer. They could not answer because Jesus did nothing evil. The mob just continued to shout out for His blood. Verse 23 said, *"But they kept shouting all the more, saying, 'Let Him be crucified!'...."*

VERSES 24-25: *"And when Pilate saw that he was accomplishing nothing, but rather that a riot was starting, he took water and washed his hands in front of the multitude, saying, 'I am innocent of this Man's blood; see to that yourselves.'* 25 *And all the people answered and said, 'His blood be on us and on our children!'"*

Here is a classic example of worldly hypocrisy. Pilate's first and foremost concern is not to prevent the death of an innocent man, but instead he is concerned about his own political standing.

> "The verdict of the NT is that he [Pilate] was a weak man, ready to serve
> expediency rather than principle, whose authorization of the judicial murder of
> the Saviour was due less to a desire to please the Jewish authorities than to fear
> of imperial displeasure if Tiberius heard of further unrest in Judaea. This is
> made abundantly evident by his mockery of the Jews in the wording of the
> superscription (John. 19:19–22). It is most unfortunate that we do not know
> anything of his record apart from his government of the Jews, towards whom
> he would appear to have shown little understanding and even less liking."[540]

When he saw a riot was starting, he decided he would give them what they wanted so that he would not be inquired of by Rome as to why a riot broke out.

Hand washing:
It is typical of human nature to come up with its own remedy for sin. False religions incorporate atonement of sin through religious works, ceremonies, or rituals. You can go to many churches today that will tell you a certain religious rite will grant forgiveness. Here we see Pilate engaging in a symbolic ceremony. He believes by pouring water over his hands he has become innocent of the blood of Jesus when he allows His execution. Needless to say, pouring water on his hands did nothing to remove his sin. Likewise, baptism does not cleanse the sins of the unrepentant who have not put their faith in Christ.

His statement to the people that they were responsible for Jesus' death did not make him sinless either. Notice how evil mankind is by the mob's response in verse 25 where it says, *"His blood be on us and on our children!"* The Jews were saying that if there was guilt or sin in this matter, they would take total responsibility for it and not Rome. Their rebellion and hatred of God and their desire for His murder was so great that they are willing to call down a curse on themselves and their own children (Matthew 27:25). The spiritual reality is that every person is responsible

---

[540] Wood, D. R. W., and Marshall, I. H. (1996). *New Bible dictionary* (3rd ed. /) (pp. 929-930). Leicester, England; Downers Grove, Ill.: InterVarsity Press.

for the murder of Jesus. It is because of our sin and rebellion that Christ paid the penalty for those who believe.

VERSE 26: *"Then he released Barabbas for them; but after having Jesus scourged, he delivered Him to be crucified."*

The hypocritical judgment hammer has fallen and the Son of God is handed over to evil men to be killed. He is whipped before He is crucified. The type of whip used is described below:
> "The whip used for scourging had a short wooden handle, to the end of which were attached several leather thongs. Each thong was tipped with very sharp pieces of metal or bone. The man to be scourged was tied to a post by the wrists high over his head, with his feet dangling and his body taut. Often there were two scourgets, one on either side of the victim, who took turns lashing him across the back. Muscles were lacerated, veins and arteries were torn open, and it was not uncommon for the kidneys, spleen, or other organs to be exposed and slashed. As would be expected, many men died of scourging before they could be taken out for execution. We do not know the full extent of Jesus' wounds, but He was so weakened by them that He was not able to carry His own cross (Mark 15:21)."[541]

Summary and Application

In these Scriptures, we see the evil of mankind and the danger of man-pleasing. Even though no guilt was found in Jesus, it did not stop His murder. Ryle describes Pilate, and politicians like him, this way:
> "We see in this miserable man a living pattern of many a ruler of this world! How many there are who know well that their public acts are wrong, and yet have not the courage to act up to their knowledge. They fear the people; they dread being laughed at; they cannot bear being unpopular. Like dead fish, they float with the tide. Human praise is the idol before which they bow down, and to that idol they sacrifice conscience, inner peace and an immortal soul."[542]

The religious leaders sought His death because of jealousy, hatred, and political expediency. We must be Christians who live by the book. We must live by convictions and judge righteously and not just follow the crowd. I have seen those who call themselves Christians make their decisions based on what is approved by worldly standards. This may keep them in good standing with the world, but they are fruitless and not used by God.
> **1 John 4:4-6:** *"You are from God, little children, and have overcome them; because greater is He who is in you than he who is in the world. [5] They are from the world; therefore they speak as from the world, and the world listens to them. [6] We are from God; he who knows God listens to us; he who is not from God does not listen to us. By this we know the spirit of truth and the spirit of error."*

---

[541] MacArthur, J. (1989). *Matthew* (Matthew 27:24). Chicago: Moody Press.

[542] *Matthew* / Ryle, J.C. p.277 (Expository thoughts on the Gospels) (Crossways classic commentaries: v.1)

MATTHEW 27:27-31
(THE WHIPPING, BEATING AND MOCKING
OF THE SON OF GOD BY MANKIND)

"Then the soldiers of the governor took Jesus into the Praetorium and gathered the whole Roman cohort around Him. ²⁸ *And they stripped Him, and put a scarlet robe on Him.* ²⁹ *And after weaving a crown of thorns , they put it on His head , and a reed in His right hand; and they kneeled down before Him and mocked Him, saying , 'Hail , King of the Jews!'* ³⁰ *And they spat on Him, and took the reed and began to beat Him on the head.* ³¹ *And after they had mocked Him, they took His robe off and put His garments on Him, and led Him away to crucify Him."*

Introduction

In the previous section (Matthew 27:22-26), Pilate held a judicial determination that Jesus did nothing worthy of death. Despite that finding, Pilate succumbed to the crowd's demand to murder Jesus. Pilate then had Jesus severely whipped and taken away (v. 26-27). The whipping Jesus received is part of our healing:

> <u>Isaiah 53:5-6:</u>
> *"But He was pierced through for our transgressions,*
> *He was crushed for our iniquities;*
> *The chastening for our well-being fell upon Him,*
> *And by <u>His scourging we are healed</u>.*
> ⁶ *All of us like sheep have gone astray,*
> *Each of us has turned to his own way;*
> *But the Lord has caused the iniquity of us all*
> *To fall on Him."*

In Matthew 27:27-32 we see the long, painful, physical abuse Jesus underwent prior to being hung on the cross. The pain was not just physical; there was mental abuse from the mocking soldiers. This mocking came by way of the crown of thorns, royal robe, and false homage (v.29-30). Jesus' greatest pain came from the fact that He was about to be separated from the Father and bear all the sin of the world. The One who was in perfect union with the Father and without sin would take on our sin and receive our punishment.

There is an important factor we must remember when looking at the ghastly murder of Jesus. His death is not to be looked upon as some melancholy lesson about caring. Neither is Jesus' death the act of a martyr for a cause. It must be remembered that JESUS IS LORD! He is the DIVINE SON OF GOD! He was innocent in every way and completely without any sin. Jesus' death and resurrection represents infinite power, glory, and love. His death was about an ultimate and loving God who willingly paid the price for the sins of an incredibly evil and defiled mankind who wanted to kill Him! Yes, it was an evil mob that partook in Jesus' murder, but He was not the victim of an evil mob. Jesus is God and thus, He was in complete control of everything. He willingly laid His life down to pay for our sins.

> **John 10:17-18:** *"For this reason the Father loves Me, because I lay down My life that I may take it again. "No one has taken it away from Me, but I lay it down on My own*

initiative. I have authority to lay it down, and I have authority to take it up again. This commandment I received from My Father."

VERSE 27: *"Then the soldiers of the governor took Jesus into the Praetorium and gathered the whole Roman cohort around Him."*

Pilate's soldiers took Jesus to the **Praetorium,** which means the governor's house.[543] There were about 600 soldiers (a cohort) who surrounded Jesus.[544]

VERSE 28-30: *"And they stripped Him, and put a scarlet robe on Him. [29] And after weaving a crown of thorns, they put it on His head, and a reed in His right hand; and they kneeled down before Him and mocked Him, saying, 'Hail, King of the Jews!' [30] And they spat on Him, and took the reed and began to beat Him on the head."*

Here we read of the physical abuse and mocking that the cohort of soldiers engaged in. The scarlet robe in verse 28 was a purplish color (John 19:2). Although the soldiers saw the scarlet robe as a mocking version of a royal cape, some commentators believe, "Christ being clad in a scarlet robe, signified His bearing our sins, to His shame, in His own body upon the tree."[545]

> **Isaiah 1:18:**
> *"Come now, and let us reason together,*
> *Says the Lord,*
> *<u>Though your sins are as scarlet,</u>*
> *<u>They will be as white as snow;</u>*
> *Though they are red like crimson,*
> *They will be like wool."*

We see them mocking Christ and causing great physical pain and injury by jamming the "crown of thorns" on His head. Anyone who has been pricked by a tiny thorn on a rose stem knows how much it hurts. Imagine what it would feel like if many long thorns were being pressed into your head. It is not known what type of thorn plant it was since, "there are a number of plants with sharp spines which grow in Palestine."[546] "The purpose was to mimic the wreath Caesar wore on

---

[543] "Originally the tent of the commander, or praetor, and, in consequence, the army headquarters (Livy, 7. 12; Caesar, *Bellum Civile* 1. 76). By extension the word came to mean the residence of a provincial governor (Matthew 27:27; Mark 15:16; John 18:28 , 33; 19:9; Acts 23:35)" Wood, D. R. W., and Marshall, I. H. (1996). *New Bible Dictionary* (3rd ed.) (p. 946). Leicester, England; Downers Grove, Ill.: InterVarsity Press.

[544] "The Praetorium was a large area, for 600 soldiers were there ('company of soldiers' is lit.'cohort' one-tenth of a legion)" Walvoord, J. F., Zuck, R. B., and Dallas Theological Seminary. (1983-c1985). *The Bible Knowledge Commentary: An Exposition of the Scriptures* (Matthew 27:32). Wheaton, IL: Victor Books.

[545] Henry, M. (1996, c1991). *Matthew Henry's Commentary on the Whole Bible: Complete and Unabridged in One Volume* (Matthew 27:26). Peabody: Hendrickson.

[546] Wood, D. R. W., and Marshall, I. H. (1996). *New Bible Dictionary* (3rd ed.) (p. 1183). Leicester, England; Downers Grove, Ill.: InterVarsity Press.

official occasions and that could be seen on Roman coins that bore his image."[547] The thorn can also represent the sin that Jesus was bearing. Remember that part of the curse on the earth as a result of Adam's sin was thorns and thistles:

> **Genesis 3:17-18:** *"Then to Adam He said, 'Because you have listened to the voice of your wife, and have eaten from the tree about which I commanded you, saying, 'You shall not eat from it'; <u>Cursed is the ground because of you;</u> In toil you shall eat of it All the days of your life.* [18]<u>*Both thorns and thistles it shall grow for you;....*</u>*"*

The earth also suffered from the curse of man's sin. The earth itself will be set free from corruption at the revealing of the sons of God.[548] "The revealing of the sons of God will occur when Christ returns for His own. They will share His glory (Romans 8:18; Colossian 1:27; 3:4; Hebrews 2:10), and will be transformed (Romans 8:23). All of nature (inanimate and animate) is personified as waiting eagerly for that time."[549]

> **Romans 8:19-23:** *"For the anxious longing of the creation waits eagerly for the revealing of the sons of God.* [20] *For the creation was subjected to futility, not of its own will, but because of Him who subjected it, in hope* [21] *that the creation itself also will be set free from its slavery to corruption into the freedom of the glory of the children of God.* [22] *For we know that the whole creation groans and suffers the pains of childbirth together until now.* [23] *And not only this, but also we ourselves, having the first fruits of the Spirit, even we ourselves groan within ourselves, waiting eagerly for our adoption as sons, the redemption of our body."*

They put a reed in His hand to be a scepter. A scepter was, "a staff or baton borne by a sovereign as an emblem of authority."[550] The soldiers used the reed as a symbol of a weak ruler. A reed is something that can be blown and bent simply by the wind. Jesus explained John the Baptist was

---

[547] MacArthur, J. (1989). *Matthew* (Matthew 27:38). Chicago: Moody Press.

[548] "<u>Manifestation of the sons of God.</u>— Believers are even now The sons of God, but the world knows them not, 1 John 3:1 . In this respect they are not seen. Their bodies, as well as their spirits, have been purchased by Christ, and they are become His members. Their bodies have, however, no marks of this Divine relation, but, like those of other men, are subject to disease, to death, and corruption. And although they have been regenerated by the Spirit of God, there is still a law in their members warring against the law of their mind. But the period approaches when their souls shall be freed from every remainder of corruption, and their bodies shall be made like unto the glorious body of the Son of God. Then this corruptible shall put on incorruption, and then shall they shine forth as the sun in the kingdom of their Father. It is then that they shall be manifested in their true character, illustrious as the sons of God, seated upon thrones, and conspicuous in robes of light and glory." Haldane, R. (1996). An Exposition of Romans (electronic ed.) (Romans 8:23). Simpsonville SC: Christian Classics Foundation.

[549] Walvoord, J. F., Zuck, R. B., and Dallas Theological Seminary. (1983-c1985). *The Bible Knowledge Commentary: An Exposition of the Scriptures* (Romans 8:19). Wheaton, IL: Victor Books.

[550] Webster's Collegiate Dictionary.

a powerful man and not weak when He said:

> <u>Luke 7:24</u>: *"And when the messengers of John had left, He began to speak to the multitudes about John, What did you go out into the wilderness to look at? <u>A reed shaken by the wind?"</u>*

The soldiers did not know Jesus' scepter is one of righteousness and strong like iron!

> <u>Hebrews 1:8</u>:
> *"But of the Son He says,*
> *'THY THRONE, O GOD, IS FOREVER AND EVER,*
> <u>*AND THE RIGHTEOUS SCEPTER IS THE SCEPTER OF HIS KINGDOM.'"*</u>

> <u>Revelation 19:15-16 (NIV)</u>:
> *"Out of his mouth comes a sharp sword with which to strike down the nations. <u>He will rule them with an iron scepter.</u> He treads the winepress of the fury of the wrath of God Almighty. ¹⁶ On his robe and on his thigh he has this name written: KING OF KINGS AND LORD OF LORDS."* [551]

In <u>Matthew 27:29</u> we see the mocking homage to Jesus as King: *"...and they kneeled down before Him and mocked Him, saying, 'Hail, King of the Jews!'"* Scripture is clear that these soldiers, as well as everyone, will have to bow before Him and glorify Him as king.

> <u>Philippians 2:8-11</u>: *"And being found in appearance as a man, He humbled Himself by becoming obedient to the point of death, even death on a cross.⁹ Therefore also God highly exalted Him, and bestowed on Him the name which is above every name,¹⁰ <u>that at the name of Jesus every knee should bow, of those who are in heaven, and on earth, and under the earth,¹¹ and that every tongue should confess that Jesus Christ is Lord,</u> to the glory of God the Father."*

The treatment of Jesus was hideous. In verse 30 we read how they beat Him on the head with the reed and spit on Him. In John 19:3 we know they hit Him with their hands. John also points out that after all the abuse and beatings Jesus received from the soldiers, Pilate again brought Him out for the religious leaders to view Him. One could speculate Pilate possibly wanted them to see how severely beaten, bloodied, and mangled Jesus was so their demand for death would be pacified. The chief priest and officers made it clear they would not be satisfied with anything short of death!

> <u>John 19:1-6</u>: *"Then Pilate therefore took Jesus, and scourged Him. ² And the soldiers wove a crown of thorns and put it on His head, and arrayed Him in a purple robe; ³ and they began to come up to Him, and say, 'Hail, King of the Jews!' and to give Him blows in the face. ⁴ <u>And Pilate came out again, and *said to them, 'Behold, I am bringing Him out to you, that you may know that I find no guilt in Him.' ⁵ Jesus therefore came out, wearing the crown of thorns and the purple robe. And Pilate *said to them, 'Behold, the Man!'</u> ⁶ When therefore the chief priests and the officers saw Him, they cried out, saying, 'Crucify, crucify!' Pilate *said to them, <u>'Take Him yourselves, and crucify Him, for I find no guilt in Him.'"</u>*

---

[551] *The Holy Bible: New International Version*. 1984. Grand Rapids: Zondervan.

If we continue to read John's account, we get some more details about what transpired:

John 19:7-15: *"The Jews answered him, 'We have a law, and by that law He ought to die because He made Himself out to be the Son of God.' ⁸ When Pilate therefore heard this statement, he was the more afraid; ⁹ and he entered into the Praetorium again, and *said to Jesus, 'Where are You from?' But Jesus gave him no answer. ¹⁰ Pilate therefore *said to Him, 'You do not speak to me? Do You not know that I have authority to release You, and I have authority to crucify You?' ¹¹ Jesus answered, 'You would have no authority over Me, unless it had been given you from above; for this reason he who delivered Me up to you has the greater sin.' ¹² As a result of this Pilate made efforts to release Him, but the Jews cried out, saying, 'If you release this Man, you are no friend of Caesar; everyone who makes himself out to be a king opposes Caesar.' ¹³ When Pilate therefore heard these words, he brought Jesus out, and sat down on the judgment seat at a place called The Pavement, but in Hebrew, Gabbatha. ¹⁴ Now it was the day of preparation for the Passover; it was about the sixth hour. And he *said to the Jews, 'Behold, your King!' ¹⁵ They therefore cried out, 'Away with Him, away with Him, crucify Him!' Pilate *said to them, 'Shall I crucify your King?' The chief priests answered, 'We have no king but Caesar.'"*

By Jesus not speaking to Pilate, He was fulfilling a prophecy in Isaiah:

Isaiah 53:7-9:

⁷ *"He was oppressed and He was afflicted,*
<u>*Yet He did not open His mouth;*</u>
<u>*Like a lamb that is led to slaughter,*</u>
<u>*And like a sheep that is silent before its shearers,*</u>
<u>*So He did not open His mouth.*</u>
⁸ *By oppression and judgment He was taken away;*
And as for His generation, who considered
That He was cut off out of the land of the living,
For the transgression of my people to whom the stroke was due?
⁹ *His grave was assigned with wicked men,*
Yet He was with a rich man in His death,
Because He had done no violence,
Nor was there any deceit in His mouth."

Severe treatment of Jesus was prophesied by Isaiah:

Isaiah 50:6:
"I gave My back to those who strike Me, And My cheeks to those who pluck out the beard; I did not cover My face from humiliation and spitting."

VERSE 31: *"And after they had mocked Him, they took His robe off and put His garments on Him, and led Him away to crucify Him."*

Note they took the valuable robe off Him, put His clothes back on Him, and then headed on to the road to Golgotha where they would crucify Him.

Summary and Application

From this lesson we see it was the ultimate cost for God to purchase our salvation: The perfect, sinless, almighty God, taking the death sentence for fallen, sinful and evil man. When we realize what He has done for us, we should be humbled by His great love. Even though we can never do anything to pay Him back, we can, out of love, obey and serve Him as led by His Holy Spirit. A secondary lesson to learn from Jesus is how we should respond when we undergo some persecution for our faith.

> **1 Peter 2:21-25:** *"For you have been called for this purpose, since Christ also suffered for you, leaving you an example for you to follow in His steps,* [22] *who committed no sin, nor was any deceit found in His mouth;* [23] *and while being reviled, He did not revile in return; while suffering, He uttered no threats, but kept entrusting Himself to Him who judges righteously;* [24] *and He Himself bore our sins in His body on the cross, that we might die to sin and live to righteousness; for by His wounds you were healed.* [25] *For you were continually straying like sheep, but now you have returned to the Shepherd and Guardian of your souls."*

I have one final point. Even though Jesus came to earth as a humble servant, He will return as the All-Powerful Lord and God! Scripture tells us that His head will not be beaten down with thorns but instead have many diadems on it. His hand will not hold a reed for a scepter but rather He will rule the nations with a rod of iron!

> **Revelation 19:11-16:** *"And I saw heaven opened; and behold, a white horse, and He who sat upon it is called Faithful and True; and in righteousness He judges and wages war.* [12] *And His eyes are a flame of fire, and upon His head are many diadems; and He has a name written upon Him which no one knows except Himself.* [13] *And He is clothed with a robe dipped in blood; and His name is called The Word of God.* [14] *And the armies which are in heaven, clothed in fine linen, white and clean, were following Him on white horses.* [15] *And from His mouth comes a sharp sword, so that with it He may smite the nations; and He will rule them with a rod of iron; and He treads the wine press of the fierce wrath of God, the Almighty.* [16] *And on His robe and on His thigh He has a name written, 'KING OF KINGS, AND LORD OF LORDS.'"*

Ryle points out that:

> "Last, but not least, let us learn from the story of the passion always to hate sin with a great hatred. Sin was the cause of all our Savior's suffering. Our sins twisted the crown of thorns; our sins drove the nails into his hands and feet; on account of our sins his blood was shed. Surely the thought of Christ crucified should make us loath all sin."[552]

---

[552] *Matthew* / Ryle, J.C. p.281 (Expository Thoughts on the Gospels) (Crossways Classic Commentaries: v.1)

MATTHEW 27:32-37
(THE CRUCIFIXION OF JESUS—PART 1)

"And as they were coming out, they found a man of Cyrene named Simon, whom they pressed into service to bear His cross. ³³ And when they had come to a place called Golgotha, which means Place of a Skull, ³⁴they gave Him wine to drink mingled with gall; and after tasting it, He was unwilling to drink.³⁵ And when they had crucified Him, they divided up His garments among themselves, casting lots; ³⁶ and sitting down, they began to keep watch over Him there. ³⁷ And they put up above His head the charge against Him which read, 'THIS IS JESUS THE KING OF THE JEWS.'"

Introduction

In Matthew 27:26-31 we read of the brutal beating of Jesus. Now in Matthew 27:32-37, we read of how Jesus was driven to Golgotha, where He will be crucified. The crucifixion and resurrection of Jesus are not just important events in the Christian faith, but are the very cornerstone of Christianity.

> **1 Corinthians 2:2:** *"…For I determined to know nothing among you except Jesus Christ, and Him crucified."*

> **Romans 4:25:** *"He who was delivered up because of our transgressions, and was raised because of our justification."*

VERSE 32: *"And as they were coming out, they found a man of Cyrene named Simon, whom they pressed into service to bear His cross."*

> By reviewing the parallel passages of this account we learn some additional facts about the man named Simon of Cyrene. Cyrene was a port city in Northern Africa[553] (near modern Libya).

> Mark's gospel tells us Simon had two sons named Alexander and Rufus.
>> **Mark 15:21:** *"And they pressed into service a passer-by coming from the country, Simon of Cyrene (the father of Alexander and Rufus), to bear His cross."*

---

[553] Wood, D. R. W., and Marshall, I. H. (1996). *New Bible Dictionary* (3rd ed.) (p. 250). Leicester, England; Downers Grove, Ill.: InterVarsity Press.

Cyrene: "A port in N. Africa, of Dorian foundation, rich in corn, silphium, wool and dates. It became part of the Ptolemaic empire in the 3rd century BC, and was bequeathed to Rome in 96 BC, becoming a province in 74 BC. Josephus quotes Strabo as stating that Cyrene encouraged Jewish settlement, and that Jews formed one of the four recognized classes of the state (Ant. 14.114). Josephus mentions also a Jewish rising there in Sulla's time, and Dio Cassius (68) another in Trajan's. To this Jewish community belonged Simon the cross-bearer (Mark 15:21 and parallels), some of the missionaries to Antioch (Acts 11:20) and the Antiochene teacher *LUCIUS . It was also represented in the Pentecost crowd (Acts 2:10) and evidently had its own (or a shared) synagogue in Jerusalem (Acts 6:9)."

The book of Romans mentions a man named Rufus. **Romans 16:13:** *"Greet Rufus, a choice man in the Lord, also his mother and mine."* Although we cannot be sure this is the same Rufus Mark mentions as the son of Simon of Cyrene, there is a reasonable chance it is. The fact that Mark mentions the actual names of Simon's children indicates that they might have been known by his readers. Many commentators believe Mark's gospel was written to Gentiles in Rome. (Notice also that the book of Romans mentions Rufus.) In summary, there may be good reason to believe Simon's sons became believers and were known by the Christians in Rome. It is for that reason that Mark mentions them.

The text states Simon was, *"pressed into service to bear His cross."* Simon did not voluntarily help, but was forced to by the Romans. Simon was probably in Jerusalem for Passover at that time. From Matthew 27:32 and John 19:17 we see Jesus was carrying His cross at the beginning of the march to Golgotha. As a result of the severe beating He underwent, Jesus was not able to carry both Himself and the cross. It was typical of Roman crucifixions to require the person being crucified to carry his own cross to the location of his execution.[554] We get more information of what transpired on the way to the cross in Luke's gospel:

> **Luke 23:27-31:** *"And there were following Him a great multitude of the people, and of women who were mourning and lamenting Him.[28] But Jesus turning to them said, 'Daughters of Jerusalem, stop weeping for Me, but weep for yourselves and for your children.[29] For behold, the days are coming when they will say, Blessed are the barren, and the wombs that never bore, and the breasts that never nursed [30] Then they will begin TO SAY TO THE MOUNTAINS , FALL ON US, AND TO THE HILLS , COVER US.[31] "For if they do these things in the green tree, what will happen in the dry?"*

This section is explained by one commentator as meaning:

> "Jesus' reference to the green and dry tree related to a popular proverb that meant if something bad occurred under good circumstances, it would be much worse under bad. His point was that if the Romans did such a terrible thing as to crucify one innocent Jewish man, what could they be expected to do to the guilty nation of Israel? If they executed a man who had committed no offense against them, what would they do to a people who rebelled?... The Lord was, of course, referring to A.D. 70, when the Temple would be utterly destroyed and the majority of its inhabitants slaughtered by the Roman legions of Titus."[555]

Upon arrival at Golgotha, we see that next Jesus' hands were nailed to the cross.

> **John 20:25:** *"The other disciples therefore were saying to him, 'We have seen the Lord!' But he said to them, 'Unless I shall see in His hands the imprint of the nails, and put my finger into the place of the nails, and put my hand into His side, I will not believe.'"*

Jesus' feet were also nailed to the cross:

---

[554] There seems to be some debate among commentators as to whether the cross being carried was the crossbeam or the entire cross.

[555] MacArthur, J. F., Jr. (1985). *Matthew*. MacArthur New Testament Commentary (p. 249). Chicago: Moody Press.

Luke 24:38-40: *"And He said to them, 'Why are you troubled, and why do doubts arise in your hearts? 39See My hands and My feet, that it is I Myself; touch Me and see, for a spirit does not have flesh and bones as you see that I have.' 40 [And when He had said this, He showed them His hands and His feet.]"*

The Roman executioners would then hoist the vertical pole into its raised position. To hasten death, they might break a leg of the one being crucified. That was not the case with Jesus. They ran a spear through Him after He died, just to make sure He was dead. This also fulfilled Scripture in the Old Testament that stated not a bone of the Messiah's body would be broken (Psalm 34:20).

> **John 19:31-37:** *"The Jews therefore, because it was the day of preparation, so that the bodies should not remain on the cross on the Sabbath (for that Sabbath was a high day), asked Pilate that their legs might be broken, and that they might be taken away.32 The soldiers therefore came, and broke the legs of the first man, and of the other man who was crucified with Him;33 but coming to Jesus, when they saw that He was already dead, they did not break His legs;34 but one of the soldiers pierced His side with a spear, and immediately there came out blood and water.35 And he who has seen has borne witness, and his witness is true; and he knows that he is telling the truth, so that you also may believe.36 For these things came to pass, that the Scripture might be fulfilled, 'Not a bone of Him shall be broken.' 37 And again another Scripture says, 'They shall look on Him whom they pierced.'"*

VERSES 33-34: *"And when they had come to a place called Golgotha, which means Place of a Skull, 34 they gave Him wine to drink mingled with gall; and after tasting it, He was unwilling to drink."*

We read the place Jesus was executed is called, "Place of the Skull" (Mark 15:22, Luke 23:33). In Hebrew it is called Golgotha (John 19:17). The King James uses the term Calvary (Luke 23:33), which is the Latin word for skull.[556] "Three possible reasons for such a name [the Skull] have been propounded: because skulls were found there; because it was a place of execution; or because the site in some way resembled a skull. All we know of the site from Scripture is that it was outside Jerusalem, fairly conspicuous, probably not far from a city gate and a highway, and that a garden containing a tomb lay nearby."[557]

Verse 34 states they offered Jesus wine mingled with gall (myrrh—Mark 15:23). "The anodyne ['serving to alleviate pain'[558]] offered to Christ during His crucifixion (Matthew 27:34 ; cf. Mark

---

[556] "The word comes from the Vulgate, where the Latin calvaria translates the Greek. kranion; both words translate Aramaic gulgoltâ, the 'Golgotha' of Matthew 27:33, meaning 'skull'." Wood, D. R. W., and Marshall, I. H. (1996). *New Bible dictionary* (3rd ed.) (p. 160). Leicester, England; Downers Grove, Ill.: InterVarsity Press.

[557] Wood, D. R. W., and Marshall, I. H. (1996). *New Bible Dictionary* (3rd ed.) (p. 160). Leicester, England; Downers Grove, Ill.: InterVarsity Press.

[558] Merriam-Webster's 11th Collegiate Dictionary - anodyne

15:23) was a diluted wine containing stupefying drugs."[559] The drink was made to lessen the pain of one who was being crucified. When Jesus tasted it and realized what it was, He refused to drink it. Jesus subjected Himself to the complete pain and torture as the penalty of our sins.

VERSES 35-36: *"And when they had crucified Him, they divided up His garments among themselves, casting lots;* [36] *and sitting down, they began to keep watch over Him there."*

One of the spoils of executioners in the Roman army was the clothes of those who were being executed. In verse 35, we read of the soldiers gambling among themselves to determine who would get His clothes. John provides more detail of this event:

> **John 19:23-25:** *"The soldiers therefore, when they had crucified Jesus, took His outer garments and made four parts, a part to every soldier and also the tunic; now the tunic was seamless, woven in one piece.* [24] *They said therefore to one another, 'Let us not tear it, but cast lots for it, to decide whose it shall be;' that the Scripture might be fulfilled, 'They divided My outer garments among them, and for My clothing they cast lots.'* [25] *Therefore the soldiers did these things. But there were standing by the cross of Jesus His mother, and His mother's sister, Mary the wife of Clopas, and Mary Magdalene."*

The crucifixion of Jesus fulfilled prophecy in detail regarding the Messiah:

> **Psalm 22:16-18:**
> *"For dogs have surrounded me;*
> *A band of evildoers has encompassed me;*
> *They pierced my hands and my feet.*
> [17] *I can count all my bones.*
> *They look, they stare at me;*
> [18] *They divide my garments among them,*
> *And for my clothing they cast lots."*

VERSE 37: *"And they put up above His head the charge against Him which read, "THIS IS JESUS THE KING OF THE JEWS."*

From John's gospel we read that Pilate had this inscription written in the three major languages of that area: Hebrew, Latin, and Greek. The religious leaders were mad that Jesus was labeled as the king of the Jews, so they went to Pilate to get it removed. Pilate did not relent, but stated, *"What I have written I have written."* Pilate no doubt saw the statement as a mockery of Jesus and the Jewish leaders. He did not know God was in complete control and let the truth be proclaimed that Jesus was, "The King of the Jews."

> **John 19:19-22:** *"And Pilate wrote an inscription also, and put it on the cross. And it was written, 'JESUS THE NAZARENE, THE KING OF THE JEWS.'* [20] *Therefore this inscription many of the Jews read, for the place where Jesus was crucified was near the city; and it was written in Hebrew, Latin, and in Greek.* [21] *And so the chief priests of the Jews were saying to Pilate, 'Do not*

---

[559] Wood, D. R. W., and Marshall, I. H. (1996). *New Bible Dictionary* (3rd ed.) (p. 395). Leicester, England; Downers Grove, Ill.: InterVarsity Press.

write, *The King of the Jews; but that He said, 'I am King of the Jews.'"* [22] Pilate answered, *'What I have written I have written.'"*

Summary and Application

We see from the main text the great punishment that Jesus undertook to pay for our sins. We have a very awesome and loving God who gave His life to save the very evil men who were murdering Him. During the crucifixion, Luke records the words of Jesus: *"...Father, forgive them; for they do not know what they are doing."* <u>**Luke 23:34**</u>.

At the cross Jesus purchased our salvation. Upon being converted by Christ, we become His disciples. We do nothing to earn salvation and we can do nothing to preserve it. Salvation is a gift from God that cannot be lost (John 6:37-39; Romans 8:29-39). Those who have been saved understand they are now slaves to a loving Master with whom nothing in life compares. Just as Christ willingly went to the cross for us, we willingly carry the cross in our life. The cross represents death. For the Christian, the cross represents death to the world and a life lived for Christ. Look at what Jesus said:

> <u>Luke 14:27-28:</u> *"Whoever does not carry his own cross and come after Me cannot be My disciple. [28] For which one of you, when he wants to build a tower, does not first sit down and calculate the cost, to see if he has enough to complete it?"*

> <u>Galatians 6:14:</u> *"But may it never be that I should boast, except in the cross of our Lord Jesus Christ, through which the world has been crucified to me, and I to the world."*

What was Jesus' reaction when He was offered the wine, *"mingled with gall,"* to lessen the pain? He rejected it, and endured the full pain of our sins. It was not symbolism, but rather the torture He experienced as the payment for our evil against God. It was the Father's will: *"...and fell on His face and prayed, saying, 'My Father, if it is possible, let this cup pass from Me; yet not as I will, but as You will.'"* <u>**Matthew 26:39.**</u>

What is your typical reaction to pain when it comes your way? Do you just run to your regular painkiller? Do you complain and make accusations against God while you search for the *"gall"* to deaden the pain? Instead, ask yourself whether the pain could be allowed from the loving and gracious God of all creation? We will have times in our lives when we walk through deep pain as part of the will of God. This is not from a God who is trying to hurt us. It is from a God who endured far greater pain on our behalf so that we would never experience the pain of the judgment of hell. It is from a loving God whose will is to draw you close to Him and conform you to His image: *"...if indeed we suffer with Him so that we may also be glorified with Him."* <u>**Romans 8:17**</u>. The secret is to walk through the pain, not in bitterness and complaining, but close to the Lord saying, *"My Father, if it is possible, let this cup pass from Me; yet not as I will, but as You will."*

MATTHEW 27:38-44
(THE CRUCIFIXION OF JESUS—PART 2)

"At that time two robbers *were crucified with Him, one on the right and one on the left. [39] *And those passing by were hurling abuse at Him, wagging their heads,* [40] *and saying, 'You who are going to destroy the temple and rebuild it in three days, save Yourself! If You are the Son of God, come down from the cross.'* [41] *In the same way the chief priests also, along with the scribes and elders, were mocking Him, and saying,* [42] *'He saved others; He cannot save Himself. He is the King of Israel; let Him now come down from the cross, and we shall believe in Him.* [43] *He trusts in God; let Him deliver Him now, if He takes pleasure in Him; for He said, I am the Son of God.'* [44] *And the robbers also who had been crucified with Him were casting the same insult at Him."*

Introduction

In this passage we see the ridicule and mocking of the Son of God by evil men. The sinfulness of man is demonstrated in this passage. It does not matter what one's status is or self-proclaimed religion, the unregenerate man is a rebel and hater of God. The mockers in this passage include commoners who passed by (v.39), the religious chief priests, scribes and elders who had Him condemned (v.41), and even condemned criminals who had but a few hours to live (v.44).

We will also see the unending love of God from this text and its parallel passages. We will see the unfathomable forgiveness of God for those who truly believe on Him. Maybe we will better understand what Jesus meant when He stated in the temple:

 Luke 4:18-21: *"'THE SPIRIT OF THE LORD IS UPON ME ,*
BECAUSE HE ANOINTED ME TO PREACH THE GOSPEL TO THE POOR.
HE HAS SENT ME TO PROCLAIM RELEASE TO THE CAPTIVES,
AND RECOVERY OF SIGHT TO THE BLIND,
TO SET FREE THOSE WHO ARE DOWNTRODDEN,
TO PROCLAIM THE FAVORABLE YEAR OF THE LORD.'
And He closed the book, and gave it back to the attendant, and sat down; and the eyes of all in the synagogue were fixed upon Him. And He began to say to them, 'Today this Scripture has been fulfilled in your hearing .'"

VERSE 38: *"At that time two robbers *were crucified with Him, one on the right and one on the left."*

We do not know a lot about these two criminals except they were robbers. Obviously the specifics of their crimes were very serious as demonstrated by their sentences resulting in capital punishment (death). The fact that Jesus was being executed with criminals fulfilled prophecies:

 Isaiah 53:11-12:
"...My Servant, will justify the many, As He will bear their iniquities.
[12]*Therefore, I will allot Him a portion with the great,*
And He will divide the booty with the strong;
Because He poured out Himself to death,
<u>*And was numbered with the transgressors;*</u>

> *Yet He Himself bore the sin of many,*
> *And interceded for the transgressors."*

We are told in verse 44 that the criminals also engaged in the mocking of Jesus (see also Mark 15:32). In John we read of the Roman soldiers breaking the legs of the two robbers to hasten their deaths (John 19:31-32). Crucifixion was not the end of the story for at least one of them. Even though both were engaged in the mocking, after some time, one repented. In Luke's parallel passage we get more detail about what transpired between Jesus and the other two on the crosses.

> **Luke 23:39-43:** *"And one of the criminals who were hanged there was hurling abuse at Him, saying, 'Are You not the Christ? Save Yourself and us!' [40] But the other answered, and rebuking him said, 'Do you not even fear God, since you are under the same sentence of condemnation? [41] And we indeed justly, for we are receiving what we deserve for our deeds; but this man has done nothing wrong.' [42] And he was saying, 'Jesus, remember me when You come in Your kingdom!' [43] And He said to him, 'Truly I say to you, today you shall be with Me in Paradise.'"*

This is truly one of the awesome examples we see in scripture regarding God's forgiveness. It also obliterates the concept of purgatory.[560] We see what John meant when the Holy Spirit led him to describe Jesus:

> **John 1:16-18:** *"For of His fulness we have all received, and <u>grace upon grace</u>. For the Law was given through Moses; <u>grace and truth were realized through Jesus Christ.</u>"*

The repentant robber on the cross had absolutely nothing "good" to claim as merit. He himself stated that he was getting what he deserved by being executed: *"And we indeed justly, for we are receiving what we deserve for our deeds;...."* **Luke 23:41.**

What about a person who was not like the robber? Scripture is clear that even a good person cannot earn heaven by his "goodness."

> **Isaiah 64:6 KJV:** *"But we are all as an unclean thing, and all our righteousnesses are as filthy rags;..."*

Matthew Henry addressing Isaiah 64:6, states:

> "We have all by sin become not only obnoxious to God's justice, but odious to his holiness; for sin is that **abominable thing which the Lord hates**, and cannot endure to look upon."

Paul states plainly that trying very hard to obey God's law and the Ten Commandments will not result in our entrance into heaven.

> **Romans 3:20:** *"...because by the works of the Law no flesh will be justified in His sight; for through the Law comes the knowledge of sin."*

Still others believe they are saved because they engage in certain religious rituals or ceremonies. Some religions claim a person is assured heaven simply because he was baptized as a baby or

---

[560] *Purgatory:* To find out more on this false doctrine go to the end of Matthew 22:33 (see footnote there also).

was a member of a certain church. From Luke 23:39-43 it is clear the repentant robber did not have a religious claim to bring to God on why he should enter heaven. Nowhere do we read of the robber being baptized before he died either. This man went to "paradise" unbaptized. External baptism alone often confers no benefit, as the case of Simon Magnus plainly shows. Although Simon Magnus was baptized, he remained, *"full of bitterness and captive to sin."* <u>Acts 8:23</u> (NIV). [561] The one criminal on the cross has a different story. We see that this repentant thief admitted his sin (Luke 23:41) and he acknowledged Jesus as Lord and God when he said, *"...Do you not even fear God, since you are under the same sentence of condemnation?"* <u>Luke 23:40</u>. He also sought forgiveness and grace when he asked Jesus to remember him *"...when You come in Your kingdom"* <u>Luke 23:42</u>. Notice Jesus' response was not one of condemnation. He did not point out how the robber had been living a life of extreme wickedness and was now asking forgiveness just moments before he dies. Jesus' response to the repentant robber was grace and forgiveness. Jesus told him, *"...Truly I say to you, today you shall be with Me in Paradise."* (Luke 23:43). This is a clear example of salvation by grace through faith in Jesus.

> <u>John 3:16-18:</u> *"For God so loved the world, that He gave His only begotten Son, that <u>whoever believes in Him should not perish, but have eternal life.</u> [17] For God did not send the Son into the world to judge the world, but that the world should be saved through Him. [18] <u>He who believes in Him is not judged; he who does not believe has been judged already, because he has not believed in the name of the only begotten Son of God.</u>"*

> <u>Ephesians 2:8-9:</u> *"For by grace you have been saved through faith; and that not of yourselves, it is the gift of God; [9]not as a result of works, that no one should boast."*

<u>VERSES 39-40:</u> *"And those passing by were hurling abuse at Him, wagging their heads, [40] and saying, 'You who are going to destroy the temple and rebuild it in three days, save Yourself! If You are the Son of God, come down from the cross.'"*

Verses 39-40 give us insight into the arrogance and evil of mankind. God Almighty is sacrificing Himself for their sins. Their response is mocking His divinity, and great pride in accomplishing His murder. The crowd pointed out that their great temple was not being destroyed, but He was. The destruction of the temple was an allegation the religious leaders used against Jesus in His trial before Caiaphas:

> <u>Matthew 26:59-62:</u> *"Now the chief priests and the whole Council kept trying to obtain false testimony against Jesus, in order that they might put Him to death; [60] and they did not find any, even though many false witnesses came forward. But later on two came forward, [61] and said, 'This man stated, I am able to destroy the temple of God and to rebuild it in three days.'[62] And the high priest stood up and said to Him, 'Do You make no answer? What is it that these men are testifying against You?'"*

---

[561] *Matthew* / Ryle, J.C. p.294 (Expository Thoughts on the Gospels) (Crossways Classic Commentaries: v.1)

Eventually they found a witness who said Jesus stated that He was, *"able to destroy the temple of God and to rebuild it in three days."* That statement is neither what Jesus said, nor what He meant. We read what Jesus actually said in the Gospel of John. Jesus was referring to His bodily resurrection.

> **John 2:18-22:** *"The Jews therefore answered and said to Him, 'What sign do You show to us, seeing that You do these things?' ¹⁹ Jesus answered and said to them, 'Destroy this temple, and in three days I will raise it up.' ²⁰ The Jews therefore said, 'It took forty-six years to build this temple, and will You raise it up in three days?' ²¹ But He was speaking of the temple of His body. ²² When therefore He was raised from the dead, His disciples remembered that He said this; and they believed the Scripture, and the word which Jesus had spoken."*

In **Matthew 27:40**, the regular people passing by stated, *"If You are the Son of God, come down from the cross."* It was no secret to the common people that Jesus stated He was the Son of God. As we will read in verse 43 the religious leaders all clearly understood, *"He said, I am the Son of God."* Jesus could have taken Himself down from the cross if He wanted to, but it would not have been the will of the Father, and He would not have paid the sacrifice needed for mankind.

> **John 10:17-18:** *"For this reason the Father loves Me, because I lay down My life that I may take it again . ¹⁸ No one has taken it away from Me, but I lay it down on My own initiative. I have authority to lay it down, and I have authority to take it up again. This commandment I received from My Father."*

Jesus was perfect in every way and He always submitted wholly to the will of the Father. Jesus' sacrifice purchased our redemption:

> **Ephesians 1:7-9:** *"In Him we have redemption through His blood, the forgiveness of our trespasses, according to the riches of His grace, ⁸ which He lavished upon us. In all wisdom and insight ⁹ He made known to us the mystery of His will, according to His kind intention which He purposed in Him."*

VERSES 41-43: *"In the same way the chief priests also, along with the scribes and elders, were mocking Him, and saying, ⁴² 'He saved others; He cannot save Himself. He is the King of Israel; let Him now come down from the cross, and we shall believe in Him. ⁴³ He trusts in God; let Him deliver Him now, if He takes pleasure in Him; for He said, I am the Son of God.'"*

Now we see it is not just the common people mocking Jesus, but the religious leaders finally jump right in. They spent a lot of time fearing Him and plotting for His murder.

> **Luke 20:19-20:** *"And the scribes and the chief priests tried to lay hands on Him that very hour, and they feared the people; for they understood that He spoke this parable against them.²⁰ And they watched Him, and sent spies who pretended to be righteous, in order that they might catch Him in some statement, so as to deliver Him up to the rule and the authority of the governor."*

In Matthew 27:42 we see the religious leaders mocked Jesus by claiming He was not as powerful as the people thought: *"He saved others; He cannot save Himself."* In their blindness they could not understand that His sacrifice on the cross would save believers for eternity:

Hebrews 7:25 (NKJV): *"Therefore He is also able to save to the uttermost those who come to God through Him, since He always lives to make intercession for them."*

The false religious leaders also thought His murder would be the end of His glory. Jesus' obedience to the cross is beyond words in glory and power for eternity:

Revelation 5:11-14: *"And I looked, and I heard the voice of many angels around the throne and the living creatures and the elders; and the number of them was myriads of myriads, and thousands of thousands,[12] saying with a loud voice, 'Worthy is the Lamb that was slain to receive power and riches and wisdom and might and honor and glory and blessing.' [13] And every created thing which is in heaven and on the earth and under the earth and on the sea, and all things in them, I heard saying, 'To Him who sits on the throne, and to the Lamb, be blessing and honor and glory and dominion forever and ever.'[14] And the four living creatures kept saying, 'Amen.' And the elders fell down and worshiped."*

Look back at our main text, in Matthew 27:42, when the religious leaders said: *"He is the King of Israel; let Him now come down from the cross, and we shall believe in Him."* It was a lie for the religious leaders to claim if He came down from the cross they would believe that He was the King of Israel. The religious leaders had not believed Moses or the prophets who taught about Christ (John 5:39-40). They would never have believed in Him as Messiah, whether He came down from the cross or even rose from the dead. Jesus pointed this out during His teaching:

Luke 16:19-31: *"Now there was a certain rich man, and he habitually dressed in purple and fine linen, gaily living in splendor every day. [20] And a certain poor man named Lazarus was laid at his gate, covered with sores, [21] and longing to be fed with the crumbs which were falling from the rich man's table; besides, even the dogs were coming and licking his sores . [22] Now it came about that the poor man died and he was carried away by the angels to Abraham's bosom; and the rich man also died and was buried. [23] And in Hades he lifted up his eyes, being in torment, and * saw Abraham far away, and Lazarus in his bosom. [24] And he cried out and said, 'Father Abraham , have mercy on me, and send Lazarus , that he may dip the tip of his finger in water and cool off my tongue; for I am in agony in this flame.' [25] But Abraham said, 'Child, remember that during your life you received your good things, and likewise Lazarus bad things; but now he is being comforted here, and you are in agony. [26] And besides all this, between us and you there is a great chasm fixed, in order that those who wish to come over from here to you may not be able, and that none may cross over from there to us.' [27] And he said, 'Then I beg you, Father, that you send him to my father's house — [28] for I have five brothers —that he may warn them, lest they also come to this place of torment.' [29] But Abraham * said, 'They have Moses and the Prophets; let them hear them.' [30] But he said, 'No, Father Abraham, but if someone goes to them from the dead, they will repent!' [31] But he said to him, ' If they do not listen to Moses and the Prophets, neither will they be persuaded if someone rises from the dead .'"*

In our main text of **Matthew 27:43** we read more about the religious leaders mocking Him when they say: *"He trusts in God; let Him deliver Him now, if He takes pleasure in Him; for He said, I* *am the Son of God."* They did not know they were fulfilling a prophecy David gave about the Messiah almost a millennium before:

> **Psalm 22:7-8:**
> *"All who see me sneer at me;*
> *They separate with the lip, they wag the head, saying,*
> *⁸ Commit yourself to the LORD; let Him deliver him;*
> *Let Him rescue him, because He delights in him."*

It is important to point out again: Jesus Himself stated clearly that He was the Son of God. This fact is undisputable. Read Jesus' own words:

> **Luke 22:70:** *"And they all said, 'Are You the Son of God, then?' And He said to them, 'Yes, I am.'"*

VERSE 44: *"And the robbers also who had been crucified with Him were casting the same insult at Him."* One robber's eternal destiny ended up to be eternal hell and the other's eternal heaven. What was the difference? Please review the notes for verse 38 (Matthew 27:38) set out previously.

Summary and Application

It was mentioned in the introduction section that the mockers of Jesus included commoners (v.39), the false-religious (v.41) and the condemned criminals (v.44). They all had one thing in common—an inward hatred of God. Because they hated God, they hated His Son Jesus. Because the unsaved hate Jesus, they will hate His true disciples. How about you—have you been mocked for being a true follower of Jesus? If not, I would suggest there is something very deficient in your Christian walk. Jesus warns if you are truly His follower, you can expect the world's hatred and persecution. In **John 15:18–25** Jesus says:

> *"If the world hates you, you know that it has hated Me before it hated you. ¹⁹ If you were of the world, the world would love its own; but because you are not of the world, but I chose you out of the world, because of this the world hates you. ²⁰Remember the word that I said to you, 'A slave is not greater than his master.' If they persecuted Me, they will also persecute you; if they kept My word, they will keep yours also. ²¹ But all these things they will do to you for My name's sake, because they do not know the One who sent Me. ²² If I had not come and spoken to them, they would not have sin, but now they have no excuse for their sin. ²³ He who hates Me hates My Father also. ²⁴ If I had not done among them the works which no one else did, they would not have sin; but now they have both seen and hated Me and My Father as well. ²⁵ But they have done this to fulfill the word that is written in their Law, 'They hated Me without a cause.'"*

We are to not be mocked for our own bad behavior, but for godly behavior in Christ:

> **1 Peter 3:16–17:** *"...and keep a good conscience so that in the thing in which you are slandered, those who revile your good behavior in Christ will be put to shame. ¹⁷ For it is better, if God should will it so, that you suffer for doing what is right rather than for doing what is wrong."*

When you are mocked, slandered and excluded for being a godly witness, your response should be to not feel sad, ashamed or neglected. Your response should be one of forgiveness and rejoicing:

> **Luke 6:23:** *"Be glad in that day and leap for joy, for behold, your reward is great in heaven. For in the same way their fathers used to treat the prophets."*

<u>MATTHEW 27:45-50</u>
(THE CRUCIFIXION OF JESUS—PART 3)

"Now from the sixth hour darkness fell upon all the land until the ninth hour. [46] *And about the ninth hour Jesus cried out with a loud voice, saying, 'Eli, Eli, lama sabachthani?' that is, 'My God, My God, why hast Thou forsaken Me?'* [47] *And some of those who were standing there, when they heard it, began saying, 'This man is calling for Elijah.'* [48] *And immediately one of them ran, and taking a sponge, he filled it with sour wine, and put it on a reed, and gave Him a drink.* [49] *But the rest of them said, 'Let us see whether Elijah will come to save Him.'* [50] *And Jesus cried out again with a loud voice, and yielded up His spirit."*

Introduction

This section involves the closing hours of the crucifixion. The mocking from the onlookers continues through verse 49. In verse 50 Jesus gives up His spirit. The remainder of the section begins the miraculous manifestation of the Son of God having completed His mission of bearing the sin of mankind.

> <u>Hebrews 10:12</u>: *"…but He, having offered one sacrifice for sins for all time, sat down at the right hand of God,"*

<u>**VERSES 45-49:**</u> *"Now from the sixth hour darkness fell upon all the land until the ninth hour.* [46] *And about the ninth hour Jesus cried out with a loud voice, saying, 'Eli, Eli, lama sabachthani?' that is, 'My God , My God , why hast Thou forsaken Me?'* [47] *And some of those who were standing there, when they heard it, began saying, 'This man is calling for Elijah.'* [48] *And immediately one of them ran, and taking a sponge, he filled it with sour wine, and put it on a reed, and gave Him a drink.* [49] *But the rest of them said, 'Let us see whether Elijah will come to save Him.'"*

From Mark 15:25 we know the crucifixion started at the third hour (i.e. 9 a.m.). Verse 45 tells us that everything became dark from the sixth hour to the ninth (i.e. between twelve noon till three o'clock in the afternoon.) Some try to argue this was an eclipse, but that is not the case:

> "… [T]he great intensity of darkness caused by an eclipse never lasts for more than six minutes, and this darkness lasted for three hours. Moreover, at the time of the Passover the moon was full, and therefore there could not be an eclipse of the sun, which is caused by an interposition of the moon between the sun and the earth."[562]

Jesus is, for this time period, "forsaken" by the Father because He is bearing the sin of all mankind. <u>**2 Corinthians 5:21:**</u> *"He made Him who knew no sin to be sin on our behalf, that we might become the righteousness of God in Him."* Jesus states in verse <u>**Matthew 27:46:**</u> *"…My God, My God, why hast Thou forsaken Me?",* which is a direct quote from Psalm 22:1. MacArthur provides the following insights:

---

[562] Easton, M. G. (1996). *Easton's Bible Dictionary,* Eclipse. Oak Harbor, WA: Logos Research Systems, Inc.

"In this unique and strange miracle, Jesus was crying out in anguish because of the separation He now experienced from His heavenly Father for the first and only time in all of eternity. It is the only time of which we have record that Jesus did not address God as Father.... In some way and by some means, in the secrets of divine sovereignty and omnipotence, the God-Man was separated from God for a brief time at Calvary, as the furious wrath of the Father was poured out on the sinless Son, who in matchless grace became sin for those who believe in Him."[563]

Verse 47 tells us some thought Jesus was calling out for Elijah to save Him. Still other evil onlookers saw the entire crucifixion as an entertaining spectacle as shown by their statement in verse 49, *"Let us see whether Elijah will come to save Him."*

In verse 48 we read that someone provided Jesus "sour wine" to drink. If you read the event in **John 19:28-29** you will get more detail:

"After this, Jesus, knowing that all things had already been accomplished, in order that the Scripture might be fulfilled, said, 'I am thirsty.' 29 A jar full of sour wine was standing there; so they put a sponge full of the sour wine upon a branch of hyssop, and brought it up to His mouth."

VERSE 50: *"And Jesus cried out again with a loud voice, and yielded up His spirit."*

We read from John, *"When Jesus therefore had received the sour wine, He said, 'It is finished!'...."* **John 19:30.** Jesus then addresses the Father as we read from Luke, *"And Jesus, crying out with a loud voice, said, 'Father , into Thy hands I commit My spirit.' And having said this, He breathed His last."* **Luke 23:46**. At this moment Jesus died,[564] but His body did not suffer the decay and judgment of sin because He had no taint of sin. Notice it says He, "yielded up His spirit." This is not a situation where the spirit was yielded up because the body expired. Jesus was in complete control. One must remember Jesus did not get overrun and killed by an evil mob. Even though we read of many times these evil men plotted to kill Him (see John 7:1), Jesus was in complete control of when and how He would die.

John 10:17-18: *"For this reason the Father loves Me, because I lay down My life that I may take it again. 18 No one has taken it away from Me, but I lay it down on My own initiative. I have authority to lay it down, and I have authority to take it up again. This commandment I received from My Father.'"*

---

[563] MacArthur, J. F., Jr. (1985). *Matthew*. MacArthur New Testament Commentary (p. 249). Chicago: Moody Press.

[564] EKPNEŌ (ἐκπνέω , (1606) lit. , to breathe out (ek, out, pneō, to breathe), to expire, is used in the N.T. , without an object, "soul" or "life" being understood, Mark 15:37, 39, and Luke 23:46 , of the Death of Christ. In Matthew 27:50 and John 19:30, where different verbs are used, the act is expressed in a way which stresses it as of His own volition: in the former, "Jesus ... yielded up His spirit (pneuma); in the latter, "He gave up His spirit." Vine, W., and Bruce, F. (1981; Published in electronic form by Logos Research Systems, 1996). *Vine's Expository Dictionary of Old and New Testament Words* (p. 146). Old Tappan NJ: Revell.

> **John 10:14-15:** *"I am the good shepherd; and I know My own, and My own know Me, ¹⁵ even as the Father knows Me and I know the Father; and I lay down My life for the sheep."*

We studied in a previous section what happens to man when he dies. That section explains **Genesis 2:7:** *"Then the LORD God formed man of dust from the ground, and breathed into his nostrils the breath of life; and man became a living being."* Upon death, the physical body of humans, underlines returns to "dust" (i.e. undergoes decay). We read about this in the curse of man in **Genesis 3:19,** which says, *"For you are dust, And to dust you shall return."* Immediately upon death, the soul returns to God (i.e. all souls belong to God; see Ecclesiastes 12:7). The believer's soul goes to the presence of God in Paradise and then, in the end, to live forever in the new heaven (Revelation 21:1-5). The unbeliever's soul is justly ordered by God to go to torment in Hades (Luke 16:23). In the end, the unbeliever ends up in hell (i.e. the Lake of Fire - 15). This whole concept of the body's decay and the soul's return to the Lord is set out in **Ecclesiastes 12:7:** *"…then the dust will return to the earth as it was, and the spirit will return to God who gave it."* We see Jesus returning the spirit back to the girl He resurrected from the dead in **Luke 8:53-56:**

> *"And they began laughing at Him, knowing that she had died. ⁵⁴ He, however, took her by the hand and called, saying, 'Child, arise!' ⁵⁵ And her spirit returned, and she rose immediately; and He gave orders for something to be given her to eat. ⁵⁶ And her parents were amazed; but He instructed them to tell no one what had happened."*

Jesus' body did not suffer decay and return to the dust because He was perfect and without any taint of sin. Because of His perfection, He was not under the curse of sin set out in **Genesis 3:19:** *"…For you are dust, And to dust you shall return."* Scripture tells us that the curse of death came to all through one person, Adam; and the salvation available to all came through only one person, Jesus.

> **1 Corinthians 15:20-28:** *"But now Christ has been raised from the dead, the first fruits of those who are asleep. ²¹ For since by a man came death, by a man also came the resurrection of the dead. ²² For as in Adam all die, so also in Christ all shall be made alive. ²³ But each in his own order: Christ the first fruits, after that those who are Christ's at His coming, ²⁴ then comes the end, when He delivers up the kingdom to the God and Father, when He has abolished all rule and all authority and power. ²⁵ For He must reign until He has put all His enemies under His feet. ²⁶ The last enemy that will be abolished is death. ²⁷ For He has put all things in subjection under His feet. But when He says, 'All things are put in subjection,' it is evident that He is excepted who put all things in subjection to Him. ²⁸ And when all things are subjected to Him, then the Son Himself also will be subjected to the One who subjected all things to Him, that God may be all in all."*

Jesus came to earth and lived in a body of human flesh and blood so He could redeem our bodies that are subject to death and decay.

> **Hebrews 2:14-15:** *"Since then the children share in flesh and blood, He Himself likewise also partook of the same, that through death He might render powerless him who had the power of death, that is, the devil; ¹⁵ and might deliver those who through fear of death were subject to slavery all their lives."*

Summary and Application

To be a Christian you absolutely need to understand the concept of the substitutionary death of Christ. A person must understand:

1. He is sinful and justly deserving to receive a judgment of eternal damnation by a righteous God.
2. Jesus, God's Son, took on a human body and overcame all sin. He never sinned once in thought, deed or action.
3. Because Christ is perfect, He is the only one who can be our substitute and take our eternal death penalty.
4. The Christian puts his faith only in the substitutionary death of Christ on the cross to pay for his sins.

MATTHEW 27:51
(THE CRUCIFIXION OF JESUS - PART 4 - THE VEIL IS REMOVED!)

"And behold, the veil of the temple was torn in two from top to bottom, and the earth shook; and the rocks were split,"

Introduction

Matthew 27:45-50 sets forth the final moments of the crucifixion (**Matthew 27:50**: *"And Jesus cried out again with a loud voice, and yielded up His spirit."*). In the verses immediately following that, we read of some of the supernatural acts performed by God that demonstrated the awesomeness of this event.

VERSE 51: *"And behold, the veil of the temple was torn in two from top to bottom, and the earth shook; and the rocks were split,…"*

The term "veil" means a large curtain that separated the holy place from the "holy of holies" in the Temple. The holy of holies was entered one day a year by the high priest during Passover. This day was called the Day of Atonement.

> "The Day of Atonement served as a reminder that the daily, weekly and monthly sacrifices made at the altar of burnt offering were not sufficient to atone for sin. Even at the altar of burnt offering the worshipper stood 'afar off', unable to approach the holy Presence of God, who was manifest between the cherubim in the holy of holies. On this one day in the year, atoning blood was brought into the holy of holies, the divine throne-room, by the high priest as the representative of the people…The high priest made atonement for 'all the iniquities of the children of Israel and all their transgressions in all their sins.' Atonement was first made for the priests because the mediator between God and his people had to be ceremonially clean. The sanctuary was also cleansed, for it, too, was ceremonially defiled by the presence and ministration of sinful men."[565]

Here are the directions God gave Israel regarding the veil.

> **Exodus 26:31-37:** *"And you shall make a veil of blue and purple and scarlet material and fine twisted linen; it shall be made with cherubim, the work of a skillful workman. 32 And you shall hang it on four pillars of acacia overlaid with gold, their hooks also being of gold, on four sockets of silver. 33 And you shall hang up the veil under the clasps, and shall bring in the ark of the testimony there within the veil; and the veil shall serve for you as a partition between the holy place and the holy of holies. 34 And you shall put the mercy seat on the ark of the testimony in the holy of holies. 35 "And you shall set the*

---

[565] Wood, D. R. W., and Marshall, I. H. (1996). *New Bible Dictionary* (3rd ed. /) (p. 104). Leicester, England; Downers Grove, Ill.: InterVarsity Press.

table outside the veil, and the lampstand opposite the table on the side of the tabernacle toward the south; and you shall put the table on the north side. 36 And you shall make a screen for the doorway of the tent of blue and purple and scarlet material and fine twisted linen, the work of a weaver. 37 And you shall make five pillars of acacia for the screen, and overlay them with gold, their hooks also being of gold; and you shall cast five sockets of bronze for them."

Scripture describes the room called the Holy of Holies and its function. Items located in the holy of holies included: the Ark of Testimony (Exodus 26:33; 40:3, 21); the Mercy-seat (Exodus 26:34); Cherubim (Exodus 25:18-22; 1 Kings 6:23-28); the Golden censer (Hebrews 9:4); Pot of manna (Exodus 16:33, Hebrews 9:4); Aaron's rod (Numbers 17:10; Hebrews 9:4); written copy of the divine law (Deuteronomy 31:26; 2 Kings 22:8). [566] The high priest had specific instructions of when he was to enter the holy of holies and the functions he was to do while there. As mentioned above, the High Priest was to enter the holy of holies alone, one time a year (Hebrews 9:7). If he entered at some other time, he would die (Leviticus 16:2). He made atonement for the holy place, himself, and the people (Leviticus 16:15-17, 20).[567] "The instant Christ's work was accomplished the veil of the temple was rent in twain, and the whole typical sacrificial system was discharged as functus officio. — Matthew 27:50, 51." [568]

Many people today misunderstand the concept of salvation in the Old Testament as compared to the New Testament. They <u>erroneously think God set up an Old Testament system as follows:</u>
- You were required to obey certain rules to earn your way to heaven.
- When you sinned, you were to go to the temple and give the required sacrifice to be forgiven.
- God changed His mind and set forth the salvation by faith system in the New Testament.

The truth is God never changed His mind! His standard then and now has always been only absolute perfection can enter heaven. Jesus said in **Matthew 5:48:** *"Therefore you are to be perfect, as your heavenly Father is perfect."* Because all people are sinners, no one can be good enough to enter heaven (Romans 3:23). People in the Old Testament were not saved by ritualistic/legalistic obedience to the Law, because even the "best" people were sinners and thus failed God's standard. The only perfect person is the divine Messiah Jesus, the God-Man. (See footnote below for more on the divinity and humanity of Christ.)[569] Those saved in the Old

---

[566] Torrey, R. (1995, c1897). *The New Topical Textbook: A Scriptural Textbook For The Use of Ministers, Teachers, And All Christian Workers.* Oak Harbor, WA: Logos research Systems, Inc.

"Functus officio" is Latin and means: "...of no further official authority or legal efficacy —used of an officer no longer in office or of an instrument, power, or agency that has fulfilled the purpose of its creation." *Merriam-Webster's Collegiate Dictionary-* online edition.

[567] Ibid

[568] Hodge, A. (1996). *Outlines of Theology.* Index created by Christian Classics Foundation. (electronic ed. based on the 1972 Banner of Truth Trust reproduction of the 1879 ed.) (p. 410). Simpsonville SC: Christian Classics Foundation.

[569] Here are some short notes of mine on Jesus' humanity and divine nature as shown in Scripture. Examples of His manhood are that He was: tempted (Luke 4:1-13), tired (John 4:6), hungry (Matthew 4:2), thirsty (John 19:28), slept (Matthew 8:24) and died (Mark 15:39-45, Matthew 27:50). Examples of His divine nature are that He was born of a virgin (Luke 1:30-38), did miracles, (John 11:38-44, Luke 7:21-23), never sinned (2 Corinthians 5:21), and rose from the dead (1 Corinthians 15:3-8, Matthew 28:5-15, John 21:14).

"Christ is God and man by a <u>hypostatic</u> or personal union, both natures, divine and human, remaining distinct without composition or confusion, in one and the same person."

> Vincent, T. (1996). *A Family Instructional Guide*. Index created by Christian Classics Foundation. (electronic edition based on the first Banner of Truth ed., 1980.) (p. 73). Simpsonville SC: Christian Classics Foundation.

"This union also was not established by mixing these two natures, with a third type of person coming forth. Rather, this union was established *without change and without mixture* , each nature retaining its own attributes; each nature contributes its attributes to the Person. Thus, the same Christ has divine as well as human attributes by virtue of the union of these two natures in Him. However, the one nature does not have the attributes of the other nature. The union of these two natures in one Person has three consequences— *communication of: 1) gifts and honor, 2) attributes,* and *3) activity and office. a* Brakel, W. (1996, c1992)."

> *The Christian's reasonable service, Volumes 1 and 2: In which Divine truths concerning the covenant of grace are expounded, defended against opposing parties, and their practice advocated as well as the administration of this covenant in the Old and New Testaments*. Published in electronic form by Christian Classics Foundation, 1996. (electronic ed. of the first publication in the English language, based on the 3rd edition of the original Dutch work.) (Vol. 1, Page 505-506). Morgan PA: Soli Deo Gloria Publications.

<u>THE HUMANITY AND DIVINITY OF CHRIST</u> by Sproul, R. C. (1996, c1992). *Essential Truths of the Christian faith*. Wheaton, Ill.: Tyndale House.

> <u>#27 The Humanity of Christ:</u> "That God the Son took upon Himself a real human nature is a crucial doctrine of historic Christianity. The great ecumenical Council of Chalcedon in A.D. 451 affirmed that Jesus is truly man and truly God and that the two natures of Christ are so united as to be without mixture, confusion, separation, or division, each nature retaining its own attributes. Christ's humanity was like ours. He became a man "for our sakes." He entered into our situation to act as our Redeemer. He became our substitute, taking upon Himself our sins in order to suffer in our place. He also became our champion, fulfilling the law of God on our behalf. In redemption there is a twofold exchange. Our sins are imparted to Jesus. His righteousness is imparted to us. He receives the judgment due to our imperfect humanity, while we receive the blessing due to His perfect humanity. In His humanity Jesus had the same limitations common to all human beings, except that He was without sin. As a human being Jesus was restricted by time and space. Like all human beings He could not be in more than one place at the same time. He sweated. He hungered. He wept. He endured pain. He was mortal, capable of suffering death. In all these respects He was like us."

> <u>#25 THE DIVINITY OF CHRIST</u>: "Faith in the deity of Christ is necessary to being a Christian. It is an essential part of the New Testament gospel of Christ. Yet in every century the church has been forced to deal with people who claim to be Christians while denying or distorting the deity of Christ.... As the Logos Incarnate, Christ is revealed as being not only pre-existent to creation, but eternal. He is said to be in the beginning *with* God and also that He *is* God (John 1:1-3). That He is *with* God demands a personal distinction within the Godhead. That He *is* God demands inclusion in the Godhead. Elsewhere, the New Testament ascribes terms and titles to Jesus that are clearly titles of deity. God bestows the preeminent divine title of *Lord* upon Him (Philippians 2:9-11). As the Son of Man, Jesus claims to be Lord of the Sabbath (Mark 2:28) and to have authority to forgive sins (Mark 2:1-12). [Note continued on the next page.]

Testament were saved the same way people are in the New Testament, by faith in God. Jesus destroyed the manmade, false religion of external self-righteousness. All of God's people have been and will be saved by faith in Jesus' sacrificial and substitutionary death on the cross. If one understood the Old Testament, he would have known that it spoke of Jesus the Messiah. Jesus confronted the false religious of His time regarding this when He said:

> **John 5:39**: *"You search the Scriptures because you think that in them you have eternal life; it is these that testify about Me;"*

Jesus told His disciples:

> **Luke 24:44**: *"Now He said to them, 'These are My words which I spoke to you while I was still with you, that all things which are written about Me in the Law of Moses and the Prophets and the Psalms must be fulfilled.'"*

On the road to Emmaus He told two of His disciples:

> **Luke 24:27**: *"Then beginning with Moses and with all the prophets, He explained to them the things concerning Himself in all the Scriptures."*

God's plan of salvation by faith in God is no different in the Old Testament or the New Testament. Look at the following Old Testament passage:

> **Habakkuk 2:4**: *"Behold, as for the proud one, His soul is not right within him; But the righteous will live by his faith."*

Salvation by faith was God's way even before the Law was given to Moses:

> **Genesis 15:6**: *"Abram believed the LORD, and He credited it to him as righteousness."*

So why did the Old Testament have a temple, priests and blood sacrifices? These served as a mere "shadow" of the coming perfect Messiah who intercedes for sinful man. The Messiah's own blood would serve as their payment for sin:

> **Hebrews 10:1-5:** *"For the Law, since it has only a shadow of the good things to come and not the very form of things, can never by the same sacrifices year by year, which they offer continually, make perfect those who draw near. [2] Otherwise, would they not have ceased to be offered, because the worshipers, having once been cleansed, would no longer have had consciousness of sins? [3] But in those sacrifices there is a reminder of sins year by year. [4] For it is impossible for the blood of bulls and goats to take away sins. [5] Therefore, when He comes into the world, He says,*
> *'Sacrifice and offering Thou hast not desired,*
> *But a body Thou hast prepared for Me;....'"*

There is no longer any need for priests, temples and ongoing sacrifices because Jesus paid the complete price on the cross.

[Note continued.]
He is called the *"Lord* of glory" (James 2:1) and willingly receives worship, as when Thomas confesses, "My Lord and my God!" (John 20:28). Paul declares that the fullness of the Godhead dwells in Christ's form bodily (Colossians 1:19) and that Jesus is higher than angels, a theme reiterated in the book of Hebrews. [Note that all of Creation was made by Jesus – Colossians 1:15-17].
[End of note.]

Hebrews 10:14-18:
"For by one offering _He has perfected for all time_ those who are sanctified.
15 And the Holy Spirit also bears witness to us; for after saying,
16 'This is the covenant that I will make with them
 After those days, says the Lord:
 I will put My laws upon their heart,
 And upon their mind I will write them,' He then says,
17 'And their sins and their lawless deeds
 I will remember no more.'
18 _Now where there is forgiveness of these things, there is no longer any offering for sin._"

"It should be observed that the Old Testament sacrifices really derive their significance from the sacrifice of Christ, and not the reverse. In other words, the types are but the shadow of the reality of the anti–type. Yet, since we have much more detail given to us regarding these sacrifices, we turn to them in order to discover the meaning of the sacrificial work of Christ.

As one considers the whole ritual of sacrifice, it appears that one of the most significant ideas seen in it is that of substitution. The worshipper comes desiring to enter into the presence and fellowship of God. His sins bar him from doing this directly. Consequently he brings a substitute for himself. As prescribed by the Mosaic law the laying on of hands was required in all kinds of blood sacrifices. 'This is a natural and expressive symbol of transfer from the person imposing to the person or thing upon which they are imposed. Thus it is used to designate a personal substitute or representative.' In particular reference to sins, the sins are said to be transferred to the sacrifice, which then bore the penalty of the sinner." [570]

Jesus is the substitute for those who put their faith in Him. A Christian trusts the substitutionary sacrifice of Christ on the cross as the complete and final payment for his sins.

Romans 3:21-27: "_But now apart from the Law the righteousness of God has been manifested, being witnessed by the Law and the Prophets, 22 even the righteousness of God through faith in Jesus Christ for all those who believe; for there is no distinction; 23 for all have sinned and fall short of the glory of God, 24 being justified as a gift by His grace through the redemption which is in Christ Jesus; 25 whom God displayed publicly as a propitiation in His blood through faith. This was to demonstrate His righteousness, because in the forbearance of God He passed over the sins previously committed; 26 for the demonstration, I say, of His righteousness at the present time, that He might be just and the justifier of the one who has faith in Jesus. 27 Where then is boasting? It is excluded. By what kind of law? Of works? No, but by a law of faith._"

Propitiation means Jesus' sacrifice on the cross satisfied God's righteous anger against sinful man

---

[570] Smith, M. H. (1999). _Systematic Theology, Volume One: Prolegomena, Theology, Anthropology, Christology_ (electronic ed.) (p. 381). Escondido, CA: Ephesians Four Group.

(i.e. *"pacifying of the wrath of God."*).[571] Some people do not like the idea that God has righteous anger against sinners. They suppose that since God is so loving, He could not be angry. That is a nice sentiment, but it is unsupported by scripture. One can love a person and yet be angry and punish his bad behavior…*ask any parent* (Hebrews 12:5-11). Scripture is clear: God's anger is against those who rebel against Him.

> **Romans 1:18:** *"For the wrath of God is revealed from heaven against all ungodliness and unrighteousness of men, who suppress the truth in unrighteousness,…"*

For those who believe in Christ for their salvation, the penalty and judgment from God's holy anger was paid in full by Jesus.

> **Romans 5:9:** *"Much more then, having now been justified by His blood, we shall be saved from the wrath of God through Him."*

> **John 3:36:** *"He who believes in the Son has eternal life; but he who does not obey the Son shall not see life, but the wrath of God abides on him."*

So the question remains, what does all this teaching on atonement and propitiation have to do with the veil being torn in Matthew 27:51? Remember the veil separated the people from the holy of holies (i.e. God's presence). The veil was immediately and supernaturally torn upon Christ's giving up His spirit. More specifically the verse says, ***"And behold, the veil of the temple was torn in two from top to bottom, and the earth shook; and the rocks were split…."*** Note that with the full payment of sin having been paid by Christ, man had access to the Father. No longer was there need for the shadows or the sacrificial system. The complete payment was once and finally paid through Christ. Man now had direct access to God through Christ. Charles Spurgeon further explains the tearing of the veil and the completion of the temple's sacrificial system as follows:

> "…. in the rending of so strong and thick a veil; … it was not intended merely as a display of power—many lessons were herein taught us. The old law of ordinances was put away, and like a worn-out vesture, rent and laid aside. When Jesus died, the sacrifices were all finished, because all fulfilled in him … That rent also revealed all the hidden things of the old dispensation: the mercy-seat could now be seen, and the glory of God gleamed forth above it. By the death of our Lord Jesus we have a clear revelation of God, for he was 'not as Moses, who put a veil over his face.' Life and immortality are now brought to light, and things which have been hidden since the foundation of the world are manifest in him. The annual ceremony of atonement was thus abolished. The atoning blood which was once every year sprinkled within the veil, was now offered once for all by the great High Priest, and therefore the place of the symbolical rite was broken up. No blood of bullocks or of lambs is needed now, for Jesus has entered within the veil with his own blood. Hence access to God is now permitted, and is the privilege of every believer in Christ Jesus."[572]

---

[571] Packer, J. (1973; Published in electronic form by Christian Classics Foundation, 1996). *Knowing God – Chapter 18: The Heart of God.* Index created by Christian Classics Foundation. (electronic ed.). Downers Grove IL: InterVarsity.

[572] Spurgeon, C. H. (1995). *Morning and Evening: Daily readings* (April 19 AM). Oak Harbor, WA: Logos Research Systems, Inc.

The concepts set out above are explained in Scripture:

> **Hebrews 10:19-23:** *"Since therefore, brethren, we have confidence to enter the holy place by the blood of Jesus, ²⁰ by a new and living way which He inaugurated for us through the veil, that is, His flesh, ²¹ and since we have a great priest over the house of God, ²² let us draw near with a sincere heart in full assurance of faith, having our hearts sprinkled clean from an evil conscience and our bodies washed with pure water. ²³ Let us hold fast the confession of our hope without wavering, for He who promised is faithful;"*

> **1 Timothy 2:5:** *"For there is one God, and one mediator also between God and men, the man Christ Jesus, ⁶ who gave Himself as a ransom for all, the testimony borne at the proper time."*

VERSE. 51c *"and the earth shook; and the rocks were split,...."*

One supernatural event that immediately took place at the death of Christ was an earthquake. When attempting to determine the significance of the earthquake we should look to other incidences in scripture where they occurred. We do know that in the past God caused an entire mountain to violently quake when He spoke to Moses (Exodus 19:18). We also see God caused earthquakes when He was angry:

> **2 Samuel 22:8:** *"Then the <u>earth shook and quaked,</u>*
> *The foundations of heaven were trembling*
> *And were shaken, because He was angry."*
> (See also Jeremiah 10:10 and Isaiah 29:6.)

As for the earthquake that occurred at Christ's death, it can be assured God was making a statement about His Son and confirming statements He had made before. We see the Roman military leader understood the impact of that statement:

> **Matthew 27:54:** *"Now the centurion, and those who were with him keeping guard over Jesus, when they saw the earthquake and the things that were happening, became very frightened and said, '<u>Truly this was the Son of God!</u>'"*

Remember that when Jesus was making His triumphal entry into Jerusalem, the followers of Christ were hailing Him as Messiah. The religious leaders told Jesus to make the people stop declaring Him as Messiah. Jesus responded by affirming His Messiahship as such a truth that if it was not declared, the rocks would cry out, and that is what happened at the Cross! Let's look at that text:

> **Luke 19:37-40:** *"And as He was now approaching, near the descent of the Mount of Olives, the whole multitude of the disciples began to praise God joyfully with a loud voice for all the miracles which they had seen, ³⁸ saying, 'Blessed is the King who comes in the name of the Lord; Peace in heaven and glory in the highest!' ³⁹ And some of the Pharisees in the multitude said to Him, 'Teacher, rebuke Your disciples.' ⁴⁰ And He answered and said, '<u>I tell you, if these become silent , the stones will cry out!</u>'"*

Summary and Application

No longer is there the separation between sinful man and a perfect and holy God. What an awesome event it was when the veil was permanently removed. The tearing of the veil means we have access to the perfect and holy God. That access is granted to us by the grace of God through faith in Christ's payment for our sins on the cross!

The false religions do not like this. They are constantly trying to reestablish that veil through heretical doctrine. They will tell people that they have to obey certain rules or engage in certain religious rituals to enter into the presence of God. They set up veils by requiring people to go through priests and thus deny them the access we have to the Father in Christ (see 1Timothy 2:5-6). These veils of legalism, ritualism, or the mixing of faith with works for salvation are a direct attack on the sufficiency of Christ's atoning work on the Cross. These manmade veils, say, "Yes, it is very good what Jesus did, but it is not enough." Their veils always say you have to "earn your part." This type of thinking is anti-Christian. The only way you can be saved is to have true faith in Christ's payment for your sins on the Cross as the sole basis of your forgiveness (**1 Peter 2:24:** *"...and He Himself bore our sins in His body on the cross, that we might die to sin and live to righteousness; for by His wounds you were healed."*). God's forgiveness is available to all-even to the vilest sinner who repents and turns to Christ in faith for his forgiveness. That is the Gospel! Now go and tell others so the veil of false religion can be removed from them.

Mark 1:14-15: *"...Jesus came into Galilee, preaching the gospel of God, [15]and saying, 'The time is fulfilled, and the kingdom of God is at hand; <u>repent and believe in the gospel</u>.'"*

- To *REPENT* means to turn from your sins and forsake them by the power of God.
- To ***BELIEVE THE GOSPEL*** means that one who is "born again" by the Spirit of God (John 3:3-8) will:
  - Believe in Jesus Christ as Almighty God, who is without sin;
  - Believe in Jesus' sacrificial death on the cross as the only and complete payment for your sins;
  - Believe in Jesus' bodily resurrection from the dead on the third day;
  - Believe in Jesus as Lord over all things and confesses this fact to others.

It is that straightforward. <u>It has nothing to do with your righteousness, good works or engaging in a religious ceremony or cleaning yourself up first to win God's acceptance</u>. If you reject God's loving gift of forgiveness in Jesus Christ, you remain a guilty sinner waiting to be punished in eternal hell. The Bible says *in* **John 3:36:** *"He who believes in the Son has eternal life; but he who does not obey the Son will not see life, but the wrath of God abides on him."* Repent and believe the gospel TODAY, before it is too late!

MATTHEW 27:52-56
(THE CRUCIFIXION of JESUS – PART 5)

"...and the tombs were opened; and many bodies of the saints who had fallen asleep were raised; [53] *and coming out of the tombs after His resurrection they entered the holy city and appeared to many.* [54] *Now the centurion, and those who were with him keeping guard over Jesus, when they saw the earthquake and the things that were happening, became very frightened and said, 'Truly this was the Son of God!'* [55] *And many women were there looking on from a distance, who had followed Jesus from Galilee, ministering to Him,* [56] *among whom was Mary Magdalene, along with Mary the mother of James and Joseph, and the mother of the sons of Zebedee."*

Introduction

In the previous lesson we began to see the impact of the death of Christ on the cross. The first manifestation is set out in verse 51 where we read that the veil outside the holy of holies was torn from top to bottom. We next read of an earthquake. Now we will see in verses 52 and 53 that the power of death is destroyed with the resurrection of many believers.

> **John 11:25:** *"Jesus said to her, 'I am the resurrection and the life; he who believes in Me shall live even if he dies,....'"*

VERSES 52-53: *"...and the tombs were opened; and many bodies of the saints who had fallen asleep were raised;* [53] *and coming out of the tombs after His resurrection they entered the holy city and appeared to many."*

Here is a quick review of what happens when a person dies. Upon death, immediately a person's physical body returns to dust and his soul returns to God (i.e. all souls belong to God). **Ecclesiastes 12:7:** *"...then the dust will return to the earth as it was, and the spirit will return to God who gave it."* The soul does not sleep as some falsely claim. Jesus Himself told the criminal on the cross, *"Truly I say to you, today you shall be with Me in Paradise."* **Luke 23:43**. The believer's soul goes to the presence of God in Paradise and then, at the end, to live forever in the new heaven (Revelation 21:1-5). The unbeliever's soul is justly ordered by God to go into torment in Hades (Luke 16:23). In the end, the unbeliever is sent to hell (i.e. the Lake of Fire – Revelation 20:14-15).

Upon resurrection an individual is given a heavenly body which is different from his earthly body of flesh and blood. Our old bodies are raised and changed. A.A. Hodge explains it this way:

> "...There are many changes in the material elements and form of the human body between birth and death, and yet no one can for a moment doubt that the body remains one and the same throughout all. There is no difficulty in believing, upon the authority of God's Word, that, in spite of the lapse of time and of all the changes, whether of matter or of form, it undergoes, the body of the resurrection will be in the same sense and to the same degree one with the body of death as the body of death is one with the body of birth...These

changes will doubtless be very great. The body of the believer is to be made 'like unto Christ's glorious body.' Philippians 3:21...not a new body substituted for the old, but the old changed into the new." [573]

Scripture explains to us this concept of the transformed, glorified body:

1 Corinthians 15:42-44, 50-55: *"So also is the resurrection of the dead. It is sown a perishable body, it is raised an imperishable body; [43] it is sown in dishonor, it is raised in glory; it is sown in weakness, it is raised in power; [44] it is sown a natural body, it is raised a spiritual body....*

[50] Now I say this, brethren, that flesh and blood cannot inherit the kingdom of God; nor does the perishable inherit the imperishable. [51] Behold, I tell you a mystery; we shall not all sleep, but we shall all be changed, [52] in a moment, in the twinkling of an eye, at the last trumpet; for the trumpet will sound, and the dead will be raised imperishable, and we shall be changed. [53] For this perishable must put on the imperishable, and this mortal must put on immortality. [54] But when this perishable will have put on the imperishable, and this mortal will have put on immortality, then will come about the saying that is written, 'DEATH IS SWALLOWED UP in victory. [55] O DEATH, WHERE IS YOUR VICTORY? O DEATH, WHERE IS YOUR STING?'"

[For more on the concept of the resurrection and the chronology of the various resurrections, see this author's notes under the section set out in Matthew 22:30.]

Part of our text for this study is **Matthew 27:52-53**, which states, *"and the tombs were opened; and many bodies of the saints who had fallen asleep were raised; [53] and coming out of the tombs after His resurrection they entered the holy city and appeared to many."* Read verse 53 carefully. Note that there is a little break in chronology. The resurrection of these, *"saints who had fallen asleep were raised,"* took place, *"after His resurrection."* One might argue that they were raised at Christ's death and then came out of the tombs after His resurrection. The problem with that scenario is that one would be claiming that a person is "raised" from the dead and also left in the tomb. The King James Version and New American Standard make it clear that they came out of their tombs after Jesus' resurrection, whereas the NIV is equivocal.[574] Many believe that these

---

[573] Hodge, A. A., and Hodge, C. (1996). *The Confession of Faith: With questions for theological students and Bible classes* (p. 386). Simpsonville, SC: Christian Classics Foundation.

[574] Notice the distinction between the KJV, NASV and the NIV. The KJV and NASV make it clear that the Saints did not come out of their graves and enter the holy city until after Jesus' resurrection. The NIV suggests that the Saint's resurrection took place before Jesus' resurrection but they did not enter the holy city until after the resurrection.

The Holy Bible: King James Version. 1995. **Matthew 27:53:** *"And came out of the graves after his resurrection, and went into the holy city, and appeared unto many."*

The New American Standard Bible. 1986. La Habra, CA: The Lockman Foundation. **Matthew 27:53:** *"and coming out of the tombs after His resurrection they entered the holy city and appeared to many."*

[Note continued on the next page.]

two verses are meant to be read that the earthquake broke open the tombs and these Old Testament saints were raised up a few days later, immediately after Jesus' resurrection. We read from Scripture that Jesus' was the first resurrection: **1 Corinthians 15:20** *"But now Christ has been raised from the dead, <u>the first fruits of those who are asleep.</u>"* (See footnote about resurrection chronology below.)[575] Addressing the issue of the chronology of Matthew 27:52-53, John Walvoord write:

> "Many others, however, say that since Christ is the first-fruits of the dead (1 Corinthians 15:23), their [i.e. the saints mentioned in Matthew 27:52-53] resurrection did not occur till He was raised. In this view, the phrase 'after Jesus' resurrection' goes with the words **were raised to life** and **came out of the tombs.** This is possible in the Greek, and is suggested in the KJV and the NASB. The tombs, then, **broke open** at Christ's death, probably by the earthquake, thus heralding Christ's triumph in death over sin, but the bodies were not raised till Christ was raised. These people returned to Jerusalem (**the Holy City**) where they were recognized by friends and family." [576]

It should not be assumed that all Old Testament saints were raised at this time. This was merely a representation of the resurrection of that group who will later be raised. (For more on the chronology of the various resurrections, see this author's notes under the section set out in Matthew 22:30.)

Regardless of the chronology debate, one thing is certain, the events in Matthew 27:52-53 are a manifestation of the sacrificial death of Christ and His complete victory of sin, death, and the corruption of the body!

[Note continued.]

> *The Holy Bible: <u>New International Version</u>.* 1984. Grand Rapids: Zondervan. **Matthew 27:53:** *"They came out of the tombs, and after Jesus' resurrection they went into the holy city and appeared to many people."*

This author leans firmly to the NASV because it is known for being *"a monumental work of scholarship and a very accurate translation."* Comfort, P. W. (1991). *The complete guide to Bible versions.* Wheaton, Ill.: Living Books. The general concept of a "word by word" translation type of the NASV is distinguishable to the NIV which is a dynamic equivalent. A dynamic equivalent translation is one in which the translators take a view of what was the "thought" behind the scripture rather than a literal word for word translation. The weakness I see in the "dynamic equivalent" is the possibility of the scholar having the wrong "thought" about a text and that thought becomes so slightly manifested in the text. I am much more interested in a word for word literal translation despite the difficulties it may cause in readability. For more on this subject See the foot note in the <u>Summary and Application</u> section after Matthew 4:8-11.)

[End of note.]

[575] One might ask, "Did not Jarius' daughter, Lazarus, or the resurrection of the widow's son occur before Jesus' resurrection?" The answer is no, they are not of the same resurrection as Jesus'. These other people would eventually die again. Jesus is the resurrection that was to eternal life (i.e. the first resurrection of one who would never die again.)

[576] Walvoord, J. F., Zuck, R. B., and Dallas Theological Seminary. (1985). *The Bible Knowledge Commentary: An Exposition of the Scriptures* (v. 2, p. 90). Wheaton, IL: Victor Books.

VERSE 54: *"Now the centurion, and those who were with him keeping guard over Jesus, when they saw the earthquake and the things that were happening, became very frightened and said, 'Truly this was the Son of God!'"*

The centurion and his soldiers had the cold hard job of killing people. They were bloody, hard-boiled men. Definitely not men of mercy, emotion, or sentiment. They were professional executioners. The centurion and his soldiers had been present during the entire crucifixion. They would have heard the mocking of the people and the religious leaders about Jesus being the Son of God (39-43). They would have heard Jesus forgive the thief on the cross (Luke 23:41-43). But when Jesus died and they heard the roar of the earthquake, they knew they were not simply guarding another crucifixion. With great fear, the centurion leader and the guards said, *"Truly this was the Son of God!"*

VERSES 55-56: *"And many women were there looking on from a distance, who had followed Jesus from Galilee, ministering to Him, ⁵⁶ among whom was Mary Magdalene, along with Mary the mother of James and Joseph, and the mother of the sons of Zebedee."*

These verses tell us some of the women who were believers witnessed His crucifixion. No doubt they had provided meals and other provision for Him since it states in verse 55 they had ministered to Him. We read in the book of Luke there were women who provided for Jesus.

> Luke 8:2-3: *"...and also some women who had been healed of evil spirits and sicknesses: Mary who was called Magdalene, from whom seven demons had gone out, ³ and Joanna the wife of Chuza, Herod's steward, and Susanna, and many others who were contributing to their support out of their private means."*

The women mentioned in Matthew 27:55-56 included Mary Magdalene, who Jesus healed from demonic possession (Luke 8:2).

> "The second woman mentioned is **Mary the mother of James and Joseph** . This **James** was one of the apostles and was commonly referred to as James the Less (Mark 15:40) or James the son of Alphaeus (Matthew 10:3; Acts 1:13) to distinguish him from the other James, who, with Peter and his brother John, constituted the inner circle of the Twelve. John identifies this Mary as the wife of Clopas (John 19:25), apparently a variant of Alphaeus. The third woman is identified as Salome by Mark (15:40) but is referred to by Matthew simply as **the mother of the sons of Zebedee**, in other words, Zebedee's wife. The **sons of Zebedee** were James and John (Matthew 4:21) and were nicknamed by Jesus 'Sons of Thunder' (Mark 3:17).... Salome and was a sister of Mary, the Mother of Jesus (see Matthew 27:56; Mark 15:40; John 19:25), making her Jesus' aunt and James and John His first cousins."[577]

If you remember from an earlier lesson, Jesus' "Aunt" Salome was the lady who approached Him about giving her sons, James and John, thrones next to Jesus in heaven.

> Matthew 20:20-23: *"Then the mother of the sons of Zebedee came to Him with her sons, bowing down, and making a request of Him. ²¹ And He said to her, 'What do you wish?' She *said to Him, 'Command that in Your kingdom these*

---

[577] MacArthur, J. (1989). *Matthew* (Matthew 27:55). Chicago: Moody Press.

two sons of mine may sit, one on Your right and one on Your left.' 22 But Jesus answered and said, 'You do not know what you are asking for. Are you able to drink the cup that I am about to drink?' They *said to Him, 'We are able.'
23 He *said to them, 'My cup you shall drink; but to sit on My right and on My left, this is not Mine to give, but it is for those for whom it has been prepared by My Father.'"

We also know that earlier Jesus' mother, Mary, along with the apostle John, had been near the cross itself. At that time Jesus charged John with the duty to care for her.

> **John 19:26-27:** *"When Jesus therefore saw His mother, and the disciple whom He loved standing nearby, He *said to His mother, 'Woman , behold, your son!' 27 Then He *said to the disciple, 'Behold, your mother!' And from that hour the disciple took her into his own household."*

Summary and Application

In this section we read of different onlookers at the cross. These onlookers included the centurion and his guards, as well as a group of women. The group of women were, *"looking on from a distance."* The women had known who Jesus was for a long period of time, and, *"had followed Jesus from Galilee, ministering to Him."* The soldiers, on the other hand, had this brief encounter with Jesus but quickly realized, *'Truly this was the Son of God!'*. Where would you fit in here? Have you followed the Lord a long time, or have you just recently realized who He is? If you are a Christian, you should evaluate where you are on your spiritual journey, and seek the Lord on how to finish in a way that honors Him.

> **Matthew 24:12–13:** *"Because lawlessness is increased, most people's love will grow cold. But the one who endures to the end, he will be saved."*

This will not be done by your efforts, but by His Spirit and power.

MATTHEW 27:57-61
(JESUS' BURIAL)

"And when it was evening, there came a rich man from Arimathea, named Joseph, who himself had also become a disciple of Jesus. 58 This man went to Pilate and asked for the body of Jesus. Then Pilate ordered it to be given over to him. 59 And Joseph took the body and wrapped it in a clean linen cloth, 60 and laid it in his own new tomb, which he had hewn out in the rock; and he rolled a large stone against the entrance of the tomb and went away. 61 And Mary Magdalene was there, and the other Mary, sitting opposite the grave."

Introduction

This section deals with Jesus' burial. We will review parallel passages to obtain additional information about this event. An important principle to be gained from this study is the ongoing fulfillment of Old Testament prophecies regarding Jesus.

VERSE 57: *"And when it was evening, there came a rich man from Arimathea, named Joseph, who himself had also become a disciple of Jesus."*

Who is this man called Joseph of Arimathea? The term "Arimathea" refers to the town in which this Joseph was from. It was a town about five miles north of Jerusalem and was also called RAMAH.[578] We learn from **Mark 15:43** that he was, *"a prominent member of the Council, who himself was waiting for the kingdom of God;..."* (i.e. a member of the prestigious Sanhedrin). The Sanhedrin was considered the Great Council located in Jerusalem. The Council had 71 members. These members were composed of mostly, "prominent members of the families of the high priest, elders and scribes. The Jews trace the origin of this to Numbers 11:16 [579]." [580] Notice from the reference in Mark 15:43 that Joseph was not just an influential man because he was a member of the council, but that he was a *"prominent member"* in the council itself. Luke 23:50 tells us that he was a *"good and righteous man."* It must be remembered that the Sanhedrin is the

---

[578] Swanson, J., and Nave, O. (1994). *New Nave's*. Oak Harbor: Logos Research Systems.

[579] The 71 members of the Sanhedrin has its roots in Numbers 11:16 where God told Moses to gather 70 men to be elders and help him judge Israel. So if you take 70 elders, plus Moses, you end up with a total of 71. The Sanhedrin then applied this concept to make 71 members.

Numbers 11:16-17: *"The Lord therefore said to Moses, 'Gather for Me seventy men from the elders of Israel, whom you know to be the elders of the people and their officers and bring them to the tent of meeting, and let them take their stand there with you. 17 Then I will come down and speak with you there, and I will take of the Spirit who is upon you, and will put Him upon them; and they shall bear the burden of the people with you, so that you shall not bear it all alone.'"*

[580] Vine, W., and Bruce, F. *Vine's Expository Dictionary of Old and New Testament Words* (p. 245) 1996. Old Tappan NJ: Revell.

council that sought Jesus' death (Mark 15:1). Luke 23:50-51 tells us that Joseph did not agree to their evil decision, *"he had not consented to their plan and action."*

Joseph is described in Mark as one who, *"was waiting for the kingdom of God;...."* This description informs us that Joseph was a sincere Jewish man who had faith that God would send His Messiah to Israel. We read in John 19:38 that he was, *"a disciple of Jesus, but a secret one, for fear of the Jews."*

VERSE 58: *"This man went to Pilate and asked for the body of Jesus. Then Pilate ordered it to be given over to him."*

Joseph wanted to provide Jesus a respectful burial. This was not a sentimental act, but one of true Christian courage. No longer could it be said that Joseph was a "secret" disciple. He laid down his reputation, political standing, and everything else to be publicly identified with Christ. We read in **Mark 15:43**, *"...he gathered up courage and went in before Pilate, and asked for the body of Jesus."* The account in Mark gives us more detail regarding Pilate's response:

> **Mark 15:44-45:** *"And Pilate wondered if He was dead by this time, and summoning the centurion, he questioned him as to whether He was already dead. ⁴⁵ And ascertaining this from the centurion, he granted the body to Joseph."*

It is important to note that Pilate wanted to make sure Jesus was indeed dead before he released the body. Some speculate that Pilate may have doubted Jesus had died so quickly. What Pilate failed to realize is that it was Jesus who was in charge of when He would die—not Pilate or his executioners. In Matthew 27:50 we read it was Jesus who, *"yielded up His spirit."* Jesus also explained:

> **John 10:17-18:** *"For this reason the Father loves Me, because I lay down My life that I may take it again. ¹⁸ No one has taken it away from Me, but I lay it down on My own initiative. I have authority to lay it down, and I have authority to take it up again. This commandment I received from My Father."*

Taking a stand for Christ that truly costs is part of the Christian life. Joseph was courageous and experienced that. It says in **2 Timothy 3:12**: *"And indeed, all who desire to live godly in Christ Jesus will be persecuted."* Some people believe that they are doing God a big favor when they make lukewarm acknowledgement of Him. Others believe that taking a stance for Christ means speaking proudly of their particular denominational affiliation. These types of religious platitudes are not what Scripture speaks of as the believer's bold, uncompromising confession of Christ. Do you remember what Jesus said in Luke 6:46 to the cowards who called him Lord? *"And why do you call Me, 'Lord, Lord,' and do not do what I say?"* Jesus also told those who falsely call Him Lord that, *'I never knew you; DEPART FROM ME, YOU WHO PRACTICE LAWLESSNESS'*. **Matthew 7:23**.

VERSE 59: *"And Joseph took the body and wrapped it in a clean linen cloth,*

Here we read of how Joseph provided a proper burial for our Lord. When you look at the extensive preparations that were made for the burial, it appears obvious that Joseph, like some of the other disciples, did not fully realize that Jesus was going to rise from the dead. We get more details of burial preparations from John's Gospel:

> John 19:38-42: *"And after these things Joseph of Arimathea, being a disciple of Jesus, but a secret one, for fear of the Jews, asked Pilate that he might take away the body of Jesus; and Pilate granted permission. He came therefore, and took away His body. [39] And Nicodemus came also, who had first come to Him by night; bringing a mixture of myrrh and aloes, about a hundred pounds weight. [40] And so they took the body of Jesus, and bound it in linen wrappings with the spices, as is the burial custom of the Jews. [41] Now in the place where He was crucified there was a garden; and in the garden a new tomb, in which no one had yet been laid. [42] Therefore on account of the Jewish day of preparation, because the tomb was nearby, they laid Jesus there."*

In the previous passage, we read Nicodemus also went with Joseph. John 19:39 also tells us Nicodemus is the one, *"who had first come to Him by night;...."* In that statement, John is referencing the first time Nicodemus came to Jesus. We read of this account in John 3:1-21:

> *"Now there was a man of the Pharisees, named Nicodemus, a ruler of the Jews; [2] this man came to Him by night, and said to Him, 'Rabbi, we know that You have come from God as a teacher; for no one can do these signs that You do unless God is with him.' [3] Jesus answered and said to him, 'Truly, truly, I say to you, unless one is born again, he cannot see the kingdom of God.' [4] Nicodemus *said to Him, 'How can a man be born when he is old? He cannot enter a second time into his mother's womb and be born, can he?' [5] Jesus answered, 'Truly, truly, I say to you, unless one is born of water and the Spirit, he cannot enter into the kingdom of God. [6] That which is born of the flesh is flesh, and that which is born of the Spirit is spirit. [7] Do not marvel that I said to you, You must be born again. [8] The wind blows where it wishes and you hear the sound of it, but do not know where it comes from and where it is going; so is everyone who is born of the Spirit.' [9] Nicodemus answered and said to Him, 'How can these things be?' [10] Jesus answered and said to him, 'Are you the teacher of Israel, and do not understand these things? [11] Truly, truly, I say to you, we speak that which we know , and bear witness of that which we have seen; and you do not receive our witness. [12] If I told you earthly things and you do not believe, how shall you believe if I tell you heavenly things? [13] And no one has ascended into heaven, but He who descended from heaven, even the Son of Man. [14] And as Moses lifted up the serpent in the wilderness, even so must the Son of Man be lifted up; [15] that whoever believes may in Him have eternal life .*
>
> *[16] For God so loved the world, that He gave His only begotten Son, that whoever believes in Him should not perish, but have eternal life. [17] For God did not send the Son into the world to judge the world, but that the world should be saved through Him. [18] He who believes in Him is not judged; he who does not believe has been judged already, because he has not believed in the name of the only begotten Son of God. [19] And this is the judgment, that the light is come into the world, and men loved the darkness rather than the light; for their deeds were evil. [20] For everyone who does evil hates the light, and does*

not come to the light, lest his deeds should be exposed. [21] But he who practices the truth comes to the light, that his deeds may be manifested as having been wrought in God.'"

We also learn Nicodemus made a somewhat courageous stand for Christ when he protested that Jesus was being condemned without a hearing (John 7:50-51).

In John 19:39-40 we read Nicodemus also brought, *"...a mixture of myrrh and aloes, about a hundred pounds weight. [40] And so they took the body of Jesus, and bound it in linen wrappings with the spices, as is the burial custom of the Jews."* When it talks about the mixture being *"about a hundred pounds weight,"* the measurement is 100 Roman litra. The term litra is translated into the English word "pound." A litra is about 12 ounces. If you convert 100 Roman pounds to our English pounds it would be about 75 English pounds. In the NIV text, the conversion is made to U.S. pounds and that is why you will read 75 pounds for John 19:39 in the NIV. The reason Nicodemus brought this mixture had to do with a burial custom:

> "When bodies were being prepared for burial it was customary for spices to be placed in the grave-clothes as a form of embalming. They included mixtures of myrrh and aloes (John 19:39), or, more generally, 'spices and ointments' (Luke 23:56). While they did not significantly inhibit putrefaction, they served as deodorants and disinfectants."[581]

VERSE 60: *"...and laid it in his own new tomb, which he had hewn out in the rock; and he rolled a large stone against the entrance of the tomb and went away."*

We read Joseph of Arimathea owned a tomb. We get more information about the tomb from John:

> **John 19:41-42:** *"Now in the place where He was crucified there was a garden; and in the garden a new tomb, in which no one had yet been laid. [42] Therefore on account of the Jewish day of preparation, because the tomb was nearby, they laid Jesus there."*

When it makes reference to the *"Jewish day of preparation,"* it is referring to the day before the Sabbath (Saturday). So John 19:42 is explaining that the, *"wrappings with the spices, as is the burial custom"* **John 19:40**, of Jesus' body was done quickly so that it would be "completed before the Sabbath began at nightfall."[582] "The fact that it was the day before the Sabbath proves conclusively that Jesus was crucified on Friday, commonly referred to by Jews as "the day of preparation."[583] We also read in **Matthew 27:60** that they, *"rolled a large stone against the entrance of the tomb."* This would seal the tomb to prevent it from being robbed by scavengers or entered by animals.

[581] Wood, D. R. W., and Marshall, I. H. (1996). *New Bible Dictionary* (3rd ed.) (p. 465). Leicester, England; Downers Grove, Ill.: InterVarsity Press.

[582] Walvoord, J. F., Zuck, R. B., and Dallas Theological Seminary. (1983-c1985). *The Bible Knowledge Commentary: An Exposition of the Scriptures* (Mt 27:62). Wheaton, IL: Victor Books.

[583] MacArthur, J. (1989). *Matthew* (Matthew 27:61). Chicago: Moody Press.

There is one more aspect of the crucifixion and burial of Jesus we must never overlook. We read Jesus was crucified along with two wicked men: **Matthew 27:38**: *"At that time two robbers were crucified with Him, one on the right and one on the left."* Compare that to the man he was with when he was buried. In Matthew 27:57 we read that Joseph of Arimathea was, *"a rich man."* It was Joseph who owned the tomb he gave to Jesus. Now compare these two facts with the prophecy Isaiah made about the Messiah several hundred years before Christ:

> **Isaiah 53:9:** *"His grave was assigned with wicked men,*
> *Yet He was with a rich man in His death,*
> *Because He had done no violence,*
> *Nor was there any deceit in His mouth."*

VERSE 61: *"And Mary Magdalene was there, and the other Mary, sitting opposite the grave."*

We do not see any of Jesus' eleven remaining disciples present at His grave, but we do see two courageous and loyal women there. The women are *Mary Magdalene* and *"the other Mary."* Both of these women were at the crucifixion (Matthew 27:55-56). Mary Magdalene is the woman *"whom He had cast out seven demons."* **Mark 16:9**. The "other Mary" is Mary the *mother* of Joses *[Joseph]* and James the Less (Mark 15:40 and 47).

Summary and Application

This section is one that demonstrates courage, devotion, and love for God by men and women. It is also one that continues to manifest the sovereignty of God in all things.

<u>MATTHEW 27:62-66</u>
(SECURING THE TOMB)

"Now on the next day, which is the one after the preparation, the chief priests and the Pharisees gathered together with Pilate, ⁶³ and said, 'Sir, we remember that when He was still alive that deceiver said, 'After three days I am to rise again.' ⁶⁴ Therefore, give orders for the grave to be made secure until the third day, lest the disciples come and steal Him away and say to the people, 'He has risen from the dead,' and the last deception will be worse than the first.'" ⁶⁵ Pilate said to them, 'You have a guard; go, make it as secure as you know how.' ⁶⁶ And they went and made the grave secure, and along with the guard they set a seal on the stone."

Introduction

The religious leaders were not content to be successful in their murder of Jesus; they now wanted to make sure they never heard from Him again. Notice Scripture tells us that not only did the tomb have guards watching it, but the leaders also had a seal put on the stone.

<u>**VERSE 62:**</u> *"Now on the next day, which is the one after the preparation, the chief priests and the Pharisees gathered together with Pilate,"*

> We know that the preparation day is Friday, so the next day would be the Sabbath. This was the Passover Sabbath, so it was a special holy day on the Jewish calendar (John 19:31). On that day the religious leaders came together to ask another favor from Pilate. Note they were so driven to wipe away any remembrance of Jesus that they actually went to see Pilate on such a high, holy day. Remember that a mere day before they would not go in to see Pilate, but had Pilate come to them. The reason they claimed that they could not go see Pilate was that if they did so, they would have entered a Gentile building. They claimed that by entering a Gentile building they would have "defiled themselves" and wrecked their Passover festivities.[584]
>
> > <u>John 18:28-29:</u> *"They *led Jesus therefore from Caiaphas into the Praetorium, and it was early; and they themselves did not enter into the Praetorium in order that they might not be defiled, but might eat the Passover. ²⁹ Pilate therefore went out to them, and *said, 'What accusation do you bring against this Man?'*
>
> Now, a day later, the idea of being defiled was not half as important as stopping Jesus altogether. Ryle provides an important prospective on the religious leaders' conduct:

---

[584] *"…lest they should be defiled,* but kept out of doors, *that they might eat the Passover,* not the paschal lamb (that was eaten the night before) but the Passover-feast, upon the sacrifices which were offered on the fifteenth day, *the Chagigah,* as they called it, the Passover-bullocks spoken of Deuteronomy 16:2 ; 2 Chronicles 30:24 ; 35:8 , 9. These they were to eat of, and therefore would not go into the court, for fear of touching a Gentile, and thereby contracting, not a legal, but only a traditional pollution." Henry, M. (1996, c1991). *Matthew Henry's Commentary on the Whole Bible: Complete and Unabridged in One Volume* (John 18:28). Peabody: Hendrickson.

"The restless enmity of these unhappy men could not sleep, even when the body of Jesus was in the grave. They recalled the words which they remembered he had spoken about 'rising again:' they resolved, as they thought, to make his rising impossible. They went to Pilate and obtained from him a guard of Roman soldiers;...they placed a seal upon the stone... unwittingly they were providing the most complete evidence of the truth of Christ's coming resurrection. They were actually making it impossible to prove that there was any deception of imposition. Their seal, their guard, their precautions, were all to become witnesses, in a few hours, that Christ had risen."[585]

VERSE 63: "...and said, 'Sir, we remember that when He was still alive that deceiver said, After three days I am to rise again.'"

Notice the religious leaders were back to acting very respectful to Pilate by calling him *"Sir."* It is also important to note that they confirmed Jesus was *indeed dead* by their statement, *"when He was still alive."*

"By his overruling providence he ordered things so that the death and burial of Jesus were placed beyond a doubt. Pilate [gave] consent to his burial [after he independently has Jesus death confirmed]...the chief priests themselves set a guard over the place where His body was deposited. Jews and Gentiles, friends and enemies all alike testify to the great fact that Christ did really and actually die and was laid in a grave. It is a fact that can never be questioned."[586]

They blaspheme Jesus to Pilate by calling Him a *"deceiver."* Notice that they are concerned about one thing—Jesus' rising after three days. How could they have known about that? Jesus had told them plainly on another occasion:

Matthew 12:38-40: *"Then some of the scribes and Pharisees answered Him, saying, 'Teacher, we want to see a sign from You.' [39] But He answered and said to them, 'An evil and adulterous generation craves for a sign; and yet no sign shall be given to it but the sign of Jonah the prophet ; [40] for just as Jonah was three days and three nights in the belly of the sea monster, so shall the Son of Man be three days and three nights in the heart of the earth.'"*

VERSE 64: *"Therefore, give orders for the grave to be made secure until the third day, lest the disciples come and steal Him away and say to the people, 'He has risen from the dead,' and the last deception will be worse than the first."*

---

[585] *Matthew* / Ryle, J.C. p. 287 (Expository Thoughts on the Gospels) (Crossways Classic Commentaries: v.1)

[586] *Matthew* / Ryle, J.C. p. 285 (Expository Thoughts on the Gospels) (Crossways Classic Commentaries: v.1)

Here the religious leaders set forth to Pilate the great reason why he had better do something. They allege that if left unchecked Jesus' *"last deception will be worse than the first."* So what is the first deception that the religious leaders are so concerned about? There is none. They are really only concerned about their own power. That reason is not a good one to sell to Pilate, so they reformulate the claim to be one of interest to Pilate and Rome. Remember at Jesus' trial before Pilate, the religious leaders made claims against Christ they thought would appeal to Pilate. These claims regarded the threat Jesus was to Rome. Read from Luke some of the charges against Him:

> Luke 23:2: *"And they began to accuse Him, saying, 'We found this man* <u>*misleading our nation*</u> *and forbidding to pay taxes to Caesar, and saying that He Himself is Christ, a King.'"*

Look how they manipulated Pilate by making the bogus claim they were concerned about the welfare of Rome and Caesar.

> John 19:12 : *"As a result of this Pilate made efforts to release Him, but the Jews cried out, saying, 'If you release this Man, you are no friend of Caesar; everyone who makes himself out to be a king opposes Caesar.'"*

The real concern the religious leaders had about the resurrection of Christ was the impact on their own power, glory, and manmade religious structure.

VERSE 65-66: *"Pilate said to them, 'You have a guard; go, make it as secure as you know how.' ⁶⁶ And they went and made the grave secure, and along with the guard they set a seal on the stone."*

Here Pilate continues to grant the religious leaders what they want—a guarded tomb with the strength of the Roman Empire behind it. They did not merely post a guard, but they also set a seal on the stone. Again, the religious leaders' schemes continue to build up ironclad evidence of Jesus' resurrection.

"The tomb was sealed by the Pharisees and chief priests for the purpose of making sure that the disciples would not come and steal the body away (verses 63, 64). The mode of doing this was probably by stretching a cord across the stone and sealing it at both ends with sealing-clay."[587]

> [See the section after the Summary below for a comment on the Apostle's Creed statement that Jesus *"descended into hell."*]

Summary and Application

We need to remember that all things are under the sovereign hand of God. In the section in Matthew 27:62-66 we see evil men working hard in their continued plot against Jesus. Despite their plotting, God is in control. The religious leaders got the tomb guarded and sealed. The result of their actions was the further verification of Jesus' resurrection. Ryle states it this way:

> "Let all true Christians lay these things to heart, and take courage. We live in a world where all things are ordered by a hand of perfect wisdom, and where in all things God works for the good of those who love Him (Romans 8:28). The powers of this world are only tools in the hand of God: He is always using them for His own purposes, however

---

[587] Easton, M. G. (1996). *Easton's Bible Dictionary, Seal.* Oak Harbor, WA: Logos Research Systems, Inc.

little they may be aware of it. They are the instruments by which He is forever cutting and polishing the living stones of His spiritual temple, and all their schemes and plans will only turn to His praise. Let us be patient in days of trouble and darkness, and look forward. The very things which now seem against us are all working together for God's glory. We only see half now: a little while longer, we shall see all; and we shall then discover that all the persecution we now endure was, like 'the seal' and 'guard' (verse 66), tending to God's glory. God can make the 'wrath of man praise Him" (Psalm 76:10, KJV).'[588]

COMMENT ON THE APOSTLES' CREED

What about the portion of the Apostles' Creed that states Jesus went to hell?

Apostles' Creed

"I believe in God the Father Almighty, Maker of heaven and earth. And in Jesus Christ His only Son our Lord; who was conceived by the Holy Ghost, Born of the Virgin Mary, suffered under Pontius Pilate, was crucified, dead, and buried; he descended into hell; the third day he rose again from the dead; he ascended into heaven, and sitteth on the right hand of God the Father Almighty; from thence he shall come to judge the quick and the dead. I believe in the Holy Ghost; the holy *catholic Church; the communion of saints; the forgiveness of sins; the resurrection of the body; and the life everlasting. Amen."
(* "catholic" means universal – not the Roman Catholic Church)

The issue is whether Jesus *"descended into hell"* after His burial. We will start the analysis by reviewing the history of the Apostles' creed. There is no evidence the Apostles' Creed was written by the Apostles, although legend claim otherwise. (There is the legend the Apostles wrote this creed on the 10th day after Christ's ascension into heaven. Another legend states that each of the 12 Apostles composed a clause that composed the Apostles' Creed.) Some wrongly claim the Apostles' Creed is the standard for the fundamentals of the Christian faith. MacArthur corrects that view when he states,
> "The Creed is by no means a complete statement of all the doctrines essential to genuine Christianity. For example, since there is no statement about the deity of Christ, a Jehovah's Witness, who denies Christ's deity, could give full assent to the Creed as it stands. In fact, the ancient forerunners of Jehovah's Witnesses, the followers of a heretic named Arius, defended themselves by appealing to the Creed." [589]

Note also that the creed makes no mention of repentance and faith in Christ for salvation. This is why tens of thousands can stand up each week and mumble through the creed and remain unsaved. As R.C. Sproul wrote: *"It is one thing to believe in God; it is another thing to believe God."* There are many versions of the Creed. The earliest is the Interrogatory Creed of Hippolytus A.D. 215. The Creed had revisions drawn up in the first and second century that emphasized the true humanity of Christ including a material body.

---

[588] *Matthew* / Ryle, J.C. p. 287-88 (Expository Thoughts on the Gospels) (Crossways Classic Commentaries: v.1)

[589] MacArthur, J. (1994). *Reckless Faith: When the church loses its will to discern* (p.103). Wheaton, Ill.: Crossway Books.

These revisions took place because the Gnostics, along with the Marcionites and Mancheans, denied the humanity and materiality of Christ. [590] Gnostics said that the physical universe was evil and therefore God did not make it. They said Jesus became the sin-bearer only after the Spirit came upon Him at baptism, and left before the crucifixion so that the Spirit had as little association with the human or material man as possible. John condemned the Gnostic heretics in his epistle:

> **1 John 4:1-3:** *"Beloved, do not believe every spirit, but test the spirits to see whether they are from God; because many false prophets have gone out into the world. [2] By this you know the Spirit of God: every spirit that confesses that Jesus Christ has come in the flesh is from God; [3] and every spirit that does not confess Jesus is not from God; and this is the spirit of the antichrist, of which you have heard that it is coming, and now it is already in the world."*

There were other changes and creeds that occurred in the 4th century. The Nicene Creed version affirmed the Deity of Christ since Arians were denying that Jesus was fully God. The current form of the Creed has its basis in the writings of Caesarius of Arles (d. 543).

One line of the creed states that Jesus, *"was crucified, dead, and buried; he descended into hell; the third day he rose again from the dead;…."* What does it mean *"He descended into hell?"* We will see that the Greek term, "Hades" was translated to English as, "hell." "Hell" in the English language is commonly seen as the realm of the Devil and his demons, a place of punishment and fire. Hades is more correctly defined as the

---

[590] <u>What does it mean to "have faith?"</u> Does it merely mean you have an opinion in which you will agree that Jesus lived and died and rose from the dead? The answer to that question is no! Even the demons acknowledge the facts of Jesus' perfect work on the cross, yet they are not saved. **James 2:19:** *"You believe that God is one. You do well; the demons also believe, and shudder."*

R.C. Sproul wrote: "Faith includes believing in God. Yet that kind of faith is not particularly praiseworthy. James writes, 'You believe that there is one God. You do well. Even the demons believe—and tremble!' (James 2:19). Here sarcasm drips from James's pen. To believe in the existence of God merely qualifies us to be demons. <u>It is one thing to believe in God; it is another thing to believe God.</u> To believe God, to trust in Him for our very life, is the essence of the Christian faith." (emphasis added).

As you can see, *saving faith* is much more than just having an opinion about who Jesus is. Jesus states in the Bible that every single person is guilty of sin, which is punished by receiving *eternal judgment in the fires of hell.* Jesus preached that the only way to escape from hell is to *<u>"repent and believe in the gospel."</u>* **Mark 1:15.**

- To **_REPENT_** means to turn from your sins and forsake them by the power of God.
- To **_BELIEVE THE GOSPEL_** means that one who is "born again" by the Spirit of God (John 3:3-8) will:
  - Believe in Jesus Christ as Almighty God, who is without sin;
  - Believe in Jesus' sacrificial death on the cross as the only and complete payment for your sins;
  - Believe in Jesus' bodily resurrection from the dead on the third day;
  - Believe in Jesus as Lord over all things and confesses this fact to others.

It is that straightforward. <u>It has nothing to do with your righteousness, good works or engaging in a religious ceremony or cleaning yourself up first to win God's acceptance.</u> If you reject God's loving gift of forgiveness in Jesus Christ, you remain a guilty sinner waiting to be punished in eternal hell. The Bible says *in* **John 3:36:** *"He who believes in the Son has eternal life; but he who does not obey the Son will not see life, but the wrath of God abides on him."* Repent and believe the gospel TODAY, before it is too late! **John 14:21:** *"He who has My commandments and keeps them is the one who loves Me; and he who loves Me will be loved by My Father, and I will love him and will disclose Myself to him."*

place for departed spirits of the damned, as well as the blessed dead who died before the Ascension of Christ. Walvoord states that:

> "Neither sheol nor hades ever refer to the eternal state and should not be considered equivalent to the English word 'hell,' which properly is the place of eternal punishment." [591] In other words, Hades is the general name given for the location of the spirit beings of those whose physical bodies have died. Hades can include both the place of punishment and the place of comfort, with an impassable divide between the two. Note that Luke 16:19-31 is a true story and not a parable. It shows this concept that Hades is a general name for the place of those who have died. Those who are God's people go to Paradise; those who are not have torment in Hades. We see that Abraham speaks from Paradise to one of the wicked under torment in Hades.

> Luke 16:22-31: *"Now it came about that the poor man died and he was carried away by the angels to Abraham's bosom; and the rich man also died and was buried .*[23] *And in Hades he lifted up his eyes, being in torment, and * saw Abraham far away, and Lazarus in his bosom.* [24] *And he cried out and said, 'Father Abraham , have mercy on me, and send Lazarus , that he may dip the tip of his finger in water and cool off my tongue; for I am in agony in this flame.'* [25] *But Abraham said, 'Child, remember that during your life you received your good things, and likewise Lazarus bad things; but now he is being comforted here, and you are in agony.* [26] *And besides all this, between us and you there is a great chasm fixed, in order that those who wish to come over from here to you may not be able, and that none may cross over from there to us.'* [27] *And he said, 'Then I beg you, Father, that you send him to my father's house —* [28] *for I have five brothers —that he may warn them, lest they also come to this place of torment.'* [29] *But Abraham said, 'They have Moses and the Prophets; let them hear them.'* [30] *But he said, 'No, Father Abraham, but if someone goes to them from the dead, they will repent!'* [31] *But he said to him, 'If they do not listen to Moses and the Prophets, neither will they be persuaded if someone rises from the dead .'"*

Some denominations use this phrase, *"descended into hell"* in their Apostle's Creed and some do not. A. Hodge states that:

> "Some (as Pearson on the Creed, pp. 333–371) have held that as Christ died vicariously as a sinner, so, in order to fulfill the law of death, His soul went temporarily to the place where the souls of those who die for their own sins die the second death forever.

> The Lutherans teach that the descent of the God–man into hell, in order to triumph over Satan and his angels in the very citadel of his kingdom, was the first step in His exaltation. (Form. Of Concord, part 2., chap. 9.)

> The Romanists teach that Christ went, while His body was in the grave, to that department of Hades (invisible world) which they call the Limbus Patrum, where the believers under the old dispensation were gathered, to preach the Gospel to them, and to take them with Him to the heaven He had prepared for them. (Cat. of the Coun. of Trent, part 1., art. 5.)

---

[591] Walvoord, J. F., Zuck, R. B., and Dallas Theological Seminary. (1983-c1985). *The Bible Knowledge Commentary: An Exposition of the Scriptures* (Revelation 20:13). Wheaton, IL: Victor Books.

In his being buried, and continuing under the power of death for a time. In the Creed commonly called the Apostles' Creed, and adopted by all the Churches, this last stage of the humiliation of Christ is expressed by the phrase, 'He descended into hell' (Hades, the invisible world). <u>This means precisely what our Confession affirms, that while the body of Jesus remained buried in the sepulcher his soul remained temporarily divorced from it in the unseen world of spirits."</u>[592]

This phrase, **"He descended into hell"** appeared in the fourth century and was derived slightly from Ephesians 4:9-10, Romans 10:7-9, and more specifically from 1 Peter 3:18-20.

> **Ephesians 4:9-10:** *"Now this expression, 'He ascended,' what does it mean except that He also descended into the lower parts of the earth? [10] He who descended is Himself also He who ascended far above all the heavens, that He might fill all things."*

Some believe that the phrase, *"descended into the lower parts of the earth"* makes reference only to Christ's descent from His heavenly throne to the earth (<u>Philippians 2:5-9</u>). It is probably better viewed as its literal meaning, His death and burial in the grave. We know Christ descended to Sheol/Hades (realm of the dead), and declared HIS VICTORY to demons who were confined there (Colossians 2:15; 1 Peter 3:18-20) (Sheol-Hebrew; Hades-Greek). This descent to Sheol/Hades does not support the view Jesus went to hell.

> **Romans 10:7-9:** *"... or 'Who will descend into the abyss?' (that is, to bring Christ up from the dead). [8] But what does it say? 'The word is near you, in your mouth and in your heart—that is, the word of faith which we are preaching, [9] that if you confess with your mouth Jesus as Lord, and believe in your heart that God raised Him from the dead, you shall be saved;'"*

> **1 Peter 3:18-20:** *"For Christ also died for sins once for all, the just for the unjust, in order that He might bring us to God, having been put to death in the flesh, but made alive in the spirit; [19] in which also <u>He went and made proclamation to the spirits now in prison, [20] who once were disobedient, when the patience of God kept waiting in the days of Noah, during the construction of the ark,</u> in which a few, that is, eight persons, were brought safely through the water."*
>
> [This verse will be discussed below.]

Other verses dealing with the concept of descending are as follows:

> **Matthew 12:40:** *"...for just as JONAH WAS THREE DAYS AND THREE NIGHTS IN THE BELLY OF THE SEA MONSTER, so shall the Son of Man be three days and three nights in <u>the heart of the earth</u>."*

> **Acts 2:24-25 and 27:** *"And God raised Him up again, putting an end to the agony of death, since it was impossible for Him to be held in its power. [25] 'For David says of Him,... [27]BECAUSE THOU WILT NOT ABANDON MY SOUL TO HADES, NOR ALLOW THY HOLY ONE TO UNDERGO DECAY.'"*

---

[592] Hodge, A., Hodge, C., and Hodge, A. (1996). *The Confession of Faith: With Questions for Theological Students and Bible Classes.* With an appendix on Presbyterianism by Charles Hodge. Index created by Christian Classics Foundation. (electronic ed. based on the 1992 Banner of Truth reprint.) (p. 146-147). Simpsonville SC: Christian Classics Foundation.

Summary and Application

Let's review the meaning of the term "Hades." The Greek term "Hades" means the "underworld" (i.e. place of those who have died). It does not exclusively mean a place of torment, but includes that:

> "HADĒS (αδης , (86)), <u>the region of departed spirits of the lost (but including the blessed dead in periods preceding the Ascension of Christ).</u> ... It corresponds to 'Sheol' in the O.T. In the A.V. [Authorized Version – also known as the King James Version] of the O.T. and N.T.<u>, it has been unhappily rendered 'hell,' e.g., Psa. 16:10; or 'the grave,' e.g. , Genesis 37:35; or 'the pit,' Numbers 16:30, 33 ;</u> in the N.T. the Revisers have always used the rendering 'Hades;' in the O.T. they have not been uniform in the translation, e.g. , in Isaiah 14:15, 'hell' ('Sheol'); usually they have 'Sheol' in the text and 'the grave' in the margin. It never denotes the grave, nor is it the permanent region of the lost; in point of time it is, for such, intermediate between decease and the doom of Gehenna.
>
> For the condition [of Hades] see Luke 16:23-31. The word is used four times in the Gospels, and always by the Lord, Matthew 11:23; 16:18; Luke 10:15; 16:23; it is used with reference to the soul of Christ, Acts 2:27, 31; Christ declares that He has the keys of it, Revelation 1:18; in Revelation 6:8 it is personified, with the signification of the temporary destiny of the doomed; it is to give up those who are therein, 20:13, and is to be cast into the lake of fire,...."[593]

Although Jesus is God and can go anywhere He wants, there is not a strong argument to support the claim Jesus descended into hell (i.e. when hell is defined as the eternal "lake of fire"). Note Hades itself will eventually be thrown into the *"lake of fire"* **Revelation 20:14**. There is no justification to claim Jesus underwent torment or punishment in Hades. In Hades "the righteous and the wicked are separated. The blessed dead are in that part of Hades called Paradise (Luke 23:43). They are also said to be in Abraham's bosom (Luke 16:22)"[594] and the unredeemed are in torment.

So what occurred after Jesus died on Good Friday? We know He preached to those in prison (1 Peter 3:19). There are two possibilities regarding His preaching to those in prison. The first possibility is that He went to the place of torment to preach to those in prison. Under that scenario one must understand Jesus was victorious over Hades and would not experience torment if He were there. The second possibility is that He preached to those in prison from His abode in Paradise. We know that Abraham was in a place of peace and comfort when he spoke to one in torment (Luke 16:22-30).

In conclusion, to determine where Jesus was after He died, we need only to look at His words. *Jesus, Himself stated that on the day He died He would be in Paradise* (i.e. the abode of God and the righteous).

> **Luke 23:39-43:** *"And one of the criminals who were hanged there was hurling abuse at Him, saying, 'Are You not the Christ? Save Yourself and us!'* [40] *But the other answered, and rebuking him said, 'Do you not even fear God, since you are under the same sentence of condemnation?* [41] *And we indeed justly, for we are receiving what we deserve for our deeds; but this man has done nothing wrong.'* [42] *And he was saying, 'Jesus,*

---

[593] Vine, W., and Bruce, F. (1981; Published in electronic form by Logos Research Systems, 1996). *Vine's Expository Dictionary of Old and New Testament Words* (p. 188). Old Tappan NJ: Revell.

[594] Easton. *Easton's* (electronic ed.).

remember me when You come in Your kingdom!' [43] *And He said to him, 'Truly I say to you, <u>today you shall be with Me in Paradise</u> .'"*

MATTHEW 28:1-17
(RESURRECTION)

*"Now after the Sabbath, as it began to dawn toward the first day of the week, Mary Magdalene and the other Mary came to look at the grave. ² And behold, a severe earthquake had occurred, for an angel of the Lord descended from heaven and came and rolled away the stone and sat upon it. ³ And his appearance was like lightning, and his garment as white as snow; ⁴ and the guards shook for fear of him, and became like dead men. ⁵ And the angel answered and said to the women, 'Do not be afraid; for I know that you are looking for Jesus who has been crucified. ⁶ He is not here, for He has risen, just as He said. Come, see the place where He was lying. ⁷ And go quickly and tell His disciples that He has risen from the dead; and behold, He is going before you into Galilee, there you will see Him; behold, I have told you.' ⁸ And they departed quickly from the tomb with fear and great joy and ran to report it to His disciples. ⁹ And behold, Jesus met them and greeted them. And they came up and took hold of His feet and worshiped Him. ¹⁰ Then Jesus *said to them, 'Do not be afraid; go and take word to My brethren to leave for Galilee , and there they shall see Me.'*

¹¹ Now while they were on their way, behold, some of the guard came into the city and reported to the chief priests all that had happened. ¹² And when they had assembled with the elders and counseled together, they gave a large sum of money to the soldiers, ¹³ and said, 'You are to say, His disciples came by night and stole Him away while we were asleep. ¹⁴ And if this should come to the governor's ears, we will win him over and keep you out of trouble.' ¹⁵ And they took the money and did as they had been instructed; and this story was widely spread among the Jews, and is to this day. ¹⁶But the eleven disciples proceeded to Galilee, to the mountain which Jesus had designated. ¹⁷ And when they saw Him, they worshiped Him; but some were doubtful."

Introduction

We are about to begin to study the hallmark of the Christian faith: THE BODILY RESURRECTION OF JESUS CHRIST!

> **1 Corinthians 15:3-4:** *"For I delivered to you as of <u>first importance</u> what I also received, that Christ died for our sins according to the Scriptures, ⁴ and that He was buried, and that <u>He was raised on the third day</u> according to the Scriptures,"*

> **Romans 1:4:** *"…who was declared the Son of God with power by the resurrection from the dead, according to the Spirit of holiness, Jesus Christ our Lord,…"*

To those who are converted by faith in Jesus Christ, His victory at the cross is the victory over death, the grave and the judgment to an eternity in hell.

> **Romans 5:12 -19:** *"Therefore, just as through one man sin entered into the world, and death through sin, and so death spread to all men, because all sinned — ¹³ for until the Law sin was in the world; but sin is not imputed when there is no law. ¹⁴ Nevertheless death reigned from Adam until Moses, even over those who had not sinned in the likeness of the offense of Adam, who is a type of Him who was to come. ¹⁵ But the free gift is not like the transgression. For if by the transgression of the one the many died, much more did the*

grace of God and the gift by the grace of the one Man, Jesus Christ, abound to the many. *[16] And the gift is not like that which came through the one who sinned; for on the one hand the judgment arose from one transgression resulting in condemnation, but on the other hand the free gift arose from many transgressions resulting in justification. [17] For if by the transgression of the one, death reigned through the one, much more those who receive the abundance of grace and of the gift of righteousness will reign in life through the One, Jesus Christ. [18] So then as through one transgression there resulted condemnation to all men, even so through one act of righteousness there resulted justification of life to all men. [19] For as through the one man's disobedience the many were made sinners, even so through the obedience of the One the many will be made righteous."*

When He rose from the dead, He was not a ghost or spirit. True Christianity speaks of the bodily resurrection of Christ.[595] Although the body was transformed to an eternal body that was able to appear

---

[595] For a more in-depth view on the doctrine of the bodily resurrection of Christ and believers, see the section of this outline just after Matthew 22:33. We know scripture teaches a body of flesh cannot live in heaven so God gives us a glorified body.

> **1 Corinthians 15:50-53:** *"Now I say this, brethren, <u>that flesh and blood cannot inherit the kingdom of God</u>; nor does the perishable inherit the imperishable. [51] Behold, I tell you a mystery; we shall not all sleep, <u>but we shall all be changed,</u> [52] in a moment, in the twinkling of an eye, at the last trumpet; for the trumpet will sound, and the dead will be raised imperishable, and we shall be changed. [53] For this perishable must put on the imperishable, and this mortal must put on immortality."*

View the above comments in light of 1 Corinthians 15 and Philippians 3.

> **1 Corinthians 15:40-44, 50-55:** *"There are also heavenly bodies and earthly bodies, but the glory of the heavenly is one, and the glory of the earthly is another. [41] There is one glory of the sun, and another glory of the moon, and another glory of the stars; for star differs from star in glory. [42] So also is the resurrection of the dead. It is sown a perishable body, it is raised an imperishable body; [43] it is sown in dishonor, it is raised in glory; it is sown in weakness, it is raised in power; [44] it is sown a natural body, it is raised a spiritual body....*
> *[50] Now I say this, brethren, that flesh and blood cannot inherit the kingdom of God; nor does the perishable inherit the imperishable. [51] Behold, I tell you a mystery; we shall not all sleep, but we shall all be changed, [52] in a moment, in the twinkling of an eye, at the last trumpet; for the trumpet will sound, and the dead will be raised imperishable, and we shall be changed. [53] For this perishable must put on the imperishable, and this mortal must put on immortality. [54] But when this perishable will have put on the imperishable, and this mortal will have put on immortality, then will come about the saying that is written, 'DEATH IS SWALLOWED UP in victory.' [55] 'O DEATH, WHERE IS YOUR VICTORY? O DEATH, WHERE IS YOUR STING?'"*

> **Philippians 3:20-21:** *"For our citizenship is in heaven, from which also we eagerly wait for a Savior, the Lord Jesus Christ; [21] <u>who will transform the body of our humble state into conformity with the body of His glory,</u> by the exertion of the power that He has even to subject all things to Himself."*

Sproul summarizes it this way: "However, just as Jesus returned from the grave with His body, albeit changed, so shall our present bodies be resurrected though changed. A body may change its state without thereby destroying its identity." Sproul, R. C. (1996, c1992). *Essential Truths of the Christian Faith*; #73. *THE LAST RESURRECTION*, Wheaton, Ill.: Tyndale House.

and disappear, it was His body. One could feel His flesh and bones. He still had nail holes in His hands and feet and He could eat food. MacArthur states that:

> "…from Jesus' post-resurrection appearances we get some idea of the greatness, power, and wonder of what our own resurrection bodies will be like. Jesus appeared and disappeared at will, reappearing again at another place far distant. He could go through walls or closed doors, and yet also could eat, drink, sit, talk, and be seen by those who He wanted to see Him. He was remarkably the same, yet even more remarkably different." [596]

A.A. Hodge explains the glorified body this way:

> "The very same bodies that are buried in the earth shall be raised and reunited to their souls—their identity preserved, although their qualities are changed. This is explicitly declared in Scripture: 'Our vile body is to be changed.' (Philippians 3:21.) 'This corruptible is to put on incorruption.' (1 Corinthians 15:53,54.) 'All that are in the graves shall hear His voice, and shall come forth.' John 5:28. 'They who are asleep, ... the dead in Christ shall rise.' (1 Thessalonians 4:13–17.) Our bodies are now members of Christ, and they are to be raised in a manner analogous to His resurrection, which we know to have been of His identical body by the print of the nails and of the spear. It was seen and handled for the space of forty days in order to establish this very fact. (Luke 24:39; Acts 1:3; 1 Corinthians 15:4.)…*There are many changes in the material elements and form of the human body between birth and death, and yet no one can for a moment doubt that the body remains one and the same throughout all.* There is no difficulty in believing, upon the authority of God's Word, that, in spite of the lapse of time and of all the changes, whether of matter or of form, it undergoes, the body of the resurrection will be in the same sense and to the same degree one with the body of death as the body of death is one with the body of birth…These changes will doubtless be very great. The body of the believer is to be made 'like unto Christ's glorious body.' Philippians 3:21 '…not a new body substituted for the old, but the old changed into the new.'" [597]

Jesus explains this Himself when the disciples mistakenly think they see His spirit:

> **Luke 24:36-43:** *"And while they were telling these things, He Himself stood in their midst. [37] But they were startled and frightened and thought that they were seeing a spirit. [38] And He said to them, 'Why are you troubled, and why do doubts arise in your hearts? [39] See My hands and My feet , that it is I Myself; touch Me and see, for a spirit does not have flesh and bones as you see that I have.' [40] [And when He had said this, He showed them His hands and His feet.] [41] And while they still could not believe it for joy and were marveling, He said to them, 'Have you anything here to eat?' [42] And they gave Him a piece of a broiled fish; [43] and He took it and ate it before them."*

There is no doctrine more hated by the Devil than the resurrection of Christ. It is at Christ's resurrection that the works of the Devil were destroyed!

---

[596] MacArthur, J. (1996, c1984). *1 Corinthians*. Includes indexes. (1 Corinthians 15:45). Chicago: Moody Press.

[597] Hodge, A. A., and Hodge, C. (1996). *The Confession of faith: With Questions for Theological Students and Bible Classes* (pp. 386–387). Simpsonville, SC: Christian Classics Foundation.

1 John 3:8: *"...The Son of God appeared for this purpose, that He might destroy the works of the devil."*

It is with great zeal that atheists and other non-Christians attack the Bible and the resurrection of Christ. They will go to great pains to find the slightest variations in a Gospel account and make a grandiose claim that there is a contradiction. Sure, there can be difficulties that require more than surface level study to understand, <u>but contradictions there are not!</u> The entire Bible is inspired by God.

2 Timothy 3:16: *"All Scripture is inspired by God and profitable for teaching, for reproof, for correction, for training in righteousness;...."*

God used men and their individual personalities to write His word, but understand that they did not write whatever they wanted, but rather what the Holy Spirit had them say:

2 Peter 1:21: *"...for no prophecy was ever made by an act of human will, but men moved by the Holy Spirit spoke from God."*

I am amazed unbelievers get so excited over little distinctions in the four Gospel accounts. They approach Scripture with the view that each Gospel account should be a photocopy of the other. I have been a trial attorney for many years. When I have a case that involves several witnesses to a criminal act, I receive multiple accounts of what transpired. If the witnesses are uninterested parties (i.e. just happened to be there) all the accounts prove true, but each witness will have his own distinctions, impressions and emphases to the crime. For example, one witness will have particularly noticed the clothes the suspect was wearing more than other facts. Another witness who was actually being threatened by a weapon, will report very exacting details regarding the weapon and the specific threat made, often to the neglect of other important events that were happening. When this happens, it appears one witness account is contradicting another. For me to get an accurate picture of the event, I will bring all the witnesses together. Once together, each witness explains his account and I begin to see how it all fits together and realize there was never a dispute about what happened. For example, say there was a holdup in which three men were working together to commit the crime. Witness 'A' gives an extensive written report about a single robber. Witness 'B's' written report mentions three robbers. So which is it, one robber or three? When I later asked witness 'A' "How many robbers were there?" He will say, "Three." I will then ask why he only mentioned one in his report. I will get a response something like this: "Even though there were three robbers, only the one guy asked me for money and I thought he is the guy the police would really be interested in, so that is why I wrote about him."

I conducted a demonstration of this phenomenon in my junior high Sunday school class. Unbeknownst to my class, I asked a couple of Sunday school teachers from a different class to drop into my class and view a short video about a mission trip. They also brought five boys from their class who just came in and stood quietly in my classroom. While the video was being shown, one of the visiting teachers did a few odd things. He took off his shoe like he was trying to get a rock out of it. He then banged the shoe a couple times against the TV. When the video was over, I handed out pieces of paper and pens to my class and asked them to write down what they saw. All nine students wrote almost exclusively about what they saw on the video. A couple may have mentioned the name of one of the teachers who dropped in. Since I had seen the video before, I discussed what was going on apart from what was on the video. My description appeared to be a complete contradiction to the other nine "eye witnesses." My report mentioned how strange the teacher acted when he hit the TV with his shoe. I also mentioned that five boys came with him and stood in the room. The skeptic would quickly turn to the fact that the other nine reports never mention the TV being hit by a shoe. Then the skeptic would howl that I was claiming five boys were standing in a small room and no one else saw them. The skeptic could only resolve this matter by deciding I was making up my facts because my report was not identical to the other nine. If you asked my nine students if there were five boys standing in our class, they would all acknowledge that there were. It is for this reason that it is intellectual dishonesty to call a different emphasis, a "conflict."

Although this is a weak human example, we must understand God can have one Gospel writer focus on a particular event and a separate writer show a different emphasis of the same event. Look at how some commentators describe the different emphasis of the person of Jesus in each of the Gospel accounts: Matthew shows Jesus as the <u>King</u>; Mark shows Jesus as the <u>Servant</u> who sacrificed Himself for mankind; Luke shows Jesus as the <u>Perfect Man</u>, and John reveals Jesus as the <u>Divine Son of God</u>. R.C. Sproul states,

> "Although Scripture came to us from the pens of human authors, the ultimate source of Scripture is God. That is why the prophets could preface their words by saying, 'Thus says the Lord.' The word inspiration also calls attention to the process by which the Holy Spirit superintended the production of Scripture. The Holy Spirit guided the human authors so that their words would be nothing less than the word of God. How God superintended the original writings of the Bible is not known. But inspiration does not mean that God dictated his messages to those who wrote the Bible. Rather, the Holy Spirit communicated through the human writers the very words of God."[598]

VERSE 1: *"Now after the Sabbath, as it began to dawn toward the first day of the week, Mary Magdalene and the other Mary came to look at the grave."*

> So we see that on Sunday *(the first day of the week)*, Jesus rose from the dead. Note, that for at least a few minutes there was darkness (John 20:1) as the dawn light was coming *"…It <u>began</u> to dawn."* Mary Magdalene and the other Mary came to the grave. Mark also mentions Salome was present (Mark 16:1). Luke tells us Joanna was there (Luke 24:10). We also know that the reason they came was to, *"look at the grave"* (Matthew 28:1) and they, *"bought spices, that they might come and anoint Him."* (Mark 16:1, Luke 24:1). Since they brought spices to anoint the body, they clearly did not come to see a resurrection. (See footnote below regarding these women.)[599]

---

[598] Sproul, R. C. (1992). *Essential truths of the Christian faith; #4 SPECIAL REVELATION AND THE BIBLE* Wheaton, IL: Tyndale House.

[599] The women were **Mary Magdalene** and *"the other Mary."* Both of these women were at the crucifixion (Matthew 27:55-56). <u>Mary Magdalene</u> is the woman, *"whom He had cast out seven demons"* (Mark 16:9). The "other Mary" is Mary the *mother* of Joses [Joseph] and James the Less (Mark 15:40 and 47) the wife of Clopas see Matthew 27:56; John 19:25. Although Matthew focuses on Mary Magdalene and the "other Mary," Scripture tells us that two other women were also there at that time. These women were Salome (Mark 16:1) and Joanna (Luke 24:10). "Salome was a sister of Mary, the Mother of Jesus (see Matthew 27:56; Mark 15:40; John 19:25), making her Jesus' aunt and James and John His [Jesus'] first cousins. MacArthur, J. (1989). *Matthew* (Matthew 27:55). Chicago: Moody Press." Joanna was…"one of several women, healed by Jesus, who assisted in maintaining the Lord's itinerant company. Her husband, Chuza, was a responsible official of Herod Antipas; whether in the household ('a steward of Herod's', NEB) or in government ('the chancellor', Moffatt) is uncertain (Luke. 8:1–3)." Wood, D. R. W., and Marshall, I. H. (1996). New Bible Dictionary (3rd ed.) (p. 588). Leicester, England; Downers Grove, Ill.: InterVarsity Press.

VERSE 2: *"And behold, a severe earthquake had occurred, for an angel of the Lord descended from heaven and came and rolled away the stone and sat upon it."*

A quick reading of this verse in comparison with the other Gospels could give the appearance of a contradiction in the story. I will show you what I mean. If you read Matthew 28:1-2 it says: *"… Mary Magdalene and the other Mary came to look at the grave. ² And behold, a severe earthquake had occurred, for an angel of the Lord descended from heaven and came and rolled away the stone and sat upon it."* Now if you read this from a perspective that things are always written in a linear-chronological manner, you would say (1) the women came to the grave and then, (2) there was an earthquake, (3) then the angel rolled away the stone. That chronology is incorrect. The stone was removed by the time they arrived. Look what John tells us in **John 20:1:** *"Now on the first day of the week Mary Magdalene *came early to the tomb, while it *was still dark, and *saw the stone already taken away from the tomb."* Luke also states the stone was rolled away before they arrived. **Luke 24:2:** *"And they found the stone rolled away from the tomb,…."* Mark likewise confirms this same point that the stone was already rolled away:

> **Mark 16:2-4:** *"And very early on the first day of the week, they *came to the tomb when the sun had risen. ³ And they were saying to one another, 'Who will roll away the stone for us from the entrance of the tomb?' ⁴ And looking up, they *saw that the stone had been rolled away, although it was extremely large."*

When you read from a cultural perspective that assumes events are always written chronologically, you end up making assumptions Matthew did not make. If you go back and carefully read Matthew 28:2 you will see Matthew <u>did not say</u> the earthquake and the removal of the stone occurred after they got there. **Matthew 28:1-2** says, *"… Mary Magdalene and the other Mary came to look at the grave. ² And behold, a severe earthquake <u>had occurred</u>, for an angel of the Lord descended from heaven and came and rolled away the stone and sat upon it."* Note that the earthquake <u>*had occurred.*</u> It did not say that it occurred while they were there.

We make the quick and erroneous assumption the women were there when the stone was rolled away because there is a description of the angel descending and the guard's reaction.

> **Matthew 28:2-4:** *"…an angel of the Lord descended from heaven and came and rolled away the stone and sat upon it. ³ And his appearance was like lightning, and his garment as white as snow; ⁴ and the guards shook for fear of him, and became like dead men."*

Without thinking of other possibilities, we assume the women witnessed this event. If the women did not see these events, how could they have been known? Could it be that the angel of the Lord told them later what had happened before they arrived? Although that is possible, there is a source of this information that has been ignored— the guards themselves. Scripture actually informs us the guards themselves told the chief priests, *"all that had happened"* when they were at the grave. Jump down to **Matthew 28:11:** *"Now while they were on their way, behold, some of the guard came into the city and reported to the chief priests all that had happened."* We know from the next verse that elders were then told what happened since they were called to a meeting to figure out a cover-up:

> **Matthew 28:12-15:** *"And when they had assembled with the elders and counseled together, they gave a large sum of money to the soldiers, ¹³ and said, 'You are to say, His disciples came by night and stole Him away while we*

were asleep. [14] And if this should come to the governor's ears, we will win him over and keep you out of trouble.' [15] And they took the money and did as they had been instructed; and this story was widely spread among the Jews, and is to this day."

I wonder if Joseph of Arimathea, as an elder, was at that meeting of the chief priests and elders. Is it possible Joseph heard the story first hand or possibly even later on from a fellow elder who was there? Being a member of the Council was very exclusive and Joseph was more than a mere member of the Council. He was a *"prominent"* member of the Council as set forth in **Mark 15:43:** *"Joseph of Arimathea came, <u>a prominent member of the Council</u>,...."*

We do not read that the stone was rolled away so Jesus could get out of the tomb. Although it is possible Jesus came out from the grave opening, nowhere in Scripture does it say that. Remember that after His resurrection, Jesus was not subject to physical boundaries (i.e. **John 20:26:** *"After eight days His disciples were again inside, and Thomas with them. Jesus came, the doors having been shut, and stood in their midst and said, 'Peace be with you.'"*). We do know the stone was rolled away allowing the women who remained to go into the tomb, at the angel's request, to see Jesus was not in there.

> **Matthew 28:5-6:** *"And the angel answered and said to the women, 'Do not be afraid; for I know that you are looking for Jesus who has been crucified. [6] He is not here, for He has risen, just as He said. <u>Come, see the place where He was lying.</u>'"*

Now that we understand the stone was rolled away before the women arrived, we need to realize all the women did not react to that event in the same way. We read from John that Mary Magdalene, upon seeing the stone removed, immediately left the group and took off running to find Peter and John.

> **John 20:1-3:** *"Now on the first day of the week Mary Magdalene *came early to the tomb, while it *was still dark, and *saw the stone already taken away from the tomb. [2] And so she *ran and *came to Simon Peter, and to the other disciple whom Jesus loved, and *said to them, 'They have taken away the Lord out of the tomb, and we do not know where they have laid Him.' [3] Peter therefore went forth, and the other disciple, and they were going to the tomb."*

This point is very important. Some nonbelievers try to claim a conflict in the resurrection accounts because of the story of Mary Magdalene in John 20:1-18. They mistakenly do not realize that she left the group to find Peter and John before the angel spoke to the remaining women about Jesus' resurrection. Note that some may want to argue that Mary Magdalene was at the angel's announcement based on Luke 24:10. One must realize Luke is recording a condensed version of the story involving the women who went to the tomb. Luke's condensed version does not even mention John running with Peter to the tomb. It is at the end of the story (Luke 24:10) that Luke identifies the women who went to the tomb and eventually met with the disciples. The reason all the women tell the apostles (Luke 24:10) is that, by this time, they all have had an encounter with Jesus. Mary Magdalene was the first to encounter Jesus (Mark 16:9). The rest of the women were second to encounter Him. These women were returning from the tomb carrying the information they received from the angel when Jesus appeared to them (Matthew 28:8-10).

The point is that despite the condensed nature of the resurrection accounts, no one gives us more information about Mary Magdalene than John. He gives the most detail regarding her specific actions. Rules of Biblical interpretation require that the *general* be interpreted in light of the *specific*, and thus we look to John on the issue of Mary Magdalene's actions. (See John 20:1-18.) Here is a summary of the events of the resurrection.

- John tells us Mary Magdalene saw the stone was moved and immediately left the group to tell Peter and John (John 20:1-2).
- When she gets back, she tells Peter and John the stone was rolled away and she thinks the Lord's body has been stolen (John 20:2).
- Peter and John take off for the tomb and see it is empty. Mary was following Peter and John to the tomb (John 20:3, 11-13).
- Peter and John leave the tomb and return to their homes with Peter marveling at what he saw (John 20:2-10 and Luke 24:12).
- Peter and John have left the tomb by the time Mary Magdalene arrives. It is after she is back at the tomb alone that Jesus first appears to her (John 20:11-17). She then takes off to tell the disciples she has seen the Lord (John 20:18).
- Jesus then appears to the rest of the women as they continue home from their first visit to the tomb on resurrection day (Matthew 28:8-10). Jesus tells the women to go and report to the disciples (Matthew 28:10). Now we see why in Luke 24:8-10 all the women are mentioned as together telling the disciples what they knew. The disciples did not believe them and thought it all nonsense (Mark 16:9-11; Luke 24:9-11).

Now that you have a summary of the events, let us rewind back to the point where Mary sees the stone rolled away and leaves. Also at that time, the rest of the women stay and are told by an angel that Jesus has risen from the dead. This announcement is set forth below in Matthew 28:3-6.

VERSES 3-7: *"And his appearance was like lightning, and his garment as white as snow; 4 and the guards shook for fear of him, and became like dead men. 5 And the angel answered and said to the women, 'Do not be afraid; for I know that you are looking for Jesus who has been crucified. 6 He is not here, for He has risen, just as He said. Come, see the place where He was lying. 7Go quickly and tell His disciples that He has risen from the dead; and behold, He is going ahead of you into Galilee, there you will see Him; behold, I have told you.'"*

Have you ever had the experience of being in a thunderstorm and a stroke of lighting hits closer than expected? Imagine being these guards. They are literally working the "graveyard shift." It is still dark and they are spending the night guarding a "dead man." Suddenly, there is an earthquake and descending from heaven is an angel, appearing like lightning and clothed in pure white! No wonder these guards were scared half to death!—(*"shook for fear of him, and became like dead men"* v. 3.). We will read below in Matthew 28:11-15 how the guards were bribed by the chief priests into not telling the people their story.

As mentioned in Matthew 28:2, the first angel sighted was the one sitting on the rolled-away stone. This sighting could well have been described by the guards. We next see an angel speaking to the remaining women and telling them in verses 5 and 6, *"...Do not be afraid; for I know that you are looking for Jesus who has been crucified. 6 He is not here, for He has risen, just as He said. Come, see the place where He was lying."* There are two angels who speak to the women inside the tomb:

> **Luke 24:3-8:** *"...but when they entered, they did not find the body of the Lord Jesus. 4 And it happened that while they were perplexed about this, behold, two*

men suddenly stood near them in dazzling apparel; [5] and as the women were terrified and bowed their faces to the ground, the men said to them, 'Why do you seek the living One among the dead? [6] He is not here, but He has risen. Remember how He spoke to you while He was still in Galilee, [7] saying that the Son of Man must be delivered into the hands of sinful men, and be crucified, and the third day rise again.' [8] And they remembered His words,"

From Mark we get the impression the women were again spoken to in the tomb. This angel seems to be reiterating what they had been told, but he also gives them additional instructions about what to tell the disciples.

Mark 16:5-8: *"And entering the tomb, they saw a young man sitting at the right, wearing a white robe; and they were amazed. [6] And he *said to them, 'Do not be amazed; you are looking for Jesus the Nazarene, who has been crucified. He has risen; He is not here; behold, here is the place where they laid Him. [7] But go, tell His disciples and Peter, He is going before you into Galilee; there you will see Him, just as He said to you.' [8] And they went out and fled from the tomb, for trembling and astonishment had gripped them; and they said nothing to anyone, for they were afraid."*

We read in John 20:2-10 (below) that while the remaining women get the message from the angel, Mary Magdalene reports to Peter and John someone must have taken His body.

John 20:2-10: *" And so she *ran and *came to Simon Peter, and to the other disciple whom Jesus loved, and *said to them, 'They have taken away the Lord out of the tomb, and we do not know where they have laid Him.' [3] Peter therefore went forth, and the other disciple, and they were going to the tomb. [4] And the two were running together; and the other disciple ran ahead faster than Peter, and came to the tomb first; [5] and stooping and looking in, he *saw the linen wrappings lying there; but he did not go in. [6] Simon Peter therefore also *came, following him, and entered the tomb; and he *beheld the linen wrappings lying there, [7] and the face-cloth, which had been on His head, not lying with the linen wrappings, but rolled up in a place by itself. [8] So the other disciple who had first come to the tomb entered then also, and he saw and believed. [9] For as yet they did not understand the Scripture, that He must rise again from the dead. [10] So the disciples went away again to their own homes."*

From the above description we read Mary Magdalene, Peter and John all run to the tomb. John gets there first. John does not enter the tomb but looks in from its entrance. John sees the burial cloth (John 20:4-5). Peter then arrives at the tomb and heads right in (v.6), and finds Jesus' grave clothes. John notes the face cloth that had been put on Jesus' head was not with the other burial clothes, but was all rolled up at a different place in the tomb (v.6-7). John then enters the tomb and sees the grave clothes. The grave clothes are another evidence of the resurrection. As Matthew Henry stated:

"Robbers of tombs have been known to take away the clothes and leave the body; but none … ever took away the body and left the clothes, especially when it was fine linen and new, Mark.15:46. Anyone would rather choose to carry a dead body in its clothes than naked. Or, if those that were supposed to have stolen it would have left the grave-clothes behind, yet it cannot be supposed they should find leisure to fold up the linen."[600]

John and Peter do not run out and tell everyone what they saw, but instead remain stunned and head back to their own homes. Note that we find out more about Peter's reaction from **Luke 24:12**: *"...he went away to his home, marveling at that which had happened."*

When John and Peter took off running to the tomb, Mary Magdalene followed them. She arrived at the tomb after Peter and John left it and returned to their homes. Mary then enters the tomb, probably for the first time. She is met by two angels who do not speak to her. Realize that she is not given any message from the angels, unlike the other women who were there earlier.

> **John 20:11-12:** *"But Mary was standing outside the tomb weeping; and so, as she wept, she stooped and looked into the tomb; [12]and she *beheld two angels in white sitting, one at the head, and one at the feet, where the body of Jesus had been lying."*

Mary Magdalene is confused, upset, and weeping when the angels finally speak to her:

> **John 20:13-18:** *"And they said to her, 'Woman, why are you weeping?' She said to them, 'Because they have taken away my Lord, and I do not know where they have laid Him.' [14]When she had said this, she turned around, and beheld Jesus standing there, and did not know that it was Jesus. [15]Jesus *said to her, 'Woman, why are you weeping? Whom are you seeking?' Supposing Him to be the gardener, she *said to Him, 'Sir, if you have carried Him away, tell me where you have laid Him, and I will take Him away.' [16]Jesus *said to her, 'Mary!' She *turned and *said to Him in Hebrew, 'Rabboni!' (which means, Teacher). [17]Jesus *said to her, 'Stop clinging to Me, for I have not yet ascended to the Father; but go to My brethren , and say to them, I ascend to My Father and your Father , and My God and your God .' [18]Mary Magdalene *came, announcing to the disciples, 'I have seen the Lord,' and that He had said these things to her."*

In reference to John 20:17, J. C. Ryle states:

> "There is something deeply touching in those simple words, 'my brothers'...weak frail, erring as the disciples were, Jesus still calls them 'brothers'...Glorious as He was in himself - a conqueror over death and hell, and the grave – the Son of God...He still calls his disciples 'brothers'." [601]

The first person Jesus reveals Himself to after His resurrection is Mary Magdalene. This is further proof of the gospel account. Men of the culture of that time would not have written a story with such an awesome event being first revealed to a woman rather than to one of His male disciples who had followed Him for three years.

---

[600] Henry, M. (1996, c1991). *Matthew Henry's Commentary on the Whole Bible: Complete and Unabridged in One Volume* (John. 20:1). Peabody: Hendrickson.

[601] *Matthew* / Ryle, J.C. p. 292 (Expository Thoughts on the Gospels)(Crossways Classic Commentaries: v.1)

We read in John 20:18 that Mary Magdalene went out from her encounter with Jesus to find the disciples. While she is doing that, Jesus appears to the other women on the road. (See Matthew 28:8-10 below.)

VERSES 8-15: *"And they left the tomb quickly with fear and great joy and ran to report it to His disciples. ⁹And behold, Jesus met them and greeted them. And they came up and took hold of His feet and worshiped Him. ¹⁰Then Jesus said to them, 'Do not be afraid; go and take word to My brethren to leave for Galilee, and there they will see Me.' ¹¹Now while they were on their way, some of the guard came into the city and reported to the chief priests all that had happened. ¹²And when they had assembled with the elders and consulted together, they gave a large sum of money to the soldiers, ¹³and said, 'You are to say, His disciples came by night and stole Him away while we were asleep. ¹⁴And if this should come to the governor's ears, we will win him over and keep you out of trouble.' ¹⁵And they took the money and did as they had been instructed; and this story was widely spread among the Jews, and is to this day."*

While these women were heading to the city, some of the guards had already arrived and reported to the chief priests what had happened. The chief priests and the elders got together and told the guards to tell people that the disciples stole the body while the guards slept (v.13). This bribery-based conspiracy between the guards and the religious leaders was quickly created for damage control. I have found in my own work as a trial attorney that if someone on the other side is trying to cook up a story, the quicker he comes up with the lie, the dumber it will sound. This is what happened to the religious leaders and the guards. They needed to get a story out quickly and they needed to keep the guards from telling anyone what they saw. Think about the story they came up with (i.e. the guards were instructed, *"...to say, 'His disciples came by night and stole Him away while we were asleep."* [v.13]). There is an obvious problem with that story: How would the guards know that the body was stolen by the disciples if the guards were asleep? It is like the young child who tells his parents that his little brother did not have his eyes closed during prayer time. The parent will then ask, "How do you know that your little brother's eyes were not closed?" The child will respond, "While we were praying I saw that he had …..um."

The guards did not have a lot of bargaining power since the penalty for a guard losing the person in his custody was death (Acts 27:42, see also Acts 12:19 and 16:27).[602] The religious leaders told the guards they would talk to the governor and keep them out of trouble (i.e. from being killed) if they just stuck to the story about being asleep and the disciples stealing the body. To provide the guards an added bonus, they gave them, *"a large sum of money,"* which could be taken back to the rest of the guard to guarantee their silence. When I say, "rest of the guards," we need to realize not all of the guards came to the chief priests, but just some representatives. Note in verse 11 it says, *"some of the guard."*

> **Matthew 28:11:** *"Now while they were on their way, behold, some of the guard came into the city and reported to the chief priests all that had happened."*

---

[602] "The concern of the soldiers that the prisoners might escape is understandable…. Roman law held guards personally responsible for their charges, and those who allowed prisoners to escape could pay with their own lives…." Polhill, J. B. (1995). *Vol. 26 Acts.* The New American Commentary (p. 529). Nashville: Broadman and Holman Publishers.

One would think that after hearing the guards' story, the religious leaders would start to believe that Jesus was the Messiah. One must not underestimate the power of hate and unbelief. They did not care about the facts; they only wanted to stop anyone else from believing in Christ. Their entire agenda was about maintaining their power and control over people. Jesus speaks prophetically of this type of person when He tells the story of the Rich Man and Lazarus. At the end of that story, Jesus says in <u>**Luke 16:31:**</u> *"But he said to him, If they do not listen to Moses and the Prophets, <u>neither will they be persuaded if someone rises from the dead</u>."*

It is important to note that despite the talk of the disciples stealing the body, we never read of the religious leaders trying to prove it. They knew the "stolen-body" story never happened. MacArthur states,

> "In the first place, if their story had been true, the Jewish leaders could surely have found the stolen body with little difficulty. <u>They had the resources of hundreds of men, including military men, and even the power of Rome behind them in this instance.</u> It would have been utterly impossible for eleven unlearned and unsophisticated men to have succeeded in eluding a search for any length of time. <u>The simplest way to have disproved the resurrection was to locate the body and put it on display for all the world to see. Yet there is no evidence that the Sanhedrin even attempted to find the body they claimed the disciples had stolen.</u>" [603]

When Mary Magdalene finally caught up with the disciples, she told them of her encounter with Jesus. The response of the disciples was disbelief.

> **Mark 16:9-11:** *"Now after He had risen early on the first day of the week, He first appeared to Mary Magdalene, from whom He had cast out seven demons. [10] She went and reported to those who had been with Him, while they were mourning and weeping. [11] And when they heard that He was alive, and had been seen by her, they refused to believe it."*

Look again at another proof of the gospel. Scripture does not hide the failures and warts of its heroes. The gospels do not portray these men (at this time) as great examples of faith in the resurrection. Rather, to their shame, it shows their lack of belief. Look how Luke describes the disciples' response to the women telling them of the resurrection: *"And these words appeared to them as nonsense, and they would not believe them."* **Luke 24:11.** This further shows that there was no plan by the disciples to steal the body because they were not looking forward to Jesus' resurrection, even though He told them on other occasions He would rise.

Additional Post-Resurrection Appearances in Scripture

Jesus revealed Himself first to Mary and then to the other women on Sunday (Resurrection Day). He then continued to reveal Himself to others. Here is a chronology that Scripture shows us:

1. Jesus appeared to Peter on Sunday (Luke 24:34; 1 Corinthians 15:5).

> **Luke 24:34:** *"...saying, 'The Lord has really risen, and has appeared to Simon.'"*

2. Jesus appeared to two disciples on the road to Emmaus on Sunday (Luke 24:13-35; cf. Mark 16:12).

---

[603] MacArthur, J. F., Jr. (1985). *Matthew.* MacArthur New Testament Commentary (p. 249). Chicago: Moody Press.

Luke 24:13-35: *"And behold, two of them were going that very day to a village named Emmaus, which was about seven miles from Jerusalem. [14] And they were conversing with each other about all these things which had taken place. [15] And it came about that while they were conversing and discussing, Jesus Himself approached, and began traveling with them. [16] But their eyes were prevented from recognizing Him. [17] And He said to them, 'What are these words that you are exchanging with one another as you are walking?' And they stood still, looking sad. [18] And one of them, named Cleopas, answered and said to Him, 'Are You the only one visiting Jerusalem and unaware of the things which have happened here in these days?' [19] And He said to them, 'What things?' And they said to Him, 'The things about Jesus the Nazarene, who was a prophet mighty in deed and word in the sight of God and all the people, [20] and how the chief priests and our rulers delivered Him up to the sentence of death, and crucified Him. [21] But we were hoping that it was He who was going to redeem Israel. Indeed, besides all this, it is the third day since these things happened. [22] But also some women among us amazed us. When they were at the tomb early in the morning, [23] and did not find His body, they came, saying that they had also seen a vision of angels, who said that He was alive. [24] And some of those who were with us went to the tomb and found it just exactly as the women also had said; but Him they did not see.' [25] And He said to them, 'O foolish men and slow of heart to believe in all that the prophets have spoken ! [26] Was it not necessary for the Christ to suffer these things and to enter into His glory?' [27] And beginning with Moses and with all the prophets, He explained to them the things concerning Himself in all the Scriptures. [28] And they approached the village where they were going, and He acted as though He would go farther. [29] And they urged Him, saying, 'Stay with us, for it is getting toward evening, and the day is now nearly over.' And He went in to stay with them. [30] And it came about that when He had reclined at the table with them, He took the bread and blessed it, and breaking it, He began giving it to them. [31] And their eyes were opened and they recognized Him; and He vanished from their sight. [32] And they said to one another, 'Were not our hearts burning within us while He was speaking to us on the road, while He was explaining the Scriptures to us? ' [33] And they arose that very hour and returned to Jerusalem, and found gathered together the eleven and those who were with them, [34] saying, 'The Lord has really risen, and has appeared to Simon.' [35] And they began to relate their experiences on the road and how He was recognized by them in the breaking of the bread."*

3. Jesus appeared to ten of His disciples as they were together on the evening of the resurrection (Sunday) (Luke 24:36-49). Notice that Jesus has them touch His hands and feet to show He had a bodily resurrection. John also mentions that He showed them His side, which is where the spear was thrust in (John 20:20, John 19:34). Jesus also ate food in front of them, proving the bodily resurrection (Luke 24:42-43); (See also John 20:19-23.).

Luke 24:36-49: *"And while they were telling these things, He Himself stood in their midst. [37] But they were startled and frightened and thought that they were seeing a spirit. [38] And He said to them, 'Why are you troubled, and why do doubts arise in your hearts? [39] See My hands and My feet, that it is I Myself; touch Me and see, for a spirit does not have flesh and bones as you see that I* have.' *40* [*And when He had said this, He showed them His hands and His feet.*] *41* *And while they still could not believe it for joy and were marveling, He said to them, 'Have you anything here to eat?'* *42* *And they gave Him a piece of a broiled fish;* *43* *and He took it and ate it before them.*

44 *Now He said to them, 'These are My words which I spoke to you while I was still with you, that all things which are written about Me in the Law of Moses and the Prophets and the Psalms must be fulfilled.'* *45* *Then He opened their minds to understand the Scriptures,* *46* *and He said to them, 'Thus it is written, that the Christ should suffer and rise again from the dead the third day;* *47* *and that repentance for forgiveness of sins should be proclaimed in His name to all the nations, beginning from Jerusalem .* *48* *You are witnesses of these things.* *49* *And behold, I am sending forth the promise of My Father upon you; but you are to stay in the city until you are clothed with power from on high.'"*

Here is John's account of that event.

John 20:19-23: *"When therefore it was evening, on that day, the first day of the week, and when the doors were shut where the disciples were, for fear of the Jews, Jesus came and stood in their midst, and *said to them, 'Peace be with you.'* *20* *And when He had said this, He showed them both His hands and His side. The disciples therefore rejoiced when they saw the Lord.* *21* *Jesus therefore said to them again, 'Peace be with you; as the Father has sent Me, I also send you.'* *22* *And when He had said this, He breathed on them, and *said to them, 'Receive the Holy Spirit.* *23* *If you forgive the sins of any, their sins have been forgiven them; if you retain the sins of any, they have been retained .'"*

(Note: Thomas was not with them at that time—see the next verse below—John 20:24.)

4.   Eight days later Jesus appeared to the eleven (that is, all the disciples) (John 20:26-31). This is where Thomas saw the risen Lord.

John 20:24-29: *"But Thomas, one of the twelve, called Didymus, was not with them when Jesus came.* *25* *The other disciples therefore were saying to him, 'We have seen the Lord!' But he said to them, 'Unless I shall see in His hands the imprint of the nails, and put my finger into the place of the nails, and put my hand into His side, I will not believe.'*

26 *And after eight days again His disciples were inside, and Thomas with them. Jesus *came, the doors having been shut, and stood in their midst, and said, 'Peace be with you.'* *27* *Then He *said to Thomas, 'Reach here your finger, and see My hands; and reach here your hand, and put it into My side; and be not unbelieving, but believing.'* *28* *Thomas answered and said to Him, 'My Lord and my God!'* *29* *Jesus *said to him, 'Because you have seen Me, have you believed? Blessed are they who did not see, and yet believed.'"*

5.   Jesus then appeared to the seven disciples fishing on the Sea of Galilee (a.k.a. at the Sea of Tiberias) (John 21:1).

John 21:1-14: *"After these things Jesus manifested Himself again to the disciples at the Sea of Tiberias, and He manifested Himself in this way.* *2* *There were together Simon Peter, and Thomas called Didymus, and Nathanael of Cana in Galilee, and the sons of Zebedee, and two others of His disciples.* *3*

Simon Peter said to them, 'I am going fishing.' They said to him, 'We will also come with you.' They went out, and got into the boat; and that night they caught nothing. ⁴ But when the day was now breaking, Jesus stood on the beach; yet the disciples did not know that it was Jesus. ⁵ Jesus therefore *said to them, 'Children, you do not have any fish, do you?' They answered Him, 'No.' ⁶ And He said to them, 'Cast the net on the right-hand side of the boat, and you will find a catch.' They cast therefore, and then they were not able to haul it in because of the great number of fish. ⁷ That disciple therefore whom Jesus loved *said to Peter, 'It is the Lord.' And so when Simon Peter heard that it was the Lord, he put his outer garment on (for he was stripped for work), and threw himself into the sea. ⁸ But the other disciples came in the little boat, for they were not far from the land, but about one hundred yards away, dragging the net full of fish. ⁹ And so when they got out upon the land, they *saw a charcoal fire already laid, and fish placed on it, and bread. ¹⁰ Jesus *said to them, 'Bring some of the fish which you have now caught.' ¹¹ Simon Peter went up, and drew the net to land, full of large fish, a hundred and fifty-three; and although there were so many, the net was not torn.

¹² Jesus *said to them, 'Come and have breakfast.' None of the disciples ventured to question Him, 'Who are You?' knowing that it was the Lord. ¹³ Jesus *came and *took the bread, and *gave them, and the fish likewise. ¹⁴ This is now the third time that Jesus was manifested to the disciples, after He was raised from the dead."

6. He then "appeared to <u>more than five hundred brethren at one time</u>" (1 Corinthians 15:6.).

    <u>**1 Corinthians 15:3-6:**</u> *"For I delivered to you as of first importance what I also received, that Christ died for our sins according to the Scriptures, ⁴ and that He was buried, and that He was raised on the third day according to the Scriptures, ⁵ and that He appeared to Cephas, then to the twelve. ⁶ After that He appeared to more than five hundred brethren at one time, most of whom remain until now, but some have fallen asleep;…"*

7. Jesus appeared to James, who was the brother of Jesus. This is the James that wrote the Book of James.

    <u>**1 Corinthians 15:7:**</u> *"…then He appeared to James,…."*

8. Jesus also appeared to all even disciples in Galilee as we read in Matthew. At this event Jesus gave them the Great Commission.

    <u>**Matthew 28:16-20:**</u> *"But the eleven disciples proceeded to Galilee, to the mountain which Jesus had designated. ¹⁷ And when they saw Him, they worshiped Him; but some were doubtful. ¹⁸ And Jesus came up and spoke to them, saying, 'All authority has been given to Me in heaven and on earth. ¹⁹ Go therefore and make disciples of all the nations, baptizing them in the name of the Father and the Son and the Holy Spirit, ²⁰ teaching them to observe all that I commanded you; and lo, I am with you always, even to the end of the age .'"*

9. Jesus appeared to all the disciples in Jerusalem 40 days later.

    <u>**Acts 1:3-11:**</u> *"To these He also presented Himself alive, after His suffering, by many convincing proofs, appearing to them over a period of forty days, and*

speaking of the things concerning the kingdom of God. ⁴ And gathering them together, He commanded them not to leave Jerusalem, but to wait for what the Father had promised, 'Which,' He said, 'you heard of from Me; ⁵ for John baptized with water, but you shall be baptized with the Holy Spirit not many days from now.'

⁶ And so when they had come together, they were asking Him, saying, 'Lord, is it at this time You are restoring the kingdom to Israel?' ⁷ He said to them, 'It is not for you to know times or epochs which the Father has fixed by His own authority; ⁸ but you shall receive power when the Holy Spirit has come upon you; and you shall be My witnesses both in Jerusalem, and in all Judea and Samaria, and even to the remotest part of the earth.'

⁹ And after He had said these things, He was lifted up while they were looking on, and a cloud received Him out of their sight. ¹⁰ And as they were gazing intently into the sky while He was departing, behold, two men in white clothing stood beside them; ¹¹ and they also said, 'Men of Galilee, why do you stand looking into the sky? This Jesus, who has been taken up from you into heaven, will come in just the same way as you have watched Him go into heaven.'"

10. Jesus appeared to Paul.

> **1 Corinthians 15:8-9:** *"...and last of all, as it were to one untimely born, He appeared to me also. ⁹ For I am the least of the apostles, who am not fit to be called an apostle, because I persecuted the church of God."*

VERSES 16-17: *"But the eleven disciples proceeded to Galilee, to the mountain which Jesus had designated. ¹⁷ And when they saw Him, they worshiped Him; but some were doubtful."*

The proof of the resurrection is enormous...unless you do not want to believe it. As a prosecutor, I have been amazed at times when a juror refuses to truly balance the evidence. If the juror wants to reach a 'not guilty' conclusion, the person will go so far as to even ignore a confession given by the defendant. I recall a murder trial that I prosecuted. The evidence included a taped confession. Even though the jury verdict ended up guilty, I later found out one juror was holding up the process and wanted to acquit. It took a great effort for the other 11 jurors to convince her the evidence pointed no other direction but guilty. Later on, after the trial was over, this particular juror engaged in writing intimate letters, sending gifts and visiting the convicted murderer in prison. She had become so emotionally connected to him during trial she had a very hard time just looking at the facts honestly and objectively. This same mentality can exist today. If one does not want the resurrection to be true, it does not matter how solid the evidence is for it, a person will ignore the evidence and create his own version of truth. The reason the non-Christian dismisses the evidence of the resurrection typically boils down to three main reasons:

(1) He is intimately connected to the worldly system, and thus, does not
    want to repent of his sin;
(2) He does not want to be accountable to God and,
(3) In his pride, he naively thinks he can escape the evidence of the
    resurrected Christ, by just ignoring God.

Simon Greenleaf, who was a famous nineteenth-century professor of law at Harvard, wrote,

> "All that Christianity asks of men ... is, that they would be consistent with themselves; that they would treat its evidences as they treat the evidence of other things; and that they would try and judge its actors and witnesses, as they deal with their fellow men, when testifying to human affairs and actions, in human tribunals. ... The result ... will be an undoubting conviction of their integrity, ability and truth" [604]

Sir Edward Clarke wrote:

> "As a lawyer I have made a prolonged study of the evidences for the events of the first Easter Day. To me the evidence is conclusive, and over and over again in the High Court I have secured the verdict on evidence not nearly so compelling. Inference follows on evidence, and a truthful witness is always artless and disdains effect. The Gospel evidence for the resurrection is of this class, and as a lawyer I accept it unreservedly as the testimony of truthful men to facts they were able to substantiate." [605]

Summary and Application

The first sermon of the Church after Pentecost was about the resurrection, and it should be so today:

> **Acts 2:22-24:** *"Men of Israel, listen to these words: Jesus the Nazarene, a man attested to you by God with miracles and wonders and signs which God performed through Him in your midst, just as you yourselves know— [23] this Man, delivered up by the predetermined plan and foreknowledge of God, you nailed to a cross by the hands of godless men and put Him to death. [24] And God raised Him up again, putting an end to the agony of death, since it was impossible for Him to be held in its power."*

Jesus asks you the same question He asked Martha after her brother Lazarus had been dead for four days.

> **John 11:25-26:** *"Jesus said to her, 'I am the resurrection and the life; he who believes in Me shall live even if he dies, [26] and everyone who lives and believes in Me shall never die. Do you believe this?'"*

No matter how much one may want to avoid it, there will come a day when *everyone will believe the resurrection* and bow before the feet of Jesus. Some will be doing it from heaven and others from hell. Which will it be for you? Repent and turn in faith to the Lord Jesus Christ.

> **Philippians 2:8-11:** *"And being found in appearance as a man, He humbled Himself by becoming obedient to the point of death, even death on a cross. [9] Therefore also God highly exalted Him, and bestowed on Him the name which is above every name, [10] that at the name of Jesus every knee should bow, of those who are in heaven, and on earth, and under the earth, [11] and that every*

---

[604] *Testimony of the Evangelists, Examined by the Rules of Evidence Administered in Courts of Justice* [Grand Rapids: Baker, 1965; reprint], p. 46.

[605] J. R. W. Stott, *Basic Christianity* [Downers Grove, IL: InterVarsity, 1971], p. 47.

tongue should confess that Jesus Christ is Lord, to the glory of God the Father."

What type of faith must one have to be saved? The faith must be in the finished work of Jesus' substitutionary death on the cross. One must realize that he cannot do anything to help pay the penalty of his sin. Jesus alone, on the cross, has paid the price *once*[606] for our sins and saved His redeemed from judgment and hell.

> **Romans 10:9-13:** *"...that if you confess with your mouth Jesus as Lord, and believe in your heart that God raised Him from the dead, you shall be saved;* [10] *for with the heart man believes, resulting in righteousness, and with the mouth he confesses, resulting in salvation.* [11] *For the Scripture says, 'Whoever believes in Him will not be disappointed.'* [12] *For there is no distinction between Jew and Greek; for the same Lord is Lord of all, abounding in riches for all who call upon Him;* [13] *for 'Whoever will call upon the name of the Lord will be saved.'"*

---

[606] Jesus does not remain on the cross as Roman Catholicism exhibits on its crucifix. He paid the price once on the cross and the sacrifice does not need to be paid over and over again. **Hebrews 9:27–28** states, *"And inasmuch as it is appointed for men to die once and after this comes judgment, so Christ also, having been offered once to bear the sins of many, will appear a second time for salvation without reference to sin, to those who eagerly await Him."*

> **Hebrews 7:24–27:** *"...but Jesus, on the other hand, because He continues forever, holds His priesthood permanently. Therefore He is able also to save forever those who draw near to God through Him, since He always lives to make intercession for them. For it was fitting for us to have such a high priest, holy, innocent, undefiled, separated from sinners and exalted above the heavens; who does not need daily, like those high priests, to offer up sacrifices, first for His own sins and then for the sins of the people, because this He did once for all when He offered up Himself."*

Romanism teaches the perpetual sacrifice:

> Catechism of the Catholic Church 1367: "The sacrifice of Christ and the sacrifice of the Eucharist are *one single sacrifice*: "The victim is one and the same: the same now offers through the ministry of priests, who then offered himself on the cross; only the manner of offering is different." "And since in this divine sacrifice which is celebrated in the Mass, the same Christ who offered himself once in a bloody manner on the altar of the cross is contained and is offered in an unbloody manner. . . this sacrifice is truly propitiatory."

R.C. Sproul explains Romanism's mass and the crucifix as follows: "The sacrifice of the Mass "participated" in the death of Christ on Calvary. The body of Christ was broken again, and His blood was again poured out. Roman Catholic imagery and theology kept Christ on the cross, even as the crucifix hangs at the front of the church. This picture the Reformers rejected. Jesus' atoning death was completed after the hours of suffering on Calvary. That Jesus was raised from the dead showed that His atoning work was complete forever." Sproul, R. (1994). *Before the face of God: Book 4: A Daily Guide for Living from Ephesians, Hebrews, and James* (electronic ed.) (p. 254). Grand Rapids: Baker Book House; Ligonier Ministries.

MATTHEW 28:18-20
(THE GREAT COMMISSION)

"And Jesus came up and spoke to them, saying, 'All authority has been given to Me in heaven and on earth. [19] Go therefore and make disciples of all the nations, baptizing them in the name of the Father and the Son and the Holy Spirit, [20] teaching them to observe all that I commanded you; and lo, I am with you always, even to the end of the age .'"

Introduction

This section sets forth The Great Commission. The Great Commission is often preached from the pulpit, but very neglected in practice. The average committed man at church will be happy to get together with other guys to hammer and saw on a church building project, but be unavailable to carry the *sword of the Spirit* by going door-to-door to evangelize. Many of the dedicated women in the church are content to bring food to a potluck, yet they are unavailable when it comes to public evangelism. This occurs for many reasons, running the spectrum from being inadequately trained, to the worst scenario, not really being a Christian in the first place.[607] We should take seriously the words of the English aristocrat C.T. Studd (1860-1931) who liquidated his wealth and his life to spread the gospel to the nations. Late in his life he said:

> "Too long have we been waiting for one another to begin! The time for waiting is past! … Should such men as we fear? …before the sleepy, lukewarm, faithless, namby-pamby Christian world, we will dare to trust our God,…. We will a thousand times sooner die trusting only in our God than live trusting in man. And when we come to this position the battle is already won, and the end of the glorious campaign in sight. We will have the real Holiness of God, not the sickly stuff of talk and dainty words and pretty thoughts; we will have the Masculine Holiness, one of daring faith and works for Jesus Christ."[608]

VERSE 18: *"And Jesus came up and spoke to them, saying, 'All authority has been given to Me in heaven and on earth.'"*

Listen to the extreme magnitude of this statement! It is a statement that cannot be made by anyone except Almighty God, *"All authority has been given to Me in heaven and on earth."* One either believes this or does not.

The statement of ultimate power and authority is set out right before He commands us to, *"make disciples of all the nations…."* The fact He has ultimate and complete control of all things should annihilate any fears or misgivings we have about going out to, *"make disciples of all the nations…."* Look at the verses below regarding this authority:

---

[607] Regarding false converts or the self-deceived review the comments in the section on Matthew 7:21-23.

[608] Grubb, Norman, 2001; *C.T. Studd: Cricketer and Pioneer* p. 120-121 (CLC Publications)

Matthew 11:27: *"All things have been handed over to Me by My Father; ...."*

John 3:35: *"The Father loves the Son and has given all things into His hand."*

When Jesus speaks of, *"All authority,"* He means, as God, He controls all that was created, and all things are subject to His judgment. He has all authority to forgive sins and grant eternal life, as well as all authority to condemn to eternal damnation. Look at the following:

- Jesus is the Creator of everything that exists:
  Colossians 1:16: *"For by Him all things were created, both in the heavens and on earth, visible and invisible, whether thrones or dominions or rulers or authorities—all things have been created through Him and for Him."*

- Jesus is the Judge of everything that exists:
  John 5:22: *"For not even the Father judges anyone, but He has given all judgment to the Son,...."*

- Jesus has all authority to forgive sins:
  Matthew 9:6: *"But so that you may know that the Son of Man has authority on earth to forgive sins."*

- Jesus is the Resurrection, having all authority to give eternal life to His own:
  John 11:25: *"Jesus said to her, 'I am the resurrection and the life; he who believes in Me will live even if he dies....'"*

  John 6:40: *"For this is the will of My Father, that everyone who beholds the Son and believes in Him will have eternal life, and I Myself will raise him up on the last day."*

- Jesus has all authority to condemn to hell:
  Matthew 25:31–32,41: *"But when the <u>Son of Man comes in His glory, and all the angels with Him, then He will sit on His glorious throne.</u> All the nations will be gathered before Him; and He will separate them from one another, as the shepherd separates the sheep from the goats;....*
  41Then He will also say to those on His left, <u>'Depart from Me, accursed ones, into the eternal fire which has been prepared for the devil and his angels;....'"</u>

Our Lord told us ahead of time that He is sending us out as defenseless sheep among ravenous wolves that will rip us apart. Yet He is in such ultimate control that He tells us that we are not to be concerned or fearful of being maligned, hated, disowned by family, arrested, beaten, or even murdered (e.g. Matthew 10:25, 21-22, 17-19, 28).[609]

---

[609] Please go to the comments in the section for Matthew 10:38-39 to read the story of missionary John Paton. In 1858 he and his wife sailed to the New Hebrides islands in the South Pacific (they are now called the Vanuatu Islands). It is a story of listening to Christ instead of the wisdom of man, or one's own fleshly desires.

Matthew 10:16–39: *"Behold, I send you out as sheep in the midst of wolves; so be shrewd as serpents and innocent as doves. ¹⁷ But beware of men, for they will hand you over to the courts and scourge you in their synagogues; ¹⁸ and you will even be brought before governors and kings for My sake, as a testimony to them and to the Gentiles. ¹⁹ But when they hand you over, do not worry about how or what you are to say; for it will be given you in that hour what you are to say. ²⁰ For it is not you who speak, but it is the Spirit of your Father who speaks in you. ²¹Brother will betray brother to death, and a father his child; and children will rise up against parents and cause them to be put to death. ²² You will be hated by all because of My name, but it is the one who has endured to the end who will be saved. ²³ But whenever they persecute you in one city, flee to the next; for truly I say to you, you will not finish going through the cities of Israel until the Son of Man comes. ²⁴ A disciple is not above his teacher, nor a slave above his master. ²⁵ It is enough for the disciple that he become like his teacher, and the slave like his master. If they have called the head of the house Beelzebul, how much more will they malign the members of his household! ² ⁶Therefore do not fear them, for there is nothing concealed that will not be revealed, or hidden that will not be known. ²⁷ What I tell you in the darkness, speak in the light; and what you hear whispered in your ear, proclaim upon the housetops. ²⁸ <u>Do not fear those who kill the body but are unable to kill the soul; but rather fear Him who is able to destroy both soul and body in hell.</u> ²⁹Are not two sparrows sold for a cent? And yet not one of them will fall to the ground apart from your Father. ³⁰But the very hairs of your head are all numbered. ³¹ So do not fear; you are more valuable than many sparrows .³² Therefore everyone who confesses Me before men, I will also confess him before My Father who is in heaven. ³³ But whoever denies Me before men, I will also deny him before My Father who is in heaven. ³⁴ Do not think that I came to bring peace on the earth; I did not come to bring peace, but a sword. ³⁵ For I came to set a man against his father, and a daughter against her mother, and a daughter-in-law against her mother-in-law; ³⁶ and a man's enemies will be the members of his household. ³⁷ He who loves father or mother more than Me is not worthy of Me; and he who loves son or daughter more than Me is not worthy of Me. ³⁸ And he who does not take his cross and follow after Me is not worthy of Me. ³⁹ He who has found his life will lose it, and he who has lost his life for My sake will find it."*

The reality is many modern U.S. evangelicals will appear bold when talking about *standing up for Christ*, but cower when confronted with a *costly stand* for Him. I watched as a church quashed a very fruitful mission project for the youth in a risky area to assure no youth would get hurt and specifically that the church would not lose donations or get sued. (Donations? Sued? Property loss *or* reaching the lost?) A couple of weeks later, during the Sunday service, the same church was singing a praise song about its unwavering devotion to Christ that contained the following words: *"If this life I lose, I will follow you."*[610] A. W. Tozer put it well when he said tongue-in-cheek: "Christians don't tell lies, they sing them." We must encourage each other that the standard is scripture and not society.

---

[610] *I Will Follow* by Chris Tomlin. For more on *risk* see John Piper's comments later in this section.

Hebrews 10:34: *"For you showed sympathy to the prisoners and <u>accepted joyfully the seizure of your property</u>, knowing that you have for yourselves a better possession and a lasting one."*

The unspoken view in much of the church is that, "I am more than willing to send a check to the mission field, but I am not willing to let Christ send me." This is tragic, and a denial of the faith. I can already hear the disdain by some for the previous sentence (i.e. that it is *a denial of the faith*). The offended will proudly tell you how they stand for the faith and immediately begin reciting orthodox tenants of the faith they claim to believe. They do not realize, "*...the kingdom of God does not consist in words but in power.*" **1 Corinthians 4:20.** They also forget the demons *fearfully* believe the orthodox tenants of the faith ... *they just do not obey them.*

James 2:19–20: *"You believe that God is one. You do well; the demons also believe, and shudder.* [20] *But are you willing to recognize, you foolish fellow, that faith without works is useless?"*

Many are those who are content to raise their hands during worship or to get out their notepad for the sermon, but are not willing to obey the commands of Christ. Why are they comfortable this way? The answer is simple—this is the acceptable standard for most of the modern church. It is acceptable to state your love for Christ, sing a praise song, pay a tithe and give a reverential nod to His commands, yet all the while neglecting to obey them. This may be acceptable for a church membership/leadership, but it is not the Christianity Christ sets forth when He said:

John 14:15: *"If you love Me, you will keep My commandments."*

I have been involved with evangelism for more than 40 years and I write this note in hopes that my descendants might learn from my experiences. Specifically, I believe there are two lessons to keep in mind when engaging in true evangelism. The first lesson to learn is to not be surprised at the fierceness of opposition you will face when you are involved in *true evangelism.* [611] The attacks will occur from both inside and outside the visible church. The most discouraging attacks will be from those within the church (and possibly even from church leadership). Sometimes it may be false-brethren (cf. Galatians 2:4). Don't be discouraged; remember that the Lord gave us

---

[611] When I say true evangelism, I mean the proclamation of the true gospel which Paul makes clear will be an offense to the unbeliever and many times will result in ridicule and persecution. Biblically, a mission trip is first and foremost the *proclamation of the gospel*. Unfortunately this is not the case in the modern church in which a mission trip focuses on building repair/construction or some other social need or issue. By resorting to social needs instead of presenting the Gospel, one will more likely be commended by others and not criticized. Instead of warning others on how to escape the judgment to come, many churches are a religious version of "the peace corps." Often they will combine their social project with a kiddie program to pretend that we are being obedient to The Great Commission. [Yes, *God definitely wants us to reach children with the gospel and I often help with kids' evangelism programs!*] My point is that I have observed adults and young people in the church who want to avoid the ridicule and persecution that comes from public evangelism to their peers, by helping with kids programs. If you doubt me, ask yourself how many will show up to help for a "vacation Bible school" as compared to those who show up for a time of "door-to-door evangelism." It must be remembered that each day, tens of thousands of people enter eternity in hell having left this earth with *a full stomach and adequate housing*. We must first share the Gospel with people since salvation for their eternal soul is their greatest need. Then, alongside that, we meet the needs of food, water, housing, medical, educational and justice, as a natural outflow of the Gospel—not a substitute for it.

Judas as the example of *the false* functioning (with great camouflage) among the elect. Other times it may be spiritually immature brothers/sisters who are leading the attack. You need to forgive all and go on. Do not give the devil a foothold by being arrogant. Remember that you too regret some of your own unscriptural or fleshly decisions that have hindered the gospel. Also remember that in the Lord you can be "strong and courageous."

> **Joshua 1:9:** *"Have I not commanded you? Be strong and courageous! Do not tremble or be dismayed, for the Lord your God is with you wherever you go."*

Do not become distracted by their comments, criticisms and slanders. Paul himself experienced the call by God to effective service while simultaneously facing strong opposition by others: *"...for a wide door for effective service has opened to me, and there are many adversaries."* **1 Corinthians 16:9.** Understand that in most cases, you will never satisfy your detractors by trying to answer all their *concerns.* It becomes a shell-game of sorts, if you answer one question well, you will be rewarded with two new *concerns* demanded to be addressed. Seriously, do not waste a lot of time discussing their complaints, but graciously stay focused on the call you have been given (Matthew 28:19-20).[612] Remember that in the end, you serve and answer to an audience of one ... the Lord. Despite the disappointment and discouragement, do not let your heart be troubled because there is a great peace that the Holy Spirit will give to those who are obedient to the will of God.

The story is told of a Christian young man who was busy evangelizing his community. He would speak of the judgment of hell, repentance, Christ's resurrection and salvation only by faith in Christ's death on the cross as the payment for sin. This did not settle well with a proud church elder who told the young man that his "negative message" was giving the church a "bad name." He went on to say, "You should tell people to *ask Jesus into their heart* and then leave it at that!" The church elder could see the young man was clearly unpersuaded. The elder became angrier and pointed his finger at the young man and said, "You have set back evangelism in this community by 10 years!" The young man dropped his head and said, "I am very sorry to hear that — I was hoping to set it back 2,000 years."

J. C. Ryle addresses the issue of complainers in the church clearly when he stated:
> "The spirit of these narrow-minded fault-finders is unhappily all too common. Their followers and successors are to be found in every part of Christ's visible church. There is never any lack of people who decry what they call 'extremes' in religion, and are incessantly recommending what they term 'moderation' in the service of Christ. If someone devotes time, money and affection to the pursuit of worldly things, they do not blame him. If he gives himself up to the service of money, pleasure or politics, they find no fault. But if the same person devotes himself and all he has to Christ, they can scarcely find words to express their sense of his folly. 'He is beside himself.' 'He is out of his mind.' 'He is a fanatic.' 'He is an enthusiast.' 'He is too righteous.' 'He is an extremist.' In short, they

---

[612] **Nehemiah 6:2–4:** *"...then Sanballat and Geshem sent a message to me, saying, "Come, let us meet together at Chephirim in the plain of Ono." But they were planning to harm me. [3] So I sent messengers to them, saying, "I am doing a great work and I cannot come down. Why should the work stop while I leave it and come down to you?" [4] They sent messages to me four times in this manner, and I answered them in the same way."*

regard it as 'waste.' Let charges like these not disturb us if we hear them made against us because we strive to serve Christ. Let us bear them patiently, and remember that they are as old as Christianity itself. Let us pity those who make such charges against believers. They show plainly that they have no sense of obligation to Christ. A cold heart makes a slow hand. Once a person understands the sinfulness of sin and the mercy of Christ in dying for them, they will never think anything too good or too costly to give to Christ. They will rather feel, 'How can I repay the Lord for all his goodness to me?' (Psalm 116:12). They will fear wasting their time, talents, money, affections on the things of this world. They will not be afraid of wasting them on the Saviour. They will fear going to extremes about business, money, politics or pleasure, but will not be afraid of doing too much for Christ." [613]

The second lesson to learn, is that deep down, most of those in the church pews do not really want any part of suffering or persecution for the sake of the gospel. To avoid this persecution, they default from the clear commands regarding evangelism and discipleship and create their own user-friendly version of evangelism. I see the excuse called *friendship evangelism* is the technique of choice for most Christians who are either untrained, fearful, immature, or false-christians within the church. *Friendship evangelism*, in its simplest form, means you act real nice to someone so that over time he will trust you and like you. After you have his attention, *some year* down the road [hopefully before either of you die, move away, or he decides to end the friendship] you will have impressed him so much he will ask you why you are so *nice and happy*. You then tell him it is because you are a Christian and then you either invite him to church or tell him he can be *happy too* if he *asks Jesus into his heart*. Obviously there are different slants on this, but the unspoken technique remains the same: I am holding back the truth of the Gospel until someone is so impressed with me that he will listen to me. When this cowardly view is espoused, it is often supported with the deep saying, *"Preach the gospel at all times; when necessary use words."* Not only does this statement have no basis in scripture, it is almost always wrongfully attributed to Francis of Assisi. Biographer Mark Galli authored the book **Francis of Assisi and His World** and he points out that, "...no biography written [about Francis] within the first 200 years of his death contains the saying. It's not likely that a pithy quote like this would have been missed by his earliest disciples." [614] Obviously scripture teaches that all believers are to live godly lives before unbelievers, but a godly life is to be lived out of love for Christ and not to escape the responsibility of telling others the truth of the gospel. "Good News can no more be communicated by deeds than can the nightly news." [615] This *silent preaching of the gospel* is a denial of the scriptural mandate to preach with words! God has chosen the foolishness of preaching to bring people to the knowledge of Him.

> **1 Corinthians 1:21:** *"For since in the wisdom of God the world through its wisdom did not come to know God, God was well-pleased through the foolishness of the message preached to save those who believe."*

---

[613] Ryle, J. C. (1993). *Mark*. Crossway Classic Commentaries (pp. 220–221). Wheaton, IL: Crossway Books.

[614] See *Speak the Gospel* by Mark Galli, *Christianity Today*, post 5/21/2009.

[615] Ibid

Romans 10:13–15: *"...for Whoever will call on the name of the Lord will be saved. [14] How then will they call on Him in whom they have not believed? How will they believe in Him whom they have not heard? And how will they hear without a preacher? [15] How will they preach unless they are sent? Just as it is written, 'How beautiful are the feet of those who bring good news of good things!'"*

One writer points out that in scripture, the gospel is spread through proclamation. You really need to look up these verses and see this fact: Matthew 4:23, 9:35, 11:5, 24:14, 26:13; Mark 1:14, 13:10, 14:9, 16:15; Luke 9:6, 20:1, 3:18, 8:1, 4:15, 43, 16:16; Acts 8:12, 25, 40, 10:36, 14:7, 21, 15:7, 16:10; Romans 1:15, 10:15, 15:20,16:25; 1 Corinthians 1:17, 9:14-18, 15:1; 2 Corinthians 2:12, 8:18, 10:16, 11:4; Galatians 1:8-9, 11; 2:2, 3:8, 4:13; Ephesians 6:19; Colossians 1:23; 1 Thessalonians 1:5; 2:2, 9; 1 Peter 4:6; Hebrew 4:2.

The true gospel informs the friend, enemy, family member or stranger you just met, <u>that he is a sinner for whom hell awaits unless he repents and believes in Christ's atoning death on the Cross as the only basis for him to be forgiven</u> (see comment for Matthew 5:17-20 on how to accurately share the gospel). Understand that when you do this (via conversation, gospel tract, etc.) the *friendship evangelism* people will berate you for *turning people away* and being *unloving*. They have this viewpoint because they are ultimately concerned about how they appear in public and not how they appear through the eyes of Christ.

I have had many meaningful conversations about the gospel with complete strangers. If you simply talk to them, you find most people are very concerned about what happens to them after they die. Maybe you struggle with talking to people – no problem, just give out high-quality tracts that <u>accurately</u> state the gospel. Hand them out to the clerk at the check-out or drive-through or wherever you go. After you do it, you will wonder why you were so disobedient in the past.

I cannot think of anything more unloving than knowing the only truth for deliverance from eternal hell and not telling another about it because he might be offended. Let me provide you an example:

> Let us say that I am your neighbor and it is about 1:30 a.m. and I see your house is on fire. I know if I go over and pound on your door yelling and screaming I will disturb your family's sleep and the neighborhood will wonder who is being so obnoxious in the middle of the night. To protect my image of being a good guy — who is not extreme, I just call the fire department. They arrive 15 minutes later. The firemen then break into the house and you barely survive. Unfortunately, the firemen were just a little too late to save your children who are 7, 3 and 6 months. They were burned to death along with your wife. What will you think of me when you find out that I was aware of the extreme danger the family was in 15 minutes before help arrived … *and said nothing.* You will not dismiss my lack of warning when I explain that I was surprised that the fire spread so fast, and that I thought you had more time. You will not accept my defense that I did not want to look like some neighborhood wacko yelling and screaming at 1:30 in the morning.

The story above represents the fallacy of *friendship evangelism.* Scripture does not tell me to withhold the Gospel from others until I have proved myself either winsome, cute or trusted enough to earn the right to tell him. We are commanded to go and tell the truth in love. The saving message of the Cross stands on the merits of Christ, not me. D. Martin Lloyd-Jones stated: "Evangelism must start with the holiness of God, the sinfulness of man, the demands of the law, and the eternal consequences of evil." [616]

Many church attenders will be happy to quote John 3:16 to you, but they act like they have never read Jesus' words that were recorded a mere 20 verses later:

> **John 3:36:** *"He who believes in the Son has eternal life; but he who does not obey the Son will not see life, but <u>the wrath of God abides on him.</u>"*

We would do well to warn others of the wrath of God abiding on them. To simply tell a person "God loves him" is true, but in his darkened understanding of God, he misinterprets that to mean God accepts him as he continues to live in an unrepentant state of disbelief.

The comments in this section are not about legalism. Good works or trying hard to obey will not save a person in any way, shape, or form. It is equally true that a person *who has been saved* by God's grace will engage in good works and seek to obey Christ. MacArthur states it this way:

> "Good works are certainly not the *cause* of our election. They are not *grounds* for justification. They are not in any sense the *basis* for our salvation. But they are the inevitable *evidence* of it. If we are truly 'His workmanship,' if He chose us and sovereignly prepared good works that we should walk in them—then there is no way God's elect can live an earthly life devoid of obedience to Jesus Christ. To suppose such a possibility is to attack the sovereignty and omnipotence of the One who chose us so that we might obey Jesus Christ."[617]

In summary, keep a correct perspective in reference to the fear of man compared to the fear of God. Realize that the day will come when all mankind will fear the Living God and bow before His majesty and authority:

> **Philippians 2:9–11:** *"For this reason also, God highly exalted Him, and bestowed on Him the name which is above every name, ¹⁰ so that at the name of Jesus every knee will bow, of those who are in heaven and on earth and under the earth, ¹¹ and that every tongue will confess that Jesus Christ is Lord, to the glory of God the Father."*

The point to take away from Matthew 28:18 is that our Lord is in complete control of ALL THINGS. Since He has ABSOLUTE AUTHORITY, we have no need to fear man when going out to spread the Gospel. Remember, *"the best of men are but men at best."*[618] Scripture sets forth the fact of man's frailty:

> **Isaiah 2:22:** *"Stop regarding man, whose breath of life is in his nostrils; For why should he be esteemed?"*

---

[616] Lloyd-Jones, Martin *Studies in the Sermon on the Mount"* (See more of Lloyd-Jones'comments on this subject set out in the comment section of Matthew 5:27-30 of this commentary.)

[617] MacArthur, J. (1993). *Ashamed of the Gospel: When the Church Becomes Like the World* (p. 169). Wheaton, Ill.: Crossway Books.

[618] The proverb was first recorded in John Aubrey's Brief Lives (1877), as a saying of General John Lambert (1619-84). Manser, Martin H. *The Facts On File Dictionary of Proverbs* p. 22.

John Piper writes in his book, *Don't Waste Your Life*, a section on what our view of risk and danger should be in service to God. He points out that risk includes the potential loss of money, reputation, health, life and even *endangering other people* (p. 79). Piper goes on to say:

"Why is there such a thing as risk? Because there is such a thing as ignorance. If there were no ignorance there would be no risk. Risk is possible because we don't know how things will turn out. This means that God can take no risks! He knows the outcome of all His choices before they happen....[b]ut not so with us. We are not God, we are ignorant. We don't know what will happen tomorrow. He does not tell us in detail what He intends to do tomorrow or five years from now. Evidently God intends for us to live and act in ignorance and in uncertainty about the outcome of our actions.... Therefore, risk is woven into the fabric of our finite lives. We cannot avoid risk even if we want to. Ignorance and uncertainty about tomorrow is our native air. All of our plans for tomorrow's activities can be shattered by a thousand unknowns whether we stay at home under the covers or ride the freeways. One of my aims is to explode the myth of safety and to somehow deliver you from the enchantment of security. Because it's a mirage. It doesn't exist. Every direction you turn there are unknowns and things beyond your control.... The way I hope to explode the myth of safety and to disenchant you with the mirage of security is simply to go to the Bible and show that it is right to risk for the cause of Christ, ...and not to is to waste your life."[619]

Piper then points to the Apostle Paul as an example. Paul was told by the Holy Spirit *"in every city that imprisonment and afflictions await me."* Read about those tribulations in 2 Corinthians 11:24-28. Piper concludes by stating;

"Every day [Paul] risked his life for the cause of God.... He had two choices: waste his life or live with risk. And He answered this choice clearly: **Acts 20:24:** *"But I do not consider my life of any account as dear to myself, so that I may finish my course and the ministry which I received from the Lord Jesus, to testify solemnly of the gospel of the grace of God."*

MacArthur states the following about persecution and fear of death:

"The worst that can happen to a believer suffering unjustly is death, and that is the best that can happen because death means the complete and final end of all sins. If the Christian is armed with the goal of being delivered from sin, and that goal is achieved through his death, the threat and experience of death is precious (cf. Romans 7:5,18; 1 Corinthians 1:21; 15:42,49). Moreover, the greatest weapon that the enemy has against the Christian, the threat of death, is not effective."[620]

---

[619] Piper, John, *"Don't Waste Your Life"* p. 80-81 (Crossway Books, 2003).

[620] *The MacArthur Study Bible*. 1997 (J. MacArthur, Jr., Ed.) (electronic ed.) (1 Peter 4:1). Nashville, TN: Word Pub.

One summed up this concept of *safety* and our service to God well when he said: "A man of God, in the will of God, *is immortal* until his work on earth is done." [621]

VERSE 19 (first part of the verse): *"Go therefore and make disciples of all the nations...."*

It is clear we are to *go* make disciples. Where are we to go? The answer is clear; we are to go throughout the entire world. **Mark 16:15** states, **"And He said to them, 'Go into all the world and preach the gospel to all creation.'"** I have heard many a pastor comfort the congregation by downplaying this command via inferring that if they are being good people on the job and serving in the church, they are doing all the Lord expects. The pastor will often conclude by saying that, "we need people to stay here to make money to send others; after all, *we can't all go.*" We can't? It is more accurate to say that we choose not to go. Yes, it is true, you are to be a good witness where you are planted (that assumes you are actually witnessing—which is rarely the case) but that does not excuse you from going out. Nowhere does scripture tell us that *only* certain people are supposed to make money to pay for missions and only certain others are the ones to go. Whether it is long or short-term, near or far, we are all to go and help others to go!

Another line you will hear from the religious while they question/discourage you from going out is that: *"There is plenty of work to do right here in our community. Why do you need to go to _____ (fill in the blank)?"* If the questioners were busy doing real evangelism in their community, that *work* they are *so concerned* about would have been done long ago. The point is clear, Jesus tells us to go, *and go we must*, whether it makes sense to family or so-called church people. The martyr Jim Elliot wrote of his call to the Quichuas Indians in South America despite the counter-calls by many church people who said it was too risky:

> "Consider the call from the Throne above, 'Go ye,' and from round about, 'Come over and help us,' and even the call from the damned souls below, 'Send Lazarus to my brothers, that they come not to this place.' Impelled, then, by these voices, I dare not stay home while Quichuas perish. So what if the well-fed church in the homeland needs stirring? They have the Scriptures, Moses and the Prophets, and a whole lot more. Their condemnation is written on their bank books and in the dust on their Bible covers. American believers have sold their lives to the service of Mammon, and God has His rightful way of dealing with those who succumb to the spirit of Laodicea."[622]

---

[621] *The Handwriting on the Wall: secrets from the prophecies of Daniel.* p.127 1992 (David Jeremiah) Thomas Nelson

[622] Elliot, Elisabeth, 1979, *Shadow of the Almighty: The Life and Testament of Jim Elliot*, p. 132 HarperCollins. (See Extra note below).

Extra note: Jim Elliot makes reference to different Bible verses in the quote above. See (a)-(f) below:

a. "to Throne above, 'Go ye,'"
Derived from **Matthew 28:18-20** (AV): **"Go ye therefore, and teach all nations, baptizing them in the name of the Father, and of the Son, and of the Holy Ghost: [20] Teaching them to observe all things whatsoever I have commanded you: and, lo, I am with you alway, even unto the end of the world. Amen."**

[Note continued on the next page.]

    b.   "...from round about, 'Come over and help us,'"

        Derived from <u>**Acts 16:9**</u>: *"A vision appeared to Paul in the night: a man of Macedonia was standing and appealing to him, and saying, <u>'Come over to Macedonia and help us.'"</u>*

    c.   "even the call from the damned souls below, 'Send Lazarus to my brothers, that they come not to this place.'"

        Derived from <u>**Luke 16:23–31**</u>: *"In Hades he lifted up his eyes, being in torment, and saw Abraham far away and Lazarus in his bosom. 24 And he cried out and said, 'Father Abraham, have mercy on me, and send Lazarus so that he may dip the tip of his finger in water and cool off my tongue, for I am in agony in this flame.' 25 But Abraham said, 'Child, remember that during your life you received your good things, and likewise Lazarus bad things; but now he is being comforted here, and you are in agony. 26 And besides all this, between us and you there is a great chasm fixed, so that those who wish to come over from here to you will not be able, and that none may cross over from there to us.' 27 <u>"And he said, 'Then I beg you, father, that you send him to my father's house—</u> 28 <u>for I have five brothers—in order that he may warn them, so that they will not also come to this place of torment.' 29 "But Abraham said, 'They have Moses and the Prophets; let them hear them.' 30</u> But he said, 'No, father Abraham, but if someone goes to them from the dead, they will repent!' 31 But he said to him, 'If they do not listen to Moses and the Prophets, they will not be persuaded even if someone rises from the dead.'"*

    d)   "...They have the Scriptures, Moses and the Prophets,..."
        See Luke 16:29 above.

    e)   "American believers have sold their lives to the service of Mammon..."

        Derived from <u>**Luke 16:13 (AV)**</u> *"No servant can serve two masters: for either he will hate the one, and love the other; or else he will hold to the one, and despise the other. <u>Ye cannot serve God and mammon."</u>*

    f)   "His rightful way of dealing with those who succumb to the spirit of Laodicea."

        Derived from <u>**Revelation 3:14–15:**</u> *"To the angel of the <u>church in Laodicea</u> write: The Amen, the faithful and true Witness, the Beginning of the creation of God, says this: 15 'I know your deeds, that you are neither cold nor hot; I wish that you were cold or hot. 16 So because you are lukewarm, and neither hot nor cold, I will spit you out of My mouth. 17 <u>Because you say, "I am rich, and have become wealthy, and have need of nothing," and you do not know that you are wretched and miserable and poor and blind and naked,</u> 18 I advise you to buy from Me gold refined by fire so that you may become rich, and white garments so that you may clothe yourself, and that the shame of your nakedness will not be revealed; and eye salve to anoint your eyes so that you may see. 19 Those whom I love, I reprove and discipline; therefore be zealous and repent.'"*

[Note ended.]

As you grow in Christ, your love for Christ will give you a vision much bigger than your little area of life. You will truly develop a progressing heart for missions similar to the seven expanding steps below:

Your heart will stir for those who do not know Christ. The reason your heart stirs is due to the fact that you really believe that the unsaved are heading to a fiery hell for all eternity.

> **Revelation 20:11–15:** *"Then I saw a great white throne and Him who sat upon it, from whose presence earth and heaven fled away, and no place was found for them. ¹² And I saw the dead, the great and the small, standing before the throne, and books were opened; and another book was opened, which is the book of life; and the dead were judged from the things which were written in the books, according to their deeds. ¹³ And the sea gave up the dead which were in it, and death and Hades gave up the dead which were in them; and they were judged, every one of them according to their deeds. ¹⁴ Then death and Hades were thrown into the lake of fire. This is the second death, the lake of fire. ¹⁵ And if anyone's name was not found written in the book of life, he was thrown into the lake of fire."*

1) You will have a heart for those serving on the mission field.

> **Colossians 2:5:** *"For even though I am absent in body, nevertheless I am with you in spirit, rejoicing to see your good discipline and the stability of your faith in Christ."*

2) Your heart will skip when you hear on Sunday morning that someone is giving a mission report. Those without a heart for missions will roll their eyes and think, "what a bore", or that the missionary just wants their money:

> **Acts 14:27:** *"When they had arrived and gathered the church together, they began to report all things that God had done with them and how He had opened a door of faith to the Gentiles."*

3) You will look for ways to help missionaries with their work and serve them:

> **Philippians 4:16–18:** *"...for even in Thessalonica you sent a gift more than once for my needs. ¹⁷ Not that I seek the gift itself, but I seek for the profit which increases to your account. ¹⁸ But I have received everything in full and have an abundance; I am amply supplied, having received from Epaphroditus what you have sent, a fragrant aroma, an acceptable sacrifice, well-pleasing to God."*

4) You will pray for those who are persecuted for the gospel:

> **1 Corinthians 12:26:** *"And if one member suffers, all the members suffer with it; if one member is honored, all the members rejoice with it."*

> **Colossians 4:18:** *"I, Paul, write this greeting with my own hand. Remember my imprisonment….."*

5) You will pray for the Lord to add workers to the mission field:

> **Matthew 9:37–38:** *"Then He said to His disciples, 'The harvest is plentiful, but the workers are few. ³⁸ Therefore beseech the Lord of the harvest to send out workers into His harvest.'"*

6)   Finally, you will go yourself. It may be nearby or far away; it may be long-term or very short-term; it may be a big work or a small work; *but you will go and continue to go!* On the mission you will experience trials, tribulations, persecution along with spiritual fruit and GREAT JOY!

Now that we have established we are to go, what are we to accomplish? Jesus said we are to *"make disciples of all the nations"* (not simply build and repair stuff). A disciple is a learner/follower. We are to make disciples of Jesus Christ and not of ourselves or our church denomination. It is very unbecoming when those in the church try to create subgroups/groupies around a leader.

> **1 Corinthians 1:12–13:** *"Now I mean this, that each one of you is saying, 'I am of Paul,' and 'I of Apollos,' and 'I of Cephas,' and 'I of Christ.' ¹³ Has Christ been divided? Paul was not crucified for you, was he? Or were you baptized in the name of Paul?"*

A man of God will use his influence to constantly point people to Christ and not himself. Paul said in **1 Corinthians 11:1:** *"Be imitators of me, just as I also am of Christ."*

VERSE 19 (second part of the verse): *"...baptizing them in the name of the Father and the Son and the Holy Spirit,...."*

We also are to see that the new disciples in Christ are baptized. I am always highly suspect of people who say they are Christians but will not be baptized. Such a view is highhanded rebellion against the words of Christ (Matthew 28:19). Baptism is expected for those who believe unto salvation.

> **Acts 8:36–38:** *"As they went along the road they came to some water; and the eunuch said, 'Look! Water! What prevents me from being baptized?' ³⁷ [And Philip said, 'If you believe with all your heart, you may.' And he answered and said, 'I believe that Jesus Christ is the Son of God.'] ³⁸ And he ordered the chariot to stop; and they both went down into the water, Philip as well as the eunuch, and he baptized him."*

Baptism is to be done in the name of the Holy Trinity (*"the name of the Father and the Son and the Holy Spirit,...."*). This makes clear the error of "oneness theology." Oneness theology (also known as, "Jesus only" or "modalism")[623] denies the fundamental doctrine of the Trinity and claims you must baptize in the name of *Jesus only* (directly contrary to the words of Jesus in Matthew 28:19). Many people have heard the term Holy Trinity but they seldom understand it.

---

[623] "The church has rejected the heresies of 'modalism' and 'tritheism'. 'Modalism' denies the distinction of persons within the Godhead, claiming that Father, Son, and Holy Spirit are just ways in which God expresses Himself. 'Tritheism,' on the other hand, falsely declares that there are three beings who together make up God." Sproul, R. C., *Essential Truths of the Christian Faith*, Wheaton, Ill.: Tyndale House (1996, c1992).

Here is an explanation. The word "Trinity" means "a group of three." The "Trinity" can be explained in part by 3 concepts:

1. There is but one God.
2. The Father, the Son and the Spirit is each God.
3. The Father, the Son and the Spirit is each a distinct Person.[624]

Realize there are not three Gods **but ONE GOD** (Deuteronomy 6:4), but in that unity of ONE God there are three eternal and co-equal persons.

Being baptized into the body of Christ is not a magical rite obtained through a special man with special water. Remember, baptism does not save you, only faith in Christ can do that.
R. C. Sproul states it this way:

> "Baptism was instituted by Christ and is to be administered in the name of the Father, Son, and Holy Spirit. The outward sign does not automatically or magically convey the realities that are signified. For example, though baptism signifies regeneration, or rebirth, it does not automatically convey rebirth. The power of baptism is not in the water but in the power of God."[625]

Just as some make the great error in believing the ritual of water baptism instills eternal salvation, others error in thinking water baptism is insignificant. Water baptism is very important for the Christian. During water baptism, an individual publicly identifies himself with Christ and the body of Christ (i.e. the church). It outwardly symbolizes the spiritual baptism/conversion that has taken place inwardly. (See 1 Corinthians 12:13, Romans 6:2-11.)

VERSE 20 (first part of the verse): *"...teaching them to observe all that I commanded you;...."*

The obedient Christian equips the new disciple who has come to faith in Christ: *"...teaching them to observe all that I commanded you;..."* Jesus did not say to go and teach them all the great *life lessons* He told us about. He said to teach them what He *commanded*. Obedience to Christ is a manifestation of the converted: **John 14:15:** *"If you love Me, you will keep **My** commandments."* The Commandments of God are summed up by our Lord:

> **Matthew 22:36–39:** *"Teacher, which is the great commandment in the Law?"* [37] *And He said to him, "You shall love the Lord your God with all your heart, and with all your soul, and with all your mind."* [38] *This is the great and foremost commandment.* [39] *"The second is like it, 'You shall love your neighbor as yourself.'*

Some have tried to twist the teachings of Christ into a life-enhancement program. This view sees the gospel as helping converts improve their marriage, get a promotion at work and be better people. The true gospel is about escaping the well-deserved judgment of hell through faith in Jesus Christ's substitutionary death on the cross. The believer is set free from sin and death and can live joyfully for the glory of God. **John 10:10:** *"...I came that they may have life, and have it abundantly."* Once a person comes to the revelation of what Christ has done for him, he is never the same. Nothing else matters but The King and His Kingdom.

---

[624] The New Bible Dictionary

[625] Sproul, R. C. (1996) *Essential Truths of the Christian Faith; #80 Baptism*, Wheaton, Ill.: Tyndale House.

> **Matthew 13:44–46:** *"The kingdom of heaven is like a treasure hidden in the field, which a man found and hid again; and from joy over it he goes and sells all that he has and buys that field.* [45] *Again, the kingdom of heaven is like a merchant seeking fine pearls,* [46] *and upon finding one pearl of great value, he went and sold all that he had and bought it."*

VERSE 20 (second part of the verse): *"...and lo, I am with you always, even to the end of the age."*

Jesus states at the end of verse 20: *"and lo, I am with you always, even to the end of the age ."* The last section in Matthew 28:20 sets out the promise of comfort and security in Christ... to the very end. As some writers have pointed out, our Lord calls us *friends* in John 15:15; our Lord calls us *brothers* in Hebrews 2:11; but what is even more awesome is that He tells us that He is *Immanuel—God with us...."* (Matthew 1:23) *"always, even to the end of the age."*

Summary and Application

Do not miss that Matthew 28:18-20 is composed of an introduction, a command, and a conclusion. The introduction starts with Jesus setting forth the reality of His complete sovereignty over all that exists when He states, *"All authority has been given to Me in heaven and on earth."* The section concludes with the fact of His constant care and comfort: *"and lo, I am with you always, even to the end of the age."* Note that in between the introduction and conclusion is the command: *"Go therefore and make disciples of all the nations, baptizing them in the name of the Father and the Son and the Holy Spirit,* [20] *teaching them to observe all that I commanded you;...."* It could not be made clearer: God is in complete control, and He is with us to the end, so we can confidently go out and spread the gospel and not be hindered by selfish concerns. Will you obey The Lord?

Let me leave you with a quote from John MacArthur:

> "The supreme way in which God chose to glorify Himself was through the redemption of sinful men, and it is through participation in that redemptive plan that believers themselves most glorify God."[626]

---

[626] MacArthur, J. (1985). *Matthew* (p 249). Chicago: Moody Press.

SUMMARY OF THIS COMMENTARY ON MATTHEW

Two matters to always remember:

Nothing else matters but THE KING and HIS KINGDOM.
(cf. Matthew 13:44-46)
and
Apart from Jesus Christ, you can do nothing.
(cf. John 15:5)

One last matter addressing all that Jesus taught:
"If you know these things, you are blessed if you do them."
(John 13:17 - see context John 13:10-20)

BIBLIOGRAPHY

a Brakel, W. *The Christian's Reasonable Service, Volumes 1 and 2:* electronic ed. of the first publication in the English language, based on the 3rd edition of the original Dutch work. Morgan PA: Soli Deo Gloria Publications, 1996, c1992.

Alexander, T. D., and Rosner, B. S. *New Dictionary of Biblical Theology* (electronic ed.). Downers Grove, IL: InterVarsity Press, 2001.

American Heritage Dictionary of the English Language 3rd ed., Houghton Mifflin Co., 1992.

Arndt, W., Gingrich, F. W., Danker, F. W., and Bauer, W. *A Greek-English lexicon of the New Testament and other Early Christian literature: A Translation and Adaption of the Fourth Revised and Augmented Edition of Walter Bauer's Griechisch-deutsches Worterbuch zu den Schrift en des Neuen Testaments und der ubrigen urchristlichen Literatur.* Chicago: University of Chicago Press, (1996, c1979).

Augustine, Saint, Bishop of Hippo. *Letters, The Works of Saint Augustine,* Augustinian Heritage Institute, Hyde Park, New York: New City Press, 2005.

Bimson, J. J., and Kane, J. P. *New Bible Atlas* (electronic ed.) Wheaton, IL: InterVarsity Press, 2000.

Blomberg, C. *The New American Commentary Vol. 22: Matthew.* (electronic ed.) Nashville: Broadman and Holman Publishers, 2001.

Brand, C., Draper, C., England, A., Bond, S., Clendenen, E. R., Butler, T. C., and Latta, B. *Holman Illustrated Bible Dictionary.* Nashville, TN: Holman Bible Publishers, 2003.

Catholic Church. *Catechism of the Catholic Church.* 2nd ed. Vatican: Libreria Editrice Vaticana, 2000.

Chambers, O. *My Utmost for His Highest: Selections for the Year* (September 9). Grand Rapids, MI: Discovery House Publishers, (1993, c1935).

Douglas, J. D., Comfort, P. W., and Mitchell, D. *Who's Who in Christian History.* Wheaton, IL: Tyndale House, 1992.

Easton. *Eastons Bible Dictionary* (electronic ed.).

Edwards, Jonathan. *The Works of Jonathan Edwards,* Vol. 2. Carlisle, Pa.: Banner of Truth, reprint, 1986.

Elliot, Elisabeth. *Shadow of the Almighty: The Life and Testament of Jim Elliot.* New York: HarperCollins, 1979.

Elwell, W. A., and Comfort, P. W. *Tyndale Bible Dictionary.* Wheaton, IL: Tyndale House Publishers, 2001.

Enhanced Strong's Lexicon, (Oak Harbor, WA: Logos Research Systems, Inc.) 1995.

Enns, P. P. *The Moody Handbook of Theology.* Chicago, Ill.: Moody Press, (1997, c1989).

Fuller, R. H. *The Cost of Discipleship*. 2nd rev. ed. New York: Macmillan, 1960.

Geisler, Norman L. "The Essential Doctrines of the Christian Faith (Part 2)." *Christian Research Journal* Vol. 28, No. 6, 2005.

Green, J. B., McKnight, S., and Marshall, I. H. *Dictionary of Jesus and the Gospels.* Downers Grove, Ill.: InterVarsity Press, 1992.

Grubb, Norman, *C.T. Studd. Cricketer and Pioneer*. Fort Washington, PA: CLC Publications, 2001.

Haldane, R. *An Exposition of Romans* (electronic ed.). Simpsonville SC: Christian Classics Foundation, 1996.

Henry, M. *Matthew Henry's Commentary on the Whole Bible, Complete and Unabridged in One Volume*. Peabody: Hendrickson, 1996, c1991.

Hodge, A. (1996). *Outlines of Theology*. Index created by Christian Classics Foundation. (electronic ed. based on the 1972 Banner of Truth Trust reproduction of the 1879 ed.) Simpsonville SC: Christian Classics Foundation, 1972.

Hodge, C. *Systematic Theology.* Oak Harbor, WA: Logos Research Systems, Inc. 1997

Hodge, A. *The Confession of Faith*. Simpsonville, SC: Christian Classics Foundation, 1997.

Hughes, R. Kent. *The Sermon on the Mount*. Crossway, 2001.

Josephus. *Antiquities of the Jews*. Peabody, MA: Hendrickson Publishers, 1987.

Keith, Kent, *The Silent Revolution: Dynamic Leadership in the Student Council.* (Terrace Press) 2003.

Kittel, G. *Theological Dictionary of the New Testament*. Translation of Theologisches Worterbuch zum Neuen Testament. Grand Rapids, Mich.: W.B. Eerdmans, (1995, c1985).

Lawson, Steve. J. *Made in Our Image – What Shall We Do With a User-Friendly God?* Multnomah Books 2006.

Lloyd-Jones, D. Martin. *Studies in the Sermon on the Mount*. Grand Rapids, MI: Wm. B. Eerdmans Publishing Co., 1971.

Louw, J. P., and E. A. Nida. *Greek-English Lexicon of the New Testament: Based on Semantic Domains*. New York: United Bible Societies, 1996, c1989.

Luther, Martin. *Commentary on Galatians*. Escondido, CA: Ephesians Four Group, 1999.

Luther, Martin. *Letter of St. Paul to the Romans.* Translated by Bon Andrew Thomton, OS Bed Hans Volz and Heinz Blanke, 1972.

MacArthur, J. *The MacArthur New Testament Commentary, - Acts*. Chicago: Moody Press, 1994, 1996.

MacArthur, J. *The MacArthur New Testament Commentary, - Matthew*. Chicago: Moody Press, 1987.

MacArthur, J. *Reckless Faith: When the Church Loses its Will to Discern.* Wheaton, Ill.: Crossway Books, 1994.

MacArthur, J. F. Jr. *1 and 2 Thessalonians. MacArthur New Testament.* Chicago: Moody Press, 2002.

Manser, Martin H. *The Facts on File Dictionary of Proverbs,* 2007.

McGarvey, J. W., and Pendleton, P. Y. *The Four-Fold Gospel.* Cincinnati, OH: The Standard Publishing Company, 1914.

Merriam-Webster's 11th Collegiate Dictionary, electronic ed., Fogware Publishing, 2008.

Morgan, R. J. *Nelson's Complete Book of Stories, Illustrations, and Quotes* (electronic ed.) Nashville: Thomas Nelson Publishers, 2000.

Morris, Henry. *The Defender's Study Bible.* World Publishing,, 1995.

Moyer, Elgin S. *Who Was Who in Church History.* New Canaan, Conn.: Keats, 1974.

Nelson's Quick Reference Topical Bible Index. Nelson's Quick Reference. Nashville, TN: Thomas Nelson Publishers, (1996).

New American Heritage Dictionary.

Oden, Thomas C. *Ancient Christian Commentary on the Scriptures, Romans, Vol. 6.* Downers Grove, Il. IVP Academic, 2005.

Osbeck, K. W. *Amazing Grace: 366 Inspiring Hymn Stories for Daily Devotions.* Grand Rapids, Mich.: Kregel Publications, 1990.

Packer, J. *Knowing God.* Index created by Christian Classics Foundation. (electronic ed.). Downers Grove IL: InterVarsity Press, 1973.

Paton, John G., *Missionary to the New Hebreds, An Autobiography Edited by His Brother.* Edinburgh: The Banner of Truth Trust, 1965, orig. 1889, 1891.

Piper, John, *Don't Waste Your Life.* Wheaton, Ill. Crossway Books, 2003.

Polhill, J. B. *The New American Commentary Vol. 26: Acts.* Nashville: Broadman and Holman Publishers, 1995.

Ryken, L., Wilhoit, J., Longman, T., Duriez, C., Penney, D., and Reid, D. G. *Dictionary of Biblical Imagery.* Downers Grove, IL: InterVarsity Press, 2000.

Ryle, J.C. *Holiness,* Simpsonville, SC: Christian Classics Foundation, 1997

Ryle, J.C. *Mark (Expository Thoughts on the Gospels),* Wheaton, Ill.: Crossways Classic Commentaries: v.2, 1993.

Ryle, J.C. *Matthew (Expository Thoughts on the Gospels)*. Wheaton, Ill.: Crossways Classic Commentaries: v.1, 1993.

Ryrie Study Bible - Expanded edition: New American Standard Version. Chicago: Moody Press, (1996).

Smith, M. H. *Larger Catechism of the Westminster Confession Standards. Index created by Christian Classics Foundation. (electronic ed.)* Greenville, SC: Greenville Presbyterian Theological Seminary Press. 1996, c1990.

Smith, M. H. Published in electronic form by Christian Classics Foundation, 1996). *Systematic Theology, Volume One: Prolegomena, Theology, Anthropology, Christology*. Index created by Christian Classics Foundation. (electronic ed.). Greenville SC: Greenville Presbyterian Theological Seminary Press, 1994.

Smith, M. H, *Systematic Theology, Volumes I and II*. Simpsonville, SC: Christian Classics Foundation, 1997.

Soanes, C., and Stevenson, A. *Concise Oxford English Dictionary* (11th ed.). Oxford: Oxford University Press, 2004.

Sproul, R. C. *Essential Truths of the Christian Faith*. Wheaton, Ill.: Tyndale House, 1996, c1992.

Spurgeon, C. H. *A Collection of Sermons* (electronic ed.). Logos Library Systems, Simpsonville SC: Christian Classics Foundation, 1996.

Spurgeon, C. H. *Metropolitan Tabernacle Pulpit, V. 28,*

Spurgeon, C. H. *Morning and Evening: Daily Readings*. Oak Harbor, WA: Logos Research Systems, Inc., 1995.

Stott, J. R., *Basic Christianity*. Downers Grove, Ill. InterVarsity, 1971.

Swanson, J., and Nave, O. *New Nave's Topical Bible*. Logos Research Systems, 1994.

Tan, P. L. *Encyclopedia of 7700 Illustrations: Signs of the Times*. Garland, Tex. Bible Communications, Inc., 1996.

Testimony of the Evangelists, Examined by the Rules of Evidence Administered in Courts of Justice. Grand Rapids, MI: Baker, 1965; reprint,.

The New American Standard Bible. La Habra, CA: The Lockman Foundation, 1986.

The New International Version of the Bible. Grand Rapids, MI: Zondervan Publishing House, 1984.

The Treasury of Scripture Knowledge: Five Hundred Thousand Scripture References and Parallel Passages. Introduction by R.A. Torrey. London: Samuel Bagster and Sons Ltd. 1995.

Thomas, I. *The Golden Treasury of Puritan Quotations*. Maywood, CA: Simpsonville, SC: Christian Classics Foundation, 1997.

United States Supreme Court: United States v. George Wilson, (Jan 1833 term 7 p. 150)

Utley, R. J. D. *Vol. 9: The First Christian Primer: Matthew*. Study Guide Commentary Series. Marshall, Texas: Bible Lessons International, 2000.

Vincent, T. *A Family Instructional Guide*. electronic edition based on the first Banner of Truth ed., 1980. Simpsonville SC: Christian Classics Foundation, 1996.

Vine, W. E., *Vine's Expository Dictionary of Old and New Testament Words*. Grand Rapids, MI: Fleming H. Revell, 1981.

Walvoord, J. F., R. B. Zuck, and Dallas Theological Seminary. *The Bible Knowledge Commentary: An Exposition of the Scriptures*. Wheaton, IL: Victor Books, (1983, c1985).

Weber, S. K. *Vol. 1: Matthew*. Holman New Testament Commentary. Nashville, TN: Broadman and Holman Publishers, 2000.

Webster's 11th Collegiate Dictionary, electronic ed., Fogware Publishing, 2008.

Whitaker, R., Brown, F., Driver, S. and Briggs, C. A. (1997, c1906). The Abridged Brown-Driver-Briggs Hebrew-English Lexicon of the Old Testament: From A Hebrew and English Lexicon of the Old Testament by Francis Brown, S.R. Driver and Charles Briggs, based on the lexicon of Wilhelm Gesenius. Edited by Richard Whitaker (Princeton Theological Seminary). Text provided by Princeton Theological Seminary. Houghton, Mifflin and Co., 1906.

Wiersbe, W. W. *Be Satisfied*. Wheaton, Ill: Victor Books., 1996.

Wiersbe, W. W. *The Bible Exposition Commentary*. Wheaton, Ill.: Victor Books, 1996.

Wood, D. R. W. and Marshall, I. H., *New Bible Dictionary*. 3rd ed. Leicester, England; Downers Grove, Ill.: InterVarsity Press, 1996.

Attitude of the Obedient Slave.

Luke 17:7–10

"Which of you, having a slave plowing or tending sheep, will say to him when he has come in from the field, 'Come immediately and sit down to eat?' But will he not say to him, 'Prepare something for me to eat, and properly clothe yourself and serve me while I eat and drink; and afterward you may eat and drink?' He does not thank the slave because he did the things which were commanded, does he? So you too, <u>when you do all the things which are commanded you, say, 'We are unworthy slaves; we have done only that which we ought to have done.'</u>..."

NOTES

NOTES

NOTES

NOTES